INTEGRATED COURSE OPTIONS

Other new financial accounting products for your course:

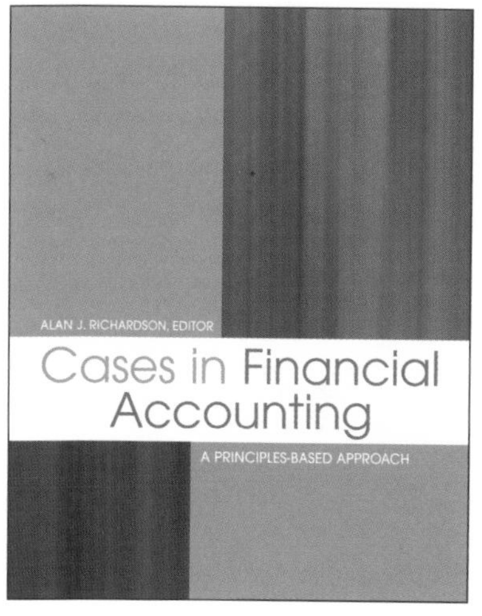

Cases in Financial Accounting: A Principles-Based Approach
Alan J. Richardson (Editor)

Homework Management System for *Financial Accounting*

Accounting Practice Sets

Blue Wave Fishing Supplies: An Accounting Practice Set

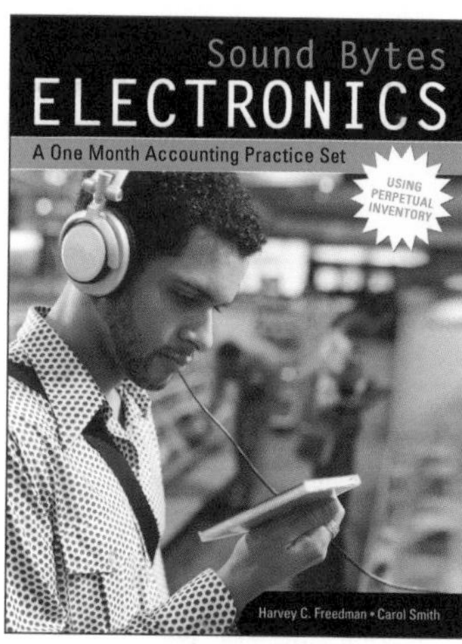

Sound Bytes Electronics: A One Month Accounting Practice Set

Harvey C. Freedman and Carol Smith

To the Student

Thomson Nelson's Financial Statement Tutorials are designed to help you learn the basic preparation of and concepts behind financial statements. These modules will help you understand how financial statements are used to evaluate a company's economic performance. These visually impressive modules also include quizzes and many practical examples from well-known companies to provide relevance to the discussion of financial statements.

The tutorial modules include:

- the Balance Sheet
- the Income Statement
- the Cash Flow Statement

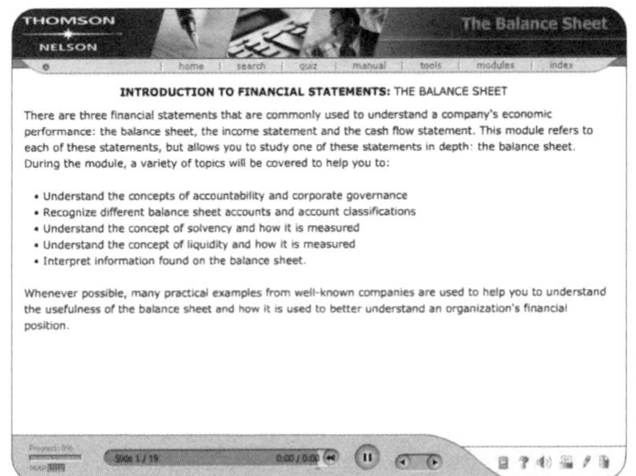

Log-in Instructions for Thomson Nelson's Financial Statement Tutorials

- Visit **www.gibbins6e.nelson.com/tutorials**
- Complete the online registration form
- Enter the access code, provided below
- Follow the instructions for creating your unique user ID and password

ACCESS CODE: **PPQBXZ6P3FS69J**

If you have purchased a used book, a passcode booklet (0-17-610402-X) is available through your bookstore or by contacting Thomson Nelson Customer Support at 1-800-268-2222 or by visiting **www.nelson.com** — click on Customer Support.

FINANCIAL ACCOUNTING

AN INTEGRATED APPROACH

Sixth Edition

Michael Gibbins, PhD, FCA
Winspear Professor of Professional Accounting
University of Alberta

Contributing author:
Rick Bates, MBA, CA
Associate Professor, University of Guelph

Australia Canada Mexico Singapore Spain United Kingdom United States

Financial Accounting: An Integrated Approach
Sixth Edition

by Michael Gibbins with contributing author Rick Bates

Editorial Director and Publisher:
Evelyn Veitch

Publisher:
Rod Banister

Senior Marketing Manager:
Charmaine Sherlock

Developmental Editor:
Natalie Barrington

Photo Researcher/Permissions Coordinator:
Kristiina Bowering

Senior Production Editor:
Julie van Veen

Proofreader:
Laurel Sparrow

Indexer:
Andrew Little

Production Coordinator:
Cathy Deak

Design Director:
Ken Phipps

Interior Design Modifications:
Katherine Strain

Cover Design:
Rocket Design

Cover Image:
Digital Vision/Getty Images

Compositor:
Kyle Gell Design

Printer:
Quebecor World

Printed and bound in Canada
3 09 08 07

For more information contact Nelson, 1120 Birchmount Road, Scarborough, Ontario, M1K 5G4. Or you can visit our Internet site at http://www.nelson.com

ISBN-13: 978-0-17-640725-4
ISBN-10: 0-17-640725-1

Library and Archives Canada Cataloguing in Publication

Gibbins, Michael, 1942–
Financial accounting : an integrated approach / Michael Gibbins; contributing author, Rick Bates. — 6th ed.

Includes bibliographical references and index.

ISBN 0-17-640725-1

1. Accounting—Textbooks.
2. Financial statements—Textbooks.
I. Bates, Rick II. Title.

HF5635.G5 2006 657'.044
C2005-907836-7

To all students of the art of accounting

M.G.

To Bill Braithwaite, teacher,
mentor, and friend.

M. (R.) B.

Sections 2.9–2.11 may be read ahead of Sections 2.4–2.8.

Sections 3.4–3.7 may be read in any order.

Sections 10.7 and 10.8–10.9 may be read independently of Sections 10.2–10.6.

This Sixth Edition marks a significant milestone in the evolution of *Financial Accounting: An Integrated Approach;* its publication marks the fifteenth anniversary since the book was first published. Since that time more than 100,000 students have been introduced to financial accounting through the use of this Canadian textbook. The world has changed a great deal during these 15 years and the book has kept pace with changes in how we do business, how accounting practice has evolved, and how the profession has reacted to the scandals that plagued both the accounting profession and the business world in recent years.

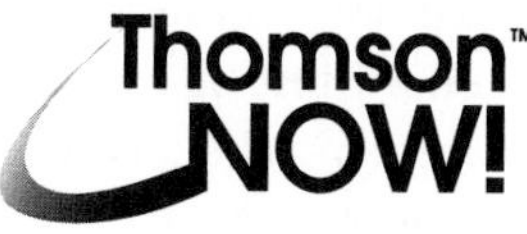

This new edition was developed in response to requests from adopters and reviewers of the book for fresh assignment material, more current examples and excerpts from financial statements, and information on recently released accounting standards, and to introduce two new tools for technology-enhanced learning: ThomsonNOW!™ homework management system for *Financial Accounting* and Thomson Nelson's Financial Statement Tutorials. For 15 years this book has set the standard for providing a balanced perspective of financial accounting; we believe the improvements in the Sixth Edition and the addition of our on-line learning tools will take our *Integrated Approach* to a new level.

This book is designed to help prepare future accountants for success in meeting their responsibilities and enjoying their careers, to help prepare future managers, investors, and other users of accounting information for success in their interactions with accounting, and to show everyone what an interesting and subtle subject accounting is. To do that, this book presents a balanced and integrated view of financial accounting, marrying business issues and good accounting principles throughout. The *hows* (preparation procedures and techniques), the *uses* (analysis and decisions), and the *whys* (concepts and principles that link preparation and use) are given explicit attention in all chapters. The balance among the three varies with topics, but all are present because none can stand without the others.

Financial accounting is presented as a utilitarian discipline, producing accounting information that is to be used and that is responsive to the people who use it and to changes in those needs over time. This presentation is aimed *both* at students who want to become managers or other users of accounting information *and* at students who want to become accountants, because intelligent use and intelligent preparation of financial accounting information require a balanced understanding of both preparation and use.

Financial Accounting: An Integrated Approach provides a strong conceptual foundation and includes insights from accounting and related research. It also grounds the subject in the practicalities that make financial accounting a challenging discipline and accounting an interesting profession. While providing structure to the learning task to help the student gain understanding, it avoids excessive structure that might give the student the impression that financial accounting is more straightforward and less subtle than it is. The student must do the cognitive work of integrating the ideas into a personal understanding, because otherwise the understanding won't last.

This sixth edition carries forward the best features from the previous edition while adding new strengths that make the text and its learning package even better.

Changes in the Sixth Edition

- The financial statements and excerpts from the 2004 and previous annual reports of both Canadian Pacific Railway Limited and Enbridge Inc. are used with permission.
- Introductory-level references are made to recent accounting standards from the *CICA Handbook.* This includes coverage of Section 1530 Comprehensive Income, mentioned briefly in the early chapters, and Section 3855 Financial Instruments, dealt with at length in Chapter 9. This section came about because of the Enron failure and deals with the classification and accounting for short-term investments.

Both of these sections were introduced in April 2005 and are required for periods beginning on or after October 1, 2006.

- Numerous references are made to the survey findings from *Financial Reporting in Canada 2005*. This information reflects up-to-date information on the current accounting practices of Canadian companies.
- To complement the improved problem material within the chapters, the homework and discussion problems are now tied more clearly to the various sections of each chapter. Approximately half of the problems are new or revised in this edition. Integrated problems are grouped separately. Homework problems that are more challenging, or more time-consuming, or both, are identified to assist instructors and students in selecting homework.

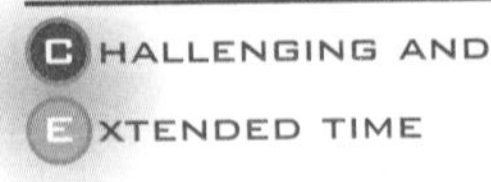

- With the purchase of a new book, each student will receive free access to Thomson Nelson's Financial Statement Tutorials that accompany this textbook. These on-line tutorials are designed to help students learn the basic preparation of and the concepts behind financial statements. Students will learn how financial statements are prepared and used to understand a company's economic performance. These tutorials primarily reinforce the textbook topics presented in Chapters 2, 3, and 4. A unique password is required to access the tutorials and can be purchased separately (0-17-610402-X) by students who have opted to purchase a used book.
- ThomsonNOW!™ for *Financial Accounting* is a highly interactive on-line homework management resource available to accompany this textbook. Students can solve problems for practice and/or grading and all problems are machine marked. Students can practise the same problem several times by generating new numbers using the algorithmic feature of this program. It is a great resource to ensure your students master the material in the text. A unique password is required and is available for purchase (0-17-610449-6). Visit **hed.nelson.com** or contact your Thomson Nelson representative to include ThomsonNOW!™ in a reduced package price with your textbook.
- To further bring the material to life, each chapter is introduced using a vignette drawn from business to illustrate what the chapter is all about. The vignette is followed by specifics of what will be learned from studying the chapter. Some of these vignettes are new and some have been revised for the Sixth Edition.

Strong features carried forward

- The material has been integrated from the beginning, so that preparation, use, and linking principles are presented together or in close sequence. For example, the transactional basis of financial accounting is presented in the first chapter, along with information about users and some introductory analysis, and these are integrated into the conceptual base of accrual accounting. In later chapters, as each financial statement is presented, its purpose and principles are explained, its preparation is illustrated fully (including necessary accounts and recordkeeping procedures), and its use is examined.
- The accounting cycle mechanics are integrated into the explanation of the financial statements in Chapters 1–3. The book's considerable practical content, including demonstration of example forms (Chapter 7) and procedures (throughout), has been written to fit with the principles and uses being explained in parallel to present the student with a broad integrative view of financial accounting.
- A Canadian company is used to illustrate financial statement format, analysis, and other issues throughout the book, both bringing the book's content down to earth and helping to integrate the various topics by relating them to the same company. In the Sixth Edition, we have continued to use Canadian Pacific Railway Limited and now include excerpts from its 2004 annual report. Numerous other company examples help to fill out the story and reflect current practice.

- The Book Overview in Chapter 1 illustrates the book's contents with reference to a Canadian company, Enbridge Inc., and uses excerpts from its 2004 annual report. This use of immediate real-company examples continues throughout in greater frequency than in the previous edition.
- Because there are differing views about the best sequence for the topics in introductory financial accounting, *numerous topics have been written to be studied in alternative orders.* The book's full financial statement analysis material is presented in Chapter 10 (along with present value and "what if" analysis), but can be used any time after the financial statements have been set out in the first four chapters. These alternative potential orders are noted at various points in the book, including in the Table of Contents.
- A number of For Your Interest boxes have been inserted to present interesting quirks, research findings, and managerial implications. The book makes numerous connections to current issues such as stock market gyrations, scandals, manipulation of information, e-commerce, international standards harmonization and other standards developments, and management's motivations in disclosing financial accounting information.
- Point-form material, graphs and charts, information about useful Web sites, and real-world examples have been used frequently. Web sites are given for all companies and organizations used as examples.
- Much of the material in the book has an informal style, directed toward easing the student into the material and generally lightening up what students feel is serious stuff. It is hoped that students and instructors will enjoy themselves, and especially that students will find financial accounting to be a lot more interesting than they might have expected. The book is written in the second person, talking directly to student readers.
- Numerous sidebars are presented beside text material to help students keep track of their learning, and the How's Your Understanding? questions at the end of each chapter section allow students to check their comprehension of the section's material. Each chapter also includes an installment of the Mato Inc. Continuing Demonstration Case, which tells the story of a small company operating at a scale with which students may be able to identify. The story develops with the topics covered throughout the book and thus provides a progressive (mostly preparation-oriented) illustration of the ideas.
- Chapter 4's approach to the cash flow statement takes advantage of the "direct" method of preparing to present the cash flow analysis in a more natural way as coming from receipts and disbursements, then shows how that does the same job as the traditional "indirect" method. The indirect method cash flow statement is also analyzed and interpreted when it is presented, just as the balance sheet and income statement were. As a result, the cash flow statement fits well with the presentation of the other financial statements in the first half of the book.
- A large number of Demonstration Problems and Mini-Demonstration Problems are provided to help students see how to apply each chapter's material.
- The homework and discussion material provides a large number of "asterisked" problems with fully worked-out solutions that are available in the Student Solutions Manual, plus regular homework material and cases with solutions in the separate solutions manual for instructors. All problems, including the asterisked ones, cover the book's topics at various levels of difficulty and with various numerical and narrative styles.
- Important terms (printed in coloured type in the chapter material) have been collected together into a list at the end of each chapter and all those terms have been explained further in an expanded glossary at the end of the book.
- When advanced topics have been included (to meet the book's objective of connecting preparation, use, and principles), they have been included at an introductory level, avoiding complexity. The book is thus a complete summary of important

topics in financial accounting, providing some knowledge to students who do not go on in accounting, but also introducing the ideas to students who will see them again more fully in later courses.
- A Student Solutions Manual is packaged free with the purchase of a new textbook and provides solution outlines to selected (asterisked) homework problems.

The book's purpose is to help students develop their own understanding of financial accounting, not to deliver "the answer"—financial accounting's answers are many and varied. Examples and the homework solutions, for example, reinforce thoughtful analysis, rather than suggesting that only one answer is to be expected. Students can purchase the Study Guide (ISBN 0-17-610411-9) to accompany *Financial Accounting: An Integrated Approach,* Sixth Edition, through their campus bookstore. With the purchase of a new book, each student will receive a free copy of a Student Solutions Manual that includes solutions to all of the problems identified by an asterisk. This Student Solutions Manual (ISBN 0-17-610442-9) can also be purchased separately by students who have opted to purchase a used book. An accounting Web site has been developed to support *Financial Accounting: An Integrated Approach,* Sixth Edition. It can be accessed at **www.gibbins6e.nelson.com** and contains updated Test Yourself questions, five Extended Projects that guide the student to real financial statements from Canadian companies, Case Study exercises, Chapter Weblinks, Exam Practice, Glossary, Audio Flashcards, and Microsoft® PowerPoint® slides.

Material for instructors has been prepared to assist in course delivery. This includes an Instructor's Resource CD (0-17-610412-7) containing the Instructor's Manual, a Test Bank, Computerized Test Bank, Exam Bank, and Microsoft® PowerPoint® slides. An Instructor's Solutions Manual (0-17-610413-5) for all homework and discussion problems, and an Exam Bank (0-17-610403-8), are also available in print.

Michael Gibbins is the Winspear Professor of Professional Accounting and Director of the Centre for Enhanced Corporate Reporting in the School of Business, University of Alberta. He was born and raised in British Columbia, where he married Betty, earned a B.Com. from the University of British Columbia, and obtained his chartered accountancy designation in the Prince George office of what is now Deloitte & Touche. Wending his way east, he worked for the Canadian Institute of Chartered Accountants in Toronto, getting an MBA from York University and becoming a father along the way to Stefan and Tanis. After a trial at teaching as an assistant professor at Queen's University School of Business, he obtained his Ph.D. at Cornell University. A return to the West as assistant professor at the University of British Columbia preceded his move to Alberta.

The author's research and teaching interests lie in how people make decisions and judgments, and in the way accounting information is used in making important decisions in business and other economic spheres. A particular interest is in the professional judgment of public accountants, managers, and other professionals who cope with the pressures and risks of modern business life, including in how such professionals "negotiate" the content of financial reports by applying their judgment and expertise. He has published widely on judgment, accounting, financial disclosure, negotiation, and educational subjects, is past editor of the Canadian accounting research journal *Contemporary Accounting Research*, and is active in various academic and professional bodies. He has received a number of education and teaching awards. In 1988 he was made a Fellow of both the Alberta and British Columbia Institutes of Chartered Accountants.

Balancing his professional and academic interests, the author collects beer bottles, ceramic frogs, and other art featuring frogs. He also enjoys hiking, snorkeling, cross-country skiing, and spending time in the Canadian wilderness, the Australian outback, and other less-trodden parts of the world.

Martin R. (Rick) Bates is an Associate Professor in the College of Management and Economics, University of Guelph. Born and raised in northern Ontario, he earned a B.A.(Econ.) at the University of Guelph and an MBA from York University. After a period of employment with a consumer finance firm, then a life insurance company, he obtained his chartered accountancy designation in the Toronto office of what is now KPMG. Leaving public accounting, he spent a brief time in the trust industry before returning to Guelph as an Assistant Professor in a teaching-only position.

Rick has co-authored an introduction to business text, as well as a number of cases and classroom materials. He has recently begun research on the effect of class size and technology on learning in undergraduate courses.

Married to Wanda with two grown children, he leads a quiet rural life. Leisure time is filled with antiquing, needlework, and woodworking. A passionate motorcyclist since his high school days, he spends as much of the summer as possible on a Gold Wing with Wanda touring Canada and the United States.

ACKNOWLEDGMENTS

All material originally published elsewhere is used with permission. Thanks are due to all the people and companies who gave their permission and therefore helped bring the book to life. For the large contribution their materials have made to the book, we particularly thank Canadian Pacific Railway Limited, Barcol Doors & Windows (especially Rosalie Laibida), all the companies whose financial material has been used in the book's cases and examples, and Bill Scott. David Baboneau and Mark Polak should be credited for their input into an earlier edition; it would have been much impoverished without them.

This book began in development work done as a project for the Centre for the Advancement of Professional Accounting Education (later called the Chartered Accountants' Centre), School of Business, University of Alberta. Michael Gibbins is grateful for the Centre's assistance.

Many people helped along the way, as this book developed over several years. Michael Gibbins is grateful to them all, and apologizes to those not mentioned specifically. Special thanks are due to the students of Accounting 311 at the University of Alberta for their patience, and especially for all their ideas and criticisms, as the book developed. Michael is especially indebted to past co-authors of the annual "Accounting 311 Course Package," who helped him work out many of the ideas in the book: Laurie Beattie, Philip Beaulieu, Richard Chandler, Anona Lukawiecki, Christine Newton, and Duncan Sinclair. For other assistance and support, Michael is grateful to Loretta Amerongen, David Annand, Elaine Aultman, David Baboneau, Peggy Barr, Andrea Berman, Allison Brooks, Dwayne Budzak, Mike Chiasson, Lane Daley, Wendy Degner, Ross Denham, Tad Drinkwater, Don Easton, Joan Finley, Jim Gaa, Stefan Gibbins, Duncan Green, Mary Hemmingsen, Karim Jamal, Dave Jobson, Jocelyn Johnston, Henry Kennedy, Rosalie Laibida, Janet LeBlanc, Tracey Lee, Mary Lea McAnally, Sandra Namchuk, Jim Newton, Linda Olsen, Simone Phillips, Mark Polak, Remi Racine, Steve Salterio, Brent Schmidt, Tom Scott, Lorraine Sherwood, Tanis Stamatelakis, Ken Sutley, Jerry Trites, Shirley Varughese, John Waterhouse, Kathy West, and Heather Wier.

Michael Gibbins would like to thank the late Francis Winspear, who supported him as the Winspear Professor and gave much other support to the University of Alberta. He was a fine example of the combination of conceptual strength and practicality that this book attempts to transmit. Finally, Michael would also like to thank his parents for the example of care and thoughtfulness they set; and his wife, Betty, and children, Stefan and Tanis, for their support over the years.

Rick Bates would like to thank Sharon Sinclair; without her support it wouldn't have happened.

We are also grateful to the following people for their suggestions and constructive comments in preparation for the Sixth Edition: Teresa Anderson (University of Ottawa), Peter Cunningham (Bishop's University), Chris Graham (University of Victoria), Walter Krystia (Ryerson University), Anita Lakra (University of Calgary), Valorie Leonard (Laurentian University), and Berndt Sigloch (Thompson Rivers University).

Thanks also go to the following people who have contributed to this project over the years and whose suggestions have proven invaluable: Asgar Ally (York University), Paul Berry (Mt. Allison University), Stuart Jones (University of Calgary), Karen Lightstone (Saint Mary's University), Valerie Leonard (Laurentian University), Robert Madden (St. Francis Xavier University), Jeanbih Pai (University of Manitoba), R.B. Schenk (Bishop's University), Julia Scott (McGill University), Laurie Tucker (York University), Shu-Lun Wong (Memorial University), Marilyn Adams (McMaster University), Robert Anderson (Brock University), H. Donald Brown (Brock University), Ray F. Carroll (Dalhousie University), Roger Collins (Thompson Rivers University),

Judy Cumby (Memorial University), Maureen Fizzell (Simon Fraser University), Leo Gallant (St. Francis Xavier University), Duncan Green (University of Calgary), Charlotte Heywood (Wilfrid Laurier University), Al Hunter (University of Lethbridge), George Kanaan (Concordia University), Margaret Kelly (University of Manitoba), Terry Litovitz (University of Toronto, Scarborough Campus), Don Lockwood (University of British Columbia), Carol McKeen (Queen's University), Cameron Morrill (University of Manitoba), Richard Pedlar (Wilfrid Laurier University), Neville Ralph (Mount Allison University), Connie Reed (University of Toronto), Catherine Seguin (University of Toronto), and Nicola M. Young (St. Mary's University).

The enthusiasm and support of Thomson Nelson has been great; thanks to Rod Banister, Natalie Barrington, Julie van Veen, Cathy Deak, Kristiina Bowering, Charmaine Sherlock, and Laurel Sparrow for all their work on this edition. Special thanks to Prem Lobo for his work on the technical review, Study Guide, Instructor's Manual, and Microsoft® PowerPoint® slides; to Catherine Byers for her work on the problems and Student Solutions Manual; and to Roger Collins for his revision of the Test Bank and Web quizzes.

PART ONE

1

Introduction to Financial Accounting

Chapter 1 gets you started. It begins with an overview of the whole book and then introduces the people who prepare and use financial accounting's information and the way accounting measures an enterprise's performance. The chapter also introduces financial accounting's underlying system and ideas about the kinds of analysis that are central to using financial statements and to accountants' value in society.

CHAPTER ONE

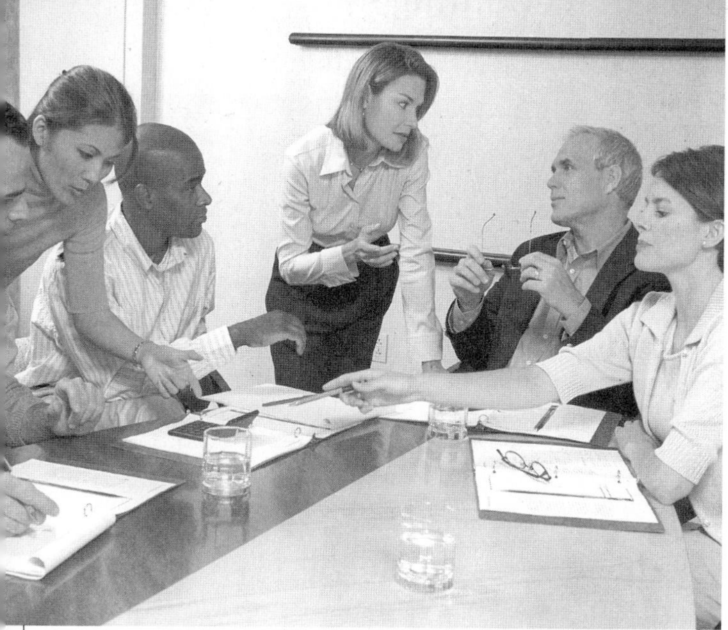

Introduction: Linking Financial Accounting's Production and Uses

1.1 Book Overview: Financial Accounting's Illumination of the World

Welcome!

Welcome to this exploration of an interesting and thought-provoking subject: financial accounting, which provides information about companies and other enterprises. To illustrate the role accounting plays in lighting the way for investors, managers, and other decision makers, or should play if it is done properly, we will use the Canadian company Enbridge Inc.'s financial statements throughout the book. Before we move to Chapter 1, this book overview will explain how Enbridge illustrates this concept and explain how the book is organized.

FYI

Financial accounting's reports tell a financial story about the organization.

In an introductory course, learning terminology is important. To help you with that, this book has a Glossary of Terms at the back. Any term printed in light brown, such as *financial accounting*, is included in the glossary. Marginal comments, such as the one on the left, highlight important ideas, and at the end of each chapter there is a list of new terms from that chapter. If you're not sure what a term means, look it up right away.

Enbridge Inc. and Financial Accounting's Illumination

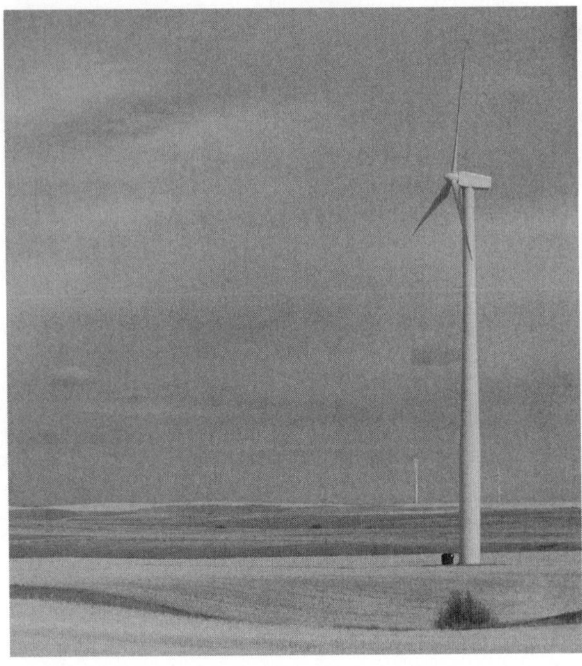

Let's start by thinking about the Canadian company Enbridge Inc. (**www.enbridge.com**). This company, which began as an interprovincial oil pipeline operator, now runs businesses all over the world. It still has its oil pipeline business, but it also owns natural gas pipelines, and engages in gas distribution, wind power, and many other energy activities. Its brands and business interests include Enbridge Pipelines in Western Canada and the United States, Enbridge Gas Distribution and Gaz Métropolitain in Central Canada, Enbridge Gas New Brunswick in Eastern Canada, Enbridge Energy Partners' natural gas pipelines in the United States, Inuvik Gas in the North, Sunbridge Wind Power in Saskatchewan, and numerous energy development projects in Canada, the United States, South America, and elsewhere.

There are ten components that make up financial accounting: seven concepts and three foundations. Let's see how they apply to Enbridge, beginning with the light that financial accounting is designed to produce.

Financial position, income, and cash flow are financial accounting's main reports.

Financial Position Financial accounting produces three major reports. The first, the "*balance sheet*," or statement of financial position, describes the resources ("*assets*") and debts ("*liabilities*") of the enterprise at a specified date. Here is a summary of how Enbridge looked at the end of 2004. When you finish this book, you'll be able to pick up the balance sheet of a company like Enbridge and know where its information comes from and what it means. To equip you to do this, we'll touch on a few complex topics like aggregating data for corporate groups, but they're covered more fully in later courses.

ENBRIDGE

FINANCIAL POSITION
DECEMBER 31, 2004

Total assets	$14.9 billion
Total liabilities	10.9 billion
Shareholders' equity	$ 4.0 billion

INCOME FOR THE YEAR ENDED
DECEMBER 31, 2004

Revenues	$6.5 billion
Expenses	5.9 billion
Net income	$0.6 billion

Income Financial position is only part of the story. The second major accounting report tells you how the company has performed in making income for the owners (Enbridge's shareholders) during a specific period. Here is a summary of how Enbridge did in 2004. By the end of this book, you will also be able to pick up the *income statement* of a company like Enbridge and understand it. To equip you, we'll touch on a few complex topics like depreciation and income tax, which are also covered more fully in later courses.

Cash Flow Even knowing that Enbridge is earning income doesn't tell us all we'd like to know. Income is all very well, but how does the company manage its cash? The third major report tells you where the enterprise's cash came from in the year and what the company did with it. Here is a summary of Enbridge's cash generation and use for 2004. By the end of this book, you'll be familiar with this report and its particular format.

ENBRIDGE

CASH FLOW FOR THE YEAR ENDED DECEMBER 31, 2004

Cash from operations	$ 0.9 billion
Cash from financing	0.1 billion
Cash for investments	(1.0 billion)
Net change in cash	$ 0.0 billion

Good disclosure is central to financial accounting.

Disclosure The three financial reports aren't all the information that financial accounting produces. Those three reports are full of numbers, but there is a lot of judgment and effort put into how the numbers are described and organized. Beyond that, a huge amount of narrative information is included with financial accounting's reports because the bare numbers don't tell us enough. Here is an example: an excerpt from a note on acquisitions that Enbridge attached to its 2004 financial reports to describe the company's acquisitions of other companies during 2004. Financial *disclosure* has become a very controversial topic in recent years, with some people tracing the failure of Enron Inc. in the United States and other recent financial debacles to poor financial disclosure. This book will introduce you to some significant disclosure issues and help "vaccinate" you against being misled by poor disclosure.

ENBRIDGE

EXCERPT FROM 2004 NOTE 5 ON ACQUISITIONS

In September 2003, the Company acquired 90% of the outstanding shares of CCPC Transportation L.L.C., owner of the Cushing to Chicago Pipeline System. Of the total purchase price of $145.8 million, $78.3 million was paid on the date of acquisition and $67.5 million, plus interest of $5.5 million, was paid in December 2004.

Financial analysis is important to interpreting financial accounting information.

Financial Analysis Let's go back to those financial reports, which accountants call "*financial statements.*" Is Enbridge financed more by its creditors (debt) or by its owners (equity)? A common "ratio" to address this question is shown here: you can see that Enbridge's creditors have contributed almost three times as much money to the company as its owners have. There are other ways to calculate the debt-equity and other ratios, as we will see later in the book. Does Enbridge make a good return on its sales (revenue)? Another common ratio used to address this question is shown here: you can see that the company's 2004 net income was 9% of its revenue. The *cash flow statement* summary given earlier shows that the company generated most of the cash it

ENBRIDGE

Dec. 31/04 Debt-equity ratio:
$10.9/$4.0 = 2.73
2004 sales return ratio:
$0.6/$6.5 = 0.09

needed for investments by borrowing rather than by day-to-day operations, and the Note 5 excerpt tells us something about what the company did with the cash it raised. Is a debt-equity ratio of 2.73 good? Is a 9% return on sales commendable? This book will show you how to use *financial statement analysis* to help evaluate the financial strength, profitability, and other characteristics of enterprises.

Internal Control Accounting information is not only used to produce financial statements. It is also very important in managing the business. It is so important that there are separate books and courses on "*management accounting*." To give you an idea of how accounting information can help management and to show you that much more goes on than preparing financial statements, this book introduces two topics. The first is *internal control*: management's use of information to keep track of important resources, debts, and business processes. Here is how Enbridge described this in its 2004 "*annual report*," which includes the financial statements, notes, and other disclosures. By the end of this book, you'll know about several internal control methods and something about preventing fraud.

EXCERPT FROM MANAGEMENT'S REPORT IN THE 2004 ANNUAL REPORT

Management has established systems of internal control that provide reasonable assurance that assets are safeguarded from loss or unauthorized use and produce reliable accounting records for the preparation of financial information. The internal control system includes an internal audit function and an established code of business conduct.

Financial accounting information is an input to good management.

Management The second connection this book draws to managing the enterprise is the general role that management plays in directing the enterprise's accounting activities, along with the other functions management performs. Financial statements are representations by management, as Enbridge noted in this report excerpt. Enbridge is not a single company but rather a large group of companies, the financial information for which is "*consolidated*" so as to represent the group as if it were a single company. This book will refer frequently to management's role, responsibilities, and motivation to show you how financial accounting fits into the enterprise.

EXCERPT FROM MANAGEMENT'S REPORT IN THE 2004 ANNUAL REPORT

Management is responsible for the accompanying consolidated financial statements and all other information in this Annual Report.

Accounting System Financial accounting draws its information from events in the world surrounding the enterprise as it buys, sells, borrows, invests, gains, and loses. There's an accounting system underneath all the financial statements and analyses, gathering data about economic events. For example, when Enbridge makes a $1,000 cash donation

ECONOMIC EVENT: ENBRIDGE DONATES $1,000 CASH TO A COMMUNITY ACTIVITY

The accounting system records this event by adding $1,000 to its record of donation expenses, and deducting $1,000 from its record of cash.

to a community activity, that economic event is tracked by the accounting system as illustrated on p. 6. This book will show you how the accounting system works and how it generates the information needed to produce the financial statements that give management needed internal control and other information.

The accounting system and its methods are financial accounting's foundation.

Methods Enbridge experiences thousands of economic events every day. All the data gathered by the accounting system has to be organized and checked, and some events that are missed by the system or that take a long time to happen have to be added in somehow. Financial accounting has many methods to deal with the task of making sure that the financial statements and other information is complete and correct. For example, when preparing the financial statements, various records are checked for accuracy. If Enbridge discovers that a trademark asset costing $5,000 is now worthless, someone has to decide how to insert this information into the accounting system. There is a method for doing this, the result of which is illustrated here. This book demonstrates many accounting methods to help you understand how the underlying data are shaped and corrected in forming the financial statements.

A $5,000 TRADEMARK ASSET IS DISCOVERED TO BE WORTHLESS

The accounting records are adjusted to remove the amount from the company's assets and transfer it to expenses, thus reducing assets on the balance sheet and reducing income on the income statement.

Standards and principles are essential to quality output from the accounting system.

Standards, Principles Accounting information doesn't just happen. Financial accounting follows principles and standards, some of which apply generally to enterprises and some of which are chosen as policy by each enterprise. At the right is what Enbridge said about its adherence to general principles and about how it calculates depreciation (the straight-line method is one of several methods the company could use). *Accounting principles* involve a lot of judgment and expertise, and because many are not hard and fast, they also involve a lot of controversy. Enterprises might be tempted to choose their accounting policies, or not to follow some usual principles, so that the financial statements show better results. Manipulation of accounting information is also said to be behind numerous corporate failures and disasters. The news media remind us frequently that people whose ethics are a bit loose can get into serious trouble in accounting just as in the rest of business and society. When you have finished this book, you will understand *generally accepted accounting principles*, know about typical *accounting policy* choices, and understand some of the ethical and professional challenges involved in producing appropriate financial statements and disclosures.

EXCERPTS FROM THE COMPANY'S 2004 ACCOUNTING POLICY NOTE

(General principles) The consolidated financial statements of the Company are prepared in accordance with Canadian generally accepted accounting principles...

(Specific policy) Depreciation of property, plant, and equipment generally is provided on a straight-line basis over the estimated service lives of the assets.

This Book's Integrated Approach

Well, this is a lot of information! But, this book will develop the concepts introduced above in manageable bites, so that your understanding and competence will develop throughout. There will be many illustrations and examples, much use of real companies like Enbridge to demonstrate topics, and other aids to your learning that are described in the preface that will be part of each chapter. But one important feature of the book to stress now is that, as the title states, it is *integrated.* The various topics illustrated for Enbridge above are all tied together and some of them appear many times in the book, so that you can see how financial statements are *prepared,* how they are *used,* and how preparation and use *fit together.* To illustrate this integration, the illumination image in Figure 1.1 shows where in the book the ten topic areas appear. You can see that some are in nearly every chapter and that the seven kinds of output and the three foundation inputs are represented throughout the book.

Integration of Use, Preparation, and Concepts

Another way to view integrating your knowledge is to think of the people wanting to use accounting's information, the people preparing it, and the concepts that link them.

USE. Financial accounting has value because the information it produces is used in many and varied ways. Users include managers, stockbrokers, bankers, financial analysts, and many others. Such people study accounting to learn how to use the information effectively and do their jobs better. Accountants also need to know how the information is used so they can understand the demand for their services and do their jobs better too.

FIGURE 1.1

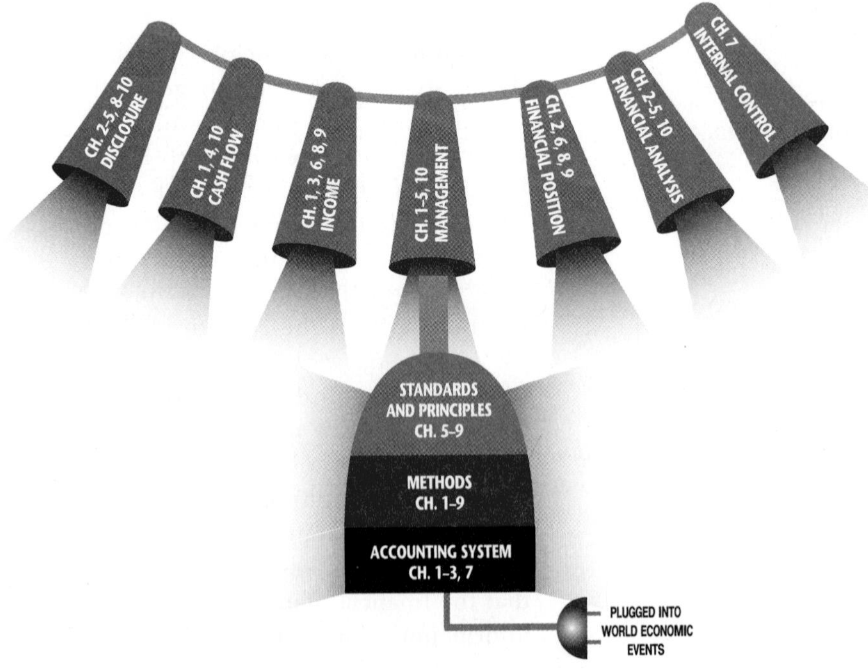

Preparation, use, and concepts are integrated throughout the book.

PREPARATION. Accounting is a complex human activity. Accounting information doesn't just happen; it's produced by people. It is a human creation just as much as a skyscraper, a video, or a sweater is. To be effective users of the information, people need to know something about how and why the information is prepared. Accountants' expertise is all about the how and the why.

CONCEPTS. Users, accountants, and accounting are a connected system. The demand for useful information shapes how financial accounting information is prepared, for example, in producing annual or quarterly performance reports. How accounting is prepared shapes its use, for example, in financial analysis and managerial decisions. Tying accounting all together are the whys: the reasons it is used and prepared, and the principles that lie behind it. Many of these principles are quite interesting and controversial, but they are important in this book not so much for themselves as for the way they explain and connect the preparation with uses.

The *hows* (preparation procedures and techniques), *whys* (concepts and principles), and *uses* (analysis and decisions) of financial accounting are examined throughout this book. Sometimes one of the three concepts is emphasized for a while, but the others are never far removed, because none can stand without the others. See the diagram in Figure 1.2, which links the three concepts.

Accounting uses numbers but requires many skills beyond number work.

Accounting is a challenging discipline that requires many skills: assigning numbers to represent financial phenomena, providing explanations of those numbers, analyzing and verifying others' number work and explanations, understanding the needs of those who use accounting's reports to make decisions, engaging in oral and written communication with the many people involved in an organization's financial activities, having familiarity with computers and other electronic media, and maintaining judgment that is sound, objective, and ethical.

Much of the challenge of accounting is in figuring out which numbers to use, deciding what "story" the numbers should tell. Adding and subtracting the numbers is often the easy part. This challenge makes accounting both easier and harder to learn than you might have thought. Accounting is rooted in business and has its own vocabulary and viewpoints, so don't expect it all to make perfect sense at the beginning. It will take a while for you to acquire a full understanding of accounting and the business world it serves. This understanding will be based on your knowledge of both concepts and techniques, and of the viewpoints of both accountants and the users of accounting.

Accounting is an unfinished human creation, continuing to change as conditions change.

Accounting is a human artifact, an art, a work in progress. It can be viewed up close or from a distance, critically or with enthusiasm. It changes as human tastes and societies change, and, like a kaleidoscope, its shapes and colours change if you twist it a bit. Though referring to a great writer, *The Economist* magazine could have been talking about accounting when it said: "… the saga is not finished. But no work of art ever is."[1] Enjoy this book's exploration of accounting; relax about the occasional difficult parts of accounting, and be prepared to be surprised at how sophisticated your knowledge will become.

FIGURE 1.2

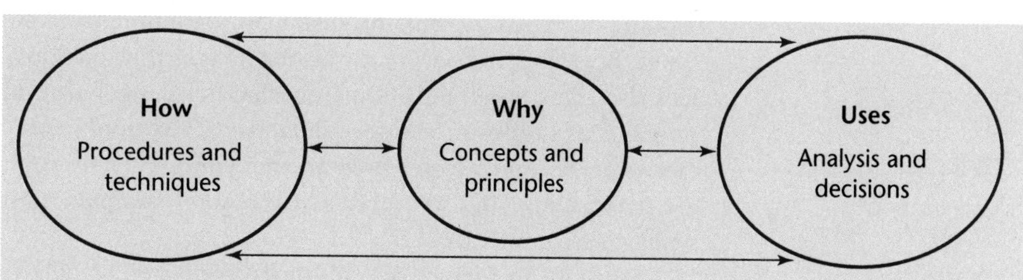

Accounting reports contain many examples of art, humour, and sophisticated design. Chicken producer Tyson Foods structured a recent annual financial report around its cover, which featured a close-up of a chicken crossing the road, and remarks in the report like "Who's Chicken?" The CBC used pictures of its newscasters, puppets, and other radio and TV characters in its financial reports. Big Rock Brewery used pictures of beer bottles and labels to jazz up its numbers, and reported its results using pictures of beer steins. Coors also likes to use pictures of beer bottles, but also uses pictures of fresh Rocky Mountain water. You might enjoy looking at the companies' Web sites to see how they do their financial reporting. Within company sites, try searching under Investor Relations, Investing, Annual Report, and Financial. Tyson is at **www.tyson.com,** CBC is at **www.cbc.ca,** Big Rock is at **www.bigrockbeer.com,** and Coors is at **www.coors.com,** or **www.molsoncoors.com.**

The Book's Organization

The book's chapters are grouped into four parts. This first chapter is an introduction. Chapters 2–5 show you how the financial statements are prepared and why they are prepared (what their uses are). Chapters 6–9 delve into more specific accounting methods and policies that are important to anyone preparing financial statements or trying to understand them. Chapter 10 focuses on financial statement analysis. (It can be covered any time after Chapter 4, when the set of financial statements has been introduced.)

This book's goals are to help you

- understand the subject of financial accounting well enough to be able to use accounting statements and explain them to others; and
- acquire the basics of how accounting works and how to prepare the statements.

Meeting these goals will benefit you whether or not you become an accountant. Nonaccountants are affected by accounting in many ways, as this book will show. For their part, accountants need to know how and why accounting reports are used, as well as how to prepare them. The going will not always be easy, but if you give it your best effort, you may be surprised at the level of understanding you reach.

Now let's turn to the rest of Chapter 1. We'll begin with a business vignette and an outline of what you can expect to get from the chapter. All chapters will start the same way.

1.2 Chapter Introduction: Linking Financial Accounting's Production and Uses

Canada is a large country, sea to sea to sea, as they say. It's essential that we be able to get around our country, but the distances are immense. You can probably think of folk songs, beer commercials, and various images that portray the vastness of Canada. Now, let's also think about the companies that help us get around this country. Three of many possible examples are Air Canada (**www.aircanada.com**), Canadian Pacific Railway (**www.cpr.ca**), and WestJet (**www.westjet.com**). How do you tell how well such companies are performing, and whether each is a good company to invest in or lend to? Here's a manager's comment:

"We have to finance an equipment refit and small expansion project next month. We know what we have to do to operate safely and keep our customers happy, and we hope we know what to do to fend off our competitors. But to raise the money we need,

we have to convince our lenders and investors that putting money into the company is good for them. We have to show that we can perform well with the money we get, and can make enough money to give the lenders and investors the return they expect. It's not easy! To make our case, we have to figure out what revenues and expenses will result from the project, figure out our cash flows so that we know there will be enough cash to pay our bills, and reconcile the various numbers to make sure there aren't any mistakes. And we have to remember to allow for enough margin to pay income tax on the profit we hope to make!"

Learning Objectives

This chapter begins to build your ability to deal with the issues the manager raised. You will learn

- Who the people are in the world of financial accounting: lenders, investors, accountants, managers, and others, and in doing so what the social setting of financial accounting is;
- How financial accounting "filters" the masses of information in the world and selects the data that enter the foundation accounting system (whether the washroom of the bus or plane is clean is very important to customers, but is not part of accounting's data, though accounting certainly shows the results of having unhappy customers);
- How financial accounting goes beyond the exchange of cash to portray the enterprise's economic position and performance;
- How to do some basic "reconciliation" analysis and recognize the impact of income tax on analyses for decision making.

1.3 Financial Accounting

Financial accounting measures an enterprise's performance *over time* and its position (status) *at a point in time*, and does so in Canadian dollars, US dollars, yen, euros, or whatever currency is judged relevant to the enterprise. This measurement of *financial performance* and *financial position* is done for all sorts of enterprises: large and small businesses, governments from local to national levels, universities, charities, churches, clubs, international associations, and many others. The *financial statements*, which are financial accounting's reports, summarize the measurements of financial performance and position in standard ways thought to be useful in evaluating whether the enterprise has done well and is in good shape. These financial statements include **notes** (sometimes dozens of pages) that contain many words of explanation and interpretation in addition to the numbers. For companies listed on stock markets, the financial statements and notes are included in a package of more words and numbers called the *annual report*. (Listed companies report more often than annually, in *quarterly reports* or other "interim" reports.) The statements report on the economic and financial side of things and are largely for the use of people outside the enterprise, such as investors, club members, regulatory agencies, and taxation authorities.

Financial accounting focuses on financial performance, position, and explanation.

In summary,

- *financial performance* means success (or failure!) in generating new resources from day-to-day operations over a period of time;
- *financial position* is the enterprise's set of financial resources and obligations at a point in time;
- *financial statements* are the reports describing financial performance and position;
- *notes* are part of the statements, adding explanations to the numbers;
- *annual* and *quarterly reports* include the statements and notes and much more.

Financial position and financial performance are closely related.

As we will see throughout the book, financial performance and position are highly related. Good performance is likely to lead to a healthy financial position: if you make money at your job, you are more likely to have money in the bank. Furthermore, a healthy financial position facilitates performance: if you have money in the bank, that helps you afford the activities that lead to good performance and avoid the risks and worries that come from being broke. The relation between performance and position, which we will see repeatedly in later chapters, can be illustrated with the diagram in Figure 1.3.

FIGURE 1.3

Performance–Position Relation

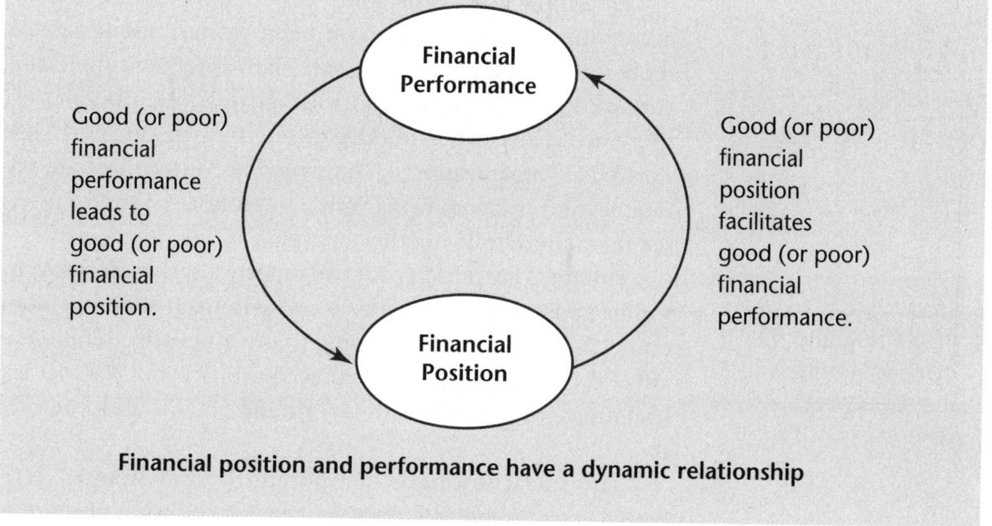
Financial Performance
Good (or poor) financial performance leads to good (or poor) financial position.
Good (or poor) financial position facilitates good (or poor) financial performance.
Financial Position
Financial position and performance have a dynamic relationship

Management accounting focuses on helping managers operate the enterprise.

Another branch of accounting, *management accounting*, is oriented toward helping *managers* and others inside the enterprise, in contrast to financial accounting's more external focus. While management accounting is not examined in this book, students interested in how financial accounting measures managerial performance will find frequent references to the relationship between managers and financial accounting. In the end, all forms of accounting exist to help people, such as managers, investors, bankers, and legislators, make decisions. As the book overview in Section 1.1 portrayed, decision making by management and other users of accounting's reports is important to all aspects of accounting, and is therefore examined throughout this book.

HOW'S YOUR UNDERSTANDING?

Here are two questions you should be able to answer based on what you have just read. If you can't answer them, it would be best to reread the material.

1. What are the two main things that financial accounting measures?
2. How are these two main things connected to each other?

1.4 The Social Setting of Financial Accounting

This book will show you the many ways in which financial accounting has been shaped by the development of business and society. Some of the numerous functions of financial accounting include the following:

- It helps stock market investors decide whether to buy, sell, or hold shares of companies.
- It helps managers run enterprises on behalf of owners, members, or citizens (in addition to the help provided by management accounting and other sources of information).
- It provides basic financial records for the purposes of day-to-day management, control, insurance, and fraud prevention.
- It is used by governments in monitoring the actions of enterprises and in assessing taxes, such as income tax and sales taxes.

We could go on for some time listing major and minor functions of financial accounting. Whole books have been written about each of the many functions! And, though this book emphasizes externally oriented financial accounting for business firms (to avoid overwhelming you with all of accounting's uses at once), don't forget that there are many other organizations that use, and are affected by, accounting. When words like "organization," "company," or "enterprise" are used, the implications often go well beyond business firms. You'll get a taste of those implications in this book and will see them more fully in other courses.

Accounting is active, affected by, and affecting, business and society in general.

Financial accounting for the enterprise, the centre of interest in this book, operates within and serves a complex social setting. It seeks to monitor and report on financial events initiated by or happening to the enterprise. These events come from and, in turn, affect the social setting, so that accounting is not passive: it tells us what is going on, but in doing so it affects our decisions and actions and, therefore, also affects what is going on.

The social setting is composed of many people. There are at least four parties directly concerned with what financial accounting says about the enterprise:

This book focuses mostly on the perspectives of owners, managers, and auditors.

1. the owners (for example, *shareholders* of a *corporation*)
2. the managers, who are running the company on behalf of the owners
3. the external *auditors*, who are employed by the owners to evaluate the accounting reports presented by the managers
4. all levels of government for taxation and regulatory purposes

Shareholders own portions of the corporation—shares that can be bought and sold—but the corporation is a legal entity existing separately from its shareholder owners. Auditors report on the credibility of the enterprise's financial statements on behalf of owners and others.

These parties have relationships with each other, as well as with financial accounting.

Owners, managers, and auditors forge many relationships, including through accounting.

- Managers, for example, may work for a company throughout their careers and, therefore, may have as much a feeling of ownership as do shareholders who may, through buying and selling shares on the stock market, be part owners of the company for only a few months before moving on to another investment.
- In smaller companies, managers and owners may be the same people.
- The external auditors are formally appointed by the owners, for example, at the annual shareholders' meeting, but they work with the managers day-to-day and may also offer advice on tax, accounting, and other topics of practical interest to managers, separately from the knowledge they use in their role as auditors.
- But an enterprise's external auditor is not permitted to be an owner or manager of the enterprise too. This is to ensure that the auditor is financially and ethically independent and can therefore be objective about the enterprise's financial affairs. *Independence* and *objectivity* are fundamental ideas that are encountered frequently in this book.

Many people are involved in financial accounting, but not all necessarily have common interests.

In addition to these three central parties, and often hard to distinguish from them, is a host of other groups, companies, institutions, and parties interested in or having an influence on the company's financial accounting. As we will see many times in this book, these parties do not share the same interest in the company's accounting and may even be in competition or conflict with each other. Most will be in the same country as the company and its management, but, increasingly, companies and other enterprises are operating internationally. So, the other groups interested in and affecting the company's financial accounting may be all over the planet. Let's see a little more about who all these people are.

Accounting and auditing can actually be quite controversial, as you're probably aware from the extensive media coverage given to such recent examples as the Enron bankruptcy in 2001, then the largest bankruptcy in US history, and the subsequent attacks on Enron's auditor, Arthur Andersen LLP. Much of the argument about what went wrong at Enron and Andersen focused on allegations about Enron's accounting methods, and the effects of Enron's business relationships with Andersen on Andersen's objectivity. We'll see more about accounting problems like those at Enron later in the book. Here are just three other examples. (1) IBM's shares lost billions of dollars in value in one day in November 1999 when the company was accused of mixing one-time gains it had made in with its regular operating income. The numbers were right, but it was alleged they were in the wrong place in the report. IBM's accounting troubles did not go away; on April 29, 2002, *Business Week* commented that "convulsions in share prices of General Electric and IBM" earlier that month were "flare-ups" over the companies' accounting **(www.ibm.com)(www.ge.com).** (2) Also in November 1999, conglomerate Tyco International Ltd. lost 23% of its total stock market value in two quick blows, first, on allegations that it was using "accounting gimmicks" to make itself look better than it was, and second, on rumours that the company's auditors, embarrassed by all the fuss, would resign. In the general controversy about accounting that resulted from the collapse of Enron, Tyco's accounting methods have come up for more scrutiny. *Business Week* reported in January 2002 that rumours of an investigation of Tyco's accounting had contributed to a further large drop in Tyco's share price **(www.tyco.com).** (3) Accounting for movies has been as much an art form as making movies for a long time. Many famous movies, seen by zillions of people, haven't made any money for the people who invested in them. Said a commentator: "Some of Hollywood's greatest special effects never make it to the screen. They're found in studio accounting books." [2]

1.5 The People Involved in Financial Accounting

Users: decision makers; Preparers: decision facilitators; Auditors: credibility enhancers.

There are many participants in the art of financial accounting. The main ones are

- the information *users* (the decision makers);
- the information *preparers*, who put the information together to facilitate the users' decision making; and,
- the *auditors*, who assist the users by enhancing the credibility of the information, providing a professional opinion that the information is fair and appropriate.

These groups of people interact with and influence each other, and the dynamics among them shape financial accounting. In turn, financial accounting affects their interests and their behaviour. All these interactions are important to accounting, as the diagram in Figure 1.4 illustrates.

FIGURE 1.4

People and Financial Accounting

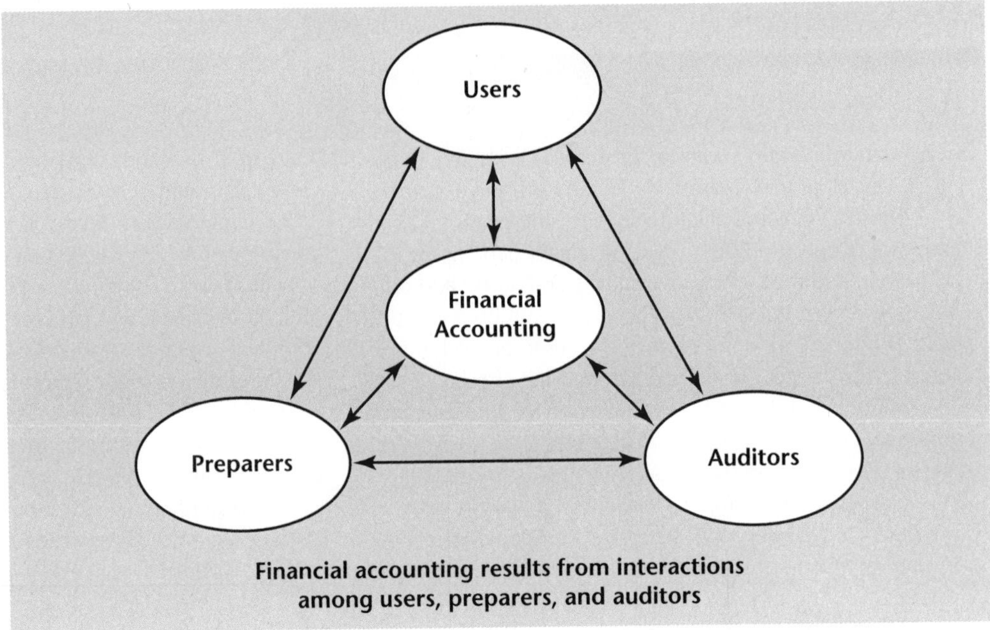
Users
Financial Accounting
Preparers
Auditors
Financial accounting results from interactions among users, preparers, and auditors

Users (Decision Makers)

User demand is the reason financial statements exist

In financial accounting, a user or decision maker is someone who makes decisions on the basis of the financial statements, on his or her own behalf, or on behalf of a company, bank, or other organization. Financial accounting is utilitarian: ultimately, the nature and contents of financial statements are functions of the demand for decision information from users. This is not to say that such people are the only ones who matter in the process, nor are they always clear about what information they need, or necessarily satisfied with what they get. User demand, however, is the fundamental reason for financial statements; therefore, understanding the demand is important.

A user's main demand is for *credible, periodic reporting* of an enterprise's financial position and performance.

Financial accounting supplies a demand for credible, periodic information.

- *Credible* means that the information in the reports (the financial statements) appears to be sufficiently trustworthy and competently prepared for it to be used to make decisions. There is a *cost–benefit* issue here: huge amounts of money could be spent trying to make the reports absolutely perfect, but since that money would have to come out of the enterprise's funds, spending it would make the enterprise's performance and position poorer. Users, such as owners and managers, may not want that to happen, so credibility is a relative condition, not an absolute one. Accounting information has to be worth its cost.
- *Periodic* means that users can expect reports on some regular basis (for example, yearly or quarterly). The longer the wait, the more solid the information is. But waiting a long time for information is not desirable; users are usually willing to accept some imprecision in the information in return for periodic reports with timely, decision-relevant information. As illustrated in the diagram in Figure 1.5, the events in the world are ongoing so accounting information takes a periodic snapshot of events.

FIGURE 1.5

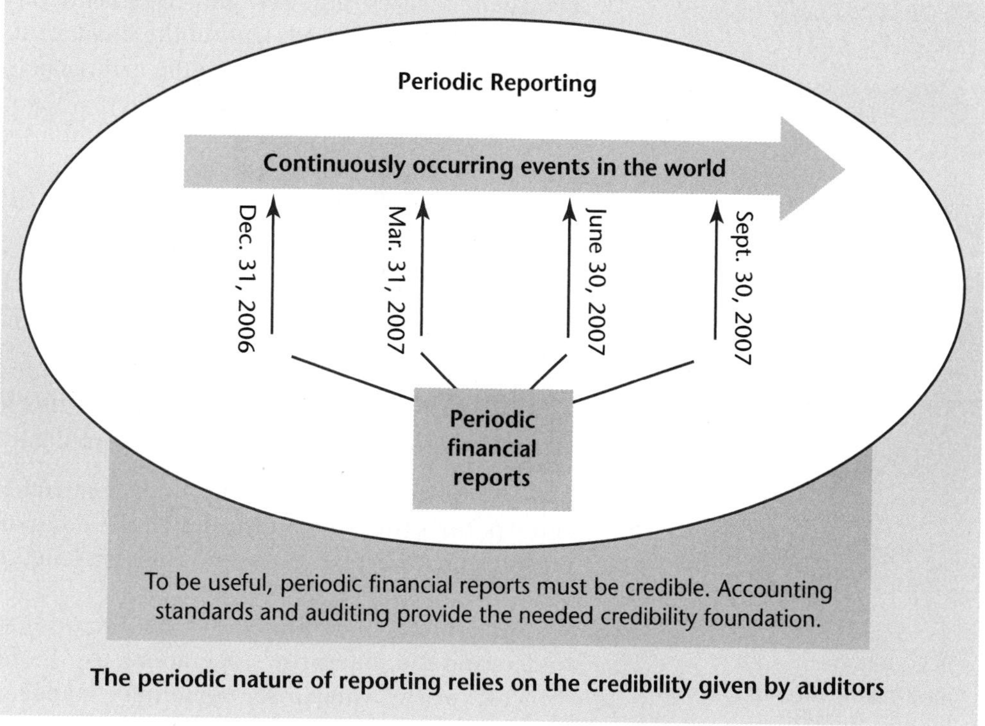

The periodic nature of reporting relies on the credibility given by auditors

The main groups of users are:

Owners: individual business **owners**, such as proprietors, partners, and other entrepreneurs; individual investors (shareholders) in shares on stock markets who can vote on company affairs; companies that invest in other companies; pension plans and other institutions that invest in companies; people with quasi-ownership interests, such as members of clubs or voters in municipalities; and so on.

Owners and potential owners are examples of users with different interests.

Potential owners: people, of the same sort as the owners listed above, who do not at present have a financial interest in the enterprise, but may be considering making an investment. Because potential owners often buy shares from present owners, for example, by trading shares on the *stock market* rather than investing directly, there is often a significant difference in outlook between present owners, who would like to sell their shares for as much as possible, and potential owners, who would like to pay as little as possible. Saying that accounting responds to demands from users does not mean that all the users will have the same demands!

Creditors often have a substantial interest in an enterprise and a say in its decisions.

Creditors and potential creditors: suppliers, banks, bondholders, employees, and others who have lent money to the enterprise, or who are owed funds in return for supplying something of value, or who are considering taking on such a role. *Creditors* do not have the legal control of the enterprise that owners have, but they often have a large say in enterprise decisions, especially if the enterprise gets into difficulty. In cases of extreme difficulty, creditors may have the right to take control of the enterprise from the owners. Sometimes the difference between creditors and owners is hard to discern because it may depend on subtle legalities about who has what rights, and some people may play both roles for a given enterprise; for example, an owner invests money in a business, but also may lend the business further money, becoming a creditor as well.

Managers are very interested in what financial accounting says about their performance.

Managers: those who run the enterprise on behalf of the owners. They have a great interest in the way accounting reports on their activities and results. Often, managers' salaries, bonuses, and the likelihood of staying in their jobs are directly affected by the contents of the financial statements. Especially in small businesses, the owner may also be the main manager.

Employees: nonmanagement employees and their unions or other associations. These groups are interested in the enterprise's ability to pay wages, maintain employment levels, and keep such promises as paying pensions.

Taxation authorities and other government bodies and agencies: groups that may use the financial statements to calculate taxes payable or to evaluate whether the enterprise is following various rules and agreements.

Government stock market regulators, stock exchange administrators, and accounting standard setters: groups that establish rules and regulations affecting accounting and monitor enterprises' compliance with them.

Financial and market analysts: people who study companies' performance and prepare reports for others by analyzing those companies. Analysts often make recommendations about whether to invest, lend, or do neither.

Accounting information intended for one group of users may inform others also.

Competitors: some of the people who get the financial statements may be trying to understand the enterprise's operations for the purpose of making life more difficult for the enterprise. Sometimes managers are reluctant to disclose information to shareholders, for example, because competitors can then also obtain it and act to reduce the enterprise's prospects.

Accounting researchers: people (mostly university professors, but also some based in public accounting firms and other organizations) who study accounting with the objective of understanding it and contributing to its improvement.

Miscellaneous third parties: various other people who may get access to an enterprise's financial statements and use them in various ways. Once statements have been issued, many people may make use of them. Politicians may make judgments about industry efficiency or taxation levels, for example. News reporters may write stories about employment practices. Judges and juries may evaluate enterprises' ability to pay damages in the course of lawsuits.

If you plan to be an accountant, the value of studying financial accounting is clear. It may not be so clear, however, if you have other plans, such as a career in management, marketing, finance, engineering, law, human resources, or production. To provide some perspective for those of you not planning an accounting career, and to help you understand the managers you will work with if you do become an accountant or auditor, comments will be made frequently about managers and financial accounting. Financial accounting is directly relevant to managers because it reports on their performance as decision makers, as caretakers of the enterprise, as representatives of the owners, as legal officers of the enterprise, and so on. Any manager cannot help but be interested in how her or his performance is being measured and in how that performance is analyzed, projected, and evaluated. Managers' bonuses, promotions, dismissals, transfers, and other rewards and penalties are often directly based on the numbers and commentaries prepared by accountants. Every manager should have an intimate understanding of how accounting is measuring his or her performance and should be able to conduct a "reasonableness check" of the information being provided to her or him and have a comfortable understanding of the accounting implications of what is going on.

Financial accounting serves many users with many interests and decisions to make.

Think about all these users and decisions! It is a great challenge to develop one set of periodic financial statements for an enterprise so that they can be useful for all. Perhaps you will not be surprised that there is much controversy about whether financial statements do this well, and whether financial accounting methods serve some users or decisions better than others.

Preparers (Decision Facilitators)

Three main groups are responsible for the information in the financial statements:

Managers are both preparers and users of financial accounting information.

Managers: people responsible for running an enterprise, including issuing accounting and other information and controlling its financial affairs. The fact that managers are also users, vitally interested in the results, has created a fundamental conflict of interest for them and has led to the development of the auditing function, as will be discussed below. Managers, as a group, are often referred to as "management."

Bookkeepers and clerks: those who, under the direction of management, keep the enterprise's basic records and create the data upon which financial accounting is built. Many bookkeeping and clerical functions are now performed by computers with all the benefits and frustrations those machines provide.

Professional accounting designations include CA, CGA, CMA, and CPA.

Accountants: people whose job it is to shape the financial statements by applying the principles of accounting to the enterprise's records under the direction of management. Many *accountants* are members of professional societies and are accredited as CAs (chartered accountants), CGAs (certified general accountants), CMAs (certified management accountants), and CPAs (certified public accountants, the largest group in the United States). Often, accountants and their societies also have auditing experience and interests, and sometimes auditing roles, but the task of preparing the financial statements is quite different in principle from the task of verifying those statements once they are prepared.

Auditors (Credibility Enhancers)

Professional accountants may act as accountants or auditors—very different roles.

Auditors have the job of assisting the users by providing their professional opinion that the financial statements have been prepared fairly, competently, and in a manner consistent with accepted principles. The auditing role is a very old one, arising because users demanded some assurance that managers' reports on their performance were not self-serving, biased, or downright untruthful. This book refers frequently to *external auditors*, who report on the financial statements on behalf of external users, but there are also *internal auditors*, who work within the enterprise to support the credibility of information being used by management, and other auditors (such as tax auditors, who verify taxpayers' computation of tax). While external auditors may be asked for advice in preparing the statements, especially for small companies, they must avoid responsibility for the statements because their role is to scrutinize the preparation process. They cannot credibly audit statements they have prepared! (Professional accountants often do prepare financial statements, but in doing so they are not acting as external auditors, and they should make this clear in covering letters and footnotes attached to the statements.)

External auditors are expected to be objective and expert professionals.

The external auditor's role falls between those of the preparer and the user, so he or she must be acceptable to both. Such acceptability is helped if the auditor is an independent professional who will collect his or her fee whether the financial results are good or bad—or whether the managers or users are happy or unhappy. The external auditing function is considered so important that the right to perform it is usually restricted to members of recognized professional accountants' societies who have auditing expertise and experience.

Public accounting firms offer a wide range of services beyond external auditing.

External auditors may work alone, but most work with other auditors in *public accounting firms*. Some of these firms are very large, having thousands of partners and other senior people, tens of thousands of employees, and offices in many cities and countries. Public accounting firms offer their clients not only external auditing, but also "consulting" advice on income tax, accounting, computer systems, and other issues. In offering such other advice to enterprises that they also audit, public accountants are not supposed to get so involved that they are in effect auditing their own work, or creating any conflict-of-interest problems. Managing this requires considerable professional skill and attention to ethics and rules of professional conduct, and whether this is being done successfully is a matter of much controversy at present. Beginning in 2000 to 2001, large US companies were required to disclose how much they pay their auditors for auditing and for various kinds of consulting. These disclosures indicated that many companies paid their auditors much more for consulting than to be auditors. Can auditors be independent scrutineers when there is more money in being consultants? In March 2002, for example, *Business Week* reported a survey of top financial managers indicating that many managers thought auditors of a company should not also be consultants to the company.[3] In December 2003 chartered accountants voted to adopt new, more rigorous independence requirements. Intended to ensure auditor independence, the new standard prohibits the provision of certain non-audit services to audit clients. These non-audit services include bookkeeping, valuation, actuarial, internal audit outsourcing, IT design or implementation, HR functions, and corporate finance activities.[4]

Figure 1.6 shows the accounting flow among the people involved. The information starts with the preparers, who fashion periodic financial statements from the underlying data, then the auditors add credibility to the statements, which are then provided to the many users.

FIGURE 1.6

People Involved in Financial Accounting

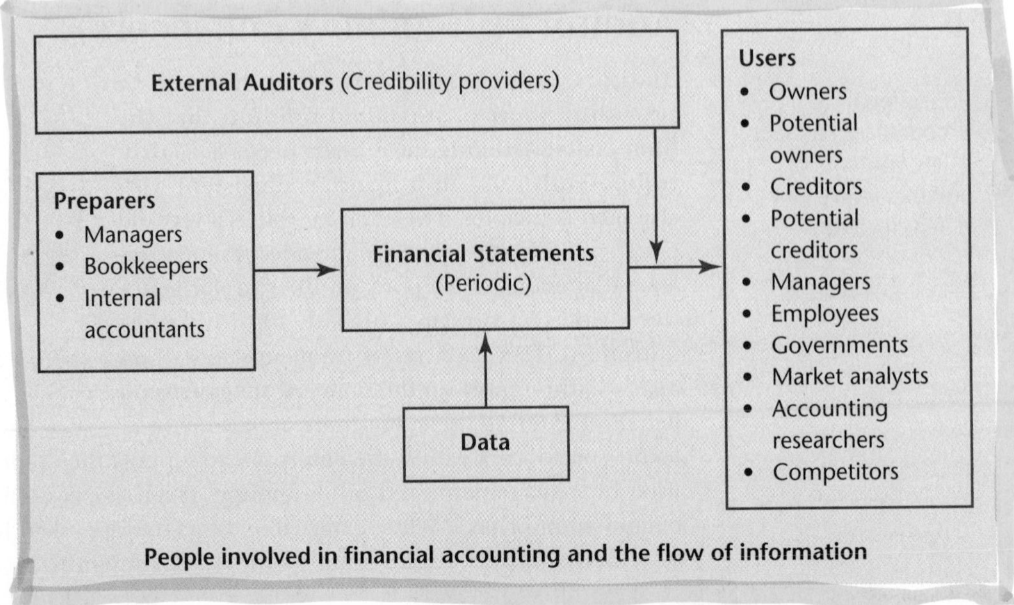

People involved in financial accounting and the flow of information

People and Ethics

Should the financial statements provide information that could damage the enterprise?

Ethics, mentioned above, will be raised throughout this book. Ethical issues can arise in just about any area of accounting. Here are some examples, all of them real:

- An enterprise has been sued by a recently fired employee, who claims that the firing was based on the employee's age and so broke employment laws. The enterprise's president denies any impropriety. The enterprise's chief accountant, who personally feels the former employee's claim is justified, has suggested to the boss that the lawsuit should be mentioned in a note to the financial statements, so that users of the statements will know there is a potential for loss if the former employee wins. The president feels the chief accountant should ignore the lawsuit in preparing the financial statements to avoid embarrassment and the appearance of admitting guilt. The president fears that such an apparent admission could be used against the enterprise in court and so could cause the enterprise to lose the lawsuit. What should the chief accountant do?
- While doing the audit, another enterprise's external auditor learns that the enterprise may have been cheating one of its customers. The customer, who is unaware of this and quite happy with things, is another client of the auditor. The auditor, who is bound by rules of conduct designed to protect the confidentiality of information gained during the audit, knows that saying anything to anyone could result in lawsuits in all directions. Should the auditor just keep quiet about what was found?
- A third enterprise's president is paid a bonus each year, calculated as a percentage of the enterprise's income. The president is considering a proposed change in an accounting method that, among other things, will raise income and increase the president's bonus. So the proposal would put money in the president's pocket. Should the president refuse to implement the accounting change, or request that the bonus calculation ignore the change, or just go ahead and enjoy the higher bonus?

What if the auditor's responsibilities to different clients conflict?

Should managers implement an accounting method that makes them better off?

These illustrative problems do not have easy answers, so none are offered at this point. They are dilemmas for the chief accountant, the auditor, and the president. This book will address ethical issues from time to time and so help you sharpen your ethical sense along with your accounting knowledge, for the two are inseparable.

In an effort to understand and help with problems, many people conduct research into accounting issues, such as: choosing appropriate accounting methods; maintaining auditor independence; stock market responses to accounting information; disputes about accounting among contending parties; exercising professional judgment about accounting; ethics of professional accountants; history of accounting methods; social issues, such as the role of women in accounting; practical solutions to computing management bonuses and other performance incentives; income tax calculation; and even the use of graphs and pictures in accounting reports. A lot of *accounting research* is going on and there are many accounting research journals with titles such as *Accounting, Organizations and Society, The Accounting Review, Contemporary Accounting Research, Journal of Accounting and Economics*, and *Journal of Accounting Research*. In this book, references to helpful research results are often made.

HOW'S YOUR UNDERSTANDING?

Here are two questions you should be able to answer based on what you have just read. If you can't answer them, it would be best to reread the material.

1. Who is a "user" of financial reports, and why would such a person want them?
2. What is the difference between a "preparer" and an "auditor," why is the difference important, and where does company management fit into the picture?

1.6 An Example: Grades

To outline how financial accounting works, let's use an analogy: the example of students going to university and getting grades for their efforts. The parallel with financial accounting isn't exact, but it will illustrate the main issues.

Students go to university to learn, among other reasons, and they get grades as a measure of their learning. Grades are not a perfect measure of learning, but they are a very important part of the process in modern universities.

Grades are used, for better or worse.

- Grades are used by the students themselves and by others, including parents and university administrators, to assess students' knowledge at various stages and to monitor their performance over time. They are also used by employers to predict future job performance, by scholarship agencies to allocate awards, and so on. Many good and bad things can happen because of a student's grades, even though the student and other people who use grades may feel that they are not necessarily the best measure of learning.

Grades have standard features thought to make them more useful.

- Grade reports come out at standard times of the year and in standard formats, and preparing them occupies much of professors' time. Great effort goes into minimizing error and fraud. For example, official transcripts are prepared carefully and certified so that anyone using them can be confident that they have not been tampered with.

Grades may affect students' learning choices; they don't just report on results.

- Because grades are important, students may choose courses and make other choices in the expectation that these choices will mean better grades, whether or not they care much about what they are learning. Sometimes the grades, which are only supposed to reflect the learning, seem so important that they drive the system instead!

Here are some parallels between the grade example and financial accounting:

1. The student is in university to learn about particular topics, but not only for that reason. Similarly, businesses and other organizations are concerned about the financial position and performance accounting measures, but not only those.
2. Learning has many dimensions, and course grades represent only some of them. Financial performance and position also have many dimensions. Financial accounting keeps track of several of these dimensions, but not all. They are not perfect, but grades and financial accounting have been with us for a long time and continue to be important.
3. Grades are measures of performance. Good grades may be used to predict good performance in the future. In accounting, good financial performance is expected to accumulate to provide a healthy financial position, and a healthy financial position is expected to lead to good subsequent performance. While they are useful to have, such expectations do not always work out, either for students or enterprises.

Grades and financial accounting are information systems with many parallels.

4. Like grades and grade reports, which summarize the results of many tests, projects, and other activities, financial accounting's reports (financial statements) are summaries of a large number of individual events. In a course, the final exam may matter more than the term paper does in calculating the course grade. In accounting, too, some events may be more important than others in compiling the financial report.
5. Knowing how employers, student loan offices, graduate schools, parents, students, and others use grade transcripts helps us to understand why they are as they are. Similarly, the use of financial accounting's reports must be understood to appreciate the role they play. A company president may be just as anxious about how people will interpret and use an accounting report as a student is about people's reaction to a grade transcript. Factors like career prospects and salary may be in the minds of both president and student.

6. Grade transcripts summarize the student's performance over specific periods of time, such as the school year. Comparisons to performance in other years are made easier by the format of the transcripts. Financial statements also appear at regular intervals (at least once a year and often on a quarterly or even monthly basis) and are prepared using a fairly standard format to increase their usefulness as a tool of comparison for different companies or the same company in different years. Grades may appear in slightly different formats, such as a four-point scale, percentage, or letter grade, just as the financial statements of companies are adapted to individual circumstances. Both offer consistent and comparable measures of results within the university or company, but sometimes create problems when comparing grades against the standards of other universities, or comparing financial statements against other companies or industries.
7. Much trouble is taken to minimize error and fraud in both grading and the preparation of financial statements. So that people may rely on the statements, auditors verify that they are prepared in a fair manner and in accordance with accepted principles.
8. It is unfortunate, but understandable, that some students choose courses not because they will learn much, but because a high grade can be easily obtained. Because financial statements are so important, some managers similarly seem to worry more about making their accounting numbers look good than about running the business properly. They may avoid investing in long-term projects or research and development that may hurt short-term results but create longer-term benefits.

HOW'S YOUR UNDERSTANDING?

Here are two questions you should be able to answer based on what you have just read. If you can't answer them, it would be best to reread the material.

1. Why are students interested in the grades they receive for courses taken?
2. What are some parallels between students' interest in grades and people's interest in accounting reports?

1.7 Financial Accounting's Transactional Filter

Accounting is an information system, filtering and summarizing data.

Accounting is an *information system* to filter and summarize data. Information systems select observations from the world, collect those results into data banks, and organize and summarize the data to produce specific kinds of information. This is useful because decision makers cannot cope with masses of raw, unorganized observations, and it is economically efficient to have one system organize data into information on behalf of various users.

Information systems are choosy, designed to select and present relevant data.

An everyday example of filtering and summarizing is the daily newspaper: the editors group stories and features so that you know where to look for what you want. There's a sports section, an entertainment section, a page for letters to the editor, and so on. No newspaper contains exactly what you want, but it gets close enough to what most people want so that it can be published at a low cost compared to what it would cost you to hire reporters to get information just for you. In order to make this work, every information system has to be choosy; it has to filter all the available data and pick what is relevant to its purpose. You don't expect the newspaper or accounting reports to contain glossy reproductions of Rembrandt paintings suitable for framing or to print the grades you got in your university courses; you go to other information sources for such things.

An information system such as financial accounting is inherently limited. It can report only what its sensors pick up as it seeks out or filters data from the mass of ongoing events. No information system tells you "*the truth*" and certainly not "*the whole truth*"; it passes along information based on the data it has been designed or permitted to gather as data.[5] See Figure 1.7.

- The gaps in the wall are the system's filter or "window on the world."
- Once a piece of raw data is admitted, it is recorded and stored in a bank of data (in accounting it is stored on paper or in computerized files with names like accounts, ledgers, journals, the *books*, which we will learn about later).
- The data in this bank are then organized to produce usable information (financial statements and reports).
- Users receive and interpret the information that has been funnelled from a large number of events into concise statements.

In accounting, we generally refer to the left part of the diagram, the data recording and some routine classifying and summarizing, as "*bookkeeping*." We refer to the right part, the turning of data into information for users, as "accounting" or "reporting." Financial accounting information is contained in the system's final product, the financial statements and notes.

The transaction is financial accounting's window on the world.

Accounting reports are based on and limited by the data collected. Therefore, if you are to understand the reports, you have to understand how accounting filters, notices, and chooses events to record into its data bank. Financial accounting's filter, its window on the world, is the *transaction. Generally*, if an event is a transaction, it is recorded into financial accounting's database; if it is not, the routine accounting system ignores the event. (Later on, we will see how accounting can incorporate some kinds of nontransactional data.)

The following are examples of accounting transactions. They should be recorded routinely by the financial accounting system.

The financial accounting system should record transactions routinely.

a. The payroll department issued a cheque to pay an employee.
b. A customer paid, in cash, an account owing since last month and gets a receipt.
c. A sales clerk prepared an invoice for a customer for the sale of goods the customer took with her and promised to pay for.
d. The head cashier deposited the day's receipts into the bank.
e. The stockroom received a shipment of spare parts for the delivery trucks, along with an invoice from the parts supplier.

There is no limit to the number or kinds of transactions that human ingenuity can devise. Accounting has to deal with them, and must change as they change. Nowadays, many companies are scrambling to handle Internet transactions, those happening through Web pages and other areas of *e-commerce*, all of which are promising to fundamentally change many accounting systems. Transactions are partly defined by the legal

FIGURE 1.7

Accounting's Transactional Filter

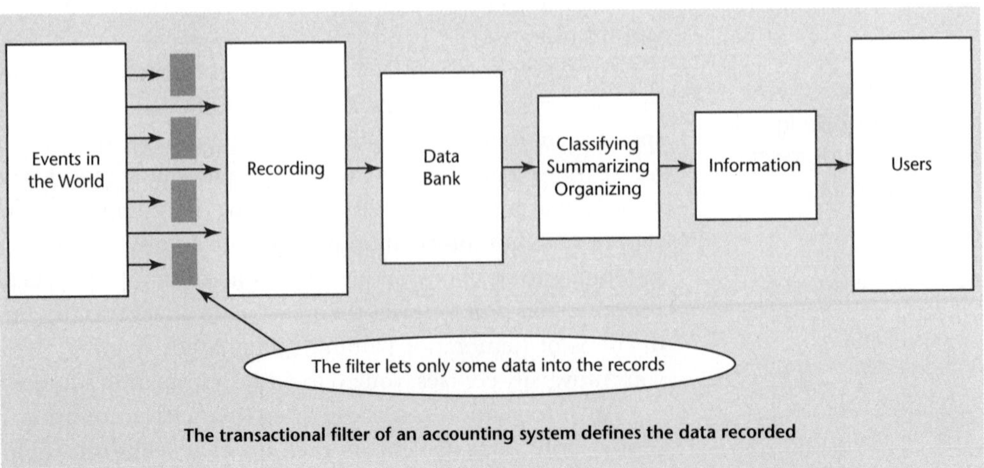

The transactional filter of an accounting system defines the data recorded

and economic system. In our society, promises to pay can be enforced in the courts, so they are considered transactions, as in example (c) above. Speaking very roughly, there are two general kinds of transactions important in accounting—*cash transactions*, in which cash is exchanged immediately, and *credit transactions*, in which there is a promise to exchange cash in the future.

Events that are not transactions will not be recorded routinely, if at all.

The following are examples of events that are *not* accounting transactions and that will therefore *not* be recorded routinely, if at all, by the accounting system.

i. The president of the company broke her leg while skiing.
ii. The credit department manager decided that a particular customer is probably never going to pay the account the customer owes.
iii. The main warehouse burned to the ground overnight.
iv. A customer ordered a machine to be delivered next month.
v. Real estate reports indicate the company's land has gone up in value by 14% since last year.

The transactional records can be "adjusted" to incorporate nontransactional data.

Some such events may be brought into the system by special *adjustments* to the routine recording system that we will learn about later. Events (ii) and (iii) are examples. But many are never included in financial accounting's information system. Event (i) is an example. Other events are recorded only after something more has happened. Event (iv) is recorded by the accounting system only when the machine is delivered, and in Canadian accounting, event (v) is recorded only if the land has been sold. (Some countries, such as Australia and the United Kingdom, have permitted such events to be reported in financial statements.)

Some large or innovative companies have accounting systems that routinely record events that are not transactions, which other or smaller companies ignore or leave to be done as special adjustments. Examples of nontransactions recorded by some companies are internal transfers of goods from department to department in the company, changes in the market values of investments, estimated income earned on partially completed construction contracts, and revisions in estimates for warranty payments. These may be included for various reasons; for example, other information systems in the company provide the necessary data, or management believes more finely tuned accounting information to be useful in internal decision making.

What distinguishes accounting transactions, such as those in the first list above, from the sorts of events in the second list? All of those in the second list may be important economically, but they are not routinely recorded by the accounting system. In order to qualify as a financial accounting transaction, an event must normally have *all five* of the following characteristics:

Three fundamental economic and legal characteristics

1. *Exchange:* the event must involve an *exchange* of goods, money, financial instruments (such as cheques or bonds), legal promises, or other items of economic value.
2. *Past:* The exchange must have *happened*, even if just seconds ago (financial accounting is essentially a historical information system).
3. *External:* the exchange must have been between the entity being accounted for and someone else, such as a customer, an owner, a supplier, an employee, a banker, or a tax collector (the exchange must have been across the entity's boundary, so to speak).

Two supplementary characteristics, needed for accounting's recordkeeping

Financial accounting transaction: exchange, past, external, evidence, dollars.

4. *Evidence:* there must be some documentation of what has happened (on paper, or electronically recorded).
5. *Dollars:* the event must be measurable in dollars, or the currency unit relevant in the country where the transaction happens.

The following transaction characteristics indicate the nature and value of financial accounting information:

Transactions are based on the legal and economic concept of exchange.

- First, transactions are linked to the legal and economic concept of an *exchange*: completing a contract by giving or receiving consideration in return for goods or services. The transactional basis of financial accounting thus has roots in the fundamental legal and economic processes by which society and business operate. It is no accident that accounting recognizes as transactions events that have a broader legal and business importance too. Transactions are the basis of financial accounting as a historical information system.
- Second, they constitute a large part of the underlying rationale for the *historical cost* basis of accounting, which is firmly founded on the transaction. If a transaction has *happened*, it should be in the accounting system and in the financial statements. It is history. If it has not happened, it is not the same sort of legal event and will not be in the historical accounting system. We can figure out how to get some events that have not happened into accounting anyway, but they often do not fit in well and can be controversial because reasonable people often disagree about whether and how to bring them in.
- Third, the characteristics of the transaction provide the basis on which the records can be verified (audited) later as part of the process of ensuring that the accounting information is credible. Events that do not have these characteristics would be difficult to verify later, and therefore inevitably lack credibility as measures of financial performance or position.

Transactions are documented and therefore make verifiable accounting records.

Let's look at the events from the first list above (list a–e, page 24) and see if they fit the set of transaction characteristics:

	Exchange	Past	External party	Evidence	Dollars
a.	money	yes	employee	cheque	cheque
b.	money	yes	customer	receipt	cash
c.	goods, promise	yes	customer	invoice	price
d.	money	yes	bank	deposit slip	cash
e.	goods, promise	yes	supplier	invoice	price

The events in the second list (i–v, page 25) lack several characteristics, especially that they are not past economic exchanges. Event (iv), for example, is not yet an exchange; the machine hasn't been delivered.

HOW'S YOUR UNDERSTANDING?

Here are two questions you should be able to answer based on what you have just read. If you can't answer them, it would be best to reread the material.

1. Why is a "transaction" important in financial accounting?
2. How do we distinguish transactions from events that are not transactions?

1.8 Demonstration Problem: Transactions

Use the five transaction criteria to determine whether each of the following events would be recorded routinely by Inglewood Electronics Inc.'s accounting system:

1. A customer brought back a faulty TV set and got a credit towards buying another TV.
2. Inglewood Electronics had a new sales promotion of "Buy Now and Don't Pay for Six Months." A customer bought a new car stereo system and had it installed immediately.
3. A hacker invaded the company's Web site and sent crazy messages to anyone using the site.
4. A customer agreed to buy a DVD player for cash as soon as the sales manager agreed to the price the customer wanted to pay.
5. The company received a loan of $350,000 from a bank toward an expansion and renovation of its existing store. The loan will be paid back over 10 years.
6. A judge awarded a settlement of $1,500 to Tom Loudish after he sued Inglewood Electronics claiming the company's "Battle of the Bands" event violated city noise regulations and damaged his hearing. In the original lawsuit, Tom had sought $3,000 from the company.
7. An employee used company cash to bribe an electrical inspector to ignore a problem in the company warehouse.
8. In writing, the company promised a customer who had just bought a new home entertainment system that it would provide a 100% warranty on the system as part of the deal.

Answers:

1. Yes, it should be recorded routinely. The customer is an external party, and the faulty TV and promise of future credit are an exchange that has happened. There would have to be evidence, such as a note, that specified how many dollars of credit the customer had toward another TV.
2. Yes, such an event would be a transaction since the customer is an external party, the car stereo system has been exchanged, and there is a promise to pay in the future. There would be evidence of this promise to pay, such as a bill or other document, signifying payment is required in six months.
3. No, such an event would lie outside accounting's domain, even if serious. There is no exchange as the company has not given the hacker anything, and there would be no routine document specifying the dollar amount of damage. The cost of fixing the Web site would be a subsequent transaction, as would any cash the company got later from suing the hacker.
4. No, the exchange has not been completed, and there is as yet no dollar amount to assign to the event. Agreeing to the dollar amount and exchanging the player for cash are still to come.
5. Yes, this is a transaction because the company has received the full amount of the loan for renovation and promises to repay. An external party has supplied the loan and it is measurable in dollars. The future loan payments are not yet recorded as transactions.
6. Yes, the judge's awarding the $1,500 settlement is a transaction since the event occurred in the past, and, by law, there is a promise for Inglewood Electronics to pay Tom Loudish. The original $3,000 claim would not have been recorded as a transaction since the amount of the settlement was not certain at that time. The outcome of the lawsuit is necessary for a transaction to occur.
7. Yes, this should be recorded. Company cash was used, creating an exchange between it and the inspector. The exchange was cash for "helping" the company, as

the employee saw it. Documentation of the dollar amount might be difficult, but if the company had a good internal control system (Chapter 7), the employee would have had to fill in some sort of document in order to get the cash. Accounting takes no moral position here: the whole thing may have been illegal or immoral, but it was still a transaction. Determining legality or morality would be a separate process. However, the dishonesty involved might cause the transaction to be recorded misleadingly, for example, as a donation or repair expense.

8. This is a difficult one. It is a proper economic exchange between the company and the external party in that the warranty promise is part of the value the customer got in exchange for agreeing to buy the system. There is evidence of the warranty, but the value of the warranty is likely unknown until the warranty period has expired. The lack of a dollar figure would cause the warranty part of the exchange to be left out of the routine accounting system. To reflect such warranties, someone would have to estimate their value once in a while and record them as "adjustments" in preparing financial statements.

Here is a summary of the eight examples using the five transactional criteria. The summary allows you to trace why events 1, 2, 5, 6, and 7 are transactions and why the other events do not meet the criteria, at least not yet.

Exchange	Past	External party	Evidence	Dollars
1. TV for credit note	yes	customer	credit note	value of TV
2. stereo for promise	yes	customer	purchase document	stereo price
3. no	yes	hacker	damage to Web site	unknown
4. not yet	yes	customer	none yet	none yet
5. money for promise	yes	bank	loan document	cash
6. legal requirement	yes	customer	judge's ruling	judge's ruling
7. "service" for money	yes	electrical inspector	payment record?	bribe amount
8. promise for money	yes	customer	warranty card	none yet

1.9 Accrual Accounting

Financial accounting must deal with large amounts of data, not all of it clear or complete.

Financial accounting's task of producing financial statements is a complex one. For even a small business, thousands of transactions have to be recorded and their financial effects evaluated. For large corporations like Inco, McDonald's, Bank of Montreal, Wal-Mart, and Toyota, or organizations like the University of Calgary, the City of New York, the United Nations, or the Red Cross, the number of transactions runs into the millions or billions. Frequently, when the time comes to prepare the financial statements, transactions have not been completed, are in dispute, or have an otherwise unclear status.

Here are examples in which appropriate figures may be difficult to determine:

- The University of Calgary provides courses in return for tuition from students. This meets the criteria for transactions we saw in the previous two sections. But figuring out who owes how much, when, and which students might not get around to paying, and allowing for course cancellations, etc., is very complicated. The transactional records are really only the starting point for figuring out the university's revenue from tuition.
- The value of Inco's supply of nickel ore depends on the cost of digging it out, smelting and finishing it, and on international nickel prices that can vary significantly from day to day.

- The value of the Bank of Montreal's loans to foreign governments (that is, the money actually to be received back from those loans) depends on the health of the borrowing countries' economies, stability in international money transfer arrangements (often disrupted by wars, politics, and natural disasters), and the relative values of various countries' currencies, which, like nickel prices, can fluctuate from day to day.

Important business complexities must somehow be fitted into financial statements.

To cope with these complexities, financial accounting for most businesses and organizations uses the *accrual accounting* approach to financial accounting. This means that in preparing the financial statements, attempts are made to

Accrual accounting's objective is to provide economically meaningful information.

- include all the cash receipts and payments that have already happened,
- incorporate future cash receipts and payments that should be expected based on existing transactions (such as the lawsuit payment in the previous section),
- measure the value of incomplete transactions (such as the warranty in the previous section),
- estimate figures when exact amounts are unknown, and generally make an economically meaningful assessment of awkward problems.

Accrual accounting thus builds on the transactional records to produce a more complete measure of financial performance and position. The simplest transactional records are just cash receipts and payments, and accrual accounting's basic job is to incorporate economically meaningful information beyond cash transactions. Some of that information, such as the customer's promise to pay, is already in the transactional record, but needs a review to see if the promise is still valid. Other information, such as wear and tear on the company's equipment or the company's promise to honour warranties, may not be in the transactional records at all. Figure 1.8 illustrates accrual accounting's task. For example:

- Someone analyzes the University of Calgary's tuition cash receipts and course records and estimates how much has been earned from courses fully or partly taught, and how much of the students' promised tuition might not be collected.
- Someone determines from the cash transaction records how much money Inco spent on nickel ore and from other records how much it cost Inco to produce nickel, and estimates whether nickel prices are higher or lower than Inco's cost to produce more nickel, in order to determine whether Inco's supply of nickel is worth what it cost to produce.
- Someone studies the loan repayment transactional records for various countries for the Bank of Montreal and estimates how much money the bank will be able to collect, in order to judge the value of the bank's uncollected loans.

Accrual accounting uses estimates and judgment to produce meaningful information.

Accrual accounting has been developed because financial statements cannot be based just on the routine accounting records of what has happened. Measuring economic performance is more complex than that, and the appropriate measures can be elusive, or can depend on one's point of view. Many augmentations to the transactional record (estimates, adjustments, judgments, and verbal explanations) must be made so that the statements will be meaningful. The resulting statements, therefore,

FIGURE 1.8

Accrual Accounting Builds On Transactional Records

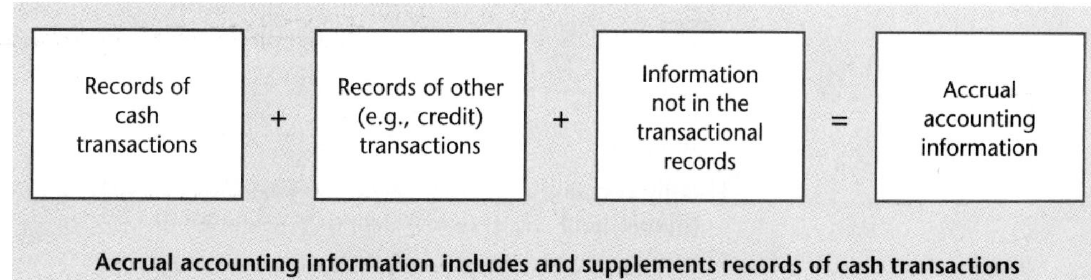

depend to a great extent on the quality and fairness of such augmentations. Managers, accountants, and auditors must use their judgment constantly.

Financial statements are meaningful and useful, and therefore not necessarily precise.

Financial accounting, because it relies on many judgments, is far more imprecise than most people, even many regular users of financial statements, realize. To help you understand the reality of modern financial accounting, much time must be spent on the real-life imprecision of preparing and using financial statements. Accrual accounting is therefore the presumed method in this book, though there will be some comparisons between it and simple cash-based accounting. Modern financial accounting starts with cash receipts and payments and then builds a very large accrual accounting process *in addition to* the cash records in order to provide the sophisticated measures of financial performance and position that today's world demands.

The chart in Figure 1.9 summarizes and gives examples of the way accrual accounting information is assembled. The foundation is cash transactions, which even the simplest accounting records include. Most accounting systems also include credit transactions, because most enterprises extend credit to customers and/or use credit from their suppliers and employees. Short-term and long-term adjustments are needed in preparing financial statements, unless the company's accounting system is sophisticated enough to have already built those in (some are, though there are always new issues to be dealt with as the world keeps changing). Finally, extensive narrative and supplementary disclosures (especially the "notes" to the financial statements) are made, sometimes using many more pages than the statements themselves do. The result is that accrual accounting is a very complex information system, and it will take the rest of this book to introduce you to it properly.

FIGURE 1.9

Accrual Accounting

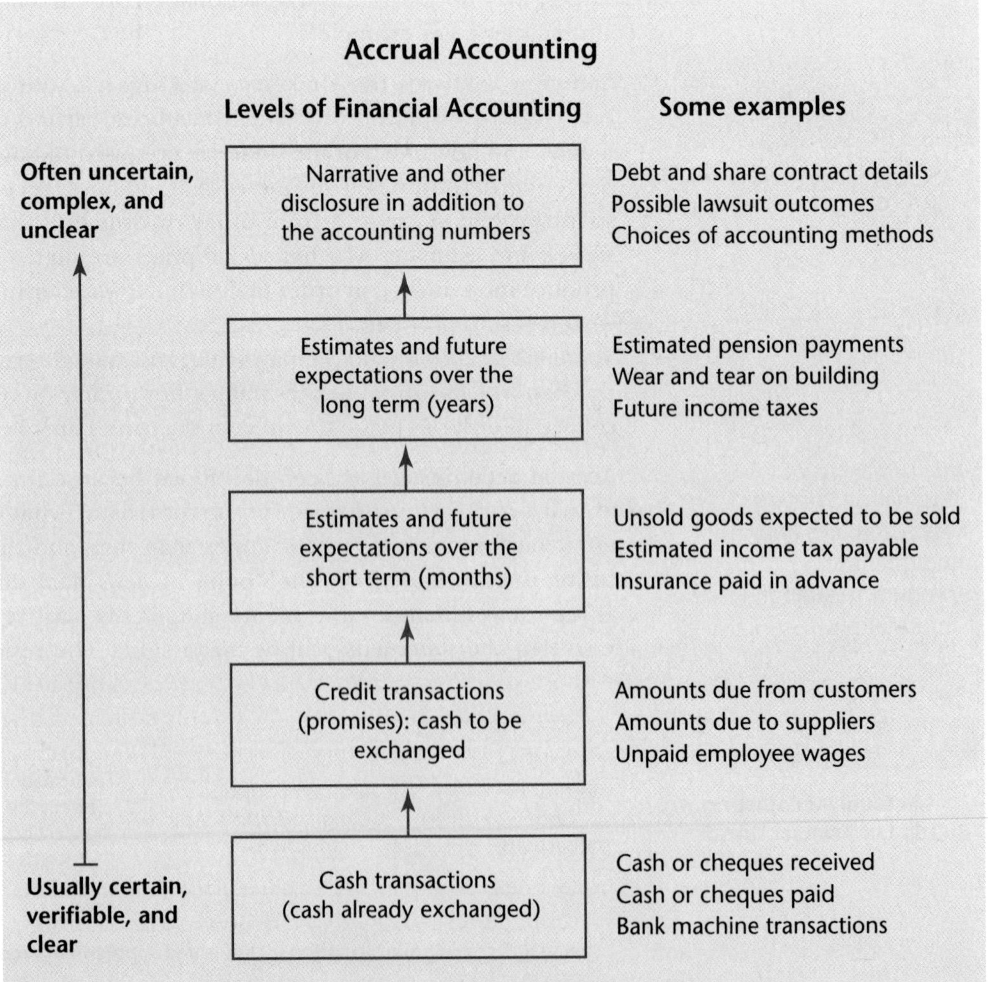

HOW'S YOUR UNDERSTANDING?

Here are two questions you should be able to answer based on what you have just read. If you can't answer them, it would be best to reread the material.

1. Does accrual accounting ignore cash transactions, or, instead, build on the record of them?
2. Why is accrual accounting thought necessary even though a record of transactions already exists?

1.10 An Accrual Accounting Example: Simone's Jewellery Business

Here is an example of how accrual accounting works. The example is of a small business, one you should be able to imagine easily, but the accounting issues it raises are exactly the same as those faced by big businesses.

Simone works in an office during the day, but in the evenings and on weekends she makes silver jewellery in a studio she has set up in her basement. The jewellery is sold in local craft stores, and Simone keeps a separate bank account to deposit the cash from her sales and to pay the bills for supplies.

Financial statements must be fitted to each business's circumstances.

Accounting is a way of portraying an enterprise. Another portrayal is a visual image: try to picture her working in her studio, driving around to craft stores to deliver her products and collect cash, and relaxing with her friends when things are going well. It is important that accounting's reports be consistent with the reality of her business, so keep the image in mind as this example develops.

Simone's accrual income for 2006, her first year in business:

Cash income equals cash receipts minus cash payments for day-to-day business events.

Last year, 2006, was Simone's first year in business, and she received $4,350 in cash from the craft stores for sales of her jewellery and paid $1,670 in cash for silver and for other supplies and expenses. How much money did she make from her business in 2006? Well, a simple, understandable answer is that she made a *cash income* of $2,680 ($4,350 cash collected, minus $1,670 cash paid out). Her bank balance increased by that amount during the year.

The notion behind accrual accounting is that the simple calculation is too simple, that it really does not properly measure what Simone accomplished during the year. Accrual accounting tries to take into account a number of things, such as the following:

Accrual accounting: uncollected sales.

- At the end of 2006, Simone was still owed $310 for sales by one craft store because the owner had been out when she stopped by. The store paid her a few weeks later, but shouldn't that amount be counted as revenue and therefore income for the year the sales were made? It was a credit transaction in that year, not a cash transaction. The amount was legally owed to Simone at the end of the year and she expected to collect the cash.

Accrual accounting: unused goods.

- At the end of the year, Simone had supplies and both finished and unfinished jewellery on hand that had cost $280. These were paid for during the year, but because they will be used to produce sales in the next year, shouldn't their cost be deducted next year instead? This is an example of a short-term expectation represented by the middle box of Figure 1.9. Simone expects to be able to use the supplies and sell the jewellery, and this expectation should be taken into account, because otherwise the economic value represented by the goods would not be recognized.

Accrual accounting: unpaid bills.

- At the end of the year, Simone had some unpaid bills for business **expenses** totalling $85. She paid those early in the next year, but aren't they really expenses for the year in which she incurred them, rather than for the year in which she paid them?

She has bills for these so they represent other credit transactions, only this time involving promises by Simone to pay her suppliers rather than by her customers to pay her.

Accrual accounting: wear and tear on equipment.

- In making the jewellery, Simone used some equipment she had bought earlier for $1,200. The equipment is expected to last about ten years, so shouldn't the wear and tear on it during the year 2006 be counted as an expense? It is not easy to figure out how much wear and tear results from a particular period, but say that she feels the year was a normal one of the ten years the equipment should last. The cost of the wear and tear, therefore, is about 10% of the $1,200 equipment cost, or $120. (This $120 figure is what accountants call "*amortization.*" It can be calculated in several ways, as we will see later on.) This is an example of a long-term estimate or expectation. Because it involves prediction of an uncertain future, and for other reasons we'll see, people have all sorts of disagreements about amortization.

FYI

Amortization is accounting's estimate of the consumption of economic value in a period.

Accounting is continually evolving, an example of which can be seen in the shift from the use of the term *depreciation* to *amortization*. Both terms denote the measurement of "consumption" of the economic value of long-term resources such as equipment. However, amortization is slowly supplanting depreciation as the more common term for this idea, but you will see both terms (and other terms) used in companies' financial reports and in this book.

Just using these four additional pieces of information, accrual accounting would calculate Simone's business income for the year 2006 (her first year in business) in the way shown in Exhibit 1.1, taking into account the various estimates and incomplete transactions described:

Simone's Jewellery Business

Calculation of Accrual Income for the Year 2006

Revenue*	
($4,350 collected, plus $310 still to be received)	$4,660
Expenses**	
($1,670 paid, minus $280 deducted because the goods are still on hand, plus $85 unpaid, plus $120 estimated amortization)	1,595
Accrual income* based on the information provided**	**$3,065**

Notes:

* **Revenue** is the benefit received or expected from the sale of goods or services during the year, so it goes beyond cash received.

** **Expenses** are costs incurred or resources consumed during the year in order to earn the revenue, so they go beyond cash paid.

*** **Accrual income** for the year is the difference between revenue and expenses.

Accrual accounting measures performance with revenues, expenses, and resulting income.

Accrual income is more complete than cash income.

Accrual accounting can and does handle many more complexities than the four included above. Even with this uncomplicated example, you can see that the $3,065 accrual income is a more complete measure of Simone's business performance than is the cash income of $2,680, which is the change in cash balance alone. (By the way, **accrual income** is not necessarily higher than cash income—it just happens to be so in this example.)

But there are some difficulties:

Accrual income is more complicated than cash income.

- The accrual income requires extra calculation and so is more complex, as portrayed with the long vertical arrow in Figure 1.9. This might confuse some people, and it leaves more room for error than the simpler calculation.
- The accrual income doesn't match the change in bank account balance anymore, so Simone might be less sure of how much she can take out of the bank for her next holiday. The accrual income and cash income can always be reconciled, however. We'll see how to do this later.
- Accrual accounting is a bit of a "slippery slope." Once you start trying to add and subtract things in calculating income, where do you stop? For example, should there be some deduction for the cost of Simone's time in making all the jewellery? The accrual income calculation seems to imply that her time was free, yet she would probably not agree with that. (Accounting for the value of the owner's time in a small business like Simone's would make economic sense, but it is generally not done because it is not based on transactions, is hard to measure, and is not allowable in Canadian income tax calculations.) What about the costs of using the room in her basement for her studio and her car for deliveries? Should some calculation of such costs be made even though it would be hard to be exact about them? What about income tax? If she has to pay income tax on what she earns from her business, should that tax also be deducted as a business expense? Or is it a personal expense that does not belong in the business's financial statements?

The more we try to accomplish with it, the more complex accrual accounting becomes.

Let's not get mired in such complexities! For now, just remember that accrual accounting tries to provide a more thorough measurement of financial performance and other aspects of an enterprise than simple cash-based accounting. In order to do so, it incorporates more complex ideas, as well as estimates and judgments. Much of your task is to understand the complexities, estimates, and judgments so that you will be able to understand the resulting financial statements and what they say about the enterprise.

Simone's accrual income if 2006 was not her first year in business:

Let's look at Simone's business again. Suppose 2006 was *not* her first year in business. That means she may have had uncollected sales, unused goods on hand, and unpaid bills at the end of 2005 (beginning of 2006). Would those make any difference to the cash income calculation for 2006? No, they wouldn't—they don't involve any change in cash receipts or payments during the year. Would they make any difference to the accrual income calculation for 2006? Yes, they would. Let's see how.

To keep the example uncluttered, let's use exactly the same numbers again, but add three new items as at the end of 2005: uncollected sales of $240; unused goods costing $230; and unpaid bills of $50. What effect does this have on the accrual income calculation?

1. Some of the $4,350 cash received in 2006 was not for that year's activity, but rather was the collection of $240 revenue that was part of the accrual income calculation in the previous year, 2005. That amount has to be subtracted from $4,350 in the 2006 accrual income calculation because it was already in 2005's accrual income and shouldn't be counted twice.
2. The unused goods costing $230 at the end of 2005 have to be added to the expense calculation for 2006, because they were there at the beginning of 2006 and so got used up during the year.
3. The unpaid bills totalling $50 at the end of 2005 were included in the cash payments in 2006 and so counted in the 2006 expenses above even though they had already been included in the 2005 expenses. So they are deducted from the 2006 expenses because they don't belong in 2006 and we don't want to count them twice.

You may wonder what the effect would be if some amounts left over from 2005 were still left over at the end of 2006. An amount owing by a customer in 2005 might still be owed at the end of 2006. Goods unused at the end of 2005 might still be on hand unused at the end of 2006. Well, these 2005 amounts must still be adjusted for as indicated above, because they were in the 2005 calculation and if not taken out of the 2006 calculation, would be included twice. For example,

- Customer Jones owed Simone $50 at the end of 2005, so this $50 would be added to 2005 accrual income.
- Customer Jones still owes the $50 at the end of 2006. Following the same logic, we would add the $50 to the 2006 accrual income. But now the $50 has been added to both years' accrual incomes. To avoid this double counting, we deduct the $50 owing at the beginning of 2006, ensuring that it is counted only in 2005's accrual income, regardless of when it is finally collected. If it is collected in 2006, this deduction removes the $50 that is in 2006 cash income; if it is not collected at the end of 2006, this deduction cancels it from the amounts owing at the end of 2006 that are added to 2006 accrual income.

Using the information above, Exhibit 1.2 shows Simone's accrual income *if 2006 was not her first year.*

Simone's Jewellery Business

Revised Calculation of Accrual Income for 2006

Revenue	
($4,350 collected, minus $240 from 2005, plus $310 still to be received)	$4,420
Expenses	
($1,670 paid, minus $50 from 2005, plus $230 unused brought forward from 2005, minus $280 unused taken forward to 2007, plus $85 unpaid at the end of 2006, plus $120 estimated amortization for 2006)	1,775
Accrual income based on the information provided	**$2,645**

Accrual income is affected by adjustments at both the beginning and end of the year.

Cash income is still $2,680, unaffected by the new information. But accrual income is changed, *as it always is,* by noncash items existing *both* at the beginning and end of the year.

HOW'S YOUR UNDERSTANDING?

Here are two questions you should be able to answer based on what you have just read. If you can't answer them, it would be best to reread the material.

1. Your cousin, a medical student, says, "In our course on managing a medical practice, we were told that our financial reports will use accrual accounting. What does that mean?"
2. Fred started his delivery business a few years ago. This year, he collected $47,000 from his customers and paid $21,000 in expenses. At the beginning of this year, his customers owed him $3,500, and he owed his suppliers $700. At the end of this year, his customers owe him $3,200, he owes his suppliers $1,450, and his truck amortization (depreciation) for the year was $4,600. Using just this information, what is this year's cash income? What is this year's accrual income?

You should get cash income $26,000 ($47,000 cash receipts minus $21,000 cash payments) and accrual income $20,350 (revenue of $47,000 – $3,500 + $3,200 = $46,700; expenses of $21,000 – $700 + $1,450 + $4,600 = $26,350; income = $46,700 – $26,350 = $20,350).

1.11 Demonstration Problem: Accrual Accounting

Artistic Supplies Inc. has the following information. From it, calculate Artistic's cash income for 2006 and accrual income for 2006.

- Cash received from customers during 2006: $789,000
- Cash paid to suppliers and employees during 2006: $717,000
- Customers owed $45,000 at the end of 2005 and $53,000 at the end of 2006 ($2,000 of which was still owed from 2005)
- Artistic owed its suppliers $31,000 at the end of 2005 and $37,000 at the end of 2006
- Artistic owed its employees $5,000 at the end of 2005 and $10,000 at the end of 2006
- Unsold art supplies costing $82,000 were on hand at the end of 2005
- Unsold art supplies costing $63,000 were on hand at the end of 2006, $7,000 of which had also been on hand at the end of 2005
- Artistic calculated its amortization for 2006 to be $37,000
- Just for fun, let's add in 35% income tax, all unpaid at the end of 2006, and assume that the amortization amount is also deductible in calculating income tax

Answers:

Artistic Supplies Cash and Accrual Income for 2006

Cash revenue and expenses:		
Revenues from customers		$ 789,000
Expenses		717,000
Cash income		$ 72,000
Noncash items:		
Owing from customers	($53,000 end of 2006 – $45,000 end of 2005)	$ 8,000*
Owing to suppliers	($37,000 end of 2006 – $31,000 end of 2005)	(6,000)
Owing to employees	($10,000 end of 2006 – $5000 end of 2005)	(5,000)
Unsold supplies	($63,000 end of 2006 – $82,000 end of 2005)	(19,000)**
Amortization		(37,000)
Total noncash items		$ (59,000)
Accrual income before tax		$ 13,000
Income tax (35% x $13,000)		4,550
Net accrual income after tax		$ 8,450

* Both the $53,000 and the $45,000 include $2,000 uncollected from 2005, which therefore does not affect the difference between the two numbers.
** Both the $63,000 and the $82,000 include $7,000 unsold from 2005, which therefore does not affect the difference between the two numbers.

1.12 Introductory Examples of Accounting Analysis: Reconciliation and Change Effects

The ability to do *analysis* is one of the most important skills accountants have. Doing it, or at least understanding it, is central to decision making. This book often focuses on analysis because it is so important to accountants and users alike, and because it is generally useful, beyond any single course. In this section, two kinds of analysis will be introduced: *reconciliation* and what we will call *change effects analysis* or *"what if" analysis.*

Reconciliation

Reconciliation is a very useful technique in general because if you can't make two numbers reconcile when they should, that may mean there are errors in one or both of them. This idea is used in business in many ways. Here are three examples.

1. *Reconciliation of cash and accrual income.* In Section 1.10, when 2006 was Simone's first year in business, we calculated her cash and accrual income. Here's a way to reconcile the two numbers (accountants often designate subtraction by putting brackets around the number, as in (205) below):

Cash income (day-to-day cash receipts minus payments)	$2,680
Add revenue not yet received in cash	310
Add back cost of goods paid for, but not yet sold	280
Deduct expenses not paid in cash in 2006 ($85 + $120)	(205)
Equals accrual income for her first year in business	$3,065

Accrual income and cash income can always be reconciled.

We should have more confidence in both cash and accrual income because we see that they do connect in a logical way. (Below, we'll also do a reconciliation for Simone when 2006 was not her first year, and for the Artistic Supplies example in Section 1.11.)

Your bank account record and the bank's record often differ.

2. *Bank reconciliation.* Here, the idea is to figure out what the bank thinks you have in your account, and what you think you have, and identify any differences. The differences usually arise because the bank has not yet deducted all the cheques you have written, since it takes time for them to work through the system, but there may be other reasons, some of which are errors by you or the bank.

Reconciliation is a method of figuring out the ways the two records may differ.

Suppose you have kept careful track of your bank deposits, cheques, and cash withdrawals from the bank machine, and your record shows that you have $534 in the bank. You get a statement from the bank showing that you have $613. Are both records right? Reconciliation will tell you. Let's get some more data. You check your cheques and withdrawals off against the bank statement and determine that two cheques are still "outstanding" (not deducted by the bank yet), one for $43 and one for $28. There are no outstanding deposits: the bank has credited you with all the deposits your own record shows. You also see on the statement that the bank has charged you $7 for some bank charges you didn't know about. And you discover that the bank has deducted someone else's cheque for $55 from your account. Finally, there is a deposit for $70 you can't remember making. From this information you can do a bank account reconciliation:

EXHIBIT 1·3

Bank's records		**Your records**	
Balance according to the bank	$613	Balance in your record	$534
Add back error made by bank	55	Deduct bank charges not recorded	(7)
Deduct cheques still outstanding	(71)	Add deposit not recorded	70
Revised balance according to bank	$597	Revised balance in your records	$597

Now you know exactly why the two amounts differ, and you can make sure that errors in both records are corrected. You also know that you can't spend the whole amount the bank's statement shows because you have written cheques that the bank has not deducted yet, but will.

Reconciliation provides information for corrective action.

3. *Credit card reconciliation.* The idea is exactly the same as for the bank reconciliation. Suppose your Spendthrift Card statement's balance is $492 owing, and you have credit card slips totalling $688. Is the $492 correct? You take your pile of credit card slips, check them off the statement you got from Spendthrift Card and identify the differences. You find out that you have $302 of slips whose charges have not yet

appeared on the statement and that the statement includes $106 in charges for which you don't have slips.

The two balances reconcile: $492 + $302 – $106 = $688. So now you know what to check into further. You can ask the card company for evidence about the $106, or maybe look around for slips you forgot to file. You can expect the card company to bill you for the other $302 next month, which helps you predict your cash needs next month.

FYI

Use common sense when solving accounting problems.

Reconciling your bank and credit card accounts is an important procedure you should be doing to help control your financial affairs. You may feel these examples are routine, hardly worth the space they take, just common sense, but much of accounting is just common-sense techniques like these reconciliation examples. You may find you are already using accounting techniques without having labelled them as accounting! As you work through the book, use your common sense—it will often help you see how to handle problems that at first glance seem complicated.

Change Effects Analysis ("What If" Analysis)

To simplify the comparison of alternatives, focus on what differs between them.

This type of analysis depends on some accounting knowledge and a lot of common sense. Here is a taste of it. The central idea is to focus just on what changes or differs between two situations, thereby simplifying the analysis by leaving out everything that doesn't change. It is a form of *marginal analysis* that you may have seen used in economics.

1. *Comparison of cash versus accrual accounting.* Suppose Simone asked "What would be the effect on my income measure if we used accrual accounting instead of cash basis accounting?" A good way to answer this is to use the same sort of reconciliation analysis, but focusing on what would *change* between the two methods of calculating income.

   Here's a demonstration, which works equally well for both examples of Simone's business, which we'll call "Simone" for when 2006 was her first year, and "Simone revised" for when it was not her first year. (This is where accounting knowledge comes in: we know that some items are positive in their general effect on accrual income and some are negative. Those are noted below.)

		Simone		**Simone revised**
Cash income		$2,680		$2,680
Changes over the year in:				
Uncollected revenue (positive)	($310 – $0)	310	($310 – $240)	70
Unused goods (positive)	($280 – $0)	280	($280 – $230)	50
Unpaid bills (negative)	($(85) – $0)	(85)	($(85) – $(50))	(35)
Amortization (negative)	($(120) – $0)	(120)	($(120) – $0)	(120)
Accrual income		$3,065		$2,645

So if 2006 was her first year in business, the answer to her question would be that accrual income would be $385 higher than cash income ($310 + $280 – $85 – $120). We don't even have to know what the accrual and cash income figures were, because we can use just the changes to answer the question. If 2006 was not her first year in business, the answer would be that accrual income would be $35 lower than cash income ($70 + $50 – $35 – $120).

1. *Comparison of cash versus accrual accounting, second example.* Let's do the same sort of "changes" analysis of the Artistic Supplies demonstration problem from Section 1.11. What difference would it make to use accrual income rather than cash income for 2006? The answer is the sum of all the changes (differences) between the two methods, again remembering that some items normally add to accrual income and some reduce it:

Change in what customers owe ($53,000 – $45,000)	$ 8,000
Change in what Artistic owes its suppliers ($37,000 – $31,000)	(6,000)
Change in what Artistic owes its employees ($10,000 – $5,000)	(5,000)
Change in the unsold goods on hand ($63,000 – $82,000)	(19,000)
Amortization for 2006, not included in cash income	(37,000)
Income tax owing on accrual income, not included in cash income	(4,550)
Accrual income would be lower than cash income for 2006 by	$(63,550)

Again, we don't need to know either income figure to answer the "what if" question. But we'd feel better if our answer also reconciled the two figures, so let's check that:

Cash income from Section 1.11	$ 72,000
Difference we calculated above	(63,550)
Accrual income from Section 1.11	$ 8,450

2. *Net-of-tax analysis.* Here's another example of "what if" analysis, incorporating that factor we all love to hate: income tax. Suppose Kamble Manufacturing Inc. has annual revenue of $11,310,200 and expenses of $9,774,800. Its income tax rate is 40%. The president of the company wants to know, "What would be the effect on *net income* (after tax) if we revised our selling prices, which would increase revenue by $230,000 per year?"

Well, we can laboriously figure out the net income now and the net income then and answer the president's question. Let's do that.

Long Approach

	Before Revision	**Revision**	**After Revision**	**Change**
Revenues	$11,310,200	230,000	$11,540,200	$ 230,000
Expenses	(9,774,800)		(9,774,800)	0
Income before tax	$ 1,535,400		$ 1,765,400	$ 230,000
Tax @ 40%	(614,160)		(706,160)	(92,000)
Net income	$ 921,240		$ 1,059,240	**$138,000**

Net-of-tax analysis focuses on what *changes* and just applies the tax to that. It then goes a bit further and notes that what we are usually interested in is what we have left after tax. If we have $100 and it is taxed at 40%, we pay $40 and are left with $60. What we are left with is $100 × (1 – the 40% tax rate). We can apply this to the president's question. As soon as the president stops for breath, we can say, "The effect on income is $230,000 × (1 – 0.4) = $138,000." We have the same answer but with far fewer steps. Pretty impressive, there is no worn-out pencil, little chance of calculation error, and there may be a raise for being so quick off the mark. We'll see net-of-tax analysis in various forms as the book proceeds. (This example was a simple one, which assumed that nothing else changed. For example, we assumed that to get the increased revenue the president expected, the company didn't have to spend more on advertising to persuade customers to pay higher prices.)

Short Approach (Net-of-tax analysis)

Net effect = $230,000 x (1– 0.4) = **$138,000**

HOW'S YOUR UNDERSTANDING?

Here are three questions you should be able to answer based on what you have just read. If you can't answer them, it would be best to reread the material.

1. Jeanette's accounting records show that she has $32,412 in her business bank account at June 30. The bank statement dated June 30 shows a balance of $41,985. What sorts of things might account for the difference?
2. Jeanette received a credit card statement asking her to pay $2,888. She had an envelope containing credit card slips totalling $3,226. When she checked the slips off against the statement, there were $594 worth of the slips that had not yet been billed by the credit card company. She also discovered that the company had billed her for a purchase made by someone else. How much was that purchase? How much should she pay the credit card company?

The other person's purchase was $256 ($2,888 + $594 – $3,226) and she should pay $2,632 ($2,888 – $256 not hers).

3. North Country Resorts Ltd., which pays income tax at a rate of 35%, is thinking of increasing its mosquito-control expenses by $48,300. What will that do to the company's net income?

It will decrease net income by $48,300 x (1 – 0.35) = $31,395. Note that to answer this, we don't need to know present income, revenue, mosquito-control expenses or anything else. They don't change so don't affect the answer.

1.13 Terms to Be Sure You Understand

The following important terms were used in this chapter. Make sure you know what they mean *in financial accounting*. If any are unclear to you, check the chapter again or refer to the glossary of terms at the back of the book. Most will be used many times as the book proceeds, so your understanding of them will deepen.

Accountant(s)
Accounting
Accounting policy
Accounting principles
Accounting research
Accrual accounting
Accrual income
Adjustment(s)
Amortization
Analysis
Annual report
Assets
Auditor(s)
Balance sheet
Bookkeeping
Books
Cash flow statement
Cash income
Cash transaction(s)
Change effects analysis
Consolidated
Corporation
Cost–benefit
Credit transaction(s)
Creditor(s)
Depreciation
Disclosure
E-commerce
Exchange
Expense(s)
External auditor(s)
Financial accounting
Financial performance
Financial position
Financial statement analysis
Financial statements
Generally accepted accounting principles (GAAP)
Historical cost
Income statement
Independence
Information systems
Internal auditor(s)
Internal control
Liabilities
Management accounting
Managers
Marginal analysis
Net income
Net-of-tax analysis
Notes
Objectivity
Owner(s)
Preparer(s)
Public accounting firms
Quarterly report
Reconciliation
Revenue(s)
Shareholders
Stock market
Transaction(s)
User(s)
"What if" analysis

INSTALLMENT 1

Toward the end of each chapter in this book is an installment of the "Continuing Demonstration Case." The case describes the founding and initial growth of wholesale distribution company Mato Inc. and develops as the chapters' topics develop. Each installment presents additional data and then shows the results of using that data. The main purpose is to illustrate the technical side of the chapter's topics, so that you can use it to reinforce your learning. Make whatever use of the case is helpful to you, but remember to think about the data provided each time and sketch out what you would do with it before you look at the suggested results. If you look at the results before thinking about them, the case will be less helpful to you.

This first installment provides background information about the two people who run Mato Inc. The founding of the company will be dealt with in Installment 2.

DATA FOR INSTALLMENT 1

"Hi, Tomas, this is Mavis. Just calling to thank you for attending my grandfather's funeral last week. I appreciate the support. Gramps was a great person and always encouraged me to make my mark in the world. Even now he's encouraging me, because in his will he left me some money that he said was to help start my own business. Maybe in a while we could get together and talk about that."

Mavis Janer and Tomas Brot have been friends for several years, ever since their days studying business together at university. They have often talked about going into business for themselves. Mavis majored in marketing and, since graduation, has worked for a national retailer, moving up the ladder to become a department head in one of the retailer's local stores. While she likes the company and seems to be doing well, she would really prefer to be on her own, making decisions and taking risks. She is full of ideas that cannot be implemented at her level in the retailing company and is afraid that if she stays there too long she will lose her entrepreneurial zeal.

Tomas majored in finance and has worked as a commercial loans officer for a bank since graduating. As he puts it, "After I'd seen a hundred business plans from people wanting to borrow money, I was sure I could put together a better plan for myself, if only I had the opportunity. The local economy hasn't been terribly encouraging, but I have seen lots of good ideas and know there's room for mine to succeed too."

With the catalyst of Mavis's inheritance, and being a careful pair, the two decided to get together and get started on a business plan by writing down (a) the objectives they would have for any business they might operate together, such as making money, and (b) the risks, constraints, and worries they'd want to avoid or minimize, such as losing their own money. Tomas was more interested in list (b) than Mavis was; he already saw himself playing the role of keeping her entrepreneurial enthusiasm "within bounds," as he called it. Their two lists are given below. Before looking at them, jot down some of the things you think they might have listed.

RESULTS FOR INSTALLMENT 1

Below are the lists summarizing what Mavis and Tomas agreed on. The lists will help determine the context within which the accounting for their eventual business will operate and the uses to which the business's financial statements will be put. Financial statements and the accounting system behind them must fit the needs of the company, its owners, its managers, and other interested parties.

a. Objectives

- Be a source of personal pride and satisfaction.
- Be able to continue as an independent business indefinitely.

- Be a business both can contribute to, so both will want to be fully involved.
- Be a challenge to their skills and even be fun to be involved in.
- Provide enough cash income to support both Mavis and Tomas (moderate support now, but greater support in the future, when both expect to have families).
- Grow in value so that it will be a future source of wealth for financing a desired comfortable lifestyle and eventually selling out at retirement.
- Be a useful learning experience that will help them restart their careers if it does not work out.

b. Risks and constraints

- Disagreements or problems that will strain their friendship or make it difficult for them to continue working together in the business.
- Catastrophic financial loss (they don't want to lose what they will invest, but they especially don't want to lose even more than that).
- Environmental degradation related to the business or its products.
- A weak start by being undercapitalized (having too little money invested to give the business a good chance to succeed—a problem Tomas had often seen in his banking work).
- Loss of control because of having to raise significantly more capital than they can find themselves.
- Excessive initial business growth that may be hard to handle.
- Excessive time demands that will damage their family lives and other life quality factors.
- Physically difficult or dangerous products.
- Distant physical locations, which will mean frequent, long commutes.
- Unethical products or services (they did not define what they meant, but thought they would know something was unethical when they saw it).

1.15 Homework and Discussion to Develop Understanding

- To assist you in relating the homework and discussion problems to the chapter's material, problems are organized roughly according to the chapter's sections.
- To further assist you, some homework and discussion problems have informal solution outlines in the Student Solutions Manual. *Such problems are marked with an asterisk (*).*
- Their solution outlines are intended to facilitate self-study and additional practice: *don't look at the solution for any of these without giving the problem a serious try first,* because once you have seen the solution it always looks easier than it is. Please note that *a problem can have several solutions*—it is possible for your answer to differ in some details from the solution outline provided and still be a good answer, especially if you have made valid, alternative assumptions or happen to know a lot about the particular situation in the problem.
- Some of the more difficult problems are marked CHALLENGING.
- Finally, some problems are marked EXTENDED TIME. These have been designed to take longer to complete than other problems. They are not necessarily harder, but typically feature a thorough examination of material and may integrate understanding from various sections of the book.

Introduction to Financial Accounting • Sections 1.2–1.6

Accounting Issues

*** PROBLEM 1.1** Professional ethics

Accountants must follow ethical guidelines prescribed by their professional societies. What are these guidelines designed to produce? Why is this goal important? What would be the probable effect on the economy if these standards ceased to exist or accountants did not adhere to them?

PROBLEM 1.2 Should management be able to choose accounting methods?

Do you think professors should have the right to use their own judgment in determining course grades, or should those grades be based on objectively set exams administered by someone other than professors? Why? Do you think companies' management should have the right to choose the accounting policies and methods by which their performance is measured? Why? How do these two cases differ, if at all?

PROBLEM 1.3 Preparer self-interest and statement reliability

The self-interests of the preparers of accounting information can influence both what is reported and how it is presented. What allows the users of financial statements to rely on fair and full disclosure in the reports they receive?

People Involved in Financial Accounting

*** PROBLEM 1.4** What are various people's interests in financial accounting?

Describe briefly what each of the following people would likely want to learn from the financial statements of BrandX Inc., and how each might be affected if the statements showed a good or bad financial performance or financial position.

a. The president of the company.
b. The company's chief accountant.
c. The chairperson of the company's board of directors (the board evaluates the president's performance on behalf of the shareholders).
d. The partner of auditing firm Dimbleby & Co., for whom BrandX Inc. is a client.
e. The local manager of tax collections for the Canada Revenue Agency.
f. John Flatstone, who owns 100 shares of BrandX Inc.
g. Mildred Evans, who is thinking of buying some shares of the company.
h. The local manager of Big Bank, which has made a large loan to BrandX Inc.

PROBLEM 1.5 Company performance and interests in financial accounting

ImproveIT Inc. manufactures agenda books and other stationery supplies for distribution across Canada. Describe how each of the following people or companies might be affected if the company showed a good or poor financial performance or financial position.

a. The company's vice-president of marketing.
b. Bill Stevens, a mailroom clerk who just started in his position two months ago.
c. SBP Inc., a supplier for ImproveIT. ImproveIT has a credit account with SBP for supplies purchased throughout the year.
d. The company's external auditor.
e. Linda Mahoney, president of Creative Impressions Ltd., which is ImproveIT's main competitor.
f. Samuel Snyder, the chief market analyst at The Atlantic Bank who is responsible for issuing reports that explain whether or not the company's stock is a strong investment or not based upon his analysis.
g. The Competition Bureau of Canada, which had been hearing a complaint against ImproveIT from a competitor, ExPaper Inc., claiming the company was employing predatory pricing. The case claimed that ImproveIT unfairly lowered prices to drive competitors out of the industry.

PROBLEM 1.6 The impact of a proposal on different stakeholders

ABC Systems is deciding whether to implement a new accounting system to handle its financial records. The new computer software would improve inventory control and ensure that statements are more accurate than at present. Buying, installing, and training employees on the new system will require an initial investment, so only after two years will the company realize significant savings from the new system.

Explain the impact that an improved accounting system will have upon the following stakeholders:

a. Management
b. Shareholders
c. Auditors

CHALLENGING AND EXTENDED TIME

PROBLEM 1.7 Uses and users of accounting information

Identify five users of accounting information. Discuss their information needs and list decisions for which each user would find accounting information helpful.

Transactions • Sections 1.7, 1.8

Identify Accounting Transactions

*** PROBLEM 1.8** Is the event a transaction?

The following things happened to Bartlett Inc. last month. Decide if each is an accounting transaction and explain briefly why it is or isn't.

a. A customer ordered $6,000 of products, to be shipped next month.
b. Another customer paid $528 for some marketing advice from the company.
c. Bartlett's share price went up by $0.50. As there are 100,000 shares outstanding, this was a value increase of $50,000.
d. Bartlett ran an ad on TV, and promised to pay the TV station the $2,000 cost next month.
e. One of the company's employees worked overtime earning $120 that would be paid next pay period.
f. The company paid a teenager $50 to compensate for a ripped shirt suffered when the teenager tried to run away after being accused of shoplifting.
g. Bartlett received a shipment of new goods for sale, paying $1,000 cash and agreeing to pay the other $12,250 in a few days.
h. Bartlett paid the other $12,250.
i. The company made a donation to a political party of $500. (The donation turned out later to have been against the election law, to the company's embarrassment.)
j. Grand Bank made the company a $20,000 short-term loan.

PROBLEM 1.9 Identify transactions

Gould Inc. experienced the following events. For each, say whether or not it is an accounting transaction and why or why not.

a. A painter repainted the reception lobby bright blue.
b. A customer who had owed Gould money for several years finally paid, to everyone's surprise.
c. The president decided that the company's main factory would be reorganized next month.
d. The company received shop supplies it had ordered earlier.
e. The company signed a new five-year lease on its Windsor warehouse.
f. The company sold some land, for which it would receive 10 annual payments starting next year.
g. The company acquired a new truck for cash plus the trade-in of an old truck.
h. An employee was discovered to have stolen a large amount of cash.
i. The company received a bill from the supplier for the shop supplies in item (d).
j. A customer who fell down in the parking lot sued the company for a large amount.

PROBLEM 1.10 Identify whether or not events are accounting transactions

The following events happened at the Guzzle Beer Corporation. For each, indicate whether or not it is an accounting transaction for Guzzle Beer Corp. and state, in five or ten words, why.

a. A large tank containing beer mixture broke and all of the mixture spilled.
b. A major shareholder sold 50,000 shares on the stock exchange.
c. The corporation paid $60,000,000 for a Mexican brewery.
d. An invoice for next week's TV advertising arrived.
e. A pub took delivery of its weekly shipment of Guzzle Beer.

Identifying Events that Constitute a Transaction

*** PROBLEM 1.11** What part of the event constitutes an accounting transaction?

The following events took place on February 1, 2004. For each event, state what part(s) of the event are accounting transaction(s), and why.

a. Smith Ltd. purchased supplies to be used immediately. The purchase price of the supplies was $5,000. Only $2,000 was paid in cash on delivery. The balance is due in 30 days.
b. The company decided to rent a service vehicle for $4,800 per year. A rental contract was signed February 1, 2004, to take effect March 1, 2004. Smith Ltd. paid $400 cash to the rental company on February 1, 2004, which represented the rent for March 2004.
c. Some of Smith's repairmen were not busy on February 1. The manager had them paint the inside of a storage room. The repairmen's salaries of $300 were paid in cash at the end of the day.
d. A shareholder sold her car to the company. The vehicle cost her $15,000 two years ago. An equivalent used vehicle would have been worth about $8,000 on February 1, 2004. No cash changed hands, but the shareholder expects the company to pay her for the car eventually.
e. An invoice for $5,000 was received relating to repairs and maintenance work done in December 2003. The company's year-end is December 31. This expense was not recorded in the 2003 financial statements.

PROBLEM 1.12 Identify parts of events that are transactions

Southward Stores Ltd. is a general merchandise retailer operating in the suburbs. During a recent month, the events listed below happened. For each event, decide if all or part of it is an accounting transaction and state briefly why or why not.

a. Southward borrowed $500,000 from the Great Pacific Bank (Canada). Payment is due in three years, but the loan can be called on ten days' notice if Southward fails to make any of the monthly interest payments, which begin next month.
b. Southward ordered goods for resale costing $300,000, to be delivered in 40 days, and sent a deposit of $10,000 with the order.
c. Southward renewed its lease on the store premises, signing an agreement that provides for a monthly rent increase from $21,000 to $23,000 beginning in three months.
d. Southward was charged with unfair pricing of its main line of merchandise. News of this sent the company's shares (listed on a stock exchange) down in price from $10 to $8.50 each. The company has 1,000,000 shares outstanding, all publicly traded.
e. The company paid a dividend of $0.50 per share, on each of its 1,000,000 issued shares. This news sent the company's shares up by $0.40 each on the stock exchange.

PROBLEM 1.13 Find accounting transactions

Bill Matthews is the vice-president of finance for FlyAway Corp., an upstart charter airline. Since the company has few employees, he must handle a large amount of the day-to-day accounting activities. Help Bill decide whether the following events from his day should be recorded as accounting transactions. For each event, explain why it is or is not a transaction.

Bill arrives for work in the morning on February 15, 2004, to hear that the company's president will not be coming to work today because she sprained her knee in the company softball match last night. Sitting at his desk in the morning, he notices the company's stock price is up $0.21 on the day. (The company has 15,000,000 outstanding shares.) Bill begins to work through the pile of paper in his inbox. The first paper is an invoice (a bill) from a supplier for $2,872 and the date for FlyAway's receipt of the goods is February 6, 2004. The next is a report from the chief mechanic requesting the approval of an order for a part costing $15,329. A new part was needed for the company's turboprop plane and it would be delivered next week. The part supplier would extend FlyAway credit for one month. A knock at the door, and Mary from the maintenance department drops by to tell Bill that she phoned a plumber to come tomorrow to fix a problem with the sink in the lunchroom. The plumber would charge $65/hour for labour and she wanted to make sure Bill approved. Finally, Bill signs the cheque for the payment of this month's lease on the company building. He must mail the cheque by the end of today.

CHALLENGING

PROBLEM 1.14 Explain the transactional basis of financial accounting

Your boss has just returned from a breakfast meeting of her small business association. The meeting had had as speaker an accountant who explained quite a few things about how accounting worked, but made a comment your boss is unclear about. As best your boss can remember the comment, the accountant said, "Every information system has to start somewhere in getting its data. Accounting starts with business transactions, and as a result financial accounting is really a careful history of the business, not a measure of the business's current value."

Explain the accountant's comment to your boss.

Accrual Accounting • Sections 1.9, 1.10, 1.11

Calculating Accrual Income

*** PROBLEM 1.15** Cash balance and accrual accounting income

Calculate (1) the cash in bank as at the end of 2007, and (2) the 2007 accrual accounting income for Dawn's Diving Trips according to the following information:

Cash in bank as at the end of 2006	$16,390
Owing from customers as at the end of 2006 (collected in 2007)	2,000
Cash collected from customers during 2007 for 2007 trips	78,480
Owing from customers as at the end of 2007 (collected in 2008)	960
Payable to suppliers as at the end of 2006 (paid in 2007)	1,620
Cash paid to suppliers during 2007 for 2007 expenses	41,830
Payable to suppliers as at the end of 2007 (paid in 2008)	3,230
Amortization on diving equipment during 2007	2,610
Cash used by Dawn for personal purposes during 2007	26,000

PROBLEM 1.16 Calculate accrual income and change in cash

"I just don't understand it!" Dwight Benat had received his accountant's calculation of Dwight's business income, showing an accrual income for his first year in business of $50,280. "If I made so much money, why don't I have that much in the bank? My bank account shows only $8,205 on hand!"

Dwight operates Benat Supply, which provides stationery and office supplies to business customers. He has no store, just a small rented warehouse, and only one employee. Here are the data he and his accountant used. Explain clearly to Dwight (1) how the accountant calculated the $50,280 income and (2) why there is only $8,205 on hand.

Collected from customers during the year	$159,680
Still owing from customers at the end of the year (collected next year)	16,900
Paid for products to resell and for other expenses, including wages, during the year	142,975
Owing for products and other expenses at the end of the year (paid next year)	10,050
Cost of unsold products on hand at the end of the year (all sold next year)	28,975
Amortization (depreciation) on equipment during the year	2,250
Personal withdrawals by Dwight during the year	8,500

PROBLEM 1.17 Effect of more items on Simone's cash and accrual incomes

Suppose the following were discovered about Simone's business (Section 1.10). For *each* item, show the dollar effect (if any) and the direction (up or down) that *correcting* the item would have on (1) Simone's cash income for her *first year in business,* and (2) Simone's accrual income for that year. Explain each of your answers briefly.

a. It was discovered that another $100 of unsold goods were on hand at the end of 2006.
b. It turned out that Simone had paid $45 more in expenses in 2006 than she thought.
c. Amortization should have been $135 for 2006, not $120.
d. Simone determined that a $30 sale, not yet collected, had accidentally been recorded twice.
e. Included in the cash receipts was a $75 customer deposit on a future sale.

PROBLEM 1.18 More effects of additional items of information on Simone's cash and accrual incomes

This problem is like Problem 1.17 but involves items this chapter has not illustrated. Use your common sense to compare the items below to Simone's results in Section 1.10 and, for *each* item, show the dollar effect (if any) and the direction (up or down) that *correcting* the item would have on (1) Simone's cash income for her first year in business, and (2) Simone's accrual income for that year. Explain each of your answers briefly.

a. Simone agreed to give a customer a refund of $110 for faulty jewellery sold in 2006. The refund will be paid in 2007. The jewellery had cost Simone $67 in material, but she will not recover any of that cost because the jewellery has to be thrown away.
b. One of the amounts Simone paid out in 2006 was $160 for some more equipment. That should not have been recorded as an expense. On the other hand, there should have been amortization of 10% on that equipment, the same as for the other equipment.
c. Simone decided she should charge her business rent for the basement studio space, but to avoid reducing the business cash, Simone would delay paying the rent to her personal bank account for a few years. She decided the rent for 2006 should be set at $500.

* PROBLEM 1.19 Reconciliation of cash income and accrual income

Turku Services Company had cash income for its first year in business of $67,450 and accrual income of $53,270. Show how the two amounts reconcile using the following information:

a. Uncollected revenue at the end of the year was $18,730.
b. Unpaid bills for expenses at the end of the year totalled $24,880.
c. Unsold supplies on hand at the end of the year totalled $3,410.
d. Expenses for the next year, paid already, totalled $2,300.
e. Amortization on the company's equipment was $13,740 for the year.

EXTENDED TIME

PROBLEM 1.20 Find the company's cash position

IlluminateU Industries manufactures specialty light bulbs. Some financial information follows.

1. Calculate the company's accrual and cash income for 2006.
2. Reconcile its cash and accrual income for the year.
3. How much cash does the company have at the end of 2006?

Cash in the bank at the end of 2005	$ 59,798
Cash collections from customers in 2006	178,690
Payments to suppliers during 2006 for 2006 expenses	86,700
Owing to suppliers at the end of 2006 (paid in 2007)	5,000
Rent paid for 2006 during 2006	7,598
Rent paid during 2006 for the first 3 months of 2007	1,850
Amount owing from customers at the end of 2005 (collected in 2006)	17,610
Amount owing from customers at the end of 2006 (collected in 2007)	27,345
Amortization on the company's equipment	11,022

PROBLEM 1.21 Calculate and reconcile cash and accrual income

Leslie has a part-time business, Quick Crack-Fix, repairing small cracks and stars in car windshields using a special polymer filler that makes the damage almost invisible and stops the cracks from spreading. The repair takes only a few minutes using equipment and supplies stored in the trunk of Leslie's car. The main customers are used car lots, car rental companies, service stations, and insurance companies, but some business is done with individual customers in the driveways of their homes.

For the current year, Leslie's business records show the following:

Collections from customers during the year	$38,562
Payments to suppliers during the year	6,538
Royalty payments to owner of Crack-Fix trademark during the year	3,265
Money taken out of the business by Leslie during the year	25,000
Amortization on business equipment and car for the year	4,800
Amounts owing by customers at the end of the previous year	2,680
Amounts owing by customers at the end of the current year	910
Amounts owing to suppliers at the end of the previous year	615
Amounts owing to suppliers at the end of the current year	927
Supplies on hand at the end of the previous year	0
Cost of supplies on hand at the end of the current year	465

Leslie's business bank account showed a balance of $1,654 at the end of the previous year.

a. Calculate the business's cash income for the current year, explaining whether you have treated the money Leslie took out of the business as a business expense (deducting it in calculating cash income for the business) or a personal withdrawal (not deducting it in calculating cash income for the business).
b. Calculate the bank account balance at the end of the current year, using your answer from part (a).

c. Calculate the business's accrual income for the current year.
d. Reconcile your answers to parts (a) and (b).

CHALLENGING

PROBLEM 1.22 Why is accrual accounting valued?

An executive of an international economic consulting firm recently said, "I find it interesting that as companies, or even countries, grow in sophistication, they tend to move from simple cash-based financial reports to accrual accounting reports." If this observation is valid, why would you suppose this movement to accrual accounting is happening?

Accounting Analysis • Section 1.12

Bank Reconciliation

*** PROBLEM 1.23** Reconcile a bank balance

Wayne has been facing some cash flow problems. Specifically, he has been having trouble keeping his bank account straight. He went to the bank to find out his balance and was told that it was $365 as of September 15. As far as he could remember, he had made a deposit of $73 that had not yet been credited by the bank and had written cheques of $145, $37, $86, and $92 that had not yet been deducted from his account by the bank.

At the same time, a good, but impatient, friend is demanding repayment of a loan of $70. Does Wayne have enough money in his bank account to repay it?

PROBLEM 1.24 Reconcile a bank statement to personal records

Reconcile Henry's month-end bank account balance and indicate what corrections you would make to Henry's records based on your analysis.

Month-end bank balance according to the bank's statement, $9,682.
Month-end bank balance according to Henry's records, $8,347.
Outstanding cheques (not processed by the bank yet), $1,937.
Outstanding deposit (not processed by the bank yet), $375.
Bank charges Henry had not known about, $58.
Someone else's cheque put through Henry's account by the bank, $205.
Interest on the bank balance credited by the bank but not known to Henry, $36.

PROBLEM 1.25 Perform a bank reconciliation to make a decision

David is considering whether or not to buy a used car for $9,500 on May 1, 2006. The only problem is that he does not know if he has enough cash to pay for the car in full or whether he needs to take out a bank loan. According to his records, he has $9,710 in his account but his bank balance according to the bank is $8,870. Using the following information, (1) reconcile David's bank account balance and (2) decide whether or not he will need a bank loan to pay for the car.

David's cash records for April:

1. Loan given to his brother by cheque, which had not been deposited yet	$1,500
2. Paycheque from his employer for April; it was deposited yesterday but had not cleared through the bank yet.	2,330
3. Rent paid by cheque for the month of April. David knew the landlord did not deposit the cheque until May 1.	850
4. Food purchased with a debit card (instant account withdrawal)	285
5. Purchases on his credit card for the month of April (to be paid in May)	840
6. Bank charges that David had not known about	25
7. Proceeds from the sale of a government bond that the bank had not credited to his account yet	835

Credit Card Reconciliation

*** PROBLEM 1.26** Credit card bills reconciliation

Dave was in an awful tangle over his Vista credit card. He had just received a bill from Vista that was much larger than he'd expected and thought the company must have made a mistake. After he calmed down, he got out all his credit card slips and other documents. This is what he found:

Amount owing according to Vista, $1,285.
Total unpaid credit card slips in Dave's pile, $954.
Two slips that, as far as Dave could tell, Vista had not yet billed him for, $118.
A cash advance that Dave had taken against the card but had forgotten about, $200.
One charge on the Vista bill that Dave did not have a slip for and did not remember, $249.

Does Dave have it all sorted out now? What do you think would be the right amount to pay Vista?

PROBLEM 1.27 Reconcile a credit card statement to a cardholder's records

Sue has just received her monthly credit card statement from MonsterCard. It says she owes $2,730. She is horrified, not having anticipated such a large amount, though she does have an envelope full of credit card slips that total a net of $1,830 (adding up all the charges and deducting some credits for goods returned to stores). Using the following information, reconcile the statement to Sue's envelope of slips and determine how much you think Sue should pay MonsterCard this month.

a. Three of Sue's slips, totalling $217, have not yet been included in the MonsterCard statement because she charged the amounts after the statement date.
b. One of the items on the statement was $628 for a major car repair that Sue remembers having done, though she can't find the credit card slip.
c. MonsterCard charged Sue $85 to renew the card for another year and added that amount to her other charges for the month.
d. One of the items on the statement was for a $225 meal in a city Sue has never even been to.
e. Sue had returned an item costing $179 to Retail Emporium Co. three months ago, but has not yet been credited for the return on MonsterCard's statement.

PROBLEM 1.28 Reconcile a credit card statement with the cardholder's records

The Christmas season was a hectic, busy, and expensive one for Ted. He just received his American Expression Credit Card bill for the month of December with a total due of $3,964. Ted cannot believe that he managed to spend such a large amount on Christmas presents over the holidays since he had only budgeted $3,000 for presents in all of December. Using the following information, reconcile the credit card statement with Ted's set of credit card slips and figure out whether he actually exceeded his budget for presents or not.

a. Ted had slips totalling $2,638 for his December present purchases.
b. Ted had taken a cash advance for $530 out on his card to pay for emergency repairs on his car. He forgot that American Expression charged him interest from the time the cash advance was taken. The charge was $7.
c. Due to the Christmas rush, Ted had not paid his November bill in full, thus charges of $328 plus $11 in interest carried over to his December bill.
d. Ted realized he had accidentally thrown out the slip for a present purchased in December that came to $365.

e. American Expression had billed him $85 for the renewal of his Member Super Plus Gold Card for the next year and the charge appeared on his December statement.

Change Effects and Net-of-Tax Analysis

*** PROBLEM 1.29** Calculate the change in net income

Mountain Crest Enterprises Inc. has revenue this year of $5,645,231, expenses other than income tax of $4,889,811, and an income tax rate of 30%. The president is considering a new marketing plan that is expected to add $342,500 to expenses and $645,000 to revenue.

a. Calculate the plan's expected effect on net income.
b. Show that your answer to part (a) is correct by (i) calculating the expected total revenue, total expenses other than income tax, income before tax, income tax expense, and net income, and (ii) subtracting the present net income from the expected net income to show that the result is your answer in part (a).

PROBLEM 1.30 Find the effects of various events on net income

Grandiloquent Gestures Inc. is a major supplier of costumes and party supplies and will plan any affair for a customer, such as a romantic evening for popping the question, or a celebration of many years of marriage, or a congratulations party for finding employment. The company's income tax rate is 35%. The company is considering some changes in its operations. Calculate separately the effect on the company's net income of each of the following proposals.

a. The company might spend more on advertising, adding $140,000 to its advertising expenses.
b. The company might raise some selling prices, adding $52,000 to revenue.
c. The company might fire the chief accountant, and use a cheap computer program instead. The chief accountant is paid $75,000 per year, and the cheap computer program will cost $4,450 a year.
d. If the company fires the chief accountant, it will incur additional losses due to shoplifting and employee theft of $15,000 per year.
e. The company might make a $75 donation to the Poor Accountants' League.

PROBLEM 1.31 Effects and net-of-tax analysis

Authors Agency Inc. manages many best-selling authors in their relations with publishers, movie companies, TV producers, and so on. In the current year, its revenues total $15,452,200 and its expenses (not including 40% income tax) total $13,222,500. The company is negotiating with famous author Stephen Queen to take on Queen's account. This is a big deal: if Authors Agency manages Queen's account, its revenues will increase by $5,300,000 and its expenses (Queen likes limos and 5-star hotels) will increase by $4,800,000.

a. What is Authors Agency's net income for the current year?
b. What would the company's net income be if it took Queen's account on?
c. Show that your answer to part (b) is right. If you did part (b) the long way, do it the short way here. If you did it the short way, do it the long way here.

PROBLEM 1.32 Effects of losing a contract on net income

Economy Chicken Inc. sells poultry to discount grocery stores, restaurants, the army, and other customers. The company's income statement for 2006 follows:

Economy Chicken Inc.
Income Statement for the Year 2006

Revenues		$67,455,892
Expenses:		
Cost of poultry sold	$ 32,555,678	
Operating, selling, and administrative expenses	21,223,590	
Interest and other financial expenses	3,210,443	
Amortization	6,789,420	63,779,131
Income before income tax		$ 3,676,761
Income tax expense		1,323,634
Net income for the year		$ 2,353,127

The army wants to renegotiate its contract with Economy Chicken, and proposes that if the company spends $2,500,000 per year more on quality control, the army will buy $2,100,000 more in chicken from the company. If the company does not agree to this, the army will likely take its considerable business elsewhere. Calculate the company's revised net income if the army's proposal is accepted.

Integrated Problems

* PROBLEM 1.33 Review of some basic ideas

Answer the following questions:

1. What is the difference between an accountant and an auditor?
2. What is the difference between accrual income and cash income?
3. Are users of financial accounting information all the same in their information needs? Why or why not?

CHALLENGING AND EXTENDED TIME

PROBLEM 1.34 Factors in comparing companies' performance

The president of Gobble Gobble Foods Inc., which makes everything from soup to nuts out of turkey meat, is comparing Gobble Gobble's performance to that of Curdled Products Inc., which does much the same using tofu and other bean curds. The president has the following data for Curdled Products, which she saw in the *Glower and Flail* newspaper yesterday (note that figures inside brackets indicate a loss):

Income for 2000	$1,565,000
Income for 2001	2,432,000
Income for 2002	(985,000)
Income for 2003	123,000
Income for 2004	1,249,000
Income for 2005	2,915,000
Income for first half of 2006	873,000

Without knowing much about accounting except the introductory ideas of this chapter, use your intelligence and experience in comparing things to make a list of the factors you think the president of Gobble Gobble should take into account in comparing her company's performance to that of Curdled.

CHALLENGING

PROBLEM 1.35 Objectives and risks in investment

Suppose you had a few thousand dollars on hand and were offered a chance to invest in a small local business. What would be the objectives you would like to see such an investment meet? What risks would you want reassurance about before committing your funds? (You can get some hints about this from the Continuing Demonstration Case.)

CASE 1A

ACCRUAL AND CASH INCOME IN MEASURING PERFORMANCE

Manitoba Wings is an airline services company with a plant near the Winnipeg airport and service centres in several provinces. It provides meals, napkins and other food-related items, airplane cleaning, interior maintenance, and several other services to various airlines. The company has been fairly successful, though recessions and deregulation of air services have put significant pressure on its operations. When the company began in the late 1970s, it had a relatively weak financial position (mainly because of borrowing to get set up) and its financial performance, while satisfactory, has not enabled it to reduce its debt load very much. It seems that every time the company gets a little ahead, new equipment must be purchased or new product lines developed, and the company finds itself borrowing again.

A recent year provides a good example. The company's accrual income was $188,000 and its cash income was $241,000. (The difference was due to amortization expense of $96,000 and uncollected revenue being $43,000 higher at the end of the year than at the beginning. In the company's financial statements, the phrase "net income for the year" was used to describe the accrual income and "cash generated by operations" described the cash income.) The president had looked forward to using some of the cash to pay down debts, but late in the year the company had to buy new food-handling and food-wrapping equipment for $206,000 to meet revised standards announced by its airline customers. Therefore, the company ended up only a few thousand dollars ahead in cash, not enough to make much of a dent in its debts.

The president has a regular half-yearly meeting with the company's external auditor to discuss accounting and auditing issues. After the above results were known, the president phoned the auditor and made the following comments: "I thought I'd ask you to think about a few things before our meeting next week. When it comes to our accounting, I think the company has too many masters and too many measures. What I mean is, first, too many people are concerned with what our financial statements say. Why can't we just prepare financial statements that meet my needs as president—why do we have to worry about all the other people outside the company? Sometimes I'm not even sure who all those other people are, since you accountants and auditors often just talk about 'users' without being too clear about what you mean. Also, I'm confused by the existence of both a 'net income' figure and a 'cash generated by operations' figure in our financial statements. Why can't we just have one or the other to measure our performance?"

The president raised issues that will be addressed frequently as this book develops your understanding. But for now, what would you say to the president?

CASE 1B

PEOPLE INVOLVED IN FINANCIAL ACCOUNTING

Bedford Road Productions Inc. (BRP) is a Nova Scotia media company that has begun to be noticed nationwide, in Europe, and the United States. BRP buys media space, especially on TV and in magazines, for various customers, and has its own design and production staff so that it can suggest ads to customers and media outlets and then go on to produce some ads itself. The company is recognized for its irreverent humour and zany approach to advertising, as well as for its ability to create ad placements that have a strong impact on customers' sales and reputation.

Here are some of the people involved in BRP:

- Kathy Barsnable, one of the two original founders of BRP and now the company's president as well as a main shareholder, is very ambitious for the company and wants to see it become a real international player, with expanded production facilities that would allow it to begin producing TV shows, special events, and even small movies. She is insistent that the company show growth and success in all its ventures.
- Greg Thom is the other original founder and is now the company's chief financial officer. Using some family money, Greg provided the company's initial financing, and he is still the company's largest shareholder, though he owns less than half the shares and so does not control the company. He also is a creditor, having provided some of the financing in loans as well as in shares. Greg is in favour of slow, careful growth, and often disagrees with Kathy's grander plans, but he and Kathy have a lot of respect for each other and work well together most of the time. Greg would be happy if others largely ran BRP, so that he could focus more on family investments and some other ventures he would like to start.
- Brent Siddhu is the company's production head. Brent, who owns some shares of the company but less than Kathy or Greg, has been pushing for expansion into TV production. He is very bright and good with people, but is bored with the media placement business that is still the foundation of BRP's success. Brent likes to travel to Los Angeles, and rumour has it that he would leave if a more creative opportunity arose.
- Hendrick Argot owns one of BRP's major customers, a much bigger company than BRP. Hendrick has been very supportive of BRP's efforts and, in addition to being a good customer, has often suggested to Kathy and Greg that he would like to buy into BRP, maybe even buy control and wrap BRP into his own media operations. Kathy used to work for Hendrick, leaving to start BRP with Greg, and although she gets along very well with Hendrick, she wants to run her own business.
- Susan Dohn is a partner in the public accounting firm that is BRP's external auditor. In addition to doing the auditing, Susan provides tax and financial advice to Kathy and Greg. BRP is one of her main clients, which she has seen grow from its small beginnings, and she was promoted to partner partly because of her success in serving BRP. There have been some controversies over some of BRP's accounting methods, which have tended to show higher income than Susan was comfortable with, but she has managed to smooth out the problems, convincing Kathy to agree to some less optimistic accounting. Kathy has agreed but still, were Greg not there to add his more cautious views, Susan might have had more difficulty retaining BRP as a client.
- Clarice Xiao is the Nova Scotia loans manager for a big Canadian bank. Clarice has also been involved with BRP for several years, approving steadily increasing bank financing as the company grew. She is rewarded by the bank for growth in her loans portfolio, but also is penalized if loans go bad, so she is interested in helping to further the company's ambitions as long as they are supported by solid business plans, including strong cash flow from which loans' interest can be met and principal repaid on schedule. Clarice, following standard bank procedure, has required that, as long as the bank has significant loans to BRP, the main shareholders must agree not to sell their shares to each other or anyone else without the bank's permission.

Discuss the different points of view these people have of BRP and their likely different interests in what the company's financial statements show about its position and performance.

NOTES

1. "Patrick O'Brian," *The Economist* (January 15, 2000): 88.
2. Eric Auchard, "IBM Financial Reporting Criticized, Shares Drop," Reuters, 24 November 1999. "Tyco: Aggressive or Out of Line?" *Business Week* (November 1, 1999): 160–65. David Henry, "Still Spooked by the Market," *Business Week* (April 29, 2002): 88. Monica Roman (ed.), "Taking Aim at Tyco—Again," *Business Week* (January 28, 2002): 50. Michael Fleeman, "Opening the Book on the Weird World of Movie Math," *The Edmonton Journal* (September 13, 1999): C4.
3. Joseph Weber et al.,"The CFOs Weigh in on Reform," *Business Week* (March 11, 2002): 30–31.
4. CICA Media Release December 4, 2003, as reported on December 6, 2005, at www.cica.ca/index.cfm.ci_id/18853/la_id/1.htm.
5. Thanks to Robert H. Crandall, "Information Economics and Accounting Theory," *The Accounting Review* (July 1969): 457–66 for the original ideas used in this section. Since the 1960s, much work has been done in the fields of management information systems, accounting information systems, decision analysis, and the Internet to develop accounting and other systems that are properly responsive to decision-making needs.

PART TWO

Preparing and Using Financial Accounting's Reports

C2 *Measuring and Evaluating Financial Position*

C3 *Measuring and Evaluating Financial Performance*

C4 *Measuring and Evaluating Cash Flow*

C5 *Standards and Principles Surrounding the Financial Statements*

The four chapters in this group introduce the set of financial statements and the principles and environment that influence, even determine, their nature.

- *Chapter 2 examines the balance sheet, the reflection of the accounting system's accumulation of information over the life of the enterprise. The history and present nature of the "double-entry" system and its "debits and credits" are covered, as is how to interpret the resulting financial statement. The balance sheet's depiction of the enterprise's legal structure and sources of financing is reviewed.*

- *Chapter 3 uses the same approach to introduce the income statement, which is accrual accounting's fundamental measure of financial performance, and the statement of retained earnings, which connects the income statement to the balance sheet.*

- *Chapter 4 introduces the cash flow statement, which is both the fourth regular financial statement and a major example of user-oriented accounting analysis.*
- *Chapter 5 completes the introduction of the financial statements by dealing with a variety of preparation and use principles and environmental forces (such as auditing, ethics, international agreements, and the stock market) acting on financial accounts.*

CHAPTER TWO

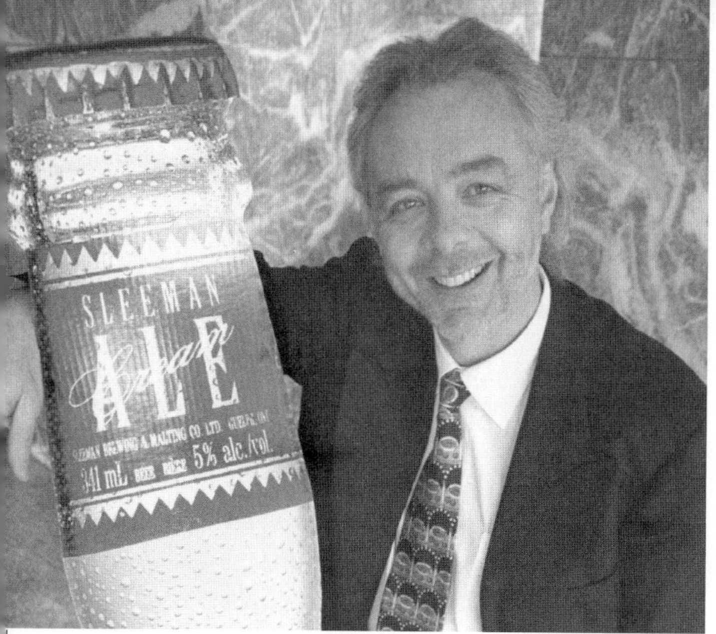

2 Measuring and Evaluating Financial Position

For information on this topic, please visit the online tutorial at www.gibbins6e.nelson.com

2.1 Chapter Introduction: Measuring and Evaluating Financial Position

"I am pleased that Sleeman continues to move in a positive direction and I am confident we will continue to make strategic decisions that benefit both our customers and our shareholders."[1]

There are two significant strategic investments disclosed in Sleeman's 2004 annual report. The first is the investment in capital projects expected to reduce operating costs at the Guelph brewery by $1.5 million annually. The second, aimed at growth in sales and income, is the acquisition of Unibroue, considered Quebec's premier brewer of craft beers and the largest microbrewery in the province. Both of these investments were made in management's ongoing quest for growth not only in sales but also in returns to the shareholders.

To achieve these goals, the return earned on these assets must be sufficient to pay the interest costs on the funds borrowed to make the investments, return the capital invested, and add to the earnings of the shareholders. Shareholders benefit from these returns either through the receipt of dividends or the through an increase in the market value of their shares.

If the investments are to add value for the shareholders, the level of risk must be reasonable. History has shown that a firm that is too highly leveraged—that is, that has too much debt relative to the assets owned—faces increased risk of financial failure. The market reacts to this situation by lowering the price offered for shares.

Even before you study the ratios used by financial analysts, the first of which are introduced in this chapter, some evaluation of Sleeman's financial position can be made by reading the Annual Report.

The Statements of Cash Flow reveal that $15,375,000 was invested in the capital projects and $40,265,000 in the acquisition of Unibroue. The statement also reveals that approximately $40 million of this was financed by increased debt and the remainder came from funds generated (earned) by Sleeman's business operation during the year. Sleeman actually reduced the proportion of assets provided by debt, a reduction of financial risk, while making these large investments. The company's profit and earnings per share increased in 2004. The increase of approximately 50% in share value during 2004 gives some indication that the strategic decisions mentioned by John Sleeman are resulting in progress towards the stated goals of benefit for the shareholders.

Learning Objectives

Chapter 1 introduced accrual accounting and its transactional base. Now we turn to four chapters that set out financial accounting's *results* and outline the *recordkeeping system* that leads to those results. Chapter 1 introduced this book's integrative approach. Chapters 2–4 focus on various financial statements and the underlying accounting system that is common to all, and Chapter 5 pulls it all together by examining the accounting principles also common to all.

This chapter focuses on the first of the set of financial statements outlined in Chapter 1: the balance sheet or statement of financial position. You will learn:

- Why the balance sheet is important, why it is arranged as it is, and some interesting history about where it came from;
- How the balance sheet is put together to answer questions about an enterprise's financial structure and strength;
- How the underlying accounting system generates the information used to assemble the balance sheet (and other statements covered later);
- How to interpret the balance sheet's representation of an enterprise's financial position and so help information users use it in decision making (this is part of the book's overall objective for your understanding of the financial statements, and, as in other chapters, this means brief introductions to some complex issues covered more fully in later courses).

Because courses may cover topics in different orders, Sections 2.9–2.11 may be read ahead of Sections 2.4–2.8 if you wish. Section 2.9 may be read at any point after Section 2.3.

2.2 A Brief History of Early Accounting

Accounting has served society for thousands of years.

Here is a brief review of some accounting history. Understanding how we got to where we are helps in understanding why and how we do the things we do now. Financial accounting is an ancient information system indeed, with many of its ideas originating hundreds or thousands of years ago.

Like other complex human inventions, financial accounting did not just appear one day fully formed. It has developed over thousands of years and has been thoroughly intertwined with the development of civilization. A science writer, quoting a brewery owner, had this to say on the topic of accounting and beer:

> Whatever the reason, the early farmers in Mesopotamia grew grain and "if you have grain, you need storehouses; if you have storehouses, you need accountants; if you have accountants, bang—you're on the road to civilization" (or the world's first audit).[2]

Accounting changes as the demands on it change, though not always smoothly.

Our focus here is on accounting, not on history. Nevertheless, the past has a bearing on accounting in that accounting evolves as business, government, and other institutions in society evolve. As the needs for information change, accounting changes to meet those needs. Accounting's evolution is not always smooth, and not always efficient; at any given time there are aspects of accounting that may not seem to fit current needs well, but over time, we can expect that accounting will, as it has in the past, meet those needs if they persist.

The need for verifiable records of resources and debts is very old.

When commerce consisted mainly of trading among families or tribal units, information demands were not complicated. Money had not been invented, so even simple financial reports could not have been prepared. People would want to know what they had on hand and would need some sort of documentation to accompany shipments, so that they and their customers would agree on what was being traded. To meet such needs, accounting began as simple list making. Especially important would be lists of the family or tribe's resources and, later, lists of debts to traders or other families. Later still, as commercial activities became more complex, families began to employ others to run aspects of their businesses and began also to create large business units with several locations. Accounting had to become more complex too, providing records that could be used to monitor the activities of employees and businesses in far-flung locations. People found that they needed to be able to verify what employees and traders said was happening. Because of these needs, the practice of having systematic records that could be audited later was begun.

To help you understand how present-day financial accounting concepts and techniques arose, a brief history, taking us from about 4500 B.C. in Mesopotamia to the 15th century Italian Renaissance, will be explored. Later, we will focus on more recent history. Keep in mind that the purpose of the review is to help you understand accounting, not to explain general history.

This history review focuses on the West; the rest of the world has interesting stories too.

Because modern accrual accounting, as practised in North America and much of the rest of the world, has its roots in the development of Western civilization, our review of accounting history is oriented to that development. The interesting stories of the development of accounting in other parts of the world, such as China, India, and Africa, are therefore not included. The comments below are necessarily brief. If you would like to read further, some reading suggestions on accounting history are provided at the end of the chapter.[3]

Mesopotamia to Rome: 4500 B.C. to A.D. 400

Today's balance sheets owe much to the list making of earlier times.

For a society to demand accounting, it must have active trade and commerce, a basic level of writing, methods of measuring and calculating, and a medium of exchange or currency.[4] The civilization that flourished in Mesopotamia (now Iraq and Syria) is usually thought to be the earliest society with an active recordkeeping system, though there is also some evidence of early records in Egypt, prepared, wouldn't you know it, for tax purposes.[5] Generally, a common language (such as Babylonian) existed for business, and there was also a good system of numbers and currency and of recordkeeping using clay tablets. As far as we know, ordinary merchants and general traders did not keep official records. Officials of the government and religious leaders of the temples decided what records were to be maintained for official purposes, and scribes did the recordkeeping. A scribe apprenticed for many years to master the craft of recording taxes, customs duties, temple offerings, and trade between governments and temples. Records consisted of counts and lists of grain, cattle, and other resources, and of obligations arising from trade. We can still see that today; the balance sheet of any enterprise includes items like unsold products and equipment, and trade obligations, such as amounts due from customers and due to suppliers. All of these balance sheet figures are summaries supported by detailed lists.

Some sort of audit was needed in earlier times, just as today.

When a scribe determined that a particular record was complete and correct, the scribe's seal was pressed into a clay tablet to certify that this was so, and the tablet was baked to prevent alteration.[6] The scribe was a forerunner of today's accountants and auditors; today's auditor writes a report instead of attaching a seal, but the function of providing assurance is an old one. This scribe-based form of recordkeeping was used for many years, spreading across land and time to Egypt, Greece, and Rome. Media other than clay tablets, such as papyrus, were used as time passed.[7] (Do you suppose people accustomed to clay tablets resisted the introduction of papyrus, just as some people accustomed to pencil and paper now resist the introduction of computers for accounting?)

Trade and commerce grew over thousands of years, from small, family operations to very large activities involving kings, religious leaders, and various levels of government.

FIGURE 2.1

A rare example of an early system of accounting, this marble slab documents the disbursements of the Athenian state, 418 B.C. to 415 B.C. Reproduced by courtesy of the Trustees of the British Museum.

The auditor heard the local manager's story, then gave a judgment. Not so different from today!

For example, as the Greek civilization spread, and the Roman Empire grew, administrative regions were organized in conquered lands in order to simplify governing them. Local administrators or governors, who managed these regions, generally could neither read nor write. When an accounting of their management was required, an official of the central government would come out and listen to an oral report. This event was, therefore, a "hearing," and the listening official was there to "audit" (from the Latin word for "hear"). Today, the person who comes to inspect and approve the financial statements of an enterprise is called an auditor, though a lot more goes on today than just listening!

The Dark Ages to the Renaissance: A.D. 400 to A.D. 1500

The Crusades helped merchants and banks to develop in the Mediterranean area.

With the fall of the Roman Empire in about the 5th century A.D., both trade and associated recordkeeping became stagnant in Europe, though activities still continued in Constantinople, North Africa, the Middle East, India, China, and elsewhere. Many ideas and inventions that we now take for granted slowly seeped into Europe: algebra from Arabia, gunpowder from China, and bookkeeping from India by way of Arabia and Constantinople. In Europe, great stimulus to trade began with the period of the Crusades, around the 11th century, when kings and princes could not themselves provide the material to support their retinues of crusaders bound for the Holy Land. This was a prosperous time for the lesser nobles and private merchants who supplied the crusaders from ports such as Venice. A shift of supply and economic power from governments to the private sector began, and large merchant banks developed, such as the Medici in Florence. These banks got heavily involved in the businesses and governments they helped to finance.

Much of the development of arithmetic needed by accounting happened in Arab countries.

Because of all these activities, a more exact system of recordkeeping was developed in order to keep track of materials supplied, cash received and spent, and especially who owed whom how much money.[8] For the traders, merchants, and bankers, the stimulus provided by the Crusades set recordkeeping off in a more organized and systematic direction. The new direction was made possible also by refinements in the use of numbers and arithmetic that had taken place in Arab countries during Europe's Dark Ages. The number system we use in accounting and in our daily lives originated from these refinements.

Modern bookkeeping still uses the double-entry system Pacioli described 500 years ago.

The exact way that accounting—or more precisely, the recordkeeping basis of accounting we call *bookkeeping*—evolved during this busy time is a subject of debate among accounting historians. A major event, however, was the publication in 1494, using the newly invented printing press, of a treatise on "double-entry" bookkeeping by Friar Luca *Pacioli* of Tuscany and Venice, in Renaissance Italy. In the book, he referred to the method as an established procedure that had been in use in the Medici banks of Italy and in other businesses for some time. Pacioli's book was an important contribution to the knowledge of algebra and arithmetic, and had value specifically because of its detailed description and codification of the double-entry system. It was rapidly translated into all the major European languages, and, using these translations, European scholars extended Pacioli's ideas. Major international celebrations of Pacioli's work were held in 1994, to mark 500 years since his book was published.

Double-Entry Bookkeeping

Pacioli's concepts were revolutionary and sound: they form the fundamental basis of modern financial accounting, providing a method of pulling together all the lists of resources and obligations in a way that helps to prevent errors. The idea is that each trade or other commercial transaction is recorded (entered) twice, hence the *double entry:*

- once to recognize the resource involved in the transaction; and
- once to recognize the source or effect of that resource change.

Double entry is designed to ensure both aspects of transactions are recorded.

Instead of the disconnected lists that existed before double-entry bookkeeping was invented, the lists of resources and sources were now connected to each other. Now a balance sheet of the modern kind could be prepared. Double-entry bookkeeping, which might be seen as a pretty humdrum sort of activity, turns out to have a solid conceptual basis and a long and important history.

Once a dollar amount (or that in any other medium of exchange—pounds, euros, yen and so on) is assigned to a transaction, that amount can be used to record both sides of the transaction. The two sides, and the sums of the two sides of all the transactions recorded, act as a check on each other. If errors are made, they are likely to be found because the two sides will not add up to the same amount. If they do add up, we say they "balance" (hence the "balance sheet" shows that the two sides do add up). The recordkeeping system Pacioli described to the world is one of the most far-reaching of human inventions.

2.3 Introduction to The Balance Sheet

The diagram that follows, which was introduced in Chapter 1, is a reminder that following this book's integrative approach, the hows, whys, and uses of the balance sheet are woven together into an overall portrayal in this chapter.

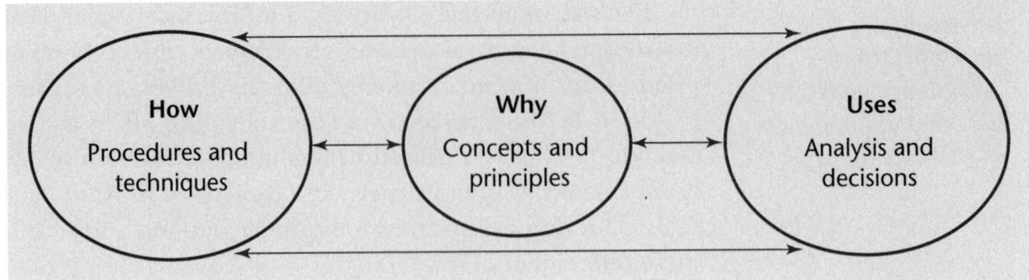

The *balance sheet*, financial accounting's oldest and most basic report, measures the enterprise's financial position at a particular date and is the basis for much financial analysis. This statement is sometimes called the *statement of financial position*, because the longer title describes exactly what the statement shows. (This book mostly uses the older, shorter, and more popular title. As in other areas of accounting, be prepared for variation in terminology!) The balance sheet summarizes, at a particular date, the enterprise's *financial position* as accounting measures it, in three categories:

The balance sheet accounts measure financial position at a point in time.

1. resources (cash, products on hand, land, buildings, etc.), called *assets*
2. obligations (loans owing, debts to suppliers, etc.), called *liabilities*
3. owners' interests (what's left after subtracting the obligations from the resources), called *equity*

The individual items in these lists are called *accounts*, and over the centuries the task of preparing them has been named account*ing*, and the people who do it are account*ants*. All these words come from *count*, which is where accounting began, just counting things and listing them.

The balance sheet portrays the enterprise by arranging its lists of accounts so that the assets sum to the same total as the other two lists, and setting them beside each other, something like this:

EXHIBIT 2·1

Assets	
Item a	$$
Item b	$$
Etc.	$$
Total	T$$

Liabilities and Equity	
Item x	$$
Item y	$$
Etc.	$$
Total	T$$

Double-entry accounting produces a balanced balance sheet, anchoring the financial statements.

Because the left total equals the right total, accountants say that they *balance*. Hence, the name balance sheet. The accounting system maintains this balance by making sure that any changes in one side of the balance sheet are matched by changes in the other side. This requires that each change be recorded twice, so the accounting system is called *double-entry*. The balance sheet turns out to be the accumulation of everything financial accounting has recorded about the enterprise since the day the enterprise began, so it is the fundamental cumulative accounting record and is the anchor to which all the other financial statements are tied.

Assets are useful financial resources.

The left side in the above portrayal of the balance sheet's list of accounts represents the enterprise's financial *resources* at that date, as measured by the financial accounting methods you will learn. These resources, called *assets*, include the enterprise's cash, money customers have promised to pay, goods for sale, land, buildings, equipment, and many other resources that the enterprise has accumulated and can use in the future.

Liabilities are existing and estimated obligations; equity is the owners' investment.

The right side of the balance sheet's list of accounts represents the *sources*, or financing, of those resources at that date, again as measured by financial accounting methods. These financing sources include existing obligations that will have to be paid in the future, such as loans from the bank, amounts due to be paid to employees and suppliers, mortgages and other long-term borrowings, and many other *debts*. Some estimates of future payments are included also, even though they may not be legally owed just yet, such as promises to pay employee pensions, and estimated future income taxes based on income already earned but not yet taxed. All these legal obligations and estimates together are called *liabilities*. The list of sources also includes amounts received from owners, which normally involve permanent financing and do not have to be repaid, plus any past accrual incomes that have not been paid out to the owners. Owners can finance an enterprise by contributing money *to* the enterprise, or by *not* taking income *out* of the enterprise, as we will see. The owners' investment is called *owners' equity*, or just *equity*. (For corporations, which are owned by shareholders, the term is usually *shareholders' equity*, while for unincorporated businesses the terms *owner's capital* or *partners' capital* is likely used, but all of these terms just mean owners' equity.)

Because the balance sheet balances, the total amount of *assets* must equal the total of *liabilities* plus *equity*. Arithmetically, the *balance sheet equation* therefore is:

Sum of Assets	=	Sum of Liabilities + Sum of Equity
Resources list	=	Sources (financing) list

The balance sheet equation, $\Sigma A = \Sigma L + \Sigma E$, or just $A = L + E$, is maintained at all times.

This equation is fundamental to financial accounting. Accounting procedures are designed to create and maintain this equality at *all* times. For example, if you get \$100 by borrowing from the bank, your balance sheet would list the \$100 cash you got as a resource and the \$100 obligation to repay as a liability. By maintaining this equality, financial accounting ensures that all the financing sources that go with the resources are identified, and vice versa. This balanced pair of lists is one of the main reasons for financial accounting's value as an information system, though, as we will see, keeping the lists always in balance produces some difficulties for accounting too. To emphasize how financial accounting works, we can restate the balance sheet equation this way (where A, L and E are all sums of their components):

$$A \textit{ must} = L + E$$

The two lists, resources and sources, are put side by side, or the first above the second, as in the standard style shown below.

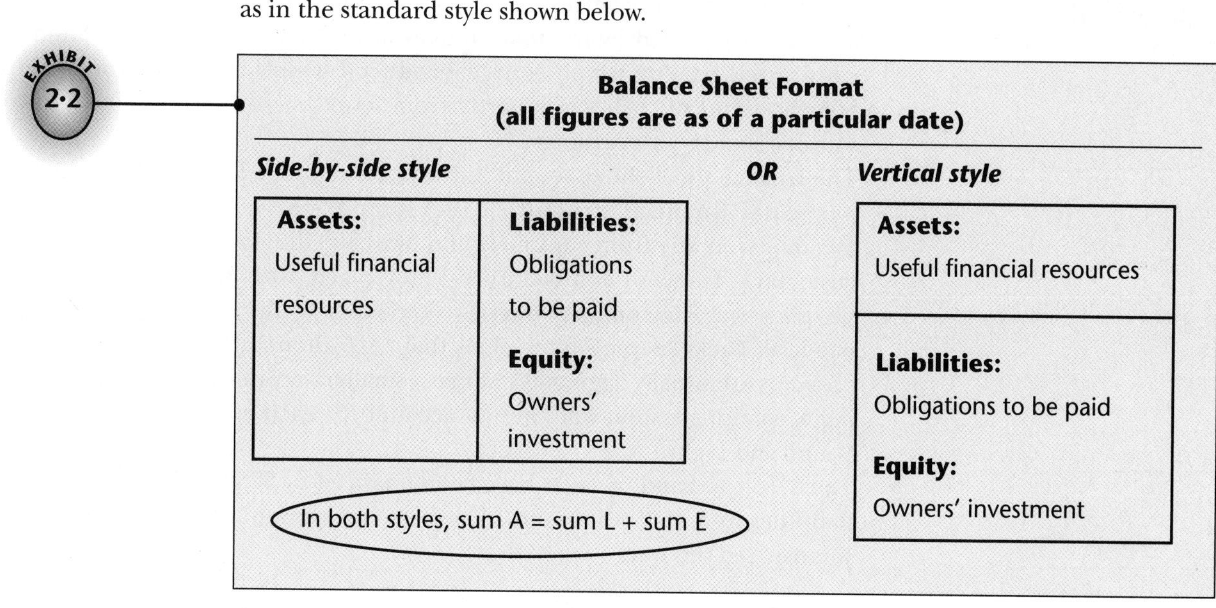

EXHIBIT 2·2
Balance Sheet Format
(all figures are as of a particular date)
Side-by-side style
OR
Vertical style
Assets:
Useful financial resources
Liabilities:
Obligations to be paid
Equity:
Owners' investment
Assets:
Useful financial resources
Liabilities:
Obligations to be paid
Equity:
Owners' investment
In both styles, sum A = sum L + sum E

Example Balance Sheet: Sound and Light Corporation

Below is a simple example balance sheet using the side-by-side style to emphasize the equality of the two lists, with assets on the left and liabilities and equity on the right. Explanations of the terms used in the balance sheet follow the example.

EXHIBIT 2·3

Sound and Light Corporation
Balance Sheet as at April 30, 2006
in Thousands of Dollars

Assets			**Liabilities and Equity**		
Current assets:			Current liabilities:		
Cash	$ 65		Owing to the bank	$ 50	
Due from customers	95		Owing to suppliers	96	$146
Unsold products	180	$340	Noncurrent liabilities:		
Noncurrent assets:			Land mortgage owing	$ 99	
Land (cost)	$200		Future income tax estimated	15	114
Factory (cost)	392		Total liabilities		$260
Accum. amort.*	(167)	425	Shareholders' equity:		
			Share capital issued	$260	
			Past income retained	245	505
TOTAL		$765	TOTAL		$765

* Accum. amort. is the total amortization on the factory recorded so far (accumulated). It is bracketed because it is negative, as will be explained below.

The balance sheet describes the financial structure at a particular date.

Let's review some features of this balance sheet:

- The title identifies the enterprise (Sound and Light Corporation), the point in time at which the balance sheet is drawn up (April 30, 2006), and the currency in which amounts are measured (thousands of dollars).
- The balance sheet balances! As of April 30, 2006, total resources of $765 thousand are exactly equalled by the total sources of these resources. It is a summary, so we cannot tell exactly which source produced which resource; for example, the $65 thousand of cash came partly from bank borrowing and partly from other sources, such as past earnings.
- The balance sheet shows several individual *accounts*, telling us about the company's particular financial structure. For example, the company expects to receive $95 thousand due from customers and owes $96 thousand to its suppliers (it is their customer). The land and factory are mortgaged, with $99 thousand still owing on the *mortgage*. The company owes $50 thousand to the bank but has chosen not to pay it all back, keeping more than that ($65 thousand) on hand as cash. (These accounts are usually aggregates of many smaller accounts; for example, the underlying accounting system will have an account for each customer who owes money to Sound and Light.)
- The $765 thousand of assets have been financed by $260 thousand ($146 + $114) of liabilities and $505 thousand of owners' investment. The balance sheet can be summarized this way:

Sound and Light Balance Sheet Summary

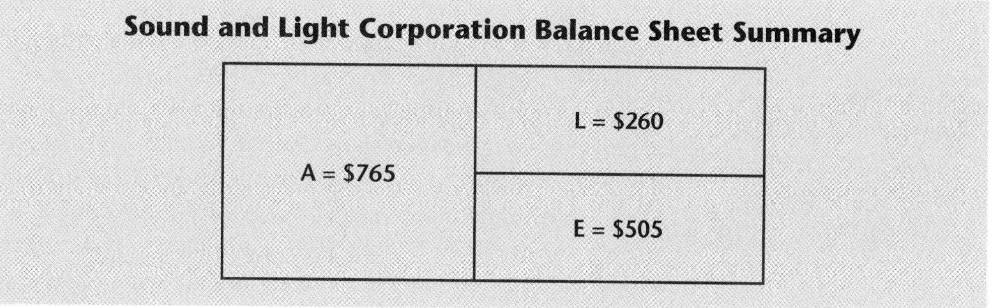

Explanations of the Three Balance Sheet Categories

Assets are resources that are owned or controlled and expected to bring future benefits.

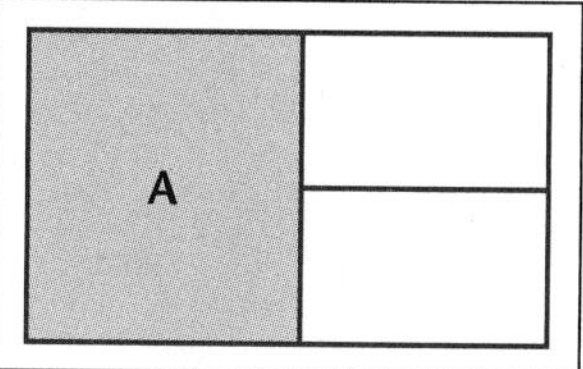

Assets. These are a mixture of the resources that the company needs to do business; for instance, products to sell or a building to operate from, and the resources that it has accumulated as a result of doing business, including amounts due from customers for past sales. *An asset is a resource, owned or controlled by the enterprise, that is needed or available to do business in the future, and which has value because it is expected to bring benefits as it is used, sold or collected.* Sound and Light's assets include cash, amounts due from customers (*accounts receivable*), unsold products (*inventory*), land, and the factory. (The "accumulated amortization" will be explained later.)

Accounting's definition of an asset doesn't include everything that has a future benefit.

Other "assets" of Sound and Light might include happy employees and a safe working environment, yet these do not appear on its balance sheet. There is a distinction between the assets that accounting recognizes and these other "assets." There are objective, standard measures for and economic control of the kind that accounting recognizes. An accounting asset like inventory of machine parts is owned by the enterprise and has a dollar cost that can be verified by anyone. A happy employee is, in theory, more productive than an unhappy employee, but it is difficult to measure with any consistency how much more productive a very happy employee is compared with an only mildly happy employee. Moreover, at least in our society, an enterprise does not own its employees! Accounting generally records assets only where there is economic control and where there can be a reasonable level of consistency in measurement techniques and results. This places limits on the scope of the financial statements.

Current assets are expected to provide benefits within a year; noncurrent assets provide benefits further into the future.

Assets are usually separated into shorter-term ones (*current assets*) and longer-term ones (*noncurrent assets*). Current assets are those that are expected to be used, sold, or collected within the next year, and noncurrent assets therefore are expected to have benefits for more than a year into the future. Sound and Light has $340 thousand in current assets and $425 thousand in noncurrent assets.

Liabilities arose in the past and represent legal or estimated claims on the assets.

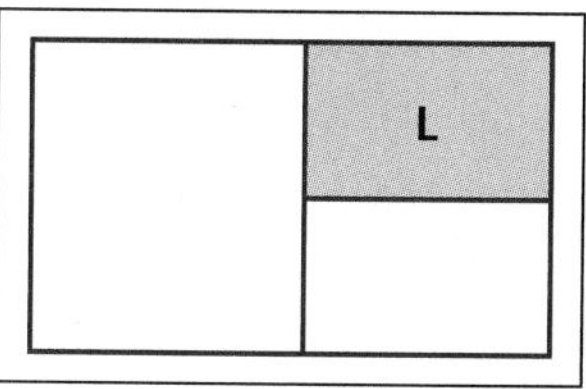

Liabilities. These are amounts due to creditors, such as to banks and suppliers, or amounts estimated to be due later, such as future pension payments to retired employees, estimated future income taxes, or interest building up on a bank loan. *A liability is a legally existing or estimated debt or obligation of the enterprise to another party, arising from a past transaction and so representing a claim on the assets at the balance sheet date.* Not all liabilities are expected to be paid in cash; some are "paid" by providing goods or services. An example is a deposit received from a customer for goods to be shipped later. The enterprise has the money (an asset) and records a corresponding liability for the deposit, but expects to give the customer the agreed-upon goods to discharge the liability. In the meantime, the customer has a claim on the enterprise, expecting to get either the goods or the cash back if the goods are not supplied. Sound and Light's liabilities include amounts owing to the bank and owing to suppliers (*accounts payable*), a mortgage on its property, and estimated future income taxes.

Accounting's definition of a liability doesn't include all possible future payments.

Following the same rule as for assets, liabilities generally include only obligations with objective and usually standard measures. If you are in debt to a friend for $10, it appears on your balance sheet. But, if you are "in debt" to a friend for saving your life, that does not appear on your balance sheet. Requiring that the obligation has arisen from a past transaction means that a promise to pay is a liability if the enterprise has already received the benefit (for example, has received cash from the bank, or goods from a supplier, or hard work from an employee expecting a pension). An expectation to pay later is *not* a liability if the transaction bringing the benefit has not happened (for example, an agreement to borrow before the cash has been received is not a liability, nor is an order to purchase something before the goods have arrived). Because some of these expected or possible future events may result in future payments even if they do not meet the definition of a liability and so do not appear in the balance sheet, they are sometimes described in the *notes to the financial statements* so that the users of the financial statement are aware of them.

Current liabilities are due within a year; noncurrent liabilities are due further into the future.

Like assets, liabilities are usually separated into shorter-term ones (*current liabilities*) and longer-term ones (*noncurrent liabilities*). Current liabilities are those that are due (expected to be paid or otherwise discharged) within the next year, and noncurrent liabilities therefore are due more than a year into the future. Some liabilities, such as many house mortgages, extend for years into the future but are partly paid each year, so the balance sheet would show both a current and a noncurrent portion for them. Sound and Light has $146 thousand in current liabilities and $114 thousand in noncurrent liabilities.

Equity is the owners' interest and equals the assets minus the liabilities.

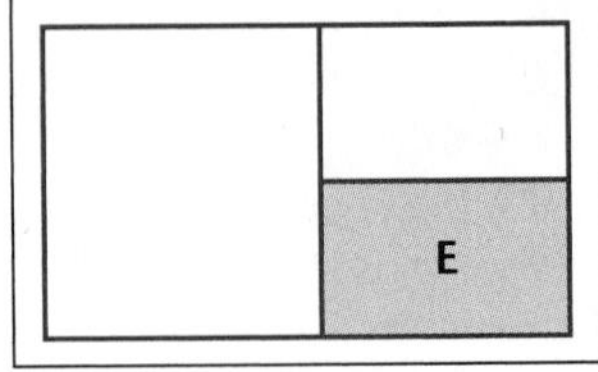

Equity. This is the owners' interest in the enterprise. That interest can come from direct contributions the owners have made, or from the accumulation of earnings that the owners have chosen not to withdraw. The details of the owners' equity section of the balance sheet depend on the legal structure of the enterprise and its ownership arrangements, which will be examined further later in this chapter.

The balance sheet does not distinguish between assets whose sources are liabilities and assets provided by owners. Complex financial events make this impractical, so the assets represent a pool of resources provided by all sources.

The owners' equity (book value) is not likely to equal the market value of the enterprise.

The owners' interest can be considered as a "residual" of the sum of the assets minus the obligations the enterprise has taken on: since A = L + E, the balance sheet equation can also be written E = A – L to focus on the equity amount.

- Because the balance sheet's equity figure equals assets minus liabilities, this residual or net concept of equity is often referred to as the *book value* of the whole enterprise.
- Book value is arithmetically valid, as the equation above shows. It is whatever accounting has measured as assets minus whatever it has measured as liabilities.
- However, book value may not tell us much about the value of the whole company right now. For example, if Sound and Light suddenly went out of business, the owners would be unlikely to receive exactly the equity of $505 thousand, because who knows what the assets would fetch if they had to be sold off all at once, and the liabilities perhaps would be settled for something other than the expected future payments used to record them.
- Similarly, if the owners decided to sell the business, the price they'd get would depend on their and the buyers' views as to the future success of the business, not just on the accumulated assets and liabilities recorded in the balance sheet. Thus, it is very unlikely that the price would equal the balance sheet equity figure.

- To summarize, owners' equity is based on historical transactions, and does not, except by coincidence, equal the current *market value* of the whole business.

Equity book value ← Assets – Liabilities according to accounting information

Equity market value ← Market forces only partly reflecting accounting information

Price to book ratio = Current price per share / Book value per share.

Before the high-technology and Internet companies lost their lustre in the early 2000s, many had small equity amounts in their balance sheets, but huge *stock market* values (*market capitalization*, share price times number of shares outstanding). The stock market was expecting strong future performance from such high-tech companies, and when those prospects dimmed, the stock market values plunged. Some of the plunge might have been predicted from analyzing the financial statements of individual companies, but much of it was due to investors' reduced expectations for success in the whole high-tech sector. The essential point is that a company's balance sheet's amounts and its overall value if sold or as measured by stock market prices come from different sets of information. The impact of these different sets may be gauged by the *price to book ratio*, which compares share price to book value (equity book value divided by the number of shares issued). A high or low ratio may indicate an over- or under-valued company. We'll tease out some of the connections between book values and current values, but others have to be left to finance and more advanced accounting courses.

Share capital is a major kind of corporations' owners' equity.

Contributions from owners can come in many forms, which we will look into a little later. For a corporation like Sound and Light, the most usual contribution is *share capital*: people give the corporation money in exchange for *shares*, which are portions of ownership interest. Sound and Light owners (shareholders) have contributed $260 thousand to the corporation. For example, some owners probably contributed cash to get Sound and Light started, so they would be among the sources of the cash asset. It is a coincidence that $260 thousand is also the total liabilities amount.

Share capital is the investment contributed by shareholders *directly* to the corporation.

Many corporations' shares, also called *stocks*, are traded on stock markets. In such markets, shares are traded between owners (investors). The corporations issuing the shares get money only when they issue the shares directly to the first owners. Therefore, trades subsequent to the initial share issue are not reflected in the corporation's share capital—these trades are transactions for the owners, but not for the corporation.

Retained earnings are the investment that owners have made by not withdrawing income.

Past income retained, usually called *retained earnings*, represents past accrual income not yet given to owners. (The terms *earnings*, *income*, and *profit* are used pretty much interchangeably, but they all refer to accrual income, as described in Chapter 1.) As we'll see in later chapters, earning income means that there will be more assets (such as cash) and/or fewer liabilities, so income is a source of assets. Sound and Light has $245 thousand in retained earnings, which means it has $245 thousand more in assets than it would have had if those earnings had all been paid out. The owners could have withdrawn cash or other assets from the company (for instance, by declaring themselves a *dividend*, which is a payment of some of the retained earnings to the owners), but they have chosen instead to leave the assets in the corporation. Thus, those assets are resources of the corporation and retained earnings are their source. The corporation can use the assets to earn more income in the future.

Retained earnings = $\sum$ Net incomes earned – $\sum$ Dividends declared since company began

Retained earnings = One of the sources of all the assets, not just cash

Negative equity is a sign of serious trouble.

Since E = A – L, it is arithmetically possible, and unfortunately seen sometimes in real enterprises, for equity to be negative. If the assets are *less* than the liabilities, which would indicate an enterprise with more obligations than resources (not a good position to be in!), the equity, and, therefore, the enterprise's book value, will be negative. Such a situation is a sign of serious financial problems and is likely to be followed by bankruptcy or other unpleasant results.

Probably you are getting tired of all the terms and definitions being introduced in this section! Getting the vocabulary of accounting across is a main function of an introductory textbook, and of these early chapters in particular. The vocabulary can be important, with much confusion if it is not used clearly. Here's an example, prompted by the possibility of negative equity just mentioned. Let's look at the term "deficit." It has several meanings, all negative versions of items we usually prefer to be positive:

A deficit is negative equity, retained earnings, income, or cash flow.

- negative accrual income (a loss)
- or negative retained earnings
- or negative equity
- or negative cash income (cash flow)

It's useful to be sure which meaning is intended when you're reading a newspaper article or watching a talking head on TV.

In the equity section of Barrick Gold Corporation's 2004 and 2003 balance sheets, the term "deficit" meant negative retained earnings. At December 31, 2004, the company had a retained earnings deficit of $624 million, but because its share capital was $4,129 million, the company's equity was still positive.[9]

These different meanings of deficit relate to one another. Large or persistent negative income can overcome any past retained earnings and produce negative retained earnings (retained losses, you might say). This could be large enough to overwhelm share capital and produce negative equity: assets must have become less than liabilities. During all this trouble, the enterprise likely also had negative cash flow.

Some Preliminary Analysis of the Sound and Light Balance Sheet

From the Sound and Light balance sheet, we can answer some questions about the corporation's financial condition:

Debt-equity ratio equals liabilities divided by equity.

1. *Financing*. Is the enterprise soundly financed? Sound and Light has financed its $765 thousand in assets as shown in the table at the right. So, it does not have a lot of debt, proportionately.

   What would you think if the creditors were owed $700 thousand, and the owners' equity was only $65 thousand? This would be a debt-equity ratio of $700 / $65 = 1,077% (10.8:1), a lot more risky for the creditors, because a lot more of their money than the owners' money would be at risk if the company ran into trouble.

Creditors	
$146,000	**short-term**
+ 114,000	**long-term**
$260,000	**34.0% of assets**
Owners	
$260,000	**contributed**
+ 245,000	**earnings not paid out**
$505,000	**66.0% of assets**
Debt-Equity Ratio	
$260,000 / $505,000	**= 51.5% (often written 0.52:1)**

Working capital equals current assets minus current liabilities. W/C ratio is CA/CL.

2. *Working Capital.* Can the enterprise pay its bills on time? Sound and Light owes $146 thousand in the short term and has only $65 thousand in cash. Therefore, to pay its bills it will have to collect cash from its customers either by getting them to pay what they already owe or by selling them some unsold products for cash.

Working Capital

$340,000	current assets
− 146,000	current liabilities
$194,000	**working capital**

There is likely no problem here: collections and sales and payments to creditors are probably going on continuously. The company has $340 thousand of current assets that it should be able to turn into cash to pay the $146 thousand of current liabilities. The *working capital* is positive, and the *working capital ratio* (also called the *current ratio*) indicates there is more than twice as much in current assets as current liabilities, so Sound and Light appears to be all right.

Working Capital Ratio

$$\frac{\$340{,}000}{\$146{,}000} = 2.33$$

The quick ratio compares near-cash assets to current liabilities.

3. *Quick Ratio.* Inventory of unsold goods is part of the current assets and so part of the working capital. But the company has to sell that inventory to get cash to pay its bills. So, if the company had trouble making its sales so that its inventory was building up, it could have difficulty paying its bills, even with positive working capital. If you were concerned about the company's ability to sell unsold goods to pay its bills, you could calculate the *quick ratio* (also called the *acid test ratio*). It is like the W/C ratio, but has only cash, very short-term investments that could be sold, and amounts due from customers in its numerator, no inventory. For Sound and Light, the quick ratio is greater than 1. We know the company could pay its current liabilities without having to sell unsold goods.

Quick Ratio

$$\frac{\$65{,}000 + \$95{,}000}{\$146{,}000} = 1.10$$

What would you think if the company had only $10 thousand in cash and $235 thousand in unsold products? In that case, though its working capital and working capital ratio would be the same, it would likely be overstocked and cash short, and might have trouble paying bills. Now the quick ratio would be 0.72. The company would have to sell some goods to meet its current liabilities.

Revised Quick Ratio

$$\frac{\$10{,}000 + \$95{,}000}{\$146{,}000} = 0.72$$

All ratios are only indicators. They require interpretation of the specific circumstances of each enterprise, so we don't know from our calculations if the company is in trouble, but a low quick ratio would be a signal to look further into the situation.

Ability to pay dividends depends on the amounts of both cash and retained earnings.

4. *Dividends.* Should the owners receive a dividend? If so, how large should it be? Legally, the *board of directors* (who manage Sound and Light on behalf of the shareholders) might be able to declare a dividend to shareholders of $245 thousand, the full amount of the retained earnings. But there is not nearly enough cash for that. Those past earnings have been reinvested in inventory of unsold products, building, equipment, and so on, and are therefore not sitting around in cash waiting to be paid to owners. This is true of nearly all corporations: they invest past earnings in operating assets and so do not have a lot of cash on hand. Probably a dividend of more than about $35 thousand, only one-seventh of the retained earnings, would cause Sound and Light some cash strain.

What would you think if the corporation had no buildings or equipment but $300 thousand in cash instead? It would appear to be cash-rich in that case and should either invest the cash productively or pay a dividend to the owners so they can do what they like with the money.

An amortized asset's book value is its cost minus its accumulated amortization.

5. *Accumulated Amortization.* What is that negative "accumulated amortization" item on the asset side of Sound and Light's balance sheet? In the example of Simone's jewellery business in Section 1.10, we deducted amortization from Simone's revenue in calculating accrual income, so that there would be an expense to represent the wear and tear on her equipment. Sound and Light has done the same: in calculating its income, it has deducted amortization expense on its factory. The income that is in the retained earnings part of the equity is, therefore, smaller than it would have been without this deduction. The accumulated amount of that expense, built up over the years, is deducted from the assets in the balance sheet to show how much of the economic value of the assets is estimated to have been used up so far.

Accumulated amortization is, therefore, a "negative asset" used to reduce the amounts of other assets. It corresponds to the amortization expenses that have been deducted in calculating income over the years, which in turn have reduced the retained earnings in equity. (Some balance sheets report only the net amount and give cost and accumulated amortization amounts in the notes.)

Book Value	
$392,000	factory cost
– 167,000	accumulated amortization
$225,000	**book value**

Comparing the cost and the accumulated amortization tells us something about the age of the factory. The $167 thousand accumulated amortization is less than half the factory's cost, so the company estimates that less than half the economic value of the factory has been used. What would you think if the accumulated amortization was $350 thousand? The factory would be nearing the end of its estimated life.

There we go again! The term "book value" can refer either to the net value of amortized assets (cost minus accumulated amortization) or to the equity of the enterprise (assets minus liabilities). As with the term "deficit," you need to know the context to know what book value means.

Three Common Balance Sheet Presentation Styles

So you see that the balance sheet provides interesting information if you know how to read it. Your skill in reading it will grow as you work with it. There are different styles of presentation of the balance sheet. All have the same information, but it is arranged differently. Three common styles, including the side-by-side and vertical formats we saw earlier, are illustrated below using the Sound and Light figures.

Sound and Light Corporation
Balance Sheet as at April 30, 2006
in Thousands of Dollars

Side-by-side style

Assets		**Liabilities and Equity**		
Current assets	$340	Current liabilities		$146
Noncurrent assets	425	Noncurrent liabilities		114
		Total liabilities		$260
		Owners' equity:		
		Contributed capital	$260	
		Retained earnings	245	505
TOTAL	$765	TOTAL		$765

Vertical style

Assets		
Current assets		$340
Noncurrent assets		425
TOTAL		$765
Liabilities and Equity		
Current liabilities		$146
Noncurrent liabilities		114
Total liabilities		$260
Owners' equity:		
Contributed capital	$260	
Retained earnings	245	505
TOTAL		$765

Working capital style

Net Assets		
Current assets		$340
Less current liabilities		146
Working capital		$194
Noncurrent assets		425
TOTAL		$619
Financing Sources		
Noncurrent liabilities		$114
Owners' equity:		
Contributed capital	$260	
Retained earnings	245	505
TOTAL		$619

HOW'S YOUR UNDERSTANDING?

Here are two questions you should be able to answer based on what you have just read. If you can't answer them, it would be best to reread the material.

1. The balance sheet is a summary of certain things at a point in time. What things?
2. Assemble a balance sheet for Northern Inc. from the following information and comment on the company's financial position at that point in time:

   Payable to suppliers, $2,100; Cash, $500; Share capital, $1,000; Receivable from customers, $1,100; Equipment, $2,000; Retained earnings, $2,200; Inventory of unsold products, $1,700

You should get current assets $3,300; noncurrent assets $2,000; total assets $5,300; current liabilities $2,100; noncurrent liabilities $0; contributed capital $1,000; retained earnings $2,200; total liabilities and equity $5,300. Working capital is $1,200 and the working capital ratio is 1.57, so, currently, it is not as strong as Sound and Light. The quick ratio is 0.76, not strong either. Liabilities of $2,100 are 39.6% of total sources, with a debt-equity ratio of 0.656, so the company's financing is similar to Sound and Light's, though all of its liabilities are current, which is unusual. With $500 cash, it does not have enough cash to pay all of its $2,200 retained earnings to owners as dividends.

TO THE READER: The next eight sections cover the accounting methods underlying the balance sheet and give examples of real companies' balance sheets. You can start with the methods (Sections 2.4–2.8), with Section 2.9, which has useful preliminary information about forms of business and financing, or with the examples in Sections 2.10 and 2.11.

2.4 Recording Transactions: Double-Entry Bookkeeping

There is more than one way to see how the double-entry system works. We'll start with a balance sheet view and then focus on the transactions themselves. Both are equivalent, but perhaps one will work better for you than the other.

A Balance Sheet View of Double Entry

One way to understand double entry is to start with the balance sheet, which is the summary of all the transactions and adjustments recorded in the accounts. The balance sheet balances; that is, the dollar value of all the resources on the left is equal to the dollar value of all the sources on the right. If the balance sheet is to *balance*, then *every transaction and adjustment must also balance*, that is, their effects on the two sides of the balance sheet must be equal:

A balanced balance sheet requires a balanced double-entry recording system.

- If a resource (asset) is increased, a source (liability or equity) must be increased by the same amount, or another resource decreased by the same amount, or there must be some mixture of source increases and other resource decreases that equals the original resource's increase.
- Conversely, if a resource is decreased, a source must be decreased by the same amount, or another resource increased by the same amount, or some mixture of source decreases and other resource increases that equals the original resource's decrease.

This is just arithmetic. Double entry is a form of algebraic notation, really, in which an equation (the *balance sheet equation*) must be maintained. This diagram may help you see the arithmetic:

Maintaining the balance sheet equation A = L + E
A change in the left side total requires an equal change in the right side total.
A change in the right side total requires an equal change in the left side total.
Either side can be rearranged internally without affecting the other side, as long as neither side's total is changed.

For reasons that are now largely lost in the mists of time, increases to resources (assets), on the left side, are called *debits*, and increases to sources (liabilities and equity), on the right side, are called *credits*. Perhaps confusingly, *negatives* on the left side are also called credits, and *negatives* on the right side are also called debits. Financial accounting uses only two names to cover the four kinds of effects, which will turn out to have some advantages as we learn more about the way accounting works. Thus the balance sheet looks like this:

Debit: assets up, or liabilities or equity down.

Credit: liabilities or equity up, or assets down.

Left side: Resources (Assets)	Right side: Sources (Liabilities, Equity)
Positive items: debits Negative items: credits	Positive items: credits Negative items: debits

Sum of resources	=	**Sum of sources**
Assets	=	**Liabilities + Equity**
Debits	=	**Credits**
(negative) Credits	=	**Debits (negative)**

For now, look at two simple examples of double entry.

1. Purchasing, on credit, goods for resale:
   a. The resource (an asset) is an addition to the enterprise's unsold products.
   b. The source (a liability) is an obligation created to pay the supplier.

   If the goods cost, say, $452, we have
   - a *debit* of $452—an addition to the *account* for the resource, in this case the *inventory* of unsold products; and
   - a *credit* of $452—an addition to the account for the source, in this case the obligation to the supplier, usually called *accounts payable*.

   The balance sheet stays in balance due to this double entry, because both resources and sources are increased (are "up") by $452:

The debit of $452 equals the credit of $452, so the balance sheet stays in balance.

Resources		***Sources***
Up (debit) $452		Up (credit) $452
Assets up $452	=	Liabilities up $452 (no change in equity)

2. Borrowing money from the bank on a long-term loan:
   a. The resource (asset) is an addition to the amount of cash on hand.
   b. The source (a liability again) is that an obligation is created to repay the bank.

If the borrowed cash is, say, $1,000, we have

- an addition to the asset "cash," so total resources go up $1,000; and
- an addition to the liability "long-term bank loan," so the total sources also go up $1,000.

The debit of $1,000 equals the credit of $1,000, so the balance sheet stays in balance.

Again, the balance sheet stays in balance:

Resources	***Sources***
Up (debit) $1,000	Up (credit) $1,000
Assets up $1,000 =	Liabilities up $1,000 (no change in equity)

If we sum the two records, we get:

Assets up $1,452 total =	Liabilities up $1,452 total (no equity change)
Total debits are $1,452	Total credits are $1,452

A Transaction Recording View of Double Entry

Double entry recognizes an exchange as something received and something given.

Recording transactions keeps the balance sheet in balance, but we might also focus on the transactions themselves. In a transaction, there is an *exchange*, as we saw in Chapter 1. Two parties are involved, and each gives something to and gets something from the other. The genius, and that's the right word, of double-entry bookkeeping is that it records the two aspects of the exchange at once, from the point of view of the enterprise whose records are being created. We might think of it this way, just a little simplified:

a. What has happened to the enterprise's resources (assets)?

Assets are the enterprise's wealth, so you can think of this as the reason the enterprise engaged in the transaction: gaining some resources or, if necessary, giving some up.

b. What is the other side of the resource change?

In an exchange, a resource is only gained if something else is given: another resource, or a promise to pay later, or an investment by owners. Was the resource, say cash, gained because it was provided by a customer, or borrowed, or obtained by selling or collecting another asset, or provided by an owner? Was the resource, say cash, lost because it was given to a supplier or employee, used to reduce a debt, used to obtain another asset, or given to an owner as a dividend?

As we saw above, the system used for recording transactions uses debits and credits:

Double entry means that debits always equal credits.

	Assets	**Liabilities and/or Equity**
Increase	Debit =	Credit
Decrease	Credit =	Debit

We will focus on recording revenues and expenses in Chapter 3. For now, if you're curious:

- Revenues increase income, and therefore equity (via retained earnings), so they are *credits.*
- Expenses decrease income, and therefore equity (via retained earnings), so they are *debits.*

Both parties record the transaction, both using double entry.

An interesting aspect of a transaction is that, because it is an exchange, *both parties* to the exchange would record it, each from that party's point of view. If Enterprise A gains cash for a loan from Enterprise B, Enterprise A would record an increase in cash (a debit) and an increase in a loan liability (a credit), while Enterprise B would record a decrease in cash (a credit) and an increase in an asset for the loan *receivable* (a debit).

Here are examples of some exchanges and of how both parties would record the two aspects of each.

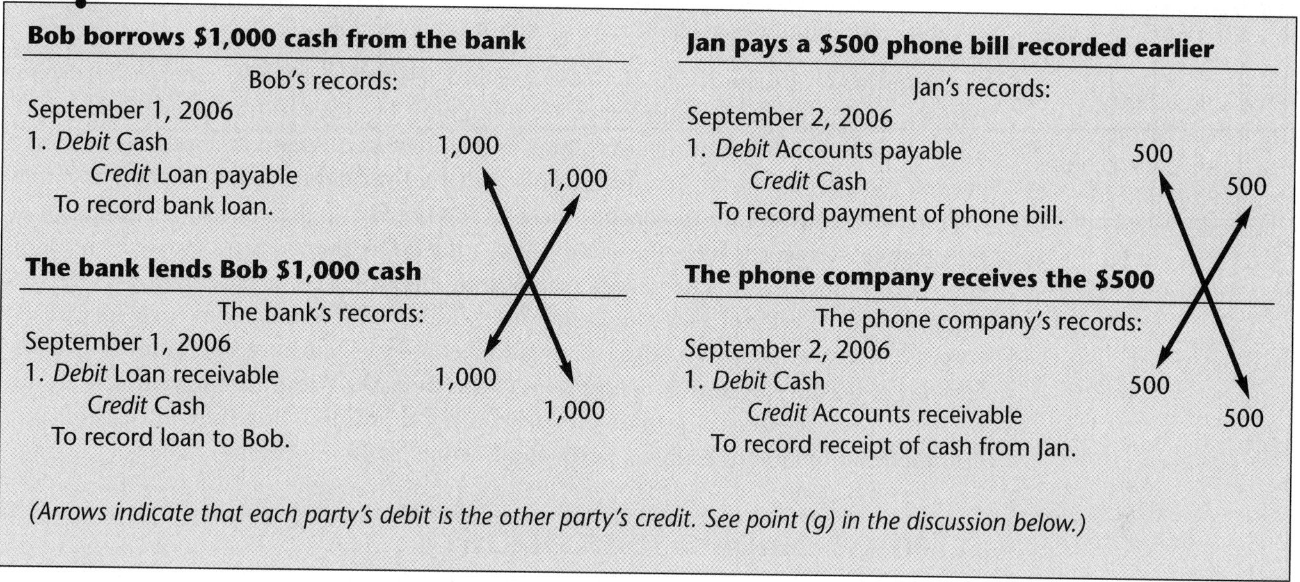

Bob borrows $1,000 cash from the bank

Bob's records:

September 1, 2006

1. *Debit* Cash 1,000

   Credit Loan payable 1,000

   To record bank loan.

The bank lends Bob $1,000 cash

The bank's records:

September 1, 2006

1. *Debit* Loan receivable 1,000

   Credit Cash 1,000

   To record loan to Bob.

Jan pays a $500 phone bill recorded earlier

Jan's records:

September 2, 2006

1. *Debit* Accounts payable 500

   Credit Cash 500

   To record payment of phone bill.

The phone company receives the $500

The phone company's records:

September 2, 2006

1. *Debit* Cash 500

   Credit Accounts receivable 500

   To record receipt of cash from Jan.

(Arrows indicate that each party's debit is the other party's credit. See point (g) in the discussion below.)

These are simple examples, but they illustrate several features of the **bookkeeping** system. (For hundreds of years, accounting records were kept in bound books. In spite of the advent of computers, "books" are still used by many enterprises, as we will see.) Some features illustrated by the Bob and Jan examples include:

Transactions are recorded into accounts, the basis of the financial statements.

a. Each double-entry record names one (or more) accounts to be *debited*, and one (or more) to be *credited*. *Accounts* contain all the transaction records and any adjustments, and therefore reflect everything recorded in the system. The Cash account, for example, lists all transactions and adjustments that have affected cash. Accounts are used directly in preparing the balance sheet and other financial statements to be examined in Chapter 3.

For each journal entry, the sum of the debits must equal the sum of the credits.

b. The double-entry records shown in the example are called *journal entries*. A journal entry can list as many accounts as are needed to record the transaction, but for *each* journal entry, *the sum of the debits must equal the sum of the credits*. If not, the balance sheet equation will not be maintained (the "books" will not balance).
c. It is traditional for the debits to be listed first in each journal entry, and for the debits to be written to the left and the credits to the right. Neither of these is arithmetically necessary, but keeping a consistent style reduces mistakes and helps keep the records understandable.
d. It is customary to omit the dollar signs in writing the entries. The transaction has to be measurable in dollars, so putting in dollar signs is thought redundant.
e. It is also customary to write a short explanation below each entry, as a memorandum of what the recorded transaction was about. Again, this is not necessary but it helps to make the record understandable and assist any follow-up or error correction.

Bookkeeping involves several useful procedural details.

f. Every journal entry should also be dated and is usually numbered so that there is no doubt when the transaction was recorded. The date can have important legal and tax implications, and, of course, it is necessary to know which fiscal period a transaction belongs in when financial statements are being prepared.

g. There's a saying that "Every person's debit is another person's credit." You can see that in the Bob and Jan examples in Exhibit 2.5. Bob's debit (increase) in cash goes with the bank's credit (decrease) in cash. The bank's cash has become Bob's. Conversely, Jan's cash has become the phone company's. These reflect the exchange that lies behind the accounting concept of a transaction.

Both parties to the transaction record it, because it is an exchange for both.

The journal entry function may be performed by records specialized by type of transaction.

Enterprises with many transactions to record, which means most enterprises, do not create a separate journal entry for each transaction, but instead use specialized records for each general kind of transaction, such as a sales record, a cash receipts record, and a cheque record. A company could list only cash receipts debits in one record, and only cash sales revenue credits in another record. The books (the balance sheet) will balance only if the two records have the same totals, so keeping them separate may be a useful control to reduce error. The people maintaining the two records have to be very careful or their records will not have the same totals. (More will be said about such specialized records in a later chapter.) Also, many bookkeeping systems are computerized; many versions of accounting software exist to perform the task. These systems may or may not produce records that look like the preceding examples, but they have the same arithmetical function of keeping all the debits equal to all the credits.

A More Complex Journal Entry

The Bob and Jan examples were rather simple. Here is an example of a more complex transaction, just so you can see how the rules set out above are maintained *no matter how complex the transaction.*

On August 14, 2005, Sorhem Inc. acquired a factory and equipment from another company. The land cost Sorhem $1,260,000, the factory building cost $12,356,000, and the factory equipment cost $7,322,000. Inventories of supplies and partially completed products were also acquired, at a cost of $1,100,000. Sorhem financed the acquisition by borrowing $12,000,000 from the bank, due in five years, issuing shares for $5,000,000 cash and paying the rest out of cash Sorhem already had.

Here is a journal entry to record the acquisition and its financing:

EXHIBIT 2·6

August 14, 2005		**Debits**	**Credits**
DR Cash	(current asset)	17,000,000	
CR Bank loan	(noncurrent liability)		12,000,000
CR Share capital	(equity)		5,000,000
DR Inventory	(current asset)	1,100,000	
DR Land	(noncurrent asset)	1,260,000	
DR Factory building	(noncurrent asset)	12,356,000	
DR Factory equipment	(noncurrent asset)	7,322,000	
CR Cash	(current asset)		22,038,000
To record the purchase and financing of the factory.			

Quite a long journal entry!

- It meets the arithmetic requirement: the sum of the debits equals the sum of the credits ($39,038,000: you might like to add the two sides and see).
- It uses whatever account names make sense to record the transaction (different companies or bookkeepers could well have named the accounts differently).
- Debits are abbreviated DR, and credits as CR, as is customary.

HOW'S YOUR UNDERSTANDING?

Here are two questions you should be able to answer based on what you have just read. If you can't answer them, it would be best to reread the material.

1. What are the effects on the balance sheet of the following transaction? Whatzis Inc. received $20,000 cash from a shareholder in return for $5,000 in newly issued shares and promised to pay the shareholder the other $15,000 back at the end of three years.

Cash asset up $20,000; Share capital equity up $5,000; Noncurrent debt liability up $15,000. Result is total increase to assets $20,000, total increase to sources of assets $20,000.

2. What is the journal entry to record the following transaction in which Whatzis Inc. used the cash from the shareholder? The company bought a large truck, which cost $89,000, by putting $20,000 down in cash and financing (borrowing) the rest from the truck dealer's finance company.

DR Truck asset 89,000, CR Cash asset 20,000, CR Truck loan liability 69,000. Result is net total increase to assets $69,000; total increase to sources of assets $69,000. Total debits 89,000, total credits 89,000.

2.5 More About Accounts

Accounts collect all the transactions and adjustments and underlie the financial statements.

The balance sheet and further statements (to be described in Chapter 3) are prepared from the underlying accounts, which have been recorded using the double-entry system so that the sum of the dollars in all the debit accounts equals the sum in all the credit accounts. But what is an account exactly? Let us use the following working definition: an account is a record of the dollar amounts comprising a particular asset, liability, equity, revenue, or expense. The net effect of these amounts is a debit or credit and is called the account's *balance*.

Another term used more than one way! Accountants use the word "balance" to refer to the equality of the assets, liabilities, and equity, as in "the balance sheet balances." They also use it to refer to the net sum of the debits and credits recorded in an account, as in "the cash account's balance is $xxx."

Here is an example of the "Cash in bank" account for a company:

EXHIBIT 2·7

CASH IN BANK

Date	Description	Entry No.	Debits	Credits	Balance
Dec. 1/05	First deposit	1	10,000		10,000 DR
Dec. 2	Deposit	3	1,146		11,146 DR
Dec. 2	Cheque	7		678	10,468 DR
Dec. 2	Cheque	8		2,341	8,127 DR

The general ledger contains all the accounts and it balances (debits equal credits).

A trial balance is a list of all the account balances, used to make sure the general ledger does balance.

You see the idea. Each account is really just a convenient summary of the entries affecting it. The *general ledger* is the complete set of all the accounts (assets, liabilities, equity accounts, revenues, and expenses) that lie behind the financial statements. In turn, the balance sheet is a summary of all the account balances for assets, liabilities, and equity.

Because the general ledger contains all the accounts, all of which came from balanced journal entries, it must balance (sum of debit-balance accounts equalling sum of credit-balance accounts) and it leads to a balanced balance sheet. Because errors might have been made, a standard bookkeeping procedure is to check that the ledger does balance by adding up all the debit and all the credit account balances to make sure the two totals are equal. There is always a little uncertainty that this will work, so the calculation is called a *trial balance.*

You might think of the ledger as a set of account pages like the Cash account above (real pages, such as in the bound books the bookkeepers of old used, or representations in a computer system). The sum of all the accounts with debit balances equals the sum of all the ones with credit balances. The diagram in Figure 2.2, using the Cash in bank example account above, might be useful:

FIGURE 2.2

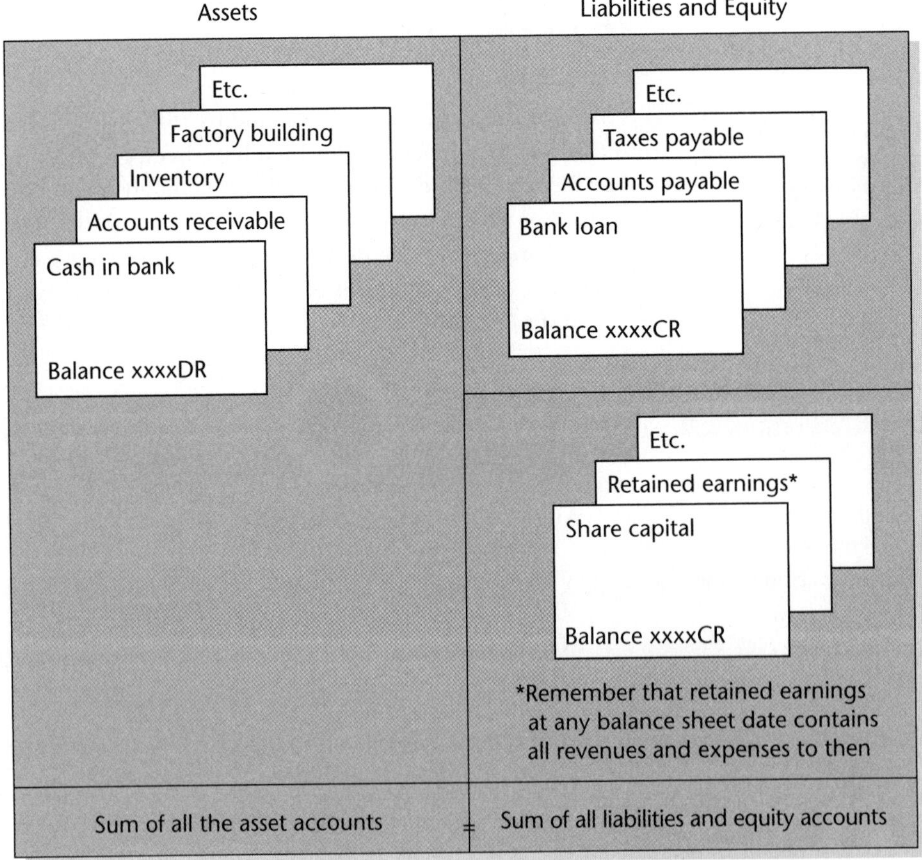

A T-account is a representation of a ledger account used in analysis or demonstration.

For demonstration and analysis purposes, accountants and accounting instructors often use a simplified version of an account called a "T-account," which includes only the debits and credits columns of the account, without calculating the balance after every entry. A T-account version of the above "Cash in bank" account example would look like this:

CASH IN BANK	
10,000	678
1,146	2,341
11,146	3,019
8,127	

Below are some examples of how account balances are calculated. Modern computerized accounting systems can produce accounts in various formats thought to be useful, but they all use the arithmetic illustrated below.

a. If the enterprise's cash began at $500 and there was a receipt of $400 and one of $750, and a payment of $300 and one of $525, the Cash asset account would show a balance of $825 (a debit because there is a positive balance in this asset account).

Cash = $500DR + $400DR + $750DR – $300CR – $525CR
= $825DR

Cash	
500	300
400	525
750	
1,650	825
825	

b. If share capital began at $1,000 and more shares were sold for $400 (which, let's say, caused the cash receipt above), the Share capital equity account would show a balance of $1,400 (a credit because there is a positive balance in this equity account).

Share capital = $1,000CR + $400CR = $1,400CR

Share capital	
	1,000
	400
	1,400
	1,400

c. If amounts owing to trade creditors began at $950 and a creditor was paid $300 (the first payment above), the Accounts payable liability account would show a balance of $650 (a credit because there is a positive balance in this liability account).

Accounts payable = $950CR – $300DR = $650CR

Accounts payable	
300	950
300	950
	650

d. If a cash collection from a customer was made for $750 (the second cash receipt above), the Accounts receivable account, with a balance of say $2,000 prior to the collection, would show a balance of $1,250 (the $750 reduces the accounts receivable asset, which has been transformed into cash through the collection transaction).

Accounts receivable = $2,000DR – $750CR = $1,250DR

Accounts receivable	
2,000	750
2,000	750
1,250	

e. If a $525 cash payment (the second cash payment above) was made on the company's bank loan, a liability account with a name like "Bank loan" would be debited with this payment. Suppose the loan had a balance of $15,000 before the payment. Then the account balance would be calculated to show the deduction of the payment.

Bank loan	
525	15,000
525	15,000
	14,475

Bank loan (part of liabilities) = $15,000CR – $525DR
= $14,475CR

Balance sheet accounts continue indefinitely.

Balance sheet accounts continue indefinitely, as long as events happen that affect them.

Financial statement amounts often are aggregates of several ledger account balances.

The figures on the financial statements may be made up of various individual account balances. The financial statements are summaries, often of many accounts. For example, a company's balance sheet showed "Accounts receivable $145,290," which turns out to be the sum of four account balances in the company's detailed accounting system:

• Accounts receivable from customers	$129,300
• Loans to employees	5,000
• Travel advances	3,860
• Due from associated company	7,130
Figure on the balance sheet	$145,290

HOW'S YOUR UNDERSTANDING?

Here are two questions you should be able to answer based on what you have just read. If you can't answer them, it would be best to reread the material.

1. How do transactions and adjustments, recorded by journal entries, find their way onto the financial statements?
2. Amble Corp.'s general ledger has the following account balances at January 31: Cash, 550 DR; Inventory, 2,200 DR; Accounts receivable, 1,750 DR; Land, 1,000 DR; Factory, 4,100 DR; Noncurrent debt, 2,400 CR; Share capital, 1,000 CR; Bank loan, 900 CR; Retained earnings, 2,550 CR; Accumulated amortization on factory, 1,320 CR; Accounts payable, 1,430 CR

What are the sums of debits and credits from the ledger trial balance, and the balance sheet totals at that date?

Sum of debits = sum of credits = 9,600; balance sheet's net total assets = total liabilities and equity = 8,280. The difference in the two totals is accumulated amortization, a credit balance account that is deducted as a negative amount on the assets side of the balance sheet.

2.6 How Debits and Credits Make the Accounting System Work

This section offers an example of how financial accounting uses debits and credits to record events and, from those records, to produce financial statements. The focus will be on the balance sheet for now. In Chapter 3, the example will be extended to cover more financial statements.

CappuMania Inc. is a small corporation that operates a coffee bar in the concourse of an office building. The company's balance sheet at the end of March 2005 follows.

CappuMania Inc.

Balance Sheet as at March 31, 2005

Assets		**Liabilities and Shareholders' Equity**	
Current assets:		Current liabilities:	
Cash	$ 4,000	Owing to suppliers	$ 1,200
Inventory of unsold food	800	Sales and other taxes owing	600
Inventory of supplies	1,900		$ 1,800
	$ 6,700	Noncurrent liabilities:	
Noncurrent assets:		Loan to buy equipment	5,000
Equipment cost	$ 9,000		$ 6,800
Accumulated amortization	(1,500)	Shareholders' equity:	
	$ 7,500	Share capital contributed	$ 3,000
		Retained earnings	4,400
			$ 7,400
	$14,200		$14,200

These accounts are assets and so have debit *balances:*

- Cash, Inventory of unsold food, Inventory of supplies, and Equipment cost.

This account is a negative asset and so has a credit *balance:*

- Accumulated amortization.

These accounts are liabilities and equities and so have credit *balances:*

- Owing to suppliers, Sales and other taxes owing, Loan to buy equipment, Share capital contributed, and Retained earnings.

We already know the accounts are in balance because the balance sheet balances (left side total = right side total). But let's do a trial balance anyway, to demonstrate that the sum of all the debits equals the sum of all the credits (we will drop the $ signs):

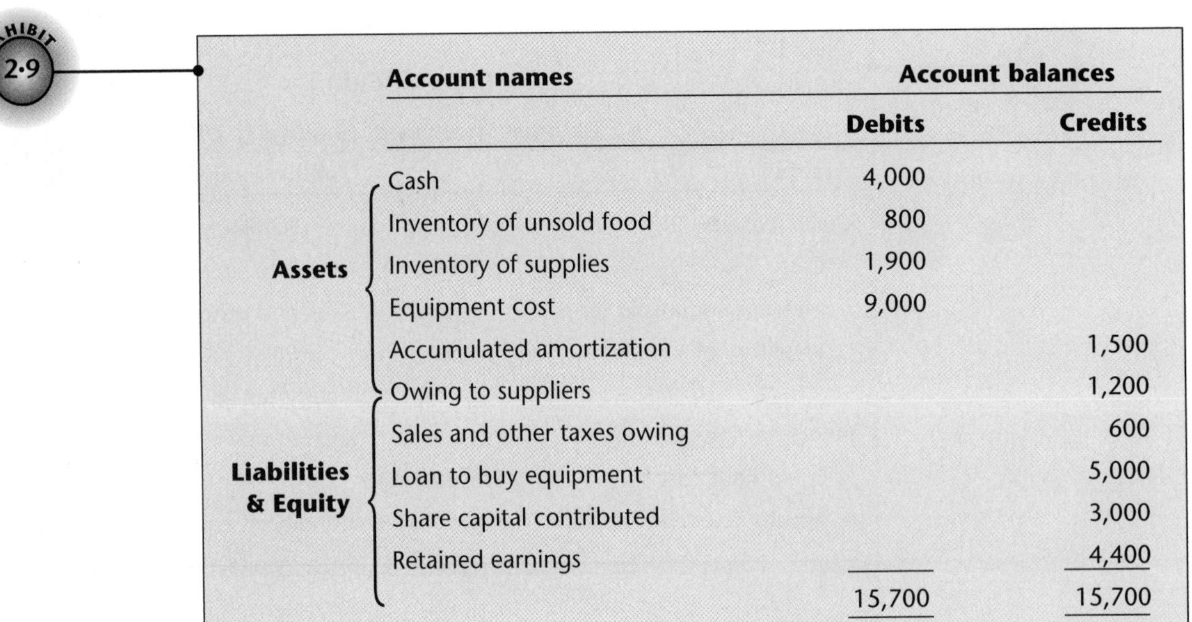

EXHIBIT 2·9

	Account names	Account balances	
		Debits	Credits
Assets	Cash	4,000	
	Inventory of unsold food	800	
	Inventory of supplies	1,900	
	Equipment cost	9,000	
	Accumulated amortization		1,500
Liabilities & Equity	Owing to suppliers		1,200
	Sales and other taxes owing		600
	Loan to buy equipment		5,000
	Share capital contributed		3,000
	Retained earnings		4,400
		15,700	15,700

The balance sheet may rearrange the ledger's accounts, but the balance is maintained.

So it balances! Accumulated amortization, a credit balance account, is deducted from the Equipment cost on the balance sheet, so the sum of the debits is not the same amount as the total of the assets side of the balance sheet, nor is the sum of the credits the same as the total of the liabilities and equity side of the balance sheet. But this sort of rearrangement of the presentation of accounts in the balance sheet still keeps the accounts in balance even though totals change, because any such rearrangement always retains the debit or credit signs.

Now let's see how the following four transactions, all happening on April 1, 2005, are recorded using accounting's double-entry method (ignoring the details of the particular computer or manual recordkeeping system):

1. CappuMania pays $500 of its taxes owing.
2. CappuMania buys $450 of more supplies, paying $100 cash and owing the rest.
3. A shareholder is given more shares in return for personally paying $1,100 on the equipment loan.
4. CappuMania buys a new coffee urn for $200 cash.

Here are the journal entries, all dated April 1, 2005:

Transaction 1 reduces an asset and a liability.

Transaction 2 increases one asset, decreases another, and increases a liability.

Transaction 3 reduces a liability and increases an equity, having no effect on assets.

Transaction 4 increases one asset and reduces another, with no other effect.

	Debit	Credit
1. *Resource effect:* Cash is reduced. Cash is a debit, so a negative effect on cash would be a credit.		
Source effect: Tax liability is reduced. A liability is a credit, so a negative effect would be a debit.		
Entry:		
DR Sales and other taxes owing (liability)	500	
CR Cash (asset)		500
Double-entry method: There is both a DR and a CR and the two are the same. (The tradition is to list the DR(s) first in an entry, but all that really matters is that for each entry, \$DR = \$CR.)		
2. *Resource effects:* Inventory is increased \$450. It is an asset, so this is a debit. Cash is decreased \$100, so this is a credit, as above.		
Source effect: The liability to suppliers is increased \$350, so this is a credit.		
Entry:		
DR Inventory of supplies (asset)	450	
CR Cash (asset)		100
CR Owing to suppliers (liability)		350
Double-entry method: There are both DRs and CRs and the sum of the DRs equals the sum of the CRs. (An entry can have any number of DRs and CRs as long as the sums of each are equal.)		
3. *Resource effect:* None.		
Source effects: The equipment loan, a liability, is decreased \$1,100, so this is a debit. The share capital, an equity, is increased \$1,100, so this is a credit.		
Entry:		
DR Loan to buy equipment (liability)	1,100	
CR Share capital contributed (equity)		1,100
Double-entry method: This transaction affects only the right side of the balance sheet, but the balance sheet stays in balance because one account on the right side goes up and another goes down.		
4. *Resource effects:* Equipment, an asset, is increased \$200, so this is a debit. Cash is decreased \$200, which is a credit as in transactions 1 and 2.		
Source effect: None.		
Entry:		
DR Equipment cost (asset)	200	
CR Cash (asset)		200
Double-entry method: This transaction also affects only one side of the balance sheet, this time the assets side, but again the balanced entry keeps the balance sheet in balance.		

Posting means entering the journal entries into the ledger accounts.

These entries are recorded (*posted*) by adding them to or subtracting them from the previous (March 31) balances in the accounts. This is done below, using a computer spreadsheet format (in this case, *Microsoft Excel®*, but the particular spreadsheet does not matter). Each set of columns (March 31, transactions, and April 1) is in balance because the sum of the debits equals the sum of the credits.

EXHIBIT 2·10

	A	B	C	D	E	F	G	H	I
1	CappuMania Inc. Trial Balance								
2									
3			Balances					Balances	
4			March 31, 2005			Transactions		April 1, 2005	
5		ACCOUNT	DR	CR	#	DR	CR	DR	CR
6									
7	Assets	Cash	4,000		1		500	3,200	
8					2		100		
9					4		200		
10		Inventory of unsold food	800					800	
11		Inventory of supplies	1,900		2	450		2,350	
12		Equipment cost	9,000		4	200		9,200	
13		Accumulated amortization		1,500					1,500
14									
15	Liabilities & Equity	Owing to suppliers		1,200	2		350		1,550
16		Sales and other taxes owing		600	1	500			100
17		Loan to buy equipment		5,000	3	1,100			3,900
18		Share capital contributed		3,000	3		1,100		4,100
19		Retained earnings		4,400					4,400
20									
21			15,700	15,700		2,250	2,250	15,550	15,550
22									

In practice, it is unlikely that another balance sheet would be prepared just one day after the March 31 balance sheet, but to complete the example, let's see what the balance sheet, after recording the four transactions, would be.

EXHIBIT 2·11

CappuMania Inc.

Balance Sheet as at April 1, 2005

Assets		**Liabilities and Shareholders' Equity**	
Current assets:		Current liabilities:	
Cash	$ 3,200	Owing to suppliers	$ 1,550
Inventory of unsold food	800	Sales and other taxes owing	100
Inventory of supplies	2,350		$ 1,650
	$ 6,350	Noncurrent liabilities:	
Noncurrent assets:		Loan to buy equipment	3,900
Equipment cost	$ 9,200		$ 5,550
Accumulated amortization	(1,500)	Shareholders' equity:	
	$ 7,700	Share capital contributed	$ 4,100
		Retained earnings	4,400
			$ 8,500
	$14,050		$14,050

In summary, the CappuMania example shows how accounting works.

- First, transactions are recorded in a two-sided (double) entry in a journal.
- Next, the journal's entries are recorded (posted) in the accounts.
- Then, the ledger of accounts is checked for balancing via a trial balance.
- Last, the trial balance is used to prepare the balance sheet.

Accounting systems have the same basic design, but vary in their formats and details.

There are many choices, judgments, and details in accounting, and most accounting systems have their own particular formats for entries and accounts, but now you have the basics.

Recordkeeping is important for managers. To a large extent, management decision making and evaluations of management performance depend on accounting information. Such decisions and evaluations may be constrained by the nature of the underlying data. For example, a principal characteristic of the transaction is that an exchange *has happened.* The basis of the financial accounting system, therefore, is a historical record of events. This can be awkward for managers seeking to look forward and predict future choices and events. Though accounting's historical focus improves its reliability, many managers wish financial accounting were more forward looking. Top managers often want to override the routine transactional system with special adjustments and accruals, but because such action has a manipulative flavour, it is often ineffective in convincing users, and management's frustration remains. When we make predictions for the future, we are guided by the past. Managers' predictions are guided by the historical results of financial accounting; however, managers must have a lot of other information beyond accounting to make their predictions accurate. Probably, that is as it should be; there is no reason to expect accounting to tell managers everything they need to know. If accounting does its job well, it provides managers a good base on which to add other information, so the managers can do their jobs well.

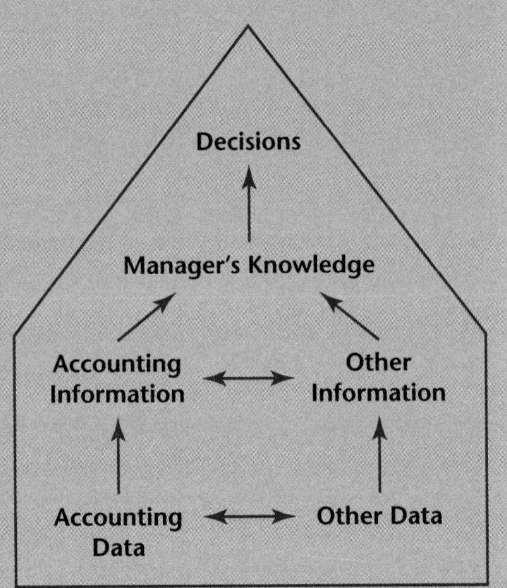

HOW'S YOUR UNDERSTANDING?

Here are two questions you should be able to answer based on what you have just read. If you can't answer them, it would be best to reread the material.

1. On April 1, 2005, a fifth transaction occurred. CappuMania paid $800 on its equipment loan. Write a journal entry to record this event.

DR Loan to buy equipment 800, CR Cash 800

2. A sixth transaction also occurred on April 1, 2005: CappuMania acquired new equipment costing $1,550 from a shareholder who was issued share capital in that amount. What would the following revised figures have been on the April 1 balance sheet after both the fifth and sixth transactions: cash, current assets, total assets, total liabilities, total equity, total liabilities, and shareholders' equity?

$2,400, $5,550, $14,800, $4,750, $10,050, $14,800.

2.7 Arranging Accounts on the Balance Sheet

In the Sound and Light and CappuMania examples, there were two important aspects of arranging accounts on the balance sheet:

The balance sheet's classification of accounts into categories conveys information.

1. Accounts were organized into the balance sheet's main categories: current assets, noncurrent assets, current liabilities, noncurrent liabilities, and equity. This was done because the arrangement of accounts is meant to convey information beyond the account balances themselves. The placement of each account tells the reader of the balance sheet what kind of account it is: a short-term asset or a long-term one, a short-term liability or a long-term one, or an equity. This enables the calculation of

meaningful ratios and other analyses. The balance sheet is said to be *classified*, because accounts are classified into meaningful categories. This means that the accountant preparing the balance sheet has to look into an account with a title like "bank loan," for example, and determine whether it should be included in current liabilities or noncurrent liabilities. (We'll see that the other financial statements also classify figures into categories.) Moving items around within the balance sheet (or within other financial statements) is called *reclassification* and is done by accountants whenever they believe it will make the financial statement more informative.

Both debit and credit balance accounts can appear anywhere on the balance sheet. Credits on the left side are negative; debits on the right side are negative too.

2. The accumulated amortization account, though having a credit balance, is not put on the right side of the balance sheet, but instead appears as a negative amount on the left side. As long as the accountant remembers whether an account is a debit or credit, it can be put anywhere on the balance sheet, to produce the most useful presentation of the information, without throwing the statement out of balance. Accounting is just arithmetic, and if you think of the balance sheet equation (A = L + E) as a real algebraic equation, you can move things around from one side to the other, just as in algebra, and when you move something that is positive on one side, it becomes negative on the other side, just as in algebra. A reminder of this use of credits on the left and debits on the right is the word *net* often used in accounting. It tells you that something has been deducted from something else: a debit account minus a smaller credit account results in a net debit, and a credit account minus a smaller debit account produces a net credit. The assets total is the net of all the positive assets minus any negative amounts, and the liabilities and owners' equity total is the net of all the positive liabilities and equity items minus any negative amounts.

Three Examples of Account Classification

a. Current and noncurrent portions of noncurrent liabilities. Many noncurrent liabilities, such as *mortgages*, *bonds*, and *debentures*, require regular payments, and although most of the debt is noncurrent, not all of it is. Accountants therefore reclassify the amount to be paid on the principal of the debt within the next year into current liabilities, and show only the residual (the part due more than a year away) as noncurrent. (The interest to be paid in the next year is not included in this, because it is not due until the future time passes.)
b. Bank *overdrafts* are another example. Suppose a company has a bank overdraft of $500, which means that its cash-in-bank asset is negative (the bank has allowed the company to remove $500 more cash from the account than there was in it, in effect, lending the company the $500). The company's other assets total $12,400. Its net assets are therefore $11,900, and this is also the total of its liabilities and owners' equity. There are at least two ways of presenting this information:

   Other assets of $12,400 minus bank overdraft of $500 = Liabilities and owners' equity of $11,900

   OR

   Other assets of $12,400 = Liabilities and owners' equity of $11,900 plus bank overdraft of $500

   For bank overdrafts, it is customary to use the second method, to move the negative bank amount to the other side of the balance sheet. Even if the company normally has cash in the bank so that the account is normally an asset, the account is a liability at this point because the bank has, in effect, lent the company $500 and will want the money back.

Reclassification is used to move items around and make the balance sheet informative.

c. Some negative amounts are left as deductions, not moved to the other side to make them positive as was done with the overdraft. Accumulated amortization is an important example of a negative-balance account. It is the amount of all the amortization calculated to date on assets such as buildings and equipment. For accumulated amortization, there are at least three ways of presenting the information, all of which maintain the balance sheet equation:

- Accumulated amortization could be shown on the right side of the balance sheet (in former times, it was, and in some countries, still is). In North America, most accountants feel that it is more informative for users to deduct it from the asset figures so that the net book value of the assets is shown. Remember that the net book value is the assets' original value (cost) minus their accumulated amortization; it tells the user how much of that original value has yet to be amortized.
- Accumulated amortization could be separately disclosed as a deduction on the left side of the balance sheet, as it was in the Sound and Light and CappuMania balance sheets. This is very common, but if there are a lot of different kinds of assets and amortization amounts, it can make the balance sheet a little cluttered.
- Just the amortized assets' net book values (cost minus accumulated amortization) could be disclosed on the balance sheet, so that accumulated amortization is not mentioned on the face of the statement. In the Sound and Light example, the noncurrent assets would be listed in the following sort of way: Noncurrent assets (net) $225. CappuMania's April 1, 2005, balance sheet would show Noncurrent assets (net) $7,700. This method, which is becoming quite popular, would be accompanied by a *note* to the financial statements listing the cost and accumulated amortization amounts separately, and so keeping the balance sheet uncluttered and allowing some additional explanations of the figures if that were thought useful.

Notes to the statements provide useful details that would clutter the statements.

This discussion illustrates an important characteristic of the balance sheet equation. It is an invention maintained by the double-entry system and thought to be useful as a conceptual tool for the measurement of financial position. It is an arithmetical result, not some sort of basic truth. The task of recording balanced journal entries to make sure that the balance sheet is in balance is really just the starting point for the fundamental accounting question of how to measure and describe financial position most appropriately.

Accounting and finance research, like any other use of the balance sheet, is dependent on how accounts are classified. Much research is done using large databases prepared from companies' published financial statements, and those databases depend on the accounting judgments made in preparing the statements. A few years ago, a major set of national financial statistics contained errors when the people putting the statistics together did not realize that accumulated amortization was a negative asset and so added it on to the assets, rather than subtracting it. As a result, the data were seriously out of balance and all the ratios calculated from the data were wrong! Accounting researchers regularly have to scrutinize their data for such errors. To add to the research challenge, various databases classify balance sheet information slightly differently, for example, sometimes adding the current portion of noncurrent debt onto the noncurrent portion. Everyone using databases of financial information has to be aware of what the databases have done with the information.

HOW'S YOUR UNDERSTANDING?

Here are two questions you should be able to answer based on what you have just read. If you can't answer them, it would be best to reread the material.

1. Why are accounts classified as they are on the balance sheet, and why are they sometimes reclassified?
2. Prepare a balance sheet for Mike's Tire Repair from the following amounts:

   Cash on hand, $90; Bank overdraft, $120; Due from customers, $640; Owner's equity, $880; Equipment cost, $890; Unsold goods (inventory), $210; Accumulated amortization on equipment, $470; Due to suppliers, $360

You should show $90, $640, $890, and $210 as positive assets and $470 as a negative asset, with (net) total assets of $1,360. The $120 and $360 are liabilities, totalling $480, and equity equals $880, so that the total of liabilities and equity is also $1,360.

2.8 Demonstration Problem: Journal Entries and Accounts

On the next page is the December 31, 2004, balance sheet of Petro-Canada (**www.petro-canada.ca**), from which you may have bought gas for your car. The balance sheet is exactly as Petro-Canada issued it (including the comparative figures for 2003), except that various notes and the signatures of members of the board of directors have not been included. Don't worry about accounts you may not recognize yet or the word "consolidated"—we'll get to such issues later, and this example doesn't involve them.

Petro-Canada Consolidated Balance Sheet
(stated in millions of Canadian dollars)

As at December 31,	*2004*	*2003* (Note 2)
Assets		
Current assets		
Cash and cash equivalents (Note 13)	$ 170	$ 635
Accounts receivable (Note 11)	1,254	1,503
Inventories (Note 14)	549	551
Prepaid expenses	13	16
	1,986	2,705
Property, plant and equipment, net (Note 13)	14,783	10,943
Goodwill (Note 12)	986	810
Deferred charges and other assets (Note 16)	345	316
	$18,100	$14,774
Liabilities and Shareholders' Equity		
Current liabilities		
Accounts payable and accrued liabilities	$ 2,223	$ 1,822
Income taxes payable	370	300
Short-term notes payable	299	—
Current portion of long-term debt (Note 17)	6	6
	2,898	2,128
Long-term debt (Note 17)	2,275	2,223
Other liabilities (Note 18)	646	306
Asset retirement obligations (Note 19)	834	773
Future income taxes (Note 7)	2,708	1,756
Commitments and contingent liabilities (Note 25)		
Shareholders' equity (Note 20)	8,739	7,588
	$18,100	$14,774

Assume that the list of transactions that follows these instructions happened the next day, January 1, 2005.

1. Record the transactions, using Petro-Canada's account names if possible.
2. Post the transactions to the company's accounts.
3. Prepare a balance sheet as at January 1, 2005.
4. Calculate three ratios to indicate if the company's financial position has changed since December 31, 2003.

Transactions on January 1, 2005:

a. Petro-Canada collected $96 million in accounts receivable.
b. The company issued new share capital to some senior managers for $4 million cash.
c. The company paid $22 million in accounts payable and all but $154 million of its income taxes payable.

d. The company bought a new refinery for $164 million, $30 million of which was paid in cash and the rest was to be paid in five years.

e. The company took delivery of a large shipment of oil and gas products for resale. These cost $5 million, which was to be paid in 30 days.

f. The company decided to repay $120 million of long-term debt in 30 days. Petro-Canada's chief financial officer decided that the debt should be reclassified as a result.

1. **January 1, 2005, journal entries to record the transactions (in millions of dollars)**

a. DR Cash and cash equivalents	96	
CR Accounts receivable		96
Collection of some accounts receivable.		
b. DR Cash and cash equivalents	4	
CR Shareholders' equity		4
Issuance of shares to senior managers.		
c. DR Accounts payable and accrued liabilities	22	
DR Income taxes payable ($370 – $154)	216	
CR Cash and cash equivalents		238
Payment of some accounts and income taxes payable.		
d. DR Property, plant and equipment, net	164	
CR Cash and cash equivalents		30
CR Long-term debt		134
Acquisition of new refinery.		
e. DR Inventories	5	
CR Accounts payable and accrued liabilities		5
Delivery of a shipment of oil and gas products for resale.		
f. DR Long-term debt	120	
CR Current portion of long-term debt		120
Reclassification of debt that is to be repaid in 30 days. (A new account called Short-term debt or some similar name could also be used.)		

2. **Posting the transactions to Petro-Canada's accounts (and calculation of new balances)**

	Balances December 31, 2004		Posted Transactions		Balances January 1, 2005	
	DR	CR	DR	CR	DR	CR
Cash & cash equivalents	170		96	238		
			4	30	2	
Accounts receivable	1,254			96	1,158	
Inventories	549		5		554	
Prepaid expenses	13				13	
Property, plant & equipment	14,783		164		14,947	
Goodwill	986				986	
Deferred charges	345				345	
Accounts payable & accrued liabilities		2,223	22	5		2,206
Income taxes payable		370	216			154
Short-term notes payable		299				299
Current portion debt		6		120		126
Long-term debt		2,275	120	134		2,289
Deferred credits		646				646
Asset retirement obligations		834				834
Future income taxes		2,708				2,708
Shareholders' equity		8,739		4		8,743
	18,100	18,100	627	627	18,005	18,005

3. **Balance sheet as at January 1, 2005**

The balance sheet would be prepared from the revised account balances shown above. Here are the summary figures from that balance sheet—make sure you can trace how each was derived.

Petro-Canada
Summary of Consolidated Balance Sheet as at January 1, 2005
(stated in millions of Canadian dollars)

Assets		**Liabilities**	
Current assets	$ 1,727	Current liabilities	$ 2,785
Noncurrent assets (net)	16,278	Noncurrent liabilities	6,477
		Equity	
		Shareholders' equity	8,743
	$18,005		$18,005

4. **Comparative ratios**

These are the same ratios used to analyze Sound and Light Corporation in Section 2.3. Make sure you can reproduce the details behind each.

	January 1, 2005	December 31, 2003
Debt-equity ratio	9,262/8,743 = 1.06	7,186/7,588 = 0.95
Working capital ratio	1,727/2,785 = 0.62	2,705/2,128 = 1.27
Quick (acid test) ratio	1,160/2,785 = 0.42	2,138/2,128 = 1.01

All three ratios have changed. The debt-equity ratio indicates less reliance on debt in financing Petro-Canada, and the other two ratios indicate a weaker short-term position. The large cash flows in the January 1, 2005, transactions may have been for good business reasons, but they did reduce the company's current strength.

2.9 Proprietorships, Partnerships, Corporations, and Financing

The balance sheet is a summary of much of the organization's financing: it shows what sources of debt and equity were used to produce the list of resources (assets). Just in case you are unfamiliar with the main kinds of business organizations and their financing, this section provides a few explanations. Remember the balance sheet equation:

Assets = Liabilities + Owners' Equity

This section considers the right-hand terms, outlining how the form of the business organization determines the way owners' equity is shown on the balance sheet and how both right-hand terms indicate how the assets are financed. This short introduction will help you deal with the material in this book. While such information is explored more deeply in books or courses on corporate law and finance, many details will also necessarily come up here as we proceed. This book's glossary will also provide help in understanding terminology.

There are many important forms of organization, such as businesses organized as partnerships, corporations, or cooperatives, and nonbusiness organizations, such as clubs, charities, governments, and political parties. They cannot all be described here. Instead, we focus on the four main kinds of business organization, and their main methods of financing.

Four Kinds of Business Organization

We have seen that each balance sheet has an owners' equity section, and that for a business enterprise there are two general kinds of equity:

1. *Directly* contributed equity (investments), in which owners have provided money or other assets to the enterprise; and
2. *Indirectly* contributed equity (retained earnings), in which owners have allowed income earned by the enterprise to remain there, to help earn more income in the future.

Equity exists only when owners have contributed to the enterprise. Trading shares among owners, such as on a stock market, provides no equity for the enterprise, as it is not involved in such trading (no transaction).

The balance sheet's equity section reflects the legal form of the organization.

The legal meaning of being an owner depends on the way the enterprise is legally organized. The equity section of the balance sheet reflects that legal meaning, so that owners and other users will understand the status of their equity. Four main kinds of business organizations are the **proprietorship**, the **partnership**, the **corporation**, and the **corporate group**.

Proprietorship

A proprietorship's equity ("capital") does not separate investment and retained earnings.

A proprietorship, like Simone's venture in Section 1.10, is a business owned by one person (the *proprietor*) and does not legally exist separately from the owner. Because the business does not exist as a separate legal entity, it is said to be *unincorporated.* If Simone just starts up a jewellery business one day, without further legal steps, the business is a proprietorship. Legally, such a business is not distinguishable from Simone's nonbusiness affairs. If she wishes, she can use the business cash to buy groceries, and if she does not pay her business bills, her creditors can claim against any nonbusiness assets she has.

A proprietorship has no legal existence separate from the owner, so direct contributions by the owner and indirect contributions by leaving income in the business are not legally distinguishable. Accordingly, the equity section of the proprietorship's balance sheet does not distinguish between the two. Both kinds of equity are simply lumped together as **owner's capital**. A proprietorship's balance sheet can list whatever assets and liabilities the owner considers relevant to the business (there being no separate legal entity to own any assets or owe any liabilities), and the owner's equity section of the balance sheet just says:

Owner's equity (or Proprietor's equity):	
Owner's capital (equity)	$XXXX

Because the proprietorship balance sheet is arbitrarily distinguished from the owner, it is usual to specify who the owner is and whether the owner's other financial affairs affect the business.

Partnership

A partnership's equity should show the capital attributable to each partner.

A partnership is also unincorporated, but it has more than one owner. Again, the owners' personal assets can generally be claimed by business creditors, so there is the same somewhat arbitrary distinction between business affairs and personal affairs. But the fact that there is more than one owner introduces some formality into the business. For example, there is (or should be) an agreement about how the earnings of the business are to be split among the partners and about how much each partner can withdraw from the business. Because stress can develop in partnerships (as with friendships), provinces, states, and countries have partnership laws that provide some structure if the partners do not do so themselves.

A recent development is that of the limited liability partnership (LLP). Used for professional business, the LLP protects each partner from personal liability for the negligent acts of another partner or of employees not under his or her direct control.

A partnership's balance sheet may, like a proprietorship's, list whatever assets and liabilities the owners consider relevant to that business. Also, the owners' equity section, like that for a proprietorship, does not distinguish between owners' direct contributions and retained earnings. The only difference is that each owner's total capital is identified on the face of the balance sheet (or, if there are many partners, as in firms of lawyers, accountants, or engineers, in a note or separate schedule). Therefore, the *partners' capital* section of the partnership's balance sheet shows:

Partners' equity:	
Partners' capital:	
Partner A	$XXXX
Partner B	XXXX
Partner C	XXXX
Total capital (equity)	$XXXX

Corporation

Financial accounting recognizes that a corporation is legally separate from its owners.

A corporation is an incorporated entity that has a legal existence of its own, separate from that of its owners. The corporation continues to exist even if the owners die or quit working, and if the business fails, owners' losses are limited to their equity in the business. Unless they have signed personal guarantees to creditors such as banks, owners will not lose personal assets if the business goes under. A corporation can own property, employ people, and otherwise conduct business just as a person can. It can even sue and be sued.

You can usually tell that a business is incorporated because it will have some indication at the end of its name, like "Limited," "Ltd.," "Inc.," or other symbols that the incorporating jurisdiction (province, state, or country) specifies. A corporation's balance sheet usually calls its equity section *shareholders' equity* to emphasize the nature of its ownership.

Corporations can be very complex. Just a few complexities are mentioned here.

A. FORMS OF SHARE CAPITAL

The share capital part of equity is the historical amount contributed to the corporation.

People become owners of a corporation by buying *shares* (called *stock* in the United States) that give them voting or other powers in it. When a corporation first issues a share, the money received for it is put in the corporation's bank account and the source of that asset is called *share capital*, which is an owners' (shareholders' or stockholders') equity item. Innovations are always being made in corporations' ownership structures. For example, some corporations are owned through "trusts" that provide tax or other advantages. If you wanted to invest in The North West Company, a Winnipeg-based retailer, or Luscar Coal, an Edmonton-based coal mining company, you would buy shares in the trusts, which own the companies.

Canadian companies usually have *no-par* shares, which means they can issue their shares for whatever amount seems appropriate. *Par value* (or *stated value*) shares, rare in Canada, but used elsewhere, have a legal minimum issue price, the par or otherwise stated value. Such a minimum share price was used in the past to prevent corporations from abusing present shareholders by selling newly issued shares cheaply, but other protections exist nowadays, so corporations now tend to have no-par shares.

There are several classes of shares, including the following:

- *Common shares* or *ordinary* shares. Owners of these vote; they are the corporation's basic (*residual*) owners, the ones who decide who shall be on the board of directors that manages the corporation for the owners and declares dividends to owners.
- *Preferred shares* or other special shares. Owners of these usually do not vote unless there is a problem, but in return they have rights such as receiving a fixed dividend each year or converting their preferred shares to common shares.
- Class A, Class B, and other such categorizations. Whether these are more like common shares or preferred shares depends on the specific rights they carry. Many corporations use these arbitrary terms because the complexity of rights often prevents a simple categorization into common or preferred.

The balance sheet or notes disclose any special classes of shares or rights.

The face of the balance sheet or, more usually, a note, will list all the kinds of shares the corporation is authorized to issue, specify any special rights, and show the amount of share capital obtained on the original issuance of each kind of share. The cash or other consideration received for such share capital is the property of the corporation: except in specific circumstances, the shareholders have no right to get it back.

B. RETAINED EARNINGS

The balance sheet or a note discloses the accumulated amount of retained earnings.

Earnings of a corporation belong to the corporation, not to its owners. The shareholders can receive the earnings only if the board of directors declares a dividend. The balance sheet usually shows the amount of any retained earnings (past earnings minus past dividends) as a separate owners' equity item, but some companies (such as Petro-Canada in the previous section) show only a single shareholders' equity figure on the balance sheet and show the various categories in the notes to the financial statements.

C. OTHER ITEMS IN SHAREHOLDERS' EQUITY

A corporation's equity may contain items other than share capital and retained earnings.

Shareholders' equity can contain some peculiar items, because business affairs are much more complex than just two categories, share capital and retained earnings. Because of this, American companies and some others have a whole schedule of shareholders' (stockholders') equity. Here are three equity items you are likely to see:

- *Capital in excess of par (or stated) value.* If the company's shares have a stated issue price or par value, and shares are issued for more than that, the difference is put into a special equity account with a name like "*contributed surplus*" or "capital in excess of stated value."
- *Treasury shares.* In some legal jurisdictions, companies whose shares are publicly traded on stock markets are allowed to buy some of their own shares. *Treasury shares* could have been listed with the company's assets, as an investment in itself, but that is thought to be double counting because the shares' value is represented by the other assets already. Instead, the cost of such shares is deducted from the owners' equity to produce a net equity figure, the equity of real owners, other than the corporation itself.
- *Foreign currency translation adjustment.* Companies that have international operations or financial dealings have to adjust amounts recorded in foreign currencies to Canadian dollars. This usually produces a *foreign currency translation adjustment* or *accumulated foreign currency translation adjustment.*

  This mouthful of an item arises from changes in the relative values of currencies. For example, if a company has assets in a foreign branch, purchased in the foreign currency, their values on the balance sheet will change if they are converted to Canadian dollars at current dollar exchange rates, which are different than the rates existing when they were acquired. (Conversion at current exchange rates is not the only method used, but will suffice for this example.) The conversion to Canadian dollars, necessary in preparing the balance sheet, can therefore produce a change in the assets' values. Nothing except the exchange rate has changed, so the effects of the exchange rate change are put into this equity account, so that the balance sheet will balance (double entry means that changing the assets' values requires changing something else too). This account, which can be positive or negative, accumulates all the adjustments needed over time to prepare Canadian dollar balance sheets. It is included in equity largely because there doesn't seem to be anywhere else to put it: it's not a liability because it's not owed to anyone. It is equity financing in the sense that it represents increases (so far) in the book values of assets held in foreign countries, so it accounts for some of the company's asset total. See the example calculation. Accounting principles may be changing to include more (perhaps eventually all) of this adjustment in the year's income calculation.

Example foreign currency translation adjustment

- Asset bought in the United States for US$100 in 1996 when the Canadian dollar was worth 68 US cents.
- Balance sheet is shown in Canadian dollars.
- Asset's cost was therefore Can$147.06 ($100/0.68), recorded at that amount on the 1996 balance sheet.
- At the end of 2001, the Canadian dollar was worth 64 US cents. So asset's cost should be recorded as $156.25 ($100/0.64) on the 2001 balance sheet.
- The difference, $156.25 – $147.06 = $9.19, is shown as a foreign currency translation adjustment in the 2001 equity to offset the increase in the asset value and keep the balance sheet in balance.

D. FORMAT OF A CORPORATION'S SHAREHOLDERS' EQUITY SECTION

Thus, in addition to its lists of assets and liabilities, a corporation's balance sheet has an owners' equity section showing various legal details to assist present owners and potential future owners:

Shareholders' (or stockholders') equity

Share capital:	
Authorized shares (narrative, normally in the notes)	
Issued capital received:	
Class A shares (for example)	$XXXX
Class B shares (for example)	XXXX
Capital in excess of stated value (if any)	XXXX
Total issued capital	$XXXX
Retained earnings	XXXX
Foreign currency translation adjustment (+ or –)	(XXXX)
	$XXXX
Less treasury shares, at cost	(XXXX)
Net total shareholders' equity	$XXXX

Corporate Group

Many companies we are familiar with, such as General Motors, Bombardier, Bank of Nova Scotia, Sears, Petro-Canada, and Pepsico, are not single corporations, but rather they are groups of many, often hundreds, of corporations. The balance sheet of such a corporate group attempts to represent what that group looks like as a "consolidated" *economic* entity, and so looks a lot like that of a single corporation, though it is an aggregation of many legally separate corporations. Doing this aggregation requires complex accounting techniques that are mostly beyond the scope of this book (except for brief coverage in Chapter 9). For now, there are some points worth keeping in mind about a *consolidated* balance sheet of a corporate group:

A corporate group has a consolidated balance sheet, likely with minority interest and goodwill.

- Look for the word "consolidated" at the top of the balance sheet and the other financial statements, as in the balance sheet of Petro-Canada in the previous section. This may be your main clue that you are dealing with a corporate group.
- The shareholders' equity section represents the equity of the primary (or *parent*) corporation in the group. The whole balance sheet is done from the point of view of the parent corporation and its owners, the group's controlling owners.
- Sometimes some of the other corporations in the group (called *subsidiaries*) are partly owned by other people or corporations outside the parent corporation. Such other partial owners are called *minority* or *noncontrolling interests*, and their equity in the subsidiary corporation is shown as a liability on the consolidated balance sheet, not as part of equity. You can think of this *minority interest liability* as representing the obligation of the parent company to the minority owners.
- Frequently, the parent company pays more for the equity (assets minus liabilities) of another corporation than the individual assets minus liabilities appear to be worth. The parent might do this because it values some factors not on the subsidiary's balance sheet, such as skilled employees or management, brand reputation, innovative marketing strategies, or expected savings or synergies to be realized when the two corporations combine some of their efforts. The whole of the subsidiary, you might say, is worth more than the sum of its parts. In such a case, the difference between what the parent corporation paid and the sum of the subsidiary's assets and liabilities added into the balance sheet, adjusting for such things as *minority interest*, is called *consolidated goodwill* (or just *goodwill*) and is shown on the consolidated balance sheet in the noncurrent assets section.

The balance sheet of a corporate group therefore looks something like this (goodwill and minority interest appear only if the group's financial arrangements make them appropriate):

EXHIBIT 2·13

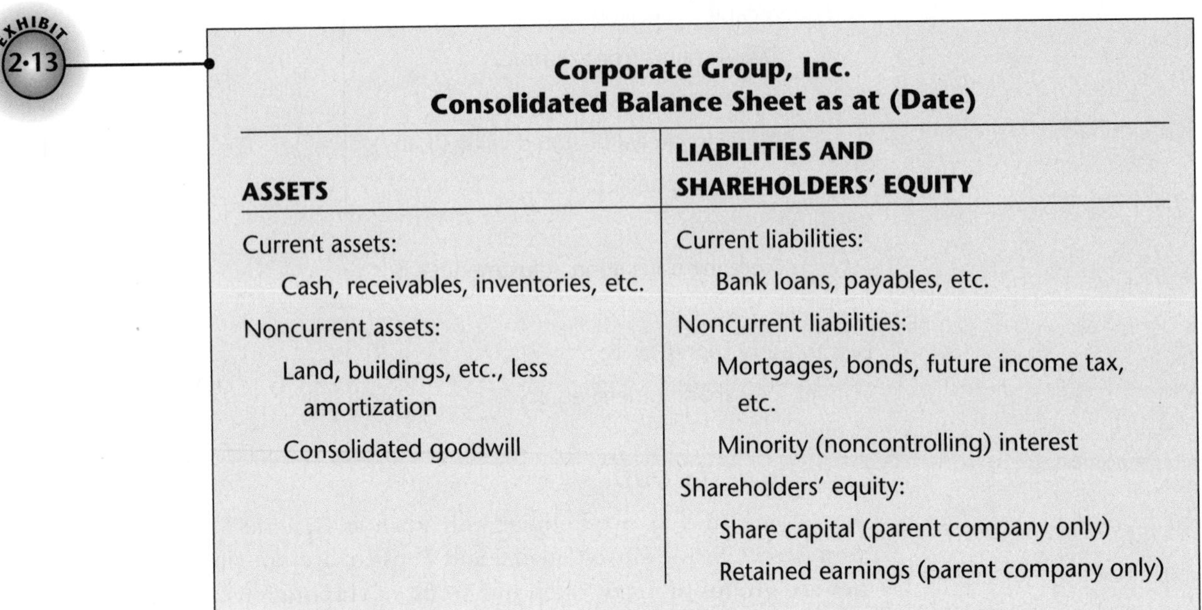

Corporate Group, Inc.
Consolidated Balance Sheet as at (Date)

ASSETS	LIABILITIES AND SHAREHOLDERS' EQUITY
Current assets:	Current liabilities:
Cash, receivables, inventories, etc.	Bank loans, payables, etc.
Noncurrent assets:	Noncurrent liabilities:
Land, buildings, etc., less amortization	Mortgages, bonds, future income tax, etc.
Consolidated goodwill	Minority (noncontrolling) interest
	Shareholders' equity:
	Share capital (parent company only)
	Retained earnings (parent company only)

Summary of the Kinds of Business Organizations

Here is a summary of the four kinds of business organizations.

EXHIBIT 2·14

Summary of Kinds of Business Organizations

Kind	Legality	Owner(s)	Equity accounts
Proprietorship	Not separate from owner	One proprietor	Capital and retained earnings are combined
Partnership	Partly separate from owners	Several or many partners	Capital and retained earnings are combined, but each partner's total is calculated
Corporation	Separate from owners	Usually several or many shareholders	Legal share capital is disclosed separately from retained earnings
Corporate Group	Consists of legally separate corporations	Usually several or many shareholders	Legal share capital of parent corporation is disclosed separately from retained earnings

BUSINESS FINANCING

The balance sheet's left side lists the assets; the right side lists the sources of the assets. Here is a list of the main sources (more information about them is in later chapters):

Current Liabilities (due within a year):

- Loans from banks due on demand or otherwise potentially payable sooner rather than later.
- Financing provided by suppliers and other trade creditors by allowing the enterprise to charge its purchases and pay for them later.
- Wages earned by but not yet paid to employees and taxes withheld from them that are to be turned over to the taxation authorities.
- Estimates of amounts owing for things such as power, interest charges, legal costs, and other debts building up but not yet actually billed to the enterprise.
- Income taxes and other taxes owed by the enterprise.
- Dividends owed by the enterprise (if it is a corporation), having been declared by the board of directors, but not yet paid to the shareholders.
- Short-term portions of longer-term debts, such as the principal payments due over the next year on long-term mortgages.

Noncurrent Liabilities (debts due more than a year in the future):

- Mortgages, bonded debt (bonds are certificates of debt issued by the enterprise that include detailed legal requirements), debentures (similar to bonds), equipment-purchase agreements, and other debts extending over several years.
- Certain long-term liabilities, such as special loans from owners in addition to their share capital, long-term tax estimates, and estimated liabilities for pensions to be paid to employees when they retire (in excess of money already put aside funded for such pensions).

Owners' Equity:

- For a proprietorship: owner's capital (contributed capital and income not withdrawn by proprietor, mixed together).
- For a partnership: owners' capital (contributed capital and income not withdrawn by partners, mixed together for each partner).
- For a corporation: share capital received for each kind of share plus retained earnings (plus some other items if legal or accounting complexities require them).

Financial Instruments:

Financial instruments may or may not be included in the balance sheet. The term describes the set of contracts, debts, shares, and other arrangements a corporation uses to conduct its business, and to protect itself against changes in prices of important supplies or in important foreign currencies. Double-entry accounting does not incorporate much of the information about these instruments and related activities like hedging (betting both ways on price changes), so the notes to the financial statements are increasingly used to summarize the company's activities, risks, and current position with regard to these. Many of the promises and other arrangements needed to run a business do not meet the accounting definition of assets or liabilities and so are often referred to as *off-balance-sheet* financing. This is a very difficult and controversial area of accounting, with alleged failure to properly report financial instruments, especially any off-balance-sheet risks, being behind some spectacular problems such as those of Enron Inc. in 2001.

When making financial decisions, managers, investors, and bankers frequently want to know what the assets, liabilities, and equity are worth today, not what they were valued at when they were recorded in a transaction that might have happened years ago. Much research has been done on alternative bases of accounting, for example, *current value accounting*, which would show assets and liabilities at current market values, not values determined by historical transactions. From the sixties to the early eighties, authors such as E.O. Edwards, P.W. Bell, R.J. Chambers, and R.R. Sterling explored how to improve financial accounting by getting closer to such current values. Considerable theoretical and other research was done into how to do current value accounting, and there have been some experiments with current values in countries, or times, when inflation was high. In Canada in the mid-1980s, for example, companies were encouraged to try it out in addition to their regular financial statements. But the research and experimentation have demonstrated fairly conclusively that nontransactional current value accounting is an idea whose time has not yet come. It becomes more attractive in times of high inflation, when historical transaction values tend to differ greatly from current values, but inflation has not been very high for some years. More seriously, people can agree on what a transaction is, but they have a lot of trouble agreeing on what current value to use, because current values are unavoidably hypothetical, being based on judgments of what values might be rather than actual events. You don't really know what your car is worth until you sell it. Most accounting researchers have concluded that the historical transaction basis of financial accounting is going to be with us for the foreseeable future.

HOW'S YOUR UNDERSTANDING?

Here are two questions you should be able to answer based on what you have just read. If you can't answer them, it would be best to reread the material.

1. The owners of Blotz Consulting Partnership wonder if they should incorporate their business as Blotz Consulting Inc. What difference would this make to the owners' equity section of the business's balance sheet?
2. What are some common examples of current and noncurrent liabilities, and how do the two types differ?

2.10 A Closer Look at Balance Sheet Content

Early in this chapter, we did some analysis of Sound and Light Corporation's simple balance sheet, and later we used Petro-Canada's balance sheet to record some transactions and illustrate how the double-entry accounting system works. Now we turn to the balance sheet of a company that will be used as an example throughout the book: Canadian Pacific Railway Limited (**www.cpr.ca**). Later chapters will examine CPR's other financial statements and notes, and in Chapter 10 a full financial statement analysis will be done so that you can see how all the ratios and other analyses fit together. The full set of CPR financial statements for 2004 are in Chapter 10—in this chapter, only the balance sheet will be presented and examined.

The CPR has been a romantic and important part of Canada. It is celebrated in one of Gordon Lightfoot's most famous songs, *Canadian Railroad Trilogy*,[10] as well as in many other songs, poems, stories, paintings and photos. The railway was built westward across the country in the late 1800s, partly to meet British Columbia's conditions for joining the central Canadian provinces and creating the country of Canada. The role of the CPR in the building of Canada is a huge and dramatic story, covered in many articles and books (such as Pierre Berton's pair of bestsellers *The National Dream* and *The Last Spike*)[11] and other media. As you read and think about the CPR, keep in mind the image of the vast Canadian country linked by steel rails.

Over the years, the CPR grew into a very large conglomerate company, Canadian Pacific Limited, which owned the railroad, but also ships, airplanes, hotels, mines, mills, and other enterprises. In 2001, a remarkable thing happened: the big company was broken up into separate companies, each focusing on just part of the big company's wide range of operations. The railway emerged in October 2001, as one of the new separate companies. That's the company we will study: it is a railway company, but you will see interesting effects of the larger corporate break-up, almost like the costs of a divorce!

CPR's 2004 balance sheet follows. (Note that the 2003 comparative figures are labelled "Restated" because the figures originally reported in 2003 were revised to calculate them the same way as in 2004. In 2004, CPR adopted several revised accrual accounting methods, and so without going back and changing the 2003 figures, they would not really be comparable to 2004. Note 2, not reproduced in this book, explains all the revised accounting methods. This kind of retrospective revision is quite common!)

Canadian Pacific Railway Limited
Consolidated Balance Sheet

Year ended December 31 (in millions)	2004	2003 (Restated– see Note 2
Assets		
Current assets		
Cash and short-term investments	**$ 353.0**	$ 134.7
Accounts receivable (Note 9)	**434.7**	395.7
Materials and supplies	**134.1**	106.4
Future income taxes (Note 7)	**70.2**	87.4
	992.0	724.2
Investments (Note 11)	**96.0**	105.6
Net properties (Note 12)	**8,393.5**	8,219.6
Other assets and deferred charges (Note 13)	**1,018.3**	907.3
Total assets	**$10,499.8**	$9,956.7
Liabilities and Shareholders' Equity		
Current liabilities		
Accounts payable and accrued liabilities	**$ 975.3**	$ 907.0
Income and other taxes payable	**16.2**	13.5
Dividends payable	**21.0**	20.2
Long-term debt maturing within one year (Note 14)	**275.7**	13.9
	1,288.2	954.6
Deferred liabilities (Note 16)	**767.8**	702.8
Long-term debt (Note 14)	**3,075.3**	3,348.9
Future income taxes (Note 7)	**1,386.1**	1,295.8
Shareholders' equity (Note 18)		
Share capital	**1,120.6**	1,118.1
Contributed surplus	**300.4**	294.6
Foreign currency translation adjustments	**77.0**	88.0
Retained income	**2,484.4**	2,153.9
	3,982.4	3,654.6
Total liabilities and shareholders' equity	**$10,499.8**	$9,956.7

Commitments and contingencies (Note 22)

See Notes to Consolidated Financial Statements.

Approved on behalf of the Board:

J. E. Newall, Director R. Phillips, Director

Comparative.

Before we get to the details, notice some standard features of CPR's balance sheet:

1. The balance sheet contains figures at two dates (2004 and 2003). The comparison is there to help the users recognize changes. It is standard practice for the more recent figures to be to the left, closer to the words describing those figures.

Not to the penny.

2. To avoid clutter, the figures are shown in millions of dollars, not exact amounts to the cent. For example, CPR had nearly $353 million in cash at the end of 2004 (nearly $135 million in 2003).

Many notes.

3. References are made to various notes. It is not possible to explain every important item on the face of the balance sheet, so extensive explanatory notes are appended to most balance sheets, and the other financial statements. To show you how many note references balance sheets often have, those references have been left in but the notes themselves are not included. (Many will be brought into later parts of this book.)

Consolidated.

4. The balance sheet is described as *consolidated*, which tells us that CPR is a corporate group, not a single corporation. Even after the break-up, CPR is a corporate group in its own right, owning railroads in the United States as well as Canada.

Fiscal year-end.

5. The balance sheet date is December 31, the end of the *fiscal* (financial) year 2004. December 31 is the most popular fiscal year-end, but many companies choose other dates.

Signed by the board.

6. The balance sheet has been signed by two members of the board of directors to show that the board approves it and to indicate the board's responsibility for it.

Here are some comments about CPR's assets, liabilities, and equity accounts.

Assets:

> *An asset is a resource that an individual, an enterprise, or a country owns or controls and that is expected to provide future benefit.*

CPR's assets rose from $9.96 billion in 2003 to $10.5 billion in 2004.

The balance sheet tells us what CPR's main assets were at the ends of 2004 and 2003, beginning with cash and short-term investments, and ending with "other assets and deferred charges." Some comments about assets:

Current assets	$ 992.0
Noncurrent assets	9,507.8
Total assets	$10,499.8

- The current assets subtotal is given ($992.0 million at end of 2004), but not the noncurrent subtotal. When you are studying financial statements, you may have to derive figures you need. Users of financial statements are expected to have some competence in understanding them, so not everything is necessarily calculated or labelled. Even the current assets subtotal is not labelled as you are expected to know what the $992.0 million is. Before long, this will be second nature to you!
- As you might expect, CPR's assets are concentrated in the noncurrent category: land, track and roadway, locomotives, freight cars, and other property. The balance sheet gives just one "net" figure for all this: $8,393.5 million at end of 2004. (Little of this cost is land, actually, because much of the land was acquired in the 1800s at very low costs compared to today's land prices.) Note 12 provides much detail that would crowd the balance sheet (note the company uses the term *accumulated depreciation* rather than accumulated amortization—they are interchangeable terms, at least for now!). Note 12 follows, describing the kinds of property the company has and showing that the net $8,393.5 million is made up of $12,876.1 million cost minus $4,482.6 million accumulated depreciation:

Canadian Pacific Railway Limited

12. Net Properties

(in millions)	**Cost**	**Accumulated depreciation**	**Net book value**
2004			
Track and roadway	$ 7,667.1	$2,482.7	$5,184.4
Buildings	319.7	128.4	191.3
Rolling stock	3,323.2	1,319.8	2,003.4
Other	1,566.1	551.7	1,014.4
Total net properties	$12,876.1	$4,482.6	$8,393.5
2003 (Restated – see Note 2)			
Track and roadway	$ 7,325.7	$2,321.0	$5,004.7
Buildings	314.6	108.1	206.5
Rolling stock	3,270.4	1,277.5	1,992.9
Other	1,535.9	520.4	1,015.5
Total net properties	$12,446.6	$4,227.0	$8,219.6

Amortized proportion of cost:
2004: $4,482.6/$12,876.1 = 34.8%
2003: $4,227.0/$12,446.6 = 34.0%

- Note 12 shows that about a third of the property's original cost had been "used up" (amortized, depreciated): 35% in 2004, 34% in 2003. The railroad has existed for over 100 years, but its property assets have been renewed regularly. If the amortized proportion had been high, say, 90%, that would indicate the property was getting old, its value having been nearly used up. Enabling you to make a judgment about the property's age is one of the reasons that companies disclose both cost and accumulated amortization or depreciation.
- CPR also expected to benefit within the next year from some tax deductions that would reduce its income tax by $70.2 million. This expectation's economic value made it an asset.
- Finally, the "other" assets are almost half employee future pension costs that CPR had already paid to the pension trustee, "prepaid pension costs." Prepaid expenses are normally current assets, because usually they apply only to the short run (few of us pay our bills very far in advance), but sometimes prepaid expenses apply to the more distant future, like pensions. Such more distant prepaid items are often called *deferred charges*, as CPR does.

Liabilities:

A liability is a presently existing commitment to transfer an individual's, enterprise's, or country's resources to others in the future.

Liabilities can be legally owed debts, but they also can be estimates of future payments based on past agreements.

- As examples of the first group, CPR had $975.3 million in accounts payable to its suppliers and accrued (estimated) liabilities at the end of 2004 and $3,075.3 million of long-term debt (plus $275.7 million of that debt due in the next year).

- As examples of the second group, CPR had $1,386.1 million of estimated future income tax (indicating that the company had been saving tax by deducting some expenses before the end of 2004 instead of later, and that later on the absence of those deductions would increase tax payments), and $767.8 million of other "deferred" noncurrent liabilities. Note 18 tells us that most of this $767.8 million was an estimate of environmental "remediation" costs to be paid plus corporate restructuring costs.

CPR's liability financing totalled $6.5 billion at December 31, 2004.

As we saw for the current assets, CPR did not add up the noncurrent liabilities for us, nor label the $1,288.2 current liabilities subtotal. The 2004 summary shown here includes all the liabilities between the current subtotal and the Shareholders' equity line as noncurrent liabilities, and indicates that the company's liabilities are primarily noncurrent. This makes financial sense: most of its assets are noncurrent, and it is sensible to finance such assets with noncurrent liabilities.

Current liabilities	$1,288.2
Noncurrent liabilities	5,229.2
Total liabilities	$6,517.4

Owners' equity:

The third term in the balance sheet equation is owners' equity, the residual ownership interest in the enterprise.

CPR's equity financing totalled $3.9 billion at December 31, 2004.

CPR had two usual items in its shareholders' equity: share capital of $1,120.6 million and retained earnings of $2,484.4 million. The company had earned income and had not paid enough dividends to distribute all of the assets representing that income to shareholders, so its retained earnings exceeded share capital at the end of 2004. (It was the other way around at the end of 2000, because CPR paid $700 million in share capital back to its former parent company, Canadian Pacific Limited, just before the corporate break-up. While share capital is normally permanent financing, sometimes it can be repaid ("redeemed"), and here is an example. As part of the break-up arrangements, all the former "ordinary" shares held by Canadian Pacific Limited were replaced by "common" shares to be traded on the stock market. CPR is traded on the Toronto and New York stock exchanges.) The company did not have enough cash and short-term investments to pay out the whole amount of retained earnings because those retained earnings had been invested in other assets, such as property. This is the normal circumstance: companies use retained earnings as "internal" financing and so do not pay all the earnings out to shareholders.

There are two other items in CPR's shareholders' equity:

CPR's equity includes contributed surplus and currency translation adjustments.

- *Contributed surplus* of $300.4 million, arising in the past from issuing the old ordinary shares at a higher price than their official value. This amount was left in CPR during the corporate break-up.
- A *foreign currency translation adjustment* of $77.0 million. *See the explanation and example of this kind of adjustment in Section 2.8.* CPR's net foreign assets, that is, assets minus liabilities, which are mostly in the United States in CPR's case, differ from their original transactional amounts by this $77.0 million. The adjustment is carried in equity because it accounts for some of the company's balance sheet assets and liabilities amounts.

Some Analysis of CPR's Balance Sheet

CPR's working capital and working capital ratio have decreased from 2003 to 2004.

Working capital: What is CPR's current financial strength? At the end of 2004, the company had negative working capital of $296.1 million and a working capital ratio of 0.77. The decrease in working capital (greater negative amount) from 2003 came about as current liabilities (largely the reclassification of the current portion of long-term debt) grew more quickly than current assets. Chapter 4 will deal in greater depth with how CPR can operate with negative working capital.

CPR's working capital

End of 2004: $992.0 – $1,288.2 = ($296.1)
End of 2003: $724.2 – $954.6 = ($230.4)

CPR's working capital ratio

End of 2004: $992.0/$1,288.2 = 0.77
End of 2003: $724.2/$954.6 = 0.75

Quick ratio red flag: Seeing that working capital is not strong, an analyst might calculate the quick ratio to see how stressed the company might be to pay its bills without having to sell inventory first. Well, all ratio calculations have to make sense for the company concerned, and a railroad, unlike a retailer, does not sell its inventory and so does not have to wait for such sales to get cash to pay bills. CPR's inventory is basically supplies for the railroad, and is not a large balance sheet amount. We would not expect the quick ratio to be much different from the working capital ratio. It is calculated here for illustration, using only cash and short-term investments and accounts receivable in the ratio numerator. The ratio was quite low for both years but the increase in cash and short-term investments both improved the ratio in 2004 and reduced the danger signal that the low 2003 ratio represented, because there was more cash to pay bills.

CPR's quick ratio

End of 2004: $787.7/$1,288.2 = 0.61
End of 2003: $530.4/$954.6 = 0.56

CPR is financed more by creditors than by owners (shareholders).

Debt versus equity financing: We can see from the balance sheet what proportion of the assets is financed by liabilities versus equity, creditors versus owners. The assets totalled $10.5 billion at the end of 2004: $6.5 billion of that was financed by debt and $4.0 billion by equity. The debt-equity ratio was thus 1.64 at the end of 2004 and 1.72 at the end of 2003. The small improvement in the ratio comes about as equity growth (through retained earnings) exceeded the growth in debt.

CPR's debt-equity ratio

End of 2004: $6,517.4/$3,982.4 = 1.64
End of 2003: $6,302.1/$3,654.6 = 1.72

CPR's market value exceeds its book equity.

Price compared to book value: At December 31, 2004, CPR's equity was $3,982.4 million. It had 158.8 million common shares issued at that date, so its book value per share was then $25.08. On December 31, 2004, its shares closed at $44.10 on the Toronto Stock Exchange, so its price to book ratio was 1.76. Investors valued CPR at about 76% more than the book value of equity.

Now that we have calculated some important ratios from CPR's balance sheet, the next step is to interpret them. Are these ratios good or bad? This requires some judgment by the user of the statement. A good starting point is to compare the ratio to a benchmark, such as the industry average or ratios of top competitors. For example, CPR's price to book ratio was above the average of 1.58 for the transportation industry and its current ratio was below the industry average of 1.41.[12] Its quick ratio was lower than Canadian National Railway Company's 0.73; however, the debt to equity ratios are similar to CN's ratio at 1.62.[13]

Why do managers care about their companies' balance sheets? The basic reason is that many outsiders do, including owners, creditors, tax authorities, and unions. Read any issue of a business newspaper or magazine, and you will see opinions like the following expressed:

- "T Inc. has a weak financial structure. Management must solve this problem before risk-shy investors can be expected to take an interest in the company."
- "H Ltd. has large cash reserves, so one can only guess that management is looking to buy another company to add to H's consolidated group."
- "The prices for corporate bonds have responded poorly to recent changes in interest rates because too many corporate balance sheets show too much debt."
- "In the current turbulent business climate, managers must pay more attention to financing short-term assets with something other than bank borrowing."

The balance sheet reports what the organization's financial position (assets, liabilities, and owners' equity) is at a point in time. It shows the assets that management has chosen to acquire for the organization, and how management has decided to finance those assets. Therefore, it provides a useful picture of the state of the company and is used by many outsiders to evaluate the quality of management's decisions on obtaining, deploying, and financing assets. For better or worse, it is the summary of all the information recognized by accounting and is, to many people, the basic scorecard of management's stewardship of the company. That's why the balance sheet is usually signed by members of the board of directors, the uppermost level of management responsible to the owners and creditors.

HOW'S YOUR UNDERSTANDING?

Here are two questions you should be able to answer based on what you have just read. If you can't answer them, it would be best to reread the material.

1. What sorts of assets does CPR have for conducting its business?
2. If CPR issued additional common shares for $250 million cash right after midnight December 31, 2004, what would be its (a) working capital, (b) working capital (current) ratio, and (c) debt-equity ratio?

(a) ($46.1) million, which equals $992 + $250 – $1,288.2; (b) 0.96, which equals ($992 + $250) / $1,288.2; (c) 1.54, which equals $6,517.4/ ($3,982.4 + $250).) All three have improved, in the sense of indicating less risk.

2.11 A Look at a Bank's Balance Sheet

To emphasize that each company's balance sheet reflects the kind of business the company does and the way the company is organized, here is the October 31, 2004, consolidated balance sheet of The Royal Bank of Canada (go to **www.rbc.com**). You'll see that there are some recognizable accounts, but in general the balance sheet is much different from CPR's. (As in the CPR example, the financial statement notes are *not* provided—the Royal's notes are very long and complex, because there is much about the bank's financing and use of financial instruments that must be explained.)

Consolidated Balance Sheet

As at October 31 (C$ millions)	2004	2003
ASSETS		
Cash and due from banks	**$ 4,758**	$ 2,887
Interest-bearing deposits with banks	**5,220**	3,126
Securities		
Trading account (pledged - $14,850 and $11,791)	**89,322**	87,532
Investment account	**38,923**	41,074
Loan substitute	**701**	325
	128,946	128,931
Assets purchased under reverse repurchase agreements	**34,862**	36,289
Loans		
Residential mortgage	**84,170**	78,817
Personal	**36,848**	32,186
Credit card	**6,456**	4,816
Business and government	**60,713**	56,630
	188,187	172,449
Allowance for loan losses	**(1,644)**	(2,055)
	186,543	170,394
Other		
Customers' liability under acceptances	**6,184**	5,943
Derivative-related amounts	**38,891**	35,612
Premises and equipment	**1,756**	1,670
Goodwill	**4,369**	4,587
Other intangibles	**523**	580
Other assets	**17,144**	13,014
	68,867	61,406
Total assets	**$429,196**	$403,033
LIABILITIES AND SHAREHOLDERS' EQUITY		
Deposits		
Personal	**$ 113,009**	$ 106,709
Business and government	**132,070**	129,860
Bank	**25,880**	22,576
	270,959	259,145
Other		
Acceptances	**6,184**	5,943
Obligations related to securities sold short	**25,005**	22,855
Obligations related to assets sold under repurchase agreements	**21,705**	23,735
Derivative-related amounts	**42,201**	37,775
Insurance claims and policy benefit liabilities	**6,838**	5,256
Other liabilities	**27,575**	21,318
	129,508	116,882
Subordinated debentures	**8,116**	6,243
Non-controlling interest in subsidiaries	**2,409**	2,388
SHAREHOLDERS' EQUITY		
Preferred shares	**832**	832
Common shares (shares issued and outstanding - 644,747,812 and 656,021,122)	**6,988**	7,018
Additional paid-in capital	**169**	85
Retained earnings	**12,065**	11,333
Treasury stock (shares held - 4,862,782 and nil)	**(294)**	–
Foreign currency translation adjustments	**(1,556)**	(893)
	18,204	18,375
	$429,196	$403,033

Gordon M. Nixon
President and Chief Executive Officer

Robert B. Peterson
Director

Each balance sheet is a picture of that particular organization's financial character.

The bank's balance sheet is just an example of how accounting adjusts to the kind of organization being accounted for. Many other kinds of organizations have balance sheets that are quite different from the standard sort of format we saw for CPR, such as governments, charities, and insurance companies. Here are some brief comments about the bank example:

- The numbers are huge: at October 31, 2004, the Royal Bank had assets exceeding $429 *billion.*
- The bank doesn't use the current and noncurrent categorizations for assets and liabilities. Using an arbitrary one-year definition for such categorization is not thought to make sense for a bank's assets or liabilities, because monies flow in and out under all sorts of frequently complex arrangements.
- The bank has little cash. If we all wanted the money in our accounts at the same time, the bank wouldn't have it. You can see that personal deposits alone (under liabilities) of $113.0 billion far exceed the bank's cash of $4.8 billion.
- The money people have in the bank is recorded as a liability (the bank owes the money to the depositors) and the money people owe the bank for loans is an asset for the bank. You can see how the bank does its business: at October 31, 2004, it had deposits from customers of $271.0 billion, had lent out $188.2 billion and invested $129.0 billion. It has hardly any money invested in property: the net book value of its premises and equipment was just $1.8 billion at October 31, 2004, far less than CPR, for example. Property is so minor that it is just included in "other" assets.
- The RBC is a corporate group. It has a small noncontrolling interest liability of $2.4 billion (arising from shares owned by minority shareholders in bank subsidiary companies included in the consolidated group). It also has some *goodwill* and *intangible assets* of $4.9 billion, included in the $68.9 billion of other assets. Goodwill arises when a company pays more for another company than the sum of the other company's assets' fair values minus its liabilities' fair values, and so represents a sort of premium paid to acquire control of the other company. Goodwill is a very controversial asset and will turn up frequently in later chapters. Intangible assets are things like trademarks, patents, and rights acquired with the goodwill.
- The bank sets its shareholders' equity section out the same way as most companies. Given the size of the bank's assets and liabilities, its equity is quite small.
- You may conclude, rightly, from all this that you cannot use standard ratios like the working capital, debt-equity, or quick ratios to analyze banks. The information for such ratios is either not provided or the ratio would not be meaningful in the ordinary way. An example is the debt-equity ratio. The RBC's ratio at the end of 2004, using the standard formula, would be 22.58 (increased from 20.93 in 2003). This is a huge ratio, and for an ordinary company would spell big risk and probably trouble, but for the RBC, it just reflects the way banks operate. They take in money and lend it out or invest it, and to do this do not need capital from owners so much as from depositors (the bank's creditors). On the other hand, banks can be precarious financially—you can see that if there were a "run" on the bank, everyone wanting their deposited money at once, the bank would have difficulty. The depositors are taking a much bigger risk, relatively, than are the bank's shareholders.

RBC's debt-equity ratio

October 31, 2004: ($270,959 + $129,508 + $8,116 + $2,409) / $18,204 = 22.58

October 31, 2003: ($259,145 + $116,882 + $6,243 + $2,388) / $18,375 = 20.93

2.12 Terms to Be Sure You Understand

A great many terms were introduced in this chapter. As suggested in Section 1.10, make sure you know what they mean *in accounting*. If any are unclear to you, check the chapter again or refer to the glossary of terms at the back of the book. Many of the terms will be used repeatedly as the book proceeds, so your understanding of them will deepen. Some particularly important terms introduced in Chapter 1 are included again here as a helpful reminder.

Account(s)
Accounts payable
Accounts receivable
Accumulated amortization
Accumulated depreciation
Accumulated foreign currency translation adjustment
Acid test ratio
Asset(s)
Balance
Balance sheet
Balance sheet equation
Board of directors
Bond(s)
Book value (asset)
Book value (equity)
Bookkeeping
Common shares
Company(ies)
Consolidated
Consolidated goodwill
Contributed surplus
Corporate group
Corporation(s)
Creditors
Credits
Current assets
Current liabilities
Current ratio
Current value accounting
Debenture(s)
Debits
Debt-equity ratio
Debts
Deferred charges
Deficit
Dividend(s)
Double entry
Earnings
Equity
Exchange
Financial instruments
Financial position
Financing
Fiscal
Foreign currency translation adjustment
General ledger
Goodwill
Income
Intangible assets
Inventory(ies)
Journal entry(ies)
Liability(ies)
Loss
Market capitalization
Market value
Minority interest liability
Minority interest(s)
Mortgage(s)
Net
Noncontrolling interest(s)
Noncurrent assets
Noncurrent liabilities
No-par
Note(s)
Notes to the financial statements
Off-balance-sheet
Overdrafts
Owner's capital
Owners' equity
Pacioli
Par value
Parent
Partners' capital
Partners' equity
Partnership
Post(ed)
Preferred shares
Price to book ratio
Profit
Proprietor's equity
Proprietorship
Quick ratio
Receivable
Reclassification
Retained earnings
Share capital
Shareholders' equity
Shares
Stated value
Statement of financial position
Stock markets
Stocks
Subsidiary(ies)
Treasury shares
Trial balance
Working capital
Working capital ratio

DATA FOR INSTALLMENT 2

In Installment 1, Mavis Janer and Tomas Brot were thinking about starting a business together and began working on a business plan by listing their objectives in having a business and the risks and constraints they were concerned about. If you have forgotten about those, you might look back to the "Results for Installment 1" in Section 1.14 to see the lists.

After much investigation and debate, Mavis and Tomas came up with a proposal for a business. They had observed a large growth in boutique-style retail stores, usually managed by families, in their region of the country, but felt such stores were not well supported either by supplies of attractive merchandise or marketing ideas. They saw a niche they could fill by setting up a regional wholesale distribution company that would provide the boutique retailers with better access to national and international suppliers of goods, and would help in both fitting their product lines to local markets and marketing the products well.

There were other such wholesale distributors in North America, but the local region did not seem well serviced by them, and Mavis and Tomas felt they had some ideas the other distributors had not thought of. The field would be very competitive, but they saw considerable opportunity for growth as baby boomers reached middle age and increased the demand for boutique retailers, and as international trade opened more opportunities for supplying interesting products at attractive prices.

Mato Inc.'s Financial Starting Point

Many things had to be done before the business could start. Here are some of the actions Mavis and Tomas took.

- They decided to incorporate a company, to provide a financing focus and some limited liability for themselves. They decided to call it Mato Inc., after the first two initials of their first names, and because it sounded vaguely exotic and international.
- They had to raise initial capital. Tomas felt they needed about $125,000 in share capital and substantial additional bank financing to support the inventory the company would carry. They planned to use modern techniques to minimize inventory levels, but, still, inventory would be a significant asset in the business as they foresaw it. After some analysis and discussion with relatives and friends, they assembled the following capital: Mavis would buy 40% of the issued voting shares with $50,000 cash from her inheritance, and Tomas would buy 24% of the shares. He did not have the $30,000 cash to make the purchase, but he would contribute his car to the business, at an agreed value of $10,000, and $20,000 in cash from his savings. Five friends and relatives agreed to contribute $45,000 cash for the remaining 36% of the shares. In addition, Tomas's father agreed to lend the business $15,000. He wanted to be a creditor of the new company; he did not want shares because he was worried about his health and wanted to be able to get the money back if he needed it.
- The company needed a management structure. It was decided that the board of directors would consist of Mavis (as chairperson), Tomas, and a representative of the five relatives and friends. Mavis would be president, and Tomas would be vice-president. Basically, Mavis was to look after business development and marketing, and Tomas would see to financing and day-to-day operations.
- They found a vacant warehouse building that could be rented at an attractive rate and was located both centrally in the region they wanted to serve and reasonably close to their homes. The building would require some renovation to meet their needs, but otherwise they could move right in and get going.

- Tomas put together a business plan and approached several banks and other financial institutions for support. On the strength of his and Mavis's background and of having their business plan and the above investments already arranged, he was able to secure the support he required: basically, a line of credit (a pre-approved borrowing limit) under which the company would have approved credit of up to $80,000 now, and further credit based on inventories and accounts receivable once operations got underway. Mavis and Tomas had to personally guarantee the line of credit to the company and pledge their shares in the company as collateral on any loan.

On March 1, 2006, the new business was established. On that day,

- the company was officially incorporated, having only one class of no-par shares;
- the company received its first bill (a fee of $1,100 to be paid to the lawyer handling the incorporation);
- the various investors paid their cash;
- a five-year lease was signed for the warehouse space;
- Tomas signed his car over to the company; and
- Mavis left her job to become the new company's only full-time employee at a monthly salary of $2,500.

Tomas would stay in his bank job for a while, and Mavis would spend most of this initial period making contacts with suppliers and retailers, supervising renovations, and doing other tasks necessary to get the business started. They felt it would be better if Tomas kept his paying job at the bank, instead of quitting and increasing the demands on the new company's cash. Until he left his bank job, Tomas would keep track of the time he put in on the company and be paid later at the same rate as Mavis, prorated over 200 hours per month, which was the number of hours per month Mavis expected to put in while getting the business started.

RESULTS FOR INSTALLMENT 2

Journal entries

These entries record the March 1, 2006, transactions:

- No entry for the company incorporation. Not an accounting transaction.
- DR Incorporation costs asset 1,100
  CR Accounts payable 1,100
  To record the lawyer's bill for incorporating the company.

- DR Cash 130,000
  CR Loan payable 15,000
  CR Share capital 115,000
  To record the initial investments in the company.

- No entry for the lease signing. Not an accounting transaction.
- DR Car asset 10,000
  CR Share capital 10,000
  To record signing Tomas's car over to the company for its agreed value in shares.

- No entry for Mavis's becoming the company's employee. Not an accounting transaction.

Company's initial balance sheet

1. Mavis and Tomas prepared two balance sheets, one with details of everyone's contributions and a second in a more standard format. The first one is shown below:

Mato Inc.
Balance Sheet Details as at March 1, 2006

Assets		Sources of Assets	
Cash:		Due to lawyer	$ 1,100
From Mavis	$ 50,000	Investments:	
From Tomas	20,000	Mavis's shares	50,000
From other		Tomas's shares	30,000
shareholders	45,000	Other shareholders	45,000
From Tomas's father	15,000	Tomas's father	15,000
Car	10,000		
Incorporation costs	1,100		
TOTAL	$141,100	TOTAL	$141,100

2. The second starting balance sheet is shown below. In it, Mavis and Tomas classified the loan from Tomas's father as a current liability because he had said he might want it back any time. The cost to the company of Tomas's car was the agreed value, as discussed above. The incorporation costs were shown as an asset because Tomas and Mavis felt there was a future benefit resulting from the incorporation of the company. However, they were not entirely sure about that because it was hard to say what the benefit actually was or for how long it would have value.

Mato Inc.
Formal Balance Sheet as at March 1, 2006

Assets		Liabilities and Shareholders' Equity	
Current assets:		Current liabilities:	
Cash	$130,000	Accounts payable	$ 1,100
Noncurrent assets:		Loan payable	15,000
Automobile (at cost)	10,000	Shareholders' equity:	
Incorporation costs	1,100	Share capital	125,000
TOTAL	$141,100	TOTAL	$141,100

2.14 Homework and Discussion to Develop Understanding

The problems roughly follow the outline of the chapter. Three main categories of questions are presented.

- Asterisked problems (*) have an informal solution provided in the Student Solutions Manual.
- EXTENDED TIME problems involve a thorough examination of the material and may take longer to complete.
- CHALLENGING problems are more difficult.

For further explanation, please refer to Section 1.15.

History of Accounting • Section 2.2

*** PROBLEM 2.1** Accounting needs and requirements

What must a society have in order to demand accounting? If there is a demand for it, what three elements are required in order to use accounting?

PROBLEM 2.2 Purpose and origin of balance sheet

You have been working at a summer job as a clerk in a small store. The new owner of the store comes over to you waving the balance sheet for the store saying, "You're studying accounting, I hear. Can you explain to me what my balance sheet is supposed to be telling me and why it is designed to have two sides? Where did such a way of measuring a business come from, anyway?" Give your reply.

PROBLEM 2.3 Evolution of accounting

What similarities are there between modern and early accounting?

PROBLEM 2.4 Pacioli's double entry

Luca Pacioli's book on mathematics and double-entry bookkeeping was a huge best-seller across Europe 400 to 500 years ago. It was translated into many languages, including English. Merchants and other business people took to double entry with great enthusiasm and it quickly became the standard method wherever Europeans did business (such as in the Americas).

Why do you think double-entry bookkeeping was (and is) so popular?

Balance Sheets • Sections 2.3, 2.10, 2.11

Preparing Personal Balance Sheets

*** PROBLEM 2.5** Personal balance sheet and debt-equity ratio

1. List your own personal resources and obligations and try to fit them into accounting's standard balance sheet format in which the resources are listed on one side and debts and claims against the resources are listed on the other, keeping in mind that total resources must balance total debts plus residual equity. In doing this, think about
   - which of your resources and obligations would or would not be reported on the balance sheet;
   - what would likely be disclosed about each;
   - which are short-term or long-term; and
   - which are easy or difficult to value numerically.

(If you have completed a credit application or student loan application, the things you reported there might be a good starting point.)

2. What decision-making information might your list of resources and obligations provide?
3. Calculate your personal debt-equity ratio (total liabilities divided by total equity). Are you soundly financed?

PROBLEM 2.6 Prepare separate and then combined balance sheets for a couple

Janet and Sam, who were engaged to be married, each made lists of their financial resources and the claims on these resources on Friday, June 16, 2006. Here are their lists:

Janet's list:	
Cash in chequing account	$ 750
Stereo	2,500
Damage deposit on hall (for wedding)	450
Sam's list:	
Cash in chequing account	$1,500
Student loan	3,200
Furniture	600
Prepaid rent on hall (for wedding)	650

1. Prepare a June 16, 2006, balance sheet for Janet using her list.
2. Prepare a June 16, 2006, balance sheet for Sam using his list.
3. On Saturday, June 17, 2006, Janet and Sam were married. Their wedding presents included:

Cash	$4,800
Household gifts	2,900
Parents' payment toward Sam's loan	2,100

The couple paid $1,000 immediately for the band that played at their wedding. There were no damages to the hall during the reception. After the party, they took a honeymoon weekend (lasting until Tuesday evening) and charged all their expenses on Janet's credit card, which they knew would be due at the end of July 2006. The honeymoon cost $900.

Prepare a balance sheet for the couple as at Wednesday, June 21, 2006. Be sure to include all the financial information given above.

PROBLEM 2.7 Prepare a comparative personal balance sheet

After graduation, Paula took a job with a large consulting firm downtown. It is a year later and Paula would like to know how much her net worth has increased now that she is making a decent salary instead of paying tuition. On the day Paula started her job, she had $600 in her chequing account and owed $900 on her credit card. The chequing account balance is $1,750 today and although she has paid off the credit card, her student loan balance has only dropped from $25,000 to $21,000. Paula sold her old car, which she had bought for $1,800 cash, and she now owes $27,000 on her new car that cost $32,000. Thinking it was time to move out of mom and dad's basement, Paula recently bought a house for $250,000 and spent another $23,000 on furniture and appliances. The balance on her mortgage is $200,000 and after living in the home for a month, Paula received a stack of bills totalling $1,200 today.

Based on this information, prepare a comparative balance sheet for today and a year ago and comment on the changes in Paula's net worth.

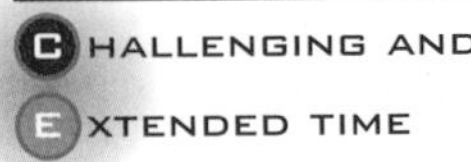

PROBLEM 2.8 Balance sheets without dollars

In the high mountains of Whimsia, two shepherds, Doug and Bob, sit arguing about their relative positions in life, an argument that has been going on for years. Doug says that he has 400 sheep, while Bob has only 360 sheep; therefore, Doug is much better off. Bob, on the other hand, argues that he has 30 acres of land, while Doug has only 20 acres. But Doug's land was inherited, while Bob traded 35 sheep for 20 acres of land ten years ago and this year gave 40 sheep for 10 acres of land. Bob also makes the observation that, of Doug's sheep, 35 belong to another man and he merely keeps them. Doug counters that he has a large one-room cabin that he built himself and claims to have been offered 3 acres of land for it. Besides these things, he has a plough, which was a gift from a friend and is worth a couple of goats; 2 carts, which were given him in trade for a poor acre of land; and an ox, acquired in return for 5 sheep.

Bob goes on to say that his wife has orders for 5 coats to be made of homespun wool and that she will receive 25 goats for them. His wife has 10 goats already, 3 of which were received in exchange for 1 sheep just last year. She also has an ox for which she traded 3 sheep and a cart, which had cost her 2 sheep. Bob's two-room cabin, though smaller than Doug's, should bring him 2 choice acres of land in a trade. Doug is reminded by Bob that he owes Ted, another shepherd, 3 sheep for bringing him his lunch each day last year.

Who is better off? State any assumptions you make. Try to develop a common numerical representation of the shepherds' situations to support your evaluation.

Preparing Business Balance Sheets

* **PROBLEM 2.9** Prepare a simple balance sheet, calculate working capital

Bluebird Bakery, a partnership that rents its bakery premises, had the following account balances at July 31, 2006. Prepare a balance sheet for the partnership by placing each account in the appropriate location in the balance sheet. From the balance sheet, calculate the partnership's working capital and working capital ratio.

Bakery equipment cost	$186,293	J. Bird partner's capital	$76,276
Demand loan from bank	21,500	Accumulated amortization	63,461
Supplies inventory cost	14,285	Cash on hand	985
Owing to suppliers	16,280	Owing by customers	4,968
B. Blue partner's capital	32,690	Cash in bank	6,832
Wages owing to employees	3,421	Unsold baked goods cost	265

PROBLEM 2.10 Prepare a balance sheet from accounts

Blue Moon Love Products Ltd. manufactures and sells various aids to middle-aged romantics, including special flower bouquets, French "beer for lovers," seductive apparel, and recipes for aphrodisiac cookies. Here are the company's balance sheet accounts as at June 30, 2006, in alphabetical order.

Blue Moon Love Products Inc.
Balance Sheet Accounts as at June 30, 2006

Accumulated amortization	$ 63,700	Owing from customers	$ 6,200
Bank account balance	14,300	Owing to suppliers	21,900
Bank loan	21,200	Retained earnings	47,500
Building	102,100	Share capital issued	25,000
Cash on hand	2,500	Short-term part of mortgage	8,000
Employees' tax not yet remitted	600	Unpaid employee wages	1,800
Fixtures and equipment	37,900	Unsold finished products	29,600
Land	48,000	Unused office supplies	1,400
Long-term part of mortgage owing	71,000	Unused product raw materials	18,700

1. Prepare the company's June 30, 2006, balance sheet from the above accounts.
2. Comment briefly on the company's financial condition as shown by the balance sheet.

PROBLEM 2.11 Prepare and comment on a simple initial balance sheet

John Graham decided to set up a business as a downtown courier, calling his business QuickJohn Courier. Before he could operate his courier service, there were a few things he needed: a bicycle, a bike lock, a delivery bag, and a good pair of running shoes. He had $200 in savings, but quickly realized that he would need more funds to purchase all of the required items. John asked his Aunt Elizabeth for a loan of $200 and promised that he would pay her back as soon as he could. She said yes.

John purchased a bike for $500, placing $275 down and promising to pay the rest later. He then bought a bike lock for $15, a pair of shoes for $60, and a delivery bag for $25, paying cash for all these items. He began his business on April 15, 2006.

John asked a friend to prepare an initial balance sheet for the new business. The friend had a couple of questions to ask first:

"John, when do you have to repay your Aunt Elizabeth?"

"She never said. But my intention is to pay her back by the end of 2007. I'm sure she would complain if I took longer than that. She wants the money for a big birthday party that year."

"How about the amount you owe on the bicycle; when is that due?"

"The store wants the money right away. I told them I would have to raise the funds by sales in my business, so they said they wanted me to pay just as soon as I could. They made me sign a form saying they could take back the bike and the other stuff if I don't pay."

With this information, prepare the initial balance sheet for QuickJohn Courier as at April 15, 2006, including any notes you think might be useful, and comment on the business's financial condition.

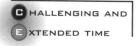

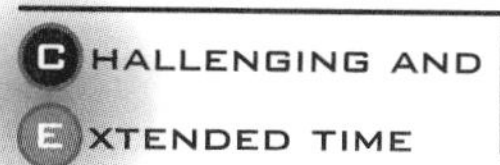

PROBLEM 2.12 Assemble a balance sheet from information fragments

You are a corporate spy trying to find out about the financial situation of Extreme Web Inc., a high-technology firm that is privately owned and does not release its balance sheet publicly. After considerable effort, you manage to be in a nightclub near a group of Extreme Web senior managers who are having too much to drink and have gotten into a discussion of financial matters. From all the confused talk, not all of which is necessarily relevant, but is recorded below, see if you can assemble the company's present balance sheet.

- "You guys are lucky, you don't have to work on our new financial plan. It's awful work, because the president wants to get our debt-equity ratio down from 2 to maybe only, gee this is great beer, half of that, and I don't think it can be done. More Buffalo wings?"
- "You think I'm lucky? I'm the person who has to collect the money from the customers that the sales department digs up from under rocks, or something. Our receivables are twice our payables, and everyone thinks it's my fault. Yeah, I'll have some wings! Didya know that the payables are only one-third of our current liabilities, but our receivables are about 90% of our current assets? My hide is on the line if I can't get the cash in. The bank says we can't have any more money than the $9 million it's already advanced us, and that it is pushing us to pay back soon. How will we do that?"
- "You two are always complaining. Get out of my calamari! Sure our working capital is the pits, but we have great people and great technology. Put that all together and we're gonna play in the big leagues yet! I bought some shares on the employee plan because I've got confidence that they'll be worth a lot more than the $10 each I paid. Some day we'll go public, and the value of the company will skyrocket. The president has good ideas and was smart to make 80% of the company's assets equipment rather than relying on those customers, who, I agree, are slow to pay."
- "Yes, but it'll be a big risk for investors. I bought some shares too, but only spent what I could afford to lose, because the company has yet to make money, and with a deficit about a quarter the size of our share capital, we aren't gonna look too great. Hey, who's that over there taking notes? Any of you guys know? Let's get out of here before we say too much!"

Recording Transactions • Section 2.4

* PROBLEM 2.13 Journal entries for simple transactions

The events listed below all took place on December 15, 2005. Provide the journal entry necessary to record each event in the accounts of Figaro Company on that date. If no entry is required, indicate that and give reasons. If you feel an assumption is necessary, state it.

a. Figaro receives a bill for television advertising in the amount of $1,800. The ads appeared the first week of December 2005.
b. Figaro receives an invoice for radio advertising that is to be broadcast on December 31, 2005. Payment is due in 30 days.
c. An interior decorator has agreed to redecorate the office of the CEO for a fee of $3,500.
d. An order for $1,600 worth of merchandise is received from a customer along with a deposit of $250.
e. A new chief accountant is hired at a salary of $85,000 per year.
f. First and last months' rent totalling $3,000 on a new shop was paid by Figaro on signing a lease for the period January 1, 2005, to December 31, 2008.

* PROBLEM 2.14 Journal entry for a business acquisition

Big Ideas Inc. decided to buy parts of the business of a competitor, which was cutting back operations. For a price of $4,200,000 (a $1,000,000 down payment and the rest in four equal annual installments plus interest at 12% per annum), Big Ideas got inventory it valued at $280,000, land it valued at $1,500,000, a retail store building it valued at $1,800,000, furniture and equipment it valued at $470,000, and some dealership rights it valued at $40,000. Big Ideas also agreed to pay a bank loan of $130,000 secured by the inventory.

Write a journal entry to record Big Ideas Inc.'s purchase.

PROBLEM 2.15 Identify transactions and write journal entries for them

LowRider Bike Rentals rents motor scooters to tourists during the summer season. For each event listed below, state whether or not it is an accounting transaction for LowRider and why. If it is an accounting transaction, write a journal entry to record it.

a. Borrowed $15,000 from the bank on January 1, 2006.
b. Paid interest on the bank loan in transaction a. on January 31, 2006. The rate of interest on the loan is 6%.
c. Purchased office furniture on January 1, 2006, for $3,800 cash.
d. Recorded amortization on the office equipment in the amount of $100.
e. Recorded service revenue for the month in the amount of $6,000. Customers had paid $5,500 of this amount and still owed the remainder.
f. Paid expenses for the month in the amount of $3,500. No other expenses had been incurred.

PROBLEM 2.16 Record transactions

The following events happened to Pooch's Pet Food Ltd. For each event that is an accounting entry:

1. write a journal entry to record the transaction in Pooch's accounts, and
2. write a journal entry to record the transaction in the accounts of the *other party* to the exchange.

a. Pooch's paid $350 for electrical utilities. The bill had been recorded as owing when it was received last month.
b. Pooch's made a sale of $4,000 on account to Bill's Pet Store.
c. Pooch's issued common shares in exchange for $5,000 cash from each of the four shareholders.
d. Pooch's borrowed $40,000 from the Regal Bank.
e. Pooch's paid its employees their salary for the week totalling $2,500.
f. Pooch's received a notice of reassessment of its income tax liability. The notice indicates an additional amount owing of $1,400 to be paid within 30 days.
g. Pooch's purchased on account inventory for resale in the amount of $3,700.
h. Pooch's paid $2,500 to the Regal Bank as partial payment of the loan received in transaction d. The payment included interest of $200.
i. Paid $2,000 of the amount owed to suppliers for the purchase of inventory for resale.

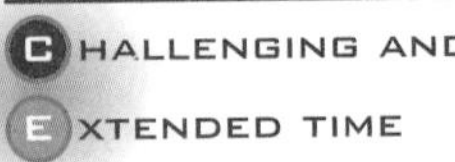

PROBLEM 2.17 Record transactions in CPR accounts

Refer to the CPR balance sheet in Section 2.10 and assume that the following events happened to CPR Limited on January 1, 2005, the day after the company's fiscal year-end.

a. CPR paid the current portion of its long-term debt, in cash.
b. CPR mailed out cheques for all dividends owed to common shareholders.
c. CPR issued no-par-value common shares for $5.2 million in cash to a group of senior managers.
d. CPR bought the rail-truck transfer facility of a large trucking company for $10 million in cash plus newly issued CPR common shares valued at $14 million.
e. CPR signed a contract for several shipments of steel at a cost of $7 million. The customer paid a deposit of $2 million and agreed to pay the balance upon delivery of the final shipment in 2005.
f. CPR refinanced $52 million of its long-term debt by exchanging present notes carrying 7.5% interest for new notes carrying 7.9% interest, but which are due several years further into the future.
g. CPR bought a patent on a new intermodal technology for $1.2 million cash.
h. CPR owed $3 million to a supplier company that also happened to be a customer owing $7 million to CPR. The two companies agreed to offset the money CPR owed against the larger amount the customer owed.

1. Record in journal entry form, in millions of dollars, any events that are accounting transactions, using the account titles in CPR's balance sheet (Section 2.10) as much as you can. Specify any appropriate additional accounts where necessary. (Only balance sheet accounts are needed to record all the transactions.)
2. Post your entries to CPR's accounts and do a trial balance after your entries to show that the balance sheet is still in balance.

Balance Sheet Accounts • Sections 2.5–2.7

* **PROBLEM 2.18** Classified balance sheet

Identify what is wrong with the following balance sheet and prepare a properly classified balance sheet instead.

Assets		**Liabilities and Shareholders' Equity**	
Inventory	$ 42,000	Bank loan	$ 30,000
Cash on hand	9,000	Accumulated amortization	54,400
Bank account	(10,600)	Mortgage due in 5 years	62,250
Account payable overpaid	400	Income tax refund expected	(2,600)
Treasury shares	2,250	Share capital	60,000
Currency translation adjustment	(1,100)	Goodwill (net of amortization)	(21,000)
Property and plant	123,000	Minority interest	3,300
Accounts receivable	46,200	Accounts payable	31,350
Deficit	8,350	Estimated interest due	1,800
	$219,400		$219,400

* PROBLEM 2.19 Examples of balance sheet categories

1. Define each of the following and choose an example of each from the CPR balance sheet in Section 2.10 of this chapter (or from the balance sheet of any company familiar or interesting to you).
   a. current asset
   b. noncurrent asset
   c. current liability
   d. noncurrent liability
   e. owners' equity item
2. Do you think the examples you selected will always be classified in the same way by all enterprises? Why or why not? Give examples if possible.

PROBLEM 2.20 Identify the other side of a transaction

Below is a series of changes in balance sheet accounts. For each, identify the one (or more) kinds of transaction that would have prompted such a change *assuming that only other balance sheet accounts are affected.* For each kind of transaction, specify the other balance sheet account(s) likely affected, and in what direction it or they would change. No other financial statements or non-balance-sheet accounts are involved in any of the items below.

a. Accounts receivable go down.
b. Share capital goes up.
c. Accounts payable go up.
d. Treasury stock goes up.
e. Goodwill goes up.
f. Prepaid expenses go up.
g. Mortgage noncurrent liability goes up.
h. Mortgage noncurrent liability goes down.
i. Inventory goes up.
j. Net book value of property and plant goes up.

PROBLEM 2.21 Identify items as asset, liability, or owners' equity

State whether or not, and why, each of the following items is likely to be an asset, liability, or equity account (perhaps more than one category in some cases) recorded in the balance sheet of the company indicated:

Company	**Item**
1. Walt Disney Co.	List of subscribers to *Discover* magazine
2. Interpacific Forest Products Ltd.	Funds collected from employees, to be repaid to them after retirement as pensions
3. Wal-Mart	Wal-Mart's satisfied customers
4. Branko Inc.	A lawsuit against the company by a plumber who alleges that Branko failed to pay for work done on the company's premises
5. Canada Safeway Ltd.	Land that Safeway has agreed to sell to a real estate developer once it has been surveyed
6. Wal-Mart	Wal-Mart's dissatisfied customers
7. Dow-Jones Inc.	The *Wall Street Journal*'s skilled group of editors and reporters
8. Imperial Oil Ltd.	Oil discovered on Imperial's property, but still underground and likely to stay there for many years
9. Edmonton Eskimos Football Club	Players under contract to the team

10. The Brick Warehouse	Deposits received from customers of The Brick for furniture not yet delivered to them
11. Torstar Corp.	Profits earned by the *Toronto Star*, but not yet paid out to the owners as dividends
12. Sears Inc.	A fleet of delivery trucks leased by Sears from several truck-leasing firms
13. Downtown Buick Sales Ltd.	A car Downtown Buick leases to real estate salesperson Don Wharton
14. Redpath Industries Ltd.	Funds owing to Redpath by a customer who recently declared bankruptcy
15. Keg Restaurants Ltd.	The phrase "The Keg" and the round logo, both registered trademarks
16. Loblaws	The parking lots surrounding the company's stores
17. Grand Centre Ltd.	A guarantee Grand Centre has made on a bank loan owed by an associated company
18. National Bioengineering Ltd.	A newly developed chemical that shows promise in curing adolescent blemishes once and for all, but that has to be approved by the government

Kinds Of Business Organizations • Section 2.9

* PROBLEM 2.22 Forms of business organization

Match each term on the left with the most fitting description on the right.

a. Owner's capital	1. Partnership equity
b. Minority interest	2. Directly contributed equity
c. Retained earnings	3. The corporation invests in itself
d. Consolidated equity	4. Can't be issued for less than the stated amount
e. Owners' capital	5. Indirectly contributed equity
f. Common shares	6. Proprietorship equity
g. Par value shares	7. Investment cost exceeds details of what was acquired
h. Consolidated goodwill	8. Parent corporation owners' interest
i. Capital in excess of par	9. Interest of owners outside the parent company
j. Treasury shares	10. Shares were issued for more than the stated amount

PROBLEM 2.23 Owner control and risk

Assuming businesses of identical size and operations, rank the following types of owners according to the level of control they are likely to have over the business and then based on the level of personal risk they face if the business fails.

- Partner
- Preferred shareholder
- Proprietor
- Common shareholder

PROBLEM 2.24 Direct equity contributions

On September 1, 2006, in order to finance an expansion into a new line of business, a company has increased equity by receiving a capital contribution of $200,000 in cash. Create separate journal entries for this transaction for a sole proprietorship, a corporation, and a partnership between Joe, Susan, and George (assume Joe currently owns 50%, Susan and George 25% each, and they have maintained this balance in the contribution made).

Integrated

Applied Problems

*** PROBLEM 2.25** Prepare simple balance sheet, notes, what-if analysis

Clambake Kate's Inc. is a Maritime eatery specializing in shellfish and soups. The premises are rented and all sales are for cash, so the company has only a few balance sheet accounts. The accounts as at May 31, 2006, are as follows.

Food supplies cost	$ 3,360	Payable to suppliers	$ 8,480
Equipment cost	103,840	Long-term loan	40,000
Other supplies cost	7,200	Wages payable	1,440
Cash in bank	3,520	Share capital issued	16,000
Accumulated amortization	43,840	Retained earnings	8,160

1. Prepare a balance sheet for Clambake Kate's Inc. as at May 31, 2006. Include any notes to the balance sheet that you think might be useful.
2. Comment on the company's financial position as shown by your balance sheet.
3. Suppose, when you were reviewing the company's accounts after preparing the balance sheet, you found an error in the records. The company had paid a supplier $4,200, but that payment had inadvertently not been deducted from the company's bank account record nor from its record of accounts payable to suppliers. You decided to record that payment. What changes therefore resulted in the balance sheet you prepared in part 1 and in your comments in part 2?

EXTENDED TIME

*** PROBLEM 2.26** Prepare a balance sheet from simple transactions

South Shore Manufacturing Ltd. had this balance sheet on July 31, 2006:

South Shore Manufacturing Ltd.
Balance Sheet as at July 31, 2006

Assets		**Liabilities and Owners' Equity**	
Current assets:		Current liabilities:	
Cash	$ 27,098	Bank indebtedness	$ 58,890
Accounts receivable	91,186	Accounts payable	87,158
Inventories, cost	123,818	Taxes payable	14,072
Expenses paid in advance	8,134	Current part of mortgage	20,358
	$250,236		$180,478
Noncurrent assets:		Noncurrent liabilities:	
Land, cost	$ 86,889	Mortgage, less current	$237,482
Factory, cost	649,123	Pension liability	75,193
	$736,012	Loan from shareholder	125,000
Accum. amortization	(220,409)		$437,675
	$515,603	Shareholders' equity:	
		Share capital issued	$ 65,000
		Retained earnings	82,686
			$147,686
	$765,839		$765,839

On August 1, 2006, South Shore Manufacturing experienced the following transactions:

1. $12,000 of the shareholder's loan was repaid.
2. A customer paid one of the accounts receivable, $13,680.
3. Additional inventory costing $5,680 was purchased on credit.
4. The company issued new shares for $30,000 cash.
5. The proceeds of the share issue were used to reduce the bank loan.
6. More land costing $50,000 was purchased for $12,000 cash plus a new long-term mortgage for the rest.
7. More factory equipment costing $34,300 was purchased on credit, with $13,900 due in six months and the rest due in 24 months.

Prepare a new balance sheet for the company as of August 1, 2006, after taking these transactions into account. You can do this directly by just reasoning out the effect of each transaction on the balance sheet accounts, or using journal entries with a computer spreadsheet, or with a set of accounts written on paper.

EXTENDED TIME

* PROBLEM 2.27 Record and post entries, do trial balance and balance sheet

Cynthia has just started a proprietorship she calls Beach Ready. She will have a six-bed tanning salon and will sell various lotions, beachwear, and other summery stuff. To get the business started, she contributed $15,000 from her savings plus a sound system for playing music in the tanning booths. She values the system at $1,500.

She bought the needed tanning beds, a computer to keep track of customers' tanning minutes and other equipment for $21,200, paying $9,200 down and agreeing to pay the rest in 24 monthly installments of $500 plus interest at 10%. After checking out several possible locations, she signed a two-year lease for space in a neighbourhood mall, costing $1,100 rent per month. Then she fixed up and painted the store at a cost of $1,600 cash. (This created an asset that you might call "leasehold improvements" because she owns the improvements although not the property she improved.) The last thing she did before the grand opening was to stock up on lotions, beachwear, and other things to sell. All that inventory cost $17,100. She paid the suppliers an initial $2,300 and promised to pay the rest within 60 days.

1. Prepare journal entries for the transactions indicated above.
2. Create a general ledger, by hand, or using a computer spreadsheet, and post your entries to it.
3. Prepare a trial balance to show that your ledger is in balance.
4. From your trial balance, prepare a properly classified balance sheet for Beach Ready.
5. Calculate the proprietorship's working capital and debt-equity ratios from your balance sheet.

* PROBLEM 2.28 Prepare a balance sheet from transactions

Fed up with her dead-end career with a big company, Tanya decided to start her own business manufacturing and selling fresh pasta and a line of associated sauces, and selling cookware and other equipment to go with the food. It took her several weeks to get set up, before she made a single sale.

Record (using journal entries and paper accounts or a computer spreadsheet) the transactions below for PastaPastaPasta Inc., which happened in the preparatory weeks, and prepare the company's balance sheet at the end of the preparatory time.

1. Tanya put personal savings of $45,000 into a new bank account opened in the company's name. She decided that $35,000 of that would go for shares of the company and the rest would be a loan she hoped the company could pay back in a few years.

2. Tanya also provided her large set of recipes and her minivan, to be owned by the new company. She thought the recipes would be worth about $500 and the minivan about $7,500. She was in no hurry to be paid for these items, but thought they should be included in the company's assets.
3. A group of friends and relatives gave her company $25,000 in cash, in return for shares.
4. The company rented space in a small strip mall and paid $2,000 as rent in advance.
5. Another friend, who had no cash but wanted to help, agreed to do some renovations and repainting in the new space, in return for some shares in the company. Tanya and the friend agreed that the work done would have cost $4,500 if she had paid someone else to do it.
6. The company bought a large amount of food processing and storage equipment for $63,250, paying $28,000 in cash and agreeing to pay the rest in five equal annual installments, beginning in six months.
7. Pasta-making supplies costing $4,720 and cookware for resale costing $3,910 was purchased for $1,000 in cash, with the remainder to be paid in 60 days.
8. The company got a $20,000 line of credit from the bank and actually borrowed $2,500 of that, repayable on demand. Tanya had to sign a personal guarantee for anything borrowed under the line of credit.
9. The company paid a lawyer $1,800 for costs of incorporation.

PROBLEM 2.29 Answer questions about balance sheet figures

Answer the question in each case below. No other statements besides the balance sheet are involved or necessary to solve each case.

a. A Ltd.'s property and plant are 45% amortized. The accumulated amortization is $675,000. What is the cost of the property and plant?

b. B Ltd.'s working capital ratio has fallen from 2.20 last year to 1.60 this year. Its current assets went up over that time from $5,104,000 to $6,152,000. What was the dollar change in current liabilities?

c. C Ltd. has the following balance sheet amounts. Current assets, $185,400; Share capital, $300,000; Noncurrent liabilities, $318,500; Noncurrent assets, $496,200; Current liabilities, $189,230. What is missing and how much is it?

d. D Ltd. has decided to borrow some cash but does not want its debt-equity ratio to go above 2. According to the balance sheet, the company has assets of $7,834,000 and liabilities of $4,673,000. How much can the company borrow?

e. E Ltd.'s debt-equity ratio has been rising even though its working capital ratio has been rising too. There has been little change in current assets or in equity, so what has been happening to cause this change in ratios?

f. F Ltd. has decided to make a major change in its financial structure by persuading some holders of its bonded debt to exchange their bonds for shares. The company's share capital is now $20,000,000 and its retained earnings (the only other item in equity) equal $42,000,000. The intention is to get the company's debt-equity ratio down from 2.1 to 1.4. How many dollars of bonds must be exchanged for shares to meet this goal?

PROBLEM 2.30 A real company's resources, sources, and debt-equity ratio

Using the Royal Bank balance sheet in Section 2.11 (or that of any other company) as an example, answer the following questions:

1. What resources does the company have?
2. How are those resources financed?

Discussion Problems

* PROBLEM 2.31 Explain some accounting terms without using accounting jargon

Explain each of the following terms in words a nonaccountant might understand (that is, with a minimum of accounting jargon):

1. transaction
2. balance
3. debit
4. to debit something
5. account
6. general ledger
7. trial balance

PROBLEM 2.32 Users and uses of the balance sheet

Consider any company you are familiar with or interested in and make a list of all the people who might be interested in its balance sheet. Make your list using the headings:

Person (decision maker) and Use (decision to be made)

Try to think about the "use" issue broadly: your list could easily be a long one. You might make it even more broad by including people you think might like to use the balance sheet but whose needs are not served by it as you understand it, or who do not have timely access to it.

PROBLEM 2.33 Double-entry transactional records: strength and weakness

In a flight of accounting passion, Professor Lump exclaimed, "The double-entry transactional recording system is financial accounting's greatest strength and its greatest weakness!" Lump went on to explain this odd comment. Write down what the professor probably said in explanation.

PROBLEM 2.34 Balance sheet information and a nonaccounting career

Write a paragraph in which you identify a nonaccounting career you or someone you know may pursue and explain the interest in balance sheet information that this career might imply. If you really cannot see any relationship between that career and anything reported in a balance sheet, explain why not.

PROBLEM 2.35 Explain balance sheet ideas to a business executive

You are the executive assistant to Stephane Solden, a particularly hard-driving and successful owner of a chain of restaurants. Not long ago, Solden and you were flying to another city and the in-flight movie was so bad the two of you ended up talking about all sorts of things. One subject was Solden's impatience with accountants and accounting, which, probably because the annual audit of the company's accounts was then taking place, seemed particularly strong. How would you respond to the following questions from Solden?

1. The main thing that sticks in my mind about the balance sheet is that the thing balances! Who cares? Why should it matter?
2. My auditor keeps wanting to talk to me about what the balance sheet says about the company's finances and how I've managed them. But I always look to the future—why should I care about the balance sheet when it's just history?
3. Last year, I had a really good idea about the balance sheet. You know, I consider our restaurant managers to be the most important asset the company has. I was going to

have the managers added to the balance sheet as assets, so it would show all our assets. But the accountants and auditors didn't seem interested in my idea. Why not?

4. Someone told me once that the balance sheet is a photograph of the business at a particular instant in time, and that you have to be careful because some accountant might have touched up the photo, airbrushed away the warts. What did they mean? Isn't the balance sheet an exact list of all the company's assets and liabilities?

PROBLEM 2.36 Users and financial statements vs. detailed data

Financial statements are highly summarized documents representing thousands of transactions. Financial newspapers and commentators produce information about companies that is even more summarized. Why would users accept, or even prefer, summarized information to detailed data? How important is it for the user to understand the procedures and assumptions behind such summarizations?

PROBLEM 2.37 General versus user-specific balance sheets

Write a paragraph giving your considered views on the following question: Can a single balance sheet ever satisfy all the users of a company's financial statements, or should there be different balance sheets prepared to meet the differing needs of users?

PROBLEM 2.38 Accountants, ethics, and balance sheets

Managers of businesses and other organizations are very concerned about how the balance sheet reflects their management of the enterprise. This is very natural, and generally appropriate too, because such concern is likely to lead managers to want to do a good job of managing. But it can also lead to a temptation to alter the information in a manager's favour. The possibility of such a temptation is part of the reason auditors are employed to examine financial statements, including the balance sheet. This temptation can also produce ethical problems for professional accountants employed by the enterprise. On the one hand, such an accountant is bound by the ethical rules of the profession to see that proper accounting methods are followed in preparing the company's balance sheet, which would imply that the information should not be altered in management's favour. On the other hand, such an accountant works for senior management and is likely bound by the contract of employment to put the enterprise's interests first. What does such an accountant (for example, the chief accountant responsible for preparing the enterprise's financial statements) do if senior management (for example, the president) wants to alter the balance sheet to make things look better and makes a good case that such an action will help the enterprise get bank loans and other assistance it needs?

Discuss this situation from the point of view of both the president and the chief accountant.

CASE 2A

FINANCIAL REPORTING ON THE INTERNET

This book mentions the Web pages for many companies. Increasingly, corporations and other organizations are putting out detailed information about themselves on the Internet. But how good is that information? Is it easy to find in the company's Web material? Is it up to date? Is it displayed usefully? Can it be downloaded easily?[14] This is a case you can construct for yourself, and discuss in class either by comparing various companies or by comparing various people's reactions to the same company.

So pick a company that interests you or that is assigned by your instructor and go to its Web site and see what is there regarding the company's balance sheet and related data. If you don't know the company's Web address, just type the company name into your search engine and you'll likely get to it easily. Once you get to the company's Web page, start your examination and consider questions such as those below, which could be addressed in a report or in a class discussion:

- How attractive and user-friendly is the initial Web page? Does it concentrate on marketing the company's products, providing general information, telling you about recent news media attention to the company, or other purposes?
- How easy is it to find the company's financial information, if it is there at all? (Many Web pages direct you to Investor Information or some such area for financial information, others specify the financial reports directly, and still others make it quite hard to find.)
- How much does the company tell you about itself to help you put the financial information in context? Can you easily relate the background to the financial stuff, or do you have to jump all over the Web site to find it?
- How useful do you find the balance sheet to be? Is it up to date? Is it analyzed or commented upon by the company? Is it related to recent events affecting the company? Or, is it just plunked on the Web as is? (You could look for a "Management Discussion and Analysis" section if the balance sheet is just included in the company's current annual report, posted as is on the Web.)
- Are the balance sheet and supporting material easy to download and/or print? Would these be readily available for insertion in an analysis of the company?

CASE 2B

IMPROVING A BALANCE SHEET

"Folks, I've called this meeting to deal with a problem: our balance sheet is too weak to enable us to withstand, and even overcome, the strong competition we're getting. I'm proud of our company. We've been successful so far, but we can't rest on our past accomplishments—we must look to the future. It's worrisome that our financial position has been weakening for a while. So—let's have ideas about how to improve our financial position. Here's our most recent balance sheet to get you thinking."

"Well, boss, I've got an idea. Why don't we just arrange with the bank for a line of credit so that we will know how much more money we can borrow? I'll bet the bank would lend us at least $10 million without difficulty, if we needed it. And if we borrowed it now, we'd have some cash to use instead of worrying about not writing cheques to pay our bills because of the overdraft."

"No, don't listen to that idea. More borrowing will just make it worse! How about we arrange with some of our major suppliers to defer paying them for a couple of years? It would cost us interest, but give us time to get those new product lines out that I'm sure will be a big hit with the customers. We've been too slow to get new stuff out, and you can see how large our inventories are getting, so we have to deal with that marketing problem if we are going to be a success. I think we could defer maybe half of the accounts payable to long-term, which would really help our working capital."

"I won't be popular for saying this, but I'm not sure what you are worrying about. Yes, we have an overdraft, but that is just temporary while we collect our receivables and sell our inventories. Look at our working capital: it is positive. We have more short-term assets than short-term debts, so we are OK. The company is also $13 million bigger than last year in total assets, so we are growing. The competition doesn't seem to be hurting us all that much! We earned income in the year—you can see that retained earnings are $1 million larger than last year."

"That comment earlier about borrowing making it worse irritates me. Our problem is short-term liabilities, not overall debt. Look at our noncurrent debt,

GoVa Fashions Inc.
Balance sheet as at the previous month-end, with last year for comparison
(All figures in millions)

Assets	**Year This**	**Year Last**	**Liabilities and Equity**	**Year This**	**Year Last**
Current assets			*Current liabilities*		
Cash	$ 0	$ 5	Bank overdraft	$ 6	$ 0
Accounts receivable	14	7	Bank loan	0	3
Inventories	28	14	Accounts payable	26	11
Prepaid expenses	1	2	Current portion debt	7	6
	$43	$28		$39	$20
Noncurrent assets			*Noncurrent liabilities*		
Property & equipment cost	$70	64	Debt, less current part	$11	$18
Accumulated amortization	(48)	(41)			
Licences (net)	2	3	*Shareholders' equity*		
	$24	$26	Share capital	$ 8	$ 8
			Retained earnings	9	8
				$17	$16
	$67	$54		$67	$54

not much of it left. We could remortgage our land and property and raise considerable long-term debt that way, which would give us cash to pay our accounts payable and give us time to get into a better competitive position. This wouldn't water down the interests of our owners by issuing more shares."

"The way I see it, our major problem is lack of equity financing. Our debt-equity ratio is high, and it got worse this year. Raising some more share capital would certainly strengthen the balance sheet, and since the company does have an income, investors should be willing to buy some new shares. It would mean reducing the control and interest of the present owners, but that would be a reasonable price to pay for financial improvement."

"I think worrying about debt and equity is wrong. That's the wrong side of the balance sheet. Our big problem is that we are not selling our products or collecting when we do sell. Our receivables and inventories have gone up 100% each since last year. We have working capital, sure, but you can't pay bills with it when it is all tied up in receivables and inventories. Our quick ratio is terrible. If we pressed our customers for collection and reduced production while our sales caught up, we could use all that cash that is now tied up."

"Maybe we should just be more creative with our balance sheet numbers. I think our property is worth a lot more than it shows on the books. We could just increase the value of the property on the asset side of the balance sheet and add that to the shareholders' equity. I read an article once that advocated that sort of asset valuation instead of cost, going beyond the usual transactional basis of accounting. Then the balance sheet would be much stronger."

"I don't know about creativity, but that comment about the property is interesting in another way. Our property and equipment are getting quite old. It's about two-thirds amortized, so that means we are going to have to look at some serious replacements soon. We had to spend $6 million this year. Our financial position is actually weaker than it looks!"

"Thank you for all the ideas. Now, what will we do?"

What do you think of the company's financial situation and the ideas for improving it? What would you suggest be done, if anything?

NOTES

1. John Sleeman, Chairman & CEO, Investor Relations website at: www.sleeman.com/en/html/invest/invest_intro.php.
2. Judith Stone, "Big Brewhaha of 1800 B.C.," *Discover* (January 1991): 14. (The words quoted in the excerpt are those of Fritz Maytag, owner of the Anchor Brewing Company of San Francisco.)
3. Information about the history of accounting and business is published in many places. A variety of professional and academic journals have shown an interest in such material, and there is a journal devoted specifically to it: the *Accounting Historians Journal*. See also the references below and at the end of Chapter 3.
4. George J. Coustourous, *Accounting in the Golden Age of Greece: A Response to Socioeconomic Changes* (Champaign: Center for International Education and Research in Accounting, U. of Illinois, 1979).
5. Report from The Associated Press, Cairo, "Earliest written words may have been taxman's," *The Edmonton Journal* (December 16, 1998), A1.
6. Orville R. Keister, "The Mechanics of Mesopotamian Record-Keeping," in *Contemporary Studies in the Evolution of Accounting Thought*, ed. Michael Chatfield (Belmont: Dickenson Publishing Company, 1968), 12–20.
7. O. ten Have, *The History of Accounting* (Palo Alto: Bay Books, 1976), 27–30.
8. Ibid., 30–46.
9. Information obtained from Barrick Gold Corporation's 2004 Annual Report at www.barrick.com/files/docs_annual/2004_AR_en.pdf
10. *Canadian Railroad Trilogy* was a hit song in 1967, Canada's centennial year. It is copyrighted by Moose Music, Inc.
11. Pierre Berton, *The National Dream: The Great Railway 1871–1881*, published 1970, and *The Last Spike: The Great Railway 1881–1885*, published 1971, both Toronto: McClelland and Stewart Limited.
12. Transportation averages obtained from FPinfomart.ca
13. Canadian National Railway Company's quick ratio and debt to equity ratio were calculated using information from the 2004 Annual Report (www.cn.ca/about/investors/pdf/Ang_081_131_CN.pdf).
14. For an article that raises numerous issues about Web-based financial reporting, see Hollis Ashbaugh, Karla M. Johnstone, and Terry D. Warfield, "Corporate Reporting on the Internet," *Accounting Horizons* 13(3), September 1999, 241–57.

CHAPTER THREE

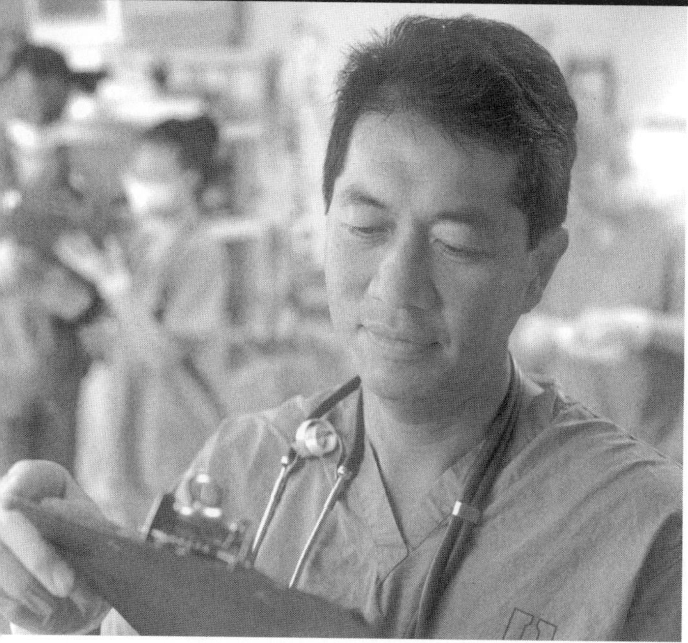

3 Measuring and Evaluating Financial Performance

For information on this topic, please visit the online tutorial at www.gibbins6e.nelson.com

3.1 Chapter Introduction: Measuring and Evaluating Financial Performance

Clarence Lee, a successful physician who has been investing in the stock market for several years, has become more and more conscious of how well (or badly) companies perform in making a profit. From an economics course he took in university, he remembered that many years ago, the famous economist John Maynard Keynes had said, "The engine which drives enterprise is not thrift, but profit."[1] Clarence clipped out several articles as he thought about profit (also commonly called income or earnings)—here are five quotes from his collection:

- "Tyco profit doubles: Manufacturing conglomerate Tyco International Ltd. said Wednesday it plans to close more than a dozen factories and possibly split up its wide-ranging businesses in efforts to boost the value of its stock. The company also reported fiscal fourth-quarter net income doubled because of a tax-rate adjustment and one-time gains."[2]
- Royal Bank profit vaults 32%: Royal Bank of Canada posted a 32% profit increase in the third quarter, despite an Enron-related charge and flat returns from its U.S. and international operations.[3]
- Hollinger Int'l reports loss: Hollinger International Inc., the newspaper publisher once controlled by Conrad Black, said Wednesday that it lost $18.5 million (U.S.) in the first quarter and it intends to file second- and third-quarter results by the end of this month.[4]
- Hollinger's financial statements have been behind schedule since 2003, when a special committee of independent directors began investigating certain fees and deals at the company.[5]
- Increased costs hit Sobey's quarterly profit: Canada's second-largest supermarket chain saw its second-quarter profit slip almost 3 per cent as costs related to changes aimed at the cutthroat Ontario market offset an increase in sales revenue.
- Enbridge profit tumbles: Oil pipeline and natural gas giant Enbridge Inc. raised its dividend Thursday while reporting a sharp drop in net profits, mainly from a one-time gain last year.[6]

It is good to see companies such as Tyco and the Royal Bank doing well. But determining earnings seems to have major challenges or companies like Hollinger would be able to report on a

Learning Objectives

Chapter 2 focused on the balance sheet, the double-entry fulcrum of financial accounting. In this chapter, we return to an idea introduced in Chapter 1, *accrual accounting*, and see how its measure of performance is reported in the income statement. You will learn:

- Why accounting's measure of income is important, and more about the history of financial accounting's development in responding to the demand for income measurement;
- How the income statement, the second major financial statement, is put together to derive the figure of income/earnings/profit that Clarence's articles were emphasizing;
- More about how the underlying accounting system works, especially how it "adjusts" the transactional data to create the accrual accounting information;
- How the income measure is connected to the balance sheet through the third financial statement, the statement of retained earnings;
- How to interpret the income statement's contents and so help users like Clarence figure out whether a particular income figure is good or not (there will be more about this in several later parts of the book, too, because it is one of the most important questions in accounting);
- What some major controversies in measuring income are about, and why companies might be tempted to misrepresent their income.

Because courses may cover topics in different orders, Sections 3.4–3.7 have been written to be studied in any order.

timely basis without needing special investigations into their own financial dealings. It is a concern, thought Clarence, that current earnings can be greatly affected by events of the past as in the case of the Royal Bank now recognizing losses related to dealings with Enron in prior years.

Clarence also wondered about the value of current earnings reports as a predictor of future performance. He had been encouraged in his decision to invest in Enbridge by the two-year-old clipping from his file that stated: "Enbridge records strong earnings gain: Enbridge Inc. reported a strong increase in quarterly profit despite the lingering impact of last year's economic slowdown, the collapse of power distributor Enron Corp., and yet another mild winter in the crucial eastern market."[7]

How can you tell if any of these numbers is a good result, a reliable measure of success, or a good indicator of future performance?

3.2 Financial Performance and the Development of Stock Markets

The idea of measuring performance didn't just appear one day. It took centuries to develop. Knowing something about that development will give you some context for the way accountants measure income, which goes back a long way, and depends on Pacioli's double-entry system just as the balance sheet does.

England and the United Kingdom: From 1500 to the Early 1800s

Managers' good stewardship of the owners' enterprise has been important for centuries.

Prior to Pacioli, English recordkeeping had much in common with Roman methods used hundreds of years earlier. "Stewards" were employed to manage the properties of the English aristocracy, much as local governors had been in Roman-held areas. In 1300, Oxford University offered an accounting course: Roman recordkeeping for stewards![8] The concept of *stewardship*, of a person managing something on behalf of someone else,

Financial accounting worldwide has grown from roots in the United Kingdom.

is still an important aspect of accounting. It is often said, for example, that an enterprise's financial statements demonstrate the quality of management's stewardship of the enterprise on behalf of its owners.

In the several hundred years since Pacioli's treatise, accounting developed to suit the social and business circumstances of each country. France, for example, had a strong, centralized government and developed a national accounting system written by a central board of administrators. On the other hand, England (which, with its neighbours, became the United Kingdom) had less government involvement in commerce and trade and a smaller civil service and relied more heavily on the initiatives of the private sector and the courts.[9] The financial accounting system now used in the United Kingdom, Canada, the United States, and many other countries relies heavily on the precedents set in England during this period. The English approach used Pacioli's double entry for the recordkeeping and built the financial statements' reporting system on that. Americans, Canadians, and others have elaborated that further. Financial accounting in continental Europe developed on a somewhat different path. Russia, China, Japan, and many other countries took different financial accounting paths too. However, the British–American approach is still gaining popularity worldwide; for example, China adopted it for much of its financial reporting in the early 1990s. Efforts are being made worldwide to "harmonize" financial accounting to assist international trade, and the sort of financial accounting set out in this book seems likely to become the international standard. International issues will be outlined further in a later chapter.

FIGURE 3.1

During the Reformation, European merchants and bankers established companies that were early versions of modern business corporations. One such merchant is the subject of this 1630 engraving by Rembrandt. The merchant's scale and ledger book demonstrate his reliance on organization, documentation, and qualification. Careful attention to these facilitates his control of capital (bags of money or gold) and trade goods (casks and chest). Reproduced by permission of the Bettmann Archive.

Until the mid-1600s accounting and recordkeeping (bookkeeping) were largely synonymous. Records were a private matter for the attention of the lord, merchant, or banker. But then a significant development occurred: the advent of companies that sold stocks (shares of ownership) to private citizens. These citizens could not all crowd into the company's office to inspect the records, even if they could understand them. This produced a demand for some form of reporting to the shareholders, for financial statements that could be relied on as accurate summaries of the records. There was a demand that the balance sheet be more detailed in its description of the owners' equity and the changes in it than had been necessary before there had been such dispersed ownership. There was even some demand for regulation of such reports; for example, in 1657 Oliver Cromwell, as regent of England, required the East India Company to publish its balance sheet.[10] Accounting was on its way to developing the standards of calculation and disclosure that are very important in modern accounting and that distinguish accounting from the underlying recordkeeping. Progress in this direction was not rapid, but it picked up steam with the arrival of the Industrial Revolution.

External financial reporting began to be important as the Industrial Revolution proceeded.

However, there were some interesting events in the interval. In 1670, a famous company was formed, namely, The Governor and Company of Adventurers of England Trading into Hudson's Bay. The Hudson's Bay Company, or The Bay, as it now calls itself in its advertisements, has played a very significant economic role over the centuries, and is still an important part of Canadian business. Many of the records kept by its far-flung employees still exist and provide detailed pictures of business and society over the years.[11] In 1720, the spectacular collapse of the South Seas Company prompted the first known written audit, conducted in order to determine the assets of the company.[12] The developing Industrial Revolution of the late 1700s and early 1800s helped to fuel the emerging commercial sector of Britain, and accounting practices became an important part of the system. In 1825, the British Parliament eased hundred-year-old prohibitions on trading shares in companies, and the modern era of stock markets and publicly owned companies began in earnest. A few years later, Parliament required annual audits of the balance sheets of some companies, though that requirement was later withdrawn and not reinstated until 1900.[13] Accounting and auditing continued to develop in response to the changing needs of the society of which they were a part.

Developments in the 19th Century[14]

Accounting was challenged by the rise of large, long-lived industrial companies.

Up to the early 19th century, most business enterprises were formed for specific ventures, were financed by a few wealthy owners, and were disbanded when the ventures were completed. The sharing of profits among the owners of the enterprise or venture took place at the end, when all of the assets were sold, the liabilities were paid off, and the net amount remaining was distributed among the owners. When, as industrialization increased, large industrial plants began replacing short-term ventures as the major form of business enterprise, the traditional method of financing and profit sharing was no longer acceptable. The large cost of constructing and maintaining these more capital-intensive enterprises was often more than a few owners could afford, and the long life of the assets made it unsatisfactory to wait for the winding up of the enterprise to share profits.

Corporations used capital markets, so they had to tell the markets about themselves.

Various pieces of legislation regarding companies were introduced in Britain in the 1830s, 1840s, and 1850s. This legislation allowed incorporated companies, also called *corporations*, to sell shares in *stock markets* (which, because the initial issuing of shares provides capital, that is to say, equity funds for the companies, are also called *capital markets*). The legislation also provided a major feature of corporations: liability of the corporation's owners to the corporation's creditors was, and still is, limited to the amount of the owners' equity in the corporation. The justification for the limited liability feature was that individual investors could not always be aware of the actions of the directors they

FIGURE 3.2

An invaluable accounting tool, the first successful European mechanical calculator was invented by Blaise Pascal in 1642 and soon became an international marvel. Pascal was already known as a scientist and mathematician when he invented the adding machine at the age of 19. Among many other things, Pascal is also known as the inventor of the barometer. Reproduced by permission of the Bettmann Archive.

elected or the managers who were in turn engaged by the directors. Therefore, investors should not be liable for any more than the amount of money they invested in the enterprise. But of course no investors would want to lose even that, so as capital markets developed, the demand for information about the corporations involved grew.

Accounting focuses on the economic entity but must also reflect legal issues.

Limited liability of its owners and an existence separate from its owners largely define the corporation. Modern laws and business practices complicate the operation of capital markets and can reduce the protection of limited liability, but the idea that a corporation is a "legal person," able to act on its own and survive changes in owners, is still central to business and to much of the rest of our lives. In financial accounting, the focus is on the *economic entity* that is exchanging physical and financial goods and promises with other entities, but since laws began to define what corporations are (and sometimes what proprietorships, partnerships, and corporate groups are, too), accounting also must reflect the legal nature of economic exchanges and the structure of the organization.

The income calculation is important in determining availability of dividends.

An important legal issue is sharing profits. The problem of how to ensure fair calculation and sharing of ownership interests led legislators to require that a corporation present its balance sheet annually to its shareholders and that an auditor be present to report to the shareholders on the validity of that financial statement. Legislation also required that any annual payments to shareholders should not come out of the sale of, or by decreasing the value of, a corporation's long-term capital assets. Such payments should be made out of monies earned yearly from these assets after all yearly debts are paid. We can think of "monies earned yearly" as revenues, and "yearly debts" as expenses, so this meant, roughly, that payments to shareholders should come out of yearly income. This is close to the dividend requirement placed on most corporations today (dividends can normally only be paid out of net income). Corporations began to compute income in statements or schedules separate from the balance sheet, so that they could demonstrate that they had performed well enough to permit the distribution of dividends or the issuing of more shares.

The income statement is a response to demand for performance measurement.

As businesses grew in size and complexity, the demand for information on financial performance increased. The static picture presented by the balance sheet was not good enough for the emerging stock markets, for the increasingly large group of nonowner professional managers, or for governments that wished to evaluate (and tax!) businesses' performance (to mention just a few of the groups interested in evaluating

FIGURE 3.3

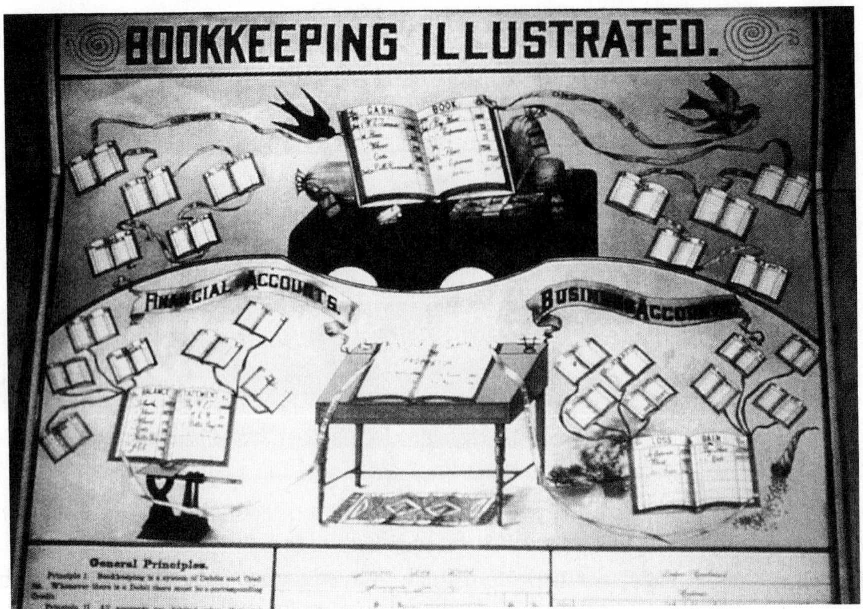

A portion of an antique bookkeeping poster. The linking ribbons in the illustration suggest the relationship between financial accounts and business decisions. Courtesy of Ursus Books and Prints Ltd., New York.

performance). The income statement came into its own as a central part of financial reporting in the last hundred years, and its measurement of financial performance is central to economic activity and performance evaluation in most of the world.

In the 19th century, financial accounting lacked a general conceptual structure.

In responding to these demands for better performance information, accountants were limited by a lack of accounting theories or conventions to illustrate and define how to prepare balance sheets and income statements. There was no nationally organized association of accountants in Britain until the end of the 19th century (although the Accountants' Society of Edinburgh received a royal charter in 1854, an event that led to the term "chartered accountant"). Financial accounting methods developed situation by situation, with no overall plan or concepts throughout this period. Some model financial statements and examples from legislation were being used, and income statements were becoming established, but it was becoming necessary to establish a rational basis, that is, principles, for preparing financial statements and for extending the principles to new settings, as business and commercial activity continued to increase. Toward the end of the 19th century, several British court cases had established that accountants and auditors had to decide what were proper and fair financial statements, and could not expect courts and legislatures to decide for them. A prominent accountant, Ernest Cooper, voiced his concern in 1894: "... the already sufficient responsibilities and anxieties of an Auditor will be extended beyond those known of any trade or profession."[15] Accounting was on its way to formulating the professional rights, responsibilities, and criteria for competence, as had the already-established professions of law, engineering, and medicine. We'll see more later on about how this has worked out in modern times. As some recent troubles have shown, the anxieties of auditors have not gone away yet!

HOW'S YOUR UNDERSTANDING?

Here are two questions you should be able to answer based on what you have just read. If you can't answer them, it would be best to reread the material.

1. Why has financial accounting become more and more sophisticated over the centuries?
2. What sort of information demands prompted the development of the income statement?

3.3 Introduction to the Income and Retained Earnings Statements

The balance sheet provides important information about the enterprise's financial structure and strength, but its description of the enterprise's financial position is not the only story to be told. Its picture is static: it tells us what the position is. Most managers, owners, and creditors also want to know how well the enterprise is performing and how it got to where it is. You could think of an enterprise's balance sheets as a set of still photos. What's needed is a video to show the action in between the balance sheets, and that is what the income statement does:

FIGURE 3.4

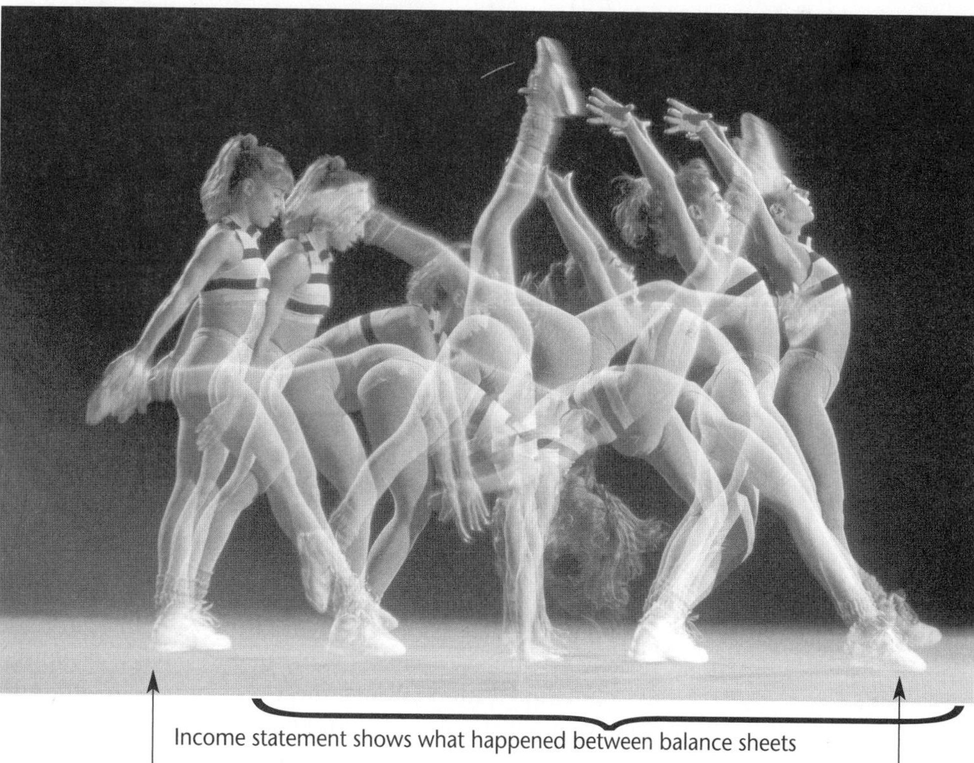

Income statement shows what happened between balance sheets

Balance sheet is a picture at a point in time

Balance sheet is a picture at a point in time

The income statement measures accrual income over a period of time.

The *income statement* measures *accrual income*. When people talk about *financial performance*, they usually mean the income statement and its summary information *net income* and *earnings per share*. These are often considered the heart of modern financial reporting.

The statement of retained earnings links the income statement to the balance sheet.

There are two other statements that also provide connections between balance sheets. This chapter includes a statement used to connect the income statement to the balance sheet, called the *statement of retained earnings*. Chapter 4 examines the other, the cash flow statement: it has its own chapter because it analyzes the company from a different perspective than the income statement does.

Balance sheet, income, and retained earnings statements are a connected system.

The income and retained earnings statements cover the time between two balance sheets, often called the beginning and ending balance sheets. Suppose a company's fiscal year-end is December 31. Then we would have a progression in which the ending balance sheet flows not only from the beginning one directly but also from the explanation of what happened during the year provided in the income and retained earnings statements:

FIGURE 3.5

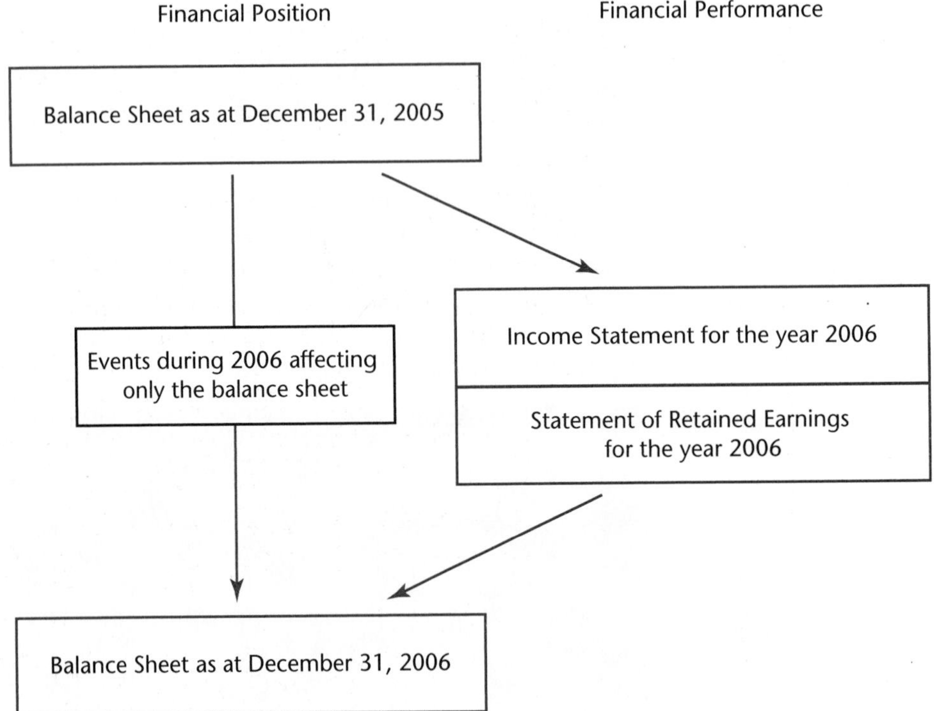

If an enterprise's owners and managers are successful, it may prosper for a long time. The Hudson's Bay Company (The Bay) was incorporated in 1670, so it is more than 330 years old! Suppose a measure of the company's financial performance were desired for comparison to other companies, for assessing income tax, for help in deciding how much to sell the company for, or for many other reasons we will come to. How could such performance be measured?

A periodic measure of performance is needed.

Well, we might measure the company's financial performance by closing it down, selling off all its assets, paying off all its liabilities, and seeing how much is left for the owners. Good performance would be indicated if the money left for the owners plus the amounts they withdrew over the years was greater than the amount they put in when they founded the company, perhaps adjusted for inflation over that time and for the owners' costs of raising the money they put in. But killing the business to measure how well it has been doing is a little drastic! Waiting until it dies of natural causes seems hardly a better solution: The Bay has outlasted many generations of owners and managers, and the Ford Motor Company has outlasted a number of Ford family members. It would be more useful to measure performance over selected shorter periods of time: annually, quarterly (every three months), or monthly. People could then make their decisions about investing in the company or getting out, and hiring managers or firing them, when they wanted to do so.

The Income Statement

The income statement measures performance as net accrual income.

This is where the income statement comes in. This statement uses accrual accounting to measure financial performance over a period of time, usually a year, three months, or one month, coming up with the "bottom line" net income for the period: its accrual income, calculated as revenues minus expenses. Remember the income calculation for Simone's jewellery business in Section 1.10 of Chapter 1:

EXHIBIT 3·1

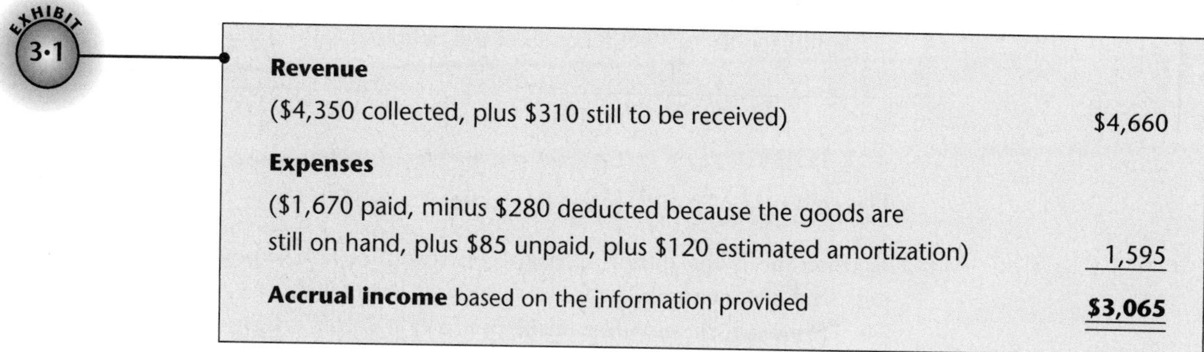

Revenue	
($4,350 collected, plus $310 still to be received)	$4,660
Expenses	
($1,670 paid, minus $280 deducted because the goods are still on hand, plus $85 unpaid, plus $120 estimated amortization)	1,595
Accrual income based on the information provided	**$3,065**

This simple income calculation illustrates the form of all business income statements as they are done in North America and much of the rest of the world:

Net accrual income for the period
= Revenues for the period – Expenses for the period

Net income means accrual income after deducting income tax expense.

Simone's income calculation shows no income tax on her income. Her business is a proprietorship, and any income tax is her personal responsibility, so proprietorships' income calculations normally do not include income tax. Corporations are responsible for their own income taxes, so their income calculations do have income tax deducted as one of the expenses. The phrase "net" income is usually used to refer to the amount of accrual income left after the income tax, which in Canada and most other countries is assessed on accrual income:

FIGURE 3.6

Net income is what is left of revenues after deducting all expenses

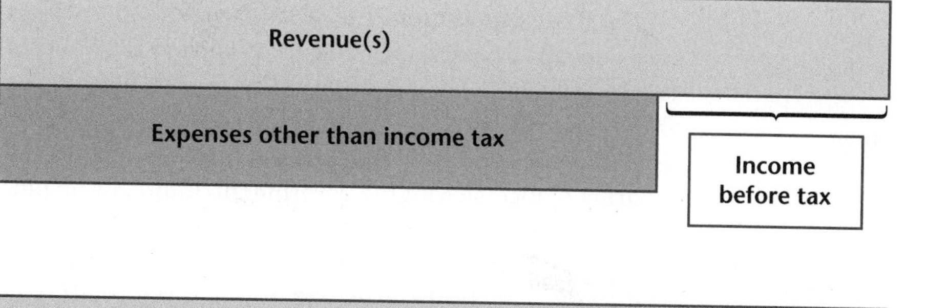

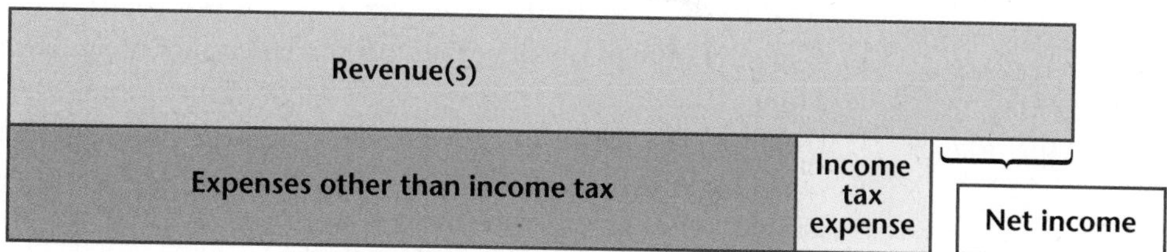

The usual format for the income statement follows this approach, showing the separation of income tax expense from the other expenses. Most income statements have much more detail!

EXHIBIT 3·2

Resulting income statement format, for a period of time

Revenue(s) for the period		Rev
Minus expenses other than income tax for the period		– Exp
Equals income before income tax	=	IBT
Minus income tax expense for the period		– Tax
Residual is accrual net income for the period	=	NI

Revenues and Expenses

Net income is the difference between revenues and expenses. So, what are these two performance measures?

Revenues are increases in the company's wealth arising from the provision of services or sales of goods to customers. Wealth increases because customers

- pay cash;
- promise to pay cash (such promises are *accounts receivable*); or
- more rarely, pay with other forms of wealth, such as by providing other assets to the company or forgiving debts owed by the company.

Revenues are increases in wealth arising from providing goods or services to customers.

So, if, *in return for services or goods,* a customer paid $1,000 in cash, another customer promised to pay $1,000 later, another gave the company $1,000 in equipment, or another forgave a $1,000 debt the company had owed the customer, these would each be called a revenue of $1,000.

Expenses are the opposite of revenues. They are decreases in the company's wealth that are incurred in order to earn revenues. Wealth decreases because operating costs have to be borne; customers have to be given the goods they have paid for; long-term assets wear out as they are used to earn revenue; and liabilities may be incurred as part of the process.

Expenses are decreases in wealth incurred in order to earn revenues.

So, if, *as part of its attempt to earn revenues,* the company paid $600 in rent, or the goods bought by a customer cost the company $600 to provide, or the building depreciated by $600, or the company promised to pay an employee $600 in wages later on, each of these would be called an expense of $600. Income tax expense is separated from other expenses partly because it is not incurred directly in order to earn revenue, being a sharing of income with the government, indirectly helping to earn revenue by supporting the costs of society.

Cost of goods sold expense is the cost to the enterprise of the goods given up to generate the revenue.

A major expense category that sometimes causes confusion is the *cost of goods sold* (*COGS*) expense. In the examples above, if the goods bought by the customer cost the company $600 to provide, then $600 is the *cost* of the goods sold that earned revenue of $1,000. The revenue is what the customer agrees to pay; the cost of goods sold is what it costs the enterprise to provide those goods. So a transaction with a customer who is buying goods has two aspects: (1) the enterprise is better off because of the revenue gained, and (2) the enterprise is worse off because of the cost of the goods that the customer takes away. When the enterprise buys the goods for sale, they begin on the balance sheet in the asset account "*inventory* of unsold goods," and when they are sold, their cost is transferred from the asset account to the expense account "*cost of goods sold.*" This is done as a separate accounting activity from recording the revenue, because it is a separate economic event. Whether the enterprise makes money on the deal depends on whether the revenue gained is greater than the cost of goods sold (plus any other expenses incurred to make the sale, such as sales commissions and shipping costs). This diagram may help you to understand cost of goods sold:

FIGURE 3.7

A. The economic exchange between company and customer

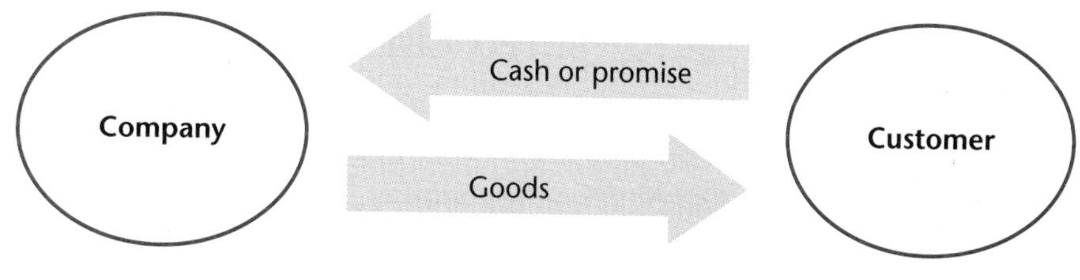

B. The company's accounting for the exchange

Revenue: company has more cash or accounts receivable.

Cost of goods sold expense: company has less inventory.

Company is better off: revenue

Company is worse off: expense

A net loss is negative net income, resulting when expenses exceed revenues.

Both revenues and expenses are measured following the concepts of accrual accounting; therefore, they represent increases or decreases in wealth, whether or not cash receipts or payments occur at the same time. As net income is the difference between revenues and expenses, it represents the net *inflow of wealth* to the company during the period. The reporting of net income means that the company has become wealthier during the period. If net income is negative, that is, if revenues are less than expenses, it is instead called *net loss* and represents a net *outflow of wealth.* In this case, the company has become less wealthy.

Transactions with owners are kept off the income statement.

Expenses include all the costs of earning the revenues, including income and other taxes, but they do *not* include payment of returns to owners (withdrawals by proprietors or partners, or dividends to shareholders of corporations). The income statement measures wealth changes resulting from customer-oriented activity, not transactions with owners. (Though, of course, sometimes people wear more than one "hat": owning shares in Coca-Cola doesn't stop you from buying a Coke when you're thirsty and so

Terminology again. As mentioned in Section 2.3, sometimes a net loss is called a *deficit*. This is especially the case when people are referring to a government, which, if its annual revenues are less than its annual expenditures, is said to be incurring a deficit. This meaning of deficit is not the same as negative retained earnings: negative earnings may eventually lead to negative retained earnings for a business corporation, but government accounting does not record retained earnings, usually just showing the difference between assets and liabilities as a residual figure, much like a proprietorship's equity. Here, the people governed are the proprietor(s)! In another difference with business accounting, governments have typically grouped their expenses together with the amounts spent on new assets under the heading of "*expenditures*," which in accounting is just another word for "payments."

being both an owner and a customer of the company.) Payments or promises of payment of returns to owners (such as when a corporation's board of directors *declares*, or promises, a dividend) are considered to be distributions of net income to owners. The undistributed remainder is kept on the balance sheet as retained earnings.

The Retained Earnings Statement

This brings us to the statement of retained earnings, which shows what has been done with the period's income. Retained earnings is the sum of past net incomes or *earnings*, measured since the company began, minus dividends declared (even if not yet paid) to owners since the beginning. The statement of retained earnings updates the balance sheet's retained earnings figure (in owners' equity) from the end of the preceding period (year, quarter, month, or whatever), which is also the beginning of the present period, to the end of the present period and so shows why the balance sheet's figure has changed from the last period:

Retained earnings on the balance sheet at end of period	=	**Retained earnings at beginning of period + net income (or – net loss) for the period – dividends declared during the period**

The retained earnings statement explains changes in the balance sheet's retained earnings.

The statement of retained earnings, therefore, shows that the net income for the period is part of the retained earnings at the end of the period by showing that the income is part of the *change* in retained earnings *over the period covered by the income statement.* The usual format of the retained earnings statement is:

Start with retained earnings, beginning of period (from prior balance sheet)	Begin RE
Add net income for the period (from income statement)	+ NI
Deduct dividends declared during the period	– Div
Add or subtract miscellaneous adjustments	+/– Adjust
Equals retained earnings, end of period (to balance sheet)	= End RE

Retained earnings can be explained in layers, period by period since the beginning.

You might be interested to know that you can, *if you have the past records*, go back year by year, figuring out how much income was added to retained earnings each year and how much in dividends was deducted. You could go all the way back to the first day of the company, when there had not yet been any income and therefore not yet any retained earnings. Retained earnings are therefore like an onion: you can keep peeling away each year's layer until you have peeled everything away and are back to zero. You can similarly peel away each year's transactions in every balance sheet account; for example, you can trace all the changes in cash back to the very beginning. For this reason, the balance sheet can be said to reflect everything that has ever been recorded in the accounts: it is the accumulation of everything that happened from when the company began until now. Accounting really is a historical information system!

Declared dividends reduce retained earnings, becoming liabilities of the corporation until paid.

In a corporation, the *board of directors* is the senior level of management, operating the company on behalf of the owners. When the board declares a *dividend*, the amount is deducted from retained earnings at that time. At that point, the corporation has a liability to the owners, which it pays off by sending the owners the promised cash, or, in some cases, something called *stock dividends*, by sending the owners more shares of the company. Dividends, like other transactions with owners, are kept off the income statement so that income can be measured *before* including them. The owners are also creditors until the dividends payable are paid.

The income-balance sheet link goes from the income statement through retained earnings.

Connecting the Income Statement to the Balance Sheet

The retained earnings statement is the link between the income statement's measure over time and the balance sheet at the end of that time. Using the standard (but simplified) formats for the income and retained earnings statements, here is the link:

FIGURE 3.8

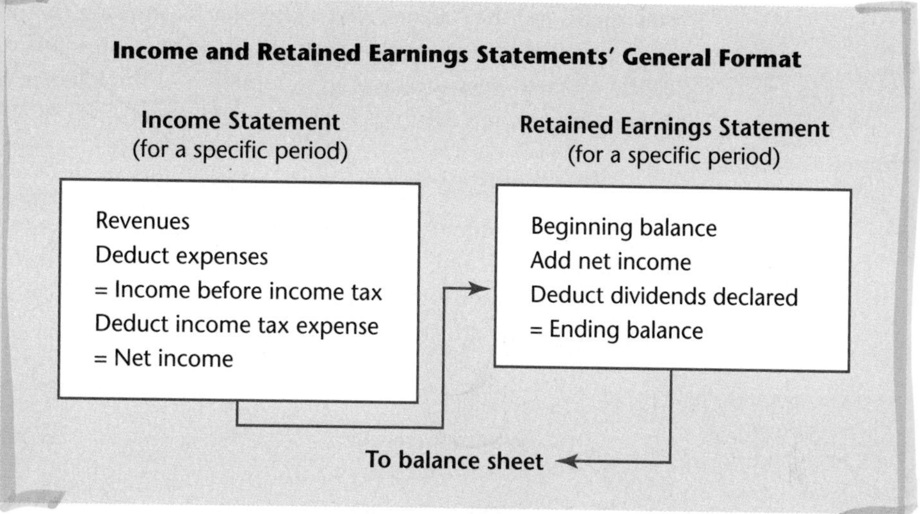

The income-balance sheet link can also be viewed from the balance sheet's changes.

This diagram began with the income calculation and transferred it to the balance sheet. Another way to look at the link between income and the balance sheet is to start at the other end, with the balance sheet. Every balance sheet balances, so we can subtract the beginning balance sheet from the ending one to calculate the changes in the balance sheet over the period:

Changes from one balance sheet to the next always balance too.

Ending Assets	=	Ending Liabilities	+	Ending Equity (including RE)
Beginning Assets	=	Beginning Liabilities	+	Beginning Equity (including RE)
Change in Assets	=	Change in Liabilities	+	Change in Equity (including RE)

Example: Suppose a corporation had assets of $1,200 at the beginning of a year and $1,450 at the end, and liabilities of $750 at the beginning and $900 at the end. We can deduce that its equity was $450 at the beginning and $550 at the end. These data produce the following calculation of the changes in the balance sheet categories:

End:	$1,450 Assets	=	$900 Liabilities + $550 Equity
Beginning:	$1,200 Assets	=	$750 Liabilities + $450 Equity
Changes:	$ 250 Assets	=	$150 Liabilities + $100 Equity

Where did the change in equity come from? Upon investigation, we find out that the company issued more share capital of $40, earned income of $185, and declared a dividend of $125. Thus:

Share capital change:		
Equity increase due to issued share capital		$ 40
Retained earnings change (which would be in the RE statement):		
Equity increase due to income	$185	
Equity decrease due to declaration of dividend	(125)	60
Change in equity between balance sheets		$100

The income statement explains the income figure in the retained earnings statement.

We know what the income was, but not what the company did to earn it. *This is what the income statement is for: describing the revenues and expenses that produced the $185 income.* But once we have that, it is useful to know how that factors into the balance sheet. The beginning and ending balance sheets define the financial position before and after the period over which the income statement measures performance. The net income is part of the change in retained earnings, which, in turn, is part of the change in the balance sheet over that period. The statement of retained earnings therefore "knits" the income statement and the balance sheet together by showing that the net income is part of the change in the balance sheet over the period. (Accountants refer to this knitting together as the *articulation* of the income statement and the balance sheet.) Income is part of the change in retained earnings for the period, therefore:

Income is part of the equity component of the balance sheet equation.

Here is a summary of the wealth effects of revenues, expenses, incomes, and losses, both from the income statement and balance sheet points of view. Make sure you understand these relationships, because they are central to how accounting measures income and how income affects the balance sheet.

FIGURE 3.9

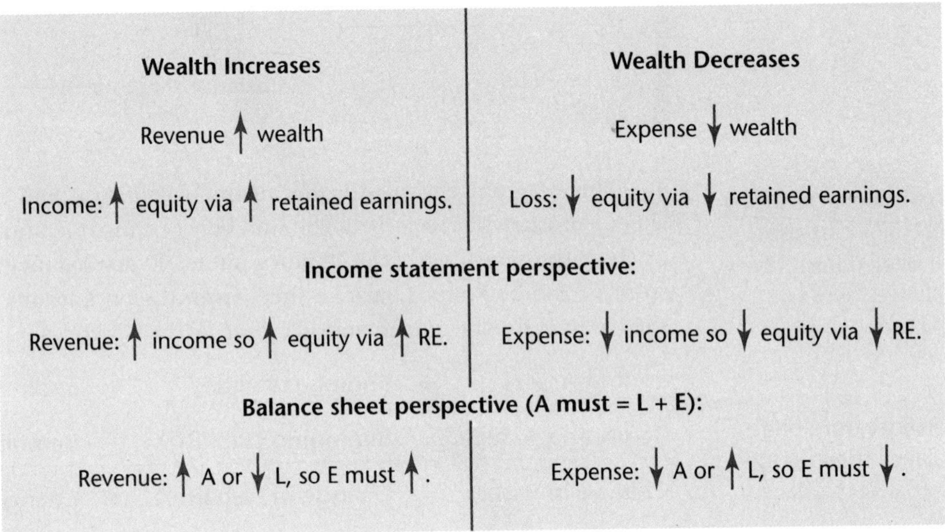

Income increases wealth, so it also increases owners' equity through retained earnings.

Later in this chapter, the double-entry debits and credits involved in this are explained. For now, focus on understanding the ideas that income is part of equity through retained earnings and that income produces an improved balance sheet. (Losses are also part of equity and they worsen the balance sheet.)

People sometimes think that the whole balance of retained earnings is available to pay dividends. Legally that may be true, but, practically, it is very unlikely to be true, because income comes from changes in all the forms of wealth on the balance sheet. A company that has made good incomes and used the money earned to invest in new plant and equipment, for example, would have to sell the plant and equipment if it were to pay out all the retained earnings as dividends. Also, since income is based on accrual accounting, it is represented by changes in noncash accounts like accounts receivable (uncollected revenues) and accounts payable (unpaid expenses), so the income in retained earnings is not all cash, and the company might have to clear up all its receivables and payables to get the cash to pay a big dividend. The owners may not even want a dividend: many companies that pay small or no dividends have excellent share prices on the stock market, because shareholders believe that the companies will grow and prosper if the money that could have been paid as dividends is instead retained by the company and used to make profitable business investments.

A Further Example of Income Statement and Balance Sheet Articulation

Bratwurst Inc. had the following balance sheet at the end of 2003 (beginning of 2004): Assets, $5,000; Liabilities, $3,000; Equity, $2,000.

- The beginning equity figure was made up of the owners' invested share capital of $500 plus $1,500 retained earnings accumulated to the end of 2003. (That $1,500 was therefore the sum of all the net incomes the company had ever had up to the end of 2003, minus all the dividends ever declared to owners up to that point.)
- During 2004, the company had revenues of $11,000 and expenses of $10,000, and declared dividends to owners of $300.
- At the end of 2004, the company had assets of $5,900, liabilities of $3,200, and equity of $2,700, made up of the owners' invested share capital of $500 plus retained earnings of $2,200.

Exhibit 3.3 shows the three financial statements reporting all this. All these statements are simplified for this example: companies report much more detail than this, but for this example the detail might confuse the main point about articulation of the statements' information.

EXHIBIT 3·3

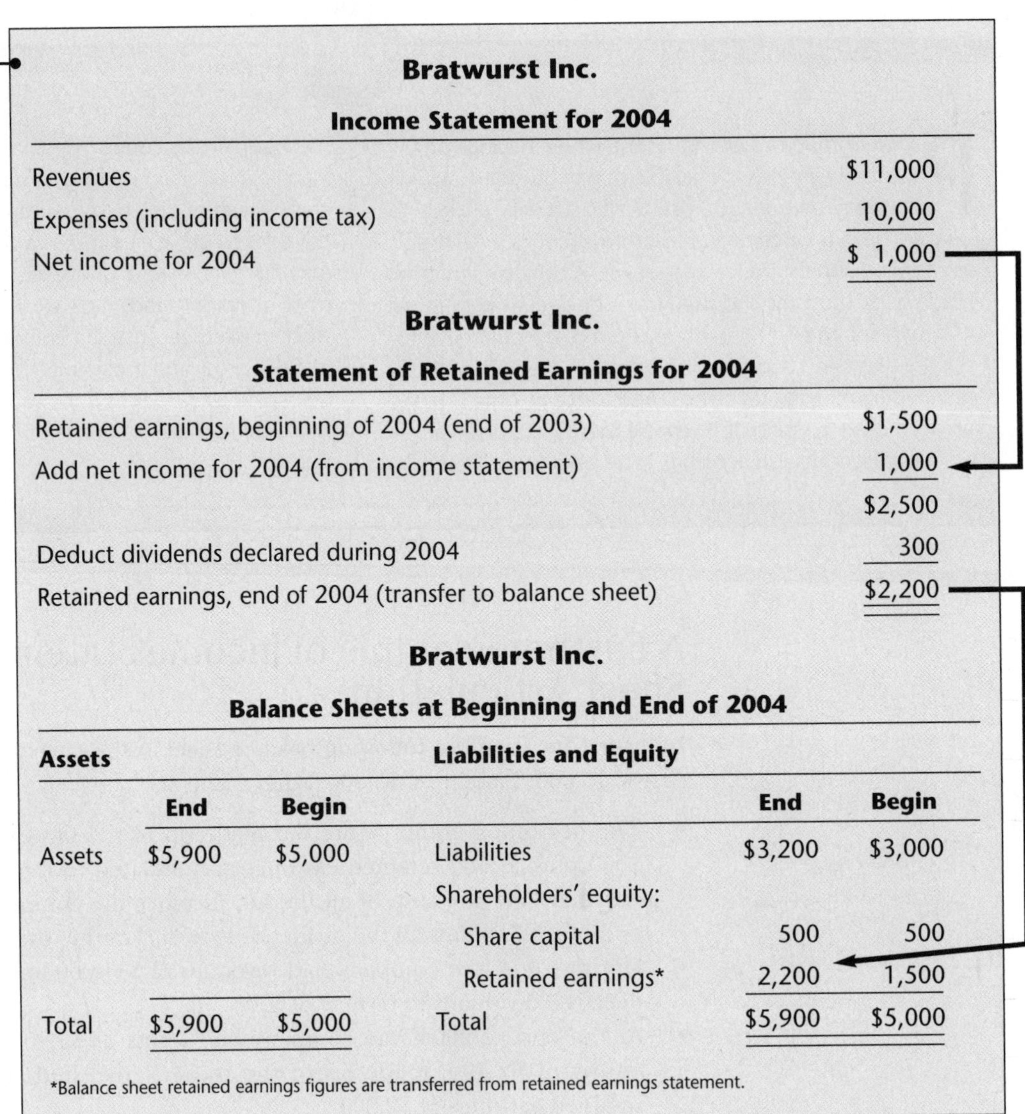

Bratwurst Inc.

Income Statement for 2004

Revenues	$11,000
Expenses (including income tax)	10,000
Net income for 2004	$ 1,000

Bratwurst Inc.

Statement of Retained Earnings for 2004

Retained earnings, beginning of 2004 (end of 2003)	$1,500
Add net income for 2004 (from income statement)	1,000
	$2,500
Deduct dividends declared during 2004	300
Retained earnings, end of 2004 (transfer to balance sheet)	$2,200

Bratwurst Inc.

Balance Sheets at Beginning and End of 2004

Assets			**Liabilities and Equity**		
	End	**Begin**		**End**	**Begin**
Assets	$5,900	$5,000	Liabilities	$3,200	$3,000
			Shareholders' equity:		
			Share capital	500	500
			Retained earnings*	2,200	1,500
Total	$5,900	$5,000	Total	$5,900	$5,000

*Balance sheet retained earnings figures are transferred from retained earnings statement.

You can see from this example that

- the income statement's bottom line is transferred to the statement of retained earnings, and
- the retained earnings statement's bottom line is transferred to the balance sheet,
- showing that the three statements tie together (articulate) through retained earnings.

The Bratwurst example shows that the income and retained earnings statements could be said to be detailed explanations of the change in the balance sheet retained earnings figure. The balance sheet could instead have had the following format under the retained earnings part of owners' equity:

EXHIBIT 3·4

Retained earnings:	
Beginning balance	$ 1,500
Add revenues	11,000
	$12,500
Deduct expenses	10,000
	$ 2,500
Deduct dividends declared	300
Ending balance	$ 2,200

The information is there, but the balance sheet would be rather cluttered, and there would hardly be room to provide details about the various revenues, expenses, and dividends. Also, the concept of income as a measure of performance would be obscured. Therefore, the income and retained earnings statements were developed to provide the detailed performance measure demanded by users of the information without complicating the balance sheet.

HOW'S YOUR UNDERSTANDING?

Here are two questions you should be able to answer based on what you have just read. If you can't answer them, it would be best to reread the material.

1. In financial accounting, what is a revenue and what is an expense?
2. Suppose Bratwurst Inc.'s accounting records showed the following for the next year, 2005: Revenues earned, $14,200; Cash collected from customers, $13,800; Expenses incurred, $12,900; Expenses paid in cash, $11,200; Dividends declared, $600; and Dividends paid in cash, $500. Can you show that Bratwurst's retained earnings as at the end of 2005 was $2,900 by calculating 2005 net income and incorporating other information we have about Bratwurst?

Begin RE = $2,200. Net income = $14,200 – $12,900 = $1,300. End RE = $2,200 + $1,300 – $600 dividends declared = $2,900.

TO THE READER: The next four sections have the following content:

- Section 3.4 has an example of a real company's income and retained earnings statements;
- Section 3.5 focuses on the way these statements are formatted to provide useful information;
- Section 3.6 shows how double-entry accrual accounting produces the accounts behind the two statements, especially revenues and expenses; and
- Section 3.7 has a demonstration problem: a double-entry accrual accounting example to help establish your intuition about how the two statements work and fit with the balance sheet.

The four sections can be read in any order. You can start with the statements in Section 3.4 and finish with the accounting entries in Section 3.7, or vice versa.

3.4 A Closer Look at Income and Retained Earnings Statements' Content

In Chapter 2, we looked at CPR's balance sheet. To continue with that company's example, Exhibit 3.5 shows the company's 2004 income statement and statement of retained earnings (called *retained income* by CPR). Like the balance sheet, both statements are consolidated because CPR is a group of corporations. The balance sheet was comparative only to 2003, but the income and retained earnings statements compare to two previous years, back to 2002.

As you review the two statements, note these points:

Periods of time (years).

1. The statements cover periods of time (years ending December 31), not a point in time as the balance sheet does. Like the balance sheet, they are shown in millions of dollars.

Many notes.

2. As for balance sheets, explanatory notes are referred to and appended. The notes are not attached here, as they are not necessary to this chapter.

Some nonoperating items.

3. The upper part of the income statement generally contains the ordinary revenues, along with the ordinary expenses incurred to earn those revenues. Below those can be various special items, as Section 3.5 will explain. CPR has several of these:
   - "Other charges" that are further described in Note 5 (not included at this point in the book). These are all forms of interest and financing costs too, in CPR's case. We will see more about them later, but for now, consider them to be kinds of interest expense.
   - "Foreign exchange gain on long-term debt." We saw in Section 2.9 how the change in the value of the Canadian dollar relative to a foreign currency in which assets are held affects the balance sheet. CPR borrowed U.S. dollars and will repay the loan using U.S. dollars. Since the Canadian dollar appreciated relative to the U.S. dollar during the year, it will cost fewer Canadian dollars to repay the loan than at the last balance sheet date. Such movements are shown as gains (in this case) or losses on the income statement.
   - Plain interest expense, which most companies separate from operating income to assist the reader to assess separately the returns (income) the company earns from its day-to-day operations and the interest costs of financing those returns.

Income tax is separately disclosed.

4. As is standard practice, CPR discloses its income tax expense separately from other expenses. CPR chooses not to calculate the subtotal "income before income tax" that most companies calculate, but that is no problem: as long as the information is there, we can calculate it if we wish to:
   - In 2004, net income was $413.0 million after tax, so if we add the $143.3 million tax to that, we can see that income before income tax was $556.3 million in 2004. The income statement could have been set out this way:

(After the Interest expense line) Income before income tax	$556.3
Income tax expense	143.3
Net income	$413.0

Canadian Pacific Railway Limited

Statement of consolidated income

Year ended December 31 (in millions, except per share data)	**2004**	**2003 (Restated – see Note 2)**	**2002 (Restated – see Note 2)**
Revenues			
Freight	**$3,728.8**	$3,479.3	$3,471.9
Other	**174.1**	181.4	193.7
	3,902.9	3,660.7	3,665.6
Operating expenses			
Compensation and benefits	**1,259.6**	1,163.9	1,143.4
Fuel	**440.0**	393.6	358.3
Materials	**178.5**	179.2	168.7
Equipment rents	**218.5**	238.5	255.4
Depreciation and amortization	**407.1**	372.3	340.2
Purchased services and other	**610.7**	583.6	555.6
	3,114.4	2,931.1	2,821.6
Operating income before the following:	**788.5**	729.6	844.0
Special charge for environmental remediation (Note 3)	**90.9**	–	–
Special charge for labour restructuring and asset impairment (Note 4)	**(19.0)**	215.1	–
Loss on transfer of assets to outsourcing firm (Note 12)	–	28.9	–
Operating income	**716.6**	485.6	844.0
Other charges (Note 5)	**36.1**	33.5	21.8
Foreign exchange gain on long-term debt	**(94.4)**	(209.5)	(13.4)
Interest expense (Note 6)	**218.6**	218.7	242.2
Income tax expense (Note 7)	**143.3**	41.6	105.9
Net income	**$ 413.0**	$ 401.3	$ 487.5
Basic earnings per share (Note 8)	**$ 2.60**	$ 2.53	$ 3.08
Diluted earnings per share (Note 8)	**$ 2.60**	$ 2.52	$ 3.06

Statement of consolidated retained income

Year ended December 31 (in millions)	**2004**	2003	2002
Balance, January 1, as previously reported	**$2,174.8**	$1,856.9	$1,441.7
Adjustment for change in accounting policy (Note 2)	**(20.9)**	(23.5)	(15.0)
Balance, January 1, as restated	**2,153.9**	1,833.4	1,426.7
Net income for the year	**413.0**	401.3	487.5
Dividends	**(82.5)**	(80.8)	(80.8)
Balance, December 31	**$2,484.4**	$2,153.9	$1,833.4

(Notes to consolidated financial statements are not included.)

- Similarly, income before income tax was $442.9 million in 2003 and $593.4 million in 2002. Make sure you see how those figures were calculated!

Net income is on the income statement and the retained earnings statement.

5. The net income from the income statement is carried down to the statement of retained earnings, as in our Bratwurst Inc. example earlier.

6. The statement of retained earnings starts with the beginning balance (note the ending balance for 2003 is the same as the beginning one for 2004), adds the $413.0 million net income, deducts $82.5 million of dividends declared, and ends with $2,484.4 million. If you refer back to the CPR balance sheet in Section 2.10, you'll see that its 2004 retained earnings figure is the same as the ending one in the statement of retained earnings. CPR has *articulated* its income statements and balance sheets through the retained earnings statements.

Ending retained earnings is on the retained earnings statement and the balance sheet.

7. Like the income statement, the retained earnings statement can contain some special items. In 2004, CPR made an adjustment for an accounting policy change. More about this sort of special item is in Section 3.5.

Retained earnings may require some adjustments and corrections.

Let's look at some of the income and retained earnings statements' content.

- Revenue, which is increases in wealth due to transactions with customers, was little changed in 2003 but grew by about 6.5% in 2004. CPR separated its revenues into two categories: its main freight business, and "Other" revenues such as from its properties. The growth in freight revenues over the three years was partially offset by the proportionately larger decline in the smaller "Other" revenue category.

Revenues as percentages of 2002

	2004	2003	2002
Freight	107.4	100.2	100
Other	89.9	93.6	100
Total	106.5	99.9	100

In the absence of cost of goods sold, operating expenses and income can be related to revenue.

- CPR does not have a cost of goods sold expense, because it is selling services, not goods. It is usual to calculate a company's *gross margin* (also called *gross profit*) by subtracting cost of goods sold from revenue, to provide an indication of how much the company "marks up" its goods for sale. We can get some idea of how CPR's revenue relates to its costs by examining its operating expenses. CPR is helpful in providing a breakdown of its operating expenses, so we can see that the largest category of expenses is paying its employees, though the compensation and benefits expense fell slightly even though revenue rose slightly, so that compensation as a percentage of total revenue went down. In the absence of a gross margin we can calculate operating income as a percentage of revenue: it declined over 13% [(23.0 – 19.9)/23.0] in 2003, recovering slightly in 2004. Compensation as a percentage of revenues declined each year so other operating expenses must have been rising. A review of the income statement reveals this to be the case for all operating expenses except equipment rentals.

Employee compensation as a percentage of revenue

2004: $1,259.6/$3,902.9 = 32.3%
2003: $1,163.9/$3,660.7 = 31.8%
2002: $1,143.4/$3,665.6 = 31.2%

Operating income as a percentage of revenue

2004: $788.5/$3,902.9 = 20.2%
2003: $729.6/$3,660.7 = 19.9%
2002: $844.0/$3,665.6 = 23.0%

Borrowing costs increased over the three years.

- CPR's borrowing cost and interest expense increased each year, both absolutely and as a percentage of total revenue. As noted earlier, "other charges" is also related to borrowing costs. While it shows a steady increase over the three years, it does not offset the decline in interest.

Interest and similar expenses

	2004	2003	2002
Interest	$218.6	$218.7	$242.2
Other charges	36.1	33.5	21.8
	$254.7	$252.2	$264.0
% of total rev.	6.5%	6.9%	7.2%

CPR's income tax rate varied across the three years.

- The company's income tax rate can be estimated from the income statement, as a percentage of the income tax expense to the total income before tax. (For CPR, the income before tax has to be calculated, as demonstrated earlier.) The rate varied from 9.4% in 2003 to 25.8% in 2004. With this, we can do the sort of net-of-tax analysis illustrated in Chapter 1. For example, if in 2004, the company increased its price on a service by $1,000 without having an increase in other expenses, the net income would go up by $742 ($1,000 × (1 – 0.258)) because the increased income would attract 25.8% increased income tax.

Income tax expense as a percentage of income before tax

2004: $143.3/$556.3 = 25.8%
2003: $ 41.6/$442.9 = 9.4%
2002: $105.9/$593.4 = 17.9%

CPR's earnings per share varied with net income.

- Below the net income figure is a ratio that is very important for public companies because financial analysts and investors use it to compare companies' performance. This is *earnings per share* (EPS), which is, roughly, net income divided by the average number of common (voting) shares outstanding. When the number of shares issued doesn't change much, EPS moves as net income does. Though CPR went through a rearrangement of its share capital in 2004, the number of shares issued grew only slightly, so the company's net income and EPS changed very similarly, as the calculation here shows. EPS is the only ratio that is a standard part of the financial statements. This per-share information is useful because it removes the company's size from the income figure and allows earnings to be compared to the particular number of shares the investor happens to own. If you know that CPR made $413.0 million in income in 2004, that is hard to relate to your own investment, say 1,000 shares, but if you know it was $2.60 per share, you can say that your investment earned $2,600 in 2004 and you can compare that to the share price to see if CPR is earning a comparable return for the price to that of other companies. Because it has made promises that could result in issuance of more shares that would therefore "dilute" the interests of present shareholders, CPR also tells us what such possible issuance would do to the EPS—you can see that the potential for dilution of the income per share is very small, only one cent in 2003, and nothing in 2004.

EPS compared to net income as a percentage of 2002

	2004	2003	2002
Net income	84.7%	82.3%	100%
Basic EPS	84.4%	82.1%	100%

CPR's dividends varied as a percentage of net income.

- The statement of retained earnings shows dividends declared, which may be related to net income, as shown here. CPR did not in the past declare dividends as a stable percentage of net income. In an analyst workshop on November 16, 2005, CPR stated its dividend policy as "ensuring shareholders' interests are balanced between dividends and share appreciation." The numbers at the right indicate that the board of directors believed the policy to be met by maintaining a constant dollar amount of dividends in the face of declining income in 2003. In 2004 it appears a shift to a policy of paying out 20% of net income as dividends may have been adopted.[16]

Dividend declared as a percentage of net income		
2004: $82.5/$413.0	=	20.0%
2003: $80.8/$401.3	=	20.1%
2002: $80.8/$487.5	=	16.6%

HOW'S YOUR UNDERSTANDING?

Here are three questions you should be able to answer based on what you have just read (the second question adds a bit of "what if" effects analysis you should be able to reason through):

1. How did CPR's 2004 performance in earning income compare to that in 2002 and 2003?
2. Suppose CPR discovered that $1 million in credit revenue had not been recorded in 2004 but should have been. The revenue wasn't recorded until January 2005. The cost of the services sold had been properly included in the 2004 expenses; it is just that the revenue was recorded in the wrong year. What would recording this revenue properly in 2004 do to: (a) the 2004 income before income tax, (b) the 2004 net income, (c) the working capital at the end of 2004, (d) the retained earnings at the end of 2004, and (e) the revenue for 2005?

(a) Income before tax for 2004 would go up by $1 million due to adding the revenue in. (b) Net income would go up by $742,000, because 25.8% income tax would have to be deducted. (c) Working capital at the end of 2004 would go up $742,000 ($1 million would be added to accounts receivable and $258,000 would be added to income tax payable). (d) Retained earnings at the end of 2004 would go up by $742,000, the increase in net income. (e) Revenue for 2005 would go down by $1 million as the revenue was removed from the 2005 year and added to the 2004 year.

3. Review the most current annual report for CPR (it can be found at www.cpr.ca). Discuss the company's approach to meeting its dividend policy in the years subsequent to 2004.

3.5 Format of Income and Retained Earnings Statements

This section elaborates the format ideas introduced in Section 3.3. Like the balance sheet, the income and retained earnings statements are designed to provide information not only through their contents but also through their contents' *classification*. There are a few principles behind the income and retained earnings statements' classification of accounts. These are shown in the illustrated format below, which is explained further in points keyed to the illustrative format. The principles are quite well established and most companies follow them in general, but each company has its own specific interpretations and wordings, so you have to be prepared to see many variations in applying the principles, and even exceptions to them.

EXHIBIT 3·6

Illustrative Format of Income and Retained Earnings Statements

Income Statement for the Period

	Revenue		$XXXX
	Operating expenses (COGS may be separately disclosed)		XXXX
a. →	Operating income		$XXXX
b. →	Nonoperating items		
	Ordinary items (interest, asset sale gains and losses, etc.)	$XXXX	
	Any unusual items separately disclosed	XXXX	XXXX
c. →	Continuing income before income tax		$XXXX
d. →	Income tax expense (current and future portions)		XXXX
e. →	Income from continuing operations		$XXXX
f. →	Any discontinued operations, net of income tax	$XXXX	
	Any extraordinary items, net of income tax	XXXX	XXXX
g. →	Net income for the year		$XXXX

Retained Earnings Statement for the Period

	Retained earnings as reported at the end of the prior period	$XXXX
h. →	Any adjustments to beginning balance for error corrections or accounting policy changes, net of income tax	XXXX
	Revised beginning retained earnings	$XXXX
	Add net income (or deduct net loss) from income statement	XXXX
i. →	Add or deduct any adjustments from transactions with shareholders, net of income tax	XXXX
	Deduct dividends declared during the period	XXXX
j. →	Ending retained earnings (to balance sheet)	$XXXX

a. *Operating revenues and expenses.* The income statement begins with the more ordinary, operating revenues and expenses, and separates those from significant (*material*) nonoperating accounts that are shown further down on the statement. As noted in Section 3.4, disclosing cost of goods sold expense (for enterprises that sell goods rather than, as CPR does, just services) makes the income statement more useful, but whether to do so is the company's choice. Enterprises may disclose individual revenues and expenses if they wish. CPR separates freight from other revenues and lists several kinds of operating expenses. A subtotal "operating income" is often identified after these revenues and expenses are set out.

b. *Nonoperating revenues and expenses.* Some revenues and expenses may be judged not to relate to day-to-day operations and so may be presented below the operating items. Interest expense is a typical example, as are gains and losses on sales of assets no longer needed. There may also be some *unusual items* that relate to operations but that are unusual in size or different from other items and so are disclosed separately. An example would be revenue from a large, never-to-be repeated special business deal. Including it in ordinary revenue would make that revenue misleadingly large. For CPR, an example of this was the "special charges for environmental remediation."

c. *Continuing income before income tax.* To signal the company's general ability to earn income, most income statements report a subtotal at this point, called Income before income tax, or Continuing income before income tax. (The word "continuing" is added if the company has discontinued operations, explained below.) CPR didn't do this, but disclosed enough information for us to figure it out.

d. *Current and future income tax expense.* Income tax expense, which includes amounts payable currently and amounts estimated to be payable in the future based on current-year events (called future tax), is deducted next. Including both current and future tax is called *interperiod tax allocation* (across time periods) because income tax estimated to be paid in the future as a consequence of present-period events should be included in this year's expense when those events are measured in this year's income.

e. *Income from continuing operations.* The total income tax expense should be calculated on the income before any discontinued or extraordinary items (see below), and then the income after this tax should be reported, so that the reader of the financial statements can see what the company's ordinary, continuing income after income tax is. This figure is thought useful for making predictions about the future as well as evaluating past performance. Many companies call this after-tax figure *income from continuing operations.* CPR had no discontinued items, so its income statement ended with net income.

f. *Discontinued operations and extraordinary items.* Then, the noncontinuing items are added or deducted. Because income tax has already been deducted on continuing operations, each of these items should have its own income tax effects shown with it, to avoid mixing those tax effects in with the income tax on continuing operations. *This means that income tax is allocated to each item that is below the continuing operations line.* This is called *intraperiod tax allocation* (limited to one period), to separate it from the interperiod (across periods) tax allocation represented by the future income tax calculation mentioned above. Each intraperiod income tax amount may be currently payable, a future estimate, or some of each. It is common to disclose both the gross effect and the income tax effect of any of these noncontinuing items. The two main such items shown at the bottom of the income statement, both shown net of their own income tax effects, are discontinued operations and extraordinary items. *Discontinued operations* are divisions or lines of business that were shut down and/or put up for sale during the year. Because such operations will not be part of the company in the future, separating them from the regular continuing operations should help in predicting future performance because they can be left out of such a prediction. For example, Molson Inc. (**www.molson.com**) had a loss from discontinued operations of $3.3 million in 2001. The majority of this loss came from operating the Montréal Canadiens hockey team and its arena, the Molson Centre. In 2001, Molson was in the process of selling the Canadiens, thus any loss from the team was not included in regular 2001 operating income because this loss would only occur in 2001, and would not continue when the team was sold. *Extraordinary items* are truly large and outside the company's control, such as a sudden expropriation of property by a government. Extraordinary items are seldom seen on income statements, but in these days of corporate restructuring and reorganization, discontinued operations have quite often been disclosed. One example of an *extraordinary item* arose due to the events of September 11, 2001. Merrill Lynch (**www.ml.com**), a large banking institution formerly headquartered in the World Trade Center in New York, reported a line on its income statement for "Expenses related to Sept. 11, net of tax" of $83 million. This extraordinary event was reported to investors outside of regular operating income because it affected the company's net income substantially. CPR had no extraordinary or discontinued items in any of 2002–2004.

g. *Net income: the bottom line.* The income statement's "bottom line" is the *net income,* which is the income from continuing operations plus or minus any discontinued operations or extraordinary items. Earnings per share, which is income divided by the average number of voting shares outstanding during the year, is usually shown both before and after extraordinary and discontinued items, to help people judge the effect of these nonrecurring items on likely future income. The nonrecurring items affect this year but should not affect future years. CPR did not need to calculate these other versions of EPS, but did calculate the diluted version of EPS, as we saw in Section 3.4.
h. *Retained earnings adjustments.* Before net income is transferred to the statement of retained earnings, the retained earnings are adjusted for the effects of three main kinds of items, *all net of any of their own income tax effects.* The first is the correction of errors in prior years' incomes discovered this year. The second is the effects on past years' results of accounting policy changes adopted this year. CPR had this sort of adjustment in each year 2002 to 2004.
i. *Transactions with shareholders.* Then net income is added into retained earnings. Two final items complete the retained earnings statement. The first is transactions with shareholders other than dividends, such as costs of redeeming shares that are kept off the income statement following the rule that income is measured by relationships with customers, employees, suppliers, and others, but not with shareholders. Following the same rule, the second and last kind of retained earnings item is dividends declared to shareholders during the period.
j. *Ending retained earnings.* Finally, ending retained earnings are transferred to the balance sheet as at the end of the period.
k. For financial statements relating to fiscal years beginning on or after October 1, 2006, Section 1530 of the *CICA Accounting Handbook* requires the disclosure of "comprehensive income," defined as the "change in equity (net assets) of an enterprise during a period from transactions and other events and circumstances from non-owner sources." We shall have to review financial statements for those years to see what formats develop from practice to satisfy the new requirement.

Determining income is one of the most important tasks of accounting. To many people, it is *the* most important. Income and its revenue and expense components are financial accounting's main measures of an enterprise's economic performance over a period of time. The way of measuring income developed by accountants over the centuries, and now pretty well defined by various accepted accounting standards and methods, is not easy to connect to economic theory about performance. There is certainly a relationship, but it is both complex and subtle. For example, accounting treats debt-holders differently from equity-holders: interest on debts is deducted as an expense in calculating income, but dividends to owners are not. Dividends are treated as distributions of income, in the statement of retained earnings. Yet both groups have invested in the company, and they both are concerned about its ability to give them the return they expect. In economics and finance, evaluations of performance, risk, and returns to investors depend on a host of factors (such as economy-wide interest rates, inflation, and overall stock market movements) that are difficult to tie to accounting's measurement of an individual company's performance. Accrual accounting's measurement of economic performance is not universally accepted, and though the accounting measure of income does correlate with such economic indicators as stock prices, it is not at all the same. We'll see more about this later.

HOW'S YOUR UNDERSTANDING?

Here are two questions you should be able to answer based on what you have just read. If you can't answer them, it would be best to reread the material.

1. Why are noncontinuing items on the income statement and retained earnings adjustments shown net of their own income tax effects?
2. Laura Inc. has the following figures for this year: revenue, $432,000; operating expenses, $375,000; interest expense, $11,000; unusual gain on sale of land, $22,000; income tax expense, $17,000; loss on discontinued operations, $50,000; income tax recovery on the discontinued operations, $12,000; beginning retained earnings, $142,000; correction of error that overstated a prior year's income calculation, $5,000; costs of a share redemption, $8,000; dividends declared, $10,000. What is the income from continuing operations, the net income, and ending retained earnings?

Income from continuing operations = $51,000 ($432,000 – $375,000 – $11,000 + $22,000 – $17,000)

Net income = $13,000 ($51,000 above – $50,000 + $12,000)

Ending retained earnings = $132,000 ($142,000 – $5,000 + $13,000 – $8,000 – $10,000)

3.6 Debits and Credits, Revenues and Expenses

In Chapter 2, we saw how entries and accounts were used to record events as transactions in the double-entry accounting system. The CappuMania Inc. example was limited to balance sheet accounts. Let's expand the example to bring in income statement accounts and to "*close*" (transfer) those to retained earnings, so that the *articulation* of the income statement and balance sheet accounts may be illustrated. Section 3.7 has a demonstration problem more focused on an intuitive understanding of the process—you can read that section before this one if you wish.

We'll continue the CappuMania example from Section 2.6. As a reminder, here is the company's April 1, 2005, balance sheet from the end of Section 2.6:

EXHIBIT 3.7

CappuMania Inc.
Balance Sheet as at April 1, 2005

Assets		**Liabilities and Shareholders' Equity**	
Current assets:		Current liabilities:	
Cash	$ 3,200	Owing to suppliers	$ 1,550
Inventory of unsold food	800	Sales and other taxes owing	100
Inventory of supplies	2,350		$ 1,650
	$ 6,350	Noncurrent liabilities:	
Noncurrent assets:		Loan to buy equipment	3,900
Equipment cost	$ 9,200		$ 5,550
Accumulated amortization	(1,500)	Shareholders' equity:	
	$ 7,700	Share capital contributed	$ 4,100
		Retained earnings	4,400
			$ 8,500
	$14,050		$14,050

Now let's add a year's business activities to that starting point. It's the year ended March 31, 2006, which will be referred to as the year 2006 below. Here is a list of ten items, a mixture of routine transactions and year-end information so that you can see they are all recorded by the same technique of balanced journal entries. A full set of entries will follow.

1. Revenue for 2006 was $89,740. The coffee bar does mostly cash business, so of this, $85,250 was in cash and the rest was on credit.
2. General expenses for 2006, not including amortization or income tax, totalled $67,230. Most of the expenses for coffee supplies and so on were on credit, so of this, only $2,120 was in cash.
3. At the end of the year (March 31, 2006), it turned out that unsold food on hand cost $550 and supplies on hand cost $1,740. Therefore, the Food inventory account has to be reduced by $250 ($800 – $550) and the Supplies inventory account has to be reduced by $610 ($2,350 – $1,740). Using up these inventories is part of the cost of earning revenue, so these reductions will be included in the company's general expenses.
4. Amortization expense for the year 2006 was $2,380.
5. The company's income tax expense for 2006 was estimated at $4,460. (It is estimated because until the income tax authorities issue a formal assessment of tax, the company does not know for sure what its tax will be for the year.)
6. The company's board of directors declared a dividend of $1,000.
7. Collections of the revenue on credit totalled $3,330 during the year.
8. Payments to suppliers for expenses on credit totalled $59,420 during the year.
9. The company paid $3,000 toward its income tax during the year.
10. Only $800 of the dividend had been paid by the end of the year.

Now we can do entries to record these activities. To help you understand the entries, here are two important points:

Revenues represent increases in equity and are therefore credits.

- Because income is a part of retained earnings, which is an equity account and therefore a credit account on the balance sheet, anything that helps income is a credit. Revenue is therefore a credit balance account.
- Conversely, anything that hurts income, reduces retained earnings and equity, is therefore a debit. An expense is therefore a debit balance account. When dividends are declared, they are deducted from retained earnings; therefore, such deductions are debits because they reduce equity.

Expenses represent decreases in equity and are therefore debits.

These points produce the following table of double-entry accounting's debits and credits (you already know this, but the table may help in making sure you understand the entries):

EXHIBIT 3·8

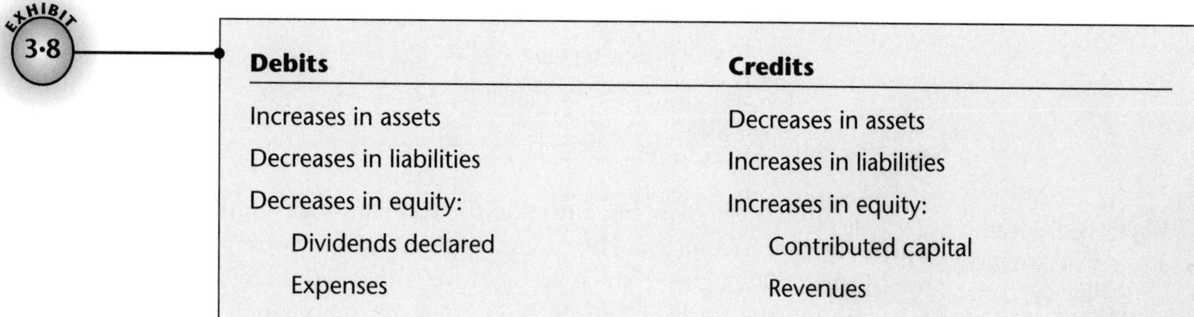

Debits	Credits
Increases in assets	Decreases in assets
Decreases in liabilities	Increases in liabilities
Decreases in equity:	Increases in equity:
Dividends declared	Contributed capital
Expenses	Revenues

Here are entries for the ten items given above. Some entries break the usual rule of putting the debits first, leading with the part of the entry that may be most readily seen from the information above. The important thing is that each entry balances:

EXHIBIT 3.9

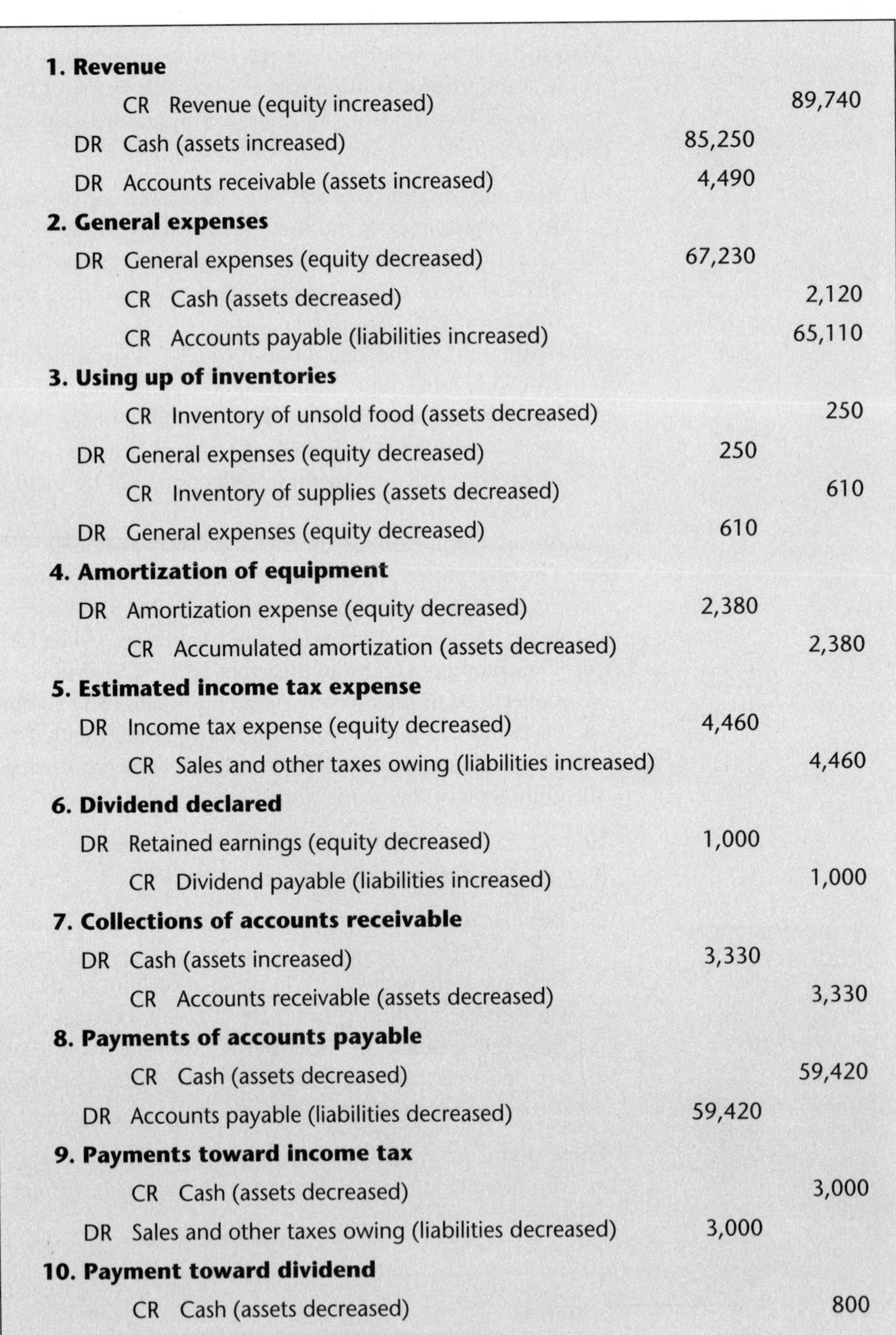

1. Revenue		
CR Revenue (equity increased)		89,740
DR Cash (assets increased)	85,250	
DR Accounts receivable (assets increased)	4,490	
2. General expenses		
DR General expenses (equity decreased)	67,230	
CR Cash (assets decreased)		2,120
CR Accounts payable (liabilities increased)		65,110
3. Using up of inventories		
CR Inventory of unsold food (assets decreased)		250
DR General expenses (equity decreased)	250	
CR Inventory of supplies (assets decreased)		610
DR General expenses (equity decreased)	610	
4. Amortization of equipment		
DR Amortization expense (equity decreased)	2,380	
CR Accumulated amortization (assets decreased)		2,380
5. Estimated income tax expense		
DR Income tax expense (equity decreased)	4,460	
CR Sales and other taxes owing (liabilities increased)		4,460
6. Dividend declared		
DR Retained earnings (equity decreased)	1,000	
CR Dividend payable (liabilities increased)		1,000
7. Collections of accounts receivable		
DR Cash (assets increased)	3,330	
CR Accounts receivable (assets decreased)		3,330
8. Payments of accounts payable		
CR Cash (assets decreased)		59,420
DR Accounts payable (liabilities decreased)	59,420	
9. Payments toward income tax		
CR Cash (assets decreased)		3,000
DR Sales and other taxes owing (liabilities decreased)	3,000	
10. Payment toward dividend		
CR Cash (assets decreased)		800
DR Dividend payable (liabilities decreased)	800	

A spreadsheet can act as an alternative format for the general ledger and its accounts.

We can *post* these ten entries to the company's accounts, using the spreadsheet basis we used in Section 2.6. The resulting spreadsheet is shown in Exhibit 3.10. Note that the April 1, 2005 figures, which are what we ended with in Section 2.6, are now in the first column, the starting figures. Some new accounts (such as accounts receivable and revenue) are needed to record the entries: the titles of these are shown in italics. *The spreadsheet represents CappuMania's general ledger. Each line (or multiple lines, for Cash) of the spreadsheet is a record of the entries to the account named in that line, so each line stands for one of the ledger accounts described in Section 2.5. Accounting systems may have different formats, but they all do the same thing!*

EXHIBIT 3·10

	A	B	C	D	E	F	G	H	I
1		CappuMania Inc. Trial Balance							
2									
3			Balance April 1, 2005			Transactions		Balance March 31, 2006	
4		ACCOUNT	DR	CR	#	DR	CR	DR	CR
5									
6		Cash	3,200		1	85,250		26,440	
7					2		2,120		
8					7	3,330			
9					8		59,420		
10					9		3,000		
11	Assets				10		800		
12		Accounts receivable	–		1	4,490		1,160	
13					7		3,330		
14		Inventory of unsold food	800		3		250	550	
15		Inventory of supplies	2,350		3		610	1,740	
16		Equipment cost	9,200					9,200	
17		Accumulated amortization		1,500	4		2,380		3,880
18									
19		Accounts payable		1,550	2		65,110		7,240
20					8	59,420			
21		Sales and other tax owing		100	5		4,460		1,560
22	Liabilities				9	3,000			
23		Dividend payable	–		6		1,000		200
24					10	800			
25		Loan to buy equipment		3,900					3,900
26									
27	Equity	Share capital contributed		4,100					4,100
28		Retained earnings		4,400	6	1,000			3,400
29									
30		Revenue	–		1		89,740		89,740
31		General expenses	–		2	67,230		68,090	
32	Income Accounts				3	250			
33					3	610			
34		Amortization expense	–		4	2,380		2,380	
35		Income tax expense	–		5	4,460		4,460	
36									
37		Totals	15,550	15,550		232,220	232,220	114,020	114,020

Debits = Credits

The spreadsheet acts as the trial balance as well as the ledger.

You can see that everything is still in balance. The sums of the debits and credits in the ten entries are $232,220, which verifies the concept of double-entry accounting. The ledger's *trial balance* is represented by the March 31, 2006, column. Since the sums of the debits and credits are equal, our accounts are balanced. The spreadsheet can be instructed to automatically sum rows and columns as you post journal entries, so that you can see immediately if you have done something arithmetically wrong.

The income statement accounts are part of the ledger and so are needed to balance it.

To highlight the calculation of income from the expanded set of accounts, a second version of the spreadsheet is shown in Exhibit 3.11. It is the same as the spreadsheet we just saw, except that the balance sheet accounts and the income statement accounts are now separately subtotalled. You will see that income (the difference between the revenue and expense accounts) equals $14,810. It is a credit, which is what equity is. You will also note that without the income statement accounts, the balance sheet accounts are out of balance by the same $14,810. We will do something about that shortly.

EXHIBIT 3·11

	A	B	C	D	E	F	G	H	I
1		CappuMania Inc. Trial Balance (with subtotals to show income calculation)							
2									
3			Balance April 1, 2005			Transactions		Balance March 31, 2006	
4		ACCOUNT	DR	CR	#	DR	CR	DR	CR
5									
6		Cash	3,200		1	85,250		26,440	
7					2		2,120		
8					7	3,330			
9					8		59,420		
10					9		3,000		
11	Assets				10		800		
12		Accounts receivable	–		1	4,490		1,160	
13					7		3,330		
14		Inventory of unsold food	800		3		250	550	
15		Inventory of supplies	2,350		3		610	1,740	
16		Equipment cost	9,200					9,200	
17		Accumulated amortization		1,500	4		2,380		3,880
18									
19		Accounts payable		1,550	2		65,110		7,240
20					8	59,420			
21		Sales and other tax owing		100	5		4,460		1,560
22	Liabilities				9	3,000			
23		Dividend payable	–		6		1,000		200
24					10	800			
25		Loan to buy equipment		3,900					3,900
26									
27	Equity	Share capital contributed		4,100					4,100
28		Retained earnings		4,400	6	1,000			3,400
29		**Balance sheet totals**	**15,550**	**15,550**		**157,290**	**142,480**	**39,090**	**24,280**
30		**Balance**				**14,810**		**14,810** ←	
31									
32		Revenue	–		1		89,740		89,740
33		General expenses	–		2	67,230		68,090	
34	Income				3	250			
35	Accounts				3	610			
36		Amortization expense	–		4	2,380		2,380	
37		Income tax expense	–		5	4,460		4,460	
38		**Income stmnt. totals**	–	–		**74,930**	**89,740**	**74,930**	**89,740**
39		**Balance**					**14,810**		**14,810** ←
40									
41		**Totals**	15,550	15,550		232,220	232,220	114,020	114,020

Exhibit 3.12 shows the company's income statement for 2006, taken from the spreadsheet's March 31, 2006, balances for the income statement accounts.

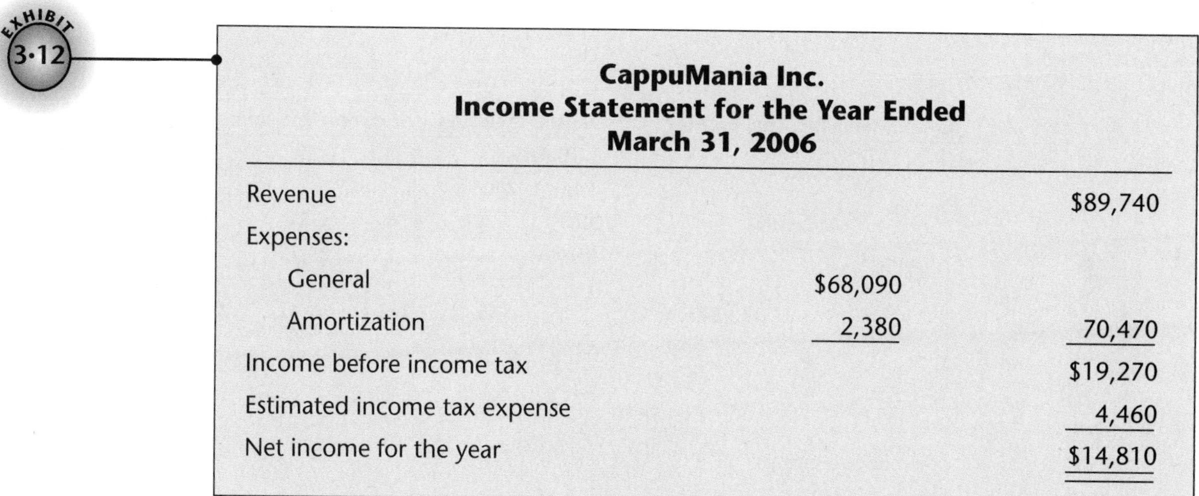

EXHIBIT 3.12

CappuMania Inc.
Income Statement for the Year Ended
March 31, 2006

Revenue		$89,740
Expenses:		
General	$68,090	
Amortization	2,380	70,470
Income before income tax		$19,270
Estimated income tax expense		4,460
Net income for the year		$14,810

Transferring revenues and expenses to retained earnings keeps the ledger in balance.

Before going on to the statement of retained earnings and the balance sheet, let's see how accountants *close* the revenue and expense accounts. The idea here is to transfer balances from those accounts to retained earnings, so that the income is transferred to retained earnings and the revenue and expense accounts are reset at zero and can then be used to record revenue and expenses for the next year (2007). The *closing entry* also illustrates how amounts can be moved from account to account, be combined in aggregate accounts, or otherwise, to rearrange balances in a desired way.

To close the revenue and expense accounts, each account with a credit balance is debited by that amount, and each account with a debit balance is credited by that amount. This brings all those accounts to zero:

DR Revenue	89,740	
CR General expenses		68,090
CR Amortization expense		2,380
CR Income tax expense		4,460
CR Retained earnings (the net income)		14,810

(Computerized accounting systems don't usually require a specific closing entry, because the computer can just reset the revenue and expense accounts to zero and adjust retained earnings automatically. But in principle, the above is what is happening.)

This entry is posted to the accounts in the spreadsheet in Exhibit 3.13, showing the closing amounts in bold italics. You will see that all the revenue and expense accounts have a zero balance now, and retained earnings now has a balance of $18,210. The March 31, 2006, balance sheet figures are now in balance, as you can see from the balance sheet subtotals line.

EXHIBIT 3·13

	A	B	C	D	E	F	G	H	I
1		**CappuMania Inc. Trial Balance (with transfer ("closing") of income to retained earnings)**							
2			**Balance April 1, 2005**			**Transactions**		**Balance March 31, 2006**	
3		**ACCOUNT**	**DR**	**CR**	**#**	**DR**	**CR**	**DR**	**CR**
4	**Assets**	Cash	3,200		1	85,250		26,440	
5					2		2,120		
6					7	3,330			
7					8		59,420		
8					9		3,000		
9					10		800		
10		Accounts receivable	–		1	4,490		1,160	
11					7		3,330		
12		Inventory of unsold food	800		3		250	550	
13		Inventory of supplies	2,350		3		610	1,740	
14		Equipment cost	9,200					9,200	
15		Accumulated amortization		1,500	4		2,380		3,880
16									
17	**Liabilities**	Accounts payable		1,550	2		65,110		7,240
18					8	59,420			
19		Sales and other tax owing		100	5		4,460		1,560
20					9	3,000			
21		Dividend payable		–	6		1,000		200
22					10	800			
23		Loan to buy equipment		3,900					3,900
24									
25	**Equity**	Share capital contributed		4,100					4,100
26		Retained earnings		4,400	6	1,000			*18,210*
27					11		*14,810*		
28		**Balance sheet totals**	*15,550*	*15,550*		*157,290*	*157,290*	*39,090*	*39,090*
29		**Balance**				–		–	
30									
31	**Income Accounts**	Revenue	–		1		89,740	–	–
32					11	*89,740*		–	–
33		General expenses	–		2	67,230		–	–
34					3	250		–	–
35					3	610		–	–
36					11		*68,090*	–	–
37		Amortization expense	–		4	2,380		–	–
38					11		*2,380*	–	–
39		Income tax expense	–		5	4,460		–	–
40					11		*4,460*	–	–
41		**Income stmnt. totals**	–	–		164,670	164,670	–	–
42		**Balance**					–	–	–
43		**Totals**	15,550	15,550		321,960	321,960	39,090	39,090

Debits = Credits

Now we can prepare the other two financial statements.

EXHIBIT 3·14

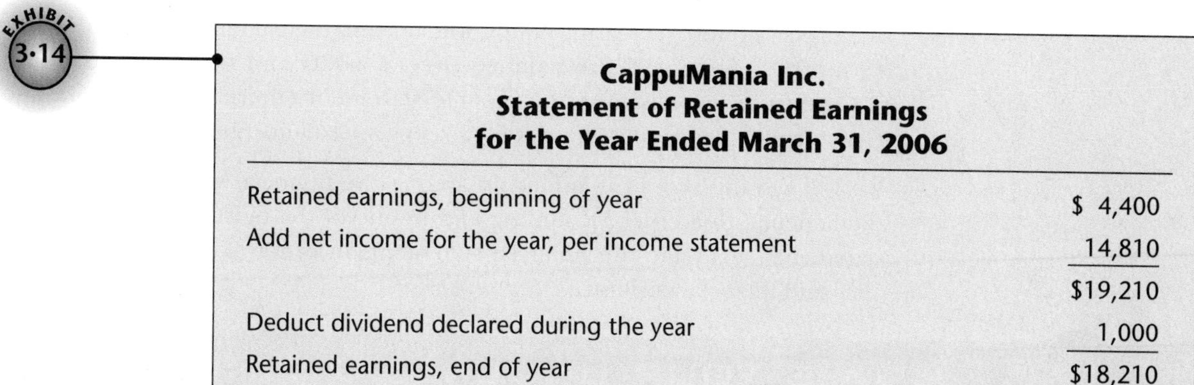

CappuMania Inc.
Statement of Retained Earnings
for the Year Ended March 31, 2006

Retained earnings, beginning of year	$ 4,400
Add net income for the year, per income statement	14,810
	$19,210
Deduct dividend declared during the year	1,000
Retained earnings, end of year	$18,210

EXHIBIT 3·15

CappuMania Inc.
Balance Sheet as at March 31, 2006

Assets		**Liabilities and Shareholders' Equity**	
Current assets:		Current liabilities:	
Cash	$26,440	Accounts payable	$ 7,240
Accounts receivable	1,160	Sales and other taxes owing	1,560
Inventory of unsold food	550	Dividend payable	200
Inventory of supplies	1,740		$ 9,000
	$29,890	Noncurrent liabilities:	
Noncurrent assets:		Loan to buy equipment	3,900
Equipment cost	$ 9,200		$12,900
Accumulated		Shareholders' equity:	
amortization	(3,880)	Share capital contributed	$ 4,100
	$ 5,320	Retained earnings	18,210
			$22,310
	$35,210		$35,210

Well, there you have it! This example has illustrated how accounting accumulates information about revenue and expense activities through journal entries posted to accounts, and how the financial statements are prepared from the accounts. The three financial statements fit together (*articulate*) because they are all based on the double-entry accounting system:

- A set of accounts is created, which is in balance (sum of all the debit account balances = sum of all the credit account balances).
- From these accounts are produced
  1. the income statement, the "bottom line" net income of which is transferred to
  2. the statement of retained earnings, the "bottom line" ending retained earnings of which is transferred to
  3. the balance sheet, which summarizes all the accounts.

Journal entries that affect income must also affect the balance sheet by the same amount.

Activities affecting income therefore affect the balance sheet through the double-entry system. Looking back at the entries above, for example,

- entry 1 increased the balance sheet's assets and increased revenue on the income statement (thereby also increasing income, which is transferred to retained earnings, therefore increasing equity, which keeps the balance sheet in balance); and
- entry 2 decreased the balance sheet's assets and increased its liabilities and increased expenses on the income statement (thereby also decreasing income, therefore decreasing equity, which keeps the balance sheet in balance).

We will see this sort of relationship among the financial statements many times. It is fundamental to accrual accounting and to one of the most important uses of financial statements: analyzing the financial statements in order to evaluate financial performance and financial position.

HOW'S YOUR UNDERSTANDING?

Here are two questions you should be able to answer based on what you have just read. If you can't answer them, it would be best to reread the material.

1. At the end of 2005, Hinton Hats Ltd. had retained earnings of $29,490. During 2006, it had revenue of $112,350, general expenses of $91,170, amortization expense of $6,210, and income tax expense of $3,420. Dividends of $5,000 were declared during 2006. At the end of 2006, the company's accounts were closed in preparation for 2007. After closing, what were the balances in the following accounts: Revenue, General expenses, Amortization expense, Income tax expense, and Retained earnings?

You should get Revenue = $0, General expenses = $0, Amortization expense = $0, Income tax expense = $0, and Retained earnings = $36,040 ($29,490 + $112,350 –$91,170 – $6,210 – $3,420 – $5,000).

2. The company's first event in 2007 was to pay $1,200 cash for the rent on its store for the first month of 2007. What did this event do to assets, liabilities, income for 2007, retained earnings, and equity?

You should get: down $1,200, no effect, down $1,200, down $1,200, down $1,200.

3.7 Demonstration Problem: Entries, Closing, and Statement Preparation

Accounting's process should make intuitive sense to you, so this example uses intuition.

Having a solid understanding of how accounts lead to the financial statements' portrayal of the enterprise's activities is very important to your understanding of accounting. Therefore, this section presents another example of preparation of financial statements, using a more intuitive approach than the previous section (but showing journal entries too).

The income and retained earnings statements report on performance over a period of time. As was shown in the diagram at the beginning of Section 3.3, there is one balance sheet at the beginning of that period, and another at the end. A sequence that will help you keep things straight is, therefore:

1. **Balance sheet at the beginning of the period, then**
2. **Income statement for the period, then**
3. **Retained earnings statement for the period, then**
4. **Balance sheet at the end of the period**

FIGURE 3.10

The income statement links the events throughout the year to the balance sheets.

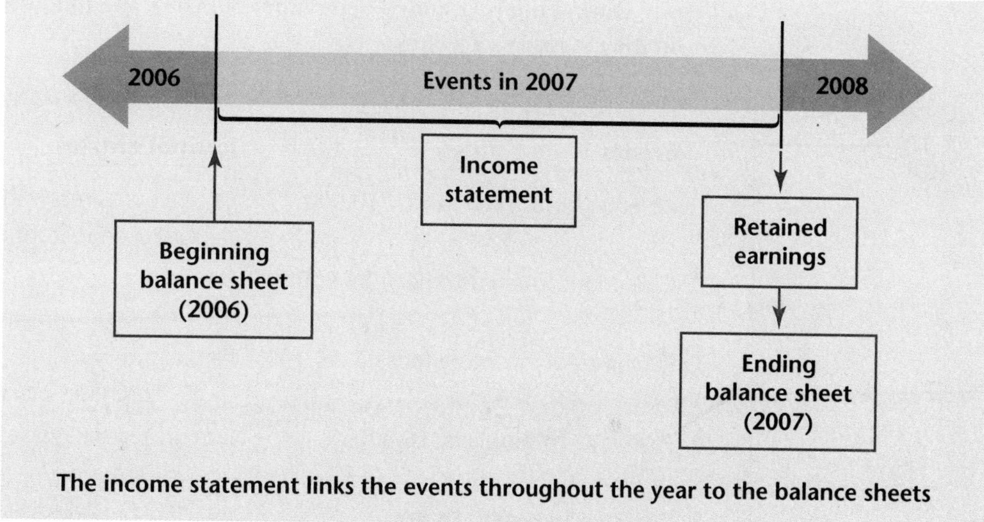

The income statement links the events throughout the year to the balance sheets

The financial statements are constructed to tell an integrated (articulated) story.

Our problem: starting with the balance sheet at the beginning of the fiscal year, record transactions for a company and from the resulting records, prepare the income and retained earnings statements for the year and the balance sheet at the end of the year. Working on this problem will further illustrate several things:

- how the income and retained earnings statements are prepared from the accounts;
- how the *accrual basis* of calculating net income works;
- how the accounts themselves reflect business events; and
- how the above sequence connects (articulates) the beginning and ending balance sheets to the other two statements.

Flashy Fashions Inc. is a small company in a coastal town. It rents its premises and its sales are all on credit (customers do not pay cash when they get the goods, but rather pay later, when billed, so a sale produces an account receivable until the cash is paid). It has only three expenses: cost of goods sold (COGS), rent, and income tax. (Remember that cost of goods sold is what the company pays to acquire and prepare for sale the goods that customers buy. It is an expense the company incurs in order to get sales revenue.)

At the end of its previous fiscal year, September 30, 2006, Flashy's balance sheet was as shown in Exhibit 3.16:

EXHIBIT 3·16

Flashy Fashions Inc.
Balance Sheet as at September 30, 2006

Assets		**Liabilities and Equity**	
Current assets:		Current liabilities:	
Cash	$ 800	Purchases payable	$ 600
Accounts receivable	400	Rent payable	300
Inventory	900	Shareholders' equity:	
		Share capital	500
		Retained earnings	700
	$2,100		$2,100

During the year ended September 30, 2007, the following information was recorded in the company's accounts:

Events	Journal entries		
1. Revenue from credit sales, $10,000	Dr Accounts receivable	10,000	
	Cr Revenue from credit sales		10,000
2. Collections from customers, $9,600	Dr Cash	9,600	
	Cr Accounts receivable		9,600
3. Purchases of inventory for sale, $6,100	Dr Inventory	6,100	
	Cr Purchases payable		6,100
4. Payments to suppliers, $6,300	Dr Purchases payable	6,300	
	Cr Cash		6,300
5. Cost of goods sold, $6,400	Dr Cost of goods sold expense	6,400	
	Cr Inventory		6,400
6. Rent charged by the landlord, $2,400	Dr Rent expense	2,400	
	Cr Rent payable		2,400
7. Rent paid to the landlord, $2,900	Dr Rent payable	2,900	
	Cr Cash		2,900
8. Income tax payable for the year, $350	Dr Income tax expense	350	
	Cr Income tax payable		350
9. Cash dividends declared, $450	Dr Dividends declared	450	
	Cr Dividends payable		450
10. Dividends paid, $450	Dr Dividends payable	450	
	Cr Cash		450

After recording these ten items, the company's accounts showed the following balances:

	Debits	Credits
Cash ($800 + $9,600 – $6,300 – $2,900 – $450)	$ 750	
Accounts receivable ($400 + $10,000 – $9,600)	800	
Inventory ($900 + $6,100 – $6,400)	600	
Purchases payable ($600 + $6,100 – $6,300)		$ 400
Dividends payable ($450 – $450)		0
Rent payable ($300 + $2,400 – $2,900)	200	
Income tax payable (owing for this year)		350
Share capital (no change)		500
Retained earnings (not changed yet by closing)		700
Dividends declared	450	
Revenue from credit sales		10,000
Cost of goods sold expense	6,400	
Rent expense	2,400	
Income tax expense	350	
	$11,950	$11,950

All the account changes should make intuitive sense.

Before we prepare financial statements, let's be sure you understand what happened in the accounts between 2006 and 2007.

a. Cash went up because of collections and down because of payments to suppliers, the landlord, and the shareholders (dividends).
b. Accounts receivable went up because of credit sales revenue and down because of collections.
c. Inventory went up because of purchases and down because the cost of goods sold was transferred to an expense account to recognize the value given up when the customers took the goods away.
d. Purchases payable went up because of purchases and down because of payments to suppliers.
e. Dividends payable went up when the dividends were declared and down when they were paid.
f. Rent payable went up because of bills from the landlord and down because of payments to the landlord. During the year, the landlord was paid more than had been billed, so rent payable reversed its sign: it's now a debit (prepaid rent). (Many accounts can be debits or credits, depending on temporary circumstances like overpaying. Even cash can be a credit: if you write too many cheques you can end up with an overdraft, in which case you have negative cash because you owe the bank instead of having money in the bank.)
g. Income tax payable went up from zero because the company owes tax on its income for this year (it did not owe any at the end of last year).
h. A new account, Dividends declared, was used to hold the dividend declared during the year. It will be transferred to retained earnings, so it is not really necessary—retained earnings could have been debited directly. However, if the company declares dividends regularly, having a separate account for them helps in keeping track and in preparing the retained earnings statement.
i. Revenue and expense accounts have only this year's revenues and expenses. Previous years' ones were transferred to retained earnings at the end of each year.

Now let's prepare the accrual basis financial statements for 2007 using the sequence given at the beginning of this section (the September 30, 2006, balance sheet was already presented above). First is the income statement, shown in Exhibit 3.19:

EXHIBIT 3.19

Flashy Fashions Inc.
Income Statement
for the Year Ended September 30, 2007

Revenue		$10,000
Operating expenses:		
Cost of goods sold	$6,400	
Rent	2,400	8,800
Income before income tax		$ 1,200
Income tax expense		350
Net income for the year		$ 850

The accrual basis income statement depends on economic events, not cash flows.

The *accrual income* (*net income*) is $850. This is not the change in cash but is rather a measure of economic events, not all of which are settled in cash during the year. Events summarized on the income statement are the following:

- Customers promised to pay $10,000. That is the accrual basis revenue, not whatever was collected ($9,600).
- Customers took goods that had cost Flashy $6,400. That is the accrual basis COGS expense, not whatever was purchased ($6,100).
- Rent of $2,400 was billed. That is the accrual basis expense, not whatever was paid to the landlord ($2,900).
- Income tax of $350 is due on the income. That is the accrual basis expense, even though no tax has yet been paid for the year.

Accrual income requires more complete accounting than keeping track of cash does.

The accrual income brings in more phenomena than the cash change does. To emphasize the nature of accrual income, we can reconcile the accrual income to the change in cash as we did back in Chapter 1:

EXHIBIT 3·20

Accrual income, according to the income statement		$850
Increase in accounts receivable (revenue not yet collected)	$(400)	
Decrease in unsold inventory (releasing tied-up cash)	300	
Decrease in unpaid purchases (this took more cash)	(200)	
Change from rent payable to prepaid rent (took more cash)	(500)	
Increase in income tax payable (an expense not paid in cash)	350	(450)
Cash income		$ 400
Dividends paid		(450)
Decrease in cash over the year (began at $800, ended at $750)		$ (50)

Dividends are not shown on the income statement. These are considered a distribution of income, not an expense of producing the income. Dividends are on the statement of retained earnings, shown in Exhibit 3.21:

EXHIBIT 3·21

Flashy Fashions Inc.
Statement of Retained Earnings
for the Year Ended September 30, 2007

Beginning balance (September 30, 2006)	$ 700
Add net income for the year, from the income statement	850
	$1,550
Deduct dividends declared	(450)
Ending balance (September 30, 2007)	$1,100

The retained earnings statement serves as a transition from the income statement to the balance sheet. We can see this in two ways. First, we can *close* the income statement accounts and dividends to retained earnings by debiting income accounts with credit balances and crediting income accounts (and dividends) with debit balances:

Dr Revenue	10,000	
Cr Cost of goods sold expense		6,400
Cr Rent expense		2,400
Cr Income tax expense		350
Cr Retained earnings (the net income)		850
Dr Retained earnings	450	
Cr Dividends declared		450

Second, we can prepare the *post-closing trial balance* to check the ledger's balance:

EXHIBIT 3·22

Post-closing List of Accounts (Trial Balance)

	Debits	**Credits**
Cash	$ 750	
Accounts receivable	800	
Inventory	600	
Purchases payable		$ 400
Rent payable (now prepaid rent)	200	
Income tax payable		350
Share capital		500
Retained earnings ($700 + $10,000 – $6,400 – $2,400 – $350 – $450)		1,100
	$2,350	$2,350

Retained earnings contains all past incomes, minus past dividends declared.

After closing, only balance sheet accounts have balances; income statement ones are zero. The accounts still balance, but now retained earnings contains all the information in the income and retained earnings statements. It is an accumulation of all the incomes (revenues minus expenses) minus all the dividends declared since the company began.

Now we can combine the September 30, 2006, balance sheet we started with and the post-closing trial balance above to prepare comparative balance sheets at the ends of 2006 and 2007:

Flashy Fashions Inc.
Balance Sheet as at September 30, 2007
(with Comparative Figures for September 30, 2006)

	2007	2006
Assets		
Current assets:		
Cash	$ 750	$ 800
Accounts receivable	800	400
Inventory	600	900
Prepaid rent	200	–
	$2,350	$2,100
Liabilities and Equity		
Current liabilities:		
Purchases payable	$ 400	$ 600
Rent payable	–	300
Income tax payable	350	0
	$ 750	$ 900
Shareholders' equity:		
Share capital	$ 500	$ 500
Retained earnings	1,100	700
	$1,600	$1,200
	$2,350	$2,100

The income statement and balance sheet are joined via double-entry accrual accounting.

The 2007 balance sheet account balances consist of the 2006 balances, plus or minus cash transactions, and plus or minus revenues and expenses. (For example, 2007 accounts receivable equal the 2006 balance plus 2007 revenue from credit sales minus 2007 cash collections.) This demonstrates again an essential feature of accrual accounting and the balanced double-entry system: the calculation of income implies the calculation of balance sheet values, and vice versa. The income statement and the balance sheet are intimately and necessarily related: one *always* implies the other. Whenever income is affected (via a change to a revenue or expense account), the balance sheet is affected by the same amount. This point is one of the most important in understanding financial accounting, and we will encounter it frequently.

HOW'S YOUR UNDERSTANDING?

Here are two questions you should be able to answer based on what you have just read. If you can't answer them, it would be best to reread the material.

1. Garf Ltd. had accounts receivable at the beginning of the year of $5,290. During the year, it had revenue from sales on credit of $39,620 and collected $41,080 from its customers. What balance did the company's Accounts receivable account show at the end of the year?

Accounts receivable = $3,830

2. Garf Ltd.'s net income for this year was $2,940, and it declared $900 in dividends to its shareholders during the year. Retained earnings were $7,410 at the beginning of the year. What are retained earnings at the end of the year, after closing?

Retained earnings = $9,450

3.8 Accrual Accounting Adjustments

The transactional records provide the foundation of the financial accounting system. In order to implement accrual accounting, such records usually require *adjustments*. Three main kinds of adjustments are needed:

Adjustments may be needed to correct errors.

Adjustments are needed for accruals that the accounting system doesn't do routinely.

1. Correction of errors discovered in the transactional record.
2. Implementation of routine accruals, *if they are not already recorded by the transactional record*. Examples are revenues earned but not yet collected, expenses incurred but not yet paid, cash received from customers prior to the related revenues having been earned, and amortization of assets. Whether accrual adjustments are needed in any accounting system depends on the sophistication of the system: sophisticated accounting systems may routinely include many adjustments that for simpler systems are made at year-end in a special set of journal entries. Most companies keep track of sales and purchases on credit: such uncollected revenue and unpaid purchases are accruals, but they are transaction-based and are frequent so they are routinely recorded. Many large companies have monthly accruals for interest expenses and other expenses as they build up, and monthly allowances for amortization of assets. Many small companies don't bother with these nontransactional items until annual financial statements are needed.

Adjustments implement other choices and estimates necessary for the financial statements.

3. Recognition of nonroutine events or estimates needed to bring the financial statements into line with what management (or the auditors) believe is the economic and business substance of the enterprise's performance and position. Examples here could include reducing the balance sheet figure for ("writing down") assets whose economic value has been impaired due to changes in market value or poor management, changing the way warranties are accounted for as a result of lawsuits about product quality, and re-estimating income tax liability on the basis of recently announced tax law revisions.

Accrual accounting adjustments follow the same double-entry format as do the transactional records:

- some account or accounts must be debited; and
- some account or accounts must be credited; and
- the sum of the debits must equal the sum of the credits.

Adjusting journal entries implement accrual accounting as needed.

Accountants call such adjustments *adjusting journal entries*. They are just the same as any other journal entries, except that they do not involve cash (except to correct errors). Their purpose is to augment the transaction-based (especially cash-based) figures, to add to the story told by the transactional records. *They implement accrual accounting.*

It is important that accrual adjustments are made if, and only if, they are appropriate.

The objective of accrual accounting is to improve the measurement of financial performance and position. However, because different choices can be made about what accounts need to be adjusted and by how much, accrual accounting can be a mechanism for manipulating results and producing misleading reports. Anyone can write an adjusting journal entry to alter the financial statements' figures; what is important is whether such an adjustment is *proper* (or whether an adjustment *not* made *should* have been). Therefore, the auditors pay particular attention to the kinds of accrual adjustments a company makes or should make, and most of the criticism of financial reporting is directed at subjective accrual adjustments, made using judgment and perhaps lacking strong documentation, rather than at the more objective, verifiable transactional records. In spite of the subjectivity and criticism, most accountants believe the accrual accounting basis to be superior to the cash basis, because it provides a more complete record that is also more representative of economic performance than the cash basis.

We can now revisit the filtering process of financial accounting introduced in Chapter 1, but with a more detailed process that illustrates the creation of usable financial statements.

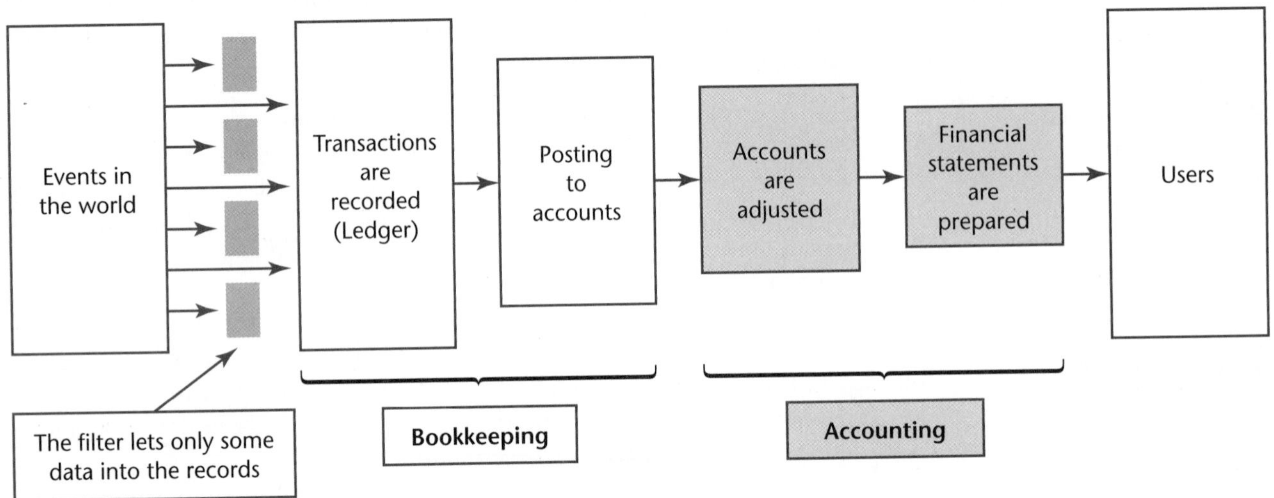

FIGURE 3.11 **The process used to construct financial statements**

An Example: The Northern Star Theatre Company

This example begins with the recording transactions and then shows the adjustments necessary to go from the records to the financial statements. To help you see how adjustments are built on the foundation of transactional records, *this example uses simple accounting records so that numerous adjustments will be necessary.* More sophisticated companies' accounting systems produce records already containing information that simpler systems include as adjustments.

Step 1: The Company and Its Initial Transactions

A group of aspiring actors from a small town decided to form a theatre company to perform in Canada's various "fringe" and other summer festivals. Here are events that happened to Northern Star Theatre Company in its first production, presented at a major Fringe Theatre Festival in 2006:

1. The theatre company (really, an informal partnership) was formed November 5, 2005, and a bank account was arranged for in the partnership's name. Six actors each agreed to put $500 into the company, but not until the money was needed.
2. The company applied in December 2005 for a place in the August 2006 Fringe, paying a fee of $400. Each actor paid $75 of the agreed amount to provide the money for the fee.
3. The Fringe notified the company in January 2006 that it had been accepted and allocated seven performances.
4. The company would have to pay a royalty to the play's author after the performances. The details were agreed with the author in March 2006.
5. Rehearsals began in March, and costumes and other props costing $470 were purchased. To pay for those items, each of the actors paid $100 more of the agreed amount, except one, Fred, who was broke at the time but promised to pay soon.
6. In early August, one of the actors, Elaine, drove to the city to see the performance venue and settle some staging details. The trip cost $290 in gas and other expenses,

all of which the company reimbursed after collecting another $100 from each member of the company except Fred, who was still broke in July.

7. In mid-August, the six actors drove to the city, a few days ahead of their performance date. They stayed with friends and spent the time constructing a set for the play and gathering up other props. The set and props cost $610 in materials to construct, all of which the company promised to pay as soon as the play was over. The cost of the car gas and motels along the way was $190, and the members who had paid for such expenses were also promised repayment after the play was over.
8. The play opened to a moderately enthusiastic audience. The Fringe collected $960 ($8 × 120 seats) and turned $897 over to the company that day after deducting $63 in sales tax. The money was deposited in the company's bank account using a city branch of the bank.

Each enterprise's accounting system should meet its needs and sophistication.

We'll now work through how these simple events are recorded (if at all) and accumulated in a very simple accounting system. Note that though this system is much simpler than what large companies would have, it probably is all this partnership of actors needs at this stage in its existence. It is important to match the accounting system to the needed level of sophistication.

Step 2: Recording the Transactions in a Journal

A *general journal* to record the transactions above is shown in Exhibit 3.24 below. Exact dates would be necessary in practice, but only the months were given above and they are used below. (Journals and ledgers are recorded to the penny, but we will ignore cents here.)

Northern Star Theatre Company
General Journal

No.	Date	Description	Debits	Credits
1.	Nov. 2005	No transaction so no entry		
2a.	Dec. 2005	Cash (Bank)	450	
		Partners' capital		450
		Initial contributions by partners: 6 × $75, per bank records.		
2b.	Dec. 2005	Performance fees expense	400	
		Cash (Bank)		400
		Fee paid to Fringe to apply for a performance venue in 2006.		
3.	Jan. 2006	No transaction so no entry		
4.	Mar. 2006	No transaction so no entry		
5a.	Mar. 2006	Cash (Bank)	500	
		Partners' capital		500
		Further contributions by five partners: 5 × $100. (No contribution from Fred.)		
5b.	Mar. 2006	Costumes and props expense	470	
		Cash (Bank)		470
		Costumes and props purchased, per suppliers' bills.		

6a.	Jul. 2006	Cash (Bank)	500	
		Partners' capital		500
		Further contributions by five partners: 5 × $100. (No contribution from Fred.)		
6b.	Jul. 2006	Travel expense	290	
		Cash (Bank)		290
		Reimbursement to Elaine for her trip to the city to check out the venue.		
7a.	Aug. 2006	Travel expense	190	
		Accounts payable		190
		Recording the liability to those partners who spent money getting the group to the city for the Fringe.		
7b.	Aug. 2006	Costumes and props expense	610	
		Accounts payable		610
		Recording the liability to various people for sets and props constructed in the city.		
8.	Aug. 2006	Cash (Bank)	897	
		Performance revenue		897
		Gate receipts for the first night.		

Step 3: Posting (Summarizing) Journal Entries in General Ledger

The recorded transactions, *posted* to *general ledger* accounts, are shown in Exhibit 3.25. The accounts are listed in the order in which they arose in the entries, not necessarily in balance sheet or income statement order.

EXHIBIT 3·25

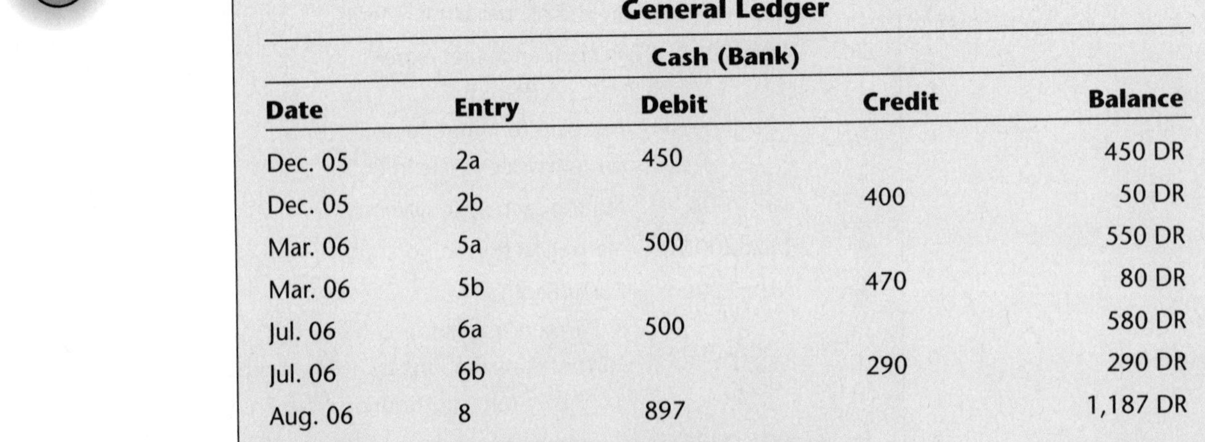

Northern Star Theatre Company
General Ledger

Cash (Bank)

Date	Entry	Debit	Credit	Balance
Dec. 05	2a	450		450 DR
Dec. 05	2b		400	50 DR
Mar. 06	5a	500		550 DR
Mar. 06	5b		470	80 DR
Jul. 06	6a	500		580 DR
Jul. 06	6b		290	290 DR
Aug. 06	8	897		1,187 DR

Partners' Capital

Date	Entry	Debit	Credit	Balance
Dec. 05	2a		450	450 CR
Mar. 06	5a		500	950 CR
Jul. 06	6a		500	1,450 CR

Performance Fees Expense

Date	Entry	Debit	Credit	Balance
Dec. 05	2b	400		400 DR

Costumes and Props Expense

Date	Entry	Debit	Credit	Balance
Mar. 06	5b	470		470 DR
Aug. 06	7b	610		1,080 DR

Travel Expense

Date	Entry	Debit	Credit	Balance
Jul. 06	6b	290		290 DR
Aug. 06	7a	190		480 DR

Accounts Payable

Date	Entry	Debit	Credit	Balance
Aug. 06	7a		190	190 CR
Aug. 06	7b		610	800 CR

Performance Revenue

Date	Entry	Debit	Credit	Balance
Aug. 06	8		897	897 CR

Step 4: Trial Balance to See if Ledger Balances

Now, as we can see from Exhibit 3.26, the ledger balances! This is an *unadjusted trial balance*, because the accounts do not yet include the adjustments necessary for financial statements.

EXHIBIT 3·26

Northern Star Theatre Company
General Ledger Unadjusted Trial Balance, mid-August 2006

Account	Debit	Credit
Cash (Bank)	1,187	
Partners' capital		1,450
Performance fees expense	400	
Costumes and props expense	1,080	
Travel expense	480	
Accounts payable		800
Performance revenue		897
TOTALS	3,147	3,147

The group of actors agreed that a set of financial statements would be a good idea, as soon as the Fringe production was over. A date of August 26, 2006, was selected for the financial statements. Before the play's production ended, however, there were three more cash transactions (continuing the numbering started above):

9. A local printing shop was paid $320 for printing programs and brochures describing the theatre company, to be handed out as people entered the venue to see the play and to be used generally to promote the play. These were available and used the first night, but were not paid for until two days later.
10. Of the amounts owing for props and set materials, the company paid $525.
11. The play was a moderate success. The audience was small after an initial bad review, but more people came to later performances. Total revenue for the remaining performances was $4,840. The group was not invited to perform at any of the "after the Fringe" events, so August 26 turned out to be as good a date as any for partnership financial statements.

Step 5: Accruals and Adjustments

Several matters required decisions and adjustments in order to prepare the August 26 financial statements. Continuing the above numbering sequence, these were:

12. The play's writer was owed her royalty; the agreed upon amount was $450.
13. Additional travel expenses for getting back to the actors' hometown, to be reimbursed to various members of the group, totalled $215.
14. Costumes and props had cost $1,080. The group estimated that costumes and props costing about $420 were not reusable, but that the rest were reusable and would last on average about five engagements, including the just-finished Fringe as one of the five. The actors agreed to keep going, and therefore agreed that the costumes and props could be accounted for on a "going concern" basis, that is, assuming there would continue to be a theatre company and therefore that the usable costumes and props had some future value. As the items had been included in Costumes and props expense, their cost would have to be "*capitalized*": removed from expense and included with the assets.
15. There were some programs and brochures left over. The programs were pretty well useless, but the brochures describing the company could be used to seek future engagements and generally advertise. Brochures costing about $80 were thought still to be useful. (This adjustment works the same way as capitalization of the costumes and props in point 14.)
16. After talking to the bank, one of the actors estimated that, to August 26, about $20 in interest would have been earned by the money in the bank account. This wasn't much, but everyone wanted to see an accurate set of financial statements, so this was deemed material (significant) enough to be included.
17. The actors agreed that they would share any income or loss equally. The one who was broke said that rather than pay any cash in, he would transfer to the other members, out of his share of the income the $200 he had not paid in, to settle his obligation. (This is an example of an adjustment that does not affect income but that is necessary to the balance sheet's *classification* of information.)

Recording and adjusting journal entries look the same; only their objectives differ.

Exhibit 3.27 shows the journal entries to *record* the three additional cash transactions and to *adjust* the accounts to recognize the effects of the additional information.

EXHIBIT 3·27

No.	Date	Description	Debits	Credits
9.	Aug. 06	Programs and brochures expense	320	
		Cash (Bank)		320
		Programs and brochures to be handed out at performances.		
10.	Aug. 06	Accounts payable	525	
		Cash (Bank)		525
		Paying some of what is owed for materials for set and props.		
11.	Aug. 06	Cash (Bank)	4,840	
		Performance revenue		4,840
		Gate receipts for the remaining performances.		
12.	Aug. 06	Royalties expense	450	
		Accounts payable		450
		Royalty owed to author.		
13.	Aug. 06	Travel expense	215	
		Accounts payable		215
		Expenses for getting back to hometown.		
14a.	Aug. 06	Costumes and props asset	660	
		Costumes and props expense		660
		Capitalizing the cost of the costumes and props having future value.		
14b.	Aug. 06	Amortization expense	132	
		Accumulated amortization		132
		Amortization of costumes and props assets: 1/5 of cost for the 2006 Fringe engagement.		
15.	Aug. 06	Brochures inventory	80	
		Programs and brochures expense		80
		Recognizing the inventory of usable brochures still on hand, at cost.		
16.	Aug. 06	Interest receivable	20	
		Interest revenue		20
		Estimated interest earned by the bank account to August 26, 2006.		
17.	Aug. 06	Partners' capital (Fred)	200	
		Partners' capital (Others)		200
		Transfer from Fred to the other partners to make up for the $200 in cash not paid in by Fred as originally agreed. *(This last entry has no effect on the summary figures in the financial statements, but is written to recognize an economic event important to the partners, Fred's agreement to settle his obligation by transferring some of his capital to the other partners. The entry's effects are on the details of partners' balances within the capital account, not on the account's total. The exact form of the entry depends on the partners' decision about how to rearrange their capital accounts.)*		

Step 6: Posting the Remaining Transactions and the Accrual Adjustments

These entries have to be posted, just as the earlier transactional ones were. Do that on your own for practice, starting with the account balances in the trial balance in Exhibit 3.26 (Step 4), and see if you agree with the August 26 trial balance in Exhibit 3.28 below.

Step 7: Another Trial Balance

Exhibit 3.28 shows the *adjusted trial balance* at August 26, 2006, using the original accounts from Step 4 and additional accounts from Step 5. Accounts are now in financial statement order.

Northern Star Theatre Company
General Ledger Adjusted Trial Balance, August 26, 2006

Account	**Debit**	**Credit**
Cash (Bank)	5,182	
Interest receivable	20	
Brochures inventory	80	
Costumes and props	660	
Accumulated amortization		132
Accounts payable		940
Partners' capital		1,450
Performance revenue		5,737
Amortization expense	132	
Costumes and props expense	420	
Performance fees expense	400	
Programs and brochures expense	240	
Royalties expense	450	
Travel expense	695	
Interest revenue		20
TOTALS	8,279	8,279

If you have trouble getting any of these account balances, here are the calculations for some, beginning with the mid-August trial balance from Exhibit 3.26 in Step 4:

Cash = $1,187 – $320 – $525 + $4,840 = $5,182
Accounts payable = $800 – $525 + $450 + $215 = $940
Performance revenue = $897 + $4,840 = $5,737
Costumes and props expense = $1,080 – $660 = $420
Travel expense = $480 + $215 = $695

Revenue and expense accounts are usually closed only at the end of the year.

The financial statements to be drawn up at August 26 are "interim" ones: they are not year-end statements, so the accounts for the year are not closed at this point. *If they were closed on August 26,* the *closing entry* would be:

DR	Performance revenue	5,737	
	CR Amortization expense		132
	CR Costumes and props expense		420
	CR Performance fees expense		400
	CR Programs and brochures expense		240
	CR Royalties expense		450
	CR Travel expense		695
DR	Interest revenue	20	
	CR Partners' capital		3,420

So far in the year, the partnership has an income of $3,420. In the details of the partners' capital, the $3,420 would be allocated to the partners under the agreement among the six actors, so each would be allocated one-sixth, $570. To August 26, none of the partners has withdrawn any share of the income, so the partnership is like a corporation that has not declared any dividends from retained earnings. The financial statements in Step 8 reflect this. (Note that the fourth member of the usual set of financial statements, the cash flow statement, is not included below because it is not covered until Chapter 4 of this book.)

Step 8: The August 26 Financial Statements

EXHIBIT 3.29

Northern Star Theatre Company
Income Statement for the Period
November 5, 2005, to August 26, 2006

Performance revenue		$5,737
Expenses:		
Amortization of costumes and props	$132	
Costumes and props not reusable	420	
Performance fees	400	
Programs and brochures	240	
Royalties	450	
Travel	695	2,337
Operating income		$3,400
Other income (bank interest)		20
Partnership income for the period (*Note 1*)		$3,420

EXHIBIT 3·30

Northern Star Theatre Company
Statement of Partners' Capital for the Period
November 5, 2005, to August 26, 2006

Beginning capital	$ 0
Capital contributed during the period	1,450
Income for the period, per income statement	3,420
Withdrawals during the period	0
Capital at end of the period (*Note 2*)	$4,870

EXHIBIT 3·31

Northern Star Theatre Company
Balance Sheet at August 26, 2006

Assets		
Current assets:		
Cash in bank	$5,182	
Bank interest receivable	20	
Inventory of brochures	80	$5,282
Noncurrent assets:		
Costumes and props, at cost	$ 660	
Less accumulated amortization	(132)	528
TOTAL		$5,810
Liabilities and Capital		
Current liabilities:		
Accounts payable		$ 940
Partners' capital (Note 2)		4,870
TOTAL		$5,810

Northern Star Theatre Company
Notes to the August 26, 2006, Financial Statements

1. The company is an unincorporated partnership of six actors who share incomes and losses equally. No provisions have been made in the financial statements for salaries to the partners or for such personal expenses as income taxes.
2. At August 26, 2006, the six partners' capital accounts are:

	Part. A	Part. B	Part. C	Part. D	Part. E	Part. F	Total
Contributed	$275	$275	$275	$275	$275	$ 75	$1,450
Transfer	40	40	40	40	40	(200)	0
Income	570	570	570	570	570	570	3,420
Capital	$885	$885	$885	$885	$885	$445	$4,870

HOW'S YOUR UNDERSTANDING?

Here are two questions you should be able to answer based on what you have just read. If you can't answer them, it would be best to reread the material.

1. Why are adjusting journal entries necessary?
2. Write adjusting journal entries for the following, decided upon by the partners of Northern Star Theatre Company after they reviewed the financial statements above, and explain what the effect of each is on income for the period since the company began. (1) An unrecorded and unpaid bill for $131 in travel expenses should have been included. (2) The inventory of brochures should have been set at $180, not $80.

The first item: DR Travel expenses 131, CR Accounts payable 131. Income down $131. The second item: DR Inventory of brochures 100, CR Programs and brochures expense 100. Income up $100.

3.9 Demonstration Problem: Accrual Accounting Adjustments

Problem: Starting with a preliminary trial balance, make adjustments to prepare the accounts for financial statements.

An unadjusted trial balance is based on the routine transactional records.

Pelforth Retail Inc. had the preliminary trial balance shown below after the completion of the year's routine recordkeeping. Accountants often refer to such a preliminary trial balance, which requires some adjustments at the year-end, as the *unadjusted trial balance*. Because not all accounts have the appropriate balances yet, the revenue and expense accounts have not yet been closed to retained earnings.

EXHIBIT 3·32

Preliminary Year-End Trial Balance for Pelforth Retail Inc.

	Debits	Credits
Cash	23,000	
Accounts receivable	78,000	
Inventories	216,000	
Prepaid expenses	6,000	
Land	80,000	
Building	240,000	
Furniture and fixtures	110,000	
Accumulated amortization		180,000
Investment in Reddy Ware Corp.	60,000	
Bank loan		70,000
Accounts payable		112,000
Mortgage payable		150,000
Share capital		75,000
Retained earnings (prior to closing)		193,000
Revenue		620,000
Cost of goods sold expense	409,000	
Operating expenses	114,000	
Amortization expense	35,000	
Interest expense	18,000	
Income tax expense	11,000	
	1,400,000	1,400,000

Adjustments are used to bring nonroutine, nontransactional information into the accounts.

The following items are not yet incorporated in the preliminary trial balance:

a. The prepaid expenses have not been adjusted since last year. The appropriate amount of prepaid expenses at the end of this year is $4,000.
b. The investment in Reddy Ware Corp. looks like a loser. Management believes it should be written down to $25,000, its current market value.
c. $2,000 in mortgage and bank loan interest should be accrued, based on the accountant's estimate of unpaid interest at the end of the year.
d. Management believes additional revenue of $15,000 should be recognized as earned, based on some special contracts with customers.
e. The cost of goods sold to go with the above additional revenue is $7,000, so that amount should be removed from inventory.
f. Management believes that an accrual for warranty expense should be made, because some of the products sold this year were unusually badly made. The likely warranty costs to be incurred in the future based on this year's sales are estimated at $3,000. All the warranty costs are expected to be incurred within the next year.
g. An old customer died while on a back-country ski trip, and the management believes the company will not ever collect the $1,000 the customer owed at the end of the year. *This will be adjusted by writing the account receivable directly off to bad debts expense. Later in the book, the more complex accounting for bad debts that is usual in Canada will be explained.*
h. A final adjustment is to the income tax expense. Because all of the above changes the company's income before income tax from the preliminary amount of $44,000 ($620,000 – ($409,000 + $114,000 + $35,000 + $18,000)) down to only $9,000 and the company revises its estimated income tax rate to 33.3%, the estimated income tax expense should be $3,000, not the $11,000 paid already. The company should expect a refund of the difference within a few months.

Adjustments have the same form as any other journal entries.

Let's write adjusting journal entries to implement the decisions and calculations above:

EXHIBIT 3·33

		DR	CR
a.	DR Operating expenses	2,000	
	CR Prepaid expenses		2,000
	To reduce prepaid expenses from $6,000 to $4,000.		
b.	DR Loss on investment (an expense)	35,000	
	CR Investment in Reddy Ware		35,000
	To reduce the investment down to market of $25,000.		
c.	DR Interest expense	2,000	
	CR Accrued interest liability		2,000
	To record estimated accrued mortgage and bank interest.		
d.	DR Accounts receivable	15,000	
	CR Revenue		15,000
	To recognize revenue earned on special contracts.		
e.	DR Cost of goods sold expense	7,000	
	CR Inventories		7,000
	To recognize the COGS for entry (d).		
f.	DR Warranty expense (or Operating expenses)	3,000	
	CR Warranty liability		3,000
	To record estimated warranty expense arising this year.		
g.	DR Bad debts expense	1,000	
	CR Accounts receivable		1,000
	To write off a receivable that will never be collected.		
h.	DR Income tax receivable	8,000	
	CR Income tax expense		8,000
	To reduce tax expense and record estimated refund.		

An adjusted trial balance provides a more complete portrayal than an unadjusted one.

Now, using the same spreadsheet approach as was done for CappuMania in Section 3.6, here are the entries posted to Pelforth's accounts. The final two columns are the *adjusted trial balance*. Note that it has accounts that the preliminary trial balance did not. Accrual accounting adjustments typically make the accounts more complex, because accrual accounting is intended to incorporate more information than the routine accounting system usually does.

EXHIBIT 3·34

	A	B	C	D	E	F	G	H	I
1		Pelforth Retail Inc. Adjustments							
2									
3			Balance April 1, 2005			Adjustments		Balance March 31, 2006	
4		ACCOUNT	DR	CR	#	DR	CR	DR	CR
5									
6	Assets	Cash	23,000					23,000	
7		Accounts receivable	78,000		d.	15,000		92,000	
8					g.		1,000		
9		Inventories	216,000		e.		7,000	209,000	
10		Income tax receivable			h.	8,000		8,000	
11		Prepaid expenses	6,000		a.		2,000	4,000	
12		Land	80,000					80,000	
13		Building	240,000					240,000	
14		Furniture and fixtures	110,000					110,000	
15		Accumulated amortization		180,000					180,000
16		Investment in Reddy Ware Corp.	60,000		b.		35,000	25,000	
17									
18	Liabilities	Accounts payable		112,000					112,000
19		Accrued interest liability			c.		2,000		2,000
20		Bank loan		70,000					70,000
21		Mortgage payable		150,000					150,000
22		Warranty liability			f.		3,000		3,000
23									
24	Equity	Share capital		75,000					75,000
25		Retained earnings (prior to closing)		193,000					193,000
26		**Balance sheet totals**	**813,000**	**780,000**		**23,000**	**50,000**	**791,000**	**785,000**
27									
28	Income Accounts	Revenue		620,000	d.		15,000		635,000
29		Cost of goods sold expense	409,000		e.	7,000		416,000	
30		Operating expenses	114,000		a.	2,000		119,000	
31					f.	3,000			
32		Bad debts expense			g.	1,000		1,000	
33		Amortization expense	35,000					35,000	
34		Interest expense	18,000		c.	2,000		20,000	
35		Loss on investment	–		b.	35,000		35,000	
36		Income tax expense	11,000		h.		8,000	3,000	
37		**Income stmnt. totals**	**587,000**	**620,000**		**50,000**	**23,000**	**629,000**	**635,000**
38									
39		Totals	1,400,000	1,400,000		73,000	73,000	1,420,000	1,420,000

Debits = Credits

Now the company's financial statements can be prepared from the adjusted trial balance. Doing that is left to you as an exercise. You should get total current assets of $336,000, net noncurrent assets of $275,000, total current liabilities of $187,000, noncurrent liability of $150,000, shareholders' equity of $274,000 (including retained earnings, after closing, of $199,000), and net income of $6,000.

HOW'S YOUR UNDERSTANDING?

Here are two questions you should be able to answer based on what you have just read. If you can't answer them, it would be best to reread the material.

1. Brazza Ltd. management wishes to record $12,000 revenue that it believes has been earned on a contract it has with a customer. No revenue for the contract has yet been collected from the customer or previously recorded. What journal entry would accomplish management's wish?

DR Accounts receivable 12,000; CR Revenue 12,000

2. Brazza Ltd. management also wishes to record an additional adjustment. This year, the company began to offer a warranty with its products. Therefore, it incurs an expense for future estimated warranty service costs each time it makes a sale. Management estimates that for the sales recorded so far this year, the warranty costs will be $3,200. What journal entry would record the estimated expense and liability incurred so far?

DR Warranty expense 3,200; CR Liability for estimated warranty costs 3,200

3.10 Managers, Investors, and Managing Earnings

The income statement is a major spotlight on management's performance.

Managers' own incomes, promotions, careers, pensions, and reputations depend on other people's decisions that, in turn, rest to some extent on information in the financial statements, particularly the income statement, and especially where capital markets, such as stock markets, are involved. Managers of large, publicly traded companies are under constant pressure because of the spotlight on earnings (net income or profit) and its components. Business and social observers often comment that this spotlight is too intense, that there is more to managerial performance than the income statement shows, and that the income statement is doubtful as a measure because it reflects the limitations of accrual-based, double-entry accounting. Nevertheless, the spotlight is there.

An indication of the importance placed on the bottom line can be found in the financial section of almost any newspaper in the regular announcements of corporations' annual and/or quarterly earnings. Below are four such announcements from a set of eight reported by the *Globe and Mail* on a single day, December 22, 2005.

Corporate Earnings

Research In Motion Ltd. (PIMM – NASDAQ, RIM – TSX)

	3 Months to Nov. 26	Year Ago
Revenues	560,596,000	365,852,000
Net profit	120,149,000	90,395,000
Net profit per share	0.63	0.48
Average shares	189,341,000	188,284,000

ATI Technologies Inc. (ATY – TSX, ATYT – NASDAQ)

	3 months to Nov. 30	Year ago
Revenues	591,000,000	210,366,000
Net profit	7,626,000	63,703,000
Net profit per share	0.03	0.25
Average shares	256,568,000	257,917,000

Funds in U.S. dollars. Per share are diluted.

Printera Corp. (PAC – TSX)

	3 months to Sept. 30	Year Ago
Revenues	31,300,000	33,500,000
Net profit	(13,400,000)	(4,400,000)
Net profit per share	(0.12)	(0.06)

Cognos Inc. (CSN-TSX)

	3 months to Nov. 30	Year ago
Revenues	560,596,000	210,366,000
Net profit	28,268,000	34,545,000
Net profit per share	0.31	0.38
Cash flow	37,952,000	41,072,000
Average shares	90,410,000	90,621,000
	9 months to Nov. 30	**Year ago**
Revenues	624,371,000	569,205,000
Net profit	80,812,000	82,259,000
Net profit per share	0.89	0.91
Cash flow	101,483,000	104,635,000
Average shares	90,744,000	90,364,000

All figures in U.S. dollars and in accordance with U.S. GAAP

Earnings announcements provide important summary information.

These announcements, which are prepared by the companies but formatted by the newspaper (frequently using the word "profit" rather than "income" or "earnings"), focus on income statement information, including earnings per share. Cash flow information is also included if available—more about this in Chapter 4. Some narrative comments are added if thought helpful.

Stock market prices and earnings tend to be correlated.

Stock market traders pay particular attention to the factors that produce good, or poor, earnings. Stock market prices and earnings are positively correlated: when earnings go up, share prices tend to be going up too, because investors want to buy the shares; and when earnings go down, share prices tend also to be going down, because investors want to sell them. During the year, investors learn about various good or poor management decisions, based on news reports, financial analysts' reports, and other sources, and form expectations about what earnings will be. There is much accounting research to show that the stock market's share price for a company's shares tends to change when the original good or poor news comes out, and then if the earnings announcement is a positive or negative surprise, they change again. The earnings per share are down for all four companies (Methanex had a loss, so negative EPS). The announcement is news, and therefore affects share prices, usually only if it varies from expectations. In general, stock market prices and earnings, as announced from time to time, tend to end up moving in the same direction and so are correlated.

Managers of public companies are very aware of their companies' financial statements.

We can conclude that the performance factors measured by accrual accounting are similar to the factors share buyers and sellers are assessing when they decide to try to buy or sell a corporation's shares. Managers of corporations with traded shares are therefore keenly aware of accounting's income measurement, because accounting is tracking factors investors are concerned about, and if the investors do not learn about these factors from other sources, they will certainly learn about them from the income statement and other financial statements. Managers of many companies, especially (but not only) larger corporations, go to great lengths to explain their performance to investors and to people on whom investors rely, such as stock market analysts and business journalists.

It is harder to tell if the income statement is as important for managers of smaller or private companies, the shares of which are not traded and about which there is less news in general, but there is no reason to think the importance is not comparable. Managers and owner-managers of smaller companies are at least as concerned as managers of larger companies are about management bonuses, income tax, and other effects of the figures in the income statement. Also, great or terrible financial results tend to change confidence of owners of all companies, large and small.

Because of income's importance to managers, they may wish to "manage" the results. Considerable accounting research has been done on *earnings management*, and what it does to share prices, managers' career prospects, and the validity of accrual accounting information. Here are five examples of earnings management.

Income Smoothing

Accrual income generally is smoother than cash income.

Many companies' senior managers choose accounting methods that have the effect of making their reported accounting income look smoother over time than it might otherwise be. "Smooth" here means that income goes up and down less than it might, so that if you plotted a company's income over time, the year-to-year variations would be smaller than they would otherwise be. There is not necessarily any "blame" to managers here, because accrual accounting generally produces a smoother measure of income than cash income does anyway. The cash receipts and payments behind cash income depend on all sorts of factors beyond the economic performance accrual accounting tries to track. For example, making an estimate of future warranty costs and using that to adjust warranty expense each year will usually produce a smoother expense (and so income) than just letting cash payments be the warranty expense, but doing so is also prudent accounting, because those future costs are really a liability that is incurred now, when the products are sold. So a manager who is smoothing income may partly be just being a good accountant!

When managers do make deliberate accounting choices that produce a smoother income, such choices are not necessarily motivated by a wish to mislead—there may be income tax and other good reasons for such choices—but the idea behind *income smoothing* is that managers would prefer the smoother trend of earnings shown in column B below to the trend in column A, even though the total income over the five years is the same and both columns show an increasing trend.

	A (original)	B (smoother)
Income for 2005	$ 1,800,000	$ 4,150,000
Income for 2006	6,570,000	4,310,000
Income for 2007	2,650,000	4,570,000
Income for 2008	8,230,000	4,820,000
Income for 2009	3,620,000	5,020,000
Sum over the 5 years	$22,870,000	$22,870,000

These data are presented in graph form in Figure 3.12. The main reason for wanting to show a smoother trend in earnings seems to be that the smoother trend makes it appear that management has a firm hold on the company, that it is competent and in control of events. The less smooth trend implies more risk, more variation. So if managers are held accountable to owners for keeping risk down, they may prefer the smoother trend.[17]

FIGURE 3.12

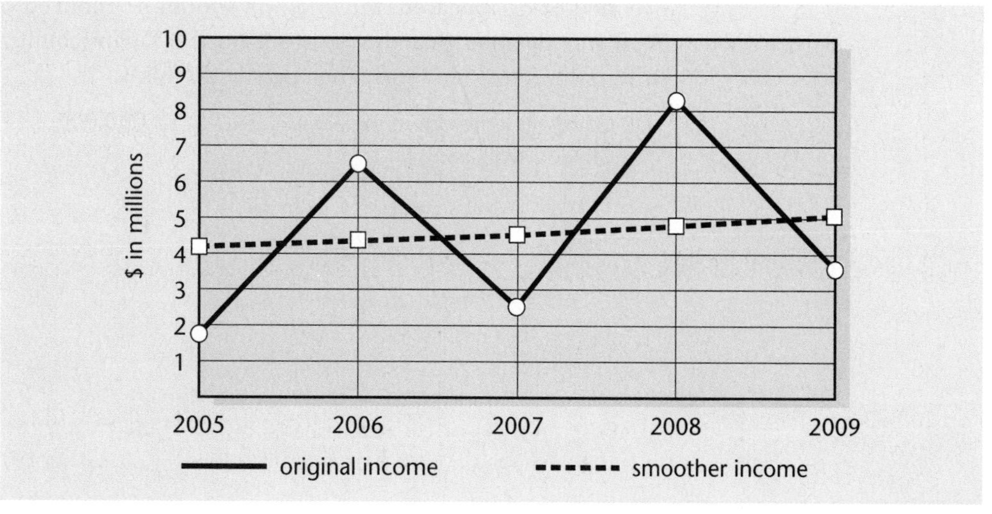

The Big Bath

Accrual accounting may also be used to make income less smooth, as in the Big Bath.

"Counter-smoothing" accounting choices have also been studied by accounting researchers. An example is the so-called *Big Bath,* in which a company having a bad year (poor earnings or even a loss) chooses accounting methods that make the results look even *worse.* Managers apparently think that they are going to be in trouble anyway, and so decide that they won't be in much worse trouble if they make the results even worse by writing off doubtful assets, recognizing future costs as expenses now, or otherwise cleaning up the accounting records. A new president may also want to blame the previous president for past trouble, and so want to clear the accounts of some assets (by charging them off as expenses) that the previous president thought were valuable but the new president thinks are not. This produces a terrible year as far as the accounting numbers go, but increases the chances that in future years, accounting results will be better than would happen without the Bath. An example is writing off the cost of an investment in a factory that the company no longer wishes to operate, rather than keeping the cost on the balance sheet and amortizing it in the future. This leaves less cost to be amortized in the future, and so should mean that future incomes will be higher than they would be otherwise because of lower future amortization expenses.

Write-offs of Consolidated Goodwill

Some recent goodwill write-offs and write-downs have been spectacular.

Consolidated goodwill arises when a company pays more (sometimes much more) for another company than the sum of the fair values of the other company's individual net assets (assets minus liabilities). For example, if High Tech Inc. issues $25 million of its shares for Upandcoming Inc., whose net assets' fair values add up to $5 million, there will be $20 million of goodwill. The entry to record such an acquisition in High Tech's books would be something like this:

DR Individual net assets	5,000,000	
DR Goodwill	20,000,000	
CR Share capital		25,000,000

Goodwill is included on the asset side of the consolidated balance sheet. But, as we will see further in Chapters 8 and 9, it is an awkward asset. Its amount really is what is *not* explained in the acquisition of one company by another (maybe the price was just too high, for example), and its value and useful life as an asset are problematic. Accepted accounting methods require that if this uncertain value should be judged to have declined or disappeared, the goodwill should be reduced or eliminated. Suppose High Tech Inc. decided that the goodwill on the Upandcoming Inc. acquisition should be written down to $2 million. The entry to do this is:

DR Goodwill write-down expense	18,000,000	
CR Goodwill asset		18,000,000

Examples of Large Write-offs

All figures in millions of dollars

Nortel Networks 2001	
Goodwill and intangible assets write-down	$12,810
Restructuring charges	3,359
Total special charges	$16,169
Lucent Technologies 2001	
Business and restructuring charge and asset impairments	$10,157
Qwest Communications 2001	
Investment write-downs	$3,294
AOL Time Warner 2002 First Quarter	
Goodwill write-down (Accounting change)	$54,239

Sometimes these goodwill adjustments can be huge. Here's an example: "AOL Time Warner, the world's biggest media company, announced the world's biggest write-off of goodwill, taking losses in the first quarter to a staggering $54.2 billion."[18] It's like the *Guinness Book of World Records*: not long before, JDS Uniphase Inc. had announced a fiscal year loss of over $50 billion, also due to writing off goodwill. A contest to the bottom, we anxious investors might say. An article commenting on the situation in the *Financial Post* in January 2002 predicted "Goodwill writedowns to hit $1 trillion."[19] Such huge write-downs and write-offs can nearly wipe out a company's equity. They usually mean that the price paid in the acquiring company's shares was much too high.

These very large write-offs and write-downs are like the Big Bath phenomenon, sort of a special case of it resulting from management's recognition that the original goodwill value and so the value of the shares issued for it were seriously wrong. Because such a correction does not affect cash, share prices may not decline very much even when the huge amounts like AOL's and JDS's are announced, but the companies' accrual income figures are devastated.

Inventing New Measures of Income

Be very cautious of newly invented replacements for net income.

Numerous companies, dissatisfied with accrual accounting's net income measure, especially when they have suffered large reversals such as goodwill write-downs, have begun to report other measures of income. Two popular ones are "*EBITDA*," which means "earnings before interest, tax, depreciation and amortization," and "*pro forma earnings*." EBITDA is invariably much more complimentary to the company and its management than net income is, because it leaves out a lot of expenses that are usually quite significant for a company, and doesn't leave out any revenues. It is sort of an *operating income before tax* measure, and you'll remember from Section 3.5 that operating income is a long way up the income statement, leaving out much. It is no replacement for a proper measure of net income that incorporates all the expenses a company must incur, even if incorporating all those makes the company's performance look worse, or makes it negative, as in AOL and JDS's cases.

Pro forma earnings is a similar more optimistic measure, used especially when the company has experienced a seriously bad year and wants investors to focus on how the company thinks it will perform in the future instead. When JDS Uniphase announced its US$50.6 billion loss, it also said it had made a pro forma profit in the same period of $67 million. Management may have hoped that investors would overlook the giant loss and focus instead on the more positive measure of performance calculated without the goodwill write-down and other unpleasant items in the 2001 results.[20]

There are no standard ways of calculating such alternative income measures, so companies can calculate them in any way that makes sense to management. Said a stock market regulator, "These measures present only part of the picture and may selectively omit certain expenses, resulting in a more positive portrayal of a company's performance."[21] So everyone who is using financial statements needs to be very cautious of such measures. Accrual net income is not perfect by any means, but its objective is to be comprehensive, not selective. As another article said, reporting comments by the head of Canada's accounting standards board, "...companies ... that place more emphasis on pro-forma results than on those produced by generally accepted accounting principles (GAAP) are confusing investors by 'inventing their own analysis.'"[22]

Stock Options as Compensation

Stock options are employee compensation.

Companies often provide motivation to managers and other employees in the form of *stock options.* These can be very complex, but essentially the idea is that the employees get the right to buy company shares at less than market value. For example, an employee might be given an option to buy a certain number of shares (let's say 100 shares) for $20 each. If the shares of the company are currently trading for $30 on the market, the employee has the right to buy 100 shares at $20 for a total of $2,000. In the open market, the employee can immediately sell the shares for $30 each or a total of $3,000 ($30 × 100) and make an instant profit of $1,000. The company has given its employee a $10 per share benefit or total compensation worth $1,000. If the shares are now worth less than $20, the option can usually be exercised some time in the future. The employee then hopes that the company's share price moves above $20, the fixed price that he or she can purchase the shares for. There is no risk for the employee since the option to buy shares does not have to be used if the share price does not increase. This form of compensation is a direct reward that is tied to the company's performance and share price.

So, why does this matter in calculating income? It's all in the way that companies account for these stock options as a form of compensation. There are two broad methods of accounting for such options. The first way is to ignore the benefit the employee gets and just record any issue of shares the usual way. In the above example, DR Cash $20, CR Share capital $20 (for each share), which has been the practice in the past. This method avoids accounting for the extra benefit that the employee could receive from exercising the option (the $10/share of profit). This way, the extra $1,000 that is effectively employee compensation is not counted on the income statement as an expense. In theory, a company could pay an employee $1,000 less in salary, grant the stock option and have earnings of $1,000 extra without hurting the employee. The consequences of the stock option compensation are a dilution of the interest of present shareholders since the number of shares has increased.

We are moving toward accounting for stock option compensation as an expense.

The second way is to record the extra benefit as an expense, as part of the wages and other compensation paid to employees. In the past, companies have not used this method, which would result in an increased wages expense thus decreasing earnings. In the above example, DR Wages expense $X, CR Options liability $X. There are several ways of coming up with $X, for example if the option above is immediately exercisable, $X would be $10. If there are some years before it can be exercised, the amount would be estimated based on what the expectation of the future market value of the shares is, and would be adjusted each year until the options were exercised or expired. The accounting details are a headache, but we are moving toward some way of recording as an expense the value provided to the employees by giving them such options. This expense would be recorded on the income statement and decrease the company's earnings by appearing as a form of compensation.

Formerly, using the first method above, these plans were not included as expenses, which was misleading since the true value of employee compensation was not disclosed. In 2002, Toronto-Dominion Bank became one of the first major Canadian companies to announce that it would expense stock options in its quarterly earnings. This reporting expense would impact earnings by "3–5 Canadian cents a share in the first year."[23] Accounting standards are now moving toward a system that will require the fair value of these options to be recorded and disclosed.

Stock options have become a popular method of compensating top executives of many major corporations. The theory is that by granting stock options, management will be motivated to increase the company's share price, benefiting all shareholders. They have come under fire recently, since they can be very large and represent a transfer of wealth from shareholders to such executives. For example, the former CEO (chief executive officer) of Nortel Networks Corp. made over $130 million in profit from stock option compensation in 2000 before Nortel's share price evaporated in 2001.[24] The CEO of Disney had total compensation in 1998, including salary, bonuses, and stock options, of U.S.$589 million with $570 million in stock option gains.[25] The CEO of JDS Uniphase received more than "$150 million US in stock option profit (before income tax and broker fees)" in 2000 even while JDS Uniphase had negative earnings.[26]

3.11 Terms to Be Sure You Understand

This chapter introduced more terms and emphasized some already introduced in earlier chapters. If you don't understand any of these, check the chapter again or refer to the glossary of terms at the end of the book.

Accounts receivable
Accrual accounting
Accrual basis
Accrual income
Adjusted journal entries
Adjusted trial balance
Adjustment(s)
Articulation
Big Bath
Board of directors
Capital markets
Capitalize(d)
Classification
Close
Closing entry
Corporation
Cost of goods sold (COGS)
Deficit
Discontinued operations
Dividend
Earnings
Earnings management
Earnings per share (EPS)
EBITDA
Economic entity
Expenditure(s)
Expense(s)
Extraordinary item(s)
Financial performance
General journal
General ledger
Gross margin
Gross profit
Income from continuing operations
Income smoothing
Income statement
Interperiod tax allocation
Intraperiod tax allocation
Inventory
Material
Net income
Net loss
Operating income before tax
Post(ed)
Post-closing trial balance
Pro forma earnings
Revenue(s)
Statement of retained earnings
Stewardship
Stock dividends
Stock markets
Stock options
Trial balance
Unadjusted trial balance
Unusual items

DATA FOR INSTALLMENT 3

Mato Inc.'s First Six Months

During the first six months of the company's existence, life was hectic for Mavis and Tomas. The main pressure was to get set up and get goods out to retailers in time for the heavy selling season from July to December. Mavis regretted several times not having started earlier, because it took much more time to make arrangements with suppliers and retailers and get goods delivered than she had expected. The first six months did generate some revenues, but the period was largely one of building.

Some important events took place in the six months to August 31, 2006.

- The warehouse space was occupied in early March, and the renovations ("leasehold improvements," consisting of partitions, shelving, and other fixtures) were completed in early June, a month later than had been desired.
- A computer was bought to handle the company's accounting, purchases, sales, inventory, and customer relations records, plus software packages suitable to these tasks.
- Tomas quit his bank job and began to work full-time for the company in July, after having devoted most of his evenings and weekends to the company since March.
- Mavis travelled around the region, to talk to retail boutique owners and line up orders, and out of the region to meet with suppliers. The company ran up large phone bills in connection with all the business development activity, but that had been anticipated in the business plan.
- Finding that they did not have enough cash to keep operating, Tomas and Mavis arranged for a demand bank loan. This money was primarily used to finance the needed level of inventory.
- In mid-August, an employee was hired to maintain all the records and help Mavis organize her activities.

RESULTS FOR INSTALLMENT 3

Journal entries to record the first six months' events follow, in summarized form.

1. Dr Leasehold improvements asset	63,964	
Dr Equipment and furniture asset	29,740	
Dr Computer equipment asset	14,900	
Dr Software asset	4,800	
Cr Accounts payable		113,404
Noncurrent assets acquired during the six months.		
2. Dr Inventory	101,816	
Cr Accounts payable		101,816
Inventory purchased during the six months.		
3. Dr Accounts receivable	42,674	
Cr Revenues		42,674
Revenues for the six months.		
4. Dr Cost of goods sold expense	28,202	
Cr Inventory		28,202
Cost of goods sold for the six months.		

	Debit	Credit
5. Dr. Salary expense—Mavis	15,000	
Dr Salary expense—Tomas	9,280	
Dr Salary expense—Other	1,200	
Dr Travel expense	8,726	
Dr Telephone expense	2,461	
Dr Rent expense	12,000	
Dr Utilities expense	1,629	
Dr Office and general expenses	3,444	
Cr Accounts payable		53,740
Remaining expenses for the six months.		
6. Dr Cash	23,951	
Cr Accounts receivable		23,951
Collections from customers for the six months.		
7. Dr Cash	75,000	
Cr Bank loan		75,000
Demand bank loan obtained.		
8. Dr Accounts payable	224,444	
Cr Cash		224,444
Cash payments for the six months.		

There was also one large adjusting journal entry. Tomas recorded amortization on the physical and nonphysical assets, improvements to leased premises, and computer software as follows: car, leasehold improvements, computer, and software: 1/2 year × 20% of cost; other equipment and furniture: 1/4 year × 10% of cost.

	Debit	Credit
9. Dr Amortization expense—auto	1,000	
Cr Accumulated amortization—auto		1,000
Dr Amortization expense—leasehold improvements	6,396	
Cr Accumulated amortization—leasehold improvements		6,396
Dr Amortization expense—equipment	744	
Cr Accumulated amortization—equipment		744
Dr Amortization expense—computer	1,490	
Cr Accumulated amortization—computer		1,490
Dr Amortization expense—software	480	
Cr Accumulated amortization—software		480
Amortization recorded for the six months.		

Posting these entries to the accounts and incorporating the beginning balance sheet figures from Installment 2 (Section 2.13) produce the following adjusted trial balance at August 31, 2006. (If you are not sure where any of these amounts come from, just take any account, start with the March 1 balance, and add/subtract the entries above that affect the account.)

Debit balance accounts		Credit balance accounts	
Cash	$ 4,507	Bank loan	$ 75,000
Accounts receivable	18,723	Accounts payable	45,616
Inventory	73,614	Loan payable	15,000
Automobile	10,000	Share capital	125,000
Leasehold improvements	63,964	Revenues	42,674
Equipment and furniture	29,740	Accum. amort.—auto.	1,000
Computer	14,900	Accum. amort.—leasehold imp.	6,396
Software	4,800	Accum. amort.—equip.	744
Incorporation costs	1,100	Accum. amort.—computer	1,490
Cost of goods sold expense	28,202	Accum. amort.—software	480
Salary—Mavis	15,000		
Salary—Tomas	9,280		
Salary—other	1,200		
Travel expense	8,726		
Telephone expense	2,461		
Rent expense	12,000		
Utilities expense	1,629		
Office and general expenses	3,444		
Amort. expense—auto.	1,000		
Amort. expense—leasehold imp.	6,396		
Amort. expense—equipment	744		
Amort. expense—computer	1,490		
Amort. expense—software	480		
	$313,400		$313,400

From that trial balance, Tomas prepared the following financial statements for the new company.

Mato Inc.
Statement of Loss and Deficit
for the Six Months Ended August 31, 2006

Revenues		$42,674
Cost of goods sold		28,202
Gross profit		$14,472
Operating expenses:		
Salaries	$25,480	
Travel	8,726	
Telephone	2,461	
Rent	12,000	
Utilities	1,629	
Office and general	3,444	
Amortization	10,110	63,850
Net loss for the six months (no tax)		$49,378
Deficit as at August 31, 2006		$49,378

Mato Inc.
Balance Sheets as at August 31 and March 1, 2006

Assets	**August**	**March**	**Liabilities and Shareholders' Equity**	**August**	**March**
Current assets:			Current liabilities:		
Cash	$ 4,507	$130,000	Bank loan	$ 75,000	$ 0
Receivables	18,723	0	Payables	45,616	1,100
Inventory	73,614	0	Loan payable	15,000	15,000
	$ 96,844	$130,000		$135,616	$ 16,100
Noncurrent assets:			Shareholders' equity:		
Equip. cost	$ 54,640	$ 10,000	Share capital	$125,000	$125,000
Equip. acc. amort.	(3,234)	0	Deficit	(49,378)	0
Leasehold (net)*	57,568	0		$ 75,622	$125,000
Software (net)**	4,320	0			
Incorp. costs	1,100	1,100			
	$114,394	$ 11,100			
TOTAL	$211,238	$141,100	TOTAL	$211,238	$141,100

* Net book value of leasehold improvements = $63,964 cost – $6,396 accumulated amortization.
** Net book value of software = $4,800 – $480 accumulated amortization.

3.13 Homework and Discussion to Develop Understanding

The problems roughly follow the outline of the chapter. Three main categories of questions are presented.

- Asterisked problems (*) have an informal solution provided in the Student Solutions Manual.
- EXTENDED TIME problems grant a thorough examination of the material and may take longer to complete.
- CHALLENGING problems are more difficult.

For further explanation, please refer to Section 1.15.

Historical Financial Performance Reporting • Section 3.2

Understanding the Historical Basis of Reporting

*** PROBLEM 3.1** Creation of the income statement

Why did the creation of long-lived corporations with dispersed ownership lead to a demand for a periodic measure of financial performance?

PROBLEM 3.2 Standards of income reporting

Why have accounting concepts, standards, and principles been developed? Why not let every company measure its financial performance in whatever way makes sense to management?

PROBLEM 3.3 Employ a historical viewpoint of financial reporting

Put yourself in the position of a shareholder in The Hudson's Bay Company in its early years. The company had major land rights in North America and traded goods from Europe for furs produced by native trappers and settlers. It was managed from England but did all of its business in North America. What would you like to know about its financial performance?

Income and Retained Earnings Statements • Section 3.3

Identification of Elements of the I/S and R/E Statement

*** PROBLEM 3.4** Basic balance sheet, income, and retained earnings ideas

Labott's Bottlery Ltd. had the following recent balance sheet:

Labott's Bottlery Ltd.
Balance Sheet as at September 30, 2006

Cash	$1,642	Mortgage	$1,000
Inventory	1,480	Share capital	3,000
Land	2,100	Retained earnings	1,222
	$5,222		$5,222

1. Why is "land" on the balance sheet, and what does it represent?
2. On October 5, 2006, the company borrowed $2,410 from the bank and used the money immediately to buy more land. What was the total dollar figure of the company's assets after this point?

3. Why did the company not just use the $3,000 share capital to buy more land instead of borrowing from the bank?
4. Explain how "retained earnings" comes to be on the balance sheet and what it represents.
5. For the year ended September 30, 2006, the company's revenues were $10,116, and its expenses (including income tax) were $9,881. What was its net income for the year?
6. During the year ended September 30, 2006, the company declared dividends of $120. Considering this and part (5), what was the balance in retained earnings at the *beginning* of that year (October 1, 2005)?
7. If the expenses for the year to September 30, 2006, were $11,600 instead of the figure in part 5, and the company did not declare any dividends, what would the retained earnings be at September 30, 2006?
8. The answer to part 7 is a negative number, which would be a deficit. Would you think such a deficit should be shown with the assets on the left side of the company's balance sheet, so that it becomes a positive number, rather than showing it as a negative number deducted from equity on the right side of the balance sheet? Why or why not?

PROBLEM 3.5 Identify common business transactions

Below are two lists. The left-hand list describes *half* of a common business transaction, and the right-hand list identifies various kinds of business transactions. Match the list on the left to that on the right.

a. Accounts payable go down	1. Acquisition of a noncurrent asset
b. Accounts receivable go down	2. Another business acquired
c. Accounts receivable go up	3. Collections from customers
d. Employee tax deducted goes down	4. Cost of goods sold
e. Factory asset goes up	5. Dividend declared
f. Goodwill goes up	6. Goods purchased
g. Inventory goes down	7. Payment of tax to the government
h. Inventory goes up	8. Payment to creditors
i. Retained earnings go down	9. Revenue earned
j. Sales tax due goes up	10. Tax collected for the government

PROBLEM 3.6 Identify items as revenues or expenses

State whether or not, and why, each of the following items is likely to be a revenue or expense for this year of the company indicated:

Company	Item
1. Noranda Inc.	Cost of advertising for new employees
2. Royal Bank of Canada	Cost of renovating its main Winnipeg branch
3. Zellers	Increased value of the land under Zellers department stores
4. Wendy's Restaurants	Food sold to customers who paid with their Visa cards
5. The Bay	A lawsuit by a customer who fell down the escalator and was injured
6. Northern Gold Mines Ltd.	Cost of issuing new shares to raise funds for exploration
7. ABC Travel Agency	Bribes paid to resorts to try to get favourable bookings for clients
8. Grand Centre Ltd.	Income taxes paid in France
9. Advanced Management Ltd.	Special good-performance bonuses promised this year but not to be paid until next year
10. Advanced Management Ltd.	Special dividends to owners, all of whom are also employees
11. Sears Inc.	Decreased value of the land under some of its inner-city locations
12. Procter & Gamble Inc.	Cost of scientific research aimed at developing new products
13. General Motors Inc.	Estimated amount of money needed to provide pensions to this year's employees when they retire
14. Hattie's Handbags Ltd.	Goods lost to shoplifting
15. Hattie's Handbags Ltd.	Salary of floor-walker who tries to catch shoplifters
16. PCL Construction Ltd.	Contract payments to be received over the next five years for construction work on a large bridge project

Format of the Income and Retained Earnings Statements • Sections 3.4, 3.5

Preparing Financial Statements from Accounts

* **PROBLEM 3.7** Prepare a simple set of financial statements from accounts.

Following are account balances of Arctic Limo Services Ltd. Prepare a 2006 income statement, a 2006 statement of retained earnings, and comparative 2005 and 2006 balance sheets. (Note that the 2006 income and dividends have not yet been closed to retained earnings.) State any assumptions you feel are necessary.

	September 30, 2006	September 30, 2005
Accumulated amortization	$ 30,000	$20,000
Cash on hand	2,000	4,000
Dividends declared	80,000	
Due from Lucky Eddie		1,000
Due to Amalgamated Loansharks		10,000
Income tax expense	35,000	
Limousines amortization expense	10,000	
Limousines cost	90,000	60,000
Long-term limousine financing	50,000	30,000
Other expenses	70,000	
Retained earnings	4,000	4,000
Revenue	300,000	
Share capital	1,000	1,000
Wages expense	100,000	
Wages payable	2,000	

PROBLEM 3.8 Prepare statements of income and retained earnings

Prepare properly classified statements of income and retained earnings from the following items listed in alphabetical order. Not all items are relevant to the solution.

Beginning retained earnings	2,527,980
Cost of goods sold	3,518,350
Cost of redeeming shares during year	27,300
Deferred revenue liability	165,000
Dividends declared during year	125,000
Error correction (prior year's expense too high)	4,400
Extraordinary gain	60,000
Gain on sale of building	40,000
Goodwill	180,000
Income tax expense	321,300
Interest expense	207,750
Interest income	20,940
Investment in marketable securities	315,000
Loss on discontinued operations	300,000
Operating expenses	1,685,300
Revenue	6,300,750

EXTENDED TIME

PROBLEM 3.9 Prepare financial statements from accounts

A list of accounts for Geewhiz Productions at November 30, 2006, is shown below, in no particular order.

Salaries expense	$ 78,000	Dividends declared	$ 14,000
Income tax payable	3,200	Accumulated amortization	108,000
Land	74,000	Cash in bank	27,000
Employee benefits expense	13,200	Income tax expense	8,100
Tax deductions payable	6,100	Credit sales revenue	402,200
Accounts receivable	18,600	Inventory on hand	78,000
Cash sales revenue	33,400	Prepaid insurance asset	3,200
Dividends payable	7,500	Beginning retained earnings	96,600
Amortization expense	37,200	Accounts payable	53,000
Cost of goods sold expense	184,100	Interest income	2,100
Insurance expense	13,800	Building	346,000
Share capital	300,000	Trucks and equipment	253,400
Office expenses	46,200	Salaries payable	5,200
Mortgage payable	169,800	Miscellaneous expenses	9,700
Bank loan owing	37,900	Interest expense	20,500

1. Decide which ones are income statement accounts.
2. Calculate net income based on your answer to part 1.
3. Calculate ending retained earnings based on your answer to part 2.
4. Prepare the following financial statements, demonstrating that your answers to parts 2 and 3 are correct:
   a. Income statement for the year ended November 30, 2006.
   b. Statement of retained earnings for the year ended on that date.
   c. Balance sheet at November 30, 2006.
5. Comment briefly on what the financial statements show about the company's performance for the year 2006 and financial position at November 30, 2006.

EXTENDED TIME

PROBLEM 3.10 Prepare month-end financial statements from accounts

Matilda Jamison runs a successful second-hand clothing shop, Waltzing Matilda's Boutique Ltd. She buys quality new and used clothes from several sources and then sells them at reasonable prices. To establish her business, Matilda invested $2,500 of her savings and her mother contributed $500. Both received shares in the company in return for their investment, so the company's share capital is $3,100. The company also took out a $4,500 bank loan.

Matilda rents retail space in a shopping mall on a monthly basis at $200 per month. She pays rent in advance for a six-month period (in other words, $1,200 twice a year) on January 1 and July 1 of every year. The company owns the display units, racks, shelving, and hangers she uses in her business, which cost $3,600 in total. She expects these items to last for five years and has, therefore, amortized them by $720 per year ($3,600/5 years = $720 per year). The resulting accumulated amortization is included on the balance sheet. The insurance policy is an annual policy purchased January 1 for $1,800.

Matilda pays her employees for work done from the 1st to the 15th of each month, on or about the 20th of each month. As a result, half of the wages earned by employees during the month have been paid (that earned from the 1st to the 15th of the month) and the remaining half is still payable. The company's income tax rate is 20%. Matilda transfers (closes) her revenues and expenses to retained earnings monthly, so revenue and expense accounts contain only one month's data at a time.

From the account balances at the end of April 2006 shown below, prepare income and retained earnings statements for Waltzing Matilda's Boutique Ltd. for the month of April 2006 and a balance sheet as at April 30, 2006. Notes to the statements are not necessary.

	Resources	Sources
Balance sheet accounts as at April 30, 2006:		
Cash	$ 960	
Accounts receivable	1,600	
Inventory of unsold goods	12,000	
Office supplies on hand	600	
Prepaid insurance	1,200	
Prepaid rent	500	
Shelving/hangers/display units	3,600	
Accumulated amortization	(1,680)	
Bank loan		$ 4,500
Accounts payable		3,200
Wages payable		750
Taxes payable		1,600
Share capital		3,000
Retained earnings March 31, 2006		3,530
Income statement accounts for April 2006:		
Revenue		11,000
Cost of goods sold		(5,500)
Wages		(1,500)
Insurance		(150)
Rent		(250)
Janitor and miscellaneous		(670)
Office supplies used		(75)
Interest		(45)
Amortization		(60)
Income tax		(550)
	$18,780	$18,780

Interpreting Financial Statement Relationships

*** PROBLEM 3.11** Derive accounting numbers

Fill in the blanks in the following schedule of financial accounting numbers for Vekeng Corporation. Start with 2004 and work forward from there.

	2004	2005	2006	2007
Revenue for the year	$ 38,000	_____	$ 61,000	$ 65,000
Expenses for the year (except income tax)	_____	42,000	50,000	_____
Income before income tax for the year	9,000	7,000	_____	4,000
Income tax expense for the year	2,000	_____	_____	1,000
Net income for the year	_____	5,500	8,000	_____
Retained earnings, beginning of the year	_____	_____	_____	_____
Dividends declared during the year	3,000	_____	4,500	0
Retained earnings, end of year	25,000	_____	33,000	_____
Other owners' equity, end of year	35,000	38,000	38,000	_____
Liabilities, end of year	_____	85,000	111,000	105,000
Assets, end of year	140,000	152,500	_____	189,000

PROBLEM 3.12 Income and retained earnings format with special items

The accounts for Prentice Retail Ltd. for last year included the following (in alphabetical order):

Correction of error in previous year's income	CR	$ 2,430
Cost of disposing of an unneeded division	DR	65,600
Dividends declared	DR	87,000
Income tax expense	DR	127,700
Income tax saved by disposing of division	CR	25,125
Loss on expropriation of land by municipality	DR	14,950
Miscellaneous revenue from investments	CR	24,810
Operating expenses	DR	1,778,170
Retained earnings, beginning of year	CR	354,290
Revenue from sales	CR	2,222,610

Prepare an income statement and statement of retained earnings for the company for last year, in as good a form as you can with the information provided.

PROBLEM 3.13 Correct a set of financial statements

WideAway Manufacturing Ltd. hired a new accountant without checking the person's qualifications too thoroughly. The accountant worked away diligently on the financial statements for 2006, but was unable to remember where everything was supposed to go, and could not get the balance sheet to balance even though the computer showed that the underlying accounts were all correct, so the balance sheet certainly should have balanced!

The accountant's financial statements are below. Redo them in correct form. (If you do, the balance sheet will balance.)

WideAway Manufacturing Ltd.
Balance Sheet as at December 31, 2006

Assets		Liabilities and Equity	
Current assets:		Current liabilities:	
Cash	$ 52,000	Bank loan	$ 35,000
Inventory	116,000	Accounts payable	98,000
Cost of goods sold	538,000	Income tax expense	41,000
Share capital	150,000	Current portion of mortgage	22,000
Current assets	$856,000	Amortization expense	74,000
Noncurrent assets:		Current liabilities	$270,000
Factory	$612,000	Noncurrent liabilities:	
Mortgage (minus current)	(242,000)	Other noncurrent liabilities	$ 16,000
Net noncurrent assets	$370,000	Shareholders' equity:	
		Land	$100,000
		Retained earnings (below)	656,000
		Equity	$756,000
Total	$1,226,000	Total	$1,042,000

WideAway Manufacturing Ltd.
Statement of Income and Retained Earnings
for the Year Ended December 31, 2006

Revenues:		
Revenue	$949,000	
Add accounts receivable	117,000	$1,066,000
Expenses:		
Operating expenses	$229,000	
Accumulated amortization	236,000	
Prepaid expenses	21,000	
Current portion of mortgage	22,000	
Dividend declared	20,000	528,000
Income before income tax		$538,000
Income taxes payable		27,000
Net income for the year		$511,000
Retained earnings—beginning of year		145,000
Retained earnings—end of year		$656,000

Income and Retained Earnings Statement Preparation • Sections 3.6, 3.7

Journal Entry Transactions

* **PROBLEM 3.14** Identify transactions and write journal entries for them

The following events took place on February 1, 2006. For each event, give the journal entry (if any) that should be made to record the transaction in the account of Smith Ltd. Indicate clearly where in the financial statements you think the accounts involved belong. State any assumptions you feel are necessary.

a. The company purchased supplies to be used immediately. The purchase price of the supplies was $5,000. Only $2,000 was paid in cash, on delivery. The balance is due in 30 days.
b. The company decided to rent a service vehicle for $4,800 per year. A rental contract was signed February 1, 2006, to take effect March 1, 2006. Smith Ltd. paid $400 cash to the rental company on February 1, 2006, which represented the rent for March 2006.
c. Some of Smith's repairmen were not busy on February 1. The manager had them paint the inside of a storage room. The repairmen's salaries of $300 were paid in cash at the end of the day.
d. A shareholder sold her car to the company. The vehicle had cost her $15,000 two years ago. An equivalent used vehicle would have been worth about $8,000 on February 1, 2006. No cash changed hands, but the shareholder expects the company to pay her for the car eventually.
e. An invoice for $5,000 was received, relating to repairs and maintenance work done in December 2005. The company's year-end is December 31. This expense was not recorded in the 2005 financial statements.

PROBLEM 3.15 Identify transactions and write journal entries for them

Southward Stores Ltd. is a general merchandise retailer operating in the suburbs. During a recent month, the events listed below happened. For each event, decide if it is an accounting transaction. If it is an accounting transaction, state briefly why and record it in journal entry form. Indicate where in the financial statements you wish each account to appear. If it is not an accounting transaction, state briefly why it is not.

a. Southward borrowed $500,000 from the Great Pacific Bank (Canada). Payment is due in three years, but the loan can be called on ten days' notice if Southward fails to make any of the monthly interest payments, which begin next month.
b. Southward ordered inventory for resale costing $300,000, to be delivered in 40 days, and sent a deposit of $10,000 with the order.
c. Southward renewed its lease on the store premises, signing an agreement which provides that, beginning in three months, the monthly rent will rise from $21,000 to $23,000.
d. Southward was charged with unfair pricing of its main line of merchandise. News of this sent the company's shares (listed on a stock exchange) down in price from $10 to $8.50 each. The company has 1,000,000 shares outstanding, all publicly traded.
e. The board of directors declared a dividend of $0.50 per share, to be paid in one week, on each of its 1,000,000 outstanding shares. This news sent the company's shares up by $0.40 each on the stock exchange.
f. A customer agreed to buy a TV for $800, to be paid in a month, and took away the TV, which has cost Southward $580.
g. Southward granted its executives stock options to buy 10,000 shares for $12 each. None of the options have been exercised yet.
h. A junior employee had a plumber come in and fix a store sink. The plumber billed Southward $200.
i. Southward purchased a new display unit on credit for $750. It has the option to buy two more units next month.

PROBLEM 3.16 Reconstruct journal entries from T-accounts

Sanderson Electronics is a new retail store that sells mainly small parts, such as switches, circuit boards, and wire. Sanderson's ledger accounts are shown below in T-account form, with entries made for the first month of business.

Cash	
(a) 30,000	(c) 1,200
(f) 1,300	(h) 1,000
(g) 650	(j) 560

Accounts Receivable	
(e) 900	(g) 650
(f) 1,400	

Prepaid Supplies	
(i) 300	

Equipment	
(c) 3,600	

Inventory	
(b) 5,000	(e) 540
	(f) 1,620

Accounts Payable	
(h) 1,000	(b) 5,000
	(d) 700

Notes Payable	
(j) 500	(c) 2,400

Common Shares	
	(a)30,000

Sales Revenue	
	(e) 900
	(f) 2,700

Supplies Expense	
(d) 700	(i) 300

Interest Expense	
(j) 60	

Cost of Goods Sold	
(e) 540	
(f) 1,620	

For each of the transactions from (a) to (j), write the general journal entry that was used to post the accounts, including an explanation of the entry.

Explanation of Account Changes

*** PROBLEM 3.17** Explain and write entries for changes in account balances

The following changes were observed in Boddin Inc.'s accounts. For each of the ten items, say in a few words what would have caused the changes and write a journal entry to account for them. Here is an example: Cash up $5,000, Bank loan up $5,000. The cause would have been that the company borrowed $5,000 from the bank. Journal entry: DR Cash 5,000, CR Bank loan 5,000.

1. Accounts payable up $573, Repairs expense up $573.
2. Revenue up $1,520, Cash up $200, Accounts receivable up $1,320.
3. Share capital up $2,000, Cash up $2,000.
4. Retained earnings down $500, Cash down $500.
5. Accounts receivable down $244, Cash up $244.
6. Mortgage payable down $1,000, Cash down $1,000.
7. Inventory up $2,320, Accounts payable up $2,320.
8. Inventory down $400, Cost of goods sold expense up $400.
9. Building up $25,000, Cash down $5,000, Mortgage payable up $20,000.
10. Revenue down $249,320 (to zero), Retained earnings up $249,320.

PROBLEM 3.18 Explain and write entries for changes in account balances

Here are more account changes that occurred to Boddin Inc. (see Problem 3.17* for others, including an example). For each of the ten items, say in a few words what would have caused the changes and write a journal entry to account for them.

1. Accounts payable down $3,220, Cash down $3,220.
2. Income tax expense up $5,900, Cash down $5,000, Income tax payable up $900.
3. Travel advances receivable up $200, Cash down $200.
4. Travel advances receivable down $200, Cash up $11, Travel expenses up $189.
5. Cash up $350, Customer deposits liability up $350.
6. Auditing expense up $3,000, Accounts payable up $2,400, cash down $600.
7. Equipment up $5,200, Share capital up $5,200.
8. Share capital down $1,000, Cash down $1,000.
9. Cash up $1,200, Accounts receivable up $3,300, Revenue up $4,500, Inventory down $2,750, Cost of goods sold expense up $2,750.

10. Cost of goods sold expense down $147,670 (to zero), Retained earnings down $147,670.

CHALLENGING

PROBLEM 3.19 Explain and write entries for incompletely described changes in account balances

BranBolter Inc. had the following changes in some of its accounts. Most changes are not completely described, so you will have to think about the rest of what happened. For each item, state in a few words what probably caused the changes and write a journal entry to account for them, consistent with your explanation. (For a simple example, see the beginning of Problem 3.17*.)

1. Inventory down $387, Inventory shortage expense up $387.
2. Retained earnings down $5,000, Cash down $2,000.
3. Investment in Bozo Mining Inc. down $40,000 (to zero), Cash up $5,000.
4. Long-term debt down $10,000, Share capital up $10,000.
5. Inventory up $3,290, Cash down $748.
6. Bonuses payable up $5,200.
7. Lawsuit loss expense up $40,200, Legal fees expense up $11,340.
8. Demand bank loan up $32,000.
9. Accounts receivable up $24,000, Inventory up $36,000, Factory assets up $100,000, Goodwill up $40,000.
10. Expenses down $743,210 (to zero), Revenues down $730,670 (to zero).

Preparing Financial Statements from Transactions

*** PROBLEM 3.20** Journal entries and statements for a small new business

Graham Cline, a second-year university student, was tired of low-paying, temporary summer work. He decided to go into business by setting up a company, Graham Cline Inc., to sell hot dogs in city parks over the summer.

The company commenced operations on January 1, 2004, and completed its first year of operations on December 31, 2004. During the year, the following events occurred:

a. On January 1, 2004, the company issued 100 shares to Graham at $1 each. In addition, Graham's father lent the company $5,000. The loan has no repayment terms and is not interest bearing.
b. On January 1, 2004, Graham Cline Inc. negotiated a contract with a local butcher shop to store its supplies in a refrigerated locker. Looking to the future, the company signed a two-year agreement that would expire December 31, 2005. The agreement called for payments of $120 on January 1, 2004 (which was made), and $130 to be made on January 1, 2005.
c. On June 1, 2004, Graham Cline Inc. purchased food for the summer for cash, consisting of 500 dozen buns at $1 per dozen and 500 dozen wieners at $3 per dozen.
d. On June 1, 2004, Graham Cline Inc. purchased two portable hot dog stands from a retiring vendor for $300 each. The company agreed to pay the former owner $100 at the purchase date, and the balance plus interest at 10% per year on December 31, 2004. The company also incurred an expense of $60 for fixing up the hot dog stands. The economic value of the stands will be "used up" by the end of the first summer and, therefore, costs related to them are all expenses for 2004.
e. During the year, sales for Graham Cline Inc. totalled $7,000.
f. The company hired another student to run one of the hot dog stands. The student was paid $800 per month for the three months she worked for the company (June through August).

Other information, not yet recorded in the accounts, is as follows:

g. The inventory at December 31, 2004, consisted of:

Buns	10 dozen
Wieners	10 dozen

These items will not last until the next year and must be thrown away.

h. The company's income tax rate is 20%. It paid its taxes owing on December 31, 2004.
i. All contractual commitments of the company have been satisfied up to December 31, 2004.
j. On December 31, 2004, the company declared and paid a dividend of $5 per share.

1. Prepare journal entries to record the foregoing events in the records of Graham Cline Inc. for the year ended December 31, 2004.
2. Prepare a balance sheet as at December 31, 2004, and statements of income and retained earnings for the year ended December 31, 2004.
3. Has Graham been successful at his venture? Would you recommend that he continue his operations next summer? Consider qualitative aspects as well as the financial statements you prepared.

EXTENDED TIME

* PROBLEM 3.21 Prepare financial statements from transactions

At the end of last year, Fergama Productions Inc., a company in the movie industry, had the following balance sheet accounts (in no particular order):

Cash	23,415	Share capital	20,000
Accounts payable	37,778	Office equipment cost	24,486
Accumulated amortization	11,134	Accounts receivable	89,455
Retained earnings	51,434	Inventory of supplies	10,240
Long-term loan payable	15,000	Taxes payable	12,250

During this year, the company's activities resulted in the following:

a. Revenue, all on credit, totalled $216,459.
b. Production expenses totalled $156,320, $11,287 of which was paid in cash and the rest charged on credit.
c. Amortization on the office equipment came to $2,680 for the year. (This produces an expense, which is a debit, and an increase in the accumulated amortization balance sheet account, which is a credit.)
d. The company bought, on credit, new supplies costing $8,657 and used up supplies costing $12,984 during the year.
e. Income tax expense for the year was estimated to be $12,319.
f. The board of directors declared a dividend of $25,000.
g. Collections from customers totalled $235,260.
h. Payments to suppliers totalled $172,276.
i. Payments of taxes totalled $18,400.
j. A $5,000 payment was made on the long-term loan.
k. The dividend was paid in cash to shareholders.

1. To get you started, prepare a balance sheet for Fergama Productions Inc. as at the end of the last year.
2. Record the activities for this year using journal entries and post those entries to accounts (using paper or a computer spreadsheet).
3. Prepare a trial balance of your accounts to show that they are in balance (if you are using a computer spreadsheet, it should do this for you).

4. From those accounts, prepare the following financial statements:
   a. Income statement for this year.
   b. Statement of retained earnings for this year.
   c. Balance sheet at the end of this year (it would be useful to prepare a comparative balance sheet for this year and last year together).
5. Comment on what the three financial statements show about the company's performance for this year and financial position at the end of this year. Would you say the company is better off than it was last year?

EXTENDED TIME

PROBLEM 3.22 Prepare financial statements from transactions

Frothingslosh Beverages Inc. began business this year with $100,000 in cash provided by the owner, Froth, in return for $35,000 in share capital and the company's promise to repay the rest in five years. The company rents its premises and equipment, so it has no noncurrent assets. Below are the transactions that occurred in the company during this first year. Record the transactions as journal entries, post them to general ledger accounts (by hand or using a computer spreadsheet), and then prepare an income statement and statement of retained earnings for the year, and balance sheet at the end of the year.

Transactions for the year:

a. The company had bought inventory costing $283,500 by the end of the year and had paid for all but $37,400 of it.
b. Employees earned $103,770 in wages during the year. Employees do not receive this entire amount since some has to be paid directly to the government for deductions such as income tax, employment insurance, and Canada pension. Of this full amount, $76,760 had been paid to employees, $15,590 in tax and other deductions had been remitted to the government, and at the end of the year, $9,790 was still owing to employees and $1,630 in deductions was still owing to the government.
c. Customers bought products for $421,270 during the year, paying $255,760 in cash and charging the rest on credit. Of the amount on credit, all but $19,160 had been collected by the end of the year.
d. The goods bought by customers had cost the company $212,398. In addition, $3,580 of inventory had mysteriously disappeared during the year, probably shoplifted.
e. Other business expenses for the year totalled $58,500, all but $1,960 paid in cash.
f. The year's income tax expense was estimated as $10,750, but because the company is a new one, none of this has to be paid until next year.
g. At the end of the year, the company declared a dividend of $10,000 to be paid early next year, and invested $50,000 of cash in a short-term investment certificate at the bank.

PROBLEM 3.23 Write a closing entry

Write an entry to close the accounts of Frothingslosh Beverages (Problem 3.22) at the end of the year and present the post-closing account balances for the company showing that they are in balance as the next year begins.

Accrual Accounting Adjustments • Sections 3.8, 3.9

Writing Adjusting Journal Entries

* **PROBLEM 3.24** Identify and describe common adjustments

The list below describes *one side* each of common accrual accounting adjustments. Describe what the purpose of the adjustment is and state what the other side of the entry is. State any assumptions you feel are necessary.

a. CR Accumulated amortization
b. CR Accrued interest liability
c. DR Noncurrent assets
d. DR Prepaid insurance asset
e. CR Warranty liability
f. CR Dividends payable
g. CR Income tax payable
h. CR Customer deposits liability
i. DR Supplies inventory
j. CR Bonuses payable

* PROBLEM 3.25 Prepare adjusting journal entries if necessary

The accountant for Super Office Supplies Inc. (SOS) is reviewing the year-end unadjusted trial balance and considering the following items of information. For each item, decide if an adjustment to the accounts is necessary; if it is, write a journal entry to make the adjustment.

a. A shipment of inventory that arrived late in the last day of the year was not recorded. The shipment cost $11,240 and was paid for routinely about three weeks later.
b. The accountant estimated that bank loan interest of $330 had built up between the last payment of interest to the bank and the end of the year.
c. In the last few days of the year, the company's share price on the Toronto Stock Exchange had fallen about $0.20 per share. The company has 500,000 shares outstanding.
d. There had been an error in calculating amortization expense during the year. To correct the error, additional expense of $14,500 would need to be recorded.
e. A customer owing $2,100 went bankrupt on the last day of the year and SOS cannot expect to collect any of the money it expected.
f. A review of the warranty liability indicated that the liability should be increased by $780.
g. At a board of directors meeting on the last day of the year, the company's president and other senior executives were awarded raises totalling $11,100 annually, to begin the next day.
h. The company had bought 12 months' building insurance two months before the end of the year, at a cost of $2,400, and debited the cost to insurance expense.
i. One of the cash receipts credited to sales revenue turned out to be a deposit of $400 made by a customer on an order that will be filled a week after the end of the year.
j. The accountant determined that a major sales order had been filled on the last day of the year, even though it was not recorded until three days later. The order was for $7,200, and the goods supplied had cost SOS $3,300. The customer paid two weeks later.

PROBLEM 3.26 Write adjusting journal entries

Write an adjusting journal entry, if required, for each of the following items, which have been encountered during preparation of Ajax Sales Inc.'s January 31, 2006, financial statements.

a. A pile of sales invoices totalling $3,124 has yet to be recorded.
b. A customer had paid a deposit of $500 on a special order, which has not yet arrived. The deposit was included in the sales amount for the day it was paid.
c. The company has a $123,000 bank loan owing. Interest at 8% was last paid 23 days before the end of the year.

d. The year-end inventory count showed that goods costing $87,943 were on hand.The inventory account showed a balance of $89,221 on the same day. These missing goods have to be written off as an Inventory Loss Expense.
e. At the end of January, the account for advances to employees for travel expenses had a balance of $3,200. Expense accounts received after that date showed that employees had spent $1,823 of this by the end of January.
f. The credit manager decided to write off, to expense, some hopeless accounts receivable totalling $320.
g. After a study of the company's employee pensions, it was decided that an additional $38,940 should be accrued for pensions earned during the year. This amount would be paid to the pension fund trustee in March 2006.
h. A court case involving another company showed that one of the company's patents was worthless, so management decided to write the patent off. It was on the accounts at a cost of $74,500 and there was accumulated amortization of $42,100 against it.
i. A search of cheque payments during February turned up $5,430 of payments that related to expenses incurred before the end of January.
j. The board of directors declared a $150,000 dividend January 25, to be paid in mid-February 2006.

EXTENDED TIME

PROBLEM 3.27 Do adjusting journal entries

The accountant for Chewie Crusts Ltd., a bakery specializing in pizza crusts for the fast-food trade, is working on the year-end accounting for the company. For each item below, decide what (if anything) needs to be done and prepare any journal entry needed to implement your decision. Use whatever account titles you like, but be clear where on the statements the accounts would be located and write clear explanations for your entries. This is the company's first year of existence.

a. The company paid $1,120 for cleaning and office supplies, all of which have been expensed. The accountant discovered that another $114 is owing but not recorded and that supplies costing $382 are still on hand and usable at the end of the year.
b. The company's sales are all on credit because its customers are restaurants, stores, and institutions, such as hospitals. All cash collections have been recorded as sales revenue. The accountant added up the customers' bills still not collected and got a total of $11,621.
c. All purchases of flour and other raw materials have been expensed, and there is no significant inventory of finished products at the end of the year because each night's production is shipped in the morning to ensure maximum freshness. However, usable raw materials costing $6,210 are on hand at the end of the year.
d. Purchases of small tools and parts (still on hand) totalling $238 were charged to expenses during the year.
e. The accountant found an unpaid invoice for $900 for advertising services on behalf of the company. The advertising campaign had been planned and advertising contracts signed before the year-end, but the campaign took place just after the year-end.
f. The president of the company directed that $2,316 originally included in repairs and maintenance expense be capitalized to recognize the creation of valuable equipment and fixtures. This is unusual for the company, but the repairs were so good that the useful life of the assets involved had been extended by several years more than originally expected.
g. All payments on the company's building mortgage had been made on time. Since the last payment, $187 of mortgage interest (the accountant's estimate) had accumulated, but the next regular payment was not due for ten days.

h. The company's board of directors declared a dividend of $14,000 to shareholders. The board meeting to declare the dividend was held three days before the year-end, but the dividend was explicitly not to be paid until two months after the year-end.
i. The general manager's employment contract specifies that at the end of the third month of each year, she is to be paid a bonus of 8% of the company's pre-tax and pre-bonus income. The accountant calculated the first year's pre-tax income, after all accruals and adjustments, to be $38,226.

Adjustments and Preparing Financial Statements

EXTENDED TIME

*** PROBLEM 3.28** Record and post adjusting journal entries, close accounts

Here are the unadjusted accounts for Tucker Northern Inc. at the end of its first year in business:

Cash	25,600	Employee deductions due	2,500
Accounts receivable	88,200	Sales taxes due	3,220
Inventory	116,900	Mortgage debt	185,780
Land	100,000	Share capital	275,000
Buildings and equipment	236,100	Revenue	349,600
Accounts payable	74,900	Cost of goods sold	142,500
		Operating expenses	181,700

The company has determined that the year-end adjustments listed below are required.

a. An uncollectible account receivable of $2,400 should be written off to expense.
b. Amortization of $13,000 should be recorded.
c. Additional revenue of $11,200 has been earned and should be recorded.
d. The COGS to go with the revenue in part (c) is $4,600.
e. Accrued interest on the mortgage at the end of the year is $900.
f. A bonus of $5,000 was awarded to the president by the board of directors.
g. Income tax for the year is estimated to be $2,700. No tax has been paid yet.

1. Record these in journal entry form.
2. Post them to the accounts (creating new accounts if you need them).
3. Prepare a balanced adjusted trial balance.
4. Close the revenue and expense accounts to retained earnings.
5. Calculate the following: net income, working capital, shareholders' equity.

PROBLEM 3.29 Preparing financial statements after adjustments

The following balance sheet has been taken from the records of Leakey Pens Inc. at the end of its first year of operations, December 31, 2006:

Cash	$ 9,900	
Short-term investment	15,000	
Accounts receivable	12,000	
Prepaid insurance	3,600	
Supplies on hand	1,500	
Truck	34,000	
Accumulated amortization		$ Nil
Accounts payable		15,000
Current portion long-term bank loan		2,000
Long-term bank loan		20,000
Unearned rent		7,200
Common stock		20,000
Revenue		40,100
Advertising expense	2,600	
Commissions expense	3,000	
Interest expense	800	
Salaries expense	21,000	
Utilities expense	900	
TOTAL	104,300	104,300

The following additional data is available:

a. Prepaid insurance at December 31 amounts to $1,800.
b. A physical count indicates $900 worth of supplies are still on hand at December 31.
c. The truck was purchased on July 1 and has a useful life of 4 years with an estimated salvage value of $2,000.
d. Employees have not been paid for working December 31. The $800 earned on that date will be included in the first Friday payment in January.
e. The unearned rent represents six months' rent received for excess warehouse space sublet to Dull Pencils Inc. The lease took effect October 31.
f. A $300 utilities bill for December telephone charges was received but has not yet been recorded.
g. Interest on the bank loan for December in the amount of $100 had not yet been deducted from the company's account by the bank.
h. A bill for a special year-end advertisement in the local paper had not yet been received. The ad appeared on December 31, at a cost of $300.

1. Record each of the above transactions in journal entry form.
2. Post them to the accounts (creating new accounts if needed.)
3. The corporate tax rate for Leakey is 25%. This tax will not be paid until April 2007. Calculate the tax owing by preparing Leakey's income statement for 2006.
4. Prepare an adjusted trial balance including all adjusted accounts and the income tax payable.

PROBLEM 3.30 Recalculating financial statements after adjustments

Using the 2004 Canadian Pacific Railway balance sheet (Chapter 2, p. 102) and income statement (Chapter 3, p. 151), (i) write journal entries for the following adjustments on Dec. 31, 2004, using account names from the company's statements, (ii) post them to the account, and (iii) rewrite the income statement (ignore earnings per share), retained earnings statement, and updated balance sheet with revised retained earnings.

a. Management decided that $35.9 million in additional freight revenue should be recorded in 2004 instead of 2005. Payment has not been received.

b. An additional amortization expense of $12.4 million had to be recorded for miscellaneous equipment. (Credit the Net properties account, which includes accumulated amortization.)

c. The interest expense on outstanding loans was $15.3 million more than previously recorded. It was accrued in a liability account.

d. CPR decided to restate its dividend on common shares and increase it by $5.2 million. The dividends have not yet been paid.

e. Additional fuel was used which had not been previously recorded for $42.3 million. The company would pay for this fuel in 2005.

f. CPR had miscalculated the income tax expense for 2005 and had to revise it upwards to $145.3 million. The additional tax has not yet been paid.

Earnings Management • Section 3.10

*** PROBLEM 3.31** Comment on income smoothing and management's motivation in measuring income

Gordon Inc. has had the following net incomes for the past several years:

2002	$2,500,000
2003	3,600,000
2004	4,700,000
2005	3,200,000
2006	5,100,000
2007	4,600,000
2008	5,500,000

1. The company is now finishing its accounting for 2009. Some items have yet to be settled, but it is possible that the net income for 2009 could be any of three figures: $6,400,000, $5,400,000, or $4,100,000. Which of the three possible 2009 net income figures would be the "smoothest" given the company's past income pattern. Why?
2. The difference between the highest and lowest net income possibilities for 2009 is in how to account for a major contract. If its revenue and expenses are included in 2009, the highest 2009 figure results; if it is postponed to 2010, the lowest 2009 figure results. It has been proposed that a portion of the contract could be included in 2009; if that were done, the middle 2009 figure, $5,400,000, results. Arguments have been advanced for all three possibilities. What support do you think might have been advanced for each?
3. Do you think a company should choose its accounting according to the net income that results, or should the company just use the most appropriate accounting, and let the net income be whatever it therefore is? Why?

PROBLEM 3.32 Measuring the effects of a large write-down

LotsoWidgets is a manufacturer of highly important widgets for the world. LotsoWidgets has been actively acquiring smaller companies in its industry over the last number of years as it attempts to grow rapidly and dominate the industry with a vast array of products. Most of these companies were acquired with the company's stock and not cash. Unfortunately, a sharp economic downturn has affected the widget industry and drastically decreased earnings. As a result, Catherine, the chief financial officer, believes the companies that LotsoWidgets acquired are no longer worth the price that they were purchased for. Of the goodwill recorded on LotsoWidgets' balance sheet, she believes it is worth only $5,000,000 today and is likely to stay at that value for the foreseeable future.

LotsoWidgets' Balance Sheet

Cash	$ 12,000,000	All liabilities	$ 80,000,000
All other assets	138,000,000	Shareholder equity	125,000,000
Goodwill	55,000,000		
Total Assets	$205,000,000	Total L + E	$205,000,000

It is three days from the end of the financial reporting period and the company's net income is projected to be an $8,000,000 loss.

1. Write out the journal entry if the company wrote down the amount of goodwill to the value estimated by the CFO and calculate the change in projected net income. (Ignore the income tax effects.)
2. Explain the effect that the write-down will have on the company's cash position.
3. Bill, the president of the company, argues that the write-down will put the company in a tough financial position because there will be a large net loss. Is Bill correct, and what are the short-term and long-term implications of such a decision?

PROBLEM 3.33 Comments by investors about large write-offs

In the chapter, there is a discussion of some of the large write-offs and write-downs that companies performed in 2001 and 2002. In the context of this information and more recent problems that may have arisen, comment on the following statements made by some investors:

> "I don't understand why companies take such a huge loss in one quarter. Wouldn't it be better to merely spread out the pain over a number of years?"

> "New CEOs entering a company need clean financial statements to deal with. I applaud those who can fix some of the company's problems by taking a bold step in one quarter rather than dragging poor performance into the future. It will give a clearer picture of earnings."

> "Most of these write-offs only deal with theoretical accounting figures anyway, not the actual cash flow of the company. I don't see why there is such a big deal made about so-called 'Big Baths' because I'm an investor who only looks at the cash flow of the company, not the games it can play with its accrual accounting."

Do you agree or disagree with these comments? Are these investors' views valid? Using these comments and other information from the chapter, discuss the concept of the "Big Bath" and its effect on managers and investors.

PROBLEM 3.34 Income smoothing and ethics

1. Section 3.10 referred to income smoothing as a way of manipulating a company's net income in order to create a desired impression of management's capability and performance. Other kinds of income manipulation by management have also been alleged. Do you think it is ethical for management to manipulate the figures by which its performance is measured? Why or why not?
2. The usual answer to part 1 is that such behaviour is unethical. Can you think of any circumstances under which such manipulation of income would be ethical? Putting it another way, are there any people, other than management, whose interests would be served by such behaviour?

Integrated Problems

Accounting Theory

*** PROBLEM 3.35** Explain terms in nontechnical language

Explain the following in nontechnical language that a person who has not read this book would understand:

1. What is net income as it is meant in financial accounting?
2. Why is net income part of owners' equity?
3. If net income is part of owners' equity, why is it necessary to have a separate income statement? Why not just report net income on the balance sheet?
4. Why are dividends to shareholders not considered to be an expense in calculating net income?

PROBLEM 3.36 Revenue recognition and accrued expenses

Lawrence Castle decided to create a limited edition chess set of the War of 1812, which he hoped to sell to chess lovers and history buffs for $500 per set. He plans to create further sets if the first is sufficiently profitable. Castle guarantees the purchaser of each set that if they are not completely satisfied they may return the set for a full refund at any time up to three years from the date of purchase. The returned sets will be destroyed rather than resold in order to increase the collectible value of the remaining sets. Each set will cost Castle $300 to produce and deliver. He estimates that half of the sets sold will be returned within the guarantee period. Assume the entire production of 10,000 sets was sold during 2006.

1. Determine the amount of income Lawrence Castle should recognize in each of the years 2006, 2007, and 2008.
2. Determine the amount of cash that Lawrence Castle will receive and pay each year and the total net cash effect over the three year period. Assume that 50% of the sets sold are returned in 2008.
3. Based on your answer to part 2, is it sensible for Castle to carry out his plan to produce further such limited edition sets at the same selling price and with the same refund guarantee if his cost stays the same?

PROBLEM 3.37 Questions about accounting asked by a businessperson

Jeanette is an electrical engineer and has been working for a large company in its technical electronics area for several years. She has decided to go into business for herself, offering electronics design and general consulting to other companies. To prepare for this venture, she has raised the necessary capital and has been reading books on business management and talking to businesspeople about running a business. She learns that you are taking a financial accounting course and says, "Maybe you can help me understand some of the peculiarities of accounting!" You protest that you have just started your course, but she asks you to try to answer her questions anyway. Without using jargon, provide brief answers to the following questions she has asked you:

1. Everyone says they will be interested to see if my company can make a profit. How will the accountants measure my profit? I know it's done on the income statement, but I really don't understand what that statement includes or doesn't include.
2. One reason I can see for wanting a good profit is that it will put money in the bank. But someone told me that accrual accounting doesn't depend on money in the bank for its measure of profit. What does that mean?
3. One of the books I've read says that a company's accounting will use the double-entry system and said that that means the balance sheets and income statements all fit together. How does that work?

4. One person told me to keep my company's accounting income low to save income tax. Another person said to keep it high to attract other investors and soothe creditors. Why is there any choice? I thought that financial accounting just reported the facts!

CHALLENGING

PROBLEM 3.38 General or user-specific income statements

Write a paragraph giving your considered views on the following question:

Do the accrual basis and the standard content and format of the income statement provide useful information to all people who are interested in companies' financial performance, or should there be different kinds of income statements prepared to suit the needs of different kinds of users?

Financial Statement Preparation

EXTENDED TIME

*** PROBLEM 3.39** Prepare income statement from transactions plus adjustments

(This problem follows from Problem 2.28*, PastaPastaPasta Inc. You should review that problem before doing this one, but it is not necessary to have answered that problem in detail before attempting this one.)

Below are events that happened to Tanya's new company during its first six months of operation. From these events, prepare an income statement for the first six months. Preparing journal entries for these events will assist you in keeping the numbers straight.

(If you did Problem 2.28*, you could also go on to record the events and prepare a balance sheet at the end of the six months.)

1. Customers took away pasta, sauces, cookware, etc. for which they promised to pay $87,340. By the end of the six months, Tanya had collected $78,670 of this, had taken back $420 of defective merchandise (which she had to just throw away), and had given up on collecting $510 so that amount has to be transferred to expense. She expected the $7,740 remainder to be collected within a month or two.
2. Tanya purchased $32,990 of food and pasta-making supplies, and $19,320 of cookware for resale. By the end of the six months, she had paid the suppliers $47,550 toward these purchases and those owing at the end of the preparatory time described in Problem 2.28*.
3. The pasta and sauces taken by customers cost Tanya $31,840 to make, so at the end of the six months, $5,870 of food and pasta-making supplies were still on hand. The cookware and other equipment taken by customers cost Tanya $9,110 to buy, so at the end of the six months, $14,120 of goods for resale were still on hand.
4. Tanya estimated the following for the six months: amortization on equipment, $3,950; amortization of improvements to rented space, $450; amortization of minivan, $750. She was not sure what to do about the recipes, because they had shown themselves to be very valuable, or the incorporation costs, because the company should last many years. She thought perhaps each could be amortized at 10% of cost per year.
5. The company paid $8,000 in rent during the six months. The landlord was charging $2,000 per month and was concerned that, while at the beginning of the period the company had paid $2,000 in advance, it had fallen behind by $2,000 at the end. Tanya promised to pay the rent more promptly in the future.
6. The company paid the first $7,050 installment on the equipment liability, plus $1,410 interest on the total debt at 8% per annum. The second installment would be due in another year.
7. The $2,500 bank loan was paid off, including $80 in interest.
8. In consultation with the other owners, Tanya set her monthly salary at $2,100. She took only $8,000 of that in cash. The company paid $950 more to the Canada Revenue Agency as income tax deductions and still owed $190 for such deductions. Tanya decided to take the remaining $3,460 in a few months, when she wanted to go on a holiday.

9. Other expenses for the six months came to $6,440, all but $760 having been paid by the end of the period.
10. Tanya's accountant said that the company did not yet owe any income tax, but that there would likely be a small tax liability by the end of the year. The accountant estimated that about $1,500 would be owed for the first six months' income.
11. Everyone agreed that no dividends to owners should be declared yet, but the hope was that about $3,000 of the first six months' income would eventually be paid as dividends.

PROBLEM 3.40 Do entries plus statements from accounts and events

To diversify his activities, hockey player Knuckles Gronsky opened a boutique for children's sportswear. He incorporated a company under the name Gronsky's Great Things Ltd., and the boutique opened for business on September 1, 2006.

Account balances and other information for the year ended August 31, 2007, for Gronsky's company follow.

Cash	$ 3,250
Accounts receivable	4,375
Inventory of clothing (after fire)	37,500
Sales revenue	300,000
Wage and salary expense	34,375
Rent paid in advance	2,500
Furniture and fixtures	19,375
Accumulated amortization	3,750
Income tax expense	8,750
Loan payable	10,000
Accounts payable	28,750
Investment in Number One Ltd.	12,500
Inventory sold (Cost of goods sold)	125,000
Supplies purchased	18,125
Rent expense	30,000
Capital from shareholder	18,750
Amortization expense	3,750
Costs associated with incorporation	2,375
Interest paid on loan	625
General operating expenses	6,250
Dividends payable	2,500
Dividends declared	5,000
Loss due to storage room fire	50,000

The following information will explain some of the preceding items:

a. On August 20, 2007, someone started a fire in the storage room and burnt $50,000 worth of inventory. There will be no insurance claim on this loss.

b. The loan is payable in yearly payments of $2,500 plus interest. Payments are to be made on August 31 each year over the next four years. The payment and interest for August 31, 2007, are already reflected in the preceding balances.

c. The investment is shares in Number One Ltd., a private company. Gronsky has no intention of selling the shares in the immediate future.

d. On August 30, 2007, the board of directors declared dividends of $5,000, $2,500 of which were paid on August 31, 2007, and the remaining $2,500 of which were to be paid September 12, 2007.

Four other events may need to be incorporated:

e. The supplies are included in expenses immediately when purchased. At August 31, 2007, supplies were counted and $11,250 remained on hand. The count has not been reflected in the above account balances.
f. On August 31, 2007, a customer brought back unused clothing the customer had paid $550 for. The customer was given a credit note, which could be used to buy clothes any time in the next year. The clothes, which had cost the company $275, were returned to inventory as they had not even been unwrapped from their packages. The above account balances do not reflect this event.
g. Late in the day on August 31, Gronsky received an offer of $25,000 for the shares in Number One Ltd. Gronsky still didn't want to sell, though the shares were obviously worth more than had been paid for them.
h. An income tax advisor estimated that the income tax expense for the year should have been $7,800, so the company should be able to get a refund of overpaid tax.

1. Write a journal entry for any of the items (e) to (h) that require an entry.
2. Prepare an income statement for 2007 for Gronsky's Great Things Ltd.
3. Prepare a statement of retained earnings for the same year.
4. Prepare the company's balance sheet as at August 31, 2007.

CHALLENGING AND EXTENDED TIME

PROBLEM 3.41 Entries and statements for a used car business

You've decided to take a job as a part-time accountant, working for a friend of yours, John Rogers, who operates a used car lot called Honest John's Used Cars Ltd. John's records consist primarily of a cheque book and a bank deposit book. He uses a cheque to pay for every purchase and always describes the purchase on the cheque stub, which remains in the cheque book. He also describes each deposit on the duplicate deposit slip, which he keeps.

John likes having things simple. He rents a small lot with a furnished sales office for $1,600 per month (including utilities). He carries no parts and provides no service on cars. His company's share capital is $50, so most of the owner's investment is retained earnings. The company has no employees except him (he gets a monthly salary of $4,000). At January 31, 2006, he had a $27,500 operating loan that carried interest at 12% (1% per month) and was payable on demand. All interest had been paid up to January 31, 2006. His inventory of unsold cars (all of which the company paid cash for) at January 31, 2006, was as follows:

Unsold Cars on Hand—January 31, 2006	Purchase Price
1996 Ford	$ 5,500
1995 Volkswagen	4,500
1994 Oldsmobile	7,000
1996 Camaro	9,000
1995 Mazda	6,400
1997 Toyota	7,600
	$40,000

John has assured you that all cash and cheques received in February 2006 were deposited in the bank. His receipts and disbursements for that month were as follows:

Cheques written during February (from cheque stubs)

Cheque #	Date	Description (Paid to, etc.)	Amount
51	Feb. 1/06	XL Property Management—Rent for February and March 2006	$ 3,000
52	Feb. 4/06	XL Property Management—Alterations to sales office	5,500
53	Feb. 10/06	Jack Yee — Purchase of 1997 Chrysler, paid in full	8,000
54	Feb. 15/06	John Rogers — Salary for February 2006	4,000
55	Feb. 22/06	Skyline Auto Auctions — Purchase of 3 cars (1994 Lincoln—$8,500; 1998 Nissan—$6,000; 1996 Honda—$4,500)	19,000
56	Feb. 28/06	Royal Bank—Payment of February interest in full	275
		Total Cash Disbursements	$39,775

Cash and cheques received in February (from duplicate bank deposit slips)

Date	Description (Received from, etc.)	Amount
Feb. 6/06	Tim Boychuk—Sale of Camaro, paid in full	$12,500
Feb. 12/06	Bob Scott—Sale of Oldsmobile, paid in full	8,800
Feb. 19/06	Downtown Dodge Used Cars—Sale of Mazda and Ford, paid in full	12,700
Feb. 28/06	Additional operating loan from bank	5,000
	Total Cash Receipts	$39,000

John has informed you that no other cars were purchased or sold during February and that no amounts are owed by or to him at January 31 or February 28, 2006. You also learned that the balance in his bank account on January 31, 2006, was $6,800. *Ignore sales taxes throughout this problem.*

1. Prepare a balance sheet for Honest John's Used Cars Ltd. as at January 31, 2006. (Deduce the retained earnings from the other account balances.)
2. Record the February 2006 transactions in journal entry form.
3. Post these transactions to the general ledger of Honest John's Used Cars Ltd.
4. Prepare a balance sheet as at February 28, 2006, and statements of income and retained earnings for the company for the one-month period ended February 28, 2006.
5. Make up a list of unsold cars at February 28, 2006, and their purchase prices. The total of these amounts should agree with the inventory account in your general ledger and balance sheet as at February 28, 2006.
6. Compare the company's net income for the month of February with the change in the bank account balance between January 31, 2006, and February 28, 2006. Reconcile them to show why they are different.
7. What are some advantages of John's having monthly financial statements? (In the past, John has prepared one set of statements each year for income tax purposes.)

Financial Statement Relationships

*** PROBLEM 3.42** Show that the financial statements articulate as figures change

Answer each of the following questions. Each one begins with the information given and derived by you for the previous ones.

a. Wanderlee Inc. began in business with cash of $100,000 and share capital of $100,000. In its first year, it showed a net income of $13,000 but declared no dividends. At the end of that year, it had liabilities of $42,000, all current. What did the company's assets total at the end of that first year?
b. If those assets were 60% noncurrent, what was the company's working capital at the end of its first year?
c. As the company began its second year, it made a big sale for $40,000, all on credit (the customer would pay in a month). The cost of goods sold to the customer, which had been in inventory, equalled $18,000. Ignoring income tax and assuming the income from the sale was added to retained earnings, what were the new amounts after the sale for current assets, total assets, equity, and total of liabilities and equity?
d. Observing the result of the big sale, the president said, "Our income from this very pleasant event is reflected in both our assets and our equity." Use your answer to part (c) to show why the president was right.

PROBLEM 3.43 Show how financial statements change and articulate

Answer the following questions about the finances of Jared's Cola Bottling Inc. Each part is related and uses answers derived from the previous sections.

1. The company began the year with $55,000 in cash and equipment assets of $50,000. To finance the venture, the company took a bank loan of $60,000 and the three owners each invested $15,000 of their own capital. What is the company's debt to equity ratio?
2. At the end of the first year, the company's net income was $8,000 and no dividends were paid out. New current liabilities were created for $12,000 while $5,000 of the bank loan was repaid. Meanwhile, cash had increased to $65,000 and the equipment was amortized by $6,000. What are the company's accounts receivable at the end of year 1?
3. The president wishes to know the company's ability to pay off its debts. If the company had to pay off all of its debt and liabilities immediately with cash, would it be able to do so? If not, how much of the accounts receivable would need to be collected in order to have enough cash?
4. The company wants to increase efficiency and output by purchasing a new piece of equipment entirely on credit. The company's owners want to make sure that their debt-equity ratio never exceeds 2. How much can the company spend on the new equipment without exceeding this limitation?

PROBLEM 3.44 Analyze some financial statement relationships

Answer each of the following *unrelated* questions. State any assumptions you feel you need to make.

a. A Ltd. has assets of $45,000, liabilities of $32,000, and a deficit of $7,000. How much have its shareholders contributed as share capital?
b. B Ltd. has current assets of $234,000, total assets of $459,000, and equity of $100,000. The company wants to reorganize its liabilities so that its working capital ratio is 2:1. If it does, what will its *noncurrent* liabilities be?

c. The board of directors of C Ltd. wishes to declare a $75,000 dividend. The company's retained earnings equal $257,000, and the company has $41,000 in the bank, a $20,000 bank loan, and $55,000 in accounts receivable. The bank will lend only $10,000 more, so the credit manager is told to collect some cash quickly from customers, *if necessary*. How much cash does the credit manager have to collect, if any?

d. D Ltd. has revenue of $783,000 and net income of $21,000 after income tax expense of $17,000. What do its other expenses total?

e. For this year, E Ltd. has net income of $43,000 and declared a dividend of $11,000. The company's beginning retained earnings totalled $217,000. At the end of the year, the company had current assets of $387,000, noncurrent assets of $414,000, current liabilities of $205,000, and share capital of $181,000. The company decides to issue new long-term bonds for cash in order to raise its working capital to $250,000. If it does so, what will the total noncurrent liabilities be?

f. F Ltd. has revenue of $540,000 and income before income tax of $59,400, which equals 11% of $540,000. After income tax of 40% on the $59,400, the company's net income is $35,640. The president is unhappy with this net income and wants to raise it to $60,000. Assuming that income tax stays at 40% and that expenses other than income tax rise proportionately with revenue, what will the revenue have to be to meet the president's net income target?

CHALLENGING

PROBLEM 3.45 Income calculation without dollars

A year has elapsed since you solved the argument between Bob and Doug, the shepherds (Problem 2.8). After studying your solution, Doug and Bob grudgingly accepted your opinion as to their relative wealth at the end of last year. The passage of time has not diminished their penchant for argument, however. Now they are arguing about who had the largest income for the year just ended.

Doug points out that the number of sheep that he personally owns at year-end exceeds his personal holdings at the beginning of the year by 80, whereas Bob's increase was only 20. Bob replies that his increase would have been 60, had he not traded 40 sheep during the year for 10 acres of additional land. Besides, he points out, he exchanged 18 sheep during the year for food and clothing items, whereas Doug exchanged only 7 for such purposes. The food and clothing have been pretty much used up by the end of the year.

Bob is happy because his wife made 5 coats during the year (fulfilling the orders she had at the beginning of the year) and received 25 goats for them. She managed to obtain orders for another 5 coats (again for 25 goats)—orders on which she has not yet begun to work. Doug points out that he took to making his own lunches this year; therefore, he does not owe Ted anything now. Doug was very unhappy one day last year when he discovered that his ox had died of a mysterious illness. Both men are thankful, however, that none of the other animals died or were lost.

Except for the matters reported above, each man's holdings at the end of the current year are the same as his holdings at the end of last year. Provide advice to the two men as to who had the higher income for the year.[27]

CASE 3A

CONCERNS ABOUT A COMPANY'S FINANCIAL PERFORMANCE

Discuss the following letter from a shareholder to a company's top financial manager, indicating how valid you think the shareholder's concerns are and pointing out any mistakes the shareholder may have made in interpreting the company's income statement and related balance sheet and retained earnings information.

Ray Rusu
114 Century Avenue
Grosport, Ontario

Ms. Debra Lazar
Vice-President, Finance
Gordon Consolidated Enterprises Inc.

Dear Ms. Lazar:

For several years, I have been a shareholder of Gordon Consolidated, longer than I have kept most of my investments. I have been concerned lately about the company's performance relative to its competitors, and because I do not wish to sell my shares, have decided to write you with my comments. Figures below come from Gordon Consolidated's recently released income statement and other financial statements.

My first concern is that top management has apparently not taken its responsibility to the shareholders seriously enough. You are supposed to operate the company profitably, but also you should use the company's accounting to put the best possible light on its performance, so as to increase the value of the shares people hold. There are three examples to illustrate my concern:

1. The income statement shows a large restructuring charge expense deducted from operating income and severely depressing earnings per share. If you are changing the way you do things, you should not deduct this as an expense, because it represents value for the future. You are making the company better by restructuring it, so it is an error to deduct such an expense and hurt my share value by hurting earnings.
2. One of the notes to the financial statements says that the company issued 1.2 million new shares during the year, for a total proceeds of $23.4 million. It appears you just added that to equity on the balance sheet instead of recording it properly as revenue and letting it increase net income and therefore equity that way. Again, you make income lower than it should be.
3. Another note says that a large liability ($18 million) for warranty costs has been estimated because of all the trouble the sports equipment line is having. While I do not suggest that the company should not meet its social obligations, I think you have vastly overestimated the likely cost of warranties. If you reduced that estimate to say $6 million, you would increase income by $12 million. Even better, if you just paid off whatever the liability is right away by offering immediate rebates to customers, you could remove the liability and warranty expense as a factor in calculating income. You're hitting income with a double whammy through your unnecessary accounting.

My second concern is with the company's revenue. It has risen 3% since last year, but I notice that the gross profit has fallen 4%. Therefore, the company must be cutting prices, or selling too many low-valued items, or going after stingy customers. You are not getting as much revenue as you should out of the products you are selling, and that looks like bad management to me. I checked the balance sheet and found that accounts receivable are up 21% since last year: if you just collected that money, you would see a much greater increase in revenue and income—more bad management.

My third concern is that the income statement badly misrepresents the company's real performance. I calculated earnings before interest, tax, depreciation and amortization, and got $184 million. Yet you show net income as only $39 million, only a little over 20% of the $184 million. It is inappropriate to deduct those things when calculating income. Interest is just a way of financing the company; income tax is confiscation by the government and has nothing to do with Gordon Consolidated's real economic performance, and depreciation and amortization are just allocations of investment costs spent years ago. Nothing to do with today. Why do you not just report EBITDA, which is a more reasonable measure? I know other companies give a lot of prominence to their EBITDA figures. Maybe this is another example of management not using the accounting to the shareholders' advantage.

My fourth concern is dividends. When you take the $39 million net income and deduct the $15 million dividends declared during the year, only $24 million of earnings are left. That's the company's real earnings power, because you have to keep the shareholders happy just as you have to pay interest to keep creditors happy. But $24 million is not much for the company to grow with. Why not just pay the dividends out of retained earnings on the balance sheet so that they don't have this depressing effect on the company's growth? Even better, if you used EBITDA instead as your performance measure, you'd have $169 million left after dividends, which would provide a much better basis for growth.

My last concern is that both net income and working capital are down from last year. Net income is down $22 million and working capital is down $45 million, over twice as much. I don't like to see a decline in performance going with a weakening balance sheet; it is double trouble. It doesn't have to be like that. As you are using what I understand is called accrual accounting, you can separate your earning power from your working capital, so that even in a poor earnings year like the last one, you could have an improvement in working capital. The working capital weakness may lead to higher interest rates on borrowing, as well as other troubles, so you should remedy that regardless of how much of a struggle it is to regain the income level of past years.

I look forward to your reply to my concerns.

Sincerely

Ray Rusu

CASE 3B

IS ACCOUNTING'S MEASURE OF EARNINGS OFF THE RAILS?

Discuss the strengths and weaknesses of accrual accounting's measure of income and its calculation as set out in the income statement, using the material from this book's first three chapters (Sections 3.5 and 3.10 may be especially helpful) plus the comments below. Is accrual accounting so flexible that it has gotten off the rails?

At this stage, your accounting knowledge should be enough to permit you to suggest several major issues in measuring and reporting income. Proposing solutions to the problems is a greater challenge, but your discussion may well incorporate solution ideas as well as identifying strengths and weaknesses.

In a 2002 article titled "Earnings: A Cleaner Look," *Business Week* magazine commented: "Shareholders have had it up to here...as calamity followed calamity. First the tech collapse, then the crash in corporate profits and the avalanche of earnings restatements, all topped off by the Enron scandal, a wave of accounting questions at even the bluest-chip companies, and the collapse of once high-flying telecoms."[28]

The article went on to ask if companies' earnings reports have been "widely inflated," if replacements for conventional net income like companies' self-defined "pro forma" income numbers have confused everyone, and if it is possible "to define more clearly what earnings are."

In another 2002 article, titled "Badly in need of repair," *The Economist* magazine remarked, "Enron and others have shown how easy it is to manipulate companies' financial statements. Can it be made more difficult?"[29]

The article listed several companies whose financial statements were questionable: famous ones like General Electric and Xerox, well-known disasters like Cendant, Enron and Waste Management, and even a little-known German company, Comroad, which *The Economist* said reported revenues 97% of which were imaginary, coming from a non-existent client in Hong Kong. The article then said, "Many investors now believe that companies can manipulate their accounts more or less at will, with the aim of producing profits that increase steadily over time. Provisions estimated liabilities such as for restructuring expenses are bumped up in good times and later released, or the value of an acquisition is slashed; there are plenty of tricks. In the dot.com years, finance directors and chief financial officers resorted to so-called pro forma numbers, which sought to strip out negative items from the income statement."

In 2002, the research journal *The Accounting Review* held a conference on Quality of Earnings. Numerous research papers were presented on various aspects of earnings quality. Such quality relates to whether accounting earnings do measure economic performance well, whether companies' income statements and earnings per share do indeed suffer from the problems *Business Week* and *The Economist* allege. Such research studies usually include a large number of companies, not just the specific "bad examples" the media may highlight, and they usually use statistical analysis of various numbers in financial statements, so their results tend to relate to how companies perform on average.

One paper reported an analysis of accrual accounting effects in working capital (accounts receivable, inventories, accounts payable) and argued that all such accruals, used to convert from cash income to accrual net income, contain unavoidable estimation error.[30] Such error need not be deliberate, because any estimation is going to be approximate to some degree. Thus net income is "wrong" in the year the estimate is made and in the next year too, in the other direction, when the estimation error is found and so the error must be corrected when the cash flow doesn't match the accrual estimate. The study found that the bigger the accrual estimates are in the first year, the lower earnings quality is that year because of the effect of these errors, and the lower longer-run earnings quality is too, as the original errors are corrected. Earnings quality is also lower the more variable companies' revenues and net incomes are, but is higher the larger the firm is. This suggests that larger firms are more stable and more accurate in their accrual estimates.

Another paper at the conference reported an analysis of "bloated balance sheets," which the paper defined as balance sheets whose accounts receivable, long-term assets (such as goodwill) and other accounts were distorted by attempts to overstate earnings.[31] The argument is that because A = L + E, and earnings are in equity, earnings cannot be overstated without also overstating assets or understating liabilities. The paper focused on "bloated" assets. The results indicated that if companies tried to overstate earnings, their balance sheets' bloated assets became a constraint on later attempts to overstate earnings (fewer ways to achieve such overstatement as balance sheet values got out of line), so early overstatement efforts were associated with less ability to overstate later. The implication is that the balance sheet operates as a control on the more ambitious earnings overstatements, at least as long as people can tell what is going on from the balance sheet's "articulation" with the income statement. (One interesting possibility not explored by the study is that a big write-off of assets, such as in the Big Bath, may wipe out the effects of earlier overstatements, releasing some of the balance sheet's constraints on future earnings optimism.)

Another 2002 article in *Business Week* wondered if people know enough accounting to understand what companies are doing, and speculated that correcting past excesses will lead to reduced earnings (echoing the second research study above), that might further depress already lower stock market prices.[32] "Experts say they're still seeing hints of exaggerated earnings that the market has yet to catch.... The reality is that accounting practices are too complex to change overnight. Players embracing the new religion of straightforward numbers find it's not as easy as scheduling a conference call or pouring more information into an annual report notes or MD&A.... Even professional money managers are scared that they don't know enough accounting.... A hoary Wall Street axiom says that any topic that attracts a crowd is old news and already priced into the market. But accounting problems are different. They are too complex to be cured simply by the realization that they are important."

NOTES

1. John Maynard Keynes, *A Treatise on Money*, 1930. Quoted in John Bartlett, *Bartlett's Familiar Quotations*, Boston: Little, Brown & Co. (1980 edition), 783.
2. Associated Press at www.theglobeandmail.com, Wednesday, November 16, 2005.
3. *National Post*, Saturday, August 27, 2005, FP3.
4. Canadian Press, at www.theglobeandmail.com, Wednesday, December 14, 2005.
5. Romina Maurino, "Increased Costs Hit Sobeys' Quarterly Profit," *The Globe and Mail* (December 14, 2005), B5.
6. Canadian Press at www.globeandmail.com, Thursday, November 3, 2005.
7. Guy Dixon, "Enbridge reports strong earnings gain," *The Globe and Mail* (May 4, 2002), B2.
8. Michael Chatfield, "English Medieval Bookkeeping: Exchequer and Manor," in *Contemporary Studies in the Evolution of Accounting Thought*, ed. Michael Chatfield (Belmont: Dickenson Publishing Company, 1968), 36.
9. O. ten Have, *The History of Accounting* (Palo Alto: Bay Books, 1976), 56–74.
10. Ibid., 67.
11. Peter C. Newman, *Company of Adventurers* (Markham: Viking/Penguin Books, 1985), xii.
12. C.J. Hasson, "The South Sea Bubble and M. Shell," in *Contemporary Studies in the Evolution of Accounting Thought*, ed. Michael Chatfield (Belmont: Dickenson Publishing Company, 1968), 86–94.
13. Ross M. Skinner and J. Alex Milburn, *Accounting Standards in Evolution, Second Edition* (Toronto: Prentice-Hall, 2001), 17.
14. Some of the ideas in this part were developed with reference to Ross M. Skinner's *Accounting Standards in Evolution* (Toronto: Holt, Rinehart and Winston, 1987).
15. Skinner and Milburn, 24.
16. www8.cpr.ca/English/Investors/Events/Investors/2005/Analyst + Workshop.htm as found on December 20, 2005.
17. For more on income smoothing, see Joshua Ronen and Simcha Sadan, *Smoothing Income Numbers: Objectives, Means, and Implications* (Reading: Addison-Wesley, 1981). Smoothing and other apparent manipulations of income figures has often been the subject of articles in business magazines such as *Forbes, Fortune,* and *Business Week.* For critical and very readable commentaries on income manipulation, see a series of articles and books by Abraham Briloff, including *Unaccountable Accounting* (New York: Harper & Row, 1972).
18. The world this week, *The Economist* (April 27, 2002), 7.
19. Steve Maich, "Goodwill writedowns to hit $1 trillion," *Financial Post* in the *National Post* (Janaury 10, 2002): FP2.
20. Michael Lewis, "Pro Forma Lingo," *CAmagazine* (March 2002), 16.
21. John Carchrae, Chair of the Canadian Securities Administrators Chief Accountants Committee, quoted in Michael Lewis, *op. cit.*, 19.

22. Richard Blackwell, "Accounting body backs GAAP use; says pro-forma results confusing investors," *The Globe and Mail* (April 19, 2002), B2.
23. Monica Gutschi, "TD Bank A Pioneer in Booking Stock Options to Bottom Line," *Dow Jones News Service* (May 17, 2002).
24. Janet McFarland, "Taking Issue, No justification for rewarding mediocre results," *The Globe and Mail* (April 27, 2002), B9.
25. "Executive Compensation, The Scorecard: Here's the definitive list of who got what," *Forbes* (May 17, 1999), 216.
26. John Gray, "Optical illusion," *Canadian Business* (March 4, 2002), 86.
27. Adapted from *Accounting Education: Problems and Prospects* (Sarasota: American Accounting Association, 1974).
28. Nanette Byrnes and Mara Derhovanesian, "Earnings: A Clearer Look," *Business Week* (May 27, 2002): 34–37.
29. "Badly in need of repair," *The Economist* (May 4, 2002): 66–68.
30. Patricia M. Dechow and Ilia D. Dichev, "The quality of accruals and earnings: The role of accrual estimation errors," working paper, University of Michigan Business School, December 2001. (Expected to appear in a special later issue of *The Accounting Review*.)
31. Jan Barton and Paul Simko, "The balance sheet as an earnings management constraint," working paper, Emory University and Indiana University, January 2002. (Also expected to appear in the special later issue of *The Accounting Review*.)
32. David Henry, "Still Spooked by the Market," *Business Week* (April 29, 2002): 88–89.

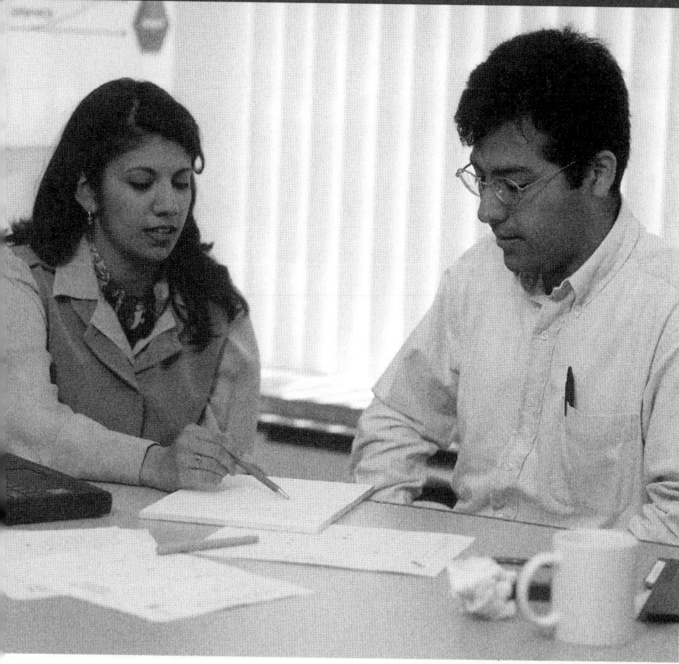

4 Measuring and Evaluating Cash Flow

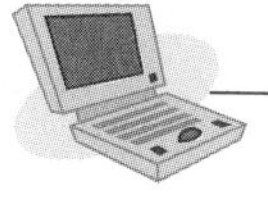

For information on this topic, please visit the online tutorial at www.gibbins6e.nelson.com

4.1 Chapter Introduction: Measuring and Evaluating Cash Flow

"Yes, I'll see him," Shelagh Frost sighed when the receptionist asked if she were able to talk to Paul Northey. Shelagh was an investment advisor, and Northey was one of her clients. He was not comfortable with risk, and whenever he showed up unannounced wanting to see her, it was always about a problem in his investment portfolio, and he tended to blame her for problems.

In stormed Northey. "I'm both angry and confused, Shelagh," he said, not waiting to sit down. "You remember last year I bought shares of Guestz Ltd., which everyone said looked like a winner. *You* said it looked like a winner," he said accusingly. "Well, the company has been reporting good income each quarter and for the whole recent fiscal year, but I just read in the paper that it is going to have serious trouble paying its debts, and may even have to make arrangements with its creditors to stave off bankruptcy! The share price tanked on this news, before I could sell, so I've lost a bundle. What the blazes is going on?"

Shelagh started to speak, but Northey didn't stop. "I thought it might be just one of those things, one of those chances you take. But another of my investments, Belhaeven Inc., which," he smiled thinly, "I picked out myself, no thanks to you, is doing quite well: it's the same size as Guestz and is making less profit, but is in no financial difficulty at all, and its price is going up a little. How can Guestz be making an income but not have any cash to pay its bills, while Belhaeven is making less income and has no trouble with cash? How can making an income lead to trouble, and making less income lead to no trouble, and how can two similar companies be so different that way?"

"Paul, believe me, I know how you feel," said Shelagh. "I recommended Guestz to some other people too, and they aren't very happy either. I've spent some time with Guestz's financial statements, trying to figure out what went wrong with its cash in spite of a rosy income number. Here, look at the company's cash flow statement with me: it shows what was going wrong."

Learning Objectives

Chapter 2 focused on the balance sheet, and Chapter 3 explained how the income statement measures performance. In this chapter, we return to the comparison of *accrual income* and *cash income* introduced in Chapter 1, which is set out in the fourth statement in the set of financial statements, the *cash flow statement*. We'll also see a lot more about cash flow besides that comparison. In this chapter, you'll learn:

- Why the cash flow statement is important, why it is arranged as it is, what story it tells about cash flow, and how it completes and complements the story told by the other statements;
- How to answer Paul's question about why a good accrual income can exist at the same time as a cash shortage (and, sometimes, a poor income or even a loss going with a cash surplus);
- How to use the cash flow information to supplement the analysis and interpretation of the balance sheet and income statement that began in Chapters 2 and 3, so that you could tackle Shelagh's task of explaining to Paul what happened to Guestz Ltd.;
- How to assemble a basic cash flow statement and make sure that it reconciles to the income statement and balance sheet. This learning will help to consolidate your understanding of those statements and to develop your analytical skill, because the cash flow statement does not come from a set of accounts in the general ledger or trial balance, as those other statements do, but rather from an analysis of those other statements.

The learning categories introduced in Chapter 1, the "How" procedures, the "Why" concepts, and the "Uses" analysis, are all important and integrated in the study of cash flow.

4.2 The Purpose of Cash Flow Analysis

The cash flow statement is a standard part of the set of financial statements.

Performance in generating additional wealth for the enterprise, as measured by the accrual accounting-based income statement, is very important to managers, investors, tax authorities, and many others. But the world is complex, and there is more to performance than generating accrual income. An additional important aspect of performance is managing the inflow and outflow of cash so that the enterprise has enough cash to pay its bills, finance its growth, and keep its borrowing under control. We all have to worry about cash flow, about how much cash is available, and where needed additional cash will come from. Businesses are no different, spending much effort on their cash management.

Managing cash flow is a central part of managing an enterprise.

Having cash to meet obligations is essential to business success.

No business enterprise can survive without cash. Nor can other organizations, such as governments, as we have seen in recent years with governments struggling to raise enough cash from taxes and other charges to meet their financial and social obligations. Employees, suppliers, and tax authorities must be paid, loans must be repaid, and assets must be kept up to date. To evaluate an enterprise's performance, it is important for present and potential investors and creditors to have information about the enterprise's cash inflows and outflows and its resulting cash position.

Solvency: ability to meet obligations when due.
Liquidity: cash to cover immediate needs.

Can the enterprise pay its debts and other financial obligations as they become due? This ability is commonly referred to as *solvency*. Does the enterprise have enough cash and short-term assets now to cover its immediate debts and obligations? This ability is commonly called *liquidity*. Enterprises can get into difficulty by not managing cash properly. Many new and established firms, like Guestz Ltd. in the previous section, have had positive net incomes, yet have still run out of cash. On the other hand, some enterprises seem to have rather a lot of cash, raising questions about why they are so well off and what might be done with the cash. Keeping a large supply of cash lying around idle is no way to earn a return for owners: the cash should be put to work by making investments, improving buildings and equipment, attracting new customers, or paying off interest-bearing debt.

Accrual income does not necessarily provide cash to be spent.

In the example of Simone's jewellery business in Section 1.10 of Chapter 1, it was shown that accrual income is not the same as cash income, because some revenues and expenses do not involve an inflow or outflow of cash in the present period. The example of uncollected revenue has already been mentioned. Amortization is another example: the cash flow happened when the asset was acquired, so the amortization expense does not involve any current cash flow. Here's an example where accrual income doesn't correspond to cash flow.

- Suppose a company like Guestz Ltd. makes a deal providing revenue of $1,000 on credit, and the customer hasn't paid yet.
- The company has expenses of $700 to generate this revenue, and the expenses have to be paid soon.
- The accrual income for the deal is the revenue minus the expenses, or $300. Looks good: a 30% return on revenue. Accrual income's measure of performance is very positive.
- But the deal provides the company no cash to pay its expenses; instead, it has $1,000 of accounts receivable, which cannot be used to pay expenses unless the customer pays or some other way is found to get cash for the receivables.
- The deal may therefore force the company to borrow money from a bank or other lender to provide it the needed cash. How much should it borrow? Or should it instead hound the customer for payment? Should it beg its creditors for more time to pay the $700 in expenses? How will it be able to afford a planned new machine to keep its product quality competitive? All of these questions are about the management of cash, and they are not answered by the positive accrual income measure.

To help answer such questions, the fourth major financial statement has been developed. The *cash flow statement* provides information about a firm's generation and use of cash and highly liquid short-term assets, and, therefore, assists in evaluating the firm's financial viability.

Even cash income does not cover all inflows and outflows of cash.

Even if accrual income were replaced by the kind of cash income measure shown in Simone's jewellery example in Section 1.10, this would not fully measure what has happened to cash. Cash income refers to operating results, from transactions with customers, suppliers, and employees. Certain inflows of cash (such as those resulting from getting a bank loan or issuing shares) or outflows of cash (such as dividends or a purchase of land) are not part of the day-to-day process of generating revenue and incurring expenses, and so are not part of cash income. They reflect management decisions beyond generation of income in the current period.

The cash flow statement therefore has a two-fold purpose:

The cash flow statement reports cash income, calling it cash from operations.

1. To produce a measure of performance based on day-to-day cash flow, cash generated by ordinary business activities, instead of accrual accounting's net income measure.

   This cash measure, which we have called cash income and which the cash flow statement calls *cash from operations, does not mean that accrual income is invalid*; rather, it provides a different perspective on performance and so enhances the information for users.

The cash flow statement also reports nonoperating cash flows from financing and investing activities.

2. To incorporate other nonoperating cash inflows and outflows, such as from investing in new assets, selling off old ones, borrowing or repaying debts, obtaining new capital from owners, or paying dividends to the owners.

   By including *nonoperating cash flows*, the cash flow statement provides a complete description of how the firm's cash was managed during the period, to tell the full story of why the enterprise has more, or less, cash at the end of the period than at the beginning.

With this information, the user can evaluate management's strategy for managing cash and make a better judgment of the company's liquidity, solvency, risk, and opportunities than could be made just from the balance sheet, income statement, and statement of retained earnings.

Things keep changing. The cash flow statement is a relatively recent addition to the set of financial statements, having become a standard part in only the last few decades. During that time, it has undergone several changes in name, format, and content. You should be alert for other titles left over from the past. Other terms and titles you may encounter are *statement of changes in financial position*, *statement of source and application of cash*, and *funds statement*.

HOW'S YOUR UNDERSTANDING?

Here are two questions you should be able to answer based on what you have just read. If you can't answer them, it would be best to reread the material.

1. What does cash flow have to do with liquidity and solvency?
2. What else is there to cash flow beyond the cash income we saw in Simone's jewellery business in Chapter 1?

4.3 The Cash Flow Statement

The cash flow statement, like the other statements, has a standard format. It is useful to know, because variations from that format may be a signal of special circumstances or problems. Here is the format, with summary figures from CPR to illustrate the categories (we'll look at CPR's cash flow statement in more detail later in the chapter).

Cash Flow Statement Standard Format (With Summary Figures for Canadian Pacific Railway for 2004, in millions)

	CPR 2004
Operating activities:	
Cash generated by operations from day-to-day cash receipts and payments related to the activities that generate income.	$ 786.0
Investing activities:	
Cash used to invest in additional noncurrent assets, including investments in other companies, minus any cash proceeds obtained by disposing of such assets.	(666.1)
Financing activities:	
Cash obtained from borrowing and from issuing share capital, minus borrowing repaid or shares redeemed. Any cash transactions in retained earnings (not included in net income) are included here, especially dividends and share issue costs.	98.4
Change in cash for the period:	
Net sum of the above three categories.	$ 218.3
Cash (and equivalents) at the beginning of the period:	
Brought forward from last period's cash flow statement and balance sheet.	134.7
Cash (and equivalents) at the end of the period:	
Equals what is shown on the balance sheet at the end of the period.	$ 353.0

Some important features of this format are:

Same period as income statement.

Cash and equivalents are defined.

Negative cash (bank overdraft) is possible.

The cash flow statement also has footnotes.

Only actual cash flows during the period are included.

1. The cash flow statement covers the same period as the income statement.
2. Cash includes some equivalents: very liquid near-cash assets that can be turned into cash without any risk of loss, such as demand bank deposits and certificates with a maturity of three months or less. CPR defined its cash as "cash and short-term investments."
3. In some cases, cash may include temporary negative bank balances (overdrafts) if they are just a result of cash management activity and the bank balances regularly vary from positive to negative. In 1999, CPR had a bank overdraft of $14.7 million, which it deducted from cash and short-term investments to produce a "net cash" amount, but has not shown an overdraft since.
4. If there is anything unusual about the enterprise's definition of cash (and equivalents), or any other category of the statement, that should be explained in the notes to the financial statements. You may even see a little reconciliation at the bottom of the cash flow statement. CPR had this in 1999 when it had the bank overdraft, showing how net cash was calculated. You can view this on CPR's website (**www.cpr.ca**).
5. The cash flow statement follows some rules to ensure that its focus stays on cash. For example, if a dividend has been declared but not all paid, only the paid part is included in the cash flow statement's financing activities section. Another example is that if there is an account payable for a noncurrent asset, the investing activities figure shows only the amount paid so far. Any asset acquisitions, borrowing, or share issues that are done without cash, such as acquiring land in return for shares, are excluded from the cash flow statement.

Operating, investing, and financing cash flows can all be either positive or negative.

6. Any of the numbers in the cash flow statement can be positive or negative, according to what happened during the period. For example, a bad year can result in cash from operations being negative, in which case it might be described as cash used in operations! As another example, a company undergoing significant restructuring could have more cash coming in from selling off assets than cash going out to buy more, so its investing section could be a positive cash inflow instead of the usual cash outflow.

Interest and tax cash payments should be disclosed.

7. At the bottom of the cash flow statement or in the financial statement notes, the amount of interest paid in cash and cash flows arising from income tax should be disclosed. CPR did this in its notes.

Cash from operations is derived indirectly from accrual income.

8. Deriving the cash flow from day-to-day operations is one of the main reasons for having the cash flow analysis. The cash from operations figure takes away accrual accounting's many adjustments, which are very important in measuring income but obscure the cash effects. To emphasize this, most cash flow statements begin with the net income figure from the income statement and then explicitly remove the effects of changes in accounts receivable, accounts payable, amortization, and other accruals. This is called the *indirect method* of deriving cash from operations, as distinct from the *direct method* of just listing operating *cash receipts* and deducting operating *cash payments* (also called *disbursements*). The direct and indirect methods of calculating cash from operations both end up with the same figure for cash from operations, they just go about the calculation differently:

FIGURE 4.1

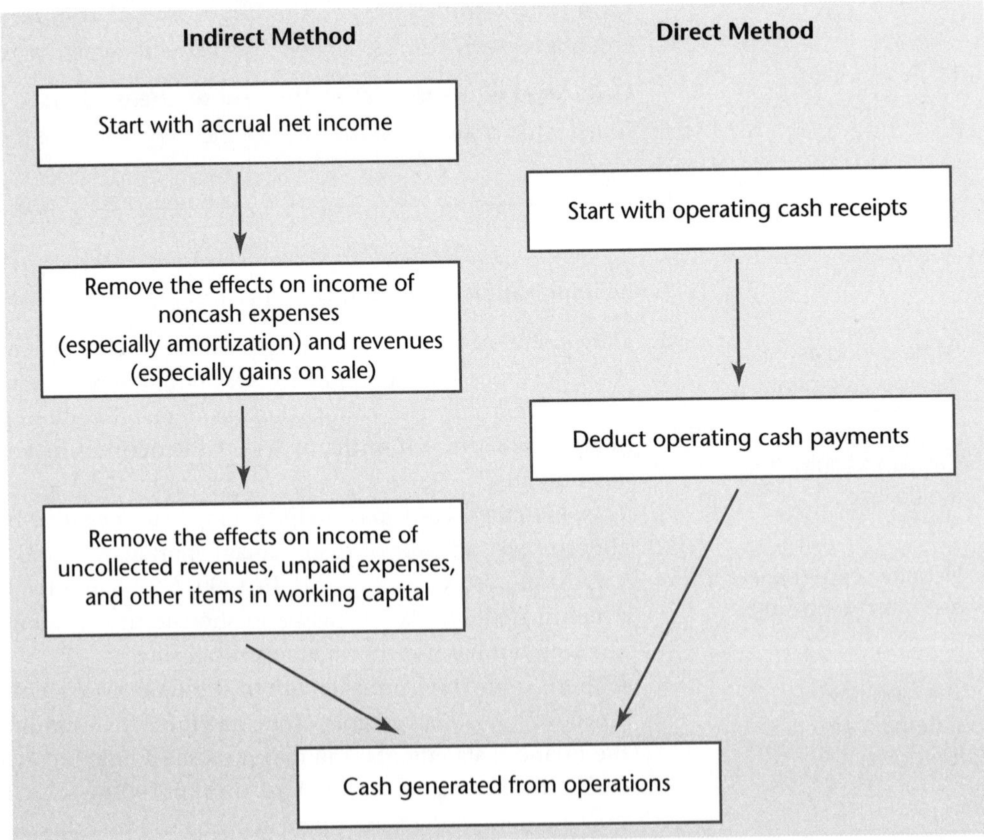

Cash flow analysis is a good way to cement your understanding of what the financial statements contain and to sharpen your analytical skills. This chapter starts with the intuitively simpler direct method of preparing the cash flow statement and then turns to the indirect method, both because it is the usual method and it allows some practice in reworking the financial statements for analysis. The chapter ends with some more complex and realistic examples.

HOW'S YOUR UNDERSTANDING?

Here are two questions you should be able to answer based on what you have just read. If you can't answer them, it would be best to reread the material.

1. What are the summary categories of cash flow used in the cash flow statement?
2. Dubroy Inc. defines its cash and equivalents to include the following (this year's and last year's figures shown in that order for each): Cash ($13,000; $4,000), Demand deposit in MegaBank ($25,000; $50,000), and Occasional bank overdraft ($7,000; $3,000).

   What is the net total change in cash that the cash flow statement for this year will explain?

Cash and equivalents at the beginning = $4,000 + $50,000 – $3,000 = $51,000. At the end they = $13,000 + $25,000 – $7,000 = $31,000. So the change in cash is negative $20,000.

4.4 Cash Flow Analysis Using Receipts and Payments

The direct method classifies information from the Cash ledger account and supporting detailed cash receipts and payments records into the cash flow statement categories shown at the beginning of Section 4.3. It's probably the way you'd expect cash flow analysis to be done, so let's begin with it. An example will show you how this works.

The following information is summarized from Roebuck Industries Inc.'s cash records for this year:

EXHIBIT 4·2

Cash on hand at the beginning of the year		$ 813,430
Cash receipts for the year:		
Cash sales	$ 73,320	
Collections from customers for credit sales	17,894,530	
Proceeds from sale of land	1,200,000	
Proceeds from issue of new bonded debt	5,300,000	
Proceeds from issue of new shares	840,000	25,307,850
		26,121,280
Cash payments (disbursements) for the year:		
Expenses paid in cash	49,210	
Payments to suppliers and employees	14,992,860	
Income tax paid	765,500	
Paid to acquire new noncurrent assets	6,733,310	
Repayments on noncurrent debt	3,112,300	
Costs of new share issue	21,340	
Dividends paid	400,000	26,074,520
Cash on hand at the end of the year		$ 46,760

The cash flow statement's categories separate day-to-day income from other cash flows.

Preparing the cash flow statement from this information is straightforward—just put the figures above into the appropriate statement categories. Note that there is no mention of accrual income; in fact there is no way to tell what it is. Two principles followed in categorizing the cash flow statement's information are reflected in the statement that follows:

- Segregate operating cash flows (those related to day-to-day income-generating activities) from the more intermittent nonoperating cash flows for investing and financing; and
- Identify cash flows related to the statement of retained earnings and put them into the financing category (for example, share issue costs and dividends paid).

Here is the resulting statement.

Roebuck Industries Inc.
Cash Flow Statement for This Year (Direct Method)

Operating activities:	
Operating cash receipts ($73,320 + $17,894,530)	$17,967,850
Operating cash payments ($49,210 + $14,992,860 + $765,500)	(15,807,570)
Cash obtained from operations	$ 2,160,280
Investing activities:	
Acquisitions of new noncurrent assets	$ (6,733,310)
Proceeds from sale of land	1,200,000
Cash used for investing	$ (5,533,310)
Financing activities:	
Proceeds from issue of new bonded debt	$ 5,300,000
Repayments on noncurrent debt	(3,112,300)
Proceeds from issue of new shares	840,000
Costs of new share issue	(21,340)
Dividends paid	(400,000)
Cash obtained from financing	$ 2,606,360
Change in cash for the year	$ (766,670)
Cash at the beginning of the year	813,430
Cash at the end of the year	$ 46,760

Positive numbers are sources of cash and negative numbers are uses of cash.

The cash flow statement's analysis is quite informative.

This analysis shows that Roebuck's cash went down almost to zero during the year, because the company spent more cash acquiring new assets than it raised through operations and financing. Though by far the largest inflows and outflows of cash were from day-to-day operations, the net contribution of operations to the company's cash supply was smaller than the net contribution through financing activities.

Some details are interesting. The company raised about a sixth of the cash needed for the new assets by selling some land. The financing was primarily debt this year, not shares, so the company is further in debt than it was (we can see that the debt-equity ratio will have gone up this year, though we don't know by how much without having the balance sheet). In paying for new assets and paying dividends, the company almost exhausted its cash. While this may have left it in a more risky position in regard to paying its bills, it is not necessarily an unwise thing to have done, because having a lot of cash sitting around earns the company little (maybe just a little bank interest), and the money may have been quite productively spent on new assets or paying off noncurrent debt.

These points illustrate two important features of cash flow analysis:

The cash flow analysis indicates financial management strategies.

- It gives insight into the company's strategy for managing its financial affairs, and at the very least suggests a list of questions that could be followed up in more detail.

For example, did the company sell the land because it was short of cash, or was it offered a price that was too good to pass up?

- For maximum usefulness, it should be combined with other information about the company, especially the information in the other financial statements. For example, what is the company's debt load, and did the increase this year put it in a difficult position? (The balance sheet can help with that question.) Or, what proportion of income is the company paying out as dividends? (The income and retained earnings statements help with that question.)

HOW'S YOUR UNDERSTANDING?

Here are two questions you should be able to answer based on what you have just read. If you can't answer them, it would be best to reread the material.

1. How can you best draw insights from the cash flow statement's analysis?
2. Suppose on the last day of this year, Roebuck experienced the following three cash transactions in addition to those already included above. What would be the resulting figures for operations, investing, financing, and change in cash for the year?
   (1) A customer who had been very slow in paying came in and paid an old account receivable of $50,000.
   (2) The company got additional bank loan financing of $120,000.
   (3) The company issued new shares valued at $75,000 in exchange for a small plot of land it wanted for expansion of its factory.

The first item is an operating receipt, increasing cash from operations by $50,000. The second is a financing inflow, increasing cash from financing by $120,000. The third doesn't involve any cash and so wouldn't be part of the cash flow statement. Results: Cash from operations up $50,000 to $2,210,280, cash for investing unchanged at $(5,533,310), cash from financing up $120,000 to $2,726,360, change in cash improved $170,000 to $(596,670).

4.5 Cash Flow Analysis Using Adjusted Accrual Income and Balance Sheet Changes

The indirect method is used in preparing most companies' cash flow statements.

The *direct method* illustrated in Section 4.4 just requires information from the cash records. But in fact the cash flow statement has traditionally been prepared, and presented, in quite a different way, by analyzing changes in the balance sheet and combining that analysis with information from the income and retained earnings statements. This is done for many reasons, including tradition and its ability to relate operating cash flow to accrual income, but also because, in practice, digging out the details of cash receipts and payments over a whole year can be a large task, especially if there are several or many cash and bank accounts, as is true for most medium to large-sized companies. The *indirect method* is explained in this section because without understanding it, you will be mystified by the format of the cash from operations section of most published cash flow statements. The analysis also will help polish your analytical skill and know-ledge of the other statements, as well as your insight about what cash flow analysis depicts.

Because of double entry, changes in cash must be explained by changes in all other accounts.

The indirect method relies on a basic property of double-entry accounting. Since cash is one of the accounts that make up a balanced balance sheet, any change in cash must be *exactly* reflected in one or more *other* balance sheet accounts. So we can analyze cash changes by looking instead at *changes in all the other accounts in the balance sheet*: those changes will tell us what the company did with its cash. Here is the balance sheet equation, to demonstrate that this must be true arithmetically (Δ stands for *change* from one year, 2004, to the next, 2005):

This year:	Cash_{2005}	+	$\text{Noncash assets}_{2005}$	=	$\text{Liabilities}_{2005}$	+	Equity_{2005}
Last year:	Cash_{2004}	+	$\text{Noncash assets}_{2004}$	=	$\text{Liabilities}_{2004}$	+	Equity_{2004}
Difference:	Δ Cash	+	Δ Noncash assets	=	Δ Liabilities	+	Δ Equity
Rearranging:	Δ Cash			=	Δ Liabilities	+	Δ Equity
						–	Δ Noncash assets

The indirect method determines changes in all noncash balance sheet accounts, eliminating those not involving cash.

The indirect method uses this basic approach: construct the cash flow statement by placing all balance sheet account changes in the appropriate categories of the cash flow statement after adjusting for (eliminating) all noncash components of those account changes. This method can handle great complexity, and accountants have procedures to ensure that no changes are forgotten in the analysis, but such complexities and procedures are beyond the scope of this book. The schedule below shows how the indirect method works for the categories of the cash flow statement. Brief additional explanations follow the schedule and then the Roebuck Industries example is redone using the indirect method. (In Section 4.7, after some practice doing the analysis, we will see how Canadian Pacific Railway did these calculations.)

Categorization of the Changes in Noncash Balance Sheet Accounts

Operating activities:

Start with net income or if different, income from continuing operations for this period (part of the retained earnings change)

Adjustments to eliminate noncash components of income:

Remove revenues and expenses (usually nonoperating) that are entirely noncash: gains and losses, write-downs and write-offs of investments and noncurrent assets in general

Remove revenues and expenses that relate to noncurrent past or future cash flows: amortization (asset cost paid in the past), and future costs to be paid (future income taxes, warranties, pension costs, etc.)

Remove the effects on accrual income of working capital account changes: accounts receivable, inventories, prepaid expenses, accounts payable, estimated accrued liabilities, etc., and investments whose trading is part of operations

Investing activities:

Additions to plant and equipment and intangible and other assets, minus any amounts not yet (or ever) paid in cash and so still showing as payable

Proceeds from disposal of plant and equipment and intangible and other assets (account changes due to elimination of cost and accumulated amortization of disposed assets are ignored because they are not cash items)

Additions to and proceeds of disposal of mainly noncurrent investments

Financing activities:

Changes in current and noncurrent debt financing, minus any parts not involving cash (such as exchanges for shares or noncash assets)

Changes in share capital, minus any parts not involving cash (such as exchanges for debt or noncash assets)

Changes in retained earnings other than net income for this period: dividends, share issue costs, etc., minus any parts not paid in cash (e.g., stock dividends or dividends payable)

Here are some comments to lead into an example of how the indirect method works.

Changes in equity and in cash: up together, down together. Same for liabilities. Opposite for noncash assets.

1. Remember the changes equation above:

$$\Delta \text{ Cash} = \Delta \text{ Liabilities} + \Delta \text{ Equity} - \Delta \text{ Noncash assets.}$$

L↑⇒Cash↑	L↓⇒Cash↓
E↑⇒Cash↑	E↓⇒Cash↓
OthA↑⇒Cash↓	OthA↓⇒Cash↑

From this equation, you can see that changes in liabilities and equity (+ signs) have the same sign as changes in cash, whereas changes in noncash assets (– sign) have the opposite sign. This should be intuitively sensible: borrowing money, for example, increases the debt liability and the cash, and paying the debt back reduces both. Issuing shares also increases cash, and dividends both reduce equity and reduce cash when they are paid. On the other hand, paying cash for a new asset increases the asset but decreases cash, and reducing an asset (say by selling land or collecting accounts receivable) increases cash. Increasing noncash assets implies using cash to do so, and decreasing noncash assets implies getting cash for them.

Income and changes in cash: up together, down together.

2. Though accrual income does not necessarily increase cash right now, *on average* earning income will increase cash. Again, the intuition should be clear. Earning income helps cash. If you find this a bit subtle, think of the opposite: surely it would not make sense to expect cash to go *down* when income goes up, or cash to go up when the company incurs a loss. Also, as income is part of equity through retained earnings, its effect on cash is the same as other equity items. Likewise, reducing equity (retained earnings) by declaring dividends reduces cash when the dividends are paid.

Income⇒Cash↑ on average
Loss⇒Cash↓ on average
Div⇒Cash↓ when paid

The indirect cash from operations calculation starts with net income and removes all the accruals that cause it to differ from cash income.

3. Given the starting point of net income, the adjustments to it in the operating activities part of the categorization schedule above just *remove* from income all the things that were done to create accrual income instead of cash income. These are the same sorts of adjustments we saw in Section 1.10 when reconciling Simone's Jewellery accrual and cash incomes. Therefore, items that *increased* accrual income are *deducted* in these adjustments, such as gains on noncurrent asset disposals, increases in accounts receivable (uncollected revenue), and increases in inventory (unused goods). Conversely, items that *decreased* accrual income are *added* in these adjustments, such as amortization expense, losses on noncurrent asset disposals, asset write-downs and write-offs, and increases in accounts payable and accrued estimated liabilities.

- Start with net income
- Deduct noncash items that increased the income (didn't increase cash)
- Add back noncash items that decreased the income (didn't decrease cash)
- The result is cash income (cash from operations)

4. The treatment of gains and losses on noncurrent asset disposals is a bit subtle to understand, but understanding it is useful because it relates to how the stock market reacts to financial information. If a company makes a gain on the sale of a noncurrent asset, it does so because it received cash (or a promise of cash) exceeding the book value of the asset, that is, exceeding the net value of the asset's cost minus its accumulated amortization. A loss on sale happens if the cash is less than book value. Such an asset sale is recorded this way:

Dr Cash	(the proceeds from the disposal)
Cr Noncurrent asset cost	(to remove the asset's cost from the accounts)
Dr Accumulated amortization	(to remove the asset's acc. amort. from the accounts)
Dr Loss on sale, *or* Cr Gain on sale	(the difference between proceeds and book value)

Gains on disposal are deducted from net income in operating activities.

Cash proceeds are included in investing activities.

Here's the subtle part. The gain or loss on disposal, which is in the income statement and so is part of accrual net income, is *not* what we want on the cash flow statement, because it is not the cash part, it is just the *difference* between the cash and the book value, as the journal entry above shows. So the gain or loss has to be removed from the net income and the cash proceeds inserted instead, but in the *investing activities* section because it is not a result of day-to-day operations. A gain helped income, so it must be deducted from net income in the operating activities section to remove it. A loss reduced income, so it must be added back to net income to remove it. (The removal of the asset cost and the accumulated amortization is ignored in the cash flow analysis because neither is a cash item.)

Noncurrent asset disposals and cash flow

Where there is a gain on disposal:
- The proceeds are a cash inflow.
- The gain is not cash and so must be subtracted from income to get cash from operations.

Where there is a loss on disposal:
- The proceeds (if any) are a cash inflow.
- The loss is not cash and so must be added back to income to get cash from operations.

Losses on disposal and write-downs are added back to net income in operating activities.

If a noncurrent asset, such as a factory or an investment in another company, is written down or written off because it is felt to have less or no value, the entry above has no "proceeds" amount, because there is no cash. So the whole amount of the write-down or write-off, which is in income, must be added back to net income in the operating activities section. This can drastically affect the difference between net income and cash from operations, because such write-downs and write-offs may be quite large (remember the Big Bath and goodwill write-downs from Chapter 3, for example). If such losses or write-downs are large, cash from operations might be quite positive even if accrual income was made low or negative by the write-down or write-off. Perhaps because of the lack of cash effect, the stock market often seems to ignore large write-offs, write-downs, or losses on disposal, not penalizing companies that report them on their income statements.

The indirect method's appeal may begin to become apparent to you from these points. By identifying the changes in noncash accounts (assets, liabilities, and equity), the analysis identifies where the company's cash came from and what the company did with the cash. This can all be done without having to go through the cash account(s) and write down what each transaction seemed to be for.

An Indirect Method Example: Roebuck Industries Again

Financial information about Roebuck Industries Inc., which we saw in the previous section about the direct method, is below. The indirect method is based on balance sheet *changes,* as indicated in the changes version of the balance sheet equation shown above, so we focus on

- balance sheet changes, including retained earnings (each change just equals this year's account balance minus last year's); and
- the income components (several are useful for the analysis, and net income is part of the retained earnings change).

All the balance sheet changes must have some connection with cash flow—a purely noncash transaction, such as issuing shares in return for land (Dr Land, Cr Share capital) is ignored, so no such purely noncash changes are included in the balance sheet changes below.

Roebuck Industries Inc.
Balance Sheet Changes
(This Year Minus Last Year)

ASSETS	
Current assets:	
Cash down	$ (766,670)
Accounts receivable up	2,875,870
Inventory down	(1,225,770)
Noncurrent assets:	
Asset cost up*	6,328,310
Accum. amortization up	(3,794,630)
TOTAL CHANGES	$ 3,417,110
LIABILITIES AND EQUITY	
Current liabilities:	
Accounts payable down	$(1,359,410)
Dividend payable up	100,000
Equipment payable** up	220,000
Noncurrent liabilities:	
Bonded debt up	5,300,000
Other debt down	(3,112,300)
Equity:	
Share capital up	840,000
Retained earnings up	1,428,820
TOTAL CHANGES	$ 3,417,110

* Cost change = $6,953,310 new assets minus $625,000 cost of land sold.
** Owing on new assets acquired.

Roebuck Industries Inc.
Income Statement for the Year

Revenue	$20,843,720
Expenses:	
COGS, etc.	$14,390,490
Amortization	3,794,630
	$18,185,120
Operating income	$ 2,658,600
Gain on land sold*	575,000
Income before tax	$ 3,233,600
Income tax expense	1,283,440
Net income	$ 1,950,160

* Gain = $1,200,000 proceeds minus $625,000 land cost.

Roebuck Industries Inc.
Retained Earnings Changes for the Year

Add net income	$1,950,160
Deduct dividends declared*	(500,000)
Deduct costs of share issue	(21,340)
NET CHANGE	$1,428,820

* $100,000 owing at year-end.

Generating the cash flow statement from these changes basically is a process of putting the changes in the appropriate categories of the cash flow statement and eliminating any noncash items from income, as explained earlier in this section. The result is a cash flow statement that has exactly the same category totals as the example in Section 4.4, and differs from that statement *only* in the way cash from operations is derived.

Here is the cash flow statement, including various explanations to help you follow what is going on—these would not usually be shown on a statement because accountants assume the reader of the statement has some understanding of how the statement is assembled. Also, in this example we have used only the changes in accounts, so the statement ends with the change in cash.

Roebuck Industries Inc.
Cash Flow Statement for This Year (Indirect Method)

Operating activities:	
Net income for the year	$ 1,950,160
Deduct noncash revenue to eliminate it: gain on land sale	(575,000)
Add back noncash expense to eliminate it: amortization	3,794,630
Deduct increase in accounts receivable to eliminate its effect	(2,875,870)
Add back reduction in inventory to eliminate its effect	1,225,770
Deduct decrease in accounts payable to eliminate its effect	(1,359,410)
Cash obtained from operations	$ 2,160,280
Investing activities:	
Acquisitions of new noncurrent assets ($6,953,310 – $220,000)	$(6,733,310)
Proceeds from sale of land	1,200,000
Cash used for investing	$(5,533,310)
Financing activities:	
Proceeds from issue of new bonded debt	$ 5,300,000
Repayments on noncurrent debt	(3,112,300)
Proceeds from issue of new shares	840,000
Costs of new share issue	(21,340)
Dividends paid ($500,000 – $100,000)	(400,000)
Cash obtained from financing	$ 2,606,360
Change in cash for the year	$ (766,670)

Using the indirect method, items in the operating section **are not sources and uses of cash** but rather the removal of noncash revenues and expenses from accrual net income.

The investing and financing sections are identical to the direct method.

Positive numbers = sources of cash

Negative numbers = uses of cash

Every balance sheet change is appropriately represented on the cash flow statement.

Take a few moments and go through the preceding set of balance sheet changes for Roebuck Industries. You'll see that every change is somewhere on the cash flow statement:

- The change in cash is the cash flow statement's "bottom line."
- Decreases in noncash assets and increases in liabilities and equity are all positive in their effects on cash. The opposites, increases in noncash assets and decreases in liabilities and equity, are all negative in their effects.
- The change in retained earnings has three components: net income, share issue costs, and dividends. They are all on the cash flow statement. Income is combined with several other changes to get cash from operations. Dividends are combined with the change in dividends payable to get dividends paid.
- The change in noncurrent assets cost is there too. The cost of new assets ($6,953,310 according to the footnote) is reduced by the change in equipment payable ($220,000) to get the cash spent on new assets, $6,733,310.
- The cost of the old land removed is also represented, because that $625,000 cost is replaced on the cash flow statement by two amounts: the positive $1,200,000 cash proceeds and the negative $575,000 gain deduction, which net to $625,000.
- The $3,794,630 change in accumulated amortization, which looks as though it increases cash on the cash flow statement, does not really do that. It is there in operating activities to *cancel out* the effect on income of having deducted the noncash amortization expense in calculating the net income.

The indirect method statement is different from the direct version only in the operations section. The operations section provides information not available from the direct version:

- The difference between accrual accounting income and cash income (cash from operations): accrual income is only slightly lower here, but in many cases is quite different. The direct method doesn't provide accrual income and so doesn't show the difference.
- Components of that difference, such as the gain on the land sale and the amortization of noncurrent assets, neither of which is provided by the direct version.
- The effect of changes in working capital accounts. Roebuck has tied up $2,875,870 of additional cash by letting the accounts receivable grow, and has used another $1,359,410 by paying off more accounts payable. On the other hand, there is $1,225,770 less cash tied up in inventory.

HOW'S YOUR UNDERSTANDING?

Here are two questions you should be able to answer based on what you have just read. If you can't answer them, it would be best to reread the material.

1. What are the kinds of adjustments the indirect method makes to net income, and why are they done?
2. Suppose Roebuck Industries Inc. experienced the following transactions on the last day of this year, in addition to those already included above. What would be the resulting figures for operations, investing, financing, and change in cash for the year?
   (1) The company bought more inventory on credit for $60,000.
   (2) The company issued more shares for $130,000 cash.
   (3) The company paid off its equipment loan, causing a temporary bank overdraft.

The first item reduces both the inventory decrease and the accounts payable decrease by the same amount, having no net effect on cash from operations, which is appropriate because there was no cash involved. The second item raises the proceeds from new shares by $130,000 and reduces the negative cash change by the same amount. The third item eliminates the equipment loan change and so increases cash paid for new assets by $220,000 to $6,953,310. The second and third items together cause a net reduction in cash of $90,000, changing the total cash change to negative $856,670. If we go back to Roebuck's cash account information in Section 4.4, we can see that cash on hand at the end of the year would now become negative ($46,760 – $90,000 = $(43,240)).

4.6 Demonstration Problem: Doing the Cash Flow Statement from Balance Sheet Changes

Here is a second demonstration of how to use balance sheet changes and net income adjustments to analyze cash flow, using the indirect method. Below are the balance sheet changes for Simplistic Enterprises Ltd., and then the cash flow statement derived from them. The cash flow statement includes some comments to help you see what each cash flow item stands for.

Simplistic Enterprises Ltd.
Balance Sheets for 2006 and 2005,
with Changes Calculated

	2006	2005	Change
Assets			
Current assets:			
Cash	$150	$130	$20
Accounts receivable	200	160	40
Noncurrent assets:			
Building cost	500	420	80
Accumulated amortization*	(180)	(130)	(50)
	$670	$580	$90
Liabilities and Equity			
Current liabilities:			
Temporary bank overdraft	$ 10	$ 25	$(15)
Accounts payable	110	65	45
Noncurrent liabilities:			
Mortgage debt	140	175	(35)
Future income tax	100	90	10
Equity:			
Share capital issued	100	85	15
Retained earnings**	210	140	70
	$670	$580	$90

* The change in accumulated amortization is due to $50 in amortization expense deducted in determining 2006 accrual income.

** According to the statement of retained earnings, the change in retained earnings is due to the 2006 net income of $95 having been added to the 2005 balance, minus dividends paid of $25.

Simplistic Enterprises Ltd.
Cash Flow Statement
(with additional comments)
for the Year 2006

Operations	
Net income for the year (accrual net income as shown in the income statement and part of the change in retained earnings on the balance sheet)	$ 95
Add back amortization expense (the change in accumulated amortization: this expense reduced accrual income but did not reduce cash income so adding it back helps to calculate cash income)	50
Add back future income tax expense (the change in the liability: as for amortization, this expense did not reduce cash income so adding it back also helps to calculate cash income)	10
Deduct the change in accounts receivable (the receivables are higher, so some of the 2006 income is from revenue that has not been collected, so cash income was lower because of the cash that has not yet come in)	(40)
Add change in accounts payable (the higher payables mean that some of the expenses deducted from 2006 income have not yet been paid, saving cash for now and meaning cash income was higher because of that)	45
Cash generated from operations (cash income)	$160
Investing	
Increased investment in the building (increasing a noncurrent asset would have taken cash, so this has a negative effect)	$ (80)
Financing	
Decrease in mortgage debt (reducing the mortgage would have taken cash)	$ (35)
Increase in share capital (this would have brought cash)	15
Dividends paid during the year (part of the change in retained earnings)	(25)
Net cash used in financing	$ (45)
Net total change in cash for the year	$ 35
Cash, beginning of the year	105
Cash, end of the year	$140
Cash consists of:	
Cash	$150
Minus temporary bank overdraft	(10)
Net cash	$140

The cash flow statement is an insightful analysis. Just by rearranging the balance sheet changes between two dates (2005 and 2006), we have produced several pieces of information:

- Simplistic increased its cash by $35 during the year: cash went up by $20 and the temporary bank overdraft went down by $15. (Positive cash went up, negative cash went down, so both increase cash.)
- This increase was entirely due to day-to-day operations because investing and financing activities both reduced cash.
- Cash from operations ($160) was nearly twice the accrual net income ($95) because the net income was reduced by noncash expenses for amortization and future income taxes. It is normal for cash from operations to exceed net income because of such expenses.
- Cash from operations would have been even higher had Simplistic collected more of its accounts receivable. On the other hand, the company hung onto some cash by not paying some accounts payable.
- The company spent $80 on its building during the year, which was more than the $50 amortization expense. This is evidence that the company is keeping its building up to date, not just letting its value decline through use.
- The company raised some cash by issuing shares ($15), but that was more than offset by the $35 needed to make payments on the mortgage principal during the year and the $25 in dividends paid.

The cash flow analysis shows us why the company's net income of $95 did not produce an equal increase in cash. Many more things were going on involving cash.

HOW'S YOUR UNDERSTANDING?

Here are two questions you should be able to answer based on what you have just read. If you can't answer them, it would be best to reread the material.

1. What does the cash flow statement's analysis show beyond the performance portrayed in the income statement?
2. Horizon Inc. has the following results and balance sheet changes from last year to this year. Calculate the three categories of the cash flow statement and determine the total change in cash for the year.
   Net income for the year, $23,950; Dividends declared and paid, $9,250; Amortization expense, $16,900; Future income tax expense, $2,200; Increase in accounts receivable, $1,205; Increase in accounts payable, $4,320; Increase in mortgage debt, $10,000; Increase in share capital, $15,000; Increase in cost of noncurrent assets, $57,260.

Cash from operations = $23,950 + $16,900 + $2,200 – $1,205 + $4,320 = $46,165. Cash used in investing = $57,260. Cash from financing = $10,000 + $15,000 – $9,250 = $15,750. Net total change in cash = $46,165 – $57,260 + $15,750 = $4,655 increase.

4.7 Interpreting A Company's Cash Flow Statement

In Chapters 2 and 3, we saw the comparative balance sheets, income statements, and statements of retained earnings of Canadian Pacific Railway. Now let's see what the company's cash flow statement has to tell us. Following it is Note 10 on changes in noncash working capital accounts, but other notes are not included in this book.

Canadian Pacific Railway Limited
Statement of consolidated cash flows

Year ended December 31 (in millions)	2004	2003 (Restated – see Note 2)	2002 (Restated – see Note 2)
Operating activities			
Net income	**$ 413.0**	$ 401.3	$ 487.5
Add (deduct) items not affecting cash			
Depreciation and amortization	**407.1**	372.3	340.2
Future income taxes (Note 7)	**131.5**	31.8	95.0
Environmental remediation charge (Note 3)	**90.9**	–	–
Restructuring and impairment charge (Note 4)	**(19.0)**	215.1	–
Foreign exchange gain on long-term debt	**(94.4)**	(209.5)	(13.4)
Amortization of deferred charges	**24.7**	20.3	19.3
Other	**–**	–	(0.8)
Restructuring payments	**(88.8)**	(107.0)	(119.3)
Other operating activities, net (Note 20)	**(112.2)**	(365.0)	(45.0)
Change in noncash working capital balances related to operations (Note 10)	**33.2**	(53.6)	–
Cash provided by operating activities	**786.0**	305.7	763.5
Investing activities			
Additions to properties (Note 12)	**(673.8)**	(686.6)	(558.5)
Other investments	**(2.5)**	(21.9)	4.0
Net proceeds from disposal of transportation properties	**10.2**	8.2	3.5
Cash used in investing activities	**(666.1)**	(700.3)	(551.0)
Financing activities			
Dividends paid	**(81.7)**	(80.8)	(80.8)
Issuance of shares	**2.5**	2.0	2.0
Issuance of long-term debt	**193.7**	699.8	–
Repayment of long-term debt	**(16.1)**	(376.6)	(405.7)
Cash provided by (used in) financing activities	**98.4**	244.4	(484.5)
Cash position			
Increase (decrease) in net cash	**218.3**	(150.2)	(272.0)
Net cash at beginning of year	**134.7**	284.9	556.9
Net cash at end of year	**$ 353.0**	$ 134.7	$ 284.9
Net cash is defined as:			
Cash and short-term investments	**$ 353.0**	$ 134.7	$ 284.9

(Notes to consolidated financial statements are not included.)

Canadian Pacific Railway Limited

10. Change in noncash working capital balances related to operations (in millions)	**2004**	**2003**	**2002**
(Use) source of cash:			
Accounts receivable	**$ (39.0)**	$ 45.2	$ 21.1
Materials and supplies	**(35.5)**	2.5	(6.6)
Accounts payable and accrued liabilities	**112.3**	(76.3)	(17.4)
Income and other taxes payable	**(4.6)**	(25.0)	2.9
Change in noncash working capital	**$ 33.2**	$ (53.6)	$ –

CPR has an uncomplicated definition of cash.

For CPR, cash is uncomplicated, being defined as just the cash and short-term investments asset, which you can verify by looking back at the balance sheet in Section 2.9.

CPR's change in cash and cash on hand have been rising.

This is a consolidated statement, as were CPR's other statements. Therefore, it describes the cash flows of the group of companies making up CPR. Like the income statement in Section 3.4, the cash flow statement covers three years, 2002–2004.

An immediately striking piece of information is that CPR's change in cash has been steadily rising, going from negative $272.0 million in 2002 to $218.3 million in 2004. The statement also reveals that the major source of cash for CPR has been operations in each year and that the company has been heavily investing in additions to property throughout the period.

A. Operating Activities.

CPR relies on internal financing.

(1) *Operations provide internal financing.* Day-to-day operations (cash income) has been a major source of cash for CPR over the last three years. While slightly less than new long-term debt ($699.8 – $376.6 = $323.2) in 2003, cash from operations is greater than the total increase in cash in all three years, indicating that CPR is reliant on *internal financing*, cash produced by the company's business operations. Shortly, we will compare this internal financing to external sources.

CPR has large noncash expenses.

(2) *Noncash expenses.* The impact of noncash expenses is significant for CPR. In 2004 and 2003, the three main noncash expenses exceeded net income, and were almost equal in 2002. This alone shows why accrual income is not a good approximation of cash income. The schedule here uses information from the cash flow statement: only the depreciation and amortization figure is also shown individually on the income statement in Section 3.4; the others are part of other items in the income statement and so we learn their amounts only from the cash flow statement, which is one of the cash flow statement's contributions.

Significant noncash expenses for CPR

	2004	2003	2002
Deprec. & amort.	$407.1	$372.3	$340.2
Future income taxes	131.5	31.8	95.0
Amort. of def. chgs	24.7	20.3	19.3
Sum	$563.3	$424.4	$454.5
Net income	$413.0	$401.3	$487.5

CPR has had large restructuring costs in most years since 1999, not actually paid for in the year incurred.

(3) *Accrual expenses and cash flows differ in timing.* Restructuring costs (mostly costs such as severance pay for employees laid off in cost-saving arrangements, but also some environmental remediation costs) are an interesting case of the use of accrual accounting. In 2003, a provision of $215.1 million for these costs was included as an expense in calculating income. The journal entry would be Dr Restructuring expense 215.1, Cr Restructuring liability 215.1. No cash was involved in recording the expense, so the $215.1 was added back to income in calculating cash from operations in 2003. The actual cash payments made each year have not equaled the expense shown on the income statement. The unpaid balance is included mainly in the "deferred liability" noncurrent liability account.

Noncash working capital changes had little net effect on CPR's operating cash flows.

(4) *Noncash working capital changes related to operations.* CPR's cash flow statement shows only small changes here: a $33.2 million increase in 2004, a slightly larger decrease of $53.6 million in 2003, and no change in 2002. This indicates that the amounts in accounts receivable, inventories, and accounts payable are being carefully controlled by CPR. We will look into this in more detail in Section 10.4.

CPR's noncash working capital changes 2003–2004

	2004 B/S	2003 B/S	Change
Accts rec'ble	$434.7	$395.7	$(39.0)
Inventories	134.1	106.4	(27.7)
Accts payable	975.3	907.0	68.3
Taxes payable	16.2	13.5	2.7
Total			$ 4.3

If you go to the balance sheet and calculate the changes in the four accounts shown in Note 10, you will see that these are not quite the same as the changes shown in Note 10, and they don't add up to the same as Note 10. You get $4.3 net changes, not the $33.2 shown in Note 10, a difference of $28.9 million. CPR's notes provide some background on this but don't make it clear what has happened. The reason appears to arise from two items in the cash flow statement: "restructuring payments" and "other operating activities, net." Both of these items involve changes to some of the four accounts, and when those changes are removed, you get the remaining changes shown in Note 10. Such complications mean that the cash flow statement contains information not obvious from the balance sheet and income statement, which are summarized from hundreds or thousands of accounts. When you try to reconstruct a company's cash flow statement, you often can't get exactly the same numbers because the company has used more detailed accounting information than in the summarized statements and hasn't provided all those details. But you can usually get close, as in this case! All this is a reminder that small net changes can come from quite large positive and negative changes, so *disclosure* of the background information can be quite useful to understanding what happened during the year. The *notes to the financial statements* can be a bit hard to read sometimes, but they are usually helpful in understanding the numbers in the statements.

Not all noncash working capital changes relate to operations.

(5) *Noncash working capital changes not related to operations.* The calculation in Note 10 to remove some noncash working capital changes not related to operations is a reminder that not all working capital accounts relate to operations. Two such accounts in particular are in CPR's current liabilities, as shown in CPR's balance sheet in Section 2.9: dividends payable ($21.0 million in 2004, and $20.2 million in 2003) and current portion of long-term debt ($275.7 million in 2004, $13.9 million in 2003). As we saw earlier in this chapter, such items are part of the Financing cash flow calculation, so CPR did not include their changes in determining cash from operations. There is one more noncash working capital account shown in Section 2.9, the change in which is not shown separately in the cash flow statement: CPR's current asset for future income taxes. That account is included in the future income tax noncash expense already described above.

There usually are miscellaneous "other" items in the cash flow analysis.

(6) *Miscellaneous stuff in operations.* In nearly every cash flow statement, there are a few "other" items that arise from various accounting calculations and don't fit the usual categories. In its 2002 cash flow figures, CPR includes $(0.8) million in its income adjustments as "Other" with no further explanation. Lower down in the Operations section, $(112.2) million in 2004 and $(365.0) million in 2003 in "other operating activities" are shown. We can't tell where the first item comes from but Note 20 (not included here) explains that "other operating activities" are cash payments in each of these years that exceed the expenses shown on the income statement relating to pensions, other benefits, and post-employment restructuring benefits. This is a second example of why you can never quite reproduce the cash flow statement from the other statements yourself: the company's accountants have used more detailed information than is disclosed in preparing the statement. In addition to its way of arranging balance sheet changes and income statement items to tell a new story, the cash flow statement also adds new information that we cannot get from the other statements.

B. Investing Activities.

CPR spent more than half a billion dollars on new property in each year.

(1) *Overall investment spending.* There was a lot of information in CPR's Operations cash flow section! The Investing section is simpler. In 2004, CPR spent $673.8 million in cash on new properties (land, track, trains, buildings, equipment) and got $10.2 million net proceeds from the disposal of transportation properties. New spending was about the same as 2003, which was up almost 20% from 2002. While in principle we could deduce these amounts from noncurrent asset balance sheet changes and related income statement information using the methods shown earlier in this chapter, in practice most companies' noncurrent asset accounts are much too complex to permit this. We have to rely on the company and its auditors to work it all out correctly.

CPR could finance all its property additions from operations in 2002 to 2004.

(2) *Internal financing of investments.* Two things about CPR's investments in properties are particularly worth noting. First, the total amount spent was less than cash from operations, so the company could have financed all its investing internally from operations, without external financing (borrowing or issuing more share capital). This was also true in 2002, but in 2003, CPR did not have enough cash from operations to finance the property additions internally.

CPR was renewing its noncurrent assets as their economic value was consumed.

(3) *Renewal of noncurrent assets as they wear out.* Second, the depreciation and amortization expense ($407.1 million in 2004: see the Operations section) was considerably less than expenditures on new properties ($673.8 million in 2004). This indicates that CPR was renewing its properties as their economic value was used up (as estimated by the depreciation and amortization expense). An important purpose of the cash flow statement is to allow us to compare these two figures and so judge whether the company is keeping its noncurrent assets renewed.

C. Financing Activities.

CPR's cash flow statement reports on the 2004 external financing.

(1) *Capital rearrangements.* The capital structure of CPR changed little during the period 2002 to 2004. The small inflows of $2.5 million in 2004 and $2.0 million in 2003 are the proceeds of issuing shares under stock option plans, 100,000 shares in 2003, and 200,000 shares in 2004.

CPR did not pay all the dividends it declared in 2004.

(2) *Dividends.* The cash flow statement indicates that CPR paid $81.7 million in dividends in 2004. The retained earnings statement in Section 3.4 indicates $82.5 million in dividends were declared. The difference of $0.8 million ($82.5 – $81.7) is dividends declared but unpaid during 2004. This tracks to the change in dividends payable of the same amount on the balance sheet in Section 2.9. Dividends payable rose to $21.0 million at the end of 2004 from $20.2 million at the end of 2003.

CPR increased long-term debt slightly in 2004.

(3) *Debt rearrangements.* CPR repaid $16.1 million of its outstanding long-term debt during 2004, slightly more than the current portion of long-term debt shown on the balance sheet at the end of 2003. New long-term borrowings totalled $193.7 million, almost $100 million more than was needed to pay dividends and retire long-term debt that came due during the year. Thus we can see that about half of the increase in cash was borrowed money, with the remainder coming from operations. CPR may have wanted to borrow now in preparation for repayment of the much larger amount ($275.7 million) of long-term debt maturing in 2005.

Cash flow analysis provides insight into business strategy as well as plain cash management.

The cash flow analysis has told us a lot, revealing several important things about CPR and its financial arrangements that were not so apparent from the balance sheets and income statements. If we'd wanted to work at those statements, we could have derived some of the information (not all, as some was included in account balance changes that we could not see readily from the other statements). But the cash flow statement saves us the trouble, as long as we know how to read it. Focusing on 2004, we have learned, among other things, the following:

- CPR's cash showed a big increase from 2003.
- CPR's cash from operations was much larger than its accrual income in 2004.
- CPR generated enough cash from operations to finance its new investments in 2004.
- CPR spent more renewing its property than the estimated value consumed as the property was used (depreciated and amortized).

- CPR borrowed during 2004 in order to increase cash holdings, possibly in preparation for debt retirement in 2005.

HOW'S YOUR UNDERSTANDING?

Here are two questions you should be able to answer based on what you have just read. If you can't answer them, it would be best to reread the material.

1. CPR relied on internal financing in 2004. How can we tell this?
2. Which figures on the cash flow statement would you compare to get an indication of whether a company appears to be renewing its noncurrent assets as they lose their value through use?

4.8 Cash Flow and The Manager

Cash flow and income are related, but not the same, especially in the short run.

Managers are responsible not only for earning income for the company, but also for managing cash so that bills can be paid on time, excess borrowing and interest costs can be avoided, and the company's liquidity and solvency can be generally protected. Effectively employing available cash so that it does not remain idle, earning nothing, is also important. Cash flow and income are generally positively correlated (good performance tends to move them both up, and poor performance tends to move them both down), and over a long enough time (years), they are almost the same. But as we saw for CPR, in any given year they are likely not the same. Their relationship can be complex, as these two examples illustrate:

Long-run profitability may depend on the short-run cash situation.

Sometimes new businesses with growing income have cash problems.

1. A few years ago, Quebec increased gasoline taxes to a higher rate than that in Ontario. This caused immediate problems for Quebec gas stations near the Ontario border: driving a few kilometres to buy gas in Ontario made a big difference in the price, unless a Quebec gas station owner decided to "swallow" the difference in tax. A CBC reporter interviewed a Quebec station owner and asked, "What are the implications of this for your long-run profitability?" The owner said, "Unless I can get some cash in the short run, there isn't going to be a long run!"
2. A problem new businesses can have is to grow too fast. Often the product demand and the entrepreneurial enthusiasm are high: the business was founded in the hope that people would want the product or service, and it is exciting to everyone when they do! The income statements of such businesses often show high profits (net incomes), but the cash flow statement and the balance sheet may tell a different story. In the enthusiasm of making sales and satisfying customers, inventory levels often get too high (making sure there is something for everyone on hand) and collections from customers often lag (receivables get too high as the entrepreneur concentrates on the pleasures of selling rather than the nuisance of collecting). The accrual income-based cash flow analysis deducts the increases in inventories and receivables from accrual-basis net income, and may show that operating cash flows are small or even negative. When this happens, you do not need a cash flow

statement to know you are in trouble: your bank balance tells you that! But the cash flow statement reports the whole story to others, so that they can see what you have accomplished in obtaining and using cash in your operating, financing, and investing activities. You then have to be prepared to explain such activities to users of the financial statements.

The cash flow statement provides a measure of managerial performance in managing cash, so smart managers must be aware of how their efforts are reflected in it, just as they are aware of the income statement and balance sheet measures of performance and position.

Stock market prices do seem to respond to cash flow information in addition to income.

There has been increasing research on the value of the cash flow statement, mostly in connection with public companies' share price changes (buy-and-sell decisions by investors). Most research, so far, defines cash flow simply as net income plus amortization (depreciation) expense. Such research usually finds that share prices do respond a little to the added information.[1] While most of the share price response is to the earnings (accrual net income) figure, some response to the cash flow information has also been found.[2]

4.9 Revisiting Cash Basis Versus Accrual Basis Accounting

This section returns to ideas first encountered in the Simone's Jewellery example in Section 1.10 and referred to since: the comparison of cash basis and accrual basis accounting. It aims to consolidate your knowledge of cash flow analysis, and should also help your understanding of how accrual accounting works by augmenting records of cash receipts and disbursements. Income tax is ignored, to avoid cluttering up the example.

Information for Goblin Consulting Ltd. for this year is:

EXHIBIT 4·11

Cash in bank, end of last year		$ 2,800
Cash receipts:		
Collections on last year's revenue	$ 1,600	
Collections on this year's revenue	75,200	
Deposit received on next year's revenue	1,000	
Long-term debt issued	6,000	
Sale of old equipment (proceeds)	500	84,300
		$87,100
Cash disbursements:		
Payment of last year's expenses	$ 900	
Payment of this year's expenses	61,300	
Advance payment on next year's expenses	2,200	
Payments on long-term debt	3,000	
Purchase of new equipment	14,000	81,400
Cash in bank, end of this year		$ 5,700
Increase in cash during the year ($5,700 – $2,800)		$ 2,900
Additional information:		
Equipment amortization for this year	$ 3,100	
Uncollected revenue at the end of this year	2,500	
Unpaid expenses at the end of this year	1,700	
Book value of old equipment at date of sale	300	
Gain on sale of equipment (proceeds – book value = $500 – $300)	200	

If we did a cash basis income statement for this year, we would get something like this:

Operating receipts ($1,600 + $75,200 + $1,000)	$77,800
Operating expenditures ($900 + $61,300 + $2,200)	64,400
Cash income for this year	$13,400

There are also:

- Nonoperating receipts of $6,500 ($6,000 debt + $500 proceeds); and
- Nonoperating expenditures of $17,000 ($3,000 debt payments + $14,000 new equipment).

If we added and subtracted those from $13,400, we'd get the total increase in cash during the year of $2,900:

Cash income	$13,400
Nonoperating receipts	6,500
Less nonoperating expenditures	(17,000)
Increase in cash during the year	$ 2,900

In contrast, the accrual basis income statement for this year would look like this, recognizing this year's earned revenues and incurred expenses:

Revenue ($75,200 cash sales + $2,500 uncollected)		$77,700
Expenses:		
General ($61,300 paid + $1,700 unpaid)	$63,000	
Amortization (specified above)	3,100	66,100
Operating income		$11,600
Gain on sale of equipment (calculated above)		200
Income for this year		$11,800

Because both cash flow and accrual figures are important, we want people to be able to understand how they are related to each other, and how they differ. That is what the cash flow statement is for. Here's what that statement for this year would look like:

EXHIBIT 4.12

Operations:		
Income for the year (accrual basis)		$ 11,800
Add back noncash expense (amortization)		3,100
Deduct back gain on sale (cash is in "proceeds" below)		(200)
		$ 14,700
Changes in noncash working capital accounts:		
Accounts receivable (up $2,500 – $1,600)	$ (900)	
Prepaid expenses ($2,200 now, none last year)	(2,200)	
Deferred revenue ($1,000 now, none last year)	1,000	
Accounts payable (up $1,700 – $900)	800	(1,300)
Cash from operations		$ 13,400
Investing:		
Purchases of new equipment	$(14,000)	
Proceeds from equipment sale	500	$(13,500)
Financing:		
Issue of long-term debt	$ 6,000	
Repayment of long-term debt	(3,000)	3,000
Increase in cash for this year		$ 2,900
Cash at beginning of this year		2,800
Cash at end of this year		$ 5,700

You can see that the cash flow statement's $13,400 "cash from operations" figure (which is derived from the $11,800 accrual basis income) is what you'd have as your cash income had you done the income statement on the cash basis. This was also demonstrated with the diagram at the end of Section 4.3 and the two ways of doing the Roebuck Industries cash flow statements in Sections 4.4 and 4.5. The cash flow statement *reconciles* the two ways of calculating income. The statement also provides the rest of the information (investing and financing) to allow you to see the total effects on cash for the year.

Therefore, with the accrual basis income statement plus the cash flow statement, you get the broader economic measure of performance that accrual accounting provides, as well as cash flow information with which to evaluate the company's cash management. The set of financial statements provides an integrated, mutually reinforcing package of information.

HOW'S YOUR UNDERSTANDING?

Here are two questions you should be able to answer based on what you have just read. If you can't answer them, it would be best to reread the material.

1. The owner of Frenzied Productions Inc. was looking at the company's income statement and said, "I understand this statement was prepared using accrual accounting. What does accrual accounting try to do, and why isn't it good enough just to report my company's cash receipts and disbursements?" Briefly answer the owner's question.
2. In 2005, Frenzied collected $53,430 from customers for sales made in 2004 and $421,780 for sales made in 2005. In 2006, it collected $46,710 from customers for sales made in 2005. At that point, all 2004 and 2005 sales had been collected. What were (a) the operating cash receipts for 2005 and (b) the accrual accounting revenue for 2005?

(a) $53,430 + $421,780 = $475,210;
(b) $421,780 + $46,710 = $468,490

4.10 Terms to Be Sure You Understand

Again, here are important terms introduced or emphasized in this chapter. Make sure you know what they mean *in accounting*. If any are unclear to you, check the chapter again or refer to the glossary of terms at the back of the book. As was the case for the terms in Chapters 1, 2, and 3, many of these will be used repeatedly as the book proceeds, so your understanding of them will deepen.

Accrual income
Cash flow statement
Cash from operations
Cash income
Cash payments
Cash receipts
Change in cash
Direct method of cash flow analysis
Disbursements
Disclosure
Financing activities
Funds statement
Indirect method of cash flow analysis
Internal financing
Investing activities
Liquidity
Nonoperating cash flows
Notes to the financial statements
Operating activities
Reconcile(s)
Solvency
Statement of changes in financial position
Statement of source and application of cash

DATA FOR INSTALLMENT 4

In order to prepare for the board of directors' meeting, Tomas thought it would be a good idea to be able to explain what had happened to the company's cash during the first six months. As a reference, here is the comparative balance sheet we saw in Installment 3:

Mato Inc.
Balance Sheets as at August 31 and March 1, 2006

Assets			**Liabilities and Shareholders' Equity**		
	August	**March**		**August**	**March**
Current assets:			Current liabilities:		
Cash	$ 4,507	$130,000	Bank loan	$ 75,000	$ 0
Receivables	18,723	0	Payables	45,616	1,100
Inventory	73,614	0	Loan payable	15,000	15,000
	$ 96,844	$130,000		$135,616	$ 16,100
Noncurrent assets:			Shareholders' equity:		
Equip. cost	$ 54,640	$ 10,000	Share capital	$125,000	$125,000
Equip. acc. amort.	(3,234)	0	Deficit	(49,378)	0
Leasehold (net)*	57,568	0		$ 75,622	$125,000
Software (net)**	4,320	0			
Incorp. costs	1,100	1,100			
	$114,394	$ 11,100			
TOTAL	$211,238	$141,100	TOTAL	$211,238	$141,100

* Net book value of leasehold improvements = $63,964 cost – $6,396 accumulated amortization.
** Net book value of software = $4,800 – $480 accumulated amortization.

Tomas decided that for his cash analysis, he would define cash and equivalents as just cash, because the demand bank loan was a source of financing the company would likely rely on for some time, and was not like a temporary bank overdraft. He began his analysis by identifying the changes in financial position since March 1, which resulted in the analysis below.

Changes in Financial Position
between March 1 and August 31, 2006

Changes in Assets		**Changes in Liabilities and Equity**	
Cash	$ (125,493)	Bank loan	$75,000
Receivables	18,723	Payables	44,516
Inventory	73,614	Loan payable	0
Equipment cost*	44,640	Share capital	0
Accum. amort.**	(3,234)	Deficit	(49,378)
Leasehold cost	63,964		
Accum. amort.**	(6,396)		
Software cost	4,800		
Accum. amort.**	(480)		
Incorp. costs	0		
	$ 70,138		$70,138

* Computer, $14,900; other equipment and furniture, $29,740.
** The changes in accumulated amortization were all due entirely to amortization expenses recorded for the period.

RESULTS FOR INSTALLMENT 4

Tomas then wrote down all the categories of the cash flow statement and filled in the appropriate figures, producing the statement shown below. *(The statement is shown in more detail than might be done in practice, so that you can trace every figure from the balance sheet change analysis above to the cash flow statement. Make sure you do this, to improve your understanding of the derivation and interpretation of the cash flow statement.)*

Mato Inc.
Cash Flow Statement
for the Six Months Ended August 31, 2006

Operations:		
Net loss for the six months		$ (49,378)
Add back amortization for the period ($3,234 + $6,396 + $480)		10,110
		$ (39,268)
Changes in noncash working capital accounts:		
Increase in accounts receivable	$(18,723)	
Increase in inventory	(73,614)	
Increase in accounts payable	44,516	(47,821)
Cash *used* in operations		$(87,089)
Investing activities:		
Equipment, computer, and furniture acquired	$(44,640)	
Leasehold improvements made	(63,964)	
Software acquired	(4,800)	(113,404)
Financing activities		
Bank loan obtained		75,000
Decrease in cash during the six months		$(125,493)
Cash on hand, March 1, 2006		130,000
Cash on hand		$ 4,507

The cash flow statement shows that the dramatic decline in cash has two causes.

- First, day-to-day operations produced a cash loss of $87,089. This was a combination of expenses exceeding revenues and the buildup of current assets, especially inventory. The increase in accounts payable helped to finance this, but even after, in essence, borrowing from suppliers, the company still fell far behind in its cash flow.
- Second, noncurrent asset acquisitions cost $113,404 in cash.

Without the bank loan, cash would have been negative $70,493. The company clearly has to get on top of its cash problems quickly.

4.12 Homework and Discussion to Develop Understanding

The problems roughly follow the outline of the chapter. Three main categories of questions are presented.

- Asterisked problems (*) have an informal solution provided in the Student Solutions Manual.
- EXTENDED TIME problems grant a thorough examination of the material and may take longer to complete.
- CHALLENGING problems are more difficult.

For further explanation, please refer to Section 1.15.

Introduction to the Cash Flow Statement • Sections 4.2 and 4.3

Purpose and Details

PROBLEM 4.1 Discussion of cash flows

In your own words, answer the following questions in a manner that would allow someone who has not read this book to understand.

a. Why are financing and investing activities of a corporation important to financial statement readers?
b. How does an increase in accounts receivable during the year affect the cash flow from operations?
c. Why is it possible that cash may have decreased during the year, even though there has been a substantial net income during the same period?
d. Why does net income (loss) for the year not normally equal the cash inflow (outflow)?
e. What effect does the declaration of a cash dividend have on cash flow? What effect does a dividend declared and paid in the same period have? What effect does payment of a dividend declared in an earlier period have?

PROBLEM 4.2 Explain what the cash flow statement tells about a company

Explain to your uncle (who has never studied accounting) what the cash flow statement tells him about a company in which he owns shares.

PROBLEM 4.3 Cash flow basics

1. What does the cash flow information in the cash flow statement tell you that you cannot get directly, if at all, from the income statement and balance sheet?
2. Beta Company's cash flow statement showed the following figures: Cash generated from operations, $127,976; Cash used in investing activities, $238,040; and Cash obtained in financing activities, $107,000. What was the net change in the company's cash for the year?

PROBLEM 4.4 Why pay attention to the cash flow statement?

A senior financial executive for a large public company remarked to a stock market analyst: "I don't know why you people worry so much about what is in our cash flow statement. Managing cash flow is our responsibility as managers; it involves paying close attention to cash on a daily basis. Why don't you pay attention to our income performance and just forget about cash flow? We'll look after that!"

Respond to the executive's comments. You do not have to agree or disagree entirely.

PROBLEM 4.5 Why not just have cash-basis accounting?

A business commentator made the following remark during a discussion of the financial performance of a large, but struggling, company: "These accountants are something to behold! They spend lots of money to create complicated financial statements, especially income statements, that use what they call 'accrual' accounting, and come up with an income number they expect us to take seriously. Then they spend a whole lot more money creating cash flow statements, which are just as complicated as the other statements, and that take away all the accruals and supposedly return us to the cash income number we would have had anyway, if they hadn't bothered with accrual accounting in the first place! Nice work! You get paid to create a dubious income measure and then more money to uncreate it. What kind of idiots do they take the business community for? Why don't they just give us the cash income and leave it at that? We can understand that, and it would make a simple income statement and no need for a cash flow statement to just cancel out the income number, as we have now."

If you were an accountant involved in the discussion and everyone turned to you for a response to the commentator, what would you say?

Preparing the Cash Flow Statement • Sections 4.4–4.6

Direct Method

* **PROBLEM 4.6** Cash flow analysis from account information

Prepare a cash flow statement from the following cash account information, which is in alphabetical order.

Bank loan obtained	60,000
Cash, beginning of year	68,920
Cash, end of year	93,620
Cash expenses	8,920
Cash sales	31,610
Collections on accounts receivable	797,640
Common shares issued	140,000
Cost of redeeming preferred shares	25,000
Dividends paid ($20,000 declared)	15,000
Employee wages and salaries paid	223,610
Income tax paid	14,920
Land purchased for cash	81,000
Payments to suppliers	513,600
Proceeds from sale of old truck	7,000
Repayments on mortgage	80,500
Truck purchased ($5,000 more still owing)	49,000

PROBLEM 4.7 Prepare a cash flow statement from account information

Based on the following cash account information (listed in alphabetical order), prepare a cash flow statement for Ryley's Dog Treats Inc.

Bonds issued	90,000
Cash, beginning of year	108,270
Cash, end of year	39,260
Cash expenses	32,400
Cash sales	65,580
Collections on accounts receivable	919,160
Common shares issued	242,000
Cost of redeeming preferred shares	44,000
Dividends paid ($50,000 declared)	33,000
Employee wages and salaries paid	365,730
Equipment purchased ($15,000 more still owing)	132,000
Income tax paid	32,490
Plant purchased for cash	233,750
Payments to suppliers	468,380
Proceeds from sale of old equipment	29,700
Repayments on mortgage	73,700

PROBLEM 4.8 Preparing a cash flow statement from account information

You are an accountant for Hannibal's Fine Dining Ltd. The owner and head chef is very upset with you because there is only $148,690 in cash on hand. He knows that there was $146,800 on hand one year ago and cash sales for the year were $850,630. Of that, $20,000 was withdrawn from the line of credit and some old equipment was sold for $6,500. He also recalls that $3,100 was collected from accounts receivable and a new investor purchased $30,000 of newly issued common shares. "Where did all this cash go?" he screams.

You show him that there were cash expenses of $168,580 plus $229,850 in wages and salaries and another $149,240 was used to reduce accounts payable. Mortgage repayments totalled $97,500, $50,000 was paid to redeem preferred shares, and the government took $63,170 in taxes. "We paid $40,000 for the new furniture and $30,000 for the kitchen equipment, and we declared $90,000 in dividends," you remind him.

Hannibal replies "Yes, but we still owe $10,000 on the equipment and $10,000 in dividends."

Fearing for more than just your job, you decide to prepare a cash flow statement to help your angry boss understand what the company did with its cash this year.

PROBLEM 4.9 Prepare a cash flow statement from information that is not all relevant

Prepare a cash flow statement from the following information for this year, presented in alphabetical order. Some of the information may not be relevant. (Hint: use the direct method.)

Account receivable written off*	1,200
Amortization expense for the year	111,120
Bank overdraft, beginning of year	0
Cash at the end of the year	43,220
Collections on accounts receivable	944,980
Customer deposits received	48,000
Dividends declared	100,000
Dividends payable, beginning of year	0
Dividends payable, end of year	20,000
Inventory purchased on credit	310,990
Investment written down**	33,000
New bonded debt issued	463,000
New equipment purchased	580,340
Old bonded debt repaid	373,000
Payments on accounts payable	832,630
Proceeds of building sold***	290,000
Shares issued in return for land	145,000
Temporary bank overdraft, end of year	17,530

* The account receivable was deemed uncollectible and was written off directly to expense.
** The investment was written down from its $50,000 cost to its market value of $17,000.
***The building sold had cost $410,000 and had accumulated amortization of $200,000.

Indirect Method

EXTENDED TIME

*** PROBLEM 4.10** Prepare a cash flow statement for Northern Star Theatre

Near the end of Section 3.8, the balance sheet for Northern Star Theatre Company was presented, along with the income statement and statement of partners' capital for the first months of the partnership's existence. Use that information to prepare a cash flow statement for the partnership for the period to August 26, 2006.

EXTENDED TIME

PROBLEM 4.11 Cash vs Accrual Income and the cash flow Statement

The year-end of Micadam Inc. is December 31, 2006. The following summarized data are taken from its accounting records (amounts are in thousands):

Cash sales	860	Wages payable:	
Credit sales	346	Balance at January 1, 2006	5
Cash purchases of inventory	610	Balance at December 31, 2006	12
Inventory purchases on account	135	Prepaid rent:	
Accounts receivable:		Balance at January 1, 2006	0
Balance at January 1, 2006	85	Balance at December 31, 2006	6
Balance at December 31,2006	110	Cash paid for expenses	145
Merchandise inventory:		Fixed assets – Equipment:	
Balance at January 1, 2006	185	Cost (purchased in 2005)	380
Balance at December 31, 2006	230	Annual Amortization	38
Accounts payable:			
Balance at January 1, 2006	50		
Balance at December 31, 2006	60		

1. Using the above information, complete the following income statements on both the accrual and cash bases.

Accrual Basis			Cash Basis		
Sales		$	Sales		$
Cost of goods sold			Cost of goods sold		
Gross profit		$	Gross profit		$
Operating expense			Operating expense		
Amortization	$		Amortization	$	
Miscellaneous			Miscellaneous		
Rent			Rent		
Wages			Wages		
Net income for the year		$	Cash income for the year		$

2. Prepare the cash flow from operations portion of the cash flow statement for Micadam Inc. at December 31, 2006.

PROBLEM 4.12 Cash flow analysis with large write-off and other adjustments

Here are the summarized 2007 and 2006 balance sheets for Saint John Enterprises Inc., showing the changes calculated by subtracting 2006 from 2007. Using them and the additional information below, prepare the cash flow statement for 2007.

	2007	2006	Changes
Cash equivalent assets	$ 17,400	$ 14,300	$ 3,100
Other current assets	164,100	123,500	40,600
Noncurrent assets, net	319,800	286,200	33,600
	$501,300	$424,000	$77,300
Cash equivalent liabilities	$ 11,200	$ 9,100	$ 2,100
Other current liabilities	117,900	90,600	27,300
Noncurrent liabilities	174,800	175,300	(500)
Share capital	80,000	60,000	20,000
Retained earnings	117,400	89,000	28,400
	$501,300	$424,000	$77,300

Additional information:

- The 2007 net income was $38,400. This was after recording a large noncurrent asset write-off of $112,000, which the company had thought necessary because an investment had gone bad during the year.
- Dividends declared during the year were $10,000.
- $1,500 of the dividends were still unpaid at the end of 2007 (there had been none unpaid at the end of 2006).
- There was an expense in 2007 for future income tax, recorded by increasing the noncurrent income tax liability by $8,800.
- The cash equivalent liabilities were temporary bank overdrafts. Some of the noncurrent liabilities were paid off during the year.
- During the year, the company sold for $8,400 a truck that had cost $25,000 and had accumulated amortization of $17,300. There was thus a gain on sale of $700 (proceeds of $8,400 – book value of $7,700 ($25,000 – $17,300)).

- Amortization expense for the year, shown on the income statement and added to the accumulated amortization account on the balance sheet, was $37,700.
- Acquisitions of noncurrent assets came to $191,000 for the year.

PROBLEM 4.13 Cash flow for Gronsky's Great Things Ltd.

If you did Problem 3.40 on Gronsky's Great Things Ltd., you will have prepared income and retained earnings statements and an ending balance sheet for the company. Use that information to prepare a 2007 cash flow statement for the company. Assume the company began the year with $18,750 cash, obtained in return for share capital issued to Gronsky.

PROBLEM 4.14 Preparation of cash flow statement

The comparative balance sheets for the Wriggle Corp. showed the following at December 31, 2006 and 2007:

Debits	**2007**	**2006**
Cash	$ 15	$ 12
Accounts receivable	27	15
Merchandise inventory	36	30
Long-term investments	15	36
Fixed assets at cost	141	90
	$234	$183
Credits		
Accumulated amortization	$21	$15
Accounts payable	24	18
Notes payable – long-term	60	48
Common shares	90	75
Retained earnings	39	27
	$234	$183

The income statement for 2007 appears below:

Wriggle Corp.
Income Statement
For the Year Ended 2007

Revenue		$450
Cost of sales		300
Gross profit		$150
Operating expenses:		
Expenses including income tax	$117	
Amortization	9	126
Income from operations		$ 24
Other gains (losses) net of income taxes:		
Gain on disposal of fixed assets		3
Loss on disposal of investments		(6)
Net income		$ 21

Additional information regarding changes in the noncurrent accounts during 2007:

a. Cash dividends paid, $9
b. Issuance of shares for cash, $15
c. Fixed assets disposed of during the year cost $9

1. Prepare a statement of cash flow in good form.
2. Comment on the operations, financing activities and investing activities of Wriggle Corp. for the year 2007.

PROBLEM 4.15 Prepare a cash flow statement from cash receipts, disbursements, and other information

Below, in alphabetical order, is information about Chantal Inc. Prepare a cash flow statement in good form.

Accumulated amortization on equipment that was sold	10,800
Advance payment on next year's expenses	8,028
Amortization for this year	42,221
Cash in bank, end of last year	63,419
Collections of this year's revenue	347,085
Collections on last year's revenue	20,516
Cost of equipment that was sold	14,400
Deposit received on next year's revenue	5,489
Noncurrent debt issued	67,500
Payment of this year's expenses (including income tax)	267,269
Payment on last year's expenses	1,701
Proceeds on sale of equipment	2,160
Purchase of new equipment	164,178
Repayment of noncurrent debt	27,000
Uncollected revenue at the end of this year	28,116
Unpaid expenses at the end of this year	26,417

* **PROBLEM 4.16** Prove given cash flow figures

The following summarized data are from Grantham Inc.'s financial statements. (CEA = cash and equivalent assets; OCA = other current assets; NCA = noncurrent assets; CEL = cash equivalent liabilities (temporary bank overdraft); OCL = other current liabilities; NCL = noncurrent liabilities; CAP = share capital; RET = retained earnings; REV = revenue; EXP = general expenses; INT = interest expense; NRE = nonoperating revenues and expenses; TAX = income tax expense; SEI = special and extraordinary items; INC = net income)

Assets			**Liabilities & Equity**			**Income**		
	2003	**2002**		**2003**	**2002**		**2003**	
CEA	$ 2,000	$ 1,000	CEL	$ 2,000	$ 3,000	REV	$125,000	
OCA	9,000	8,000	OCL	4,000	2,000	EXP	(84,000)	(amort. = $5,000)
NCA	37,000	32,000	NCL	17,000	18,000	INT	(2,000)	
			CAP	12,000	10,000	NRE	4,000**	
			RET*	13,000	8,000	TAX	(19,000)	(future = $3,000)
						SEI	(13,000)***	
	$48,000	$41,000		$48,000	$41,000	INC	$ 11,000	

* Dividend of $6,000 was declared and paid in 2003.
** $4,000 nonoperating income is a gain on an NCA sale: proceeds $7,000 minus $3,000 book value.
*** $(13,000) special item = $21,000 write-off minus $8,000 future tax reduction.

Show that the following are correct for the 2003 cash flow statement:

a.	Cash generated from operations	$ 29,000
b.	Cash obtained from financing activities	0
c.	Cash disbursed for investing activities (net)	(27,000)
d.	Increase in cash and equivalents	$ 2,000

*** PROBLEM 4.17** Correct a badly prepared cash flow statement

Fred talked his way into a job with Aragon Ltd., convincing the company's boss that he had enough accounting knowledge to do the company's accounting. All went well for a while: Fred managed to get the year's accounting done and came up with an appropriate balance sheet, income statement, and statement of retained earnings. But he just hasn't been able to get the cash flow statement to work out. He has calculated all the balance sheet changes correctly, but it just doesn't work out right. In response to a loud "Help!" you go over to Fred's desk to see if you can do anything. You find Fred's draft cash flow statement below, and you are able to determine that all his numbers are taken correctly from the other statements, so all that is needed is to rearrange Fred's draft and get everything in the right direction, and it should all work out.

Using Fred's draft, prepare a cash flow statement for Aragon Ltd. in proper format.

Aragon Ltd.
Draft Cash Flow Statement

Operations:		
Net income for the year		$ 216,350
Cash on hand		48,340
Less amortization for the year	$(218,890)	
Add deferred income tax expense	21,210	(197,680)
Working capital changes:		
Cash and equivalents	$ 62,070	
Increase in accounts receivable	(223,120)	
Decrease in inventory	80,200	
Decrease in accounts payable	91,970	
Increase in current income tax payable	(6,530)	4,590
Cash from operations		$ 71,600
Investing:		
Additions to noncurrent assets	$(393,980)	
Proceeds from sales of noncurrent assets	(11,260)	(405,240)
Financing:		
New noncurrent debt	$(250,500)	
Repayments of noncurrent debt	78,800	
Dividends paid	75,000	
Share capital issued	120,000	126,700
Change in cash for the year		$(206,940)

What If Analysis

*** PROBLEM 4.18** "What if" questions

Indicate the effect on Beta Company's cash flow statement of each of the following events, if they had occurred during the year:

a. What if a new truck had been purchased at a cost of $38,950?
b. What if $20,000 were borrowed long-term specifically to help pay for the truck?
c. What if collections of accounts receivable had been $6,000 less than actually happened?
d. What if the company had paid an additional dividend of $15,000?
e. What if the company had borrowed $25,000 from the bank as a demand loan?
f. What if the company had decided to record an additional $5,000 in amortization expense for the year?

PROBLEM 4.19 Effects analysis questions on Tamarack Systems

These two questions are based on the Tamarack Systems information in Problem 4.30*. You can do some analysis without doing that problem, but the specific answers are based on the cash flow statement required in that problem.

1. What would have changed on Tamarack's 2007 cash flow statement if the cash received for the garage sale had been $40,000 instead of $25,000?
2. What would have changed on the cash flow statement if the accumulated amortization on the garage had been $82,000 instead of $70,000? (Ignore part 1.)

PROBLEM 4.20 Effects analysis questions on CPR

The following events all occurred on December 30, 2004, and were accidentally omitted from the CPR statement of consolidated cash flows in Section 4.7. Indicate what changes to the cash flow statement would result from each event. (Note: For each event, start with the original statement and ignore the effects of the five other events.)

a. A building was purchased for $25 million.
b. $14 million of common shares were issued.
c. The chief accountant realized the depreciation and amortization expense was $10 million larger than it should have been.
d. $130 million in long-term debt was repaid.
e. An additional $7 million was received from disposal of transportation properties.
f. A company paid its bill of $5 million for a shipment of wheat that had been made in 2003. The $5 million revenue was included in net income for 2003.

PROBLEM 4.21 Effects on cash flow statement of unpaid dividends and building disposal

1. You have just prepared a cash flow statement for Frogmorton Corp., and it works out to the correct change in cash and equivalents. You then discover that included in the current liabilities is an account for dividends payable that you had not realized was there. Explain why the cash from operations and financing figures on your cash flow statement are incorrect and why the total change in cash is correct in spite of your error.
2. You are struggling with the cash flow statement for Smithwood Inc. You know that the net total change in noncurrent assets over the year is an increase of $382,500 and that amortization expense for the year was $159,400. You then learn that during the year the company sold a building for $190,000. The building had cost $790,000 and there was accumulated amortization on it of $610,000 at the date of sale.
   a. Calculate the apparent amount spent on acquisitions of noncurrent assets during the year.
   b. Calculate the gain or loss on the sale of the building.
   c. Specify the adjustments to income in the operations section of the cash flow statement arising from noncurrent assets.
   d. Specify the figures in the investing activities section of the cash flow statement.

PROBLEM 4.22 "What if" questions involving cash flow

By making certain business decisions or choosing the location of items in their financial statements, companies may be able to alter the "story" the cash flow statement tells. For each action or choice below, explain what effect (if any) would result in the cash flow statement for the present year (including cash and equivalents at the bottom) if the action or choice happened.

1. Company A arranges with the bank to let it have a temporary bank overdraft of $250,000 as a way of getting some immediately needed financing.
2. Company B decides to classify $75,000 of its accounts receivable as long-term assets instead of current assets.
3. Company C decides to buy land for $710,000, arranging for 100% long-term debt financing instead of issuing new share capital.
4. Company D decides to decrease its amortization expense for this year by $82,000.
5. Company E decides to declare a $50,000 dividend to shareholders payable immediately in cash.
6. Company F decides to donate $35,000 to the Poor Accountants' League (the donation will be included with business expenses).

Interpreting a Company's Cash Flow Statement • Sections 4.7 and 4.8

* **PROBLEM 4.23** Comment on a company's cash management

Axiomatic Inc.'s cash flow statement for last year is shown below. Make as many observations as you can about how the company managed its cash during the year.

Axiomatic Inc.
Cash Flow Statement for Last Year

Operations:		
Net income for the year		$ 94,900
Add back noncash expenses:		
Amortization expense	$ 216,800	
Deferred income tax expense	14,200	
Pension expense	38,900	269,900
Noncash working capital changes:		
Increase in accounts receivable	$(143,900)	
Increase in inventories	(71,600)	
Increase in accounts payable	87,000	(128,500)
Cash generated by operations		$ 236,300
Investing activities:		
Additions to noncurrent assets	$(429,100)	
Proceeds on disposal of noncurrent assets	27,700	(401,400)
Financing activities:		
Short-term bank loan	$ 30,000	
Additions to noncurrent debt	343,200	
Repayments of noncurrent debt	(316,000)	
Share capital issued	200,000	
Dividends paid during the year	(40,000)	217,200
Increase in cash for the year		$ 52,100
Cash, beginning of year		(93,500)
Cash, end of year		$ (41,400)

PROBLEM 4.24 Comment on a company's cash management

Last year's cash flow statement for Wemakem Inc. is shown below. Make as many observations as you can about how the company managed its cash during the year.

Wemakem Inc.
Cash Flow Statement for the Last Year

Operating Activities		
Net income for the year		$ 575,000
Add back noncash expenses:		
Amortization expense	$ 1,273,000	
Future income tax expense	104,300	
Pension expense	391,400	1,768,700
Noncash working capital changes:		
Increase in accounts payable	$ 57,400	
Decrease in inventories	31,000	
Increase in accounts receivable	(17,800)	70,600
Cash generated by operations		$ 2,414,300
Investing Activities		
Additions to noncurrent assets	$(1,526,700)	
Proceeds from disposal of noncurrent assets	18,700	(1,508,000)
Financing Activities		
Short-term debt repaid	$ (143,400)	
Long-term debt repaid	(658,900)	
Common shares issued	54,000	
Dividends paid	(598,000)	(1,346,300)
Decrease in cash for the year		$ (440,000)
Cash on hand at the beginning of the year		1,357,400
Cash on hand at the end of the year		$ 917,400

PROBLEM 4.25 Comment on a company's cash management

Make as many observations as you can about cash management at Enbridge Inc. based on its cash flow statement.

Enbridge Consolidated Statements of Cash Flows
(Millions of Canadian dollars, except per share amounts)

Year ended December 31,	2004	2003	2002
		Restated (Note 2)	Restated (Note 2)
Cash Provided by Operating Activities			
Earnings from continuing operations	**652.2**	674.1	336.9
Charges/(credits) not affecting cash			
Depreciation	**525.0**	443.0	403.9
Equity earnings in excess of cash distributions	**(39.2)**	(22.1)	(44.6)
Gain on sale of assets to Enbridge Income Fund	**–**	(239.9)	–
Gain on reduction of ownership interest	**(29.6)**	(50.0)	(10.0)
Gain on sale of investment in AltaGas Income Trust	**(121.5)**	–	–
Gain on sale of securities	**–**	–	(21.4)
Writedown of EGD regulatory receivable	**–**	26.0	–
Writedown of Enbridge Midcoast Energy assets	**–**	–	122.7
Future income taxes	**12.7**	85.8	(77.8)
Other	**28.2**	21.4	(10.2)
Changes in operating assets and liabilities (Note 19)	**(141.1)**	(569.8)	151.6
Cash provided by operating activities of discontinued operations	**–**	–	26.3
	886.7	368.5	877.4
Investing Activities			
Acquisitions (Note 5)	**(833.9)**	(78.3)	(289.3)
Long-term investments	**(16.9)**	(50.5)	(1,282.7)
Additions to property, plant and equipment	**(496.4)**	(391.3)	(729.9)
Proceeds on redemption of Enbridge Commercial Trust preferred units	**–**	24.9	–
Sale of investment in AltaGas Income Trust	**346.7**	–	–
Sale of assets to Enbridge Income Fund (Note 4)	**–**	331.2	–
Proceeds on dispositions	**–**	–	1,706.9
Affiliate loans	**–**	427.2	358.1
Changes in construction payable	**0.5**	(3.7)	(14.8)
	(999.7)	259.5	(251.7)
Financing Activities			
Net change in short-term borrowings and short-term debt	**738.0**	359.8	(1,180.9)
Long-term debt issues	**500.0**	150.0	247.4
Long-term debt repayments	**(450.0)**	(725.0)	(382.7)
Non-recourse long-term debt issued by joint ventures	**–**	538.3	–
Non-recourse long-term debt repaid by joint ventures	**(42.9)**	(663.8)	–
Non-controlling interests	**(2.4)**	(4.0)	0.2
Preferred securities	**(350.0)**	–	200.0
Common shares issued	**44.4**	70.9	293.1
Enbridge Energy Management shares issued (Note 8)	**–**	–	421.9
Preferred share dividends	**(6.9)**	(6.9)	(6.9)
Common share dividends	**(315.8)**	(283.9)	(251.1)
	114.4	(564.6)	(659.0)
Increase/(Decrease) in Cash	**1.4**	63.4	(33.3)
Cash at Beginning of Year	**104.1**	40.7	74.0
Cash at End of Year	**105.5**	104.1	40.7

19. Changes in Operating Assets and Liabilities
(millions of dollars)

Year ended December 31,	2004	2003	2002
Accounts receivable and other	**(347.4)**	(346.9)	81.5
Inventory	**35.3**	(232.4)	69.5
Deferred amounts and other assets	**(94.2)**	(78.9)	72.4
Accounts payable and other	**278.3**	93.9	(76.4)
Interest payable	**(13.1)**	(5.5)	4.6
	(141.1)	(569.8)	151.6

Changes in accounts payable exclude changes in construction payables which are investing activities.

*** PROBLEM 4.26** Interpret a simple cash flow statement and answer "what if" questions

A high-school friend of yours, Natasha Wheeler, is currently in second-year fine arts and, in addition to many other talents, happens to have an entrepreneurial flair. For the last two summers, she has operated a bicycle rental business near a local park. Last year (2006), even though the business was just getting started, she made enough money to get herself through the school year. Encouraged by this initial success, she bought several more bikes this year (2007) and constructed a movable shed out of which she operated her business and serviced the bikes.

Business was even better this summer, but Natasha is confused. While her business income was much up from last year, there is no cash for her to withdraw. She does not know how she will pay her university expenses this year.

Knowing that you are taking an accounting course, she comes to you for help. She realizes that you cannot lend her any money, but thinks that maybe you can explain what is going on with her business. (Ignore income tax throughout.)

1. Using the cash flow statement below, explain to Natasha how it is possible that the income statement can show a profit, while there is no cash for her to withdraw from the business. Explain to her where all the cash went.
2. In order to be able to pay herself a dividend, Natasha proposes to have her business borrow another $5,000 from her parents, who will not expect her to repay the money in the near future, and another $2,000 from the bank, which is looking very carefully at Natasha's cash position (and at her very saleable bicycles) and expecting to be repaid as soon as possible. Ignoring any dividend she might pay, what effect will these two events have on the cash flow statement?
3. Is it a good idea to borrow to pay a dividend? Does Natasha have any other alternatives?

Wheeler's Bicycle Rental Ltd.
Cash Flow Statement for the Year Ended August 31, 2007
with Comparative Figures for 2006

	2007	2006
Operations:		
Net income	$ 9,000	$ 5,500
Add back amortization expense	3,000	1,000
Cash from operations	$12,000	$ 6,500
Investing:		
Purchases of bikes	(15,000)	(5,000)
Purchase of shed	(5,000)	—
Financing:		
Bank loan	7,000	—
Loan from parents	—	3,000
Share capital issued	—	2,000
Dividend paid	—	(5,500)
(Decrease) or increase in cash	$ (1,000)	$ 1,000
Cash balance—beginning of year	1,000	0
Cash balance—end of year	$ 0	$ 1,000

* PROBLEM 4.27 Prepare a cash flow analysis from a narrative

You're having lunch with a family friend, the president of a local company you wouldn't mind working for some day. She starts to complain about the company's cash problems, and you decide to impress her by doing an analysis of those problems. So as she talks, you scribble the figures she mentions down on your napkin, with a plan to organize those into an analysis.

Here's what she said. Use the information to prepare a rough cash flow statement and then use that to provide helpful comments to her.

"You students often complain about being short of cash. The problem can affect companies too. Look at my company. Last year, we had $50,000 in the bank, a good solid position, and we didn't owe the bank anything. Now, we have only $5,000 and we owe the bank $90,000 in short-term loans, and I worry about how to pay the loans. It is hard to understand how we got into this difficulty. Part of it was because we had to finance a big expansion in our factory—that cost $600,000, and we only got $30,000 back from selling off some old equipment. The bank was sticky about lending money for the expansion, but we were able to increase our mortgage by $250,000, and we got another $100,000 from issuing some more shares. It was too bad we had the cash problems this year, because we had a good income, $100,000, and only paid out $40,000 of that in dividends. Our accountant said we brought in more cash than that, said it had to do with the $200,000 amortization, but I didn't really catch what that meant, because I know that amortization doesn't actually involve any cash. I do know that we have had increasing difficulty collecting from our customers, because some of them seem to have cash problems as well, so our accounts receivable are up $150,000 from last year. And the accountant said that our inventories were getting a bit high, being up $25,000 from last year. It's been frustrating—we earn income but don't seem to have cash!"

CHALLENGING

PROBLEM 4.28 Interpret trends in cash management

Apex Accessories Inc. makes, imports, and sells various goods for the fashion trade, including costume jewellery, belts and other leather goods, hats, and many kinds of apparel. The business is both seasonal and unstable, with products coming and going as fashions and availability from foreign suppliers change. During a "business issues" TV program about the fashion industry, some of Apex's financial results were displayed in an on-screen table, while a narrator gushed about the marvellous management the company had. Here is that table:

Year	Year-end total assets	Year-end total bank borrowing	Net income for the year	Year's cash flow from operations
1994	$24,400,000	$ 8,300,000	$2,100,000	$3,200,000
1995	29,100,000	9,600,000	2,400,000	3,900,000
1996	28,500,000	8,900,000	2,300,000	3,200,000
1997	34,700,000	10,300,000	2,600,000	2,500,000
1998	37,800,000	12,000,000	2,800,000	2,200,000
1999	35,400,000	14,100,000	3,000,000	1,800,000
2000	37,000,000	14,200,000	3,100,000	3,800,000
2001	39,600,000	15,200,000	3,300,000	3,400,000
2002	43,000,000	16,400,000	3,200,000	2,800,000
2003	45,700,000	18,500,000	3,400,000	1,900,000

1. Which column of figures do you suppose the narrator was referring to when gushing about the "marvellous management"?
2. Provide as many comments as you can about the company's results. Do you think the management is marvellous?

3. For this particular company (which is listed on a stock exchange), would you expect market traders to respond much to the cash flow information once they know the net income figures? Put another way, do you think the cash flow information has any added value to the net income information?

Integrated

Prepare and Comment on the Cash Flow Statement

EXTENDED TIME

*** PROBLEM 4.29** Prepare a cash flow statement from balance sheet changes

Lambic Beverages Inc. makes special high-powered beers, some fermented in the bottle, and nonalcoholic sparkling drinks. Below are the company's balance sheets for the end of this year and last year, and some information about income and dividends during this year. From this information, prepare a cash flow statement for this year and comment on what it tells you. While you're at it, calculate the company's working capital ratio and debt–equity ratio for both years and comment on those, in relation to the cash flow analysis.

Lambic Beverages Inc.
Comparative Balance Sheets for This Year and Last Year

Assets			**Liabilities and Equity**		
	This Year	**Last Year**		**This Year**	**Last Year**
Current assets:			Current Liabilities:		
Cash	$ 560	$ 1,120	Bank loan	$ 400	$ 1,500
Accounts receivable	3,210	2,060	Accounts payable	7,240	6,220
Inventory	4,440	4,910	Income tax payable	0	330
	$ 8,210	$ 8,090		$ 7,640	$ 8,050
Noncurrent assets:			Noncurrent liabilities:		
Property and plant	$26,670	$24,820	Long-term debt	$12,740	$13,280
Accumulated amort.	(7,760)	(5,130)	Future income tax	1,320	1,070
	$18,910	$19,690		$14,060	$14,350
			Shareholders' equity:		
			Share capital	$ 1,500	$ 1,200
			Retained earnings	3,920	4,180
				$ 5,420	$ 5,380
	$27,120	$27,780		$27,120	$27,780

Other information:

- The company had a net loss of $210 for this year. Not expecting that, the company paid a $50 dividend early in the year.
- Amortization expense for the year was $2,630 and future income tax expense was $250.

*** PROBLEM 4.30** Prepare the cash flow statement from complete balance sheet

Here are the balance sheet changes between 2006 and 2007 for Tamarack Systems Inc.

Tamarack Systems Inc.
Balance Sheets for 2006 and 2007, with Changes Calculated

	2007	2006	Change
Assets			
Current assets:			
Cash	$ 16,064	$ 12,440	$ 3,624
Temporary investments	0	65,000	(65,000)
Accounts receivable	220,668	143,962	76,706
Inventories	176,962	187,777	(10,815)
Prepaid expenses	9,004	14,321	(5,317)
Total current assets	$422,698	$423,500	$ (802)
Noncurrent assets:			
Land cost	$ 82,500	$ 75,000	$ 7,500
Building cost	600,898	420,984	179,914
Accumulated amortization	(243,224)	(173,320)	(69,904)
Net total noncurrent assets	$440,174	$322,664	$117,510
Totals	$862,872	$746,164	$116,708
Liabilities and Equity			
Current liabilities:			
Bank loan	$ 64,900	$ 43,200	$ 21,700
Accounts payable	199,853	163,866	35,987
Income taxes payable	17,228	16,090	1,138
Dividends payable	0	6,000	(6,000)
Current portion of bonds payable	22,000	20,000	2,000
Total current liabilities	$303,981	$249,156	$ 54,825
Noncurrent liabilities:			
Bonds payable	$213,000	$235,000	$ (22,000)
Provision for warranty costs	8,925	11,850	(2,925)
Future income tax	43,439	38,923	4,516
Total noncurrent liabilities	$265,364	$285,773	$ (20,409)
Equity:			
Share capital issued	$150,000	$100,000	$ 50,000
Retained earnings	143,527	111,235	32,292
Total equity	$293,527	$211,235	$ 82,292
Totals	$862,872	$746,164	$116,708

Further information:

1. The change in retained earnings is composed of net income $56,292 minus dividends declared of $24,000.
2. Land that had cost $35,000 was written off to expense as being worthless.
3. Payments to customers for warranty claims during 2007 equalled $7,000.
4. Land costing $5,000 was obtained in exchange for shares issued.
5. During 2007, a garage was sold for $25,000 cash. The cost of the garage was $100,000, and its accumulated amortization at the date of sale was $70,000.

From this information, prepare a cash flow statement for Tamarack for 2007 and comment on what the statement shows about the company's cash management.

EXTENDED TIME

PROBLEM 4.31 Prepare and interpret basic cash flow analysis from balance sheet changes

Another student has been having an awful time trying to prepare a cash flow statement for Greenplace Restaurants Inc. for the 2006 fiscal year. You go over to help and find the disorganized list of balance sheet changes below. About all that can be said for it is that it does balance, so the student has managed to identify all the changes from 2005.

1. Take the list below and prepare a cash flow statement for Greenplace for 2006.
2. Explain what your statement reveals about the company's 2006 cash management.

List of Balance Sheet Changes for Greenplace Restaurants Inc. for Fiscal Year 2006

	Direction	A↑, L↓, E↓	A↓, L↑, E↑
Trade payables	Up		$ 37,970
Accumulated amortization	Up		47,110
Cash in bank	Up	$ 3,030	
Receivables	Down		24,489
Bank loan	Up		24,780
Inventories	Up	37,241	
Net income	Positive		61,140
Dividends declared and paid	Positive	21,000	
Prepaid expenses	Up	8,778	
Buildings, equipment	Up	206,942	
Mortgage payable	Up		45,500
Taxes payable	Down	9,498	
Share capital	Up		35,000
Term deposits (30 days)	Down		10,500
Sums of changes		$286,489	$286,789

PROBLEM 4.32 Prepare and interpret a basic cash flow analysis from financial statements

1. Prepare a cash flow statement from the following financial statements of Fuzzy Wuzzy Wines Ltd.
2. Comment on what your statement tells you about the company's cash management during the year ended August 31, 2006. If you were a shareholder in Fuzzy Wuzzy, would you be happy with management's performance?

Balance Sheets as at August 31, 2006 and 2005

Assets			**Liabilities and Equity**		
	2006	**2005**		**2006**	**2005**
Current assets:			Current liabilities:		
Cash	$ 80	$ 175	Bank loan	$ 140	$ 100
Short-term investment	0	150	Payables	425	200
Receivables	520	350		$ 565	$ 300
Inventories	340	250	Noncurrent liabilities:		
	$ 940	$ 925	Long-term loans	225	400
Noncurrent assets:				$ 790	$ 700
Factory cost	$1,450	$ 925	Shareholders' equity:		
Accum. amort.	(475)	(350)	Share capital	$ 700	$ 500
	$ 975	$ 575	Retained earnings	425	300
				$1,125	$ 800
	$1,915	$1,500		$1,915	$1,500

Fuzzy Wuzzy Wines Ltd.
Statement of Income and Retained Earnings
for the Year Ended August 31, 2006

Revenue		$3,000
Expenses:		
Amortization	$ 210	
Building write-off*	45	
General	2,320	2,575
Income before income tax		$ 425
Income tax expense		190
Net income for the year		$ 235
Retained earnings—beginning of year		300
Dividends declared and paid		(110)
Retained earnings—end of year		$ 425

* Building written off cost $130 and had accumulated amortization of $85.

PROBLEM 4.33 Prepare cash flow statement with several accrual adjustments and comment on it

Using the following comparative balance sheets and additional information for Prairie Products Inc., prepare a cash flow statement for the year ended November 30, 2007. State any assumptions you find necessary. Comment on what your statement shows about the company's cash management for 2007.

Prairie Products Inc.
Balance Sheet at November 30, 2007
with 2006 Figures for Comparison
(in thousands of dollars)

Assets			**Liabilities and Equity**		
	2007	**2006**		**2007**	**2006**
Current assets			*Current liabilities*		
Cash	$ 31	$ 38	Bank loan	$ 25	$ 30
Marketable securities	100	200	Accounts payable	195	284
Accounts receivable	281	315	Taxes payable	34	20
Inventories	321	239	Dividends payable	20	30
Prepaid expenses	12	18		$ 274	$ 364
	$ 745	$ 810	*Noncurrent liabilities*		
Noncurrent assets			Mortgage payable	$ 240	$ 280
Land cost	$ 182	$ 70	Bonds payable	200	0
Buildings cost	761	493	Future income tax	138	111
Equipment cost	643	510	Warranty liability	126	118
	$1,586	$1,073		$ 704	$ 509
Accum. amortization	631	569	*Shareholders' equity*		
	$ 955	$ 504	Share capital	$ 600	$ 450
Investments, cost	365	438	Retained earnings	487	429
	$1,320	$ 942		$1,087	$ 879
TOTAL	$2,065	$1,752	TOTAL	$2,065	$1,752

Additional information for 2007 (all figures are in thousands of dollars):

a. Net income was $98 and dividends of $40 were declared.
b. A building was sold for $42 that had cost $110 and had accumulated amortization of $56.
c. Amortization expense for the year was $118.
d. One of the noncurrent investments, which had cost $73, was sold for $102.
e. The change in future income tax liability was entirely due to the future (deferred) portion of income tax expense.
f. The change in warranty liability was composed of warranty expense of $23 minus payouts on warranties of $15.

Assorted Problems

* PROBLEM 4.34 Cash versus accrual income and cash from operations

From the following information:

1. Calculate cash income for the year.
2. Calculate accrual net income for the year.
3. Explain why they are different by showing cash from operations as calculated by the indirect method.
4. Calculate cash from operations by the direct method.

Collections:	On last year's revenue	46,665	Cash proceeds on new shares issued		210,000
	On this year's revenue	848,911	Cost of issuing new shares		4,622
	On next year's revenue	20,000	Amortization expense for the year		114,618
Payments:	On last year's expenses	78,640	Uncollected revenue:	Beginning of year	53,116
	On this year's expenses	649,925		End of year	73,007
	On next year's expenses	14,610	Unpaid expenses:	Beginning of year	78,640
Sale of land for cash (cost $80,000)		135,000		End of year	115,304
Paid to purchase new noncurrent assets		441,486	Cash:	Beginning of year	13,023
Still owing on those noncurrent assets		61,000		End of year	84,316

PROBLEM 4.35 Effects on income and cash of big accounting changes

When the new president of Lefton Inc. took office, she decided that the previous president had made some poor business decisions and that "the balance sheet needs to be cleaned up." Accordingly, the following accounting changes were implemented at the president's instruction:

- Uncollectible accounts receivable of $645,000 were written off directly to expense.
- Long-term investments costing $12,750,000 were written down to their estimated market value of $6,000,000.
- An investment in a foreign country, costing $4,800,000, was written off altogether.
- Liability for future warranty payments was increased by $495,000 additional expense.
- Income tax savings of $3,310,000 were expected from all this.

Before the new president took office, net income for the year was $784,000 and cash from operating activities was negative $442,000.

1. Calculate the revised net income for the year.
2. Calculate the revised cash from operations for the year.
3. A commentator criticized the new president for implementing a "Big Bath." What are your views about the propriety of the president's actions?

PROBLEM 4.36 Use a cash flow statement to derive an ending balance sheet

Give your knowledge of the financial statement relationships a workout by deriving the balance sheet of TGIF Industries Ltd. at the end of 2007 from the two statements given below (the balance sheet at the end of 2006 and the cash flow statement for 2007). When you have done that, prepare some comments on what the company's cash management strategy seemed to be for 2007, and whether that left the company financially stronger or weaker at the end of 2007 than at the end of 2006.

TGIF Industries Ltd.
Balance Sheet at December 31, 2006
(in thousands of dollars)

Assets		**Liabilities and Equity**	
Current assets		*Current liabilities*	
Cash on hand	$ 19	Demand bank loan	$ 2,205
Cash in bank	238	Other bank indebtedness	840
Accounts receivable	2,868	Accounts payable, accruals	1,948
Inventories	2,916	Income, other taxes payable	213
Prepaid expenses	184		$ 5,206
	$ 6,225		
		Noncurrent liabilities	
Noncurrent assets		Mortgage payable	$ 516
Land cost	$ 416	Loans from shareholders	600
Automotive equipment cost	892	Other long-term loans	318
Buildings cost	2,411	Deferred (future) income tax	248
Equipment cost	1,020	Estimated pension liability	163
	$ 4,739		$ 1,845
Accumulated amortization	863	*Shareholders' equity*	
	$ 3,876	Share capital	$ 1,000
Investments, cost	740	Retained earnings	2,790
	$ 4,616		$ 3,790
TOTAL	$10,841	TOTAL	$10,841

TGIF Industries Ltd.
Cash Flow Statement for the Year Ended December 31, 2007
(in thousands of dollars)

Operations:		
Net income for the year		$ 614
Add expenses (deduct revenues) not involving cash:		
Amortization expense	$ 291	
Loss on sale of investments	85	
Deferred (future) income tax expense	68	
Estimated pension expense	53	
Gain on sale of land	(210)	
Gain on sale of building	(38)	249
Add (deduct) effects of changes in noncash working capital:		
Accounts receivable	$ 1,134	
Inventories	647	
Prepaid expenses	37	
Accounts payable, accruals	(587)	
Income, other taxes payable	(14)	1,217
Cash generated by operations		$ 2,080
Investing activities:		
Investment in term deposits	$ (100)	
Proceeds from sales of long-term assets:		
Investments (cost $560)	475	
Land (cost $80)	290	
Building (cost $890)	514	
Cost of acquisitions of long-term assets:		
New building	(1,670)	
New equipment	(643)	(1,134)
Financing activities:		
Decrease in demand bank loan	$(1,137)	
Decrease in other bank indebtedness	(360)	
Payments on mortgage	(103)	
Additional loans from shareholders	250	
Debenture debt issued	300	
Payments of other long-term loans	(74)	
Payments of employee pensions	(43)	
Share capital issued	250	
Dividends paid ($100 declared)	(40)	(957)
Decrease in cash (cash on hand up $6, cash in bank down $17)		$ (11)

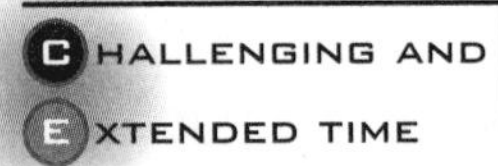

PROBLEM 4.37 Prepare a full set of statements, including cash flow

Grandin Ltd. manufactures a single product and has revenue from related service activities. The company had been growing slowly but steadily until this year (2007), when revenue, especially from services, increased substantially.

The company's bookkeeper was part way through preparing the 2007 financial statements (with 2006 for comparison) and asked you for help in completing them. When you went to the company's offices you got the information below. Assume these figures are correct.

Account Name	2007	2006
Accounts payable	$ 12,300	$ 8,900
Accounts receivable	44,200	21,300
Accumulated amortization	36,000	32,000
Administrative expenses	14,600	11,900
Bank loan—current	29,000	19,000
Cash	4,700	5,400
Cost of goods sold	103,190	71,650
Current income tax expense	5,200	3,000
Future income tax expense	250	500
Future income tax liability	4,350	4,100
Amortization	4,000	5,800
Dividends paid	4,000	6,000
Equipment	87,000	87,000
Equipment financing	20,000	24,000
Income taxes payable	2,200	1,000
Interest expense	4,800	3,900
Inventory	42,500	37,000
Packaging and shipping expense	8,100	7,500
Prepaid expenses	2,100	800
Retained earnings—beginning	37,500	33,300
Revenue—product sales	163,290	116,250
Revenue—service	73,700	32,600
Service wage expense	69,500	28,200
Share capital	25,000	25,000
Utilities expense	9,200	6,200

1. Prepare a comparative balance sheet, income statement, and statement of retained earnings for 2007 and 2006.
2. Prepare a cash flow statement for 2007 (you do not have the information to do comparative figures for 2006).

PROBLEM 4.38 Ethics of cash flow manipulation

There is an interesting ethical issue behind the very reason the cash flow statement is thought by some people to have advantages over the income statement. The reason is that people are often mistrustful of the income statement because they feel its accrual accounting methods can be used to manipulate net income as a measure of performance, and they think that the cash flow figures are more "real." For example, a company might claim large revenues, not yet collected, that make its income higher (and because the revenues are not collected, the accounts receivable are also higher), but if the cash has not been collected, the increase in accounts receivable will be deducted from net income on the cash flow statement, and the lack of "real" cash inflow will be apparent because cash from operations will be lower than would be expected from the income number. Thus, it is thought that the cash flow statement's cash from operations figure is more believable than net income and, if it is too different from net income, will unmask manipulations of the net income.

The ethical issue is that it is possible to manipulate the cash flow figures too. For example, a company might accelerate or delay receivables collections in order to change the cash flow figures, whether or not the net income is also being manipulated. There may be a difference from manipulating net income because changing cash flow figures requires real actions, affecting customers or suppliers or employees, so there are real consequences, such as irritating customers or having to offer inducements for early payment. Nevertheless, it can be done.

It seems that most people would feel that altering the accruals just to make net income better (or worse, or smoother) is ethically questionable, even if it is understandable because of the way management is evaluated and rewarded. But is altering the cash flow ethically questionable? Is there an ethical problem if management decides to put pressure on customers to accelerate collections and improve the company's cash position? Sounds like good management, not like manipulation.

Suggest two or three ways, not included above, in which operating, investing, or financing cash flows could be altered from their normal levels. For each, discuss whether, or under what conditions, you would think there is an ethical problem in such alteration.

CASE 4A

DISCUSS ISSUES RELATED TO CASH FLOW ANALYSIS

The three financial statements included in Chapters 2 and 3 are all based on accrual accounting, which generates a net income figure and related balance sheet accounts that attempt to measure the enterprise's economic performance and position. In this chapter, the cash flow statement was used to report the enterprise's results as if accrual accounting had not been used, focusing instead on cash flow. Discuss the following questions, using as an example CPR (see its statements in Sections 2.10, 3.4, and 4.7), Enbridge, Petro-Canada, TD Bank or any company whose statements you can obtain from the company Web page or the library. (For current information about CPR, go to **www.cpr.ca**.)

1. Does the cash flow statement really help the person who is trying to understand the enterprise's performance, or is it just another complicated accounting statement that is mysterious to nonaccountants? Which parts of it are most understandable and which parts are least understandable?
2. Is it a good idea to indicate, by preparing the cash flow statement, that knowing about an enterprise's income performance is not enough? What does the presence of the cash flow statement say about the value of the income measure? Conversely, what does the presence of the broader income measure say about the value of the more narrowly defined cash flow measure?
3. For CPR (or any other company you select), is the story told by the cash flow statement consistent with or supportive of the story told by the income statement? Would you expect good performance in one to imply good performance in the other, long-term or short-term? What kinds of differences in the stories the two statements tell would you expect to be significant enough for readers of the statement to react to (such as by buying or selling shares of the company and so changing its share price)?
4. Are there events you would like to see reflected, or separately disclosed, in the cash flow statement that are not? Are there things in the cash flow statement you think are unnecessary? (For example, do you think people need the reconciliation with accrual income in the cash from operations section, or would it be satisfactory to just state what cash from operations is without all the reconciling items?)
5. What sorts of clues about the enterprise's business and financial strategies can you get from the cash flow statement? Are there other issues the statement can raise questions about, even if it alone cannot answer them?

CASE 4B

DISCUSS A CONFERENCE CALL ON A COMPANY'S FINANCIAL PERFORMANCE

Serena was nervous as she walked into the boardroom for her company's quarterly conference call with financial analysts and other interested people. In a few hours, she would be on a live phone call (also Webcast) with more than a hundred people. She would be responding to analysts' questions and comments about the company's performance from the boardroom, in the company of her company's top managers: the chair of the board of directors, the president and chief executive officer, and her immediate boss, the chief financial officer. Serena was newly appointed as the company's chief accountant, after a very successful career in public accounting. She felt that she knew her accounting, but still expected the conference call would be an ordeal.

Here are the accounting-related questions and comments from the analysts. Discuss how Serena or other of the top managers might have responded to them, individually or as a set. Also discuss what the questions add up to as an overall portrayal of the analysts' concerns about the company's performance.

1. We've been expecting the company to make about $3.50 EPS, compared to last year's $3.35. It did make that, actually hitting $3.65, but I notice that the cash flow per share is down to $4.80 from last year's $5.25. Does this mean the company's performance is slipping in spite of the better accrual income?"
2. To follow the previous question, I am very concerned that cash flow per share is higher than EPS. It looks as if EPS is well below what it should be, even if you did make the EPS target.
3. We all know that in the long run, on average, earnings and cash flow correlate positively. But in this year, you have a negative correlation: EPS going up but cash flow per share going down. I suspect either your cash flow or accrual earnings figure is wrong.
4. Your cash flow statement shows a large increase in accounts receivable and inventories. This seems to be why the cash flow has fallen. The receivables increase in particular seems to indicate problems with collection, or, and this is what I am worried about, you may have recorded more revenue than you should have and just added that to the accounts receivable. I'm not accusing, but as you know we are all sensitive these days about companies trying to boost their earnings.
5. The cash flow statement also indicates that the company is bringing in many millions of dollars in cash from depreciation and amortization. What have you done with all that cash?
6. Following up on the previous question, your income statement showed a big restructuring charge, but on the cash flow statement, most of it is added to income. Does that mean the restructuring charge is just an estimate, not really incurred yet or paid out?
7. The previous questions have focused on operations. I am more concerned about the company's risk. The cash flow statement indicates significant borrowing this year, more than was issued in new shares. Such borrowing increases the debt-equity ratio and the risk. Since you did generate some cash from operations, why would you have to borrow? Even with the borrowing, your cash hardly went up at all.
8. There is another risk here. Your working capital is up, but it is largely noncash, so you don't really have the cash you need to operate properly and pay your bills.
9. An earlier question mentioned depreciation and amortization. I see that this amounts to more than a hundred million dollars this year, but your spending on new property and plant assets was only about half that. As I understand the numbers, there is a greater increase in accounts receivable and inventory than there is in property and plant. Is your strategy to shrink rather than to grow?
10. The financing information in your cash flow statement indicates that your long-term borrowing was used in part to pay dividends. That seems unwise—you should pay dividends only if you have lots of internal financing from operations.
11. On the other hand, I note that your long-term borrowing was about the same amount as your additions to property and plant, so it does make sense to finance long-term assets with long-term

borrowing. Would be even better to finance with permanent capital, though.

12. I've been looking at some patterns. Over the last three years, your cash from operations has gone steadily down, and your cash from borrowing has gone steadily up. It seems to me you are getting into some financial trouble.
13. I represent a large pension fund that has thousands of shares of the company. We are concerned that the company's share price has weakened in the last year or so in spite of growth in earnings per share. All these questions suggest to me that the share price is falling because you are having cash problems rather than earnings problems.
14. We've been talking about the past year most of the time. If I look forward, I see that you have a large debt repayment due next year. Since you were already borrowing this year, will you have to borrow to make that repayment? Your cash flow difficulties this year were in spite of not having to repay any debt, so you will need more cash flow next year to stay out of serious trouble. Do you have plans to improve cash from operations by getting those inventories and receivables down?

NOTES

1. There have been many research papers on the correlation between accrual income and operating cash flows over time. A recent paper, for example, showed that the ability to predict future cash flows from present accrual incomes appears to have been increasing from the 1980s to the 1990s. (W. Kross and M.S. Kim, "The Ability of Earnings to Predict Future Operating Cash Flows Has Been Increasing—Not Decreasing," working paper, Purdue University and University of Missouri, 2002.
2. For more information on the "cash flow" research results, see W.H. Beaver, *Financial Reporting: An Accounting Revolution*, 2nd ed. (Englewood Cliffs: Prentice-Hall, 1989), 116; or P.A. Griffin, ed., *Usefulness to Investors and Creditors of Information Provided by Financial Reporting*, 2nd ed. (Stamford: Financial Accounting Standards Board, 1987), 144–45. Accounting research journals such as *The Accounting Review*, *Contemporary Accounting Research*, *Journal of Accounting and Economics*, and *Journal of Accounting Research* occasionally have articles examining cash flow or comparing cash flow to accrual net income.

CHAPTER FIVE

5 Standards and Principles Surrounding the Financial Statements

5.1 Chapter Introduction: Accounting Standards and Principles

"Ladies and gentlemen of the jury, I put it to you that the defendants, Market Darling Inc.'s top managers on trial here, willfully circumvented accounting standards in preparing the set of financial statements that are the heart of this lawsuit. When investors, ordinary Canadians like yourselves, bought Market Darling shares, they were putting their faith in the company as well as their savings, and part of that faith was that they would get honest information in the company's financial reports. That faith was destroyed by the company's self-serving accounting, and the evidence shows that such accounting also led to the collapse of the whole business and the loss of investors' money as well as their faith. I'll summarize the main parts of this sad story:

- Market Darling began ten years ago with a solid business concept and good employees. But top managers, there at the defendants' table, wanted faster growth.
- To fuel the rapid growth those managers wanted, the company needed large amounts of money, which it got from share issues and bank borrowing, and spent on increasingly grandiose and dubious investments and acquisitions of other companies.
- To convince investors and lenders that it was doing well, and so keep their money coming in, the company had to show strong growth in earnings.
- Top managers found accounting too conservative and cautious for their liking, so they started to find ways of reporting revenues that were not real and delaying expenses, and so produced artificially high earnings, retained earnings and assets like receivables and inventories.
- The continuous and increasing demand for earnings growth became a treadmill. The company began making business deals and acquiring other companies because they made the accounting numbers look good, not because they made business sense. Trusting investors supported the company, and the share price rose more than ten-fold in a few years.
- Getting increasingly good accounting results became the whole goal. But it was a house of cards. The accounting was unfair, unreliable, unconventional, unconservative, and ultimately unbelievable. When investors realized this, they ran for cover, and the share price collapsed. Faithful investors lost their shirts, when the share price fell over 95% in a few weeks and the company was forced into bankruptcy.
- Ladies and gentlemen, this lawsuit is fundamentally about accounting standards and the company's failure to follow them. If the company had followed accepted accounting standards, instead of trying to get around them, it would not have gotten into this mess, investors would not have suffered the huge losses, and you would not be here thinking about accounting on this fine summer's day."

Learning Objectives

This is the last of the four chapters introducing the financial statements. It has few numbers. (Perhaps the break from numbers will help the previous material settle into your understanding!) Instead, this chapter focuses on the large system of standards and principles that govern the way accountants assemble the numbers. We have seen that accrual accounting and even transaction recording require judgment and managerial decisions—now we will delve into the concepts that guide the accountants and the accounting.

Doing accounting and using accounting information requires concepts as well as numbers.

Both doing accounting and making good use of accounting information requires a solid conceptual understanding, in addition to being able to work with the numbers. Accounting information doesn't just appear, it follows accepted standards of preparation, format, and disclosure, or should follow them, as the lawsuit vignette illustrates. *Accounting standards and principles are not just "theory"*: they are a set of very practical guidelines that accountants and managers follow every day. This chapter is a foundation for succeeding chapters that get into the specifics of doing accounting and making accounting choices and that use the principles from this chapter continuously.

In this chapter you will learn:

GAAP represent the system of standards and principles that govern financial accounting.

- Why financial accounting has *authoritative standards* and *generally accepted accounting principles (GAAP)*, where those have come from, and how capital markets and business contract arrangements incorporate the resulting accounting information;
- How the structure of financial accounting standards and principles provides guidance to accountants and to managers such as those in the lawsuit above;
- How those standards and principles are supposed to be connected to the circumstances of a particular company, such as Canadian Pacific Railway;
- What role *external auditors* are supposed to play in the maintenance of standards and in producing good financial reporting upon which people can rely; and
- How accounting standards are being applied beyond the usual Canadian business company, such as to international business and not-for-profit organizations and governments.

5.2 Using Principles to Produce Accounting Information

Practising accountants use accounting principles to guide their actions.

How do accountants decide what accounting is needed and then put their decisions into practice? This section outlines the conceptual background that guides accountants. Doing accounting well takes expert knowledge, considerable experience, and continuous attention to new problems and solutions. Concepts and principles are very important in accounting because they form a logical structure that practising accountants use every day to consider problems, make or recommend decisions, and explain solutions.

All the accounting revolves around the accounting entity that is its focus.

Applying accounting standards and principles depends on the particular *accounting entity*, the enterprise for which the accounting is being done. The neighbourhood cappuccino bar is just as appropriate an entity to be accounted for as are the groups of hundreds of corporations making up IBM or the Royal Bank of Canada, but decision criteria would imply different accounting needs for the cappuccino bar entity, IBM, or the bank, so GAAP would be applied differently for these entities. (More about this is in For Your Interest at the end of this section.)

Three general groups of highly related ideas lie behind the chart shown in Figure 5.1, which concerns the accounting for a company, corporate group, or other accounting entity:

1. *Decision criteria:* how to meet the needs of those who use and pay for the accounting.
2. *Generally accepted accounting principles:* financial accounting's conceptual structure.
3. *Preparation steps:* how decisions are put into practice for that entity.

FIGURE 5.1

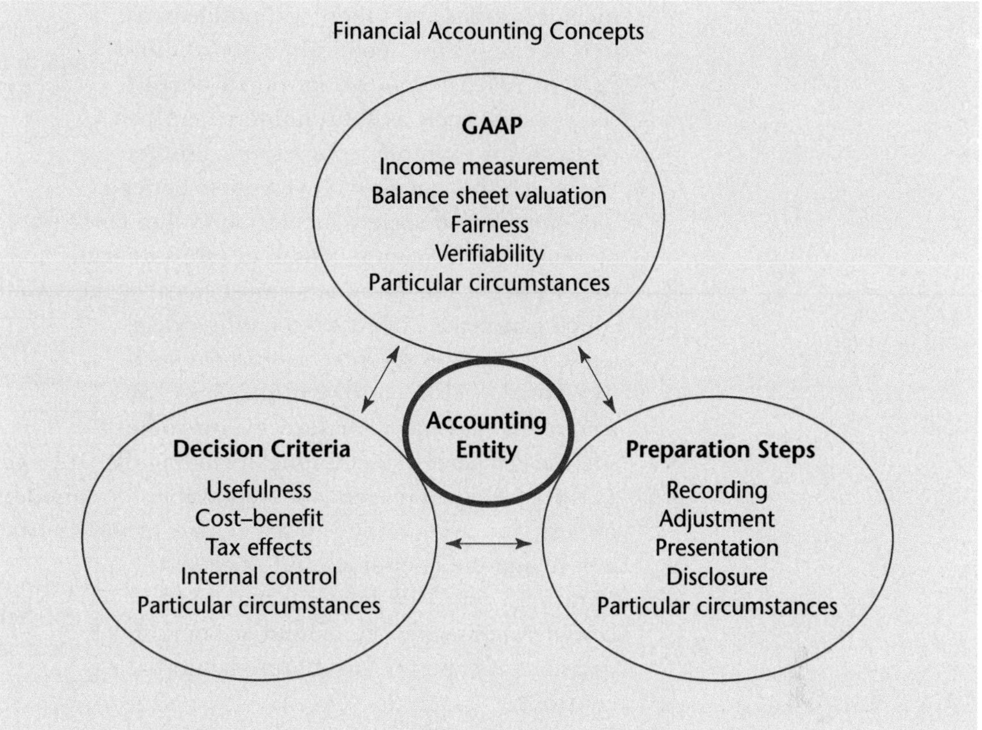

Accounting standards and principles change and adapt as the world changes.

These three groups of ideas are in constant flux, both with each other and with the changing nature of the business and professional environment. The double-headed arrows indicate this flux, and the lack of a beginning or end to the chart indicates that the accountant might start just about anywhere and work back and forth through the various issues in doing the job of making accounting work.

Here's an outline of the ideas within each of the three groups of concepts in Figure 5.1. You'll get to know them all more deeply as you use them in learning about how to do accounting in the rest of the book.

Decision criteria: These criteria refer to serving the needs of shareholders, managers, creditors, and others who use accounting information. The five sets of ideas in this group are:

Accounting information fundamentally should be useful, in numerous ways.

1. *Usefulness:* This is the fundamental reason for having financial accounting. It includes *relevance* (decision usefulness), *materiality* (size of impact on user's decisions or interests), and some ways in which accounting can be useful, including *timeliness* (getting the information in time to use it in making a decision), value in *prediction*, value in calculating various parties' *shares of results* (such as dividends and management bonuses), value in evaluating the *performance*, *accountability*, and *stewardship* of management.

> Usefulness questions about information:
> - Does it matter to anyone? *(relevance)*
> - Would it change someone's decision? *(materiality)*
> - Does it arrive when it's needed? *(timeliness)*
> - *Past:* Is it useful for evaluating performance?
> - *Present:* Is it useful in sharing the rewards?
> - *Future:* Is it useful for predicting results?

2. *Cost-benefit:* Like anything else, accounting should be worth its cost, so the usefulness criteria have to be balanced against costs, including the cost of *doing* accounting, plus, possibly, the costly *consequences* of accounting. Costly consequences might

include lawsuits and other legal problems as well as competitive, political, or social difficulties. Releasing information to benefit some users, such as shareholders, can be costly if, for example, competitors also get the information and use it to compete better.

> *Cost-benefit:* Is the information worth the cost to produce it or the cost of its consequences?

3. *Tax effects:* In our society, income and other taxes are significant considerations, and accounting information is used in assessing many taxes, so every enterprise subject to tax (on itself or its owners) must consider the tax effects of accounting methods, which can make or break accounting decisions, or even be the real reasons for such decisions. This book mentions tax frequently and has later sections on some specific tax issues in accounting, including the GST and income tax.

> *Tax:* Will the information result in more, or less, tax?

4. *Internal control:* Managers are responsible for running the enterprise on behalf of owners, and accounting is a major part of the information used in managing and controlling the operations and assets of the enterprise, so, like tax, internal control considerations often lie behind accounting decisions. Chapter 7 has more on internal control.

> *Internal control:* Does the information help management look after the assets?

5. *Particular circumstances:* Every entity for which accounting is done has its own circumstances (depending on its industry, the way it does business, its financial situation, its legal situation, and its managers' information preferences), so decision criteria have to be interpreted in the light of those circumstances.

> GAAP are a set of practical concepts intended to ensure the information is useful and fair.

Generally accepted accounting principles: GAAP form the conceptual structure of financial accounting and have been developed over the years to represent both the decision criteria above and broader social and professional criteria of appropriateness. The five sets of ideas in this group are:

1. *Income measurement:* Measuring income is fundamental to financial accounting and solutions are judged according to the central concepts of *recognition* and *matching* of revenues and expenses. Revenues and expenses should be *recognized* (entered into the accounts) only when they have been earned or incurred, and they should *match* each other so that the net income, which is revenues minus expenses, is meaningful. Chapter 6 explores these income measurement ideas in more depth.

> Questions about income measurement:
> - Are revenues and expenses measured properly? *(recognition)*
> - Are revenues and expenses measured comparably to each other? *(matching)*

2. *Balance sheet valuation:* Valuing assets, liabilities, and equity is just as fundamental as measuring income is, so solutions are judged according to the *cost principle* and *conservatism*, the two main valuation concepts. Accounting is still largely a *historical cost*-based information system (assets, liabilities, and equity all being shown mostly at values arising up to but not past the balance sheet date). Being *conservative* (prudent and cautious) about the values used in cases where historical values are not appropriate (such as when an asset's value has declined below its cost) is considered important in avoiding optimistically misleading figures. Chapters 8 and 9 focus on accounting

> Questions about balance sheet valuation:
> - Do the values arise from past events? *(cost principle; historical cost)*
> - Are the values prudent, not optimistic? *(conservatism)*

principles behind the balance sheet numbers, and because the balance sheet and income statement articulate, Chapter 6's examination of income measurement also has implications to balance sheet valuation.

3. *Fairness:* This is the most fundamental objective of financial statements. The *external auditors* report on it, stating specifically if in their opinion the financial statements are fair.

   Several principles are involved in meeting this fundamental fairness objective. One principle is *objectivity*: the information should be *neutral* (not favouring any of the users) and "*representationally faithful*," telling the story according to what really has happened and not being influenced by the interests of any party(ies), who might wish things had been different. Some of the recent controversy about accounting in cases like Enron concerns a related principle that accountants and auditors call "*form versus substance*": do the financial statements report on the economic substance of what has happened, or are they just based on following the rules to produce something that looks right but is not reality? An example of form improperly dominating substance is when a company chooses business transactions because of how they will look in the financial statements, not because they make good business sense: the accounting is then driving the business, not just reporting on it.

   Another fairness principle is *continuity* or *going concern*, the idea that the user of the information should be entitled to assume that the enterprise will continue in business unless the user is informed otherwise, and so that using principles such as cost or matching is appropriate (a "liquidation," or immediate sale, basis, for example, would be appropriate if the enterprise is not a going concern). The information should also be *reliable*: accurately compiled and free of intentional or inadvertent error. Users can be expected to want to compare the enterprise to others and to its own past history; the information should be *comparable* to others and *consistent* over time so that results can be compared to those of other enterprises or other time periods.

   All of these principles seek to ensure that the information is valid and not misleading. You will hear much about the principles in this item, so here is a list of the main ones again: *fairness, objectivity, neutrality, form versus substance, going concern, reliability, comparability,* and *consistency.*

> Fairness questions about information:
> - Does it tell it like it is? *(objectivity)*
> - Is it uninfluenced by people's wishes or hopes? *(neutrality)*
> - Does it report economic *substance*?
> - Does it (or should it) assume that the enterprise will continue? *(going concern)*
> - Is it *reliable,* free of error?
> - Does it make the enterprise *comparable* to other similar enterprises?
> - Has it been prepared *consistently* so that comparisons can be made over time?

4. *Verifiability:* If accounting information is to meet the standards indicated above, anyone should be able to go back and see, or check, how the information was put together and evaluate its appropriateness. This means that there should be documents and other evidence behind the accounting information so that it can always be verified. *Verifiability* leads to a need for documents to back up accounting records, as well as to careful records that the external auditor can check. (Such documentation is often called the "audit trail.") Section 5.8 has more about auditing.

5. *Particular circumstances:* Just as for the decision criteria, the above principles have to be interpreted, and sometimes rethought in accordance with the entity's circumstances.

> *Verifiability:* Can someone else check that the information has been properly assembled and so is fair?

What is fair for one company may not be fair for another whose financing, management, ownership interests, or prospects are different.

Accounting's preparation steps also are aimed at making the information useful and fair.

Preparation steps: Accounting involves a series of procedures for producing the information users get. These procedures are usually, though not always, done in the order below, and accountants may decide at a later stage that an earlier stage needs to be rethought. There is more about the preparation steps in Chapter 7.

1. *Recording:* This is when the business and economic events are turned into accounting data using the double-entry system of recording transactions. We saw this transaction step in Chapters 1 and 2 particularly.
2. *Adjustment:* At this stage, recorded data are changed or augmented to comply with additional information or to meet any of the criteria in the two groups above. It is the stage when the accountant is acting consciously as an interpreter of the business world. Adjustments were part of Chapter 3's coverage of accrual income.
3. *Presentation:* Here the recorded and adjusted data are organized, formatted, and fitted with captions to produce the financial statements and other reports the users get. In doing this work, the accountant has to ensure that all the information combines into an appropriate overall depiction of the enterprise, remembering, for example, that decisions about income measurement affect balance sheet valuation and vice versa because of the ways that the financial statements *articulate.* Financial statement presentation and articulation were emphasized in Chapters 2, 3, and 4.

   Information preparation:
   - Record
   - Adjust
   - Organize and format
   - Add disclosure

4. *Disclosure:* Doing the numbers appropriately is not enough. The accountant also has to decide whether to group numbers together or disclose them separately, and how to supplement the numbers with notes and other narrative, tabular, or graphic *disclosure.* There is more about disclosure in this chapter.
5. *Particular circumstances:* As in the other two groups of ideas, each entity's circumstances affect what is actually done. No two enterprises have quite the same accounting systems and problems, so the procedures followed by accountants from enterprise to enterprise are not quite the same.

The repeated mentions of "particular circumstances" above are reminders that it is very important to fit the accounting to the circumstances of the particular accounting entity. However, if you always changed everything to suit each enterprise, there would be no standards left, and no comparability to other enterprises. If every course in the university used a unique grading system, you couldn't compare how you did in different courses, or compute a grade-point average. Here, very briefly, are three examples of accounting difficulties that face accountants and managers:

- Global, CTV, and CBC have national TV networks in Canada. CBC is publicly owned, largely financed by the government of Canada, and is not generally supposed to be trying to make a profit, while CTV and Global are privately owned and are definitely trying to make a profit. Should all three use the same accounting methods, so that they may be compared, or does the CBC's public ownership and mandate mean that its accounting should be different? (In past years, CBC's accounting was very different from that of a profit-making company, but its accounting has been getting less and less different over the years.)
- Because companies cannot "own" their employees, all those great employees are not shown on the balance sheet of IBM, or the CPR, or the University of Toronto. But what about a sports team like the Vancouver Canucks, the Toronto Raptors, or Manchester United? These teams often pay millions of dollars for the right to have particular players play for them (recently soccer football team Real Madrid paid US$64.5 million just to get star player Zinedine Zidane, for example).[1] How should the team account for such sums? Are they assets or expenses? If they are assets, how long do they last? Should they be amortized over the "useful life" of the player concerned? That would be to treat the player rather like a machine or building, but maybe, in an economic sense, that's what the player is. (The actual players are not on the teams' balance sheets, but the costs to get them are, and many teams indeed amortize such costs over the length of time the players are thought to be useful—an exceedingly difficult estimation to do, when an injury, for example, can render a star player pretty well useless long before age would be expected to do the same.)
- How do you figure out the profitability of a big movie like one of the *Star Wars* series? Such a movie should attract lots of folks to the theatre soon after it comes out, but it will, or might, generate other revenues for years, such as video or DVD rentals, TV showings, product tie-ins, books, etc. Did *Casablanca* make money? It was released 60 years ago but continues to generate revenue. (This is one of accounting's hardest problems, and it has really not been solved. There are almost constant lawsuits between people who are supposed to share profits from movies and disagree about how such profits should be calculated, especially how to factor in such unknowns as future revenues. Comparing movie companies' net income to that of other companies is quite difficult.)

HOW'S YOUR UNDERSTANDING?

Here are two questions you should be able to answer based on what you have just read. If you can't answer them, it would be best to reread the material.

1. Why is the accounting entity important to the way accounting is done?
2. What is the purpose of financial accounting's GAAP conceptual structure?

5.3 An Example of Applying Accounting Principles to a Company

Well, let's bring all this down to earth. Let's see how we might think about the concepts behind financial accounting by relating them to CPR, the company whose financial statements were studied in Chapters 2, 3, and 4. We learned about CPR's balance sheet in Chapter 2, its income statement in Chapter 3, and its cash flow in Chapter 4. Please think about what sort of company CPR is and how it is performing as you read the scenarios below, and refresh your memory about CPR from the earlier chapters if you need to. For current information about CPR, consult the company's Web site (**www.cpr.ca**).

Information Use Scenarios

CPR is a transportation company with a long and important history in Canada, facing a very competitive North American environment. Let's think now about some of the users of the company's financial statements:

Scenario 1: The board has to evaluate how the CEO is doing in managing the company.

1. The company's *board of directors* manages the company on behalf of the shareholders. One function of the board that involves the financial statements is hiring and evaluating the performance of the company's top operating management, especially the president and chief executive officer (CEO). Suppose you are a member of CPR's board and are preparing for a discussion of the CEO's performance at the next board meeting. CPR's financial statements are among the information provided to the board prior to the meeting, and will be a major input to this evaluation.

Scenario 2: A financial analyst has to decide whether to recommend the company's shares.

2. The company's shares are *listed* (that is, can be bought and sold) on the Toronto Stock Exchange (CPR's trading symbol is CP, no R). (You could look in today's financial newspaper under the TSX stock price listings and see how the company's shares are doing.) Suppose you are a financial analyst for a Canadian investment dealer and are preparing a report projecting future earnings and making recommendations about whether the company's shares are worthwhile to buy, or to keep if already held, or instead should be sold. You have the company's financial statements and will use them as support to your report.

Scenario 3: A bank lending officer has to review the company's borrowing status.

3. CPR has several billions of dollars in borrowing (part of its long-term debt) and has lines of credit (pre-authorized borrowing capability) for millions of dollars more ($577.3 million at December 31, 2004, according to the financial statements' Note 22 on commitments). Suppose you are a commercial lending officer for a bank, conducting a regular review of the company's borrowing status. You must consider the quality of the company's financial performance and assets (some of which, such as railway locomotives, have been assigned as security on its debt, and, therefore, could be seized if the company didn't pay its loans back on schedule). Financial performance is important because good net income usually goes with generation of cash to pay loans, and a good past record suggests that the company is likely to be able to earn income and generate cash in the future. You have requested recent financial statements to use in your review.

Scenario 4: A supplier has to decide whether to sign a contract with the company.

4. CPR depends on a large number of suppliers to support its railway operations. The company operates in Canada and the United States, and with its commitment to meet the needs of its own customers, has to be on good terms with all sorts of suppliers. Suppose you are the sales manager of a company that manufactures locomotives, railway cars, and parts for such "rolling stock" and are considering signing a long-term supply contract with CPR. You want to sign the contract because your company would like the business, but you have to be satisfied that your shipments will be paid for and that CPR is well run, as your reputation will be tied to CPR's to some extent. More positively, you hope that if you do a good job, you will have an opportunity to grow with CPR. Most of the information you need has been received already, but you have obtained recent CPR financial statements and are reviewing them as you make your final decisions about the contract.

These scenarios have been chosen to add to your insight into the use of financial accounting information. They are not complete. *In all cases,* the financial statements would be only *part* of the set of information used in the decision making, but you can see that the financial statements can play a role in many different decisions. Also, as we saw in earlier sections, there are many other uses of financial statements, some of which might make different demands on the quality of the information than are discussed here.

Demands on the Quality of Financial Accounting Information

Let's think about what the users in these scenarios might reasonably expect of the financial statements. You'll see that important accounting concepts and principles, included in Section 5.2 above, arise. Those are described in italics below.

1. The financial statements should not be deliberately misleading. The bank loans officer would want to feel confident that the statements were not prepared in such a way as to make the company appear to be a better lending risk than it is. The board of directors similarly would want the statements to provide an objective portrayal of the CEO's performance in running the company.

The four example users all want the information they use to be fair.

   This is the criterion of fairness. It is so important that the auditors' report (see Section 5.8) refers to it explicitly. The auditors state their opinion that the financial statements "present fairly" the company's financial position and results. There is much flexibility and judgment involved in financial accounting, so the auditors cannot say that the statements are "correct," but they can testify to their fairness.

Anyone evaluating performance would expect revenues and expenses to be matched.

   As described in Section 5.2, a very important fairness-related criterion for choosing accrual accounting methods is matching: revenues and expenses should be determined using compatible methods so that the net income (which is revenues minus expenses) makes sense. Matching is central to many accounting methods, including those for income tax, inventory and cost of goods sold, amortization, pensions, and warranties. Much of the income measurement content of Chapter 6 has to do with matching. One common way of "manipulating" financial results, making them unfair, is to fail to match expenses with revenues, for example, showing revenues before they have really been earned and before the expenses to earn them have been incurred.

Users are unlikely to be concerned about insignificant errors in the information.

2. Preparing financial statements, like any other activity, costs money and takes time. Most people would be satisfied if the statements were fair as to the *important* things and would not mind a few minor errors in them, especially if preventing small errors cost the company money (reducing the company's income and cash flow) or delayed the release of the statements. The supplier sales manager would not want to wait for the statements while CPR's accountants tried to get every tiny detail in the statements just right, nor would any other user who had to make a decision soon.

   This is the criterion of materiality (significance). Financial statements are supposed to be materially fair, so that users can be confident that the statements do not contain major errors. Materiality is also explicitly mentioned in the auditor's report: the auditors say that the statements present fairly, "in all material respects," or words to that effect. Just what is or is not material is a matter of judgment and has been the subject of considerable research and study by accountants and auditors. It is generally felt that an item, error, or disclosure is material if it would change someone's decision. Usually, people judge materiality by considering the size of a possible error compared to the net income or the total assets. For example, an accountant or auditor might judge that an error over 5% of net income or 1% of total assets is material and a smaller one is not. But, as you might expect, the materiality judgment depends on any particular uses of the information that are expected, and on whether the error seems to be a unique, random problem or part of a repeated pattern of mistakes, or even fraud.

3. The criteria of fairness and materiality imply some standard against which an accounting method or number can be judged. The financial analyst would like to

know that CPR's financial statements are materially fair, *given* accepted current methods. In the income statement, for example, sales revenue should mean what a knowledgeable analyst or other user would expect for such a company. As a second example, CPR is actually a group of companies, so its financial statements are consolidated, and it would be reasonable to expect that the company's method of calculating consolidated figures is proper, in accordance with accepted practices for consolidation.

GAAP represent the quality standard against which the financial statements are held.

This is where GAAP come in. To assure the users that accepted methods have been followed, the auditor's report also says that the auditors' opinion is that the statements have been prepared "in accordance with generally accepted accounting principles." This does not necessarily mean that any one particular method has been followed: GAAP often include several acceptable methods, depending on the circumstances. Therefore, following GAAP means that the company's accounting methods and the resulting figures are appropriate to its circumstances. Remember the repeated references to the entity's particular circumstances in the previous section (5.2).

4. Accounting information should tell people the results of the business arrangements and transactions the company has made to deal with the economic forces it faces. The information should therefore be traceable back to such business phenomena. A financial statement that is fair would also thus agree with these phenomena, and the auditors should be able to trace the accounting back to the phenomena to verify that the accounting does agree. The board of directors should be able to assume that the company's figure for sales revenue is supported by sales invoices, cash records, shipping records, and other evidence of actual sales. If there is any doubt about the results, or if there are any gaps in the supporting data, the board and the other users would probably want prudence, not too much optimism, in putting all the information together.

All users want their financial statements to be substantive, reliable, and verifiable.

Several criteria are present here. The financial statements should be reliable, carefully assembled from the underlying data, and not full of mistakes or misjudgments. They should reflect economic substance, not hopes or artificial arrangements. To make sure of reliability and substance, the information in the statements should be verifiable back to the business events and documents supporting them.

Conservative accounting avoids overstating the good news in financial statements.

Caution and prudence in filling in gaps, estimating uncertain amounts such as future collections and the value of unsold inventory, and measuring expenses to go with revenues, are represented in the criterion of conservatism. This often controversial criterion states that under uncertainty, assets, revenues, and income should not be overstated and liabilities, expenses, and losses should not be understated. Conservatism should involve being careful, not deliberately biasing important numbers downward, but just where prudence ends and bias begins is a matter of judgment.

5. The previous criteria indicate that the financial statements necessarily reflect judgment on the part of the preparers. Also, the figures in the statements are summaries of many accounts: for example, "accounts receivable" and "long-term debt" may include dozens or thousands of different customers or creditors. The bank's commercial lending officer may want to know what sort of long-term debts the company has, so that those may be evaluated against past or potential bank borrowing by the company. The bank would not want other creditors to interfere with the company's ability to pay the bank back. The financial analyst may want to know if the company has made commitments to issue more shares (such as in a plan to motivate senior management by issuing shares to them cheaply if they perform well), because issuing those might reduce the equity of anyone buying the shares now.

This raises the principle of disclosure. The financial statements include a large number of notes and account descriptions intended to make it clear to the reader which important accounting methods have been followed (especially if those methods are not

Extensive disclosure beyond the numbers is helpful in many situations.

what might be expected) and to provide supplementary information on debts, share capital, commitments, lawsuits, and other things thought to be helpful, or necessary, in understanding the statements. Disclosure beyond the accounting figures is increasingly extensive: many pages of notes often accompany the set of statements, and companies disclose additional information to taxation authorities, to securities regulators (such as the Ontario Securities Commission and the U.S. Securities and Exchange Commission), and to important other parties who have a reason to get the information (such as the bank loan officer and the financial analyst). Several aspects of disclosure are explored later in this chapter.

Most users want to be able to compare the company validly to others.

6. The banker and the financial analyst are also involved with other companies. They would like to be able to compare CPR's financial statements to those of similar companies, such as CNR, Canadian National Railway, (**www.cn.ca**). It may be difficult to be sure that a company is performing well or badly in an absolute sense, but it can always be compared to others, as long as the financial statements have been prepared in a comparable way.

   Comparability is important but a difficult criterion to meet, as was illustrated with the comments in Section 5.2 about comparing CBC to CTV or Global. Since no enterprise is quite the same as any other, making valid comparisons is a tricky task. It will be important when we review techniques for financial statement analysis in Chapter 10.

7. The banker, the analyst, and the board of directors' members will also want to study the trend in financial performance and position over time. Is the net income improving over time, or deteriorating? How about liquidity? Or the ratio of debt-equity financing? It is important to know if significant events have happened to make comparisons over time difficult or even impossible. It is also important to know if the company has changed its accounting methods over time, because such changes may affect the comparability of the accounting figures from year to year.

   Keeping the same accounting methods over time is called consistency. It is usually presumed that if the company is following GAAP, that includes using consistent methods or else telling the reader of the statements what the effects of changes in accounting methods are (if they are material).

Comparisons over time are facilitated by consistency in accounting.

These "information use scenarios" should help you see that accounting principles and concepts are central to the practice of accounting. They have a big influence on the numbers you actually see in financial statements, because companies generally try to follow them in ways suitable for each company. But sometimes following one principle seems to violate another.

Tradeoffs Among Accounting Principles

The various concepts within GAAP do not always fit together well.

If you think about the criteria and principles mentioned above, you may see that they do not always fit together well. Here are five examples:

- Conservatism is often argued to be a bias that interferes with fairness.
- If a company's circumstances are unusual, conforming rigorously to GAAP as followed by other companies may mean that the company's financial statements are not a fair portrayal of that particular company.
- If some other companies with which a company is likely to be compared (such as others in its industry) change their accounting methods, the company has to decide whether to change its methods too for the sake of comparability, even though that means inconsistency in its own figures over time.
- Similarly, when a new or revised accounting standard is announced, following the new standard (that is, conforming with GAAP as they now exist) will mean inconsistency over time for all companies that did not previously use the approved new method.

- Some people argue that it does not matter a great deal if a company's revenues and expenses are not properly matched, as long as the problem and information to adjust to other accounting methods are disclosed. The idea is that users of the company's financial statements can adjust the results to improve the match, if they do not like what the company did. (Doing such an adjustment is not always easy, however, even if all the information is available—some examples of making adjustments to reflect different accounting methods are given in later chapters.)

People's information needs and interests vary and conflict, and so do GAAP concepts.

You might feel that GAAP are not very well constructed if such problems can happen. People have certainly criticized GAAP for being inadequate and inconsistent. Many studies have been done to try to remove problems, including a multi-million-dollar study for the Financial Accounting Standards Board in the United States, called the "Conceptual Framework Project." That project was launched in the mid-1970s and was largely abandoned 10 years later. It appears that one framework, one way of thinking about financial statements, cannot deal with *all* the conflicting interests and priorities of the many users, preparers, and auditors. The inherent struggle and competition among people in our economic system tend to rule out single solutions, no matter how internally logical they may be, and the result is the rather imperfect but also flexible set of principles that make up GAAP. You might say there is something for everyone in GAAP, but not everything for anyone!

Here is an example of a tradeoff that simply cannot be avoided:

- It would seem sensible that the more reliable the accounting information is, the better. You get more reliable information by being very careful about how you prepare it, checking it carefully, having the auditors come in and verify it, maybe even waiting until some major uncertainties are resolved, so you do not have to guess about them.
- It also seems sensible that decision makers need information relevant to their decisions when they are making the decisions. This means that information should be timely; people should not have to wait for the information they need. Decision relevance and timeliness are two concepts behind GAAP mentioned in the previous section of this chapter.

Let's take the example of a company trying to report on its liability for pensions to employees. It has thousands of employees who will retire at various times over the next 40 years, if they do not quit, die, or get fired first. The pensions paid will depend on how much the employees earn before they retire, and that is not known yet for most of them—the younger ones' earnings are all in the future, and who knows what the future holds? The pensions also depend on how long the employees live after they retire and on whether they will have surviving spouses to be supported as long as they live. The company is trying to put aside enough money to cover all these pensions and will earn interest on the money saved for this purpose, so the amount of money required now also depends on how much interest will be earned on it over the years before the employees retire.

A relevant figure may be unreliable, but waiting to make it reliable may make it irrelevant.

How is that for a mass of uncertainty? Any number you come up with for the pension liability will be based on all sorts of estimates of unknown future events. So to get a liability figure that is at all reliable, you really have to wait 20 or 30 years until most of the employees have retired. You can always expect to get reliability by just waiting a while, even years, to see how things turn out. But waiting 20 or 30 years will hardly provide timely information, relevant to decisions like those being made by the board of directors, investment analyst, banker, and supplier mentioned above. Such decisions require the best information we can come up with now, even if it is necessarily based on estimates and assumptions.

Therefore, there is almost never a solution that produces both the most reliable and timeliest, relevant accounting information. As time passes, reliability rises and timely relevance falls, so we have to try to find some mid-point where there is enough of both, but not as much as we would like of either! Figure 5.2 illustrates this relevance-reliability tradeoff.

FIGURE 5.2

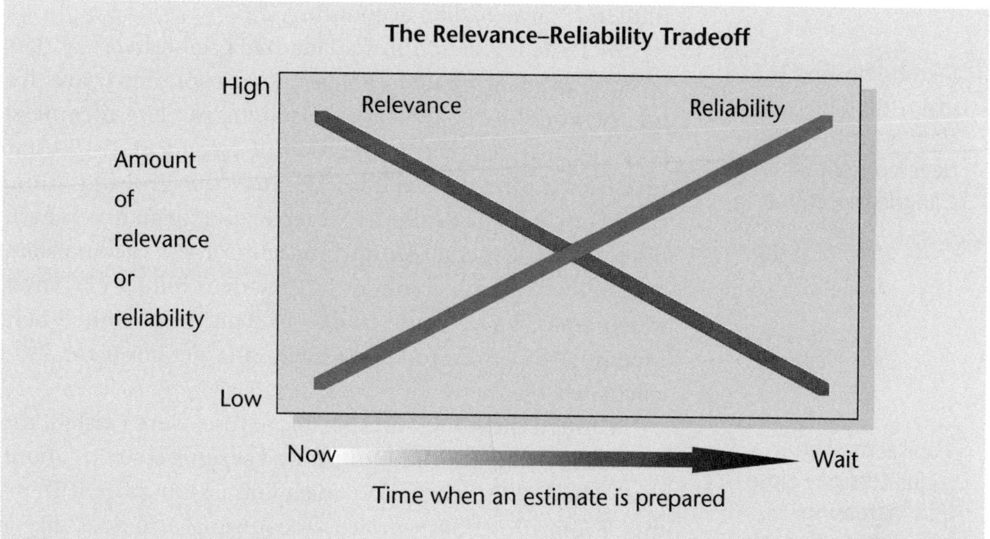

HOW'S YOUR UNDERSTANDING?

Here are two questions you should be able to answer based on what you have just read. If you can't answer them, it would be best to reread the material.

1. You have just opened CPR's annual report and found that the auditor's report says that it is the auditor's opinion that the financial statements have been prepared in accordance with generally accepted accounting principles. What concepts of information value would the auditor have assumed as part of GAAP?
2. Can accounting numbers, such as those in CPR's financial statements, be relevant, reliable, fair, and conservative all at once?

5.4 Financial Accounting Standards and Their Development

We left the review of historical developments relevant to financial accounting in Section 3.2, with the development of stock markets and the income statement. Chapter 4 added the last financial statement, the relatively recent cash flow statement. The main development in the just-ended 20th century is the great growth in official accounting standards. This section traces their growth and present nature.[2]

The OSC and the TSX are very important in Canadian financial accounting, but so is the SEC.

Canadian accounting practice has its main roots in Britain, but in the last hundred years it began to develop more independently from that in Britain, also coming under the stronger influence of events in the United States and internationally. Canada's federal system of government, different from the more centralized one in Britain, meant that legislation affecting accounting and professional accounting associations in Canada had strong provincial as well as national influences. As an example, in the early part of this century, Ontario led the rest of the country in introducing legislation that affected accounting methods. Today, the *Ontario Securities Commission* (*OSC*) (**www.osc.gov.on.ca**) is the most important regulator of capital markets in Canada and therefore has great influence on the accounting used by corporations whose shares are traded on stock exchanges (especially the *Toronto Stock Exchange*, or *TSX*, the country's largest (**www.tsx.ca**)). There is no national securities commission in Canada, while in the

United States, the national *Securities and Exchange Commission* (*SEC*) (**www.sec.gov**) plays an even more dominant regulatory role there than does the Ontario Securities Commission in Canada, and because of the influence of the United States on much of Canada's business practice, as in the rest of Canadian life, the SEC is also an important influence on Canadian accounting.

Income tax and U.S. investment have been significant to the development of Canadian accounting.

By 1920, legislation in Canada had established mandatory reporting of the financial position of incorporated companies (corporations) and had begun to set requirements for the contents of the income statement. The income statement became important both because income tax legislation passed in 1917 established rules for calculating revenues and expenses, and because the growing amount of equity investment in Canadian industry called for better performance measures and for more financial disclosure in general. Another reason for the income statement's growing prominence was the increased investment in Canadian industry by investors from the United States, which created a demand, similar to that in the United States, for disclosure of how net incomes, and therefore the dividends declared on the basis of the incomes, were calculated.

Capital market regulators pay close and increasing attention to financial accounting.

Though these pressures for more disclosure existed, the general prosperity in North America during the 1920s prevented serious concern about companies' financial disclosure. The 1929 stock market crash and ensuing Great Depression permanently changed this. From the 1930s onward, accounting practices, like many aspects of companies' financial and productive operations, attracted great, and often critical, attention from legislators and the public. The U.S. SEC was established in the mid-1930s, and securities commissions were also established in some of Canada's provinces, such as the OSC in Ontario. Their impact on business and financial accounting has steadily increased in the period since the Second World War.

In a sort of reprise of the 1920s, the 1990s also were a period of prosperity in which accounting principles and their regulation may have begun to slip, to be brought up short by the "high tech" collapse and stock market downturn of the early 2000s. Accounting's regulatory difficulties have even become the stuff of mainstream media. In 2002, *The New Yorker*, bastion of the arts, the chic, and the scene, published an exposé of a struggle between the SEC and public accounting firms titled "The Accountants' War"![3]

Regulation of Financial Accounting: Accounting Standards

The *CICA Handbook* is the main source of financial accounting standards in Canada.

Professional associations of accountants began to develop more rigorous accounting standards and auditing standards for their members to follow, and legislation began to require companies to adhere to these standards. In Canada, the Dominion Association of Chartered Accountants (now called the Canadian Institute of Chartered Accountants or the CICA) presented briefs to Parliament on accounting issues, issued bulletins making suggestions on financial accounting and auditing standards, and in the late 1960s began to issue official standards in the *CICA Handbook*.[4] *CICA Handbook* standards are given considerable authority by company legislation and securities commissions' regulations and will be referred to frequently in this book. Having a detailed set of accounting standards with legal authority is quite a recent phenomenon in Canada, as it is in many parts of the world, but this is growing rapidly worldwide.

The *CICA Handbook's* recommendations are intended to produce fair financial reporting.

The *CICA Handbook* is a looseleaf package hundreds of pages long (quite a handful!) that is continuously updated to reflect the standard-setters' judgments about how to deal with ever-changing circumstances. It's now gone electronic, and the public can get information about accounting standards through the CICA's Web site (**www.cica.ca**) and subscribers to the *CICA Handbook* receive it on-line through that site. Many professional accountants receive it as part of their professional membership. The *Handbook* consists of various discussions of accounting (and auditing) topics, accompanied by

"Recommendations" on what to do in those cases that the standard-setters have resolved. The *Handbook* recognizes that its recommendations cannot cover everything and that there may even be circumstances where following them would be misleading. Therefore, accountants and auditors must exercise their professional judgment about each accounting issue: they cannot just ignore the *Handbook*, but neither can they just follow it if it does not apply appropriately to the issue. The overriding criterion, as we have already seen, is that the financial statements should present the company's financial affairs *fairly*.

The FASB is the main source of financial accounting standards in the United States.

In the United States, the American Institute of Accountants (now called the American Institute of Certified Public Accountants or the AICPA (**www.aicpa.org**)) also began to issue pronouncements on financial accounting and auditing. The AICPA still issues auditing standards, but in the early 1970s its financial accounting standard-setting body, the Accounting Principles Board, was replaced by a new body set up to be independent of the AICPA: the *Financial Accounting Standards Board* (*FASB*) (**www.fasb.org**). (This is unlike the situation in Canada, where the *CICA Handbook* standards are set by the *Accounting Standards Board*, a committee of the CICA.) The U.S. SEC generally supports the FASB's position as financial accounting standard-setter for the United States, which gives the FASB great influence in accounting throughout much of the world, including Canada. As in many countries, there has been quite a proliferation of accounting standards in the United States, with well over 100 separate FASB standards (many of those very long and complex) and many SEC pronouncements issued over the last 20 or so years.

Financial accounting standards arise from sources other than the CICA and FASB.

There are many other voices in the setting of financial accounting standards and in the development of financial accounting. There is, for example, legislation requiring particular accounting methods for some sensitive companies, such as banks and trust companies. Standard-setting activities are also sometimes carried out by other associations, and courts often establish precedents in accounting issues as in other areas. There is much activity at the international level, such as that of the International Federation of Accountants (IFAC) (**www.ifac.org**), the International Organization of Securities Commissions (IOSCO) (**www.iosco.org**) and the *International Accounting Standards Board* (*IASB*) (**www.iasb.org.uk**), which, founded in 1973, has published a large number of international financial accounting standards. These standards have so far been less binding than such national standards as those issued by the CICA or the FASB, but there is great interest in harmonizing standards so that investors, managers, and other interested parties will be able to rely on the content and quality of financial statements no matter where in the world the statements originate. There is more about IASB and international standards in Section 5.5 on p. 304.

The Growth of Accounting Standards and Principles

Financial accounting continuously affects and is affected by society's economic activity.

The 20th century saw great growth in business and commercial activity, in stock markets and other capital markets, in international trade, in governments, in the sophistication of managers and investors, and in the communication links among them all. At any hour of the day, there is a major stock market open somewhere, with investors from all over the world trading on it. Business activity is truly a 24-hour-a-day, 365-day-a-year affair, with information about business activities flowing throughout the world via electronic, paper, and other media. Financial accounting is being continually shaped by all this activity. The basic double-entry model of financial accounting has endured for hundreds of years, but the way that model is applied and the supplementary information associated with it have developed far beyond Pacioli's description. Financial accounting's measures of financial position and performance are central to national and international economies and political structures, and financial accounting and its standards themselves are economically and politically powerful institutions in society.

Managers may be interested in accounting standards for several reasons.

Some Positives

1. Standards make reporting managers' performance clearer.
2. Standards make for easier comparisons with other companies.
3. Standards reduce the costs of accounting (each company would not have to work through and invent accounting methods on its own).
4. Standards increase the company's credibility to important users of financial statements in general.
5. Standards help to evaluate the conceptual and numerical effects of accounting choices and business decisions managers may have to make.

Some Negatives

1. Not all managers may wish to be measured clearly or have their company's performance easily comparable to that of other companies.
2. Standards specify general methods that may not work well for or even mismeasure some specific companies or situations.
3. Some complex standards may be quite costly to follow for some companies.
4. New standards may cause difficulty for loan agreements, bonus plans, or other arrangements that depend on accounting information and that were agreed to prior to the implementation of the new standards.

With reasons like these, it should be no surprise that the top managers of many companies take accounting standards very seriously. Many companies seek to influence accounting standards through lobbying standard-setters (such as CICA or FASB), securities commissions, other government agencies, and doing studies of the effects of proposed standards.

Financial accounting changes continuously as its environment changes.

Financial accounting is continuously evolving as the nation and the world evolve. This is not to say that every change is for the better, any more than it is in other human endeavours, but rather to emphasize that financial accounting is an organic, evolving discipline: the best prediction we can make about future balance sheets, income statements, and cash flow statements is that they will not be exactly the same in the future as they are now. This book attempts to develop in you an understanding of how financial accounting got to where it is and what the pressures on it are. This understanding will help you to keep in mind that financial accounting is not cast in stone and will equip you to deal with the changes that are sure to come. If you want to keep up with what is going on, accounting associations have active Web sites containing information about changing business practices, accounting developments, and professional activities. Here are some to try (some were already mentioned in the discussion above):

Both preparers and users of financial accounting should keep up with ongoing change.

- Canadian Institute of Chartered Accountants (**www.cica.ca**)
- CGA-Canada (**www.cga-canada.org**)
- Society of Management Accountants of Canada (**www.cma-canada.org**)
- American Institute of Certified Public Accountants (**www.aicpa.org**)
- Financial Accounting Standards Board (U.S.) (**www.fasb.org**)
- Institute of Chartered Accountants in England and Wales (**www.icaew.co.uk**)
- International Accounting Standards Board (**www.iasb.org.uk**)

Financial accounting concepts are based on good practice as well as theory.

Financial accounting has a surprisingly large set of concepts and principles to guide accountants in preparing financial statements, auditors in verifying them, and users in interpreting them. A very large amount has been written about the conceptual and theoretical side of accounting, and as we have seen, several groups are involved in setting financial accounting standards and otherwise regulating accounting information. All this material occupies many metres of library and office shelves and much space in computer databases and Web sites. These concepts have been deduced by accountants, researchers, and standard-setters from logic and observation of good practices, and they are used to guide everyone who prepares, audits, uses, or studies financial accounting. The *CICA Handbook*, for example, accompanies its standards with much conceptual material, including a whole section devoted to financial accounting concepts.

GAAP, including authoritative standards, always leave room for professional judgment.

GAAP are the rules, standards, and usual practices that companies are expected to follow in preparing their financial statements. They are a combination of the *authoritative standards* issued by accounting standard-setters (such as CICA in Canada, FASB in the United States, IASB internationally) and the accepted ways of doing accounting that are not included in such standards. Year by year, the set of authoritative standards grows, as does the larger set of generally accepted accounting principles that includes those standards and other accepted practices. However, the world continues to increase in complexity, so neither the standards nor GAAP are ever extensive enough to include everything. Economic complexity seems likely to keep increasing, so it is likely that there will always be a gap between the demand for good financial accounting and the authoritative and generally accepted responses to the demand. Perhaps that is just as well: accounting rules that tried to cover everything would be enormously complex themselves and might even get in the way of useful economic change. In any case, people may not follow the rules. In 2002, the head of the TSX said that "No guidelines, rules, laws or regulations can counter a lack of ethics and fraudulent minds."[5]

The existence of a gap between what is authoritative or merely acceptable practice and the demand for good accounting means that accounting professionals will continue to play an important role for society by exercising their judgment and expertise to solve financial accounting problems. And if they make mistakes, those will continue to make a lot of other people unhappy and prompt headlines like: "Hide and Seek: Accounting tricks make it difficult for investors to get a true picture of a company's finances,"[6] "Financial disclosure is good—but it doesn't always help,"[7] "The CFOs [chief financial officers] Weigh in on Reform,"[8] and "FASB: Rewriting the Book on Bookkeeping: Will broader, simpler rules prevent more Enrons?"[9]

Figure 5.3 depicts the great growth in authoritative standards and other parts of GAAP as the world's business and accounting complexities continue to grow.

FIGURE 5.3

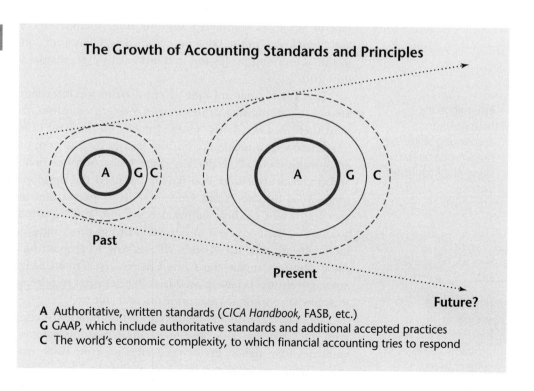

The Growth of Accounting Standards and Principles

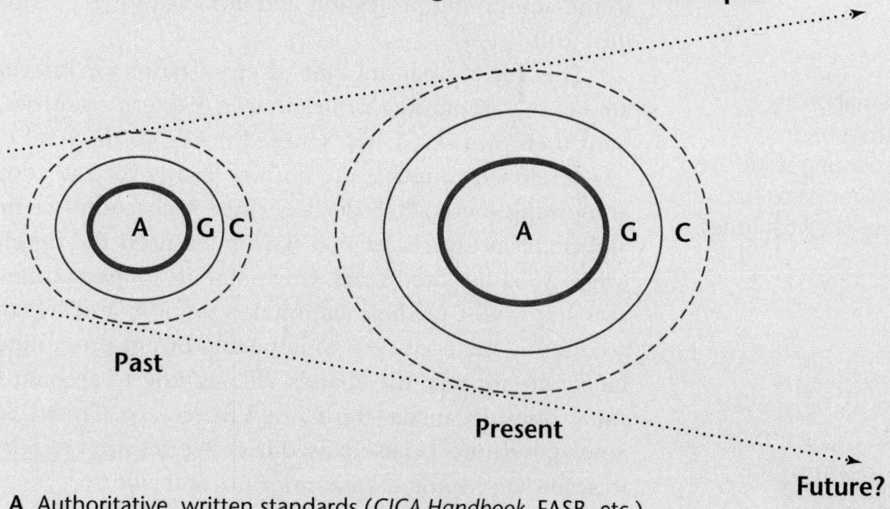

A Authoritative, written standards (*CICA Handbook*, FASB, etc.)
G GAAP, which include authoritative standards and additional accepted practices
C The world's economic complexity, to which financial accounting tries to respond

HOW'S YOUR UNDERSTANDING?

Here are two questions you should be able to answer based on what you have just read. If you can't answer them, it would be best to reread the material.

1. Why do we have accounting standards and who issues them?
2. Are these authoritative accounting standards all there is to GAAP?

5.5 International and Nonbusiness Accounting Standards

This section is a reminder that there is much more to financial accounting than implied by this book's focus on Canadian business corporations. International accounting standards were mentioned in the previous section: let's begin with them.

International Accounting Standards

International harmonization of accounting standards is a goal supported by many people.

As in business and economics generally, international issues are coming increasingly to the fore in financial accounting. So far, the standards of national bodies are still most important in each country (the CICA in Canada, the FASB in the U.S., etc.), but as was noted earlier, there has been an International Accounting Standards Board since 1973 and it issues standards too. The IASB and its predecessor body (called the International Accounting Standards Committee) have issued more than 40 individual standards. These standards cover about the same areas as the Canadian and U.S. standards: the goal is to develop common standards that could be used by companies operating in several countries, and eventually that all countries could use within their own borders. The term for this is *convergence*, meaning that accounting standards would be alike from country to country so that international trade, stock markets, transfers of funds, and other international business could be assisted, or at least not impeded. As it is, each country's accounting standards are often quite different from those of other countries. Horror stories of companies showing huge incomes according to one country's rules and huge losses, in the same year, according to another country's rules are embarrassing to the accounting profession and awkward for regulators such as the SEC and OSC to deal with.

Internationally harmonized accounting standards may not be to the liking of all countries.

There is a great amount of enthusiasm for international standards convergence among the accounting professions in Western countries, though such countries do not want their own standards "watered down" to the level of less-developed countries. The less-developed countries are not necessarily keen to adopt the complex Western accrual accounting methods, especially since such countries may lack the legal, professional, and financial structures that have influenced the development of Western accounting over several hundred years. Governments in many countries see financial accounting as very important to their national economic and business goals, and do not support accounting methods seen as impeding or not promoting such goals. And many governments do not take the "hands off" attitude to accounting standards that has been the usual case in Canada, the United States, the United Kingdom, and similar countries. Some governments have passed laws that set strict requirements for financial accounting in accordance with national priorities and culture.

International standards harmonization will probably increase, in spite of many difficulties.

An illustration of the challenge to international standards is the attempt to make even the Canadian, U.S., and Mexican accounting systems similar, given that the three countries have signed the North American Free Trade Agreement (NAFTA). A recent study, *Significant Differences in GAAP in Canada, Chile, Mexico and the United States*, tackles the three countries' (and Chile's) financial accounting and finds a great many differences.[10] (Chile's accounting has been added since the signing of the American Free Trade Agreement.) Canadian companies wishing to do business in the United States already must pay close attention to U.S. standards, but even between Canada and the United States, there are accounting differences. Some of these differences are being addressed by various national standard-setters, but it will take a while to iron out all of them. It may be optimistic to think they can ever all be removed, given that the three (or four) countries are different in important legal and business ways that affect accounting.

More than 100 countries used to set their own accounting standards, but in recent years a large number have decided to adopt IASB standards as their national standards. The only major countries not having done so yet are Japan, Canada, and the United States. In Canada, CICA has recently decided to adopt IASB standards as of about 2012, and in the United States, FASB is working actively on convergence of its standards with those of the IASB. In 2002, *The Economist* referred to adoption of international standards in North America as "the impossible dream."[11] In spite of the difficulties, there seems to be momentum toward strong and common international standards, accepted in all major countries, so it seems a good bet to say they will exist some day.

An Example: Disclosures of Changes in Equity

FASB standards in the United States require more attention to changes in shareholders' equity than is typical under CICA standards in Canada. As a result, U.S. companies do not have just a Statement of Retained Earnings, but rather roll that statement, along with explanations of changes in all the other equity accounts, together into a Statement of Stockholders' (or Shareholders') Equity. Exhibit 5.1 is an example, for the large U.S. company Tyson Foods, Inc. (**www.tysonfoodsinc.com**).

Is the U.S. standard for more disclosure about equity changes preferable to the Canadian practice?

There is more information than we've seen in Canadian examples. Each equity account is shown, just as the retained earnings changes were in the examples in Chapter 3. If accounting standards were harmonized even just between these two countries, would you want the more-informative U.S. version, or prefer to stay with just the retained earnings changes reported in Canada? The principle of disclosure would suggest that the more information the better, and so support the U.S. version. On the other hand, some people feel that adding information to already-complex financial statements would not help all the users who already struggle with trying to understand them. (Because of the United States' importance in Canada, quite a few Canadian companies use something like the U.S. disclosure, which more than satisfies Canadian standards.) There is an additional U.S. calculation called "comprehensive income." It is an altered measure of income, and the difference between it and net income is accumulated over the years in an equity account called "Accumulated Other Comprehensive Income (Loss)." As part of the international convergence mentioned above, Canadian standards will soon require a comprehensive income calculation too (see item *k* on page 157).

EXHIBIT 5·1

Consolidated Statements of Shareholders' Equity
Tyson Foods, Inc. 2005 Annual Report

Three years ended October 1, 2005 in millions	Common Stock Class A		Common Stock Class B		Capital in Excess of Par Value	Retained Earnings	Treasury Stock		Unamortized Deferred Compensation	Accumulated Other Comprehensive Income (Loss)	Total Shareholders' Equity
	Shares	Amount	Shares	Amount			Shares	Amount			
Balance – September 28, 2002	267	$27	102	$10	$1,879	$2,097	16	$(265)	$(37)	$(49)	$3,662
Comprehensive Income:											
Net Income						337					337
Other comprehensive income (loss) net of tax of $8 million											
Derivative gain recognized in cost of sales (net of $(1) million tax)										(2)	(2)
Derivative unrealized gain (net of $7 million tax)										11	11
Unrealized gain on investments (net of $1 million tax)										1	1
Currency translation adjustment										21	21
Additional pension liability (net of $2 million tax)										3	3
Total Comprehensive Income											371
Purchase of Treasury Shares							4	(41)			(41)
Restricted Shares Issued					(19)		(4)	55	(37)		(1)
Restricted Shares Canceled					1			(1)	1		1
Dividends Paid						(54)					(54)
Amortization of Deferred Compensation									16		16
Balance – September 27, 2003	267	27	102	10	1,861	2,380	16	(252)	(57)	(15)	3,954
Comprehensive Income:											
Net income						403					403
Other comprehensive income (loss) net of tax of $(13) million											
Derivative gain recognized in cost of sales (net of $(26) million tax)										(40)	(40)
Derivative unrealized gain (net of $12 million tax)										19	19
Currency translation adjustment										23	23
Additional pension liability (net of $1 million tax)										1	1
Total Comprehensive Income											406
Purchase of Treasury Shares							4	(72)			(72)
Stock Options Exercised					(2)		(3)	44			42
Restricted Shares Issued					1			6	(7)		–
Restricted Shares Canceled					1			(4)	2		(1)
Dividends Paid						(55)					(55)
Amortization of Deferred Compensation									16		16
Reclassification and Other	1				(12)			14			2
Balance – October 2, 2004	268	27	102	10	1,849	2,728	17	(264)	(46)	(12)	4,292
Comprehensive Income:											
Net income						353					353
Other comprehensive income (loss) net of tax of $11 million)											
Derivative loss recognized in cost of sales (net of $13 million tax)										21	21
Derivative unrealized loss (net of $0 tax)										(1)	(1)
Unrealized loss on investments (net of $(1) million)										(2)	(2)
Currency translation adjustment										23	23
Additional pension liability (net of $(1) million tax)										(1)	(1)
Total Comprehensive Income											393
Purchase of Treasury Shares							3	(45)			(45)
Stock Options Exercised					14		(3)	37			51
Restricted Shares Issued							(2)	38	(35)		3
Restricted Shares Canceled					1			(4)	1		(2)
Dividends Paid						(55)					(55)
Dividends Accrued						(13)					(13)
Amortization of Deferred Compensation									25		25
Other					3						3
Balance – October 1, 2005	268	$27	102	$10	$1,867	$3,013	15	$(238)	$(55)	$28	$4,652

See accompanying notes.

There can even be lack of harmonization within one country! In Canada, as in other countries, there has been a controversy over whether the financial accounting appropriate for large traded corporations like Emerson and CPR is also appropriate for small businesses. Such accounting is expensive and may be overly complex for reporting on simpler enterprises. In 1999, a CICA study group came down on both sides of the issue, recommending that small business enterprises ("SBEs") follow GAAP to ensure that their financial statements are credible to bankers and taxation authorities, but that where the financial reporting needs of SBEs are clearly different than those of larger public corporations, different accounting standards be developed for them.[12] Such standards have now been issued in *CICA Handbook Section 1300*, effective for fiscal years beginning after January 1, 2002. The new "Little GAAP" is permitted only for carefully defined SBEs, and such small businesses can instead keep using the regular "Big GAAP" if they wish.[13] No one is sure how having two sets of standards within one country will work out. The controversy will doubtless continue.

Governments

This book emphasizes business organizations because they provide quite enough complexity for an introductory study of financial statements! But there are many other kinds of organizations that produce financial statements, and because these organizations are often structured as they are for particular reasons, their accounting must adapt to their legal, organizational, and financial peculiarities. Two common nonbusiness organizations are *governments* and *not-for-profit organizations.*

Governments represent people but do not have owners, nor are they created to earn income or retain earnings. Exhibit 5.2 shows the Government of Canada's 2005 versions of an income and retained earnings statement ("Condensed Statement of Revenues, Expenditures and Accumulated Deficit"), balance sheet ("Condensed Statement of Assets and Liabilities") and cash flow statement ("Condensed Statement of Changes in Financial Position"). The "Significant Accounting Policies" note is also in the exhibit, but other notes have not been included. For more about the Government of Canada's financial results, see (**www.fin.gc.ca**) and look for the topic "Economic and fiscal information" as part of the Department of Finance's Web page.

Condensed Financial Statements of the Government of Canada

The fundamental purpose of these condensed financial statements is to provide an overview of the financial affairs and resources for which the Government is responsible under authority granted by Parliament. Responsibility for the integrity and objectivity of these statements rests with the Government.

These financial statements are extracted and condensed from the audited financial statements included in the *Public Accounts of Canada*, which are tabled in Parliament each year. As these condensed financial statements are, by their nature, summarized, they do not include all disclosure required for financial reporting by governments in Canada. Readers interested in the disclosure of more detailed data should refer to the audited financial statements in the *Public Accounts*.

Government of Canada
Condensed Statement of Operations and
Accumulated Deficit for the Year Ended March 31, 2005

	2005		2004
	Budget[1]	**Actual**	**Actual**
	($ millions)		
Revenues			
Income tax	125,200	132,037	123,530
Other taxes and duties	41,700	42,857	41,365
Employment insurance premiums	17,000	17,307	17,546
Other revenues	16,900	19,457	16,106
Total revenues	***200,800***	***211,658***	***198,547***
Expenses			
Transfer payments			
Old age security and related payments	27,900	27,871	26,902
Other levels of government	30,600	41,955	29,392
Employment insurance benefits	15,700	14,748	15,058
Other transfer payments	32,800	33,689	31,026
Total transfer payments	*107,000*	*118,263*	*102,378*
Other program expenses	54,400	57,647	51,317
Total program expenses	***161,400***	***175,910***	***153,695***
Public debt charges	35,400	34,118	35,769
Total expenses	***196,800***	***210,028***	***189,464***
Annual surplus	**4,000**[2]	**1,630**	**9,083**
Accumulated deficit, beginning of year	501,500[3]	501,493	510,576
Accumulated deficit, end of year	**497,500**	**499,863**	**501,493**

1 Derived from Budget 2004 and adjusted to a gross basis.

2 Budget 2004 disclosed the budgetary surplus as $4 billion before deducting reserves for contingency ($3 billion) and economic prudence ($1 billion).

3 Adjusted to the actual closing amount of previous year.

Condensed Statement of Financial Position as at March 31, 2005

	2005	2004
	($ millions)	
Liabilities		
Accounts payable and accrued liabilities	90,473	79,964
Interest-bearing debt		
Unmatured debt	435,460	440,231
Pension and other liabilities	179,808	180,898
Total interest-bearing debt	*615,268*	*621,129*
Total liabilities	***705,741***	***701,093***
Financial assets		
Cash and accounts receivable	76,281	70,921
Foreign exchange accounts	40,871	44,313
Loans, investments and advances	33,860	29,548
Total financial assets	***151,012***	***144,782***
Net debt	***554,729***	***556,311***
Non-financial assets		
Tangible capital assets	48,207	47,745
Other	6,659	7,073
Total non-financial assets	***54,866***	***54,818***
Accumulated deficit	**499,863**	**501,493**

Government of Canada
Condensed Statement of Cash Flow
for the year ended March 31, 2005

	2005	2004
	($ millions)	
Cash provided by operating activities		
Annual surplus	1,630	9,083
Items not affecting cash	4,508	4,031
	6,138	**13,114**
Cash used for capital investment activities	**(4,475)**	**(4,444)**
Cash provided by (used for) investing activities	**3,157**	**(2,425)**
Total cash generated	***4,820***	***6,245***
Cash used to repay unmatured debt	**(4,771)**	**(2,185)**
Net increase in cash	**49**	**4,060**
Cash at beginning of year	20,546	16,486
Cash at end of year	**20,595**	**20,546**

Notes to the Condensed Financial Statements

Significant Accounting Policies

The Government of Canada reporting entity includes all departments, agencies, corporations and funds which are owned or controlled by the Government and which are accountable to Parliament. The financial activities of all these entities are consolidated in these statements, except for enterprise Crown corporations and other government business enterprises, which are not dependent on the Government for financing their activities. These corporations are reported under the modified equity basis of accounting. The Canada Pension Plan is excluded from the reporting entity as it is under the joint control of the Government and participating provinces.

The Government accounts for transactions on an accrual basis. Financial assets recorded on the Condensed Statement of Financial Position can provide resources to discharge liabilities or finance future operations and are recorded at the lower of cost or net realizable value. Non-financial assets cannot normally be converted into cash to finance future operations without disrupting government operations; they are recorded at cost less accumulated amortization. Liabilities are recorded at the estimated amount ultimately payable, with pension and other similar benefits being determined on an actuarial basis. Valuation allowances are established for loan guarantees, concessionary and sovereign loans, and other obligations.

Some amounts in these statements are based on estimates and assumptions made by the Government. By their nature, such estimates are subject to measurement uncertainty, although all of them are believed to be reasonable.

Perusing the three financial statements will show you several similarities to and differences from the sort of business accounting you have seen in this book so far:

- The statements do have many familiar components: revenues, liabilities, assets, cash from operations, and notes. The Significant Accounting Policies note tells us that a lot of the government's agencies are consolidated into the figures, but not all. In particular, the Canada Pension Plan is not included.
- The government's revenues are nearly all from taxation. No surprise there!
- The government's financial role is to manage the country, not to make a "profit" by incurring expenses to earn revenue. It is the other way around; the government is supposed to spend its revenue on worthwhile activities in accordance with the official budget. Consequently, there is no "net income" number on the statement of operation but rather something called a "surplus": the difference between this year's revenues and expenditures.
- You can see what the money is spent on: transfers to provincial governments, old age security and employment insurance benefits, and "program expenditures" for things like the military. Somewhere in there are the CBC, student loan programs, and so on.
- The government has a huge deficit! At the end of March 2005, it stood at $500 *billion* (about $15,000 for every citizen of Canada). The balance sheet shows that the deficit is about three times the government's assets, high for an individual or small business. But the government can borrow against future revenues and as long as it can keep the money coming in to pay its debts, it can hang on. In 2005 there was a surplus of $1.6 billion, so the accumulated deficit went down by that amount—a good sign financially. However, that accumulated deficit will take over 300 years to recover at the rate of $1.6 billion per year—a very long-term mortgage indeed. This represents past overexpenditures and has to be recovered, if at all, from future taxpayers.
- The cash flow statement shows that the government did indeed keep ahead of its debts in 2005, repaying its Canadian dollar borrowings by a net amount of almost $5 billion—another good sign financially.
- The government has no shareholders, no owners, so the balance sheet has no equity section, just giving the accumulated deficit where we might expect the equity to be. Or is it where we would expect it to be? It is shown with the assets section—because it is a debit, like the assets. This placement doesn't mean the deficit is a good thing!
- The balance sheet starts with the government's liabilities. If you buy a Canada Savings Bond or other government bonds or treasury bills, you are lending to the government and so as an investor in such items, you are a creditor of the government as well as a taxpayer.
- Almost a quarter of the liabilities are for "pensions and other liabilities." This amount is largely for pensions promised to government employees. Given the deficit, these pensions can only be paid by taxing Canadians in the future.

Financial accounting for governments reflects governments' differing circumstances.

Government accounting in Canada has changed over the last decade. Beginning in April 1999, the federal government phased in accrual accounting. The process was completed in April 2001. Since then the government's transactions have been recorded on an accrual basis. The format of the government's financial statements still differs from those we have seen to date for businesses such as CPR and Enbridge to accommodate the different objectives of government. However, because governments are the makers of the laws, a private organization's set of standards (such as the *CICA Handbook*) can have only a persuasive effect, not an authoritative one. It is likely that over the next decade or so, many government financial balance sheets will come to resemble business ones; however, the business concept of "net income" is probably too different from the objectives of government to make it likely we'll see a governmental income statement along business lines.

Not-for-Profit Organizations

Financial accounting for not-for-profit organizations is becoming more business-like.

An enormous range of organizations, including private clubs, charities such as the Red Cross, sports teams, universities, political parties, research units, the Girl Guides, churches, and unions, are classified as not-for-profit (or nonprofit) organizations. The members of such organizations do not own them as do owners of businesses and do not have a right to a share of any equity (assets minus liabilities). Members of such organizations are not usually as oriented to making income as are business owners, because most such organizations are created to perform a specific service or other function. Some of the accounting methods used by these organizations are similar to those of governments, but many such organizations, especially those close to being businesses, use fairly complete accrual accounting, including amortization.

Not-for-profit organizations often have special funds, such as capital funds raised from donation appeals, government grants, and bequests made in people's wills. Keeping various designated funds separate and accounting for operations separately from other activities (like fund-raising) requires accounting methods that can be more complex than those used by private businesses. Amortization and other accrual accounting procedures can also be more complex. The trend, encouraged by the *CICA Handbook*, is to bring the accounting for such organizations as much as possible under the same GAAP structure as that for businesses, without removing such important features as keeping designated funds separate and without obscuring the fair reporting of nonprofit activities by reporting them as if they were intended to generate profit.

To illustrate these points, Exhibit 5.3 shows the balance sheet ("Statement of Financial Position") of the Canadian Academic Accounting Association, the association of Canadian accounting professors and instructors. You'll see that its balance sheet segregates three different "funds" but does not separate current and noncurrent assets or liabilities. It has no equity, but instead just "Fund Balances." Its General fund includes the CAAA's initial capital obtained from members and donors, and a sort of retained earnings, "Accumulated excess of revenues over expenditures." The CAAA is in much better financial shape than the Government of Canada, having assets more than three times its liabilities, instead of only a seventh of them.

The Canadian Academic Accounting Association
Statement of Financial Position

Year Ended December 31

	General Fund	Research Funds	Education Fund	**2004 Total**	2003 Total
Assets					
Cash	$ 11,622	$ –	$ –	**$ 11,622**	$ 10,963
Receivables	66,439	–	–	**66,439**	2,838
GST	11,406	–	–	**11,406**	8,574
Investments (Note 3)	390,271	92,640	15,070	**497,981**	479,382
Prepaids	8,209	–	–	**8,209**	7,267
	$487,947	$92,640	$15,070	**$595,657**	$509,024
Liabilities					
Payables and accruals	$ 66,138	$ –	$ –	**$ 66,138**	$ 40,483
Grant commitments outstanding	–	62,000	–	**62,000**	27,000
Fees and subscriptions received in advance	16,576	–	–	**16,576**	46,633
	82,714	62,000	–	**144,714**	114,116
Fund Balances					
General					
Capital	82,787	–	–	**82,787**	82,787
Accumulated excess of revenues over expenditures	322,446	–	–	**322,446**	266,075
Research (Schedule 5)	–	30,640	–	**30,640**	43,151
Education (Schedule 5)	–	–	15,070	**15,070**	2,895
	405,233	30,640	15,070	**450,943**	394,908
	$487,947	$92,640	$15,070	**$595,657**	$509,024

(Notes to the financial statements are not included.)

HOW'S YOUR UNDERSTANDING?

Here are two questions you should be able to answer based on what you have just read. If you can't answer them, it would be best to reread the material.

1. What might make international harmonization of accounting standards difficult?
2. What might lead the financial statements of governments and not-for-profit organizations to differ from those of businesses?

5.6 The Annual Report and the Set of Financial Statements

Financial reporting is important for many organizations. All incorporated companies, and most other legally constituted organizations, are required to prepare a set of financial statements at least annually, explaining their financial performance and position. Public companies, which are those whose shares are traded on a stock exchange or in more informal "over-the-counter" markets, usually also issue some *interim* or *quarterly* financial information, especially on the subject of earnings. Proprietorships, partnerships, and closely owned "private" corporations prepare annual financial statements, at their bankers' request or for inclusion with personal or corporate income tax returns, even if there are no other reasons for doing so. Such enterprises usually do not go to the lengths of disclosure and explanation that public companies do, or prepare *annual reports*, as the set of financial statements and notes are sufficient.

The standard set of financial statements has four statements plus notes.

In Canada, the standard set of financial statements has five components:

1. Balance sheet (statement of financial position) *(Chapter 2)*.
2. Income statement (*Chapter 3*).
3. Statement of retained earnings *(Chapter 3; also the U.S. Statement of stockholders' equity in this chapter's Section 5.5)*.
4. Cash flow statement *(Chapter 4)*.
5. Notes to the financial statements *(more on these in Section 5.7)*.

The external auditor's report covers all five components of the set of statements.

A sixth item accompanies the financial statements and notes: the *auditor's report* on the fairness of the set. The contents of the statements and its notes are the responsibility of management, and the auditor's report consists of the auditor's opinion about those statements and notes. You should be skeptical of financial statements that have not been audited or those whose audit report is not attached. Letters or reports providing less than the audit assurance are often attached to financial statements; you should read any such assurances carefully because they usually are very careful about what level of assurance they do—and don't—provide. *(More about the auditor's report is in Section 5.8.)*

Here's a quick review of how the statements relate. The income statement displays what happened to the company during a period of time (commonly one year in the annual report) and produces a bottom line net income figure. The retained earnings statement uses the net income figure and shows whether it was distributed to owners (dividend) or put back into retained earnings. The ending retained earnings number goes onto the balance sheet, which displays the company's financial position in terms of its financial sources and resources at the end of the year. Thus, all three statements articulate. Finally, the cash flow statement is the link from accrual accounting to the actual cash flows of the company. Notes are behind these four statements and provide further information to aid in *disclosure*. Finally, the auditor's report is the encircling watchdog of the statements by providing an evaluation that judges whether they fairly represent the company.

FIGURE 5.4

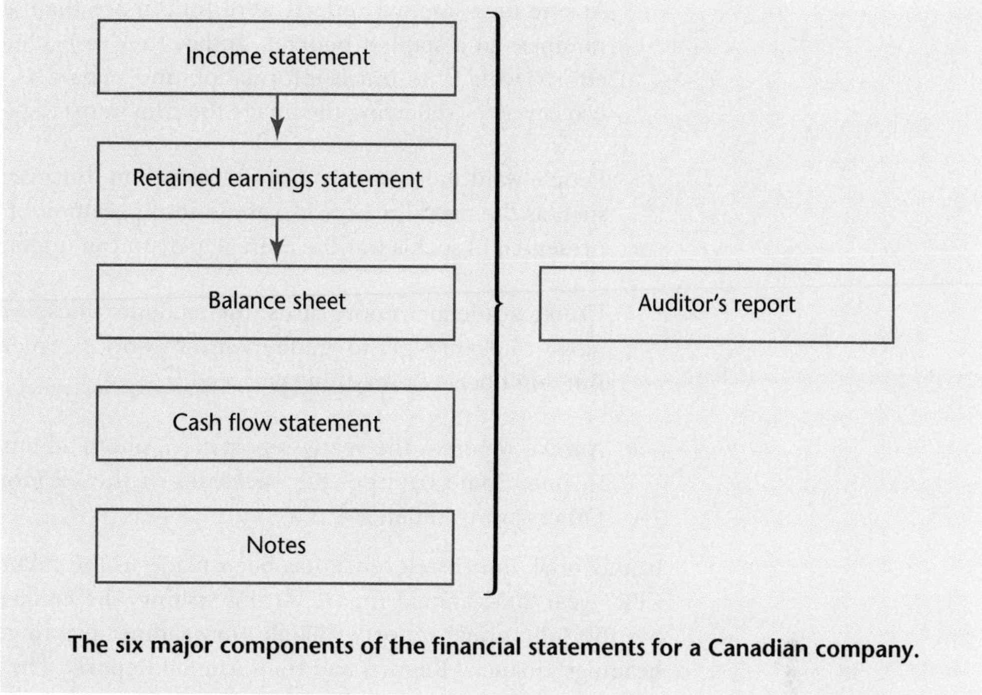

The six major components of the financial statements for a Canadian company.

Public companies and many other organizations include their set of financial statements in a much larger *annual report*. This report usually contains (in approximately the following order):

1. summary data on the company's performance for the year, usually in a graphical or other easy-to-read form, and comparisons going back five or ten years;
2. a *letter to the shareholders* from the company's chief executive officer, who is usually its president or chairperson of the board of directors;
3. information about the company's history, strategies, plans, products, locations, employees, and other matters to help the reader understand the company and put the rest of the annual report in context;
4. an often extensive "*management discussion and analysis*," including a description of the economic, financial, and other factors behind the company's business, usually broken down by its main products or departments;
5. a short section explaining that the financial statements and the general internal control of the business are the responsibility of management;
6. the set of financial statements, with extensive notes, and the auditor's report;
7. various details about the company's legal status, names of its directors and officers, and other information the company thinks is important.

The annual report contains much in addition to the four financial statements and notes.

The following comment is from an article about the annual report:

> Although recent years have ushered in many changes in corporate financial reporting ... the annual report remains the centrepiece of the whole reporting process.... The world of financial reporting is changing. Recognition of users' needs has expanded such reporting far beyond the financial statements.[14]

Many people besides the company's accountants and the external auditors are involved in preparing the annual report. The top managers set its tone, and advertising and public relations staff design its presentation, often using photos and attractive graphs. Overall, the annual report can be quite a fancy document, and 75 or more pages long! Here are some comments about annual reports:

> At one time, annual reports were little more than a collection of financial numbers in a stapled booklet. Today, they've become full-blown magazine efforts, with ... as much information and pizzazz as they can pack between two covers ... reflecting the image the firm wants to project.[15]

> People want more, more, more information. But some things don't change, such as the need for honest, candid interpretation of company performance presented in such a way the average person can understand it.[16]

> Unlike academic report cards, the students whose work is assessed in these glossy catalogues get to grade their own work.... So enjoy the pretty pictures. But don't believe everything you read.[17]

> Annual reports—the yearly report card, photo album, and corporate promo in one. Some trumpet the successes of the 12 months past, real or not. Others just trumpet.[18]

In this book, much reference has been made to the financial statements contained in CPR's year 2004 annual report. At this writing, the company's Web page (**www.cpr.ca**) has the full annual report available for reading, printing, or downloading under the headings Financial Reports and then Annual Reports. The annual reports for the previous five years were also on the Web page, facilitating comparisons across years, starting from when CPR was still part of the former conglomerate Canadian Pacific Inc.

Annual reports, news, and other current information are on companies' Web pages.

Most companies, and many other organizations, have active Web sites. Your Web search engine can usually find the home page you want if you just type in the company or organization name. *Please give accessing a company you're interested in a try*, and when companies are mentioned in this book, try their Web pages for current information. Look for the financial reports, investor relations, or shareholders' information sections in companies' pages. With the advent of the Web, some companies have questioned the necessity of printing an expensive glossy annual report and have put more information on their Web pages. Such pages also often have quarterly reports and other "interim" news. Data services available through libraries and commercial services like business newspapers have thousands of annual reports available for electronic access and downloading.

HOW'S YOUR UNDERSTANDING?

Here are two questions you should be able to answer based on what you have just read. If you can't answer them, it would be best to reread the material.

1. What kinds of information would you expect to see in the annual report of a large public company like IBM, Bank of Nova Scotia, McDonald's, or Microsoft?
2. What parts of the annual report are normally included in the assurance provided by the external auditor's report?

5.7 Notes and Other Supplementary Information

The financial statement notes are an integral part of the set of statements.

Because the four standard financial statements are not enough to transmit all the information required by users of the statements, a variety of supplementary narrative and tabular data is appended to the statements. This is true whether or not the company prepares a full annual report with even more data, as described above. Accepted accounting practices provide that, at a minimum, certain added pieces are sufficiently important that they are considered an integral part of the statements and are covered by the auditor's report. Here are outlines of the kinds of information typically covered by the notes and supplementary disclosures.

1. Normally required and covered by the auditor's report:
   a. A description of the company's significant accounting policies, necessary in interpreting the statements' figures (usually the first note following the statements).
   b. Backup details on any statement figures needing further explanation, typically the amortization figures, long-term debts, share capital, pension liability, and any accounts unusually calculated or very significant for the particular company.
   c. Information on some things not included in the figures, such as "contingent" (potentially possible) liabilities, purchase commitments, lawsuits, relationships with associated companies or persons, and significant "subsequent" events since the official balance sheet date (for example, a major fire).
   d. Analysis of revenues and contributions to income of any significant product-line or geographical "segments" of the company's business (for example, contribution of a lumber product line versus a food line, or operations in Canada versus the United States).
2. Also fairly standard, especially for larger companies:
   a. Comparative income and balance sheet figures going back at least five years, often ten. If a company changes any important accounting policy, it has to go back and change such trend analyses to keep past figures comparable.
   b. An explanation of the different responsibilities of management and the external auditors for the financial information and of management's responsibility to maintain control over the company's assets.
   c. The *MD&A* ("management discussion and analysis") of the decisions and results for the year, providing an important background for the numbers and notes in the financial statements. Look for the MD&A whenever you are reading an annual report like CPR's.
3. Still largely voluntary:
   a. Graphs and other pictorial supplements.
   b. Details of employment contracts, product specifications, business policies, donations, business objectives, and other such details.
   c. Lists of subsidiary and associated companies, senior managers, office addresses and the home Web page.
   d. Reports on pollution control, excellent employees, customer relations, human resource management, trade with unpopular countries, and other socially sensitive information.

HOW'S YOUR UNDERSTANDING?

Here are two questions you should be able to answer based on what you have just read. If you can't answer them, it would be best to reread the material.

1. What kinds of footnoted information are covered by the auditor's report?
2. What is the MD&A? (A good way to answer this is to go to an annual report on the Web and see what is in the MD&A. Try CPR (**www.cpr.ca**) Financial Reports, or Microsoft (**www.microsoft.com**) About Microsoft, Investor Relations, or any other company you are interested in.)

5.8 The External Auditor's Report

The External Auditor's Professional Opinion

The external auditor provides a professional opinion on the financial statements' fairness.

TYPES OF AUDITOR OPINIONS
- *Clean* or *unqualified* (the best kind)
- *Qualified* (specific problems mentioned)
- *Adverse* (auditor says statements are not fair)
- *Denial* (auditor cannot say if statements are fair)

Several references to the external auditor (who normally is actually a firm of auditors) have been made already. The external auditor is a professional accountant engaged to provide *assurance* about the *fairness* of the financial statements. Assurance refers to adding credibility to the financial statements by doing an expert examination of them and so adding the auditor's reputation to the statements. Fairness has a variety of components, as discussed in Section 5.2. The *auditor's report* is normally a routine statement by the auditor, saying that in the auditor's opinion, the financial statements are fair. Such a routine report is often referred to as a *clean opinion* because it is not cluttered by problems or special circumstances. But if it is not routine, the auditor is trying to tell the users something important. The auditor may report a *qualified opinion*, indicating that the auditor has some concern about the statements; in extreme cases, the report may even say that the financial statements are not fair (*adverse opinion*), or that the auditor cannot say one way or the other (*denial of opinion*). These result from some very serious objection by the auditor to the contents of the statements or to restrictions on the auditor's ability to do a good job.

The standard audit report wording is the best kind, because it doesn't warn of problems.

Always check to see if the financial statements you are using have been audited, and if so, what the auditor's report says. The more boring and standard the opinion is, the better. Any variation from standard wording is a "red flag" for the reader of the statements. So you can see a standard clean opinion, here is the auditors' report that accompanied the CPR financial statements we studied in earlier chapters. There are international differences in auditing as well as in accounting, so here also is the CPR auditors' "comment" to their report for U.S. readers: CPR changed its accounting in 2001 because Canadian accounting standards changed. Canadian generally accepted auditing standards ("GAAS") do not require that the auditors qualify their opinion for such a change as long as it is explained in the financial statement notes (Note 3 in this case), but U.S. GAAS do require such a qualification.

Auditors' Report
To the shareholders of Canadian Pacific Railway Limited

We have audited the consolidated balance sheets of Canadian Pacific Railway Limited as at December 31, 2004 and 2003, and the consolidated statements of income, retained income and cash flows for each of the three years in the period ended December 31, 2004. These consolidated financial statements are the responsibility of the Company's management. Our responsibility is to express an opinion on these financial statements based on our audits.

We conducted our audits in accordance with generally accepted auditing standards in Canada. Those standards require that we plan and perform an audit to obtain reasonable assurance whether the financial statements are free of material misstatement. An audit includes examining, on a test basis, evidence supporting the amounts and disclosures in the financial statements. An audit also includes assessing the accounting principles used and significant estimates made by management, as well as evaluating the overall financial statement presentation.

In our opinion, these financial statements present fairly, in all material respects, the financial position of Canadian Pacific Railway Limited as at December 31, 2004 and 2003, and the results of its operations and its cash flows for each of the three years in the period ended December 31, 2004, in accordance with generally accepted accounting principles in Canada.

Pricewaterhousecoopers LLP
Chartered Accountants
Calgary, Alberta
February 11, 2005

Comments by auditors for U.S. readers on Canada–U.S. reporting difference

In the United States, reporting standards for auditors require the addition of an explanatory paragraph (following the opinion paragraph) when there is a change in accounting principles that has a material effect on the comparability of the Company's financial statements, such as the changes described in Notes 2 and 25 to the consolidated financial statements. Our report to the shareholders dated February 11, 2005, is expressed in accordance with Canadian reporting standards, which do not require a reference to such a change in accounting principles in the Auditors' Report when the change is properly accounted for and disclosed in the financial statements.

Pricewaterhousecoopers LLP
Chartered Accountants
Calgary, Alberta
February 11, 2005

The form and content of the auditor's report change every few years, as auditors rethink how best to communicate with the users of financial statements. Because the auditors are formally reporting to the owners of the company, not to management, the report is usually specifically addressed to the owners (the shareholders). The CPR auditor's report uses the current standard format, which has three paragraphs:

The external auditor's report usually has three standard paragraphs for its findings.

1. The first paragraph identifies the company and the set of statements and their date and states that they are the responsibility of management and that the auditors' responsibility is to express an opinion on them. It doesn't hurt to be sure you know what set of statements the auditor is reporting on!
2. The second paragraph outlines what the auditors did to enable them to express an opinion, stating in particular that they followed GAAS in assessing the accounting principles and estimates used by management. Any problems here, or restrictions on the evidence the auditor was able to examine, will be noted by the auditor and could be significant to the users of the statements.
3. The third paragraph states what the auditors' opinion is concerning the fairness of, and adherence to, generally accepted accounting principles of the statements (or, if there are problems, the lack thereof).

Financial statements are not necessarily audited fully—or even at all.

Often, smaller companies have something less than a full audit done on their financial statements. An example is a "*review*," in which a professional accountant has scrutinized the financial statements and conducted some more limited verification intended to catch major problems. In such a case, instead of an auditor's report, there will be a letter from the accountant or accounting firm stating that somewhat less has been done: read such a letter *carefully* so that you know how much assurance the accountants are offering. Even less review is provided by a "*compilation*," in which the professional accountant has assembled the financial statements from information provided by the enterprise and takes no responsibility at all for the validity of that information. You may well see financial statements that are entirely *unaudited*, accompanied by no professional assurance of any kind. Your reliance on such statements depends entirely on your reliance on the people who prepared the statements.

The External Auditor's Professional Role

What does an external auditor or auditing firm do? External auditing refers to the evaluation of an organization's financial statements by an auditor who is supposed to be unconnected with and so independent of the management of the organization. The role of the external auditor has two fundamental parts:

1. To have an independent, unbiased, and professional perspective; and
2. To render a competent opinion on the fairness of the financial statements according to accepted accounting and auditing standards.

Many companies, governments, and other organizations also have *internal auditors*. Such auditors work within the organization and help management operate the organization. Their work is not dealt with in this book.

External auditors are almost always members of professional associations.

Let's begin with independence and professionalism. Auditors are members of professional associations, such as the Canadian Institute of Chartered Accountants and the corresponding provincial institutes (*CAs*), and, in the United States, the American Institute of Certified Public Accountants and corresponding state societies (*CPAs*). Other professional accounting associations also have auditing components, such as the Certified General Accountants' Association of Canada (CGA-Canada) and provincial associations (*CGAs*) and the Society of Management Accountants of Canada and provincial societies (*CMAs*). Laws usually restrict the right to be an external auditor, especially of public companies and other large enterprises, to members of specified professional associations. But there is no restriction on who can act as an accountant to prepare the financial statements.

A fundamental objective of these professional associations is to protect society by ensuring the *professionalism* and *independence* of the external auditors who belong to them. Protecting society should be consistent with protecting the association's members' professional reputations. To this end, there are complex rules of *professional ethics* that prohibit the external auditor from having a financial interest, directly and in most indirect ways as well, in the client companies or other organizations being audited. (More about professional ethics is in the next section.) These rules and similar ones related to other relationships between the auditor and the client are intended to ensure that the auditor has no personal interest in whether the financial statements report one kind of performance or another. In other words, the auditor should be an unbiased, professionally skeptical reviewer of the financial statements and not someone who wants the result to turn out one way or another. Another term for this desirable state is *objectivity*, the same idea as the objectivity principle of GAAP discussed in Section 5.2. Here's what the rules of professional conduct say CAs in Alberta must do on any professional engagement, including an audit. CAs are told that they must be:

> ... free of any influence, interest or relationship which, in respect of the engagement impairs the member's professional judgment or objectivity or which, in the view of a reasonable observer, would impair the member's [the CA's] professional judgment or objectivity.[19]

Professional ethics require the external auditor to be independent and skeptical.

CGAs, CMAs, and American CPAs have similar independence rules of conduct to follow when doing audits and other professional engagements. Such rules do not yet exist in every country.

Maintaining independence and objectivity is not easy, because the auditors are business entrepreneurs themselves and their clients pay them for doing the audit. The idea is that independence is maintained because the auditor is appointed by and reports to the shareholders, not management. Since the financial statements are reports on management's stewardship performance, the auditor is presumed to be working for the shareholders in verifying management's reports. In practice, however, external auditors must have a close working relationship with client management.

Also, managers are in a strong position to recommend a change in auditor if the relationship is not to their liking. Maintaining independence under these circumstances is difficult and is complicated further by the fact that auditing (public accounting) firms offer tax, consulting, and many other nonauditing services, the revenue for which may exceed the fee for doing the audit. It is also complicated by the fact that if users of financial statements suffer losses, they can and often do sue the auditor, so the auditor must be very careful not to be compromised by the relationship with management.

The auditor's report is a professional opinion—not a guarantee—that the financial statements are fair.

The second part of the auditor's role is to render a competent opinion on the financial statements. In some of the above situations, there may have been more of a problem with competence than objectivity! The auditor's report is an opinion, not a guarantee, nor does it say that the company has performed well or badly. It simply says that the performance and the position have been measured and presented in a generally accepted and unbiased way. Given the complexity of accounting, auditing, and business in general, the auditor's opinion is fundamentally a professional judgment. The auditor must be competent, but, in addition, must weigh all sorts of factors in determining whether the overall result is fair. Concerned about the quality of their judgment, auditing firms in North America have sponsored a great deal of research into the professional judgment of auditors.

The auditor focuses on detecting any material problems.

An external auditor tends to focus on issues that could have a significant effect on the financial statements (the "*materiality*" or significance criterion), because most people consider it uneconomical to have the auditor concern herself or himself with the many small errors and irregularities that may crop up during the year. Auditors plan their

External auditor independence is a continuously controversial issue. Articles abound with titles like "Who Can You Trust? Auditors, Analysts and Earnings Reports Are Supposed to Help You. Too Often They Don't,"[20] "Ethics Be Damned, Let's Merge"[21] (talking about mergers between big accounting/auditing firms and law firms, intended to provide broader services to clients), and "Certified Public Accomplice"[22] (criticizing U.S. CPAs who offer services like selling life insurance on which they may earn higher fees than as auditors). As the big professional firms get bigger and more global, they are often as big as many of their clients, with complicated business arrangements. Capital market regulators and the accounting professions are frequently embroiled in independence problems, especially when particular embarrassing examples occur. In an article titled "Where Are the Accountants? Why Auditors End Up Missing So Many Danger Signs," this comment was made:

> It all seems so straightforward ... the role accountants are supposed to play in keeping the financial system honest. The problem is, it doesn't seem to happen as often as it should. As one apparently prosperous company after another saw earnings crumble in the wake of an accounting scandal over the past year, the auditors—at least in their public statements—often acted as surprised as investors to see years of reported profits go up in smoke. None of the major accounting firms has emerged unscathed.[23]

The above comment was made in 1998, before the most recent scandals involving Enron and numerous other companies revived serious concerns about auditors' performance and about their perhaps too-close relationships with the management they audit, including doing consulting projects for management. A strengthening of auditor independence rules seems likely to come.

work so that they have a reasonable likelihood of detecting material misstatements and errors. This criterion has been claimed by auditors to apply to fraud and misrepresentation by management or employees, and so only those instances of fraud that are large enough to materially affect the overall financial information should be caught by the external auditors. For a large company, one with a net income of $100,000,000 or more, that would have to be a very large case of fraud indeed—in the millions of dollars. In practice, however, many client companies wish their external auditors to assist them in protecting and controlling cash and other assets subject to theft or misappropriation, so the auditors often spend significantly more time verifying cash and other such assets than would be warranted by the size of such assets in the financial statements.

HOW'S YOUR UNDERSTANDING?

Here are two questions you should be able to answer based on what you have just read. If you can't answer them, it would be best to reread the material.

1. The external auditor's report on a company's financial statements refers to "generally accepted auditing standards." Why is the auditor referring to GAAS?
2. The president of a small company recently said, "We need to have an external auditor for our financial statements so we can guarantee their accuracy to our bank." Will that be the result if an auditor is appointed?

5.9 The Nature of a Profession and Professional Ethics

Professionals and professional ethics are important in financial accounting.

Ethics came up in the above discussion of the auditor's report. But ethics involve more people than the auditors. Evolving systems of standards, such as GAAP and GAAS, work reasonably well partly because professionals, who are both expert and ethical, are involved. Ethical behaviour comes from personal standards plus various written codes of ethical conduct, all of which we might group together as *professional ethics*. Those who may be tempted not to be ethical know that severe penalties (including fines, penalties assessed by professional associations, and even imprisonment) can result from unethical behaviour.

Professional accountants are bound by standards of competence and ethics.

For many people today, there is strong concern about being professional. There are, however, certain occupations that have established status as the professions. In today's world, some groups that have this status are physicians, lawyers, engineers, architects, and professional accountants. Part of the reason these groups stand out is that entry into each of them requires a post-secondary education, including training and examination by practitioners, and members are bound by a code of conduct or professional ethics. Members of each professional group usually enjoy a monopoly in their particular area of expertise. Associations of architects, physicians, engineers, lawyers, and other members of legally recognized professions can all prevent people from calling themselves members of their particular professions and practising in that capacity. Such groups have to convince the public (as represented by governments, for example) that they have expertise and appropriate codes of ethical conduct, but also that entrance to their area of expertise should be regulated for the public good. In Canada, CAs, CGAs, and CMAs, and in the U.S., CPAs, all have entrance examinations, codes of ethical conduct, and other professional trappings. The same is true for professional accountants in many countries.

Professional accountants have a legally protected status and responsibilities to go with it.

Uncertified accountants do not enjoy the same powers or privileges that members of the above professions do. You, your friend, or anyone can all call yourselves "accountants." There are no restrictions preventing you or anyone else from advertising in the paper, yellow pages, or any other publication to attract clients. However, if you want to call yourself a CA, CGA, or CMA, you must meet various requirements, for these titles are professional designations protected by law, as are other professional designations. For professional accountants, there are both powers and restrictions (for example, advertising must meet certain standards of content and decorum). The rights that a particular profession enjoys come in return for promises made about the quality and ethics of its members' work. If a professional accountant has not lived up to the standards of conduct held by the profession, he or she can be reprimanded or expelled by the profession and/or sued in court. Anyone can be sued, of course, but professionals are usually held to a higher standard of performance than are nonprofessionals.

All told, being in a profession has many advantages (including service to society, monopoly over an area of work, collegial support, social prestige, and good pay), but one must remember that in return there is the social responsibility of discharging one's duties competently and in accordance with the profession's code of ethics. Professional codes of ethics involve not only behaving in a professional manner (for example, with integrity and objectivity), but also maintaining the level of expertise required in order to perform skilfully. This involves following procedures (often as set out in documents like the *CICA Handbook*) and exercising informed judgment that will, or should, ensure that high standards of work and performance are met.

Professional accountants may encounter many ethical dilemmas.

Here are examples of ethical problems that may be faced by professional accountants. What would you, as a member of society or as someone who may rely on accounting information or auditors' reports, think would be appropriate ethical behaviour in each case?

- Mary works for a public accounting firm and is part of the team doing the external audit of Westward Industries Inc. Staff at Westward are all very friendly, and Mary is offered the chance to buy one of the company's high-quality sound systems for only half the usual price. Should she accept the deal?
- Karim is also on the Westward external audit team. He is a member of a bowling league. During a game, he hears a member of another team boast of cheating Westward systematically by overbilling on printing invoices. Should he tell Westward?
- Joan and Henry fall in love and decide to marry. Both are professional accountants: Joan is the chief accountant of Westward, responsible for preparing all the company's financial statements, and Henry is a partner of the public accounting firm and is in charge of the external audit of the company. Should Henry turn the audit over to another partner, or perhaps even ask the accounting firm to resign as auditor (because as a partner, he shares in the firm's income from all audits)?
- Michel is another member of the Westward external audit team. During some audit tests, he discovers that Westward engaged in some business activities that appear to be illegal. Breaking that particular law can bring large fines and even jail terms. Should Michel go to the police?
- Erin works for the same public accounting firm. During the audit of Basic Electronics Ltd., she discovers that an employee of Basic is overcharging Westward by applying too high a markup to services contracted with Westward. Documents indicate that Basic's management is aware of this and is happy to be getting away with it, because it has a material effect on Basic's income. Should she tell the management of Basic that she knows what they are doing? Should she tell Henry, the partner responsible for the Westward audit? Should she tell Westward?
- Giorgio is a partner of the same public accounting firm. For years, his father has owned a few shares of Westward, among a whole portfolio of shares of many companies. His father has just died and willed all the shares to Giorgio. Should he sell the Westward shares?

Ethical rules help in these dilemmas, but professional judgment is also required.

Well, we could go on for some time. One of the more interesting and challenging aspects of being a professional is dealing with such ethical issues. Some of the examples above do not have clear answers, but here are some ideas:[24]

- The external auditors are supposed to be independent scrutineers of their clients' financial affairs. Mary should probably not accept the deal, unless it is available to anyone who turns up at a retail store, because accepting it would undermine her independence. Being friendly with clients is fine, but auditors also have to maintain some distance from clients to protect their independence and integrity.
- Karim should tell Westward what he heard and suggest they look into their printing costs. When doing their work, auditors acquire much confidential information about their clients and must be very careful about how they use it. In this case, the information was not acquired under circumstances of confidentiality. He may find himself in court over the issue, however, so he may need to seek legal advice before speaking to Westward.
- Henry needs to take some action to remove himself from the job of auditing his wife's work, to protect both her and his integrity. The public accounting firm probably has rules about such relationships, which likely involve transferring the job to another partner and keeping Henry entirely ignorant of the work on the Westward audit. The firm might have to resign the audit (this would likely be expected in the United States, for example); Westward might even ask the firm to do so to protect the credibility of its audited financial statements.
- Michel's situation is very complex. There is a mixture of confidentially acquired information and a duty to society. Much more has to be known before any advice could be offered to Michel. At the very least, Michel and the public accounting firm

would have to get legal advice immediately. The board of directors of most large companies has an *audit committee* (usually composed of directors who are not also officers or employees of the company) to give the auditors a way to bring criticisms of management to the board's attention. Michel's firm would likely raise this with Westward's audit committee.

- Erin's is another very complex situation. Erin is responsible for protecting the confidentiality of her client, Basic, and would be in trouble if she told another company what she learned on the audit. But her firm is responsible to both clients. Again, she and the firm would need immediate legal advice.
- Most public accounting firms have rules prohibiting members of the firm from having an interest in any clients audited by the firm. Giorgio would probably have to sell his shares of Westward.

HOW'S YOUR UNDERSTANDING?

Here are two questions you should be able to answer based on what you have just read. If you can't answer them, it would be best to reread the material.

1. Why do professional accountants have to abide by codes of ethics, and what difference might that make to the users of their services?
2. What ethical issues do you see in the following situation? During the audit of Westward Industries Inc., Sonya discovered that an accounting clerk, needing money for a child's operation, had temporarily taken some cash collected from customers. The clerk had returned the money a short time later, before anyone had known it was missing, and was otherwise a very competent and valued employee. The company's controls over cash have since been tightened, and it is unlikely that the clerk would be able to repeat the theft. Sonya is the only person, other than the clerk, who knows about the theft.

5.10 Capital Markets

Frequent references have been made to stock markets and their investors/traders, and the importance such markets have for financial accounting, both directly and through the influence of regulators such as the OSC in Canada and the SEC in the United States. This section provides some background on *capital markets* (which include stock markets) and their connection with financial accounting. Nearly everyone is affected by how these markets work, through pension plans, retirement savings plans, and individual investments, and they have provided a powerful impetus to research in economics, finance, and accounting.[25]

Stock Markets and Other Markets for Financial Capital

Stock markets facilitate the exchange of shares by investors.

As business corporations developed, ownership rights in them were sold more and more broadly. The owners (shareholders) began to invest in several businesses at once and to buy and sell their shares from and to each other. To facilitate such buying and selling ("trading") of shares among these *investors*, *stock markets* organized as *stock exchanges* developed. Today there are many such exchanges, including the major international ones in New York, London, Tokyo, Paris, and Toronto, as well as specialized or regional exchanges. There are also "over-the-counter" markets and other alternatives to the major exchanges. Brokers, investment banks, market analysts, and others conduct, assist in, and advise on trading.

Many bonds and other kinds of financial instruments are also traded on exchanges.

Trading goes on in more than just shares of companies. There is also trading of rights (using terms such as "warrant" or "options") to buy or sell shares in the future, to convert from one kind of share to another, to receive dividends, and to perform a wide variety of other future actions. New rights and *financial instruments* to convey such rights are being invented and traded all the time. Special markets have been developed for some of these, such as an options exchange in Chicago, but many are traded on regular stock exchanges. Corporate and government bonds are also traded, and there is such a variety of financial instruments that the distinction between ownership shares, creditorship bonds, and other rights and instruments is often blurred. For example, some bonds carry the right to be converted into shares at the option of the holder.

All kinds of securities and exchanges make up the world's capital markets.

Many exchanges and over-the-counter markets use computerized trading systems for the listed companies whose shares and other *securities* (the usual general name for all these shares, bonds, and other financial instruments) trade on the exchanges and other markets, and, increasingly, investors can buy or sell securities pretty well 24-hours-a-day somewhere in the world. Taken together, all these exchanges, markets, and buying and selling activities are usually called capital markets. They include both share (stock) trading and trading of all the other securities that corporations and governments use to finance their assets.

Capital markets follow their own paths, separate from the issuers of securities.

These markets operate quite separately from the companies and other organizations that initially issue the securities.

- For example, when a company (a corporation) decides to issue some bonds or shares, these securities are offered to the market(s), and the company receives the proceeds of the initial sale of them (less commissions to brokers and others involved). After that, however, the company ceases to be a direct participant. Investors buy the securities from each other and sell them to each other with no participation from the company.
- Investors may even act in the face of opposition from the company. For example, an investor may try to get enough shares together to get voting control of the company (a "takeover"). There is always a risk for so-called *public companies* (companies whose shares members of the public are able to buy or sell from each other without permission of the companies) that the markets will behave in ways the companies do not like.
- There are other examples of investors acting in ways not desired by the company. One is that the company may announce a new management team that it expects will improve the company's performance, only to see the price of its shares fall because the people buying and selling the shares do not like the new team and more people want to sell their shares than want to buy them, producing a fall in the share price.
- The markets often create new securities out of the ones the company initially issued and then trade those. For example, a share may carry the right to buy another share in the future. That right may be bought and sold separately on the market, so that you could own the share without any such right, or the right without any such share. You might even be able to buy an "option" consisting of a bet as to whether the share price will rise or fall in the next month or year, or buy a bet as to the overall price of the market's shares in the future. (Overall price measures, such as the Dow Jones Industrial Average, the NASDAQ, the S&P 500 or the S&P/TSX Composite Index (the primary Canadian index), are closely watched by many people. At this writing, for example, the Web sites of the CBC (**www.cbc.ca**), the *National Post* (**www.nationalpost.com**), the *Globe and Mail* (**www.globeandmail.com**), and many other organizations report these averages and other stock market information daily.)

Security Trading and Security Prices

Capital markets work about the same as any market. People trade (buy and sell) what they own for something else, usually money or a promise of it.

- There are people who own securities, such as shares of CPR, Bombardier, IBM, or any other public company. Some of these people will be willing to sell their shares, if the price is right. If no one was willing to sell at any price, there would be no trading!

- There are people who don't own the securities, but who are willing to buy them from the above people, if the price is right. If no one was willing to buy at any price, there would be no trading! Let's call the first group the "sellers" and the second group the "buyers." Suppose we had the following list of possible prices of CPR shares (hypothetical, but in the range of CPR's recent trading prices on the Toronto Stock Exchange):

Price	Sellers' Willingness to Sell	Buyers' Willingness to Buy
$50	Everyone would sell	No one would buy
$40	Most would sell	A few would buy
$30	Half would sell	Half would buy
$20	Some would sell	Most would buy
$10	None would sell	All would buy

Securities' prices on capital markets are set by supply and demand forces, like any market.

You'll recognize from this list of prices that we have a supply curve and a demand curve. Capital market prices are set by the interaction between those wanting to sell and those wanting to buy. At a price of $50, there'd be lots of shares for sale but no buyers; at a price of $10, there'd be lots of buyers but no sellers. Each day's market price for the shares is set by the balance between people willing to buy and people willing to sell:

- If there are more sellers than buyers, the price will fall, roughly down to the level at which there is an equal number of buyers and sellers (or at least, shares demanded and shares for sale); and
- If there are more buyers than sellers, the price will rise, roughly up to the level at which there is an equal number of sellers and buyers (or shares for sale and shares demanded).

In the above example, we'd expect the buyers and sellers to agree to trade (buy and sell) at a price around $30. So if we looked up CPR's shares in the newspaper's listing of TSX prices, we'd expect today's price to be about $30. But the daily price is set by the pressures of supply and demand, so it will vary depending on how many buyers and sellers make offers to buy or sell, and, therefore, it will vary around $30 as those pressures vary.

Role of Information in a Capital Market

Why would the pressures of supply and demand vary? Broadly speaking, there are three kinds of reasons that are of interest in understanding the role financial accounting information plays:

Part of the capital market's supply and demand is not particularly related to information.

1. *Noninformation-based trading.* The circumstances of some buyers and sellers may require them to sell, or even buy, almost regardless of anything to do with the particular company whose shares are being traded. An owner of some shares may die and the estate may have to sell the shares in order to distribute the money to the beneficiaries of the owner's will. Or an "institutional" investor, such as a pension plan, may need some cash to pay pensions or other payments. Or a person may win a lottery and buy shares in a mutual fund (an investment consisting of a sample of shares of many companies), so that the mutual fund in turn has to buy some shares. Therefore, some trading is likely to be occurring continuously for reasons of raising or spending available cash. Such trading is referred to as "liquidity trading."

Part of the capital market's supply and demand is related to general information.

2. *General information-based trading.* Companies whose shares are traded are part of a general economic system, and some general events may change people's views on the wisdom of investing in anything and so cause changes in all or most shares traded on an exchange. The share price of companies such as CPR may therefore change along with the rest. Examples of such general events are changes in national interest rates, announcements of trends such as inflation or consumer confidence, wars, illness, or death of important people, and elections that change the party in power. If the Canadian federal government announced a new special tax on corporations' incomes, we might expect pretty well every company's share price to fall, including CPR's, because investors would see this as hurting every company's future incomes and, therefore, the returns investors would get from owning shares in any company. Market-wide price changes coming from the economic system are often called "systematic" effects. It is not clear theoretically why general information generates trades, because if all companies are affected, why bother to trade? Some of the trades may happen because investors think some companies will be hurt or helped more than others, and some investors may be getting out of that market altogether, such as by selling their shares and buying gold or real estate.

Much of the capital market's supply and demand relates to security-specific information.

3. *Specific information-based trading.* Information specifically about CPR's future prospects may also cause changes in the willingness of people to buy or sell its shares. For example, if the company announces that it is going to buy another company, some people may like that idea (and, wanting to buy, increase the demand for shares) and other people may dislike the idea (and, wanting to sell, increase the supply of shares). If most people think buying the other company is a good idea, the share price will rise; if most people think it is a bad idea, the share price will fall. This phenomenon, in which share prices reflect people's evaluation of the impact or meaning of an event on the wisdom of holding a company's shares, is very important to understanding share prices and accounting's information role. We can say that the stock market "prices" the information, in that the change in the trading price of the shares (up, down, or not at all) is a measure of the value of the information to the market. We might say that *decision-relevant information* is *material* to the market if knowing about it changes, or would change, a security's market price or, perhaps, would prompt trading (buying and selling) even if the net effect on price were zero.

A great amount of analysis and research in accounting, finance, and economics uses this third role of information to measure the apparent value of all sorts of company-specific and security-specific information, such as the company's annual announcement of its net income ("earnings announcement"), announcements of changes in management, and news about other events initiated by or affecting the company. (Using change in capital market prices as a measure of information value requires some faith in the market system, and confidence in the market's ability to respond appropriately to information.)

Return and Risk

The return from holding a security is part current cash flow and part price change.

The return you earn by owning a security such as a CPR share is the sum of

- the cash you get (from dividends or interest payments), and
- the change (hopefully an increase) in the market price of the security.

So you get a cash return plus a holding gain or "capital gain" (or loss).

Price change risk may be systematic (general) or unsystematic (security-specific).

If the security you own varies in market price, that variation is, according to capital market theory, a measure of the *risk* from owning the security, since price could go up or down. Risk is calculated as the variance or standard deviation of the prices around the average price, or trend in average price, of that security. A risky security, therefore, is one whose price varies all over the place. As described above, a security's price may vary because the whole stock market or bond market is going up or down, or because of information specific to that security, or to the company issuing the security. So, analytically, the price change risk is separated into

- *systematic risk*: the portion of the security's variation that relates to or correlates with variation in the overall market; and
- *unsystematic risk*: the security's own residual variation not related to the market. "Beta" (a term coming from the mathematical model used to relate a firm's returns to those of the market overall) is a measure of the security's relationship to overall market variations. Securities can be classified according to this relationship: a *low-beta* security's prices vary *less* than overall market prices do, while a *high-beta* security's prices vary *more* than the market.

Accounting information has modest value in predicting prices and price change risk.

A natural question at this point might be, "Does accounting information (especially income or cash flow) help to predict security prices and, therefore, risks and returns?" Market prices are pretty hard to predict, period. Therefore, accounting information isn't much help, but neither is anything else. However, accounting information can be helpful indirectly. When important events that do affect security prices are also represented in the accounting information (perhaps later on, since accounting reports come out only quarterly or annually), then the accounting information will indirectly be predictive too. It depends on how well accounting does represent the original event: it seems that if phenomena reported in the accounting information have a clear economic meaning (such as when they represent an impact on cash or risk), they do have some incremental predictive value.

Accounting information does relate to actual price changes that happen.

After the fact, however, it is clear that accounting information (especially earnings) does correlate highly with market prices. The longer the accounting-price relationship is measured, ordinarily the better it is: accounting earnings, for example, usually correlate better with stock prices over several years than over a few months. Accounting does relate to whatever affects markets, though calling the shots in advance is hard!

Aggregates

A portfolio of investments has less unsystematic risk than individual securities have.

Securities markets involve aggregate behaviour. To reduce risk, investors will invest in a group of securities, termed a *portfolio*. By choosing securities with differing risks, the investor can assemble a portfolio with whatever overall risk the investor wishes. Generally, a portfolio is less risky than any individual security because, by adding together a group of securities with different unsystematic risks, the unique variations in each partially cancel out. When one's price goes up, another's may go down. Thus, a portfolio is a way of "diversifying away" the unsystematic risk.

Portfolio thinking has become pervasive in the investment community. Most research on the impact of accounting information presumes that investors have portfolios of securities, and when companies are accounting for their *own* investments (marketable securities and pension funds, for example), they increasingly make the same presumption.

Market Informational Efficiency

An efficient capital market revises its prices properly and quickly for any information.

Efficiency of information use means that markets respond so quickly and smoothly to information that, once the information becomes public, its effects are immediately reflected in prices through the trading of securities. People who think the information implies that they should buy, do so, from people who think they should sell. This fast response means that if the market is efficient, you can't use publicly available information (such as public financial statements everyone can read) to "beat" the market; by the time you have the information and can act, the market will already have reacted to the information and produced a new trading price that reflects the information. You, as an individual trader, don't have the power to do much about the price that the overall sum of buys and sells has produced, so, unless you can trade on your information before anyone else knows it, you will find that the price already reflects the information. If everyone gets an accounting report at the same time, probably only those traders nimble enough to act immediately will be able to take advantage of any news in the report.

An efficient capital market responds to information it does not expect.

Capital markets operate on information, but they do so in light of expectations already formed, in accordance with what was already known. Therefore, the markets tend to respond to new information only if it is *unexpected.* The argument can be made that for an efficient capital market, only the unexpected portion of earnings (or of any other such item or announcement) is information to the market. The market will not respond much to financial results that are exactly as everyone expected. There always is some response, though, because of liquidity trading and because various market traders have different expectations and beliefs—these differences make the markets work!

Capital market efficiency is a hypothesis, not a fact, but is supported by research.

Research indicates that some markets (for example, the New York Stock Exchange) are quite efficient with respect to publicly available information, but many people doubt these findings. The research is by no means conclusive, and the behaviour of many markets is not well understood. Because informational efficiency is a difficult phenomenon to demonstrate conclusively, it is often called a hypothesis about how markets work: the *efficient market hypothesis.*

Fair trading requires a fair distribution of information.

Securities commissions and other market regulators are responsible for ensuring that securities trading is as fair as possible. One problem securities commissions worry about is so-called asymmetric information: some market traders know more than others do about a security and, therefore, potentially can take advantage of the more ignorant traders. If you know that bad things are ahead, you sell to people who don't know that the price will fall when everyone learns about the bad things, or if you know that good things are ahead, you buy from people who don't know their shares are worth more than they think. A major role of financial accounting is to reduce information asymmetries by producing information that informs everyone.

Insiders may know more than other traders, so their trading is scrutinized by regulators.

An example of the effects of asymmetric information is that people on the "inside" of the company might use their private knowledge to take advantage of other investors. Such insiders can buy or sell before other investors learn about something and, therefore, before the market can reach a new price based on the information. If you were a senior executive of CPR, and you knew that tomorrow the company would release an unexpectedly poor earnings report that will cause the share price to fall, you could sell out today to share buyers who are ignorant of what you know. Securities commissions require that any significant information be released quickly and to everyone at once, and they keep an eye on "insider trading."

Accounting standards that require companies to release significant information as soon as it is known, along with other efforts to remove information asymmetries, probably assist the markets to behave fairly in that prices will be set by buyers and sellers all equally knowledgeable about the company. However, even if someone less knowledgeable is being unfairly taken advantage of, the market will still be efficient in that its prices will still reflect whatever the various people know.

Corporate disclosure is a continuous process, of which financial accounting is only a part.

Financial statements are one of the ways that companies provide information about themselves to outsiders. Capital markets certainly pay attention to financial accounting information, but in a world in which many people buy and sell bonds, shares, and options several times a day, quarterly or annual financial statements are only helpful infrequently. *Disclosure* is a continuous and varied process. Much of the information in the financial statements leaks out over the year, in press releases, announcements, and official information filings with securities commissions or stock exchanges. For example, the audit of a company's December 31 financial statements may be completed in February and the financial statements printed and issued in April, but throughout the prior year there will have been announcements about important events, of quarterly per-share-earnings figures and, as early as January (before the audit has been completed), the final earnings per share for the year. Not surprisingly, accounting research shows that stock price changes generally happen before the official earnings reports are released, and this is more likely to happen for larger firms, about which there tends to be more information available between accounting reports. An efficient capital market may be able to make sense out of narrative disclosure, such as a management discussion, even if its implications are not built into the accounting numbers, so such disclosure has become almost as important as the numbers for many companies.

Immediate disclosure helps to keep capital markets fair.

There is, therefore, a continual flow of financial statement-related and other significant information from public companies to capital markets. The general idea is that information should be released as soon as it is known, so that general market traders are not disadvantaged compared to insiders. This helps to keep the system fair for all, but also it assists the market's pricing system to reflect informed evaluations of companies' prospects, so that the market prices are consistent with society's overall interest in appropriate allocation of economic resources. A recent study reported that "Disclosure activity reveals credible, relevant information not in current earnings and this information is incorporated into the current stock price." [26]

The above discussion emphasized the role of information in capital markets. Information can only have a role if market traders use it. In the aftermath of the Enron disaster, a lot of blame has been directed at auditors and Enron executives. But there have also been some voices saying that if only investors had used the information available to them, they would not have been so surprised at Enron's difficulties. Two examples are "Did Enron's Investors Fool Themselves?" which reported that a study of Enron's financial statements should have "triggered warning bells long before the share price started falling," and "The value of a good audit," which argued that "Unregulated market forces can fix audit and accounting issues. But it requires knowledge and understanding from all participants in the market for accounting services. They must know what they are paying for."[27]

HOW'S YOUR UNDERSTANDING?

Here are two questions you should be able to answer based on what you have just read. If you can't answer them, it would be best to reread the material.

1. Why might a particular piece of accounting information, such as an announcement of the year's earnings per share, often not have much impact on share prices?
2. If a capital market is described as being "efficient," what does that imply about the usefulness of financial accounting information and narrative disclosure in that market?

5.11 Contracts and Financial Accounting Information

Financial accounting has many roles besides providing information to capital markets.

Reporting to capital markets is not all that financial accounting is good for, or that managers worry about. Financial accounting plays many other roles that are important to managers and other parties. Such accounting information is used in resource-allocation decisions made by governments, in assessing income taxes, in negotiations with and by labour unions, and perhaps also in enhancing or attacking the political power of certain groups (such as the corporate sector) in society.

This section has some ideas about the contractual relationships among people involved in a business, and about a consequent role of accounting information in how such *contracts* work. There has been much research on contracts, as on capital markets, so this section only summarizes what is known.[28] The area goes by several other names, with differences that aren't important to this discussion, including "agency theory," "principal-agent theory," and "positive accounting theory."

Contracts are formal or informal, in which one party agrees to act on another's behalf.

In a contract, people agree to do things on each other's behalf and to be compensated for doing so properly. For example, managers, auditors, lawyers, or physicians are entrusted with acting on behalf of one or more other people (the owners, creditors, defendants, or patients). Contracts may be formally written ones (such as legally binding "indentures" providing protection to bondholders), less formal employment contracts or supplier agreements, or informal arrangements such as a handshake between partners. The person who is to do something and be compensated is often called the *agent*, and the person who wants it done is the *principal*. Many contracts involve both parties doing things for the other, and in any case, it is usually assumed that a valid contract requires that both parties entered into it freely, because both expect to benefit.

The parties to a contract generally will not have the same interests.

There is a fundamental characteristic of contracts among self-interested participants: *the people are unlikely to have the same interests.* Conflict of interests is not viewed as being bad, but rather as being the natural state of affairs. For example, if the agent is to provide effort on behalf of the principal, it would be natural for the agent to want to work less hard than the principal wishes. For the agent, effort is costly and might therefore be minimized, whereas the principal would want the agent's effort to be maximized.

Managers are stewards with their own interests, running the company for the owners.

In the contract setting, accounting has a major role in reporting on what the agent did on behalf of the principal. This is the *stewardship* role of accounting information (in monitoring the past stewardship of the agent, such as company managers, on behalf of the principal, such as the owners or shareholders), as distinct from the future-oriented, decision-making role of such information in capital markets. Now the focus is on how the managers behave, rather than on how the capital market, consisting of shareholders and potential shareholders, behaves. You can think of the information produced by financial accounting as resulting from the wish by the various parties to provide incentives and controls over each other's behaviour, especially agents' behaviour. This wish exists because agents are assumed to want to act in their own interests, and, in the absence of appropriate incentives and controls, their interests are assumed not necessarily to coincide with those of their principals.

Accounting information is appropriate if it helps in the contractual relationship.

From this point of view, accounting information is a part of the contract and should serve the monitoring and other needs of the contracting parties. Principals and agents specify what they need and accounting serves that, so accounting is useful, and not in any sense "right" or "wrong." If conditions change between various parties, accounting (and auditing) will change to meet the new conditions. Principals and agents will demand whatever information they require to manage the contractual relationship between them, and information, therefore, can be judged only in terms of that specific relationship. Is it what they need, or isn't it?

Owners and managers may have different views about how to pay the managers.

Here is an example. Suppose the shareholders of Lakewood Inc. wanted management to work hard to maximize the price of Lakewood's shares, which are traded on a stock exchange. The higher the price, the better the return to the owners from owning the shares and the higher their wealth. The owners might, through their representatives on Lakewood's board of directors, propose a management contract that specifies that the top managers get no salary, but instead get 20% of the change in the company's share price over each year. The top managers might well reply that this is too risky for them because all sorts of things might affect share price, including things they have no control over such as wars, recessions, or other unexpected problems. The share price could go up, but it might as likely go down. The managers may then propose that they should be paid a flat salary of $200,000 each, regardless of changes in share price, believing that the owners should take the risks. This isn't what the owners want, because they are concerned that the managers will not be sufficiently conscientious if they are guaranteed a salary regardless of performance.

The managerial compensation is negotiated between owners and managers.

Therefore, the two parties negotiate. Finally, a contract is agreed upon. Suppose it says that the managers will get $150,000 each plus performance bonuses of 5% of the annual net income and 3% of the increase in share price, with no penalty for negative income or negative change in share price, but with no bonuses then either. (The owners, interested in maximizing the share price, and the managers, feeling that they have more control over net income than share price, would in this case have agreed to include both factors in the bonus calculation.) Management compensation contracts are often very complex and a subcommittee of the board of directors may be created specifically to design and monitor such contracts. Securities commissions increasingly require public companies to disclose the nature of such contracts and the compensation that results from them, especially for the chief executive officer and other senior managers. Management compensation contracts in which pay depends on performance and that pay off in shares, or options to buy shares cheaply, in addition to cash have become very common in recent years.

Both parties to the contract are interested in relevant accounting information.

The result is that the managers, as agents for the owners (the principals), have agreed to work for the owners, and the owners have agreed to employ the managers. Both parties entered into the contract for their own reasons, and both are satisfied with it (or they would not have agreed). Now the owners can use financial accounting information to monitor the managers' performance and to calculate their bonuses based on net income. Both parties, because of their contract, are interested in the accounting information; neither would be satisfied without accounting. They may specify in their contract that GAAP be used to calculate net income, for the sake of convenience or because they prefer it that way. They also may specify other ways of calculating net income that they think are to their mutual advantage.

GAAP play a role in measuring managers' performance on behalf of owners.

If many companies have these sorts of bonus arrangements or other incentive contracts in which financial accounting information plays a role, there can be strong pressures on the development of GAAP or official accounting standards in directions that improve the effectiveness of such contracts. These pressures are likely to be in similar directions to those of, say, capital markets, because the owners are trading their shares on such markets. They will not be exactly the same, though, because the managers have to agree to the contracts too and may not want, for example, to bear as much risk as the capital market might like them to.

Auditors evaluate the managers' accounting information on behalf of owners.

There is also a clear role for auditors in the smooth functioning of contracts. If the managers are responsible for the accounting information and are being paid on the basis of it, the owners (who are perhaps some distance from the company's offices and in any case would not want to have to show up to ask questions about accounting) may not be inclined to trust the managers' figures and would prefer having an outside auditor evaluate them. Adding credibility to management's information is the oldest reason for auditing, and still central to it.

Some contracts may be very specific about accounting information.

There are many kinds of formal and informal contracts, with many parties other than managers (such as suppliers, associated companies, foreign business partners, and governments) that may use financial accounting information. The parties to such contracts will necessarily have an interest in the financial statements, in GAAP, in auditing, and in the other aspects of financial accounting. They will, therefore, act as part of the system of information demand and use that shapes accounting. Some of the contracts that are likely to be of interest from a financial accounting point of view include management compensation contracts, as illustrated above, labour contracts, contracts with suppliers and/or customers, and financial contracts such as those drawn up for issuance of bonds, other debt, or equity. One reason for written contracts is the conflict of interests mentioned earlier. For example, bondholders receive a claim on the company, or its assets, that has a higher legal priority than the shareholders' residual claim. A contract, such as a "bond indenture," is written specifying the exact rights of the bondholders. The indenture might say that if the company's working capital falls below a certain level, the bondholders have the right to demand early payment or some other penalty. This doesn't remove the conflict of interests, but clarifying the situation makes everyone's assessments of the company's performance and prospects more informed.

HOW'S YOUR UNDERSTANDING?

Here are two questions you should be able to answer based on what you have just read. If you can't answer them, it would be best to reread the material.

1. What is the "contractual" view of the value of financial accounting information?
2. Green Inc. has a set of management bonus contracts for its senior executives, specifying that their pay will be based partly on how well the company performs. Brown Inc., however, just pays its managers a flat salary. What differences would you expect in the attitudes of the two groups of managers to their company's financial statements?

5.12 Terms to Be Sure You Understand

Here is this chapter's list of terms introduced or emphasized. Many will reappear in later chapters, so make sure you know what they mean *in accounting*, and if any are unclear to you, check the chapter again, or refer to the glossary of terms at the back of the book.

Accounting entity
Accounting principles
Accounting standards
Accounting Standards Board
Adverse opinion
Agent
Annual report
Assurance
Audit committee
Auditor's report
Authoritative standards
Board of directors
CA
Capital markets
CGA
CICA Handbook
Clean opinion
CMA
Compilation
Conservatism
Consistency
Contracts
Cost principle
CPA
Denial of opinion
Disclosure
Efficiency (of information)
Efficient capital market
Efficient market hypothesis
External audit
External auditor(s)
Fairness
FASB
Financial Accounting Standards Board
Financial instruments
Financial reporting
Form versus substance
GAAP
GAAS
Generally accepted accounting principles
Generally accepted auditing standards
Going concern
Government
Harmonization
Historical cost
IASB
Independence
Interim financial reporting
International Accounting Standards Board
Investors
Letter to the shareholders
Listed
Management discussion and analysis
Matching

Materiality
MD&A
Neutrality
Not-for-profit organizations
Objectivity
Ontario Securities Commission
OSC
Principal
Professional ethics
Professionalism
Public companies
Qualified opinion
Quarterly financial reporting
Recognition
Relevance
Reliability
Review
SEC
Securities
Securities and Exchange Commission
Stewardship
Stock exchanges
Stock markets
Timeliness
Toronto Stock Exchange
TSX
Unaudited
Verifiability

DATA FOR INSTALLMENT 5

The preparation of the standard set of financial statements for Mato Inc. to August 31, 2006, has been illustrated. We left Mavis Janer and Tomas Brot preparing for the board of directors' meeting and thinking about how to get their company out of trouble. As they reviewed their financial statements, Mavis and Tomas had some questions about their accounting. They are not accountants, remember, and are anxious to get on with running the business. Here, then, are some of their questions:

1. Should they hire an accountant to "do their books" so they will not be responsible for that job?
2. Do their financial statements have to follow the *CICA Handbook*'s standards?
3. What things, if any, in the financial statements will require policy decisions by them as the owners/managers?
4. Should their company appoint an external auditor?

RESULTS FOR INSTALLMENT 5

1. Hiring an accountant is really a matter of preference and money. If they do not want to do the job and feel strongly enough about it to want to pay someone else, and can afford to do so, they should go ahead. Their new employee may be able to do what is needed, with the help of the software they already have. However, this does not absolve them of their ultimate managerial responsibility for the accounting and financial statements.
2. No, their statements do not *have* to follow the *CICA Handbook*. The *Handbook* is a guide, not law. However, their company is incorporated and the statute under which it is incorporated will require that annual financial statements be prepared following accepted principles. The statute may even state or imply that the *Handbook* is the source of what is acceptable. Also, groups of people such as their bankers, the other investors, prospective purchasers of their business, income tax authorities, and external auditors will object to their financial statements if they diverge much from the guidelines in the *Handbook*.
3. From the financial statements in Installments 3 and 4, some possible financial accounting issues are:
    - Amortization seems to be calculated in a simple way. While this is not a bad thing, the simple calculations may not provide figures that are useful in evaluating the performance of this particular business.
    - Inventory is getting large. If the customers are boutique retailers who are likely to be sensitive to seasonal and other changes in demand, the company may have to deal with obsolete or out-of-style inventory items and may need an accounting policy for valuing such items (reducing their value to some estimate of market value).
    - The balance sheet does not say much about the company's authorized and issued share capital, such as the number of shares or rights of shareholders. A note to the statements giving this information would be a good idea (and expected by GAAP).
    - The company may have made commitments to purchase various items, such as those intended for the Christmas season. Users of the financial statements might like to know about any such commitments.
    - The company is operating in leased premises and has spent a large amount of money to improve those premises. Users of the financial statements may find some information about the lease useful, especially its term and any renewal privileges.

- Users of the financial statements might like more information about the loan made by Tomas's father, such as confirmation of the fact that it is repayable on demand, as it appears to be (and so may be more like the bank loan than it now seems) and what interest is payable on the loan, if any.
- The income statement shows no interest expense at all, yet there is a significant bank loan. There appears either to be an error or an unrecorded liability. (Or perhaps interest has been paid and is included in the office and general expenses.)
- It is likely that the bank can seize the inventory and accounts receivable to collect on its loan: this and other security on the bank loan should be disclosed.
- It is common to disclose salaries paid to directors and officers (in other words, those of Mavis and Tomas) separately from other salaries.

4. There is probably little need to have their financial statements audited at this point. Auditing does cost money! However, they will have to satisfy the income tax authorities, their banker, and the other investors as to the credibility of their financial statements, so they should keep careful records and look into hiring an outside accountant at least to review the financial statements and report that no substantial errors appear to have been made. (There are several levels of external help, including simple advice, a more substantial review, and even a full audit.)

5.14 Homework and Discussion to Develop Understanding

The problems roughly follow the outline of the chapter. Three main categories of questions are presented.

- Asterisked problems (*) have an informal solution provided in the Student Solutions Manual.
- EXTENDED TIME problems grant a thorough examination of the material and may take longer to complete.
- CHALLENGING problems are more difficult.

For further explanation, please refer to Section 1.15.

Accounting Structure • Sections 5.2–5.4

Concepts

*** PROBLEM 5.1** Explain why various organizations are accounting entities

Explain briefly why each of the following is an "accounting entity," for which financial statements may be prepared.

1. Simone's jewellery business in Chapter 1.
2. The Royal Bank in Chapter 2.
3. The group of corporations making up the oil company Exxon.
4. The University of Lethbridge.
5. Continuing Case company Mato Inc.
6. The large accounting partnership firm Ernst & Young.
7. The City of Moose Jaw.
8. International fast-food giant McDonald's Corporation.

EXTENDED TIME

*** PROBLEM 5.2** Identify some accounting concepts and principles

Identify the accounting concepts or principles that relate to each of the following sentences and explain what effect the concepts or principles have on financial statements:

1. Users of financial statements should be able to believe that the numbers represent real events.
2. Financial statements should avoid undue optimism about the future.
3. It is hard to say absolutely that a company is performing well or badly, but you can evaluate its relative performance.
4. Financial accounting should be helpful both in understanding the past and looking ahead to the future.
5. The content of financial statements should not depend on who prepares them.

EXTENDED TIME

*** PROBLEM 5.3** The need for accounting standards

Explain the need for recognized accounting standards.

* PROBLEM 5.4 Explain the relevance-reliability tradeoff

Nonna is a financial analyst, responsible for making recommendations to clients of her employer, investment broker MEB Securities, about which companies would make good investments. She studies the characteristics of each company's shares and other securities and is particularly careful to understand what each company's balance sheet, income statement, and other financial statements indicate about the company's performance and prospects. She has been concerned lately about the reliability of some of the numbers in financial statements, particularly estimates of future consequences of past transactions, such as accounts receivable for uncollected revenues and long-term pension liabilities. While she believes that knowing about such things is important to her analyses, she feels that some of these important numbers have low reliability and thus are less useful to her than they would be if she could believe in them more.

Explain to Nonna why financial accounting numbers may be reported even if they are not entirely reliable.

PROBLEM 5.5 Usefulness of accounting concepts and principles

Bob is a hard-driving, impatient business executive. You work for him and can feel the grey hair sprouting on your head from all the pressure. One day, he returns from a lunch meeting with his accountant and says, "That accountant told me that there are accounting concepts and principles that tell me important things about why my financial statements are useful, why they are worth all the money they cost to produce and audit. I'm not convinced."

Choose any five of the concepts and principles in Sections 5.2 and 5.3 and explain to Bob why those five are useful. Make your explanations brief and to the point: Bob hates long-winded answers!

PROBLEM 5.6 Can one criterion of materiality suit different users?

The president of a public corporation recently commented:

> Our auditor says that our financial statements present fairly our financial position and the results of our operations. I challenged her as to how she determined such fairness. She replied that fairness means that the financial statements are not misstated in amounts that would be considered material, that is, significant.
>
> I believe that there is some confusion with this materiality concept, since different users of our financial statements may have different ideas as to what is material. For example, bankers, institutional investors, small investors, and tax assessors all have different perceptions of materiality.

Discuss the issues raised by the president.

CHALLENGING AND EXTENDED TIME

PROBLEM 5.7 Reasons for and value of accounting standards

During a speech to a business club, an accounting professor, who was describing the benefits of business competition, remarked:

"Over the last 200 years, there has been a large increase in the regulation of financial accounting by professional associations and government agencies. This has led to a large political component in the setting of financial accounting standards: accounting thus has to respond to the concerns of the time, rather than being objective and stable.

This sort of thing is part of what has made measuring each company's financial performance quite complicated and expensive. In my opinion, financial accounting costs a company more than it is worth to the company."

Exercise your knowledge of the world, as well as of accounting, by answering the following questions briefly. There are not any definitive answers to these questions, but the issues are important.

1. Why do you think society appears to desire that financial accounting be regulated—that there be standards a company has to follow in its financial accounting?
2. Is it possible that a company's financial accounting may cost more than that company feels it is worth, but be worthwhile doing anyway?
3. Should accounting standards be set as part of society's political processes, or should such standards be stable and uninfluenced by changes in society?
4. If the professor is right in saying that financial accounting and its standards are complicated and expensive, why do they not prevent such questionable phenomena as income smoothing and the Big Bath?

GAAP

* PROBLEM 5.8 International accounting standards – harmonization

Discuss the advantages and disadvantages of any movement toward convergence of various countries' national accounting standards to international accounting standards.

* PROBLEM 5.9 Measurement, valuation, and articulation of balance sheet and income statement

> "When an accountant is preparing a balance sheet and income statement, the principles behind balance sheet valuation and income measurement affect each other because the two statements articulate through double-entry accounting."

Explain what this statement means by reference to the set of generally accepted accounting principles described in Section 5.2.

* PROBLEM 5.10 Is having no GAAP worse than the present GAAP complexity?

Write a paragraph or two discussing the following topic: "The only thing worse than the large and complex set of practices, standards, and theories that make up GAAP would be if there were no such thing as GAAP."

PROBLEM 5.11 Which principles from GAAP apply and how are they applied?

You happen to be walking past your boss's office and you hear her exclaim, "These generally accepted accounting principles give me a headache! How can I figure out which ones apply to my business and decide how to apply them?" Wanting to impress your boss, you rush into her office and blurt out some answers to the questions. What do you say?

EXTENDED TIME

PROBLEM 5.12 Apply financial accounting principles to a company

In Section 5.3, some accounting principles were applied to the use of CPR's financial statements. Using another company, indicate why and how the following principles might be important to an investor who is using the company's financial statements to help in deciding whether to buy the company's shares. (If you have trouble thinking of a company, you could use the one that makes or sells your favourite car, beverage, cereal, designer clothes, takeout food, entertainment products, or home products.)

1. Fairness
2. Materiality
3. Comparability
4. Consistency
5. Going concern
6. Conservatism
7. Timeliness
8. Disclosure

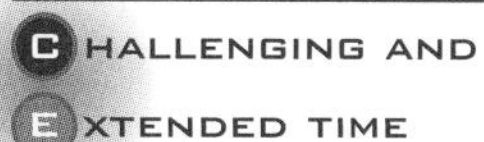

PROBLEM 5.13 Should small businesses have different GAAP?

Several people or groups, such as the CICA study group mentioned in Section 5.5, have addressed the question of whether small business enterprises should have their own set of GAAP rather than being required to comply with all the "Big GAAP" recommendations in the *CICA Handbook.* The writers reason that many current accounting principles seem to be geared to large businesses and that small ones should not be asked to implement recommendations that are irrelevant or that do not justify their costs through greater benefits.[29]

1. Give arguments for having one set of GAAP for all sizes of businesses.
2. Now argue for small businesses having their own set of GAAP.

PROBLEM 5.14 What if top managers disagree with GAAP?

Should top managers be held responsible for their companies' accounting if authoritative standards prescribe accounting methods they disagree with? Why or why not?

PROBLEM 5.15 Purpose and consequences of accounting standards

Quite often, proposed or even published authoritative accounting standards are controversial. An example is changing the way some forms of share capital are distinguished from debt, such as in considering whether shares that have a limited life, and are scheduled therefore for redemption on a specific date, should really be considered to be debt rather than equity. This may be an apparently sensible, even innocuous, idea, but implementing it changes a corporation's debt-equity ratio for the worse and may change the way the owners of such shares (or is it debt?) view their relationship with the corporation. When such a controversy arises, the idea of accounting standards as objective, neutral ways of doing accounting "best" is raised by defenders of the standards. Opponents argue that standards should not complicate or spoil sensible business arrangements, but merely ensure that such arrangements are reported clearly so that users of financial statements can make their own judgments about what matters. Standard-setting committees get caught in the middle, trying to find a way to have standards that matter (that is, that do change the way financial accounting is done, at least for some enterprises), but that do not put unnecessary burdens on enterprises, their owners, their accountants, or other parties.

Should accounting standards impose solutions on enterprises, or instead should they just be guidance to the "best practice" that enterprises can use or not use?

International

*** PROBLEM 5.16** Reasons for and objections to standards harmonization

Suppose two countries, Canada and a country less economically developed, are meeting to consider harmonizing their accounting standards. There is much willingness on both sides to succeed with the harmonization, but several serious obstacles to it have arisen during the meeting.

1. Why would standards harmonization be a good idea?
2. What obstacles to it are likely to have arisen during the meeting?

EXTENDED TIME

PROBLEM 5.17 Are international accounting standards a good idea?

There is always a tension between making accounting the same for every enterprise and allowing flexibility. The more sameness, the less each enterprise can present itself on the basis of its own particular characteristics. Not every enterprise will fit into the same mould. But if each enterprise can choose its own accounting, comparability is lost and users of financial statements have to learn anew each enterprise's accounting methods. The opportunity for misleading information may be increased.

If these points are put on the global stage, and "country" is substituted for "enterprise" above, we have the same problem but on a large scale. Does it make sense for every country to use the same accounting methods? Some differences among countries go very deep, affecting the legal rules under which enterprises operate, affecting what is considered good and poor managerial performance, and even affecting what the objectives of accounting and business are taken to be.

Do you think it makes sense to try for international accounting standards? Would such standards have to be so general that they would have less real impact on enterprises than more specific national standards? Would they be unwieldy and slow to change as global conditions change? Can they be the basis for regulation of capital markets, for the administration of various contracts, and for the objective assessment of performance? Discuss the question of whether international accounting standards are desirable, and if they are, how detailed or specific they should be.

PROBLEM 5.18 Should Canada set its own accounting standards?

There has been considerable debate in Canada about whether Canada should be setting its own accounting standards. Canada is not a large country and is close to the United States, so some people argue that Canada should just use U.S. accounting standards (FASB). Other people say Canada should adopt international standards (IASB). Still other people say that Canada is big enough to carry its weight in standard setting and should not hand the job over to any other country or group of countries.

Do you think Canada should set its own accounting standards or instead use FASB or IASB standards? Take a position and give a few reasons to support your position.

PROBLEM 5.19 Should NAFTA countries use the same accounting?

Canada, Mexico, and the U.S. are all signatories to the North American Free Trade Agreement (NAFTA). Other countries are likely to join NAFTA as full or partial members. Do you think all members of NAFTA should use the same financial accounting principles and financial statement formats? Why, or why not?

Nonbusiness

*** PROBLEM 5.20** Suggest nonbusiness characteristics of some organizations

The organizations below all have some characteristics that lead their financial accounting to be different from that of ordinary business enterprises. Identify one or two such characteristics for each:

1. The Government of Canada.
2. Large retailer YourStore that is being operated by a bankruptcy trustee while it is being wound up and its useful assets are being sold off.
3. Any student club in your university.
4. Sick Children's Hospital.
5. Banff National Park.

PROBLEM 5.21 Users of an association's financial statements

Section 5.5 showed the balance sheet of the Canadian Academic Accounting Association, which is the "learned society" for accounting professors. The CAAA puts on conferences, publishes two academic research journals, distributes some donated research funds, and does numerous other things of interest to its members. Members pay fees to belong and to attend conferences, but the cost of the journals and some other services are included with the membership fee.

Think about the professor or instructor you have in this course: what kind of financial information do you think such a person would want to have about the CAAA, to which the professor or instructor belongs? How well do you think the normal transaction-based financial accounting method you have learned about so far meets such a person's needs? (If you prefer, answer the questions for another not-for-profit association about which you are more familiar or to which you belong, such as a fishing club, your local church, or a community association.)

PROBLEM 5.22 Answer accounting questions from the treasurer of a club

Ron has just been elected treasurer of Snow Trails Club, a snowmobiling club, and has been handed the club's accounting records by the previous treasurer. The club accounts for its revenue on the accrual basis, but records expenditures from cash, not accrual expenses. Ron has taken a course in business accounting, but feels his accounting skills are quite modest and he is nervous about the accounting he will be responsible for as treasurer. Answer the following questions Ron has asked you:

1. "Will I have to follow GAAP in doing the club's financial statements?"
2. "The club has not had an income statement, but has had a 'statement of revenue and expenditure' that shows how much revenue excess (or deficit) is left over each year. Why is there no income statement as a business would have?"
3. "The club members are concerned about several things—like the number of members we have, the sources of grants we've received, and the success of various snowmobiling tours we've taken. Can I include these sorts of things in the financial statements?"
4. "Do we have to have the financial statements audited?"

PROBLEM 5.23 Should nonbusiness organizations use business accounting approaches?

There is debate over the extent to which nonbusiness organizations should use the accrual accounting approach that is the basis for business accounting. Questions have been raised over such topics as

- whether amortization, which is used to help measure business income by accounting for the economic consumption of assets, makes sense for public assets like roads, parks, and waterways;
- whether it makes sense to think of nonbusiness organizations as having anything like the "accrual net income" that is the measure of business performance;
- whether a balance sheet that, in business, balances owners' equity against assets and liabilities makes sense for an organization that has no owners, but instead has members, voters, or citizens;
- whether the whole idea of using accrual accounting in nonbusiness organizations represents a mind-set about economic efficiency, performance, and "the bottom line" that is inappropriate to organizations that may not exist for the economic reasons that businesses do.

Choose any one of the following organizations and list factors favouring, and opposing, the use of accrual accounting methods for that organization's accounting:

a. The Government of the province of Ontario.
b. York University.

c. A place of religious worship.
d. Any club you belong to or know about.
e. Parks Canada.

Annual Report and Financial Statements • Sections 5.6 and 5.7

* PROBLEM 5.24 Connections among the financial statements

Why should the set of financial statements that is included in the annual report be interpreted as a set? Putting it another way, does the income statement tell you anything about the balance sheet; does the balance sheet tell you anything about the cash flow statement, etc.?

PROBLEM 5.25 The value of notes and supplementary information

An investor in CPR received the annual report and was horrified at the many pages of notes and other information supplementary to the financial statements. "All this stuff should not be necessary. If the company did its accounting right, all this information would be incorporated into the financial statement numbers and descriptions, so I could make much better sense of what it all means. All I need to know is that the financial statements are fair, and the auditors' report tells me that, so spare me all the details!"

Explain to the investor why all the notes and other information is necessary.

PROBLEM 5.26 Are annual reports obsolete?

In this Internet age, many people have suggested that companies stop issuing annual reports and periodic financial statements and replace them with continuously updated information on their Web pages. If you wanted to see how a company was doing, you could go to the Web page and find out its up-to-date revenues and expenses, assets and liabilities, information from top management, explanatory notes, plans for the future, and so on. There would be no, or little, delay getting such information onto the Web page and so out to investors and others, and no need for companies to wait until the end of the year to put all the information together into an annual report. Users of the Web information could assemble whatever parts of the available data they wanted into whatever sort of report they wanted, whenever they wanted it.

Using your knowledge of the financial statements, accounting standards and other topics so far, outline the advantages and disadvantages of replacing the annual report with continuously updated information on a company's Web page.

PROBLEM 5.27 What is important in the annual report's financial information

A busy businessperson said, "I've made some investments in Canadian companies, so I receive their annual reports. The reports are many pages long—I don't have time to read all that. Everyone knows the income statement is the most important statement. The rest of the financial statements are meant to confuse and overwhelm readers."

Defend or refute this statement.

The External Auditor's Report • Section 5.8

* PROBLEM 5.28 Reasons for and difficulty of auditor independence

Auditors play an important role in the financial reporting system, and their independence from their clients is an essential feature of this system.

1. Why is such independence considered necessary?
2. Why is it difficult to maintain?

PROBLEM 5.29 Purpose, value, and limitations of the auditor's report

1. What purpose is served by the external auditor of a corporation?
2. Review the auditor's report included with the financial statements of any company you like. What is the report telling you?
3. To an investor, what value has been added to the financial statements by the auditor's report? Why?
4. Suggest some limitations on the value of the auditor's report that an investor should be aware of.

PROBLEM 5.30 Threats to an auditor's independence

Roger is the partner on the audit of Rugs Unlimited Ltd. Comment on whether or not, and why, each of the following may be a threat to Roger's independence.

1. Roger and the chief financial officer of Rugs Unlimited play golf together every few weeks.
2. During the audit, Roger notices that the company has a serious problem with its computer system. Roger's accounting firm is then hired by Rugs Unlimited to do a major redesign of the system, for a large fee.
3. As part of the completion of the audit, Roger works with the company to determine its likely income tax liability for the year, including helping to prepare the company's income tax returns. Roger bills the company for the tax advice separately from the audit fee.
4. Roger's former assistant on the Rugs Unlimited audit is hired by the company as the chief financial accountant, responsible for preparing all the company's financial statements.
5. Roger is asked to submit a bid on the next year's Rugs Unlimited audit fee, in competition with several other accounting firms. Roger decides to submit a very low bid because the income from tax and consulting services would make up for the lower audit revenue.

PROBLEM 5.31 Participants' roles and responsibilities

Briefly explain each of the following:

1. The role and responsibilities of management in the financial accounting process.
2. The role and responsibilities of the independent auditor.
3. Why information must be reliable and relevant to be useful.

Professionalism and Ethics • Section 5.9

Nature of a Profession

* **PROBLEM 5.32** Describe the role of accounting professionals in financial accounting

Why is it important that professional accountants are involved in financial accounting? Answer by outlining the characteristics of professionalism that you think have an impact on the nature of the financial accounting information.

PROBLEM 5.33 Discuss some statements about the accounting profession

1. "When accountants claim to be using professional judgment, they are just avoiding committing themselves to the right answer, or may be showing their lack of competence in solving the problems they face."

2. "CAs, CGAs, and CMAs are not really professionals because they are required to serve their clients or employers and do not have a responsibility to the public, as real professionals like physicians and lawyers do."

CHALLENGING

PROBLEM 5.34 Public responsibilities and private rights of professional accountants

Two true stories:

- A professional accountant got into trouble with the law and was charged with "conduct unbecoming to the profession" by the accountant's professional organization. After a hearing, the accountant was ejected from the professional organization, forbidden ever to use the professional designation again, and forced to pay the costs of the hearing. However, the university degree the accountant had earned was not taken away, because a degree, unlike a professional designation, cannot be removed once legitimately earned.
- A public accounting firm discovered that two of its employees were running a sex-oriented Web site. They were doing this on their own private time, with their own private money and their own private computers. They had broken no laws. Nevertheless, the accounting firm fired both of them, for "conduct unbecoming to employees of the firm." Their professional organization took no action against them.

With these two incidents as background, discuss how the line could be drawn between a professional accountant's responsibility to society through the profession and the accountant's rights as a private citizen. Should a professional accountant be held to a higher standard than other citizens?

Ethics

* **PROBLEM 5.35** Discuss some statements about professional ethics

1. "Professional ethics is rather an empty phrase when applied to accountants, because accounting is a technical task that has right or wrong answers, not ethical dilemmas."
2. "Ethical people have a strong sense of morals and a conscience. While accountants may well have these, when the professional associations write down ethical rules, they undermine accountants' ethical sense by turning them into rule-followers."

PROBLEM 5.36 Discuss an ethical issue: independence versus expertise

It is generally expected that external auditors should be independent of their clients, so that they will be objective and neutral in considering the fairness of the financial statements. It is also expected that the external auditors should be expert and knowledgeable about their clients, so that their work will be done with necessary competence.

Suppose you have been appointed as the external auditor of the widely owned public company Losser Inc., which will be one of several clients you have. Losser has been struggling in recent years, and senior management has been criticized in the media. The audit of Losser will bring you an annual audit fee of about $75,000. Soon after your appointment, the president of Losser takes you out to a nice restaurant and offers you a consulting contract with the company. The contract would bring an annual fee of $250,000, and would be in force as long as you were auditor. In return for the fee, you would advise the president about business and financial strategies—you can see that you would really be a personal advisor to the president. However, doing the consulting would make you much more knowledgeable about the company, and you could doubtless put that knowledge to use in doing your audit work.

The president asks you to think about the consulting offer. Discuss the factors favouring and opposing your doing the consulting and indicate whether you think you should accept the contract.

PROBLEM 5.37 Does considering ethics add to understanding accountants and financial statements?

Discuss the following comment, made by a businessperson after hearing a speech on professional ethics in accounting.

> Professional ethics in accounting has always seemed a doubtful subject to me, because I don't see that there is much to it beyond good business sense. Being independent, for example, means that the external auditor offers a better service because the auditor's opinion on the financial statements means more than if the auditor was not independent. It doesn't require an ethical sense to see that. In general, we all try to be ethical in what we do, and an ethical accountant will command a higher pay than an unethical one as a consequence. So an accountant will do the right thing because it is good business, it makes the accountant better off to do that. Please don't take this as cynicism: I genuinely wonder what talking about ethics really adds to the understanding of what accountants should do and what their financial statements should be like.

Capital Markets and Contracts • Sections 5.10 and 5.11

*** PROBLEM 5.38** Capital markets, contracts, and accounting

1. Briefly describe two important connections between accounting information and capital market behaviour.
2. Briefly describe two important connections between accounting information and the behaviour of parties who have business or employment contracts with other parties.

PROBLEM 5.39 Settle an argument about financial accounting's purpose

Two students are arguing. One says that financial accounting exists in order to provide information to outsiders (for example, capital markets) for assessing company performance. The other says that it exists in order to provide a monitoring and control system over managers who are running the company as the agents of the owners. Settle the argument.

CHALLENGING

PROBLEM 5.40 Capital markets

On October 31, 2006, analysts predicted that the earnings per share of Laurel Oakes Corp. would equal $4.80 for the year ended December 31, 2006. Actual results were announced on February 27, 2007. Earnings per share for 2006 came to $3.95. Consider the three dates noted above (October 31, 2006, December 31, 2006, and February 27, 2007). At which of these dates would you expect to see share prices react to earnings information? Why? Can you predict the direction in which share prices would react on any of these dates? If yes, explain why; if no, explain why not.

Integrated

*** PROBLEM 5.41** Explain the origin and present importance of some terms

Explain where the following terms came from in the history of business and accounting and indicate what importance each might still have now in the new millennium's financial accounting:

1. Stewardship
2. Securities regulation
3. Authoritative accounting standards
4. Harmonization
5. Independence
6. Disclosure

PROBLEM 5.42 Authoritative standards, capital markets, and contracts

Many of the accounting methods we study in this book are based on authoritative standards (*CICA Handbook*, FASB *Statements*, and so on) that attempt to specify how companies' financial accounting should be done. Such standards don't cover everything: companies must still make many choices when they are preparing their financial statements.

Why are there authoritative standards for companies to follow? Why don't they cover everything? Should we have more or less of them? Put your answer in the context of this chapter's ideas about auditing, capital markets, and contractual uses of information.

CHALLENGING

PROBLEM 5.43 Is accounting neutral?

A speaker at a recent conference stated:

> Many groups, including governments, financial institutions, investors, and corporations in various industries, argue that their interests are affected by present and proposed accounting pronouncements. The sometimes contradictory interests of these groups are recognized by the accounting profession. However, accounting is neutral and is not influenced by the self-interest of any one group.[30]

Discuss the above quotation.

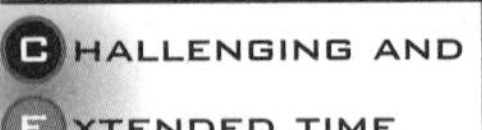

PROBLEM 5.44 Auditors and forecast information

Recently, there has been pressure to expand the role of auditors because investors and other groups are demanding more forward-looking information. If these demands are met, auditors may be expected to review the plans and forecasts of a company that will be reporting to the public, and to determine the fairness of such forward-looking financial statements.

Discuss the implications of this expanded role for auditors, using such concepts as fairness, independence, information value, comparability, relevance, reliability, objectivity, efficient capital markets, contracts, and any other concepts that you feel are important.

CASE 5A

INTERPRET NON-CANADIAN FINANCIAL REPORTS

Financial accounting has different standards all over the world and as a result, companies' financial statements are presented differently depending on the country. For the following companies, visit the Web to find their annual reports and other information provided to investors. (The annual reports are usually under the "Investor Relations," "Company Information," or "About us" link. Use your navigation skills to find them.)

- Microsoft (**www.microsoft.com/msft/**)
- Nokia—parent company (**www.nokia.com**)
- Toyota (**www.global.toyota.com**)
- Sony (**www.sony.com**)
- Starbucks (**www.starbucks.com/aboutus**)
- BMW (**www.bmw.com**)
- Royal Dutch Shell (**www.shell.com**)
- Ericsson (**www.ericsson.com**)

Read the material and discuss the companies' results. The statements are not in the usual Canadian format and use somewhat different terminology, but your accounting knowledge, and some questioning and discussion, should lead you to figure out what they are telling you. In your discussion consider issues such as the following:

- How is the company's financial information presented on the Web site?
- How informative is the other country's reporting format for financial statements compared to the Canadian one?
- Are there any significant differences in the presentation of the financial statements between other countries? Are other countries' statements more informative?
- Would international harmonization of accounting standards and reporting be advantageous to the average investor?
- What assurances do you get from the auditor's report?
- Do you see any differences in the application of the sorts of accounting principles outlined in Sections 5.2 and 5.3?

CASE 5B

SHOULD GAAP BE TIGHTENED UP?

An accountant decided to clean out his office and found an article from a number of years ago about the quality and consistency of accounting information. It made him start thinking about more recent accounting controversies. At coffee that morning, he discussed it with his colleagues. Here is the editorial.

IT'S TIME TO NARROW THE GAAP GAP

Financial reporting in Canada is just not good enough. There is too much deliberate, legally sanctioned, holier-than-thou confusion. It's pleasantly called the GAAP gap.

The Ontario Securities Commission is scrutinizing one side of the reporting issue — getting the company to put out the "facts." And hopefully, public companies will soon become liable for continually good disclosure.

But good reporting also embraces the way in which the so-called "facts" are colored, or spun, on the way out of the company's mouth. And that's the notorious GAAP gap.

GAAP stands for Generally Accepted Accounting Principles. Every public company must report according to GAAP, by law.

Well, GAAP is too elastic. Like a child's balloon, a company can make its earnings or assets grow bigger or smaller under GAAP, provided its accountants blow or suck hard enough.

In other words, public companies can adopt a careful, conservative approach to financial reporting or one that's freewheeling. It's up to them.

Well, this won't do. The accounting profession and the regulators must narrow the GAAP gap, so that investors can understand what's going on in companies into which they put their precious savings.

Here are some examples of companies riding horses through the GAAP gap. In all cases, the company's accounting falls within GAAP's legal limits.

A trust company conglomerate reports a $16-million profit, which could also be interpreted as a $12-million loss.

A holding company suddenly reclassifies some short-term investments as long term, raising a morass of valuation and liquidity issues.

A beverage company capitalizes some of its expenses, controversially. This practice maximizes assets and profits at the same time.

Some companies account for subsidiaries by cost accounting, which does not recognize the subsidiaries' losses, when they could use equity accounting, which does.

Another company has used slower depreciation schedules than the rest of its industry without explaining why. And so it goes on.

When confronted with these cases, the accounting profession argues, loftily, that GAAP must be elastic enough to allow for the reporting of unusual situations.

Well, some regulators paint a darker picture. Too many company accountants have become rule oriented, they say. When challenged about a loose presentation, the accountant often replies: "Show me where it says I can't do that?"

Well, if the accountants are becoming rule-oriented, give them tighter rules, within GAAP. That's the answer.

Investors are too often led into confusion through the GAAP gap. It must be narrowed.

Source: "It's Time to Narrow the GAAP Gap," *Financial Post*, January 29–31, 1994, S1.

Here are some comments the accountants made. What do you think?

"Those journalists are always after accountants and auditors. Don't they realize that we are professionals and exercise our judgment carefully, so that there were undoubtedly circumstances that made the editorial's examples sensible to the accountants and auditors involved? Even if they were not sensible, they are only a few examples—what about some examples of all the times the accountants and auditors did the right thing? Not newsworthy, I guess."

"Don't be too hard on the media. They're an important part of the workings of GAAP—after all, we find out that way if what we do really is generally accepted! Remember some of the media attention that led to improvements in accounting? Like the trouble over pooling of interests consolidation, and poor accounting by governments and nonprofit organizations?"

CASE 5B (CONTINUED)

Should GAAP be tightened up?

"This editorial may have been a good foreshadowing of what was coming. There have been a lot of recent examples where accounting practices have led to the downfall of major companies. Look at the result of Enron, which collapsed, costing investors billions, partly due to accounting irregularities or other recent problems over information disclosure. There has been a major crisis of confidence over the validity of many companies' financial reporting and it all centres on GAAP."

"I tend to agree that GAAP are too loose. Look at the situation of companies that compete in the same industry. It's hard to compare these companies when GAAP allow them to create unique financial statements. Major media companies like Global, CTV, and CBC do not even report in the same way. How is one supposed to evaluate these companies with such significant differences in reporting?"

"You know, the editorial does make me wonder just what advantage GAAP provide society. I remember an editorial somewhere after a plane crash, where the claim was that air regulations weren't strong enough to prevent crashes, and the counterclaim was that anytime you take off in an aluminum tube that is heavier than air, you're taking a chance and sooner or later someone will crash, regulations or not. Investing in businesses and managing them is at least as risky as flying, and people shouldn't expect GAAP to remove that risk. People need to become familiar with accounting principles and with the companies they invest in, so they can tell if something is amiss."

"I'll bet you could make an argument that having flexible GAAP to permit companies to tell their financial stories to the public in ways that fit those companies is cheaper for society in the long run than trying to control every accounting number with detailed rules. The rules would cost so much in accounting time, computers, and paper to administer that the cost of a few bad apples in the accounting barrel would be small in comparison."

"The editorial makes a good point about the dark side of the rules. If you have detailed rules, the accountants and auditors just turn into rule-followers rather than professionals. You could extend that argument to say that GAAP are already too detailed."

"That's not what the editorial means. It is saying that accountants view rules as constraints, preventing them from doing things, not as guides to appropriate behaviour. It says that the accountants seem to think that unless a rule exists, they can do anything, so I think it means that the accountants don't exercise professional judgment at all."

CASE 5C

DISCUSS ETHICS OF AN ACCOUNTING MANAGER'S BEHAVIOUR

Discuss the ethical issues involved in the situation described below.

Leslie was chief accountant for a municipality. The job included responsibility for the municipality's computer systems, which are mostly used for financial records such as tax billings and collections, budgets, operating expenditures, payrolls, and services such as parks and swimming pools, but also are used by the police, fire department, welfare office, and other municipal operations. Recent budget pressures and technological developments have created some information system challenges, so the municipal Council set up a task force to respond to the challenges and put Leslie in charge. The task force was specifically directed to find ways to save money that the municipality desperately needed elsewhere, in particular for services to several kinds of disadvantaged citizens.

Leslie was recently fired by Council for "insubordination and incompetence" resulting from the task force's work. Two problems were especially irritating to Council.

1. The task force developed an integrated computer system for recording and responding to emergency calls. The system would connect the emergency response system to tax records and other information about citizens, to discourage abuse and ensure that the municipality billed people for all services provided. Considerable financial benefit to the municipality would result, but at the cost of delays in responding to emergency calls and substantially reduced privacy for callers. Leslie was concerned about these costs, because delays could cost lives and loss of privacy might discourage needy people from calling. However, a meeting of the task force with the Finance Committee of Council, chaired by the mayor, resulted in instructions to Leslie to disregard those concerns because the efficiencies gained would allow other needy people to be helped with the funds saved. Leslie was not satisfied with this, feeling that the impact on emergency response was too high a price to pay, and as the person responsible for computer systems and head of the task force, wrote a confidential memo to the mayor stating that the Finance Committee's instructions were inappropriate and giving careful reasons. Someone leaked the memo to the local media, with sensational results that were quite embarrassing to Council.
2. As Council investigated the first problem, a second one came to light. Earlier in the task force's work, a list of abuses of municipal resources and services had been developed, so that the new system could be designed to reduce or eliminate them. The list included such things as people avoiding property taxes on home improvements, plowing and cleaning streets of important citizens first, people making multiple welfare claims, municipal employees taking unauthorized holiday leaves, sending several ambulances to one emergency call because of duplications in recording calls, senior citizens receiving more than authorized discounts on recreation fees, and gifts by some contractors to municipal employees who send business their way. In the interests of task force efficiency, because not everything could be solved at once, Leslie had shortened the list and asked the task force to focus only on the remaining abuses. Leslie had thought a lot about which abuses to keep on the list and had eliminated several that potentially involved large dollars but seemed to Leslie to be socially acceptable, like the seniors' discounts. Council members questioned Leslie's judgment on these issues and criticized Leslie for presuming to make the eliminations in the first place.

NOTES

1. *The Economist,* "A survey of football" (June 1, 2002): 4.
2. Some of the ideas in Section 5.4 were developed with reference to George Murphy, "Corporate Reporting Practices in Canada: 1900–1970," *Working Paper Series,* Vol. 1 (The Academy of Accounting Historians, 1979).
3. Jane Mayer, "The Accountants' War," *The New Yorker* (April 22 & 29, 2002): 64, 66, 68–70, 72.
4. For a description of accounting standard-setting in Canada in the 130 years from 1864 to 1992, see G. Baylin, L. MacDonald, and Alan J. Richardson, "Accounting Standard-Setting in Canada, 1864–1992: A Theoretical Analysis of Structural Evolution," *Journal of International Accounting & Taxation,* 5 no. 1(1996): 113–31.
5. Alan Toulin, "Don't expect Enron-free world: Stymiest," *Financial Post* in the *National Post* (June 6, 2002): FP11. Barbara Stymiest spoke as CEO of the TSX.
6. John Gray, "Hide and Seek," *Canadian Business* (April 1, 2002): 28, 30–32.
7. Matthew Ingram, "Financial disclosure is good—but it doesn't always help," *The Globe and Mail* (February 5, 2002): B16.
8. Joseph Weber, "The CFOs Weigh in on Reform," *Business Week* (March 11, 2002): 30–31.
9. Mike McNamee, "FASB: Rewriting the Book on Bookkeeping," *Business Week* (May 20, 2002): 123–124.
10. American Free Trade Agreement (AFTA) Committee for Cooperation on Financial Reporting Matters, *Significant Differences in GAAP in Canada, Chile, Mexico and the United States, Third Edition,* Toronto: Canadian Institute of Chartered Accountants, 2001.
11. "The Impossible Dream," *The Economist* (March 2, 2002): 69.
12. A. Lavigne, "Standards with a Differential," *CA Magazine* (October 1999): 49–50.
13. A. F. Budlong, "Differential Reporting," a *Regulation Update* published by the Institute of Chartered Accountants of Alberta (May 2002). See www.icaa.ab.ca.
14. Gerald D. Trites, "Read It in the Annual Report," *CA Magazine* (December 1990): 45–48.
15. B. Gates, "Reports Deliver Message with Style and Pizzazz," *Financial Post* (November 27, 1990): 17.
16. S. Noakes (quoting P. Creighton), "Reports Gain New Prominence," *Financial Post* (December 2, 1993): 16.
17. D. Olive, "Watch Out for Glossy Truths," *National Post* (April 10, 1999): B10.
18. G.M. Kang, "It's Corporate America's Spring Hornblowing Festival," *Business Week* (April 12, 1993): 31.
19. Quoted by D. Vansen, in "Objectivity...," *Monthly Statement* (Alberta: Institute of Chartered Accountants of Alberta, March 1999): 8.
20. S. Bartlett, "Who Can You Trust?" *Business Week* (October 5, 1998): 133.
21. J.E. Garten, "Ethics be Damned, Let's Merge," *Business Week* (August 30, 1999): 26.
22. J. Novack, "Certified Public Accomplice," *Forbes* (November 15, 1999): 282–83.
23. R. Melcher, "Where are the Accountants?" *Business Week* (October 5, 1998): 144, 146
24. For ideas on how to deal with such ethical dilemmas, see L.J. Brooks, *Professional Ethics for Accountants* (West Publishing, 1995), or L.A. Ponemon and D.R.L. Gabhart, *Ethical Reasoning in Accounting and Auditing* (Vancouver: CGA-Canada Research Foundation, 1993).
25. For good summaries of accounting implications of capital market concepts and research, see W.H. Beaver, "Perspectives on Recent Capital Market Research," *The Accounting Review* (April 2002): 453–474; W.R. Scott, *Financial Accounting Theory* (Scarborough: Prentice-Hall Canada, 1997), especially Chapters 3, 4, and 5; C.M.C. Lee, "Measuring Wealth," *CA Magazine* (April 1996): 32–37; G. Foster, *Financial Statement Analysis,* 2nd ed. (Englewood Cliffs: Prentice-Hall, 1986), especially Chapters 9 and 11; R. L. Watts and J.L. Zimmerman, *Positive Accounting Theory* (Englewood Cliffs: Prentice-Hall, 1986), especially Chapters 2 and 3; W.H. Beaver, *Financial Reporting: An Accounting Revolution,* 2nd ed. (Englewood Cliffs: Prentice-Hall, 1989); or T.R. Dyckman and D. Morse, *Efficient Capital Markets and Accounting: A Critical Analysis,* 2nd ed. (Englewood Cliffs: Prentice-Hall, 1986).
26. R.J. Lundholm and L.A. Myers, "Bringing the Future Forward: The Effect of Disclosure on the Returns-Earnings Relation," *Journal of Accounting Research* (forthcoming 2002).

27. Chris Higson, "Did Enron's Investors Fool Themselves?" *Business Strategy Review* (vol. 12, no. 4, 2001): 1–6; Daniel B. Thornton, "The value of a good audit," *National Post Online* (April 23, 2002): 5 pages.
28. For more ideas about contracts and their relationship to accounting, see R.L. Watts and J.L. Zimmerman, *Positive Accounting Theory* (Englewood Cliffs: Prentice-Hall, 1986), Chapters 8 and 9; J.E. Butterworth, M. Gibbins, and R.D. King, "The Structure of Accounting Theory: Some Basic Conceptual and Methodological Issues," in *Research to Support Standard Setting in Financial Accounting: A Canadian Perspective*, ed. S.J. Basu and A. Milburn (Toronto: The Clarkson Gordon Foundation, 1982): 9–17, especially. This article was reprinted in *Modern Accounting Research: History, Survey, and Guide*, ed. R. Mattessich (Vancouver: Canadian Certified General Accountants' Research Foundation, 1984), 209–50.
29. Adapted from the 1979 National CA Uniform Final (Qualifying) Examination. By permission of the Canadian Institute of Chartered Accountants, Toronto, Canada.
30. Adapted from the 1984 National CA Uniform Final (Qualifying) Examination. By permission of the Canadian Institute of Chartered Accountants, Toronto, Canada.

PART THREE

Doing Financial Accounting

The four chapters in this group delve into various practices important to anyone preparing financial statements. These practices are presented to show their importance both to future accountants and to people not planning to become accountants.

- *Chapter 6 focuses on the way accrual accounting measures income, accounting's "bottom line," as the difference between revenues and expenses.*
- *Chapter 7 outlines recordkeeping and internal control considerations that exist separately from the financial statements but significantly influence those statements.*
- *Chapters 8 and 9 examine the accounts on the two sides of the balance sheet in more detail. Chapter 8 focuses on the left "assets" side and Chapter 9 on the right "liabilities and equity" side.*

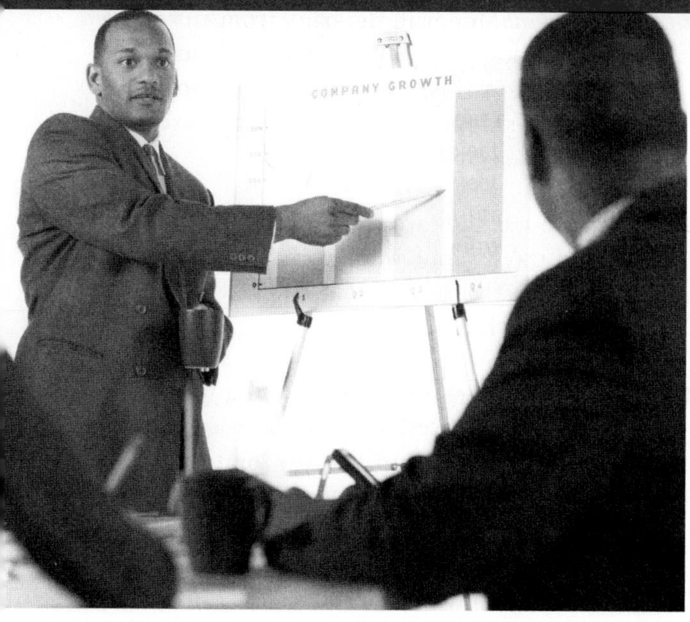

6 Revenue and Expense Recognition

6.1 Chapter Introduction: Revenue and Expense Recognition

Every public company has an annual meeting at which top management reports on performance and prospects for the future, and shareholders are able to ask questions. Here's some of what went on at a recent annual meeting.

Chief executive officer (CEO): ... and I hope you have found my report useful. While the company faces many challenges, there is much strength here too, and we look forward to improved prosperity. I now invite questions from shareholders present today.

Shareholder A. Benoit: Thank you for your informative comments. My question is about the company's revenues. I note that revenues have failed to grow much this year while inventories have risen. Can you explain what is going wrong?

CEO: We are facing much stronger competition in some product lines, so products we expected to sell have not sold, depressing revenue and increasing inventories because those products were available to sell but just did not move out the door.

Shareholder A. Benoit: Have the product markets collapsed? If not, then having the products available is still a good thing. Unless you doubt you will sell them, why not add them to revenue when you have them ready to sell? Otherwise you make the company look worse than it is, which hurts the company's share price and so the value of my shares.

Shareholder B. Hutchence: Please also tell us why the company's accounts receivable are up along with inventories. This doesn't make sense when revenues have not grown.

CEO: I'll ask our chief financial officer (CFO) to address those questions.

CFO: The company's accounting policy is to record revenue only when a legal customer order has been received, so we cannot show revenue for products no one has yet ordered. The accounts receivable are up, I agree, and frankly it is because in the face of competition, we have taken orders from some lower-quality customers than we used to, and some of those customers are slower to pay than we had hoped.

Shareholder J. Ranu: Hold on, here! You record revenue when you get an order? You don't wait until you fill the order? Sounds like even though this has not been a good revenue year, your accounting has made it better than it should have been. Are you covering up a real decline in revenue?

CFO: I don't like your language. We're not covering up anything. But once we receive an order, it is as good as money in the bank, so we mark it down as revenue.

Shareholder J. Ranu: Money in the bank from customers who are slow to pay? Do any other companies like ours do this? It sounds fishy. Since you have not shipped the products yet, are they still in inventory?

CFO: Well, of course they are still in inventory. We only record the revenue when we get the order. We record cost of goods sold when we ship the products, a few days later.

Shareholder B. Hutchence: You guys are trying to pull the wool over our eyes! You are showing revenue you should not, and are not matching the expenses with the revenues. Sounds like the company's books are a mess, and the income figure is a fabrication! I'll bet it helps you make your bonuses, but it doesn't help us!

Several shareholders shout: Are you cooking the books?

CEO: Order, please! All of this can be explained if you will be kind enough to listen....

Learning Objectives

Most annual meetings are not this confrontational, though controversy does erupt at many companies' meetings from time to time, but the vignette illustrates several important points. In this chapter you will learn:

- How accrual accounting works to make sure that revenues and expenses are measured in the appropriate period so that each period's income is valid (so there is no impropriety, "cooking the books" as in the vignette);
- How advancing or delaying the measurement of revenues and expenses, done to get income right, affects past and future income measures as well as the balance sheet (such as the receivables and inventories in the vignette);
- How to determine when it is the appropriate time to record revenues and related expenses (the company in the vignette is recording revenues too soon, before goods are shipped);
- How to set good accounting policies for measuring revenues and expenses so that the results are not "fishy" as in the vignette, and why users of financial statements need to be vigilant just in case the company is using improper accounting policies (most companies are quite scrupulous about their accounting, but some that are not have been prominent in recent years, to the embarrassment of all principled accountants, auditors, and managers).

6.2 What Is Accrual Accounting?

This chapter begins four chapters on *doing* financial accounting by focusing on how accrual accounting's measures of revenue and expense are constructed and matched to provide the measure of income. It is all based on double-entry accounting and on the concepts of revenue and expense, and the ways of adjusting accounts that were introduced in Chapter 3. With the conceptual and technical background provided by the first five chapters, this whole chapter is devoted to *revenue* and *expense recognition*, because *accrual accounting* is at the heart of financial accounting and is absolutely essential to understanding the income statement. Also, in many ways, the balance sheet is a "residual" of the measurement of revenues, expenses, and income, so this chapter extends your understanding of the balance sheet as well. Later chapters examine various parts of the balance sheet in more depth, using this chapter's explanation of accrual accounting.

Accrual accounting is all about choosing *when* to recognize phenomena in the accounts.

The key to accrual accounting is that it frees financial accounting from having to follow cash transactions only. With accrual accounting, revenues, expenses, assets, and liabilities can be recorded (*recognized*, as accountants say) before or after cash transactions happen. This can be done by the familiar method of debiting something and crediting something. The big question is *when* to recognize these income statement and balance sheet amounts by recording them in the accounts. For example, if revenue can be recorded at another time than when cash changes hands, such as by debiting accounts receivable and crediting revenue before the customer pays, when is it appropriate to do that? What evidence, principles, or assumptions support recognition before the cash changes hands, or after?

Accrual accounting involves estimates, judgments, and subjectivity.

Accrual accounting is the dominant form of financial accounting in the world today. It exists because cash flow information is simply not complete enough to assess financial performance or financial position. Keeping track of cash flow is crucial for business success, but it is not enough. We have to go beyond cash flow to assess economic performance more broadly and to assess noncash resources and obligations. We do this even though it forces us to make estimates, judgments, and other accounting choices that, in turn, make the results less precise than we would wish, and more subjective than transaction-based cash flow figures.

As a reminder of the ideas about accrual accounting introduced in Chapters 1 and 3, let's imagine the following conversation between a student and a relative who is also a professional accountant:

Accountant: Well, you spent the summer working at High-Class Boutique. How did you do?

Student: I had a great time. Met some great people, learned a lot about retailing, and so decided to major in marketing.

Accountant: No, I meant how did you do financially?

Student: Let's see. I received $6,460 over the four months. I have $4,530 left in the bank; so, I guess I must have spent $1,930. Gee, $4,530 doesn't make me rich after a summer's work! But the Boutique still owes me for my last week of work.

Accountant: What did you spend the $1,930 on?

Student: I blew some of the money on burgers and evening entertainment, and on that trip to the lake. But also, I bought clothes for the fall term, and I have the answering machine, and the fancy calculator I got so that I might be able to pass accounting.

Accountant: Don't forget you have to pay your Uncle Al back the money he lent you in May. That's in your bank account too, so it looks as if you spent more than $1,930. You promised to pay him, plus interest, at the end of the summer. There's also your university tuition for next year, and didn't you say once that you owed a friend something for gas for that trip to the lake?

Student: I don't think we should count the tuition because it doesn't really apply until I register. Although I guess that *is* why I was working. Now I'm not sure if I had a good summer or not!

Accrual accounting incorporates many phenomena besides the period's cash flows.

This example illustrates many of the issues accrual accounting tries to deal with, including:

1. The more you think about it, the more complex measuring performance and position seems to be, and the less satisfactory cash by itself seems to be as a measure.
2. Some of the revenue earned may not yet have been received in cash (payment for the last week of work).
3. Similarly, some costs incurred may not yet have been paid (the gas for the lake trip).
4. Some cash payments result in resources still having economic value at the end of the period (the answering machine, the calculator, and maybe the clothes).
5. Some cash receipts result in obligations still outstanding at the end of the period (Uncle Al's loan).
6. The longer-term resources may have deteriorated during the period (not all the clothes purchased during the summer will still be valuable because fashions change, and the answering machine and calculator are now used items).
7. Obligations may build up during the period (the interest on Uncle Al's loan).
8. There is often doubt about whether some things should be included in measuring performance for a given period or position at a given point in time (the university tuition), leading to necessary judgments and decisions that make accrual accounting's measurements often subjective and even controversial.

Illustrative Accrual Issues

Why accrual accounting?

1. Complexity leads to a demand for accrual basis rather than cash basis.

Some complexities:

2. Uncollected revenues.
3. Unpaid expenses.
4. Asset values extending beyond this period.
5. Some cash receipts that have to be repaid.
6. Deterioration of asset values during this period.
7. Obligations that build up during this period.

It's not straightforward.

8. Judgments and decisions are often required.

Accrual accounting's tradeoff: aiming for relevance without losing too much reliability.

Think of accrual accounting as an attempt to measure economic performance and financial position in a more complete way than just using cash. *There is always a tradeoff here:* the closer to cash, the more precise the measure is, but also the more limited and less informative it is. The more accountants try to make the financial statements economically relevant, the more they must include estimates and other sources of imprecision or error. Referring back to the relevance-reliability tradeoff diagram in Section 5.3, *accrual accounting aims for more relevance but the price paid*

Relevance-Reliability Tradeoff
More relevance → Less reliability
More reliability → Less relevance

is less reliability. To minimize the damage to reliability, there are many rules and standards surrounding accrual accounting, as we saw already in Chapter 5, and considerable evidence is normally required to back up the accrual figures. Companies are expected to choose sensible policies for doing their accrual accounting, and to stay with those policies over the years unless there is good reason for changing them.

Mini-Demonstration Problem

We're about to launch into conceptual material you might find difficult. Remembering that it is all based on the accrual accounting examples we already saw might help you with it. So let's make sure you have the earlier examples straight. If you have any trouble with this little demonstration, please look back to Chapter 1, Sections 1.10 to 1.12, and Chapter 4, Section 4.9.

In its first year, new company Affleck Inc. collected cash from its customers of $85,000, paid cash bills of $74,000, and bought a truck for $50,000, borrowing $40,000 from the bank in order to do that and so ending the year with $1,000 in the bank. At the end of the year, the company had uncollected revenues of $13,000 and unpaid expenses of $4,000, and $5,000 of the truck's value was thought to have been used (amortization).

a. What was the company's accrual income for the year?
The accrual income figure incorporates some cash figures (cash collections and payments) adjusted for some noncash or not-yet-cash figures (uncollected revenues, unpaid expenses, and amortization), and does not incorporate some cash figures (the truck purchase and the bank loan). So accrual income = $85,000 – $74,000 + $13,000 – $4,000 – $5,000 = $15,000.

b. What was the company's cash income for the year?
Just the day-to-day cash flows: $85,000 – $74,000 = $11,000.

c. What was cash from operations for the year?
Accrual income adjusted for noncash revenues and expenses and noncash working capital changes: $15,000 + $5,000 amortization – $13,000 uncollected revenue + $4,000 unpaid expenses = $11,000, which is cash income.

FIGURE 6.1

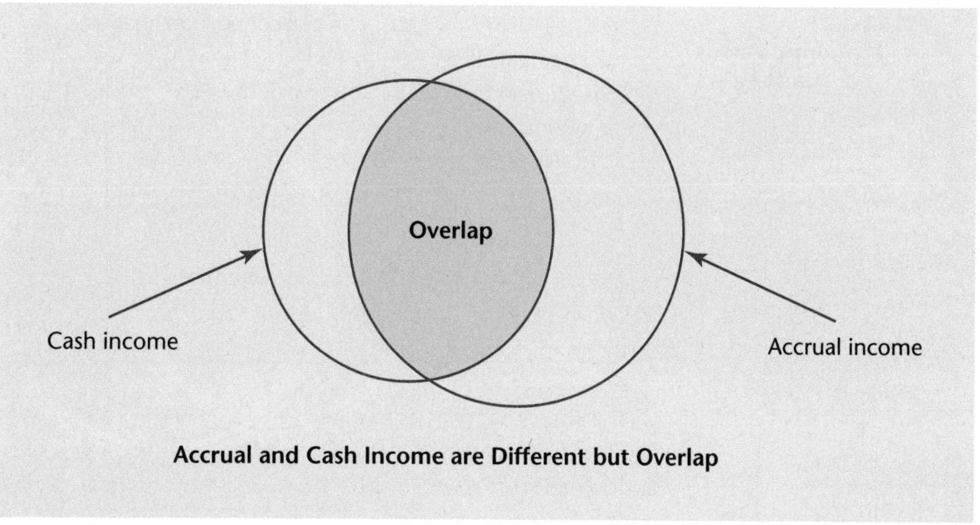

Accrual and Cash Income are Different but Overlap

HOW'S YOUR UNDERSTANDING?

Here are two questions you should be able to answer based on what you have just read. If you can't answer them, it would be best to reread the material.

1. If accrual accounting produces less precise figures than just using cash transactions would, why is accrual accounting used?
2. Suppose it was discovered that Affleck Inc. had inventories costing $9,000 on hand at the end of its first year. This amount had been included in the $74,000 of cash bills paid. What are the revised figures for (a) accrual income, (b) cash income, and (c) cash from operations?

(a) Accrual income will be $9,000 higher because there is an asset that had been recorded as an expense, so $15,000 + $9,000 = $24,000. Calculating it the long way, income = $85,000 – $74,000 + 13,000 + $9,000 – 4,000 – $5,000 = $24,000.

(b) Cash income is unaffected, still being $11,000. Nothing has happened to cash.

(c) Cash from operations will now have a $9,000 inventory increase to deduct from accrual income, so it will be $24,000 + $5,000 – $13,000 – $9,000 + $4,000 = $11,000, unchanged from before. This confirms that cash income is unaffected.

6.3 Conceptual Foundation of Accrual Accounting

Accrual accounting recognizes economic phenomena whether or not realized in cash.

Accrual accounting is based on the idea that events, estimates, and judgments important to the measurement of financial performance and position should be *recognized* by entries in the accounts (and therefore reflected in the financial statements), whether they have not yet, or have already, been *realized* by cash received or paid out. Adapting the diagram in Section 6.2 (Figure 6.1), we might say in Figure 6.2 that *the objective is to recognize economic flows separately from cash flows.* The result affects income, through the revenue and expense figures, but also affects the balance sheet, through accounts like accounts receivable and accounts payable that are used to create the appropriate revenues and expenses. The income statement and balance sheet *articulate* through accrual accounting.

FIGURE 6.2

Economic Versus Cash Flows

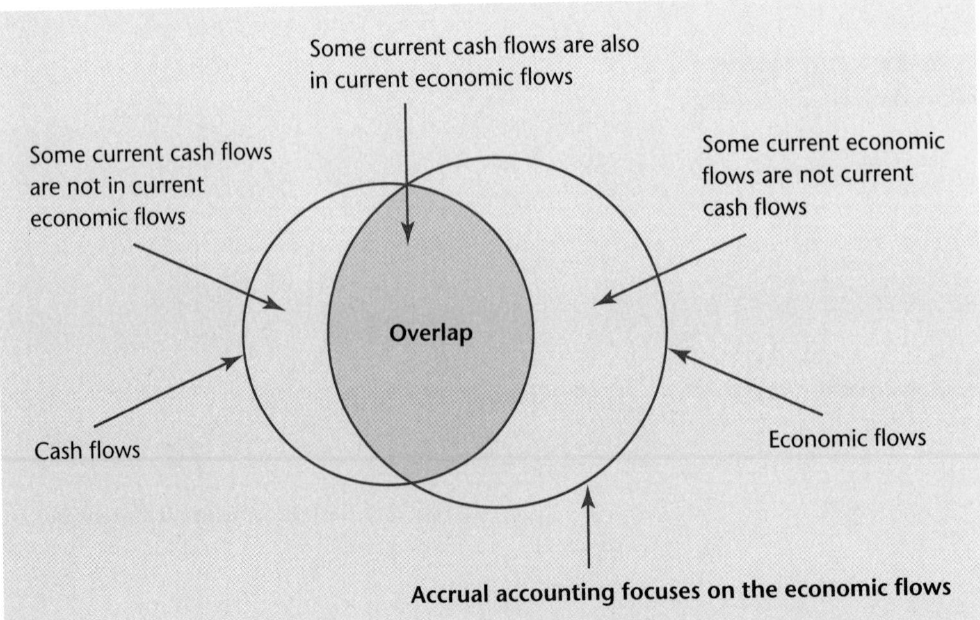
Some current cash flows are also in current economic flows
Some current cash flows are not in current economic flows
Some current economic flows are not current cash flows
Overlap
Cash flows
Economic flows
Accrual accounting focuses on the economic flows

Let's build the accrual accounting approach from some basics. These four cornerstones (which are shown in Figure 6.3) have come up already in this book, but we'll give them brief definitions again and build from there:

Revenues: economic inflows.

Expenses: economic outflows.

Net income: economic success.

Matching revenues and expenses is supposed to produce a logical net income measure.

- *Revenues* are *inflows* of economic resources from customers. We might say that earning revenues is the reason a company is in business.
- *Expenses* are *outflows* of economic resources to employees, suppliers, taxation authorities, and others, resulting from business activities to generate revenue and serve customers. We might say that incurring expenses is the cost of earning revenues.
- *Net income* is the *difference* between revenues and expenses over a period of time, such as a month, a quarter, or a year. We might say that net income is the measure of success in generating more revenues than it costs to generate those revenues.
- *Matching* is the *logic* of income measurement, ensuring that revenues and expenses are measured comparably, so that deducting the expenses from the revenues to calculate net income produces a meaningful result. We might say that matching ties accrual accounting together into a coherent system.

Note some features of these cornerstones:

Revenues and expenses are economic concepts extending beyond transactions.

Properly measured revenues and expenses should lead to proper net income.

Many criteria besides matching help ensure that revenues, expenses, and income are proper.

- Revenues and expenses refer to inflows and outflows of economic resources. These flows may be represented by the kinds of events recognized by the transactional recordkeeping system, but they may also involve nontransactional phenomena. In particular, they may involve phenomena that arise *before* or *after* cash changes hands, as well as *at the time of* the cash flow.
- Net income depends on how revenues and expenses are measured, and is not well defined separately from revenues and expenses. Accountants don't, or shouldn't, choose the income number first and force the calculation of revenues and expenses to result in that income. Instead, they measure revenues and expenses as properly as they can. Net income then is just the difference between these revenues and expenses.
- Matching involves trying to line up measures of economic inflows with those of economic outflows. It is logical, but not the only logic one could imagine applying. For example, if revenues are overestimated and then expenses are overestimated to match, the net income figure may be about right because the overestimations roughly cancel out, but the figures for revenues and expenses will be misleading, as will any balance sheet accounts related to them, such as accounts receivable and accounts payable. If the method of recognizing revenue is poor, it hardly makes sense to argue for a poor expense recognition method for the sake of matching. So, many other criteria enter into revenue and expense recognition and income measurement to fine-tune the system and ensure that the matched measures are sensible. Examples of such criteria are fairness, comparability, consistency, conservatism, and other concepts in Chapter 5, plus various detailed methods for determining how much revenue has been earned and how much expense has been incurred, which we will see.

FIGURE 6.3

The Four Cornerstones of Accrual Accounting

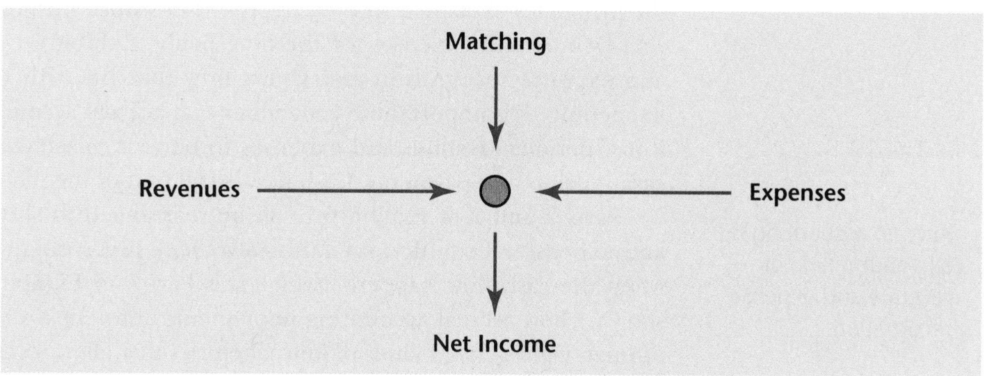

FYI

Revenue-expense matching gives income measurement priority over balance sheet valuation.

The discussion above indicates that matching is a central criterion in accrual accounting, used to get the income right by lining up the revenues and expenses properly. The balance sheet is a sort of residual of the matching process: you record whatever receivables, payables, amortization, etc., you need to get the income right, so the balance sheet figures are secondarily important to getting a valid income number. Matching's central place is increasingly challenged by people who argue that this is wrong. They have two primary arguments. One is that putting things on the balance sheet, or leaving them off, to get the income statement right is improper because financial statement users then may be misled by the balance sheet.

Using fair values for the balance sheet is gaining popularity, including for measuring income.

The second argument is that a *better way to measure income* is to measure changes in the fair values of the balance sheet assets and liabilities, and take the net of those changes as the income for the period. Comparing your assets and debts, if you are better off at the end of the period than at the beginning, you have made an income; if you're worse off, you've made a loss. You then focus on getting the balance sheet right, in fair values, and the income statement becomes the residual, the resultant of getting the balance sheet right. *Fair value accounting* is gaining popularity worldwide, and although it is not close to replacing the matching principle yet, there is some possibility it will win out some time in the future. It is used already in some areas of accounting, as we will see in later chapters.

Accrual accounting can handle matching or fair value accounting, or a mixture.

The accrual accounting model given below can accommodate either the matching principle or the fair value approach, or a mixture of the two: the difference is in how the numbers used in the various entries are calculated, with matching emphasizing the income statement side of entries, and fair value emphasizing the balance sheet side. In any case, the income statement and balance sheet must still articulate somehow.

A Conceptual System for Accrual Income Measurement

Accrual accounting includes cash flows plus both earlier and later economic phenomena.

Accrual accounting's purpose is to extend the measurement of financial performance and position by recognizing phenomena prior to and subsequent to cash flows, as well as at the point of cash flows, making accrual accounting more complete than just using transactions, especially just cash transactions. (In sophisticated companies, many of the routine noncash parts of accrual accounting, such as recognizing uncollected revenue as accounts receivable, are handled with transactional records, but those are still based on the principles explained in this chapter.) Let's work through how this is done, focusing on revenues and expenses for the time being. Exhibit 6.1 summarizes accrual revenue and expense recognition and shows how that fits with the cash flows that are also happening. It is important to remember that accrual accounting *does not ignore cash flows*; it just permits revenues and expenses to be recognized *earlier* or *later* than the related cash receipts and payments. Cash flow is still part of the picture.

Accrual accounting is all about *timing* of revenue and expense recognition.

Parts 2 and 3 of Exhibit 6.1 can be rearranged to show the four possible revenue and expense recognition scenarios *other than* just recognizing revenues and expenses when the cash flow happens (which was Part 1 of Exhibit 6.1). Exhibit 6.2 does this, showing how accrual accounting implements different *timing* than that of the cash flows through eight general kinds of journal entries that allow revenue and expense recognition

Summary of Accrual Accounting Revenue and Expense Recognition

	Revenues	Expenses
(1) Start with cash transactions	DR Cash CR Revenues	DR Expenses CR Cash
(2) Stretch the time out so that revenues and expenses are recognized *before* the cash transactions		
(a) Recognition	DR Accounts receivable CR Revenues	DR Expenses CR Accounts payable#
(b) Cash transactions	DR Cash CR Accounts receivable	DR Accounts payable# CR Cash

Note that the sums of entries 2(a) and 2(b) equal the entries in (1). The accounts receivable and payable accounts are temporary accounts used to allow earlier recognition of revenues and expenses and are eliminated when the cash flows.

	Revenues	Expenses
(3) Stretch the time out the other way so that revenues and expenses are recognized after the cash transactions		
(a) Cash transactions	DR Cash CR Deferred revenue**	DR Assets* CR Cash
(b) Recognition	DR Deferred revenue** CR Revenues	DR Expenses CR Assets*

Note that the sums of entries 3(a) and 3(b) equal the entries in (1). The assets* and deferred revenue** accounts are temporary accounts used to allow later recognition of revenues and expenses and are eliminated by that recognition.

Other liabilities than accounts payable may be involved, such as accrued interest, income tax payable, warranty liability, pension liability, and deferred income tax.

* Example asset accounts that might be debited at the cash transaction stage include inventories, prepaid insurance, and factory. These are eliminated (over time) by entries that credit such accounts and debit cost of goods sold, insurance expense, and amortization expense.

** Deferred revenue is a temporary liability account used to record cash received before the revenue has been earned, such as with customer deposits.

to happen before or after the cash transactions. In this exhibit, the "current accounting period" is the one in which the accounting is now being done—the "past" period has already finished and the "next" period has not started. "Period" can be any period over which income is being measured: a year, a quarter, a month, or whatever. The arrows indicate accounts used to allow the revenue or expense recognition to diverge from the cash flow. As noted in Exhibit 6.1, these accounts are temporary in concept, and eventually are eliminated by later cash flow or later recognition.

EXHIBIT 6·2

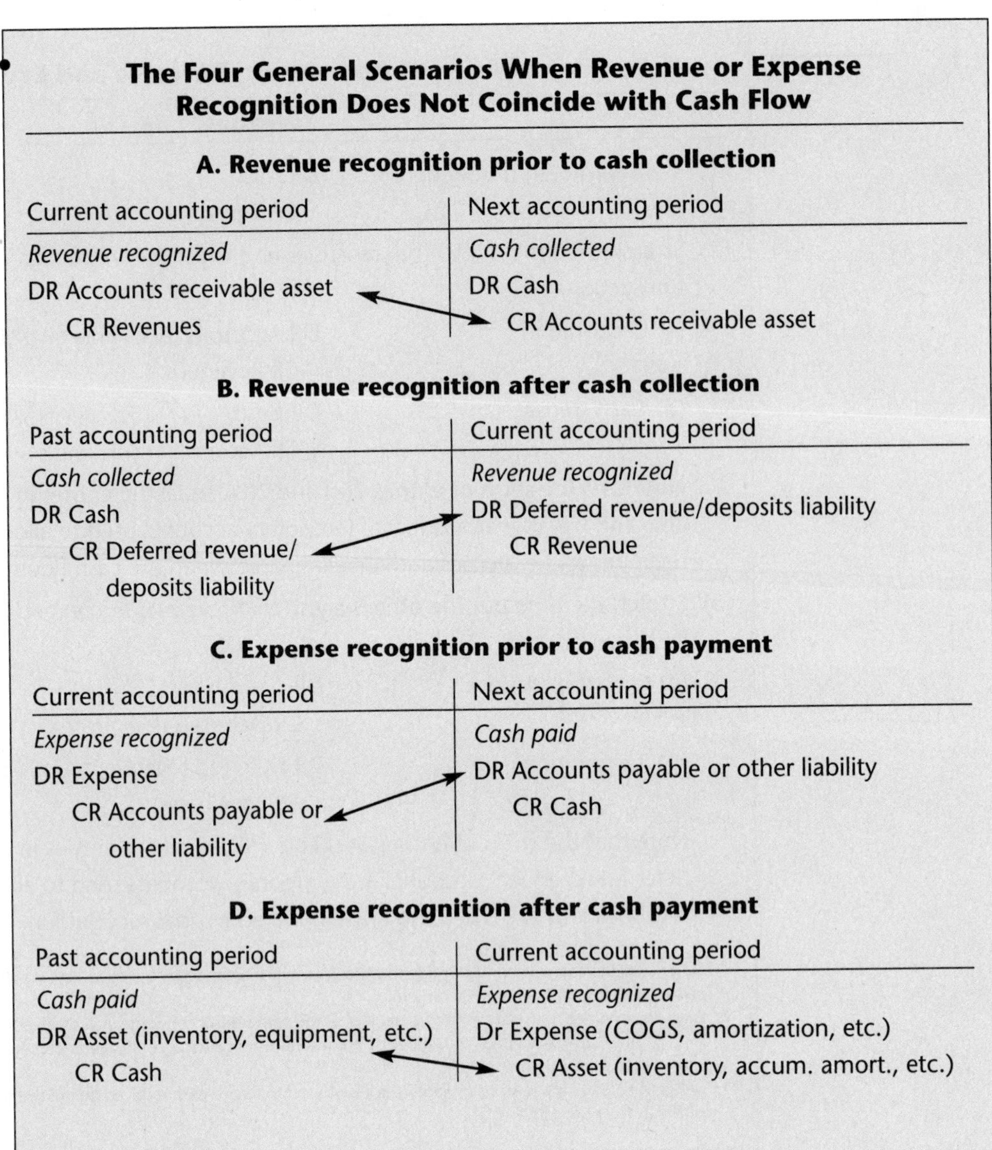

The Four General Scenarios When Revenue or Expense Recognition Does Not Coincide with Cash Flow

A. Revenue recognition prior to cash collection

Current accounting period	Next accounting period
Revenue recognized	*Cash collected*
DR Accounts receivable asset	DR Cash
CR Revenues	CR Accounts receivable asset

B. Revenue recognition after cash collection

Past accounting period	Current accounting period
Cash collected	*Revenue recognized*
DR Cash	DR Deferred revenue/deposits liability
CR Deferred revenue/ deposits liability	CR Revenue

C. Expense recognition prior to cash payment

Current accounting period	Next accounting period
Expense recognized	*Cash paid*
DR Expense	DR Accounts payable or other liability
CR Accounts payable or other liability	CR Cash

D. Expense recognition after cash payment

Past accounting period	Current accounting period
Cash paid	*Expense recognized*
DR Asset (inventory, equipment, etc.)	Dr Expense (COGS, amortization, etc.)
CR Cash	CR Asset (inventory, accum. amort., etc.)

Accrual accounting separates recognition from cash flow, incorporating both in a logical *system* of entries.

Accrual accounting reflects practical complexity as well as its conceptual base.

Following in Exhibit 6.3 are some examples to help you see how the accrual accounting system works. We'll use types of entries you've already seen in earlier chapters. The example entries involve manufacturer Northern Gear Ltd. Now you should be able to see how the records and adjustments you already know how to do aggregate into an overall structure that makes accrual accounting a *system.*

As you know, Canada has a system of GST and provincial sales taxes in most provinces. To make the examples in Exhibit 6.3 more realistic, some such taxes are also included in the example entries; the basic idea is that when tax is charged to customers, it has to be paid to the government and so is a liability, and when tax is incurred on the company's purchases, it can be claimed back from the government and so reduces the liability. Companies also must deduct income taxes and other deductions from employees' pay, so the examples include that too. Don't get hung up on them now. In Chapter 7, more time will be devoted to how these practical tax considerations work. They are included to illustrate that accrual accounting adapts to whatever the business and legal requirements are, and so can become quite complex. Some modern accounting procedures are very complex indeed. *But the conceptual structure in Exhibits 6.1 and 6.2 underlies whatever complex procedures an enterprise uses.*

Recognition prior to cash flow			
Revenue			
Northern Gear made a sale on credit	DR Accounts receivable	2,464	
	CR Revenue		2,200
	CR Sales taxes due		264
Expense			
Employees worked for wages paid later	DR Wages expense	1,860	
	CR Deductions due		340
	CR Wages payable		1,520
Interest was due on a bank loan	DR Interest expense	240	
	CR Interest payable		240
Legal advice was obtained, plus GST	DR Legal advice expense	500	
	DR Sales taxes due	35	
	CR Accounts payable		535
Cash flows related to prior recognition			
Collection			
A customer made a payment on account	DR Cash	1,100	
	CR Accounts receivable		1,100
Payment			
The company paid a supplier	DR Accounts payable	775	
	CR Cash		775
The company remitted employee deductions	DR Deductions due	825	
	CR Cash		825
Cash revenues and expenses			
Cash revenue			
A customer made a minor purchase	DR Cash	90	
	CR Sales taxes due		10
	CR Revenue		80
Cash expense			
Northern Gear made a donation to charity	DR Donations expense	100	
	CR Cash		100
The company bought supplies, plus GST	DR Supplies expense	210	
	DR Sales taxes due	15	
	CR Cash		225
Cash flows related to later recognition			
Collection			
A customer paid for an order in advance	DR Cash	784	
	CR Deferred revenue		784
Payment			
Northern Gear bought new machinery	DR Machinery asset	5,200	
	CR Cash		5,200
The company bought inventory, plus GST	DR Inventory asset	2,300	
	DR Sales taxes due	161	
	CR Cash		2,461
The company paid for insurance in advance	DR Prepaid insurance asset	840	
	CR Cash		840

Exhibit 6.3 continues on next page

EXHIBIT 6·3 (continued)

Recognition after cash flow

Revenue			
The customer's prepaid order was shipped	DR Deferred revenue	784	
	CR Sales taxes due		84
	CR Revenue		700
Expense			
Cost of goods sold on a week's sales	DR COGS expense	23,611	
	CR Inventory asset		23,611
Amortization for a year	DR Amort. expense	41,500	
	CR Accum. amort.		41,500
Insurance used during a month	DR Insurance expense	70	
	CR Prepaid insurance		70

Accrual accounting is a flexible system that can handle many phenomena.

These entries don't cover quite everything accrual accounting can do, and you might be able to think of events that combine some of the above entries. An example is buying inventory on credit. That is a debit to Inventory and a credit not to Cash, but to Accounts payable. This entry allows both recognition of the expense later *and* payment of the cash later. Buying machinery or other noncurrent assets on credit would work the same way. Accrual accounting is quite flexible and can handle all sorts of events and adjustments. All you need to do is figure out what to debit and what to credit.

Does accrual accounting matter? Here are some comments about research results: "Accrual accounting can be viewed as one potentially cost-effective compromise between merely reporting cash flows and a more ambitious system of fuller disclosure."[1] ("Fuller disclosure" might include reporting all the company's transactions and other events and just letting the user of the information construct his/her own version of income, assets, etc., in whatever way that person thinks appropriate. You can think of accounting principles as decisions on behalf of presumed users of what they would like to know, so there is always, at least conceptually, the possibility of not making such a decision and just reporting everything.) "There is a significant, positive correlation between (share) price changes and earnings changes."[2] "Price changes appear to be more highly correlated with earnings changes than with changes in 'cash flow'."[3] "The research provides clear evidence that investors and creditors can use accounting information to predict many phenomena of interest."[4] (So the principles, entries, and other efforts by accountants do make a difference. A good thing for accountants!)

HOW'S YOUR UNDERSTANDING?

Here are two questions you should be able to answer based on what you have just read. If you can't answer them, it would be best to reread the material.

1. How do accrual accounting entries work to separate the earning of revenue from the receipt of cash, and is it always necessary to separate them, or can they happen at the same time?
2. In what way can it be said that amortization expense and cost of goods sold expense are examples of the same thing?

6.4 Accounting Policy Choices

There are complications, but we have seen that the general pattern behind accrual accounting's revenue and expense recognition system is:

- *Recognition of revenue prior to cash collection:* Create an asset, usually called accounts receivable, to hold the economic value gained through the revenue until the cash is collected.
- *Recognition of revenue after cash collection:* Create a liability, usually called customer deposits or deferred revenue, to hold the cash value until the revenue has been earned.
- *Recognition of expense prior to cash payment:* Create a liability account, such as accounts payable, wages payable, pension liability, or future income tax liability, to hold the economic value lost through the expense until the cash is paid.
- *Recognition of expense after cash payment:* Create an asset account, such as inventory or buildings and equipment, to hold the economic value until it is consumed, when it is then transferred to an expense such as cost of goods sold or amortization expense.

Accrual accounting uses a variety of accounts to represent noncash economic values.

Since accrual accounting is a system, decisions about when and how to record the various recognition and other entries described above and in the previous section should not be made in an unorganized way. Instead, the enterprise should make *accounting policy choices* about how its accrual accounting is to be conducted.

What Is an Accounting Policy?

Management needs to provide direction about how the accounting is to be done.

Imagine the following scenario: the bookkeeper for MegaMega Stores Inc. has to decide whether or not each sales invoice should be recorded as revenue (credit revenue, debit cash, or accounts receivable) and so, each time, phones the president and asks whether that invoice should be recorded. Pretty silly, eh? What the company needs to do is decide, *in advance and in general*, what sort of transaction constitutes a sale that is to be recorded as revenue. Then this decision can be communicated to the bookkeeper, who can apply the criteria to each invoice and so decide what to record without phoning the president. The president can run the company instead of talking to the bookkeeper every few minutes.

An accounting policy is a decision made in advance about how, when, and whether to record or recognize something. Typically, companies make policy choices in many areas. The following are only a few examples:

- when and how to recognize revenue
- how to compute amortization on plant and equipment assets
- how to value inventories and calculate cost of goods sold
- how to value receivables, including how to estimate the effects of bad debts
- which expenditures on noncurrent assets should be added to the asset accounts and which should be included with expenses such as repairs and maintenance

Accounting policies apply to everything in the financial statements.

Many choices are needed in assembling meaningful financial statements. When you choose the location of an account in the financial statements (such as putting it in current liabilities rather than noncurrent liabilities), you are making an accounting policy choice!

Accounting policy choices are very important to the interpretation and analysis of the financial statements. Without knowing how the statements were assembled, it is difficult to use them intelligently. For this reason, the first of the notes following the financial statements is usually a summary of the company's *significant accounting policies.* These are the topics covered in CPR's year 2004 "Summary of significant accounting policies note:[5]

- Consolidation method
- List of principal subsidiaries
- How revenue is recognized
- What are cash and short-term investments
- How foreign currencies are translated
- Accounting for pensions, other benefits
- What is in inventories
- What kinds of property are owned
- How property is depreciated
- Accounting for financial instruments
- Accounting for restructuring charges
- Accounting for income taxes
- Calculation of earnings per share
- Accounting for stock options

In an immediately following note, CPR also describes *changes* in the company's accounting policies for hedging transactions, legal obligations arising from asset retirement, stock-based compensation, guarantees that require payment contingent on specified types of future events, impairment of the value of long-lived assets, and the cost of severance and termination benefits.[6] The company stated that all these changes were made to comply with changes in the CICA accounting guidelines. Details of the effect of the changes on the financial statements are also provided.

Other notes to CPR's statements provide further details on important policies. Companies do not overwhelm the reader with descriptions about every accounting policy: those that are obvious or that follow standard rules that an informed reader (you're becoming one!) should know about are usually not described. For example, the definitions of current assets and current liabilities are well known and would be mentioned only if something unusual was being done.

Why Is There a Choice?

Accrual accounting requires that accounting policy choices be made.

Accrual accounting forces the preparers of financial statements to make choices, whether they like it or not.

1. The basis of accrual accounting is to augment the transactional records to produce a more complete economic picture of the enterprise's performance and position. How to do this is a matter of judgment and of criteria such as fairness and matching. Accrual accounting therefore *necessitates* choices about accounting figures, notes, and methods.
2. Even the basic transactional records of accounting require decisions about what is a transaction, which accounts to use, and how and when transactions are to be recorded.
3. In Canada, the United States, Britain, Australia, New Zealand, and many other countries, governments and professional accounting standard-setters (such as the CICA and the FASB) have been reluctant to try to specify all solutions and require all enterprises to follow them. Such authorities appear to believe that choices in accounting are appropriate to fit the accounting to each enterprise's circumstances, and perhaps inevitable in our free enterprise economic system. Stock market participants, financial analysts, and others who rely on financial statements are expected to attain sufficient knowledge of accounting and the enterprise to make informed decisions, just as they would when buying the enterprise's products or having other interactions with the enterprise.

Why Is There a Choice Among Accounting Policies?

1. Accrual accounting makes it necessary.
2. Even recording transactions requires policies.
3. Accounting standards do not specify all possible solutions.
4. Format and disclosure also involve choices and policies.

Not all countries give as much policy choice to companies as Canada does.

Authorities in many countries (such as China, France, Germany, and Japan) specify accounting methods more strictly than in Canada. In such countries, the material covered in this chapter would put more emphasis on how to implement the approved accounting methods and less on how to choose among a variety of acceptable methods.

Recording something in the accounts, having a narrative disclosure, or both, is a choice.

4. Because the complete financial statements include the titles and classifications of figures and the footnotes and other narrative disclosures, there is frequently a decision to be made as to whether to adjust the figures for something or to disclose it in the narrative material instead, or give it a special title, or even all of these. For example, if the company has been sued by a disgruntled customer, should that be recorded as a liability? If recorded, should it be listed separately in the balance sheet? Should it instead just be disclosed in the notes, or perhaps in a note even if it is recorded?

General Criteria for Accounting Policy Choices

When deciding how to account for revenues, inventories, amortization, and other matters (*including* what to say in footnote disclosures), companies have to consider the following kinds of criteria and work out how they apply to the specific policy choice situation. These criteria were examined in depth in Sections 5.2 and 5.3.

The principles in Chapter 5 are essential to making accounting policy choices.

1. *Fairness* (objectivity, lack of bias, correspondence with economic substance).
2. *Matching* (fitting revenue recognition to the economic process, fitting expense recognition to the economic process and to the revenue).
3. *Consistency* over time.
4. *Comparability* to other companies (especially in the same industry).
5. Conformance with *authoritative standards*, and less formal aspects of *GAAP*.
6. *Materiality* to (significance to decisions of) known or presumed users of the information.
7. *Conservatism* (taking anticipated losses into account before the transaction happens, but not taking anticipated gains into account until the transaction happens).

In addition, various criteria specific to the particular accounting policy choice issue must be considered. Examples are the cost of implementing the policy, tax effects, internal control considerations, and other business implications and consequences. These criteria will be indicated as topics are covered in this and later chapters.

How Much Freedom of Choice Is There?

Accounting policy choices are constrained by authoritative standards and broader GAAP.

Accounting policy choices are made within the standards set out by the *CICA Handbook*, the FASB, and other standard-setters and regulators as described in Chapter 5. While companies ordinarily do not *have* to follow these standards, or the less-formal parts of GAAP, they can get into considerable trouble if they do not. Stock markets may refuse to list their shares. Taxation authorities may refuse to accept their financial statements as evidence of income for tax purposes. Shareholders and creditors may sue for alleged misrepresentation. Embarrassing newspaper articles may be written about them. So many policy choices are highly constrained, and are expected to be made with reference to standard criteria. There are some areas of accounting that are new or controversial enough that there is no or little guidance from standard-setters, and then the company is a little more free to make its own policy decisions.

Even when there is an authoritative standard or a clear tradition, the necessity of fitting the accounting policy to the particular circumstances of the enterprise necessitates, in turn, the exercise of professional judgment by the preparers and auditors of the information. As the *CICA Handbook*'s Introduction to Accounting Standards says:

Standards cannot cover everything, so people still have to use their heads.

"Accounting Handbook Sections emphasize principles rather than detailed rules and, therefore, cannot be phrased to suit all circumstances or combinations of circumstances that may arise."[7]

Does accounting policy choice provide a way for company management to alter the picture presented in the financial statements—to present the story they want to tell rather than the "truth"? The short answer is yes. The whole idea of accrual accounting is to permit a company to choose how its performance and position are to be depicted. There is a fine line between choosing the accounting policies that suit the company's circumstances and therefore produce fair reporting, and choosing policies that tell a desired story that may not be fair. *The vast majority of companies and their managers are scrupulous about their accounting* and consider producing fair financial statements to be both ethical and good business practice. But we do learn of companies that have stepped over the line and "doctored" their accounts to make themselves look better or to hide some embarrassing result. The following shows some types of doctoring:

- What accountants and the business press often call *aggressive accounting*: seeking out accounting methods and policy choices that serve management's objectives for growth, financing, bonuses, or other purposes that seem to violate fairness or conservatism.
- The examples of income manipulation in Chapter 3, Section 3.10: *earnings management*, the *Big Bath* and *income smoothing*.
- The recent high-profile examples of following accounting standards in a way that confuses more than informs—a contributing factor to Enron's downfall was strong negative stock market reaction to perceived self-serving accounting policy choices.

Manipulation dangers can be overrated. Few managers are crooked in their accounting; most are honest and anxious that their accounting be fair and truthful. Most believe that good financial reporting is important to the company's reputation and ability to borrow, raise share capital, and generally do business. Most consider good financial reporting to be part of good business and professional ethics. However, the danger of manipulation is always there, so accountants, auditors, and users who rely on financial statements for their decisions must be vigilant.

A Few Technical Points

Accounting policy choices generally do not affect cash and cash flow.

1. *Cash flow.* Generally, accounting policy choice does not affect cash flow. Policy choices are made by accrual accounting entries, which are intended to go beyond cash and so seldom affect cash directly. There may be indirect or eventual effects, especially through income tax. But, at the instant an accounting policy choice is implemented, there is no cash or cash flow effect except in the rare case where a cash account is involved. The cash flow statement is useful partly because its analysis helps to identify accounting policy choices that may have taken the income a little too far from cash flow.

Accounting policy choices that affect income must also affect the balance sheet.

2. *Dual effects of changes.* Because the financial statements are fundamentally connected through double-entry accounting, most accounting policy changes affect both the balance sheet and the income statement. *They must affect both if they are to affect net income.* This is financial statement *articulation*. Here are some examples:

Balance Sheet Accounts		Main Income Statement Accounts
Temporary investments	⟷	Nonoperating revenue or expense
Accounts receivable	⟷	Revenue, bad debts expense
Inventories	⟷	Cost of goods sold expense
Prepaid and accrued expenses	⟷	Various expense accounts
Property and plant assets	⟷	Amortization expense
Intangible and leased assets	⟷	Amortization expense
Liabilities	⟷	Various expense accounts
Equity	⟷	None*

* Transactions with owners, such as share capital issues and redemptions and dividends, are ordinarily not considered part of the measurement of income. However, there are some technicalities in which this may be violated—this book will not cover such technicalities.

Classification and disclosure choices are part of accounting policy choice.

3. *Classification and disclosure.* There are accounting policy choices in three areas, besides the example of Equity accounts above, that are important even though they do not directly affect the current period's income:
   - *Classification* policies (decisions about where within the balance sheet or where within the income statement to show accounts) do not affect income because they do not involve both the balance sheet and income statement, as do *recognition* policies, but instead affect only one statement or the other.
   - *Disclosure* policies relate to what is said about the figures in the words used in the statements and in the notes to the statements.
   - *Changes* in accounting policies are also disclosed, including a description of the change and a calculation of the effect the change has had on the financial statements. Many changes have to be given retroactive effect; for example, if the revenue recognition method is changed, past years' financial statements have to be recalculated to show them on the new basis. Therefore, if a company has changed its accounting policy in some area, the *prior years'* figures in this year's annual report may not be the same as the ones you would have seen in last year's annual report.

HOW'S YOUR UNDERSTANDING?

Here are two questions you should be able to answer based on what you have just read. If you can't answer them, it would be best to reread the material.

1. Sue Wong, an experienced investor, reacted in frustration on having difficulty comparing the financial statements of two companies she was considering investing in, because the companies had made different choices about accounting for some items. Why do enterprises make choices, and why might they be different choices?
2. The president of Burning Issues Ltd., a political polling firm, is concerned about how to account for large expenditures on developing mailing and phone lists. The question is whether these expenditures should be included in the assets of the firm or deducted as expenses. What criteria should the president use in deciding how to account for the expenditures?

6.5 The Fiscal Period

Measuring financial performance and position requires defined fiscal periods.

Financial statements all have a time dimension. Balance sheets are prepared as at specific points in time, and the other three statements cover specified periods of time. Business and other economic activities go on continuously, so if the financial statements are to be at or begin and end at particular dates, financial accounting must somehow find a way to separate all those activities into *fiscal periods*. Accrual accounting is the method, because it is designed to incorporate economic phenomena that happen before or after the cash transactions. *You could say that without the need for periodic reporting for fiscal periods, accrual accounting would be unnecessary.* But how does accrual accounting separate the records and adjustments into periods?

Here's an example of the problem. Quantum Inc. earns its revenue through a series of projects, done one at a time. Cash receipts for revenues happen once or twice during each project, and cash payments for expenses happen about a month after expenses are incurred.

Accrual accounting must cut continuous business activities into fiscal periods.

To calculate net income for, say, 2006 using accrual accounting, we can use the various categories of entries set out in Section 6.3. We can recognize revenues and expenses before or after cash inflows and outflows. But how much of these apply to 2006 rather than to other years? We need to find a way to "*cut off*" the accounting records of what are continuous activities, so that 2006 can be separated from 2005 and 2007. The 2006 net income is a measure of the economic value added by the projects *during that year*. By the *matching* criterion, that measure is produced by calculating the increase in resources (revenues) minus the decrease in resources (expenses), determined using comparable methods so that their difference is a meaningful income figure.

Exhibit 6.4 and Figure 6.4 show Quantum's projects affecting 2006:

EXHIBIT 6·4

	Receipts	Payments
Project #39		
Work began on the project		Nov. 05
Some cash received from the customer	Dec. 05	
Disbursements for expenses began		Dec. 05
Work completed on the project		Feb. 06
Disbursements for expenses ended		Mar. 06
Remaining cash received from the customer	Apr. 06	
Project #40		
Work began on the project		Mar. 06
Disbursements for expenses began		Apr. 06
All cash received from the customer	Sep. 06	
Work completed on the project		Oct. 06
Disbursements for expenses ended		Nov. 06
Project #41		
Some cash received from the customer	Nov. 06	
Work began on the project		Nov. 06
Disbursements for expenses began		Dec. 06
Work completed on the project		Mar. 07
Disbursements for expenses ended		Apr. 07
Remaining cash received from the customer	Apr. 07	

FIGURE 6.4

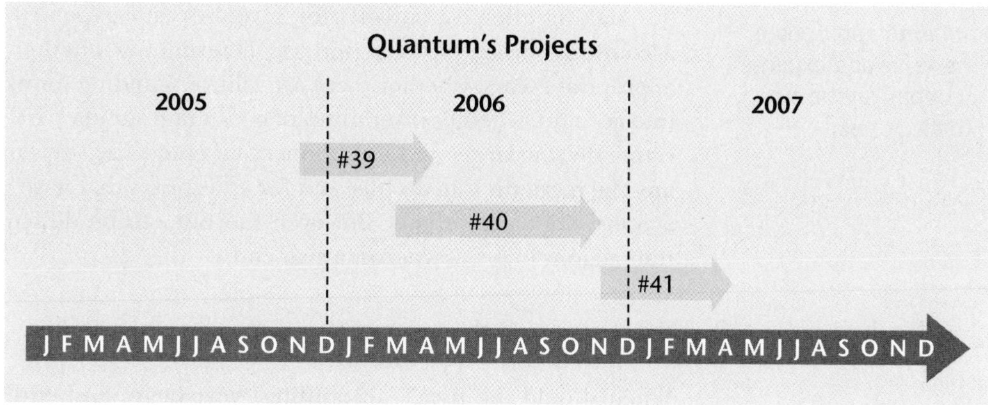

Let's try to do this project by project.

- Project 40 is easiest. The project began and ended in 2006. All the receipts and payments happened in 2006, and all the revenue was earned (and collected) and expenses were incurred (and paid) in 2006. The cash basis works fine here because there is no "cut off" needed between 2006 and any other year.

Income measurement requires that revenues and expenses be cut off in appropriate and matching ways.

- Project 39 is more awkward. There were two cash inflows, Dec. 2005 and Apr. 2006. The project was completed in 2006, so there is no problem at the end of 2006. The accounting problem arises at the beginning of 2006, in the transition from 2005. For the project revenues, the accounting depends on whether the cash inflows to the end of Dec. 2005 coincided with the revenue earned to that point:
  a. If the Dec. 2005 inflow was less than the amount of revenue earned by the end of the year, then there should be a Dec. 31, 2005, *account receivable* created for the rest of the revenue earned but not collected.
  b. If the Dec. 2005 inflow was *greater* than the amount of revenue earned by the end of the year, then there should be a Dec. 31, 2005, *deferred revenue liability* created for the unearned portion.
  c. If the Dec. 2005 inflow equalled the amount of revenue earned by the end of the year, then there is no problem: cash and accrual accounting coincide.

  For the Project 39 expenses, there are two problems.
  1. The expenses incurred in December would not be paid until January, so a Dec. 31, 2005, account payable should be created for those.
  2. The amount of expenses recognized in 2005 should match the revenue recognized for 2005, so that the revenue-expense difference, net income, is meaningful.
- Project 41 has the same sort of awkwardness as Project 39, except that since it extends into 2007, it has to be cut off properly at the end of 2006, in the transition to 2007.

Allocation of revenues and expenses to a period affects other periods too.

- So 2006 revenues, expenses, and resulting net income will be a combination of the part of Project 39's revenues and expenses *not* recognized in 2005, all of Project 40's revenues and expenses, and the part of Project 41's revenues and expenses recognized in 2006. You can see that *both* the cut off at the end of 2005 and the one at the end of 2006 have to be appropriate if the 2006 revenues, expenses, and net income are to be fair. Because of this, the 2006 results involve estimates on Projects 39 and 41 that also affect the fairness of the results for 2005 and 2007. The revenues and expenses for those projects have to be properly *allocated* among the years they involve, and the results for all those years will be affected by the quality of the allocations. Lots of work for accountants!

Making appropriate revenue and expense cut offs can be a difficult task.

Making effective cut offs for revenues and expenses is a major task for accrual accounting. Much effort is put into determining whether revenues are placed in the appropriate years, whether there are bills outstanding for expenses that should be taken into account, whether inventories of goods and supplies are actually on hand, and so on. Generally, the larger and less frequent an enterprise's revenue and expense transactions are, the harder it is to do this, and for enterprises that have many short and simple transactions, the easier it gets. But even there it can be difficult if there are thousands of transactions in process across a year-end.

Choice of Fiscal Period

Most companies have a December 31 fiscal year-end, but many other dates are used too.

When should the fiscal (accounting) year begin and end? Companies have an initial choice, but once they make it, reasons of habit and legal and tax rules usually force them to stay with that choice indefinitely. They may select a fiscal year-end that is a relatively quiet time, so that there aren't many unfinished transactions in process and the revenue and expense cut offs can be made more cleanly. However, in practice, most companies select December 31 as their fiscal year-end.

In Chapters 6–9 of this book, frequent references will be made to statistics about Canadian companies included in *Financial Reporting in Canada 2005*, the 30th edition of a survey of company annual reports published by CICA. The sample of 200 companies is taken from the Toronto Stock Exchange, and it changes every edition as companies start up, merge, and go out of business. The publication includes not only statistics, but also many examples of how these companies did their accounting and wrote their footnote disclosures. For example, the samples of 200 companies included 126 December 31 year-ends in 2001, 124 in 2002 and 133 in 2003 and 2004. The popularity of December 31 declined slightly in the companies sampled.[8]

Every other month-end was represented in the sample, and sometimes a date other than a month-end was used (such as 52 or 53 week fiscal periods). Though history, tradition, and income tax reasons make December 31 the majority choice, the minority, still a substantial number, choosing other fiscal periods has many reasons for other dates, including a better fit with the company's "natural" business year (some food companies choose dates just before or after the harvest season, and some retailers prefer dates other than December 31 because they like to avoid the hectic Christmas season), but choosing other dates may just be traditional too. "Regardless of the reasons for odd fiscal years, this much is certain for many firms. The business calendar quickly becomes engraved in stone. Procter & Gamble, for example, closes its books at the end of June. No one remembers why. Is a change likely? Not on your life."[9]

HOW'S YOUR UNDERSTANDING?

Here are two questions you should be able to answer based on what you have just read. If you can't answer them, it would be best to reread the material.

1. Why is the fiscal period an important issue in financial accounting?
2. Sheaf Farm Products Ltd. is considering changing its accounting policy for revenue recognition, to match the revenue better to expenses. It is now 2006. The policy being considered would increase revenue in 2006 by $53,200. Accounts receivable at the end of 2005 would increase by $38,900 and at the end of 2006 would increase by $92,100, the difference being the $53,200 revenue effect in 2006. If the policy change were made, how much revenue would be moved from 2006 to 2005, and how much from 2007 to 2006?

Revenue changes: $38,900 moved from 2006 to 2005; $92,100 moved from 2007 to 2006.

6.6 Revenue Recognition

Accuracy Versus Decision Relevance

Income for the life of the enterprise can be determined from cash flows, without accruals.

Income over the life of an enterprise is based on cash flows. At the end of the enterprise's life, all expenses have resulted in cash outflows and all the revenue earned has resulted in cash inflows. There is no need for accrual accounting, or for estimates of any kind; the results are known with certainty. Income over the life of the enterprise is simply the sum of the cash on hand at the end plus any cash withdrawn by the owners over the enterprise's life (such as dividends), minus any cash contributed by the owners over that time (such as share capital).

Decision making cannot wait until the firm's life ends, so we have accrual accounting.

Decision makers want information about performance earlier than at the end of the enterprise's life. It is difficult, though, to cut the essentially continuous operations of a company into discrete time periods. Income determined before the end of the company's life, so that it is relevant for evaluating the enterprise's performance over shorter decision periods, is unavoidably subject to estimates and judgments because the whole story is never known until the end.

This takes us back to the ever-present tradeoff between reliability and relevance in income measurement, illustrated in Section 5.3 as relevance versus reliability of estimates, and mentioned in Section 6.2 also. If revenues and expenses are recognized earlier, so that they are more relevant for decision making, then they will not be as reliable (accurately measured) as they would be if recognition were delayed until later, when outcomes of the various economic activities are better known. Because the tradeoff is very important to accrual accounting, Figure 6.5 illustrates it again, now relating it to *when* phenomena are recognized in the accounts.

Critical Event Simplification

If we are to describe the firm's operations for a given period by calculating the income for that period, we must define a means by which to measure the amount of income that can be attributed to that period. We accomplish this by

- defining how much revenue can be *recognized* in that period; and, then
- *matching* to that revenue the expenses which were incurred to generate the revenue.

FIGURE 6.5

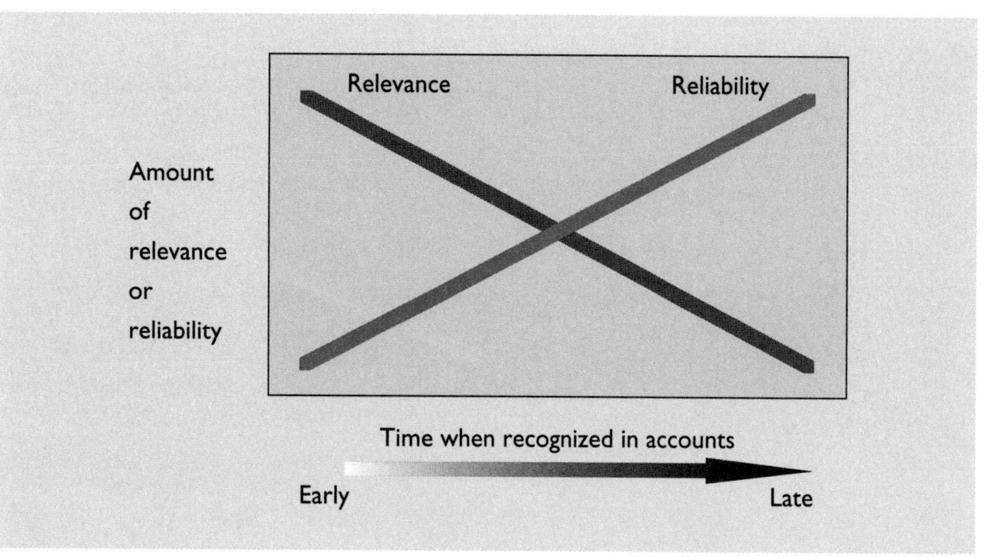

Income is the result of revenue recognition matched by expense recognition.

Income, the value added by the activities of the firm, is just the *difference* between the recognized revenue and the recognized expenses. Revenue recognition is important because, by the matching criterion, expense recognition and therefore income measurement should correspond with the revenue. This can get rather messy in practice, as you might imagine. For example, some expenses, often called *period expenses*, are only indirectly related to revenue, being incurred as time passes (interest is an example). Others, often called *discretionary expenses*, arise more haphazardly or as other business decisions are made by management (such as donations, research and development, or maintenance). But for simplicity, let's assume that revenue recognition is the primary driver of income measurement.

What are the revenues, or the expenses, for a period? From an economic and business point of view, income is earned by a wide variety of actions taken by the enterprise. There is a whole sequence of activities intended to help generate income, which therefore generate revenue and incur expenses, including, for example:

1 Organizing the firm in the first place
2. Building the factory
3. Buying or making inventory
4. Advertising
5. Selling
6. Delivering to a customer
7. Billing
8. Collecting cash
9. Providing warranty service

How should we recognize revenue when there is such a series of activities as those listed above? Recognizing it a bit at a time as each activity is carried out would approximate the economic process underlying the business. This would be relevant, all right, but by the same token it would be very subjective and imprecise, because it is difficult to say what each activity actually adds. How do you tell, when the company is just being organized, what revenue that form of organization will help to generate, for example? It would also be expensive to implement, with armies of accountants scurrying about measuring the small value change generated by each of the various activities and writing masses of journal entries to recognize each value change. The upward-sloping solid line in Figure 6.6 illustrates the presumed increase in value generated by the sorts of activities listed above.

FIGURE 6.6

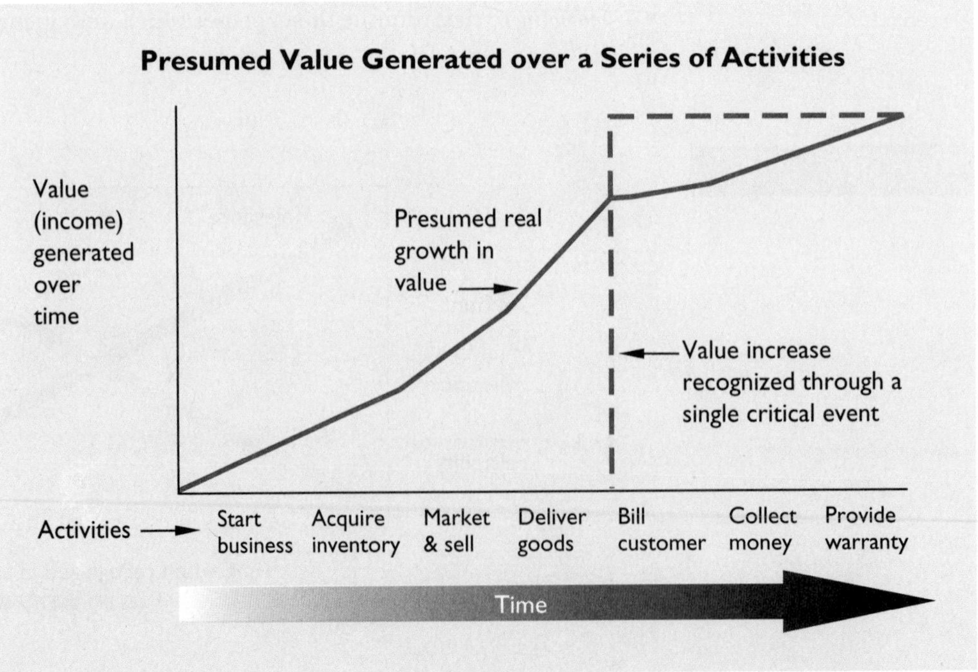

Recognizing revenue at a single critical event is practical, but theoretically awkward.

Instead, for greater objectivity and verifiability and less accounting cost, accountants usually choose *one* activity in the sequence of value-producing activities above as the *critical event* in the revenue generation sequence that can be readily documented, and recognize all of the revenue at that point. This is a simplification, because clearly some revenue could have been recognized when earlier activities were carried out, and probably some should be recognized when later activities take place. In theory, revenue is under-recognized prior to that point and over-recognized after it. Figure 6.6 also illustrates this. The critical event is designated by the vertical dotted line at the end of the delivery activity. Income earned prior to this event is not recognized by the accounting system, so the value produced by the activities to the left of it is not recognized until, all at once, 100% of the value is recognized. Until the rest of the activities are completed, the result (to the right of the dotted line) is over-recognition of the value because there are still things to be done. Using the critical event simplification is an accounting policy choice, a fairly obvious and practical one made by most companies, but still a choice.

Delivery of goods or services is the most common critical event for recognizing revenue.

The most common critical event used is the point of completing delivery of the goods or services to the customer. To recognize the earning of revenue when that event has taken place, we make a *recognition* entry to record the asset (or liability reduction) obtained for the revenue:

DR Accounts receivable, or Cash, or Deferred revenue liability	XXXX	
CR Revenue		XXXX

For some companies, such as those building big projects like power stations or pipelines, or project-based companies such as Quantum Inc. in Section 6.5, it is worthwhile and fair to make a different accounting policy choice: to estimate revenue at several points along the sequence illustrated in Figure 6.6. That means chopping the amount of revenue up into pieces and recording *each* piece with an entry like the one above, instead of all at once. Later, we'll see examples of how to recognize revenue, and therefore income, in smaller steps that more closely fit the continuously increasing value. However, most companies use the practical simplification of the critical event.

Criteria for Revenue Recognition

Revenue Recognition Criteria

All four should be met:

1. Goods/services provided
2. Related costs known
3. Revenue measurable
4. Revenue receipt promised

Revenue recognition, then, is the usual first step in determining income for the period. The revenue recognition criteria discussed here have been formulated for the purpose of making sure that revenue will be recognized only when there is objective evidence that revenue has indeed been earned. This is an attempt to ensure that the result is reliable. The following four criteria must normally *all* be met in order that revenue may be recognized. For most enterprises, the activity nearest to fitting these criteria is chosen as the critical event, and for most of them that is delivery. However, as we'll see, there are exceptions (as usual!).

These four criteria must normally all be met before revenue is recognized.

1. All or substantially all of the goods or services to be provided to customers have been provided or performed (the "delivery" criterion mentioned above).
2. Most of the costs to generate the revenue have been incurred, and those remaining can be measured with reasonable accuracy.
3. The amount of the revenue can be reasonably measured in dollar terms (for example, if some customers are likely to return goods for a refund, such returns can be reasonably estimated).

4. Cash, a promise of cash (a receivable), or another asset that can be measured with reasonable precision has been received.

Although the above criteria seem fairly clear, there are still many judgments to be made about when the criteria are met. For instance, how should the "delivery" criterion be defined? Is it when 100% of the services have been performed? 90%? 80%? People must use their heads and exercise good judgment. In the vignette at the beginning of this chapter, the company was not following good practice, because it recognized revenue when an order was received, not waiting for delivery.

HOW'S YOUR UNDERSTANDING?

Here are two questions you should be able to answer based on what you have just read. If you can't answer them, it would be best to reread the material.

1. Why is the "critical event" a simplification and why is it used anyway?
2. Suppose Friendly Construction earned $1,000,000 revenue from a building contract, progressively, as follows: 10% when the contract was signed, 20% when the foundation was finished, 40% when the building exterior was finished, 20% when the interior was finished, and 10% after the owner had moved in and final adjustments and corrections were made. The company's expenses on the contract were $850,000, incurred according to the same progression as the revenue. If delivery were used as the critical event, how much revenue, expense, and net income would be recognized at that point, and how much would really have been earned/incurred then?

100% of revenue, expense, and income would be recognized: $1,000,000; $850,000; $150,000. Assuming delivery was when the owner moved in, only 90% of all the above would really have been earned/incurred: $900,000 revenue earned, $765,000 expenses incurred, $135,000 income earned. Using a single critical event would have understated income until that event and then overstated it after the event.

6.7 Revenue Recognition Methods

Look again at the journal entry to recognize revenue shown just above the revenue recognition criteria in Section 6.6. With this entry in mind, let's take a closer look at five commonly used methods of *revenue recognition.*

> **Revenue recognition:**
> DR Receivables, Cash or other balance sheet account,
> CR Revenue, on the income statement

1. At Delivery (Point of Sale or Shipment)

> Point of delivery usually meets the revenue recognition criteria given in Section 6.6.

For most retail, service, and manufacturing businesses, revenue is recognized when the product or service is sold. "Sold" is usually defined as being when the goods or services have been delivered, or at least shipped to the purchaser, when legal title passes to the purchaser. It's a single critical event.

- At that point substantially all of the service has been performed, terms and price have been set, and cash has either been received, or is reasonably certain to be received.
- Even though there is some risk involved in extending credit, this can usually be adequately estimated and adjusted for by creating an allowance for doubtful accounts receivable and a corresponding bad debts expense. More about this is in Chapter 7.
- Another risk at the point of sale is the possibility of returns and the likely service obligation under the warranties for the product or service sold. These can usually be

adequately estimated and recognized as an expense of the business and matched against the revenue of that period.

Delivery (point of sale) is so common a revenue recognition method that most companies do not mention in their financial statements that they are using it. You are expected to assume it is the one being used if you are not told otherwise. In accordance with this, you should be told if one of the other methods below is being used. CPR's year 2004 annual report has a revenue recognition policy note stating: "Railway freight revenues are recognized based on the percentage of completed service method. Other revenue is recognized as service is performed or contractual obligations are met."[10] (More about CPR's method is under heading 2 below.) Here are two other examples:

- From Canadian Tire's 2004 annual report: "The Corporation's shipments of merchandise to Associate Dealers (retail store owner-operators) are recorded as revenue when delivered. Revenue on the sale of petroleum products is recorded upon sale to the consumer."[11]
- From the Bombardier Inc. 2004–05 annual report: "Revenues from the sale of commercial aircraft and narrow-body business aircraft (Learjet) are recognized upon final delivery of products and presented in manufacturing revenues."[12]

2. During Production

Recognizing revenue only once for multi-period projects distorts income in all periods.

Sometimes the earnings process extends well beyond one fiscal period, as is the case in building construction, road building, shipbuilding, and other lengthy processes. In such situations, if a company waited until the point of delivery to recognize revenue, it might report no revenue for one or more years, and then, when the project was complete, would report all the revenue. This would distort the performance picture for the duration of the project: some years with no revenue, then one year with huge revenue, even though the company was working faithfully on the contract all along. The "How's Your Understanding?" item above illustrated this.

Recognizing revenue during production is fair if applied conservatively.

In the case of construction and similar operations, there are not likely many projects going on at once (few, anyway, in comparison to the number of hamburgers making up a burger bar's revenue), and these projects include enough documentation that the value added can usually be estimated and verified. Therefore, in an attempt to provide users with relevant information and reflect the economics of what is happening, revenue may be recognized during production. (With matching, this also means recognizing expenses and therefore income during production.) A typical description of this is from the 2004 annual report of Aecon Group Inc., Canada's largest public construction and infrastructure development company: "Revenue and income from fixed price construction contracts, including contracts in which the Company participates through joint ventures, are determined on the percentage of completion method, based on the ratio of costs incurred to date over estimated total costs."[13] We saw above that CPR uses the "percentage of completed services method" to recognize its main kind of revenues, railway freight revenues. This early-recognition approach is applied in a *conservative* way: if a project looks as if it will make money (project revenues greater than expenses), a portion of that income is recognized in the period in which the portion seems to have been earned, but if a project looks as if it will lose money (project revenues less than expenses), the whole anticipated loss is recognized right away.

Recognizing revenue during production requires a great deal of judgment.

Percentage of completion, mentioned by Aecon Group and CPR, is the most common method of recognizing revenue during production. This method entails determining what proportion of the project, or in CPR's case, promised freight shipments, has been completed during the year and recognizing that proportion of total expected revenue, expenses (costs), and, therefore, income, as was done in the "How's Your

Understanding?" item above. Often, this is done by measuring the proportion of expected total costs incurred during the period (Aecon Group's method). It may also be done by using physical estimates of completion, shipping records (for CPR), architects' estimates of project completion, and similar methods using evidence other than the proportion of total estimated costs spent so far. In order to recognize revenue using percentage of completion, the contract price (total revenue) must be reasonably certain, total costs must be reasonably determinable, and there must be reasonable assurance of payment. The frequent use of the word "reasonable" here shows that a lot of judgment is required in using this method!

Example of Percentage of Completion Method

Percentage of completion spreads revenues and income out over several fiscal periods.

Let's assume Greenway Construction had a large, three-year project with total revenue of \$4,000,000 and total costs of \$3,400,000. (Prior to expense recognition, project costs are charged to an inventory account for costs of construction in process. Like other inventories, this account holds costs until they are matched to revenues.) Total estimated income for the project over the three years was therefore \$600,000. The project was 20% completed at the end of the first year, 65% completed at the end of the second year, and 100% completed at the end of the third year. Ignoring complications that arise when revenues and costs do not work out as expected, Exhibit 6.5 shows journal entries to implement percentage of completion revenue (*and matched expense*) recognition during production. (All amounts are in thousands of dollars.)

EXHIBIT 6.5

	Year 1		Year 2		Year 3	
Percentage of contract done in the year	20%		45%		35%	
Revenue recognition:						
DR Accounts receivable	800		1,800		1,400	
CR Revenue		800		1,800		1,400
Percentage earned each year.						
Expense recognition:						
DR Cost of goods sold expense	680		1,530		1,190	
CR Construction in process inventory		680		1,530		1,190
Percentage matched to revenue.						
Resulting income each year	\$120		\$270		\$210	

You can see the *timing* effect of accrual accounting here. The annual entries have the effect of *spreading the \$600,000 project income out over the three years*: 20% to the first year, 45% to the second, 35% to the third.

3. Completion of Production

This method defers all revenue and income until the end of the process.

In the percentage of completion method, revenue is recognized as the work proceeds. But it is also possible to wait until the work is all done and recognize the revenue then. Waiting until the end is like the point-of-sale method, except if the work takes a long time, perhaps several accounting periods, then it is *very conservative* because no revenue would be recognized for a long time, then all of it at once. The distortion mentioned above would be implemented deliberately, because it is believed that no revenue or income can be said to be earned until everything is done, even if that takes a long time. It would be like not getting any grades for your years of courses until the last day of the last class, when you'd get all the grades at once and find out if your four years had been a success or a failure.

Example of Completion of Production Method

In the Greenway Construction example above, if revenue and the associated expenses were recognized on the completion of production, the project income would be:

- $0 in Year 1;
- $0 in Year 2; and
- $600,000 in Year 3.

This method differs greatly from the more economically appropriate percentage of completion method.

Compared to the percentage of completion method, income would be:

- $120,000 *lower* in Year 1;
- $270,000 *lower* in Year 2; and
- $390,000 *higher* in Year 3.

So if Greenway wanted to know "what if" it changed to the completion of production (or *completed contract*) method, there's the answer, ignoring income tax.

If there is no customer yet, even the completed contract method is likely inappropriate.

If there is no customer yet, but the production is done, is that a legitimate time to recognize revenue? That is appropriate only under very limited circumstances, such as when there are ready or guaranteed markets for the product, stable prices, and minimal marketing costs. It would not be appropriate for a construction company building houses in standard styles and selling them later. Revenue recognition should wait until the sale happens, so that the criteria listed in Section 6.6 are met. Historically, revenue from gold mines was recognized at the point of completion of production; producers could expect to sell all they produced since there was a world price for gold and Western governments provided a ready market. This is no longer the case for all gold mines, and today almost the only time revenue is recognized at time of completion when there is no customer yet is in agricultural concerns that produce within government quotas.

4. When Cash Is Received

Waiting for the cash to recognize revenue is an exception, not the rule.

If there is serious doubt as to the collectibility of cash from a revenue-generating transaction, revenue recognition is delayed until the collection has taken place. This does not mean that revenue recognition is delayed every time a business extends credit to a customer. In the vast majority of cases, revenue is recognized before the cash is received. Most businesses have accounts receivable, which are recognized but uncollected revenue. Revenue recognition is only delayed when the risk is great and the amount collectible cannot be reasonably determined, or is not sufficiently predictable. Delay is proper until the revenue recognition criteria have been met.

Examples of Revenue Recognition on a Cash Received Basis

Particular business circumstances may require cash basis revenue recognition.

- An example of waiting for the cash is in the case of certain real estate transactions that are speculative in nature and/or for which the collection of cash is contingent upon some future condition (such as the purchasers of a shopping mall successfully leasing a certain percentage of the space).
- Another example of revenue recognition at time of collection is the "Installment sales" method. When the majority of the revenue will come in over a long series of installments, and there is substantial uncertainty that a given customer will actually make all the payments, the revenue is recognized in stages as the cash comes in. The Installment sales method has some complexities, but in principle it is just a way of recognizing revenue on a *cash received basis*.

- A final example is that many businesses do not extend credit to their customers, but deal only on a cash basis. Fast-food restaurants, coffee shops, some movie theatres, and numerous other "cash only" businesses recognize revenue on a cash basis because that is the only basis they have. (By the way, if customers pay with credit cards, those payments are normally treated as cash. If there is any receivable, it is a bulk one with the credit card company related to delays in processing the credit card slips, not resulting from extending credit to individual customers.)

5. At Some Point After Cash Has Been Received

Circumstances may require delaying revenue recognition past when cash is received.

Revenue recognition methods 1, 2, and 3 use accrual accounting, while method 4 essentially uses the cash basis for recognizing revenue. It is also possible to defer recognition for some time *after* the cash has been collected. Even though cash has been received, all revenue may not be recognized immediately because of some circumstance, such as a guaranteed deposit refund policy or a policy of "satisfaction guaranteed or money back." Here's how this method works:

1. A current liability account (Deferred revenue) is credited when the cash is collected:

   DR Cash
   CR Deferred revenue or Deposits received liability

2. Revenue will be recognized at a point in the future, normally after the refund time has expired or the required after-delivery service has been performed:

   DR Deferred revenue or Deposits received liability
   CR Revenue

(We saw this pair of entries in the conceptual discussion in Section 6.3.)

Customer deposits are not revenue until the goods or services are delivered.

Deferring revenue recognition to a point after cash has been received is standard practice if, for some reason, a customer has paid in advance. Examples are magazine subscriptions or fitness club memberships, which are prepayments by the customers for service to be received later. This is a very conservative method, but that is really not the reason it is used. It is used because until the services or goods have been delivered, the revenue and therefore the income have not yet been *earned.* The revenue recognition criteria have not been met. Fairness requires waiting until they have been met.

HOW'S YOUR UNDERSTANDING?

Here are two questions you should be able to answer based on what you have just read. If you can't answer them, it would be best to reread the material.

1. What circumstances make each of the five revenue recognition methods appropriate?
2. During the year, Smokey Inc. completed and billed projects having total revenue of $150,000, one of which had a $10,000 "return if not satisfied" promise. At the end of the year, one more project with revenue of $14,000 was complete but it had not been billed because the client had not yet taken possession of the goods. At the end of the year, further projects with eventual revenue of $45,000 were 60% complete. Cash of $150,000 had been collected on the billed projects, $10,000 on the completed but undelivered project, and $20,000 on the incomplete ones. What would be the revenue for the year on each of the five methods in this section?

---

1. *Delivery: $150,000;*
2. *Percentage completion: $191,000 ($150,000 + $14,000 + 0.60 × $45,000);*
3. *Completion of production: $164,000 ($150,000 + $14,000);*
4. *Cash received: $180,000 ($150,000 + $10,000 + $20,000) or just a conservative $132,000;*
5. *After cash was received: $140,000 ($150,000 – $10,000).*

This is quite a variety of revenue figures, and more combinations of the given data could be imagined!

6.8 Expense Recognition and Matching

Usually, expenses incurred in a period are assumed to match revenues for that period.

According to the "matching" criterion, *expense recognition* should be timed to match the revenue recognition method. The basic idea is that expense accounts should be debited in parallel to the crediting of revenue accounts. In practice, this is done quite routinely for most expenses. When expenses such as wages, interest, heat, property taxes, or advertising are incurred, they are recognized as expenses on the assumption that they were incurred to help earn revenues in the same period. Sometimes this assumption is a bit strained; for example, advertising may stimulate revenue over more than the current period, but the subjectivity of estimating multi-period effects and the simplicity of just expensing such costs when incurred lead most companies to just expense them, matching them to current revenues.

A franchisee buys the right to use the franchiser's brand, etc., under specified conditions.

There are cases, however, when the accounting has to be more refined. We saw expense matching to the revenue recognized during production in the Greenway Construction example above. Just to help you see the potential accrual accounting offers for fine-tuning revenue and expense recognition, here's another example, from the diverse field of *franchising*.

WonderBurgers Ltd. is a franchiser, which means it sells the right to sell its products in particular geographic areas. For example, a franchisee might pay $25,000 for the right to set up a WonderBurgers fast-food restaurant in Sudbury, and no one else would be able to use the WonderBurgers brand name and other features, such as its recipes, in Sudbury.

Revenue from selling franchises is recognized over time, like construction revenue.

Let's suppose that the management of WonderBurgers estimates that it takes three years for a franchise to become viable and knows that during that time it will have to provide a lot of help. Suppose the sort of schedule of cash flows and economic activity that WonderBurgers has experienced for a typical $25,000 franchise fee is much like the one shown in Exhibit 6.6 below. The "percent-of-fee-earned" amounts could have been determined by how much revenue was collected or how much support cost was spent, but because of the kinds of effort the company and its franchisees go through in getting a franchise going, management has worked out a general policy of recognizing 40% of the revenue in the first year of a franchise and 30% in each of the next two years. (It's a lot like the percentage of completion method we saw above, which is no accident. Franchise accounting is a form of the percentage of completion method.)

EXHIBIT 6·6

Year	Cash Paid by Franchisee	Cash Cost to Help Franchisee	Percent of Fee Earned
1	$15,000	$4,000	40%
2	5,000	3,000	30%
3	5,000	1,000	30%
	$25,000	$8,000	100%

Using management's estimates of percent of fee earned as the basis of revenue recognition, the revenue recognized from the typical franchise sale would be

- Year 1, $10,000 (40%); and
- Years 2 and 3, $7,500 each (30% each).

Expenses related to the franchise are recognized so as to match the revenue.

According to the matching criterion, the expense of helping the franchisee should be recognized on the same schedule, so the expense recognized would be

- Year 1, $3,200 (40%); and
- Years 2 and 3, $2,400 each (30% each).

Expense matching produces income that follows the same pattern as revenue.

This matching process means that the income from the contract follows the same pattern. The total expected income is $17,000 ($25,000 minus $8,000), and the matching process produces an income pattern of

- Year 1, $6,800 (40% of $17,000, which is $10,000 revenue recognized minus $3,200 expense recognized); and
- Years 2 and 3, $5,100 (30% of $17,000 each, which is $7,500 revenue minus $2,400 expense).

The resulting income schedule and differences between the accrual basis (percentage of completion) and cash basis income are in Exhibit 6.7 below.

	Accrual Basis Income			Cash Basis Income		
	(a)	(b)	(c)	(d)	(e)	(f)
Year	Revenue	Expense	Income	Received	Spent	Income
1	$10,000	$3,200	$ 6,800	$15,000	$4,000	$11,000
2	7,500	2,400	5,100	5,000	3,000	2,000
3	7,500	2,400	5,100	5,000	1,000	4,000
	$25,000	$8,000	$17,000	$25,000	$8,000	$17,000

Difference

Year	(a)–(d)	(b)–(e)	(c)–(f)
1	$(5,000)	$ (800)	$(4,200)
2	2,500	(600)	3,100
3	2,500	1,400	1,100
	0	0	0

The accrual and cash bases eventually produce the same total income, by different routes.

You can see the point again about accrual accounting being a matter of *timing*. Both the accrual and the cash basis get to the same point, $17,000 income over the three years, but they take different routes to get there. In Year 1, the accrual income is $4,200 less than the net cash inflow of $11,000, but in Years 2 and 3, the accrual income is greater than the net cash inflows.

The cash flow statement's Operations section reconciles accrual income to cash flow. To refresh your knowledge of the cash flow statement and show how the accrual and cash bases reconcile, the Operations section of WonderBurgers Ltd.'s cash flow statements would show the following (ignoring tax and other complications):

Year 1	Accrual income	$ 6,800
	Add increase in deferred revenue ($15,000 collected minus $10,000 recognized as revenue)	5,000
	Deduct increase in prepaid expense ($4,000 spent minus $3,200 recognized as expense)	(800)
	Cash from operations (cash income)	$11,000
Year 2	Accrual income	$ 5,100
	Deduct decrease in deferred revenue ($5,000 collected minus $7,500 recognized as revenue)	(2,500)
	Deduct increase in prepaid expense ($3,000 spent minus $2,400 recognized as expense)	(600)
	Cash from operations (cash income)	$ 2,000
Year 3	Accrual income	$ 5,100
	Deduct decrease in deferred revenue ($5,000 collected minus $7,500 recognized as revenue)	(2,500)
	Add decrease in prepaid expense ($1,000 spent minus $2,400 recognized as expense)	1,400
	Cash from operations (cash income)	$ 4,000

If you look back to the Difference section of Exhibit 6.7 above, you will see that the cash flow statement's adjusting items are those same differences.

All methods of managing the accounts, so that the accrual income can be different from the cash flow, involve creating balance sheet accounts to hold the differences until they disappear. Accounts for doing this have names like accounts receivable, inventory, contract work in process, deferred revenue liability, and accounts payable. The details of their workings are often complicated, and each company has its own system.

Accrual accounting's purpose is to move beyond cash flows toward a broader economic concept of earnings and financial position. From a manager's point of view, this has several implications:

- As a more inclusive way of measuring performance and position, accrual accounting reflects more of what a manager is trying to do than cash flow can. This should make accrual accounting attractive to managers who want to be evaluated fairly and who are interested in comparing their companies to others.
- Financial accounting reports the results of actions, not the reasons for them (except by implication). Managers may therefore feel that the accounting statements are incomplete because they miss the "why" behind the revenues, expenses, assets, and liabilities.
- To many people, earnings should be defined as changes in the market value of the company. Managers may be compensated using market-value mechanisms like bonuses and stock options. The evidence-based accounting procedures for revenue recognition, expense recognition, and matching them to measure income may not relate very well to managers' efforts to increase the market value of their companies.
- Accrual accounting's procedures require evidence to support entries and conservatism in estimating the effects of future events (provide for expected losses, but not for expected gains until they occur). To managers seeking an even-handed evaluation of their performance, accounting may seem overly skeptical about the future and downwardly biased in its measures. Managers may wish that accrual accounting recognized their optimism about the future more than it does.
- The criteria as to when and how to recognize revenues and expenses are inescapably judgmental and, therefore, to many managers' tastes, are both arbitrary and subjective. Many managers find accrual accounting too loose and flexible and would prefer less estimation and subjectivity.

Managers should take financial accounting seriously so that they can know when the accounting measures seem appropriate and when they do not. Accrual accounting has many advantages and is very widely used, but managers should not accept it uncritically.

HOW'S YOUR UNDERSTANDING?

Here are two questions you should be able to answer based on what you have just read. If you can't answer them, it would be best to reread the material.

1. Why is matching revenues and expenses important?
2. Suppose everything was the same in the WonderBurgers example except that the percentages of fees earned and expenses incurred over the three years were determined by how much revenue was collected or how much support cost was spent. Calculate the following for both methods: accrual income for Years 1, 2, 3, and total; difference from cash basis income for Years 1, 2, 3, and total.

Based on revenue collected

	Year 1	Year 2	Year 3	Total
Accrual incomes (60%, 20%, 20% of $17,000)	$10,200	$3,400	$ 3,400	$17,000
Cash incomes (as before)	11,000	2,000	4,000	17,000
Differences	$ (800)	$1,400	$ (600)	$ 0

Based on support cost spent

	Year 1	Year 2	Year 3	Total
Accrual incomes (50%, 37.5%, 12.5% of $17,000)	$ 8,500	$ 6,375	$ 2,125	$17,000
Cash incomes (as before)	11,000	2,000	4,000	17,000
Differences	$ (2,500)	$ 4,375	$(1,875)	$ 0

6.9 Demonstration Problem: Revenue and Expense Recognition

Nakiska Fabricating Inc. produces large pressure vessels, pipeline pumping stations, and related equipment for the oil and gas industry. Its products are all made to order and can cost its customers millions of dollars. The company keeps its accounts on a project basis, grouping a set of items ordered by one customer and due at a similar time into a single project account. For each project, there are extensive initial design costs, then the costs of producing the items ordered, then large delivery costs (delivering its largest vessels involves closing highways, paying for police escorts, cutting overhead electrical wires, etc.), and finally significant on-site service costs to make sure the items are installed properly and work to specifications. A major project can therefore take several years from the receipt of the order to the end of the on-site service, and to maintain its reputation and learn from any mistakes, Nakiska always responds to customer complaints even if they arise years later. All contracts specify payment to Nakiska of 25% of the contract price when project work begins, 60% upon delivery, and 15% when on-site service is finished. The company's fiscal year-end is April 30.

Here is information about the company's recent projects (ignoring income taxes and nonproject revenues and expenses). "Costs" are those incurred to the date given.

	Projects					
	N38	**N39**	**N40**	**N41**	**N42**	**N43**
Order received	May 05	Sep 05	Oct 05	Mar 06	Jul 06	Dec 06
Project work begun	Jun 05	Nov 05	Dec 05	May 06	Sep 06	Feb 07
Project delivered to site	Mar 06	May 06	Aug 06	Oct 06	May 07	Oct 07
On-site service finished	May 06	Jun 06	Oct 06	Jul 07	Jul 07	Apr 08
Contract price (millions)	$3.2	$1.9	$5.4	$4.5	$2.3	$4.2
Costs to Apr 30, 2006	2.5	1.2	2.1	0.0	0.0	0.0
Costs to Apr 30, 2007	2.6	1.6	4.8	4.6	1.7	0.7
Costs to Apr 30, 2008	2.7	1.6	4.8	4.9	2.0	3.5

1. Assuming the future costs are known or can be estimated, and that customers pay on time, calculate the company's project income for the year ended April 30, 2004, on the
   a. delivery basis;
   b. percentage of completion basis;
   c. finishing of on-site service basis;
   d. cash received basis.
2. After attending an accounting workshop at which prudent accounting was emphasized, Nakiska's project accountant wondered if the company should postpone revenue and expense recognition until all possible customer complaints had been dealt with. Contracts N38 and N41, for example, had continued to cost the company money after the on-site service had been completed. Address the accountant's concern.

Answers:

1. Project incomes for year ended April 30, 2007 (in millions):
   a. Delivery basis:

N38	All in previous year	$0.0
N39	100% because delivered during year ($1.9 – $1.6)	0.3
N40	100% because delivered during year ($5.4 – $4.8)	0.6
N41	Anticipate the eventual loss ($4.5 – $4.9)	(0.4)
N42	Not delivered during year	0.0
N43	Not delivered during year	0.0
	Total project income for the year	$0.5

b. Percentage of completion basis:

N38	($2.6 – $2.5)/$2.7 × ($3.2 – $2.7)	$0.0185
N39	($1.6 – $1.2)/$1.6 × ($1.9 – $1.6)	0.075
N40	($4.8 – $2.1)/$4.8 × ($5.4 – $4.8)	0.3375
N41	Anticipate the eventual loss ($4.5 – $4.9)	(0.4)
N42	($1.7 – $0.0)/$2.0 × ($2.3 – $2.0)	0.255
N43	($0.7 – $0.0)/$3.5 × ($4.2 – $3.5)	0.14
	Total project income for the year	$0.426

c. Finishing of on-site service basis:

N38	100% because completed during year ($3.2 – $2.7)	$0.5
N39	100% because completed during year ($1.9 – $1.6)	0.3
N40	100% because completed during year ($5.4 – $4.8)	0.6
N41	Anticipate the eventual loss ($4.5 – $4.9)	(0.4)
N42	Not completed during year	0.0
N43	Not completed during year	0.0
	Total project income for the year	$1.0

d. Cash received basis:

N38	15% of contract price received: 15% x ($3.2 – $2.7)	$0.075
N39	75% of contract price received: 75% x ($1.9 – $1.6)	0.225
N40	75% of contract price received: 75% x ($5.4 – $4.8)	0.45
N41	Anticipate the eventual loss ($4.5 – $4.9)	(0.4)
N42	25% of contract price received: 25% x ($2.3 – $2.0)	0.075
N43	25% of contract price received: 25% x ($4.2 – $3.5)	0.175
	Total project income for the year	$0.6

Note that these incomes differ because of the facts of the situations. The four bases do not necessarily line up in any particular order in any particular year.

(2) Postponing all recognition of revenues and expenses (and therefore income) until all possible complaints have been dealt with is unnecessarily conservative. As long as the company has carried out the terms of the contract and can estimate possible future "warranty" costs, the revenue recognition criteria have been met and project revenues and expenses, including a provision for estimated warranty costs, should be recognized and used to calculate project incomes. Postponing the whole because of uncertainty about a small part would seriously under-report the company's earnings.

HOW'S YOUR UNDERSTANDING?

Here are two questions you should be able to answer based on what you have just read. If you can't answer them, it would be best to reread the material.

1. Generally, under which of the four recognition bases shown above would income be affected by (a) a delay in the project work that delayed delivery but not completion of on-site service, or (b) a delay in payments by customers?

(a) Income would be affected under the delivery basis if delivery is delayed, and probably under the percentage of completion basis because it uses the proportion of costs incurred to any point. (b) Income would be affected only under the cash received basis.

2. Which basis would show the highest *accumulated* income to any date (say April 30, 2004) for Nakiska, and which would show the lowest accumulated income?

The highest accumulated income in this example would be shown by the delivery basis, because the other three all postpone some revenue and expense recognition past the delivery date. The lowest accumulated income in this example would be shown by the percentage of completion basis, because some costs continue to be incurred past the finishing of on-site service (which is also the date of the last customer payment) and so percentage of completion would postpone some revenues and income past that date.

6.10 Prepaid and Accrued Expenses

Prepaid and accrued expenses serve to line expense recognition up with the fiscal period.

This section is about a very common use of accrual accounting: to line up expenses such as insurance, interest, rent, and property taxes with the fiscal period to which they apply, whether or not they were paid for before, during, or after that period. The ideas in this section apply most usually to current assets and liabilities, adjusting for fairly short-term differences between the expense and the cash payment, but they can also apply to longer-term deferred assets and liability accruals.

Prepaid and accrued expenses result from two factors (which we saw in the conceptual discussion in Sections 6.2 and 6.3):

1. Matching expense recognition to the fiscal period over which the expense is incurred (and during which revenue is recognized); and
2. Cash flow for paying the expense not coinciding with the expense recognition.

Only two journal entries are needed to implement the two factors:

1. *Expense recognition:* An annual or more usually monthly adjustment to the accounts to create an expense account and recognize that *either* a prepaid asset has been consumed *or* an accrued liability has been incurred:

   DR Some expense account
   CR Some balance sheet account (prepaid expense or accrued liability)

2. *Cash payment:* Recorded whenever the payment is made for the expense:

   DR The balance sheet account (prepaid expense or accrued liability)
   CR Cash

Prepaid Expenses Asset

Prepaid expenses arise when expenses are paid *prior* to the period to which the expenses apply.

Prepaid expenses are assets that arise because expenditures have been made, but there is still value extending into the future, so that the expenditure isn't all an expense yet. They are usually classified as current assets because the future value usually continues only into the next year. But sometimes the value extends beyond a year, and the company may then appropriately show a noncurrent prepaid expense or "deferred charge" if it is a significant enough amount to warrant such classification. Prepaid expenses arise whenever the payment schedule for an expense is ahead of the company's fiscal period, such as for annual insurance premiums when the policy's ending date is past the fiscal year-end, or property taxes that are based on the municipality's tax assessment schedule and cover a period past the company's fiscal period.

Prepaid expense assets have value in reducing future cash payouts.

Prepaid expenses are not assets in the same way as are receivables (to be collected in cash) or inventories (to be sold for cash). They arise from accrual accounting, in cases where the expense recognition follows the cash flow. As was indicated earlier in this chapter, this is conceptually the same reason inventories and factory assets are on the balance sheet: something of value exists and therefore its cost should not yet be deducted as an expense. Here, the value is in the fact that, having spent the money already, the company will not have to spend it in the next period. They have an economic value because future resources will not have to be expended.

Pure Prepaid Expenses Asset Case

The purest case of a prepaid expense arises where entry #1 above always *follows* entry #2: payment is always in advance. In Figure 6.7, *the horizontal arrow is fiscal periods and the vertical axis has prepaid expense asset above the arrow and accrued liability below it.* The cash payments are made at times X, Y, and Z, and *after* each of those times, the prepaid expense is transferred to expense by entries like #1 over the period to which it applies. In this pure prepaid case, there is no accrued expenses liability.

FIGURE 6.7

Pure Prepaid Expenses Asset Case

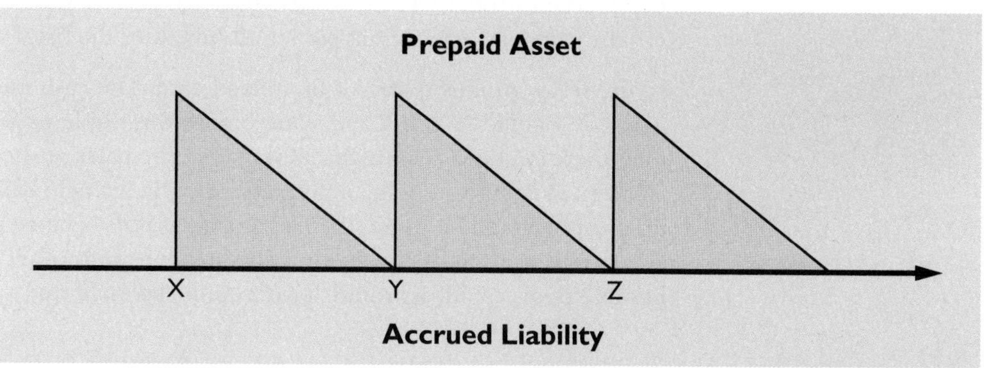

Accrued Expenses Liability

Accrued expenses arise when expenses are paid *after* the period to which the expenses apply.

Accrued expenses are liabilities, usually current, that arise from exactly the same timing difference as do prepaid expenses, but in their case the cash flow happens *after* the economic value has been obtained. An example is accruing interest that is building up on a bank loan. Another is paying for an audit only after the work has been done for the present fiscal year.

Pure Accrued Expenses Liability Case

The purest case of an accrued expense arises where entry #1 above always *precedes* entry #2: payment is always afterwards ("in arrears"). In Figure 6.8, the horizontal arrow is still fiscal periods, with prepaid expense asset above it and accrued liability below it. The cash payments are still made at times X, Y, and Z, and *prior to* each of those times, the expense is created by building up the accrual to expense over the period to which it applies. In this pure accrued expenses case there is no prepaid expense.

FIGURE 6.8

Pure Accrued Expenses Liability Case

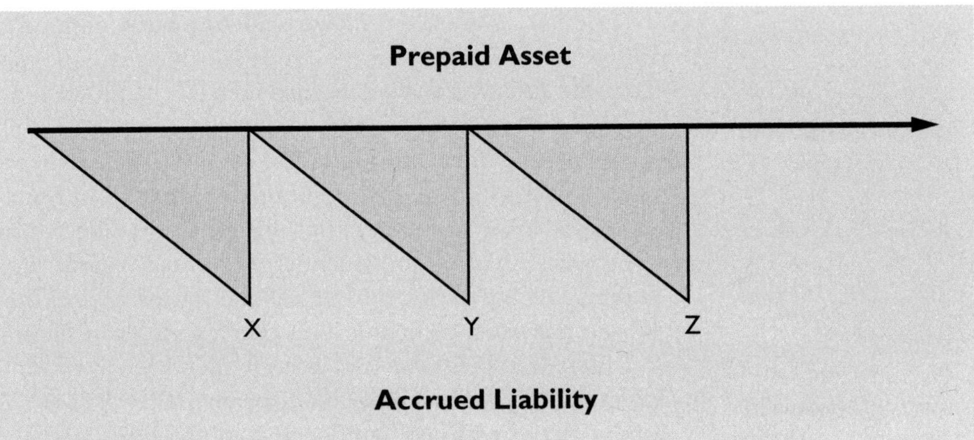

The Balance Sheet Account Can Vary Between Being an Asset and a Liability

Mixed Asset–Liability Case

A mixed case is also common, in which sometimes the cash paid is prior to the incurrence of the expense, and sometimes follows it. Suppose a company has a June 30 fiscal year-end and pays property taxes to the local municipality. Property taxes apply to the calendar year:

- Prepaid property taxes at the fiscal year-end of June 30 arise if property taxes for the whole of the calendar year are paid in June, before the end of the fiscal year.
- Accrued property taxes at the fiscal year-end of June 30 arise if property taxes for the calendar year are not paid until July, after the fiscal year-end.

Figure 6.9 is an illustration of the mixed case. The cash payment times X, Y, and Z are now not regular: X and Y are made before the whole expense has been incurred, and then there is a long delay before Z is made. The balance sheet account varies from being an accrued liability to being a prepaid expense. A single balance sheet account could be used, and it could be put in the current assets if its balance is a debit, and in the current liabilities if its balance is a credit. (This happens with other accounts, too. If an account payable is overpaid, it would have a debit balance and would be included with the accounts receivable, on the assumption the overpayment would be refunded or used to purchase more goods. Conversely, if an account receivable is overpaid by the customer, it would have a credit balance and would be shown with the accounts payable, on the same assumption.)

FIGURE 6.9

Mixed Asset–Liability Case

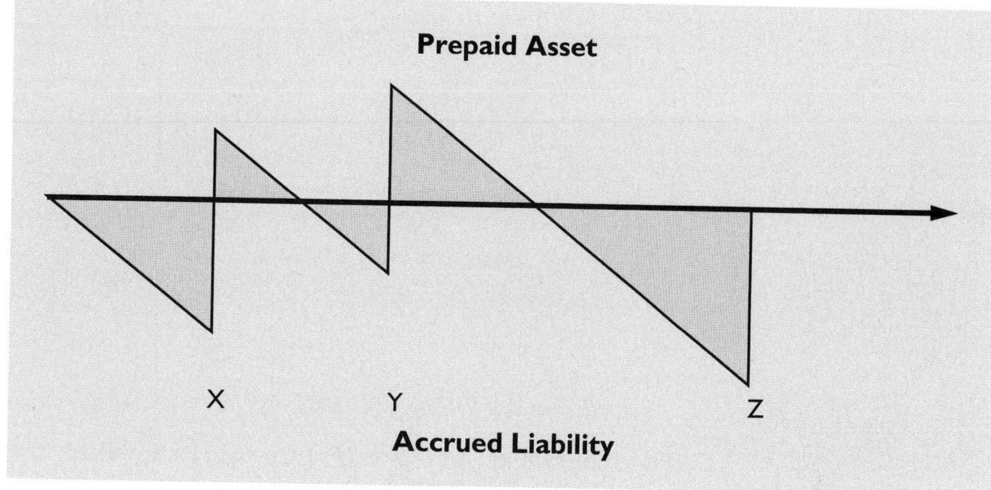

Depending on payment timing, an expense may be either accrued or prepaid.

Therefore, *accrued (unpaid) expenses and prepaid expenses are just opposite sides of the same coin*, reflecting a mismatch between the cash payment and the expense (use of the economic value). They arise as accrual accounting tries to arrange the expenses to reflect economic use rather than cash flow. They are assets or liabilities depending on how the cash flow and the expense recognition happen to mismatch, so you often see similar kinds of items as prepaid expense assets and as accrued expense liabilities, or even as an asset one year and a liability the next. Common examples include insurance, property taxes, sales commissions, interest, licences, and current income taxes (payable if owing, or refundable if overpaid).

Example

Here is an example. Day and Night Inc. has ten local corner stores that are part of a national chain. Each year, it pays a franchise fee to the chain for use of the chain's logo and other rights during the calendar year. No matter when the fee is paid, its economic value applies to the calendar year. The company's fiscal year-end is September 30, however, so it is measuring expenses over the period October 1 to September 30, not the calendar year to which the payments apply. This is the kind of mismatch of periods that gives rise to prepaid and accrued expenses. *The expense is allocated to fiscal periods regardless of when it is paid.*

Illustration 1: The fee is paid on August 31 every year.

The diagram of this case in Figure 6.10 shows the payment made at A (end of August) each year. This pays off an accrued expense that had been building up since the beginning of the year and creates a prepaid expense for the rest of the year. By S (end of September), there is still some prepaid expense, and by D (end of December) there is neither a prepaid expense nor an accrued liability. The expense for any fiscal year is a combination of the consumption of the three-month prepaid existing at the end of September last year, the eight-month January to August accrual for this year, and one month's consumption of the prepaid existing at the end of August this year.

FIGURE 6.10

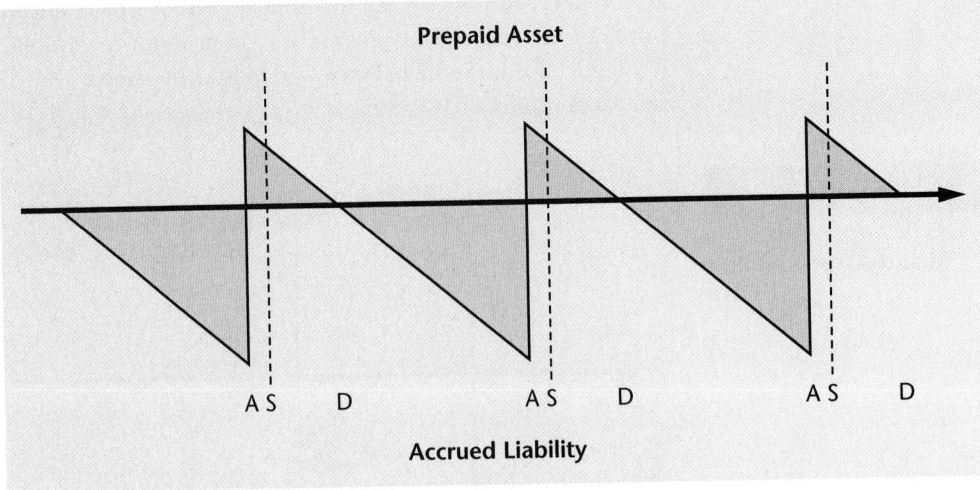

Illustration 2: The fee is paid on November 30 every year.

The diagram of this case (Figure 6.11) shows the payment made at N (end of November) each year. This pays off an accrued expense that had been building up since the beginning of the year and creates a prepaid expense for only one month. By S (end of September), there is an accrued expense, and by D (end of December) there is neither a prepaid expense nor an accrued liability. The expense for any fiscal year is a combination of the two-month accrual from the end of September to the end of November last year, the consumption of the one-month prepaid existing at the end of November last year, and the nine-month January to September accrual for this year.

FIGURE 6.11

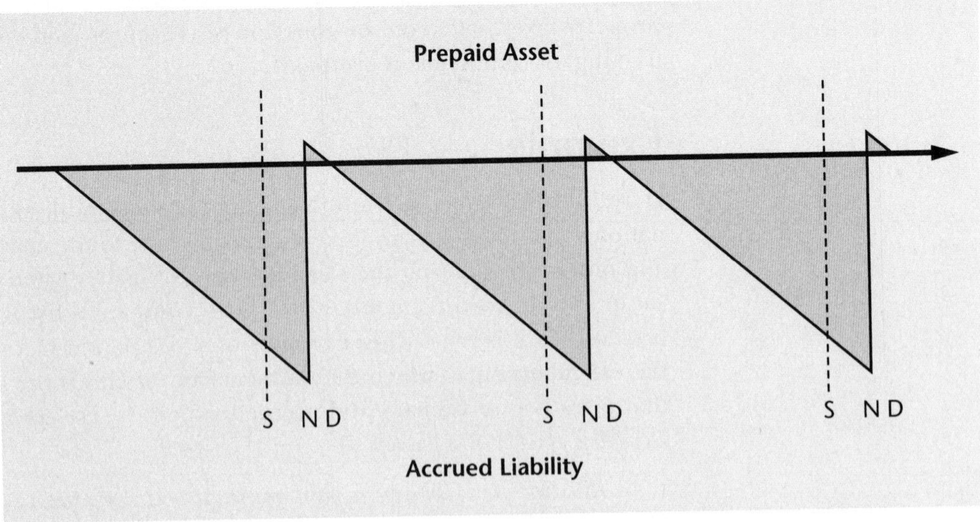

The expense is independent of payment timing; together expense and payment make an asset or liability.

Accrual accounting has used a prepaid expense asset in the first case and an accrued expense liability in the second case to produce the same calculation of expense: 3/12 of last year's fee (the October to December part) plus 9/12 of this year's (the January to September part). *The happenstance of the payment date does not affect the expense, but it does affect the balance sheet.* The balance sheet's asset or liability accounts arise as a consequence of accrual accounting's method of measuring expenses (and therefore income) properly, in combination with the timing of the payment of the fee. For such prepaid and accrued accounts, we could say that the balance sheet values are just residuals of the particular combination of expense incurrence and cash payment and don't have any deeper meaning.

Mini-Demonstration Case: Prepaid and Accrued Expenses

Let's put some numbers into the Day and Night Inc. example used in the charts above. The company's fiscal year-end is September 30. Suppose the annual franchise fee, which applies to the calendar year, is $12,000 the first year, $15,000 the second year and $18,000 the third year.

Illustration 1: The fee is paid on August 31 every year.

Prepaid asset Sept. 30 Year 1: 3/12 × $12,000 = $3,000
Expense for year ended Sept. 30 Year 2: 3/12 × $12,000 + 9/12 × $15,000 = $14,250
(This equals the last 3 months of the previous calendar year's fee plus the first 9 months of this calendar year's fee, to fit the annual fees to the company's fiscal year.)
Prepaid asset Sept. 30 Year 2: 3/12 × $15,000 = $3,750
Expense for year ended Sept. 30 Year 3: 3/12 × $15,000 + 9/12 × $18,000 = $17,250
(Again, this equals the last 3 months of the previous calendar year's fee plus the first 9 months of this calendar year's fee, to fit the annual fees to the company's fiscal year.)
Prepaid asset Sept. 30 Year 3: 3/12 × $18,000 = $4,500

Illustration 2: The feel is paid on November 30 every year.

Accrued liability Sept. 30 Year 1: 9/12 × $12,000 = $9,000
Expense for year ended Sept. 30 Year 2: 3/12 × $12,000 + 9/12 × $15,000 = $14,250
(Same as Illustration 1: expense is unaffected by payment date.)
Accrued liability Sept. 30 Year 2: 9/12 × $15,000 = $11,250
Expense for year ended Sept. 30 Year 3: 3/12 × $15,000 + 9/12 × $18,000 = $17,250
(Again, same Illustration 1: expense is unaffected by payment date.)
Accrued liability Sept. 30 Year 3: 9/12 × $18,000 = $13,500

HOW'S YOUR UNDERSTANDING?

Here are two questions you should be able to answer based on what you have just read. If you can't answer them, it would be best to reread the material.

1. Why might the balance sheet account related to a particular expense be a prepaid expense asset at the end of one year and an accrued expense liability at the end of another year?
2. Mah Stores Inc. pays its insurance premium in advance every year on September 30 for the year beginning that date. This year, the premium (paid last September) was $5,280 and next year it is estimated to be $5,400. If the company's fiscal year-end is July 31, what is the prepaid insurance asset or accrued insurance liability at this July 31? If the company failed to pay its premium for next year until November 1, what would be the prepaid insurance asset or accrued insurance liability on its quarterly balance sheet at October 31?

July 31: Asset = $880 (2/12 × $5,280);
Oct. 31: Liability = $450 (1/12 × $5,400).

6.11 Terms to Be Sure You Understand

Here is this chapter's list of terms introduced or emphasized. Make sure you know what they mean *in accounting*, and if any are unclear to you, check the chapter again or refer to the glossary of terms at the back of the book.

Accounting policy choices
Accrual accounting
Accrued expenses
Aggressive accounting
Articulate
Articulation
Authoritative standards
Big Bath
Cash received basis
Classification
Comparability
Completed contract
Conservatism
Conservative
Consistency
Critical event
Cut off
Delivery (point of sale)
Disclosure
Discretionary expenses
Earnings management
Expense recognition
Expenses
Fair value accounting
Fairness
Fiscal periods
Franchising
GAAP
Income
Income smoothing
Matching
Materiality
Net income
Percentage of completion
Period expenses
Prepaid expenses
Realized
Recognition
Recognized
Revenue recognition
Revenues
Significant accounting policies

CONTINUING DEMONSTRATION CASE

INSTALLMENT 6

DATA FOR INSTALLMENT 6

The Continuing Case is intended to give you a little extra practice, mostly on preparation of accounting information. It has been a while since sets of journal entries were illustrated, so this installment presents the entries for the second six months of Mato's operation. You can see that the ideas behind accrual accounting, especially cutting the business's activities into fiscal periods, are present in the standard entries to record revenues and expenses. Later installments will deal with the company's accounting policy choices and analysis of its first year's financial statements.

Here again is the August 31, 2006, general ledger trial balance produced in Installment 3 and used to produce the financial statements for the first six months of the company's existence.

Debit balance accounts		Credit balance accounts	
Cash	$ 4,507	Bank loan	$ 75,000
Accounts receivable	18,723	Accounts payable	45,616
Inventory	73,614	Loan payable	15,000
Automobile	10,000	Share capital	125,000
Leasehold improvements	63,964	Revenues	42,674
Equipment and furniture	29,740	Accum. amort.—auto.	1,000
Computer	14,900	Accum. amort.—leasehold imp.	6,396
Software	4,800	Accum. amort.—equip.	744
Incorporation costs	1,100	Accum. amort.—computer	1,490
Cost of goods sold expense	28,202	Accum. amort.—software	480
Salary—Mavis	15,000		
Salary—Tomas	9,280		
Salary—other	1,200		
Travel expense	8,726		
Telephone expense	2,461		
Rent expense	12,000		
Utilities expense	1,629		
Office and general expenses	3,444		
Amort. expense—auto.	1,000		
Amort. expense—leasehold imp.	6,396		
Amort. expense—equipment	744		
Amort. expense—computer	1,490		
Amort. expense—software	480		
	$313,400		$313,400

Alarmed by the company's loss for the six months ($49,378 per Installment 3) and negative cash generation (decrease in cash of $125,493 per Installment 4), Mavis and Tomas took strong action over the next six months. They put extra effort into sales, pressed the boutiques for collection as much as they could without damaging their new relationships with these customers, reduced inventory levels, and generally tried to run "a lean shop," as Tomas put it.

Here are events for the six months ended February 28, 2007, grouped and identified for later reference:

a. Revenue for the six months totalled $184,982, all on credit. (It will turn out later that they had been collecting and paying GST during this time—that will be dealt with in a later installment, to avoid complicating this one.)
b. Collections from customers during the six months were $189,996.
c. Purchases for the six months were $71,004, all on credit.
d. Payments to suppliers during the six months came to $81,276. (To conserve cash, the company continued to rely on the patience of its suppliers more than Tomas liked. But doing so did save interest expense, because the suppliers did not charge interest while the bank did!)
e. Cost of goods sold for the six months was $110,565.
f. An inventory count on February 28, 2007, revealed inventory on hand costing $33,612. (This allowed Tomas to deduce that there had been a shortage in inventory, because there was a little less on hand than expected based on the cost of what had been sold. There was inventory of $73,614 on hand at the end of August, $71,004 more was purchased, and the cost of goods sold was $110,565. $73,614 + $71,004 – $110,565 = $34,053 which should have been on hand. The count showed $33,612 so there was a shortage of $441.)
g. Tomas decided to combine the three salary expense accounts into one, effective September 1, 2006.
h. Salaries for the six months to February 28, 2007, totalled $42,000. The company had paid all of this, except that it owed the government $2,284 in income tax and other deductions, and the employees $2,358 in net salaries at the end of February.
i. Various operating expenses for the six months were: travel, $1,376; phone, $1,553; rent, $12,000; utilities, $1,956; office and general expenses, $2,489. All of these were paid by February 28, except for $1,312.
j. The company bought further necessary equipment at a cost of $2,650 cash on November 3, 2006.
k. The company's bank loan rose and fell during the period. A total of $32,000 in further borrowing was incurred, and $59,500 was repaid.
l. Bank loan interest of $4,814 was paid during the six months (including a portion for the period prior to August 31, 2006, that had not been included in the accounts to that date).
m. Unfortunately (personally and financially), Tomas's father's health had deteriorated over the autumn and so he requested that his loan be repaid. The company did that on December 15, 2006, including interest of $1,425.

The employee (mentioned in an earlier installment) had been hired in August and looked after the bookkeeping for the company. The above events were made up of hundreds of individual transactions recorded by the employee, but they are summarized by the journal entries that follow. *See if you can do them before you look at the results!*

RESULTS FOR INSTALLMENT 6

Journal entries for the period September 1, 2006, to February 28, 2007, follow, corresponding with the events listed previously. To save clutter, they are not accompanied by explanations or DR and CR indications, other than in the placement of the figures (the debits to the left). Since they are summary entries, their dates are also omitted.

a. Accounts receivable	184,982	
Revenue		184,982
b. Cash	189,996	
Accounts receivable		189,996
c. Inventory	71,004	
Accounts payable		71,004
d. Accounts payable	81,276	
Cash		81,276
e. Cost of goods sold expense	110,565	
Inventory		110,565
f. Inventory shortage expense	441	
Inventory		441
($73,614 + $71,004 – $110,565 – $33,612)		
g. Salaries Expense	25,480	
Salary—Mavis		15,000
Salary—Tomas		9,280
Salary—Other		1,200
h. Salaries expense	42,000	
Deductions payable		2,284
Salaries payable		2,358
Cash (deduced)		37,358
i. Travel expense	1,376	
Phone expense	1,553	
Rent expense	12,000	
Utilities expense	1,956	
Office and general expense	2,489	
Accounts payable		1,312
Cash (deduced)		18,062
j. Equipment and furniture	2,650	
Cash		2,650
k. Cash	32,000	
Bank loan		32,000
Bank loan	59,500	
Cash		59,500
l. Interest expense	4,814	
Cash		4,814
m. Loan payable	15,000	
Interest expense	1,425	
Cash		16,425

Posting these journal entries results in the following general ledger account balances at February 28, 2007 (arranged in balance sheet order, as is usually, but certainly not always, done in a trial balance). Credits are shown in brackets.

Account	Balance Aug. 31/06	Transactions for period to February 28, 2007	Balance Feb. 28/07
Cash	4,507	189,996 (81,276) (37,358) (18,062) (2,650) 32,000 (59,500) (4,814) (16,425)	6,418
Accounts receivable	18,723	184,982 (189,996)	13,709
Inventory	73,614	71,004 (110,565) (441)	33,612
Automobile	10,000	0	10,000
Accum. amort.—auto	(1,000)	0	(1,000)
Leasehold improvements	63,964	0	63,964
Accum. amort.—leasehold imp.	(6,396)	0	(6,396)
Equipment and furniture	29,740	2,650	32,390
Accum. amort.—equip.	(744)	0	(744)
Computer	14,900	0	14,900
Accum. amort.—computer	(1,490)	0	(1,490)
Software	4,800	0	4,800
Accum. amort.—software	(480)	0	(480)
Incorporation cost	1,100	0	1,100
Bank loan	(75,000)	(32,000) 59,500	(47,500)
Accounts payable	(45,616)	(71,004) 81,276 (1,312)	(36,656)
Deductions payable	0	(2,284)	(2,284)
Salaries payable	0	(2,358)	(2,358)
Loan payable	(15,000)	15,000	0
Share capital	(125,000)	0	(125,000)
Revenue	(42,674)	(184,982)	(227,656)
Cost of goods sold expense	28,202	110,565	138,767
Salary—Mavis	15,000	(15,000)	0
Salary—Tomas	9,280	(9,280)	0
Salary—other	1,200	(1,200)	0
Salaries expense	0	25,480 42,000	67,480
Travel expense	8,726	1,376	10,102
Phone expense	2,461	1,553	4,014
Rent expense	12,000	12,000	24,000
Utilities expense	1,629	1,956	3,585
Office and general expense	3,444	2,489	5,933
Interest expense	0	4,814 1,425	6,239
Inventory shortage expense	0	441	441
Amortization expense—auto.	1,000	0	1,000
Amortization expense—leasehold	6,396	0	6,396
Amortization expense—equipment	744	0	744
Amortization expense—computer	1,490	0	1,490
Amortization expense—software	480	0	480
Net Sums	0	0	0

6.13 Homework and Discussion to Develop Understanding

The problems roughly follow the outline of the chapter. Three main categories of questions are presented.

- Asterisked problems (*) have an informal solution provided in the Student Solutions Manual.
- EXTENDED TIME problems involve a thorough examination of the material and may take longer to complete.
- CHALLENGING problems are more difficult.

For further explanation, please refer to Section 1.15.

Accrual Accounting • Sections 6.2–6.3

What Is It and Why Do We Use It?

*** PROBLEM 6.1** Discuss the basis of accrual accounting

Discuss the following:

1. Speaking positively, it might be said that accrual accounting improves on the cash flow information. Speaking negatively, it might be said that accrual accounting messes up the picture by introducing noncash flow factors. Whether or not you like the result they achieve, how do accrual accounting entries work to alter the cash flow story?
2. Why can it be said that timing is at the centre of accrual accounting?

PROBLEM 6.2 Explain why accrual accounting diverges from cash flow

Respond in point form to the following complaint by a businessperson:

> "I find modern financial accounting really annoying. The basis of financial strength is the availability and use of real resources, like cash and machinery, yet accrual accounting produces an income measure that is deliberately different from the cash return earned by the business. Why is this so? Why should accrual accounting diverge from the measurement of cash flow?"

PROBLEM 6.3 Why accrual accounting is needed

Discuss the following statement: "Over the life of a business entity, it matters little which basis of revenue recognition is used. It is only because investors and others such as taxation authorities demand periodic income measurement that problems of revenues and expense recognition arise."

PROBLEM 6.4 Is accrual accounting a tool of management?

A professor recently said that accrual accounting was invented because managers wanted something they could manipulate to their own purposes more than was possible with transaction-based, cash-based data. Accrual accounting, the professor continued, is a tool of management and has driven accounting away from the goal of producing information that is representative of any real phenomena and toward fanciful reports largely devoid of real meaning.

1. What do you think of the professor's views? Are there any better reasons for accrual accounting?

2. The professor said that academics and practitioners tend to differ in their responses to his views. What do you think the differences would be?
3. If the professor is right, what does that say about the dictum that management bears the responsibility for providing financial information about an enterprise?

Conceptual Foundation

*** PROBLEM 6.5** Explain how revenues and expenses differ from cash flows

1. Explain the difference between a revenue and a cash receipt.
2. Give examples of items that are revenue of a given period but not receipts of that period, items that are receipts but not revenue, and items that are both revenue and receipts.
3. Explain the difference between an expense and a cash disbursement (payment).
4. Give examples of items that are expenses of a given period but not disbursements of that period, items that are disbursements but not expenses, and items that are both expenses and disbursements.

PROBLEM 6.6 Match accrual accounting terms

Match the terms on the left with the most appropriate phrases on the right.

1. Accounts receivable	a. Consumption of long-term assets
2. Inventory	b. Revenue recognized after collection
3. Cash	c. An estimate of what the government wants soon
4. Prepaid expense	d. Goods waiting to be expensed
5. Deferred revenue	e. Revenue recognized before collection
6. Pension liability	f. Usually unaffected by accounting policy choice
7. Future tax liability	g. Expense paid before being consumed
8. Accrued expense liability	h. An estimate of what the government wants much later
9. Income tax payable	i. Promises to employees expensed already
10. Amortization	j. Expense paid after economic value has been obtained

PROBLEM 6.7 Examine some accrual accounting phenomena

1. On December 31, the end of the accounting period of Major Corp., the company accountant is about to make some adjustments. Describe a set of circumstances where, in making the typical year-end adjustments
   a. an expense is debited and a liability is credited
   b. an expense is debited and an asset contra account is credited
   c. an asset is debited and a revenue is credited
   d. a liability is credited and a revenue is debited
2. A business executive remarked, "Accountants use a dual standard for measuring assets. Some are on the balance sheet because they have real future economic value. Others are there only because they're left over from the income measurement process ... sort of expenses waiting to be deducted. Similarly with liabilities: some are really owed but some are just leftovers of the accrual accounting process for measuring income."

Discuss the remark, citing examples of assets and liabilities that might fit the executive's four categories.

PROBLEM 6.8 Conversion from cash to accrual basis

Temporary Help Ltd. is a company offering specialized personal services (for example, secretarial assistance, delivery of advertising, errands, shopping for gifts). The company's accounts have been kept on a cash basis, but its banker has asked that the accounting be changed to the accrual basis. Income for 2006 on the cash basis was $169,000. Using the following figures (note the order of the years), calculate the company's 2006 income on the accrual basis.

	Assets		Liabilities	
	2006	**2005**	**2006**	**2005**
Cash basis:				
Current	$ 96,000	$ 83,000	$37,000	$37,000
Noncurrent	—	—	—	—
Accrual basis:				
Current	174,000	144,000	78,000	55,000
Noncurrent	30,000	36,000	16,000	—

PROBLEM 6.9 Explain accrual concepts to a businessperson

A businessperson you know has just received the financial statements of a company in which that person owns shares. Answer the following questions asked by the person. Try to answer without jargon and use examples that will make your answers clear.

1. I've been told that these accrual accounting numbers are "mainly a matter of timing." What does that mean?
2. I see the company has a note in its financial statements describing its "revenue recognition" method. Why would I want to know that?
3. I know from my business experience that sometimes you collect cash sooner or later than you expect. Customers may have cash, or not, for all sorts of reasons that have nothing to do with you. I understand that accrual accounting takes this into account so that it doesn't matter when cash is collected; you get the same revenue figure anyway. Is this true?
4. I understand that accountants try to be sure that revenues and expenses "match" each other so that the income you get by subtracting expenses from revenues makes sense. Seems quite appropriate. But what effect, if any, does this matching procedure have on the balance sheet figures?

Accounting Policy Choices • Section 6.4

* PROBLEM 6.10 Can the auditor prevent unfair accounting policies?

A commentator on the accounting scene remarked, "Management makes its accounting choices to serve its own interests, and there's no way the poor lonely auditor can hold the fort of fairness when you consider how vague and judgmental accrual accounting's criteria for accounting policy choices are."

What are your views on the commentator's remarks?

PROBLEM 6.11 Whose role should it be to choose accounting policies?

Should management have the responsibility and authority to choose companies' accounting policies, or should that role be someone else's (for example, the government's, the auditor's, an independent board's)? If you think it should be management's role, why? If you think it should be someone else's role, whose? Why?

PROBLEM 6.12 Comment on various remarks about accounting policies

Comment briefly on the following remarks by a businessperson:

1. "No one cares what our accounting policy choices are because they have no effect on the price of the company's shares."
2. "Our accounting policies are mainly a signal about the kind of company we are (conservatively managed, careful to follow authoritative rules) and so they are fairly consistent overall."
3. "Once we have established proper accounting policies, all those notes at the end of the financial statements are really an irrelevant nuisance."

*** PROBLEM 6.13** Discuss the conflict between flexible and standard accounting

As you have seen, there is a general conflict between two financial reporting objectives. The first objective is to fit the accounting to each company's circumstances so that the resulting reports are relevant to understanding or evaluating that company. The second is to make accounting consistent from company to company so that intercompany comparisons may be facilitated and the overall credibility of the information maintained.

Give your views on how important this conflict is and how (if at all) it should be dealt with.

PROBLEM 6.14 Issues about the significant accounting policies note

1. What is the purpose of the significant accounting policies note that usually is the first note to a company's financial statements?
2. How should a company decide what to include in that note?
3. A business commentator suggested that, when a company uses an accounting policy that is unusual, its significant accounting policies note should include a calculation of the effect on income of using that policy as compared to the more usual practice. What do you think of that idea?

PROBLEM 6.15 Questions on auditors, judgment, and accounting policies

Write a paragraph on each of the following topics, using the perspective on accounting policy choice and methods provided in this chapter:

1. Why the auditor's report refers to whether the company's financial statements have been prepared in accordance with GAAP.
2. Why professional judgment is needed in preparing financial statements.
3. Whether it is justifiable to use an aggressive revenue recognition policy (recognizing revenue early in the production-sale-collection cycle process).

PROBLEM 6.16 Comment on a newspaper article critical of accounting

On page 405 there is a newspaper article critical of managing earnings through aggressive accounting.[14] The article does not talk about revenue and expense recognition directly, but implies it through the techniques it mentions:

- The Big Bath, which we have seen before, which depresses current income by moving expenses forward from the future in order to make the future income higher.
- Immediately writing off part of the costs of acquiring another company, rather than keeping them on the balance sheet and amortizing them against future income.

- Paying managers with stock options; giving them cheap shares instead of cash and thereby not showing the real cost of employing them, because instead of an expense that reduces income, there is just a lower amount of share capital in the equity section of the balance sheet.
- Capitalizing research and development costs as assets to be amortized instead of deducting them as expenses now, which has the opposite effect to those of the first two income management methods.

Comment on the issues raised in the article. Some of these are: Do you think the problems are particularly serious in high-tech companies that rely on R&D, give big incentives to creative people, and sell ideas more than goods? Would it solve anything to have Canadian companies follow American practices more closely, even though there are problems in the United States too? Is it possible for a company to use aggressive accounting practices and still be conservative?

Tech firms' accounting methods assailed

Aggressive practices boost earnings, but may not be sustainable in long term: report

SIMON TUCK

Technology Reporter, Ottawa

Some of Canada's largest technology companies are boosting their earnings through the use of aggressive accounting practices, according to a report from Merrill Lynch Canada Inc.

The report warns that earnings created by the aggressive methods, which are far more widespread in the United States, are not sustainable in the long term. That would be especially perilous for the companies if the economy weakens and investors become more skittish.

"In these times of turbulent markets," the report says, "we feel this may be the time to take a more critical look at earnings quality issues in the sector."

The report says Canadian technology heavyweights Northern Telecom Ltd., Newbridge Networks Corp., JDS Fitel Inc., ATI Technologies Inc. and Mitel Corp. were the companies reviewed and "almost all could see a reduction to their reported and estimated [earnings] after adjusting for some accounting practices."

The report is careful to point out that the accounting practices are not illegal, or even inappropriate. But it does state that such methods are "a red flag worth monitoring."

However, many analysts and investors are ignoring the red flag, said Tom Astle, senior technology analyst at Toronto-based Merrill Lynch Canada. "Technology companies have discovered that Wall Street and Bay Street tend to ignore writeoffs."

The report points out four areas of concern:

- "Big-bath accounting" that loads write-offs onto quarters where a company would record a loss in any case. That increases expenses in one quarter, but boosts income in future quarters, creating the impression of a brightening financial picture.
- Writing off "research and development in process" from acquisitions. That also has the effect of transferring costs from future quarters to the current one, and boosting earnings in subsequent periods.
- Unrecorded costs for employee stock options. The report says that such options have a value that should be recorded as an expense at the time of issue, but rarely is.
- Recording expenditures on research and development as assets that are then subject to amortization, rather than as expenses. This pracitce increases profit in the short term, but reduces it in subsequent quarters as the asset is amortized. Such expenditures should be recorded as expenses as they occur, the report says.

Tim Saunders, Mitel's vice-president and corporate controller, said the report addresses an important and timely issue, but he said his Kanata, Ont.-based firm uses conservative accounting practices.

Marc René de Cotret, a spokesman for Nepean, Ont.-based JDS Fitel, said his company uses "very clean" accounting methods. "We have very, very conservative accounting practices."

ATI's accounting practices are also conservative, said spokeswoman Jo-Anne Chang, adding that Canadian high-tech firms are not as aggressive as their U.S. counterparts.

Northern Telecom, of Brampton, Ont., and Newbridge, of Kanata, Ont., did not comment. However, the report itself states that all the firms are operating within the law and within generally accepted accounting principles.

But the report says that just obeying the rules does not provide an entirely clear picture for investors. "Simply complying with generally accepted accounting principles in either Canada or the United States does not guarantee earnings quality."

The silver lining for Canada's technology industry is the report's even heavier criticism of the accounting practices of U.S. firms.

The report suggests that Canadian companies begin following accepted American accounting practices "so that we can compare apples to apples."

Reprinted from *The Globe and Mail,* 29 March 1999, by Simon Tuck.

Revenue Recognition • Sections 6.6–6.7

*** PROBLEM 6.17** Recommend revenue recognition policies

What revenue recognition policy would you recommend for each of the following companies? Why?

a. Harry's Hamburgers, an all-night fast-food joint on the highway.
b. EngSoft, a designer and installer of high-priced, custom-fitted software for engineering and other high-tech companies.
c. Nevada Gold, a miner of gold in northern Nevada.
d. Fast Furniture, a seller of cheap furniture, which has the slogan "buy now and pay nothing until a year from now."
e. Goldenrod Construction, which does building contracts with governments and large corporations.
f. Handsome Homes, which builds homes in the new part of town and hires agents to sell the homes upon completion.

EXTENDED TIME

PROBLEM 6.18 Likely revenue recognition policies for various cases

For each of the following independent cases, identify at what point revenue should be recognized:

Case 1. Tim Hortons sells coupon books for ten dollars. Each of the two-dollar coupons can be used in the restaurant at any time during the next 12 months. The customer must pay cash for the coupon book.

Case 2. In 2005 Snowdon Construction Company started a long-term construction project to build a large office block. The project was completed in 2007. At the end of 2007 the building had still not been sold as Snowdon was seeking a premium price. Snowdon is confident that it will be able to sell the building for the full asking price given the high demand and short supply of office space in the area.

Case 3. The Korean Kar Kompany has always recognized revenue at the point of sale of its vehicles. Recently, it extended its warranties to cover its vehicles for a period of ten years. A recent B.Comm. graduate working in the accounting department now questions whether Korean Kar has completed the earnings process at the time of sale. She suggests that the warranty obligation for ten years means that a significant amount of additional work must be carried out in the future. Korean Kar's engineers estimate the cost of warranty work will average about 5% of the vehicle's selling price.

Case 4. Allan Alls has just opened his real estate brokerage business, Allsold, and is unsure when he should recognize revenue for the business. It is his opinion that he has earned at least half of the commission when the sale listing is signed since he receives this amount even if another agent sells the property. He argues the remainder of the commission revenue should be recognized when an offer of purchase and sale is accepted by the owner of the property. His accountant has told Allan that the proper timing of revenue recognition for this business is when the real estate sale has closed; that is, when the new owner takes title to the property.

PROBLEM 6.19 Choose suitable revenue recognition policies

In each of the following independent cases, indicate when you think the company in question should recognize revenue. Support your decision with reference to the generally accepted criteria for revenue recognition.

a. Alaska Gold Co. mines and refines gold. The company waits to sell the gold until it feels the market price is favourable. The company can, if it wishes, sell its entire inventory of gold at any time at the prevailing market price.
b. Crazy Freddie sells cheap, ugly furniture on the installment plan. His customers take delivery of the furniture after making a down payment. In the course of the past year, Crazy Freddie has had to repossess over 50% of the furniture that he sold, due to customers defaulting on payments.
c. Tom and Mark's Construction Co. undertakes long-term construction contracts. The company only accepts contracts that will pay a fixed fee. Costs can be estimated with reasonable accuracy, and there has never been a problem collecting from customers.
d. Cecily Cedric Co. is a toy manufacturer, producing toys that are shipped to various retail customers upon receipt of their purchase order. Sales are billed after shipment. The company estimates that approximately 2% of credit sales prove to be uncollectible.

* PROBLEM 6.20 Revenue recognition policy for a fashion house

Molloy House Inc. makes and sells high-priced made-to-order clothing. All sales are one-time-only designs, made to the buyer's specifications after much consultation and demonstrations of fabrics and styles. Prices average over $10,000 for a dress and more than that for gowns, suits, and other larger items. Sales volumes are not high, but profit margins are: gross margin is usually over 60% and net income is usually over 20% of sales. Customers are promised absolute satisfaction, and about 10% of sales are returned or need costly adjustment. Customers pay about 25% of the price before work begins and are billed for the rest upon delivery, which is normally some weeks or months later. Most customers pay within a month or two of delivery, but some long-time customers are slower than that. Occasionally, due to death or bankruptcy, the remaining 75% is never paid—this happens in about one in 50 sales.

a. Specify the revenue recognition policy that you would recommend Molloy House use and explain why that policy is appropriate.
b. Most deliveries are made during three periods: the spring (coming out balls, graduations, and horse races), the summer (weddings), and the fall (opera and charity balls), but the company's staff are busy all year filling orders, which are often made far in advance and so allow the company to maintain fairly steady production. All fabric and other materials and supplies are purchased only as each order requires them; the company has no significant general inventory.
   (i) An unfilled order is both an asset and a liability for Molloy House. Explain why this is true.
   (ii) When would be a good date for the company's fiscal year-end? Why?

PROBLEM 6.21 Accounting for a health club

Carrot Club is a local health club, with exercise machines, a health food bar, and other features. The club offers a membership package of $400 for 100 visits. The package has to be paid for $100 down plus $100 per month over the next three months. A few new members fail to pay the $300 they owe. The company uses accrual accounting, and therefore its financial statements have accounts receivable for unpaid memberships and deferred revenue liability for members' unused visits.

- At the end of the 2005 fiscal year, members' unused visits totalled 85,000. At that date, members owed $22,000.
- During the 2006 fiscal year, the club sold 1,200 new memberships and experienced 140,000 visits by members. Bad debts of $1,400 were written off against the accounts receivable.

- At the end of the 2006 fiscal year, the club estimated that $1,500 of the $17,500 members' accounts owing then were doubtful.

1. Ignoring the possibility that some members may never use visits they've paid for, calculate:
   a. Revenue for the 2006 fiscal year.
   b. Deferred revenue liability for unused visits, as at the end of the 2006 fiscal year.
2. The company's auditor suggested that the financial statements should take into account the fact that some paid-up members move, lose interest, or otherwise end up never using all the visits they have paid for. If the company adopted this accounting policy, indicate the effect (up, down, or no effect) on each of the following, and say why you chose the answer you did.
   a. Accounts receivable at the end of 2006.
   b. Revenue for 2006.

PROBLEM 6.22 Franchise revenue amounts and policies

Clucky Chicken Corp. (CC) and Poulet Chicken Inc. (PC) are competitors. Both sell franchises for their chicken restaurants. The purchaser of the franchise (the franchisee) receives the right to use CC's and PC's products and benefit from national training and advertising programs for ten years. The buyers agree to pay $750,000 for a franchise. Of this amount, $150,000 is paid upon signing the agreement and the remainder is payable in five equal annual installments of $120,000 each.

Clucky Chicken recognizes all franchise revenue when franchise agreements are signed. Poulet Chicken recognizes franchise revenue as cash is received. In 2004 the companies each sold eight franchises. In 2005 they each sold six. In 2006 and 2007 neither company sold a franchise.

1. Determine the amount of franchise revenue recognized by each company in 2004, 2005, 2006, and 2007.
2. Do you think that revenue should be recognized when the franchise agreement is signed, when cash is received, or over the life of the franchise agreement? Why? Fully support your answer.

* PROBLEM 6.23 Answer a question about revenues

The Rosemead Nursery raises trees intended for sale to landscape suppliers and contractors. The trees normally take five years to reach saleable size. What special problems of income determination does Rosemead face if it is to prepare annual financial statements?

* PROBLEM 6.24 Revenue recognition for an airline

Redneck Airlines recognizes revenue when transportation is provided. Passengers who cancel tickets prior to the day of departure are given nonrefundable credits for future flights. The airline then charges a $20.00 change fee when another flight is booked. Passengers who miss a flight or cancel on the day of departure forfeit their fare.

On January 2, 2005, John purchased a round-trip ticket from Edmonton to Victoria for $300.00 and paid for it three days later. The flight was to leave Edmonton on January 24, 2005, and return on January 26, 2005. On January 17, John learned that he would have to work on the following weekend so he cancelled his ticket.

On February 7, 2005, John called and booked a round-trip flight to Winnipeg, departing February 21, 2005, and returning February 23, 2005. John used his credit towards the fare of $400.00 and paid cash for the change fee and difference in fares. John caught the flight on the 21st but slept in on the 23rd and missed his return flight. He arrived at the airport that afternoon and paid $200.00 cash for a one-way ticket on a plane leaving immediately.

Prepare journal entries to record Redneck's revenue from John.

PROBLEM 6.25 Accounting versus economic view of revenue

An economist might argue that revenue is created or earned continuously by a wide variety of the firm's activities (such as production, sales, delivery), yet the accountant in a typical case selects only one of these steps (the "critical event") to signal the time at which all revenues are to be recognized.

a. Assuming that the economist's view is correct, under what circumstances would the accountant's method lead to an undistorted measure of periodic income? In other words, under what conditions will the opinion that income is continuously earned agree with income as determined by accountants?
b. What are the obstacles to the practical implementation of the economist's view as the basis for accounting income determination?

Fiscal Period, Expense Recognition and Matching • Sections 6.5, 6.8, 6.9

* **PROBLEM 6.26** Revenues, expenses, and income for a construction contract

Rockheads Inc. is a construction contractor specializing in roads and other large constructions of earthworks, rocks, and concrete. Here is information about one of its multi-year contracts, Job 48.

Total revenue agreed in the contract: $5,200,000
Rockheads' estimate of its total costs over the life of the contract: $4,300,000
Year 1: Spent $900,000, billed $1,300,000, collected $1,000,000
Year 2: Spent $1,990,000, billed $1,800,000, collected $2,030,000
Year 3: Spent $1,410,000, billed $2,100,000, collected $2,170,000

Calculate the revenue, expense, and income from Job 48 for *each year* and for the *whole contract* on each of the following bases:

a. Completed contract basis.
b. Percentage completion basis (using proportion of cost spent as the measure of percentage completed and rounding percentages to the nearest whole percent).
c. Cash received basis (hint: match expense recognition to the proportion of total cash received each year).

PROBLEM 6.27 Construction accounting

Rimrock Construction Ltd. has several contracts to construct buildings:

Contract No.	Expected Revenue	Expected Expense	Expected Income	Percentage Completed End of 2005	Percentage Completed End of 2006
48	$1,000,000	$ 800,000	$200,000	60%	100%
49	1,500,000	1,300,000	200,000	20%	80%
50	860,000	710,000	150,000	0%	100%
51	2,430,000	1,950,000	480,000	0%	90%
52	1,600,000	1,320,000	280,000	0%	20%

1. Assuming all revenues, collections, expenses, and payments are as expected, calculate income before income tax for 2006:
   a. Using the completed contracts basis to recognize contract revenues and expenses.
   b. Using the percentage of completion basis to recognize contract revenues and expenses.
2. Which of these two bases is the more conservative? Why?

3. No revenue has yet been collected on Contract #50, but all expenses related to it have been paid. Contract #50 has run into legal trouble. Rimrock now expects to receive only $100,000 of the expected revenue. Write the journal entry, if any is needed, to recognize this information. (Assume the completed contract basis if necessary.)

PROBLEM 6.28 Revenue, expenses, and income for a construction contract.

The information below relates to an individual long-term construction contract of Tamarack Construction Ltd.

Year	Costs Incurred	Cash Received
2004	$1,500,000	$2,025,000
2005	2,750,000	3,150,000
2006	1,600,000	2,325,000
Total	$5,850,000	$7,500,000

Assume that the contract price was $7,500,000 and that the original cost estimate on the contract was $6,000,000. Calculate the revenue, expenses, and income for each year 2004 to 2006 and for the whole contract on each of the following bases:

a. Completed contract basis
b. Percentage of completion basis (using proportion of cost spent as the measure of percentage completed and rounding percentages to the nearest whole percent).
c. Cash received basis (hint: match expense recognition to the proportion of total cash received each year).
d. How would your answer to b. change if the contract were not yet completed?

* PROBLEM 6.29 Answer a question about expenses

In 2006, Flimsy Construction Ltd. has recognized 38% of the total expected revenue from a contract to build a garage onto Professor Blotz's house. The total contract price is $43,000 and Flimsy expects its costs for the contract to be $29,500. Costs so far have been in line with expectations. How much contract expense should Flimsy recognize for 2006 and what would be the resulting contract income for 2006?

* PROBLEM 6.30 Calculate accrual net income from various accounts

Pottery Galore Ltd. has just finished its 2006 fiscal year. From the following data, calculate net income or loss for 2006:

Collections from customers during 2006	$174,320
Accounts receivable, end of 2005	11,380
Accounts receivable, end of 2006	9,440
Bad debts (written off to expense directly from accounts receivable in 2006)	520
Payments to suppliers and employees during 2006	145,690
Accounts and wages payable, end of 2005	12,770
Accounts and wages payable, end of 2006	15,510
Inventory of unsold goods, end of 2005	21,340
Inventory of unsold goods, end of 2006	24,650
Bank loan, end of 2006	12,000
(The loan was taken out a month before the end of 2006 at an interest rate of 8%. No interest has yet been paid.)	
Income tax payable, end of 2006 (none end of 2005)	2,340
Income tax paid during 2006	3,400
Future income tax liability, end of 2006 (none end of 2005)	1,230

PROBLEM 6.31 Contract cash flow and income calculations

The Swazy Construction Company has secured a contract with the Alberta government for the construction of 15 km of highway at a contract price of $125,000 a kilometre. Payments for each kilometre of highway are to be made according to the following schedule:

- 35% at the time the concrete is poured
- 45% when all work on that kilometre is completed
- 20% when all 15 km of highway have been completed, inspected, and approved

At the end of the first period of operation, 5 km of highway have been entirely completed and approved, concrete has been poured on a second stretch of 5 km, and preliminary grading has been done on the third 5-km stretch.

The job was originally estimated to cost $100,000 a kilometre. Costs to date have coincided with these original estimates and have totalled the following amounts: on the completed stretch, $100,000 a kilometre; on the second stretch, $80,000 a kilometre; and on the third stretch, $12,500 a kilometre. It is estimated that each unfinished stretch will be completed at the costs originally estimated.

1. How much should the Alberta government have paid Swazy during or at the end of the first period of operation under the terms of the contract? Show computations.
2. How much income would you report for this period? Show your calculations and justify your method.

PROBLEM 6.32 Income on various revenue recognition bases

The Latanae Company produces a single product at a cost of $8 each, all of which is paid in cash when the unit is produced. Selling expenses of $4 a unit are paid at the time of shipment. The sale price is $15 a unit; all sales are on account. No customer defaults are expected, and no costs are incurred at the time of collection.

During 2005, the company produced 150,000 units, shipped 120,000 units, and collected $900,000 from customers. During 2006, it produced 120,000 units, shipped 135,000 units, and collected $1,425,000 from customers.

1. Ignoring income tax for now, determine the amount of income that would be reported for each of these two years:
   a. If revenue and expense are recognized at the time of production.
   b. If revenue and expense are recognized at the time of shipment.
   c. If revenue and expense are recognized at the time of collection.
2. Would the asset total shown on the December 31, 2006, balance sheet be affected by the choice among the three recognition bases used in part 1? What would be the amount of any such difference?
3. Redo part 1, assuming that the company's income tax rate is 30%.

PROBLEM 6.33 Real company's revenue, expense recognition

Using the financial statements, MD&A, and other information of any company you are interested in, write a comprehensive review of the company's revenue and expense recognition policies. (This information can be found on the Web page of most public companies, or check **www.sedar.com** for the companies' filings.) Cover such points as

a. What the nature of the company's business is and how it earns its revenue and incurs its expenses;
b. What the company's financial statements and notes disclose about its important revenue and expense recognition policies;
c. Based on (a) and (b) and on your own thinking about the company, the appropriateness of the company's revenue and expense policies and what questions or concerns you have about them; and

d. What the company's cash flow statement tells you about how close the company's accrual net income is to cash income.

Prepaid and Accrued Expenses • Section 6.10

*** PROBLEM 6.34** Calculate prepaid and accrued expense

A local company pays its property taxes on a rather erratic basis. Here is a schedule of its property tax bills and payments over the last few years:

- Was billed in April 2004 for the calendar 2004 taxes of $4,500.
- Paid those taxes September 20, 2004.
- Was billed in April 2005 for the calendar 2005 taxes of $4,800.
- Paid those taxes November 30, 2005.
- Was billed in April 2006 for the calendar 2007 taxes of $5,100.
- Paid those taxes August 15, 2007.

Calculate the prepaid or accrued property taxes and the property tax expense *for the fiscal years 2005 and 2006*, if the company had *each* of the following fiscal year-ends:

a. April 30
b. June 30
c. September 30
d. December 31

PROBLEM 6.35 Prepaid and accrued expenses

For each of these examples, calculate whether the company had a prepaid asset or an accrued liability at the end of 2005, what the amount of that was, and what the related expense for 2005 was.

1. Westridge Manufacturing Inc. has significant costs for worker training. These costs are sometimes paid in advance and sometimes after they have been incurred. At the beginning of 2005, the company had paid $148,560 in advance. During 2005, the company incurred training costs of $960,370 and paid $808,760. In addition, the company suffered injury costs totalling $127,530 in spite of the training.
2. Athabasca Eco-Tours pays for some of the costs of its tours in advance, some during the tours, and some later, after the tours have occurred. At the beginning of 2005, the company owed $62,380 on prior tours. During 2005, the company incurred $875,320 in tour costs and paid $814,630.

PROBLEM 6.36 Prepaid and accrued expenses

Papa Jack's Pizza has an account with a local media company for television and radio advertisements. On January 1, 2006, Papa Jack's Pizza had a positive balance of $8,000 in its advertising account. Papa Jack's Pizza ran ads costing $11,000 in January and made a payment of $13,000 at the end of the month. February's ads cost $16,000 and a payment of $9,000 was made at the end of the month. Prepare journal entries for these transactions and a chart to reflect the account activity for the first two months of 2006. (Use the format of Figures 6.10 and 6.11 in Section 6.10.)

Integrated

*** PROBLEM 6.37** Discuss some terms

Discuss what each of the following terms has to do with income measurement and related balance sheet valuation:

a. aggressive accounting
b. articulation
c. deferred revenue
d. matching
e. period expenses
f. conservatism

*** PROBLEM 6.38** Adjusting journal entries

It is the end of International Fabrics Inc.'s fiscal year. You are working on the company's financial statements, and have discovered the items listed below. For each item:

1. State whether or not the item requires that an adjustment be made in the company's accounts according to the principles of accrual accounting; and
2. If the answer to part 1 is yes, write a journal entry to adjust the company's accounts.

a. Sales of $3,200 made on account just before the end of the fiscal year were not recorded until the beginning of the next year.
b. The cost of goods sold for those sales, totalling $1,900, has not yet been recognized.
c. During the year, deposits of $5,300 were made by customers on special orders and were credited to the deposit liability account. Deposits of $1,400 are still being held, but all the other special orders have been completed and the customers have paid the rest of the price for those orders (those payments are included in sales revenue).
d. Maintenance expenses seemed rather high, and on investigation it turned out that an addition to the company's store, constructed over a period of several months at a cost of $62,320, had been included in the maintenance expenses.
e. Just before the year-end, the company was sued by a customer whose expensive curtains lost their colour as soon as they were exposed to sunlight. The lawsuit was for $4,300 to replace the curtains and $50,000 in pain and suffering damages. Legal advice indicates that the curtains should be replaced (which would cost the company about what it is being sued for) but that the customer will not succeed with the pain and suffering damages.
f. The company's auditors sent a bill for $2,350 for the year's audit work.
g. Just before the year-end, the company bought an automobile from a major shareholder for $17,220, agreeing to pay in three months.
h. At the beginning of the year, the company had paid $2,000 for the exclusive right to distribute in Canada fabrics made by Silk Dreams Inc. of Pennsylvania. The exclusive distributorship is for a period of four years.

*** PROBLEM 6.39** Explain some accrual accounting topics

Explain to a businessperson who is not an accountant and is impatient with jargon what each of the following topics has to do with accrual accounting, what impact it has on companies' financial statements, and how important it is in understanding the financial statements.

a. Recognizing revenue when it has been earned.
b. Using the balance sheet to hold the "residual" effects of income measurement.
c. Matching expense recognition to the fiscal period in which the expense was incurred.

PROBLEM 6.40 Calculation of accrual income from cash records

Mike Stammer is a private investigator. He keeps his accounting records on a cash basis and has produced the following income statement, *as he calls it.*

Mike Stammer Income Statement for the Year Ended June 30, 2006	
Fees collected in cash	$85,000
Less cash expenses	34,600
Net income	$50,400

An examination of Mike's records shows these balances at the beginning and end of fiscal 2006:

	July 1, 2005	June 30, 2006
Fees receivable	$12,460	$ 3,900
Client deposits on continuing investigations	—	1,800
Accrued expenses	4,250	5,250
Prepaid expenses	1,900	2,500

1. a. What amount of the fees Mike collected in fiscal 2006 were received for investigations he actually completed in fiscal 2005?
   b. What amount of the fees received in 2006 will he earn in 2007?
   c. How much in fees did he earn in 2006, but not collect?
2. a. What amount of the expenses Mike paid in fiscal 2006 should be matched with his efforts in fiscal 2005 or 2007?
   b. What amount of expenses paid in previous years should be matched with revenues Mike earned in 2006?
3. Use your answers to parts 1 and 2 to prepare an accrual basis income statement for Mike Stammer for the year ended June 30, 2006.
4. Add or subtract whichever adjustments to the cash income statement are necessary to reconcile Mike's $50,400 "income" to your figure.
5. Compare the two income statements. Why might Mike Stammer (or others using his financial information) prefer to use the cash basis of accounting? Why might he (or others) prefer the accrual basis?

PROBLEM 6.41 Recommend revenue and expense recognition policy

Bob Basquit Productions Ltd. (BBPL) acquired the rights to use the names of a number of basketball players on life-sized stuffed dolls it purchases from a toy manufacturer. The dolls are marketed through mail order advertisements in the TV-listings inserts of large newspapers. When an order is received (with a money order, cheque, or credit card number), BBPL contacts the toy manufacturer. The toy manufacturer is responsible for manufacturing and shipping the doll to the lucky boy or girl. BBPL is notified at the time of shipment. The customer has the option of returning the doll within two weeks of the day it is received. BBPL pays the toy manufacturer within 30 days after delivery. Response to the dolls this Christmas has been overwhelming. In fact, the toy manufacturer is working extra shifts to try to keep up with the demand.

1. Identify three points in time that BBPL could recognize revenue on the dolls. Which would you recommend? Why?
2. Identify two different points in time that the toy manufacturer could recognize revenue on the dolls.

3. Discuss how BBPL should account for its payments to basketball players for the right to use their names. (Assume that each player is paid a lump sum initially and a royalty on each doll sold that uses his name.)

PROBLEM 6.42 Accounting methods for a frequent buyer program

Heather, the owner of Blue Books, has been struggling with the competition from big bookstore chains and has decided to offer customers a reward points plan to encourage repeat business. The plan is free, and if a customer joins, every dollar spent on a book earns the customer 5 cents toward future books. This is not a discount on future purchases, but has to be used to obtain books just on points. For example, if a customer wants to get a $20.00 book on points, she would have to have spent $400.00 before then. If she has only spent, say, $350.00, she cannot use the points accumulated so far to get a discount on the book but must wait until she has spent another $50.00, and then she will get the book free.

1. *Ignoring the possibility that some customers may never redeem their points,* describe the accounting policy you would recommend the company use for this new points plan. Your policy should be the one you think is conceptually sound—don't worry here about the practical implications of your policy, such as keeping track of needed information. Answer in two parts:
   a. How would you account for points earned by customers before they redeem any free books?
   b. How would you account for the redemption of points for free books?
2. Bert observed that some customers will never redeem their points. Explain how, if at all, you would modify the policy you recommended above in accounting for this factor.
3. The bookstore's auditor observed that both conservatism and matching are important to the policy choice. Explain why both are important in this case.

PROBLEM 6.43 Revenue and expense recognition for a franchiser

The Pie Place, Inc. (TPP) was started in 2005 to franchise a chain of fast-food outlets that would sell only pies: meat, mince, pecan, sugar, and the like. A specialty was to be "pi-pie," a recipe made from various roots (ginger, ginseng, etc.) and invented by Janet Randolph, the founder and owner of TPP.

Janet has divided each major city into population sectors of about 200,000 each and plans to sell one franchise per sector. For smaller cities, franchises will cover rural areas as well. The franchises will be good for ten years, renewable for at least two more ten-year periods, and will sell for $20,000 each. Each franchisee must pay TPP $5,000 down in cash, pay the remainder in three equal annual installments (with no interest charges), and agree to buy various ingredients from TPP. In return, TPP will provide expert advice (Janet's), recipes, help with locating and constructing the food outlet, management training, and some national advertising. (Most advertising costs will be charged back to the franchises on a pro rata basis.)

Here are data for TPP's first year, ended August 31, 2006:

Franchise agreements signed	28
Down payments received	26
Fast-food outlets opened	18
Franchise-related costs	$230,000
Other general expenses	$55,000

One of the franchises has already gone out of business (having paid only the initial $5,000), two others of those that have opened do not look as if they are going to make it, and one of the unopened franchises looks as if it will never get going.

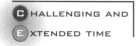

1. List as many methods as you can think of for recognizing revenue from franchise sales.
2. Rank those methods from least conservative to most conservative.
3. List as many methods as you can think of for recognizing expenses from franchise-related costs.
4. Match each expense recognition method to the revenue recognition method that seems most appropriate.
5. Compare the income before tax for 2006 that would be produced by two or three of the more reasonable matched methods of recognizing revenue and expense.
6. Choose a matched method that you think would be most appropriate for TPP.
7. Draft an "accounting policy" footnote describing your chosen revenue/expense recognition method for TPP's August 31, 2006, financial statements.

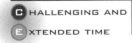

PROBLEM 6.44 Comprehensive revenue and expense issues

Programs Plus Inc. (PPI) is engaged in developing a computerized scheduling, shipping, maintenance, and operations system for the North American logistics industry.

PPI has spent the last five years conducting systems development work and this year (ended November 30, 2006) sold its first systems. Initial funding of $3,000,000 came from the founder, who invested $1,500,000 for shares and $1,500,000 in the form of a loan. In the past, the company was not very concerned about accounting issues and financial statements, but now it is seeking external financing and is required to prepare financial statements to obtain this financing.

It is now December 19, 2006. The president is very concerned about how the company's results for the year ended November 30, 2006, will appear to investors. She understands that GAAP allow choices to be made regarding accounting policies and is interested in the choices available for the following two issues:

- Costs totalling $2,500,000 have been incurred evenly over the last five years in developing systems. Of these costs, $1,000,000 relate to failed efforts on a system that was found this year to be unmarketable. The rest of the costs are attributable to the development of a system that is currently being sold. The company expects to be able to sell the system for five years before it becomes technologically obsolete. The system is expected to become more obsolete and therefore, harder to market as the five years progress. Right now, the company anticipates selling the system as follows:

Fiscal year ended Nov. 30, 2006	2 systems already sold
Fiscal year ended Nov. 30, 2007	4 systems expected to be sold
Fiscal year ended Nov. 30, 2008	3 systems expected to be sold
Fiscal year ended Nov. 30, 2009	2 systems expected to be sold
Fiscal year ended Nov. 30, 2010	1 system expected to be sold

- Sales commenced in the last half of 2006. Each sales contract is priced to provide a $250,000 margin over estimated contract costs. Sales arise as follows: a contract is negotiated covering the services to be provided; a nonreturnable deposit of 15% of the negotiated price is required before work commences; as work continues, regular billings are made at specific stages of completion of the system. To November 30, 2006, the following sales have occurred:

Sold To	Total Contract Price	Deposit	Contract Billings So Far	Cash Rec'd Including Deposit	Completed So Far	Cash Paid for Costs So Far
Co. A	$2,000,000	$300,000	$750,000	$600,000	40%	$500,000
Co. B	2,250,000	337,500	Nil	337,500	Nil	Nil
	$4,250,000	$637,500	$750,000	$937,500		$500,000

Prior to making any accounting decisions involved in the above issues, the company's account balances at November 30, 2006, are:

	Debit	Credit
Cash	$ 937,500	
Contract costs paid	500,000	
Contract receipts		$ 937,500
Development costs	2,500,000	
Share capital		1,500,000
Shareholder loan		1,500,000
	$3,937,500	$3,937,500

The following additional information is relevant:

a. Of the costs to date, $500,000 has been paid in cash and an additional $200,000 has been incurred but not paid. The only cash inflow this year has been from contract deposits and billings.
b. The company is still in the development stage and is not required to pay income tax for 2006 or prior years.
c. The founding shareholder's loan is interest-free and due on demand, but the shareholder has signed a letter confirming that he will not withdraw the funds over the course of the next year.

Given all of the above information, answer the following:

1. Suggest two different methods of recognizing revenue from sales of the systems. (No calculations are needed—just describe the methods.)
2. Choose a revenue recognition method for CompCom and state why you prefer it.
3. Based on the method you chose in part 2, calculate the company's revenue and contract cost expense for the year ended November 30, 2006.
4. The president wants to capitalize the development costs. How much would you recommend be capitalized, and why?
5. Explain to the president why amortization of any such development cost asset is necessary.
6. Choose a method of amortizing the development cost asset that makes sense to you and calculate the amortization expense for 2006 and the accumulated amortization at November 30, 2006.
7. Based on your answers to the previous parts, prepare an income statement and statement of retained earnings for 2006 and a balance sheet as at November 30, 2006, with appropriate notes.
8. If you're not exhausted, also prepare a cash flow statement for 2006.

CASE 6A

A VARIETY OF REVENUE AND EXPENSE RECOGNITION PROBLEMS IN REAL COMPANIES

Much of this book has involved large companies in the public eye. But income measurement is important in all kinds of enterprises. Discuss the accounting methods, ethics, and business practices in the following examples, *all real companies* with their identities disguised. In each example, try to figure out which accounts in the income statement and balance sheet are involved so that you can say what the effects are on the financial statements.

1. Great Chicken was founded to sell fast-food franchises using the name of a well-known entertainer. Quite a few retired couples and other hopeful people signed up to buy franchises, usually putting up their savings and promising to pay the rest out of the profits of their franchise. Great Chicken recorded the total value of each franchise as revenue on the day the deal was signed. The company had no expenses to speak of at the beginning (except advertising and promotion), so its income statement showed high profits, which encouraged more people to sign up for franchises, which produced more profits. The company's profit growth was huge. But then it became apparent that the franchisees had not chosen good locations, didn't know much about running a chicken shop, couldn't cook and serve the food properly, and so couldn't pay their promised franchise payments. It also became apparent that Great Chicken really didn't know how to help them. To the despair of everyone, the whole operation, franchiser and franchisees, went out of business.
2. Intensive Research Inc., located next to a major university, raised funding to develop some drugs for treating serious illnesses. During several years of research and development, the company had very small revenues (interest and some research grants and fees for consulting to other companies) and very large R&D expenses. The president believed it would be inappropriate accounting to match the high R&D to zero revenues yet from the drugs, and bad for the company's image to have losses all this time, so the company capitalized R&D (removed it from expense and put it on the balance sheet as a long-term asset). Enough was capitalized each year to bring the company's net income to just above zero.
3. Central Community Association rented out its hall on weekends for weddings and other functions. The money earned by these rentals was a major part of the association's funding, largely paying the salary of the association's manager. However, a fair number of renters managed to disappear from town or otherwise avoid paying, so the association instituted a policy of payment in advance. In the first year of this policy, the association showed a large increase in income, because rental reservations often well into future months had been included in the revenue. An argument broke out at the association's regular board of directors meeting when an accountant suggested that each function's reservation revenue be deferred until the function had been held. It turned out that the association's manager, flush with cash, had spent a lot more on repairs and cleaning than usual, and if the revenue was deferred, the association would show a loss for the year, contrary to its by-laws. The manager argued that the deferral of revenue was unnecessary because after the first year of the new policy, things would pretty much even out, revenues coming in at about the same rate as expenses, and so the policy of requiring payment in advance brought in effect a permanent gain for the association.
4. The president of Morgan Lumber always kept the results of the annual inventory count secret. Even the company's chief accountant was not told how much inventory was on hand until a preliminary income figure had been determined for the year. Then the president would consult the records of the inventory count and provide a year-end inventory cost figure, from which the chief accountant deduced the cost of goods sold (beginning inventory plus purchases minus ending inventory equals the cost of what must have been sold). Each year, the final income turned out to be just about what the president wanted, in line with indications given to the bank and with installments paid on the company's income tax.

5. Western Business Bank had a large portfolio of loans receivable, all secured by property mortgages. Some of these loans were not being repaid very well, or at all, but the bank did not worry about this much as long as the market values of the mortgaged properties exceeded the loans amounts. So each month, the bank added interest on the loans to interest revenue and to the loans receivable, which therefore continued to rise because many were not being repaid by borrowers. Therefore, the bank's reported assets and revenue (and income) grew even if the borrowers were not keeping up their payments. The bank reasoned that it could always seize the mortgaged properties, sell them, and recover its money. Then, to everyone's horror, the real estate market collapsed, driving market values of mortgaged properties down below the accumulated "loans plus accrued interest" receivables. The bank went out of business soon after, leaving many shareholders and depositors without their money.
6. Brilliant Software had a small but innovative set of software to be sold in the educational market. Having made promises to investors that the company would succeed, the president was disappointed at the great competition the company faced and resultant slow sales. The company's sales force was therefore issued with "sales call reports" that looked just like sales invoices. When a salesperson made a call, the report was filled in with the number of software packages the potential customer had expressed an interest in, though not actually agreed to buy. These reports came back to head office, where signatures were forged onto them to turn them into sales orders, which were then booked as revenue. To complete the process, the software had to be shipped, but to where? The so-called customer had not actually ordered it. So Brilliant Software quietly rented a warehouse in an obscure part of town, and "shipped" the software there. Somehow no one seemed to question the consequent growth in accounts receivable, and the "shipped" software gathered dust in the warehouse until the whole mess was uncovered.[15]

CASE 6B

"LESSONS OF THE '90S"

Discuss the lessons for preparing and using accrual accounting information that are suggested in the article below, "Lessons of the '90s."[16] As some "disaster stories" mentioned in the article (Enron, Global Crossing, and WorldCom) will continue to unfold after this book has gone to press, your discussion could be updated by events that have happened since the article was written.

LESSONS OF THE '90S

If there is anything Wall Street and the rest of us should have learned from the '90s, it's that the fixation on earnings reports is what got us into this mess in the first place.

By Harris Collingwood

Investors, pummelled financially by a two-year drop in stocks and psychologically by the atrocities of Sept. 11, 2001, are said to be chastened now.

A newly sober Wall Street shudders when recalling the stock market bubble, as a groggy party-goer regrets the excesses of the night before. The day traders have taken their optimism and margin accounts and chat-board rants and disappeared down the same hole that swallowed the age of irony.

That's what we're told. But then we get a day like May 8. After the close of trading the previous day, Cisco Systems, the former Internet titan, disclosed a modest profit of $729 million, or 10 cents a share, and the markets went wild.

The Nasdaq composite index, thick with technology stocks, soared 7.8 per cent, its biggest gain in more than a year and the eighth-biggest ever. The Dow Jones industrial average posted its best performance since September. And why? Because Cisco beat its modest earnings-growth target by a slim two cents a share.

Never mind that Cisco's quarterly revenue was basically flat, and that analysts and Cisco's own management attributed the profits to cost cutting rather than to an upturn in business. Cisco beat its forecast, and that's all that matters.

If there is anything Wall Street and the rest of us should have learned from the '90s, it's that the fixation on earnings reports is what got us into this mess in the first place.

It's not by coincidence that the bull market's disaster stories—Enron, Global Crossing and WorldCom, to name just three—concern the companies that were most adept at conjuring market-pleasing numbers. Their handsome earnings statements disguised enterprises too rotten to stand unsupported, and their collapse took lives, businesses and portfolios down with them.

It would be comforting to think that the damage was confined to Enron and a handful of other companies that got up to tricks no respectable corporation would even consider.

Public companies and investors alike were obsessed with earnings growth

Yet during the stock market boom, nearly every public company, from the most admired to the most reviled, was gripped by an unhealthy obsession with earnings growth.

In its early phases this fixation may have stimulated corporate innovation and efficiency, but by the time the bull market was in full cry, the pressure for endless growth was driving corporations to fudge the facts, mortgage the future and work against their own best interests and those of their customers, employees and shareholders.

Obsessions die hard. As the market's one-day frenzy over Cisco illustrates, the earnings fixation withstood the bursting of the stock market bubble, and it will withstand whatever reform measures eventually emerge from Washington.

It is a matter of some urgency, then, to figure out how business fell under this corrosive spell—before it undoes another big company, obliterates billions more dollars in shareholder wealth and throws thousands more people out of work.

A little like the Public Broadcasting System, the earnings game owes its survival to corporate sponsorship, as well as to the support of viewers (or investors) like you. Corporate executives, for their part, are almost compelled to play.

Continued earnings growth ensures their company's access to affordable sources of capital. It also lets executives keep their jobs and collect stock options and other earnings-related incentives.

But executives aren't the only ones playing the earnings game. Over the years, an entire earnings infrastructure has developed, including corporate executives and directors, accountants and analysts, fund managers and kitchen-table stock players.

These interested parties play mutually reinforcing roles in sustaining the fiction that continuous profit growth is either possible or desirable.

And it is a fiction. Even in the 1990s, an exceptionally good period for business, only one in eight large companies managed to achieve continuous, year-upon-year earnings growth.

According to a recent report by Credit Suisse First Boston, average earnings growth during the '90s, the up years and the down years taken together, was little better than seven per cent.

Nonetheless, most large companies currently predict that their earnings will grow by about 15 per cent a year, every year. And no company in the CSFB study forecasts even a single year of declining profits.

The companies that do achieve continual growth aren't necessarily better off for it, nor are their investors. Over the years, economists have come to two widely shared conclusions about corporate earnings: First, higher earnings this quarter do not presage higher earnings next quarter.

The second conclusion is that rapidly growing profits are not necessarily a symptom of robust corporate health. They're just as likely to indicate a corporate management that is more adept at fancy accounting tricks than at running a business.

In recent years, earnings have so dominated the financial conversation that it's hard to remember that there are other ways to judge and compare corporate performance.

Some professional investors, the legendary Warren Buffet among them, evaluate companies by their return on invested capital. Others, like the mutual fund manager Robert Olstein, consistently make money by focusing on the cash generated by a company's continuing operations.

Baruch Lev, an accounting professor at New York University's Stern School of Business, argues against relying on any single data point. He advocates ranking companies on everything from patent filings to the amount they invest in employee training.

But in a sound-bite era, the subtle and complex lose out to the simple and obvious every time. As the long bull market recouped the losses of the early-'90s downturn, a single, stark equation took firm hold in the minds of the mass of investors: More earnings equals more shareholder value. All business news was reduced to earnings news, and growth forecasting emerged as an industry in its own right.

Left to their own devices, corporate managers during the boom weren't about to abandon the earnings game. The rewards for playing were too great and the penalties for nonparticipation too severe.

But in theory at least, two groups of professionals—audit firms and securities analysts—had a duty to investors to restrain corporate managers' most self-serving impulses and subject their actions to skeptical scrutiny.

Instead, far too many analysts and auditors connived with management to conceal the true condition of some of the market's most dysfunctional companies.

The litany of the professionals' failures has been well chronicled, so regular readers of the business pages will recognize a few of the more egregious examples.

Watchdogs lost their effectiveness trying to serve two masters

As early as February 2001, auditors from Arthur Andersen were aware that Andrew Fastow, Enron's chief financial officer, was serving two masters: Enron and the partnerships with which the company had an ostensibly arm's-length relationship. The auditors discussed the blatant conflict among themselves but did nothing to check it.

Auditors at another firm, KPMG, supposedly allowed Xerox to produce a deceptively cheery picture of its revenue growth. The company's European, Latin American and Canadian units booked all the revenue from the long-term copier leases up front, even though customers paid over several years.

The pressures that drove the accounting firms to bend their principles are clear enough. In the 1980s and 1990s, the firms aggressively sold consulting services to their existing audit clients.

Consulting revenue soon surpassed audit revenue at the Big Five firms, leading them to regard auditing not as a function in its own right but as a marketing tool.

Aware that corporate clients could simply fire an unco-operative auditor—as Xerox did when KPMG refused to certify the company's 2000 financial report—audit firms became more and more lenient toward their clients.

Like the accounting firms, analysts suffer from hopelessly divided loyalties. Although in theory analysts' primary task is to provide reliable information to investors, their primary constituency is actually their colleagues in investment banking, who earn multimillion-dollar fees for underwriting and distributing securities of corporate clients.

None of these conflicts of interest should come as news to reasonably informed investors. It was not exactly a secret in the 1990s that many corporations were straining the limits of acceptable accounting, and that several of the companies with the most questionable accounting, including Waste Management and Sunbeam, were clients of Arthur Andersen.

The standards that govern corporate accounting—known as generally accepted accounting principles—are far more flexible than the public would imagine.

In general, this is a desirable and necessary quality. It brings, say, an airline, which collects its payment as soon as it sells a ticket, and a software company, where payment lags far behind the sale, into the same financial universe.

The trouble is, that same flexibility gives corporate managers the latitude to summon earnings out of this air if they're so inclined. It enabled companies like Xerox to claim most of their revenue all at once, even though their clients usually paid over a period of several years.

For now, at least, investors do seem to be scrutinizing earnings reports with a new diligence. But it will be interesting to see if their caution survives the next stock market rally, and whether they can resist the hype of ratings-starved financial channels spewing earnings reports by the minute, all day every working day.

In the end, corporate managers are probably the best hope for breaking the grip of the earnings obsession.

Gillette's chief executive, James Kilts, has disavowed his predecessor's promises of 18 per cent annual earnings growth, saying it led the company to increase prices, cut ad spending and otherwise cripple its own long-term prospects.

The stock market and human nature being what they are, such realism isn't likely to become the majority view. But even a sizable minority could help ensure that the next boom doesn't end as badly as the last one.

Harris Collingwood, a former senior editor of The Harvard Business Review, writes frequently on business and finance.

NOTES

1. W.H. Beaver, *Financial Reporting: An Accounting Revolution*, 2nd ed. (Englewood Cliffs: Prentice-Hall, 1989), 8.
2. Ibid., 105.
3. Ibid., 105.
4. P.A. Griffin, ed., *Usefulness to Investors and Creditors of Information Provided by Financial Reporting*, 2nd ed. (Stamford: Financial Accounting Standards Board, 1987), 14.
5. CPR notes to consolidated financial statements, 2004 Annual Report, 48–51.
6. Ibid., 51–53.
7. Canadian Institute of Chartered Accountants, "Introduction to Accounting Standards," in *CICA Handbook* (Toronto: Canadian Institute of Chartered Accountants, revised to April 2005), as posted on the *Handbook* Web site **http://www.knotia.ca.**
8. C. Byrd, I. Chen, and J. Smith, *Financial Reporting in Canada, 2005* (Toronto: Canadian Institute of Chartered Accountants, 2005), 6. (The 2005 30th edition surveys annual reports of 200 Toronto Stock Exchange companies for 2004, 2003, 2002 and 2001.)
9. Christopher Power, "Let's Get Fiscal," *Forbes* (April 30, 1984): 103.
10. CPR, 2004 Annual Report, 48.
11. Canadian Tire 2004 Annual Report, 87.
12. Bombardier Inc. 2004–05 Annual Report, 97.
13. Aecon Group Inc. 2004 Annual Report, 34.
14. S. Tuck, "Tech Firms' Accounting Methods Assailed," *The Globe and Mail* (29 March 1999): B1, B9.
15. Based on the article "Anatomy of a Fraud," by M. Maremont, *Business Week* (16 September 1996): 90–92, 94.
16. H. Collingwood, "Lessons of the '90s," *The Edmonton Journal* (June 16, 2002): D5. Reprinted from *The New York Times Magazine.*

CHAPTER SEVEN

Recordkeeping and Control

7

7.1 Chapter Introduction: Recordkeeping and Control

Episode 42 in the Adventures of …drum roll… Forensic Man!

The caper. It was a dark night in the city. In an alley behind the jewellery store, the famous cat burglar struggled into her tight Mauve Menace costume with "If You've Got It, Flaunt It" stencilled on the back. "Oof," she muttered, "gotta lay off the ice cream bars." But then it was an easy climb up to the store's roof and in through a heating duct.

The insider. It was also easy to find the safe. "Canoodling with that doofus Meek Mike from the store's office was no fun, but at least I got the store layout and part of the safe combination out of the jerk for my trouble." She evaded the security system with her usual agility, then after only five hours of fiddling with the safe's lock, got it open.

The loot. The safe was full of just what she was looking for: very expensive custom-made jewellery. She scooped it out into her special loot bag and closed the safe.

The getaway. She returned to the roof through the heating duct, the way she had come, and jumped down to the alley, spraining only one ankle. She tossed the loot to her sidekick, Freddie the Fence (who had fallen asleep waiting), struggled back out of her costume, and limped nonchalantly away. Another perfect crime!

The superhero. Next day, at her day job, her way to the water cooler was suddenly blocked by the massive frame of Forensic Man. (Forensic Man liked to block people's way because if he had to chase anyone, he was sure he'd get a hernia or have a heart attack, or muss his hair.) "We've got you now, Mauve," he said. "You got nothing on me, Forensic Man," she laughed, knowing that she had left nothing behind at the store and that Freddie the Fence would be careful when selling the jewellery.

The crooks are foiled. "You picked the wrong store, Mauve," said Forensic Man. "This store has an internal control system that can identify every item you took and can specify the value of all your loot. We can trace everything back to Freddie the Fence, and we know he couldn't get into that store through the roof in a thousand years. And colluding with Meek Mike didn't help you much—he had access to the jewellery, but not to the inventory records, so he couldn't cover up the theft. We caught him in the store trying to trash the computer, but the internal control system did an automatic back-up of the records every evening, so all he did was draw attention to his guilt. And to top it off, the store has a new tiny video camera that caught you climbing back up to the heating duct—you really should lay off the ice cream bars!"

Learning Objectives

This silly little story introduces *internal control,* an important feature of accounting that is in the background, not as obvious as the financial statements, but absolutely essential to good business management. This chapter illustrates that producing financial statements is not the only reason for having accounting (which you will also see when you take a course in management accounting). In this chapter you will learn:

- Why internal control is important to managers (such as those of the jewellery store above);
- How accounting records are set up to provide the documentation that is at the heart of internal control (the jewellery store can trace every item the Mauve Menace took);
- How accounting records are used to provide control information against which to compare physical assets and so minimize errors, loss of assets, and even fraud (the jewellery store's records provided a control that even insider Meek Mike could not compromise);
- How to keep track of funds collected or deducted on behalf of others, especially GST and other sales taxes, and employee deductions like income taxes and union dues (it's not part of the Mauve Menace story, but the jewellery store would have to collect GST on every item sold and turn the tax collected over to the government);
- How "contra accounts" are used to record estimates necessary to the financial statements, such as bad debts and amortization, without disturbing the internal control accounting for the related assets, accounts receivable, and noncurrent assets (the jewellery store would have more assets to keep under control than just the contents of the safe).

7.2 Accounting's "Books" and Records

The Importance of Good Records

Records provide essential knowledge for managers and people evaluating managers.

Complete and accurate records are important: they provide the observations behind the accounting information and the history of the enterprise. Without knowing what has happened, investors and managers cannot make plans for the future, evaluate alternatives properly, or learn from past actions. In today's complex business environment, especially since enterprises have become very large, the number of business events is much too great for anyone to keep track of without having accurate records (written or, these days, computerized records). Records provide the basis for extrapolations into the future, information for evaluating and rewarding performance, and a basis for *internal control* over the existence and quality of an enterprise's assets. Internal control, furthermore, not only provides systematic protection from theft and loss, but also documentation for legal and insurance purposes. Recordkeeping, however, does cost money, and therefore records should be worth their cost. How complex and sophisticated to make one's records is a business decision, just as is how to price or market one's product.

These are fundamental points about records:

Without good records, the enterprise's managers are flying blind.

- Records are the basis of accounting information, as we have seen beginning with the transactional base of financial accounting in Chapter 1. Therefore, the better the records, the better the accounting.
- Records also provide essential evidence of what people do, request, and promise. They are the backbone of managing what happens in and to the enterprise and therefore are fundamental to managers. Without good records, managers are flying blind.
- Many outside parties, like auditors, bankers, and tax authorities, want to scrutinize records that support the enterprise's claims about the income it has earned, the sales it has made, the bills it has paid, the tax it has collected for the government, the tax it owes on its own income, and so on. Records are so important to income tax, for example, that the law requires enterprises (and individuals) to keep records and allows the taxation authorities to make their own judgments about tax liability in the event good records haven't been kept.
- And, last but not least, it is very expensive to catch and correct errors, prepare proper financial statements, or any other reports, or uncover fraud, if good records have not been kept. Without good records, enterprises can get into spectacular messes! Here are some real examples:
    - A big American life insurance company called Equity Funding suffered multimillion-dollar losses because its records of issuing life insurance were so unreliable that some fraud artists high up in the company's management induced it to pay out vast sums for insurance policies that did not exist.
    - A charitable organization in Western Canada let its records get into such terrible shape that it could not even figure out what cash and bank balances it should have. While there did not seem to be any fraud, the charity had to go through the embarrassment and expense of trying to reconstruct events that had happened years earlier, and ended up having to have its board of directors pass a special motion to declare that the charity had to give up trying to sort out the mess and would

Examples of bad records
- Phony documents
- Tangles in cash and bank
- No back-up copies
- Computer system chaos

deem its bank and cash balances to be whatever the current best guesses were.

- A fired employee took a magnet to the electronic records of a large wholesale company, destroying its records of what customers owed it. There were no back-up copies of the electronic files. The company was forced to rely on the honesty of many customers to pay what they said they owed.
- A large Canadian university implemented a faulty computerized record-keeping system, one of the highly integrated "ERP" (enterprise resource planning) systems that have become popular in recent years. The system generated mysterious information that didn't seem to make sense, and any errors seemed to multiply like rabbits. By the end of the first year of the new system, the university's departments had little good information about how much of their budgets had been spent or how much could be carried over from year to year, and the university's internal financial statements were a tangle, with amounts being added to and subtracted from accounts seemingly at random. Armies of clerks had to be employed to try to connect the documents the university had to the information the computers were producing.

Summary of Financial Accounting's Procedures

Financial accounting information should be prepared through a well-defined set of procedures.

The general steps that should be followed in coming up with a set of audited financial statements, outlined in previous chapters, but repeated here as reminders, are

Accounting steps
1. Record
2. Post
3. Set policies
4. Adjust
5. B/S, I/S, R/E
6. Cash flow
7. Notes
8. Audit
9. Approve
10. Release
11. Close

1. Record transactions as individual journal entries or in specialized records for various routine transactions, such as cash receipts or cheques written.
2. Summarize the transactions by posting them to accounts.
3. Choose accounting methods and policies to be followed consistently in reporting performance and position.
4. In accordance with those methods and policies, make end-of-period accruals, corrections, and other adjustments.
5. Prepare the balance sheet, income statement, and retained earnings statement from the accounts.
6. Prepare the cash flow statement from the other three statements and additional information about changes in noncurrent assets and liabilities and owners' equity.
7. Prepare the accounting policy notes and other footnote disclosures, and add comparative figures for last year.
8. Have the full set of statements and notes audited (usually, the auditing process begins earlier, before the year-end and before the statements have been prepared).
9. Append the auditor's report to the set of statements and notes and have the balance sheet signed as approved by the board of directors.
10. Release the statements, notes, and auditor's report as a set.
11. Somewhere after step 5, close the income, dividends, and retained earnings adjustments accounts to retained earnings to make all those accounts' balances zero in preparation for next year's step 1 (the balance sheet accounts continue into the next year and so are not closed). Computerized accounting systems usually do this step automatically.

The Underlying Accounting System

All of these procedures require evidence. We've seen some examples already, such as in the evidence needed of an exchange for a transaction to be recorded and of delivery for revenue to be recognized. To help you see the role that the underlying accounting system and the evidence supporting it play in producing the account information we've been using in the text, this section shows you examples of how the evidence is assembled, and what some of it looks like. This will also prepare you for the internal control topic later in the chapter, because internal control both depends on and contributes to the enterprise's recordkeeping system.

a. Source Documents and the Transactional Cycle: A Real Example

Recordkeeping requires documents to originate and verify the records.

Accounting recordkeeping depends upon sets of *source documents* to show that transactions have occurred. Such documents trigger the initial recordkeeping and are kept so that the accounting records can be checked and verified to correct errors, permit auditing, be used in case of dispute, and support income tax claims and other legal actions. The transactions themselves reflect various events in operating the business. Examples below were supplied by an Edmonton company, Barcol Doors & Windows Ltd. (**www.barcol.com**), which is a manufacturer and supplier of doors and windows to the building, retail, and home trade.[1] *Keep in mind that these are examples only: every company has its own system and documents, and many of the "books" people refer to are actually electronic records in computer systems.*

At Barcol, a work order agreed to by the customer starts the recordkeeping process.

1. Barcol sells products made from components and raw materials that it buys from other companies. The first step is to determine what the customer wants and get the customer's agreement to the product and costs. This is done via a *work order*, which is Barcol's record of what it is to make and what will be charged for it. This is not an accounting transaction, as there has been no exchange yet, but it is important evidence in case the customer and Barcol disagree later on what the customer wanted and how much would be paid. See Figure 7.1 for Barcol's work order form. It is dated and prenumbered, and has spaces for details like the agreed terms of payment.

Barcol uses purchase orders and expects that others will use them too.

2. The next step is ordering any raw material not on hand but needed to complete the work order. Like the work order stage, ordering raw materials is not an accounting transaction, so orders are not recorded in the accounts. However, documenting and keeping track of orders is very important to Barcol, so it uses "*purchase order*" forms for this. Figure 7.2 provides an example. You'll see that it is dated and prenumbered, so that it may be followed up in case of problems, and the items ordered are listed in detail so they can be checked against what actually arrives from the supplier. If you look back at Figure 7.1, you'll see that near the top it has a space for the "Customer P.O.#" so Barcol is expecting its customers (those that are other businesses, at least) to use purchase orders too.

When Barcol accepts a delivery, the packing slip is evidence of an accounting transaction.

3. When ordered items arrive, they are checked against purchase orders and the supplier's packing slips, to ensure the order is correct. A copy of a *packing slip* from one of Barcol's suppliers is shown in Figure 7.3. It has no financial details but is evidence that the transaction happened in case there is any disagreement when the supplier bills Barcol or when the customer wonders how the work is going on the product ordered. This document, prepared by Barcol's supplier, is headed Sales Order because it is the supplier's version of the same sort of evidence Barcol wanted when it prepared the purchase order in Figure 7.2. The packing slip even quotes Barcol's purchase order number: you can see what a complete, cross-referenced set of records Barcol, its customers, and its suppliers are creating.

FIGURE 7.1

Work Order

CONDITIONAL SALES CONTRACT

BARCOL
DOORS & WINDOWS
"Serving Albertans Since 1952"

WORK ORDER
G 08384

☐ HEAD OFFICE
14820 - YELLOWHEAD TRAIL
EDMONTON, ALBERTA T5L 3C5
TELEPHONE (780) 452-7140
FAX (780) 451-0724

☐ SOUTHSIDE BRANCH
2854 CALGARY TRAIL S.
EDMONTON, ALBERTA T6J 6V7
TELEPHONE (780) 440-3667
FAX (780) 463-6061

☐ FORT SASKATCHEWAN
8732 - 112 STREET
FORT SASKATCHEWAN, AB T8L 2S7
TELEPHONE (780) 998-9759
FAX (780) 998-9760

Date

How did you Hear of BARCOL?
Yellow Pages ☐ Referral ☐ Coupon ☐ Other ☐

BILL TO
POSTAL CODE
CUSTOMER No.

LOCATION
JOB #
CUSTOMER P.O. #

ORDERED BY:
SEE:

BUSINESS PHONE
CELL PHONE
RESIDENCE PHONE

QTY. ORDERED	QTY. SHIPPED	SIZE	DESCRIPTION	AMOUNT	TOTAL

X
Customer Signature
By placing my signature on this Conditional Sales Contract, I understand and agree that it is subject to the terms and conditions on the reverse side

BARCOL Representative

Loaded by

Materials received in good order as requested by X
Customer Signature

SUB TOTAL	
G.S.T. #R100395565	
TOTAL	
DEPOSIT	
BALANCE DUE ➤	

TERMS: COD ☐ NET 30 ☐ CASH ☐ CHEQUE ☐ MC ☐ AMEX ☐ VISA ☐

DATE COMPLETED:

CARD NUMBER:

EXPIRY DATE:

FOR OFFICE USE ONLY

DATE	INSTALLER	INSTALLATION/TRAVEL TIME	P.O. No.	SUPPLIER	DATE	REC'D		
							32	
							33	

PT. 1 (WHITE) - H.O. PT. 2 (YELLOW) - CUSTOMER PT. 3 (PINK) - OFFICE PT. 4 (GREEN) - REQUISITION PT. 5 (YELLOW) - CUSTOMER

A sales invoice is Barcol's formal evidence that a revenue transaction has happened.

4. Selling the products is what Barcol is in business to do. When the product is complete and delivered to the customer, a *sales invoice* is prepared, specifying various useful details as in the example in Figure 7.4, which is the invoice for the goods involved in the previous three figures. A copy of this invoice supports the sale transaction recorded as DR Accounts receivable and CR Sales revenue. You can see there is $294.56 *GST* on the total, so the invoice also supports a debit to Accounts receivable and a credit to GST payable for the tax, which is not part of Barcol's revenue, but instead is collected on behalf of the government. (We'll see more about accounting for sales taxes like GST later in this chapter.)

Barcol keeps track of its purchases and payables as well as its sales, and ties those to cheques written to suppliers.

5. Barcol's suppliers also send invoices to it for payment of the raw materials it has ordered. At the top of Figure 7.5 is an example of the accounts payable record Barcol creates from these invoices (which it has checked back to its purchase orders, Figure 7.2, and suppliers' packing slips, Figure 7.3). Barcol uses this record to explain to the supplier which invoices it is paying. The top of Figure 7.5 has room to

FIGURE 7.2

Purchase Order

BARCOL
DOORS & WINDOWS
14820 YELLOWHEAD TRAIL, EDMONTON, ALBERTA T5L 3C5
TELEPHONE (780) 452-7140 FAX (780) 451-0724
"Your Door Specialists Since 1952"

W. W. W SUPPLY

PURCHASE ORDER
45319

DATE: OCT 10/02
TERMS: ☒ Net 30 ☐
CONFIRMATION ONLY ☐
ORDER PLACED WITH: FAX
DATE ORDERED: OCT 12/02

PLEASE SHIP THE FOLLOWING MATERIALS SUBJECT TO CONDITIONS SHOWN ON THIS ORDER.
SHIP TO ☒ 14820 YELLOWHEAD TRAIL, EDMONTON, ALBERTA
☐ 8732 - 112 STREET, FORT SASKATCHEWAN, ALBERTA
☐ 2854 CALGARY TRAIL SOUTH, EDMONTON, ALBERTA

VIA ☐ TRUCK ☒ PICK-UP ☐ COURIER ☐
☐ DELIVER ☐ MAIL ☐ UPS

SHIPMENT REQUIRED: 2 WEEKS?

QUANTITY	DESCRIPTION	QUAN. REC'D	DATE REC'D	AMT. PAID
1	13'6" x 16'9¼" (T0134) 3" HARDWARE (16x10) 3415x.416			1417.23
	— 7' HIGH LIFT TRACK CUSTOM 110x.416			45.65
	266x.54			143.64
				$1606.52 TOTAL
	<NO WRAP>			

1. ALL INVOICES MUST BE RENDERED IN DUPLICATE.
2. Acknowledge receipt of order with shipping date.
3. Delivery Slip must accompany all shipments.
4. Bill of Lading or Express Receipt must accompany Invoice.
5. No changes or alterations without consent of Purchasing Agent.

BARCOL DOOR LTD.
PURCHASING AGENT

WHITE - SUPPLIER BLUE - COSTING COPY PINK - FILE COPY CANARY - RECEIVING COPY

list several invoices. Only one is given in this example, which also says that cheque #6777 is to pay for the invoice total of $130.54. With this record, both Barcol and the supplier can readily track down any missing or disputed shipments or invoices. The *cheque* is attached to this record when Barcol pays the amount indicated.

Cash receipts complete the cycle: order, purchase, payment, sale, collection.

6. Collecting from customers is the last event in Barcol's revenue generation cycle. Three kinds of collection are illustrated here.
   a. Figure 7.6 shows a list of cash received from customers that is being deposited. This is from Barcol's cash receipts record, which supports the cash records and the credits Barcol posts to reduce customers' accounts receivable for the payments they have made. Details are given of the customers for tracing to cash sales or accounts receivable records, and the form even specifies that all the cash is in Canadian dollars. Barcol prepares the same sort of list for cheques received from customers (not illustrated).

FIGURE 7.3

Packing Slip

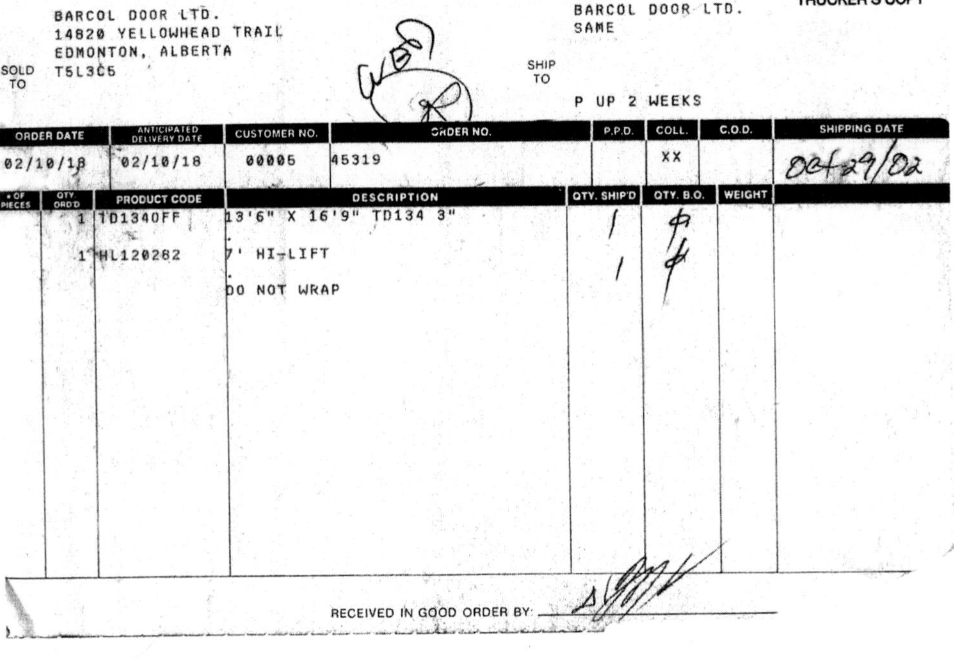

TRUCKER'S COPY

SOLD TO: BARCOL DOOR LTD.
14820 YELLOWHEAD TRAIL
EDMONTON, ALBERTA
T5L3C5

SHIP TO: BARCOL DOOR LTD.
SAME

P UP 2 WEEKS

ORDER DATE	ANTICIPATED DELIVERY DATE	CUSTOMER NO.	ORDER NO.	P.P.D.	COLL.	C.O.D.	SHIPPING DATE
02/10/18	02/10/18	00005	45319		XX		02/29/02

# OF PIECES	QTY ORD'D	PRODUCT CODE	DESCRIPTION	QTY. SHIP'D	QTY. B.O.	WEIGHT
	1	1D1340FF	13'6" X 16'9" TD134 3"	1	0	
	1	HL120282	7' HI-LIFT	1	0	
			DO NOT WRAP			

RECEIVED IN GOOD ORDER BY:

FIGURE 7.4

Sales Invoice

Head Office
14820 - Yellowhead Trail
Edmonton, Alberta T5L 3C5
Phone: (780) 452-7140
Fax: (780) 451-0724

ACC#XYZ110

SOLD TO:
XYZ LTD.

SHIP TO:

INVOICE NUMBER	INVOICE DATE	DATE SHIPPED	SHIPPED VIA	FOB
IN26526	11/14/02	11/10/02	27	SITE

P.O. NUMBER	PREPAID/COLL	SALESPERSON	WO#	EXEMPTION NO.
36352	N/A	BM	G06355	NA

TERMS: NET30

QTY	ITEM NO.	DESCRIPTION	PRICE	TOTAL
1		13'6"X16'9" TD134 C/W 3" HARDWARE	$3,472.00	
		7' HIGH LIFT TRACK		
		C/W STEEL DOOR CHANNEL		
1		H5023 1/2hp*208v*3ph OPERATOR	$736.00	
		C/W PNEUMATIC REVERSE EDGE		
		INSTALLED		
		TOTAL THIS INVOICE		$4,208.00

PLEASE MAKE CHECKS PAYABLE TO:
BARCOL DOORS & WINDOWS
14820 YELLOWHEAD TRAIL
EDMONTON, AB T5L 3C5

GST #R100395565

SUBTOTAL	$4,208.00
TAX RATE 7% GST	$294.56
SHIPPING AND HANDLING	N/A
Rush order or other expense	N/A
TOTAL	$4,502.56

FIGURE 7.5

Accounts Payable Record and Cheque

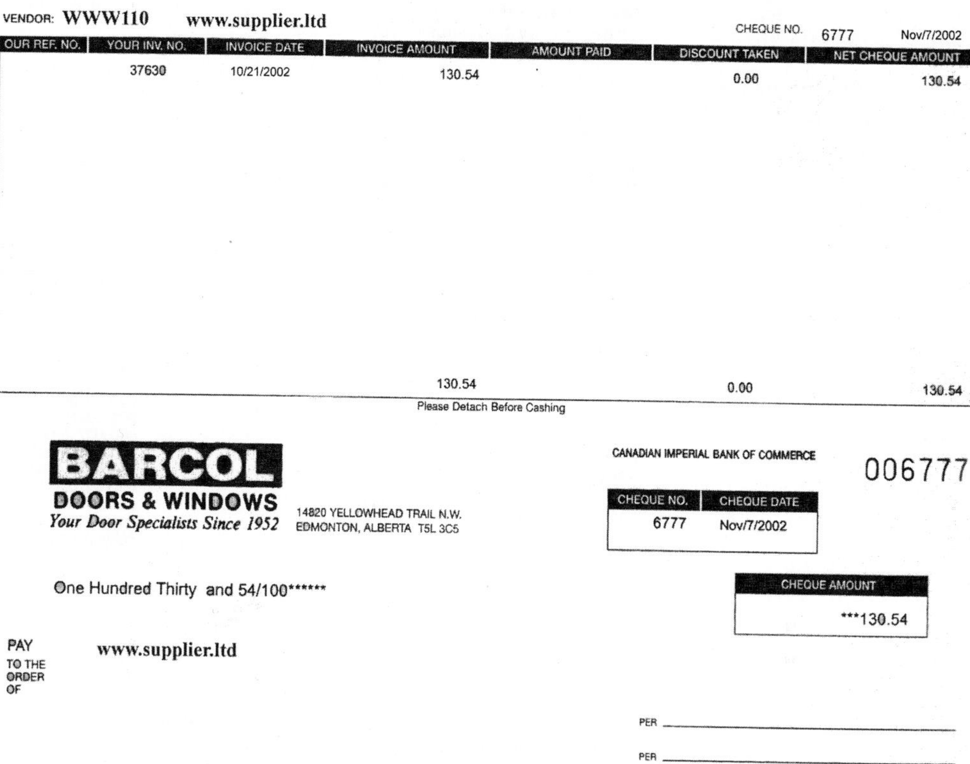

VENDOR: WWW110 www.supplier.ltd CHEQUE NO. 6777 Nov/7/2002

OUR REF. NO.	YOUR INV. NO.	INVOICE DATE	INVOICE AMOUNT	AMOUNT PAID	DISCOUNT TAKEN	NET CHEQUE AMOUNT
	37630	10/21/2002	130.54		0.00	130.54
			130.54		0.00	130.54

Please Detach Before Cashing

BARCOL DOORS & WINDOWS *Your Door Specialists Since 1952* 14820 YELLOWHEAD TRAIL N.W. EDMONTON, ALBERTA T5L 3C5

CANADIAN IMPERIAL BANK OF COMMERCE 006777

CHEQUE NO.	CHEQUE DATE
6777	Nov/7/2002

One Hundred Thirty and 54/100******

CHEQUE AMOUNT ***130.54

PAY TO THE ORDER OF www.supplier.ltd

PER

PER

b. These days, Barcol, like many businesses, relies on credit cards for customers' payments on many sales. The proportion of sales paid by credit card is continuously growing. When a customer pays by credit card, the credit card slip is deposited into the bank just like cash or a cheque (the credit card company bills Barcol for its fee monthly). Figure 7.7 shows a little form that Barcol's credit card computer record prints out to go with all the credit card slips: you'll see that Barcol would be depositing slips from three different credit card companies. You'll also notice the "Inst paymnt" amount, small on that day but also growing. That is the record of "Interac" direct-withdrawal payments by customers.

c. More electronic, some customers pay Barcol by just notifying their and its banks to transfer the money to pay, without bothering with cheques or credit cards. This sort of *electronic funds transfer* (*EFT*) is becoming more common at Barcol, especially by large regular customers. Figure 7.8 is the form a customer faxed to Barcol to tell it that a transfer had been made.

Barcol's cash receipts have little actual cash in them in today's world of electronic and plastic payments.

Without keeping track of EFTs, credit card payments, and Interac payments, Barcol would have little idea of what its bank balances should be, because these three forms of customer payment are much more important for Barcol now than cash and cheques combined.

Barcol uses other kinds of documents also. It has more electronic transfers, for example, to pay all employees by direct deposit into their bank accounts. There are many kinds of documents used by various companies. Each company adapts documents to its own needs, especially to provide legal evidence and support accounting transactions records. You can count on two things about any company, government, sports club, or other organization: (1) it will have various documents to back up its accounting system, and (2) those documents will be suited to that organization and so might not be quite like any other organization's.

FIGURE 7.6

List of Customer Cash Receipts for Deposit

Date: Monday, October 07, 2002 2:17PM
A/R Bank Deposit Slips (ARDPST01)

Barcol Doors and Windows

Page 1

From Batch No. [2700] To [2700]

Bank ID: 1 Account: 1110 Date: 10/04/02
Batch Number: 2,700 Deposit Slip Number: 2,118 Currency: CAD

3

Customer Number	Payer	Check/Remittance Number	Amount
KEL025	MR. A	000002700-0000001	3,156.50
LEC104	MR. B	000002700-0000002	124.92
DUT040	MS. C	000002700-0000003	234.06
FOR046	CASH SALE	000002700-0000004	132.95
BIR038	MR. D	000002700-0000005	48.10
COU090	MS. E	000002700-0000006	102.19
HAY024	CASH SALE	000002700-0000007	487.43
KUN099	CASH SALE	000002700-0000008	396.97
PAR007	F LTD	000002700-0000009	1,169.51
LIE040	G LTD	000002700-0000010	839.95
CLA112	MS. H	000002700-0000011	1,075.35
CAR0064	MR. I	000002700-0000012	1,245.48
MAC0013	MR. J	000002700-0000013	390.55
ARM037	MR. K	000002700-0000014	860.28
ALY099	CASH SALE	000002700-0000015	1,850.39
MAC017	M LTD	000002700-0000016	377.22
ALL070	A LTD	000002700-0000017	1,000.00
INV111	B INGO LTD	000002700-00018	2,068.31
		3 Total:	15,560.16

Date: Monday, October 07, 2002 2:17PM
A/R Bank Deposit Slips (ARDPST01)

Barcol Doors and Windows

Page 2

	Cash	
______	X 1	______
______	X 2	______
______	X 5	______
______	X 10	______
______	X 20	______
______	X 50	______
______	X 100	______
______	Coins	______
	Total 3	15,560.16
	Total Deposit	15,560.16

b. Books of Original Entry

Specialized paper or electronic journals are used to record routine repetitive transactions.

Based on source documents, accounting transactions are recorded. Because this is when the business event first is recorded by the accounting system, these basic transactional records are often called "*books of original entry.*" These records specify the accounts to which transactions are to be debited or credited. Typically, transactions of a similar nature are grouped together, and separate, specialized records are used to record frequent routine transactions. Some examples of specialized records are

- a *sales journal*, listing all sales in sales invoice order;
- a *cash receipts journal*, listing payments received from customers (Barcol's collections lists are forms of this); and

FIGURE 7.7

Credit Card Deposit Slip

```
        BARCOL OVERDOOR 1980 LTD
         14820 YELLOWHEAD TRAIL
            EDMONTON      AB
STORE 991364       TERM A0991364
       *** END OF DAY REPORT ***
BATCH 002 SHIFT 001 DAY 189 EMPL=
SEPT/27/02 15:42
          * * * * * * * * * *
DAILY SUMMARY
                     SHIFT     ACCUM. TOTAL
INST PAYMNT      $1,352.38      $1,352.38
VISA            $15,560.16     $15,560.16
M/C              $6,641.08      $6,641.08
AMEX             $1,599.16      $1,599.16
TOTAL           $25,152.78     $25,152.78
          * * * * * * * * * *
HOST REPORT
DAY IN BALANCE
ACCOUNT CREDITED               $25,152.78
```

FIGURE 7.8

Remittance Advice

XYZ INC

REMITTANCE ADVICE
Date: 30 SEP 2002

BARCOL DOORS & WINDOWS LTD
14820 - YELLOWEAD TRAIL
EDMONTON, AB T5L 3C5
Attention To: Accounts Receivable
Fax: 7804510724

This statement is to notify you of an electronic deposit that will be made to your bank account for the following transaction(s).

Transaction number : 144443
Deposit date : 02-OCT-02
Supplier number : 65313

Invoice Date	Invoice Number	Description	Discount	Amount
31-AUG-00	IN40351			763.00
			Total:	763.00

- a cheque register or *cash disbursement journal*, recording all cheques issued, in cheque number order. Companies usually have separate cheque registers (and bank accounts) for major areas, such as payment of accounts payable, general payroll, executive payroll, and dividend payments. Records for cash disbursements using EFT or other automatic payment systems are generated automatically by the system.

The general journal is used for adjustments and less routine transactions.

Each company will also have a "*general journal*," used mainly to originate journal entries for transactions that are not provided for in specialized journals, and for accruals and adjustments of any kind. No adjustments are just written into the ledger accounts: all must originate with journal entries in the general journal. Journal entries, like the rest of accounting's records, must be organized and kept on hand for later reference, and they must be supported by documents or calculations of some kind so that they may be verified later (or even just plain understood after the original reasons for the entries have faded from people's memory).

c. Ledgers

Ledgers are books (or computer records) having a separate page or account code for each individual account referred to in the books of original entry. Each area or page contains a summary of all the transactions relating to that particular account and therefore "posted" to it. (Remember the set of accounts in page format illustrated in Section 2.5.)

The general ledger includes all the accounts behind the financial statements.

General ledger—the collection of all the asset, liability, equity, revenue, and expense accounts, summarizing the entire operations of the business. The general ledger is the central record of the financial accounting system and is the basis on which the balance sheet, retained earnings statement, and income statement are prepared. The ledger may be a "book" or it may be space on a computer disk or server. Many companies now keep their records on the computer and print out information only as they require it. As we saw in earlier chapters, a "trial balance" of all the general ledger accounts and their balances is prepared periodically (such as at the end of each month) in order to demonstrate that the ledger is in balance, that the sum of its debit-balance accounts equals the sum of its credit-balance accounts. (A listing of just the account names without balances, useful in designing or redesigning the accounting system and relating it to the financial statements' format, is called a "*chart of accounts*.")

Subsidiary ledgers list details backing up general accounts such as accounts receivable.

Specialized (or subsidiary) ledgers—accounts receivable and accounts payable ledgers are two examples of specialized ledgers. For instance, if a company extends credit to its customers, it may want to keep a separate ledger account for each customer. These ledgers are balanced by making sure that their accounts add up to the same amount as is shown in the relevant general ledger account (for example, the accounts receivable "*control*" *account* in the general ledger, which is the account used to prepare the financial statements, should have the same balance as the list of customers' individual accounts). A subsidiary ledger does not "balance" by having its debits equal its credits, but rather by having its sum equal the amount in the primary account in the general ledger. Making sure this is true is an important way of ensuring that individual customer accounts receivable, for example, are correct. Subsidiary ledgers, therefore, are part of the *internal control* system; their details are not in the financial statements, but they support the validity of the main "control" account that does appear in the financial statements. (More about control accounts is in Sections 7.6 and 7.7.)

d. Electronic Commerce

Barcol's receipts and payments are becoming more and more electronic.

With the advent of sophisticated interconnected computer systems, especially via the Web, many business transactions are now being conducted entirely electronically. *Electronic commerce* (*e-commerce* or *e-business*) is quite a challenge to financial accounting, and to internal control, because its essence is the absence of the painstaking "paper trail" that has traditionally supported accounting records. Many people, not just accountants, think some sort of credible trail, even if not in paper, needs to be continued in some form, but how? Enterprises still need good records for all the reasons outlined at the beginning of this section, but clearly the form of those records is changing dramatically. These days, Barcol sees little cash and not as many cheques as it used to from customers, with most payments, even by other businesses, being made by credit card or electronically. It doesn't pay its own employees by cash or cheque, just deposits their pay directly into their personal bank accounts.

E-commerce has other interesting implications for accounting. Here are examples.

1. There needs to be some compatibility between computer systems if the accounting systems on both sides of a transaction are to recognize it properly, and some trust in the electronic media to make the system work. The Web is developing interfaces that provide the compatibility and credibility mechanisms with names like "encryption" and "Web Trust" beginning to appear.
2. There can be a lot of "in-transit" activities, because physical transfers (shipments, deliveries, etc.) are usually slower than the electronic system. If you order a book from an on-line retailer, you, the retailer, and your credit card company will have all the electronic records completed long before the book shows up. The tendency of records to be speedier, and separated from the physical movements, means that it can be a challenge to control and reconcile in-transit items.
3. The parties to e-commerce can be bound together quite closely, with the ability to make enquiries into each other's computer systems to find out order specifications, progress on production of goods, and other things to smooth the business relationship. This means that not only must the financial statements be right, but the underlying records must be good too, so that business partners' enquiries are answered reliably. Some external parties, like banks, tax authorities, or securities regulators, may want to go straight to the underlying records without waiting for financial statements. There's a bit of a paradox here: e-commerce both operates without paper *and* demands a good trail of evidence.

E-commerce binds companies together, in both accounting and their underlying records.

E-commerce and the Web are part of big changes coming in accounting and financial reporting.

Financial reporting itself is going on-line and becoming continuous rather than waiting for ritual quarterly or annual reporting dates: numerous references to companies' Web pages have been made in this book, and many versions of on-line and even interactive financial reporting are being developed.[2] E-commerce and electronic financial reporting are likely to change accounting and financial reporting dramatically in future years. Maybe in the future, books like this will be on-line to match the on-line accounting they will then be describing!

Like most smaller companies, Barcol Doors & Windows has computerized its accounting system, meshing that with the sort of electronic collection and payment methods mentioned above. Rosalie Laibida, in charge of the company's accounting, said that it seemed to be the right thing to do, and has had many benefits, but it was a huge step to take, and there were many problems getting it all to work; for example,

- Since Barcol is a small company, it didn't seem feasible to have a custom accounting system developed, so standard commercial accounting software was purchased. Endless trouble resulted in trying to make the software fit the company's needs. At the beginning, the system wouldn't produce some needed reports and produced others that made no sense!
- The system wouldn't allow a change in fiscal year. Not bad—forever stuck in 2001 or whatever: income statement for the period ending in infinity!
- An accident nearby wrecked a transformer, leading to a power surge that wiped out three weeks' worth of data! The classic "it could happen to you" happened to Barcol! Now the records are backed up on tapes nightly, and the disks are stored off-site. For extra protection, the essential accounts receivable records are burned onto CDs and also stored off-site.
- Finding that the system was producing ever more paper, Barcol has largely stopped printing out accounting records at all. Queries and analyses are conducted on-screen, which works very well now that the system is working properly. However, the important "aged" list of accounts receivable is still printed out frequently so that it can be used to keep on top of collections, which are Barcol's lifeblood.
- The human element continues to complicate everything. Barcol keeps lists of work orders, purchase orders and similar documents, because people keep forgetting to complete the things set out in such documents and need reminders if documents seem to get old without action or customers complain that orders have not been filled.

HOW'S YOUR UNDERSTANDING?

Here are two questions you should be able to answer based on what you have just read. If you can't answer them, it would be best to reread the material.

1. Why are good records and careful documentation important to an organization with and without e-commerce?
2. What are each of the following documents and records for? Purchase order. Sales invoice. Cash receipts journal. Cash disbursements journal. General journal. General ledger. Accounts receivable subsidiary ledger.

7.3 Internal Control

Financial accounting has several important uses.

We have so far identified several different uses for financial accounting information, including,

a. evaluation of management's performance, for the purpose of deciding whether to reward or punish managers;
b. prediction of future performance, for the purpose of deciding whether to invest in or lend to the company; and
c. division of the company's returns (incomes) into portions for various parties: management bonuses, income taxes, dividends to owners, and so on.

The rest of this chapter focuses on another important use:

d. maintenance of internal control over assets and such day-to-day activities as making sales, collecting cash, and incurring expenses.

Accounting records are important for control as well as for preparing financial statements.

An appropriate recordkeeping system for any organization is one that can be used to keep track of resources, thus discouraging misappropriation of the organization's property or inefficient use of resources and helping management safeguard assets. Yet, it should not be overly cumbersome or bureaucratic. Records also help management meet its responsibility to run the enterprise effectively, and generally to control what is going on. Such *internal control* is not only a matter of recordkeeping: physical protection, insurance, and proper supervision of employees are also important to internal control. The Barcol Doors & Windows documents in Section 7.2 were part of the company's internal control system; they were numbered and dated, and contained several details that could be used to follow up if problems arose.

This is a brief introduction to an interesting area of management responsibility that accountants and auditors consider part of their area of expertise. The *CICA Assurance Handbook* (paragraph 5141.02) provides the following definition for internal control:

> *Internal control* is the process designed and effected by those charged with governance, management, and other personnel to provide reasonable assurance about the achievement of the entity's objectives with regard to reliability of financial reporting, effectiveness and efficiency of operations and compliance with applicable laws and regulations. It follows that internal control is designed and implemented to address identified business risks that threaten the achievement of any of these objectives.[3]

Main Components of Internal Control

As the *CICA Assurance Handbook* excerpt above points out, internal control is the responsibility of management. Here are some ways that management can establish proper control over the enterprise's affairs. After the points have been made, they will be related to a recent really spectacular fraud.

Control: Manage competently.

1. *Run the enterprise competently.* Looking after the enterprise's assets and making sure various activities, including recordkeeping, are done well is just part of being a good manager. A well-run enterprise has a climate of efficiency and records that cross-check each other, as well as competent managers who are likely to realize quickly when something is going wrong. Having a good internal control system contributes to the profitability and efficiency that good managers seek.

Control: Have good records.

2. *Maintain effective records.* Having a comprehensive, connected set of records, as was illustrated for Barcol Doors & Windows, provides an early warning system and helps to motivate good performance by everyone, because the records provide routine monitoring and act as the basis for hourly pay, performance appraisals, bonuses, and other parts of the motivation system. Records also provide an audit trail of events that can be traced back to identify the causes of problems. An effective recordkeeping system goes well beyond accounting transactions (we saw the example of Barcol's purchase order system), but accounting records are likely to be at the heart of it. Many modern organizations have integrated their accounting and other records into a decision-oriented *management information system* that can be used to support a wide range of management decisions and evaluations.

Control: Use the records and learn from them.

3. *Use the records to act and learn.* It is an unfortunate fact of life in many organizations that many records seem to be maintained just for the sake of doing that. We all have chafed at bureaucratic form filling and having to prepare multiple copies of things for no apparent good reason. If management allows records to grow of their own accord, money is wasted, and perhaps equally important, people in the organization learn that the records don't matter, that mistakes and worse will not be acted upon or corrected. This can seriously undermine the control aspect of recordkeeping, and is likely to produce records that are useless for managers to learn from events, because the records either have too many errors or have become irrelevant to the organization's current needs.

Control: Segregate duties.

4. *Keep recordkeeping separate from asset handling.* An effective way of providing security over assets like cash, accounts receivable, and inventories is to have records showing how much of each asset is supposed to be on hand at any time. But if the person who handles assets (say, cash) also keeps the records, then errors or fraud can be hidden by altering the records. Accountants call separation of recordkeeping from handling assets "*segregation of duties.*" One person collects the cash, and another person maintains the cash records. So if one or the other makes a mistake, a difference will arise between the count of cash on hand and what the record shows should be on hand. This difference then can be investigated and the cause corrected. Segregation of duties can also be used within the recordkeeping system: for example, one person can maintain the general ledger, with the total accounts receivable account, and another can maintain the accounts receivable subsidiary ledger, with the detailed list of customer accounts. It is hard for smaller enterprises with few employees to spread the jobs around enough to segregate all the important tasks, but it should be done as much as is sensible. If segregation of duties doesn't exist, the boss needs to keep a close eye on important assets, such as cash and inventories.

Control: Treat employees well.

5. *Adequately pay and motivate employees.* A more positive side of internal control is to pay and reward people for their efforts on behalf of the enterprise, so that they try to do a good job and are not tempted to subvert recordkeeping and other control systems. Disgruntled employees may not care if things go wrong or may even take some pleasure when the enterprise suffers losses. As you can imagine, the control provided by

Internal control components

1. Be competent
2. Keep track
3. Learn
4. Segregate duties
5. Manage people
6. Insure
7. Protect assets
8. Scrutinize
9. Be ethical

segregation of duties is destroyed if the people involved "collude" (work together) to cover up errors or fraud, and while such actions can never be wholly prevented, their probability is reduced if people feel good about the enterprise and feel they are fairly treated.

Control: Carry insurance.

6. *Carry insurance on assets.* Like anything else, internal control has to be worth its cost. It is probably worth the cost to have a careful control system for the main part of the enterprise's activities (for example, buying and selling goods), but there will be some unusual circumstances that are not anticipated or for which setting up elaborate controls doesn't seem worthwhile. Some events, such as earthquakes or fires, may be entirely or mostly beyond management's control. So it makes sense to protect the owners' investment by carrying insurance for some events against which internal control systems cannot provide adequate protection. There is a side benefit of insurance: insurance companies tend to want to know a lot about how the enterprise is protecting and managing its assets, and satisfying the insurance company about this can result in improvements in controls.

Control: Physically protect assets.

7. *Physically protect sensitive assets.* This control method is rather obvious, but it's easy to overlook too. Sensitive assets, such as cash, inventories, and tools, should be behind lock and key, kept in particular storage areas, or otherwise protected from unauthorized or casual access. Many enterprises are sloppy about access to their inventories in particular, and sometimes protection is a good idea for assets you might not think of. For example, many manufacturers produce scrap as a by-product, and the scrap can be very valuable. One Canadian manufacturer put its scrap in the backyard and found out later that thousands of dollars' worth had been lifted over the back fence and sold on the scrap market.

Control: Independent scrutiny.

8. *Welcome independent scrutiny of accounting and governance.* An important, even crucial, aspect of good internal control is a willingness to undergo careful independent scrutiny of the organization's procedures and governance. The ultimate responsibility is borne by the board of directors (for a corporation; other organizations should have corresponding bodies), which is responsible to the shareholders/owners for the governance of the organization. If others in the organization are to believe that the sorts of controls mentioned in this section are important, the people at the top have to live by them also. Those people at the top should welcome scrutiny of their policies, priorities, performance, and general behaviour. Letting the external auditors do their job is part of this scrutiny, as is having a good internal audit operation within the organization. The board of directors should have an *audit committee* composed of directors who are not also members of management, and both external and internal auditors should have full and frank access to the audit committee to discuss top management's behaviour. Even if such scrutiny were not useful in itself, having gone through it is very helpful to top management and the board of directors when problems do arise—as they tend to do, because no organization is going to be flawless.

Control: Set an ethical example.

9. *Take ethics seriously and set an example.* This ties back to the first point, and connects to every other point as well. Top management sets the tone and provides the example that determines whether the whole organizational culture emphasizes ethical behaviour or not. Reacting to one of the latest corporate scandals (WorldCom) in June 2002, US President Bush said, "There is a need for renewed corporate responsibility in America. Those entrusted with shareholders' money must strive for the highest of high standards."[4] No internal control system, no *corporate governance* structure, will work if the people who operate it are not ethical. There is a great deal of controversy about what sorts of ethical standards are appropriate, and to what extent they should include broader responsibilities, such as for the environment, poverty, and human rights. This book cannot even make a start on resolving this controversy, because it goes to the heart of what society and business are all about, but it is clear

that broad principles beyond either the company's or the manager's direct self-interest are involved. Being known by others in the organization for following ethical principles and expecting others to do so too is essential.

Effective internal control is common-sense management.

There is much more to internal control, governance, and ethics. Designing effective control systems requires an understanding of management's objectives, a sensitivity to the cost-benefit balance needed between tight but costly controls and loose but cheap controls, knowledge of computer systems and other recordkeeping methods, considerable insight into the subtleties of human motivation and behaviour, and more than a little understanding of the human society and culture that allows the organization to exist. It also requires some common sense: complete protection is not possible, and tying the enterprise up in red tape in order to try to get complete protection is not what a good internal control system does.

In 2002, a truly massive fraud (US$691 million; over a billion Canadian dollars) was discovered at Allfirst Financial Inc., a Baltimore branch of international bank Allied Irish Banks PLC of Dublin. The fraud was allegedly perpetrated by a currency trader working in Baltimore but trading largely on Asian currency markets. It involved making very large bets on currency fluctuations and covering up losses due to bad bets by making more bets, just like a gambler who wants to play one more round of poker to cover losses already incurred.[5] Here are some comments on some internal control implications of this huge fraud:

- There is some question about the competence of those supervising the trader. Banks have to watch their traders carefully because any trade can be a very large risk to the bank. If anyone had been in any doubt, a fiasco a few years earlier, in which a Singapore currency trader bankrupted Barings Bank, should have been instructive to everyone.
- Records appeared to have been prepared, so later on, the amount of the losses could be measured. Recordkeeping was not a problem, it seems.
- But learning from the records was a problem. Though the trader's activities could be tracked later on, there apparently was little attention during those activities that might have alerted senior management.
- The trader was responsible for preparing some records of his own activities, and so could disguise what was going on. Not segregating the recordkeeping from the trading behaviour was an elementary error, but it is unfortunately commonly made by managers who are impatient with such procedures or feel they need to trust people.
- We don't know how well paid or motivated the trader was. It seems the trading losses just started to grow and were not motivated by trying to make personal gains. But the trader was perhaps led astray by being given too much freedom with others' money.
- Insurance can be hard to get for such potential catastrophes, because insurers would believe good management should prevent them and do not want to underwrite poor management!
- The assets in this case were financial ones, not physical ones, and the real problems came from the potential losses (liabilities) arising from such trading. All of these should have had more careful protection so that a single employee could not risk them.
- Internal audit procedures should have identified the weaknesses noted above. It is not known why they did not.
- There are no apparent ethical problems, other than the overall issue of how top management carried out its governance and stewardship roles and what sort of tone was set for the bank's internal culture to allow the trader to behave as he did for long enough to create such a catastrophe.

HOW'S YOUR UNDERSTANDING?

Here are two questions you should be able to answer based on what you have just read. If you can't answer them, it would be best to reread the material.

1. What should a good internal control system do?
2. What are some components of an internal control system?

7.4 Top Management's Responsibility for Internal Control

Section 7.3 stated that management, especially top management, is responsible for internal control. Top management's responsibility for the ethical climate of the organization and the soundness of its accounting and controls cannot be overemphasized, especially in the light of the serious problems in corporate governance that have turned up repeatedly in recent years. Exhibit 7.1 details what top management of CPR said about their responsibility for financial reporting and internal control in the company's 2004 annual report:

Canadian Pacific Railway Limited
Management's Responsibility for Financial Reporting

The information in this Annual Report is the responsibility of management. The consolidated financial statements have been prepared by management in accordance with Canadian generally accepted accounting principles and include some amounts based on management's best estimates and careful judgment.

Management maintains a system of internal accounting controls to provide reasonable assurance that assets are safeguarded and that transactions are authorized, recorded and reported properly. The internal audit department reviews these accounting controls on an ongoing basis and reports its findings and recommendations to management and the Audit, Finance and Risk Management Committee of the Board of Directors.

The Board of Directors carries out its responsibility for the consolidated financial statements principally through its Audit, Finance and Risk Management Committee, consisting of five members, all of whom are outside directors. This Committee reviews the consolidated financial statements with management and the independent auditors prior to submission to the Board for approval. It also reviews the recommendations of both the independent and internal auditors for improvements to internal controls, as well as the actions of management to implement such recommendations.

Michael T. Waites
Executive Vice-President and
Chief Financial Officer
February 21, 2005

Robert J. Ritchie
President and
Chief Executive Officer

Top management sets the internal control tone for the whole company.

The connection between internal control and financial reporting is important. CPR's top managers are taking responsibility for the whole financial reporting system in this statement, including internal control. Even the auditors' access to the board of directors through the Audit Committee, which is part of the board's control at the very top of the company, is mentioned. Control really means that top management knows what is going on around the company, knows what is going on inside the company, and manages the company well in whatever climate of change or turbulence management finds itself. At best, this means prudent management at the top, setting the tone for the whole company and leading to informed and appropriate actions throughout.

Good internal control is just good management.

For most companies, this works pretty well. But there are many dramatic examples of what happens to companies whose management is not in control: banks fail because of over-lending to questionable borrowers or poorly supervised currency trading (as we saw in Section 7.3); sports stadiums and government buildings cost far more than expected because of loss of control over construction processes; big retail chains lose control over their buying and marketing and so lose their customer base; fast-food chains build more outlets than there are stomachs to fill; and many growing companies let their receivables and inventories get too large as they try to serve all possible customers. About the failure of Enron, a writer commented that the company culture "... led to Enron's demise: the frenetic pace, the lure of riches and the lack of controls."[6] After WorldCom admitted its financial statements had been manipulated to produce higher earnings, the US SEC immediately charged the company with fraud.[7] These are examples of bad management, not just bad control, because in essence, management and control are the same thing. As we turn now to specific control areas, the overriding role of top management in running the business properly should be kept in mind.

HOW'S YOUR UNDERSTANDING?

Here are two questions you should be able to answer based on what you have just read. If you can't answer them, it would be best to reread the material.

1. Why is internal control a top management responsibility?
2. Where does CPR say the ultimate responsibility for the financial statements lies?

7.5 Internal Control of Cash

Cash is the asset usually most susceptible to theft because of its liquid and generally anonymous nature.

> A real case: Mike, a junior auditor in a northern town, was assigned to do a surprise count of the cash on hand at a local clothing store. The cash counted was short as compared to what was expected based on the auditors' projections of cash from sales and bank deposit records. The store's accounting clerk accused Mike of stealing the cash himself while counting it, and so he had to call the police from the store and insist that they search him and so demonstrate that he had not stolen it. It turned out that the accounting clerk had been stealing cash and covering up the thefts by changing the sales records—a classic case of poor internal control through lack of segregation of duties, because the clerk had access to both the cash and the records of the cash. The theft was discovered only because Mike's surprise cash count referred to sales records that the clerk had not yet altered to cover up the shortage. The clerk was fired, and he promised to make restitution, though it was difficult to tell how much had been taken because sales records had been

altered for several years. The owner of the store was quite critical of the auditors for "not preventing the loss," but the auditors showed that they had indeed warned the owner, who had said that it would be too expensive to employ someone else to keep the sales records or control the cash.

The general principles in Section 7.3 apply to the specific cash control situation.

For cash sales, one of the most common controls is to have locked-in sales registers or other carefully controlled records. Registers (such as those you would see at any supermarket) usually print a consecutive number on the locked-in tape for each transaction. The access key is kept by a single person, perhaps a supervisor, who balances cash to sale records. The proceeds that should have been received will be recorded on the tape. The person who keeps the key should count the cash with the cashier, compare it to the sales proceeds, and check that the tape numbers are consecutive from one person's shift to that of the next person. If this sort of system is to work, there has to be no collusion between the people controlling the cash and checking the records—often collusion is difficult to prevent, so having yet another person provide overall monitoring of the process is a good idea. And as we saw in the Barcol example in Section 7.2, there are many forms of "cash" needing control attention besides currency and cheques, including "Interac" direct payments to the company, credit cards, and electronic funds transfers.

A real case: A large company established a "*petty cash*" fund in its front office to be used to pay for small purchases, such as office supplies and courier charges. The receptionist was given a fund of $1,000 in cash, and when most of that was spent, submitted all the receipts in an envelope and was reimbursed for the cash spent to bring the petty cash fund back up to $1,000. The internal control therefore was that, at any time, the receptionist should have cash on hand plus receipts for payments totalling $1,000. What the company did not know was that the receptionist was involved with the delivery driver from the store from which the company got most of its office supplies, and nearly all invoices from that company paid through petty cash were inflated. The company paid far more than it should have for the supplies, but no one knew because the people who got the supplies did not see the invoices, which were kept by the receptionist as evidence of cash payouts. The people who reimbursed the receptionist had not seen the office supplies and so did not know the invoices were inflated. The thefts and the collusion between the receptionist and driver were discovered long after the two had moved to another city: someone noticed that after the receptionist and driver left, office supplies costs were lower than they used to be! The company has no good idea of how much was stolen, but it probably exceeded $10,000 over the years.

Prenumbering documents is an example of a control technique that helps to catch errors.

Another way to control cash from sales is to have multi-copied, prenumbered sales invoices, as Barcol has. The invoice copies are then removed by one person: for cash sales, the amounts are crosschecked to cash records, and for credit sales, the amounts are crosschecked to accounts receivable records. Any gaps in the invoices' numerical continuity are investigated. For this control to work, supervisors must ensure that an invoice is prepared for each sales transaction. An additional control is to regularly check inventory and compare it with the sales records. This should prevent, or at least detect, someone selling inventory and pocketing the cash.

Take, for example, the Mayfield Pro Shop, which accumulated $10,000 in sales at the end of a month according to the invoice copies in the locked box. If the inventory at the start of the month was worth $25,000 and at the end of the month was worth $14,000 (based on the retail price of the goods), the shop should have sold $11,000 worth of goods. The $1,000 difference could be due to one of the following:

1. Someone could have kept $1,000 worth of cash from sales and not written any invoices for those sales.
2. Someone could have shoplifted $1,000 worth of goods.
3. The inventory could be inaccurate, or other errors could have occurred.

Combining cash and inventory controls is useful for both assets.

Point 3 is a reminder that there are usually other reasons for shortfalls besides theft, but keeping track of cash and inventory together is one method of highlighting the possibilities and investigating them.

These examples of cash-control problems are presented to illustrate that accounting records are important beyond their use in preparing financial statements. The examples are not intended to suggest that employees or customers are crooks, but to show that management must be prudent in meeting its responsibility of good stewardship in taking care of the owners' assets. Part of that responsibility lies in not putting employees or others in such poorly controlled situations that they are tempted to steal, and paying people with responsibility for cash well enough that they do not start thinking of themselves as underpaid and therefore deserving of more money from the company!

> A real case: An armoured truck company had developed a good business picking up cash from supermarkets and other stores and delivering it to banks. The company trusted its employees and had never had problems. Usually the trucks were staffed by two people, a driver and a second person that rode in the back. The two had to sign various forms and, in a sense, they kept an eye on each other so no one got tempted: there was often a million dollars or more in unmarked, untraceable cash in the truck. Sometimes, though, one of the two people was sick, or on vacation, or called away on some errand for the company, and there would be just one person to drive the truck and collect the money. On one day like that, there was a particularly large amount of money in the truck, and the driver, apparently on impulse, just took it and departed for foreign parts!

Before leaving the subject of cash control, a major additional control warrants mention. Cash on hand is important, but as we saw with Barcol, most of the company's cash is likely to be in, or going in and out of, its bank accounts. It is central to cash control to prepare a formal *bank reconciliation* frequently, at least monthly. This example of *reconciliation* was outlined in Chapter 1, Section 1.12. Keeping close track of bank accounts is important not only to prevent (or at least catch) errors and fraud, but also to ensure that managers have accurate accounting information when they are making decisions. A company that is not sure how much cash it has in the bank is likely to be poorly managed, and because errors and other problems are always possible, regular bank reconciliation is essential. (The banks themselves can have trouble with their cash, not just because of robbers toting masks and guns. Banks have very elaborate cash controls, including careful and frequent reconciliations. But sometimes, plain common sense is useful: in April 2000, a branch of government-owned ATB Financial in St. Albert, Alberta, received a deposit of US$7.5 billion, more than the total assets of ATB Financial! It won't surprise you that the deposit was part of a scam that was exposed by an alert, and amazed, clerk at the branch.)[8]

HOW'S YOUR UNDERSTANDING?

Here are two questions you should be able to answer based on what you have just read. If you can't answer them, it would be best to reread the material.

1. John is in charge of a $200 petty cash fund. When he counted his cash today, he had $45.95 on hand, and decided that he should replenish the fund. He therefore requested a cheque to "cash" from the company, submitting receipts in support of the request. What amount did he request, and what was the total of the receipts he included with his request?

$154.05 is the answer to both questions.

2. The Mayfield Pro Shop began this month with cash of $1,200 and inventory (priced at retail) of $26,700. The shop had sales of $9,500 this month, received more inventory on credit having a retail price of $7,800, and had $2,300 cash on hand at the end of the month. How much cash did the shop deposit this month and how much inventory, at retail prices, should there have been on hand at the end of the month?

Cash deposited = $8,400, which = $1,200 + $9,500 – $2,300;

Inventory at month-end = $25,000, which = $26,700 + $7,800 – $9,500.

You can see the integration of cash and inventory control because the $9,500 sales appear in both calculations.

7.6 Control of Sales Taxes Collected and Employee Deductions to Be Remitted

Accrual accounting has been described so far as a method of going beyond cash flow to produce a more comprehensive measure of income and valuation of balance sheet accounts. But by going beyond cash, accrual accounting also creates records that are very important from an internal control point of view. Here are three general examples:

Accrual accounting provides very useful noncash control accounts.

- The journal entry "DR Accounts receivable, CR Revenue" recognizes revenue that has been earned but not yet collected in cash. While it does that, it also creates the accounts receivable account, which then becomes a record of what customers owe the enterprise. This account, which is often called the accounts receivable *control account*, is supported by a subsidiary ledger or list of what individual customers owe, and is a very important part of the control system. It should be difficult to forget about a customer or to forget to give a customer credit for paying, because the control account should reflect everything customers have promised to pay, minus everything they have paid, at any date.
- The journal entries (a) "DR Inventory, CR Accounts payable or Cash" and (b) "DR Cost of goods sold expense, CR Inventory" also produce a control account for inventories, telling us what should be on hand at any date. We saw a retail-priced example of this in the Mayfield Pro Shop in the previous section; more explanation about the use of the accounting records for inventory control will be given in Section 7.8.
- The journal entry "DR Expense or Inventory, CR Accounts payable" produces a control account for accounts payable, showing what is owed to suppliers at any date.

For many chapters of this book, we have been preparing and using accounts to generate financial statements. The above examples illustrate that the accounts also play another role: providing internal control information. As we saw with the various top management examples in Sections 7.3–7.5, the resulting financial statements also reflect the internal control within the enterprise: poor control is very likely to lead to unreliable financial statements, or worse. Figure 7.9 illustrates the dual role that accounts play.

FIGURE 7.9

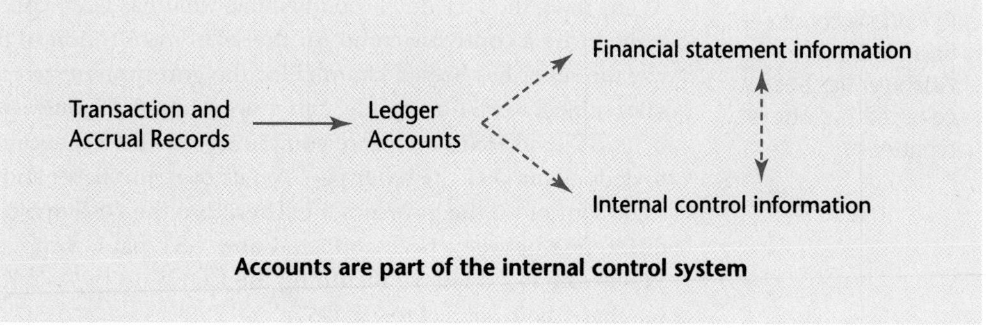

To illustrate the use of accounts for control, this section examines a very important use of accounting records for keeping track of some important current liabilities other than the accounts payable in the last example above. This use is in keeping track of *money the enterprise owes on behalf of others.* Two examples that occur in practically every business and most other organizations as well are:

Collecting sales taxes creates a liability to the government(s).

a. Collecting *sales taxes* from customers on behalf of the government. The taxes are not the enterprise's money—it is acting as a tax collector on behalf of the government and so is required to turn it over to the government. When you buy something in a store and the store adds provincial sales tax (*PST*), the federal goods and services tax (*GST*), or the blended PST-GST combination used in some provinces (harmonized sales tax, or *HST*, which works essentially the same way as the GST, from an accounting viewpoint), this is your contribution to the government and the store is just a channel to get it from you to the government.

Making deductions from employees' pay creates liabilities to various outside parties.

b. Deducting income tax, pension contributions, union dues, medical insurance fees, and many other possible deductions from employees' pay. You've probably experienced these *employee deductions*: you think you have earned, say, $250, but your paycheque is perhaps only $180 because of all the deductions. Here again, the employer is acting as a channel to get your income tax and other contributions to the government, the union, the medical insurer, or wherever.

Let's examine each of these examples, so you can see how the accounting records create control totals, and how each example incorporates its particular economic and legal circumstances.

Collecting Sales Taxes

The simplest example here is the collection of PST. When a sale, say $100, is made and, say, 6% PST is added, the following journal entry records the transaction:

DR Cash or Accounts receivable	106	
CR Revenue		100
CR PST due (a current liability account)		6

Legally, the customer must pay $106, now or later, but only $100 is the seller's revenue. The $6 is owed to the government. You can see that the "PST due" account can be used to accumulate all the PST collected on all the applicable sales. When the PST due is paid to the government, the liability account is reduced:

DR PST due	xxx	
CR Cash		xxx

PST due account's balance shows whatever has been collected but not yet remitted.

At any date, the PST due account shows what has been collected but not yet remitted. It is therefore a control account for the seller's obligation to the government. It shows the way the seller has been a channel for the government's money, because it goes up when sales subject to PST are made, and down when the money is sent to the government.

GST (and HST) are more complicated than PST, because the seller is normally able to deduct any GST the seller pays (on its own purchases and expenses) from the amount to be sent on to the government. Therefore the GST due to the government is only the difference between GST collected and GST paid. Suppose we have the following: a $1,000 sale (we'll ignore recording the COGS on the sale for this example), and a $400 purchase, both subject to 7% GST:

DR Cash or Accounts receivable	1,070	
CR Revenue		1,000
CR GST due		70
DR Inventory	400	
DR GST due	28	
CR Cash or Accounts payable		428

Now the seller owes only $42 in net GST, as shown by the GST due control account. When it is remitted to the government, the GST due liability is debited and cash/bank is credited. (It is possible for the GST due account to be a debit (an asset) if the company makes particularly large purchases and has small sales in a given period, but this would be rare.) As you can see from the debit to Inventory in the second entry, the inventory control account and COGS expense are maintained at the goods' cost *without* GST, because GST is controlled in a separate account.

GST due account's balance is the net of GST collected and paid, minus remittances.

The journal entries for PST and GST can be combined to show the total tax in a province that has both taxes or the HST's blended PST/GST. The point of the example is to show you how the accrual accounting system produces useful control accounts for the PST, GST, or whatever, due to the government. The control accounts can be as sophisticated as the tax law requires (many complications have been left out of these examples).

Deducting from Employees

Accounting has to keep track of deductions plus any fringe benefits.

Employee deductions have some complications that the accounting system has to handle. One is that each deduction normally has to be sent to a different place: for example, income tax deducted goes to the government, union dues deducted go to the union, United Way donations go to the United Way. A second complication is that the employer often has to pay "fringe benefits" in *addition* to the amount deducted from the employee. Pensions, Canada Pension, employment insurance, and many kinds of medical and other insurance are examples. Therefore, the wages the employee earns are not the only expense the employer incurs. The accounting system can handle these without difficulty, using control accounts for all.

Example

Employee's earnings: during a period, an employee earned wages of $1,100.
Deductions: income tax, $200; employment insurance, $40; union dues, $50; medical coverage, $65; totalling $355.
Take-home pay: a net of $745 ($1,100 wages minus $355 deductions).
Fringe benefits to be paid by the employer: employment insurance, $45; workers' compensation insurance, $15; medical coverage, $67; totalling $127.
Total cost to the employer: $1,100 wages plus $127 benefits = $1,227 for the period.

The accounting records would show this in the two entries below or one combined entry:

Account	DR	CR
DR Wages expense	1,100	
CR Income tax deductions due liability		200
CR Employment insurance due liability		40
CR Union dues due liability		50
CR Medical premiums due liability		65
CR Wages payable liability		745
DR Fringe benefits expense (or include in Wages expense)	127	
CR Employment insurance due liability		45
CR Workers' compensation insurance due liability		15
CR Medical premiums due liability		67

All the accounts credited in the example are control accounts for payments to be made.

The control accounts show how much is due to be remitted:

- $200 income tax,
- $85 employment insurance ($40 + $45),
- $50 union dues,
- $132 medical premiums ($65 + $67), and
- $15 workers' compensation insurance.

As in the sales tax examples, the control account balances show how much has been deducted and/or is due as fringe benefits owed by the employer, minus the amounts remitted to the appropriate bodies. It is the company's legal responsibility to remit these to the outside parties involved. The wages payable account is also a control account, showing how much is to be paid to the employee. Its balance is therefore the sum of the net take-home pay the employees have earned, minus amounts paid to the employees.

The above example was for only one employee: the employer would not likely record each employee separately this way, but would calculate the sums for all employees for the period and record them all together. The control accounts would still work the same way, but would be backed up by detailed wage records showing every employee.

HOW'S YOUR UNDERSTANDING?

Here are two questions you should be able to answer based on what you have just read. If you can't answer them, it would be best to reread the material.

1. Last month, Apex Retailing had cash sales of $18,000 and collected PST of $1,080 and GST of $1,260 on those sales. In addition, Apex paid GST of $680 on its own cash purchases of $9,700. How would the sales and purchases be recorded, and how much PST and GST were owing for the month?

DR Cash 20,340, CR Revenue 18,000, CR PST due 1,080, CR GST due 1,260.

DR Inventory 9,700, DR GST due 680, CR Cash 10,380.

PST due = $1,080; GST due = $580 ($1,260 – $680).

2. In the same month, Apex employees earned wages of $9,000, from which various deductions totalling $2,200 were made. Apex was responsible for fringe benefits of $2,400 on these wages. What was the total expense of having the employees for the month? What was the employees' take home pay? What were the total remittances due for the month?

Total expense = $11,400 ($9,000 + $2,400);

Take-home pay: $6,800 ($9,000 – $2,200);

Total remittances due: $4,600 ($2,200 + $2,400).

7.7 Control Accounts and Contra Accounts

Balance sheet accounts are control accounts.

Just about every balance sheet account can be considered to be a *control account.*

- Cash is a record of the cash that should be there if counted.
- Accounts receivable is the sum of all the individual customers' accounts.
- Inventory is the amount that should be found if the company lists or counts all the unsold goods physically on hand.
- GST due is the net amount of GST collected on all sales minus GST paid on all purchases and any remittances to the government.
- The number of shares outstanding should be traceable to the share capital account. (The particular owners may change, for example, due to trading on the stock market, but the company should always know how many shares it has issued and what it originally received for them.)
- Even the property, plant, and equipment asset accounts are controls, as all the assets whose costs are included should be physically present.

The usefulness of all these balance sheet accounts as control accounts is that the amounts in them should be supported by or reconcilable to detailed lists or subsidiary ledgers, or some such background data. What do we do, then, when we want to make a change in a balance sheet account without changing the underlying records and lists? Here are examples of when we might *want* to change the balance sheet account and at the same time be *reluctant* to do it:

- There has been an overall decline in the market value of the inventory, so for conservatism we want to reduce the inventory asset account on the balance sheet and record an expense for the loss in value, but do not want to change the inventory control account because it should equal the sum of the costs of all the goods on hand.
- We are worried that we might not collect all the accounts receivable, so for conservatism and proper income measurement, we want to recognize that the value of the accounts receivable has gone down, and record an expense for the "bad debts" implied in this loss of value. But we do not want to change the accounts receivable control account because it should correspond to the list of all customers' accounts and we are not yet giving up on collecting any. The control feature is still useful.
- The property and plant assets are being used up economically, so we want to record amortization expense as part of our income measurement, but we do not want to change the accounts for the asset costs. Their costs are not changing, but rather their economic values are being consumed.

Can financial statement adjustments be made without interfering with internal control?

In all these examples, the financial statement objectives of proper balance sheet valuation and income measurement seem to conflict with maintaining the accounts for control purposes.

Contra accounts solve the apparent conflict between financial statements and control.

What to do? Well, accrual accounting is very flexible. A perhaps peculiar kind of account called a *contra account* has been invented to allow us to recognize expenses and value changes without changing the control account. It is useful both for income measurement and to preserve the internal control aspects of the accounts, and so provides a bridge between accounting's roles in internal control and in financial statement preparation. Referring back to Figure 7.9 in Section 7.6, a contra account is part of the vertical dotted arrow connecting financial statement information and internal control information.

Contra accounts' balances have the opposite sign to the control accounts they match.

Contra accounts have balances that are in the *opposite direction* to that of the control account with which they are associated; for example, contra asset accounts have credit balances that are "contra" the assets' debit balances. They are used for managing accruals, usually for expenses, separately from the asset, liability, or equity accounts to which they relate, and therefore they keep the accruals from being mixed into those accounts.

Contra accounts only have meaning in conjunction with the control accounts to which they are matched. We'll see below how this works.

Contra accounts are used to avoid making expense adjustments to control accounts.

In this section, we will focus only on the two most common uses of contra accounts: accumulating amortization (depreciation) and allowing for doubtful accounts receivable. Virtually all enterprises have both. These accounts illustrate how the accounting system can meet one objective (expense recognition) and *avoid* compromising another objective (control) by creating accounts that recognize expenses but do not change the control accounts related to those expenses (asset costs and accounts receivable).

FIGURE 7.10

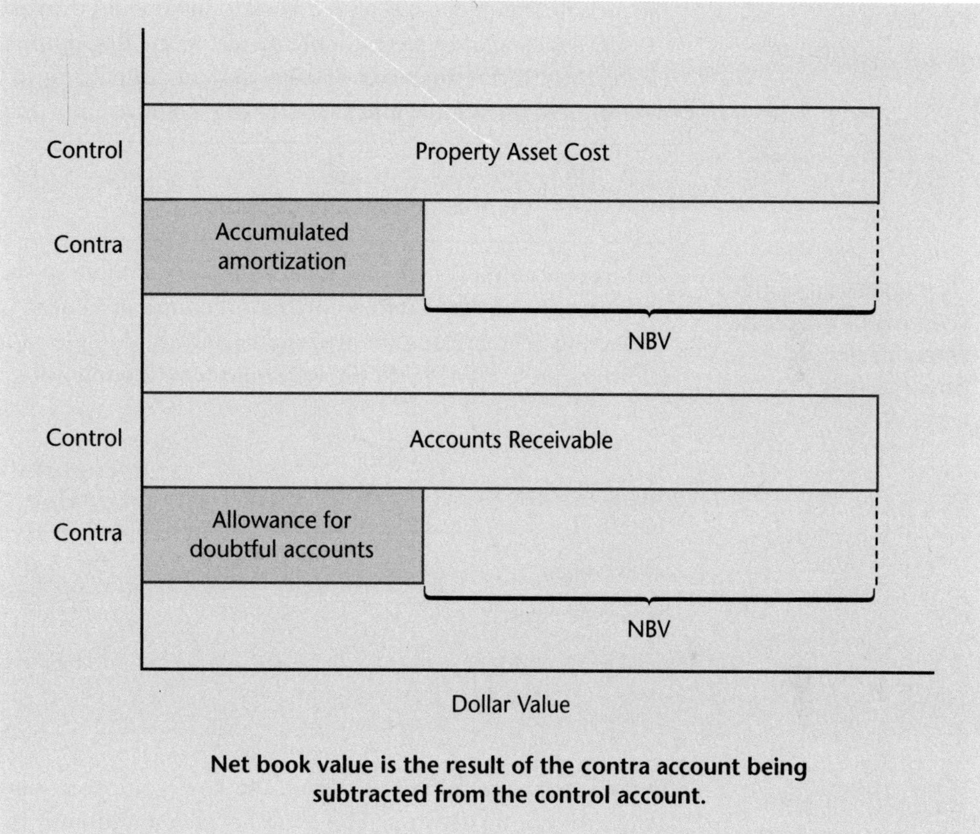

Net book value is the result of the contra account being subtracted from the control account.

Accumulated Amortization (Depreciation)

Amortization is a general word that includes depreciation.

The *accumulated amortization* contra accounts are used to accumulate *amortization* on fixed assets, such as buildings and equipment. The terminology is changing here: until recently, such amortization was called "depreciation" and the word "amortization" was used for intangible assets, such as goodwill, leasehold improvements, and patents. Many companies still use the word "depreciation," and call the contra account "accumulated depreciation."

In the case of amortization, a contra account is created when the periodic expense for using the asset is recognized. For example, the annual amortization charge of $100,000 on a building would be recognized this way:

The amortization expense entry's credit is to the contra account, not the asset account.

DR Amortization expense	100,000	
CR Accumulated amortization		100,000

- The debit is an expense account in the income statement.
- The credit is a contra asset account.

The credit side of the journal entry could have been to the asset account "Building." Instead the contra account is used, to leave the asset cost account and its control role untouched.

The balance sheet can present the acquisition cost of the asset along with the accumulated amount of expense previously recognized. Showing both of these items allows users to make a rough guess as to how long the asset has been in service.

The accumulated amortization contra is the sum of amortization expenses over time.

Accumulated amortization on the balance sheet is the *amount of amortization accumulated over the life of the asset to date,* whereas the *amortization expense* recorded *this year* (to match the revenues the asset consumption is presumed to have helped generate) is on the income statement and added back to income on the cash flow statement.

Let's look at a simple example involving the dog pound's purchase of a new truck to catch strays. If the truck cost $50,000 and an annual amortization expense of $8,000 was determined, the annual journal entry to recognize amortization would be:

DR Amortization expense	8,000	
CR Accumulated amortization		8,000

Net book value is the cost minus the contra accumulated amortization.

The asset account for the truck's cost would continue to show a balance of $50,000, but each year the accumulated amortization contra asset account would increase by $8,000. Deducting accumulated amortization from the long-term asset account leaves a figure known as the *net book value.* So, we would have the following:

Date	Cost	Accumulated Amortization Contra	Net Book Value
Purchase	$50,000	$ 0	$50,000
End of first year	50,000	8,000	42,000
End of second year	50,000	16,000	34,000

In a disposal, both the asset cost and its accumulated amortization are removed.

If the truck were sold at any time, the cost would be removed from the ledger, but so would the contra account. The contra is meaningful only in comparison to the cost, and when the truck is gone neither account is needed anymore. Suppose the truck was sold for $37,000 at the end of the second year. Then we would have the following entry:

DR Cash (the proceeds)	37,000	
CR Truck asset (*removing the cost*)		50,000
DR Truck accumulated amortization (*removing the contra*)	16,000	
CR Gain on sale of truck (on the income statement)		3,000

A gain or loss on sale is the difference between proceeds and net book value.

The gain on sale is just the difference between the proceeds and the net book value at the date of sale, as was explained in Section 4.5, cash flow analysis.

- If the proceeds had been $29,000 instead, the debit to Cash would have been $29,000, and there would have been a $5,000 debit to Loss on sale (perhaps included with an account such as "other expenses" in the income statement). The loss is the difference between the $29,000 proceeds and the $34,000 net book value.

Gains and Losses on Sale
Proceeds > Net book value: *Gain* on sale
Proceeds < Net book value: *Loss* on sale
No proceeds: *Write-off* of net book value

A write-off can be thought of as a disposal without proceeds.

- Let's suppose that at the end of the second year the truck was used to pick up a particularly ornery bunch of dogs, and they turned out to have a highly contagious disease. The truck had to be junked, and the insurance company refused to pay anything because such a risk was not contemplated when the insurance was written. Now we have what accountants call a "*write-off*": a disposal without proceeds. The journal entry would still credit Cost for $50,000 and debit the Accumulated amortization contra for $16,000, and there would now be a $34,000 debit to a Loss on disposal or write-off account (probably still included in a line such as "other expenses" on the income statement, unless it was considered material enough to warrant being shown separately). The whole net book value is said to have been written off.

DR Loss on disposal or write-off *(on the income statement)*	34,000	
CR Truck asset (*removing the cost*)		50,000
DR Truck accumulated amortization (*removing the contra*)	16,000	

There will be more examples and discussion of amortization and gains and losses in Chapter 8.

Accumulated amortization for intangible assets may be deducted from the asset cost.

When *intangible assets* (noncurrent, nonphysical assets, such as goodwill, patents, franchise rights, or *capitalized costs* such as development costs or incorporation costs) are amortized, the accumulated amortization is often just deducted from the asset cost on the balance sheet, not shown separately (or disclosed in a footnote) as it is for physical assets' accumulated amortization. If there is not seen to be an internal control reason for keeping the cost and accumulated amortization accounts separate, the amortization entry may just debit expense and credit the asset account. If there are internal control reasons (keeping track of asset costs), there may well be an accumulated amortization account in the ledger, which is deducted from the asset cost account when the balance sheet is being prepared. Gains, losses, and write-offs on such assets are calculated the same as for the physical assets.

Enterprises may have hundreds of ledger accounts, kept separate for internal control purposes, which are aggregated into the relatively few figures on the balance sheet. Accumulated amortization is a contra account that is typically kept separate in the ledger and disclosed on the balance sheet. We now turn to an example account that is typically kept separate in the ledger but *not* disclosed on the balance sheet: the allowance for doubtful accounts receivable.

Doubtful Accounts Receivable

Allowing customers to buy on credit carries the risk that they will not pay.

Now, let's look at the other most common use of contra accounts, the *allowance for doubtful accounts.* When a company sells to a customer on account, there will always be some risk that the customer will fail to pay. Therefore, a portion of the sales on account will be doubtful, and that portion should be deducted from revenue on the income statement in the period of sale to match the *bad debts expense* (resulting from the probable failure to collect) to the revenue recognized that period.

Let's assume that a company determines, by past experience or current evidence of customers' troubles, that about $500 of sales on account will likely not be paid. The journal entry to recognize the expense is:

The credit side of the bad debts expense entry is to the allowance contra account, leaving the control account untouched.

DR Bad debts expense	500	
CR Allowance for doubtful accounts		500

The credit in this entry is again to a contra asset account, just as it was for amortization. (That account was in the noncurrent assets section of the balance sheet, while this one is in the current assets section.) The reason for not deducting the amount directly from the accounts receivable asset is to maintain the asset account as a control: even if collection is doubtful, the company may still try to collect on the accounts and therefore doesn't want to alter the accounts receivable control total, which should tally with the list of individual customer accounts.

The expense and contra are created when collection is doubtful, while there is worry but still hope.

We might say that when the bad debts expense and the allowance account are created, this is the "worry stage": there is doubt about collectibility of some accounts, and that doubt is recorded as an expense because it is thought that some economic value has been lost, but the company has not yet given up on trying to collect all the accounts.

The main difference between this situation and that of amortization is that only the net amount of the accounts receivable minus the allowance for doubtful accounts is usually disclosed on the balance sheet. This contra account is deemed to be less useful for readers of the balance sheet than the accumulated amortization contra account, and perhaps more sensitive if disclosed. Somewhere in the notes, the amount of accumulated amortization is disclosed, but the allowance for doubtful accounts, even that there is such an allowance, is usually not disclosed anywhere. Also, the income statement always discloses the amortization expense but seldom discloses the bad debts expense, which is just included with other expenses somewhere.

The allowance and the bad debts expense are seldom disclosed in the financial statements.

At the write-off point, doubt about collection has been replaced by lack of hope.

Eventually, after pursuing a nonpaying customer for some time, a company may decide to *write the account off*, to give up keeping the account in the list of customer accounts and the accounts receivable control account. The hope of collecting is now being abandoned, and it is thought not necessary to keep the receivable in the list of accounts whose collection is being pursued and whose total equals the balance in the accounts receivable control account.

Another journal entry is needed because the expense recognition entry above did not touch the accounts receivable control account, and now we *do* want to change that account because we are not going to bother including it in the list of accounts under control. Suppose the bad account in question equals $100 (it was one of the risky ones contemplated when the allowance was created above), then the *write-off* entry is:

DR Allowance for doubtful accounts	100	
CR Accounts receivable		100

Writing off a bad debt reduced the receivable and the allowance without affecting income.

This entry eliminates the account from the books of the company completely, but you'll notice that it does not affect expenses (or, therefore, income): that effect was created when the allowance and expense were recorded earlier, at the "worry stage." The power to write off an account is usually quite tightly controlled and great care is taken to keep track of payments received. The reason should be fairly obvious: if you write an account off it is no longer on the books anywhere, and then, if the deadbeat customer pays, the person who receives the money could simply keep it and no one else in the company would know.

The write-off entry assumes the account was among those allowed for earlier.

You'll note that this write-off is handled differently from the noncurrent asset write-offs described above. The reason is that the allowance for doubtful accounts is considered to apply to the whole list of accounts receivable, in aggregate. We don't necessarily know *which* specific accounts receivable were allowed for: for example, the $500 allowance for doubtful accounts was probably based on an average experience, such as that, say, 15% of accounts over 40 days old will not be collected. We don't need to know exactly which accounts are doubtful in order to make such an allowance for the aggregate risk being taken. There was a contra accumulated amortization for each building or truck, but there is no particular contra for each account receivable, so both the account receivable asset and an equal amount of the allowance for doubtful accounts contra are just eliminated in the above bad debt write-off. It's like assuming that the written-off receivable had been 100% allowed for. (We'll see in Chapter 8 that amortization can be done on a "group basis," in which case things work much like they do for bad debts.)

Bad debt write-offs can throw the system off if they are large enough. For example, in the above case, what if a customer account for $800 had to be written off? That's more than there is in the allowance! There are methods for adjusting the allowance to take such problems into account, but this book will not include them beyond a brief comment in the Jellyroll Sweets example at the end of this section.

It is possible to operate the accounting without an allowance for doubtful accounts. Bad accounts can be written off directly to accounts receivable, by the so-called *direct write-off* method. Suppose an account totalling $1,500 is to be written off directly. Then the entry would be:

DR Bad debts expense	1,500	
CR Accounts receivable		1,500

Using an allowance contra is usually more conservative than using the direct write-off method.

This is equivalent to allowing for it first and then *immediately* writing it off, using the "worry stage" and "write-off" entries shown earlier:

Worry:	DR Bad debts expense	1,500	
	CR Allowance for doubtful accounts		1,500
Write-off:	DR Allowance for doubtful accounts	1,500	
	CR Accounts receivable		1,500

As this example shows, the allowance can be seen as a temporary holding account for amounts the company worries about, to be cancelled out if the account is ever written off. But during the holding period, an expense has been recognized and the asset value on the balance sheet has been reduced. Using an allowance is thought usually preferable to direct write-off, not only because of the internal control advantages the contra account provides, but also because the allowance provides for a way to have an expense *before* the company gives up on collection, and so is generally more conservative in its effects on the balance sheet and income statement. Using such an allowance is part of GAAP and is accepted for income tax purposes in Canada, so the direct write-off method is rare, used when a company has few accounts receivable or when a large account not contemplated in the allowance suddenly goes bad.

Example: Allowance for Doubtful Accounts

Here is a final example of the use and effect of an allowance for doubtful accounts.

Accounts receivable minus allowance equals estimated collectible amount.

- Jellyroll Sweets Inc. sells confections to retail stores. At the end of 2006, it had accounts receivable of $53,000 and an allowance for doubtful accounts of $3,100. *Therefore, the estimated collectible amount of the accounts receivable was $49,900 at the end of 2006.*
- During 2007, the company had credit sales of $432,800 and collected $417,400 from customers. Therefore, at the end of 2007, the accounts receivable stood at $68,400 ($53,000 + $432,800 – $417,400).
- At that point, the sales manager went through the list of accounts receivable and determined (1) that accounts totalling $1,200 were hopeless and should be written off, and (2) that an aggregate allowance of $4,200 was required at the end of 2007.

At the end of the year, write-offs and necessary further allowance are determined.

Here are journal entries to accomplish what is needed.

Write off the bad ones:		
DR Allowance for doubtful accounts	1,200	
CR Accounts receivable		1,200
Allow for the doubtful ones:		
DR Bad debts expense	2,300	
CR Allowance for doubtful accounts		2,300
Balance in allowance = $3,100 – $1,200 =	$1,900	
Allowance needed at the end of 2007 =	$4,200	
Additional allowance = $4,200 – $1,900 =	$2,300	

Year-end adjustments take into account any prior allowances and write-offs.

The allowance and write-off entries could be done in the other order, but in this case, the sales manager was thinking of really old receivables, from last year, to write off, and newer ones to allow for. The order of entries does not matter as long as the final balances are adjusted to be the same, so the calculation for the allowance entry takes into account any preceding or planned write-off. If the entries were done in the opposite order, the calculation of the allowance entry would start with $3,100 and subtract that from ($4,200 + $1,200 = $5,400) to provide for the planned write-off. The entry would still be for $2,300 more bad debts expense and then the write-off would reduce the allowance from $5,400 to the desired $4,200.

No matter what order the entries were made in, the accounts receivable balance is now $67,200 ($68,400 – $1,200) and the contra balance is $4,200.

- Therefore, the estimated collectible value of the accounts receivable (the net balance sheet value or net book value) is $63,000 at the end of 2007 ($67,200 – $4,200).
- Bad debts expense for 2007 is $2,300.
- The write-off of the hopeless ones cleaned them out of the list of receivables, but did not affect either income or the net book value on the balance sheet. You can see this by redoing the calculation of the allowance and expense entry with no write-off of the hopeless ones:
    - If none had been written off, the allowance balance would still be the $3,100 from last year.
    - But now the allowance needed would be $4,200 for the doubtful ones and $1,200 for the hopeless ones (still in the receivables), totalling $5,400.
    - Subtracting the $3,100 from that total leaves $2,300, so the second journal entry and therefore the bad debts expense would be the same.
    - Now the accounts receivable would be $68,400, and the allowance would be $5,400. So, the estimated collectible amount of the accounts receivable (the net book value) would still be $63,000.

A write-off against the allowance has no effect on the net receivable amount in the balance sheet.

HOW'S YOUR UNDERSTANDING?

Here are two questions you should be able to answer based on what you have just read. If you can't answer them, it would be best to reread the material.

1. Argyll had a building that cost $438,000. At the beginning of the year, the accumulated amortization on the building was $233,000. The building was sold for $190,000 late in the year, after a further amortization expense of $34,000 was recorded. What were the journal entries to record (1) the amortization expense and (2) the disposal?

(1) *DR Amortization expense 34,000, CR Accumulated amortization 34,000.*

(2) *DR Cash (proceeds) 190,000, CR Building cost 438,000, DR Accumulated amortization 267,000, CR Gain on sale 19,000. The gain on sale is the proceeds of $190,000 minus the book value of $171,000 ($438,000 – $267,000).*

2. Argyll also has accounts receivable. At the end of the year, the total in the accounts receivable control account is $321,000 and the balance in the allowance for doubtful accounts is $22,000 (after recording bad debts expense for the year of $11,000). Upon examination of the accounts, management decides that $5,000 of the accounts is hopeless and should be written off, and that the allowance should be increased by $7,000 after that. What is (1) the bad debts expense for the year, (2) the accounts receivable control account balance at the end of the year, (3) the allowance for doubtful accounts at the end of the year, and (4) the estimated collectible amount at the end of the year (net book value)?

(1) *$18,000 ($11,000 already + $7,000 more needed);*

(2) *$316,000 ($321,000 – $5,000 written off);*

(3) *$24,000 ($22,000 – $5,000 + $7,000);*

(4) *$292,000 ($316,000 control – $24,000 contra).*

7.8 Demonstration Problem: Contra Accounts

This problem demonstrates that the two contra account examples in Section 7.7, accumulated amortization and allowance for doubtful accounts, are very similar in intent and interpretation. If you understand this well, you will be able to make sense out of other contra accounts you might encounter.

Strand Cable Inc. serves the residents of a medium-sized Ontario city. Among its assets are a building and accounts receivable. Data for a recent year, prior to recording any amortization or bad debts expense for the year, include

- equipment cost: $2,670,000 at beginning of year;
- cost of new equipment acquired during the year: $473,000;
- equipment sold during the year: cost $93,000, accumulated amortization $63,000, cash proceeds $25,000;
- accumulated amortization at the beginning of the year: $1,105,000;
- estimated economic value of equipment lost during the year: $339,000;
- obsolete equipment to be scrapped at the end of the year: cost $51,000, accumulated amortization $37,000;
- accounts receivable from customers at the beginning of the year: $3,762,000;
- credit sales of cable service during the year: $16,973,000;
- collections from customers during the year: $16,438,000;
- doubtful accounts receivable at the beginning of the year: $53,000;
- accounts receivable that became doubtful during the year: $78,000;
- hopeless accounts receivable at the end of the year: $62,000.

An analysis of the various accounts is shown below, followed by some observations and then the journal entries to record the data. Before you read further, see if you can do the journal entries, and calculate the year-end net book value of the equipment and the accounts receivable.

(a) Account analysis

	Control Account	**Contra Account**	**Net Book Value**
Equipment			
Beginning of year	$ 2,670,000	$ 1,105,000	$ 1,565,000
New equipment	473,000		473,000
Equipment sold	(93,000)	(63,000)	(30,000)
Amortization expense		339,000	(339,000)
Write-offs	(51,000)	(37,000)	(14,000)
End of year	$ 2,999,000	$ 1,344,000	$ 1,655,000
Accounts receivable			
Beginning of the year	$ 3,762,000	$ 53,000	$ 3,709,000
Credit sales	16,973,000		16,973,000
Collections	(16,438,000)		(16,438,000)
Bad debts expense		78,000	(78,000)
Write-offs	(62,000)	(62,000)	0
End of year	$ 4,235,000	$ 69,000	$ 4,166,000

(b) Some observations

- Only business events and write-offs affect the control accounts.
- Accruals for consumption of the assets are put through the contra accounts.
- A write-off has no effect on net book value if the asset is fully allowed for or amortized (the equipment scrapped had $14,000 unamortized book value).
- For the equipment, book value indicates the portion of the asset's cost not yet amortized, therefore thought to have economic value into the future.
- For the accounts receivable, the book value is also economic value into the future, being the estimated amount of the accounts receivable that will be collected.

(c) Journal entries

Equipment				Accounts Receivable		
			Additions			
Dr Control	473,000			Dr Control	16,973,000	
Cr Cash		473,000		Cr Revenue		16,973,000
			Collections			
Dr Cash	25,000			Dr Cash	16,438,000	
Cr Control		93,000		Cr Control		16,438,000
Dr Contra	63,000					
Dr Loss expense	5,000					
			Asset consumption			
Dr Expense	339,000			Dr Expense	78,000	
Cr Contra		339,000		Cr Contra		78,000
			Write-offs			
Dr Contra	37,000			Dr Contra	62,000	
Cr Control		51,000		Cr Control		62,000
Dr Loss expense	14,000					

HOW'S YOUR UNDERSTANDING?

Here are two questions you should be able to answer based on what you have just read. If you can't answer them, it would be best to reread the material.

1. What is represented by the amount calculated by subtracting the contra account from the control account?
2. If an asset is fully allowed for or amortized on the date it is written off, the write-off has no effect on income. Why is that?

7.9 Inventory Control

This chapter has emphasized the importance of keeping records to provide information to both internal and external users. Many of the records kept have to do with the control of inventory. Inventory control is important for management because a high percentage of working capital may be tied up in inventory, the inventory items may be perishable or become obsolete if held too long, and, due to the physical attributes of some types of inventory, there may be a great potential for theft.

Inventory control is separate from reporting inventory in the financial statements.

Several different inventory control systems may be used, depending on the nature of the inventory and the objectives of management. The methods explained below are the three most commonly used by businesses. Each provides a different amount of information at a different cost. It is important to note that the choice of inventory control system is a recordkeeping choice as opposed to a reporting choice: management is simply deciding how to record the inventory. How inventory is reported in the financial statements will be dealt with in Chapter 8.

The Perpetual Accounting Control Method

When an order of inventory items is received, the quantity received is added to the quantity recorded as being already on hand. When items are sold, they are deducted from the recorded quantity. Therefore, the perpetual method shows how many items are supposed to be on hand at any time:

FORMULA

Start with the quantity on hand at the beginning of the period.

Add the quantity purchased during the period.

Deduct the quantity sold during the period.

Equals the quantity that should be on hand at the end of the period.

The perpetual control method's records show how much inventory should be on hand.

The name *perpetual inventory control method* comes from the idea that the accounting system has a continuously updated figure for the amount that should be on hand. If a physical count of the inventory fails to show that quantity, the company knows that something has been lost or stolen, or that there has been an error in the records. Just as for cash, bank accounts, accounts receivable, and GST due, the records provide *accounting control* in addition to any physical protection. The accounting records tell the company what to expect to be on hand.

If the cost of items is included in the count along with the quantity, the perpetual record can be used to estimate the total cost of inventory at any time, without having to bother counting and pricing everything.

FORMULA

Beginning inventory cost (support with physical count if desired)

+ Cost of purchases of inventory (records)

– Cost of inventory sold (records)

= Ending inventory cost (support with physical count if desired)

In the perpetual method, COGS is known and is removed from inventory when there is a sale.

The perpetual control method has been assumed in most of the examples so far in the text, because purchases have been recorded as debits to inventory asset and cost of goods sold has been credited to the asset and debited to *COGS expense*.

The perpetual method provides additional management information.

- Suppose that after the above calculation, the expected ending inventory cost was $100,000, but a count to support that showed only $96,500 of inventory on hand.
- Management would know there had been a $3,500 shortage or other error, and could intensify controls over inventory if that was thought to be cost-effective.
- If it cost $10,000 to improve the controls, management might well conclude that losing $3,500 was the cheaper option.
- The inventory asset account would be adjusted to the count by an adjusting entry to CR Inventory $3,500 and DR Inventory shortage expense. This is a write-off entry, reducing the control account. The accounts would then show the expense being incurred by the imperfect controls. (If there were *more* inventory on hand than expected, there could instead be an inventory overage account, a credit balance so a sort of negative expense, though this would probably indicate an error somewhere as it is unlikely any thieves were breaking in and adding inventory!)

- The overage/shortage expense account would probably be included with COGS in the income statement, as management would usually consider this information to be an internal matter, and it would not likely, we hope, be large enough to be material in its effect on COGS.

The Retail Accounting Control Method

This is like the perpetual method, except that records are based on selling prices of goods rather than just quantities or costs. In the *retail inventory control method*, a department or branch is charged with the total selling value (sales price times quantity) of all items for sale delivered to it. Revenue from sales is then deducted from this total value as the items are sold. This ties inventory control to cash control, as in the Mayfield Pro Shop example in Section 7.5. At any point in time, the department or branch should have inventory, plus cash from sales made since the last revenue report, plus records of sales on credit or via credit cards, equal to the current total retail value:

FORMULA

Start with the retail price of all goods received by the department on hand at the beginning of the period.

Add goods received during the period, also valued at retail price.

Deduct the department's sales (connected to cash, cheque, electronic funds transfer, and credit card control procedures).

Equals inventory that should be on hand, priced at retail.

The retail method is like the perpetual method, but using selling prices instead of costs.

If a physical count, with items priced at retail, fails to show the expected total retail value, the company knows that some items have been lost or stolen, or that there has been an error in the records. An adjustment for the shortage or overage can be made in the same way as for the perpetual method. Total cost of the inventory can be estimated at any time by deducting the average markup from the current total retail value. The retail method is, however, a little complicated in practice because of the need to keep track of markdowns, returned goods, special sale prices, and other price adjustments if the method is to work accurately.

The Periodic Count Method

The periodic count method lacks records to show how much inventory should be on hand.

When goods are bought, they are put on the shelf or in the storeroom, and when they are sold or used, they are taken off the shelf or out of the storeroom. With the above two control systems, records are kept of these movements, to provide expected quantities or values on hand.

But if complete records of such inventory changes are not kept, the enterprise does not have records to indicate what should be on hand. The only way to tell what is on hand is to go and count it. Because this sort of counting tends to be done only periodically, when an inventory figure is needed for financial statements or insurance purposes, this *lack* of accounting control is called the *periodic inventory control method*. While there may be other features of internal control present, such as physical protection and insurance, it lacks the parallel recordkeeping that gives the above two methods their value. There is no way to reconcile counts to records in order to discover errors as in the other two methods because records created for this purpose do not exist, but it is simple and cheap to operate because no continuing records are kept. Recordkeeping does cost money!

The periodic system works this way:

> **FORMULA**
>
> **Beginning inventory (count), priced usually at cost (or retail minus markup)**
>
> **+ Purchases (records) at cost**
>
> **– Ending inventory (count), priced at cost**
>
> **= Cost of goods sold expense (deduced)**

In the periodic count method, COGS is deduced: inventory not on hand is assumed sold.

The cost of inventory apparently sold is *deduced* (rather than known from records). It might not all have been actually sold. Some could have been lost, stolen, evaporated, etc. So under the periodic method, cost of goods sold expense (cost of counted beginning inventory + cost of purchases – cost of counted ending inventory) includes all these other possibilities. They cannot be separated because the necessary records were not kept. *This is not a flaw,* it is just that management did not believe the extra recordkeeping was worth the money it would cost. The adjustment to a separate account for inventory shortage or overage, shown for the perpetual method above, cannot be made, because the deduced COGS includes the "real" COGS plus/minus any shortage/overage. This will be demonstrated below.

Cost and Benefit of Controls

The greater the value of inventory control, the more likely the perpetual method is to be used.

The perpetual method can be costly in terms of recordkeeping. (So can the similar retail method, though probably sales records have to be kept anyway, so the extra cost of the inventory control may not be large.) Management must pay someone to record, sort, and compile the information. What type of business uses a perpetual system? The local car dealership is a good example of one. Cars are expensive—therefore a large investment must be made if a good supply is to be on hand for customers to choose from. The high value of cars and the need to keep track for licence and insurance purposes means that serial numbers and other identification information is easily available and usually recorded in various places. Automobiles have a high risk of becoming obsolete because consumer preferences change, and the cost of theft is high even if only one car is stolen. Because of the relatively small quantity of cars sold by most dealerships, recordkeeping costs are not high.

Perpetual records should be reconciled with physical counts: the more valuable the items, the more frequent the reconciliation.

Whenever an accounting control system is used, there must be regular *reconciliation* between the accounting records and any other evidence available. The idea of reconciliation as a useful technique was introduced in Section 1.12 and the value of bank reconciliation in particular was pointed out in Section 7.5. There is no real value to accounting control unless the resulting records are compared to other evidence, such as physical counts for inventories. But valuable though reconciliation is, it does cost time and money to do. Most businesses reconcile sensitive items, such as bank accounts, cash on hand, and high-value inventories, very frequently, but leave other items, such as building assets and low-value inventories, to less frequent reconciliations, often based on just a sample of items.

Inventory Control Journal Entries: Bransworth Ltd.

Bransworth Ltd. uses a perpetual accounting control system for its inventory. It has the following data for a recent period:

Beginning accounts receivable	$ 40,000	Beginning inventory	$ 23,000
Purchases during period (all cash)	114,000	Sales (all credit)	150,000
Cash collected in period	115,000	Ending inventory count	28,000

The company's markup is 50% on cost (that is, selling price is 150% of cost, so the company can calculate COGS from sales revenue). Just to make it easier, we'll assume all sales, purchases, and collections were in single transactions. Here are summary journal entries for the company's system:

EXHIBIT 7·2

a. Purchases	DR Inventory asset	114,000	
	CR Cash		114,000
	Purchases during the period.		
b. Sales	DR Accounts receivable	150,000	
	CR Sales revenue		150,000
	Sales on credit during the period.		
c. Cost of goods sold	DR Cost of goods sold expense	100,000	
	CR Inventory asset		100,000
	COGS expense: $150,000 revenue minus 50% markup on cost.		
d. Count adjustment	DR Inventory shortage expense	9,000	
	CR Inventory asset		9,000
	Shortage: record indicates inventory should be $23,000 + $114,000 – $100,000 = $37,000, but only $28,000 is on hand.		
e. Collections	DR Cash	115,000	
	CR Accounts receivable		115,000
	Customer collections during the period.		

Let's review two accounts here, to ensure you see how the accounting figures help with the control:

EXHIBIT 7·3

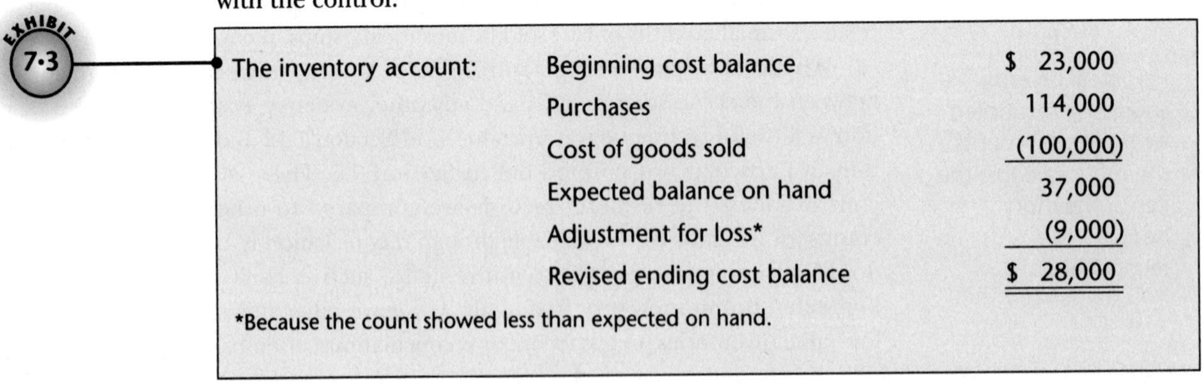

The inventory account:	Beginning cost balance	$ 23,000
	Purchases	114,000
	Cost of goods sold	(100,000)
	Expected balance on hand	37,000
	Adjustment for loss*	(9,000)
	Revised ending cost balance	$ 28,000

*Because the count showed less than expected on hand.

EXHIBIT 7·4

The accounts receivable account:	Beginning	$ 40,000
	Sales	150,000
	Collections	(115,000)
	Ending balance	$ 75,000

There is accounts receivable control here. The company can check with the customers or otherwise verify that this amount really is a collectible asset. Cash control follows from this, too. The collections figure from the accounts receivable account is part of the deposits to cash, so it becomes part of the record-based control system for cash.

For comparison, let's see how the entries above would change if Bransworth used the periodic system, *without* accounting control. Using the same journal entry references as above, we'd have:

EXHIBIT 7·5

a.	Purchases	DR Purchases expense (or similar account name)	114,000	
		CR Cash		114,000
b.	Sales	Same entry as for perpetual method		
c.	COGS	No entry: the company does not record COGS when sales are made		
d.	Count adjustment	DR Beginning inventory expense	23,000	
		CR Inventory asset		23,000
		Transferring beginning inventory to expense.		
		DR Inventory asset	28,000	
		CR Ending inventory "expense"		28,000
		Recording ending inventory by removing its cost from expense (that is, from Purchases + Beginning inventory).		
e.	Collections	Same entry as for perpetual method		

The cost of goods sold must be deduced as the net sum of the three expense accounts above:

Beginning inventory	$ 23,000
+ Purchases	114,000
– Ending inventory	(28,000)
= COGS	$109,000

This is the same as the perpetual method's *total* of COGS $100,000 + Shortage expense $9,000. So there is no effect on the net income of choosing between the two control methods, because each contains an adjustment to the actual amount counted at the end of the year. There is no effect on the balance sheet either, because both adjust to the same $28,000 ending amount. *The differences between the methods are in their control and management information.*

HOW'S YOUR UNDERSTANDING?

Here are two questions you should be able to answer based on what you have just read. If you can't answer them, it would be best to reread the material.

1. What is the role of recordkeeping in internal control?
2. Granot Inc. uses the perpetual inventory method. At the beginning of the month, inventory costing $145,890 was on hand. Purchases for the month totalled $267,540 and cost of goods recorded as sold totalled $258,310. At the end of the month, a count showed inventory costing $152,730 to be on hand. What, if anything, was the inventory shortage for the month?

$145,890 + $267,540 – $258,310 = $155,120 expected to be on hand, minus $152,730 counted = $2,390 shortage.

7.10 A Procedural Review

By this time, you should be "thinking double-entry": aware that when one account is affected, another must be too. This is fundamental to accrual accounting, and to internal control provided by the double-entry accounting records. Consider the following examples:

EXHIBIT 7·6

a. *Revenue cycle*

Recognition:	DR Accounts receivable CR Revenue
Collection:	DR Cash CR Accounts receivable

b. *Doubtful account cycle*

Allowance:	DR Bad debts expense CR Allowance for doubtful accounts
Write-off:	DR Allowance for doubtful accounts CR Accounts receivable

c. *Purchases cycle (perpetual method)*

Purchase:	DR Inventory CR Accounts payable
Payment:	DR Accounts payable CR Cash
Recognition:	DR Cost of goods sold expense CR Inventory

d. *Capitalization/amortization/disposal cycle*

Acquisition:	DR Noncurrent asset CR Cash or liability account
or Capitalization:	DR Noncurrent asset CR Expense
Amortization with a contra account:	DR Amortization expense CR Accumulated amortization contra
or Amortization without a contra account:	DR Amortization expense CR Noncurrent asset account
Disposal:	DR Cash (proceeds) CR Noncurrent asset (cost) DR Accumulated amortization contra CR Gain or DR loss on sale
Write-down or write-off:	CR Noncurrent asset (cost) DR Accumulated amortization DR Write-down or write-off loss

HOW'S YOUR UNDERSTANDING?

Here are two questions you should be able to answer based on what you have just read. If you can't answer them, it would be best to reread the material.

1. The term "write-off" is used with reference to both long-term assets and accounts receivable. What does the term mean in those cases and how does it differ between the two?
2. Flimsy's accounts receivable at the end of 2006 totalled $78,490. The allowance for doubtful accounts had been $2,310, but it was decided that this would be increased by $1,560 and then that $1,100 in hopeless accounts would be written off. What was the net collectible value of the receivables as shown on the balance sheet at the end of 2006 and the bad debts expense for 2006?

Collectible value = $78,490 – ($2,310 + $1,560) = $74,620 (The $1,100 in hopeless accounts would be deducted from the control account and the allowance and so has no effect on the collectible value.); Bad debts expense = $1,560

7.11 Terms to Be Sure You Understand

Here is this chapter's list of terms introduced or emphasized. Make sure you know what they mean *in accounting*, and if any are unclear to you, check the chapter again or refer to the glossary of terms at the back of the book.

Accounting control
Accumulated amortization
Allowance for doubtful accounts
Amortization
Amortization expense
Audit committee
Bad debts expense
Bank reconciliation
Books of original entry
Capitalized costs
Cash disbursements journal
Cash receipts journal
Chart of accounts
Cheque
COGS expense
Contra account
Control account
Corporate governance
Direct write-off
E-commerce
EFT
Electronic commerce
Electronic funds transfer
Employee deductions
General journal
General ledger
GST
HST
Intangible assets
Internal control
Management information system
Net book value
Packing slip
Periodic inventory control method
Perpetual inventory control method
Petty cash
PST
Purchase order
Reconciliation
Retail inventory control method
Sales invoice
Sales journal
Sales taxes
Segregation of duties
Source documents
Specialized ledgers
Subsidiary ledgers
Work order
Write-off (bad debts)
Write-off (noncurrent assets)

INSTALLMENT 7

DATA FOR INSTALLMENT 7

After recording the transactions to February 28, 2007, in Installment 6, the trial balance of Mato Inc.'s general ledger was (credits are bracketed):

Cash	6,418	Revenue	(227,656)
Accounts receivable	13,709	Cost of goods sold expense	138,767
Inventory	33,612	Salary—Mavis	0
Automobile	10,000	Salary—Tomas	0
Accumulated amortization —auto.	(1,000)	Salary—other	0
Leasehold improvements	63,964	Salaries expense	67,480
Accumulated amortization — leasehold	(6,396)	Travel expense	10,102
Equipment and furniture	32,390	Phone expense	4,014
Accumulated amortization —equipment	(744)	Rent expense	24,000
Computer	14,900	Utilities expense	3,585
Accumulated amortization —computer	(1,490)	Office and general expense	5,933
Software	4,800	Interest expense	6,239
Accumulated amortization —software	(480)	Inventory shortage expense	441
Incorporation cost	1,100	Amortization expense—auto.	1,000
Bank loan	(47,500)	Amortization expense—leasehold	6,396
Accounts payable	(36,656)	Amortization expense—equipment	744
Deductions payable	(2,284)	Amortization expense—computer	1,490
Salaries payable	(2,358)	Amortization expense—software	480
Loan payable	0		0
Share capital	(125,000)		

It was time to prepare the financial statements for the year ended February 28, 2007. Before that could be done, the following adjustments had to be made:

a. Based on the amortization calculations made during the first six months, the amounts for the second six months would be:
   - Car, leasehold improvements, computer, and software: 1/2 year × 20% of cost.
   - Equipment and furniture: 1/2 year × 10% of cost.

   The expenses for the second six months would therefore be: car, $1,000; leasehold improvements, $6,396; computer, $1,490; software, $480; equipment and furniture, $1,620.

b. Estimated unpaid bank loan interest to February 28 was $230.

c. Unfortunately, some of the boutique customers had run into financial difficulty. One customer who owed $894 had gone bankrupt and other accounts totalling $1,542 were doubtful.

d. Tomas had been getting some accounting assistance from a local public accountant. No bill had yet been received for this help, but Tomas estimated that the company owed about $280 at the end of February.

e. It turned out that included in the revenue figure was a deposit of $500 made by a customer on a special order from Africa that had not yet arrived.

f. Included in the office and general expenses was an insurance policy costing $1,050, good for two years from March 1, 2006.

g. Mavis and Tomas decided that they should pay the company back about $200 for Mavis and $425 for Tomas for personal use of the company automobile. Automobile expenses were included in the travel expense account.

h. Mavis was concerned that the accounts receivable list "didn't look right," as she put it. Upon checking, she discovered that shipments totalling $2,231 in revenue had been made in late January and early February, but had not yet been billed. The cost of the goods shipped had been correctly removed from the inventory account and charged to cost of goods sold.

i. Tomas decided that the sales taxes due to the government, which had been included in accounts payable, should be put in a separate account. The amount due at February 28 was $1,843. Beginning March 1, this account would be used for all GST and PST collected and remitted.

Results for Installment 7

Adjusting journal entries at February 28, 2007, to take the above information into account:

a. Amortization expense—auto.	1,000	
Accumulated amortization—auto.		1,000
Amortization expense—leasehold	6,396	
Accumulated amortization—leasehold		6,396
Amortization expense—computer	1,490	
Accumulated amortization—computer		1,490
Amortization expense—software	480	
Accumulated amortization—software		480
Amortization expense—equipment and furniture	1,620	
Accumulated amortization—equipment and furniture		1,620
b. Interest expense	230	
Accounts payable		230
c. Bad debts expense	2,436	
Allowance for doubtful accounts		2,436
($894 + $1,542 = $2,436)		
Allowance for doubtful accounts	894	
Accounts receivable		894
d. Office and general expenses	280	
Accounts payable		280
e. Revenue	500	
Customer deposits liability		500
f. Prepaid insurance	525	
Office and general expense		525
($1,050 over two years = $525 per year)		
g. Accounts receivable	625	
Travel expense		625
($200 + $425 = $625)		
h. Accounts receivable	2,231	
Revenue		2,231
i. Accounts payable	1,843	
Sales taxes due		1,843

After posting the adjusting journal entries to the trial balance given at the beginning of this installment, the following adjusted February 28, 2007, account balances were produced (credits are bracketed as usual):

Account	Balance	Account	Balance
Cash	6,418	Revenue	(229,387)
Accounts receivable	15,671	Cost of goods sold expense	138,767
Allowance for doubtful accounts	(1,542)	Bad debts expense	2,436
Inventory	33,612	Salary—Mavis	0
Prepaid insurance	525	Salary—Tomas	0
Automobile	10,000	Salary—other	0
Accumulated amortization —auto.	(2,000)	Salaries expense	67,480
Leasehold improvements	63,964	Travel expense	9,477
Accumulated amortization — leasehold	(12,792)	Phone expense	4,014
Equipment and furniture	32,390	Rent expense	24,000
Accumulated amortization —equipment	(2,364)	Utilities expense	3,585
Computer	14,900	Office and general expense	5,688
Accumulated amortization —computer	(2,980)	Interest expense	6,469
Software	4,800	Inventory shortage expense	441
Accumulated amortization —software	(960)	Amortization expense—auto.	2,000
Incorporation cost	1,100	Amortization expense —leasehold	12,792
Bank loan	(47,500)	Amortization expense —equipment	2,364
Accounts payable	(35,323)	Amortization expense —computer	2,980
Customer deposits liability	(500)	Amortization expense —software	960
Sales taxes due	(1,843)		0
Deductions payable	(2,284)		
Salaries payable	(2,358)		
Loan payable	0		
Share capital	(125,000)		

That's enough for now! We'll do some more work with these balances, including preparing financial statements, in later installments.

7.13 Homework and Discussion to Develop Understanding

The problems roughly follow the outline of the chapter. Three main categories of questions are presented.

- Asterisked problems (*) have an informal solution provided in the Student Solutions Manual.
- EXTENDED TIME problems grant a thorough examination of the material and may take longer to complete.
- CHALLENGING problems are more difficult.

For further explanation, please refer to Section 1.15.

Accounting and Recordkeeping • Section 7.2

Explaining Accounting Documentation

*** PROBLEM 7.1** Describe accounting's documents and books of original entry

The financial statements are prepared from account balances from the general ledger. Behind these balances, however, are numerous documents and books of original entry. Describe the main kinds of documents used to support financial accounting and the books of original entry that are prepared from those documents.

PROBLEM 7.2 Necessary source documents and purpose of trial balance

1. Make a list of the source documents you expect would be needed to back up the transactional records in an accounting system and describe in ten words or so why each document would be useful.
2. Why does the bookkeeper (or the computer system) produce a trial balance of the general ledger regularly?

PROBLEM 7.3 Accounting documentation in e-commerce

Musi.ca, the on-line CD seller, takes orders and collects payments via credit card numbers supplied by customers on its high-security Web page. Orders are transmitted automatically to CD warehouser Disko Inc., which ships the CDs to customers and receives payment from Musi.ca electronically as each CD is shipped. Musi.ca makes its money by charging just a little more to customers' credit cards than Disko Inc. charges it.

One day, you go to Musi.ca's Web page, order the new hit album from Sing'em, type in your credit card number, and your CD arrives in the mail less than a week later. Outline the source documents and "books of original entry" that this e-commerce transaction would probably generate for all four parties involved: you, Musi.ca, Disko Inc., and your credit card company.

Explaining the Reasons For Recordkeeping

*** PROBLEM 7.4** Recordkeeping differences in large versus small businesses

Identify some differences you might expect to find between the transaction filters and accounting books and records of a large corporation and those of a corner store run by one person. What effects might those differences have on the company's accounting policies?

PROBLEM 7.5 Explain the value of recordkeeping to a businessperson

At a recent Student Accounting Club wine and cheese party, local businesspeople mixed with students. One small business entrepreneur was heard to say, "All that financial accounting information you students learn about is not relevant to me. I just started up my business. I only have five employees: four people in the shop building the product and one person in shipping/receiving. I'm out on calls, drumming up business, so I have my finger on the real pulse of the firm—that's sales. My brother pays the bills and does up the payroll every two weeks. Once in a while I write cheques too. It's all simple and smooth, so why add a lot of time-consuming, costly recordkeeping to it all? All those books and financial statements are fine for the big public companies. I can do without the complications."

Prepare an appropriate response to the businessperson.

PROBLEM 7.6 Recordkeeping differences in nonprofit groups

Mike and Ted have been friends since their university days. After graduation, Mike took a job at a large head office in the city while Ted opted to work for a small nonprofit charity. The two regularly meet for lunch to discuss their experiences in the two jobs.

Today, Ted explains his frustrations; "I don't understand why I have to fill out all of these accounting forms each day. There always seems to be a mountain of paperwork to complete. I feel like I spend all day creating copies of forms, filing them, and entering information into the computer. Why is all this paperwork necessary?"

Mike explains his situation, "At my work, we have a detailed control system. Transactions are carefully recorded and we keep a long list of source documents to verify what is occurring. It often seems like a lot of paperwork but I'm beginning to see how important it is to keep good records."

1. Explain to Ted why a strong underlying accounting system would be needed for a nonprofit organization. Examine the issue from the point of view of:
   a. a donor
   b. a beneficiary of the charity
   c. the charity's board of directors
   d. the government
2. Would a nonprofit organization differ from a large corporation in the way it needs to keep detailed accounting records?

Internal Control • Sections 7.3– 7.5

Identification of Internal Control Problems

* **PROBLEM 7.7** Identify violated components of internal control

In each of the following cases, what component of good internal control is being violated (if any)? (See Section 7.3 if you can't remember the components.)

a. Tough Inc. pays all its employees minimum wage and does not have pleasant working conditions.
b. Fred is a very conscientious employee and does such a good job that he does pretty much all of Whisp Ltd.'s office tasks.
c. Garand Inc. has a sophisticated internal control system that prints out various reports on discrepancies, which company management gets the accounting clerks to investigate and resolve.
d. John runs a small warehousing business. He's proud of saving money on accounting. For example, he doesn't keep track of purchases and shipments of goods because he can "look at the shelves and see if everything is all right."
e. Wildwood Restaurant is proud of its "family approach" to its employees, taking great care to make them feel important and trusted. Everyone has a key to the restaurant and several employees can often be found there in off hours, helping to clean and prepare for the next day.

f. Hadlee Corp's founder, getting on in years, has turned the president's job over to his playboy son, who is quite interested in horse racing and turns up at the office only occasionally.

EXTENDED TIME

* PROBLEM 7.8 Identify missing features of internal control

Read the following description of a sports club and indicate what features of good internal control seem to be missing. Are any of those offset by strength in other features?

> The club earns revenue from members' fees, and from selling tickets to its games and advertising in its programs. Advertising receipts are mainly by cheque; other receipts are primarily cash, with an increasing percentage by credit card. Most expenditures are in cash, except for equipment, facility rentals, and the three employees' pay, all done by cheques. One employee does some coaching, schedules games, and coordinates players and officials. The second employee (who is married to the first) looks after equipment, prepares rental facilities for games, makes travel arrangements, and does various miscellaneous jobs. The third employee looks after cash, payroll, and accounting. The club's board of directors meets monthly and always has monthly (or annual) financial reports to scrutinize. All three employees are members of the board and other board members rely on them.
>
> The club has a rented office/storeroom, where all employees work most of the time and where all the club's equipment and various supplies are stored. Cash, cheques, and credit card slips are deposited into the bank every two weeks, and payment cheques are issued as needed. Cash expenses are paid out of cash collected from members' fees and ticket sales, so often there is not enough cash to bother depositing. Sometimes there is not enough cash to pay cash expenses, in which case the third employee, who is authorized to sign all cheques, just writes a cheque to "cash" and cashes it at the nearby bank where the club's bank account is maintained. The board of directors discusses all major trips, equipment purchases, and other large expenditures in advance, and gives general approvals (or denials) to the employees to then look after the details.

PROBLEM 7.9 Earnings management or internal control problem?

According to *The Economist*, June 2002, "Almost 1,000 American companies have now restated their earnings since 1997, admitting in effect that they had previously published wrong or misleading numbers."[9] In Chapter 3 or 6 of this book, we might have noted this situation as earnings management or general misuse of accrual accounting. But 1,000 companies is a lot, so it is plausible that such problems were not always deliberate.

Explain how the restatements *The Economist* referred to could be evidence of internal control problems, referring to the ideas in Sections 7.3 and 7.4.

PROBLEM 7.10 Top management responsibility for internal control

The proud owner of Beedle Inc., a successful high-tech company, is very good at hiring and motivating excellent people to develop and sell products. Delegation is the key, says the owner: "Hire good people and get out of their way!" As part of this philosophy, the owner hired the best accountants available and turned over to them all accounting, control, and finance functions. The owner concentrates on strategy and business planning, and the company has grown steadily for several years.

Explain to the owner what top management responsibilities are being neglected here. Given that the company is so successful, does such neglect really matter?

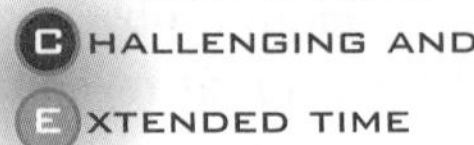

PROBLEM 7.11 Identify cash control problems

Many companies put a great amount of effort into controlling their cash, both that on hand and in banks, often more than for any other asset.

1. Why do you think such great effort is required to control cash?
2. List the control problems you'd expect in each of the following cases. To answer, try to visualize how the cash would probably flow into and out of the company and its bank accounts:
   a. Cash collected at the sales counter of the local dollar store.
   b. Wages being paid to construction employees working on a large highway project.
   c. Donations to the local charity being collected by door-to-door volunteer canvassers.
   d. Money deposited into vending machines.
   e. Cash provided to the receptionist by the company at the main entrance, to be used to pay for deliveries, buy emergency supplies, and other minor things.

Components and People Involved in Internal Control

***PROBLEM 7.12** Explain components of internal control

Ingram Inc. has the following features in its internal control system. Explain why each is a useful component of the company's controls:

a. One person looks after the accounts receivable records and another person is in charge of receiving and depositing cash.
b. The receptionist has a petty cash fund.
c. The company uses the retail inventory method.
d. The company keeps its inventory in a locked warehouse.
e. Each month, the bookkeeper reconciles the balances in the liability accounts for various employee deductions to payroll and payment records.

PROBLEM 7.13 Explain the nature and purpose of internal control to a manager

A friend, Janet, has accepted a job as president of a local company. During a meeting you attended, an accountant mentioned to Janet that she would be responsible for internal control of the company. When the accountant left the room, Janet turned to you and asked, "What is internal control, and why should I care about it?" Answer Janet's question, using clear language without technical jargon.

PROBLEM 7.14 List factors for evaluating whether to improve internal control

You work for Sydney Industries Ltd. The president has been reading other companies' annual reports and has become concerned that the company's internal controls may not be adequate. On the other hand, the president does not want to spend the company's money unnecessarily.

List the factors you would suggest the president consider in evaluating whether better internal controls would be worthwhile.

PROBLEM 7.15 Internal control — theatre admissions

Your date has taken you to a classical music concert. More interested in your financial accounting course than the music, you begin to think about the appropriate internal controls needed to ensure that all cash is received by the theatre operator and that all patrons pay for their admission. You and your date purchased your tickets at the box office paying cash, but you noted on entering the theatre that other people had purchased their tickets earlier. When you moved from the foyer to the theatre, a theatre employee examined your ticket, advised you of the location of your seat, tore your ticket, and returned the stub to you. You then proceeded to the auditorium entrance where an usher checked your ticket and directed you to your seat.

Ignoring the sounds coming from the stage, list the control procedures you observed and any you think should be in place.

Sales Tax and Employee Deductions to Be Remitted • Section 7.6

Calculating Sales Tax and Employee Deductions

*** PROBLEM 7.16** Record sales taxes and employee deductions

Montane Tours Inc. provides guiding services in high alpine areas and operates Mountain Crest souvenir shops in some resort towns. Two groups of transactions the company recently had are described below. The payments indicated were for the amounts due before the transactions, because such remittances follow the transactions creating the amounts due.

a. The company earned sales revenue of $72,000, on which it charged PST of $4,320 and GST of $5,040. Customers paid $69,030 of the total during the month, and the company expected to collect the rest within 60 days. The company paid the provincial government $3,900 on account of PST and the federal government $3,100 on account of GST. GST paid was lower because the company incurred $1,840 GST on its own $26,286 purchases.
b. Employees earned $39,250 in wages, from which the company deducted income tax of $11,180 and other deductions of $4,990. The company incurred fringe benefit costs of $6,315 on those wages. During the month, the company remitted $12,668 to the government on account of income taxes and remitted $11,894 to various government bodies, pension trustees, and other organizations on account of other deductions and fringe benefits.

Record the transactions described.

PROBLEM 7.17 Calculating GST and PST due

Kate's Cards & Gifts is a small retail outlet. At the end of the year, Kate needs your assistance in calculating the amount of GST and PST that she still needs to remit to the governments. For the following transactions, write out the journal entries and then calculate the total GST due and PST due.

a. Kate's Cards & Gifts had sales of $493,000 for the period. Included in this amount were GST at 7% for $30,009 and PST at 8% for $34,295. Cash collected was $361,760 and the remainder is owing to the company.
b. The store made its own purchases of inventory in the period that came to $297,000. Included in this amount was GST of $19,430 while the company is exempt from paying PST. An initial cash payment of $190,000 was made while the remainder was on credit.
c. The company paid the federal and provincial governments $8,000 of GST and $20,000 of the PST, respectively.

PROBLEM 7.18 Answer questions about sales taxes and employee deductions

A partial list of Havefun Wedding Planners Ltd.'s accounts is below.

Sales taxes payable	$ 7,620
Employee tax deductions due	10,480
Other employee deductions and fringe benefits due	6,530
Wages payable	22,460
Revenue	629,530
Wages expense	315,210
Fringe benefits expense	26,870

1. The company has no expense account for sales taxes, though it does have expense accounts for corporate income tax and property taxes on its building. Why is that?
2. The company also has no expense account for employees' income taxes, even though it has to pay such taxes to the government. Why is that?
3. Over a period of time, will the amounts debited to wages expense equal the amounts credited to wages payable? Why or why not?
4. After the above balances were determined, the company recorded revenue on a wedding plan of $40,000 and charged 7% GST and 8% PST on that sale. Which of the above accounts were affected by the sale, in what direction(s), and by how much?
5. Also after the above balances were determined, the company paid its accountant $6,420, on which it paid GST of 7%. Which of the above accounts were affected by the payment, in what direction(s), and by how much?
6. The company accountant wanted to write cheques to the provincial and federal governments for all PST and GST due. Taking into account items 4 and 5, how much would the cheques total?
7. Again, after the above balances were determined, some employees turned in extra time sheets, showing they had overtime totalling $2,200. The company incurred $570 in holiday pay, pension contributions, and other fringe benefits in addition to this, and deducted $760 in income tax and $93 in other deductions. Which of the above accounts were affected by all this, in what direction(s), and by how much?

Contra Accounts • Sections 7.7 and 7.8

Calculating Doubtful Accounts Receivable

* **PROBLEM 7.19** Answer questions about doubtful accounts receivable

Dragon Designs Ltd. had the following general ledger accounts for last year, using the T-account format. All the company's sales are on credit to retail stores across the country. The first amount in each account is the balance at the beginning of the year; the last amount, under the solid line, is the balance at the end of the year. Other amounts are transactions and adjustments during the year.

Accounts Receivable		Allow. for Doubt. Accts.		Bad Debts Expense	
244,620			11,914	0	
1,693,784					
	1,599,005				
			9,117	9,117	
	8,293	8,293			
331,106			12,738	9,117	

Answer these questions:

1. What was the company's revenue for the year?
2. How much was collected on account of revenue for the year?
3. How much of the uncollected revenue did the company give up on during the year?
4. What was the expense the company incurred from taking the risk of extending credit to customers during the year?
5. On average, how much did the company lose on each dollar of sales? Answer this two ways: by looking at the bad debts expense, and at the bad debts written off. What are the values of each way from management's point of view?
6. What was the estimated collectible value of the accounts receivable at the end of the year?
7. What was the estimated collectible value of the accounts receivable *prior* to the year-end write-off of uncollectible accounts?

PROBLEM 7.20 Calculate bad debt allowance and expense

Windhook Technologies Ltd. has been having difficulty collecting its accounts receivable. For the year 2006, the company made provisions for bad debts of $66,650, bringing the balance in the allowance for doubtful accounts to $110,000. At the end of 2006, accounts receivable equalled $643,250. When the year-end audit was being done, it was decided that a further $83,700 of accounts receivable were doubtful and that $55,800 of accounts receivable previously deemed doubtful should be written off altogether.

Calculate the following:

a. Bad debts expense for 2006.
b. Allowance for doubtful accounts at the end of 2006.
c. Estimated collectible value of accounts receivable at the end of 2006.

PROBLEM 7.21 Accounting for doubtful accounts and bad debt expense

Coldlink Company uses an aging of accounts receivable to estimate the needed allowance for doubtful accounts on the basis that the more delinquent an account becomes, the less likelihood of collection. The following is the result of the aging of accounts receivable at December 31, 2007, and the proportion of the balances that Coldlink believes is needed for proper matching of bad debts expense to the period:

Account Status	Account Balance Total	Estimated Loss Percentage
Not yet due	$200,000	1%
Past Due:		
1–30 days	100,000	3%
31–60 days	50,000	4%
61–90 days	120,000	5%
Over 90 days	30,000	30%
Total	$500,000	

1. Calculate the required ending balance in the doubtful accounts allowance at December 31, 2007.
2. Assuming the balance in the allowance for doubtful accounts is $2,500 prior to the year-end adjustment, calculate the bad debt expense that Coldlink will report in 2007.
3. Write the journal entry to adjust the doubtful accounts allowance account at December 31, 2007.
4. On January 4, 2008, the company is informed that customer John Henry, who went bankrupt while owing the company money, has been discharged in bankruptcy and

no further payments will be received from him. It is decided to write off Mr. Henry's account balance of $642. Write the journal entry to record this write-off.

PROBLEM 7.22 Analysis of effects of decisions on net accounts receivable

Gallumphing Gourmet Inc. sells imported fancy kitchenware to retailers. Lately, the company has been having increasing problems collecting its receivables and has been forced to consider increasing its allowance for doubtful accounts. Accounts receivable at the end of last year were $922,000 and at the end of this year are $1,332,000. The allowance for doubtful accounts was $40,000 at the end of last year and has not been revised yet for this year's experience. Instead, the company has just written off some accounts receivable directly to bad debts expense; the expense therefore shows a balance of $34,000 of these write-offs for this year. The company is considering three different actions to take its current poorer collection experience into account:

a. Directly writing off additional, apparently hopeless accounts totalling $51,000.
b. Adjusting the allowance for doubtful accounts to $92,000 to include the accounts in (a) and some doubtful accounts, but not giving up on the hopeless ones just yet.
c. Combining (a) and (b) by increasing the allowance to include all the hopeless and doubtful ones and then writing off the hopeless ones.

Analyze the three possible actions, calculating for each what the revised balances are in (1) accounts receivable, (2) allowance for doubtful accounts, and (3) bad debts expense, and showing what the effect of each is on (4) net collectible value of the accounts receivable, (5) working capital, and (6) income for the year.

Amortization and Write-offs

* **PROBLEM 7.23** Answer questions about factory assets and amortization

Aaron Manufacturing Inc. had the following general ledger accounts for last year, using the T-account format. The first amount in each account is the balance at the beginning of the year; the last amount, under the solid line, is the balance at the end of the year. Other amounts are transactions and adjustments during the year.

Factory Assets		Accumulated Amortization		Amortization Expenses	
5,497,888			1,977,321	0	
1,032,568					
	843,992	411,883			
			793,220	793,220	
	89,245	59,200			
5,597,219			2,299,458	793,220	

Answer these questions:

1. What was the portion of the factory assets estimated to have been consumed economically in earning revenue during the year?
2. How much was spent acquiring additional factory assets during the year?
3. The assets that cost $843,992 brought $350,000 in proceeds. Did their sale result in a gain or a loss on disposal? Write the journal entry that would have recorded the sale.
4. The assets that cost $89,245 were retired and written off, bringing no proceeds. Write the journal entry that would have recorded the write-off.
5. What was the net book value of the factory assets at the end of the year?

PROBLEM 7.24 Calculating net book value

An air cargo supply company decides to purchase a new jumbo cargo plane for $145,000,000. The plane will be in use for a period of 20 years. For the following events, write out the applicable journal entries. Treat each event individually.

a. Five years after purchase, the company sells the plane for $85,000,000. To date, amortization on the plane was $35,000,000.
b. Eight years after purchase, the company sells the plane for $95,000,000. At this point, total accumulated amortization on the plane was $56,000,000.
c. The plane catches fire on the ground in a country where a war is going on and is destroyed. Unfortunately, the insurance company refuses to pay anything because the insurance excludes war-related damage. The company has to write off the plane. At the point of the fire, the plane had been amortized $42,500,000.

PROBLEM 7.25 Answer questions about contra accounts and write-offs

A partial list of Boomber Inc.'s asset and income statement accounts is below.

Accounts receivable control account	$ 8,423,119
Allowance for doubtful accounts	113,402
Investment in Magnifico Manufacturing Inc. (cost)	1,560,000
Equipment and furniture (cost)	10,399,163
Accumulated amortization on equipment and furniture	3,725,021
Bad debts expense	56,286
Amortization expense on equipment and furniture	1,025,120

1. What did it cost Boomber this year to extend credit to customers who are unlikely to pay?
2. What did it cost Boomber this year to use equipment and furniture in its revenue-generating business activities?
3. What is (a) the net collectible value of the accounts receivable and (b) the net book value of the equipment and furniture?
4. After seeing the above figures, Boomber's chief accountant decided that $69,579 of worthless accounts receivable should be written off. What effect would doing this have on: (a) accounts receivable, (b) allowance for doubtful accounts, (c) bad debts expense, and (d) net collectible value of accounts receivable?
5. The chief accountant also decided that some of the furniture had no use in the business anymore and should be written off. No proceeds were expected on selling the furniture; instead, it would be donated to a local charity. The furniture had cost $55,250 and had accumulated amortization of $50,950. What effect would this decision have on (a) the cost of equipment and furniture, (b) accumulated amortization on equipment and furniture, (c) net book value of equipment and furniture, and (d) income for the year?
6. The chief accountant, while she was at it, suggested that 80% of the investment in Magnifico be written off. Magnifico was in serious financial trouble and it looked as if Boomber would be unable to sell it for much more than 20% of cost. What effect would this decision have on (a) total assets of Boomber, and (b) income for the year?

Inventory Control • Section 7.9

Calculating Inventory Using the Periodic and Perpetual Methods

***PROBLEM 7.26** Periodic and perpetual inventory control calculations

You are the senior accountant for a shoe wholesaler that uses the periodic inventory method. You have determined the following information from your company's records, which you assume are correct:

a. Inventory of $246,720 was on hand at the start of the year.
b. Purchases for the year totalled $1,690,000. Of this, $1,412,000 was purchased on account; that is, accounts payable were credited for this amount at the time of the purchase.
c. The ending balance in accounts payable was $47,500 higher than the opening balance.
d. A year-end inventory count revealed inventory of $324,800.

1. Calculate cost of goods sold according to the periodic inventory method.
2. Assume now that your company uses the perpetual method of inventory control, and that your records show that $1,548,325 of inventory (at cost) was sold during the year. What is the adjustment needed to correct the records, given the inventory count in item (d) above? What might the need for this adjustment indicate about company operations?
3. If the perpetual method generally provides more control over inventory for management, why don't all companies use it?

PROBLEM 7.27A Recording inventory and sales-related transactions

Edenvale Toys Inc. had the following transactions relating to its inventory held for resale in its first month of operations:

Date	Transaction
June 3	Edenvale purchased from Southern Novelties Inc. 200 cases of toys at $25 per case plus GST at 7% on account.
June 7	Edenvale sold 55 cases of toys to Tiny Tots Stores at $60 per case plus GST at 7% on account.
June 12	Tiny Tots returned 10 cases of defective toys to Edenvale.
June 14	Edenvale returned the 10 cases of defective toys to Southern Novelties Inc.
June 20	Edenvale received a payment on account from Tiny Tots in the amount of $1,800.
June 22	Edenvale paid Southern $4,000 on account.
June 28	Edenvale sold another 75 cases of toys to Tiny Tots on account at $70 per case plus GST at 7%.

1. Write journal entries to record each of the transactions above assuming Edenvale uses the perpetual inventory control method.
2. Calculate the balance on Edenvale's books at June 30 for:
   a. Accounts receivable from Tiny Tots.
   b. Accounts payable to Southern.
   c. Inventory purchased from Southern held for resale.
   d. The amount of GST due resulting from these transactions.

PROBLEM 7.27B Interpreting financial statements—cost of goods sold

The Consolidated Statements of Operations in the 2004 Annual Report for Gap Inc. show the following:

$ in millions	52 weeks Ended Jan. 29, 2005	52 Weeks Ended Jan 31, 2004	52 Weeks Ended Feb. 1, 2003
Net sales	$ 16,267	$ 15,854	$ 14,455
Cost of goods sold and occupancy expenses	9,886	9,885	9,541
Gross profit	6,381	5,969	4,914

Note A to the financial statements reveals the following:

Cost of Goods Sold and Occupancy Expenses

Cost of goods sold and occupancy expenses include the cost of merchandise, inventory shortage and valuation adjustments, inbound freight charges, purchasing and receiving costs, certain payroll costs associated with our sourcing operations, inspection costs, warehousing costs, rent, occupancy, and depreciation for our stores and distribution centres.

1. Why do you think Gap Inc. reports cost of goods sold in this manner?
2. Calculate Gap Inc.'s gross profit as a percentage of sales, using Gap's figures.
3. Using your result from part 2, but additionally assuming that only 75% of Gap's "Cost of goods sold and occupancy expenses" actually relate directly to inventory costs, determine the cost to Gap Inc. of an item it sells for $100.
4. Based on your own research, does your answer in part 3 seem reasonable? Explain.

PROBLEM 7.28 Calculations and entries for various control account transactions

Parts 2 and 3 may be done independently of part 1, and vice versa.

You have the following information for Blue Mountain Products Inc.:

- Balances beginning of year: Cash, $328,600; Accounts receivable, $721,310; Inventory, $806,220; Prepaid expenses, $93,760; Accounts payable, $518,640; GST due, $33,260.
- Transactions for the year: Sales on credit, $4,218,140 plus GST, $295,270; Collections, $4,602,380; Purchases (all on credit), $2,289,715 plus GST, $160,280; Payments to suppliers, $2,186,410; GST remitted, $163,200.
- The company's selling prices are determined by adding 100% to its cost for products.
- All the prepaid expenses were consumed during the year, and a further $14,220 were incurred but unpaid by the end of the year.
- The company operates a perpetual inventory system. At the end of the year, the inventory count showed inventory costing $968,320 to be on hand.

1. Based just on the above data, calculate the year-end balance in the following:
   a. Cash control account
   b. Accounts receivable control account
   c. Inventory control account
   d. Prepaid expenses
   e. Accounts payable control account
   f. GST due control account
2. Write journal entries to record all the transactions and other relevant information.
3. Assume the company used the periodic inventory method instead. Identify which entries from part 2 are different and write the periodic method entries.

Integrated Problems

Recordkeeping and Control Accounting

***PROBLEM 7.29** Explain accounting terms in plain English

Your aunt, a prominent businessperson, learns you are studying accounting and, one evening, asks you to explain the following terms to her. Your aunt is smart and successful and, maybe for that reason, is impatient with jargon, so she wants the answers to be short, to the point, and in jargon-free English.

a. Adjustments
b. Contra accounts
c. Internal control
d. Control accounts
e. Books of original entry
f. Write-off of uncollectible accounts
g. Accounting control

PROBLEM 7.30 Match terms to descriptions

Match each term on the left with the most appropriate phrase on the right.

1. Allowance for doubtful accounts	a. Says what should be there
2. Intangible assets	b. Not a control method
3. Chart of accounts	c. Look them up to verify
4. Periodic inventory method	d. Provides an expense without changing the asset
5. Segregation of duties	e. Based on selling prices
6. Bad debt write-off	f. Don't let anyone do too much
7. Source documents	g. Trial balance with no numbers
8. Books of original entry	h. A contra account is not usually used for these
9. Control account	i. The basis for amounts posted to ledgers
10. Retail inventory method	j. Doesn't change the financial statements

PROBLEM 7.31 Evaluate statements about accounting and recordkeeping

State whether or not you agree with each of the statements below and, in a few words, tell why.

a. HST due is not a true liability of the company because it is the government's money.
b. Internal control is the sole responsibility of the accountants in an organization.
c. If an event satisfies all four of the transaction criteria, you can be sure it will be recorded by the entity's accounting system.
d. E-commerce transactions between a company and its customers are not accounting transactions in the company's records because no cash is ever involved.
e. The perpetual method of accounting for inventory provides better internal control than the periodic method.
f. A properly designed system of internal control over cash will prevent employee theft of cash.

CHALLENGING AND EXTENDED TIME

PROBLEM 7.32 Write a paragraph each on various topics

Write a paragraph on each of the following topics. Feel free to go beyond this chapter's specific content to add your own experiences or views.

a. The relationship between corporate managers' responsibility for internal control and their responsibility to earn income for the shareholders.
b. The value of financial accounting's double-entry system in assisting with internal control.
c. The importance of documents to the credibility of financial accounting information.
d. The relationship between the way the enterprise records transactions and the kinds of adjustments required to meet the objectives of accrual accounting.
e. The role of the enterprise's accounting system in meeting its legal obligation to collect taxes on behalf of governments.

Contra and Control Account Issues

*** PROBLEM 7.33** Outline how internal controls mutually reinforce each other

Outline how, in accounting for routine purchase and sale transactions, double-entry accounting can provide control accounts for cash, accounts receivable, inventories, accounts payable, and GST that interrelate and mutually reinforce each other.

PROBLEM 7.34 Answer questions about control topics

Answer the following questions briefly in nontechnical language.

1. Why is an accumulated amortization contra account standard practice for physical noncurrent assets but not for intangible noncurrent assets?
2. Why is using an allowance for doubtful accounts considered preferable to just writing bad debts directly off to expense?
3. Since the perpetual inventory approach provides better internal control than the periodic method, what are the advantages of the periodic method that prompt many companies, especially smaller ones, to use it for all their inventories and even large companies to use it for supplies inventories?
4. Why does the purchase of goods for resale result in the reduction of GST liability?
5. The chief accountant for a company that has a lot of short-term investments suggests setting up a contra account for market value declines in such investments. Such a contra account, which some companies use, has not been mentioned in the chapter: using the chapter's content, give some likely reasons why it would be proposed.

PROBLEM 7.35 Discuss some issues in contra accounts and sales taxes

1. Most companies net the contra account for accounts receivable (allowance for doubtful accounts) against the accounts receivable balance in their balance sheet and so show only the net collectible value of the receivables. On the other hand, it is standard practice under GAAP to report the contra account for factory assets (accumulated amortization) separately on the balance sheet, or in a note, so that the reader can see the cost of the assets, the amortization accumulated, and the net book value of the assets. The contra accounts for other noncurrent assets, such as amortization on patents or goodwill, are usually not disclosed, so the reader of the financial statements can see only the net book value, much as for accounts receivable. Do these differences strike you as awkward, or unnecessary? Can you make a case for disclosing either all contra accounts or none of them?
2. It is usual to argue that since sales taxes, such as PST and GST, are collected on behalf of the government with no discretion by the company collecting them, they are not expenses of the company. The company is acting as a tax collector and just transferring the money from customers to governments. But the customers likely consider the sales taxes to be part of the cost of buying the goods or services, and if the company reduces the price of what it sells, the customers are glad to see the

taxes go down too. In fact, if the company didn't even charge the tax explicitly but just sent a portion of its revenue in to the government as the tax (such as in a "no GST sale" where the customer pays say $10.00, the company's revenue is only 100/107 of that, or $9.35, and the tax is 7% of $9.35, or $0.65), the customers would be even happier. Can you make a case for such sales taxes being considered as expenses of the company, which would be shown on the income statement?

Preparing Adjusting Journal Entries

*** PROBLEM 7.36** Write journal entries to adjust accounts

Write a journal entry, if any is needed, to adjust the accounts for each of the following independent items. State any assumptions you find necessary.

a. The allowance for doubtful accounts was $2,800 too low.
b. Amortization of $7,200 was needed on a truck.
c. GST of $420 was paid on the purchase of inventory and debited to the Inventory asset account.
d. Employee tax deductions of $39,650 were remitted to the government and debited to Wages expense.
e. It was decided to give up trying to collect an old account receivable of $235.
f. A machine with a cost of $72,600 and book value of $19,700 was sold for $14,200.
g. Upon comparing the inventory count to the perpetual records, a shortage of $4,620 was discovered.
h. An employee stole $35,000 cash that customers had paid on their accounts receivable. Insurance will cover $10,000 of the loss.
i. A storage shed that cost $89,000 and had accumulated amortization of $63,000 blew over in a storm and had to be scrapped.
j. Accounts receivable were studied and it was determined that the net collectible value was $787,000. The accounts receivable control account showed $813,000 and the allowance stood at $26,000.

PROBLEM 7.37 Write entries to adjust accounts for various items

Write a journal entry, if any is needed, to adjust the accounts for each of the following independent items.

a. $23,500 amortization of goodwill is needed.
b. The development costs asset stands at $185,000, before considering $380,000 more spent this year and charged to expense. It is decided to capitalize half of this year's expense and then amortize the resulting asset evenly over five years.
c. A truck with a book value of $38,650 and accumulated amortization of $73,250 is sold for $45,000, to be paid by the purchaser in 30 days.
d. A building that cost $800,000 and has accumulated amortization of $250,000 has increased in value on the real estate market, going up from $600,000 last year to $675,000.
e. Another building, costing $300,000 and having accumulated amortization of $40,000, is sold for $320,000 cash.
f. An employee stole inventory costing the company $20,000 and hid the theft by altering the company's perpetual inventory record. Caught red-handed, the employee has promised to repay the company within 60 days if no legal action is taken by the company. The company agrees.
g. Fringe benefits costing $93,210 are paid to various outside parties and the total is debited to Wages expense.
h. GST of $16,260 added on to purchases by suppliers is deducted from the $47,380 GST added to sales by the company, and the net $31,120 is remitted to the government.

i. Land costing $236,640 that has become swampy and unusable is written off.
j. A large customer that the company was worried about went bankrupt. The $69,800 account receivable had been half allowed-for already because the company had believed it would collect half. Now the bankruptcy trustee advises that creditors of the bankrupt company will receive only 10% of the amounts owing.

CHALLENGING

PROBLEM 7.38 Correct accounts for errors by bookkeeper

The bookkeeper for Granny's Goodies Inc. (GGI) was recently appointed to that position after years as chief goodie taster. The president is not interested in accounting and thinks it is not important, so the goodie taster got the job in spite of having little accounting knowledge. Below are some items about the company and the journal entries the bookkeeper made in relation to those items. For each item, complete or correct what the bookkeeper has done.

a. The company issued some shares and sold them to employees. The bookkeeper debited cash and credited revenue $50,000.
b. The company bought a truck at a price of $38,000, paying $15,000 down and financing the rest over 5 years with a bank loan. The bookkeeper debited truck asset and credited cash $15,000.
c. The bookkeeper recorded amortization expense for the year of $10,200, which included 10% amortization on the truck, in accordance with company policy. The amortization was debited to amortization expense and credited to accumulated amortization.
d. The company sold a cookie cutter machine it no longer needed for $200. The machine had cost $2,100 and had accumulated amortization of $1,660. The bookkeeper decided that $200 should be credited to cash and did that, but did not complete the entry, throwing the general ledger out of balance. Knowing the ledger should be in balance, the bookkeeper added an account to the ledger called "imbalance revenue" and put $200 in it so everything would balance.
e. During the year, the company deducted $78,200 in income taxes from employees' pay and remitted it all to the government. When the taxes were remitted to the government, the bookkeeper debited income tax expense and credited cash. The company's wages payable account showed a rather large balance at the end of the year because employees had been paid only the net amounts.
f. At the end of the year, the company's perpetual inventory asset account showed a balance of $6,400. The bookkeeper thought that was a little high, because the company pretty well sold its goodies as it made them—there's little market for old goodies! Sure enough, when the goodie inventory was counted on that day, it had a cost of only $3,700. The rest appeared to have been eaten by employees, rats, customers, or whatever. The bookkeeper had no idea whether any entry should be made and so didn't do one.
g. At the end of the year, the company owed $150 in unpaid interest on its bank loan. The bookkeeper debited interest expense and credited interest payable for $150.
h. GGI sold some of its goodies on credit to coffee shops. It had never had any bad debts or had to make any allowance for them. But at the end of this year, two coffee shop customers were in financial trouble. One had been closed down by the health department and had gone out of business, owing GGI $320. The other had become very slow in paying since a national coffee chain had opened next door, and the bookkeeper doubted the $405 it owed would be paid. The bookkeeper recorded all this by debiting bad debts expense and crediting accounts receivable $85 ($405 – $320).

i. A customer, making a big order for goodies to be delivered later, came in and gave the company a $400 deposit on the last day of the year. This was included in the cash revenue for the day.
j. On the last day of the year, the company declared a dividend of $5,000 to be paid 20 days later. The bookkeeper debited dividends expense and credited retained earnings $5,000.
k. Net income for the year worked out to $52,340, as the bookkeeper calculated it. This amount was credited to retained earnings and debited to cash.

Calculating the Income Effects of Various Events

* PROBLEM 7.39 Calculate income effects of various phenomena

Calculate any effect on income of each of the following independent cases.

a. A building cost $250,000. Accumulated amortization on it was $240,000. Building sold for $28,000.
b. An account receivable was $7,800. There was an allowance of $5,000 on it. Collection abandoned.
c. Goodwill cost $800,000, amortized down to book value $350,000. Remainder written off.
d. Inventory control account showed $2,850,000. Inventory count showed $2,698,000.
e. A machine cost $37,000. Accumulated amortization on it was $29,000. Machine written off.
f. Inventory purchased for $180,000 on credit. GST of 7% added on.
g. Building cost $250,000. Accumulated amortization on it was $240,000. Sold for $6,000.
h. Development expenses total $700,000. Half of these were capitalized.
i. Employees earned $110,000 plus $19,000 fringe benefits. Deductions from employees were $34,000.
j. An account receivable was $14,000. Payment of $12,000 received by electronic funds transfer.

PROBLEM 7.40 Calculate financial statement effects of various events

For each item below, give the dollar amount and direction of the effects on current assets, noncurrrent assets, and net income (ignoring income tax).

a. A Ltd. writes off $2,500 of previously allowed-for accounts receivable.
b. B Ltd., which has a perpetual inventory system, counts its year-end inventory and determines its cost to be $739,600. The inventory control account has a balance of $746,400.
c. C Ltd. sells for $179,000 cash a building that cost $690,000 and has accumulated amortization of $438,000.
d. D Ltd. is surprised by the bankruptcy of a major customer and has to record a direct accounts receivable write-off of $149,000.
e. E Ltd. writes off an old building that cost $420,000 and has accumulated amortization of $420,000.
f. F Ltd. discovers a fraud by an employee. The loss is $58,000 in cash, $30,000 of which will be covered by the company's insurance.
g. G Ltd. buys a shipment of inventory, paying $60,000 cash plus 7% GST. The company has considerable GST due, collected on its own sales.

PROBLEM 7.41 Identify and determine effect on net income of a group of adjustments

The accountant for Discher Industries Inc. made a number of year-end adjustments to the accounts. Here are the company's balance sheet accounts before and after the adjustments. Identify what adjustment was probably behind each account change and specify its effect on net income for the year.

	Unadjusted	Adjusted
Cash	17,500	17,500
Accounts receivable	84,900	80,400
Allowance for doubtful accounts	6,400	7,900
Inventory	115,600	109,200
Prepaid expenses	4,200	3,500
Land	35,000	35,000
Factory	248,200	245,200
Accumulated amortization	103,700	100,900
Investments	65,500	65,000
Bank loan	74,000	74,000
Accounts payable	81,600	85,000
Accrued liabilities	2,100	3,400
Wages and deductions payable	13,400	16,300
Sales taxes due	2,800	2,800
Income taxes payable	600	9,200
Mortgage payable	74,000	74,000
Future income tax liability	32,100	34,300
Warranty liability	17,500	18,200
Share capital	100,000	100,000
Retained earnings	62,700	19,800

PROBLEM 7.42 Inferring missing amounts based on income statement relationships

In each of the following independent cases, use your knowledge of income statement relationships to calculate the missing values.

Case	Sales Revenue	Beginning Inventory	Purchases	Total Available	Ending Inventory	Cost of Goods Sold	Gross Profit	Expenses	Pretax Income Or (Loss)
A	$850	$150	$800	$?	$200	$?	$100	$25	$?
B	900	?	750	?	100	?	?	50	75
C	800	?	650	975	?	?	75	?	(50)
D	?	200	?	?	325	775	425	150	?
E	950	100	650	?	?	?	?	150	125

CASE 7A

INTERNAL CONTROL REQUIREMENTS OF TWO ORGANIZATIONS

Tiffany recently graduated with a business degree and got a job with local plumbing, electrical, heating and air conditioning distributor Mountain Crest Supply Inc., working in the company's office. Her new employer has asked her to review its internal control systems and suggest ways of improving their effectiveness and efficiency. She also has been a member of Earth Friends, an environmental awareness group and, with her studies behind her, will be taking a more active role in the group, having just been elected president and head of the group's board of directors.

Mountain Crest Supply buys most of its goods (ranging from large air conditioning and lighting units all the way down to nuts, bolts and cleaning rags) from manufacturers worldwide and sells them to building contractors, tradespeople, government agencies, hydroponic gardeners, general businesses and home renovators locally and in the region. It has a small manufacturing operation of its own, making some plastic piping and other simple parts. The company has a strong reputation in the region as the place to go when you need a part no one else can supply, and has even fabricated parts for such occasional exotic uses as hot air balloons and beer brewing. The quality of its piping and electrical systems is so good that, to the company's distress, its products keep turning up in places raided by the police for pot growing.

Virtually all of the company's sales are on credit it extends (after a credit check for new customers), or paid for by customers' credit cards, but some is on Interac and a little is for cash. For a fee, deliveries are made to just about anywhere in the region, and the company is known for getting parts to a customer within hours of receiving an order. To maintain its competitive position, the company cheerfully takes back products that turn out not to meet the customer's needs, or that are in excess of need. Many of its contractor customers therefore buy in bulk and return significant proportions of what they originally bought. Given all this service, the company's prices are a little higher than competitors' and to compete, it will offer lower prices on the condition that customers pay a restocking fee on returned goods that are not defective. Its inventories are also larger than competitors' and include numerous items that are one-of-a-kind products or parts for products sold years ago.

Mountain Crest Supply's employees are known for their product knowledge and their eagerness to help customers. Many employees have worked in sales, the parts room, the office and delivery, and tasks in those areas are regularly done by whichever employee happens to be available at the moment. It's quite common for a single employee to take down a customer order, locate the items needed in the storeroom, complete the customer invoice, and even deliver the goods. (Nearly all employees are licensed to drive the delivery trucks and vans, keys for which are kept on pegs at the back of the storeroom.) The company encourages employees to go out on delivery, see the customers' job sites, show an interest, and suggest additional products the customer might find useful. Tiffany has already been out on several deliveries and has helped on the sales floor and in tracking down parts and supplies, as part of getting to know the business.

Earth Friends has a history of low-key effectiveness in local and regional environmental issues. It publishes an environmental watch newsletter, has an active Web site, and arranges numerous one-on-one sessions of its members with people thought to be opinion leaders or decision makers. Its efforts were largely responsible for the diversion of several highways around sensitive wetlands, for revision of several municipal water and air standards, for effective environmental awareness campaigns in the schools, and for a series of useful conferences bringing local environmentalists, business leaders and politicians together. Meeting the president of Mountain Crest Supply at one of those conferences led eventually to Tiffany's job with the company.

Earth Friends' activities are financed through memberships, donations from bodies and businesses thought not to be harming the environment, occasional government grants, and occasional fundraising from the general public. The revenues come in by cash or cheque (recently some donations by credit card have been accepted), and the expenses are paid mostly by cheque, much of that to reimburse members who have used their own funds to meet people or to travel to environmentally sensitive sites, but a good part also to pay increasingly significant office costs, such as for the newsletter and Web site. Only recently, the group has begun to pay people as part-time staff, for Web services, newsletter production and conference organizing.

An elected board of directors manages Earth Friends' activities and performs required tasks such as certifying that funds have been spent as promised to donors or granting agencies. All directors are volunteers like Tiffany, and most put in considerable time on this labour of love.

Discuss the internal control needs, practical constraints and likely control weaknesses of Mountain Crest Supply and Earth Friends. How similar, or different, are these, and how similar, or different, are Tiffany's roles in the two organizations? In addressing these issues, refer explicitly to the kind of organization each is and the likely objectives of the people involved in it.

CASE 7B

INTERNAL CONTROL AND TOP MANAGEMENT

Top management of modern businesses faces increasingly challenging problems. The business must be managed day-to-day and there should be some sort of coherent strategy to guide this managing. Earnings and cash flow must be sufficient to satisfy investors and creditors, and to keep the business on track when tough times occur. An internal culture that is ethical and effective in meeting corporate goals and society's expectations should be nurtured and supported. Through all of this, top management is responsible for exercising effective control over the whole business and has to answer to owners, employees, creditors, customers and society at large if problems arise. As we have seen in recent years, many problems do arise!

Discuss top management's role in exercising control over the business and meeting the expectations of others. If it is helpful, place the discussion in the context of a specific interesting company. Just to get you started, below are some remarks heard on phone-in shows and in other conversations about the recent corporate disasters and related issues.

"The pressure on top management to generate returns for shareholders leads to a natural attempt to maximize those returns and ignore control and social responsibility. In fact, since top management works for the shareholders, it would be irresponsible and unethical not to behave this way."

"Ascribing all the recent problems to shareholder pressures for earnings maximization overstates management's willingness or ability to manipulate accounting. Many problems are just a result of insufficient control, of a buccaneer culture where the ends are valued no matter what the means, so the company's people get themselves and the company into trouble."

"We have seen some problems recently, all right, but most of them are the result of overexuberance, mainly in the technology sector, and in spite of them the results for society have been positive. It is certainly preferable to have a wide-open, entrepreneurial culture in the company than to put it in charge of conservative, control-minded bureaucrats."

"What we have is a moral failure. Top managers have been setting a poor example for their people, in paying themselves huge salaries, taking stock options and generally behaving as if they had no responsibility for the shareholders' money, or the employees' future."

"It's 'that vision thing,' as President Bush the First used to say. The problem is that top managers who are thought to be visionary leaders are appointed and then operate by charisma rather than competence. Poor management is bound to include poor control and stewardship of other people's interests. It doesn't have to be malicious, just incompetent. Boards of directors should start appointing dull, careful top managers who know their stuff."

"Much of our economy runs on confidence: the confidence of shareholders, employees, customers and suppliers. If that confidence is eroded because companies are out of control, the whole economic system grinds to a halt."

"Our Western economic system depends on self-policing. We have loose controls on companies because we assume they have good control on themselves. If that is not true, society will impose regulations and conditions that will hurt all companies, not just the bad eggs. Top management therefore has a responsibility to keep their part of free enterprise under control, or someone else will do it for them to the cost of all of us."

"Managers are people, and if they misbehave, it is ultimately their personal choice to do so. Therefore it comes down to the personal ethics and responsibility of each manager. If a company is not well managed or controlled, it is because individual managers have made bad choices."

"Managers are people, so they get trapped by the demands of their jobs. If you have a mortgage, kids, aged parents, even a desire for the good life yourself, you can't just act according to your own preferences, no matter how moral. You can't just quit when you feel like it. You have to fit in, and this is just as true for top managers as it is for the mailroom clerk. If you are in a go-go company in which the poorer performers are fired each year (as seems to have been the case in Enron), you can't put control concerns first. You won't survive doing that, so you won't be around to be a sober manager anyway."

"It's a matter of incentives. If top managers fail to exercise sufficient control over their companies and their accounting, it is because their incentives don't lead them to that. They are rewarded for short-term results, so they maximize those. They are penalized for investments in office costs, controls, caution, so they minimize those. If you want to make top managers pay more attention to their control responsibilities, you have to change their incentives."

NOTES

1. Thanks to Rosalie J. Laibida, the accountant at Barcol Doors & Windows Ltd., for providing the examples of the company's documents and permission to use them.
2. See a recent CICA research study, *The Impact of Technology on Financial and Business Reporting,* described in G. Trites, "Democratizing Disclosure," *CA Magazine* (October 1999): 47–48.
3. Canadian Institute of Chartered Accountants, Assurance Handbook Section 5100, Paragraph 5141.042 as posted on the Web site http://www knotia.ca.
4. President Bush was quoted by B. McKenna, "WorldCom charged with fraud," *The Globe and Mail* (June 27, 2002): B1.
5. The basic description of the fraud was taken from A. Galloni, M. R. Sesit and B. Pedley, "Allfirst may have lacked adequate risk controls," *The Wall Street Journal* (reprinted in *The Globe and Mail,* March 6, 2002, p. B9).
6. M. Moffeit, "The collapse of the temple of cool," written from Houston for Knight-Ridder Newspapers, in *The Edmonton Journal* (June 2, 2002): D4–D5.
7. B. McKenna, "WorldCom charged with fraud," *The Globe and Mail* (June 27, 2002): B1.
8. C. Rusnell, "ATB target of $7.5B US scam," *The Edmonton Journal* (April 24, 2002): A1, A16.
9. "An economy singed: The markets' mood reflects a poor outlook for America's economy," *The Economist,* (June 2, 2002): 13.

CHAPTER EIGHT

Assets Accounting

8.1 Chapter Introduction: Accounting for the Left-Hand Side of the Balance Sheet

"Well, Mr. Groven, for us to determine the value of your business, we have to consider both what is in the financial statements and what is not. We also have to consider a lot of other things, especially income tax considerations for you and the potential buyer.

"Essentially, your company has value partly because of what it has now, but mainly because of the earnings and cash it can generate in the future. How do the financial statements help with this? Well, some assets and liabilities on the balance sheet can be taken at their accounting values: cash, most of the accounts receivable, accounts payable and specific debts, such as to the bank. And the income and cash flow statements give us a pattern of resource inflows that we might be able to extrapolate into the future. So we have to look carefully into how you measure earnings and cash flow in your company's financial statements, and so how you calculate cost of goods sold, depreciation and amortization, and other important earnings components. Knowing all this, we can do some calculations to tell us whether the company makes more money than similar companies or similar investments—its ability to generate such excess earnings would add a lot to its value.

"But in many ways, the financial statements are of limited help in valuing the business. Accountants measure most assets at historical values, and those old values are likely a poor indication of either immediate cash value or future earnings power. And then there are the intangible assets that really give your company its value—reputation, location, brand name, quality of employees, and you, Mr. Groven. To a large extent you are your company, and without you, the company would be worth much less. Unless you have outlived your usefulness, ha, ha. Some companies' values go up when their founders die, but I'm sure you're not one of those dinosaurs! We have another client, who runs a popular and pricey restaurant; she wants to sell, but finds that without her and her skills, the restaurant is just a bunch of pots and pans. There are many intangible assets in a business like yours, and they are essential to the company's value and ability to make money in the future, but you won't find them in the balance sheet.

"Now, let's get on with doing the valuation...."

Learning Objectives

Valuing Mr. Groven's business raises questions about how to value the balance sheet's assets, and whether there are assets not on the balance sheet that are important to the business's future. The connection between the asset values and the income and cash flow measures is also raised. (Let's remember right away that most *accounting policy choices* don't change the net cash flow for the year, though they may rearrange some of the details in the cash flow statement.) In this chapter, you will learn:

- That there are several methods for determining asset values on the balance sheet besides the historical transaction cost basis covered in the book so far and criticized by the person valuing Mr. Groven's business;
- How accountants determine what the "cost" of an asset is (there is more to it than you might think);
- How the balance sheet values are determined for the three main current assets: cash, accounts receivable, and inventories;
- That there are several methods for determining amortization expense, reflecting rather different assumptions about how property and plant assets help to generate income;
- How the balance sheet values are determined for property and plant assets and the associated effects on income via amortization expense and gains or losses on disposal;
- How accounting deals with the difficult and increasingly controversial problem of accounting for the sorts of intangible assets that the person valuing Mr. Groven's business mentioned, and with the effects on income that result if costs are "capitalized" (put on the balance sheet as assets, making the company look better) rather than "expensed" (put on the income statement as expenses, making the company look worse).

8.2 Balance Sheet Valuation

Asset accounting affects income as well as the balance sheet.

This chapter's focus is on *accounting policy choices* for the assets on the balance sheet, and we continue to centre attention on such choices introduced in coverage of revenue and expense recognition in Chapter 6, and part of the coverage of internal control in Chapter 7. Knowing about the choices behind the balance sheet's assets is important in understanding the balance sheet's figures and disclosures about them in the notes, but also is important in understanding the income statement because balance sheet accounting usually affects the income statement too, through double-entry accrual accounting and the *articulation* of the two statements. Here's an example. There are several methods of calculating amortization on the enterprise's assets. The company's choice among those methods affects amortization expense on the income statement and so net income, and therefore equity on the balance sheet, as well as accumulated amortization and therefore net book value of assets on the balance sheet. Analyzing financial statements and the effects of management decisions, covered in Chapter 10, depends on a good understanding of the balance sheet numbers and their effects on income.

Asset accounting involves many choices and some controversy.

When we look at a balance sheet, what do the numbers, the numeric values assigned to assets (and liabilities and equity, for that matter), mean? The *asset valuation* (or, more generally, *balance sheet valuation*) question is both complex and controversial. You may intuitively think that the assets should be valued at what they are worth, but what does that mean? There are many choices to be made, as it turns out.

There are seven basic methods often suggested for valuing assets and liabilities, all of which have been used in some contexts:

Seven main methods have been proposed and used for valuing assets and liabilities.

- Historical cost
- Price-level-adjusted historical cost
- Current or market value
- Lower of cost or market
- Fair value
- Value in use
- Liquidation value

No one valuation method is best for everything.

Because the financial statements articulate through double-entry accrual accounting, asset valuation usually also affects income measurement, so choosing a valuation method implies a decision about income measurement too. As you read the description below of each balance sheet valuation and therefore income measurement method, think about which one you believe is appropriate, and in which circumstances. There is much variety and judgment within generally accepted accounting principles, and no one method, even the main one (historical cost), is best in all circumstances. You will see versions of some methods in most financial statements, as examples below will show.

Historical cost valuation may produce too much of an emphasis on the past.

Balance sheet valuation is often controversial, partly because of a concern that the values should be useful in people's decision making and a suspicion that historical cost values are not as useful as those that look more to the future. Historical cost, coming from the transactional base of financial accounting, does not reveal the changes in market conditions which can help in predicting the future, and decision makers who believe this is a problem may not think that accrual accounting adjustments go far enough to overcome the problem. Would you drive your car looking only in the rear-view mirror to see where you have been and not look out the front window to see where you are going?

Let's see the perspective the seven balance sheet valuation methods bring to the task of choosing the numbers for the balance sheet.

Historical Cost

The general historical cost basis is interpreted specifically for each balance sheet account.

Historical cost, otherwise known as *acquisition cost*, values assets at the amounts of the payments made or promised to acquire the assets, and values liabilities at the amounts of any associated promises. These amounts usually come from transactional evidence, such as invoices, receipts, or contracts. Equity amounts come from past share issues and incomes retained. While we normally think of "cost" as applying to assets, the transaction-based values that cost produces for assets are also produced for liabilities and equity, hence the whole balance sheet can be described as a "historical cost" statement. Here is a brief summary of what historical cost is normally interpreted to mean for various balance sheet accounts, with the chapter sections that provide more details:

Cash	Cash and bank balances produced by prior cash transactions (Section 8.5)
Accounts receivable	Revenue already recognized but not yet collected (Sections 6.6, 8.6)
Inventories	Cost of making the goods available for sale (Sections 8.4, 8.7)
Prepaid expenses	Costs paid but not yet transferred to expenses (Section 6.10)
Investments	Cost incurred when each investment was acquired (Sections 8.5, 9.6)
Property and plant	Cost to make the assets suitable for their intended use (Section 8.4)

Intangible assets	Cost incurred when each asset was acquired or produced (Section 8.14)
Accounts payable	Already recognized, but unpaid expenses and purchases (Section 9.2)
Accrued liabilities	Estimated expenses already recognized but not yet paid (Sections 6.10, 9.2)
Debt	Legal promises to pay specified in past borrowing transactions (Sections 9.2, 9.3)
Share capital	Cash or other value received when each share was originally issued (Section 9.4)
Retained earnings	Past incomes earned minus past dividends declared (Section 3.2)

Historical cost valuation is the usual method under GAAP.

The ability to document the cost (see "verifiability" in Sections 5.2 and 5.3) is a major reason that historical cost is the usual valuation method for most assets and liabilities. Another principal reason is that an enterprise will rarely purchase assets or make promises for more than the enterprise believes them to be worth. If you believe that an asset will provide you with $10,000 worth of productive capacity, you will not rationally pay or promise more than $10,000 for it. Under this method, an asset valued at historical cost is valued at its expected lowest (or most conservative) value of future benefits at the date of acquisition. In most cases, *GAAP* imply the use of historical costs, unless some other valuation basis is more appropriate and is specifically disclosed in the financial statements.

Some additional points in connection with this method are worth noting.

Historical cost reflects value *at the date of acquisition.*

- *At the date of acquisition of an asset,* historical cost = market value = value in use, in most cases. Rational people would pay only what the asset is worth to them if used in their business and such value in use should tend to determine the market value of the asset, as various people consider how useful the asset would be to them.

Historical cost does not reflect value changes since acquisition.

- Much of the criticism of historical cost has to do with what happens after the date of asset acquisition. Suppose a piece of land was purchased 10 years ago for $50,000. Is the land worth $200,000 or $100 today on the market, or if used in the business? The historical cost does not seem as relevant as more current information to managers' decisions about whether to replace assets and investors' evaluations of management's performance.

Historical cost is not good enough if market value or value in use is seriously impaired.

- GAAP deem historical cost to be an inadequate valuation if an asset's market value or usefulness to the enterprise has been seriously impaired. Largely because of *conservatism*, unproductive assets should be "written down" or "written off," and the "lower of cost or market" rule is used in valuing inventories and some other current assets. We will see more about these later in the chapter.

Historical cost examples

- Cash and accounts receivable are based on past transactions, as are most liabilities and share capital
- Cost of inventories, investments, property and plant, and land
- Prepaid expenses and net book value of assets being amortized are unexpired costs
- Many intangibles lack a clear cost and so are not on balance sheet

Many assets are really unexpired costs, to be deducted from income as expenses.

- Accrual accounting's income measurement produces some asset accounts that are not particularly meaningful as *values* in that they don't represent a real asset so much as they do the residual effect of trying to get the income number right. Prepaid expenses and net book value of assets being amortized are examples of "costs waiting to be deducted from revenue in the future" or "unexpired costs." Using amortization to allocate the cost of an asset as an expense deducted from income may get a good income measure, but does not necessarily produce a meaningful balance sheet figure for the asset being amortized.

The historical cost basis may not handle intangible and high-tech assets well.

- Some items that could be assets and do have value to the enterprise, and even a market value, do not appear on the balance sheet because they do not have a clear historical cost. Such economic assets as skilled employees, innovative use of technology, or clever business methods are usually not on the balance sheet, yet are apparently used by the stock market and others in valuing the whole business. In this time of high-tech, dot-com, and Internet developments, many people feel that the historical cost basis, at least as it is currently interpreted using GAAP, seriously misrepresents the real economic assets of many companies and the income derived from them. Terms such as "economic value added," "measuring value added," "balanced scorecard," "nonfinancial performance measurement," and "strategic performance measurement" are just some that are used in discussions of how to improve or replace historical cost and GAAP. More on this controversy is in Section 8.14 on "intangible" assets.

Concerns over how assets are valued using historical cost have led people to suggest alternative methods for valuing assets and liabilities on the balance sheet. Some of the more popular alternatives are below.

Price-Level-Adjusted Historical Cost

Adjusting historical costs for inflation is an old but so far unsuccessful idea.

Price-level adjustments
Rise in popularity in times or countries of high inflation, when the historical cost is made unstable by the inflation.

Price-level-adjusted historical cost adjusts for changes in the value or purchasing power of the dollar (the measuring unit), rather than for changes in the values of particular assets. The historical cost values of the assets and liabilities are adjusted for changes in the value of the dollar (using economy-wide indices such as the Consumer Price Index) since the assets were acquired or liabilities were incurred. Though this is a venerable idea, first proposed early in the last century, and has been used by some companies (for example, the Philips electronics company in the Netherlands) and by some countries that had high inflation (Brazil for one), it has not found much favour in North America. One reason for its lack of popularity is that if historical cost is unsatisfactory compared to current values, adjusting the cost for inflation still leaves it unsatisfactory, only now less understandable.

Current or Market Value

Current value accounting is a good theoretical idea and appeals to people's intuition.

Current or market value
Intuitive and theoretically sensible, but may be too volatile and may increase managers' focus on the short run.

Current or *market value* accounting would record the individual assets and liabilities at their current particular market value. It focuses on the individual values of the balance sheet items, not on changes in the dollar itself, as price-level-adjusted accounting does. It assumes that value is market-determined and that income should be measured using changes in market values over time. The argument, which is intuitively reasonable to most people who aren't accountants, is that if, for example, your house's market worth is greater today than yesterday, you have made money on it today, even if you have not sold it. If its market worth is less, you have lost money on it, even if you have not sold it. This method has been the subject of much writing and experimentation in the United States and Canada and has some theoretical attraction in economics and finance, but it does not seem likely to replace historical cost as the most popular method for most assets. The biggest problem comes from the assumption that an asset's market value is relevant even if it is not being sold or replaced. Also, as we have seen in stock market prices in recent years, market values can be very volatile, so if they were used, asset values and income measures might be highly variable. Using such values might increase the already-criticized tendency of some managers to focus on the short run instead of building and managing for the long run.

Market value accounting is increasingly being used for financial assets of some companies.

Recently, there has been some impetus to market value accounting for assets that really do have a ready market, and are traded frequently: so-called *financial assets*, such as traded shares, bonds, and some kinds of loans and other financial instruments. It is becoming part of GAAP. The *CICA Accounting Handbook* Section 3855 requires that for interim or annual statements for fiscal periods beginning on or after October 1, 2006, financial assets should be measured at their fair values (see "fair value" below).

Current value accounting can use either input or output values, or a mixture of the two:

Market values can be determined on either a buying or selling basis.

a. *Input market value*, or entry value, refers to the amount it would cost to bring the asset into the company if it were not now in, usually measured by estimating "*replacement cost*" to purchase it again or "reproduction cost" to make it again. The same idea holds for the hypothetical reborrowing of liabilities.
b. *Output market value*, or exit value, is the amount an asset is worth if sold now (in other words, its "*net realizable value*") or the amount that a liability could be paid off at now, usually measured by quoted prices, appraisals, and similar estimates.

Lower of Cost or Market

Lower of cost or market is required by GAAP for all current assets.

Though using market value as the basis of valuing assets is restricted to financial assets, market value plays a role in a fundamental asset valuation method that is central to GAAP: *lower of cost or market*. Following the principle of *conservatism*, lower of cost or market is used to value all current assets, as we will see later in this chapter. The version of market used can be either replacement cost or net realizable value, depending on the kind of current asset.

Lower of cost or market
Used for current assets, especially inventories and temporary investments.

Fair Value

Fair value is likely to see increased use in financial statements.

Fair value is an alternative asset valuation method that you will see more and more often. It is very similar to market value, except does not require a market value to exist and so is a little more hypothetical. The *CICA Handbook* defines fair value as "the amount of the consideration that would be agreed upon in an arm's length transaction between knowledgeable, willing parties who are under no compulsion to act."[1] This is a hypothetical amount ("would be agreed") but is supposed to represent a potential market transaction between two free agents, both knowledgeable and willing, and not related to each other ("arm's length"). The use of fair value is gaining ground internationally for valuing stock options granted to employees in particular, as will be discussed in Chapter 9. There is support in some countries for using it to value inventories of things like unsold agricultural produce.

Fair value
The fair value of a stock option would be the difference between what someone would pay for the shares involved and the price the employee given the option has to pay.

Fair value is also a logical method for valuing assets (and liabilities) of discontinued operations, waiting for a buyer, unless historical costs are used. The choice of balance sheet valuation method is not prescribed by GAAP but disclosing the method is required.

Value in Use

Value in use is important in managers' decision making.

This approach considers that value flows from the way the company will *use* the asset to generate future cash flows (cash generated from revenues net of expenses). *Value in use* is often estimated by calculating the "*net present value*"[2] of future cash inflows generated or outflows made unnecessary by the asset. (If you don't know what present value is, see chapter endnote 2. It is also covered in Chapter 10, Section 10.7.) For example, a machine might be valued according to the products that it will make and that will be sold: the cash flow it will bring in, discounted back to the present. Modern theories of finance and management accounting presume that value in use, measured by discounting future cash flows to get net present value, is an appropriate method for managerial decisions about asset acquisition and financing, and many people presume it underlies market values.

Value in use
Examples of its use: capital leases and impaired assets like bad investments, reduced goodwill, or discontinued operations.

Value in use is the accounting method for *capital leases*, which are included in Section 8.14. Present value calculations are used and form the numbers used in the financial statements for such leases. Value in use is also implied in the case of *impaired assets*, which are written down from their original cost because such assets are deemed to have lost value and so their cost is thought to be unrepresentative of their future value to the company. This is like the lower of cost or market rule, but applied to noncurrent assets. An example would be an investment in another company that has gone bad, a discontinued operation, or goodwill that has turned out not to have the value originally thought (see Section 8.14). In such cases, value in use could be approximated by fair value or output market value if the asset is to be disposed of, or by a present value calculation in the less likely case that the asset is to be kept in its impaired state.

Liquidation Value

Use of liquidation value indicates a company in trouble, *not a going concern.*

Liquidation value
Used for a company being wound up by a bankruptcy trustee.

Liquidation value is like output market value, but used on a "going out of business, sell it for what you can" basis. It is the value that the company's assets would bring upon being sold and that liabilities would be paid off for, if the whole company went out of business. It is used when the company is not felt to be a *going concern*, that is, if its continued viability cannot be assumed. When a trustee in bankruptcy is administering the winding up of a company, the liquidation values are used in negotiations with creditors and other parties. You are unlikely to see the financial statements of such a company, unless you are directly involved.

Therefore, the reader of financial statements prepared on the historical cost basis should be entitled to presume that the company in question *is* a going concern. This presumption is an important part of financial accounting, but every year it turns out to be wrong for some companies that unexpectedly fail. Such bad outcomes remind us that good judgment is required in selecting the balance sheet valuation basis, as with other aspects of financial accounting. A judgment that a company is a going concern and so should use historical cost accounting will turn out to have been wrong if the company fails. On the other hand, a judgment that it is not a going concern might be self-fulfilling: it might panic creditors and investors, and spark a failure no one wants.

HOW'S YOUR UNDERSTANDING?

Here are two questions you should be able to answer based on what you have just read. If you can't answer them, it would be best to reread the material.

1. The owner of Staely Industries Inc. is grumbling about the limitations of historical cost accounting for valuing the company's assets and liabilities. Tell the owner what other valuation or measurement methods might be used and what each does that the historical cost basis does not do.
2. Why are historical costs often thought to be more "real," even if less relevant, than market value or fair value?

8.3 Demonstration Problem: Current Market Value as an Alternative To Historical Cost

Let's look at a realistic and relevant example. Canada has many companies that specialize in acquiring and developing real estate for office buildings, shopping centres, industrial plants, housing developments, and many other uses. As you probably know, real estate values are highly variable, with frequent booms and busts. Consider two real estate development companies operating in the Toronto market. Let's call them Oxbridge and Bramview:

The two companies are the same except for the cost paid for the similar parcels of land.

- Oxbridge has undeveloped land, bought during a downturn in the Toronto real estate market, that cost $5,000,000 and has an estimated current market (output) value of $8,000,000. The company's net income has been about $700,000 per year in the last few years.
- Bramview also has undeveloped land, comparable to Oxbridge's except bought during an overheated period of the Toronto market at a cost of $11,000,000. Its estimated current market value is also $8,000,000, and the company's net income has also been about $700,000 per year.

The two pieces of land are about the same, but the companies' historical-cost-based balance sheets certainly do not look the same:

- Oxbridge: Undeveloped land, at cost $5,000,000
- Bramview: Undeveloped land, at cost $11,000,000

Should income be related to current market value rather than historical cost?

Also, Oxbridge will show a higher ratio of net income to total assets, indicating apparently stronger performance than Bramview, because its total assets will be lower than Bramview's. Now, we could argue that this is as it should be, that Bramview has not really done as well because too much was paid for the land, in hindsight. But another argument is that since the two pieces of land are comparable economic assets, net income should be related to the economic value (e.g., market value) of the assets, not to costs that depend on historical happenstance rather than currently relevant economic conditions.

Let's consider the idea of changing both companies' balance sheet valuations for the land to current market value. Using the concepts from the previous section and earlier in this book, what might be some pros and cons of this idea?

Pros:

- More relevant valuation for users in assessing company's value.
- More useful in comparing companies with similar economic assets.
- Fairer way of relating performance (income) to the economic value that managers are managing on behalf of owners.
- More timely data than the "obsolete" cost figures.
- Not costly to implement (unless real estate appraisers have to be paid).
- Understandable to users who know something about real estate.

Cons:

- Less reliable numbers because they are based on estimated selling value of land that has not been sold.
- Less consistent balance sheet values because real estate values tend to vary a great deal over time.
- Not transaction-based and therefore not verifiable.
- Not conservative in the long run because land values have tended to rise over time, especially as measured in dollars subject to inflation.
- Not a generally accepted procedure, so users accustomed to GAAP would have to adjust their performance evaluation methods and rewrite contracts, such as for lending agreements and management compensation, that depend on financial statement information.
- No effect on cash flow directly or through income tax because the land has not been sold, so there might be doubt that moving the financial statement numbers around in the absence of real economic effects would be very helpful to anyone.

Well, you can probably add more pros and cons. We don't know the significance (materiality) of the land valuation issue to the companies' financial statements or the income tax and other consequences of changing the accounting numbers. But you should see that the accounting concepts are useful in figuring out what would be the appropriate accounting procedure to use.

How might changing to market values be implemented in the accounts? Here are some possibilities (all ignoring income tax considerations):

Possibility 1: Adjust land to market value and put the difference into income.

1. Any difference between current market value and the value on the companies' balance sheets (cost, so far) could be just included in the current year's net income:
   - Oxbridge's land asset would be debited $3,000,000 to bring it up to the $8,000,000 market value, and the credit would go to an income statement account like "Other revenue," raising the current year's income by more than 400% to $3,700,000.
   - Bramview's land asset would be credited $3,000,000 to bring it down to the $8,000,000 market value, and the debit would go to an income statement account like "Other expense," changing the current year's income to a loss of $2,300,000 (more than three times the current income).

Possibility 2: Adjust land to market value and put the difference into retained earnings.

2. The difference could be put directly into retained earnings. Oxbridge's retained earnings would rise by $3,000,000, and Bramview's would fall by $3,000,000. Oxbridge would appear more able to pay a dividend; Bramview would appear less able. As would also happen with method 1, this could paradoxically hurt Oxbridge more than Bramview, because the accounting change could produce pressure from shareholders for increased dividends, even though there is no additional cash to pay such dividends.

Possibility 3: Adjust land to market value and put the difference in a special equity account.

3. The difference could be put into owners' equity but not into retained earnings, by creating a new equity account called something like "Unrealized changes in asset valuations." This would increase Oxbridge's equity by $3,000,000 with a new credit balance account, but would decrease Bramview's equity by $3,000,000 with a new debit balance account. Since it would not be part of retained earnings, the new account might not affect the owners' demand for dividends, thus avoiding the implication that the valuation change is similar to the kinds of events behind the revenues and expenses that form net income and retained earnings. (Some methods of implementing current value and price-level-adjusted accounting that have been developed, and adopted by a few companies and countries, have used such an "Unrealized gains and/or losses" account.)

Possibility 4: Adjust land to market value only if market value is lower than cost.

4. Perhaps the principle of conservatism should be invoked, whereby one of the above methods (most likely the first) would be followed only when the market value is less than the present balance sheet value. In this case, only Bramview would adjust its figures, because its cost is higher than current market value. The other side of the adjustment would probably go to income as in the first possibility but could also go to retained earnings or a special equity account. Though the companies' accounting would still show different figures for the same sort of land, using "lower of cost or market" would be conservative, so users could rely on the balance sheet values not being overstated relative to current conditions. This might be done particularly if a decline in market value indicated a serious impairment in the land's value. GAAP already require such a write-down if there is a permanent or long-term impairment in an asset's value.

Possibility 5: Don't adjust the accounts; just disclose the information.

5. Perhaps the historical cost numbers should not be changed, but each company could disclose the current market value of the land on its balance sheet or in a note:
   - Oxbridge: Undeveloped land (current market value estimated at $8,000,000), at cost $5,000,000.
   - Bramview: Undeveloped land (current market value estimated at $8,000,000), at cost $11,000,000.

   This method provides users with information about the market values, but does not presume what they mean, as the other methods do. Users can probably make intelligent use of information as long as they know about it (that is, if it is disclosed). With full information and "what if" analytical skill, they can adjust the financial statements to reflect the information in whatever way they consider relevant to their needs, using any of the above adjustment methods they think appropriate.

Because any change from historical cost in the absence of actually selling the land would not affect cash flow (no proceeds) and, we will assume, would not affect income tax either, there is no net effect on the cash flow statement. Cash from operations would not be affected, nor would any of the other cash flow categories. Net income at the top of the cash flow statement might change, but the change would be cancelled out by adding back any reduction of income, or subtracting any gain, because such gains or losses would be noncash items.

HOW'S YOUR UNDERSTANDING?

Here are two questions you should be able to answer based on what you have just read. If you can't answer them, it would be best to reread the material.

1. What would changing from the historical cost method to the current market value method for valuing the companies' assets do to cash flow?
2. Greyhurst Land Development Inc. has large landholdings. The company's president said recently that historical cost valuation for the company's land is correct according to GAAP, but is nevertheless inappropriate for the company. Is this possible?

8.4 The Cost of an Asset: The Basic Components

There's more to "cost" than meets the eye!

Section 8.2 gave considerable space to historical cost, and cost is an important part of much of the rest of this chapter. Before going further, let's tie down what financial accounting actually means by the word *cost*, particularly for *tangible assets* such as inventories and fixed assets. (As was indicated at the beginning of Section 8.2, other balance sheet accounts are also examined in this chapter and Chapter 9.) As in other areas of accrual accounting, conceptual and practical considerations make cost a little more complex than might be thought. The principles about assigning costs to assets are important in recognizing expenses and valuing assets, because a debit added to expense reduces present income, while the same debit added to an asset increases assets now and reduces future income via amortization, cost of goods sold, or other expenses arising from consumption of assets. How then is it determined whether to assign a debit, say for an expenditure on a building, to the building asset or to repairs expense?

Many costs may be incurred on an asset besides the simple invoice cost.

On the surface, figuring out the cost of an asset looks simple. You buy a truck for $25,000 and value the truck on the balance sheet at $25,000. However, there is often more to the cost of an asset than just the simple invoice cost or direct cost. You might pay to have your company name painted on the truck. Is that part of the truck asset, or advertising expense? What about the tires, which will wear out a lot sooner than the rest of the truck and will be replaced several times over the truck's useful life?

As another example, when you purchase a big computerized manufacturing machine, it may cost you $500,000 for the actual machine. But, in order to use the machine, certain other things must be added, such as temperature control, a raised floor for wiring, and a fire protection system. Therefore, a section of the factory must be renovated to meet these specifications. Is all that part of the cost of the machine? What about the cost of training people to use the machine?

Cost includes all the costs to get the asset ready for using it as the enterprise intends.

Such installation or preparation costs are a good example of expenditures that are a component of the asset's cost. Overall, the *cost* of an asset includes *all the costs required to make it suitable for its intended purpose, particularly those costs incurred prior to putting the asset into service.* This definition works for all assets, but is most readily understood for longer-lived assets like buildings and equipment. For inventories, putting the asset into service mainly means selling it or using it in the business, because inventory is not held for long. Determining the cost of inventories parallels the way it is done for longer-lived assets like buildings and equipment, but there are more complexities for the longer-lived assets. Some comments are made about inventories in this section, but most of the focus is on longer-lived assets.

Asset cost includes expenditures to make it ready for service or better it later.

For longer-lived assets, costs are accumulated and added to the asset's overall cost until the asset is put into service. After that, its cost is *amortized* against the revenue the asset helps to earn. In the years following acquisition, the question of whether the asset cost should be changed will crop up again when repairs must be made. When a major repair or apparent improvement in the asset is done, the question is whether the asset's productivity or efficiency has been improved, or its useful life extended. If so, there has been a *betterment* of the asset and the cost of that should be *capitalized* (added to the cost of the asset). If not, the cost should just be charged to expense, such as to an account called repairs and maintenance expense. Expenditures that might be betterments are often expensed anyway, because they may just serve to maintain the asset on its expected pattern of declining value through use, rather than unambiguously making the asset better than expected.

These ideas are summarized in Figure 8.1. The solid line rising up on the left is the accumulation of expenditures until, at the point the asset is put into service, the asset's cost has been established. After that, net book value goes down as the asset is amortized. A betterment exists and is recorded by adding an expenditure to the asset's original cost

FIGURE 8.1

Asset Cost, Amortization, and Betterment

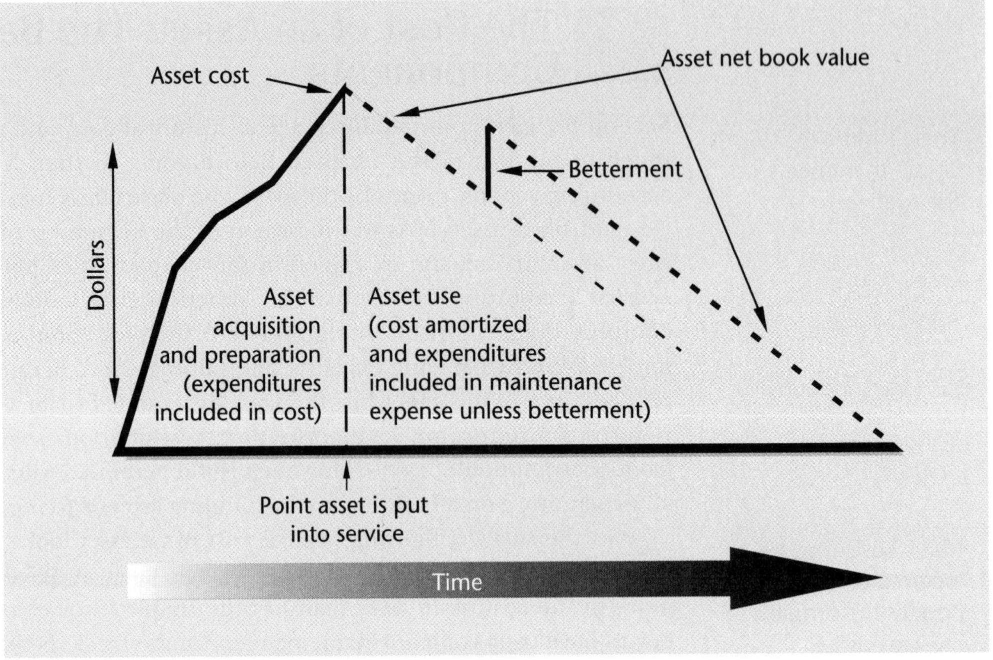

if, and only if, the expenditure adds to the asset's economic value or extends its life (the latter is illustrated in the figure, showing the new amortization line above and extending to the right of the old one).

It can be difficult to decide whether some expenditures really added value to the asset.

What exactly *are* the costs that are necessary to make an asset suitable for its intended use? That can sometimes be difficult to determine. For example, suppose an enterprise constructs a specialized new manufacturing machine, using some of its regular employees and resources:

- The cost of an asset that the enterprise constructs for itself, rather than buying finished, will obviously include the cost of raw materials and direct labour needed to make it.
- But should the salaries of supervisors, who would have been paid anyway, be included? Capitalizing such costs involves a debit to the asset account and a credit to the expense account, reducing the latter and therefore increasing current income. Supervision salaries during construction probably would be included in the asset cost only if the supervisors clearly helped produce a good asset and could not be doing other things for the enterprise at the same time.
- How about interest on monies borrowed to finance the project? Did the enterprise borrow because by paying earlier it could get a better price for materials, so that the interest really is related to the cost of the asset? Or was the enterprise just short of money, so that the interest is more a cost of a weak financial position rather than of the asset itself? It is a matter of judgment and depends on the situation. Because of conservatism, most enterprises do not include interest on borrowed funds in the cost of assets, but some do, such as electric utilities, which borrow money over the several years it takes to construct power plants. Interest would only be included if incurred prior to putting the asset into service, not after.

The problems of deciding whether to capitalize costs like supervision and interest are part of a larger issue, mentioned in Section 8.2 and examined in Section 8.14, of how and whether to capitalize internal costs on intangible assets like goodwill and research and development.

The choice of whether to capitalize or expense certain costs can be significant to the financial statements.

Capitalize or expense a cost?

Decision This Year	Effects on: This Year's Income	Future Years' Incomes
Capitalize	Higher	Lower
Expense	Lower	Higher

Deciding what to include in an asset's cost, which is to say whether to *capitalize or expense* a given cost, can make quite a difference to the enterprise's balance sheet and income statement. Suppose Gondola Inc. has spent $100,000 this year on supervisors' salaries in connection with setting up a new mountain gondola ride in the Rockies. If that cost is just deducted from revenue as an expense this year, it will reduce income and income tax expense. But if the cost is added to the gondola ride asset instead, total assets will be higher, and this year's income and income tax expense will be higher too. Over the next several years, incomes and income tax expenses will be lower because of higher amortization on the higher asset cost. So, aside from accounting appropriately and fairly for the asset, the decision about how to handle the supervisors' salaries will affect income, assets, and income tax expenses this year and in several future years. Thus, a *capitalization* entry is opposite an *amortization* entry: capitalizing reduces the expense and increases the asset, while amortizing does the opposite. And capitalizing this year means that the capitalized cost will have to be amortized or otherwise deducted from income in future years.

Inventory costing requires similar judgments and policies about indirect costs.

The capitalizing versus expensing choice can arise with just about any asset. Inventory is an example. Purchased inventory can be straightforward. It is basically the invoice cost plus transportation, storage, and handling costs. Manufactured inventory, on the other hand, requires some decisions. As with other assets constructed by the enterprise, the cost of raw materials and direct labour are usually included. But what about overhead? *Overhead costs* are indirectly related to production, such as accountants' and supervisors' salaries, and building operating costs, including electricity, rent, depreciation, and insurance. Most manufacturing companies include some or all of such costs in determining the cost of unsold manufactured goods.

When telecom giant WorldCom got into trouble in late June 2002, it was because of capitalizing costs that would normally be expensed, treating such costs as "capital expenditures" rather than as expenses. In the journal entry to record such costs, the debit went to assets, not to expenses, and great hullabaloo resulted. What might seem to be a little difference in an entry can have great consequences. The media's reporting of the problem was interesting and dramatic:

- "WorldCom said Tuesday it has documented about US$3.8 billion in improperly accounted for expenses after an internal investigation uncovered what appears to be one of the largest cases of accounting fraud in history."[3] So, how the entry is recorded can be described as a fraud, even if no money goes to the person recording the entry. Or does money go to the person? The decision to capitalize expenses will increase net income in the present period, and management's bonuses and stock options may well be increased as a result, so maybe there is money going to the people involved, so it may be more like taking money from the cash register than it seems.
- "WorldCom ... confirmed that US$3.8 billion in expenses were improperly booked as capital expenditures during 2001 and the first three months of this year 2002. The effect of such a manoeuvre is to boost reported cash flow and profit, at least in the short term."[4] This comment gets the effect on income right: higher in the present, and at least implied lower in the future. However, there is no boost to cash flow from such an entry: cash is not affected by debiting an asset rather than an expense. If anything, cash might soon be hurt by such an entry because reporting a higher income might attract higher income tax and higher bonuses to management.

Accounting policies are used for asset costs just as for other areas of accounting.

Enterprises should have *accounting policies* for how to determine whether expenditures, such as supervision and interest, are included in assets' costs. These policies are designed to ensure consistency in calculating cost, to fit the accounting to the enterprise's particular circumstances, and to meet other criteria, such as conservatism. They meet the same needs and follow the same rules as any policy choice (see Sections 6.4 and 5.2). For example, suppose a company spends money improving leased space. Should those costs be included in a "leasehold improvements" asset or just deducted as expenses? The enterprise will make the choice according to GAAP principles such as fairness, conservatism, and matching, plus such other criteria as income tax rules, cost of gathering necessary data, and materiality.

In summary, the components of the cost of an asset include all those acquisition and preparation costs that are judged to be required to make it suitable for the purpose intended, whether it be making a computer usable in the information-gathering process or bringing inventory into saleable condition. Some common components of the cost of an asset are listed in Exhibit 8.1.

Common Components of Asset Cost

a. Inventory
- Raw materials costs;
- Labour costs;
- Storage costs;
- Handling costs prior to sale;
- Indirect overhead costs of production, such as heat, power, and supervisors' salaries.

b. Land
- Purchase price, including real estate agent commissions;
- Costs of obtaining clear title, such as legal fees and title searches;
- Costs of clearing, removing unwanted structures, draining, and landscaping.

c. Building (purchased)
- Purchase price;
- Renovation or upgrading costs to make it suitable for the intended use;
- Initial painting and decoration.

d. Building (self-constructed)
- Materials costs;
- Labour costs;
- Excavating, surveying, engineering, and design costs;
- Insurance while constructing the building;
- Perhaps some overhead costs and even financing costs incurred during construction.

e. Purchased Equipment
- Purchase price, including taxes;
- Transportation costs;
- Installation costs;
- Testing costs;
- Overhauls that extend equipment's life or increase its value (betterments).

f. Leasehold Improvements on Rented Property
- Materials costs, labour costs, and other costs to construct the improvements;
- Initial painting and decoration of the rented premises.

HOW'S YOUR UNDERSTANDING?

Here are two questions you should be able to answer based on what you have just read. If you can't answer them, it would be best to reread the material.

1. Magnus Fabricators Ltd. has constructed a new factory building, using company employees and equipment for most of the work. The company's accountant said, "Various costs must be capitalized to produce an appropriate balance sheet figure for the building's cost." What did the accountant mean and what sorts of costs were likely meant?
2. How does a company determine when to stop adding expenditures to the cost of a new building and instead to add those expenditures to repairs and maintenance expense?

8.5 Cash and Temporary Investments

As explained in Chapter 4, cash and very near-cash assets are generally considered to be "cash and equivalents," and changes in them are the focus of the cash flow statement's analysis of cash flows. This section describes some financial accounting principles that affect accounting for cash and so affect what the balance sheet and cash flow statement report.

Cash and Very Near-Cash Assets

Cash includes all varieties of unrestricted cash on hand and in banks anywhere in the world.

The main principle in accounting for *cash* and very near-cash assets grouped with cash on the balance sheet is that what is called "cash" should be available for immediate use, such as paying bills. So the following are included in Cash:

- Cash on hand, including petty cash and undeposited cash receipts and credit card slips, in any of the company's offices worldwide.
- Cash in savings and chequing accounts in the company's bank or banks, worldwide, as long as its use is unrestricted.
- "Cash in transit" that is on its way from other banks or countries (if there are complexities in such transit items, as there might be with some e-commerce and international businesses, the company will have to judge whether these are really not available for use at balance sheet date and so should be included in accounts receivable).

Cash does *not* include any amounts not available for immediate use.

The following are *not* included in Cash on the balance sheet:

- Bad cheques received from customers and refused by their banks, and therefore not really cash, but instead accounts receivable (doubtful ones), because the customers have to be chased down for the money.
- Cash that is not available for immediate use, such as a trust account holding a deposit on a planned land purchase, or a term deposit or investment certificate that cannot be cashed until a particular date (this would be a "temporary investment").
- Cash subject to other countries' exchange or currency controls that limit its availability for immediate use.

Cash includes the ledger account balance, if positive, converted to Canadian dollars.

Some details to note:

- The Cash amount on the balance sheet is the balance according to the ledger account(s), not the balance given in the bank's statement of the account(s). As was shown way back in the demonstration of

Cash: what the company's accounts show can be readily used in the business (converted to Canadian dollars if foreign).

bank account reconciliation in Section 1.12, this means that items that have not yet cleared through the bank, but are in process of doing so, are included in calculating Cash. Examples are outstanding deposits and outstanding cheques, which have left the company and are still working their way through the banking system.

- This means, as pointed out also in Section 7.5, that bank reconciliation is an essential practice in accounting for cash. The company must be sure that the cash records are correct, with errors identified and dealt with, so that the figures in the balance sheet (and cash flow statement) are proper.

A bank overdraft is included with liabilities, not deducted from the Cash asset.

- A bank overdraft, which is a credit (negative) balance in the ledger record for the bank account, happens when the company has written more cheques than there is money in the bank, according to the ledger. This credit balance is really a bank loan, and so is *reclassified* to current liabilities and shown together with the official bank loans, and is not subtracted from other positive cash or bank balances or shown as a negative asset. (As was noted in Chapter 4, a temporary overdraft may be deducted from cash to get a net cash figure for the cash flow statement.)
- Cash in foreign currencies has to be converted to the currency being used as the basis of the financial statements (Canadian dollars for most Canadian companies). This requires reference to foreign exchange rates as of the balance sheet dates and can be a little complicated for currencies that are not readily exchangeable for Canadian dollars or that are rising or falling rapidly in comparison to the Canadian dollar.

Temporary Investments

a. Temporary Investments and Marketable Securities

Temporary investments are used to provide a better return than bank deposits do.

Temporary investments: putting excess cash to work until it is needed.

Having plain cash on hand earns no interest, and bank account balances usually pay little interest, so enterprises use *temporary investments* primarily to put extra cash to work. Such investments include stocks, bonds, commercial paper (such as notes issued by financial companies), government bonds and treasury bills, and investment certificates and term deposits in banks. Guaranteed investment certificates (GICs) are a common form of the last kind.

Temporary investments are valued on the balance sheet at lower of cost or market.

Because there is no intention to hold such investments for long or to try to influence the operations or policies of the organizations that issued the securities, such investments are included in current assets. Like other current assets, these investments are valued at the *lower of cost or market* (market is measured as current market (net realizable) value, what the investments would receive if sold in an ordinary, nonpanicked way). The reader of the balance sheet should be able to assume that the value shown is not higher than what would be obtained by selling the investments. Dividends and interest from such investments are usually also included in nonoperating revenues. If the investments are *marketable securities* having a quoted market value, such as shares in public companies, that value is usually disclosed if it is different from the amount at which they are valued on the balance sheet.

You are expected to assume GAAP are being followed if you are not specifically told.

Because cash and temporary investments are often considered by management to be part of the enterprise's overall supply of cash, the two may be reported together on the balance sheet, especially if temporary investments are cashable, very short-term, or not large in comparison to cash. *Financial Reporting in Canada*, 2005, reports that 194–197 of the 200 companies it surveyed in 2001–2004 reported a cash asset, and that the most common titles were: Cash and Cash Equivalents, Cash, Cash and Short-Term Investments. A declining number of these companies (20%–25%, down from 40% in the 2001 survey) reported bank overdrafts. A few (3–7) did not report any cash, positive or negative. Around 80% of the companies reported temporary ("short-term") investments. About half did not say how they valued temporary investments, while about 20% said temporary investments were carried at cost and a further 15% reported using lower of cost or market valuation[5]. Such lack of disclosure is an example of an assumption that the reader of the financial statements should be sufficiently knowledgeable about financial accounting principles to know what basis is used if it is not specified. Developing your knowledge about *GAAP* is one of this book's main objectives.

b. Example of Effects of Accounting Method

Wildrose Inc. has temporary investments costing $520,000.

1. Suppose the investments' market values slipped to $484,000 on the balance sheet date. What would happen to income if the company followed the lower of cost or market rule?
2. Suppose instead that the investments' market values went up to $585,000 on the balance sheet date. How much better off would the company appear to be if it reported the investments at market value instead of lower of cost or market?

Part 1:

A write-down reduces income but does not affect cash flow unless the investment is considered part of cash.

- The company should write the investments down to $484,000, because current assets are assumed to be liquid and conservatively valued.
- The entry would be to debit an expense with the difference, $36,000 and credit either the investment account or a contra account with a title like "Allowance for decline in investments' market value."
- The $36,000 expense would probably be a nonoperating one and the write-down would reduce income tax expense if the write-down were a tax-deductible expense. Net income would go down by $36,000, minus any tax saving.
- The working capital would be reduced by the write-down, also minus any reduction in income tax payable.
- Cash flow would not be affected as no cash is involved, unless (as used to be the case and still may be for some companies) the investments are considered part of cash—in that case, cash from operations would go down too.

Part 2:

If information is disclosed, you can estimate the effects of alternate accounting policies.

- The company's current assets would be $65,000 higher, and net income and working capital would be higher by that amount less any likely income tax on the increase in value.
- Writing assets up above cost is generally not permitted in Canada due to two principles: conservatism and the lack of a transaction to establish the market value (echoing the revenue recognition criteria). Management may still get the message across by disclosing the market value, which the *CICA Handbook* recommends. Then readers of the financial statements can do the above sort of effects analysis if they wish.

HOW'S YOUR UNDERSTANDING?

Here are two questions you should be able to answer based on what you have just read. If you can't answer them, it would be best to reread the material.

1. What is the difference between cash and temporary investments, and why might they be grouped together on the balance sheet even if different?
2. Xie Inc. bought some shares on the stock market at a cost of $230,000 to employ some excess cash temporarily. At the balance sheet date, these shares had a current market value of $210,000. At what value would they be shown on the balance sheet, what effect would this have on income, what is the rule you followed to answer the previous questions, and why does this rule exist?

Balance sheet valuation: $210,000

Income reduced by $20,000 before any income tax effect

Lower of cost or market rule

Reasons include assumed liquidity of current assets and conservatism

8.6 Accounts Receivable

Trade Accounts Receivable

Trade accounts receivable are revenue that has been recognized but not yet collected.

Most *accounts receivable* are *recognized but uncollected revenue*, created by the accrual accounting entry: DR Accounts receivable, CR Revenue. Such receivables arise from the company's day-to-day business or "trading" activities and so are often called *trade receivables*. They are included in current assets because they're usually expected to be collected within one year. Any interest charged to slow payers is added to the balance by an entry like this: DR Accounts receivable, CR Interest revenue (nonoperating revenue).

Valuation of Accounts Receivable

Receivables are reduced by an allowance contra if their collectible value has fallen.

GAAP's lower of cost or market rule requires that current assets which are to be turned into cash soon must be reduced in value if it does not appear they will fetch the expected cash. With receivables, there's often collection uncertainty, and many enterprises experience difficulties in collection, especially as time passes after the sale. So, if the collectible amount is now expected to be lower than originally anticipated, the receivable must be reduced to an estimated collectible amount. The method for doing this, by subtracting an allowance for doubtful accounts contra account from the accounts receivable control account, was described in Section 7.7.

The entry to record the allowance for doubtful accounts receivable is: DR Bad debts expense, CR Allowance for doubtful accounts. How to determine the required allowance is an accounting policy decision too. Broadly, there are two methods:

If the entry debits an expense and credits the balance sheet, which is more important to be accurate, the debit or the credit?

Focus on the debit in the entry: Match the expense debit to revenue by a study of the typical bad debt losses incurred according to revenue. You might, for example, determine that 0.5% of credit sales are not collected and base the expense on that estimate. This method emphasizes the matching criterion for income measurement and is good for estimating bad debt expenses for management's scrutiny of credit policies during the year. But because it doesn't focus on the balance sheet, the credit in the entry, it doesn't necessarily result in a good estimate of the collectible value of the receivables at any point, so the objective of reporting the receivables at the cash they should fetch may not be met.

Focus on the credit in the entry: Instead, the credit part of the entry's effect on the balance sheet valuation can be the focus. A traditional method, "aging" of the receivables to determine which ones are getting old and therefore more doubtful or even hopeless, is used by most companies. But as there may be a very large number of receivables (think of how many the MasterCard, Visa, or American Express credit card operations must have!), the aging analysis is often done using samples or using analysis that identifies the most doubtful ones, such as analysis of customers' payment patterns to identify customers who have run into trouble paying.

Do both: Many companies use the first method for internal control, marketing strategy, and credit analysis purposes during the year, and the second method whenever a balance sheet is prepared. GAAP generally give precedence to the second method and its balance sheet focus—not the only time you will see the income measurement matching criterion superseded by the demands of balance sheet valuation.

In a contest between revenue-expense matching and balance sheet valuation, valuation usually wins.

What you see on the balance sheet is usually just the net estimated collectible value.

The estimated collectible amount is the net of accounts receivable minus the allowance: the allowance functions to adjust the net value down to the lower of cost (original sale value) and market (current estimated collectible amount). On the balance sheet, accounts receivable are valued at this net amount: most companies do not disclose either the original value or the allowance, just the net. They probably don't want competitors to know what proportion of their accounts receivable are in trouble! *Financial Reporting in Canada 2005* indicates that less than 25% of the 200 companies surveyed even disclosed that there was an allowance. Again, the reader is to assume that if GAAP are followed, an allowance must have been made if necessary. When the existence of an allowance was disclosed, its amount was given also.[6]

Other Receivables

Other receivables are separated from trade receivables if important.

If large, nontrade receivables are shown separately from trade receivables. But if not, they are usually just lumped in with the trade receivables. *Financial Reporting in Canada 2005* reports that, in 2004, the most recent year surveyed, 112 of the 200 companies indicated that they had more than one type of receivable and disclosed the amount of each type, 86 just gave one figure for receivables, one said it had receivables but didn't disclose the amount, and one did not report any receivables.[7]

There are two main kinds of other receivables.

Notes receivable arise from revenue transactions, but there are other receivables that don't.

1. *Notes receivable.* These usually arise from revenue transactions and are supported by a signed contract between buyer and seller that specifies a payment schedule, an interest rate, and often other legal details. Such notes are often used for large and/or long-term receivables, such as sales of automobiles, houses, or appliances, and loans by banks and finance companies. Notes are shown at *present value* (only interest that has built up so far is included in the asset, not future interest: see this chapter's endnote 2 or Section 10.7). An "allowance for doubtful notes" is used if necessary.
2. Loans to employees, officers, shareholders, and associated companies, tax refunds the company is waiting for, expense advances not yet accounted for by employees, and other receivables not arising from revenue transactions. They are accounted for and valued much as normal trade receivables and notes receivable are, but because some may arise from peculiar circumstances, companies often disclose the reasons for them and explain other circumstances about them.

HOW'S YOUR UNDERSTANDING?

Here are two questions you should be able to answer based on what you have just read. If you can't answer them, it would be best to reread the material.

1. What does the balance sheet's net figure for accounts receivable represent?
2. Are you likely to see separate disclosure of the allowance contra or nontrade receivables? Why or why not?

8.7 Inventory Valuation and Cost of Goods Sold

Inventories, like other current assets, are valued at lower of cost or market.

Inventory accounting, like accounting for other current assets, follows the lower of cost or market rule. It starts with the historical cost of the inventory. But, because inventory is expected to be turned into cash (sold), or otherwise consumed within the next year, it is a current asset, and because it is a current asset, GAAP require that any impairment in the asset's value be recognized in the period when the impairment occurred, not left until later when the asset is sold or used.

Inventory accounting affects both balance sheet values and income (via COGS).

This section explains how to determine cost. The following section, Section 8.8, explains how to determine market value and calculate the lower of the two. Inventory accounting affects both the balance sheet (*inventory valuation*) and the expense recognized for the use of inventory (*cost of goods sold expense, COGS*). Inventories include raw materials, work still in process and not yet ready for sale, finished or purchased goods held for sale, and supplies held for use within the business. *Financial Reporting in Canada 2005* indicates that 165 of its 200 surveyed companies in 2004 reported having inventories and about a third each reported all inventories in one figure, some inventory categories separately, or all inventory categories separately.[8]

Inventory Cost Flow Assumptions

Total cost is just the sum of quantity times unit cost for all items of inventory.

- We can get the quantity by counting the items, estimating the quantity, or using records (remember inventory control in Section 7.8).
- We know that unit cost includes the invoiced cost plus inward shipping, preparation, and so on (Section 8.4).
- Finding total cost, therefore, seems easy: just identify each item in inventory, trace it back to the purchase records, figure out its cost, and add all the costs together.

Attaching cost to actual items of inventory is likely difficult and costly, even impossible.

But is it so easy? Imagine the trouble you'd have keeping track of the invoiced cost, shipping, and other cost components for every item in a hardware store's inventory, or the impossibility of keeping track of individual barrels of oil in an oil refinery. Even if it were possible to do it somehow, the value of the resulting "precise" costing would be unlikely to be worth the trouble and cost to do it.

Few companies use actual cost for their inventories.

In practice, the actual cost of inventory items is tracked only for high-value items (houses, automobiles, airplanes, expensive jewellery) that can be identified by serial numbers and other methods. As the cost of keeping records decreases due to computerization, more items can be tracked this way. Still, serial numbers or other ways to identify specific inventory items would be needed for this tracking. According to *Financial Reporting in Canada 2005*, only four of the 200 companies in its survey for 2004 (unchanged from 2003) said they used actual, or "*specific identification*," cost for any inventories, and all used it only for some inventories, using assumed cost flow methods for other inventories.[9]

Inventory costing usually assumes how inventories and costs flow through the business.

For most inventories, because it is not worthwhile or even possible to keep track of the cost of individual items in inventory, most companies figure out their balance sheet inventory cost and cost of goods sold expense by *assuming* some flow of inventory items and their costs through the business. Management can't know or doesn't want to have to know exactly which ones are on hand, or which have been sold, so assumptions are used.

Assumptions about inventory cost flow lead to calculations of inventory and COGS amounts. The more information used in those calculations, the more precise (closer to "actual" cost) the result is. Usually more information is available about more important or more valuable inventories, and if the company has a perpetual inventory control system, that provides more information than a simpler periodic system does. The examples below use whatever information is available, or else ignore some of it to simplify the conceptual points about comparing the methods. Later in this section, the assumptions' relative effects on the balance sheet inventory asset and the income statement's COGS expense are summarized.

Example of the assumed cost flow problem:

We'll start with a simple example of how *assumed cost flow* works. The example involves inventory purchased for resale (such as for a retailer), but the ideas work just as well for inventory manufactured by a company: in that case, cost of *purchases* is replaced by cost of *goods manufactured*. Here is an example of the problem that *assumed cost flow* deals with:

- One item in Viking Inc.'s inventory is helmets with horns on them.
- At the beginning of the period, there were 25 helmets on hand, costing $85 each.
- During the period, Viking purchased 72 more helmets, 30 at $80 each, then 42 at $90.
- So 97 helmets were *available for sale* during the period. The total *available cost* for the period = cost of beginning inventory + cost of purchases = 25 × $85 + 30 × $80 + 42 × $90 = $8,305.
- During the period, 78 helmets were sold, so there were 19 left at the end.
- The problem is how to figure out the cost of the 78 helmets sold and the 19 still on hand: allocating the $8,305 between cost of goods sold (*income measurement*) and the cost of ending inventory (*balance sheet valuation*). If Viking used specific identification as its inventory costing method, we'd know which ones were which, but if not, we have to *assume* which ones are sold and which ones are still on hand.

Viking helmets

	No.	Unit Cost	Total Cost
Begin	25	$85	$2,125
Purchased:	30	$80	2,400
	42	$90	3,780
Available	97		$8,305

Divide the $8,305 between:
Cost of goods sold expense
Ending inventory asset

- Some *assumptions* that could be made (more about each is explained later):
  a. Assume that the 19 helmets were among the 42 bought in the second purchase (cost $90 each). In that case:
     - Ending inventory cost = 19 × $90 = $1,710.
     - Cost of goods sold expense = $8,305 available – $1,710 = $6,595. (We'll see below how to calculate COGS directly, but it will always equal the difference between available cost and ending inventory cost.)
     - *This is the "first-in, first-out" or "FIFO" assumption.*
  b. Just divide $8,305 by 97, getting $85.62 as the average cost, and use that to calculate cost of goods sold and ending inventory. In that case:
     - Ending inventory cost = 19 × $85.62 = $1,627.
     - Cost of goods sold expense = 78 × $85.62 = $6,678.
     - Sum of ending inventory cost and COGS = $8,305, the available cost.
     - *This is the "weighted annual average" or AVGE assumption.*

c. Assume that the 19 helmets were among the 25 on hand at the beginning (cost $85 each). In that case:
   - Ending inventory cost = 19 × $85 = $1,615.
   - Cost of goods sold expense = $8,305 available – $1,615 = $6,690. (We'll see below how to calculate COGS directly, but it will always equal the difference between available cost and ending inventory cost.)
   - *This is the "last-in, first-out" or "LIFO" assumption.*

The chart in Figure 8.2 depicts the derivation and allocation of available cost. In all cases acceptable under GAAP, the sum of cost of goods sold expense and ending inventory cost equals the available cost ($8,305 in the example above).

FIGURE 8.2

Derivation and Allocation of Available Cost

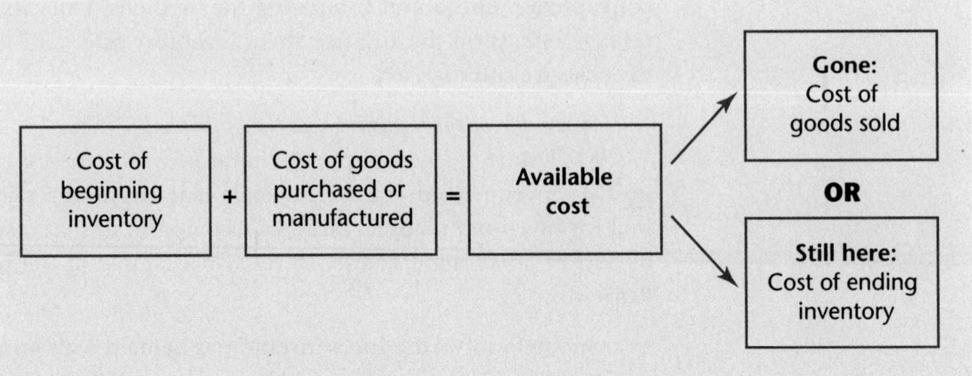

More About Inventory Cost Flow Assumptions

The choice of inventory method matters only if purchase or manufacturing costs change.

The above example introduced three cost flow assumptions, FIFO, AVGE, and LIFO. These three assumptions are a traditional part of GAAP. If costs of purchases or manufacturing don't change much, then there won't be much difference between the inventory costs and COGS produced by the assumptions, as was the case in the Viking helmets example. In recent years, inflation in most Western countries has been low, so the different methods do not currently matter much to the reported income and assets of most companies, but most companies will still tell you what method is being used, because each company may experience cost price changes that matter for it. It's therefore useful to know how the assumptions work; also, inflation may return some day.

Viking helmets example

	COGS Expense	Ending Inventory
FIFO	$6,595	$1,710
AVGE	6,678	1,627
LIFO	6,690	1,615

The cost flow assumption need not match the physical flow of the inventory.

Let's examine these assumptions further. Remember that, because each assumption *allocates* the available inventory cost between the inventory asset and the cost of goods sold expense differently, the choice of assumption has an effect on *both* the balance sheet and the income statement. The significance of the effect depends on how much purchase (or manufacturing) costs per unit rise or fall during the period. Companies don't have to use a cost flow assumption that matches the physical way inventory is managed, though it makes sense if there is such a match, so choosing inventory accounting policy usually takes physical flow into consideration.

FIFO is a convenient, popular, sensible inventory flow assumption.

FIFO assigns the more recent purchase costs to the balance sheet inventory asset account, and, therefore, older costs to the COGS expense account. FIFO means "*first in, first out*," but it might help you to think of it also as "last in, still here" because the method uses the costs of the most recently acquired items to get the balance sheet cost.

- FIFO is used because it is convenient and produces inventory asset values that are close to current costs, which seems to many people to be appropriate for a current asset.

- It is convenient because all you really need to do is keep your purchase invoices and, when you know how many units are on hand, just go through recent invoices to find the costs. For example, suppose there are 620 boxes of chocolates on hand at Dec. 31, and recent purchase invoices showed the following costs: Dec. 29, 260 boxes at \$3.20; Dec. 14, 310 boxes at \$3.35; Dec. 1, 210 boxes at \$3; and so on. The FIFO cost is found by starting with the most recent purchase and going back in time until all the ones on hand are accounted for (working on assumption, since we do not really know when any particular box on hand was purchased). The reasoning is this:

Amount on hand:	620 boxes		
Most recent purchase	260 boxes: invoice cost = \$3.20 × 260	=	\$ 832.00
Leaves (from prior purchases)	360 boxes		
Next most recent purchase	310 boxes: invoice cost = \$3.35 × 310	=	1,038.50
Leaves (from prior purchase)	50 boxes: invoice cost = \$3.00 × 50	=	150.00
Total FIFO cost		=	\$2,020.50

You don't need complicated records, just a pile of invoices. It doesn't matter what the internal control method is, because it doesn't provide any further necessary information: all you need to know is the quantity on hand at the balance sheet date, whether determined by count or by perpetual records.

- Using FIFO, COGS can be calculated just by subtracting the ending inventory determined from the purchase invoices (or manufacturing cost records) from the available cost. You can reason COGS out separately, and that will be demonstrated below, but one of the advantages of the FIFO method is that you don't have to bother.
- *Financial Reporting in Canada 2005* indicates that in 2004, 51 of the 147 companies that disclosed their cost determination method used FIFO alone, and another 23 companies that used more than one method used FIFO.[10] The total of 74 is 50% of the companies that disclosed their method, so FIFO is popular.
- FIFO is considered appropriate for a current asset by many people because it is the most reasonable method of physically moving inventory, especially inventory that is perishable or subject to changes in style or features, such as groceries, clothing, and other retail products. Picture a shelf in a grocery store: FIFO assumes that new stock is placed behind older stock on the shelf, so that the inventory keeps moving forward on the shelf. That way older items sell first and do not just collect dust and mould at the back of the shelf. It's the way we hope perishable inventory would actually be managed!

AVGE is sensible and popular for bulk products and raw materials.

AVGE assigns the available cost equally to the inventory asset and to cost of goods sold expense. In the Viking helmet example above, both inventory asset and cost of goods sold used the same \$85.62 average cost per helmet.

- Average cost is used largely for inventories that are a mixture of recent and older purchases and that are not particularly perishable, such as lumber, metals, oil, gas, and other bulk products and raw materials. The AVGE assumption that the inventory items are all mixed together makes sense for such inventories.
- The AVGE method is not just an average of the prices paid for the inventory items. Rather, the average is calculated by *weighting* the prices by the amount of inventory acquired at each price. Therefore, a small batch of items affects the average less than a large batch. The word "weighted" is sometimes used with the word "average" to emphasize this approach.
- The average calculation is affected by the amount of information available about inventory changes during the period. The most common average method is called

"*moving weighted average*": using it, the average cost of the inventory on hand is recalculated every time there is a purchase (or an additional batch manufactured). The average thus moves up and down as cost prices change, and the average at the balance sheet date is whatever the most recent moving average was. The balance sheet date is nothing special, just another date in the continuing sequence of inventory changes. Calculating a moving average is very tedious when done by hand, but a computer-based perpetual inventory system can do it easily, so moving average is more likely for important or computer-controlled inventories. Let's take the following scenario:

Prior to any purchase, we have H1 units on hand at a unit cost of C.

Purchase (or manufacturing) batch 1 costs P1 per unit, and there are N1 units.

Some units are then sold, leaving H2 units on hand.

Purchase (or manufacturing) batch 2 costs P2 per unit, and there are N2 units.

And so on.

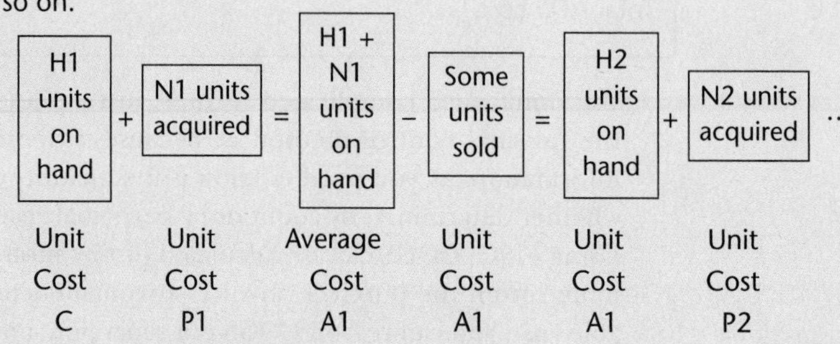

Using the above diagram, a moving weighted average is calculated like this:

- The first moving average assumes the H1 units on hand and the N1 units added are mixed together, so their average cost is $(C \times H1) + (P1 \times N1) / (H1 + N1)$.
- This average, called A1 above, is used for the cost of any items on hand or COGS of any sold after that, prior to the next purchase or manufacturing batch.
- Prior to the next purchase or manufacturing batch, there are H2 units on hand.
- Second moving average is $(A1 \times H2) + (P2 \times N2) / (H2 + N2)$, call it A2.
- Average A2 is used for inventory on hand or COGS, until the next purchase.
- And so on.

Financial Reporting in Canada 2005 says that in 2004 the (weighted) average cost method was the most popular among its 200 companies, with 56 companies using it alone and 25 using it in combination with other methods. The total of 81 is 55% of the 147 companies disclosing their inventory costing method, just beating out FIFO's 50%.[11] This popularity reflects the Canadian economy's emphasis on natural resources, such as gas, oil, lumber, and coal: companies in these sectors are very likely to use average cost.

LIFO is not a sensible flow assumption, but it saves tax in the United States (although not in Canada).

LIFO is, on the face of it, a strange valuation method. It assumes that the *newer* items are sold first and, therefore, the ones left on hand are *older*. In the extreme, this would imply that the grocery store's first loaves of bread are still at the back of the shelf, years later. LIFO means "*last in, first out*," but you could also think of it as "first in, still here" as a reminder of its odd assumption.

- LIFO is used for one very practical reason: in the United States, it is an allowable method for income tax purposes. In a period of rising purchase costs (inflation), which is pretty much constantly the case even though at a reduced rate in recent years, it produces a higher cost of goods sold expense and a lower inventory asset value than do FIFO or AVGE. Therefore, LIFO also produces lower income and lower income tax, *if* it can be used for tax purposes.
- In Canada, LIFO is *not* an allowable method for income tax purposes, so a Canadian company using it for the financial statements would have to compute inventory values all over again using one of the other methods when doing its income tax return.
- *Financial Reporting in Canada 2005* indicates that only two companies disclosed using LIFO exclusively, with another three using it for only some inventories.[12] (It would make sense to use it for inventories held by U.S. subsidiaries of Canadian companies, or if a U.S. parent company used it and required it of a Canadian subsidiary.)
- It can be argued that LIFO matches revenues with expenses better than the other two methods do. For example, if a company changes its selling prices as its purchase costs change, its revenues reflect recent price changes and it then seems appropriate to deduct the more recent purchase costs as cost of goods sold expense against the revenues. The trouble is that LIFO produces inventory asset values that are based on older purchase costs and this seems awkward for valuing a current asset. As we saw for estimating doubtful accounts based on revenues, revenue-expense matching is unlikely to be used if it results in an unsatisfactory balance sheet valuation (unless there is a tax saving available!).
- It would be nice to use current purchase prices for cost of goods sold expense and for the balance sheet inventory value. But that can't be done if we stick to the double-entry historical cost accounting basis: the books wouldn't balance because some of the units would have been purchased at older costs and those costs would be in the accounts, too, in the inventory asset or expense accounts. COGS expense and ending inventory cost must sum to the period's available cost.
- LIFO calculations are affected by the amount of information available. Like AVGE, there is a more tedious calculation when there is more information, as a perpetual control method provides. This tedious calculation results in "layers" of costs that are attributable to various stages of the LIFO calculation. If you hear about "LIFO layers," that is what is being referred to. This book will not get into these details because of LIFO's low popularity and lack of tax acceptability in Canada. However, one thing to be aware of is that if inventory quantities fall, old costs in the LIFO inventory are transferred into COGS, and this can produce a sudden decline in COGS and increase in income.

Effects Analysis

The three methods' effects on assets and income are predictable if prices rise or fall.

In a period of rising purchase prices or manufacturing costs

- FIFO tends to have the highest inventory asset value and lowest cost of goods sold expense (and therefore highest net income);
- LIFO tends to have the lowest inventory asset value and highest COGS (and therefore lowest net income); and
- AVGE tends to be between the other two in asset values, COGS, and net income.

If purchase prices are falling, the positions of FIFO and LIFO reverse, with FIFO tending to have the lowest net income and LIFO the highest. AVGE tends again to be between the other two.

The size of the effects depends on turnover and patterns of price and quantity changes.

The differences among the methods are larger the more purchase cost prices rise (or fall) during the period. The differences tend to be smaller when inventory turnover is high, because price changes occurring during the time inventory is held are smaller and the size of the inventory asset relative to cost of goods sold expense is smaller. If a perpetual LIFO or moving average method is being used, the differences can also be in unexpected directions, depending on coincidental increases or decreases in inventory levels. The relationships among the methods also can stray from the typical pattern if purchase price changes and inventory quantities are moving in opposite directions (for example, if inventory levels are falling, but prices are rising, or vice versa).

HOW'S YOUR UNDERSTANDING?

Here are two questions you should be able to answer based on what you have just read. If you can't answer them, it would be best to reread the material.

1. Why are there different methods for determining the cost of inventories and cost of goods sold expense?
2. Beyond the general criteria for accounting policy choice, such as fairness, how does a company decide which method to use for its inventory costing?

8.8 Demonstration Problem: Inventory Costing

This section reviews how to calculate inventory costs and COGS using five methods:

1. FIFO.
2. A simple annual weighted AVGE, which does not require information about inventory movements during the year, used here to illustrate how the average works before showing the moving average.
3. Moving weighted AVGE, the better AVGE method if information is available about inventory movements during the year.
4. A simple periodic LIFO, which also does not require information about inventory movements during the period, used to emphasize the LIFO assumption before showing the perpetual LIFO.
5. Perpetual LIFO, the better LIFO method if information is available about inventory movements during the year.

Among the products Meeix Inc. purchases and sells is Gloop. It began last year with 1,000 units of Gloop on hand at a cost of $4 each, and during the year its purchase and sales records were as shown in Exhibit 8.2:

Date	Units Purchased	Units Sold	Units on Hand	Purchase Price
Jan. 1			1,000	$4
Feb. 15		350	650	
Mar. 20	600		1,250	$5
Apr. 30		750	500	
Sept. 12	800		1,300	$6
Dec. 11		200	1,100	
	1,400	1,300		

It is always useful to know what available cost has to be allocated.

Given the available cost, you only need COGS expense to deduce the asset or vice versa.

Let's start with *available cost*. *Regardless of the cost flow assumption to be used,* we know that the beginning inventory cost is $4,000 and that purchases costing $7,800 (600 × $5 + 800 × $6) were made. Available cost, therefore, is the sum of beginning inventory and purchases, which sum is $11,800. Consequently, as long as the historical cost basis of accounting is used, any inventory *cost allocation* method must produce $11,800 as the sum of the ending inventory asset and cost of goods sold expense.

This gives us a way to check our calculations. If we calculate cost of goods sold expense and ending inventory asset cost separately, they must add up to $11,800. As a short cut, we can calculate *either* the expense or the asset value and deduce the other by deducting it from $11,800. This is easier than doing it twice, but the calculations below will include both the expense and the asset so that you can see how it all works.

The chart in Figure 8.3 shows how the quantities of Gloop changed during the year. Before trying any of the methods' calculations, keep in mind how the methods' cost flow assumptions would treat the *ending* inventory's 1,100 units:

- FIFO: 1,100 on hand = 800 most recently bought + 300 of those bought Mar. 20.
- AVGE:

  Annual weighted: the 1,100 on hand are a proportionate mixture of those on hand at the beginning and those bought Mar. 20 and Sept. 12.

  Moving weighted:

  1. The first average is the 1,250 on hand at Mar. 20, which is a proportionate mixture of those on hand at the beginning plus those bought Mar. 20.
  2. The second average is the 1,300 on hand Sept. 12, which is a proportionate mixture of the first average (on hand Apr. 30) and those bought Sept. 12.
- LIFO:

  Periodic: the 1,100 on hand must be the 1,000 on hand at the beginning plus 100 next oldest, those bought Mar. 20 (no attention paid to changes in inventory balances during the period, because under the periodic method, such changes would not be known).

  Perpetual: during the year, the inventory hit a minimum of 500, so that's all of the beginning items that could still be on hand at the end. Therefore 1,100 on hand = 500 from the beginning plus 600 bought in the first purchase after that, Sept. 12 (the only purchase since then).

FIGURE 8.3

Inventory Balances and Changes: Meeix's Gloop

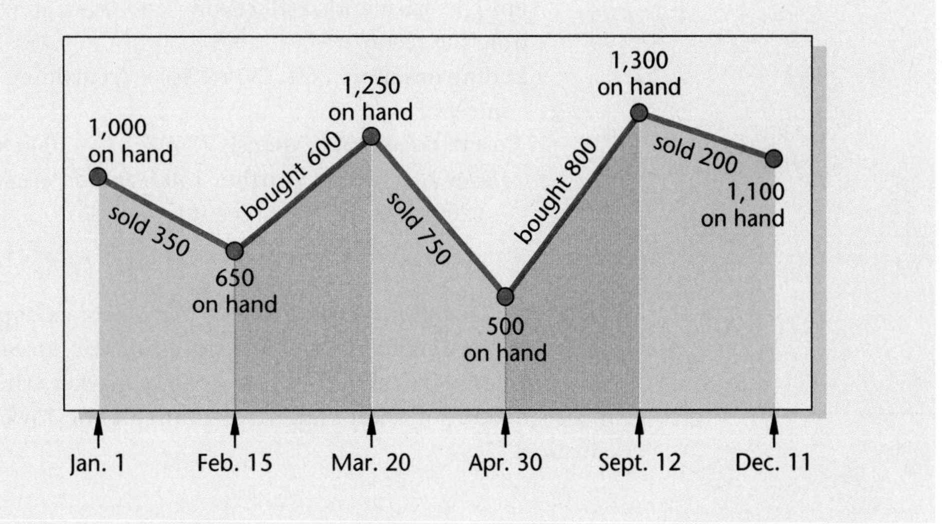

Based on the patterns shown in Figure 8.3 and the above summary of each method's assumption about the ending inventory quantity, here are the calculations for ending inventory cost and cost of goods sold.

a. **FIFO**

Ending inventory cost: (800 × $6) + (remaining 300 × $5)	$ 6,300
Cost of goods sold expense: (1,000 × $4) + (remaining 300 × $5)	5,500
	$11,800

b. **AVGE**

b.1 *Annual weighted average*

Average cost = $11,800 / (1,000 + 600 + 800) = $4.917 (rounded)	
Ending inventory cost: 1,100 × $4.917	$ 5,408
Cost of goods sold expense: 1,300 × $4.917	6,392
	$11,800

b.2 *Moving weighted average*

The average works the same way as the above weighted average, but it is recalculated after each purchase, weighted in accordance with the inventory on hand at that point.

Weighted average after first purchase
= ([650 × $4] + [600 × $5]) / (650 + 600) = $4.48

Weighted average after second purchase
= ([500 × $4.48] + [800 × $6]) / (500 + 800) = $5.415

Ending inventory cost (using average at that point): 1,100 × $5.415	$ 5,957
Cost of goods sold expense (using the average immediately preceding each sale): (350 × $4) + (750 × $4.48) + (200 × $5.415)	5,843
	$11,800

c. **LIFO**

c.1 *Periodic basis*

Ending inventory cost: (1,000 × $4) + (remaining 100 × $5)	$ 4,500
Cost of goods sold expense: (800 × $6) + (remaining 500 × $5)	7,300
	$11,800

c.2 *Perpetual basis*

The perpetual records allow us to determine whether it is reasonable to assume that all the original 1,000 units are still on hand. In this example it is not, because at one point the inventory was down to 500 units, so that "layer" of cost has been partly used up. The calculation reflects the "cost layer" information available from the records.

Ending inventory cost: (500 × $4) + (remaining 600 bought since × $6)	$ 5,600
Cost of goods sold expense: (350 × $4) + (600 × $5 [layer all gone]) + (further 150 from the original layer × $4) + (200 from the most recent layer × $6)	6,200
	$11,800

The table in Exhibit 8.3 summarizes the Meeix example's results. It demonstrates the effects on the financial statements of choosing among the inventory cost methods, *assuming* that in all cases cost is lower than market value for the ending inventory asset and so making market value irrelevant in the lower of cost or market inventory valuation.

EXHIBIT 8·3

Cost Method		Ending Inventory Asset	Cost of Goods Sold Expense	Total Cost Available
FIFO		$6,300	$5,500	$11,800
AVGE	—Annual	5,408	6,392	11,800
	—Moving	5,957	5,843	11,800
LIFO	—Periodic	4,500	7,300	11,800
	—Perpetual	5,600	6,200	11,800

HOW'S YOUR UNDERSTANDING?

Here are two questions you should be able to answer based on what you have just read. If you can't answer them, it would be best to reread the material.

1. What are the important differences among the five inventory costing methods demonstrated in this section?
2. Meeix Inc. also stocks a pet food called Dog's Breakfast. Last year, there were 200 crates of Dog's Breakfast on hand at the beginning of the year, and 1,500 crates were purchased and 1,450 crates were sold during the year. The crates on hand at the beginning cost $400 each. There were three purchases: early in the year, 500 crates costing $404 each were purchased; then 600 crates costing $390 each; and near the end of the year, 400 crates costing $384.50 each were purchased. What would be the cost of the inventory at the end of the year and the cost of goods sold expense under (a) FIFO? (b) simple annual AVGE? and (c) periodic LIFO?

Ending inventory = 250 crates (200 + 1,500 – 1,450).
Available cost = 200 × $400 + 500 × $404 + 600 × $390 + 400 × $384.50 = $669,800.

(a) FIFO ending inventory = $96,125 (250 × $384.50);
COGS = 200 × $400 + 500 × $404 + 600 × $390 + 150 × $384.50 = $573,675;
Check: $96,125 + $573,675 = $669,800 available cost.

(b) Annual AVGE = $669,800 / 1,700 = $394;
Ending inventory = $98,500 (250 × $394);
COGS = 1,450 × $394 = $571,300;
Check: $98,500 + $571,300 = $669,800 available cost.

(c) Periodic LIFO ending inventory = $100,200 (200 × $400 + 50 × $404);
COGS = 400 × $384.50 + 600 × $390 + 450 × $404 = $569,600.
Check: $100,200 + $569,600 = $669,800 available cost.

8.9 Lower of Cost or Market and Other Costing Methods

Inventory Market Value for Lower of Cost or Market Rule

There are two common perspectives on this rule:

Replacement cost makes sense for the market value of inventory to be used, not sold.

- For inventory that is not to be sold, but rather to be used up (for example, manufacturing raw materials, factory supplies, and office supplies), the *input* market value or *replacement cost* seems most relevant. *Replacement cost* is determined by obtaining prices from suppliers and making other estimates of what it would cost to replace the items on hand. The focus is on items whose supply prices are falling because, remember, we're concerned only with cases in which market (replacement cost) is *lower* than the cost originally paid, or assumed to have been paid, for the items.

Net realizable value makes sense for the market value of inventory that is to be sold.

- For inventory that is to be sold, the *output* market value or *net realizable value* seems most relevant. *Net realizable value* is determined by taking selling prices and deducting any costs to complete the items (such as putting them in a box) or selling them. Again, the focus is on items whose net realizable value is below cost, so we're concerned about items whose selling prices are falling or that have been damaged, or have become obsolete, or out of style so that we can't sell them for what we thought we could.

Lower of Cost or Market

Basically, to calculate the lower of cost or market value, we just take the cost of the items and compare those costs to the market values and use the *lower* as the balance sheet inventory value. Exhibit 8.4 shows an example:

Example of Lower of Cost or Market Calculation

Inventory Item	Quantity	Total Cost	Total Market	L of C or M
Part #493-A	500 units	$ 2,000	$ 2,600	$ 2,000 (C)
Part #499	60 kg	432	420	420 (M)
Product #239	1,000 units	60,000	75,000	60,000 (C)
Product #240	200 units	3,000	700	700 (M)
Etc.				
TOTALS (let's say)		$643,290	$858,400	$629,680

The inventory figure shown on the balance sheet is either:

a. The sum of the final column ($629,680), which is the sum of the lower of cost or market calculated on each individual item; or
b. The total cost ($643,290), on the assumption that since total market ($858,400) exceeds total cost, no adjustment down to market is needed.

Lower of cost or market comparison may be done by item (conservative) or overall.

Alternative (a) is more conservative, but (b) is likely to be used if there is no evidence of a serious problem overall with the inventory.

If any reduction from cost to market is necessary, it becomes an expense for the period.

Using the conservative method (a) for illustration, the lower values for some (Part #499, Product #240, and apparently others) bring the sum of the lower values ($629,680) to less than the total cost ($643,290) by $13,610. If we were being conservative, we'd record a loss of $13,610, debiting a Loss expense account and crediting Inventory asset, assuming the perpetual control method. (Instead of crediting Inventory directly, an "Allowance for reduction in inventory" account, like the Allowance for doubtful accounts receivable, could be used.)

The loss account would be unlikely to be disclosed separately from COGS on the income statement, because as long as it is not large (material), it is a normal sort of thing and the reader should assume any company has some such minor losses. After all, if the items had been sold during the year, such as in a clearance sale, the reduced revenue would have been part of revenue and the cost would have been in COGS, so the "loss" would have been buried in the overall revenue minus the COGS part of the income calculation.

Often, choices of cost and market methods go together.

In practice, companies usually focus mainly on items whose values are likely to be impaired (as might be identified during the physical count), rather than calculating market value for everything. Also, often the kind of inventory suggests both a cost flow assumption and a market value method. For example,

- raw materials and supplies are often shown at the lower of average cost and replacement cost (this is CPR's accounting policy),[13] while
- goods for sale are usually shown at the lower of FIFO cost and net realizable value.

Thus we tend to see the cost and market methods going together (average with replacement, FIFO with net realizable value), though there are many exceptions. The retail method of costing inventory (commented on briefly below) is an amalgamation of costs and selling prices, so it, too, is an example of costs and market values going together.

The inventory cost and market methods are both accounting policy choices.

Canadian financial accounting standards are not explicit about lower of cost or market calculations. They are left to the professional judgment of individual accountants and auditors. In the United States there are a number of rules and regulations, including the "floor–ceiling" rule (in which market equals replacement cost as long as that does not exceed a pair of floor and ceiling values calculated from selling price), which provide more specific guidance. The complexities of these rules and guidelines are best left to other books. But what you should know for now is that figuring out lower of cost or market for inventories requires management to make accounting policy decisions about cost, about market, *and* about comparing them. *Financial Reporting in Canada 2005* reports that in 2004, 80 companies of the 157 that disclosed their market value method used a version of net realizable value only, and just 12 used only replacement cost. But of the 62 reporting using more than one method, 54 used replacement cost, usually in conjunction with net realizable value.[14]

Terminology again! Here's a tiny item. This book uses the phrase "lower of cost or market," but the more common phrase is "lower of cost *and* market." *Financial Reporting in Canada 2005* reports that in its sample, 141 companies used "and" and only 11 used "or" in 2004.[15] This book's author once lost marks on an exam for using "or" and so now uses it out of stubbornness!

The Retail Inventory Method and Other Methods

In Section 7.8 on inventory control, the retail inventory method was mentioned as a way of combining retail inventory prices with cash and other controls. The method can also be used to estimate inventory costs. *Financial Reporting in Canada 2005* does not mention the retail method, but an earlier edition reported that in 1994, 12 companies (out of the 300 then surveyed) used the retail method.[16] The survey was of large companies; the retail method is probably much more common among smaller companies. The retail method, which, as you might expect, is most applicable for retailers' inventories, combines purchase costs and selling prices into a single calculation. An inventory figure is first determined by valuing items at retail prices (Section 7.8) and then cost is estimated by deducting estimated markups from the retail value. As Section 7.8 notes, the method is simple in concept but complicated in practice.

A few other inventory costing methods are used. *Financial Reporting in Canada 1995* said that in 1994, 16 companies reported methods other than the ones described here.[17] By 2005, *Financial Reporting in Canada* reported that only 7 of its 200 companies used something other than FIFO, AVGE, or LIFO.[18] One of these, "standard costing" for manufactured inventories, uses estimated costs based on standard production costs and volumes.

HOW'S YOUR UNDERSTANDING?

Here are two questions you should be able to answer based on what you have just read. If you can't answer them, it would be best to reread the material.

1. In using lower of cost or market, how does a company determine "market"?
2. Lytle Inc. has three items in inventory: A (cost $5,200, market $7,000), B (cost $6,100, market $5,700), and C (cost $11,400, market $16,600). Calculate (i) lower of cost or market, (ii) the balance sheet inventory value, and (iii) any loss incurred. For all these, do two calculations and indicate which is the more conservative.

Total cost = $22,700; total market = $29,300; individually, lower of cost or market = $5,200 + $5,700 + $11,400 = $22,300.

Answers: First calculation: (i) $22,700, (ii) $22,700, (iii) no loss. Second calculation: (i) $22,300, (ii) $22,300, (iii) $400 loss. The second is more conservative.

8.10 Amortization of Assets and Amortization Expense

Amortization allocates to expense the cost of all tangible assets except land.

Fixed assets (so-called tangible assets, including land, buildings, equipment, furniture, vehicles, computers, etc.) have value because the company intends to receive economic benefits from using them in the future. However, with the exception of land, no fixed assets have an unlimited useful life, so all must eventually be retired from service. Amortization is the process of allocating the cost over years of benefit, and the annual deduction from revenue is *amortization expense*. According to GAAP, all fixed assets except land are amortized.

Amortization is based on a prediction of the future and so is inevitably inexact.

Amortization, no matter how carefully calculated, is never exact. It involves a prediction of economic use and useful life, and such a prediction can easily be wrong. If assets are grouped together for computing amortization, the errors can be reduced because some assets for which the prediction overshoots may be offset by others for which it undershoots. Any amortization amount is fundamentally arbitrary; for that reason, most companies prefer fairly simple calculations rather than complex guesses! Correcting for errors in amortization estimates is considered so routine that such error corrections are not disclosed separately in the income statement, but are just included with amortization expense.

FYI

As was noted in Section 1.10, the terminology for amortization is changing. You'll see the terms "amortization," "depreciation," and "depletion" in newspapers, financial statements, databases, and elsewhere. Historically, *depreciation* has been used for physical assets, such as buildings and equipment; *depletion* has been used for "wasting assets," such as timber sales or ore bodies, and *amortization* has been used for various miscellaneous and intangible assets. The usage is changing: since 1990, the *CICA Handbook* has used *amortization* as the only term, and this book uses that term most of the time. *Depreciation* and *depletion* may eventually disappear from Canadian financial statements. But they may not: they are deeply entrenched terms, especially depreciation.

Why Allocate the Cost?

Amortization allocates the cost of a long-lived asset to expense over the asset's useful life.

Amortization is a technique for *measuring income* by matching an allocation of the asset's cost to the revenue it is presumed to help earn. Assets are resources of the enterprise, used in order to generate revenue for the owners and, ultimately, a return on their investment. One of the objectives of accrual accounting is to attempt to match expenses with the revenue earned, as we saw in Chapter 6. In the case of long-lived assets, the cost will benefit many periods in which revenue is earned. When purchasing a fixed asset such as a building or equipment, the rational purchaser will at least have an approximate idea of how much benefit the asset will provide. For example, when buying a piece of equipment to slice bread, the baker must have a reasonable idea of how many loaves it will slice, before it wears out or a better slicer becomes available. If the baker can estimate how many loaves it will slice, the baker can then deduct the cost of the machine from revenue a part at a time, over the number of years it will take to bake that many loaves of bread. If the whole asset cost were deducted from income in the period in which it was acquired, that would make that period's income relatively low, and subsequent periods' incomes relatively high. Amortization spreads the cost out over all the periods that share in the using up of the asset's economic value. Therefore, accounting amortization is a *cost allocation* system, used to measure income: *it is not a system to track value changes in the assets or to measure the current or market value of those assets in the balance sheet.*

Amortization's cost allocation is based on what is expected to happen in the future.

Amortization allocates cost to expense; it does not track changes in market value.

- Suppose the bread slicer mentioned above cost $5,000 and will have no value to the business after eight years. Amortization of $5,000 over eight years (for example, $625 of amortization expense each year) shows that using up the slicer's economic value over those years costs the baker something. The baker has a $5,000 economic asset now, but in eight years will have no economic asset, even if the slicer still exists physically.
- Over the years, the cost and resale value of bread slicers may keep changing due to inflation, market conditions, or technological change. The baker may be able to resell the slicer for only $3,000 after one year, so perhaps the market value used up in that year is $2,000, but if the amortization method specifies $625 per year, that is what is used in the accounts and financial statements. The balance sheet shows the net of the asset's original cost minus accumulated amortization: it does *not* mean the asset's current or market value is that net "book value" amount. In the above example, after one year the balance sheet shows the bread slicer at $4,375 ($5,000 cost less $625), not at $3,000 or any other measure of current value. Knowing what is happening to market values may be very important. If so, the manager has to look elsewhere than financial accounting for the information.

Why Not Amortize Land?

Land is not amortized because its value is not considered to be consumed as it is used.

The basic answer is that land's economic value is not considered to decline through use. Land is considered immune to physical or economic decline. As a machine is used in a production process, it wears out, like the soles of your shoes as you walk. But such wear and tear, and other natural processes, such as wind, rain, rust, fatigue, and corrosion, are not thought to affect the economic value of land, nor are nonphysical causes of economic amortization. A machine can become obsolete with the advent of newer and faster machines, economic conditions in an area can result in the closure of a plant that has many productive years left but cannot be profitable anymore, and the whims of fashion can cause retail merchants to change display racks every two years when they were built to last for 10. But land continues on.

However, land can collapse, turn to swamp or otherwise lose its value, so if evidence of a loss of land value *does* appear, the land's cost can be reduced to a revised value, but that is a special case and is a write-down or write-off "loss" rather than amortization.

When Does the Cost Allocation (Amortization Expense) Begin?

The cost determined for the asset is amortized after the asset goes into service.

Amortization is meant to provide an expense to match the economic benefit obtained from the use of the asset. Therefore, when the asset is put to use and the benefit begins to be realized, amortization expense should begin. The general pattern is to capitalize costs incurred on the asset prior to putting it into service, and when the asset is put into service, to amortize those costs.

This pattern is illustrated in the chart in Figure 8.4, which is similar to Figure 8.1 used in Section 8.4 to explain the components of asset cost. *The line sloping downward from cost need not be a straight one, as we will see.*

Amortization for Partial Periods

It would be convenient if all assets were bought and sold at the fiscal year-end. Of course that seldom happens, so companies have to decide what to do about amortization for such periods as

- the time between the asset going into service and the fiscal year-end or other financial statement date such as for a quarterly report; and
- the time between the beginning of the fiscal period and the date at which an asset is sold, junked, or written off.

Companies must make accounting policy choices about partial periods. Usually such choices are not disclosed in the accounting policy note because they are not likely to be important to people reading the financial statements. Other than ignoring the issue, there are basically two choices:

- Calculate the amortization for the partial period as a proportion of the annual amount. For example, if a machine's amortization would be $3,500 for a year and it is sold seven months into the year, calculate amortization as 7/12 of the annual amount.

FIGURE 8.4

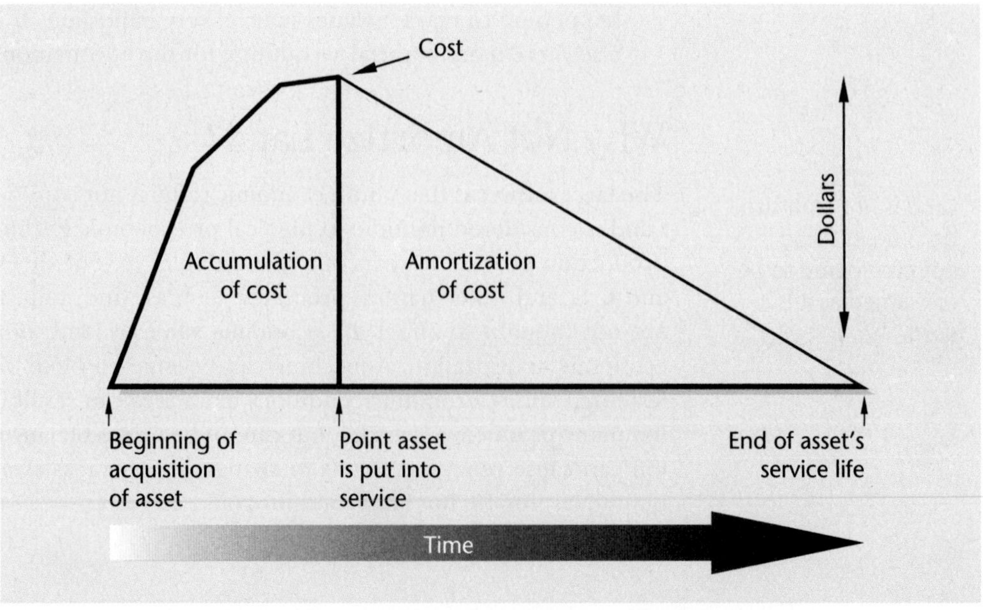

- Have a standard policy of amortizing say 50% of the usual amount in the year the asset is purchased and 50% in the year it is sold. This is arbitrary but will be reasonable if assets are bought and sold fairly steadily during the year, and it saves having to do special computations for every asset bought and sold. (Canadian income tax law prescribes that capital cost allowance be deducted at only half the usual rate in the year the asset is acquired. No capital cost allowance is deductible in the year the asset is sold.)

Amortization, Income Tax, and Cash Flow

Amortization in the accounts is irrelevant for income tax purposes in Canada.

Amortization has no effect on cash or cash flow.

In Canada, amortization calculated in the accounts is irrelevant for income tax purposes because the federal and provincial income tax laws require companies (and individuals) to follow their rules, not GAAP, in computing taxable income. A company can use whatever GAAP amortization method it likes in its financial statements, but whatever that is, it is still irrelevant for income tax purposes.

The amortization entry (Dr Amortization expense, Cr Accumulated amortization) has no cash component, so amortization has no cash effect. The fact that amortization appears on the cash flow statement using the traditional indirect method (Section 4.5) often misleads people: because it is added to income, it seems to be a source of cash. But amortization and adjustments in it to correct errors in estimation have no effect on cash one way or the other. Amortization is added back to income at the beginning of the cash flow statement to remove its effect from accrual accounting income and so to help convert that income to cash income.

Amortization Is a Useful Part of Historical Cost Accounting

Amortization is a useful but inexact allocation of asset cost to expense, to match revenue.

Amortization does not match actual market value changes in assets, it has no cash effect, it is an estimate only, and it has no income tax effect! What good is it? That's a question often asked, and the answer goes back to the matching criterion and historical cost basis of accrual accounting. We know that some economic value is being used up as a depreciable asset is used in earning revenue. Since we are limited to using cost in measuring that value, we end up with a way of spreading the cost out over the useful life to match the presumed consumption of that cost to the benefits (revenue) gained from the use. If we didn't have the historical cost basis or matching, we probably wouldn't need amortization as it is conventionally calculated. But, since we do have them, we have it!

HOW'S YOUR UNDERSTANDING?

Here are two questions you should be able to answer based on what you have just read. If you can't answer them, it would be best to reread the material.

1. What is amortization of long-lived assets supposed to accomplish?
2. Why is the basis of amortization used by financial accounting controversial, misunderstood, and/or limited in its usefulness?

8.11 Gains and Losses on Noncurrent Asset Disposals and Write-Offs

Gains, *losses*, and *write-offs* have been covered already, particularly in Section 7.7 on contra accounts and Section 4.5 on the indirect method of cash flow analysis. This section is a short summary to relate these items to what amortization is and does.

Gains and losses on noncurrent asset sales are separated from revenues and expenses.

When a noncurrent asset is sold, the sale could be handled as ordinary revenues are: the proceeds could be added to revenue and the asset's book value (cost minus accumulated amortization) could be added to the cost of goods sold. But this would mix usually infrequent noncurrent asset sales with day-to-day revenues, obscuring both and allowing one to offset the other, confusing the income statement's measure of performance.

A gain or loss is just the difference between proceeds and book value.

A gain or loss results when the book value of an asset is not equal to the proceeds obtained for it. The gain or loss is just the difference between the proceeds and the book value (cost minus accumulated amortization, if any), resulting in the following entry, described in Section 7.7:

DR Cash or nontrade receivables (proceeds)	XXXX		
CR Cost of the noncurrent asset			XXXX
DR Accumulated amortization to date on that asset	XXXX		
DR Loss or CR Gain on sale	XXXX	or	XXXX

Here is an example: Company X has a truck that cost $84,000. The accumulated amortization at the date of sale is $46,000. Therefore, book value is $38,000 at the date of sale. If the company:

a. sells it for $52,000, there is a gain on sale of $14,000 ($52,000 – $38,000);
b. sells it for $30,000, there is a loss on sale of $8,000 ($38,000 – $30,000);
c. throws it away, there is a loss on disposal of $38,000 ($38,000 – $0).

Gains and losses are corrections to the estimates involved in amortization.

The previous section mentioned that amortization is never exact, and so corrections in amortization estimates are routine. This goes for gains and losses on sale, too. You can think of gains and losses as *amortization corrections*. They're pretty well inevitable, given the inexactitude of estimates of useful life and eventual proceeds:

- If the company knew in advance what the proceeds would be and when the sale would happen, it could have amortized the asset down exactly to the proceeds amount by that date, and by the calculations above, there would be no gain or loss.
- If the proceeds are less than book value, there is a loss: in effect, more amortization is needed and that's what the loss really is. (Therefore, the loss is added back to income on the cash flow statement, just as amortization is.)
- If the proceeds are more than book value, there is a gain: in effect, too much amortization was taken and the gain is really just that excess (which caused the lower book value) being recognized. (Therefore, the gain is deducted from income on the cash flow statement; it's just negative amortization.)

These ideas are depicted in Figure 8.5.

Group Amortization

A gain or loss cannot be recorded if the asset's book value is not known.

Many assets, especially lower value ones like furniture and equipment, and aggregates like fleets of rental cars or delivery trucks, are amortized as a group. Canadian income tax law requires that most assets be amortized for income tax purposes ("capital cost allowance") in groups called asset classes. In such cases, there is usually no gain or loss recognized on the sale of one asset of the group, because its individual book value is not known. The gain or loss is in effect buried in accumulated amortization by the following journal entry (which is the same as the one above but with no gain or loss):

FIGURE 8.5

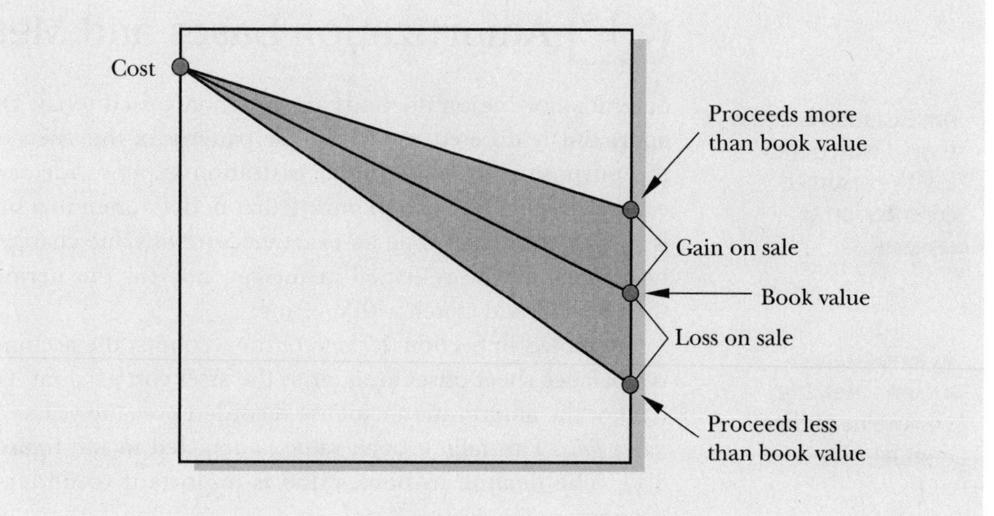

DR Cash or nontrade receivables (proceeds)	XXXX	
CR Cost of the noncurrent asset		XXXX
DR Accumulated amortization (cost minus proceeds)	XXXX	

This entry wouldn't work very well if proceeds exceeded cost, but we'll leave that complication out. Burying any gain or loss in accumulated amortization assumes that such gains or losses average out to zero over time. If they do not, the accumulated amortization will get out of line over time. Dealing with this is a subject for more advanced accounting courses.

Write-Offs and Write-Downs

Write-offs and write-downs are recorded as asset disposals without proceeds.

The above ideas also work for three other situations, referred to earlier in this text: (1) sales of nonamortized noncurrent assets (investments or land, for example) and (2) write-offs or (3) write-downs of noncurrent assets, whether already amortized or not:

- In (1), the gain or loss on sale is just the difference between cost and proceeds because there is no accumulated amortization.
- In (2), the asset is being removed from the balance sheet, without any cash proceeds, as when the truck was thrown away in example (c) above. The write-off amount is just cost, or book value if there is accumulated amortization, because there is no "proceeds" line in the journal entry.
- In (3), the write-down amount similarly involves no proceeds. It is the same as a write-off except that not all of the asset is removed from the balance sheet.

HOW'S YOUR UNDERSTANDING?

Here are two questions you should be able to answer based on what you have just read. If you can't answer them, it would be best to reread the material.

1. In what way is a gain or loss on a noncurrent asset disposal just an amortization adjustment?
2. A company disposed of a whole factory that cost $12,500,000 and had accumulated amortization of $8,700,000. What was the gain or loss on disposal (or loss on write-off) under each of the following cases: (1) proceeds $4,500,000, (2) proceeds $2,400,000, (3) proceeds zero (write-off)?

Book value is $12,500,000 – $8,700,000 = $3,800,000.

(1) $700,000 gain ($4,500,000 – $3,800,000).

(2) $1,400,000 loss ($2,400,000 – $3,800,000).

(3) Write-off loss $3,800,000, the book value.

8.12 Amortization Bases and Methods

Amortization expense should match the asset's presumed contribution to revenue.

Several amortization methods are commonly used today. Different methods attempt to approximate different economic use patterns of the assets over their lives. In each case, the purpose is to *match* the amortization expense for each period to the presumed economic benefit obtained during that period, often in a simple way, since amortization is an estimate rather than an exact measure of value changes. That presumed economic benefit should be reflected in the revenue for the period, so amortization expense therefore should match with revenue.

As amortization accumulates, the book value of the asset falls.

As noted in Section 7.7 on contra accounts, the accumulated amortization account is a balance sheet offset account to the asset cost account. Over time, it accumulates the total of the amortization expense recorded over the years. *As this accumulation rises, book value falls.* This falling book value is depicted in the figures in Sections 8.4, 8.10, and 8.11. The decline in book value is important to understanding the methods and diagrams in this section.

Amortization methods follow four general assumptions about assets' economic benefits.

There are four basic assumptions about how an asset brings economic benefit, and a kind of amortization (cost allocation) for each (the third one, included for completeness, is rarely seen):

Assumption About Benefit	Kind of Cost Allocation
1. *Evenly over the asset's life* The asset is assumed to be equally valuable in earning income in each year of its useful life.	*Straight-line* Expense is the same each year of the useful life.
2. *Falling over the asset's life* The asset's value in its early years is assumed to be greater than that in its later years.	*Accelerated, declining balance* Expense is larger in the earlier years than in the later years.
3. *Rising over the asset's life* Opposite to assumption 2 above.	*Decelerated* Opposite to accelerated.
4. *Variable over the asset's life* The asset's value in earning income varies according to how much production is achieved each year.	*Units of production, depletion* Expense depends on each year's volume of production.

Amortization expense is a cost allocation representing the asset's economic use.

These four general kinds are compared graphically in Figure 8.6. Each has a different amortization expense per period, *the expense being designed to represent the estimated value of the asset in generating revenue per period,* and a different pattern of book value. Book value equals cost minus accumulated amortization, so, because cost is constant, the book value pattern comes from the accumulation of the amortization.

FIGURE 8.6

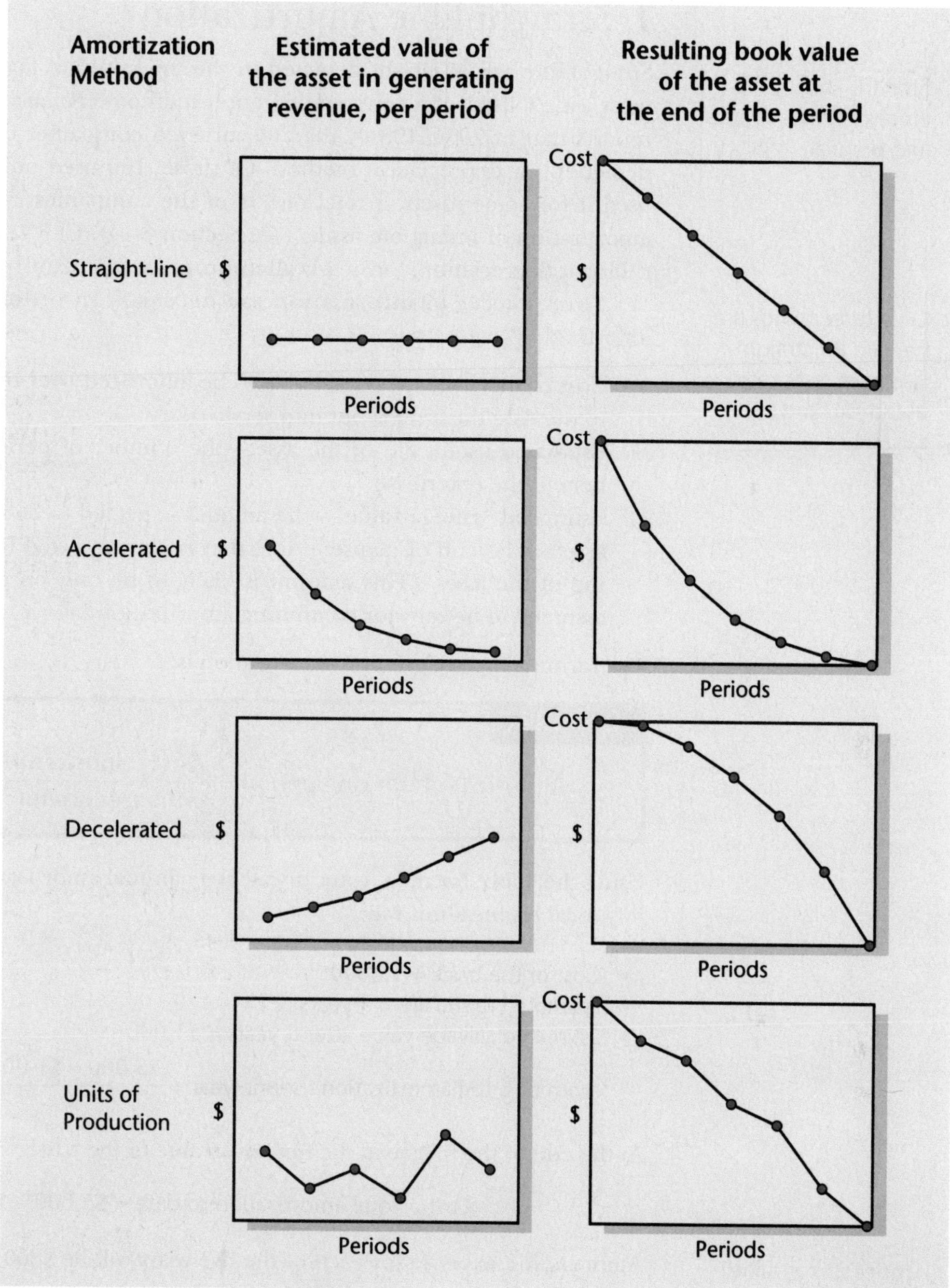

Amortization Method	Estimated value of the asset in generating revenue, per period	Resulting book value of the asset at the end of the period
Straight-line		
Accelerated		
Decelerated		
Units of Production		

Terminology. You may be wondering where the names "accelerated" and "decelerated" amortization come from. They are from comparisons with straight-line amortization.

- Accelerated amortization is accelerated (higher expense) in comparison with straight-line amortization in the early years of the asset's life (compare the accelerated expense pattern with the straight-line one in the left-hand diagrams in Figure 8.6).
- Decelerated amortization has a smaller expense than straight-line amortization in the early years of the asset's life (compare the decelerated expense pattern with the straight-line one in Figure 8.6).

The reason for the name "units of production" is explained later.

1. Straight-Line Amortization

Straight-line amortization is simple and popular.

Straight-line amortization, depicted in the top panel of Figure 8.6, is the simplest and most widely used of all the amortization methods. *Financial Reporting in Canada 2005* reports that in 2004, 198 of the 200 surveyed companies disclosed their amortization, depletion, or depreciation method. Of those, 100 used only straight-line and 81 more used it for some assets, a total of 181 of the companies.[19] It is nearly always used for amortization of intangible assets (see Section 8.14). CPR uses the straight-line method, calling it depreciation, for nearly all its property and plant.[20]

Only three things are needed for straight-line: cost, estimated useful life, and salvage.

Three pieces of information are necessary in order to compute straight-line amortization.

a. Cost of the asset—the total cost to be amortized over time (the amount capitalized to the date the asset is put into service).
b. Estimated useful life of the asset—the number of periods the asset is expected to benefit the enterprise.
c. Estimated "salvage value"—the amount expected to be recovered via the sale of the asset at the end of its useful life, that is, the expected future proceeds from disposing of the asset. (This amount is likely to be only an educated guess and is often assumed to be zero for computing amortization over long periods of time.)

The formula for straight-line amortization is:

FORMULA

$$\text{Amortization for one period} = \frac{\text{Cost minus estimated salvage value}}{\text{Estimated useful life (no. of periods)}}$$

Using the above formula, you can calculate annual amortization on a delivery truck used by a local business this way:

- Cost of the truck = \$5,000
- Estimated useful life = 5 years
- Estimated salvage value after 5 years = \$1,000

From this, the amortization for one year = $\frac{\$5{,}000 - \$1{,}000}{5} = \$800$

At the end of the first year, the net book value of the truck will be:

Cost – Total amortization to date = \$5,000 – \$800 = \$4,200

Under straight-line, annual expense is constant, and book value declines linearly.

Amortization expense for each of the five years will be \$800, reducing the book value by \$800 per year. As shown in Figure 8.6 above, the constant expense produces a linear increase in accumulated amortization and so a linear decline in book value.

Straight-line is made even easier by reducing to a simple rate, if salvage is assumed zero.

A common practice for many enterprises is to assume the salvage value of the asset to be negligible or zero, which then enables amortization to be expressed in terms of percentages instead of years. For example, a company might use straight-line amortization expressed as 20% of historical cost, rather than as a term of five years. In the above example, 20% straight-line would be an annual amortization of \$1,000.

2. Accelerated Amortization

Some assets contribute more in the early years of their useful life than later.

Some assets contribute most of their benefit to the enterprise in the early parts of their lives. For example, a new computer may benefit the company greatly when it is first purchased, but due to quickly changing technology and changing needs as the company grows, this same computer may be relegated to less important tasks within a few years of its purchase, as better computers are acquired. Therefore, even though the computer will continue to benefit the company, most of its economic value has been consumed near the beginning of its life.

Declining balance accelerated amortization is the second most popular.

In Canada the *declining balance* method, also called *diminishing balance*, is not widely used. *Financial Reporting in Canada 2005* says that only two of the 200 companies reported using only declining balance amortization in 2004. A further 45 companies used it in combination with other methods, 37 of these with straight-line.[21] "Capital cost allowance," the form of amortization required to be used for income tax purposes (to come in Section 9.3), is also usually calculated using a declining balance procedure.

The method normally ignores salvage value. Therefore, the information needed is:

Only three things are needed for declining balance: cost, rate, and any prior accumulated amortization.

a. Cost of the asset.
b. Amortization rate: the *percentage of the book value* (cost minus amortization to date) of the asset that is to be amortized in the period.
c. Total amortization recorded since the acquisition of the asset (accumulated amortization).

Note the *essential difference with straight-line*: in declining balance, the rate is not applied to the cost, as it was in straight-line, but rather to the book value. Book value declines over time, and so does the amortization expense using this method, hence the name declining balance.

The formula for declining balance amortization is:

FORMULA

Amortization for one period = (Cost – Accumulated amortization) × Rate
= Remaining book value of the asset × Rate

Doubling the straight-line rate works as an approximation for the declining balance rate.

Let's use the declining balance method to compute amortization for the five-year life of the same truck we had above. We could do some complex algebra to work out the exact amortization rate that will result in the cost being fully depreciated over the asset's life. Instead of doing this, since amortization is an estimate anyway, approximate rates are usually used. For example, the amortization expense for "*double declining balance*" (a particular and very common type of declining balance) uses *double the straight-line rate.* Double declining balance works reasonably well for assets with an expected life in the ten-year range, but not for shorter lives. Canadian capital cost allowance rates used in computing taxable income were originally based on double declining balance estimates.

Since the truck is expected to be useful for only five years, not in the ten-year useful life range, double declining balance is not really suitable (double the straight-line rate would be 40%), so we will use 25% instead to approximate the economic consumption pattern.

- Cost = $5,000
- Amortization to date = $0 (we're at the beginning)
- Amortization rate = 25%

EXHIBIT 8·5

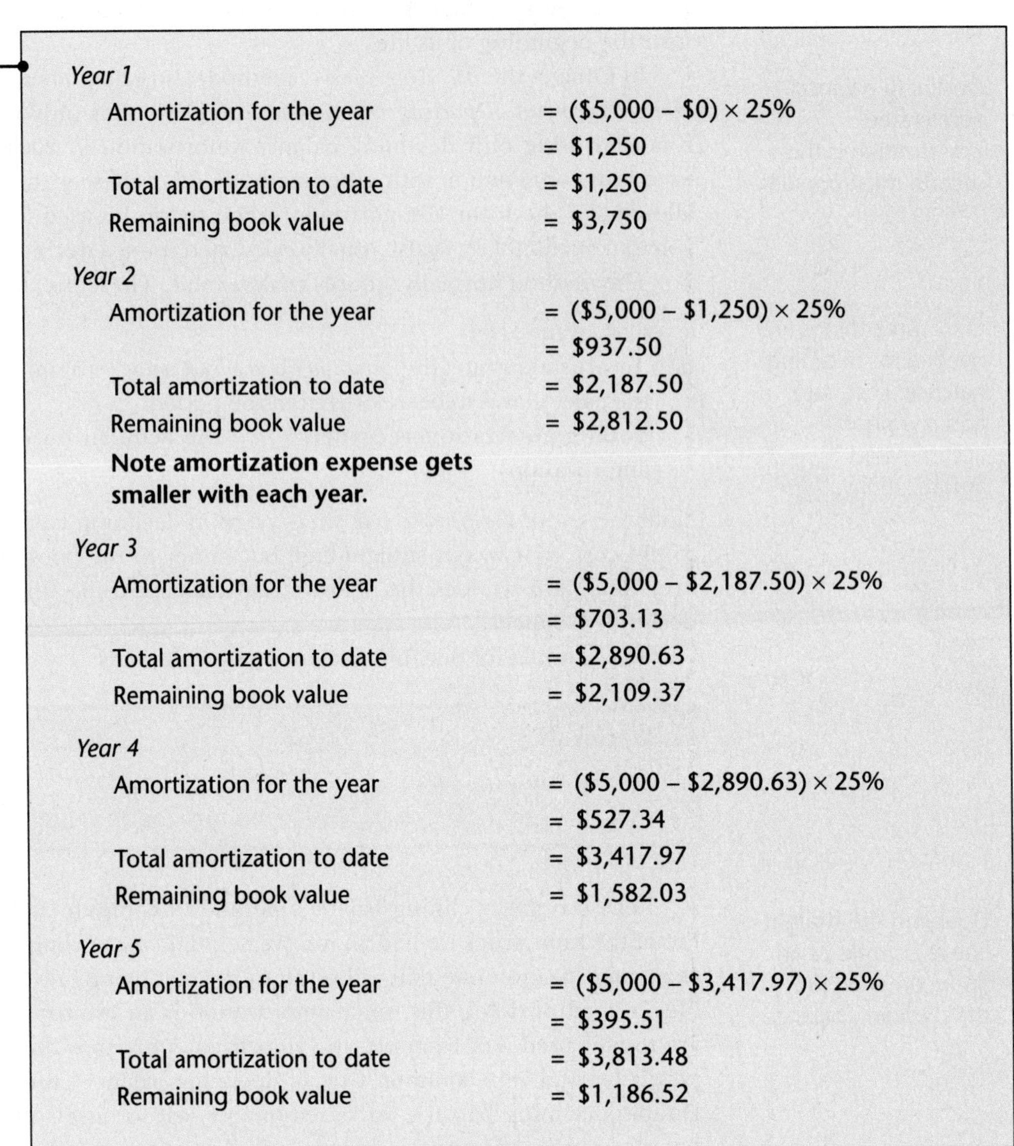

Year 1

Amortization for the year	= (\$5,000 – \$0) × 25%
	= \$1,250
Total amortization to date	= \$1,250
Remaining book value	= \$3,750

Year 2

Amortization for the year	= (\$5,000 – \$1,250) × 25%
	= \$937.50
Total amortization to date	= \$2,187.50
Remaining book value	= \$2,812.50

Note amortization expense gets smaller with each year.

Year 3

Amortization for the year	= (\$5,000 – \$2,187.50) × 25%
	= \$703.13
Total amortization to date	= \$2,890.63
Remaining book value	= \$2,109.37

Year 4

Amortization for the year	= (\$5,000 – \$2,890.63) × 25%
	= \$527.34
Total amortization to date	= \$3,417.97
Remaining book value	= \$1,582.03

Year 5

Amortization for the year	= (\$5,000 – \$3,417.97) × 25%
	= \$395.51
Total amortization to date	= \$3,813.48
Remaining book value	= \$1,186.52

Although in this example the remaining book value of the truck at the end of five years is fairly close to the expected salvage value of the truck, declining balance amortization does not normally take salvage value into account. Consequently, the book value at the end of five years would be the same whether or not the company expected to recover any of the cost of the truck.

Because the annual amortization declines, the book value goes down in a curve.

The second panel of the chart in Figure 8.6 shows the kinds of patterns of amortization expense and book value we calculated for the truck. The expense and book value lines are curves instead of straight lines. Will there be any difference in net income using one method instead of the other? Yes. Will there be any difference in the cash position of the company using declining balance rather than straight-line? No.

In the United States, a method of calculating accelerated amortization called "sum of the years' digits" is often used. This is a method of calculating accelerated amortization more exactly than by declining balance that was common before the advent of calculators and computers. Now sum-of-the-years'-digits amortization is less common. It is rare in Canada (*Financial Reporting in Canada 2005* doesn't even mention it), so in this book it is illustrated only in an endnote.[22]

3. Units-of-Production Amortization and Depletion

Either straight-line or declining balance may be too simple if annual asset usage varies.

The economic consumption of some assets may not necessarily be a function of time, but rather of use. For example, it may make more sense to say that the delivery truck is expected to last so many kilometres rather than so many years. The consumption of natural resources ("wasting assets") is also often accounted for using "depletion," a units-of-production amortization approach, because the value to the enterprise of a stand of timber, or an oil well, is tied to the number of trees remaining to be felled or the amount of oil left to be recovered. If the economic value of the asset is related to the annual usage or the physical removal of an asset, the annual economic contribution will depend on volume of usage or removal and will not necessarily be a regular amount each year, as it is with straight-line and declining balance.

To compute amortization or depletion per unit of usage, the following information is needed:

Needed for units-of-production amortization: cost, salvage, total usage, this year's usage.

a. Cost of the asset.
b. Estimated salvage value.
c. Estimated number of units to be produced during life of asset—the estimated number of board feet of lumber in the timber stand, or the estimated number of kilometres that the delivery truck will travel, or other production measures.
d. The number of units produced in the year for which the amortization is to be calculated.

The formula for computing units-of-production amortization is:

FORMULA

$$\text{Amortization or depletion for one unit of use or production (for example, a kilometre)} = \frac{\text{Cost minus Estimated salvage value}}{\text{Estimated no. of units of use or production during life}}$$

Using the delivery truck as an example one more time, amortization of the truck over its expected useful life might be calculated this way:

- Cost = \$5,000
- Estimated salvage value = \$1,000
- Estimated no. of km to be driven = 200,000

$$\text{Amortization rate} = \frac{\$5,000 - \$1,000}{200,000} = \$0.02 \text{ amortization per km}$$

From this, the annual amortization can be computed:

Year 1
Suppose the truck is driven 20,000 km during the year. The amortization expense for the year will be: \$0.02 × 20,000 = \$400.

Year 2
If the truck is driven 80,000 km during the second year, the amortization expense for the year will be: \$0.02 × 80,000 = \$1,600.

Year 3
Let's say the truck is driven 65,000 km during the year. Then the amortization charge for the year will be: \$0.02 × 65,000 = \$1,300.

Year 4
Let's suppose the truck is driven 50,000 km during the year. We can't just base the amortization expense on the 50,000, however, because this would take the total usage over the 200,000 km used above in setting the rate. The units-of-production method has the problem that the total usage is unlikely to coincide with the original estimate, and so the usage rate (\$0.02 here) is unlikely to be exactly accurate.

This may be harder to get right than it is to get the total useful life right in the straight-line method, but any amortization method is unlikely to be exactly right, as noted earlier. In this case, the fourth year's amortization expense is just the remaining $700 (cost $5,000 minus $1,000 salvage and the previous years' amortizations, $400 + $1,600 + $1,300), which is less than $0.02 × 50,000 km.

Year 5

In the earlier examples, the truck was expected to last five years. If it is still being driven in Year 5, and if salvage value is still expected to be $1,000, there will be no amortization in the fifth year, further evidence that the original 200,000 km estimate was incorrect. This could be fixed by going back and recalculating prior years' amortizations, but in practice the error would likely not be fixed because such errors are normal whenever estimates of the future are used to calculate amortization and other expenses, such as income taxes, warranties, and pensions. Such errors just make any year's amortization expense less accurate than it might theoretically be.

The annual units-of-production amortization varies with usage of the asset.

The bottom panel in Figure 8.6 illustrates units-of-production amortization. It is the only method that can result in the annual amortization expense going up and down from period to period. *Financial Reporting in Canada 2005* says that, in 2004, four of the 200 companies reported using only units-of-production amortization, and eight used it in combination with other methods.[23] CPR is one of these, calculating depreciation on "rail and other track material in the United States based directly on usage," though most of its assets are depreciated straight-line.[24]

Depletion is often subtracted from the asset, not accumulated in a contra account.

Depletion of a wasting asset and units-of-production amortization of a fixed asset are computed in the same manner, but depletion refers to the physical consumption of an asset, rather than just the economic consumption. For the timber stand mentioned earlier, salvage value may be the value of the land after all the timber has been cut. Instead of accumulating depletion in a contra account, the asset itself may be reduced by the amount of the depletion for the period. In this case, the journal entry would debit depletion expense and credit the timber stand asset, rather than crediting accumulated amortization. The asset account would then show the remaining book value at the present time, not the original cost.

4. Decelerated Amortization

If the asset's economic value is expected to decline more slowly in earlier years and more quickly in later years, a form of decelerated amortization (the *opposite* of accelerated amortization) may be used. Under decelerated amortization, amortization expense per period *rises* over the duration of the asset's life. The third panel of the chart in Figure 8.6 illustrates this method. Such an approach is rarely used, because for most assets it does not seem to follow reasonable economic assumptions. Some companies in the real estate industry use it because if the real estate, for example an apartment or office building, is financed by borrowing, the interest expense from the borrowing falls each year as the debt is repaid, and having amortization expense rise leaves the sum of interest and amortization more or less constant. This is thought to match revenue from leasing or renting the property, which is likely to be fairly stable over time. People who do not like this method argue that smoothing reported income should not be a reason for choosing an amortization method, but the arguments for it have persuaded some companies, so it does exist even though it is not "generally accepted" for most companies. *Financial Reporting in Canada 2005* indicates that only four companies in 2004 reported using a form of decelerated amortization, called the "sinking fund" method, and seven more used it in combination with straight-line amortization for other assets.[25] The calculations for this method are complex and so will not be illustrated here.

Amortization Effects

The amortization policy choice's main effect is on income.

What differences does the choice of amortization method make to the financial statements? This accounting policy choice has its main effect on income. Use of an accelerated method like declining balance increases amortization in the early years of assets' lives, relative to the amortization produced by straight-line amortization. Therefore, income will be lower in the early years if accelerated amortization is used, and higher in the later years when the accelerated amortization falls below straight-line.

A numerical example shows this. Suppose we have a machine with a cost of $10,000 and an expected useful life of 10 years with $1,000 expected salvage value. Straight-line amortization would be $900 per year (10% of ($10,000 – $1,000)). Declining balance amortization, using the double declining balance (DDB) approximation, would be 20% of book value each year (salvage ignored). The table in Exhibit 8.6 results.

Example Comparison of Straight-line and Accelerated Amortization

	10% Straight-line Amortization		20% DDB Amortization	
Year	**Beginning Book Value**	**Amortization Expense**	**Beginning Book Value**	**Amortization Expense**
1	$10,000	$ 900	$10,000	$2,000
2	9,100	900	8,000	1,600
3	8,200	900	6,400	1,280
4	7,300	900	5,120	1,024
5	6,400	900	4,096	819
6	5,500	900	3,277	655
7	4,600	900	2,622	524
8	3,700	900	2,098	420
9	2,800	900	1,678	336
10	1,900	900	1,342	268
11	1,000		1,074	
Ten-year totals		$9,000		$8,926

Using the above example and the charts we saw earlier in Figure 8.6, straight-line and accelerated amortization may be compared, as shown in Figure 8.7.

FIGURE 8.7

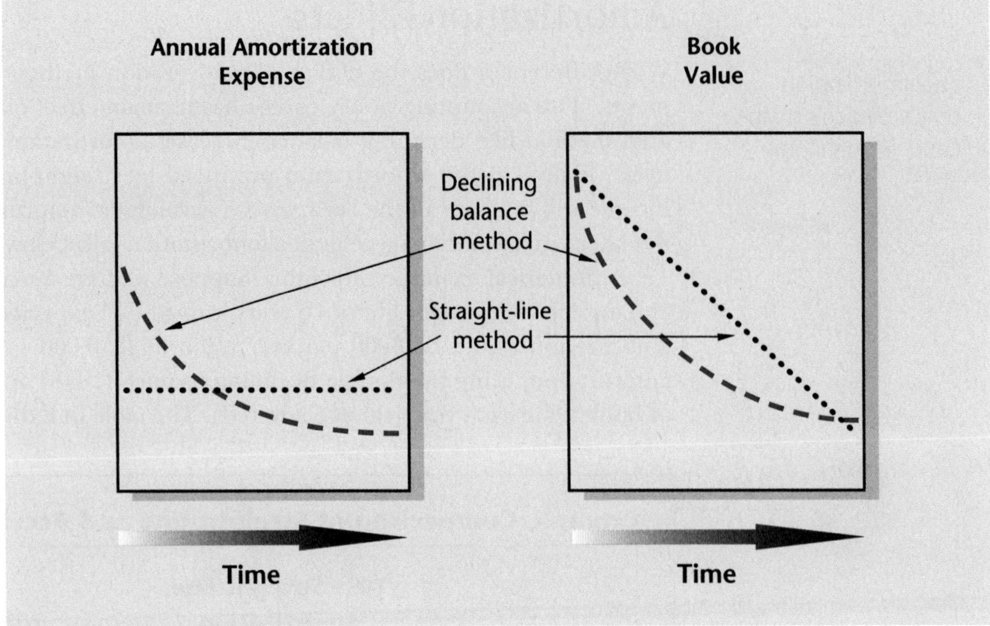

The specific effects depend on the details of each case, but the example shows the comparative pattern. Both methods produce about the same amortization over 10 years ($9,000 versus $8,926) and about the same book value at the end of that time ($1,000 versus $1,074), but their patterns are different. The accelerated amortization has a higher expense (and therefore a lower income) for the first four years, and a lower expense (and therefore a higher income) for the last six years. Compared to straight-line, accelerated amortization results in the book value falling more steeply in the early years and less steeply in the later years.

The same cost is amortized, so the methods end up at the same place by different routes, *timing* the expense differently.

No general comparison with units-of-production amortization can be made, because by design it varies with production or usage levels. But like the other two methods, it does have to amortize the same amount over time (except that declining balance ignores salvage), so the various methods all get to the same fully amortized point eventually. The choice of amortization method is therefore essentially a choice about the *timing* of the amortization expense:

- mostly in earlier years (accelerated),
- even over the years (straight-line), or
- variable (units-of-production).

Because income (via amortization expense) and noncurrent assets (book value) are affected, the choice of amortization policy does affect the ratios of income to assets and equity, which, as we will see in Chapter 10, are used to judge the company's income performance relative to its size.

HOW'S YOUR UNDERSTANDING?

Here are two questions you should be able to answer based on what you have just read. If you can't answer them, it would be best to reread the material.

1. Explain to the president of Cold Lake Manufacturing Inc., which opened for business at the beginning of this year, what amortization expense is supposed to accomplish and the criteria you would recommend the company use in choosing the most appropriate method.
2. Cold Lake management is trying to decide on its accounting policy for amortization. A manager did a rough calculation and determined that if the company used each method properly, the results for the present year would be: straight-line amortization, $238,400 expense; accelerated amortization, $389,600 expense; units-of-production, $189,200 expense. What would be the following effects if the company chose either of the other two in comparison to straight-line: (1) dollar effect on income before income tax for the present year; (2) dollar effect on cash flow for the present year; (3) dollar effect on current income tax payable for the present year; and (4) directional effect on income in future years?

Accelerated compared to straight-line: (1) income before tax reduced by $151,200; (2), (3) no effects on cash flow or income tax payable; (4) will eventually show increased income as the accelerated expense declines below the straight-line.

Units-of-production compared to straight-line: (1) income before tax increased by $49,200; (2), (3) no effects on cash flow or income tax payable; (4) will eventually show lower income because it and straight-line will amortize the same book value and it has amortized less this year so has some catching up to do.

8.13 Demonstration Problem: Amortization Methods

Asimov Petroleum Inc. has a refinery that cost $30,800,000 three years ago. The refinery has an expected useful life of 30 years and is expected to be worth $2,000,000 at the end of that life. The refinery is located near an oilfield, which is thought to have enough oil to allow the refinery to produce 20,000,000 barrels of refined product over the 30 years. Over the last three years, 1,900,000 barrels were produced, and in the fourth year, production of 900,000 is expected. Asimov has received an offer to buy the refinery at the end of the fourth year for $25,000,000.

Calculate the gain or loss on disposal that would result if the refinery were sold at the end of the fourth year, using (a) straight-line, (b) double declining balance and (c) units-of-production amortization for the refinery. Comment on what the answers indicate about the amortization methods and the meaning of the gains or losses.

(a) Straight-line basis
Annual amortization = ($30,800,000 – $2,000,000) / 30 = $960,000.
Amortization to end of fourth year will be $3,840,000 ($960,000 × 4).
Book value at that point will be $30,800,000 – $3,840,000 = $26,960,000.
Gain/loss on disposal will be $25,000,000 – $26,960,000 = $1,960,000 loss.

(b) Double declining balance basis
Rate is twice the straight-line rate. Twice 1/30 = 1/15.
Amortization for first year = $30,800,000 × 1/15 = $2,053,333.
Book value end of first year = $30,800,000 – $2,053,333 = $28,746,667.
Amortization for second year = $28,746,667 × 1/15 = $1,916,444.
Book value end of second year = $28,746,667 – $1,916,444 = $26,830,223.
Amortization for third year = $26,830,223 × 1/15 = $1,788,682.
Book value end of third year = $26,830,223 – $1,788,682 = $25,041,541.
Amortization for fourth year = $25,041,541 × 1/15 = $1,669,436.
Book value end of fourth year = $25,041,541 – $1,669,436 = $23,372,105.
Gain/loss on disposal will be $25,000,000 – $23,372,105 = $1,627,895 gain.

(c) Units-of-production basis
Amortization rate = (\$30,800,000 – \$2,000,000) / 20,000,000 barrels
= \$1.44 per barrel.
Amortization to end of fourth year = (1,900,000 + 900,000) × \$1.44 = \$4,032,000.
Book value end of fourth year = \$30,800,000 – \$4,032,000 = \$26,768,000.
Gain/loss on disposal will be \$25,000,000 – \$26,768,000 = \$1,768,000 loss.

Comments on the answers

The straight-line and units-of-production methods produce similar results, because the refinery is being used fairly close to its average production level of 666,667 barrels a year (20,000,000 barrels over 30 years). Double declining balance results in a much higher amortization in the early years than the other two methods, which would be suitable if the refinery was more valuable in its early years. There may be other indications of this early higher value, but the rate of production doesn't indicate that. Double declining balance probably is weighted too much to early years to be a reasonable match with the economic value of the refinery.

The mismatch can be seen in the differences in gains/losses on disposal were the offer accepted. Both straight-line and units-of-production show a loss approaching \$2 million, whereas double declining balance shows a gain approaching \$2 million. Because double declining balance resulted in high amortization expenses in the early years, the gain on sale is mainly a correction of the over-amortization. None of the three methods necessarily results in an economically valid gain or loss figure, because the gain or loss is the difference between two largely non-comparable amounts: the book value (based on original cost and a 30-year-horizon amortization method) and the current market value of the refinery (based on current market conditions, availability of interested buyers, cost to them of financing the deal, etc.). Gains or losses on sale are best considered as a mixture of two things: real gains or losses, and amortization adjustments. For the latter, a large gain or loss may indicate that the amortization method was poorly chosen.

HOW'S YOUR UNDERSTANDING?

Here are two questions you should be able to answer based on what you have just read. If you can't answer them, it would be best to reread the material.

1. Suppose Azimov Petroleum used double declining balance amortization for the refinery, and the president decided not to sell the refinery. Should the president be criticized for turning down a gain on sale of nearly \$2 million?

Not exactly. The gain is a result of the amortization choice, so the president might instead be criticized for using an inappropriately rapid amortization method. But substantive criticism should be based on the economics of the proposed deal, such as the price offered, not on historical amortization adjustments.

2. Suppose the company's geologist reported that the oilfield had more oil than had been thought: enough to produce 30,000,000 barrels of refined product. Engineers reported that the refinery could handle the increased production, and the marketing people said that with more effort, the increased production could be sold. What would this good news do to the calculation of refinery amortization under the three methods used above?

The news would have no effect on the first two methods. The cost to be amortized is still the same. The refinery's expected useful life is stated in years, so the calculations for straight-line and double declining balance are unaffected. For units-of-production, the per-barrel rate has to be revised, but as a lower rate will be applied to a higher production quantity, the annual amortization might not change much. For units-of-production, there would be a question of whether to recalculate the amortization for the first years, or leave those years alone and just redo it for the remaining years, starting with book value at the time the decision to increase production is made.

8.14 Other Assets, Intangibles, and Capital Leases

Most of the discussion of noncurrent assets so far has involved "fixed" assets such as land, buildings, and equipment. There are other noncurrent assets on many companies' balance sheets, however:

- "Deferred charges" and other kinds of miscellaneous noncurrent assets.
- "Intangible" assets, which have economic value but lack the same "tangible" physical existence that the fixed assets have.
- Some leased land, buildings, and equipment, which although not owned appear on the balance sheet anyway.

Deferred Charges

"Other assets" may include noncurrent prepaid expenses and various other noncurrent items.

Section 6.10 examined prepaid and accrued expenses. Prepaid expenses are expenses for future periods paid already but kept on the balance sheet as assets, to be deducted from future revenue. Most of these are short-term, and thus are included in current assets. But sometimes payments made in the current or past years are thought to provide benefit for years into the future. Such noncurrent assets may be specifically identified, for example "organization costs" or "deferred financing costs," or may be just included in a general noncurrent asset called something like "*deferred charges*" or "*other assets.*" Sometimes tax credits not expected to be obtained for some time and other kinds of long-term receivables are included.

If these are significant, they should be explained in the notes to the financial statements. CPR had $1018.3 million of these at the end of 2004, and disclosed in a note that these included $838.3 million of prepaid pension costs (noncurrent because they apply to retirement years in the future); the remaining $180.0 million is just called "other." *Financial Reporting in Canada 2005* says that 114 of the 200 companies surveyed disclosed having deferred charges, with 94 of these disclosing the main types as CPR did.[26]

Accounting standards keep changing. Until the end of 2001, companies could record losses on foreign exchange as deferred charges and then amortize them over a reasonable period. A typical source of such losses is borrowing in foreign currencies: if the Canadian dollar declines relative to such foreign currencies, then the company suffers a loss—this loss could be amortized over the period of the related debt. Starting January 1, 2002, such losses should be included with expenses as they occur, not deferred to the future. Accounting for all this is very complex, depending on various sophisticated methods for avoiding such losses in the first place, such as hedging by buying foreign exchange futures so that when repayment is due, the company has access to the foreign currency at protected rates.

Because these deferred charges are significant to CPR's balance sheet, and the accounting standards change will affect its future income statements, the company discussed the situation at some length in a financial statement note headed "changes in accounting policy." (Most significant accounting policy changes come from standards changes rather than from a real choice by companies.) CPR announced that the unamortized deferred asset would be written off to retained earnings in early 2002, and that when preparing its 2002 statements, the comparative income for 2001 would be restated lower than already reported for 2001. Specifically, the write-off to retained earnings would be $165 million (which is the $192 million mentioned above, net of income tax), and the retroactive reduction in 2001 net income would be $27 million, also net of tax.[27] This retroactive change in policy is an example of why the comparative figures for past years are often not the same as the figures reported in those years.

Intangible Assets

Intangible noncurrent assets include franchises, licences, patents, goodwill, and more.

Intangible assets are long-term assets that do not have a visible physical existence, as do land, buildings, or equipment. Intangible assets include the following:

- Patents, copyrights, trademarks, and other such legal property.
- Franchises, distributorships, and other such rights to sell someone else's products in a certain geographical area (McDonald's Restaurants, Arthur Murray Dance Studios, and Canadian Tire are examples in which the local operator has paid for the right to use the name and sell the products).
- Product development expenditures (e.g., product-testing costs or computer software development costs) that are capitalized so they can be expensed at the time they earn revenue in the future, thus being noncurrent prepaid expenses, recorded to satisfy the matching principle.
- Purchased *goodwill* (arising when more is paid for a group of assets, such as a whole business, than the assets seem to be worth individually). Goodwill arises mainly when one company purchases another and the two are combined into a corporate group with consolidated financial statements. Consolidation is in Section 9.7, but the nature of the resulting goodwill is reviewed later in this section.

According to *Financial Accounting in Canada 2005,* 130 of the surveyed companies disclosed goodwill on the balance sheet and 98 reported intangible assets other than goodwill, most commonly broadcast rights, licences, and patents.[28]

What Are Intangible Assets Worth?

Intangibles' economic value and therefore status as assets is often doubtful.

Because such assets *are* intangible, their existence and value may be doubtful. Generally, the more clearly identifiable and documented the assets are (especially via external evidence such as contracts and legal documents), the less difficulty they pose. However, even for clearly owned assets such as patents and franchises, there may be considerable doubt about their future economic value. For example, what is a Wendy's franchise worth? It depends on ever-changing consumer tastes, on whether a competitor does or doesn't open across the street, and on many other business and economic factors.

Capitalizing internal development expenditures is controversial and largely not allowed.

For assets lacking clear external documentation, such as product development expenditures, there is often a real question as to whether they belong on the balance sheet at all. Capitalizing expenditures on such items may appear to create better matching and is usually seen to be proper by those making such expenditures, but this depends on whether they will ever return future value. Will the great new product sell? Will it produce revenues greater than costs? If the expenditure is capitalized, when would amortization of the asset begin and over what period? Answering such questions requires difficult judgments, and many people have concluded that such assets should not appear; these people favour conservatism in accounting, are afraid of manipulation, or just feel that recognizing such assets is not fair or appropriate. Expenditures on such things would therefore be expensed immediately and not capitalized. For these sorts of reasons, accounting standards require that general research and development expenditures (*R&D*) be expensed as they are made, *not* capitalized as intangible assets.

Now you see them, now you don't? In the late years of the last century, there was great pressure on accounting to include more intangible assets, to represent better the circumstances of high-tech and other "new economy" companies. Managers who wished to present a positive image of their companies could include as assets "human capital," innovative production processes, various kinds of business networking arrangements, e-commerce techniques, and many other things that seem clearly to have economic value. In early 2000, the market capitalization (total number of shares times the current share price) of software company Oracle exceeded the sum of the market capitalizations of all the "big three" automakers, and Yahoo!'s exceeded that of Procter & Gamble,[29] yet Oracle's and Yahoo!'s balance sheets didn't reveal the apparent intangible assets, business smarts, excellent people, or whatever made them so popular. There were calls for major revisions of financial accounting to represent all this properly, to dump the archaic historical costs and convince the stubborn accountants to loosen up.

Then the markets crashed, especially the high-tech sector! Former high-flyers saw their share prices fall to nearly zero, and various scandals about overly optimistic accounting came up regularly, as we have seen frequently already in this book. The clamour for getting all this intangible stuff onto the balance sheet died away. It may return when the stock markets recover, but for now, there is a newly sober interest in conservative accounting, focusing on assets that can be demonstrated to have value in the traditional ways.

Accounting for research and development expenditures is part of the controversy. A recent Canadian study indicates that investors and financial analysts do want some disclosure about R&D and that in response to that, companies that do R&D are more likely to disclose information about it when they are also listed in U.S. stock exchanges, are seeking capital, or are reported on by several analysts.[30] GAAP's conservative expensing and not capitalizing R&D is most strongly required in the U.S. There is some research evidence that stock market prices behave as if this is a mismatching of revenues and expenses and therefore produces a misspecification of income.[31] However, in spite of the research to date, no movement toward capitalizing is likely any time soon: standard-setters and auditors mistrust estimates of the value of internally generated intangibles, especially in the light of recent stock market troubles.

Purchased Goodwill

Goodwill is total price minus values of assets and liabilities, for whatever reason.

Goodwill is a special case, though no less controversial. Goodwill means that the "whole" of a business purchased is worth more than the sum of the "parts" as represented by the individual assets and liabilities. More was paid for the business than you'd expect from knowing the values of assets and liabilities. The price of a business is set in the market place, and there is no reason it should tie to the accounting assets and liabilities, but still the existence of a gap between the whole and the sum of the parts raises the question of just why the gap exists. Is it because of loyal customers, good managers, good locations, reduced competition, synergy with the purchasing company, or any of many other reasons? Each of these reasons might indicate a different meaning for the goodwill asset.

From an accounting point of view, goodwill arises, in a way, because of the necessity to keep the accounts in balance. Here is an example: Great Inc. buys all the business assets of Small Ltd. for $800,000 cash. The best estimate of the fair market values of those assets are: receivables, $60,000; inventories, $110,000; land, $100,000; building, $260,000; equipment, $130,000; total, $660,000. No liabilities are assumed by Great.

Great would record the purchase as follows:

DR Accounts receivable	60,000	
DR Inventories	110,000	
DR Land	100,000	
DR Buildings	260,000	
DR Equipment	130,000	
CR Cash		800,000

No problem. Except that the entry doesn't balance! So a new account called Goodwill is created and debited with $140,000, which is the $800,000, cost of the whole, minus $660,000, the sum of the fair values of the parts. This is shown in Figure 8.8.

FIGURE 8.8

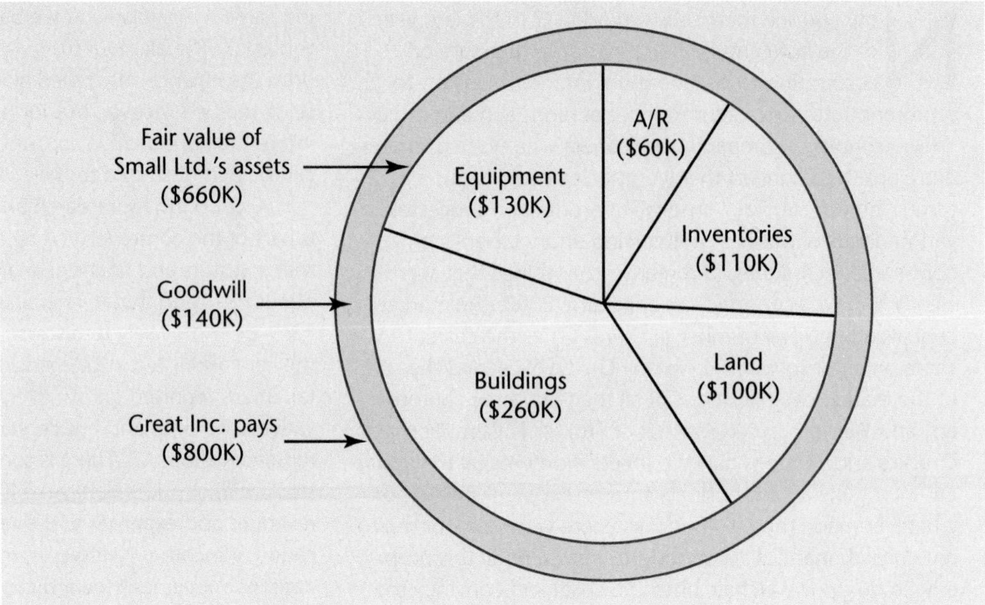

We can calculate purchased goodwill more easily than we can evaluate it.

This Goodwill account keeps the books in balance, but its value and meaning are unclear. If goodwill represents unrecorded assets, what are they? If it represents a good location, good managers, or synergy with the operations of Great, what are these things really worth? How much future value do they have? How long will this value last? Does goodwill, at least sometimes, indicate that the purchaser made a bad deal and just paid too much? That has been the likely reason for some of the more spectacularly large recent goodwill write-offs. (By the way, in the reverse situation, if the cost of the whole is *less* than the sum of the parts, no "badwill" is recorded. It would be a credit, so where would it go? It's not owed to anyone, and can't be called revenue according to any normal criteria. Instead, the amounts assigned to the parts are reduced so that they add up to the cost of the whole.)

Cost of Intangibles

The purchase cost of intangible assets is determined in the same way as for tangible assets.

Goodwill's cost is determined as illustrated above. For other intangible assets, cost is determined in the same way as that of any other asset, set out in Section 8.4: purchase cost plus other expenditures made prior to putting the asset into service (getting economic benefits from it).

There may be substantial ambiguity about the cost of internally developed assets, such as product development expenditures, because it may be difficult to determine exactly what was spent to develop the asset, separately from normal expenses. This is the same problem we saw in Section 8.4 for determining the cost of assets in general. Adding this to the general uncertainty about the value of intangible assets means that many companies decline to recognize (capitalize) such assets. Internally developed goodwill is *never* capitalized (for example, expenditures on office parties that create happy employees are expensed, not capitalized).

Amortization of Intangibles

Intangible assets are amortized over their useful lives, just like fixed assets. Determining legal useful life may be fairly straightforward for assets supported by contracts or other documents (for example, contracts such as franchises normally have a specified term, and patents are good for a specific number of years), but whether this is also the economic useful life is harder to say. For some assets, such as incorporation costs, useful life is anyone's guess. This difficulty leads many companies to just expense such costs at the outset.

Intangible assets are amortized to income over estimated useful life, using straight-line.

Because of all this ambiguity, intangibles are amortized simply, using the straight-line basis over the estimated useful life, and are usually estimated reasonably conservatively. The asset account itself is usually credited with the amortization, rather than bothering with a contra account for accumulated amortization, because such an asset is more like a prepaid expense (in which the book value represents future expense deductions) than like a tangible asset whose original cost may be usefully kept separate for control reasons.

Goodwill is a particular problem. Since it is often unclear just what it is, it is a challenge to figure out a way to amortize it. Until recently, Canadian standards specified a maximum useful life of 40 years for goodwill, surely an optimistic estimate! There was pressure to reduce this to 20 years or even less. But then, in conjunction with changes in accounting for business combinations generally, a rather different approach was taken. Effective in 2002, goodwill is not to be "amortized" at all: instead, it is to be tested each year to see if its value has become impaired. If there has been an impairment, it has to be written down to the lower value, never to be written back up. Testing impairment of an asset that is essentially unidentifiable is a challenge in itself! The recommended approach is to look at the apparent market value or fair value of the investment that produced the goodwill: if the cost to make the investment would be much less now than it was originally, then there has been an impairment and a goodwill write-down is indicated. This approach lies behind recent huge write-downs of investments in high-tech companies.

Leases

Capital Leases

Capital leases are an example of accrual accounting's inclusion of economic phenomena.

Some leased assets are included on the balance sheet because the company is deemed to have enough of the rights and obligations of ownership, the assets are significant to the company's economic performance, and leaving them off the balance sheet is thought to misrepresent the company's economic position. This is an example of accrual accounting's moving well beyond just recording transactions: there is no *legal* exchange of leased assets, but it is thought that there has been an *economic* exchange of them. Financial accounting treats *capital lease* assets essentially as if there were owned fixed assets instead of leased assets.

A capital lease's initial asset and liability amounts both equal the present value of future payments.

Such capital leases are included on the balance sheet (often just mixed in with owned fixed assets) as follows:

- The "cost" is the *present value* of the future lease payments, using an appropriate interest rate usually deduced from the lease agreement to remove the future interest from the total payments and calculate the present value. (See Section 10.7 or the discussion of present value under Value in Use in Section 8.2, or this chapter's endnote 2: the present value is the future cash flows but with any future interest removed.)
- At the same time, the present value of those payments is recorded as a liability.
- So the journal entry to put capital leases on the balance sheet is:

DR Capital lease asset	XXXX	
CR Capital lease obligations liability		XXXX

Once in the accounts, capital leases are treated just as tangible assets and debts are.

- After that:
  - The leased asset is amortized, just as the owned assets are, following a policy that is consistent with that used for any similar owned assets but also taking into account the terms of the lease.
  - The liability is reduced as payments are made on the lease. Each payment is divided into deduced principal and interest portions, so that only the principal portion is deducted from the liability and the rest is considered interest expense. This maintains the liability at the present value of the remaining lease payments.
  - The expenses for using the leased asset, therefore, are amortization and interest. Such amounts are usually combined with other amortization and interest expenses because the intent is to represent the economic situation fairly.

The payments made on a capital lease are allocated

Part goes to reducing the lease liability
Part goes to interest expense

DR Lease liability	XX	
DR Interest expense	XX	
CR Cash		XX

Operating Leases

Operating leases are not capitalized, so result only in rent expense, not assets or liabilities.

If the lease does *not* result in an economic equivalence of ownership (for example, if it is really a rental, where the owner continues to pay property tax, do the repairs and maintenance, and generally control the asset), the lease is termed an "*operating lease*." For such leases, there is no asset or lease obligation liability recognized, and the lease payments are just expensed as rent expense.

For an operating lease, there is no allocation of the payments made

DR Rent expense	XX	
CR Cash		XX

Comparison of Capital and Operating Leases

Figure 8.9 compares the accounting for capital and operating leases. For both, the cash flow over the lease term is the same; the difference is in the *timing* of the various expenses and in the *valuation* of the balance sheet.

FIGURE 8.9

	Capital Lease	Operating Lease
Balance sheet	Lease asset as part of fixed assets Accumulated amortization on leased asset Lease liability as part of debts	Nothing on balance sheet
Income statement	Amortization expense on the leased asset Interest on the lease liability	Rent expense

Over the life of the lease, the amortization and interest expense add up to the same total as the rent expense: they both equal the lease payments

Disclosure

Various particulars of significant capital leases are usually disclosed in the notes to the financial statements, so that the readers of the statements may judge the effects of such capitalization. Such separate disclosure is usual for the lease obligations liability, the terms of the lease, and related amortization and interest expenses. *Financial Accounting in Canada 2005* reports that in 2004, 72 of the surveyed companies disclosed that they had capital lease assets (down from 85 in 2000) but 16 of those only disclosed the existence of such assets without reporting the amount included in the assets. One hopes that the decrease in the number of companies reporting capital leases is a result of changing financing arrangements and not of lower compliance with disclosure requirements.[32]

If the operating lease is significant to the company, some of its particulars may be disclosed in the notes to the financial statements. *Financial Reporting in Canada 2005* indicates that in 2004, 158 of the 200 companies disclosed that they had operating leases: 99 of these had operating leases only, and 59 of the 72 disclosing they had capital leases also said they had operating leases.[33]

The *CICA Handbook* recommends that the next five years' lease payments be disclosed, regardless of lease type. Of the 158 disclosing operating leases, 153 specified the lease payments for each of the next five years. Of the 72 disclosing capital lease obligations, 42 specified the payments for each of the next five years, a smaller proportion (perhaps they felt having a lease liability recorded on the balance sheet was enough disclosure).[34] It is clear from all this that capital and operating leases are significant parts of the ways companies assemble economic assets for their use.

This chapter has focused on companies' accounting policy choices for assets. Research shows that stock market prices correlate with accounting income as measured by accrual accounting, and that extends to the results of accounting policy choices that affect income, and perhaps even potential choices such as for R&D. Policy choices that have direct cash consequences (such as through higher or lower future tax assessments) are more likely to prompt a stock market response than are choices without direct cash consequences. Inventory accounting choices (usually FIFO versus LIFO, studied with U.S. companies) do make a difference to stock prices, probably due to the income tax savings the LIFO choice provides in the United States. Amortization policy choices have little effect on stock prices, probably because there is no tax or cash flow effect. Indirect cash consequences may also exist and provoke a response. For example, if an accounting policy, such as to capitalize leases, changes the debt-equity ratio, the company's risk might appear different enough to affect interest rates on its debts and so change future interest payments.

HOW'S YOUR UNDERSTANDING?

Here are two questions you should be able to answer based on what you have just read. If you can't answer them, it would be best to reread the material.

1. What are the main similarities and differences between tangible fixed assets and (a) intangible assets and (b) capital leases?
2. A company discloses the following in its financial statements and notes: licences and patents, goodwill, capital leases, and operating leases. Specify the expense accounts you would expect to exist, related to these items.

8.15 Terms to Be Sure You Understand

Here is this chapter's list of terms introduced or emphasized. Make sure you know what they mean *in accounting*, and if any are unclear to you, check the chapter again or refer to the glossary of terms at the back of the book.

Accelerated amortization
Accounting policies
Accounting policy choices
Accounts receivable
Acquisition cost
Amortization
Amortization expense
Amortize(d)
Articulation
Asset valuation
Assumed cost flow
Available cost
AVGE
Balance sheet valuation
Betterment
Capitalize(d)
Capital lease(s)
Cash
COGS
Conservatism
Cost
Cost allocation
Cost of goods sold expense
Current value
Decelerated amortization
Declining balance
Deferred charges
Depletion
Depreciation
Diminishing balance
Double declining balance
Fair value
FIFO
Financial assets
First-in, first-out
Fixed assets
GAAP
Gains
Going concern
Goodwill
Historical cost
Impaired assets
Income measurement
Input market value
Intangible assets
Inventory
Inventory valuation
Last-in, first-out
LIFO
Liquidation value
Losses
Lower of cost or market
Marketable securities
Market value
Matching
Moving weighted average
Net present value
Net realizable value
Notes receivable
Operating lease
Other assets
Output market value
Overhead costs
Present value
Price-level-adjusted historical cost
R&D
Reclassified account
Replacement cost
Retail inventory control method
Specific identification
Straight-line amortization
Tangible assets
Temporary investments
Trade receivables
Units-of-production amortization
Value in use
Write-offs

INSTALLMENT 8

DATA FOR INSTALLMENT 8

In Installment 6, the February 28, 2007, adjusted trial balance was produced. Before preparing financial statements, Mavis and Tomas went through the accounts and decided on the accounting policies that should be used in the statements. To help you think about what policies might be needed, here again is the trial balance from Installment 7.

Cash	6,418	Revenue	(229,387)
Accounts receivable	15,671	Cost of goods sold expense	138,767
Allowance for doubtful accounts	(1,542)	Bad debts expense	2,436
Inventory	33,612	Salary—Mavis	0
Prepaid insurance	525	Salary—Tomas	0
Automobile	10,000	Salary—other	0
Accumulated amortization—auto	(2,000)	Salaries expense	67,480
Leasehold improvements	63,964	Travel expense	9,477
Accumulated amortization—leasehold	(12,792)	Phone expense	4,014
Equipment and furniture	32,390	Rent expense	24,000
Accumulated amortization—equipment	(2,364)	Utilities expense	3,585
Computer	14,900	Office and general expense	5,688
Accumulated amortization—computer	(2,980)	Interest expense	6,469
Software	4,800	Inventory shortage expense	441
Accumulated amortization—software	(960)	Amortization expense—auto	2,000
Incorporation cost	1,100	Amortization expense—leasehold	12,792
Bank loan	(47,500)	Amortization expense—equipment	2,364
Accounts payable	(35,323)	Amortization expense—computer	2,980
Customer deposits liability	(500)	Amortization expense—software	960
Sales taxes due	(1,843)		0
Deductions payable	(2,284)		
Salaries payable	(2,358)		
Loan payable	0		
Share capital	(125,000)		

RESULTS FOR INSTALLMENT 8

Here are the resulting accounting policies for Mato Inc. Some policies relate to liabilities, some details of which are covered in Chapter 9. They are included here for completeness and so that the full financial statements may be presented in Installment 9.

- Cash and equivalents were defined to be cash only. The demand bank loan was to be treated as financing (as it was in the six-month statements in Installment 4).
- The allowance for doubtful accounts would not be disclosed in the balance sheet or notes.
- Inventory would be valued at the lower of FIFO cost or net realizable value.
- The title "Prepaid expense" would be used to group together prepaid insurance and any other prepaid expenses that might arise in the future.
- The automobile, equipment, furniture, and computer would be shown in one account called "Equipment," valued at cost (total $57,290 at the end of February).
- Accumulated amortization would be shown for those three accounts together (total $7,344 at the end of February).
- The leasehold improvements and software would be shown at net book value (cost minus accumulated amortization), with neither cost nor accumulated amortization disclosed.

- Mavis and Tomas were not too sure what to do with the incorporation cost. They decided to leave the account on the balance sheet as a noncurrent asset and not to amortize it because they could see no relationship between it and the company's 2007 revenue and so thought it did not belong as an expense.
- Accounts payable, sales taxes due, deductions payable, and salaries payable would be aggregated on the balance sheet under the title "Payables" (total $41,808 at February 28).
- The customer deposits account would be titled "Deferred revenue" and would include any such revenue deferrals that arose in the future.
- Share capital details would be described in a note, not on the face of the balance sheet.
- Revenue would be recognized on a critical event basis, that event being delivery of goods to customers. Mavis and Tomas reviewed the revenue cut-off and decided that this basis had been properly used in 2007. They also decided that this basis was what readers of the financial statements would expect and so it did not have to be disclosed.
- Mavis and Tomas also reviewed the expenses, especially cost of goods sold, to ensure that the expenses cut-off had produced a proper matching of expenses to revenue.
- It was decided to disclose cost of goods sold and all the other expenses separately, so that the reader could get a full picture of the company's operations.
- Amortization expense would be a slight exception to the above, because instead of disclosing each kind of amortization separately, just a single total amortization expense would be disclosed ($21,096).
- Policy for calculating amortization expense would be straight-line, with the rates Tomas had used: car, leasehold improvements, computer and software, 20% of cost per year; equipment and furniture, 10% of cost per year.

The resulting financial statements are presented in Installment 9.

8.17 Homework and Discussion to Develop Understanding

The problems roughly follow the outline of the chapter. Three main categories of questions are presented.

- Asterisked problems (*) have an informal solution provided in the Student Solutions Manual.
- EXTENDED TIME problems involve a thorough examination of the material and may take longer to complete.
- CHALLENGING problems are more difficult.

For further explanation, please refer to Section 1.15.

Balance Sheet Valuation • Sections 8.2 and 8.3

*** PROBLEM 8.1** Consider asset valuation methods

Historical cost is the usual method of valuing assets on the balance sheet, following from the transactional basis of financial accounting. Identify the other valuation methods that have been used or proposed and indicate reasons for and against their use as alternatives to historical cost.

PROBLEM 8.2 Strengths and weaknesses of historical cost accounting

State three significant strengths and three significant weaknesses of historical cost accounting.

PROBLEM 8.3 Answer questions about asset valuation

1. What are some reasons that valuation methods other than historical cost have not replaced it in general use?
2. Greystone Inc.'s president is considering revaluing the company's land on its balance sheet to reflect current real estate market values that are much lower than the cost of the land. What might such a revaluation do to the company's assets, owners' equity, and net income?

*** PROBLEM 8.4** Is asset accounting inconsistent, and does that matter?

A financial analyst said that GAAP for assets are inconsistent, with some assets valued at the lower of cost or market, some at cost minus accumulated amortization, and some just at cost. Explain why the same valuation basis is not used for all assets, and comment on whether or not the apparent inconsistency harms the usefulness of financial statements.

PROBLEM 8.5 Effects of asset accounting change to market from cost

Beauport Inc. owns several parcels of land in the Montreal area. The area has been subject to wide swings in real estate values, and Beauport's president is doubtful that the historical cost basis is appropriate for accounting for the company's land and buildings. Give short but careful answers to the following questions asked by the president:

1. If we changed to market values for the real estate instead of cost, would that make our balance sheet look better or worse?
2. Similarly for income, would using market value instead of cost make us look more profitable or less?
3. Does it matter what we do, as long as we disclose both cost and market value somewhere in our financial statements?

PROBLEM 8.6 Questions on accounting values and income

Pull together your knowledge of how accounting numbers are derived and answer each of the following briefly:

1. Explain why balance sheet valuation and income measurement are linked.
2. Briefly discuss two of the limitations of historical cost balance sheet valuation.
3. During times of rising prices, will the following tend to be overstated or understated? Why?
   a. Assets
   b. Net income
   c. Return on equity (This is just net income divided by equity, so think about what might happen to the numerator and the denominator.)

CHALLENGING

PROBLEM 8.7 Identify possible asset valuation methods

Igor Ice Inc. (III) has recently agreed to purchase the local arena at a price of $2,000,000. The realtor had listed the property at $2,300,000, but Tom Igor, III's president, managed to talk the present owner, Melted Water Corp., down to the lower price by promising full payment in cash. Tom has seen the city's property tax assessment of the arena, which revealed that the arena's total assessed value was $1,600,000, allocated 70% to land and 30% to the building.

Tom is also aware that the arena has firm contracts (regardless of change in ownership of the arena) for the next 20 years with both a popular football team and a highly successful local hockey team. Net total cash flows from the two contracts are expected to be approximately $500,000 per year over the full term of the contracts. This is rather convenient, since the remaining expected life of the arena is projected by a professional estimator to be 20 years.

Upon consultation with a contractor, Tom learned that the cost to replace the arena in its original condition is currently $3,000,000. The president of Melted Water Corp. felt that the price offered by Tom was more than appropriate, since the net book value of the building on his company's books is only $600,000. Igor Ice Inc. can borrow or invest at an interest rate of 10%.

1. Identify all possible valuations of the arena for which sufficient information has been supplied. Where calculations are required, show your work. (Present value calculations are not required, but indicate the kind of calculation that would be needed.)
2. List the potential users of each valuation and describe how they would use the information.

The Cost of an Asset: The Basic Components

* **PROBLEM 8.8** Determine the cost of an asset

Advanced Shopping Inc. has bought some land on which it intends to build a shopping centre. Calculate the cost of the land given the following information, stating any assumptions you need to make.

a. Advanced has agreed to pay the previous owner $50,000 per year for 10 years for the land title. These payments include interest totalling $150,000 over the 10 years.
b. Advanced paid a real estate broker $20,000 for conducting negotiations with the previous owner.
c. An engineering firm was paid $9,500 for a series of tests on the land to ensure that it was not environmentally contaminated and that it had a good rock base on which to build the shopping centre.

d. Advanced paid $4,000 to have several large signs made and erected on the site, announcing that the new centre would open in 18 months.
e. The site was bulldozed to get rid of the previous owner's drive-in theatre and then levelled and filled at a cost of $35,200. Sale of scrap from the theatre brought in $1,500 cash.
f. A neighbour who did not want to live next door to a shopping centre threatened a lawsuit. Advanced settled the suit out of court for $25,000 and agreed to buy the neighbour's property too, for $110,000. That property would be held for the time being and probably sold later on, after the shopping centre had increased its value.
g. An architect was paid $66,700 for initial plans and drawings of the shopping centre, necessary to get a building permit from the municipality.
h. The president and several other senior managers of Advanced spent a total of 47 days' time on the land purchase deal, including some visits to the site. Allocating their salaries to that activity would produce an amount of $43,200. The site visits cost $7,200 in travel costs (Advanced's head office is in another city).

PROBLEM 8.9 Determine asset costs from various possible components

Determine the costs of land and building that would appear on the balance sheet of Smith Co. Ltd., based on the following information:

Purchase price of plant site	$ 150,000
Building materials (includes $15,000 in materials wasted due to worker inexperience)	800,000
Machinery installation charges	55,000
Grading and draining plant site	35,000
Labour costs of construction (Smith Co. used its own workers to build the plant rather than laying them off because business was slack. However, the labour to build the plant cost $40,000 more than outside contractors would have charged, due to inside workers' inexperience and inefficiency.)	540,000
Machinery purchase cost	1,000,000
Machinery delivery charges	18,000
Parking lot grading and paving	78,000
Replacement of building windows shot out by vandals before production start-up	8,500
Architect's fees	50,000

PROBLEM 8.10 Conceptual components of asset cost

The new accountant for Mactaggart Industries is wondering how to calculate the cost of a new machine the company just installed. Explain briefly whether or not you think each of the following items should be part of the machine's cost, and why:

a. The invoice price of the machine.
b. Sales tax paid on the machine.
c. Shipping charges to get the machine to the company's factory.
d. The cost of the factory manager's trip to the machine manufacturer's plant to choose the machine.
e. The cost of painting the machine light green, as other machines in the factory are painted.
f. Estimated revenue lost because the machine arrived late.
g. The cost of substandard products made while the factory personnel were learning how to operate the machine (all thrown away so as not to damage the company's reputation for quality products).

h. Interest cost on the bank loan used to finance the machine's purchase.
i. The cost of moving three other machines in the factory to make room for the new one.

PROBLEM 8.11 Capitalized or expensed?

There may be circumstances under which each of the following could be either part of Squelox's noncurrent asset cost or not part of it (charged directly to expense). For each, explain briefly when (if ever) the cost should be capitalized as part of the assets versus expensing it.

1. Cost of painting a machine
2. A lawyer's bill
3. Cost of substandard products produced on a new machine

Cash and Temporary Investments • Section 8.5

*** PROBLEM 8.12** Decide what items are cash or temporary investments

Decide which, if any, of the following items would likely be included in (1) cash or (2) temporary investments on the balance sheet of a large company. Explain briefly.

a. Money on deposit in a bank in Brazil, deposited by the company's Brazilian branch.
b. A 90-day guaranteed investment certificate with the company's main bank.
c. Money in transit between the company's banks in Germany and Spain.
d. Receptionists' petty cash funds in the company's various offices worldwide.
e. Three NSF ("not sufficient funds") bad cheques bounced by the customers' banks.
f. An investment in 90% of the shares of a company that supplies raw materials.
g. A deposit recorded on the last day of the year but credited by the bank three days later.
h. Money on deposit in an Indonesian bank as a guarantee of performance for a contract.
i. An investment in 0.5% of the shares of a publicly traded company.
j. An overdraft in the bank account maintained by the branch in Calgary.

PROBLEM 8.13 Basic questions about temporary investments

1. Many companies have temporary investments on their balance sheets. How do these investments differ from
   a. cash,
   b. long-term investments in associated companies?
2. Suggest why, in spite of part 1(a), such investments might be included in cash and equivalents for purposes of deriving the cash flow statement's information.
3. Why are such investments valued at the lower of cost or market?

PROBLEM 8.14 Valuation of marketable securities

Wobistics Inc. owns the following marketable securities:

	Cost Basis	Market Value
Excetera Ltd. common shares	$17,500	$29,750
PCX Corporation common shares	$26,250	$17,500
International Logistics Corp. common shares	$38,000	$52,500
Alberta Airlines Ltd. common shares	$43,750	$40,250

a. Using the lower of cost or market method, what value would appear on Wobistics' balance sheet for marketable securities?
b. Ignoring income tax, how would Wobistics' balance sheet be different if it used market values?

Accounts Receivable • Section 8.6

* PROBLEM 8.15 Answer questions about accounts receivable

Answer the following questions about accounts receivable.

1. In what way can it be said that accounts receivable follow the "lower of cost or market" rule used for other current assets?
2. Banks disclose their allowances for doubtful loans and their losses on bad loans. Why do you think they do, and why don't most other companies?
3. A company has some receivables that are not due for payment for about four years. The president wants to just include those with the regular receivables. What else might be done, and what difference would it make if your proposal were followed?
4. Another company has sold some products on sale contracts that provide for interest to be paid. For example, one contract is for $15,000 plus $1,100 interest. The sale was recorded by debiting accounts receivable and crediting sales revenue for $16,100. What is wrong with that, and how would you fix it? In your solution, how would the interest be accounted for?
5. Why would it make sense to disclose trade receivables separately from receivables like income tax refunds and employee loans?

PROBLEM 8.16 Accounting for uncollectible accounts

Gold Metal Corp. has the following unadjusted account balances at December 31, 2006:

	Account Balances	
	Debit	**Credit**
Accounts receivable	$200,000	
Allowance for doubtful accounts	4,000	
Sales		$600,000

1. Assume Gold Metal estimates that 3% of its sales will be uncollectible.
   a. What will be the amount of bad debt expense recognized by Gold Metal for 2006?
   b. What will be the balance in the allowance for doubtful accounts after the adjusting entry for bad debt expense is made?
2. Assume Gold Metal estimates that 5% of accounts receivable will not be collected.
   a. What will be the amount of bad debt expense recognized by Gold Metal for 2006?
   b. What will be the balance in the allowance for doubtful accounts after the adjusting entry for bad debt expense is made?

PROBLEM 8.17 Valuation and classification of receivables

Ferguson Ltd. has a variety of accounts receivable. They are listed below. Indicate how you would report them on the company's balance sheet, and what numbers the balance sheet would show as a result of your decisions.

a. Customer accounts receivable, $6,341,700.
b. Income tax refund due (expected within about six months), $423,000.
c. Loans to employees to buy houses (repayment not required unless an employee leaves the company or is fired; otherwise, each employee's loan will be due the earlier of 10 years from the initial date of loan or the house's sale, $813,000.

d. Long-term income tax credit expected to be realized in about five years, $156,000.
e. Allowance for doubtful customer accounts, $348,000.

Inventory Valuation and Cost of Goods Sold • Sections 8.7–8.9

LIFO, FIFO and Average Methods

PROBLEM 8.18 Effect of inventory valuation method on reported income

Choose the inventory valuation method that is best described by each of the following statements:

1. FIFO   2. LIFO   3. Average (or weighted average)   4. Specific Identification

____ Most accurate matching of costs of sales and revenues
____ Results in higher income in a period of inflation
____ Includes newest costs in cost of goods sold
____ Values inventories at oldest costs
____ Results in the same inventory valuation, regardless of whether a periodic or perpetual inventory control system is used
____ Results in the lowest net income in a period of falling prices
____ Emphasizes balance sheet valuation
____ Emphasizes income determination
____ Not acceptable for income tax purposes in Canada
____ Best matches current costs with current revenues
____ Matches old costs with newest sales prices
____ Appropriate for use with high dollar, low frequency of sales items

EXTENDED TIME

PROBLEM 8.19 LIFO, FIFO, and AVGE inventory cost calculations

The following purchases of inventory were made by Anvil Corp. in April.

Date	Number of Units Purchased	Per Unit Amount	Total Cost
April 2	150	$7	$ 1,050
April 15	250	8	2,000
April 23	75	9	675
	475		

Sales of inventory during April were:

Date	Number of Units Sold
April 6	100
April 13	240
April 18	250
	590

Anvil's inventory on April 1 consisted of 200 units valued at $6 cost each.

1. Calculate cost of goods sold for April, using periodic LIFO, FIFO, and annual weighted average inventory cost flow assumptions.
2. Calculate ending inventory values as at April 30 under each of the three methods above.
3. Suppose the market price for these units was only $7 per unit at April 30, and the lower of cost or market valuation is applied to each unit individually. Redo part 2 above.
4. (Optional) Redo parts 1, 2, and 3, assuming Anvil uses a perpetual inventory control system and therefore would calculate LIFO using the perpetual records and AVGE using the weighted moving average.

PROBLEM 8.20 Inventory cost and effects calculations

You work for a large local company as inventory manager. The company uses FIFO in accounting for inventory. In June, the company began to stock a new product, Painto. The June inventory record for Painto was:

Date	Purchase Price	Units Purchased	Units Sold	Units on Hand
June 1	$12	1,250		1,250
10	$13	1,000		2,250
12			250	2,000
17	$14	500		2,500
23			2,000	500
27	$15	1,500		2,000
30			800	1,200

1. Calculate, using FIFO:
   a. The cost of the June 30 inventory of Painto.
   b. The cost of goods sold for Painto for June.
2. Calculate, using LIFO (either perpetual or periodic):
   a. The cost of the June 30 inventory of Painto.
   b. The cost of goods sold for Painto for June.
3. Based on your calculations in parts 1 and 2, and ignoring income tax, what would be the effect of changing from FIFO to LIFO on the company's
   a. income before income tax for June,
   b. balance sheet at the end of June?

* PROBLEM 8.21 Analyze various possible inventory costing policies

Yang Inc. has been in business for three years. The company manages its inventories well, so that there are no significant inventories for which cost is less than market value. For the past three years, here are the company's inventory asset and COGS expense computed under each of three methods:

		2007	2006	2005
a. FIFO	— ending inventory	$112,000	$148,000	$115,000
	— COGS expense	636,000	867,000	585,000
b. AVGE	— ending inventory	108,000	126,000	106,000
	— COGS expense	618,000	880,000	594,000
c. LIFO	— ending inventory	104,000	118,000	92,000
	— COGS expense	614,000	874,000	608,000
Purchases in each year		600,000	900,000	700,000

1. Determine the inventory cost policy that would produce the highest and lowest income in each year and calculate the effect on income (before income tax) of choosing the former over the latter.
2. Given the variation of results you observed in part 1, how should a company choose its inventory cost policy?

PROBLEM 8.22 Using knowledge of statement relationships for analysis

Mutual Insurance Ltd. has received a fire-loss claim from Boomer Fireworks Ltd. in the amount of $180,000 for inventory destroyed in a fire at Boomer's warehouse on May 24, 2006. A review of Boomer's past financial statements reveals the company has earned an average 33 1/3% gross profit margin. (Gross profit margin = Gross profit/Sales) You have been able to find the following information from accounting records not destroyed in the fire:

Inventory May 1, 2006	$ 320,000
Purchases May 1 to May 24	600,000
Sales, May 1 to May 24	1,200,000

1. Using the information available, estimate the amount of inventory destroyed in the fire.
2. How reasonable is Boomer's claim? On what basis do you think it calculated the loss of inventory in the fire?

PROBLEM 8.23 Inventory cost and market calculations

Winedark Sea Ltd. sells prints of romantic paintings. The prints are done on expensive paper and are quite costly. Pricing the prints to sell is hard because the popularity of a print is difficult to predict. If prints don't sell well, they are disposed of in bulk for use in hotels and motels.

Here are data on two prints:

	Print X		Print Y	
	Units	Cost per Unit	Units	Cost per Unit
Inventory, January 1, 2006	8	$510	22	$750
Purchases during 2006:				
During summer	20	525	50	720
During fall	30	500	60	764
Sales during 2006	46		76	

1. Calculate the following:
   a. Inventory cost, December 31, 2006, for Print X, FIFO basis.
   b. Cost of goods sold, 2006, for Print Y, AVGE basis.
2. Print Y hasn't sold since September. No one seems to like it any more. An out-of-town hotel has offered $100 each for all that Winedark has left, if Winedark will pay the $10 per print shipping cost. What amount would you suggest be used for the inventory of Print Y on the December 31, 2006, balance sheet? Why?

Lower of Cost or Market and Other Costing Methods

* **PROBLEM 8.24** Calculate lower of cost or market on inventory items

Classy Products Inc. has the following items in its inventory. Calculate the inventory value that would be reported according to GAAP, using (1) the most conservative method and (2) an acceptable less conservative method.

Inventory item	Quantity	Cost per unit	Market per unit
Blue bombies	6,000 units	$13.50	$25.00
Red rockies	2,000 units	11.90	7.00
Yellow yallies	10,000 units	13.00	15.00
Tangerine tackies	4,000 units	24.00	5.00
Gold glammies	5,000 units	6.50	8.20

PROBLEM 8.25 Calculate lower of cost or market on inventory items

Thingamajigs Incorporated has the following items in its inventory. Calculate the inventory that would be reported according to GAAP, using (1) the most conservative method and (2) an acceptable less conservative method.

Inventory item	Quantity	Cost per unit	Market per unit
Gadgets	4,000 units	$ 78.00	$ 90
Gizmos	5,000 units	76.50	66
Widgets	3,000 units	94.50	108
Doodads	2,000 units	100.50	84
Thingamabobs	6,000 units	57.00	72

PROBLEM 8.26 Explain the effects of changing from non-GAAP to GAAP

The president of a small local company has been advised by a newly hired accountant that the company's balance sheet valuation methods are not quite appropriate. One example is that the company has been valuing inventories at cost, whereas GAAP normally requires that the lower of cost or market be used for such a current asset. Explain as carefully as you can what would be the effect on the company's balance sheet, income statement, and cash flow statement if the accounting for inventory were changed to the GAAP basis.

Amortization • Sections 8.10–8.13

Calculations, Entries, Effects, and Choice

* **PROBLEM 8.27** Amortization calculations, entries, and effects

At the beginning of 2005, Garrison Inc. acquired machinery costing $100,000 and having a useful life of 10 years. The company amortized this machinery during 2005 and 2006 using the straight-line method. During 2007, it decided to change to the declining balance method of amortization for the machinery.

1. Calculate the amortization expense Garrison has recognized for 2005 and 2006, and write a journal entry to record either year's amount.
2. Calculate the amortization expense Garrison would have recorded had it been using the declining balance method for 2005 and 2006.
3. Calculate the effects of changing from straight-line to declining balance on the following (ignoring income tax):
   a. The balance sheet at the end of 2005
   b. The income statement for 2006
   c. The balance sheet at the end of 2006
   d. The cash flow statement for 2006

PROBLEM 8.28 Amortization calculations, entries, effects, and choice

SD Corporation acquired machinery at the beginning of 2005, having a cost of $150,000 and an anticipated useful life of 10 years. It amortized this machinery for 2005 and 2006 using the straight-line method. Early in 2007, it decided to change to the declining balance method of amortization.

1. Prepare the journal entry to record amortization expense for 2006 using the straight-line method.
2. Prepare the journal entry to record amortization expense for 2006 using the declining balance method at a rate of 20%.
3. Show the effects of changing from straight-line to the 20% declining balance method on the 2006 income statement, the 2006 cash flow statement, and the balance sheet at the end of 2006. Ignore income tax.
4. In what circumstances is the use of declining balance amortization more appropriate than use of the straight-line method?

PROBLEM 8.29 Double declining balance and straight-line calculations

ACE has a very large machine used to move aircraft simulators around while they are being assembled. The machine cost $850,000 at the beginning of the 2005 fiscal year. It was expected to be useful for 10 years and to have a salvage value of only $30,000 as scrap at the end of its life.

a. Calculate the amortization on the machine for *fiscal year 2007* on the double declining balance basis.
b. ACE actually uses straight-line amortization for the machine and incorporates salvage value. Calculate whether ACE's net income *for fiscal year 2007* was therefore higher or lower than it would have been if double declining balance amortization had been used for the machine.

Gains and Losses on Noncurrent Asset Disposals and Write-offs

* **PROBLEM 8.30** Calculate gains, losses, write-offs, and write-downs

Determine the amount that is added to or subtracted from income for each of the following items.

a. A truck costing $45,000 and having accumulated amortization of $18,000 is sold for $16,000 cash.
b. An investment of $100,000 in another company turns out to have been a bad idea. It looks as if the investment can be sold for only $15,000.
c. An old building that cost $78,000 and has accumulated amortization of $78,000 is given to the fire department to burn down for practice.
d. Land that cost $50,000 is sold for 10 payments of $10,000 each, to be received over the next 10 years. The interest included in those payments will equal $27,000.
e. A machine that is part of a group of assets that are amortized as a group is sold. The machine cost $3,000 eight years ago and $500 is received for it.
f. A division is sold as a business because the company is going to get out of that line of business. The division brings $340,000 in cash proceeds, and has assets costing $670,000, accumulated amortization of $240,000, and liabilities of $120,000, which the selling company is still responsible for.

PROBLEM 8.31 Amortization calculations, entries, effects, and choice

Tonka Inc. purchased a new delivery van on January 1, 2005. The total cost of the van including provincial sales tax was $32,000. The estimated useful life of the vehicle was 5 years or 300,000 km. The estimated salvage value of the vehicle was $2,000.

1. Calculate the amortization expense and the year-end net book value for 2005 and 2006 using:
   a. The straight-line method.
   b. The units-of-production method. (The van was driven 50,000 km in 2005 and 75,000 km in 2006.)
   c. The double declining balance method.
2. Assuming the van was sold for $18,000 at the end of 2006 after amortization had been charged for the year, write the journal entry to record the sale if amortization had been calculated using:
   a. The straight-line method.
   b. The units-of-production method.
   c. The double declining balance method.
3. Calculate the total cost to Tonka of using the van under each of the alternative methods. Explain the outcome of your calculations.

PROBLEM 8.32 Gain or loss using straight-line, double declining balance, and units-of-production

Rubber Ducky Ltd. produces various products made from rubber. Three years ago it paid $150,000 for a machine that shapes rubber into hockey pucks, has an expected life of 10 years, and has a salvage value of $10,000. The machine's engineers guarantee that it can produce 5,000,000 pucks in its life. To date Rubber Ducky has produced 1,534,193.

Peter Puck Inc. just offered $100,000 for the machine. Calculate the gain or loss on disposal that would result if the machine were sold at the end of the third year, using (a) straight-line, (b) double declining balance and (c) units-of-production amortization for the machine. Comment on what the answers indicate about the amortization methods and the meaning of the gains or losses.

PROBLEM 8.33 Various amortization questions and calculations

1. Your friend Fast Eddie has just completed the first year of operating a one-truck delivery company. Fast Eddie explains to you that, because of careful care of the truck, the price the truck would fetch on the used truck market is not much different from the price paid for the truck a year ago. As a result, says Fast Eddie, no amortization expense on the truck is needed for accounting purposes this year. Next year, Fast Eddie believes the truck's value will drop a noticeable amount, but this is not a problem because the cash obtained from deducting tax amortization (capital cost allowance) and so saving income tax will compensate for the decline in market value over the year.

   Explain to Fast Eddie what the accounting concept of amortization is and how Fast Eddie's thinking is in error with respect to that concept.
2. Larry Green, another friend, is just starting a yard grooming service and has purchased a group of new lawnmowers for $10,000. Larry expects the mowers to last five years and to have negligible resale value at that point. Larry's business plan projects cutting 5,000 lawns over the five years, with per-year projections of 500, 1,000, 1,200, 1,800, and 500 lawns over the five years.
   a. Calculate the accumulated amortization balance at the end of the second year on each of the following amortization bases:
      1. Straight-line.
      2. Declining balance (25% rate).
      3. Units-of-production.
   b. Based on your calculations, which amortization basis would produce the highest retained earnings at the end of the second year?
   c. Larry has never heard of the units-of-production basis. Explain why companies use it and comment on whether it would make sense for Larry's business.
   d. If the 25% declining balance method is used, accumulated amortization will be $7,627 at the end of the fifth year. Suppose that on the first day of the sixth year, all the lawnmowers are sold as junk for $100 cash in total. Ignoring income taxes:
      1. Calculate the loss on sale that would be recorded that day.
      2. Suppose Larry objects to recording the loss on sale, pointing out that $100 more was received for the lawnmowers than had been expected five years earlier, and claims that, in any case, income for the sixth year should not be reduced by the loss when it happened on the first day on the year. Reply to Larry.

Other Assets, Intangibles, and Capital Leases • Section 8.14

Purchased Intangibles

*** PROBLEM 8.34** Answer questions about intangible assets accounting

1. Ransome Biometrics Inc. is negotiating to buy the assets and hire the employees and management of Frog Hollow Research Inc. At the moment, the deal looks like this: Ransome will pay $2,100,000 in cash and issue new shares with an agreed value of $12,000,000 to the owners of Frog Hollow, in exchange for the following assets (agreed values in brackets): accounts receivable ($200,000), inventory ($650,000), high-technology equipment ($2,210,000), and patents ($3,650,000). Explain how the acquisition would be accounted for in Ransome's books.
2. The president of Ransome is not happy with the accounting you've outlined in part 1, saying that no value has been assigned to the high-quality Frog Hollow personnel who will become part of Ransome's business. "The whole reason for the deal was to take advantage of Frog Hollow's excellent R&D record and use its people's expertise to help in Ransome's operations, but the accounting does not recognize that at all," said the president. Explain to the president whether the accounting does or does not recognize the value of the Frog Hollow people.
3. "Perhaps," mused the president, "we could assign an explicit value to the Frog Hollow people in the acquisition deal. They were the main reason for the deal, so at least half of the acquisition price should be assigned to them. That would be an asset on Ransome's balance sheet that I would be happy to defend." If the president's idea were accepted, what difference would that make to the company's balance sheet? Would that difference matter? Would it be acceptable under GAAP?

PROBLEM 8.35 Calculate any goodwill on a business purchase

Foofaraw Ltd. paid $250,000 for land, buildings, inventories, and accounts payable of another business that will become a branch. The assets (after deducting the accounts payable of $60,000) had an aggregate fair market value of $228,000.

1. What (if anything) is the resulting asset on Foofaraw's balance sheet?
2. If Foofaraw had paid $225,000, what would be your answer to part 1?

PROBLEM 8.36 Accounting for goodwill

Octuplex Inc. acquired the shares of another company for $5,180,000 cash. At the date of the acquisition, the fair values of the other company's assets totalled $7,328,000 and the fair values of its liabilities totalled $2,564,800.

1. Calculate goodwill arising from the acquisition, if any.
2. Why is any such goodwill considered to be an asset of Octuplex Inc.?
3. The president of Octuplex Inc. was perplexed by accounting rules, saying: "I don't understand why, if goodwill is an asset, our advertising is not. Advertising is essential to the future profitability of our company, and seems to me more relevant to assessing our company performance than goodwill is." Explain to the president why advertising is generally not considered to be an asset.

Internally Developed Intangibles

*** PROBLEM 8.37** Effects analysis: expensing versus capitalizing, plus tax

The controller of Squiffle, Inc., is having a disagreement with senior management about a company accounting policy. Help out by analyzing the case below, which involves income tax. The tax effect can be reasoned out without knowing anything about income tax other than the information given.

Squiffle, in business for only a year, has capitalized $67,000 in development costs. The controller argues that such costs should be expensed instead. Assume this accounting policy affects current income tax liability only and that the company's income tax rate is 30%. What would the controller's proposal do to

a. the current year's net income,
b. the current year's cash flow,
c. working capital at the end of the current year?

PROBLEM 8.38 Answer questions about intangible assets

A businessperson has asked you the following questions. Answer each as clearly as you can.

a. Why does GAAP frown on capitalizing the goodwill we generate through having good management and hiring and motivating excellent employees?
b. Anyway, what could it hurt to capitalize such goodwill? The balance sheet would show more assets, but otherwise there'd be no effect on anything, would there?
c. Our auditors have said that we are violating GAAP by not showing as an asset the lease we have signed on our main factory building. How can that be? Wouldn't we violate some pretty basic principles if we put something we don't even own on our balance sheet?
d. We've been lucky enough to sign a franchise agreement with our major supplier, so now we can be the unique source of that supplier's goods in the local market. I understand that we do account for this franchise agreement. How do we do that, and why is it done differently than the goodwill I already asked you about?

PROBLEM 8.39 Questions about intangibles and capital leases

Answer the following questions briefly:

1. Why is capitalizing costs, such as intangible assets, a reasonable idea?
2. Why is it not such a good idea?
3. Explain clearly why and how capitalizing the costs of a development project as a "deferred costs" asset affects the income statement and the balance sheet.
4. Explain why capitalizing such costs does not have any direct effect on the cash flow statement's cash from operations figure.
5. Suggest some indirect effects on cash flow that such a capitalization policy may have.
6. If an asset is leased, it is not owned. Accounting standards require creating a balance sheet asset account for some leased assets. How can that be justified?
7. If a lease is treated as a capital lease rather than an operating lease, what effects does that have on the balance sheet, income statement, and cash flow statement?

PROBLEM 8.40 Issues in accounting for tangible and intangible assets

For some years, the world economy, particularly in the more developed countries, has been undergoing what some people believe is a fundamental realignment from the "old economy" manufacturing and natural resource industries to the "new economy" knowledge-based, communications, service, and Internet-based activities. This has caused some problems for financial accounting. One is that the economic values of the knowledge and other intangible assets thought to give "new economy" companies their overall value are not explicitly represented in the companies' balance sheets. A second problem is that the tangible assets of the "old economy" companies may be overvalued in their balance sheets if those assets are not attractive for earning income as the economy shifts. A third problem is that the income measures and stock market values of "new economy" companies may be highly variable (as events in 2001 and 2002 showed), making their earnings hard to relate to their share prices and hard to compare to "old economy" companies' earnings and share prices.

Discuss the issues raised above. What sorts of changes in financial accounting might address the problems? Do you think financial accounting requires a significant overhaul? Why, or why not?

Integrated Problems

* PROBLEM 8.41 Indicate policy change effects

Indicate the probable direction of the effect of each of the following possible accounting policy changes on the account given:

Policy Change	Effect On
a. Capitalize R&D expenses	Assets
b. Recognize accounts receivable sooner	Revenue
c. Capitalize some repairs expenses	Net income
d. Change from moving AVGE to FIFO for inventories	Net income
e. Change to straight-line from declining balance for factory	Assets
f. Recognize doubtful accounts sooner	Net income
g. Write off spoiled inventories	Operating income

* PROBLEM 8.42 Answer various questions about asset accounting

Answer this mixture of narrative and numerical questions about Thuringia Inc.'s accounting.

1. Earlier in the current year, the company had sold an old building for $115,000. The building had cost $820,000 and had accumulated amortization of $762,000 at the date of sale. All that had been recorded for the sale so far was to debit cash $115,000 and credit sales revenue $115,000. Record a journal entry to correct the accounts.
2. Thuringia Inc. has been experiencing steadily rising prices for the products it purchases for resale. In this circumstance, would the moving average basis of accounting for its inventory give higher or lower net income than the FIFO basis would?
3. The company's policy is to use replacement cost for determining the market value of its inventory of goods for resale. Replacement cost is greater than cost, which in turn is greater than net realizable value. Is the company's policy appropriate?
4. An error was found in the records for December. A $14,350 sale on credit, not actually made until early in January, which is in the next fiscal year, was recorded in December. The $9,120 cost of goods sold had also been mistakenly removed from inventory because the company's perpetual inventory control system was tied to its sales recording system. Record a journal entry as of the end of December to correct the accounts.
5. An analysis of the temporary investments account (total cost $525,000) showed that the total market value of the investments was $515,000 at the end of the fiscal year. Investment market values had never been below cost before. Is there a problem?
6. To avoid all the complexities of FIFO, AVGE, or LIFO, perhaps Thuringia should just account for the actual cost of its inventories. Why might actual cost not be a solution for the company?

PROBLEM 8.43 Record noncurrent asset transactions and adjustments

Below are several information items about the first year in business of manufacturer Borzian Inc.

a. Borzian purchased a factory from another company on the first day of the year. The total price was $6,250,000, which was allocated $1,500,000 to land, $3,650,000 to the building, and $1,100,000 to equipment in the factory. To finance the purchase, Borzian obtained a 7% mortgage loan of $3,500,000 (first payment of $250,000 plus interest was due on the first day of the next year), issued shares valued at $1,000,000, and paid $1,750,000 cash.
b. To convert the factory to the uses Borzian needed, $400,000 was immediately spent on the building and $950,000 on equipment. This was all paid in cash, some of it raised from selling equipment acquired in the original purchase, but not needed by Borzian. That equipment had been allocated a cost of $500,000, and Borzian sold it for $519,000.
c. Amortization for the year was calculated to be $202,500 on the building (5% per year) and $155,000 on the equipment (10% per year).
d. Right at the end of the year, equipment that had cost $70,000 was sold for $45,000 cash. This money was to be used to help make the first mortgage payment.

1. For each item, write a journal entry or entries to record any transaction or adjustment that is indicated.
2. What was the net book value of the factory at the end of the year?
3. What impact on income for the year did the four items have?

PROBLEM 8.44 Answer questions about asset accounting

1. Starre Ltd. has a very conservative amortization policy, using higher amortization rates than most companies use. This year, the company sold a surplus building and showed a gain on sale. The president wants the gain on sale included in the calculation of her bonus pay for the year. Specify one argument for including the gain in her bonus calculation and one against doing that.
2. A business commentator said that Starre Ltd. should be praised for the conservative amortization policy "because of the income tax savings that result and the higher cash flow apparent from the large amortization added to income on the cash flow statement." Briefly evaluate the commentator's two points.
3. At a meeting of Starre Ltd.'s board of directors, the chief financial officer explained that the amortization policy was straight-line, a common policy, but the rate used was high. For example, machinery and equipment was amortized at 12 1/2 % per year with no salvage value. The directors discussed the policy at length. Give one argument for the company's policy and one against it.
4. For some years, Dobin Inc. has had a policy of recognizing an intangible asset, "development costs." The asset has been created by crediting operating expenses for some costs thought to benefit future years. The resulting asset has been amortized by 50% per year, so any capitalized costs have been deferred for only two years into the future. At the end of 2005, the asset equalled $240,000. During 2006, $120,000 was amortized and $130,000 more was capitalized from 2006 operating expenses. It has been decided to discontinue this policy, effective at the *beginning* of 2006. The asset balance at the end of 2005 is to be put into a special "unusual expenses" account for 2006. It is now the end of 2006, and financial statements for 2006 are being prepared. Record a journal entry as at the end of 2006 to accomplish the policy change.

PROBLEM 8.45 Answer questions about amortization and inventory costing

1. According to its financial statement notes, Egret Electric uses straight-line amortization, at various useful lives from 8 years to 40 years. Some competitors use accelerated double declining balance amortization, and Egret is considering changing to that method for the company's *more recently acquired assets.* (Older assets would be left on the straight-line method because they are getting close to being fully amortized in any case.) The change would be made beginning in the 2006 fiscal year.
   a. If this policy change were made, what would happen to 2006 net income (up, down, or no effect), and why?
   b. If this policy change were made, what would happen to total assets at the end of 2006 (up, down, or no effect), and why?
2. Also according to its notes, Egret uses a mixture of average cost and FIFO for its inventories. Consider the product Switching Panel 404-C. At the end of 2005, there were 4,000 panels in inventory at a cost of $89.00 each. During the 2006 fiscal year, 18,000 panels were manufactured at a cost of $93.00 each, and 17,000 were sold for a selling price of $160.00 each. Calculate the inventory cost at the end of 2006 on (a) Annual average cost basis and (b) FIFO basis.
3. Net realizable value of the panels at the end of 2006 was $160.00 each. What adjustment, if any, would be made because of this in preparing the 2006 financial statements? Why?

PROBLEM 8.46 Answer questions about inventory costing and amortization

1. Ander Oil Exploration uses a mixture of average cost and FIFO for its inventories. The company, which faces steadily rising purchase costs and inventory levels, is considering changing its policy to use average cost for all inventories. The policy change would be implemented in the current fiscal year.
   a. If this policy change were made, what would happen to current net income (up, down, or no effect), and why?
   b. If this policy change were made, what would happen to current cash from operations (up, down, or no effect), and why?
2. Ander uses the units of production method for its amortization, based on production calculations made by its engineers. One of its oil production properties cost $9 million and was acquired October 1, 2005. Its useful life was then estimated at 20 years, with a salvage value of $1 million. Oil production from the property was estimated at five million barrels over that useful life. In 2009, 280,000 barrels of oil were produced from the property, bringing the total produced by the end of 2009 to 890,000 barrels. For that property, calculate
   a. amortization expense for the year ended September 30, 2009,
   b. accumulated amortization as at September 30, 2009.
3. Assume Ander used accelerated, double declining balance amortization for the property in part 2. Calculate the amortization expense for the year ended September 30, *2007,* for that property, using that accelerated method.

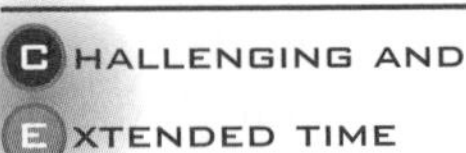

PROBLEM 8.47 Oil production balance sheet and income

The Lindleigh Company is in the business of oil production. On January 1, 2001, the company paid $1,000,000 for the lease of an area near MacDonald Lake. The lease area was known to contain 5,000,000 barrels of oil in the form of tar sands.

During the five years to December 31, 2006, the company spent $5,000,000 on exploratory work in assessing the extent of the deposits, perfecting the extraction technique, and building access roads.

1. Assuming that the company commenced with a capital stock of $3,000,000 and has borrowed $3,000,000 since then, and that the transactions specified are the only ones in which the company has engaged, present a balance sheet for the Lindleigh Company as at December 31, 2006.
2. During 2007, 500,000 barrels of oil were produced. Production costs incurred during the period were $1,000,000. At the end of the period, 100,000 barrels of refined oil remained in storage, and 400,000 barrels had been sold at a price of $4 per barrel. The company owed income tax of 35% on pre-tax income.
   a. Assuming that selling expenses were $200,000, prepare an income statement for the Lindleigh Company for 2007. Show your cost of goods sold computation.
   b. How would the Assets portion of the balance sheet appear as at December 31, 2007?

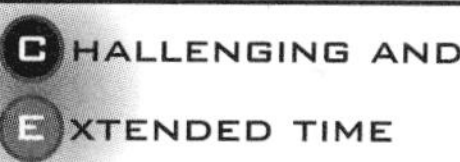

PROBLEM 8.48 Asset prices, policies, effects, and entries

Advanced Markets Ltd., a retailer, began business on November 1, 2006. The company's balance sheets then, and at October 31, 2007, were (in thousands of dollars):

	Oct. 31, 2007	Nov. 1, 2006		Oct. 31, 2007	Nov. 1, 2006
Cash	$ 26	$100	Accounts payable	$194	$180
Accts. receivable	334	300	Share capital	500	500
Allow. doubt. accts.	(30)	(20)	Retained earnings	76	—
Inventory (FIFO)	354	240			
Fixtures	40	—			
Accum. amortization	(8)	—			
Goodwill (net)	54	60			
	$770	$680		$770	$680

The company had receivables, payables, and inventories from the beginning because it was formed to take over the business of another company whose owner had decided to retire to a warmer climate. The company's premises and equipment were all rented, so the company had no fixed assets when it began. The company need not pay any income tax this year.

1. From the information given, calculate the purchase price of the business Advanced Markets purchased November 1, 2006.
2. Net income for the company's first year, to October 31, 2007, was $76 (thousand). Calculate cash generated by operations for that year (in thousands).
3. If the company changed to average cost for its inventory, the October 31, 2007, inventory asset would be $316 (thousand). If it did so, what would the following be?
   a. Retained earnings, October 31, 2007.
   b. Cash generated by operations (based on your answer to part 2).
4. The company buys its inventories in large lots. Its purchases and sales last year were:

November 1, 2006, beginning	8,000 units @ $30 = $240 (thousand)
Sales before next purchase	6,000 units
February 15, 2007, purchase	7,000 units @ $36 = $252 (thousand)
Sales before next purchase	4,000 units
July 31, 2007, purchase	7,500 units @ $40 = $300 (thousand)
Sales before October 31, 2007	3,500 units

   a. What would the company's October 31, 2007, inventory cost be on the periodic LIFO basis?

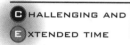

b. What would the 2007 cost of goods sold be on the LIFO basis?
c. Redo parts (a) and (b) using the perpetual LIFO basis. Why are there differences in the figures?

5. On December 31, 2007, in the company's second year of operation, several unneeded counters and tables were sold for $15 thousand cash. At that date, those assets (which had cost $18 thousand) had a book value of $12 thousand.
   a. Write a journal entry to record the sale.
   b. Explain why this sale affects the calculation of cash from operations in the company's cash flow statement for its second year of operation.

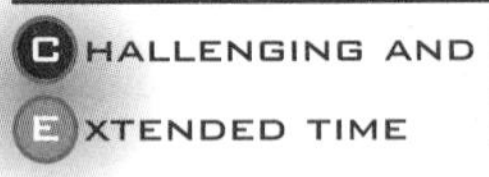

PROBLEM 8.49 Accounting calculations, effects, entries

Harriett has been making quilts, aprons, pillows, scarves, and other such items for years. Recently, she took the plunge and opened a shop to sell her products and those of other local craftspeople. Her husband, who is more interested in sports than accounting, keeps her books and prepared the draft financial statements that follow.

Draft Financial Statements for Harriett's Handmades Ltd.
Balance Sheet as at December 31, 2006

Assets		Liabilities and Owners' Equity	
Current:		Current:	
Inventory	$ 43,000	Owing to bank	$ 18,000
Owing from customers	2,140	Owing to suppliers	21,000
Cash	4,600	Income tax owing	3,200
	$ 49,740		$ 42,200
Noncurrent:		Store mortgage	110,000
Store	$187,000	Owners' equity:	
Amortization so far	3,740	Shares issued	68,000
	$183,260	Income so far	12,800
	$233,000		$233,000

Income Statement
for the Year Ended December 31, 2006

Sales		$152,000
Cost of goods sold:		
Purchases	$118,000	
Less inventory left over	43,000	75,000
Margin		$ 77,000
Expenses:		
Store operations	$ 22,000	
Wages	24,000	
Interest	15,000	61,000
Income before tax		$ 16,000
Estimated income tax owing		3,200
Income for the year		$ 12,800

1. The company's "store" assets cost the following: fixtures and shelving, $19,000; cash register and other equipment, $14,000; building, $114,000; land, $40,000; total, $187,000. Harriett's husband computed amortization at 2% of the total and included the resulting $3,740 in store operations expenses.
   a. Evaluate Harriett's husband's amortization accounting policy.
   b. Propose a more suitable amortization accounting policy, indicating any assumptions you need in order to do that.
   c. Calculate amortization for 2006, based on your proposed policy, and write a journal entry to adjust the accounts to reflect your calculation.
2. Most of the company's inventory and the cost of goods sold are recorded at actual cost because each item is tagged with the name of the person who made it plus an identification number. However, the store also sells a line of fancy wrapping paper. Purchases and sales of that paper were as follows:

Initial purchase	200 packages @ $1.20	$ 240
Sales to April 24	160 packages	
Purchase April 25	300 packages @ $1.30	390
Sales to August 15	310 packages	
Purchase August 16	500 packages @ $1.40	700
Sales December 31	450 packages	
		$1,330

   Harriett's husband, working from an old accounting text, came up with the following figures for the wrapping paper:

Unit cost:	$1,330 / 1,000 = $1.33
Cost of goods sold:	920 × $1.33 = $1,224
Ending inventory:	80 × $1.33 = $106

   a. What inventory costing method was Harriett's husband using?
   b. Is that an acceptable method for the wrapping paper? Why?
   c. Using the *perpetual LIFO* method, calculate ending inventory and cost of goods sold for the wrapping paper.
3. Harriett is thinking of capitalizing $2,000 of the year's wage expenses (spent early in 2006 to build shelving) and including that in the cost of fixtures and shelving.
   a. What does it mean to "capitalize" such expenses?
   b. What would be the effect on 2006 income (ignoring income tax) if Harriett decided to capitalize the wages?
4. When Harriett reviewed the draft financial statements, she discovered the following:
   - Net realizable value of the inventory totalled $41,600.
   - One customer account totalling $150 was uncollectible, and three others totalling $280 were doubtful.
   - Cash on hand was overstated by $1,000 because her husband had recorded a $1,000 bank loan twice.
   - A $210 bill for operating expenses not incurred until January 2007 was included in accounts payable.
   - The current portion of the store mortgage was $4,200.

   Taking these items and assuming implementation of your amortization policy (part 1 above) and Harriett's wage capitalization plan (part 3), calculate the revised income before income tax for 2006.
5. Harriett's husband estimated income taxes payable by just multiplying the income before tax by 20%. In fact, when all the above information was taken into account, the income tax payable for 2006 was $2,100. (We'll ignore any future income tax.)
   a. Write a journal entry to adjust the estimated income tax recorded by the husband to reflect the above information.

b. Taking into account (a) above and parts 1, 2, and 4, calculate the following as at December 31, 2006:
   i. Retained earnings.
   ii.. Total assets.

CHALLENGING AND EXTENDED TIME

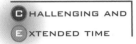

PROBLEM 8.50 Calculation of adjusting entries and effect on income and retained earnings

Andie's Confection Company
Unadjusted Trial Balance
As at December 31, 2006

	DEBITS	CREDITS
Cash	$ 12,395	
Accounts receivable	18,420	
Allowance for doubtful accounts		553
Merchandise inventory	28,650	
Prepaid rent	9,000	
Prepaid insurance	2,400	
Land	568	
Buildings	2,423	
Accumulated amortization—buildings		872
Equipment	3,268	
Accumulated amortization—equipment		643
Intangible assets	1,232	
Bank indebtedness		632
Accounts payable		391
Income taxes payable		
Current portion of long-term debt		1,385
Long-term debt		4,052
Share capital		50,000
Retained earnings		15,378
Sales		64,360
Cost of goods sold	38,616	
Rent expense	4,500	
Insurance expense	1,200	
Amortization expense	0	
Wages and salaries	15,594	
Totals	$138,266	$138,266

a. A review of the accounts receivable at the year-end indicates that 5% of the accounts are unlikely to be collected.
b. A physical count of the inventory reveals only $27 960 of merchandise on hand.
c. The prepaid rent represents six months' rent paid in advance on October 1, 2006.
d. The prepaid insurance represents the premium on a one-year policy taking effect on September 1, 2006.
e. Andie's amortizes long-term assets on the straight-line basis at 5% for buildings, 10% for equipment.
f. The accountants' review indicates that there has been no impairment of the intangible assets' value.
g. $1,500 of the long-term debt is scheduled to be repaid in 2007.
h. Employees have worked the final week of the year but will not be paid until the first payday of 2007. Total wages earned but unpaid are $300.

1. Write journal entries for any needed adjusting entries for Andie's.
2. Calculate the effect of the above entries on:
   a. net income for 2006,
   b. 2006 ending retained earnings.
3. Calculate net income for 2006.

CASE 8A

EARNINGS MANIPULATION VIA CAPITALIZING VERSUS EXPENSING EXPENDITURES

CEO Petra Scatti asked CFO Chandra Sunder to explain some accounting issues that Scatti thought might prove awkward. Scatti had been CEO of the company for two years and had been, she thought, a good leader as the company built up its business. She was proud that the company's quarterly earnings per share had grown from $0.53 to $1.12 during her time at the helm, and she had been telling analysts and the media that continued earnings growth could be expected.

But now Scatti was concerned. With all the recent accounting trouble, could her company's EPS growth, of which she was so proud, be a result of inappropriate or aggressive accounting? She had found the 2002 *Business Week* article while waiting in the dentist's office. Reflecting on her own company's accounts, she did wonder about a fairly steady growth in the company's assets. Was that growth real, or had it been engineered to make EPS grow?

CFO Sunder, the audit committee, and the external auditors had not indicated any problems with the company's accounting, but Scatti decided to review the situation anyway. After all, the company's accounting was ultimately her responsibility as CEO.

When Sunder arrived at her office, Scatti had some questions:

1. The *Business Week* article I sent to you got me thinking. But before we go further, did *Business Week* have it right? Is manipulating asset accounting so easy?
2. The article talks about not being able to manipulate cash flow, but then manipulating it anyway. What gives? And is EBITDA cash flow? News to me.
3. I know that capitalizing expenditures versus expensing them is ultimately a judgment call. Accounting standards leave that to people like you and me, and our accountants. How do we make that judgment properly? How can I assure shareholders, or regulators, or myself, that both our assets and our income are rock-solid? Or am I asking too much?

HOW TO HIDE $3.8 BILLION IN EXPENSES

PRESTO! By shifting billions in expenses from operations to investing, WorldCom made its business look much healthier

---

When WorldCom Inc. revealed on June 25 that it had uncovered a $3.8 billion accounting fraud, everyone from the smallest investors to President George W. Bush reacted with shock and outrage. How was this possible? How could such an established company have hidden such huge expenses from the investing public? Here's a look at what WorldCom did and how the company did it.

What exactly did WorldCom do?

During 2001 and the first quarter of 2002, the company counted as capital investments $3.8 billion that it spent on everyday expenses. This makes a difference because capital investments are treated differently from other expenses for accounting purposes. Capital spending is money used to buy long-lasting assets, like fiber-optic cables or switches that direct telephone calls, so the cost is spread out over several years. For example, if WorldCom spent $10 million on switches it expected to last 10 years, it would book a $1 million expense for 10 years. In contrast, if it spent $10 million on office space, it has to count all of that expense in the period in which it occurred. The company says the expenses that were counted as capital expenditures involve "line costs," which are fees WorldCom pays to other telecom players for the right to access their networks.

How does this affect profits?

Counting everyday expenses as capital investments boosts net income because expenses that are supposed to be counted in one quarter are spread out over years. WorldCom originally reported net income of $1.4 billion in 2001 and $172 million in the first quarter of 2002. Now the company says it lost money the whole time. "You do this to make your bottom line look better," says Rosemarie Kalinowski, an analyst with debt rating agency Standard & Poor's.

How is cash flow affected?

Different people use the term "cash flow" to mean different things. What WorldCom did affects cash generated from operations, a closely watched line in financial statements. WorldCom originally reported that its operating activities in 2001 produced $7.7 billion in cash. Now, it says that figure really was $4.6 billion. But WorldCom's overall cash flow isn't affected because the restatement will lower the amount of cash reported as used in investing activities, which include capital investments. So the two changes cancel each other out. It does, however, affect another measure of cash flow, something called EBITDA.

What's EBITDA?

EBITDA stands for earnings before interest, taxes, depreciation, and amortization. Investors see this as a more accurate barometer of a company's health than cash flow from operations. This is where WorldCom's accounting games had the biggest impact. The company originally reported that its EBITDA for 2001 was $10.5 billion; now it says the figure really was $6.3 billion. In the first quarter, it reported EBITDA of $2.1 billion, while the real figure was $1.4 billion. In other words, WorldCom was in much worse shape than investors and banks thought. "This is an industry where companies trade based on EBITDA," says Robert Willens, an accounting expert at Lehman Brothers Inc. "Capitalizing expenses has a direct impact on EBITDA."

Does this mean investors can no longer rely on cash flow?

Not necessarily. Capitalizing expenses is not that common because it's so easy to detect. While there are some gray areas, it's pretty clear what should be counted as everyday expenses and what should be counted as capital expenditures. "This is sort of obvious to anyone who bothers to look at it," says Willens. "This doesn't involve offshore partnerships or special purpose entities. This is Accounting 101."

So where were the auditors?

Good question. WorldCom's auditors were from Arthur Andersen LLP, which says its work for the company complied with all accounting standards. The WorldCom fraud came to light when John W. Sidgmore became chief executive in April and ordered an internal review of the company's books. The probe was conducted by WorldCom's new auditor, KPMG, as well as WorldCom employees. At its completion, WorldCom announced the restatement and fired its chief financial officer, Scott D. Sullivan. If there is a silver lining in the WorldCom fiasco, it's that this sort of accounting fraud can be uncovered quite easily—you just need accountants who are looking for it.

By Peter Elstrom in New York
BusinessWeek / July 8, 2002

CASE 8B

QUALITY OF FINANCIAL ACCOUNTING'S ASSET VALUATION

MEMO TO M. Garonne, Business Editor
FROM A. Frank, Business Reporter
RE Story idea

Here is an elaboration of the story idea I mentioned in the elevator. Should I go ahead with it? What more should I, or could I, incorporate into the story? I know that a story about accounting valuations sounds like a snooze, but I am convinced it is very important to business and to stock markets, and I know I can bring it to life.

I foresee a five-part series:

- Series title: Accounting's asset values: it's a jungle out there.
- Part 1: The balance sheet's asset values aren't what you think.
- Part 2: Change with the times: accounting's critics certainly do.
- Part 3: A better way of valuing assets and calculating income?
- Part 4: Watch out: smoke and mirrors and assets that go bump in the night.
- Part 5: Who's watching the store: where are the accountants, auditors and regulators?

Here's the flavour of what I have put together so far.

Part 1: The balance sheet's asset values aren't what you think.

People who read our business pages have some business savvy, as our surveys have shown. But I'll bet most have a fuzzy understanding of what is actually in a balance sheet, and where the numbers come from, and what is not there, for that matter. My idea here is to get at three confusing things, at least:

- When I talk to accountants about what they put on the balance sheet as assets, they usually mumble something about having future value. Assets have value in earning income in the future, something like that. But then they value these future-valued things by their historical cost. So we have the future, valued by the past. Sometimes, in the case of property assets, the past can be a long way back, and the asset is expected to have value a long way into the future. You have to wonder what we have when we look at a balance sheet—whether in the end the balance sheet numbers can be interpreted at all.
- As if that wasn't bad enough, it turns out the various assets are not all valued exactly at historical cost, anyway. To confuse us further, accountants knock the values of some assets down to "market," and others down to "impaired" value. Someone apparently figures out what some assets could be sold for or bought again for, or what they are worth in generating cash flows in the future (there's that future benefit again). The balance sheet therefore doesn't actually use historical cost all the way through, but switches to other values here and there. Seems to result in a hodgepodge—when all these numbers are added up to get total assets, what do you really have?
- Wait, it gets worse. Picture the poor investor or businessperson holding a company's balance sheet and trying to figure out the company's value from the asset values. Can't be done. Some accountants have been quite huffy about it, saying that valuing the whole company is not their job, it's for markets or business valuators to do. Balance sheet values the company's assets, not the company, something like that. You still with me?

So the first part of the series would grab people's interest by showing them that what they get now isn't what they might think it is. Perhaps suggest at the end that accountants could figure out better what people do want in their balance sheets and provide that.

Part 2: Change with the times: accounting's critics certainly do.

Which is where we get to the critics of accounting. There are zillions of these, and one of the interesting things about all this is that the critics seem to change their tunes more than accounting changes. Accounting is the rock in all this.

- There were lots of critics 20 years ago when inflation was high. Using costs was said to produce irrelevant asset numbers, because prices were changing all the time but once an asset got into the books, its cost was frozen at a price no one would pay later, such as at the balance sheet date. The critics said to change the accounting to value assets at current prices, and that was tried. But the numbers were hypothetical and no one seemed to know how to use them for anything, and then inflation died down, along with the criticism.

- Then in the '90s, when dot-coms and telecoms were riding high, the critics were on accounting's case because asset values failed to represent the revolutionary business approach of the "New Economy." New companies with hardly any assets and no track record had stock market capitalizations many times those of "Old Economy" solid performers that made cars or soap or delivered physical goods rather than hype, and that had large assets as measured by accounting. To the critics, it was clear that accounting simply missed the "intangible" values of the high-tech favourites, values that investors could see as they bid the share prices up, but that accountants were too stodgy to see.
- Now that most of those high flyers are in bankruptcy court and stock prices have crashed down, the critics are saying that accounting somehow managed to get its values too high, not too low as the critics were saying two years earlier. Companies were writing off huge amounts of goodwill as worthless, where a short time earlier the goodwill had represented the future. No one says accounting's asset values are too low now.

Through all of this, accounting plows on, steering a bit one way or the other as critics assail it, but generally valuing assets pretty much as it always has. The critics flutter about, not really making much difference. There's a story in there somewhere.

Part 3: A better way of valuing assets and calculating income?

One group of critics has maybe had more staying power. For years, some, largely in the halls of academe, have been saying that accounting has had it wrong from the start in valuing assets at cost or something close to it. These critics say that assets should be valued basically at current market values, and that income should be calculated as the change in these market values over the period of time. Your assets are worth more, you show a profit; your assets are worth less, you show a loss. Simple. Anyone could understand it. And then maybe the stock market prices for companies would bear some relation to the balance sheet values of their assets.

An accountant told me that the use of market values is gaining ground, particularly in the guise of something called "fair values," which are estimates of what an asset would be worth if sold in a fair exchange between two arm's-length parties. I understand vaguely that fair values can be estimated somehow even if there is no clear market value and no intention to sell, and that they are being used more and more. Right now, these fair values add to the hodgepodge of asset values in balance sheets, but maybe they can take over from all the other values and make life simpler again.

The accountant said that we could come up with an interesting illustration by taking the balance sheets of a couple of well-known companies and showing how they might be different if fair values were used for all their assets, and how income would be different too. When I said that would be great, the accountant backed off some, saying that no one knew what the fair values were for any company and so the illustration would have to be hypothetical.

Well what do you think? Am I on to something? Will our readers think these ideas are good ones? I haven't outlined Parts 4 and 5 here, because this memo is already getting long, and in a way those parts are easier to write. There has been so much in the news about bad accounting and counting expenses as assets and so on that it won't be hard to list the kinds of things people should watch out for when looking at a balance sheet's assets, and to list the responsibilities of accountants, auditors and securities regulators to prevent abuses. I thought the series could end with a call to the accounting profession to come up with good solutions to the problems pointed out in the series, including to limit the ways companies make themselves look better than they are.

Let me know as soon as you can, and I'll get going!

NOTES

1. Canadian Institute of Chartered Accountants, "Accounting Recommendations: Section 3870, Stock-Based Compensation and Other Stock-Based Payments, Paragraph 3870.07," in *CICA Handbook* (Toronto: Canadian Institute of Chartered Accountants, revised to June 30, 2002), as posted on the *Handbook* Web site (http://handbook.cica.ca).
2. Present value is the future cash flows minus lost future interest implied by waiting for the cash. For example, suppose you are getting $1.00 after one year. If you had the money now, you would be able to earn 10% on it, but by waiting a year, you give up that interest. The present value of the $1.00 is the amount prior to the lost interest, the amount that would build up to $1.00 in a year at 10%. That would be 91 cents. In a year, 91 cents at 10% would earn 9 cents' interest, bringing the total to the $1.00 you will get in a year. The present value (91 cents) is thus always smaller than the future cash payment ($1.00), which is said to be "discounted" to a lower amount to remove the effects of future interest. See Section 10.7.
3. The Associated Press, "Massive fraud uncovered at WorldCom," *The Edmonton Journal* (June 26, 2002): G3.
4. J. Saunders, "Massive earnings fraud rocks U.S. telecom," *The Globe and Mail* (June 26, 2002): A1, A12.
5. C. Byrd, I. Chen, J. Smith, *Financial Reporting in Canada 2005* (Toronto, Canadian Institute of Chartered Accountants, 2005), 186–187.
6. Ibid., 194.
7. Ibid., 194.
8. Ibid., 214.
9. Ibid., 215.
10. Ibid., 214.
11. Ibid., 214.
12. Ibid., 214.
13. CPR, 2004 Annual Report, 49.
14. Byrd, Chen and Smith, 241.
15. Ibid., 214.
16. C. Byrd, *Financial Reporting in Canada 1995* (Toronto: Canadian Institute of Chartered Accountants, 1995): 101.
17. Ibid., 107.
18. Byrd, Chen and Smith, 214.
19. Ibid., 240.
20. CPR, 2004 annual report, 49.
21. Byrd, Chen and Smith, 241.
22. *Illustration of sum-of-the-year's-digits amortization.* The variables needed to compute amortization using this method are
    a. Cost,
    b. Estimated salvage value,
    c. Estimated life of the asset—calculated in years,
    d. The sum of the years—for example, for a three-year life: Sum = 1 + 2 + 3 = 6.
    e. Number of years of life remaining.

    The formula for computing sum-of-the-years'-digits amortization is

    Amortization for the year = (C – S) × (N / SYD)

    Where: Cost (C) and salvage (S) are as usually defined; N = number of useful years remaining, and SYD = sum of years' digits.

    Let's look again at the delivery truck and compute the annual amortization:

    Cost = $5,000; salvage value = $1,000; years of life = 5; sum of the years = 5 + 4 + 3 + 2 + 1 = 15

Amortization for year 1 = ($5,000 – $1,000) × (5 / 15) =	$1,333.33
Amortization for year 2 = ($5,000 – $1,000) × (4 / 15) =	1,066.67
Amortization for year 3 = ($5,000 – $1,000) × (3 / 15) =	800.00
Amortization for year 4 = ($5,000 – $1,000) × (2 / 15) =	533.33
Amortization for year 5 = ($5,000 – $1,000) × (1 / 15) =	266.67
Total	$4,000.00

23. Byrd, Chen and Smith, 241.
24. CPR, 2004 annual report, 49.
25. Byrd, Chen and Smith, 242.
26. Ibid., 288.
27. CPR, 2001 annual report, 46.
28. Byrd, Chen and Smith, 255–257.
29. *Business Week* (27 March 2000): 39.
30. See two Canadian studies: G.M. Entwistle, "Exploring the R&D Disclosure Environment," *Accounting Horizons*, 13 no. 4 (December 1999): 323–41, and C.A. Carnaghan, *Factors Influencing Managerial Decisions about Intangible Asset Disclosures: The Role of Accountability Theory and Impression Management*, PhD dissertation, U. of Alberta 1999.
31. For evidence on the effects of stock market prices' response to conservative expensing and not capitalizing research and development, see B. Lev and T. Sougiannis, "The Capitalization, Amortization and

Value-Relevance of R&D," *Journal of Accounting and Economics* 21 (1996): 107–38.

32. Byrd, Chen and Smith, 276.

33. Ibid., 276.

34. Ibid., 277.

CHAPTER NINE

9 Liabilities, Equity, and Corporate Groups

9.1 Chapter Introduction: Accounting For the Right-Hand Side of the Balance Sheet

TCI News Release TCI

Thornton Cunliffe Inc.

For release to all media at 4:00 p.m. Eastern Standard Time, November 22

Henry Woo, CEO of Thornton Cunliffe Inc. (TCI), and Sebastien Cruz, CEO of West Pass Industries Ltd. (WPIL) announced today that TCI has agreed to acquire the outstanding voting shares of WPIL. The combined strengths will position TCI to be first in Canada in serving its valued customers and will create a dynamic vehicle for investors.

Both companies' boards of directors voted unanimously for this combination of two strong and highly regarded businesses. Henry Woo will remain CEO of TCI, and Sebastien Cruz will become chairman of the board. Donna Gladred will become CEO of WPIL, which will continue to operate under its own name. To achieve the operating efficiencies envisaged, some WPIL units will be merged with TCI units, and the TCI Logistics Group will be transferred to WPIL. Gaining such efficiencies will require the elimination of some jobs at both companies, but normal attrition and turnover should provide for this so that no layoffs are expected.

Under the terms of the acquisition agreement, owners of WPIL shares will receive an immediate cash dividend of $1.20 per share and will exchange their shares for newly issued voting shares of TCI on a 2.4 to 1 ratio. At current share prices on the Toronto Stock Exchange, this values WPIL at C$319 million. The fair values of WPIL's net assets are estimated to be C$233 million, therefore goodwill on acquisition is valued at C$86 million. This represents the value of the WPIL name and expertise, as well as the synergies that will be achieved in the combined businesses.

TCI will guarantee certain of WPIL's debts and will underwrite the revision of WPIL's pension plans to make them consistent with TCI's. Managers and directors of both companies will be eligible for a new stock option plan, under which benefits are contingent on increases in TCI's share price looking forward three to five years.

Contact Zoe Duran at TCI for a press kit with full details.

Learning Objectives

This chapter focuses on understanding the right-hand side of a typical corporate balance sheet.

Chapter 8 was about the "left-hand side" of the balance sheet (assets). This chapter is about the "right-hand side" (*liabilities* and *equity*), and, because Chapter 10 covers analysis of the financial statements, is the final step in meeting the book's overall objective that you be able to pick up a company's set of financial statements and understand their contents. As has happened sometimes already, meeting this objective requires brief attention to some issues that are very complex and that are dealt with more thoroughly in advanced accounting courses. Most sections in this chapter are not detailed, for two reasons: we have encountered many of the issues already when considering asset and income accounting, and the accounting practices for many liabilities and equity items are very complex, beyond what this introductory book can sensibly cover. The intent is that you will learn enough to make sense out of statements' content without drowning in details. Perhaps that will spark your interest to learn more on your own or in other courses.

In this chapter you will learn:

- How companies' legal and financial structures are reported in the balance sheet. The right-hand side of the balance sheet is where much of the complexity of modern financial arrangements has to be worked out. This adds to Section 2.9's coverage of various forms of business: proprietorships, partnerships, and especially corporations;
- The basics of accounting and disclosure for various kinds of legal debts and estimated accruals for such phenomena as income taxes, pensions, and warranties;
- The principles behind accounting and disclosure for equity, supplementing what you already know about share capital and retained earnings;
- The nature of some controversies about liabilities and equity that may not be reported very well in financial accounting, such as financial instruments and stock options of the sort to be awarded by Thornton Cunliffe in the news release above;
- The basics of accounting for corporate groups, such as the above combination of Thornton Cunliffe and West Pass Industries. Accounting for corporate groups has a significant impact on income measurement and on the asset side of the balance sheet too; however, the topic is covered in this chapter because it raises important issues that are specific to the right-hand side. It is an example of an accounting method that is very complex in practice but has principles that are understandable without the practical complexities. It is also part of the goal of understanding a corporate balance sheet, because, as we saw in Chapter 2, most companies are actually corporate groups.

As for the asset accounting in Chapter 8, many of this chapter's topics have been introduced in earlier chapters, so this chapter builds on earlier material and ties up a few loose ends.

9.2 Current Liabilities

Many accounting principles apply to both current and noncurrent liabilities.

In much of liability accounting, the principal difference between current and noncurrent liabilities is just their timing. A loan due to be repaid in five months is shown as a current liability, and one due in five years is a noncurrent liability. Their due dates may be the primary feature that distinguishes them. Similarly, an accrual for an expense that is expected to be paid in five months is a current liability, and one that is expected to be paid in five years is a noncurrent liability. Both are accruals used for income measurement; they may also differ primarily in timing. Because noncurrent liabilities tend to be harder to estimate as the future is farther away, there may be more practical complexities for noncurrent liabilities than for current ones. Therefore, this section will examine some accounting principles for liabilities, current and noncurrent, and will point out some particular current liability issues. Noncurrent liability issues are picked up again in Section 9.3.

The current–noncurrent distinction should go beyond intention to pay.

Even in such a traditional idea as separating current and noncurrent liabilities there can be controversy. The distinction should be based on the expected pattern of payment, not on intention. For example, if a company has a debt that is due in six months, it is current, even if management hopes to delay its payment for a couple of years. This simple idea has caused a fuss lately, especially in the case of "*callable debt*," which is debt that is due at the option of the creditor. An example is that most bank loans in Canada are legally "*demand loans*." For such loans, the bank can ask for its money back with just a few days' notice. Many companies have bank loans that they repay on a planned schedule, or that they constantly repay and reborrow as the need arises. Looking at the pattern of payment, you could say that such bank debt is really noncurrent because all or most of it is likely to be paid well into the future. But legally, no matter what management may intend, the creditor controls the repayment schedule and can ask for the money on short notice. There is recent pressure to call all such callable debt current, no matter what the intended repayment schedule. Doing this could result in severe apparent damage to companies' balance sheets if bank debt that had been classified as noncurrent is moved to the current liability category.

Getting current liabilities right is important in measuring income and working capital.

Getting the current liabilities right is important for several reasons. The total current liabilities are part of the calculation of *working capital* and the *working capital ratio*, very important in assessing an enterprise's financial strength. Many of the current liability accounts are accruals of expenses, so getting income measured properly requires getting the accruals right. Conservatism supports recording all legitimate liabilities, especially any due in the short run or any whose recording would increase expenses (or reduce revenue). Doing this avoids overstating income. Conservatism also supports transferring any short-term part of noncurrent debts into the current category, as in the example above of callable debt, so that the short-term demands on cash to meet those debts are recognized.

Liabilities are part of the balance sheet, but also affect income, mainly through expenses.

As is true of assets, liabilities are significant both for their effect on balance sheet valuation and their connection to income measurement. Their principal effect on income measurement is through their association with expenses. Expenses arise from consuming the economic value of assets, such as inventory or fixed assets, but also from incurring liabilities. Such liability incurrence arises from expense recognition *prior to* the cash flow, such as accounts payable, income tax payable, pension liability, and warranty liability, topics mentioned in earlier chapters and examined in this chapter. Liabilities are sometimes associated with revenues too, such as via the deferred revenue liability for revenue collected before it is earned, but their main importance to income measurement is through expenses.

When auditors are examining the accounts, they pay particular attention to ensuring that no current liabilities have been left out of the balance sheet. They ask banks to provide written confirmation of loans, they review payments in the next period to see if any are for liabilities and corresponding expenses that should have been recorded in the current period, and they check accruals for unpaid wages, income taxes, interest, and other expenses. Sometimes extensive searches are made for evidence of unrecorded liabilities, especially when there have been other indications of accounting errors or manipulations.

A scam in the other direction was uncovered when an auditor found that a client company, trying to get its income down to save tax, had recorded expenses in the current year that were not actually incurred until the next year. The company had overstated current liabilities, surprising the auditor, who had been looking for understatements of them! The supplier of the supplies and services involved had assisted with the scam by obligingly dating invoices weeks earlier than they should have been.

This section summarizes some important things you should know about *accounting policies* for liabilities, as to their valuation on the balance sheet and their connection to income measurement. Only some parts will be new to you, but you should find the summary useful.

Legal Debts

Bank loans, trade accounts payable, wages payable, Canada Pension Plan, and employees' income tax deducted from their pay due to governments, other employee deductions and fringe benefits due, sales taxes collected and due to governments, bonded debt, mortgages, asset purchase contracts, and other legal debts are recorded when incurred and are reported at the amounts incurred (minus anything paid so far). Here are just a few details:

Debts are shown at the historical value that arose when the debt was incurred.

- *Historical cost* accounting applies here too. The amounts shown are those that arose when the debt was incurred. This is normally the same amount as will actually be paid, but sometimes it is not. (An example of where it is not, bonds issued at a discount or premium, is included in Section 9.3.)
- There is no recognition of nonhistorical interpretations of the debt, even if the economic meaning of the debt would increase because of such recognition. Three things therefore that are *not* recognized are:
  - Interest that will have to be paid but has not yet accrued (for example, if a debt is due in two years, only the interest to date is added, not the interest for the next two years).
  - Inflation (even though being in debt during a period of inflation is a good idea because you pay back with dollars worth less than those you borrowed).
  - Market value changes in public debt (for example, if interest rates have risen so much that a bond issued for $1,000 but now paying an unattractive interest rate is now selling on the bond market for only $780, the debt liability is not revalued on the balance sheet to reflect the lower market value).
- Unless there is evidence to the contrary, the company is assumed to be a *going concern* and, therefore, debts are shown at the amounts that would normally be paid, and are expected to be paid, not at some other liquidation value that might be negotiated with creditors if the company got into serious financial trouble.
- For important debts, some of the legal details are disclosed (usually in the notes to the financial statements). The main details here are the interest rate on the debt (especially for noncurrent debt), any assets or other securities given, repayment terms, and any special conditions, such as being convertible to equity.

Debts do not include future interest, inflation, or market value changes.

Liabilities' valuation assumes that the enterprise is a going concern and will pay.

Notes usually contain details of important debts, especially noncurrent ones.

Current Portion of Noncurrent Debts

In one way, current and noncurrent debts are just two parts of the same debt. In order to determine current liabilities properly, and conservatively, GAAP requires that if there is a noncurrent debt on which some payment is to be made within the next year, that payment be included in current liabilities. So a single debt is split into two parts: current and noncurrent. This does not affect the legal debt in the slightest: it is just done for accounting purposes.

There's a twist here you should watch for, consistent with the principle noted above of not recognizing future interest. In accordance with the above points, it's only the *principal* portion payable in the next year that's called current. Suppose, for example

The current part of noncurrent debt is only the principal portion of next year's payments.

- Jocelyn owes $71,000 on her mortgage.
- During the next year, she must make 12 monthly payments of $1,000, including interest.

- If the interest will amount to $6,400 over the next year, then the rest of the $12,000 to be paid will be $5,600 on the principal.
- Therefore, her balance sheet will show two components of the $71,000 principal owing:
  - a current liability of $5,600, the amount of the principal to be repaid next year, and
  - a noncurrent liability of the remaining $65,400 ($71,000 – $5,600).
- The current liability is *not* $12,000, the total of the payments to be made in the next year, because that includes the coming year's interest, which is ignored in the balance sheet because it has not yet accrued.

Short-Term Accruals and Other Current Liabilities

Short-term accruals are for income measurement and are usually not controversial.

Accrued interest, estimated after-sale service costs, estimated income tax payable, and other such estimated but not yet legally payable short-term liabilities are accounted for by debiting an expense account and crediting a current liability. Although they are not yet actual debts, they are reported in the same way as the legal debts. These accruals are not controversial for current liabilities, but can be controversial if they are noncurrent, as Section 9.3 will show. Such accruals are a product of the matching process behind income measurement, and they are usually done very carefully, because if they are not, an imprecise "cut off" of the expenses involved would make both the current year's and next year's income wrong.

Current liabilities also include various miscellaneous credit balance accounts.

Current liabilities also include other credit balance accounts.

- One, already mentioned above, and explained in Chapter 6, is deferred revenue or customer deposits, which represent revenue collected before it has been earned. This is not necessarily a legal debt, but it is viewed as an economic one, in that the enterprise has not yet earned the money. In a business sense, it is a debt, because it would be a poor business practice to collect money in advance from customers and refuse to either do the agreed revenue-earning work or return the money.
- Another credit balance account, which was described in Section 6.10, is an accrued liability, the negative version of prepaid expense: an account that may usually be a prepaid expense but sometimes ends up as a credit instead, because the expense is incurred but for some reason is not paid in advance.
- Similar to this is a third kind of credit balance account, an asset that has gone negative due to an event that is not typical of the asset. Two common examples are a bank overdraft (overspent bank balance) and a credit balance in accounts receivable resulting from a customer overpaying the account. This last is like a customer deposit but usually results from inadvertent overpayment or a billing error. (The enterprise may overpay an account payable for the same reasons: if so, the debit balance in accounts payable should be transferred to accounts receivable.) Reclassification of accounts between current liabilities and current assets is important only if the amounts involved are material to the total of either category.

HOW'S YOUR UNDERSTANDING?

Here are two questions you should be able to answer based on what you have just read. If you can't answer them, it would be best to reread the material.

1. Current liabilities arise for several reasons. What are they?
2. Why is it important to get the current liabilities measured properly?

9.3 Noncurrent Liabilities

Long-Term Debts

Debts that are due more than a year into the future are included in noncurrent liabilities, minus any principal portion due within the next year that is included in current liabilities.

Noncurrent debt is usually secured in some way, and the security and other details are disclosed.

Most noncurrent liabilities are supported by specific agreements about repayment terms between the enterprise and its lenders. These usually involve some *security* to protect the lender. There are several common kinds of security, which can exist in various combinations.

- One is a *mortgage* held by the lender on the enterprise's property or equipment so that the lender can claim title to those assets if the enterprise does not make the agreed payments on time.
- A second kind of security is a *debenture*, which is a more general kind of right by the lender to take some degree of control over the enterprise if necessary.
- A third kind is an *indenture*, which is a set of specifications that the enterprise must meet otherwise the lender can demand payment or take other action. Such specifications may be that the enterprise maintain a particular level of working capital, or a particular working capital ratio, or meet other conditions defined on the financial statements. (Such indentures may tempt management to choose accounting policies designed to help the financial statements meet the agreed specifications.)
- A fourth kind of security, often used by banks with smaller company borrowers, is to ask the owners of the company to provide *personal guarantees* in case the enterprise's assets are not sufficient to repay the debt if trouble comes.

GAAP require some disclosure of important security on long-term debts, plus repayment terms and some other details, so the financial statement notes about long-term debts can be extensive. Some long-term debts, such as *loans from shareholders*, may be unsecured and have an unspecified due date, which will also be disclosed if informative.

Conditional sales contracts and capital leases are common kinds of noncurrent liabilities.

A common kind of noncurrent debt is an agreement to pay for an asset over a period of time.

- For land or buildings, such an agreement is usually a mortgage.
- Equipment and vehicles may also be acquired with such agreements, often by a *conditional sale contract*, under which the title does not pass to the enterprise until it has met all the payments. These are usually not large in comparison to other noncurrent liabilities, so there may not be much disclosure about them.
- Another way of acquiring economic assets, explained in Section 8.14, is via *capital leases*. The liability for such leases, after being recorded by the process described in Section 8.14, is included in noncurrent (and current) liabilities just as if it was a regular debt, because the accounting principle is that they are economic debts.

Discounts or Premiums on Noncurrent Debts

Discounts and premiums result from differences between bonds' interest rates and market rates.

Sometimes noncurrent debt is issued at a discount or a premium. This is easiest to explain with *bonded debt*. A *bond* is an instrument like a share that usually can be traded among investors, but instead of carrying ownership rights, carries a portion of a mortgage, indenture agreement, or other security and has a limited term before it must be repaid and has the right to interest in the meantime.

- Suppose the enterprise decides to borrow using a bond issue composed of $1,000 bonds carrying 7% interest.

- When the bond issue is all ready, interest rates in the market for such bonds may have risen a bit, say to 8%. Lenders would not want a 7% bond.
- So the enterprise sells the bonds at a *discount*, a lower price such that the amount the lender pays will earn 8%.
- The lender gives the company less than $1,000 for each bond, and that lower amount is such that the $70 interest (7% of $1,000) represents the 8% the lender wants.
- If the interest rates have fallen, say to 6%, the lender will be willing to pay *more* than $1,000 for each bond, such that the $70 interest represents the 6% return the lender wants. So the enterprise gets a *premium* for the bonds, more than $1,000 each.

(The present value calculations behind bond prices are included in Section 10.7.)

Example

- A corporation issued 10,000 $1,000 bonds, thus having a total legal debt of $10,000,000.
- Suppose the bonds sold for a total of either $8,760,000 (a discount) or $11,180,000 (a premium).
- The selling price can be said to be the appropriate price for that bond at prevailing market interest rates, so in the first case, the bond pays interest at a rate below market rates, and in the second case, pays at a rate above market rates.
- At the issue date of the bonds, the proceeds and discount or premium are recorded thus:

Discount			Premium		
Dr Cash (proceeds)	8,760,000		Dr Cash (proceeds)	11,180,000	
Cr Bonded debt		10,000,000	Cr Bonded debt		10,000,000
Dr Bond discount	1,240,000		Cr Bond premium		1,180,000

The discount or premium is included with the legal debt on the balance sheet.

The bonded debt account is a liability. But so is the discount or premium. The premium or discount account works as a *contra account*, to change the balance sheet valuation of the liability without changing the legal debt account. (The premium is a credit balance account, so it is not opposite in sign as contra accounts like the allowance for doubtful accounts and accumulated amortization are.) The legal debt is what has to be repaid; the discount or premium is just an adjustment to get the proceeds to what will bring the bond market the return it requires. So on the day of issue, the enterprise's balance sheet would show a liability called bonded debt, at the amount of:

- $8,760,000 (in the case of the discount: $10,000,000 – $1,240,000), or
- $11,180,000 (in the case of the premium: $10,000,000 + $1,180,000).

Thus the reported liability meets the historical cost criterion: it is what was received for the bonds.

Amortizing a bond discount or premium makes the interest expense approximate the market rate.

But the amount of the proceeds is *not* what will eventually be repaid to the lenders. That is $10,000,000 in both cases.

- So the discount or premium is *amortized* over the period until the bonds are due. It therefore shrinks away until on the due date it is zero and the $10,000,000 is correctly shown as the debt on that date.
- The period's amortization amount is included with interest expense reported on the income statement.
- The discount is a debit, so amortizing it adds to the interest expense, making the reported expense higher than the $70 cash interest paid per bond. This makes sense, as the reason for the discount is that the bond market demanded a rate

higher than 7%, and by selling the bonds at a discount, the enterprise provided that higher rate. The real interest cost is higher than $70.
- In the case of a premium, the amortization reduces the reported interest expense, which again makes sense because the bond market was happy with a rate lower than 7% and by selling the bonds at a premium, the enterprise provided that lower rate.
- Thus, the reported interest expense approximates the market rate demanded when the bonds were sold.
- If you already understand the concept of *present value* (Section 10.7), you will see that what is happening is that the bonded debt, adjusted by the unamortized discount or premium, is being shown on the balance sheet at the present value of the bond, calculated at the market interest rate in effect when the bond was issued.
- Methods for calculating amortization of a discount or premium are in more advanced accounting textbooks.
- Just like amortization on assets, amortization of discount or premium is a noncash expense debit or credit that has to be adjusted for in the Operations section of the cash flow statement.

Long-Term Accruals

Long-term accruals are often imprecise, but are thought relevant anyway.

These are in principle just longer-term versions of the short-term accruals.

- Like the current liability accruals, they are created by debiting an expense account.
- But, since there will not be a payment for a long time, the credit is to a noncurrent liability.
- Many of these are approximate estimates, depending on many assumptions: they are recorded in order to account for the future consequences of arrangements made to help earn income today, and so their main purpose is income measurement rather than balance sheet valuation.
- Referring to the *relevance-reliability tradeoff*, imprecise estimates of future payments are thought relevant to users of the financial statements even if they are not entirely reliable.

Long-term accruals are shown at the present value of estimated future payments.

For long-term accruals (often called *provisions*), there is no debt payable now and it's often anyone's guess as to exactly when a debt will arise and precisely how much it will be. If feasible, such accruals are based on the *present value* of future estimated cash flows because of the principle, mentioned in Section 9.2, of not recognizing future interest in the balance sheet liability figure. Using present value is more feasible for accruals based on contractual arrangements, such as pension liabilities, than those based on estimates of more discretionary cash flows, such as product warranties. (The present value represents the principal value of the liability, not including future interest, like a mortgage the total payments of which exceed the present principal because the future payments will include interest. See Section 10.7.)

Warranty Liability

- This is the estimated future cost of providing warranty service for products already sold. The revenue is already recognized, so matching requires recognizing any promises to fix problems that go with the revenue.
- In the period in which a product is sold, an expense is recognized to match to the revenue by the expense recognition entry:

  DR Warranty expense
  CR Warranty liability

- When a warranty payment is made, the liability is reduced by the payment entry:

  DR Warranty liability
  CR Cash

Or, if a replacement product is provided:

DR Warranty liability
CR Inventory

For the second payment entry to work out over time, the liability estimate would be based on the *cost* of the products being provided as replacements, not on the selling price to the customers, the likely basis if cash payouts were to be made, as in the first payment entry.

- If, as is likely, some of the warranty cost will be paid within the next year, that amount is included in current liabilities among the short-term accruals.

Here is an example of the difficulty of making a long-term accrual. Like the hippie music the radio stations play for the baby boomers, it's an oldie but goodie. In the 1960s, General Motors produced a little rear-engined car called the Corvair. It was popular and seemed trouble-free. There were Corvair clubs of devotees. It was all very sweet. GM did not have to have a very large warranty provision for the Corvair. But then Ralph Nader's famous book *Unsafe at Any Speed* came out, criticizing the Corvair as well as other cars. People returned to their car dealers in droves, complaining about their Corvairs. It was no longer so sweet. Suddenly, GM had to increase its warranty provision, current, and noncurrent, because of the cost of fixing real or imagined problems. Its warranty expense estimates had been fine under previous conditions, but were suddenly made wrong by the unanticipated event of Nader's book. It's an example of the unavoidable fact that accrual accounting estimates of the future, no matter how carefully made, can easily turn out later to have been wrong.

Pension Liability

- This is the estimated future cost of providing pensions for work already done by employees, minus cash paid to a pension trustee to be invested to fund the eventual pensions. (A pension trustee is a third party that manages the pension's assets that the company paid out to the trustee. It is responsible for investing these assets and payment of pension benefits to retired employees.)
- For example, if an employee has worked five years and is already entitled to some part of a pension 30 years from now based on that work, the estimated present value of that pension entitlement is recorded as a liability. Cash already paid to the trustee is deducted from the liability.

Pension liability is a good example of a complicated but still imprecise estimate.

- You can see the problems in trying to estimate such a liability when you think of all the things that can change in those 30 years and that must be thought about in making the estimate: the employee might die first, be fired, or quit; interest rates (used in the present value calculation) will doubtless vary; the pension plan itself might change, even retroactively; laws governing such plans may change; and so on.
- When the employee earns a pension entitlement, that is presumed to be an expense of the period in which it is earned and is recorded by the expense recognition entry:

DR Pension expense
CR Pension liability

- When a payment is made to a trustee or directly to a retired employee, the payment is recorded by:

DR Pension liability
CR Cash

This transfers the money to the trustee, and *takes it out of the company's accounts.* So a company might have a very small pension liability if it is keeping up with payments to the trustee. But it might have a *contingent liability*: having made promises to pay employees, the company normally would keep those promises even if the trustee did not earn enough money investing the funds to make the promised pension payments years later. Contingent liabilities are disclosed in notes to the financial statements—as you can see from this example, they also are based on estimates of what *might* happen.

- Pension liabilities continually need adjustment as conditions and assumptions change, and those adjustments are just included in wages or other expenses of the period of the adjustment, because they are a routine consequence of accrual accounting, just as adjustments to asset amortization, allowance for doubtful accounts, and other estimates are routinely made.
- Because they are important to understanding a company's promises to its employees and its long-term financial situation, pension plans are usually described at length in notes to the financial statements, which normally include information about the total estimated obligation and the assets to meet those obligations that are held by the trustee. CPR disclosed, in a note that took nearly two pages, that at the end of 2004, the estimated obligation (present value) was $6.827 billion, much bigger than any of its balance sheet liabilities. Because the obligation was more than covered, as CPR calculated it, the company showed an $838.3 million pension plan *asset* among its noncurrent assets.[1]
- As the CPR example shows, if the company makes more payments than are necessary to meet the estimated needs of the pension plan, the pension liability can become an asset, a noncurrent prepaid expense. The pension liability can therefore change to an asset, and back again, just like the prepaid and accrued expenses explained in Section 6.10.
- There are three awkward complications with pension plans, much in the news lately:
    - The trustee's pension assets and obligations are not included in the company's balance sheet, so that means the company may have very large off-balance-sheet assets and liabilities, as CPR does. Not only do these represent *contingent liabilities* (and *contingent assets*), but also their role in the company's financial operations may be very large and not apparent from the balance sheet, just in long technical notes.
    - If the trustee has more funds than needed to meet the estimated obligations, so that the plan is over-funded, whose money is the extra? The employees' or the company's? There have been major battles with unions and other employee groups over this, because in the go-go 1990s, many plans earned more money in interest and stock market gains than expected, and some companies took back the extra to help with their general financing. The trustee's assets and liabilities, and any surplus, are not included in the company's balance sheet (though maybe they should be). This is an example of the very controversial off-balance-sheet financing issue, about which there will be more in Section 9.5. In the early years of the 2000s, many pension plans performed badly, even losing money, so companies' contingent liabilities looked likely to become real ones in order to make up the shortfall.[2]
    - Often the pension trustee invests the funds in the company's own shares. This is how CPR does it. This means that the employees' ability to receive their pensions depends on the company's continued success. In the optimistic 1990s, this was thought to provide a good incentive to employees to want to make the company succeed, as well as being a source of equity financing for the company. But what happens if the company goes bust, so that the share values plunge or

disappear? Then the employees get no pension. The company's contingent liability becomes huge, but if it is bust, it will not be able to pay, and the employees' pension trustee is left with worthless share certificates to paper the walls with. This is what happened in the Enron case in 2001: employees lost virtually all their pensions because the trustee had invested in Enron shares, which lost all their value when Enron collapsed.[3]

According to *Financial Reporting in Canada 2005*, 142 of its 200 surveyed companies reported having some sort of pension plan in 2004. Of these, 38 disclosed a pension liability, 5 a deferred asset, and 71 both, for a total of 114 disclosing some sort of balance sheet amount, up from 98 in 2001. Changes to improve disclosure requirements related to pension benefits are required by the *CICA Handbook* for years ending on or after June 30, 2004.[4] This may, at least in part, account for the increase in companies making balance sheet disclosures.

Post-Employment Benefits Other than Pensions

- These are similar to pension benefits, including health care, dental care, life insurance and other benefits. The differences from pension promises are often subtle, and the problems of estimating the cost of such promises are similarly vexing, so most of the points made above about pensions apply here too.
- The expense recognition and payment entries follow the same pattern as for pensions.
- Recent changes in Canadian accounting standards group these benefits with pensions, and similarly complex note disclosure is called for. CPR combined these with its pension disclosures, as the revised standards recommend.
- With Canada's state support of medical costs, these obligations are usually not as large for Canadian companies as they are for companies in the United States, where the obligations can be billions of dollars. In its 2004 annual report, for example, IBM reported a noncurrent liability of $8.4 billion.[5] Several news reports have discussed the cost added to General Motors vehicles by the cost of post-retirement benefits. In this regard GM reported an accrued liability of $28.1 billion at the end of 2004.[6] CPR, by contrast, reported a liability of only $248 million.[7]
- According to *Financial Reporting in Canada 2005*, 96 of the 200 companies disclosed that they had post-retirement benefit plans in 2004 in a separate note.[8]

Future Income Taxes

The method of accounting for future income taxes has recently changed in Canada.

Accounting for future income taxes is one of the most challenging topics in financial accounting. Part of the challenge results from the complexity of income tax law, and part from great disagreements about how future income tax should be accounted for, if at all. After many years of debate, the *CICA Handbook* was revised in 1997 to provide a fundamentally different way of accounting for future income taxes than had been done until then. (The new method was fundamentally different from the prior Canadian method, but more like the U.S. and IASC methods.) To emphasize the change in method, the name of the method and of the accounts involved was changed from *deferred income tax* to *future income taxes*. This section will outline the principles behind the accounting method: you don't have to be a tax expert to understand them!

The income tax accounting problem arises because of temporary differences between accounting and the tax law.

- Here's the problem. Because income tax law differs in many ways from financial accounting principles, there are differences between the income tax liability you'd get from the accounting income and other accounting numbers, and the income tax payable to the government for the year. Suppose, for example, that the following *temporary difference* exists:

- According to the best estimates made in the company's income tax returns for this year, the company owes $800,000 in income tax for the current year.
- The company has been deducting amortization for income tax purposes (called *capital cost allowance*) on an accelerated basis whereas the amortization in the accounts is straight-line. As we saw in Section 8.12, the two amortization methods eventually get to the same book value (salvage value, or zero), but there is *temporarily* a difference.
- At the end of last year, this difference multiplied by the income tax rate the company expected to pay was $1,100,000. This was recorded as future income tax liability at the end of last year.
- At the end of this year, the difference times the income tax rate was $1,250,000. The future income tax liability therefore has to be increased by $150,000 to the new number.
- The income tax expense for the year then is $800,000 currently payable plus $150,000 to adjust the future income tax liability, totalling $950,000.
- The journal entries to record all this would be:

DR Current portion of income tax expense	800,000	
CR Income tax payable		800,000
DR Future portion of income tax expense	150,000	
CR Future income tax liability		150,000

- The income tax expense on the income statement is thus the result of adjusting two balance sheet accounts: *income tax payable* and *future income tax liability*. The expense on the income statement will be the sum, $950,000 in the example, but the two amounts, *current portion of income tax expense* and *future portion of income tax expense*, should be disclosed in the notes if not on the income statement.
- On the cash flow statement, changes in income tax payable are part of the noncash working capital adjustment in calculating cash from operations, and changes in the future income tax liability are part of the noncash expenses adjustment, like amortization and long-term accruals such as pensions.
- In practice, the way the future portion of the income tax expense is determined is by analyzing all the balance sheet accounts that could involve differences between the accounting numbers and the income tax rules. The amortization versus capital cost allowance difference illustrated above is the most common source of such differences, but the income tax law is very complex, so there can be dozens of other sources of differences. Also, income tax is usually payable, but, as may have happened to you, companies sometimes get tax refunds, so there may be an income tax receivable. The amortization versus capital cost allowance difference creates a noncurrent future income tax liability on most companies' balance sheets, but because of the income tax complexities, it is possible, even likely, that the company will have two, three, or even six income tax items on its balance sheet all at once (there may, for example, be tax payable in Canada, but a tax receivable from the United States through a branch or subsidiary):

Potential Income Tax Locations on the Balance Sheet	
Current assets Income tax receivable Future income tax (perhaps with prepaid expenses)	*Current Liabilities* Income tax payable Future income tax (perhaps with accrued expenses)
Noncurrent assets Future income tax (perhaps with deferred charges)	*Noncurrent liabilities* Future income tax (usually shown on its own)
Notes to the financial statements will usually disclose any of these that are material, especially if they are grouped with other assets or liabilities.	

- To illustrate, at the end of 2004, CPR had the following balance sheet accounts, which you can see in the balance sheet we studied earlier in Section 2.10:
  - A current asset for future income taxes of $70.2 million;
  - A current liability for income (and other taxes) payable of $16.2 million; and
  - A noncurrent liability for future income taxes of $1,386.1 million (over $1 billion!).
- Similarly, since all the income tax accounts can be assets (debits) or liabilities (credits), the income tax expenses on the income statement can be any of these four combinations (the first one is the most common and was illustrated in the example above):

Potential Combinations of Income Tax Expense Portions

Adjustment Required On Balance Sheet		Resulting Income Tax Expense		
Current Payable or Receivable	Future Liability or Asset	Current Portion	Future Portion	Total Expense
CR	CR	DR	DR	DR + DR
DR	CR	CR	DR	CR + DR
CR	DR	DR	CR	DR + CR
DR	DR	CR	CR	CR + CR

- If you're not fed up with all this complexity, there is one more issue. Combining both current and future income tax involves spreading the expected tax burden out over many years, many accounting periods. That is called *interperiod tax allocation*, which you might remember from Section 3.5. But you might also remember from Section 3.5 that there is *intraperiod tax allocation*, which involves allocating the total income tax expense to the continuing income, the discontinued operations, extraordinary items, retained earnings adjustments, etc. Well, all these intraperiod allocations must also be done for both current and future portions of the income tax expense. It keeps many accountants very busy!

The matching principle requires that income tax accounting follow the rest of the accounting.

Why go to all this trouble? The simplest solution would be just to use the income tax actually payable, $800,000 in the above example, as the expense for the year. Just DR Income tax expense and CR Income tax payable. Then pay the tax. Easy. Many people in business would not expect otherwise.

But accrual accounting doesn't let us off the hook so easily. There is a big problem: the income tax expense would then depend on an amortization method other than the one in the accounts. The expense would not match the way other expenses are accounted for in the financial statements (amortization in this example, but many others in the reality of complex modern income taxation).

The *matching principle* would be violated if income tax just included the present year's tax payable, so accounting standards specify that in the case of temporary differences like this, *the income tax expense should match the rest of the accounting.* Because the estimates of future income tax arise from balance sheet accounts (and for other reasons we won't go into, such as changes in income tax rates), they don't necessarily exactly match the way revenues and other expenses were calculated. But they are close because, after all, the revenue and expense recognition affects the balance sheet as the income statement *articulates* with it. Thus, tax allocation accounting using future income tax liabilities and assets is specified by accounting standards worldwide.

It wouldn't work to just use the income tax payable as the income tax expense.

Well, one might say, horrified by the complexity outlined above, why not just use the tax amortization (capital cost allowance) in the accounts rather than the straight-line or other accounting methods, so that no temporary difference arises and there are then no future income tax implications? Simple, too, and it is appealing to businesspeople who don't want to spend a lot of money on accounting—but too simple, unfortunately. There are many differences between accounting principles and income tax law, and so unless we are prepared to scrap GAAP and just account for everything exactly the same as the tax law, we're stuck with some differences.

Government income tax policies are likely to have nothing to do with accounting measurement.

It would be appealing to just use the tax law for accounting, but that is not thought appropriate, at least not in Canada, the United States, and many other countries. The tax law is written for all sorts of economic, political, and other reasons besides measuring financial performance and position, so it would make a poor basis for accounting. For example, the government may say that machinery bought between July and October of year 200X can be amortized for tax purposes faster than regular machinery, and then in September announce that the deadline has been extended to December. Or that machinery located in an economically depressed part of the country should get a faster tax amortization than the same machinery located somewhere else. This is all quite reasonable for the government to do. But should companies keep changing their accounting every time the government makes such a decision, and should the same machinery, with the same useful economic life, be amortized differently just because it is located in a different province? You might argue, yes, sure, the machinery is a different economic asset because it is in a different place or was bought in December rather than January. But after much study of the implications, involving many countries (with widely varying tax systems), over many years, accounting standard-setters have concluded that it would be inappropriate for financial accounting's income tax numbers and all the related numbers such as amortization to ignore GAAP and be based on arbitrary tax law variations.

Future income tax adjustments use effective tax rates.

Income tax accounting uses whatever income tax rates apply in the various provinces or countries in which the company operates. By dividing the total income tax expense, which is the combination of the current and future portions of the income tax expense, by the continuing income before income tax, the enterprise's *effective income tax rate* can be calculated. For example, if the current portion of the expense is $311,000 and the future portion is negative $(73,000), the net total expense is $238,000. If the accounting income is $680,000, then the effective income tax rate is 35% ($238,000 / $680,000). Companies are supposed to explain why their effective rate differs from the official "statutory" rate if the difference is significant. Some reasons include having nontaxable revenues (dividend income, for example, is not taxed in Canada if received from another corporation that already paid income tax in Canada), having expenses that are not tax deductible (there are quite a few of these, including portions of entertainment expenses, some political contributions, and some kinds of financing expenses), or taking advantage of special industry provisions such as tax credits for oil and gas exploration.

Mini-Demonstration Problem: Income Tax Accounting

At the end of last year, Canadian Specific Railway (CSR) had the following income tax accounts on its balance sheet:

Current assets		*Current liabilities*	
Income tax receivable	$ 75,000	Income tax payable	$ 614,000
Future income tax	$114,000	Future income tax	$ 0
Noncurrent assets		*Noncurrent liabilities*	
Future income tax	$329,000	Future income tax	$8,743,000

At the end of this year, the company's accounts showed:

Current assets		*Current liabilities*	
Income tax receivable	$ 0	Income tax payable	$ 237,000
Future income tax	$196,000	Future income tax	$ 17,000
Noncurrent assets		*Noncurrent liabilities*	
Future income tax	$612,000	Future income tax	$9,229,000

During the year, CSR paid $5,218,000 in income tax to various governments and received a refund of $75,000. According to its income tax returns, the company's estimated income tax due for this year was $4,841,000. What were the following figures on CSR's income statement for this year: (a) current portion of income tax expense, (b) future portion of income tax expense, and (c) total income tax expense? The company's income before income tax on the income statement for this year was $14,226,000, so (d) what was its effective income tax rate? (e) What income tax adjustments would appear on this year's cash flow statement?

(a) Current Portion of Income Tax Expense

This equals the estimated tax due for the year according to the tax returns: $4,841,000. The amounts paid or refunds collected are irrelevant to the income statement, which is prepared on an accrual basis, not a cash flow basis.

(b) Future Portion of Income Tax Expense

This equals the net changes in the future income tax accounts from last year to this:

Current asset: $196,000 – $114,000	$ (82,000)
Noncurrent asset: $612,000 – $329,000	(283,000)
Current liability: $17,000 – $0	17,000
Noncurrent liability: $9,229,000 – $8,743,000	486,000
Net total	$ 138,000

The future portion of the expense is the net total, $138,000. The changes in assets are netted against the changes in liabilities: the liability increases represent increases in the expense, while the asset increases represent decreases in the expense, just as is true for any other liabilities (such as accounts payable) or assets (such as inventories or prepaid expenses).

(c) Total Income Tax Expense

Sum of current and future: $4,841,000 + $138,000 = $4,979,000.

(d) Effective Income Tax Rate

Income tax expense $4,979,000 divided by income before income tax $14,226,000 = 35%.

(e) Income Tax Adjustments on Cash Flow Statement

All the adjustments below would be in the Operations section of the cash flow statement, part of the conversion from net income to cash from operations:

- The net change in the receivable and payable accounts would be shown as part of the changes in noncash working capital: the asset change of negative $75,000 would be added back to income because it helped cash, while the liability change of negative $377,000 ($614,000 down to $237,000) would be subtracted because reducing it took more cash. This would produce a net subtraction of $302,000 from income.

- The net future income tax expense (which came from changes in the four future income tax balance sheet accounts) would be added back to net income as a noncash expense along with amortization and other noncash expenses: $138,000. It is possible that the net changes in the current and noncurrent future income tax accounts would be shown separately, or the former included with the noncash working capital changes, but their sum would still add to $138,000.
- The result would be a net overall subtraction from income of $164,000 ($302,000 – $138,000). Cash flow was higher than the accrual expense, so the cash outflow for income tax = the accrual expense of $4,979,000 + $164,000 = $5,143,000 outflow, according to the cash flow statement. (This would not be shown as a separate figure on the cash flow statement, but would be part of the overall conversion from accrual net income to cash from operations.)
- Check: The net cash paid out for income tax was $5,218,000 paid – $75,000 received = $5,143,000.

HOW'S YOUR UNDERSTANDING?

Here are two questions you should be able to answer based on what you have just read. If you can't answer them, it would be best to reread the material.

1. List the main kinds of noncurrent liabilities you'd expect to see in a typical balance sheet and describe how each kind is valued (how the number representing it is determined).
2. For this year, Kite Ltd.'s tax return estimates $32,118 owing in income tax for the year, but if you applied its effective tax rate to its income statement's "income before income tax," you'd get $22,949. If you examined the differences between accounting and income tax law for its assets and liabilities, you'd get an estimated future income tax liability of $28,976 at the end of this year (it was $38,415 at the end of last year). What would be (a) the current portion of income tax expense for this year, (b) the future portion, and (c) the total income tax expense?

(a) Current portion = income tax return estimate = $32,118.

(b) Future portion = change in future tax liability = $28,976 – $38,415 = $(9,439).

(c) Total income tax expense $32,118 – $9,439 = $22,679 net.

9.4 Equity

This section reviews topics in accounting for equity of unincorporated businesses and corporations. Some of these have been mentioned earlier in the book, and complexities are left for other books. Referring back to the equity descriptions in Section 2.9 may be helpful if your memory of the various forms of business and kinds of equity is hazy. Section 9.5 outlines ideas about complex financial structures and Sections 9.6 and 9.7 are about corporate groups—all of these have some implications to equity accounting.

Unincorporated Businesses

Unincorporated businesses, sole *proprietorships* or *partnerships*, are not legal persons separate from their owners, as corporations are. But the accounting principle stated in Chapters 2 and 3 of separating the company's dealings with customers and suppliers (from which it earns income) from its dealings with owners is still followed. The result is the following set of accounting practices for unincorporated businesses. Because of double-entry accounting and the articulation of the income statement and balance sheet, such practices for assets, liabilities, revenues, and expenses affect equity too, directly or indirectly.

Unincorporated businesses have generally similar assets and liabilities to those of corporations.

- Except for specific variations, most of which are given below, the accounting for assets, liabilities, revenues, and expenses is the same as for corporations, and so is the same as has been explained in earlier chapters. Unincorporated businesses still have accounts receivable, inventories, amortization, debts, short- and long-term accruals, and other business trappings. Accounting for assets and most liabilities is virtually unaffected by the form of business.
- Five main liability differences do exist, some of which affect the accounting for equity too.
  1. Unincorporated businesses (and "private" corporations too) cannot issue debt to the public, so you will not see bonded debt on the balance sheet.
  2. Any sort of secured debt is really a debt of the owner, so it is a little arbitrary as to whether something like a mortgage is included in the balance sheet—usually it is included if the mortgaged asset is included on the other side of the balance sheet, but there should be a note about the legal circumstances.
  3. Because the business and the owner are not really separable, generally there is no such thing as an owner's loan to the business corresponding to a shareholder's loan. Any investment by the owner (or owners, in the case of a partnership) is just included in equity.
  4. Similarly, the business cannot declare a dividend, so there is no such thing as dividends payable. The owner(s) may feel that some payment should be made by the business, but until that payment is made, there has been no economic transaction. Any payments to the owner(s) are just deducted from equity when made.
  5. Consistent with all this, and with income tax law, the business is not subject to income tax. Income tax is a personal obligation of the owner(s). Therefore there is no income tax expense on the income statement and no income tax payable or future income tax liability on the balance sheet. If the business does pay income tax on behalf of the owner, that is just deducted from equity when made, because it is really just a withdrawal of cash by the owner(s), as is true whenever the business happens to pay a personal bill for the owner.

Any investment or withdrawals by the owner(s) are included in equity.

An unincorporated business's income statement can be hard to compare to a corporation's.

- Two important expenses you'd see in a corporation are missing from the unincorporated business's income statement. There is no income tax expense and there is no expense for the owner's (or owners') wages or salaries. Any payments for income tax or to owners are deducted from equity, not shown as business expenses. The lack of an income tax expense in particular means that the income number is usually just called income, not *net* income. The lack of both of these expenses, coupled with the occasionally arbitrary classification of assets like buildings and cars, and expenses like travel and entertainment, as being part of the business or part of the owner's (owners') personal affairs, can make it difficult to compare the profitability of an unincorporated business to that of a corporation.

Unincorporated businesses lump all the equity items together into a single capital figure.

- The unincorporated business's balance sheet has a simple equity section: usually shown as just one figure called *capital* and calculated as:

  Beginning capital
  \+ new investment by owner(s)
  \+ income for the year (or minus loss)
  – withdrawals by owner(s)
  = ending capital.

  There may be a statement of owner's (or owners') capital changes, something like the statement of retained earnings except including all the equity changes listed above, and for a partnership there is usually a statement or analysis of the partners' individual capital accounts, as was illustrated in Section 2.9.
- Notes to the financial statements, financial statement titles, and account names are usually used to explain the business's relationship to the owner(s) and to cover issues such as those outlined above.

Incorporated Businesses

For an incorporated company (a *corporation* or limited company), there are several mainly legal requirements that influence the accounting:

A corporation's balance sheet is accompanied by considerable legal detail about equity.

- Dividends must ordinarily be paid out of accumulated income only and not out of invested capital. Therefore, shareholders' equity is divided into invested capital (share capital) and retained earnings, and only the latter is available for dividends.
- Share capital shows the dollar amounts, for each class of shares, contributed by shareholders over the years to buy shares directly from the company, including identifying any amounts paid in excess of par values (which may be called *contributed surplus* or some other name indicating it's an extra). These amounts are all *historical* figures. CPR had a contributed surplus in its equity section of $330.4 million in 2004.
- Various legal details about classes of shares and their rights and restrictions are disclosed separately, on the balance sheet and/or in a note.
- Retained earnings shows the accumulated income minus dividends declared since the company's incorporation. Restrictions on dividends may be disclosed. Declared dividends are liabilities of the corporation until paid.

Some other items should be mentioned here:

Shareholders of a corporation may be creditors too.

1. Shareholders may lend the company money, for example, by advancing money that the shareholders want to have repaid rather than investing in permanent share capital. In a small private corporation, the owner-manager may lend by not withdrawing all the salary that has been recorded as an expense, perhaps because the company is short of money. Such a loan from shareholder(s) is shown under liabilities, not owners' equity, because the shareholder is acting as a creditor rather than an owner (though the distinction may strike you as rather slight).

Treasury shares not cancelled are shown at cost as a reduction in shareholders' equity.

2. The company may (in some jurisdictions) buy a few of its own shares. Such shares represent an interest in the assets and do not have voting rights. Therefore, such shares are either cancelled, which reduces share capital, or else called *treasury shares* and deducted from the rest of owners' equity at the cost paid for them, at least until the shares are resold or cancelled (see Section 2.9).

The foreign currency translation adjustment is in equity for lack of another place to put it.

3. Also in Section 2.9, an awkward equity account, *accumulated foreign currency translation adjustment*, was explained. It's a consequence of adjusting all the other balance sheet and income statement accounts for transactions in foreign currencies, assets purchased with foreign currencies and liabilities owed in foreign currencies. Standards are changing so that in future it is likely the equity account will be eliminated by instead putting these adjustments into the income statement. For now, however, this account is a feature of the equity sections of most companies with operations in other countries. CPR is no different as its balance sheet showed foreign currency translation adjustments of $77.0 million.
4. Two phenomena that cause a little fun in accounting for corporate equity are *share splits* and *stock dividends*. A split is when the corporation's shares are divided into twice or three times as many shares, so that their smaller value may be easier for investors to purchase. (If some venerable companies, such as IBM, had not repeatedly split their shares over the years, each one would cost thousands or hundreds of thousands of dollars on the market.) A stock dividend is when the board of directors decides to issue some new shares (a small percentage of those already outstanding) to the shareholders instead of paying a cash dividend. Note two points about these.
   (1) They are really just different versions of the same thing. A 2-for-1 share (stock) split means that if you owned 100 shares, you now own 200. A 10% stock dividend means that if you owned 100 shares, you now own 110.

(2) If the stock markets are efficient, splits and stock dividends should not affect share values: the value of split shares should fall by 50%, so that the two new ones equal the value of the one old one, and the value of shares after a 10% stock dividend should also fall so that 110% of the new shares are worth what 100% of the old shares were. But the stock markets do not always react this way. Because a split makes the shares a little easier to own, the value of split shares may fall a little less than 50%, and the value of shares after a stock dividend may be a little higher than just dividing the old value over the new number of shares.

The traditional accounting practices for splits and stock dividends depend on a judgment that may be difficult to defend given modern stock market pricing. That judgment is that share splits provide no benefit to shareholders, but that stock dividends do.

(a) So if a corporation splits its shares, there is no accounting entry. The share records and the notes to the financial statements are just changed to show the new number of shares.

(b) On the other hand, a stock dividend is allocated a value: in the case of a 10% stock dividend, an entry is made:

DR Retained earnings
    CR Share capital

This entry recognizes a deemed increase in the book value of share capital. Calculating the amount and distinguishing between a small split and a big stock dividend are explained in more advanced accounting books.

Most companies perform stock splits when there is a feeling that their stock has become too expensive. Commonly, many companies like to keep their stock value under $100 per common share. One glaring exception to this practice is Berkshire Hathaway Inc. (**www.berkshirehathaway.com**), a holding company headed by Warren Buffett, which invests in and owns a variety of companies. The company's main activities are in the insurance field but it has a variety of other subsidiaries including Dairy Queen, Benjamin Moore, and numerous others. At the end of 2001, it had more than $500 million in equity investments including 8% of the common shares of Coca-Cola and 9% of the common shares of the Gillette Company, just to name a few.[9] Berkshire Hathaway has never split its common shares and in mid-2002, a single share cost more than U.S.$70,000. For many people, purchasing one share might compose their entire investment portfolio! (To find out Berkshire's current price, go to **www.nyse.com** and search under the ticker symbol BRK.A.) From 1964 to 2001, the return on the company's shares was a staggering 194,936% (for an annual compound return of 22.6%) versus 4,742% for the S&P 500.[10] This performance has made Warren Buffett one of the most watched investors in the world and the second richest person in the United States.[11]

Nonbusiness Organizations

As described in Section 5.5, nonbusiness organizations such as governments, clubs, and churches typically have different accounting for equity because they don't have owners, share capital, dividends, and other business trappings. When you are using the financial statements of such an organization, pay particular attention to what kind of organization it is and to the way that it is represented in the balance sheet equity section, because there is enormous variation that flows from tradition as well as legal particulars of each organization.

Generally, nonbusiness organizations have equity sections that are simpler than those of corporations. Often they show just a single figure calculated as total assets minus total liabilities. But there can be complexities too, such as the legal necessity to keep track of the sources of funds and keep various kinds of funds separate (for example, operating funds versus funds donated to the organization for specific purposes), so these can lead to occasionally complex accounting for equity and related assets and liabilities. There is a whole branch of accounting called *fund accounting* developed to deal with these complexities: its basic goal is to separate the organization into segments that are accounted for separately in accordance with each segment's legal or financial situation, which, therefore, have separate equity accounting, and which frequently have accounts receivable from, accounts payable to, and even investments in each other.

HOW'S YOUR UNDERSTANDING?

Here are two questions you should be able to answer based on what you have just read. If you can't answer them, it would be best to reread the material.

1. What are typical differences between an unincorporated business's equity and other balance sheet accounting and that of a corporation?
2. What are shareholder loans, share splits, and stock dividends, and what impact do they have on a corporation's balance sheet equity section?

9.5 Complex Financial Structures

Modern ways of organizing and financing businesses, particularly corporations, have created liabilities and equities that are difficult to fit into the double-entry GAAP model of financial accounting, and that are sometimes difficult to assign as liabilities or equity even if they are recorded. As you are probably tired of reading, accounting for these matters is complicated and so is dealt with in advanced accounting books, so this section just describes some of the items to watch out for when reading a corporate balance sheet.

Financing That Is a Mixture of Equity and Debt

Some shares and bonds may be convertible or have other characteristics that are a mixture of equity and debt.

Corporations' financing arrangements are often more complex than the simple liabilities versus equity categorization traditional in the balance sheet.

- Sometimes a corporation will issue *convertible* shares or bonds. According to certain rules, and usually at the choice of the holder of the share or bond, such a security can be converted to another kind. A preferred share may be convertible to common shares, or a bond may be convertible to common shares.
- Sometimes a share is *redeemable*, so that the company has the right to buy it back from the holder, or the holder has the right to sell it back to the company, making it a little like debt rather than the permanent capital shares normally are.
- Or *term preferred* shares may "come due" at a given date, making them also a little like debt.

These sorts of securities blur the balance sheet's line between liabilities and equity. If a preferred share is more like a debt than an equity, because, for example, it is redeemable at the option of the holder, GAAP are beginning to require that it be included as a liability, not an equity, and dividends paid on such shares would be interest expense on the income statement, not dividends on the retained earnings statement.

The standard model of financial accounting is clearly creaking under the strain of such "hybrid" securities, and there are increasing views that the balance sheet should not be categorized into debt and equity but rather that the characteristics of each financing source be explained and the decision about how (or if) to categorize it should be left to the user of the financial statements. Considerable information about such securities is already included in the notes, so that the statement user can evaluate their present or potential impact on the figures.

Commitments and Options

Warrants, stock options, and other commitments to issue more shares are disclosed.

Often, a corporation will make a commitment to issue further shares under certain conditions. Convertible bonds or preferred shares, mentioned above, are such a commitment. There are other types of commitments. A typical example is *warrants*, which are issued with shares and give the holder the right to buy more shares at a specified price. Another is *stock options*, which are often awarded to senior managers as a part of their compensation, and again give the holder the right to buy shares at a specified price. This price is expected to be attractive so that the stock option motivates the executive to try to increase the corporation's share price on the stock market because a higher share price makes the stock option more valuable. The commitments that have any likelihood of being honoured are disclosed in the notes, and if issuing the potential shares could reduce the earnings per share, the potentially lower "diluted" EPS is reported. According to *Financial Reporting in Canada 2005*, all of the 200 surveyed companies reported commitments to issue shares in 2004, with all but one providing a description of their stock-based compensation plan.[12]

Stock options are included in *stock-based compensation* in accounting standards. Such options, along with employee stock savings plans, provide assistance to employees, management, and directors to own their companies' shares. Stock options are at the centre of an extremely controversial accounting problem, one of the most controversial of all. Suppose a company gives the right to buy a share for $5.00 to an employee when the fair value of that share reaches a specified value at some future date. Then the employee is getting a benefit (at least as long as it is realistic to expect that the share price will reach that value and that the employee will opt to buy the share). Suppose the expected value of the benefit is $7 (more about this below). We might expect the arrangement to be recorded something like this:

DR Compensation expense (with Wages)	7	
CR Compensation liability		7

Then, when the employee buys the share, the share issue could be recorded this way:

DR Cash	5	
DR Compensation liability	7	
CR Share capital		12

But that has not been the approach used. Instead, there has been no recognition of the compensation, just this entry when the employee buys the shares:

DR Cash	5	
CR Share capital		5

For a company that has provided generous stock options, this entry fails to record a major part of the company's compensation to employees. In particular, it fails to show the real expense being incurred for such options, and therefore shows a higher income than it would if the compensation were deducted as an expense.

Keeping a major compensation off the income statement to make the income measure higher sounds like *earnings management* to many people (see Section 3.10). In the 1990s, with great increases in share prices, stock options were the major form of compensation for many companies, especially those in the high-tech, dot-com and telecom industries. When the accounting standard-setters tried to require the compensation to be recorded as an expense, there was great opposition from many companies. There were strong opinions about this, with headlines like "Expensing options is a move forward,"[13] and "Any way you look at it, options are an expense."[14] Perhaps the controversy will die down as the great increases in share prices seen in the 1990s have stopped or been reversed, along with the attractiveness of stock options, but perhaps not!

Some of the opposition to recording the compensation came from companies who were happy to keep it out of the income calculation, but there are some other reasons:

- The entry above looks simple. Just record the $7 expected benefit given to the employee. But it is not so simple in practice.
    - How is the "expected benefit" calculated? The best solution developed so far is to use a sophisticated options-valuation formula (likely the "Black-Scholes" formula) to calculate what the option is likely to be worth at the date it is granted (assumed to be $7 above), and then update that estimate regularly, adjusting the liability and debiting or crediting expense each time an adjustment is needed.
    - What if the share price is bouncing around a lot? Is the estimated amount of the benefit so clear? The formula above takes assumptions about expected share price variation into account, but using assumptions makes the value more arguable.
    - What if the employee doesn't buy the share when he or she could, but waits until the price is higher than the expected price, or lower? Should such a decision by the employee affect the compensation expense recorded by the employer?
    - What if the share price falls instead, so that when the employee can exercise the option, the price is $3, so the employee would be better off buying the share on the open market than by exercising the option (if the employee were then interested in owning any shares at all)?
    - What if the company doesn't do as well as everyone hopes and no or few employees ever exercise their options?

  In all these cases, any compensation expense is arguable and even hypothetical at any time prior to the employee's exercising the option, and maybe even then.

Canada became the first major jurisdiction to require the expensing of all stock-based compensation awards for all fiscal periods beginning on or after January 1, 2004.

While the concept of recognizing the value of the options granted as employee compensation expenses is quite simple, though still controversial, the determination of the "fair value" can be very complex. The *CICA Handbook* illustrates the use of the Black-Scholes options pricing model for this purpose. As with some other topics we have introduced, the details of this process are best covered in a more advanced course.

Once this value of the options is determined, the accounting is much more straightforward. As a simplified example let's assume Options One, a public company, grants to its employees options to purchase 10,000 shares on January 1, 2006. The exercise price is $25, equal to the market price of the stock on the grant date. All of the options vest at the end of the three years. Using the Black-Scholes pricing model, the fair value of the options is determined to be $90,000. In the absence of a change in the calculated value, the following entry would be made in each year to recognize the compensation cost:

DR Compensation cost	30,000	
CR Contributed surplus		30,000

Assuming all the options are then exercised on the same day, the entry to record the issuance of stock would be:

DR Cash (10,000 shares x $25)	250,000	
DR Contributed surplus	90,000	
CR Common stock		340,000

Off-Balance-Sheet Financing and Contractual Obligations

Enterprises may make many financial commitments that are not recorded as liabilities.

New financial arrangements are being invented all the time, and the impacts they make on the balance sheet, or might make depending on the company's accounting policies, are likely to be a factor in their acceptability and popularity. Five examples of financing that may or may not be well reported in the balance sheet and/or in the notes to the financial statements include:

- Ordinary "operating" rental and leasing contracts (capital leases *are* included in the liabilities, as we saw in Section 8.14). In an article titled "Badly in need of repair," about alleged severe problems in accounting, *The Economist* argued in 2002 that operating leases make up most off-balance-sheet financing and many should have been recorded instead as capital leases, thus getting the assets, but especially the financing, onto the balance sheet. *The Economist* said that in 1997, one-third of the aircraft of the five biggest American airlines were treated as operating leases rather than capital leases.[15]
- The sale of rights to collect accounts receivable so as to speed up the cash inflow in return for taking on potential obligations to the party buying those rights.
- Making long-term purchase commitments to get favourable terms.
- Making commitments for abnormal expenditures, such as large commitments for fixed assets.
- Financing pensions and other post-employment benefits using trustees. The trustees' assets and liabilities do not appear in the company's balance sheet, as explained in Section 9.5, but the company is usually required to make up any shortfall in the trustee's provisions for employee pensions, and may want to take back into its own income any extra earnings made by the trustee.
- Using subsidiary or associated companies to borrow money so that the commitments do not show up on the parent company's balance sheet. Usually the parent company guarantees such debt, so there is a potentially large commitment nevertheless. This is one of the ways Enron got into trouble: using so-called "special purpose entities (SPEs)" (business partnerships) to handle much of its financing. The relationship between Enron and the hundred or more SPEs it used was not apparent to users of the company's financial statements, and they did not appear at all in Enron's liabilities, though there was some disclosure of them in Enron's notes. When the SPEs got into trouble, they helped to pull Enron down.[16]

Many, probably most, of these arrangements are made for good business reasons. But there may be a concern among users of financial statements that sometimes such sources of financing may be sought in order to avoid recording liabilities and so avoid weakening the balance sheet. As these obligations are not included in the financial statement figures, they can only be learned about by reading the notes, if then. GAAP require that significant contractual obligations be disclosed, and *Financial Reporting in Canada 2005* indicates that in 2004, 95 of the 200 surveyed companies provided disclosures of guarantees other than guarantees of subsidiary debt.[17]

Financial Instruments

Financial instruments include financial assets and liabilities, whether or not recognized in the accounts.

These were mentioned briefly in Section 2.9. The phrase *financial instruments* refers to the company's set of financial assets and liabilities. It also covers various commitments and arrangements, such as agreements to purchase currencies in advance to "hedge" against the risk of unfavourable currency fluctuations, "derivative" instruments that are based on overall market price changes in shares, currencies or commodities, or "swap" contracts in which, for example, an outside bank agrees to pay the interest on some of the enterprise's debt if the rate varies beyond some agreed upon range. In its 2004 annual report, CPR had about two pages of information about its financial instruments.[18]

- Forward selling or purchasing of U.S. dollars to manage its foreign currency risk (exposure to currency fluctuations). At December 31, 2004, CPR reported that based on futures prices then, it had a potential unrealized gain of $0.2 million on these forward contracts. Neither this gain nor the contracts themselves (about U.S.$98.3 million) appeared in the financial statement figures, just in the notes.
- Forward contracts to buy crude oil, to protect against crude oil price fluctuations (CPR uses a lot of fuel). The unrealized gain on the approximately U.S.$146.6 million of these oil futures contracts was $32 million at the end of 2004. Again, none of these were included in the financial statement figures.
- Interest rate swaps, by which someone else agrees to pay the interest on some CPR debt and CPR in turn pays the other party a different rate. This is done to make interest rates more variable, so that the company is not stuck with high-interest debt. At the end of 2004, CPR had swap agreements for a nominal amount of U.S $200 million.
- Interest rate risk and fair values of debt. As is explained in Section 10.7, interest rates and market values of bonds and other debts are intimately related. As interest rates rise, debt values tend to fall, because debt paying what had been an attractive interest rate becomes less attractive, and vice versa. CPR provided a table of all its debts, estimating fair values for each and comparing those to the book values.
- Credit risk on the various financial instruments, arising if the other parties to the various arrangements didn't live up to their side of the bargain. This can happen if one party makes a bad deal and later cannot, or will not, pay what it has promised. One of the many problems Enron's collapse created was that it became unable to live up to billions of dollars of energy contracts, leaving other companies suddenly liable or unprotected from losses. CPR reported that there was no significant risk of this kind from its financial instruments at the end of 2004.

Existence and fair values of financial instruments are generally disclosed, but the accounts are not adjusted.

There is literally no end to the kinds of financial instruments that exist, and innovations in instruments happen practically daily. Accounting standard-setters have wrestled for several years with the problem of whether and how to represent these instruments in the financial statements. Recently, GAAP have required that such instruments be disclosed in the notes, as we saw with CPR above. In April 2005, the Accounting Standards Board issued three new sections of the *Accounting Handbook* dealing with financial instruments. This new comprehensive guidance largely harmonizes Canadian GAAP with U.S. standards. The new requirements are applicable to fiscal periods on or after October 1, 2006.

Under the new guidelines, financial instruments are classified as follows:

1. **Held for trading** investments are designated as such if at the time of purchase they are acquired principally for the purpose of selling, or they are to be held as part of a portfolio of investments managed together for short-term profit. This classification is determined primarily by management intent.
2. **Held to maturity** investments must have fixed or determinable payments (such as the interest payments on a bond) and a fixed maturity date, and the investing entity must have a positive intention and the ability to hold the investment to maturity.
3. **Loans and receivables** are financial assets resulting from the delivery of cash or other assets by a lender to a borrower in return for a promise to repay on a specified date or dates, or on demand.

4. **Available-for-sale** financial assets are those financial assets that are designated as available for sale or that are not classified as one of the three categories described above.

HOW'S YOUR UNDERSTANDING?

Here are two questions you should be able to answer based on what you have just read. If you can't answer them, it would be best to reread the material.

1. Why do redeemable or convertible securities issued by a corporation cause some difficulties for the traditional balance sheet format?
2. Why is off-balance-sheet financing a controversial problem for accounting?

Many businesses are really groups of corporations.

9.6 Corporate Groups: Intercorporate Investments

Modern businesses, especially large ones, are often groups of separately incorporated companies. Such *corporate groups* were discussed in Section 2.9. This section and the next expand on that discussion, describing *consolidated* financial statements for corporate groups but also some other accounting issues involved in such groups. Accounting for corporate groups is a complicated part of financial accounting and is covered in detail in the financial accounting standards of the CICA and FASB. This book introduces you to the main principles behind it and shows you how to apply the principles to do some basic calculations.

Kinds of Intercorporate Investments

Corporations invest in other companies in many ways and for a variety of reasons. The investment may be passive in nature, or made for one of the following reasons:

1. An investment may be targeted to earn a higher return on idle cash than that provided by bank accounts. Typically of low risk and readily convertible to cash, these investments may generate income from interest or dividends, or capital gains if the price rises.
2. An actively managed portfolio of investments may be used in the normal course of business to earn returns on price changes. Such active trading investment portfolios are most often used by financial institutions who may earn further returns by acting as a dealer.
3. Cash may also be invested in longer-term securities to earn higher rates of return. While such investments may be made in equity securities, money market instruments such as bonds are more commonly used. The intent is often to hold such debt instruments to maturity.

Corporations also make strategic investments "in equity instruments issued by another entity, with the intention of establishing or maintaining a long-term operating relationship with the entity in which the investment is made."[19] Such investments may be accounted for as subsidiaries, investments subject to significant influence, interests in joint ventures.

Six common investments are summarized in Exhibit 9.1 and will be examined in this section and the next.

Classification and Accounting for Investments

Classification	Investment Type	Accounting Method
Passive	Hold-to-maturity	Cost
Passive	Available for sale	Fair value: gains & losses are recognized in other comprehensive income until sold
Passive	Trading investment	Fair value: gains & losses are recognized in net income
Strategic	Control investment	Consolidation
Strategic	Significant influence	Equity method
Strategic	Joint venture	Proportionate consolidation

Figure 9.1 illustrates a corporate group, with Corporation A at its financial centre. This section will review how to account for A's investment in Corporations B, D, and H, none of which A controls, and the next section will cover accounting for A's investment in C, E, F, and G, all of which A controls.

1. Temporary Investments (Short-Term Passive Investments)

Temporary investments are the most short-term and passive intercorporate investments.

An investment is classified as a "temporary investment" if it matures within one year or if it can be liquidated reasonably quickly and the investment is intended to be a temporary use of idle cash. Held-for-trading investments would usually be temporary in nature. Held-to-maturity investments would be classified as long-term unless the maturity falls within one year. Available-for-sale investments may be either current or long-term, the determination of which requires careful consideration of the conditions described above.

The potentially significant effect on the reported liquidity position of the entity makes proper determination of the current *vs.* long-term classification of these investments critical.

2. Long-Term Passive Investments

In a passive investment, the investor does not exercise significant influence over the investee.

As noted above, held-to-maturity investments will be long-term unless the maturity falls within one year and under certain circumstances available-for-sale investments may also be classified as long-term. Held-to-maturity investments are, by definition, debt securities. While management's intent is to hold these securities to maturity, they may be sold at any time. Available-for-sale and held for trading investments may be either debt securities or share investments.

If the investment is in voting shares then it may be classified as either passive or strategic in nature depending on the intention behind and *control* involved in the investing corporation's (investor's) ownership of the investment.

3. Long-Term Strategic Investment

The equity basis is used when the investor exercises significant influence over the investee.

In a strategic investment, the investor owns enough of the investee company to influence what it does, but may not entirely control it. A strategic investment in common shares may be classified as a significant influence investment, a control investment, or a joint venture. The investing corporation is said to exercise *significant influence* if it has more than the 20% voting interest suggested above but not voting control (not more than 50%). This is illustrated in Figure 9.1 as A's investment in D. In this case, the *equity basis* of accounting is used. Under this basis, the investing corporation includes in its income statement *and* balance sheet its share of earnings by the investee company, because it has influenced that company's performance and can take some credit for it.

Under the equity basis,

The equity basis is accrual accounting, the investor's share of the investee's income is accrued.

When the investor receives a dividend from the investee, that is collection of accrued income.

- the investor's investment asset is still valued initially at cost, as it was for passive investments using the cost basis.
- As the *investee* corporation earns income (or incurs losses), the *investor corporation's* asset is increased for the investor's share of that income (or decreased for its share of losses!) and that share is included in the investor's income. This is an accrual of income the investor is entitled to. The investor is taking credit for its share of the investee's income (increase in retained earnings). Nonoperating "other" revenue is credited with this share and the investment asset account is debited, so that asset account is treated like an account receivable for the accrued income.
- When the investee pays a dividend, the investor receives some of the accrued income as its share of the dividend, so the dividend received is deducted from the investor's investment asset account, just as collection of an account receivable would be deducted from the account receivable asset. The dividend is not called income by the investor because *the income has already been accrued*; instead, the dividend is deducted from the investment asset because it is considered a return of some of the money invested.
- There are some other more complicated features of equity basis accounting we will not get into.

Financial Reporting in Canada 2005 reports that in 2004, 124 of the 200 companies surveyed had long-term investments other than joint ventures (mentioned at the end of this section). Of these, 24 used the cost basis, 19 used the equity basis, 72 used both, 1 found some other way of accounting for their investment, and 8 did not say what basis they used.[20]

A Cost and Equity Basis Example

Exhibit 9.2 summarizes how the two methods work (ignoring complexities):

Here is an example. Grand Ltd. acquired investments in two other corporations on January 1, 2006. These acquisitions are (a) and (b) in the list below; events (c) to (e) also took place in 2006.

a. 60,000 shares (15% of the voting interest) in AA Ltd. were purchased for $1,800,000 cash. Because this was to be a fairly passive long-term investment, Grand would account for it using the *cost basis.*
b. 145,000 shares (29% of the voting interest) in BB Ltd. were purchased for $4,640,000 cash. Since Grand intended to participate in the management of BB Ltd., Grand would account for it using the *equity basis.*
c. On June 30, both investees announced their earnings per share for the first six months of 2006: $2 per share for AA Ltd. and $2.10 per share for BB Ltd.
d. On December 10, both investees paid dividends to shareholders: $1.50 per share for AA Ltd. and $1.60 per share for BB Ltd.
e. On December 31, both investees announced their earnings per share for 2006: $3.40 per share ($1.40 additional since June 30) for AA Ltd. and $3.90 per share ($1.80 additional since June 30) for BB Ltd.

FIGURE 9.1

Illustration of a Corporate Group

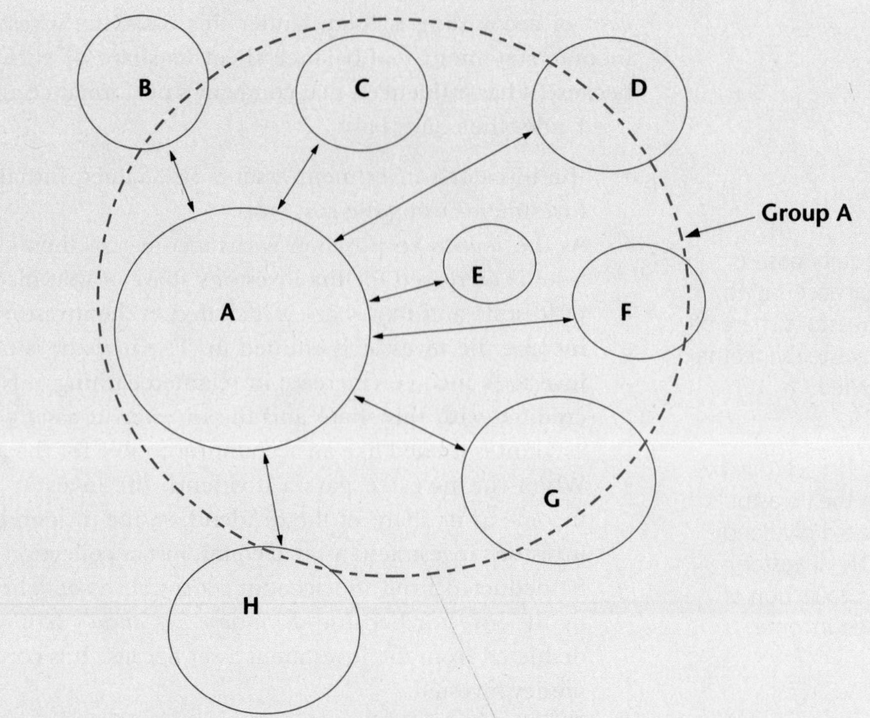

Corporation A is the main company in Group A, an economic entity greater than A by itself and encompassing the separate corporate legal entities.

A owns all of the voting shares of C and E: they are entirely part of Group A and so are combined with A in A's consolidated financial statements.

A owns more than 50% of the voting shares of F and G, so they are consolidated too, but some accounting has to be made for the parts of them A does not own.

A does not control D but has significant influence over it, so it will be accounted for as a long-term active investment (equity basis).

A has no significant portion of the voting shares of B or H, so they will be accounted for as passive investments, either short-term or long-term depending on A's intent.

Joint ventures and mergers are not illustrated here.

	Cost basis	**Equity basis**
Initial carrying value of the investor's intercorporate investment asset	Original cost	Original cost
Investor's share of income earned by investee	Nothing done	Add to asset and to other revenue
Investor's share of dividend paid by investee	Add to cash and to other revenue	Add to cash and deduct from investment asset
Resulting balance sheet value of the investor's intercorporate investment asset	Just original cost	Original cost plus accrued income share minus share of dividends paid

The effects of items (a) to (e) on the financial statements of Grand Ltd. at the end of 2006 are:

INVESTMENT IN AA LTD. (COST BASIS)

a. Long-term investment asset starts out at the purchase price of $1,800,000 (cash reduced by same amount).
b. (Concerns only BB Ltd.)
c. Earnings announcement is ignored for accounting purposes in the cost basis.
d. Cash received and dividend revenue are recorded for $90,000 (60,000 shares × $1.50).
e. Earnings announcement is ignored for accounting purposes in the cost basis.

Cost basis: no change in asset; dividend added to revenue when received.

Using the cost basis, Grand Ltd.'s financial statements as of December 31, 2006, will therefore include for AA Ltd.:

Grand Ltd. balance sheet at end of 2006
Investment in AA Ltd. (noncurrent asset) $1,800,000
Grand Ltd. income statement for 2006
Dividend revenue (in other revenue) $ 90,000

INVESTMENT IN BB LTD. (EQUITY BASIS)

a. (Concerns only AA Ltd.)
b. Long-term investment asset starts out at the purchase price of $4,640,000, the same as if the cost basis were used.
c. Upon earnings announcement, both investment revenue and investment asset are increased by $304,500 (145,000 shares × $2.10), Grand's share of BB's income.
d. Cash is increased by and investment asset is reduced by $232,000 (145,000 shares × $1.60): the dividend received is therefore deemed to be a return to Grand Ltd. of some of its investment.
e. Upon earnings announcement, both investment revenue and investment asset are increased by $261,000 (145,000 shares × $1.80), Grand's share of BB's income.

Equity basis: asset and revenue increased for income share; asset decreased upon dividend.

Using the equity basis, Grand Ltd.'s financial statements as of December 31, 2006, will therefore include for BB Ltd.:

Grand Ltd. balance sheet at end of 2006
Investment in BB Ltd. (noncurrent asset) $4,973,500
Grand Ltd. income statement for 2006
Investment revenue (in other revenue) $ 565,500
Calculations:
$4,973,000 = $4,640,000 + $304,500 – $232,000 + $261,000
$565,500 = $304,500 + $261,000

4. Joint Venture

A *joint venture* is a partnership between the investing corporation and other investors, usually formed to conduct exploration (such as in the oil and gas industry), develop new products, or pool resources in some other way. It is common in international business. Here, the investing corporation does not have control, but it does have significant influence on the joint venture because of the partnership arrangement and the business arrangements among the joint venture and the partner investors.

Joint ventures are accounted for in the investing company's financial statements using "proportionate consolidation," in which the investing company's proportionate shares of the venture's assets and liabilities (say, 50% if the venture is 50% owned) are combined with the investing company's assets and liabilities. We will not examine this method in this book.

HOW'S YOUR UNDERSTANDING?

Here are two questions you should be able to answer based on what you have just read. If you can't answer them, it would be best to reread the material.

1. If Gretel Ltd. buys a noncontrolling number of shares of Hansel Inc. for $460,000, what are the criteria by which management of Gretel should decide if the investment is to be accounted for on the cost basis or the equity basis?
2. During the year, Gretel receives a $45,000 dividend from Hansel. At the end of the year, Hansel reports a net income. If Gretel's proportion of the Hansel voting shares is applied to Hansel's net income, the resulting figure is $78,500. What income from its investment in Hansel will Gretel report if it is using the cost basis? The equity basis? What is the "Investment in Hansel" asset on Gretel's books at the end of the year on the cost basis? The equity basis?

Cost basis income = $45,000, the dividend;

Equity basis income = $78,500 (Gretel's share of Hansel's income);

Cost basis asset = $460,000 (no change from the investment in part 1);

Equity basis asset = $493,500 ($460,000 + $78,500 share of income – $45,000 dividend).

9.7 Corporate Groups: Consolidation

This section considers the remaining kind of investment summarized in Exhibit 9.1, combining the financial statements of a group of corporations into one set of *consolidated financial statements* representing the group.

5. Acquisition by One Corporation of Another

> Consolidation represents the corporate group as one economic entity.

Frequently, one corporation acquires more than 50% of the voting shares of another, becoming the majority owner of the other. This was illustrated in Figure 9.1 as A's investment in C, E, F, and G. This is done for many reasons, including to operate the two companies jointly and gain the benefits of such coordination. As long as voting control is held, the investing company can gain many benefits without having to own all the shares of the other, though it may well do so. Financial accounting uses a technique called *consolidation* to present the two companies as one *economic entity*, almost as if they were one company. As noted in Figure 9.1, the economic entity is greater than any of the individual legal entities represented by the corporations in the group.

> A corporate combination is accounted for as the acquisition of one corporation by the other.

Until recently, a *business combination* could be defined as a *merger*, a coming together of equals, instead of an *acquisition* by one of the other. To summarize a long and loud controversy, accounting standard-setters finally concluded that the accounting method for mergers, called "pooling of interests," led to too many abuses and masked what was nearly always one company dominating the other. Therefore, all corporate combinations are accounted for using a method called the "*purchase method*" to distinguish it from pooling of interests. The company that is in control is also called the *parent* and the controlled company is called the *subsidiary*.

> Consolidation portrays separate corporations as if they were a single entity.

Consolidation is imaginary: there is no legal, consolidated entity. Rather, it is legally a group of separate companies with connected ownership. The idea is to present the group of companies *as if* it were a single entity. This method is thought to represent the economic and business circumstances more faithfully than would reporting separate statements for all the legally separate companies and leaving the user to try to add them together.

> The basic idea of consolidation is to add the companies' accounts together.

Consolidation uses a simple idea: to prepare the financial statements of a group of companies, put the balance sheets, income statements, and other statements for all the companies side by side and, mostly, add them up. The consolidated balance sheet's cash figure would be the sum of all of the companies' cash figures, the consolidated income statement's cost of goods sold expense figure would be the sum of their cost of goods sold figures, and so on. But accounting is never that simple, is it? To apply this simple idea to the complexities of modern businesses, a quite complicated set of GAAP for consolidation has arisen. In this book, the complexities will be left out in favour of a focus on three main issues in consolidation accounting:

1. What to do if the parent company owns less than 100% of the subsidiary's voting shares (Corporations F and G in Figure 9.1).
2. Determining the asset and liability values that are to be added together.
3. Determining any "goodwill" arising from the acquisition price paid by the parent.

Three Basic Concepts in Purchase Method Consolidation

Noncontrolling (minority) interest liability is the part of the entity the parent does not own.

1. *Noncontrolling (minority) interest.* This arises if the parent owns less than 100% of the subsidiary, and equals the percentage of the voting shares *not owned* by the parent times the subsidiary's shareholders' equity at the date of acquisition, adjusted for changes since that date.
   - For example, if P Inc. bought 75% of the voting shares of S Ltd. on January 3, 2003, when S Ltd.'s shareholders' equity equalled $300,000, then the *noncontrolling interest,* which many consolidated financial statements refer to as the *minority interest,* would equal 25% of that, or $75,000.
   - This amount is shown as a liability on the consolidated balance sheet. The liability represents the part of the joint consolidated entity's equity *not* owned by the parent company's shareholders. *It represents someone else's equity in the group, so it is not included with the consolidated equity.* It is not a debt of the consolidated entity, because it need not be paid—you could think of it as an acknowledgment that the consolidated entity has an obligation to the minority owners of S Ltd., who did *not* sell their shares to P Inc.
   - So the noncontrolling interest is another of the accounts that blurs the distinction between liabilities and equity.
   - Over time, the noncontrolling interest liability is accounted for similarly to the way the investment asset was in the equity method in Section 9.6:
     - The liability is increased (*and consolidated net income is decreased*) each year by the minority owners' share of the subsidiary's net income;
     - It is decreased (and consolidated cash is decreased) whenever the minority owners receive a dividend.
     - So if the parent company succeeds in getting the subsidiary to earn income, some of that income is credited to the minority owners, and when the minority owners are paid a dividend, the liability is reduced just as any liability would be.

Minority's share decreases consolidated income and increases liability.

Consolidation starts by adding together all the parent's and subsidiary's accounts.

2. *Balance sheet asset and liability values.* The idea of consolidation is just to add the accounts together: the parent's accounts receivable are added to the subsidiary's accounts receivable, the land is added to the land, the accounts payable are added to the accounts payable, the revenue is added to the revenue, the income tax expense is added to the income tax expense, and so on. But four exceptions to simply adding the parent's and subsidiary's balance sheets together are important in understanding how consolidation works:
   (1) Any *intercompany balances are ignored.* If S Ltd. owes P Inc. $40,000, for example, that would be on S Ltd.'s balance sheet as an account payable and on P Inc.'s balance sheet as an account receivable. If the consolidated balance sheet is to represent the two companies as if they were one entity, then this $40,000 amount is an *internal* matter to that entity: it is not owed to or receivable from anyone outside the entity, so it is not like the other accounts payable and accounts receiv-

able. Therefore, it is just left out of the consolidated figures. Intercompany sales and expenses, such as management fees, are also left out of the income statement, and any profit made by one company in dealing with the other is left out as well. Eliminating these can be complex: we won't deal with them.

(2) The account for the parent company's investment in the subsidiary is also an intercompany account, so it is ignored in the consolidation.

At acquisition, consolidated shareholders' equity equals just the parent's equity.

(3) Another intercompany amount left out is the parent's share of the subsidiary's shareholders' equity. It is what the parent bought, so it is included in the parent's investment account and therefore is not part of the consolidated equity external to the consolidated entity. The part of the subsidiary's equity *not* bought is transferred to the noncontrolling interest liability (as noted above), so the result is that *none* of the subsidiary's equity at the date of acquisition is included in consolidated equity. *Consolidated equity at date of acquisition equals just the parent's equity alone.* The parent purchased shares of the subsidiary, and via its voting interest, its owners control the assets and liabilities of the subsidiary. The subsidiary's assets and liabilities are therefore included in the consolidated balance sheet, and to avoid double counting, the intercompany accounts for parent's investment and subsidiary's equity are eliminated.

At the acquisition date, the subsidiary's assets and liabilities are revalued only for the parent's share.

(4) The last exception to just adding the companies' accounts together is to recognize that, when it acquired the subsidiary, the parent company may have had different values in mind for various of the subsidiary's assets and liabilities than the amounts shown for those on the subsidiary's balance sheet. Because a transaction did happen (the parent bought shares of the subsidiary), the historical cost basis of accounting requires that any revised values at that date be taken into account. These are called the *fair values* at that date; they can be viewed as the cost to the parent of the subsidiary's net assets, and there was a transaction to give them validity (the purchase of the subsidiary's shares). However, because the minority owners did not sell, there was not a transaction for their share of the subsidiary's assets and liabilities, so *the minority's share is not taken into account in revaluing the subsidiary's assets and liabilities to fair values.* We know what the parent paid for what it got; we do not know what might have been paid for what it did *not* buy (the minority's share). Therefore, *at the date of acquisition*, each of the subsidiary's assets and liabilities is added into the consolidated figures using the following formula:

FORMULA

Amount used in consolidation calculation = Book value in subsidiary's balance sheet + Parent's share of subsidiary × (Fair value – subsidiary's book value)

Example of Fair Value Adjustment

- Subsidiary's land was on its balance sheet at a value (presumably cost) of $120,000.
- Parent's evaluation indicated its fair value was $180,000.
- Parent bought 85% of the subsidiary.
- Therefore, using the formula above, the land would be included in the consolidated figures at a value of $171,000 [$120,000 + 0.85 ($180,000 – $120,000)].
- The last term is the adjustment to reflect the parent's cost for the 85% interest it acquired, maintaining the historical cost basis for the consolidated financial statements. Therefore, the consolidated figures do not *fully* revalue the subsidiary's assets and liabilities: the minority owners' share of such revaluation is left out because they did not sell.

Any revaluations of assets and liabilities that are done may affect future consolidated income; for example, if the subsidiary's buildings and equipment are increased in value in the consolidation, then the consolidated amortization expense will have to be increased too, in order to take that into account. This is another complication we will not take any further!

Consolidated goodwill equals parent's investment cost minus *partially* revalued subsidiary.

3. *Goodwill arising on consolidation.* What if P Inc. paid more for the shares of S Ltd. than the sum of the fair values of S Ltd.'s assets minus its liabilities? This indicates that P Inc. is buying something else *not* on S Ltd.'s balance sheet, something in addition to all the individual parts of S Ltd. This something is called *goodwill*, or ***goodwill** arising on consolidation.* As explained in Section 8.14, it might represent good managers, a good location, faithful customers, economies of scale with the parent, reduced competition, or other factors the parent company took into account in agreeing to a price for the subsidiary's shares:

FORMULA

Consolidated goodwill asset = Cost of parent's investment – Parent's portion of (Fair values of subsidiary's assets – Fair values of its liabilities)

Example of Consolidated Goodwill Calculation

- Very Big Inc. paid $1,200,000 for 80% of the voting shares of Not So Big Ltd.
- At that date Very Big evaluated Not So Big's assets to be worth $4,300,000 and its liabilities to be $3,000,000.
- Using the above formula, consolidated goodwill at the date of acquisition would be $160,000 [$1,200,000 – 0.80 × ($4,300,000 – $3,000,000)].

Figure 9.2 illustrates the three valuations of the subsidiary company. The first layer is the company's original book value. Since the parent has less than 100% control of the subsidiary, a noncontrolling (minority) interest is recorded as a liability on the parent's balance sheet. The minority interest liability is based on the original book value of the subsidiary. The second layer is the fair value of the subsidiary, assessed by the parent when the parent purchases the subsidiary's shares. Finally, if the third layer (the purchase price) is greater than the fair value of the company, goodwill is created. Note, the fair values and goodwill portions are only calculated based upon the share the parent owns of the subsidiary (e.g. 80% in the prior example).

Consolidated goodwill is shown among the noncurrent assets on the consolidated balance sheet. As noted in Section 8.14, it used to be amortized over time but is now maintained at its historical value unless an annual review of it indicates that its value has been impaired. In that case, it is written down to its estimated fair value and the write-down is included as an expense for the year (probably separated from operating expenses).

Two wrinkles regarding goodwill might as well be mentioned.

Goodwill appears only if it is an asset (a positive difference between cost and fair values).

(1) If the difference is negative (investment cost is *less* than the parent's portion of the net sum of the fair values), you might expect this to be called "badwill" and to be shown on the consolidated balance sheet too. But under GAAP, it is assumed that there was something wrong with the subsidiary's assets for this to happen, so the fair values are reduced in the consolidation calculation until the parent's portion exactly equals the purchase price. The result is that goodwill (or badwill) is zero.

(2) If the subsidiary already had goodwill, that is wrapped into the new goodwill figure and not carried forward separately.

FIGURE 9.2

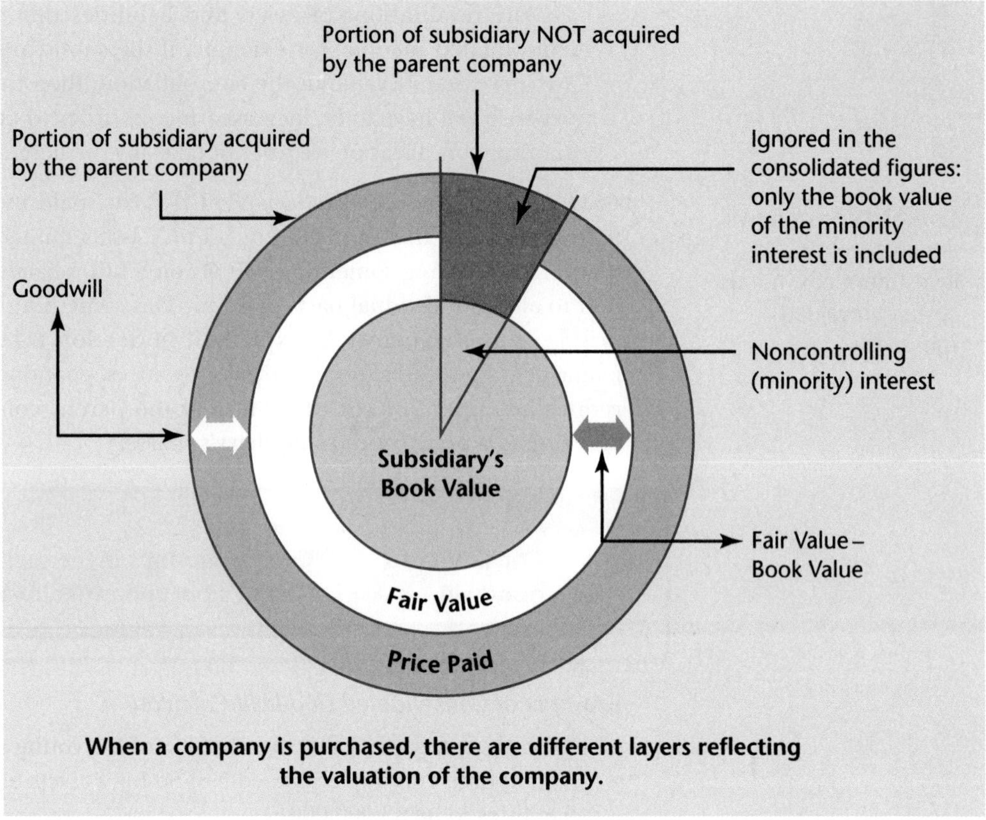

When a company is purchased, there are different layers reflecting the valuation of the company.

To summarize, the consolidated balance sheet at date of acquisition includes

- the parent company's balance sheet figures;
- the subsidiary's assets and liabilities, revalued to reflect the parent's portion of any increases and decreases to fair values;
- any noncontrolling (minority) interest in the subsidiary's equity; and
- any consolidated goodwill.

The latter two, minority interest and goodwill, do not appear on either of the individual companies' balance sheets—they arise only when the corporate group is consolidated. The revaluations of the subsidiary's assets and liabilities also appear only in the consolidated balance sheet—the subsidiary's balance sheet continues with the values it had prior to acquisition, except that usually the subsidiary's accounting policies are changed to match the parent's and that can result in changes in the allowance for doubtful accounts, inventory valuation, accumulated amortization, and so on.

The consolidated balance sheet does *not* include

- the parent's account for investment in subsidiary;
- the subsidiary's shareholders' equity; or
- any other intercompany asset and liability accounts.

An Example of Consolidation at Date of Acquisition

ABC Company purchased 80% of XYZ Company's voting shares for $500,000. We have the following information for XYZ as at the date of acquisition (no intercompany receivables or payables existed at that date):

XYZ Data	Book Values	Fair Values
Cash	$ 45,000	$ 45,000
Accounts receivable	75,000	60,000
Inventory	100,000	120,000
Property and equipment (net)	200,000	300,000
	$420,000	$525,000
Accounts payable	$ 90,000	95,000
Common shares	50,000	
Retained earnings	280,000	
	$420,000	
Sum of fair values of net assets		$430,000

a. *Goodwill arising on consolidation.* ABC paid $500,000 for 80% of $430,000 (the identifiable fair values):

Purchase price	$500,000
Minus acquired fair value (80% × $430,000)	344,000
Goodwill	$156,000

b. *Noncontrolling interest.* ABC purchased only 80% of XYZ. Therefore, the other 20% is the owners' equity of the noncontrolling owners. It is 20% of the book value of XYZ's owners' equity at the date of acquisition, or 20% × ($50,000 + $280,000) = $66,000.

c. *Consolidated figures for ABC* are shown in Exhibit 9.4.

	Balance Sheet Book Values as at Date of Acquisition		Adjust 80% of FV – BV* of XYZ	Include Goodwill and Non-controlling Interest	Consolidated Balance Sheet
	ABC	XYZ			
Cash	$ 175,000	$ 45,000	$ 0		$ 220,000
Receivables	425,000	75,000	(12,000)		488,000
Inventory	660,000	100,000	16,000		776,000
Investment in XYZ	500,000	—		Ignore	—
Property & equipment	1,700,000	200,000	80,000		1,980,000
Consolidated goodwill	—	—		$156,000	156,000
	$3,460,000	$420,000			$3,620,000
Payables	$ 730,000	$ 90,000	$ 4,000		$ 824,000
Long-term debt	850,000	0	0		850,000
Consolidated noncontrolling interest	—	—		$ 66,000	66,000
Common shares	100,000	50,000		ABC only	100,000
Retained earnings	1,780,000	280,000		ABC only	1,780,000
	$3,460,000	$420,000			$3,620,000

* FV – BV = Item's fair value – Its value on XYZ's balance sheet.

A Comment on Consolidated Net Income After Acquisition

Consolidated net income is reduced by extra amortization, etc.

Consolidated net income is the sum of the incomes earned since acquisition, with adjustments to remove intercompany balances and any subsidiary's noncontrolling owners' interest in the income earned by the subsidiary and to reflect amortization of goodwill, among other things. The calculation is as follows:

Start with the sum of the parent's and the subsidiaries' incomes	$ XXXX
Subtract:	
a. Any profits earned by any of the companies on intercompany sales.	(XXXX)
b. Any income from the subsidiaries already included in the parent's or other subsidiaries' accounts through use of the equity method of accounting on the companies' individual financial statements (these are intercompany amounts too).	(XXXX)
c. Any extra amortization and other expenses resulting from adjusting subsidiaries' assets and liabilities to fair values in the consolidation.	(XXXX)
d. Any noncontrolling owners' share of the net income earned by the subsidiary of which they remain part owners (roughly equal to the noncontrolling ownership percentage multiplied by the subsidiary's net income).	(XXXX)
e. Write-down of any impaired goodwill arising on consolidation.	(XXXX)
The result is consolidated net income	$ XXXX

You can see that consolidated net income is likely to be less than the sum of the individual companies' net incomes, perhaps substantially less if goodwill impairment is large or there are significant minority interests.

HOW'S YOUR UNDERSTANDING?

Here are two questions you should be able to answer based on what you have just read. If you can't answer them, it would be best to reread the material.

1. On January 1, 2003, Supersix Inc. bought 75% of the voting shares of Weaknees Ltd. for $231,000 cash. At that date, Weaknees's balance sheet showed assets of $784,000 and liabilities of $697,000. Supersix assessed the fair values of Weaknees's assets to be $800,000 and its liabilities to be $690,000 at acquisition date. Why do noncontrolling (minority) interest and goodwill appear on Supersix's consolidated balance sheet, and what were the figures for those items at acquisition date?

MI appears because it represents the equity that the parent did not acquire.

MI = 25% of ($784,000 – $697,000) = $21,750.

GW appears because it is part of the acquisition cost: for unidentifiable but valued assets.

GW = $231,000 – 75% of ($800,000 – $690,000) = $148,500

2. At the same date, Supersix's balance sheet showed assets of $56,782,000 and liabilities of $45,329,000. What would be the consolidated equity of Supersix after consolidating Weaknees?

Consolidated equity is just Supersix's ($56,782,000 – $45,329,000 = $11,453,000).

9.8 Terms to Be Sure You Understand

Here is this chapter's list of terms introduced or emphasized. Make sure you know what they mean *in accounting*, and if any are unclear to you, check the chapter again or refer to the glossary of terms at the back of the book.

Accounting policies
Accumulated foreign currency translation adjustment
Acquisition
Bond
Bonded debt
Business combinations
Callable debt
Capital
Capital cost allowance
Capital leases
Conditional sale contract
Consolidated
Consolidated financial statements
Consolidation
Contingent assets
Contingent liabilities
Contra account
Contributed surplus
Convertible
Corporate groups
Corporation
Cost basis
Current portion of income tax expense
Debenture
Deferred income tax
Demand loans
Discount
Earnings management
Economic entity
Effective income tax rate
Equity
Equity basis
Fair values
Financial instruments
Fund accounting
Future income tax liability
Future income taxes
Future portion of income tax expense
Going concern
Goodwill
Goodwill arising on consolidation
Historical cost
Income tax payable
Indenture
Interperiod tax allocation
Intraperiod tax allocation
Joint venture
Liabilities
Loans from shareholders
Matching principle
Merger
Minority interest
Mortgage
Noncontrolling interest
Parent
Partnership(s)
Personal guarantees
Premium
Present value
Proprietorship(s)
Provisions
Purchase method
Redeemable
Security
Share splits
Significant influence
Stock-based compensation
Stock dividends
Stock options
Subsidiary
Temporary difference(s)
Temporary investments
Treasury shares
Warrants
Working capital
Working capital ratio

INSTALLMENT 9

In this installment, we'll prepare the complete first year's financial statements and notes for the company. The statements will be analyzed in Installment 10, so make sure you are clear about how they are assembled below.

DATA FOR INSTALLMENT 9

In Installment 7, the February 28, 2007, adjusted trial balance of Mato Inc. was prepared, and in Installment 8, the company chose its accounting policies. The data are therefore the trial balance and the policies. Refer back to those installments if you are unsure about any results below.

RESULTS FOR INSTALLMENT 9

With some accounting help, Tomas prepared the set of financial statements and notes for the company's first year.

Mato Inc.
Statement of Income and Deficit
for the Year Ended February 28, 2007

Revenue		$229,387
Cost of goods sold		138,767
Gross profit		$ 90,620
Operating expenses:		
Bad debts	$ 2,436	
Salaries	67,480	
Travel	9,477	
Telephone	4,014	
Rent	24,000	
Utilities	3,585	
Office and general	5,688	
Inventory shortage	441	
Interest	6,469	
Amortization	21,096	144,686
Net loss for the year (no tax)		$ (54,066)
Retained earnings, March 1, 2006		0
Deficit as at February 28, 2007		$ (54,066)

Mato Inc.
Balance Sheets
at February 28, 2007 and March 1, 2006

Assets	**2007**	**2006**	**Liabilities and Equity**	**2007**	**2006**
Current assets:			Current liabilities:		
Cash	$ 6,418	$130,000	Bank loan	$ 47,500	$ 0
Receivables (net)	14,129	0	Payables	41,808	1,100
Inventory	33,612	0	Loan payable	0	15,000
Prepaid expense	525	0	Deferred revenue	500	0
	$ 54,684	$130,000		$ 89,808	$ 16,100
Noncurrent assets:			Shareholders' equity:		
Equipment cost	$ 57,290	$ 10,000	Share capital	$125,000	$125,000
Accum. amort.	(7,344)	0	Deficit	(54,066)	0
Leasehold (net)	51,172	0		$ 70,934	$125,000
Software (net)	3,840	0			
Incorp. cost	1,100	1,100			
	$106,058	$ 11,100			
TOTAL	$160,742	$141,100	TOTAL	$160,742	$141,100

Mato Inc.
Cash Flow Statement
For the Year Ended February 28, 2007

Operations:		
Net loss for the year		$ (54,066)
Add back amortization for the year		21,096
Changes in noncash working capital accounts:		
Increase in accounts receivable	$ (14,129)	
Increase in inventory	(33,612)	
Increase in prepaid expenses	(525)	
Increase in accounts payable	40,708	
Increase in deferred revenue	500	(7,058)
Cash used in operations		$ (40,028)
Investing activities:		
Equipment, leasehold improvements, and software acquired		(116,054)
Financing activities:		
Bank borrowing	$ 47,500	
Repayment of loan	(15,000)	32,500
Decrease in cash during the year		$(123,582)
Cash on hand, March 1, 2006		130,000
Cash on hand, February 28, 2007		$ 6,418

Mato Inc.
Notes to the Financial Statements as at February 28, 2007

1. Significant accounting policies:
   a. Inventory is valued at the lower of cost, determined by the first-in, first-out method, and net realizable value.
   b. Noncurrent assets are recorded at cost. Amortization is calculated on a straight-line basis of 20% of cost per annum on automotive equipment, leasehold improvements, and computer equipment and software, and at 10% of cost per annum on other equipment and furniture.
2. The bank loan is secured by receivables, inventories, a general charge on the company's assets, and by the personal guarantees of the shareholders.
3. The company's authorized capital is 1,000,000 shares without par value. At the beginning of the year, 12,500 shares were issued for $10 cash each.
4. No provision for income taxes has been made in the financial statements because the current loss will result in an income tax recovery only if there are future taxable incomes against which that loss may be deducted.
5. Salaries of directors and officers of the company were $54,280 for the year.
6. The company has commitments to purchase goods that will cost $23,430 on delivery, which is expected by April 30, 2007.

Discussion of the Results

The results for the year were still negative: a loss of $54,066 and a decrease in cash of $123,582. However, there was quite an improvement compared with the first six months:

- The loss for the first six months (Installment 3) had been $49,378, so the additional loss for the second six months was relatively small at only $4,688.
- The cash decrease for the first six months (Installment 4) was $125,493, so there was an addition to cash of $1,911 during the second six months.
- The working capital at the end of August (Installment 3) was negative at $38,772 ($96,844 – $135,616) and by February 28, 2007, was still negative at $35,124 ($54,684 – $89,808), but a little less negative.

Further analysis of the results will be conducted in Installment 10. However, Mavis and Tomas wonder if the financial statements have made their company's performance appear worse than necessary and if some other choice of accounting policies might make things look more optimistic.

Mavis and Tomas's concern regarding changing their accounting policies to make things look rosier is understandable. They have worked hard to make their company succeed, but the first year's results are not positive. If they had paid themselves no salaries for their year's work, the company would have shown a tiny income ($54,280 salaries per note 5 above minus the $54,066 loss would equal $214 income before income tax). But that would have been misleading because it would fail to measure the value added by their efforts—not to mention that they would have starved! Would it make sense to try to find accounting policies that would improve the picture? The answer is no, for the following reasons:

1. Such manipulation would be ethically questionable and perhaps even dangerous, if it obscured the company's real problems and reduced the pressure on Mavis and Tomas to improve Mato's performance. They may feel disappointed, but the thing

to do is to try harder to manage the company well, not "shoot the messenger" by trying to change the financial accounting "message."

2. Such a change would not likely help in dealing with the parties who are going to be most concerned about the company. The bank already has the company's assets pretty well tied up as security on its loan and is going to be interested in the company's ability to generate cash to repay the loan, as well as in its long-term viability. The bank is undoubtedly very concerned about the company and will be on the lookout for desperate actions, so optimistic reporting is unlikely to fool the bankers—or, for that matter, suppliers, other investors, and the company's employee.
3. The cash flow statement would show the same cash flow figures regardless of accounting policy changes, so users of the financial statements who know how to read the cash flow statement would see through such changes, and might even become suspicious if the income diverged too much from the cash flow from operations.
4. For this company, there is really not much that could be manipulated even if it were ethical and successful. Receivables are not large, nor is there any obvious reason for the company to recognize revenue sooner than it does without violating GAAP. Inventories are also not large, and, since FIFO is already being used, there is likely to be little room for raising inventory value to increase income. Amortization could be slowed down, but such a move would make little difference to income. Even cutting amortization in half would reduce the year's loss by less than 20%.

9.10 Homework and Discussion to Develop Understanding

The problems roughly follow the outline of the chapter. Three main categories of questions are presented.

- Asterisked problems (*) have an informal solution provided in the Student Solutions Manual.
- EXTENDED TIME problems grant a thorough examination of the material and may take longer to complete.
- CHALLENGING problems are more difficult.

For further explanation, please refer to Section 1.15.

Current and Noncurrent Liabilities • Section 9.2 and 9.3

Understanding Liabilities

*** PROBLEM 9.1** Questions about the right-hand side of the balance sheet

Answer the following questions briefly:

1. What is the difference between liabilities and equity?
2. What is the difference, if any, between liabilities and debts?
3. Suggest two examples each of short-term and long-term accruals that require difficult estimates and indicate what the difficulty is in each case.
4. Should companies avoid long-term accruals because they are likely to be inaccurate and therefore misleading, and just pay in cash costs such as warranties and pensions as they arise?

PROBLEM 9.2 Answer questions about liabilities

Respond to the question asked in each comment below.

1. "Warranties are honoured as part of good business practice: keep your customers happy. Whether to honour a claim and how much cost to incur are managerial judgments that depend on how good the customer is, what the reputation effects are, etc. Therefore, warranties are discretionary period expenses like donations. There is no accrual for future donations, so why is there an accrual for future warranty costs?"
2. "Employees take their pensions when they retire, years into the future. Whether there is any pension depends on whether the employee keeps working for the company, and how long the employee lives after retirement. Therefore pension costs can only be realistically determined when they are being paid in the future. Why shouldn't they be expensed then, rather than now?"
3. "After thinking about warranties and pensions, I have a proposal. Let's take accrual accounting to the next step and accrue all future expenses we can reasonably predict now. I mentioned donations already. We could add repairs and maintenance, interest, income taxes, and executive bonuses, to mention just a few."

PROBLEM 9.3 Effects of pension accounting on the future

Here's a problem. Suppose companies in general did not accrue enough pension liabilities to account fully for their obligations to employees, warranty liabilities to account for their obligations to customers, etc. There are persistent worries about this in these times of aging baby boomers and less complacent consumers. A commentator said, "The real costs of company obligations are not being recognized in balance sheets and so cash is being taken out of the hands of future generations of employees and consumers."

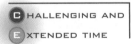

Explain how the alleged failure to accrue enough for obligations like pensions and warranties could take cash out of the hands of future generations.

Liability Calculations

*** PROBLEM 9.4** Do current and noncurrent liability calculations

In each case below, calculate (1) current liability at the end of this year; (2) noncurrent liability at the end of this year; and (3) interest expense for the *next* year.

a. John Ltd.'s factory mortgage of $842,500 requires payments of $11,200 each month. During the next year, the interest part of the payments will equal $61,232.
b. Frieda Inc.'s land mortgage of $232,200 requires payments of $60,000 over the next year. By the end of next year, the principal due on the mortgage will have gone down to $189,400.
c. Graham Ltd.'s $87,436 property mortgage requires monthly payments of $1,500 plus interest. During the next year, payments will total $25,674.

PROBLEM 9.5 Questions about long-term accruals

1. Balmer Inc. started the year with a pension liability of $42,000. During the year, employees earned pension entitlements with a present value of $147,600 and the company paid $157,400 to the pension trustee. State the amount of the pension expense for the year and the pension liability at the end of the year.
2. Balmer Inc. also has a warranty plan. Estimated warranty liability was $64,000 at the beginning of the year, and based on the company's sales for the year, warranty service costing $100,500 in wages and other costs, plus $79,400 in replacement products, was expected to have to be provided eventually. Actual expenditures for the year were $107,500 in wages and other costs and $99,800 in replacement products. Calculate warranty expense for the year and estimated warranty liability at the end of the year.
3. Write one or more journal entries to record Balmer Inc.'s warranty experience for the year.
4. For part 2, what would be your answers if Balmer Inc. accounted for warranties on the cash basis instead of the accrual basis?
5. Suppose Balmer Inc. had a real disaster with a product during the next year. For that product only, wages and other service costs totalled $150,000 and replacement products costing $210,000 had to be provided. Comment on what this disaster might do to the company's warranty accounting. Focus on the accounting issues—no numbers are needed.

PROBLEM 9.6 Calculate current and noncurrent portions of a mortgage

Tweedsmuir Land Ltd. has substantial mortgage debt. The debt was $15,254,182 at the beginning of this year. Mortgage payments of $4,394,051 were made during the year and the mortgage balance was $12,261,968 at the end of the year. No new borrowing was made this year. Next year, the payments required total $4,639,373 and if there is no new borrowing the mortgage balance will be $8,749,453 at the end of next year. Calculate (a) Interest expense for this year; (b) Current portion of the mortgage liability at the end of this year; and (c) Noncurrent mortgage liability at the end of this year.

PROBLEM 9.7 Calculate various liability and expense amounts

In each of the following cases, calculate the year-end liability and any associated expense for the year.

1. Bach Inc. has collected fees from orchestras for their performance of various symphonies to which it has the rights. During the year, it collected fees of $250,000, but by the end of the year, the orchestras had performed symphonies corresponding to only $192,000 of the fees. The rest were to be performed next year.
2. Beethoven Ltd. started the year owing $138,000 to its pension plan trustee. During the year, its employees earned pensions having an estimated present value of $439,500, and the company paid the trustee $489,900.
3. Redo part 2 changing only one number: change the present value of pensions earned to $333,200. Where would the liability figure you got appear on the balance sheet?
4. Mozart Inc. has a warranty plan for the musical instruments it manufactures. The company's prices are high and its quality is good, but musicians are a choosy lot, so the company has a substantial warranty cost, which its management feels is worthwhile to keep its reputation and repeat business up. At the beginning of the year, the estimated warranty liability was $218,320. During the year, the company incurred warranty costs of $142,280, $97,640 of that in cash and the rest in replacement instruments. This was close to the $140,000 expected on the basis of the year's sales.
5. Suppose Mozart Inc. had an unexpected problem with a new model of tuba and recalled all the tubas sold for free repairs, costing the company $75,000 in total. Knowing this, would this change either of your answers to part 4?

PROBLEM 9.8 Calculate various liability and expense amounts

Calculate the unknown figure in each of the following unrelated cases.

1. Current portion of long-term debt = $983,500. Payments due next year = $2,480,000. Total debt = $8,554,000. How much interest is to be paid next year?
2. Net bonded debt liability on the balance sheet = $22,380,720. Interest to be paid next year = $1,849,750. Discount amortization will be $67,000. What will the interest expense be for next year? What will be the net bonded debt liability on the balance sheet at the end of next year?
3. Pension liability at the beginning of the year = $899,900. Payments to the pension trustee during the year = $3,679,280. Liability at the end of the year = $323,610. What was the estimated present value of the pensions earned during the year? What was the pension expense for the year?
4. Warranty costs are accounted for on the cash basis, and this year the warranty expense = $182,920. An analysis of the sales and warranty patterns indicates that estimated warranty obligations were $62,040 at the beginning of the year and $106,490 at the end. If accrual accounting were used for warranties, what would the warranty expense be for this year? What difference would it make to income before income tax?

Bond Discounts and Premiums

* PROBLEM 9.9 Bond discount or premium calculations

In each case below, (1) calculate the amount of any discount or premium on issue of the bonds, (2) record the issue of the bonds, and (3) state whether interest expense over the life of the bonds will be higher, lower, or the same as the cash interest paid on the bond each year.

a. A Ltd. issued 10,000 $100 bonds and received $97.50 cash each.
b. B Ltd. issued 10,000 $100 bonds, but found that the planned interest rate of 7% was lower than market rates and so received $915,000 for them.
c. C Ltd. issued 10,000 $100 bonds for a premium of 5% on legal value.

PROBLEM 9.10 Record a new bond issue

Sunshine Vacations Inc. (SVI) is a large tour operator in North America. In order to finance a new expansion into the Caribbean, the company hopes to raise money by offering an 8.5% bond issue worth $42,000,000. The bonds were well received by the market and ended up raising $46,200,000 yielding the current market rate.

a. Record the bond issue.
b. When the bond premium is amortized, will it increase or decrease the overall interest expense on the bonds? (Hint: will the overall interest expense be debited or credited?)
c. Does this increase or decrease in interest expense mean that the company is paying an effective interest rate higher or lower than the coupon rate of 8.5%?

PROBLEM 9.11 Calculate or record various liability and expense amounts

1. High Risk Inc. issued $10,000 first-mortgage bonds having a total face value of $50,000,000 and carrying a 6.2% interest rate. They were not well received by the bond market, so High Risk received only $47,074,275 for them. (a) Record the bond issue, and (b) calculate the balance sheet liability for the bonds as of the issue date.
2. Regarding part 1, will High Risk's interest expense for the bonds be more or less than 6.2% times the face value ($3,100,000)? Why?

PROBLEM 9.12 Answer questions about bond discounts and premiums

The president of Redstone Inc. has just been discussing a planned new bond issue with financial advisors and has come to you with some resulting accounting questions. Answer each.

1. "We are thinking of setting the interest rate on the bonds a little above current market rates to make them more attractive. I'm told this will produce a balance sheet liability higher than the face value of the bonds. How does this happen?"
2. "Your answer to my first question is troubling. How can it make sense to show a liability higher than the amount we will have to pay when the bonds come due? What will we do with the difference then?"
3. "So I guess the amount of interest expense on the bonds, as calculated by the accountants, will be less than the actual amount of interest paid each year. That will be nice, because the reduction will improve earnings and carry through to our cash flow statement, right?"

Explaining Income Tax Accounting

* **PROBLEM 9.13** Explain some things about income tax allocation

Explain the following:

1. Why is it thought necessary to have a future portion of income tax expense and future income tax liability?
2. How does the resulting income tax allocation method fit accrual accounting?
3. Why is the calculation method of the future portion of the income tax expense sometimes described as not matching revenue very well?

PROBLEM 9.14 Temporary differences in income tax accounting

Explain what "temporary differences" are, and why the future income tax liability (or asset) depends on them but not on permanent differences between accounting and income tax calculations such as nontaxable revenues or nondeductible expenses.

PROBLEM 9.15 Explain the purpose and nature of income tax allocation

George picked up the financial statements of a company he owns shares in and noticed the following two accounts, which he didn't understand:

Future portion of income tax expense	$19,749,200
Future income tax liability	$86,293,500

Explain to George the purpose of income tax allocation accounting and what the two figures he didn't understand mean.

PROBLEM 9.16 Answer questions about income tax accounts

Answer each of the following questions:

1. Before income tax allocation accounting was introduced, the income tax expense on companies' income statements just equalled the income tax payable on each year's taxable income. For a company with new factory assets, would net income have been larger or smaller without income tax allocation? Explain.
2. Following from part 1, would net income have been larger or smaller without income tax allocation for a company with old factory assets? Explain.
3. Companies do not *have* to claim capital cost allowance deductions in calculating their taxable income if they choose not to. Thus, there are circumstances in which the full CCA available is not claimed. If a company chooses not to claim the full CCA available, what will that do to (i) current portion of income tax expense, (ii) future portion of income tax expense, (iii) total income tax expense?
4. What are the effects of each of the following on (i) current income tax expense, (ii) future income tax expense, (iii) total income tax expense?
   a. A company incurs and pays a large repair expense.
   b. A company buys a large new machine for its factory.
   c. A company buys a large shipment of inventory to be sold next year.
   d. A company receives a large nontaxable dividend from another company.
   e. A company declares and pays a dividend to its shareholders.
   f. A company makes a large sale to a good customer.

Calculating Income Tax

*** PROBLEM 9.17** Calculate income tax expense and future tax liability

At the end of 2005, Henrik Inc. had future income tax liability of $329,612 and retained earnings of $3,949,286. For 2006, the company's income statement showed income before tax of $648,960. There was only one temporary difference between the accounting and income tax calculations for 2006: capital cost allowance (CCA) exceeded book amortization expense by $343,502. There was also $29,650 of nontaxable revenue, so the company's taxable income was $275,808 for 2006. The company's income tax rate for 2006 was 32% and is expected to remain at that rate indefinitely. The company paid no dividends in 2006.

1. Calculate the following:
   a. Current portion of income tax expense for 2006.
   b. Future portion of income tax expense for 2006.
   c. Net income for 2006.
   d. Future income tax liability at the end of 2006.
   e. Retained earnings at the end of 2006.
2. Suppose the tax law changed a little in 2006, so that expected income tax rates in the future were now expected to vary from 32%, and the estimated future income

tax liability at the end of 2006 is now $420,500. Recalculate the five numbers asked for in part 1.

*** PROBLEM 9.18** Calculate net income and future income tax liability

Mars Bears Ltd. has a stable income before income tax on its income statement: $120,000 each year. Its income tax rate is also stable: 36%. It has one asset costing $350,000 that it amortizes at $35,000 per year. The capital cost allowance deductible on that asset is 10% in the first year and 20% in each year thereafter, the rate being applied to the unamortized cost (CCA is a declining balance method). Calculate the following for *each* of the first three years of the company's existence:

a. CCA deductible.
b. Taxable income (add book amortization back to income and deduct CCA instead).
c. Current portion of income tax expense.
d. Future portion of income tax expense.
e. Total income tax expense.
f. Net income for the year.
g. Future income tax liability at the end of the year.

PROBLEM 9.19 Calculate net income, future income tax liability, and other amounts

You have the following information about Gazoo Entertainments Ltd.:

Year	Income Before Income tax	Current Income Tax Expense	Future Income Tax Expense	Future Income Tax Liability at Beginning of Year
2005	$409,125	$101,250	$51,150	$142,530
2006	538,340	129,100	45,450	?
2007	217,350	47,300	27,610	?
2008	(51,100)	(27,800)	9,250	?
2009	42,775	27,480	(5,270)	?

Answer the following:

a. What is the net income in 2006, 2008, and 2009?
b. What is the future income tax liability at the end of 2009?
c. What is the total income tax expense for 2008?
d. In 2008, how could there be both a negative current income tax expense and positive future income tax expense?
e. Assuming Gazoo's future income tax arises from differences between book amortization and CCA, is amortization greater than CCA in 2005? In 2007? In 2009?
f. What was the company's effective income tax rate in 2007? In 2008?

PROBLEM 9.20 Calculate income tax expense and future tax liability

At the end of 2006, Plasticorp Ltd. had future income tax liability of $2,513,140 and retained earnings of $25,492,725. For 2007, the company's income statement showed income before tax of $2,211,305 and amortization expense of $4,382,436. Inspection of the company's income tax records showed that in 2007, $88,860 of its revenue was not subject to income tax, $50,557 of its expenses were not tax deductible, and its capital cost allowance was $4,045,730, so its taxable income was $2,1509,706. The company's income tax rate for 2007 was 35% and is expected to remain at that rate indefinitely. The company declared and paid a $500,000 dividend in 2007.

1. Calculate the following:
   a. Current portion of income tax expense for 2007.
   b. Future portion of income tax expense for 2007 (the difference between book amortization and CCA was the only temporary difference in 2007).
   c. Net income for 2007.
   d. Future income tax liability at the end of 2007.
   e. Retained earnings at the end of 2007.
2. Suppose expectations of future income taxes to be paid changed a little in 2007, so that the estimated future income tax liability at the end of 2007 is now $2,340,500. Recalculate the five numbers asked for in part 1.

PROBLEM 9.21 Journal entry for income tax payable and future tax

For 2006, Great World Air Inc. had income before income tax of $26,600 (in thousands of dollars). Taxable income for 2006 was $23,760 thousand, and an analysis of balance sheet accounts indicated that temporary differences between accounting and tax rules of $3,737 thousand arose in 2006. The company's income tax rate for 2006 was 36% and that is expected to be the rate for the future.

1. Write a journal entry to record the company's 2006 income tax expense. Show your calculations.
2 Based on your answer to part 1, what was the company's net income for 2006?

Equity • Section 9.4

Understanding Equity Accounting

* **PROBLEM 9.22** Explain some features of accounting for equity

Answer each of the following questions briefly:

1. Why does an unincorporated business have only a single equity account, Capital?
2. What does it matter that a bond or preferred share may be convertible to a common share?
3. Why is a stock split ignored in accounting whereas a stock dividend is traditionally recorded (debit retained earnings, credit share capital)?
4. Why is there so much disclosure of the legal details of shares and other equity accounts?
5. Why does it matter if a class of shares has a minimum issue price or par value?

PROBLEM 9.23 Answer various questions about equity accounting

Answer each of the following questions briefly.

1. Give some examples of distinctions made in financial accounting between equity accounts and other balance sheet accounts that are in some way problematic. For each, what is the problem?
2. Given the increasing number of hybrid and generally complex financial instruments and financing methods, should financial accounting drop the debt-equity distinction on the right-hand side of the balance sheet?
3. The business's economic earning power, assets, and liabilities are presumably what matters to external users of financial accounting information. Why then are there various rules about accounting for equity that depend on the form of the business organization (e.g., whether it is incorporated or not)?
4. The equity section of the balance sheet is recorded at historical amounts, not at the current market value of the equity, what the company could be sold for today.

Given that, what aspects, if any, of the way equity is accounted for provide useful information to the owners of the equity?

PROBLEM 9.24 Calculations of partnership equity

Big Partners is a firm of architects, whose partners are Barbara, Ian, and Gordon. The partnership agreement specifies that the first two partners get 30% each of the firm's income and the third partner gets 40%. During the most recent year, the firm earned $600,000 before any withdrawals by partners. At the end of the year, the firm's liabilities totalled $435,400. At the beginning of the year, Barbara's capital account was $105,000; Ian's was $23,900; and Gordon's was $183,200. Withdrawals for the year were: Barbara, $143,600; Ian, $150,100; and Gordon, $61,000.

1. Calculate the partners' capital accounts as at the end of the year.
2. Present the partnership's summarized balance sheet as at the end of the year.
3. Suppose Ian had withdrawn $225,000 instead during the most recent year. Would you think the partnership's balance sheet would or should be different from the one you presented in part 2? Why, or why not? This has not been covered in the chapter, but you should be able to consider the question on the basis of your knowledge of asset and equity accounting.

Financial Instruments • Section 9.5

Disclosure of Financial Instruments

PROBLEM 9.25 Investment classification

Ergometric Ltd., whose shares are broadly traded on the TSX, has numerous investments. As the newest accounting clerk, you have been assigned to classify the following investments and recommend the method to be used in accounting for each of them.

a. Various long-term government of Canada bonds maturing in ten to twenty years are acquired as a temporary investment. It is management's expectation that interest rates will fall, causing a significant price increase in the bonds within the next year.
b. An investment in bonds is held as part of an actively traded portfolio. The money invested in the bonds is obtained from loans and Ergometric is cautious in matching the maturities of the loans and the bonds acquired.
c. Ergometric holds 8%, the largest single shareholding, of the voting shares of a large public company. Ergometric is proportionately represented on the board of directors. Management intends to hold the shares for a long time, awaiting significant appreciation in the market price.
d. Ergometric owns 45% of the voting shares of a large public company. The remaining 55% of shares are widely held. Ergometric elected 4 of the 10 members of the board of directors and generally sets the operating and financing policy of the firm.
e. Ergometric holds a tiny percentage of the shares in a large, public company. The value of these shares has increased dramatically but they have not been sold. Management is convinced the shares will appreciate even more and as a result borrowed money, using the share as collateral, when cash was needed.

PROBLEM 9.26 Investment classification

The shares of Wise Inc., a manufacturer of owl figurines, are traded on the TSX. Wise has been very profitable in recent years. Rather than diversify or distribute the earnings as dividends, Wise has made a number of investments. As the new accountant, you are asked to classify the investments listed below and indicate the recommended method of accounting for each.

a. Wise holds $1,500,000, 6% bonds that mature in 25 years. Wise will sell the bonds if the market price rises sufficiently or if the money is needed for expansion.
b. Wise holds $5,000,000 in bonds of Seagull Ltd. The bonds mature in 2020 and, because of the high interest yield, management expects to retain the investment until then.
c. Wise holds 10,000 shares of the Royal Bank. These shares are held in anticipation of capital appreciation.
d. Wise holds 60% of the common shares of Garden Gnome Inc.; the remaining 40% are held by Gary Gardener. The board of directors of Garden Gnome consists of six members, four of whom are appointed by Wise Inc. All decisions of the board must be unanimously agreed to by the board members.
e. Wise holds 30% of the shares of Flightless Inc. The remaining shares are equally divided among three other investors. Each investor has equal representation on the board of directors. The other representatives are quite passive and attend meetings irregularly. All strategic decisions to date appear to have been made by the Wise appointees.

EXTENDED TIME

PROBLEM 9.27 Effects of pension assets on the financial statements

Respond to the following events at Millwood Corp.:

Millwood Corp. has a pension plan covering substantially all its employees. The pension trustee is a separate legal entity from Millwood, but a majority of its directors are also senior managers at Millwood. At the end of the year, the pension trustee calculated that its expected obligation for employees' pensions (present value of expected payouts discounted at projected rates of return on pension assets) was $778 million. At the same date, the trustee had assets of $814 million. The only pension account on Millwood's balance sheet at that date was a liability to the trustee of $6 million, representing pension deductions and employee withholdings from the latter part of the year. (The $6 million was shown as a receivable in the trustee's balance sheet; so was part of its $814 million of assets.)

1. In a speech, the CEO of Millwood referred to an "off-balance-sheet asset" of "over $800 million." A critic of the speech said the number was only $36 million. Do you think it was either? Explain.
2. In a management meeting, the Millwood CEO mentioned that the company should plan to "recover" the trustee's excess assets of $36 million and take that amount into income. What do you think about that plan?
3. Suppose all the Millwood data were the same except that the trustee's estimated obligation was $852 million at the end of the year? Does this change either of your answers above?
4. What about the liability side of the Millwood case? Using the estimated obligation of $852 million, what adjustment (if any) to the liabilities side of Millwood's balance sheet would you make? What disclosure would you make in Millwood's notes? Are there any implications for Millwood's income?

CHALLENGING

PROBLEM 9.28 Adequacy of GAAP for financial instruments

This chapter has had several topics in which controversy exists over the way GAAP do or do not deal with modern financial activities. There is the problem of financing that is not clearly either debt or equity. There is the attempt to make estimates of future income tax payments, which may be made only in the distant future. A major ongoing problem is in accounting for financial instruments. Or perhaps it would be better to say "lack of accounting for financial instruments" because while GAAP require considerable disclosure about such instruments, there is little progress on accounting for them by building them, and associated gains and losses, into the financial accounting numbers.

Is disclosure enough? Should "mark to market" accounting be required, so that the accounts reflect the kinds of calculations that financial managers make when making hedging, interest rate swap, and other financial arrangements?

Discuss the question of whether financial accounting is now too far removed from the way modern financial arrangements are made, and if so, what might be done about it. Would it be reasonable to change the accounting every time an innovative financial instrument was developed? Or is the problem deeper, involving a fundamental problem with financial accounting's historical cost base that is most apparent when financial instruments and financial arrangements are, in general, considered?

Corporate Groups: Intercorporate Investment • Section 9.6

Cost Versus Equity Investment Calculations

* PROBLEM 9.29 Cost versus equity basis for nonconsolidated investment

China Sports Ltd. purchased 40% of the voting shares of Brassy Ltd. at the beginning of this year for $4,100,000. During the year, Brassy earned net income of $600,000 and paid dividends of $250,000. China Sports, which has been accounting for its investment in Brassy on the cost basis, has income of $800,000 for this year. If the equity basis were used instead, what would China Sports Ltd.'s income be?

PROBLEM 9.30 Cost versus equity basis of an investment

Widgets-for-u Inc. increased its investment in Widgetland Inc. from 15% to 25% on January 1, 2006, the first day of the fiscal year. As a result, Widgets-for-u Inc. has changed its accounting policy to account for Widgetland Inc. on the equity basis instead of on a cost basis. For the year ended Dec. 31, 2005, Widgetland Inc. had net income of $250,000 and paid dividends of $85,000. For the year ended Dec. 31, 2006, Widgetland Inc. increased its net income to $550,000 and declared dividends of $210,000. What figure did Widgets-for-u Inc. report in its income statement as revenue from its investment in Widgetland Inc. in 2005 and 2006?

PROBLEM 9.31 Equity method

On January 1, 2006, Harrison Co. purchased 40% of the outstanding common (voting) shared of Junior Corporation for $40,000. This gave Harrison significant influence. At the date of acquisition, the balance sheet of Junior showed the following book values:

	Book Value	Market Value
Assets not subject to amortization	$50,000	$50,000
Assets subject to amortization	35,000	40,000
Liabilities	10,000	10,000
Common shares	65,000	N/A
Retained earnings	10,000	N/A

1. Prepare the journal entry to record the acquisition.
2. Show your calculation of purchased goodwill at the date of acquisition.
3. Junior reported net income for the year ended December 31, 2006, in the amount of $14,000 and paid dividends of $4,500 during the year. The assets subject to amortization have a remaining useful life of five years and straight-line depreciation is used. Goodwill has not been impaired. Prepare the entries Harrison Co. would prepare.

Corporate Groups: Consolidation • Section 9.7

Understanding Consolidation

PROBLEM 9.32 Explanation of consolidated statements

In 2006, Parent Company acquired 80% of the outstanding voting shares of Subsidiary Company, establishing control over the board of directors. Parent Company used the cost method of accounting for the investment during the year, but prepared consolidated financial statements at the end of the year. The consolidated financial statements are summarized below:

	Parent	Subsidiary	Consolidated
Cash	$ 14,000	$ 15,000	$ 29,000
Accounts receivable	27,000	24,000	45,000
Inventory	18,500	11,500	30,000
Property, plant and equipment	110,000	80,500	190,500
Investments in Subsidiary Company	92,000		
Intangible assets			5200
	$261,500	$131,000	$299,700
Current liabilities	$ 37,000	$ 11,500	$ 42,500
Long-term liabilities	5,000	3,000	8,000
Minority interest			25,200
Common shares	125,000	75,000	125,000
Retained earnings	94,500	41,500	99,000
	$261,500	$131,000	$299,700
Revenue	$110,000	$ 77,000	$167,000
Cost of goods sold	70,000	42,500	96,500
Operating expenses	22,000	21,500	43,500
Minority interest			4,500
Net income	$ 18,000	$ 13,000	$ 22,500
Retained earnings, beginning of year	$ 89,000	$ 33,500	$ 89,000
Dividends	12,500	5,000	12,500
Retained earnings, end of year	$ 94,500	$ 41,500	$ 99,000

Required:

1. Why does Parent Company use the cost method throughout the year? Could Parent use an alternative method?
2. Explain the meaning of the accounts appearing on the consolidated balance sheet that do not appear on either of the unconsolidated balance sheets.
3. Certain accounts and amounts from the unconsolidated statement do not appear on the consolidated statements. Identify these amounts and accounts and explain why they are eliminated in the consolidation.
4. Accounts receivable and accounts payable on the unconsolidated statement do not total to the amount shown on the consolidated statements. What is the most likely reason for this?

PROBLEM 9.33 Answer conceptual questions on consolidation

Chromium Furniture Ltd. wishes to expand operations by acquiring other furniture manufacturers and associated businesses. In relation to this, the president is curious about accounting methods for groups of companies. Answer briefly the following four questions the president has asked:

1. "Why does a subsidiary have to be consolidated with the parent's accounts?"
2. "Why doesn't consolidating a newly acquired subsidiary affect consolidated retained earnings? (After all, the subsidiary has retained earnings too.)"
3. "Since it is the sum of more than one company, won't a consolidated balance sheet present a stronger financial picture than the parent's unconsolidated balance sheet does?"
4. "What does 'Goodwill on consolidation' on the consolidated balance sheet mean?"

PROBLEM 9.34 Problems with goodwill on consolidation

In 2001 and 2002, there were many very large reported losses related to goodwill write-offs. JDS Uniphase and AOL Time Warner, for example, both reported losses in the U.S.$50 billion range. Both companies had recorded the goodwill from acquisitions (JDS of Uniphase, AOL of Time Warner) that had been paid for by the issuance of shares of the acquiring company, valued at the huge stock market values typical of high-flying tech companies in the late 1990s.

1. Explain how the large goodwill values in such companies' consolidated balance sheets arose. Which other figure on the balance sheet was also made very large by the acquisition?
2. What does the answer to part 1 do to the usefulness of standard ratios like debt-equity and working capital for evaluating such companies' financial position?
3. When the value of tech companies collapsed in the early 2000s, what should have been done with the apparently inflated values of (a) consolidated goodwill and (b) share capital? Did AOL and JDS really have any option but to report the staggering losses they did?

Consolidation Calculations

* **PROBLEM 9.35** Basic consolidation calculations and balance sheet

Seeking to expand its markets, Big Ltd. recently purchased 80% of the voting shares of Piddling Ltd. for $10,800,000. At the date of the acquisition, Piddling had assets of $14,600,000, liabilities of $8,200,000, and equity of $6,400,000. By the best estimate Big could make at the date of acquisition, the fair market value of Piddling's assets was $16,100,000 and that of its liabilities was $8,300,000.

1. Calculate the goodwill on consolidation as of the acquisition date.
2. Calculate the noncontrolling (minority) interest as of the acquisition date.
3. Complete the consolidated balance sheet figures below.

Account	Big Ltd.	Piddling Ltd.	Consolidated
General assets	$105,000,000	$14,600,000	$
Investment in Piddling	10,800,000		
Goodwill			
General liabilities	83,700,000	8,200,000	
Noncontrolling interest			
Equity	32,100,000	6,400,000	

PROBLEM 9.36 Basic consolidated figures

Fine Furniture has decided to purchase 65% of Steel Appliances Ltd. for $38,000,000 in cash. The two companies' balance sheets as at the acquisition date are (in millions of dollars):

Assets	Fine	Steel	Liabilities and Equity	Fine	Steel
Cash equivalent assets	$112	$10	Cash equivalent liabilities	$ 28	$ 0
Other current assets	304	45	Other current liabilities	260	10
Noncurrent assets (net)	432	25	Noncurrent liabilities	272	15
			Share capital	160	15
			Ret. earnings	128	40
	$848	$80		$848	$80

Fine Furniture has evaluated all of Steel's assets and liabilities as having fair value equal to book value except for its noncurrent assets, which Fine Furniture believes have a fair value of $28 million.

1. Calculate the consolidated goodwill that would appear on the consolidated balance sheet at the acquisition date.
2. Calculate the following consolidated figures as at the acquisition date:
   a. Consolidated total assets.
   b. Consolidated owners' equity.
   c. Consolidated total liabilities.

PROBLEM 9.37 Goodwill amount and reasons; later consolidated income

Trifecta Ltd. recently purchased a 70% interest in Mega Magazines, a small magazine wholesaler. Mega's balance sheet on the date of acquisition appears below.

Assets		Liabilities and Equity	
Cash	$ 10,000	Liabilities	$ 95,000
Accounts receivable (net)	58,000	Owners' equity	108,000
Inventory	60,000		
Fixed assets (net)	75,000		
	$203,000		$203,000

Mega's receivables have an adequate provision for doubtful accounts. Inventories are carried at cost and current replacement value is about $60,000. Land with a book value of $30,000 has a market value of $39,000. In the purchase agreement, Trifecta assumed all of Mega's liabilities. Before the sale was final, the then owners of Mega were allowed to withdraw all cash from the company as a dividend.

1. If Trifecta paid $110,000 (in addition to the $95,000 to pay the liabilities) for its interest in Mega Magazines, what was the amount of purchased goodwill? (Hint: all Trifecta got for its money were receivables, inventories, and fixed assets.)
2. Why would Trifecta have been willing to pay this amount for goodwill?
3. Assume that in the year following the acquisition, Mega made a net income of $24,000. Therefore, decide whether the following statement is true or false and state why: To record Mega's earnings, the consolidated retained earnings of Trifecta will be increased by $24,000.

PROBLEM 9.38 Equity basis of accounting versus consolidation

Accounting for intercorporate investments is subject to GAAP. Apply your knowledge of GAAP to the following situation.

Newsworthy Inc. (NI) owns 45% of the voting shares of Reportit Corp. (RC). NI acquired the shares several years ago for $8,500,000. RC lost money for a few years after acquisition but has recently begun to be profitable: since NI acquired its shares, RC has had losses totalling $750,000 and incomes totalling $1,025,000, for a total net income since acquisition of $275,000. Last year, RC paid its first dividend, $50,000.

1. NI accounts for its investment in RC on the equity basis. What does this mean?
2. What is the present figure for investment in RC on the balance sheet of NI?
3. What difference would it make to the balance sheet of NI if the RC investment were consolidated instead?
4. Suppose that NI had bought 65% of the RC voting shares for its $8,500,000 and that at that date the following values existed for RC: book value of assets, $15,000,000; sum of fair values of assets, $16,000,000; book value of liabilities, $5,000,000; sum of fair values of liabilities, $8,000,000. Calculate the goodwill that would have been shown on the consolidated balance sheet of NI if the RC investment had been consolidated at that date.

* **PROBLEM 9.39** Accounting effects of a business acquisition

Suppose that, to spread its business risk, a major brewing company decides to buy into the retail furniture business by acquiring a controlling interest in a national chain that sells furniture, appliances, and related goods at discount prices. Changing its usual policy of 100% ownership, the brewer acquires a 60% voting interest. On January 1, 2005, the brewer pays $54,000,000 cash for 60% of the chain's voting shares. At that date, the chain's balance sheet shows:

Cash	$ 2,000,000	Demand bank loan	$14,000,000
Other current assets	53,000,000	Other current liab.	26,000,000
Noncurrent assets	38,000,000	Noncurrent liab.	20,000,000
Less accum. amort.	(6,000,000)	Shareholders' equity	27,000,000
	$87,000,000		$87,000,000

The brewer's evaluation is that the fair values at January 1, 2005, are the same as the book value for all of the chain's assets and liabilities except land; it is on the chain's books at a cost of $4,000,000, but the brewer's evaluation is that its fair value is $7,000,000 at January 1, 2005.

The furniture chain is expected to report a substantial net income for the four months from January 1, 2005, to April 30, 2005 (the brewer's year-end), so the brewery managers are pleased with their decision to get into the furniture retailing business.

1. The brewer owns more than 50% of the furniture chain, so it should be consolidated with the brewer's other companies in preparing financial statements. But the chain is quite different from the brewer's other activities, so would it make sense to add apples in with oranges? Comment on this question.
2. Calculate the consolidated goodwill (if any) arising as at January 1, 2005, from the purchase of the furniture chain.

3. Evaluate each of the following items, stating assumptions or reasons if you wish. If the furniture chain were consolidated with the brewer as of January 1, 2005, what would happen on *that date* to:

	Would Go Up	Would Go Down	No Effect	Not Possible to Tell
a. Consolidated total assets				
b. Consolidated shareholders' equity				
c. Consolidated net income since May 1, 2004				

4. Looking ahead to the consolidated income for the year ended April 30, 2005, will the furniture chain's expected substantial net income contribute significantly to the brewer's consolidated net income? Comment on this question.

PROBLEM 9.40 Goodwill and consolidated net income

Foodex Inc. is increasing the vertical integration of its operations by buying out suppliers. On July 1, 2005, Foodex purchased 70% of the common shares of Grow Food Farms, an Alabama supplier of asparagus, celery, and other produce. Grow Food is itself a bit of a conglomerate because it has extensive landholdings in Atlanta and Dallas, and owns dairies in Wisconsin and Ontario.

On July 1, 2005, Grow Food's balance sheet showed a net book value of \$112,800,000. The aggregate net fair value of individual assets and liabilities was \$171,000,000 as at that date. Foodex paid \$165,000,000 (\$25,000,000 cash, the rest newly issued shares of Foodex) for its investment in Grow Food.

It is now March 31, 2006, the end of Foodex's fiscal year. For Foodex, it has been a good year. Grow Food has also done well, reporting a net income of \$39,000,000 during the nine months ended March 31, 2006, and declaring \$15,000,000 in dividends during that period. On a nonconsolidated basis, Foodex's investment in Grow Food stood at \$181,800,000 at March 31, 2006, and its net income for the year was \$74,200,000.

1. What accounting method is Foodex using for its investment in Grow Foods? How can you tell?
2. Two figures that may appear on the consolidated balance sheet of Foodex and Grow Food are "Goodwill arising on consolidation" and "Minority interest liability." Why are the fair values of Grow Food's individual assets relevant for calculating the former but not the latter?
3. Calculate consolidated net income for the year ended March 31, 2006, as well as you can with the data provided.

PROBLEM 9.41 Accounting for an acquisition

Winnipeg Merchandisers Ltd. and Red River Stores Ltd. are considering some form of business combination. Two alternatives are being studied: a purchase of all the voting shares of Red River by Winnipeg or a purchase of 75% of the voting shares of Red River by Winnipeg. Management of the two companies wants to know what the combined company's consolidated balance sheet would look like, based on their present financial information. (The final figures will depend on the actual date of the combination.) Here are the two companies' balance sheets as at a recent date:

	Winnipeg Book Values	Red River Book Values	Red River Fair Values
Assets			
Current assets	$1,124,645	$1,005,789	$1,104,311
Noncurrent assets	3,678,872	2,890,003	3,040,722
Liabilities and Equity			
Current liabilities	1,076,554	879,321	899,321
Shareholders' equity	3,726,963	3,016,471	

If Winnipeg purchases all of Red River's voting shares, it is willing to pay $3,400,000, which it will finance by borrowing against the values of its and Red River's assets. If Winnipeg purchases only 75% of the voting shares, it is willing to pay only $2,400,000, because the remaining block of 25% would be held by a single person who might interfere with Winnipeg's plans for the combined company.

1. Present the consolidated balance sheet under each of the two combinations being considered:
   a. 100% purchase of Red River by Winnipeg.
   b. 75% purchase of Red River by Winnipeg.
2. Write a brief report to the management of the two companies, explaining carefully, and avoiding accounting jargon:
   a. specifically, what the differences are in the consolidated balance sheets under the two combinations and why those differences exist; and
   b. which of the two balance sheets, in your opinion, would be the strongest.

Integrated Problems

Matching Terms

*** PROBLEM 9.42** Match liability, equity, and business combinations terms

Match each phrase on the left with the most appropriate phrase on the right.

1. Has no effect on equity at acquisition date
2. Liability arises only on consolidation
3. Left out of the income statement
4. A name that encompasses debts and some assets
5. Financing that isn't a liability or an equity
6. Accrues a share of a noncontrolled company's income
7. An expense based on analysis of balance sheet accounts
8. A promise to meet specified financial conditions
9. A usually informal kind of debt
10. Trying to give something for nothing

a. Income tax-future portion
b. Loan from shareholders
c. Stock dividend
d. Purchase method consolidation
e. Equity method
f. Proprietor's income tax
g. Minority interest
h. Financial instruments
i. Off-balance-sheet
j. Indenture

PROBLEM 9.43 Match intercorporate investment terms with their purposes

Match the list of terms in the left column with the purposes in the right column, written in deliberately brief and simple terms.

a. Consolidated	1. A buyer and a seller
b. Cost basis	2. Accounted for as one
c. Economic entity	3. Don't count it until we get it
d. Equity basis	4. No longer acceptable
e. Fair values	5. Parent and subsidiaries together
f. Goodwill	6. Take credit for influence
g. Minority interest	7. The extra we paid
h. Pooling of interests	8. We have a say but not control
i. Purchase method	9. What we didn't buy
j. Significant influence	10. Worth of individual parts

Creating and Understanding Financial Statements

PROBLEM 9.44 Outline a talk on consolidated financial statements

You have been asked to give a talk to a group of individual investors on the subject of "What to look for in consolidated financial statements and how to understand what you see." Briefly outline the main points in your talk.

PROBLEM 9.45 Effects of new complexities on financial statements

A business commentator remarked: "Double-entry accounting has been around for a long time. Maybe too long. In our complex modern world, many events can happen to an enterprise that do not meet the double-entry accounting model. When the CEO borrows money to buy a new home, that is not in the enterprise's accounting system, nor should it be. So why is anyone surprised that some financing methods don't fit the double-entry model and so aren't in the balance sheet's numbers? Accounting transactions and adjustments can't cover everything, and if we tried to make them do that, we'd end up with meaningless balance sheets. So leave the balance sheet alone and just make sure everything is fully disclosed in the notes."

Respond to the commentator's remarks.

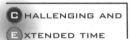

PROBLEM 9.46 Prepare a full set of statements under GAAP

Macro Ltd. services personal computers. Don Debit, the company's accountant, has compiled the following list of balances in the company's accounts at January 31, 2005, the fiscal year-end.

Macro Ltd.
List of Account Balances, January 31, 2005

Accounts payable	$ 40,000
Accounts receivable	48,000
Accumulated depreciation—building	6,000
Bank loan	100,000
Building	86,000
Cash	30,000
Depreciation on building for the year	6,000
Dividends declared	20,000
Dividends payable	5,000
General expenses	170,000
Investments	16,000
Income tax expense	3,000
Interest on bank loan for the year	12,000
Land	50,000
Service fee revenues	213,000
Share capital	15,000
Shareholders' loan	60,000
Repair supplies used during year	38,000
Retained earnings	25,000
Gain on sale of plant and equipment	15,000

Here is additional information about some of these figures:

1. Accounts payable will be paid in February 2005 except for $5,000, which will be paid February 1, 2006.
2. Accounts receivable will be collected in February or March 2005.
3. The bank loan is payable in yearly payments of $20,000, which are to be made December 31 of each year for the next five years. Interest on the loan has been paid up to January 31, 2005.
4. A dividend of $20,000 was declared on January 31, 2005, and $15,000 was paid to the shareholders on the same day. The balance will be paid on December 31, 2005.
5. "Investments" were purchased just before the year-end and consist of the following:

8% term deposits, due in April 2005	$ 4,000
Investment in shares of ABC Ltd.	12,000
	$16,000

   The shares of ABC Ltd. are not publicly traded, so there is no ready market for them. Macro Ltd. owns 3% of ABC Ltd.'s shares.
6. The shareholders' loan is due on demand, but no repayment is expected to be made in the upcoming year. This loan is unsecured.
7. The land and building are recorded at estimated market value, based on an appraisal done on January 2, 2005. The land had cost $40,000; the building had cost $96,000.
8. The bank loan is secured by a first mortgage on the land and building.
9. Of the cash, $5,000 is held in trust, as part of a recent sales agreement with a customer.
10. "General expenses" includes $50,000 of a bad-debt expense due to the bankruptcy of a major customer during the year.
11. "Income tax expense" includes $1,000 of tax related to the sale of plant and equipment during the year, future tax of $4,000, and a claim for a tax refund of $2,000. The refund claim is included in accounts receivable.

12. "Service fee revenues" includes $20,000 of revenue that should have been recorded in the prior year.
13. It turns out that retained earnings includes a future income tax liability of $6,000 ($2,000 from the beginning of the year and $4,000 from item 11 above). Don didn't know where to put it so he just included it in retained earnings.

Prepare a properly classified balance sheet, income statement, and statement of retained earnings from the above information for the year ended January 31, 2005, as well as any notes to the financial statements that you feel are necessary to satisfy user needs and disclosure requirements under GAAP. If it is helpful, assume that a prospective creditor such as a bank will use the financial statements.

CASE 9A

EVALUATE THE ACCOUNTING FOR A RECENT CORPORATE ACQUISITION

In mid-2002, Pfizer Inc., the maker of cholesterol drug Lipitor and virility drug Viagra, acquired Pharmacia Corp., another large drug company, for U.S.$60 billion. Let's look at the accounting for such a business combination. Pfizer paid for Pharmacia with its own newly-issued shares, so in Pfizer's books, the acquisition would be recorded like this (depending on the actual market values of Pfizer's shares when issued):

DR Investment in Pharmacia	60 billion	
CR Share capital		60 billion

There would be no entry in Pharmacia's books, because all that changed for Pharmacia was its owners.

In the consolidated financial statements of Pfizer, the accounting would depend on the fair values of Pharmacia's net assets. At the end of 2001, Pharmacia's balance sheet showed total assets of U.S.$22 billion, including U.S.$6 billion for the net assets of Monsanto, which Pharmacia was in the process of getting rid of, "spinning it off" to shareholders by issuing a dividend consisting of the Monsanto shares Pharmacia owned. At the end of 2001, Pharmacia's liabilities (without any of Monsanto's) were U.S.$10 billion, giving it a net equity value of U.S.$12 billion, or U.S.$6 billion without Monsanto. Pharmacia had several important products under development at the time of Pfizer's takeover, so let's say that at the middle of 2002, Pharmacia's net assets had a fair value of about $20 billion without Monsanto, which was almost entirely spun off by then. Let's say also that the U.S.$4 billion in increased fair value was due only to Pharmacia's assets, that is, that the fair values of its liabilities equalled their U.S.$10 billion book value. In the consolidated balance sheet of Pfizer at the date of acquisition, there would thus be:

An increase in consolidated assets other than goodwill of	$20 billion
An increase in consolidated goodwill of	50 billion
	$70 billion
An increase in consolidated liabilities of	10 billion
Higher Pfizer share capital of	60 billion
	$70 billion

If the acquisition had been for cash, buying Pharmacia's shares on the market, Pfizer would have had to borrow the money (at least until it could issue its own shares on the market to pay off the debt). Pfizer had only about U.S.$1 billion in cash, so it would have had to borrow the whole U.S.$60 billion. This would be quite impractical, because before the acquisition, Pfizer had assets of about U.S.$40 billion and liabilities of a little more than half that, equity a little less than half. Such borrowing would have quadrupled its liabilities and raised its debt-equity ratio from a little over 1:1 to 4:1. The risks and interest costs would have been huge. By issuing shares to Pharmacia owners instead, Pfizer transferred the risk to present shareholders, who saw their shareholdings suddenly diluted by large numbers of Pharmacia shareholders, and to Pharmacia shareholders, who would have to hope that Pfizer would make their new shares perform well. Pfizer trades on the New York Stock Exchange: its share prices had been declining steadily before the July 15, 2002, announcement of the Pharmacia deal, and they continued to decline after the announcement, picking up a little at the end of the month. (This followed the general pattern of share prices in the turbulent mid-2002 stock market.)

You can look at Pfizer's financial statements, MD&A and press releases on **www.pfizer.com** and see how the acquisition was accounted for, and how the acquisition of Pharmacia has turned out. Share prices can be seen on a number of services, or on the NYSE Web site **www.nyse.com**. If the numbers are greatly different from those above, and/or if the acquisition hit any snags (for example, problems with anti-trust competition regulators), your discussion of the issues below may change. Both companies' Web sites had news about the acquisition in mid-2002, but Pharmacia may no longer have an independent Web site by the time you read this.

A July 15, 2002, article about the acquisition commented:

> The deal comes amid unprecedented pressure on pharmaceutical companies, as the industry struggles with a dry spell in its research labs, fights rising competition from generics makers and wrestles with

> intense pressure on prices from governments and private buyers worldwide. As a result, drug companies are facing slowing or declining revenues and are watching their stocks sink to their lowest level in years.[21]

The article speculated that, as the new Pfizer would be the world's largest drug company measured by revenue, its rivals (like Bristol-Myers Squibb Co., Merck & Co. and GlaxoSmithKline PLC) would be under pressure to find merger partners to keep up with Pfizer's growth. On the other hand, the article also said that mergers in the pharmaceutical industry had generally not worked out too well (though praising Pfizer's earlier acquisition of Warner-Lambert). The stock prices of acquiring companies often decline after a merger announcement, indicating that stock market traders think promised synergies and other benefits are unlikely, or that the price paid by the acquiring company was too large. Pfizer (or its shareholders) paid quite a high price: Pharmacia's 2001 net income was U.S.$1.5 billion, including U.S.$229 million from Monsanto, being spun off. The goodwill implied in the U.S.$60 billion price was thus around 40 times Pharmacia's current earnings.

Under the new rules for accounting for goodwill, Pfizer would write a large portion of the U.S.$50 billion off as a special item if there is evidence that too much was paid. Throughout all this, and including such a write-off, there would be no effect on Pfizer's cash flow, indeed it would be increased by adding Pharmacia's cash flow. Therefore, even if there were a huge goodwill write-off (and you can check by looking at Pfizer's 2002 or 2003 annual report), there might be little apparent impact on the company's performance or share price of "paying too much."

1. Using the above information and anything about Pfizer available since, discuss the business value and impact on shareholders of the Pharmacia acquisition.
2. Discuss the accounting for the acquisition, especially the value attributed to the goodwill and how the goodwill might be accounted for in later years. How might a reader of Pfizer's financial statements judge the value and meaning of the goodwill figure? (If the accounting for the acquisition was significantly different from that outlined above, identify the differences and discuss why they arose.)
3. The amount of goodwill produced in accounting for such an acquisition could be reduced by (1) assigning more dollars to the fair values of the acquired company's net assets, or (2) reducing the credit to share capital used in recording the acquisition, or even (3) just writing the goodwill off immediately. Would any of these methods make sense?
4. Such an acquisition has either no effect or a positive effect on consolidated cash flow. The cash flow effects thus might be widely different from the effects on accrual income now or later, and on the debt-equity structure of the balance sheet. Does this divergence indicate weaknesses in the way accrual accounting accounts for business combinations?
5. Many companies struggle with high debt loads caused by acquiring other companies. Given the Pfizer example, why wouldn't all acquisitions be accomplished by issuing new shares rather than paying in cash?

CASE 9B

POOR ACCOUNTING FOR DEBT AND EQUITY?

Judge: The witness for the prosecution having been sworn in, the prosecution may begin its questions.

Prosecutor: Thank you, Your Honour. Now, Dr. Runciman, would you please state your qualifications and experience?

Witness: I have a Ph.D. in accounting and have been a professor of accounting at Local University for 12 years. Much of my research and consulting has been focused on companies' accounting for and reporting of their debt and equity.

Prosecutor: Thank you. I hereby file Dr. Runciman's curriculum vitae with the Court. Now, Dr. Runciman, please state, to begin with, how a company's accounting for debt and equity could potentially harm investors.

Defence: Objection. Calls for speculation, and a general statement may have nothing to do with the facts of this case.

Judge: Sustained. Prosecution will rephrase the question.

Prosecutor: Dr. Runciman, what are "generally accepted accounting principles"?

Witness: These principles, usually referred to as GAAP, are the aggregation of published regulations and accepted good practices. They carry official weight in that the auditor's report states whether the auditors believe the financial statements have been prepared in accordance with GAAP.

Prosecutor: So companies must follow these GAAP?

Witness: No, GAAP are not laws. There may be more than one acceptable way to do the accounting, so companies must determine which methods are most appropriate for their circumstances. Some previous court cases, such as Continental Vending in the U.S., have held that following GAAP is less important than preparing fair financial statements, so financial reporting is more complicated than just following GAAP.

Prosecutor: Dr. Runciman, what are debt and equity, as far as accounting is concerned?

Witness: Debt is money owing to parties outside the company, resulting from transactions or agreements already made. Equity is the owners' interest in the company, as built up over the years by owners' contributions and earnings retained in the company.

Prosecutor: So if the company has made a promise to pay an outsider, that promise is a debt.

Witness: Generally, yes. But if the promise depends on some other event that is yet to happen, the promise is not considered a debt. For example, a promise to pay for goods that have not yet been delivered is not a debt. But it may be disclosed in the financial statement notes as a "commitment" or "contingent liability." Also, the company has to evaluate what is likely to be paid to meet any promise and record that likelihood. For example, if a promise has been made to pay pensions, the company has to estimate how many employees will quit, get fired ,or die before retirement and so not get a pension. The balance sheet reports the best estimate of what is owed for pensions, not the higher amount that theoretically has been promised.

Prosecutor: Let's get to this case. At the March 31 date specified in the fraud charge against Scarborough Fair Inc. and its officers, the charge this court is considering, were there problems in the company's accounting for its debt and equity in your view?

Witness: There were two problems to start with. One is that the company showed as long-term debt some debts that it had to repay within the next year. I estimate the amount to be $73 million at the specified balance sheet date. The second is that the company had some preferred shares that were convertible to debt, and since the company had been performing relatively poorly, I think the preferred shareholders would intend to convert the shares, so they should have been shown as debt, not equity.

To improve the exposition, some comments by the defence are reported below even though they would be made later when the defence cross-examined the witness.

Defence: You said the shares should be shown as debt because the shareholders intended to convert them.

Witness: Yes.

Defence: Do you have any evidence of that intent?

Witness: There was no evidence at March 31, but it would have been the rational thing to do. And since the fraud charge was laid, some shareholders have done that.

Defence: So it was rational to convert. Would it also be rational for Scarborough Fair to refinance its long-term debt so that nothing would have to be paid in the next year?

Witness: Yes, I suppose so.

Defence: You claim that rationality and intent are appropriate criteria for the accounting for the preferred shares, but not for the long-term debt. Aren't you being inconsistent?

Witness: Well, ...

Prosecutor: The company and its officers are on trial here, not the shareholders. Let's turn to another issue. Scarborough Fair's balance sheet at March 31 reported a $16 million debt to an associated company, Robinson Products Ltd. Please comment on that.

Witness: There were two problems. First, Scarborough Fair had guaranteed certain of Robinson Products' debts, so a more appropriate debt figure would be the guaranteed debt of $138 million. There should have been a note disclosure of this contingent liability. Second, Scarborough Fair owned 78% of Robinson Products, so Robinson's accounts should have been consolidated with Scarborough's, which would have revealed the full extent of Robinson's debts, $320 million.

Defence: Are you saying that a potential debt should have been recorded as an actual one? This contradicts your definition of a debt.

Witness: Scarborough controlled Robinson, so in an economic sense, Robinson's debt was Scarborough's.

Defence: Professor, surely we cannot convict anyone for being a bad economist! (Laughter in the courtroom.) Legally, did Scarborough owe more than $16 million in regard to Robinson?

Prosecutor: Objection. That is a question of law, not accounting.

Judge: Objection upheld. Is the witness saying that there was not a problem in the company's debt to Robinson but rather in the way the corporate group was reported?

Witness: Yes. People relying on Scarborough's financial statements should have been told that there was much more to the relationship than $16 million.

Prosecutor: By failing to report the ownership of Robinson properly, did the defendants also report Scarborough's equity improperly?

Witness: Yes. Robinson had been suffering losses, which Scarborough did not report because it didn't consolidate Robinson, so Scarborough's equity should have been $38 million lower due to its share of those losses.

Defence: Scarborough was using equity accounting for its relationship with Robinson. Didn't that mean Scarborough did show the impact on its equity of the Robinson losses?

Witness: Yes, but ...

Defence: Thank you.

Prosecutor: Dustin Distributing Inc. is another part of Scarborough Fair's group. It was 89% owned, and was consolidated with Scarborough, was it not?

Witness: Yes.

Prosecutor: Now, Robinson owed Dustin $78 million too. What happened to that?

Witness: In the consolidated balance sheet, that $78 million was shown as an account receivable. So it looked like an asset, not a debt.

Defence: It was not a debt. In fact, if, as you say, Robinson should have been consolidated, then both the asset and the debt would be eliminated anyway as being within the group. Is that right?

Witness: Not exactly. The asset would have been eliminated, but as the debt was not there to start with, consolidating would not change that.

Prosecutor: Let's turn to Scarborough's direct debts. Was anything missing from its balance sheet?

Witness: Yes. First, the company had recognized revenue from several large contracts but had not shown the associated expenses because they had not yet been paid. Either the revenue was over-reported or the expenses were under-reported. My estimate is that income after tax was over-reported by $29 million because of this under-reporting of debt. Second, the company had made promises to issue shares to senior managers under stock option plans—those promises should have been recorded as compensation expenses and liabilities. I estimate the unrecorded liability at March 31 to be $110 million, net of some tax effects.

Defence: But the company's shares were declining in value and since the fraud charges were laid, the shares have gone down enormously. Who'd want the shares under option?

Witness: That's not the point. At March 31, the promises had been made and should have been recorded. Not only were liabilities under-stated, but also income and retained earnings were over-stated.

Defence: Did the March 31 financial statement notes disclose the potential additional share issues due to the option plan?

Witness: Yes.

Defence: And did the diluted earnings per share calculation take the potential share issues into account?

Witness: Yes.

Defence: So couldn't anyone reading the financial statements have made the calculation you just reported?

Witness: Yes, but not easily.

Prosecutor: We are about to turn to other witnesses who will show how the fraud described in the charges against the defendants was perpetrated, but I have one more question for this witness. Were Scarborough Fair's revenues for the year ended March 31 too high, in your opinion? If so, what does that have to do with the balance sheet?

Witness: Yes, the revenues were too high. Scarborough Fair had made arrangements with a supplier, Canticle Inc., to swap advertising space on their Web pages. Each company would carry ads for the other company, at no cash cost because the agreement was that the ads had the same value to both companies. Scarborough Fair recorded the swap agreement by increasing its revenue and its advertising expense at the same time. In my opinion, the dollar amount was much too high, because Web advertising is not really very valuable. Scarborough Fair recorded a receivable from Canticle for Canticle's advertising and a payable to Canticle for Scarborough's advertising. From time to time, the receivable and payable would be written off against each other. But while the two accounts existed, the important working capital ratio was affected, and the company could manipulate it by choosing when to write the receivable and payable off against each other, and by how much. The debt-equity ratio was also affected by this accounting.

Defence: How can you criticize this accounting? It made the debts higher than they would have been, not lower, and income was not affected. It sounds like good, conservative accounting.

Discuss the debt and equity accounting issues raised by this court case.

NOTES

1. CPR, 2004 annual report, 70–72.
2. E. Church, "Profits seen threatened by rosy pension numbers: Off-balance-sheet shortfall could reach statements," *The Globe and Mail* (May 7, 2002), B9.
3. Various contributors, "Enron: Running on empty," *Business Week* (December 10, 2001), 80–82.
4. C. Byrd, I. Chen, and J. Smith, *Financial Reporting in Canada 2005* (Toronto: Canadian Institute of Chartered Accountants, 2005), 365–366.
5. "Note W," IBM, 2004 Annual Report. Online, www.ibm.com.
6. Note 16, GM 2004 annual report. Online, www.gm.com.
7. CPR, 2004 annual report, 72.
8. Byrd, Chen and Smith, 365.
9. Berkshire Hathaway 2001 Annual Report, (PDF version), 1.
10. Ibid., 2
11. "Forbes 400 Richest Americans in 2001," available online at www.forbes.com.
12. Byrd, Chen and Smith, 489.
13. F. Taylor (Vox), "Expensing options is a move forward," *The Globe and Mail* (May 17, 2002), B9.
14. M. Ingram, "Any way you look at it, options are an expense," *The Globe and Mail* (May 2, 2002), B7.
15. "Badly in need of repair," *The Economist* (May 4, 2002), 66–68.
16. N. Byrnes, "Five Ways to Avoid More Enrons," *Business Week* (February 18, 2002), 36–37.
17. Byrd, Chen, and Smith, 345.
18. CPR, 2004 annual report, 63–66.
19. CICA *Accounting Handbook,* Section 3855.12.
20. C. Byrd, I. Chen, and J. Smith, *Financial Reporting in Canada 2005* (Toronto: Canadian Institute of Chartered Accountants, 2005), 223.
21. R. Frank and S. Hensley, "Pfizer to buy Pharmacia for $60 billion in stock," *The Wall Street Journal,* reprinted in *The Globe and Mail* (July 15, 2002), B5.

PART FOUR

4

Financial Accounting Analysis Wrap-Up

Chapter 10 provides analysis relevant to preparing and using financial accounting information: financial statement analysis (focusing on the illustrative case of Canadian Pacific Railway Limited, made familiar by various examples in earlier chapters and so brought together in this chapter), "present value" analysis of the time value of money, and "what if" or "effects" analysis used to help managers understand the effects of accounting changes or various financial and other business deals.

CHAPTER TEN

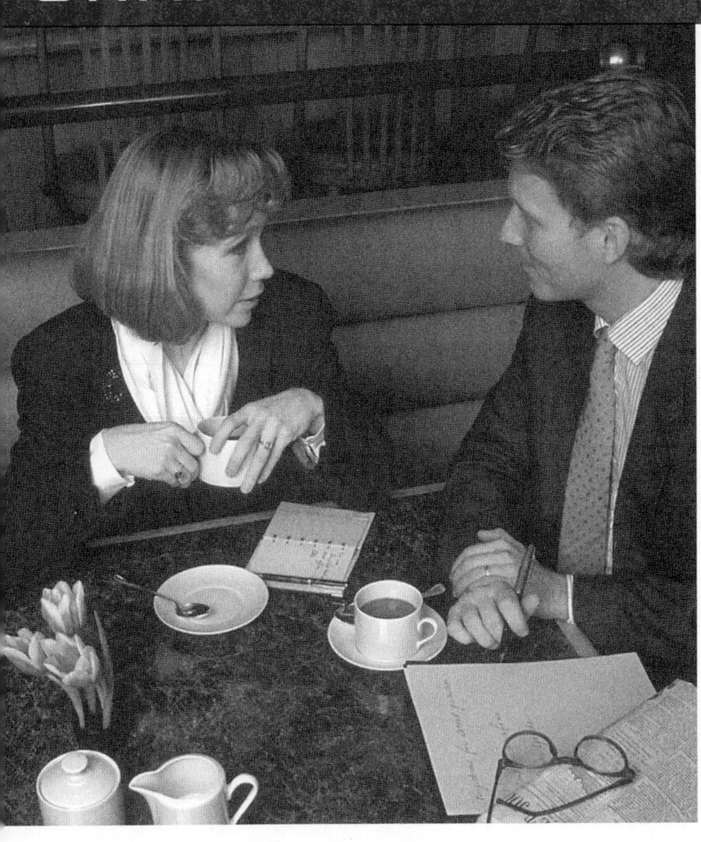

10 Financial Accounting Analysis Wrap-Up

TO THE READER: This chapter is written to be used flexibly. Its three parts (Sections 10.2–10.6, Section 10.7, and Sections 10.8–10.9) may be studied in any order, any time after Chapter 4 is covered.

10.1 Chapter Introduction: Analysis of Financial Accounting Information

Lydia and Serge are successful professionals: Lydia is in architecture and Serge is in engineering. They are beginning to accumulate significant savings and have started to think about building an investment portfolio. In preparation for a meeting with an investment advisor, they are talking over cups of frothy coffee at a local muffin and doughnut shop.

Lydia: "I believe in business fundamentals. A company that performs well should be appreciated by the stock market in the long run. In my practice, I certainly see some client companies that seem to be well-run and others that don't seem to have it together. But those are impressions from meeting the clients' people and seeing their offices. I'd like to do a more rigorous evaluation than that."

Serge: "Remember when we were deciding to buy a house? We worried about whether we were taking on an appropriate debt load, and if we were getting enough benefit out of our savings by transferring them into the house down payment. We had to balance the loss of investment income from our savings and the new cost of mortgage interest against the benefits of being house-owners. Companies have to do the same sort of calculations: we need to see how they do that and if they do it well."

Lydia: "We've both talked about companies doing things well. I'm more than a little spooked by all the upset in stock markets and companies' accounting, and am not sure how to tell who really is doing well. Look at this newspaper: one article claims that cash flow is the best measure of performance, and beside it is an article talking about net income as a good prediction of future performance, and at the bottom of the page there is an analysis of future cash flows discounted to the present to show the investment value of those cash flows. There seem to be many versions of what 'doing well' means."

Learning Objectives

This final chapter provides useful tools for analyzing and evaluating financial position and performance. For those of you who will not become accountants, this chapter will help you develop essential analytical skills. No matter where your career takes you, or what business-oriented courses you take from here, the ability to analyze a company's financial statements and determine how well the company is performing is highly valuable. If you do become an accountant, this chapter helps you develop the kind of analytical ability that the world expects accountants to have. In this chapter you will learn:

- How to calculate and interpret a full set of financial *ratios* (Sections 10.2–10.5). Various earlier chapters have presented some *ratio analysis* and interpretations: here they will be brought together using the continuing example of CPR;
- How to do *leverage analysis* to determine how a company's borrowing is contributing to the earnings it makes for the owners/shareholders (Section 10.6);
- How to do basic *present value analysis* of future cash flows to evaluate projects, bonds, and other financial matters (Section 10.7);
- How to do *"what if" (effects) analysis*, including using a framework for understanding how events and accounting policies can affect the financial statements.

Future accountant or not, you'll be pleased at how much you know about corporate performance by the time you have worked through the chapter's extensive examples and explanations.

Serge: "Yes, one of my clients is doing a major re-evaluation of a proposed project we were bidding on because they said that changes in expected rates of returns were making the project less advantageous and more risky. They said they wanted to reconsider their financing mix before deciding to go ahead. It would be useful for me to be able to incorporate relevant analysis into my project proposals so that I don't get surprised when I talk to a client. My personal investment objectives and ability to provide good professional services may overlap here."

Lydia: "You've got that right! Just yesterday, our senior partner said we should consider a change in the way our firm calculates its own profit and asked us to look at an analysis that showed what our firm's profit would be if various alternatives were used. That sort of analysis would be useful for you and me when comparing companies as investments because often they use different accounting methods and have different options for the future."

10.2 Investment and Relative Return

Investment and Relative Return

An investment forgoes current consumption in order to provide future consumption.

A fundamental economic assumption is that wealth, or capital, has value because it can be used for consumption, to get "all the ... things your little heart pines for," as Fats Waller sang. If our wealth is used up on current consumption, there'll be no consumption next period, so generally we are willing to forgo some current consumption by investing some of our wealth in order to obtain consumption in the future. We hope that the investment will earn a return that we can consume in the future.

This takes us to the business concept that an investment is made to earn a return. How much of a return? Whether the return is satisfactory depends on the size of the investment required to earn it. For example, you might be pleased with a $1,000 annual return if you had invested $2,000, but horrified if you had invested $2,000,000. One way to relate the two components is via *return on investment (ROI)*, in which the return is the numerator and the initial investment is the denominator:

$$\textbf{Relative return (return on investment)} = \frac{\textbf{Return}}{\textbf{Investment}}$$

The concept of ROI requires attention to both the return and the investment.

Later, we will examine relative returns, like return on investment, in more depth. For now, note that we have to have some way of measuring *both* return *and* investment if we are to be able to calculate (and evaluate) relative return:

- Is the return in the numerator valid? Earlier chapters commented about earnings management and other manipulations, and about earnings and cash flow as different ways of measuring return. The word "return" in ROI could be represented by several possible quantities, including net income, cash generated by operations, or interest. The appropriate quantity for the numerator depends on the context of the analysis, as we will see. Also, the roles of GAAP and other rules in making figures such as net income meaningful are very important to the conclusions that may be drawn from ratio analysis.
- Is the investment in the denominator valid? The same point about choosing the relevant quantity applies to the denominator. Also, earlier chapters commented about various alternative ways of measuring assets, about unclear distinctions between liabilities and equity, and about distortions that may result from off-balance-sheet liabilities and assets.
- Additionally, sometimes a doubtful or ambiguous accounting method can create a problem in both the numerator and denominator, bringing the whole ratio into question. An example here is that if a company chooses a revenue recognition method that makes the validity of net income doubtful, that will also make the retained earnings and equity figures doubtful, throwing into question one of the most widely used ROI-type ratios, called *return on equity (ROE)*, which is a ratio of income to equity.
- The purpose of a ratio is to produce a scale-free, *relative* measure of a company that can be used to compare to other companies, or to other years for the company. Such a measure is scale-free because both numerator and denominator are measured in the same units (dollars) and both are dependent on the size of the company. A large company will have a larger investment than a small one and should be expected to have a larger return as well, but a ratio like ROI cancels out some of the effects of size and so allows the large and small companies to be compared.

Ratios allow comparisons of different sized companies or the same company over time.

"Net-of-Tax" Analysis

Way back in Section 1.12, *net-of-tax analysis* was introduced. Please take a moment and review the Kamble Manufacturing example in that section.

Net-of-tax analysis is a way of quickly estimating the effect on net income, and on ratios that use net income, of changes in revenues, expenses, gains, or losses. If you assume income tax is paid or refunded quickly, you can use it also to estimate effects on operating cash flows. The whole idea is to focus on income statement items that *change*, take out the income tax effect, and so get the effect on net income directly without having to include all the items that do not change. The analysis illustrated by the Kamble Manufacturing example follows this formula:

$$\textbf{Net income} = (\textbf{1} - \textbf{Tax rate}) \times \textbf{Income before income tax}$$

Net-of-Tax Example

Here's another example. Suppose Alcatraz Fencing Inc. has one revenue, one expense, and an income tax rate of 35%. You can look at net income as the residual after the income tax has been deducted. But this works just as well for the revenues and expenses. Let's recast the income statement as if the revenues and expenses were taxed directly, so that they are shown net of tax and the income tax effect is, therefore, included in them rather than being a separate expense:

	Income Statement	**Net-of-Tax Version**
Revenue (net = $1,000 × (1 − 0.35))	$1,000	$650
Expense (net = $700 × (1 − 0.35))	700	455
Income before income tax	$ 300	
Income tax expense (35%)	105	
Net income	$ 195	$195

The effect of a revenue or expense change on net income is the change × (1 – Tax rate).

Suppose the president of Alcatraz has a plan to increase revenue by $200 without any increase in the $700 expense. What would that do to net income?

- Using the above formula, the new net income would be higher by $200 × (1 – 0.35) = $130.
- Therefore the new net income would be $325 ($195 + $130). There is no need to recalculate the whole income statement.
- If you are doubtful, you can always do the analysis the longer way by recalculating the income statement, as was illustrated in Section 1.12's Kamble example.
- The new revenue is $1,200, the expenses are still $700, so income before income tax is now $500. New income tax expense at 35% is $175, and so new net income is $325. Same answer, but longer, particularly for real companies that have many revenues and expenses.

Another Net-of-Tax Example, Using Interest Expense

Interest and other expenses cost less than they seem because they reduce income tax.

Another net-of-tax example, which will be important for some of the ratio analyses in this chapter, concerns interest expense. Suppose $60 of Alcatraz's expense was interest and we wanted to know what the company's net income would be *prior* to considering the interest (as if it had no debt).

- The answer is that if the interest expense were not present, the net income would go up, but not by $60, because *deducting the interest expense saves income tax.*
- The net income would rise by $60 × (1 – 0.35) = $39. Same formula again. Interest really costs the company only $39, because it brings a tax saving, as does any tax deductible expense.
- Again, we can calculate the net income effect the long way. Revenue is still $1,000, expense is now $640 ($700 – $60 interest), so new income before income tax is $360, new income tax expense is $126, and new net income is $234, which is $39 higher than the original $195.

HOW'S YOUR UNDERSTANDING?

Here are two questions you should be able to answer based on what you have just read. If you can't answer them, it would be best to reread the material.

1. The president of a company is thinking about changing the company's method of accounting for insurance expense, and wants to know what the effect of the policy will be on net income. Explain why all you need to know to estimate the effect is the amount of the expense under the present and proposed methods and the company's income tax rate.
2. A Canadian transportation company had revenues of $10.5 billion in a recent year. Its income tax rate was 37%. If its revenues increased by 2%, with no effect on expenses other than income tax, what would be the effect on net income for that year?

Revenue effect = 2% × $10.5 billion = $210.0 million more revenue.

Net income effect = $210 (1 – 0.37) = $132.3 million higher.

10.3 Introduction to Financial Statement Analysis

Financial Evaluation Is Not Just Calculation

Financial statement analysis is knowledge-based judgment, not just calculation.

The purpose of *financial statement analysis* is to use the statements to evaluate an enterprise's financial performance and position. Therefore, the value of the analysis depends on the contents of the financial statements. When you have completed Sections 10.2–10.6, you will be able to take a set of financial statements of pretty well any company and make an evaluation of its performance and prospects. Such an evaluation *is not just a calculation,* it is a *judgment* based on the calculations that make sense for that company and based on substantial knowledge of the company. The more you know about a company, its business, its management, *and* its accounting, the more useful and credible your analysis will be.

There are many sources and kinds of financial statement analysis.

Financial evaluation

- Calculations based on informed judgment.
- Techniques often specialized to suit particular companies, industries, or decisions.
- Financial statements are only part of a vast array of information.

You may have noticed that the preceding paragraph used the word "company." Analytical techniques for governments and not-for-profit organizations are more specialized than those illustrated for this book's examples, though many of the ratios and other techniques are useful there too. Some companies, such as banks and insurance companies, also have sufficiently specialized financial statements and business operations that they require particular analytical techniques in addition to or instead of those illustrated in this book. Other methods of analysis can always be developed in order to make the analysis fit the decision-making (use) objective of the user. Therefore, *this chapter is illustrative*: other techniques exist, and new ones are being invented all the time. Banks, on-line investment services, and various brokerages offer some analysis on their Web pages; the financial pages of newspapers like *The Globe and Mail, National Post,* and *The Wall Street Journal* contain analyses of companies pretty well daily, and magazines like *Canadian Business, Fortune,* and *Business Week* publish frequent comparisons of companies' performance, often of hundreds of companies at a time, using various financial statement numbers and ratios. When you use any of these, pay attention to how various numbers and ratios are defined, because these can vary significantly.

The financial statements should be analyzed given all the other available information.

Financial accounting information is not used in a vacuum, but is part of a vast array of information available to investors, creditors, managers, and others. The use of this information depends on its quality, such as whether the financial statements have been carefully prepared and are comparable to other companies' statements. Use is also affected by the availability of other sources of information that may contain all or part of what is in the financial statements. As is noted in the coverage of stock markets in Chapter 5, it is difficult to "beat the market" using financial statement information, because the statements reflect business events people already know something about and because there are many other people, all with their own sources of information, also trying to analyze what is going on and taking action on the basis of their analyses. Financial accounting information is part of a network of information; it doesn't stand alone. Consistent with this, various analytical techniques, though explained and illustrated separately in this chapter, work best together to tell an overall story. This is illustrated also.

Doing Intelligent Analysis

Ratios are indicators, given meaning by the analyst's understanding of the company.

Much of financial analysis involves ratios, which are *boiled-down summaries* of the financial statements. Ratios have little meaning on their own: they are merely *indicators*, which can be interpreted and used meaningfully only with a good understanding of the company and the accounting policies used in preparing the financial statements. The scale-free nature of a ratio means that it allows comparisons over certain periods of time, among companies of different sizes, and with other indicators such as interest rates or share prices. But it also can be tempting to think that when you have calculated a ratio, you have something meaningful in itself. While there is some fundamental meaning in each ratio, as we will see, what the comparisons mean to the analyst's decision must be added by the analyst, using knowledge and information beyond the ratios.

To do an intelligent and useful financial statement analysis, you should do the following:

The analysis depends on the decision or evaluation to be made from it.

a. Get a clear understanding of the decision or evaluation to which the analysis will contribute, who the decision maker is, and what assistance he or she requires. Helping an investor decide whether to make a long-term investment in shares requires a different set of evaluations than helping a bank manager decide whether to make a short-term secured loan. The two analyses share an interest in the enterprise's viability, economic prospects, and management quality, but the first implies an orientation to earnings performance, stock market behaviour, and investing activity by the enterprise, whereas the second is more concerned with ability to pay, quality of assets, and debt structure.
b. Learn about the enterprise, its circumstances, and its plans. This is essential in any real analysis: don't be misled by the more limited information given for the examples in this book. The annual report's *Management Discussion and Analysis (MD&A)* section and the *notes to the financial statements* will help you learn about the enterprise. Circumstances may make a big difference: for example, good performance for a new company in a troubled industry may be unsatisfactory for an established company in a prosperous industry.
c. Calculate the ratios, trends, and other figures that apply to *your specific problem.* Don't calculate indiscriminately. The examples in this chapter show you how to calculate many ratios and other comparisons, but not all are relevant to every situation.
d. Find whatever comparative information you can to provide a frame of reference for your analysis. Industry data, reports by other analysts, results for similar companies or the same company in other years, and other such information is often plentiful.
e. Use the MD&A and other explanatory sections of the annual report to deepen the insight into performance and strategy that your analysis provides.

A useful analysis is focused, selective, informed, and organized.

f. Focus on the analytical results that are most significant to the decision maker's circumstances and integrate and organize the analysis so that it will be of most help to the decision maker.

There are many sources of information about companies to help you become knowledgeable about them and be able to place your analysis in context. As you might expect, there is more information about large companies than small ones and more about public companies (those whose shares and other securities are listed on stock exchanges) than about private ones (those that are closely held by a few owners). Companies usually post their complete annual reports, including financial statements, on their Web pages and will often send you additional information, such as securities commissions filings. Many libraries have extensive sources of company, industry, and other economic information, much of it on computer-readable databases. Consult your university or public library, because new databases and other information products are coming out continuously.

Many sources of helpful financial information exist, including the Web.

The Web is increasingly important as a source of financial information: many companies have informative Web sites, and there are numerous services that point you to financial information. Just one example is the U.S. Securities and Exchange Commission's site (**www.sec.gov**), which links to the SEC's EDGAR database that contains all of the thousands of information filings to the SEC, many by Canadian and other non-U.S. companies. The corresponding site in Canada, maintained by the Canadian Securities Administrators (the provincial securities commissions) in both English and French, is **www.sedar.com**. With SEDAR, you can select the name of any public company in Canada and get access to its publicly available information. Another example is the research and analysis service offered by on-line brokers—while some of this is offered only to the brokers' customers, much is available to anyone who accesses the brokers' sites. Similarly, business magazines such as *Canadian Business, Business Week, The Economist, Forbes,* and *Fortune* offer on-line information, sometimes for subscribers only. If you are analyzing a company, type the company's name into your Web search engine and you might be surprised at the variety of articles, news releases, analyses, and commentaries that are out there.

Analysis often involves recasting the financial statements on different bases.

As you know, the preparer of financial statements has a choice from among a number of accounting policies on which to base the financial information. You, as the analyst of these statements, may wish to recast them using other policies that you prefer before computing any of the ratios. For example, some analysts deduct intangible assets, such as goodwill, from assets and owners' equity before computing ratios. They reason that because these assets are not physical in nature, some people may doubt their value; deleting them, therefore, may improve comparability with companies that don't have such assets. Sections 10.8–10.9 illustrate how to do "what if" analysis that considers possible changes, including changes to the way the company does its accounting.

Use ratios with care and intelligence.

The validity of financial analysis based on accounting ratios has been challenged. Among the criticisms are that:

(1) future plans and expected results, not historical numbers, should be used in computing ratios, especially liquidity ratios;
(2) current market values, not historical numbers, should be used for assets, debts, and shareholders' equity in computing performance ratios; and
(3) cash flow, not accounting income, should be used in computing performance ratios.

Another objection is that because, at least for public companies, stock markets and other capital markets adjust prices of companies' securities as information comes out, ratios based on publicly available information cannot tell you anything the markets have not already incorporated into security prices. While these criticisms are controversial, they are reminders to use ratios with care and intelligence. Useful additional ideas on the issues raised in this section can be found in many accounting and finance texts. Be careful when reading such material: ratio analysis may be made to appear more cut-and-dried than it is, and some nonaccounting authors do not appear to know much about the nature of the accounting information used in the analysis.

Financial Statements and Managers' Performance

Identifying managers' contribution to a company's performance can be difficult.

It can be hard to determine how much of a company's performance is really due to management and how much depends on other factors, such as economic trends, product price changes, union pressure, and even pure good or bad luck. Also, in most companies, management is a group, so it is difficult to set one manager's performance apart from the group's. The result is that evaluating a manager's performance (even the president's) with financial statements requires great care and knowledge of the company and its industry—and is always somewhat arbitrary.

The ratios and other computations used in financial statement analysis can easily compound the problem of evaluating the manager. Let's take the example of return on assets. Consider the case of two companies, "A" and "B."

- Company A has assets of \$100,000 and net income plus after-tax interest of \$20,000, for a 20% *return on assets* (*ROA* is a ratio to be explained in Section 10.4). Looks great. But the manager is not looking into the future much and so is not keeping the company's assets or maintenance up to date.
- Company B is exactly the same, except that the manager is very aware of the need to stay competitive and look after the assets, and so has spent \$10,000 on new assets and \$2,000 (after tax) on an improved maintenance program. B's assets are, therefore, \$110,000 and its net income plus after-tax interest is \$18,000, for a 16% ROA.

A ratio like ROA can make a good manager look worse than a poor manager.

Consequently, A looks better than B: ROA is reduced for B by both a smaller numerator and a larger denominator than A has. You can see that unless the person doing the financial analysis really understands the situation, the prudent and responsible manager of B will look worse than the neglectful manager of A!

HOW'S YOUR UNDERSTANDING?

Here are two questions you should be able to answer based on what you have just read. If you can't answer them, it would be best to reread the material.

1. How should a person prepare before beginning to analyze a set of financial statements?
2. What are some limitations of financial statement analysis?

10.4 Financial Statement Ratio Analysis

Canadian Pacific Railway Limited: An Example Company

The analyses in this and the next two sections use the December 31, 2004, financial information of CPR, the company you will have become familiar with through use of its financial statements as illustrations in Chapters 2, 3, 4, and elsewhere. CPR is used in this chapter because it is familiar, so you will have some of the knowledge you need to interpret the ratios, and because this chapter's analysis will be able to pull together the various bits of knowledge scattered throughout the earlier chapters' examples. For more information about CPR, and to find out how it has been doing since the year 2004, consult its Web site, **www.cpr.ca**, which has lots of financial, strategic, managerial, product, and market information, or go to the SEDAR site (**www. sedar.com**) and select Canadian Pacific Railway Limited. You can also use your search engine to find news reports and other information about the company.

To save you having to dig around in earlier chapters, here are the year 2004 financial statements of CPR. The four statements you used before are included, plus three notes (Notes 6, 10, and 12) that provide supplementary information useful in the analysis to come. *Please review these statements before you go on.*

Canadian Pacific Railway Limited
Consolidated Balance Sheet

Year ended December 31 (in millions)	2004	2003 (Restated – see Note 2)
Assets		
Current assets		
Cash and short-term investments	**$ 353.0**	$ 134.7
Accounts receivable (Note 9)	**434.7**	395.7
Materials and supplies	**134.1**	106.4
Future income taxes (Note 7)	**70.2**	87.4
	992.0	724.2
Investments (Note 11)	**96.0**	105.6
Net properties (Note 12)	**8,393.5**	8,219.6
Other assets and deferred charges (Note 13)	**1,018.3**	907.3
Total assets	**$ 10,499.8**	$ 9,956.7
Liabilities and shareholders' equity		
Current liabilities		
Accounts payable and accrued liabilities	**$ 975.3**	$ 907.0
Income and other taxes payable	**16.2**	13.5
Dividends payable	**21.0**	20.2
Long-term debt maturing within one year (Note 14)	**275.7**	13.9
	1,288.2	954.6
Deferred liabilities (Note 16)	**767.8**	702.8
Long-term debt (Note 14)	**3,075.3**	3,348.9
Future income taxes (Note 7)	**1,386.1**	1,295.8
Shareholders' equity (Note 19)		
Share capital	**1,120.6**	1,118.1
Contributed surplus	**300.4**	294.6
Foreign currency translation adjustments	**77.0**	88.0
Retained income	**2,484.4**	2,153.9
	3,982.4	3,654.6
Total liabilities and shareholders' equity	**$ 10,499.8**	$ 9,956.7

Commitments and contingencies (Note 22)

See Notes to Consolidated Financial Statements

Approved on behalf of the Board:

J.E. Newall, Director R. Phillips, Director

Canadian Pacific Railway Limited

Statement of Consolidated Income

Year ended December 31 (in millions, except per share data)	**2004**	**2003** (Restated – see Note 2)	**2002** (Restated – see Note 2)
Revenues			
Freight	**$ 3,728.8**	$ 3,479.3	$ 3,471.9
Other	**174.1**	181.4	193.7
	3,902.9	3,660.7	3,665.6
Operating expenses			
Compensation and benefits	**1,259.6**	1,163.9	1,143.4
Fuel	**440.0**	393.6	358.3
Materials	**178.5**	179.2	168.7
Equipment rents	**218.5**	238.5	255.4
Depreciation and amortization	**407.1**	372.3	340.2
Purchased services and other	**610.7**	583.6	555.6
	3,114.4	2,931.1	2,821.6
Operating income, before the following:	**788.5**	729.6	844.0
Special charge for environmental remediation (Note 3)	**90.9**	–	–
Special charge for labour restructuring and asset impairment (Note 4)	**(19.0)**	215.1	–
Loss on transfer of assets to outsourcing firm (Note 12)	–	28.9	–
Operating income	**716.6**	485.6	844.0
Other charges (Note 5)	**36.1**	33.5	21.8
Foreign exchange gain on long-term debt	**(94.4)**	(209.5)	(13.4)
Interest expense (Note 6)	**218.6**	218.7	242.2
Income tax expense (Note 7)	**143.3**	41.6	105.9
Net income	**$ 413.0**	$ 401.3	$ 487.5
Basic earnings per share (Note 8)	**$ 2.60**	$ 2.53	$ 3.08
Diluted earnings per share (Note 8)	**$ 2.60**	$ 2.52	$ 3.06

See Notes to Consolidated Financial Statements.

Canadian Pacific Railway Limited
Statement of Consolidated Cash Flows

Year ended December 31 (in millions)	**2004**	**2003** (Restated – see Note 2)	**2002** (Restated – see Note 2)
Operating activities			
Net income	**$ 413.0**	$ 401.3	$ 487.5
Add (deduct) items not affecting cash			
Depreciation and amortization	**407.1**	372.3	340.2
Future income taxes (Note 7)	**131.5**	31.8	95.0
Environmental remediation charge (Note 3)	**90.9**	–	–
Restructuring and impairment charge (Note 4)	**(19.0)**	215.1	–
Foreign exchange gain on long-term debt	**(94.4)**	(209.5)	(13.4)
Amortization of deferred charges	**24.7**	20.3	19.3
Other	**–**	–	(0.8)
Restructuring payments	**(88.8)**	(107.0)	(119.3)
Other operating activities, net (Note 20)	**(112.2)**	(365.0)	(45.0)
Change in noncash working capital balances related to operations (Note 10)	**33.2**	(53.6)	–
Cash provided by operating activities	**786.0**	305.7	763.5
Investing activities			
Additions to properties (Note 12)	**(673.8)**	(686.6)	(558.5)
Other investments	**(2.5)**	(21.9)	4.0
Net proceeds from disposal of transportation properties	**10.2**	8.2	3.5
Cash used in investing activities	**(666.1)**	(700.3)	(551.0)
Financing activities			
Dividends paid	**(81.7)**	(80.8)	(80.8)
Issuance of shares	**2.5**	2.0	2.0
Issuance of long-term debt	**193.7**	699.8	–
Repayment of long-term debt	**(16.1)**	(376.6)	(405.7)
Cash provided by (used in) financing activities	**98.4**	244.4	(484.5)
Cash position			
Increase (decrease) in net cash	**218.3**	(150.2)	(272.0)
Net cash at beginning of year	**134.7**	284.9	556.9
Net cash at end of year	**$ 353.0**	$ 134.7	$ 284.9
Net cash is defined as:			
Cash and short-term investments	**$ 353.0**	$ 134.7	$ 284.9

See Notes to Consolidated Financial Statements.

Canadian Pacific Railway Ltd.

6. Interest expense (in millions)	**2004**	**2003**	**2002**
Interest expense	$ 223.9	$ 226.4	$ 254.2
Interest income	(5.3)	(7.7)	(12.0)
Total interest expense	$ 218.6	$ 218.7	$ 242.2
Gross cash interest payments	$ 219.0	$ 228.7	$ 245.5

Canadian Pacific Railway Limited

10. Change in noncash working capital balances related to operations (in millions)	**2004**	**2003**	**2002**
(Use) source of cash:			
Accounts receivable	$ (39.0)	$ 45.2	$ 21.1
Materials and supplies	(35.5)	2.5	(6.6)
Accounts payable and accrued liabilities	112.3	(76.3)	(17.4)
Income and other taxes payable	(4.6)	(25.0)	2.9
Change in noncash working capital	$ 33.2	$ (53.6)	$ –

Canadian Pacific Railway Limited

12. Net properties (in millions)	Cost	Accumulated depreciation	Net book value
2004			
Track and roadway	$ 7,667.1	$ 2,482.7	$ 5,184.4
Buildings	319.7	128.4	191.3
Rolling stock	3,323.2	1,319.8	2,003.4
Other	1,566.1	551.7	1,014.4
Total net properties	$ 12,876.1	$ 4,482.6	$ 8,393.5
2003 (Restated – see Note 2)			
Track and roadway	$ 7,325.7	$ 2,321.0	$ 5,004.7
Buildings	314.6	108.1	206.5
Rolling stock	3,270.4	1,277.5	1,992.9
Other	1,535.9	520.4	1,015.5
Total net properties	$ 12,446.6	$ 4,227.0	$ 8,219.6

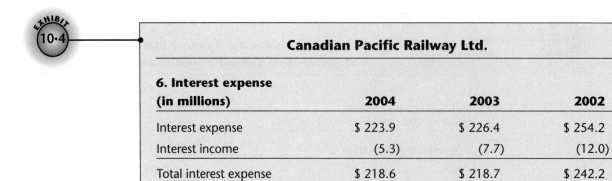

Exhibit 10.6 continues on the next page

(continued)

Included in the "Other" category at December 31, 2004, are software development costs of $596.5 million (2003 – $582.9 million) and accumulated depreciation of $202.8 million (2003 – $164.7 million). Additions during 2004 were $30.3 million (2003 – $31.7 million) and depreciation expense was $53.6 million (2003 – $55.3 million).

At December 31, 2004, net properties included $396.9 million (2003 – $387.9 million) of assets held under capital lease at cost and related accumulated depreciation of $83.5 million (2003 – $70.1 million).

During the year, capital assets were acquired under the Company's capital program at an aggregate cost of $686.3 million (2003 – $699.0 million), none of which were acquired by means of capital leases (2003 – $nil). At April 1, 2003, the Company consolidated $193.5 million in net properties of a VIE for which it is the primary beneficiary (see Note 2). Cash payments related to capital purchases were $673.8 million (2003 – $686.6 million). At December 31, 2004, $0.2 million (2003 – $12.4 million) remained in accounts payable related to the above purchases.

Included in the special charge recorded in the second quarter of 2003 was a $102.7-million write-down to fair market value of the assets of the D&H, including a $21.8-million (US$16.0 million) accrual for the impact of labour restructuring (see Note 4).

In the fourth quarter of 2003, CPR and IBM Canada Ltd. ("IBM") entered into a seven-year agreement for IBM to operate and enhance the Company's computing infrastructure. CPR incurred a loss of $28.9 million on the transfer of computer assets to IBM at the start of the arrangement.

Continue this section only after familiarizing yourself with the CPR financial statements.

To make sure you are familiar with the CPR financial statements and so are ready to start the analysis, answer the following questions:

- What were the company's total assets at December 31, 2004? Was that more or less than 2003?
- What was the total equity of the company at December 31, 2004?
- What was the company's net income for the year ended December 31, 2004? What were the main revenues and expenses that led to this income?
- How much cash was generated by operations for the year ended December 31, 2004? Did the company end up with more or less cash at the end of the year than at the beginning?
- What was accumulated amortization (depreciation) at the end of 2004? At the end of 2003?
- How much did accounts receivable changes contribute to the increases and decreases in noncash working capital used in calculating cash from operations in 2004?

This section focuses on extracting financial statement information and calculating ratios.

Ratios are only indicators, so precision to several decimal places is unnecessary.

Twenty kinds of ratios that could be used to analyze a company's financial performance and position are outlined in the following pages. Each ratio is illustrated by showing how it is calculated from the CPR statements. Some interpretive and comparative comments are made as illustrations, but the main purpose of this section is to show you how to extract the needed information from the statements and figure out the ratios.

Most figures below are given in millions of dollars, as they are in CPR's statements. Ratios are calculated arbitrarily to three decimal places. They could be done to more decimals, but that would be false accuracy, because the ratios depend on all sorts of judgments and estimates made in assembling the financial statements and, therefore, should not be thought of as precise quantities, but rather as indicators.

This section's 20 ratios are summarized in Exhibit 10.8, near the end of the section. They all should be used in combination with each other, because each has only part of the story to tell, but to help you see their main uses, they are grouped into four categories:

- Performance ratios: ratios 1–11.
- Activity (turnover) ratios: ratios 12–14.
- Financing ratios: ratios 15–17.
- Liquidity and solvency warning ratios: ratios 18–20.

Performance Ratios

ROE = Net income / Owners' equity.

1. *Return on equity* (sometimes called return on shareholders' investment or return on net worth): calculated as *Net income / Owners' equity*. ROE, a very frequently used ratio, indicates how much return the company is generating on the historically accumulated owners' investment (contributed share capital and other capital items plus retained earnings). Owners' equity can be taken straight from the balance sheet or can be computed from the balance sheet equation as total assets minus total liabilities. The denominator can be year-end equity or average equity over the year; for a growing company, you'd expect a slightly larger ROE figure for the latter.

   ROE: What return is the owners' historical investment earning?

   CPR's ROE (based on year-end equity) for the last two years was:

   - **2004:** \$413.0 / \$3,982.4 = 0.104
   - **2003:** \$401.3 / \$3,654.6 = 0.110

   CPR's 2004 ROE at 10.4% was down a little from 2003's 11%.

   The income return relative to equity was in the range of many companies' ROEs. The 2004 return was a little lower than 2003: Both income and equity were higher at the end of 2004 than at the end of 2003 but equity grew proportionally more at 9.0% ((\$3,982.4 – \$3,654.6)/\$3,654.6) than income at 2.9% ((\$413.0 – \$401.3)/401.3). The analyses to come will tell us more about how the ROE came about and how it relates to other indicators.

ROA = (Income + Interest expense) / Total assets.

2. *Return on assets* (often also called return on investment or ROI): usually calculated as *(Net income + Interest expense) / Total assets.* Income before income tax may be used instead of net income. As with the equity denominator in ROE, the total assets figure can be the year-end figure or the average over the year. *ROA* indicates the company's ability to generate a return on its assets *before considering the cost of financing those assets (interest).* It helps in judging whether borrowing is worthwhile: presumably if it costs *x*% to borrow money, the company should expect to earn at least *x*% on the assets acquired with the money. (The relationship between ROA and borrowing cost is explored further in Section 10.6.) Some financial databases calculate ROA just as income divided by total assets, but we will remove the financing cost because that provides more information.

   ROA : What return are the assets earning, before considering the interest cost of financing them?

ROA(ATI): Calculating ROA using after-tax interest.

We will use a slightly refined version of ROA: we'll calculate the interest expense *after income tax*, because if interest is just added back to income, the impact of the tax saving it brings is lost. Net income is after tax, so it makes sense to use an after-tax version of interest expense too.

Refined ROA(ATI) = (Net income + After-tax interest expense) / Total assets.

For our *refined ROA*, which will be designated *ROA(ATI)* as a reminder that it uses after-tax interest (ATI), we first have to calculate the after-tax interest cost. You will recall from Section 10.2 that *After-tax interest cost = Interest expense × (1 – Tax rate)*:

- We first have to estimate CPR's effective income tax rate. Its income statement shows net income but not income before income tax: we have to calculate that by adding the income tax expense back to net income. Doing this results in income before income tax in 2004 of $556.3 ($413.0 + $143.3) and $422.9 in 2003 ($401.3 + $41.6).
- With that information, we can estimate CPR's income tax rate: 2004 = 25.8% ($143.3 / $556.3) and 2003 = 9.4% ($41.6 / $442.9). (One of CPR's notes, not included in this book, sets out the tax rate reductions and other factors that led these rates to be lower than expected Canadian statutory rates.)
- Now we need to know CPR's interest expense. Note 6, presented earlier in this section, shows that the interest expense figure on the income statement is a net after deducting interest revenue. According to the note, the interest expense was $223.9 in 2004 and $226.4 in 2003.
- We can now calculate the company's interest cost on an after-tax basis: 2004 = $166.1 ($223.9 × (1 – 0.258)) and 2003 = $205.1 ($226.4 × (1 – 0.094)). Note: the rounded figures for CPR's tax rates in 2004 and 2003 are used in this calculation and all future calculations.

ROA: To calculate the numerator, add after-tax interest expense to net income.

CPR's refined ROA(ATI) based on year-end assets was:

- **2004:** ($413.0 + $166.1) / $10,499.8 = 0.055
- **2003:** ($401.3 + $205.1) / $9,956.7 = 0.061

CPR's 2004 ROA(ATI) of 5.5% was down from 2003's 6.1% and about half its ROE.

These ROAs were moderate: in 2004 and 2003, it was hard to get more than 5% or so on guaranteed investment certificates at the bank, on Canada Savings Bonds (CSBs), and on similar investments. CPR has earned more than that on its assets, but it is taking more risk to earn its returns than you'd take on bank certificates or CSBs, so it should be able to do better. Many companies have ROAs in this range. The calculation above also shows some interesting results along the way. First, the interest really only cost the company $166.1 million in 2004 ($205.1 million in 2003) because it was a tax-deductible expense and so saved income tax. Second, if the company had not had any interest at all, its net income, after tax, would have been $579.1 million in 2004 ($413.0 + $166.1) and $606.4 million in 2003 ($401.3 + $205.1).

CPR has positive leverage: ROE greater than ROA(ATI).

These two "relative return" ratios may be compared, as is done in the little table here. Whenever the ROE exceeds the ROA, that means the company is making extra money for the owners by borrowing to make the assets greater than they would be with just equity funding. In 2003, *leverage* (the "extra" in the table) more than doubled the ROA, and in 2004 nearly doubled it. Leverage is a main topic in Section 10.6; some other ratios that reflect leverage effects are shown later in this section.

CPR's ROE and ROA

	ROE	ROA	Extra
2004	0.104	0.055	0.049
2003	0.110	0.061	0.052

Sales return = Net income / Revenue.

3. *Sales return* (or *profit margin*): usually calculated as *Net income / Revenue.* Sales return indicates the percentage of sales revenue that ends up as income, so it is the average "bottom line" profit on each dollar of sales. For example, a 0.10 sales return would mean that 10 cents in net income are generated from each dollar of sales, on average. It is a useful measure of performance and gives some indication of pricing strategy or competition intensity. You might expect a discount retailer in a competitive market to have a low sales return, and an upscale jeweller to have a high return, for example.

   In Section 10.6, we will use an alternative version of the sales return ratio, calculated analogously to that of the refined ROA(ATI), by adding interest expense after tax back to net income in order to determine the operating return before the cost of financing that return. Here the more usual simpler version will be illustrated.

Sales return was down in 2004 compared to 2003, as were ROE and ROA(ATI).

   CPR's sales return for 2004 was 0.106 ($413.0 / $3,902.9) and for 2003 was 0.110 ($401.3 / $3,660.7). CPR earned 10.6 cents per dollar of revenue in 2004 and 11 cents in 2003.

   - **2004:** ($413.0 / $3,902.9) = 0.106
   - **2003:** ($401.3 / $3,660.7) = 0.110

   The combination of revenue growth of 7.2% (($3,728.8 – $3,479.3)/$3,479.3) while controlling operating expenses which increased only 6.2% (($3,114.4 – $2,931.1)/$2,931.1) would lead to an increase in the sales return. The positive outcome was offset by increases in nonoperating costs and lower foreign exchange gains on long-term debt.

Common size analysis converts the statements to percentages of revenue or assets.

4. *Common size financial statements*: by calculating all balance sheet figures as percentages (ratios) of total assets and/or all income statement figures as percentages of total revenue, the size of the company can be approximately factored out. This procedure assists in comparing companies of different sizes and in spotting trends over time for a single company. You can think of it as turning the whole financial statement into ratios.

   Common size comparisons can be done using a variety of assumptions. To illustrate the analysis, here are common size percentages for the three years included in CPR's income statement. Freight revenue could have been used as the baseline, because freight is CPR's main business, but to connect with other analyses being illustrated, *total revenue* is used here. This is a judgment, of the sort the analyst always has to make. To further illustrate judgment, some income statement items were grouped and others were not—different groupings may lead to different conclusions. All percentages were rounded to one decimal.

CPR Common Size Income Statements

	2004	2003	2002
Revenues:			
Freight	95.5%	95.0%	94.7%
Other	4.5	5.0	5.3
Total	100.0%	100.0%	100.0%
Operating expenses:			
Compensation	32.3	31.8	31.2
Fuel	11.3	10.8	9.8
Other	38.1	44.2	36.0
Operating income	18.3	13.2	23.0
Foreign exchange gain	(2.4)	(5.7)	(0.4)
Interest and other	6.5	6.9	7.2
Income tax	3.7	1.1	2.9
Net income (Ratio 3 percentages)	10.5%	10.9%	13.2%

The common size income statement shows the components of sales return.

Two interesting trends are immediately apparent: operating expenses as a percentage of sales have increased each year, and interest and other charges have been falling. The reduction in interest and other charges has been insufficient to offset the rising operating costs.

- Sales growth ($3728.8 – $3479.3)/$3479.3 = 7.2%
- Operating expense growth (($3,114.4 – $2,931.1)/$2931.1) = 6.2%

A similar analysis may be done of the balance sheet, dividing all assets, liabilities, and equity items by total assets. You might try that yourself as an exercise and see what is revealed by it.

Gross margin = (Revenue – COGS) / Revenue.

5. *Gross margin* (or *gross profit ratio*): calculated as *(Revenue – Cost of goods sold expense) / Revenue*. This provides a further indication of a company's product pricing and product mix beyond the business line analysis done above. For example, a gross margin of 33% indicates that a company's average markup on cost is 50% (revenue equals 150% of cost, so cost is 67% of revenue and gross margin is 33%). This is a rough indicator only, especially for companies with a variety of products or unstable markets.

Gross margin cannot be calculated from CPR's financial statements.

As we saw in Section 3.4, gross margin cannot be calculated for CPR. The company sells services, not products, so it has no "cost of goods sold" to report. Perhaps its expense categories could be grouped into a "cost of services provided" category, but the company doesn't do that. In Section 3.4, we tried other ways of relating CPR's revenues and expenses. Using the common size income statement shown above as Ratio 4, the various categories of expenses can be related to revenue, and that is about all that can be done.

It is a reminder that financial statement analysis is dependent on the contents of the financial statements. We cannot analyze information we do not have, or that would be irrelevant or inapplicable to the particular company we are analyzing.

Average interest rate = Interest expense / Liabilities.

6. *Average interest rate*: calculated as *Interest expense / Liabilities*. This ratio shows what the company pays for interest relative to its borrowing. There are various versions of this ratio:

- Interest expense can be calculated before or after income tax.
- Related expenses such as amortization of debt issue costs could be included or not.
- All liabilities may be included or just interest-bearing ones, such as bonds and mortgages.

If the ratio is calculated on an after-tax basis and applied to all liabilities, it is likely to be quite low: interest is tax-deductible, so income tax savings amount to a significant part of it, and many liabilities, such as future income tax, dividends payable, deposits on contracts, and most accounts payable, carry no interest. Interest rate calculations are discussed further in Section 10.6, where the rate is calculated on an after-tax basis.

On a before-tax basis, Note 6 reports interest expense of $223.9 million in 2004 and $226.4 million in 2003. We can calculate total liabilities two ways:

- Add up all the liabilities: 2004: $1,288.2 + $767.8 + $3,075.3 + $1,386.1 = $6,517.4; 2003: $954.6 + $702.8 + $3,348.9 + $1,295.8 = $6,302.1.
- Just subtract equity from the total of liabilities and equity: 2004: $10,499.8 – $3,982.4 = $6,517.4; 2003: $9,956.7 – $3,654.6 = $6,302.1.
- It's sometimes useful to use both methods just to check!

Therefore, the average pre-tax interest rate on all year-end liabilities was:

- **2004:** $223.9 / $6,517.4 = 0.034
- **2003:** $226.4 / $6,302.1 = 0.036

Average interest rate is low and has not changed much in the two years.

The two years had almost the same average interest rate. As some of the liabilities included in the ratio's denominator did not carry interest, it is a predictably low rate. The impact of interest on measuring leverage will be examined in Section 10.6. The very long Note 14 about long-term debt (not included in this book) indicates that the long-term debt carries interest at average rates from 6% to 9% (and that there is some "perpetual" debt created by an act of parliament in 1889—a left-over of the railway's original financing to link the country with steel). Assuming that only the long-term debt (including its current portion) bears interest, we can calculate the average long-term interest rate:

- **2004:** $223.9 / ($275.7 + $3,075.3) = 0.067
- **2003:** $226.4 / ($13.9 + $3,348.9) = 0.067

This calculation suggests that the company's interest rates have fallen. The unchanged overall average above was partly a function of a change in the mix of interest-bearing and non-interest-bearing liabilities.

Cash flow to total assets = Cash from operations / Total assets.

7. *Cash flow to total assets*: calculated as *Cash generated by operations / Total assets.* Cash generated by operations is found in the cash flow statement, and total assets may be taken from the year-end balance sheet figure or calculated as an average of the beginning and ending figures. This ratio relates the company's ability to generate cash resources to its assets, which approximately factors out size. It provides an alternative return measure to ROA, focusing on cash return rather than on accrual income return as used in ROA.

   CPR's cash flow to assets ratios were:

   - **2004:** $786.0 / $10,499.8 = 0.075
   - **2003:** $305.7 / $9,956.7 = 0.031

Cash flow to total assets in 2004 was more than double that of 2003.

Cash flow to total assets in 2004 was more than double that of 2003. A review of the statement of cash flows reveals the major cause of this change as the reduction of cash used up by "other operating activities." The cash provided by operations in 2003 appears unusually low, with 2004 being a return to a more normal level. Cash flow to total assets is also higher than ROA, which is what we should expect since operating cash flows should provide funds for new assets to replace those that are wearing out and for which amortization was deducted in calculating net income. Section 10.5 has more about this.

EPS = (Net income – Preferred dividends) / Average number of common shares outstanding.

8. *Earnings per share*: conceptually, this ratio is calculated as (*Net income – Dividends on preferred shares*) / *Average number of common shares outstanding*. *EPS* relates earnings attributable to common shares (the numerator) to the number of common shares issued, thereby providing a sort of down-to-earth performance measure. It is also another way of factoring out the company's size. If you have only 100 shares of a large company, it is not easy to understand what the company's multimillion-dollar income means to you. But if you are told that the EPS = $2.10, you know that your 100 shares earned $210 for the year and can then relate the company's returns to your own circumstances.

EPS is provided in the audited financial statements of public companies.

Calculating EPS is a little complicated, so GAAP require that publicly traded companies provide it in their financial statements. (See *price-earnings ratio* below.) Because it is part of the financial statements, it is (for public companies) the only ratio routinely covered by the auditor's report. For small, closely held companies, EPS is not meaningful, and not required by GAAP, because the owners usually cannot trade their shares readily and are likely to be interested in the value of the overall company more than in that of individual shares.

There are different versions of EPS, depending on circumstances.

More than one version of EPS can appear in the same set of statements. If a company has extraordinary items, discontinued operations, or other anomalies, EPS is calculated both before and after such items, so that the effect of such items may readily be seen. Also, if the company has potential commitments to issue further shares, such as in stock-option plans to motivate senior management or preferred shares convertible to common shares at the option of the holder of the preferred shares, the potential effect of the exercise of such commitments is calculated by showing both ordinary EPS and "fully diluted" EPS. ("Dilution" refers to the potential lowering of return to present shareholders resulting from other people's exercising rights arising from commitments already made by the company.) Adding to the variety, EPS can be calculated a little differently in the U.S. than in Canada (though country differences like that are being reduced or eliminated, as noted in the discussion of international standards harmonization in Section 5.5).

CPR had no discontinued operations, nor any extraordinary items. But it did have commitments potentially requiring it to issue more shares (stock options). Therefore, the income statement shown at the beginning of this section shows two EPS figures for each year:

- **2004:** Basic EPS = $2.60, diluted EPS = $2.60
- **2003:** Basic EPS = $2.53; diluted EPS = $2.52

The weighted average number of common shares outstanding during 2004 was 158.7 million (158.5 million for 2003). The dilutive effect of the outstanding share options is quite small: less than $0.01 in 2004 and only $0.01 in 2003. This indicates CPR has granted only a relatively small number of stock options to its employees in recent years.

Book value per share = (Shareholders' equity – Preferred shares) / Common shares issued.

9. *Book value per share*: calculated as *(Shareholders' equity – Preferred shares) / Number of common shares issued and outstanding*. Similar to EPS, this ratio relates the portion of the shareholders' equity attributable to the residual common shareholders to the number of shares outstanding, and so brings the company balance sheet down to the level of the individual shareholder. It is not really a performance ratio, but shareholders' equity does include retained earnings, so it incorporates accumulated performance. Because the balance sheet's figures do not reflect the current market value of most assets or of the company as a whole, many people feel that book value per share is a largely meaningless ratio. Other people feel that as an accumulation, it is less subject to manipulation than annual earnings, and some accounting research uses book value per share as a preferred measure to EPS. In any case, you will see it mentioned in many financial publications.

Book value per share increased from 2003 to 2004.

Using the same 158.7 million shares outstanding at the end of 2004, and the 158.5 million shares outstanding at the end of December 2003 (a small number having been issued under stock option plans) for 2004, CPR's book value per common share was:

- **2004:** $3,982.4 / 158.7 = $25.09
- **2003:** $3,654.6 / 158.5 = $23.06

Normally, book value per share increases as retained earnings accumulate and new shares are issued. Indeed, the increase in book value per share of $2.03 ($25.09 – $23.06) is very close to the increase in retained earnings per share, $2.08 (($2,484.4 – $2,153.9)/158.7).

CPR's market capitalization was 64% higher than its book value at the end of 2004.

In Section 2.10, a comparison of market value per share to book value per share was made. The company's closing share price on December 31, 2004, was $41.10, so its *price to book ratio* was 1.64 ($41.10 / $25.09 from above). Thus the company's *market capitalization* was 64% higher than book value. With 158.7 million shares outstanding, the stock market valued CPR at about $6.5 billion, compared to its equity book value of $4 billion. This is not a great premium, but then, numerous companies that had much higher premiums due to stratospheric share prices and not much book value to back them up have crashed to earth (Enron, WorldCom, Global Crossing, Nortel, and on and on). CPR is being valued as a stable, not exciting company—which fits with the stability in earnings and cash flows we have seen in earlier ratios.

PE ratio = Current market price per share / EPS.

10. *Price-earnings ratio*: calculated as *Current market price per share / EPS.* The *PE ratio* relates the accounting earnings and market price of the shares, but, since the relationship between such earnings and changes in stock market prices is not straightforward (as discussed in Chapter 5 especially), the interpretation of PE is controversial. Nevertheless, it is a widely used ratio, appearing in many publications and analyses of companies. Many newspapers include PE (or its inverse, the *earnings-price ratio*) in their daily summaries of each company's stock market trades and prices.

The PE ratio varies because of general stock market changes unrelated to the company.

The idea is that because market price should reflect the market's expectation of future performance, PE compares the present performance with those expectations, as did the price to book ratio mentioned under Ratio 9. A company with a high PE is expected to show greater future performance than its present level, while one with a low PE is not expected to do much better in the future. High-PE companies are those that are popular and have good share prices, while low-PE companies are not so popular, having low share prices relative to their present earnings. PE is highly subject to general increases and decreases in market prices, so it is difficult to interpret over time and is more useful when comparing similar companies listed in the same stock market at the same time. It is especially difficult to interpret, maybe largely meaningless, when the stock market is going through a sudden change, as happened when the dot-com bust began the long disruption in share prices in 2000 and continued throughout the early years of the decade.

CPR's PE is consistent with a stable investment of low risk.

CPR's stock price has fluctuated somewhat throughout 2003 and 2004 but the trend has been to fairly steady growth. Using the year-end closing prices, which are close to the highs for the year, gives a conservative view of the price-earnings ratio:

- **2004:** PE = $41.10 / $2.60 = 15.8
- **2003:** PE = $36.58 / $2.53 = 14.5

This is a solid PE, a little on the low side but again indicating that the market sees CPR as a good, fairly safe investment. No high flyer, but not likely to go bust suddenly, either. Many PE ratios in recent years were ridiculously high, and some observers think they are still on the high side. You can get an idea of whether the PE is too high by inverting it to get the earnings-price ratio. CPR's earnings-price ratio would be about 7%: this is the earnings return implied for an investor who bought in at $41.10. Such a return is better than bond interest rates, and CPR is probably not a risky investment, unless the stock market has a complete meltdown.

Dividend payout ratio = Dividends declared / Earnings (or Dividends per share / EPS).

11. *Dividend payout ratio*: calculated as *Annual common dividends declared per share / EPS*, or if dividends per share are not disclosed, just *Dividends declared / Net income.* This is a measure of the portion of earnings paid to shareholders. For example, if the dividend payout ratio is 0.40, 40% of income was distributed to shareholders and the remaining 60% was kept in the company (retained earnings) to finance assets or reduce debts. A stable ratio would suggest that the company has a policy of paying dividends based on earnings, and a variable ratio would suggest that other factors than earnings are important in the board of directors' decisions to declare dividends.

Though it cannot be illustrated using CPR, a wrinkle in calculating the dividend payout ratio should be mentioned. It can be calculated in various ways:

- Dividends declared per share / EPS, or
- Dividends declared per share / Continuing earnings per share, or
- Total dividends declared (on statement of retained earnings) / Net income, or
- Total dividends declared / Continuing earnings (on income statement).

The total and per-share methods should produce similar results, depending on whether, as for CPR, there have been major changes in shares issued during the year or lumpy dividends. The total method is always available, but the per-share versions depend on knowing the dividends per share figure, which is not always disclosed. Basing the ratio on continuing earnings (or continuing EPS) instead of net income or EPS is useful if the company has been divesting itself of big chunks of its business. The payout ratio would then be a better estimate of what might be expected in the future.

CPR has only a short history of dividend payouts since the reorganization in 2001. We can learn the total dividends amount each year from the statement of retained earnings. Using this information and the average number of shares outstanding, an estimate of annual dividends can be calculated.

EXHIBIT 10.7

	2004	2003	2002
Dividends declared ($ millions)	$ 82.5	$ 80.8	$ 80.8
Net income ($ millions)	$ 413.0	$ 401.3	$ 487.5
Weighted average number of shares outstanding (millions)	158.7	158.5	158.5
Basic EPS	$ 2.60	$ 2.53	$ 3.08
Dividend per share (calculated)	$ 0.52	$ 0.51	$ 0.51
Dividend payout ratio	0.200	0.201	0.165

From the information in Exhibit 10.7, we can infer that CPR appears to be conservative and stable. It appears that the board of directors has chosen to follow a policy of conservative stable dividends in the amount of about $0.13 per share quarterly or 20% of total net income.

The dividend payout ratio is usually consistent with the company's PE ratio. Fast-growing companies are often strapped for cash and so pay little or no dividends, plowing earnings back into more growth. People hold the shares of such companies because they expect growth in share price, not dividends, and because of such expectations of future growth, the PE ratios of such companies are usually high. In contrast, people invest in some more dull, but safer, companies not because they expect high share price growth but because they expect regular dividends, almost like Canada Savings Bonds. CPR pays more than zero dividends, but with its supply of cash could have paid a higher percentage of earnings than it did. This reinforces the growing conclusion from these ratios that CPR is a solid, moderate company, not a high-growth one. Just what we would expect from a railway that is more than 100 years old.

Activity (Turnover) Ratios

Total asset turnover = Revenue / Total assets.

12. *Total asset turnover*: calculated as *Revenue / Total assets.* Total assets can be the year-end figure, which is used in this book, or an average of beginning and ending assets, which relates the revenue over a period to the average assets over the same period, and may be more relevant if a company is growing or shrinking rapidly in assets. This and similar turnover ratios relate the company's dollar sales volume to its size, thereby answering the question: How much revenue is associated with a dollar of assets?

- Turnover and profit-margin ratios are often useful together because they tend to move in opposite directions.
- Companies with high turnover tend to have low margins.
- Companies with low turnover tend to have (or hope to have) high margins.
- Those extremes represent contrary marketing strategies or competitive pressures: pricing low and trying for high volume versus pricing high and making more on each unit sold.

There is more about using profit margin and turnover together in Section 10.6.

Using year-end assets, CPR's total asset turnovers were:

Total asset turnover was low but slightly improved in 2004 as revenue grew faster than assets.

- **2004:** \$3,902.9 / \$10,499.8 = 0.372
- **2003:** \$3,660.7 / \$9,956.7 = 0.368

Two observations are indicated.

(1) These turnover ratios are very low. They are much below those that most companies have: CPR takes nearly three years to earn a dollar of revenue on each dollar of assets. By comparison, Canadian Tire had a total asset turnover for the same 2004 period of 1.37[1] (more than three times CPR's) and Wal-Mart's turnover for the year ended March 31, 2004, was 2.47[2] (seven times CPR's). Well, what would we expect? CPR has miles of railroad track, thousands of engines and railcars, maintenance shops and so on. Canadian Tire owns few of its stores, letting franchisees build most of them, and Wal-Mart is a discount retailer, depending on high sales volume. It is a reminder to consider the kind of company being analyzed, and a reminder that *there are no absolute ratios*, only relative comparisons. One comparison could be to Canadian National Railway. In 2004, CN's asset turnover was 0.34,[3] less than CPR's. So this comparison puts CPR in a better relative light.

(2) CPR's asset turnover improved slightly from 2003 to 2004. This improvement is the result of higher growth in revenues, 6.6% ((\$3.902.9 – \$3,660.7)/\$3,660.7), than in assets, 5.5% ((\$10,499.8 – \$9,956.7)/\$9,956.7). While the change is small, it is another indication of the stability of CPR.

Inventory turnover = COGS / Average inventories.

13. *Inventory turnover*: calculated as *Cost of goods sold expense / Average inventory assets* (or by year-end inventory, for convenience). If cost of goods sold is not disclosed, it is often replaced by sales revenue in calculating the ratio, which is alright for comparing one year to others for one company, as long as markups and product mixes do not change substantially. This ratio relates the level of inventories to the volume of activity: a company with low turnover may be risking obsolescence or deterioration in its inventory and/or may be incurring excessive storage and insurance costs. In recent years, many companies have attempted to pare inventories to the bone, keeping just enough on hand to meet customer demand or even ordering inventory as it is demanded by customers (as in the "just in time" method of minimizing inventories without running out of stock and irritating customers).

As we have already seen, CPR doesn't have a cost of goods sold, and its balance sheet indicates its inventories are just supplies for running the railroad, not goods for sale. So we cannot calculate a meaningful inventory turnover ratio. Using CPR as the example company has this shortcoming, but it doesn't mean the inventory turnover ratio is not important or useful. It is very important for evaluating retailers and other sellers of goods.

Collection ratio = Accounts receivable / (Revenue / 365).

14. *Collection ratio* (receivables turnover, often called *days' sales in receivables*): calculated as *Accounts receivable / (Revenue / 365)*. As for the other turnover ratios, the balance sheet amount, accounts receivable, can be the year-end figure or an average over the year. This ratio indicates how many days it takes, on average, to collect a day's sales revenue. It becomes large when accounts receivable become larger relative to sales, so its interpretation is the *opposite* of those of the previous two turnover ratios: a large collection ratio is a negative signal, raising questions about the company's policies of granting credit and the vigour of its collection attempts. The ratio is subject to significant seasonal changes for many companies, usually rising during heavy selling periods, such as just before Christmas for a retailer, and falling during slow times. (It would be preferable to use only revenue from credit sales in the denominator, since cash sales are collected immediately, but few companies break their revenue figures down to separate cash revenue.)

CPR's collection ratios were:

It takes CPR a month and one-third, on average, to collect from its customers.

- **2004:** $434.7 / ($3,902.9 / 365) = 40.6 days
- **2003:** $395.7 / ($3,660.7 / 365) = 39.5 days

It takes the company about a month and one-third, on average, to collect from its customers. This is reasonable time: most customers pay monthly, and CPR has government agencies and other relatively slow payers among its customers. Its collection pattern is similar to CN Rail's: CN's collection ratio for 2004 was 44.3 days.[4]

Financing Ratios

Debt-equity ratio = Total liabilities / Total equity.

15. *Debt-equity ratio*: calculated as *Total liabilities / Total equity*, or sometimes as Total external debt / Total equity, to exclude deferred revenue, future income tax, and other liabilities that are consequences of accrual accounting's revenue and expense matching more than they are real debt. This ratio, which we saw back in Section 2.10, measures the proportion of borrowing to owners' investment (including retained earnings) and thus indicates the company's policy of financing its assets.

A ratio greater than 1 indicates the assets are financed mostly with debt, while a ratio less than 1 indicates the assets are financed mostly with equity. A high ratio, well above 1, is a warning about risk: the company is heavily in debt relative to its equity and may be vulnerable to interest rate increases, general tightening of credit, or creditor nervousness. (A high ratio also indicates that the company is *leveraged*, which means it has borrowed to increase its assets over the amount that could be acquired with owners' funds only, and it hopes thereby to increase returns and benefit the owners. See the comments on leverage at the end of the discussion of ROA earlier in this section and in Section 10.6.)

The debt-equity ratio has trended downward since 2001.

CPR's debt-equity ratios, as calculated in Section 2.10 and using the same liability totals as were calculated for Ratio 6 above, were:

- **2004:** \$6,517.4 / \$3,982.4 = 1.64
- **2003:** \$6,302.1 / \$3,654.6 = 1.72

CPR's debt-equity ratio was 2.14 in 2001, a significant increase from the 2000 level of 1.42. It now seems probable that this increase was brought about by financial needs arising from the reorganization of Canadian Pacific in 2001. The trend appears to be downward towards earlier levels, again evidencing the stability of CPR. However, the debt-equity ratio certainly shows that CPR is leveraged, relying more on debt than on equity, but that its relative reliance on debt is decreasing.

Long-term debt-equity ratio = Long-term debts / Equity.

16. *Long-term debt-equity ratio*: calculated as *(Long-term loans + Mortgages + Bonds + Similar long-term debts) / Total equity*. This ratio has many versions, depending on which specific items the analyst decides to include as debt. It is frequently referred to as *the* debt/equity ratio under the apparent assumption that longer-term debt is more relevant to evaluating risk and financing strategy than are the accrual and non-interest-bearing components of Ratio 15.

    For CPR, this ratio involves just the one long-term debt figure on the balance sheet. Not including the debt's tiny current portion, the resulting ratios were:

CPR's reliance on long-term debt is decreasing.

- **2004:** \$3,075.3 / \$3,982.4 = 0.772
- **2003:** \$3,348.9 / \$3,654.6 = 0.916

Again we see the downward trend in CPR's reliance on debt since 2001, when this ratio was at 1.18.

Debt to assets ratio = total liabilities / Total assets.

17. *Debt to assets ratio*: if calculated as *Total liabilities / Total assets*, this ratio is the complement of the debt-equity ratio discussed above (Ratio 15) and indicates the proportion of assets financed by borrowing. It may also be calculated by just comparing long-term debt or external debt to assets (complement of Ratio 16).

    Using total liabilities, the ratios for CPR were:

Over 60% of CPR's assets were financed by liabilities in 2004.

- **2004:** \$6,517.4 / \$10,498.8 = 0.62
- **2003:** \$6,302.1 / \$9,956.7 = 0.63

The same pattern as in Ratios 15 and 16 is here. Assets were financed more than 50% by liabilities and the reliance on liabilities has decreased since 2001 when the company financed its assets over two-thirds by liabilities, which is what we also learned from the debt-equity ratio being over 2.

Liquidity and Solvency Warning Ratios

Working capital ratio = Current assets / Current liabilities.

18. *Working capital (current) ratio*: calculated as *Current assets / Current liabilities*. This ratio has already been scrutinized (Section 2.10). It indicates whether the company has enough short-term assets to cover its short-term debts. A ratio above 1 indicates that *working capital* is positive (current assets exceed current liabilities), and a ratio below 1 indicates that working capital is negative. Generally, the higher the ratio, the greater is the financial stability and the lower is the risk for both creditors and owners. However, the ratio should not be too high because that may indicate the company is not reinvesting in long-term assets to maintain future productivity. Also, a high working capital ratio can actually indicate problems if inventories are getting larger than they should or collections of receivables are slowing down.

The working capital ratio's meaning depends on the company's specific circumstances.

The working capital ratio is a very commonly used indicator. Some analysts use a rough rule that says the working capital ratio should be around 2 (twice as much in current assets as current liabilities), but this is simplistic. Many large companies regularly operate with a working capital ratio closer to 1 than 2. The ratio's interpretation depends on the specific circumstances of each company, as does the interpretation of any ratio. Interpretation of it is also complex because it is static, measuring financial position at a point in time and not considering any future cash flows the company may be able to generate to pay its debts.

This ratio is most useful for companies having cash flows that are relatively smooth during the year and hardest to interpret for those that have unusual assets or liabilities or that depend on future cash flows to pay current debts. An example of the latter would be a company that owns a rented building: there may be few current assets and large current liabilities for mortgage payments, but, as long as the building is mostly rented and rental income is steady, the company is not in difficulty even though its working capital ratio is low. However, it is more at risk than a similar company with a higher working capital ratio, because that company could more easily weather a loss of tenants due to recession or the opening of a competing building.

CPR has a negative working capital position.

As we saw in Section 2.10, CPR's working capital ratio changed only slightly in 2004:

- **2004:** $992.0 / $1,288.2 = 0.77
- **2003:** $724.2 / $954.6 = 0.76

This ratio shows CPR's working capital position to be negative; that is, there are insufficient current assets on hand to repay all current liabilities. We have noted throughout that CPR is a very stable company. It is also the case that CPR generates its revenue using its long-term assets to provide service rather than selling its current assets as in the case with Wal-Mart. Thus by using its current revenues as earned and collected, CPR is able to meet the required payments of expenses and current liabilities despite the working capital deficit.

Acid test ratio = (Cash + Temporary investments + Accounts receivable) / Current liabilities.

19. *Acid test (quick) ratio*: calculated as *(Cash + Temporary investments + Accounts receivable) / Current liabilities.* This is a more demanding version of the working capital ratio and indicates whether current liabilities could be paid without having to sell the inventory (in other words, without having to convince more customers to buy what the company has for sale). There is an even harsher version of this ratio, called the "extreme acid test," which uses only cash and equivalents in the numerator. A complementary ratio, Inventory / Working capital, is often used to indicate what percentage of working capital is tied up in inventory. These ratios are all used to signal lower levels of liquidity, and so greater degrees of risk, than may be revealed by the working capital ratio alone, and so tend to be used when that ratio is deteriorating or is worrisome for some other reason. We saw that the working capital ratio for CPR may have risen only to adequacy, so the acid test ratio may tell us something further about the company's liquidity.

Using the acid test ratio is likely to be informative if a company's working capital includes large amounts of inventories that would have to be sold to pay bills, or large prepaid expenses that have drained cash. CPR doesn't have either of these, so the quick ratio will not tell us much more than the working capital ratio does, but let's calculate it anyway. The ratio was presented in Section 2.10:

CPR's acid test ratio is less than 1, indicating weak liquidity.

- **2004:** ($353.0 + $434.7) / $1,288.2 = 0.61
- **2003:** ($134.7 + $395.7) / $954.6 = 0.56

This shows CPR to have liquid assets equal to only 60% of its current liabilities. This is low but is likely adequate, assuming CPR could match its payments to at least some of its suppliers roughly to the time it takes to collect from its own customers.

Interest coverage ratio = (Income before interest expense and income tax) / Interest expense.

20. *Interest coverage ratio*: usually calculated as *(Income before interest expense and income tax) / Interest expense*. This and similar coverage ratios that are based on cash flow figures from the cash flow statement indicate the degree to which financial commitments (in this case, those to pay interest on debts) are covered by the company's ability to generate income or cash flow. A low coverage ratio indicates that the company is not operating at a sufficiently profitable level to cover the interest obligation comfortably and may also be a warning of solvency problems (difficulty in meeting obligations over the long haul).

CPR's interest coverage ratios, using the interest expense from Note 6 used in earlier ratios, were:

CPR's interest coverage was comfortable in 2004, and improving.

- **2004:** ($413.0 + $143.3 + $223.9) / $223.9 = 3.49
- **2003:** ($401.3 + $41.6 + $226.4) / $226.4 = 2.96

The result here is what we would expect from the other debt-related ratios. CPR's interest coverage is comfortable, though with its increased borrowing and the increased interest that goes with it, it is less comfortable than it was in 2003.

Concluding Comments About the Twenty Ratios

The twenty ratios are summarized in Exhibit 10.8. Each one focuses on a different aspect of performance, and the comparison of each with the previous or other years tells us something and also invites us to learn more about the company so we can understand what each ratio is indicating. Comments integrating the story told by all the ratios will be made in Section 10.6 on page 668.

Summary of the Twenty Ratios for Canadian Pacific Railway

Ratio	2004	2003
1. ROE	0.104	0.110
2. ROA(ATI)	0.055	0.061
3. Sales return (based on net income)	0.106	0.110
4. Common size	see details	see details
5. Gross margin	not available	not available
6. Average interest rate (no tax correction)	0.034	0.036
7. Cash flow to total assets	0.075	0.031
8. EPS (reported audited figure)	$2.60	$2.53
9. Book value per share	$25.09	$23.06
10. PE (approximate)	15.8	14.5
11. Dividend payout	0.200	0.201
12. Total assets turnover	0.372	0.368
13. Inventory turnover	not available	not available
14. Collection	40.6 days	39.5 days
15. Debt-equity	1.64	1.72
16. Long-term debt-equity	0.772	0.916
17. Debt to assets	0.62	0.63
18. Working capital	0.77	0.76
19. Acid test	0.61	0.56
20. Interest coverage	3.49	2.96

By the time you read this, CPR will have gone through at least one more fiscal year. To improve your understanding of the company and the ratios above, visit the company Web site (**www.cpr.ca**) and look for the year 2005 or subsequent annual reports, or its regular quarterly reports. The company's explanations of performance in the letter to shareholders, the Management Discussion and Analysis (MD&A), the notes to the financial statements, and elsewhere in the annual report, plus other items such as press releases, and speeches contained in CPR's Web site, or elsewhere such as the SEDAR site (**www.sedar.com**) are likely to be informative. Compare it to competitors such as CN Rail (**www.cn.ca**).

Here are some accounting research results relevant to the value of the kind of financial analysis included in this chapter:

1. Ratios computed from financial statements have some value in predicting bankruptcy or other financial problems. For some companies, but not all, financial problems can be predicted several years in advance using accounting ratios.
2. Even though annual reports come out rather a long time after the fiscal year-end, there is enough reaction by stock markets to them to indicate that analysis of the reports still has something to say to market traders.
3. People cannot cope with masses of disaggregated data: it takes too long and requires too much special expertise. So, summarizing techniques, such as financial analysis, play a major role in users' decision making.
4. Analysts' forecasts of earnings, based partly on financial statement data, do help to predict companies' future earnings performance. The analysts can often anticipate significant changes in earnings because they are following companies closely, so market prices regularly change before the new financial statements are released. Sometimes financial statement analysis does turn up new information, allowing people to fine-tune their expectations about future performance.
5. Financial statement analysis helps to assess risk, and thus helps investors choose the shares that seem appropriate for their risk preferences.
6. Financial statement analysis is useful to corroborate what people already believe about a company's performance, position, or risk. Even if such analysis turns up little that is "new," it acts as a check on the other flows of information about companies, because the validity of that information can be verified later when the financial statements come out.

HOW'S YOUR UNDERSTANDING?

Here are two questions you should be able to answer based on what you have just read. If you can't answer them, it would be best to reread the material.

1. How well did CPR perform in 2004 as compared to 2003?
2. How was CPR's liquidity at the end of 2004? Is that an improvement over 2003?

10.5 Interpretation of Cash Flow Information

The cash flow statement supplements the analysis of the other statements.

Both in the theory of economics and finance and in the practical relationships between businesses and their owners and creditors, cash flow is an important measure of return. Income for the company is all very well, but owners sooner or later want to receive some of it in cash dividends, and lenders want cash payments to cover interest and principal due, and so on. Income is revenue minus expenses, but the revenue may be tied up in uncollected receivables and the expenses may either not have been paid yet or have been paid in advance. In financial statement analysis, the cash flow statement's focus on cash provides important supplementary information about how the company was managed and how it performed.

To refresh your memory of the cash flow statement and help you think about using it for analysis, Exhibit 10.9 contains a summary of the kinds of effects on cash that the statement can indicate.

EXHIBIT 10·9

	Increase Cash	Decrease Cash
Net income:		
Positive net incomes	X	
Negative net incomes (net losses)		X
Noncash expenses (such as amortization of long-term assets and the deferred portion of income tax expense) are added back to net income and so *appear to*	X	
Noncash revenues (such as a gain on sale of a noncurrent asset) are deducted from net income and so *appear to*		X
Changes in noncash working capital accounts:		
Increases in noncash current assets		X
Decreases in such assets	X	
Increases in noncash current liabilities	X	
Decreases in such liabilities		X
Changes in noncurrent assets:		
Increases in cost of (investment in) such assets		X
Proceeds from disposal of such assets	X	
Changes in noncurrent debts and capital:		
Financing obtained from owners and creditors	X	
Repayments, redemptions, dividend payments		X

Here are some points about the cash flow statement, based on the above summary.

- The operations section of the statement converts income from the complex accrual basis used in preparing the income statement to a simpler cash flow basis.
- Cash from operations thus is an alternative measure of return. We saw this in Ratio 7, cash flow to total assets, in Section 10.4.
- The conversion from accrual to cash basis reveals something about how the company has managed its current assets and liabilities over the period; for example, have receivables gone up, delaying the inflow of cash from revenue?
- The investing and financing sections of the statement show what the company did with the cash it generated from day-to-day operations, and how much nonoperating cash it raised during the period.

The cash flow statement helps to evaluate earnings quality, investment and financing policies, and risks.

The cash flow statement, *in combination with the income statement and balance sheet*, can be used in at least the following ways.[5] Each point is illustrated by reference to CPR's cash flow statement, given at the beginning of Section 9.4 and already examined in Section 4.7.

a. *Evaluate the relative significance of the cash flow figures* by relating them to the size of the company's assets, liabilities, equity, and income. For CPR, we saw in Section 10.4 that the ratio of operating cash flow to total assets was larger than the return on assets in 2004 but only about half the ROA in 2003. This would seem to be the result of lower-than-normal cash flows from operations in 2003 when less than half the 2002 or 2004 cash flows were generated. The lower-than-usual cash flows from operations were offset by increased borrowings, as seen in the cash provided by financing activities.

b. *Evaluate the company's relative dependence on internally generated cash* (from operations) versus cash generated from external financing activities. Operating cash flow was the main source of cash in all three years shown in Exhibit 10.3. However, in both 2003 and 2004, CPR required long-term borrowings in excess of repayments to finance the significant additions to properties seen as cash uses in investing.

c. *Evaluate solvency* (ability to pay debts when due) *and liquidity* (having adequate reserves of cash and near-cash assets). We saw from Section 10.4 that solvency does not seem to be a problem: CPR can cover its interest payments and, based on the 2004 experience, can borrow long-term and repay it when due. Liquidity is a little strained, but the company took major action in 2004 to borrow long-term and shore up its liquidity. The cash flow statement shows that even in 2003 when the inflows from operations were unusually low, they still provided a significant portion of the funds needed for investing activities.

Nine evaluations using cash flow information

a. Significance of cash flow
b. Dependence on internal versus external financing
c. Solvency and liquidity
d. Spending on asset acquisitions
e. Debt versus equity strategy
f. Dividend policy
g. Quality of earnings
h. Possible cash flow manipulation
i. Hazards of success or benefits of decline

d. *Evaluate the level of spending on long-term asset acquisitions* in relation to the size of the company's assets and the amount of annual amortization, in order to help judge whether the company appears to be keeping its plant and equipment up to date. CPR stayed ahead of the game in 2004 as it had in 2003 by spending 60% to 80% more on new assets than was charged as the amortization on existing assets ($673.8 million spent compared to $407.1 million amortized in 2004).

Considering that there is some inflation and that the assets are expected to last a long time (amortization is only 3% of the $12,876 million property and plant costs the company had at the beginning of 2004 according to Note 12 shown in Exhibit 10.6), the spending was probably not much more than enough to replace what was wearing out. New spending totaled just 5% of the $12,876 million property and plant cost at the beginning of the year, leaving 2% to cover inflation and expansion. The company appears to be holding its own but not expanding.

e. *Evaluate the company's debt versus equity financing strategy*. We saw in Section 10.4 that CPR is leveraged, having almost twice as much in liabilities as equity at the end of 2004. Accounts payable represents 15% of the total debt at the end of 2004, but the long-term debt-equity ratio is still almost 1 but declining over time. Looking at the cash flow statement, we can infer that the financing strategy is clearly to borrow long-term to supplement operating cash flows, not to raise more equity. The marginal growth in share capital resulted entirely from employees exercising stock options. The cash flow statement reveals that equity has not been part of the financing strategy, except through letting retained earnings grow.

f. *Evaluate the company's dividend policy* by comparing dividends with both income and cash flow, and reviewing the pattern over time. The newly independent CPR is essentially a new company in financial terms, even though in operating terms it is over 100 years old. The dividend policy is probably still evolving but, as mentioned earlier, it appears that CPR is attempting to maintain a constant dividend per share. This is often done by companies to provide shareholders with a dependable cash flow in the expectation that this will encourage some stability in the share price.

g. *Determine the relationship between income and cash flow* to evaluate the "quality" of earnings (income): income should be reasonably consistent with cash flow, after adjusting for normal corrections such as amortization, and should not be so far out of line with cash flow that there's some question about its validity. Here CPR's cash flow to earnings has generally been healthy since it became independent of the parent group in 2001. Although low enough to be of possible concern in 2003, cash flow from operating activities returned to earlier levels of about twice the earnings in 2004. Note 10, at the beginning of Section 10.4, indicates that there was little net change in noncash working capital between 2003 and 2004. Reductions in accounts receivable and inventories were offset by the increase in accounts payable and accrued liabilities. The reduction in accounts receivable brought the collection ratio down during the year. This decrease supports the lack of other indications of problems with recognizing revenue prematurely. There are no indications of earnings management or other threats to earnings quality.

h. *Identify possible manipulation of the cash flow figures,* such as failing to replace inventories or delaying payment of current or noncurrent debts, by comparisons to the way cash flows were generated in past years. CPR's operating cash flows are very stable. There is no indication of anything untoward in the cash flow figures.

i. *Identify either the hazards of success,* such as drains on cash flow due to the buildup of inventories or accounts receivable, *or the benefits of decline,* such as cash increases due to shrinking inventories or receivables. There don't seem to be hazards in CPR's cash flow information. The company is emerging from the former corporate umbrella and has had to take some steps to upgrade liquidity, but its operating cash flows indicate robust performance and ability to generate enough cash flow internally to keep property and plant assets up to date.

HOW'S YOUR UNDERSTANDING?

Here are two questions you should be able to answer based on what you have just read. If you can't answer them, it would be best to reread the material.

1. What were the main components of CPR's 2004 cash flow?
2. How does cash flow information contribute to financial statement analysis?

10.6 Integrative Ratio Analysis

Pulling all the analytical results together is more art than science.

The previous two sections contained a lot of ratios and comments. To pull all the details together to form some conclusions about performance, risk, earnings quality, and other factors is more an art than a science, because the conclusions depend on the decisions made or information used to craft the analysis, as well as on the degree of knowledge or detail the analyst brings to bear. They also depend on what is found among the various ratios and cash flow data. If the analysis reveals a serious liquidity problem, for example, that may well colour all the conclusions. Similarly, if the company's accounting methods were suspect for some reason, the conclusions would likely be particularly cautious or skeptical.

To help you think about how to pull your analysis together, this section contains two illustrations:

1. An overall summary of what the previous two sections' analyses have shown about CPR.
2. An example of an integrated numerical analysis: *leverage analysis.*

Overall Conclusions From the CPR Analysis in Sections 10.4 and 10.5

Here are some conclusions to connect the various analyses in the preceding sections together into an overall portrayal of CPR's financial performance and position. The categories of Section 10.4 plus Section 10.5 are used to make some integrative comments; then a summary follows.

Performance

CPR's story is steady, stable performance showing a mixture of small improvements and small declines from 2003 to 2004. Return on equity and return on assets declined slightly, while earnings per share rose and cash provided by operations more than doubled. It should be noted, however, that this doubling of cash flow from operations really only provided a return to the 2002 level. The reasons are contained in the similar decline in sales return, and small growth in both revenues and operating expenses, resulting in little growth in net income. CPR's price-earnings ratio and price to book ratio indicate that the stock market sees the company as a solid investment, not a high flyer. Dividends will be important if share price growth is low.

Activity (Turnover)

The company's asset turnover was relatively slow: it is a large-asset railway, so that is to be expected. The bulk of its assets are noncurrent. The company's revenues grew slightly faster than its assets, providing a small improvement in the asset turnover from 2003 to 2004. The asset turnover improved, indicating that the pace of growth in income was slightly higher than that of assets. Receivables collections improved, which also improves the asset turnover, but it is still not fast. Taken together, the activity ratios are further indications that CPR is a mature company, stable and not rapidly expanding or changing.

Financing

CPR was leveraged with 60% more debt than equity. This means that about two-thirds of its assets were provided by creditors and only one-third by owners. The debt-equity ratio has been declining since CPR became independent, mainly through the growth of retained earnings. Most of its financing was long-term, like its assets: the company was following common principles of matching the financing term to the assets being financed.

Liquidity/Solvency/Warning

The company had negative working capital (ratio less than 1) in both 2004 and 2003. Despite this situation, CPR is able to meet its current liability obligations by generating cash from operations and by maintaining a balance among cash, accounts receivable, and accounts payable. Inventories were not a major part of CPR's working capital, so the quick ratio was only a little weaker than the working capital ratio. Interest coverage was comfortable, both compared to income and, as cash from operations was larger than income, compared to cash flow.

Cash Flow

Operating cash flows were stable and significant, providing enough cash to finance property and plant acquisitions without external financing in 2004. This left the external financing to provide a base increase in cash, to help liquidity. Spending on new property and plant appeared to be about enough to keep the assets up to date and to replace those wearing out, but not enough for real growth.

Overall Summary

CPR in 2004 was a stable company, putting its affairs in order and maintaining a healthy cash flow and slightly improved earnings and returns to shareholders. Long-term debt, and therefore risk, were reduced, helping improve liquidity and so reducing short-term risk. The various ratios and stock market price performance agreed in portraying the company as not extreme on any dimension, positively or negatively, and so being an attractive investment though not a high-flyer. Its market capitalization and price-earnings ratio indicated that investors expect similar performance and moderate growth in the future. Have a look at **www.cpr.ca** and **www.sedar.com** and see how CPR has performed since this evaluation!

Leverage Analysis

Leverage, also called "trading on the equity," "financial leverage," and, in Britain and some other countries, "gearing," is an important objective and consequence of borrowing money and then using it to generate returns. It works like this:

- Professor Grunion wants to invest $15,000 in a real estate project.
- Grunion has $5,000 available in personal funds.
- So, Grunion borrows $10,000 from the bank at 11% interest.
- Grunion invests the total $15,000 in the project and receives an annual return of $2,100.
- The project's return is 14% before tax ($2,100 / $15,000).
- Out of that, Grunion pays the bank interest (11% of $10,000 = $1,100).
- Grunion keeps the rest ($2,100 – $1,100 = $1,000).
- Grunion's before-tax return on the equity invested is 20% ($1,000 / $5,000).

Grunion has made extra money by borrowing at a rate less than the project earns.

Not bad! The project returns 14%, but Grunion gets 20% on the equity invested. The reason is that Grunion borrowed at 11% but used the borrowed funds to earn 14%. The extra 3% return on the borrowed funds is Grunion's to keep in return for taking the risk of investing in the project:

- Overall return = 14% on $15,000 = $2,100.
- Paid to the bank = 11% on $10,000 = $1,100 (3% less than the return).
- Kept by Grunion: 14% on $5,000 own funds + 3% on $10,000 borrowed funds.
- Grunion's return = the 14% ($700) + the 3% ($300) = $1,000, which is 20% of the $5,000, so Grunion has benefited from leverage: borrowing money to earn money.

Leverage is a good way to increase your return, as long as you can ensure that the project's total rate of return is greater than your borrowing cost. It's a double-edged sword, though, because leverage can hit you hard if returns are low or negative. Suppose Grunion's real estate project returns only 7%. Then look what happens:

- Overall return = 7% on $15,000 = $1,050.
- Paid to the bank = 11% on $10,000 = $1,100.
- Kept by Grunion: 7% on own funds minus 4% on $10,000 borrowed funds.
- Grunion's return = the 7% ($350) – the 4% ($400) = –$50, which is –1% of $5,000. Grunion has been hurt by leverage. The project earned a return, but not enough of a return to cover the cost of borrowing money to invest in the project.

Borrowing hurts if its interest rate is higher than the rate the project earns.

So, Grunion in this case loses on every dollar borrowed, because the project returns less than the cost of borrowing. It's not such a great deal anymore! Grunion is losing 1% on the equity invested, but if just that equity had been invested, with no borrowing, Grunion would have made 7%, the project's return. Leverage is now hurting, not helping.

Leverage is therefore the difference between what the project earns before any return to the lenders and the investor and what the investor earns, after paying the lenders the cost of the borrowing. Keeping the Grunion example in mind, we have the following:

- The investor's return is after all costs of borrowing, so it is the project income minus interest that is the project net income. That is related to the amount of investment the investor made, the investor's equity. Net income divided by equity is return on equity. ROE is Ratio 1, Section 10.4.
- The project return before interest is what Ratio 2, Section 10.4, was getting at: return on assets, the refined ROA(ATI) version that is calculated prior to the after-tax cost of interest.
- Any difference between ROE and ROA(ATI) is leverage. In the two Grunion examples above:
  a. ROE = 0.20; ROA(ATI) = 0.14; leverage therefore = 0.06, so Grunion has benefited by 6% from favourable borrowing;
  b. ROE = –0.01; ROA(ATI) = 0.07; leverage therefore = –0.08; so Grunion has suffered by 8% from unfavourable borrowing.

ROE – ROA = Leverage, either positive or negative.

Based on the above discussion, leverage can be defined by the following equation, in which any of the terms can be positive or negative:

ROE = ROA + Leverage

After-Tax Leverage

Before we can apply the leverage idea to CPR or any company, it is useful to consider the effects of income tax. They were included in the ROE and ROA(ATI) calculated in Section 10.4, but were not included in the Grunion example above. It's easy to do. Let's assume Grunion's income tax rate is 40%.

- In the first example, the project net income would now be $1,000 × (1 – 0.4) = $600.
- This is 12% of Grunion's $5,000 investment, so ROE = 12%. (We could calculate the after-tax ROE directly as the before-tax 20% × (1 – 0.4) = 12%.)
- In the first example, the project's return before interest would be $600 + ($1,100 × (1 – 0.4)) = $1,260, calculated the way the numerator in ROA(ATI), Ratio 2, does it. This is also the $2,100 before-interest return × (1 – 0.4).
- So ROA(ATI) = $1,260 / $15,000 = 8.4%. (As for ROE, we could calculate the after-tax ROA directly, as the before-tax 14% × (1 – 0.4) = 8.4%.)
- Following the same reasoning, the second project's ROE would be –1% × (1 – 0.4) = –0.6%, and its ROA(ATI) would be 7% × (1 – 0.4) = 4.2%. (The latter, calculated as Ratio 2 does it, is also (–$50 × (1 – 0.4) + $1,100 × (1 – 0.4)) / $15,000 = $630 / $15,000 = 4.2%.)
- Any difference between ROE and ROA(ATI) is leverage. In the two after-tax examples:
  a. ROE = 0.12; ROA(ATI) = 0.084; leverage therefore = 0.036, so Grunion has benefited by 3.6% from favourable borrowing (this is 60% of the before-tax leverage, which is what we would expect: original 6% × (1 – 0.4));
  b. ROE = –0.006; ROA(ATI) = 0.042; leverage therefore = –0.048; so Grunion has suffered by 4.8% from unfavourable borrowing (which is (1 – 0.4) × the original negative 8%).

The four Grunion versions are summarized in Exhibit 10.10, showing how in each case an adequate or inadequate ROA leads to positive or negative leverage, before or after income tax.

EXHIBIT 10·10

Summary of Grunion Examples

	Positive Leverage		**Negative Leverage**	
	Before Tax	**After 40% Tax**	**Before Tax**	**After 40% Tax**
Start with ROA	0.14	0.084	0.07	0.042
– Interest rate	0.11	0.066	0.11	0.066
= Leverage potential	0.03	0.018	(0.04)	(0.024)
× Debt-equity ratio	2	2	2	2
= Leverage obtained	0.06	0.036	(0.08)	(0.048)
+ ROA	0.14	0.084	0.07	0.042
= ROE (leveraged)	0.20	0.12	(0.01)	(0.006)

Income tax reduces the impact of positive or negative leverage.

So after-tax leverage is just like after-tax anything else: take the before-tax calculation and multiply it by (1 – Tax rate). Because of income tax, positive leverage is smaller as some of the gain is paid in income tax, and negative leverage is also smaller as some of the loss reduces income tax (assuming that the tax rate also applies to negative income, which is that there is other income against which the loss can be deducted). Leverage can be analyzed using either before- or after-tax figures. The earlier equation defining leverage can be rewritten this way, in which all terms are after-tax:

ROE = ROA(ATI) + Leverage

Expanded Leverage Analysis: The Scott Formula

What was CPR's leverage?

- According to Section 10.4, its ROE in 2004 was 0.104, and its ROA(ATI) was 0.055.
- Therefore, its leverage was 0.049 in 2004 (0.104 – 0.055).
- It was 0.049 (0.11 – 0.061) in 2003.

This is substantial: leverage made about 50% of the contribution to ROE in both years. If CPR had not borrowed, its ROE would have been halved. How did this happen?

The Scott formula is an example of integrative use of ratio analysis.

To incorporate more of the ratios in Section 10.4, and thus both integrate the ratio analyses and expand the story about leverage, Professor W. R. Scott, most recently at the University of Waterloo, developed the "*Scott formula*." This formula is a version of a group of integrative analyses (another, the "DuPont formula," has been used for nearly a century). It is based on combining ratios into a larger story. There are other approaches to numerical integrative analysis, such as using various ratios together in a "multiple regression" statistical analysis to try to predict bankruptcy or other problems, and you will probably see other ways of combining ratios because many analysts seek ways to combine them. The Scott formula is used to illustrate such expanded analysis, because it is an example of taking advantage of the double-entry nature of financial statements to increase analytical power.

This expanded analysis uses the after-tax version of leverage above, plus relies on the basic cause of leverage illustrated in the Grunion examples: leverage happens when there is borrowing and the rate of return earned on the project is different from the cost of borrowing. The impact of leverage depends on the extent of borrowing: if Grunion had positive leverage, the more borrowed, the better ROE resulted, and if leverage was negative, the more borrowed, the worse the ROE. You'll see that the Scott formula uses the same leverage logic as shown in the four Grunion examples summarized in Exhibit 10.10. Using these ideas, four definitions are important:

1. Overall return ROE is the same as Ratio 1 in Section 10.4;
2. Project return is ROA(ATI), which was Ratio 2;
3. Borrowing cost (interest rate after tax) is IN(ATI), the after-tax version of average interest rate Ratio 6, calculated as (Interest expense × (1 – Tax rate)) / Borrowing;
4. Extent of borrowing is L/E, the debt-equity ratio (Ratio 15).

As illustrated in Exhibit 10.10, leverage equals the difference between project return and borrowing cost, times the extent of borrowing:

Leverage = (ROA(ATI) – IN(ATI)) × L/E

The two terms inside the brackets on the right show the *potential* for leverage (illustrated in Exhibit 10.10), and determine whether the leverage is positive or negative. Let's call the part inside the brackets *leverage potential*. Therefore, we can write the leverage formula as:

Leverage = Leverage potential × Extent of borrowing

The expanded analysis in Exhibit 10.10 uses these ideas to show *why* the leverage was as it was. If the project return was greater than the borrowing cost, borrowing helped. If the return was less than the borrowing cost, borrowing hurt.

So we have the following expanded analysis:

ROE = ROA(ATI) + (ROA(ATI) – IN(ATI)) × L/E

The Scott formula incorporates two more ratios by breaking the first term on the right, ROA(ATI) into two ratios:

- SR(ATI), an after-tax version of sales return (Ratio 3), which uses the ROA(ATI) numerator and revenue as the denominator, and
- AT, the total assets turnover (Ratio 12), which uses revenue as the numerator and has the same denominator as ROA(ATI).

Thus the full Scott formula analysis is:

ROE = ROA(ATI) + (ROA(ATI) – IN(ATI)) × L/E

ROE = SR(ATI) × AT + (ROA(ATI) – IN(ATI)) × L/E

The Scott formula integrates six ratios into its analysis of leverage.

The analysis integrates six different ratios and also shows leverage potential:

- *ROE*, the return on equity (Ratio 1)
- *SR(ATI)*, an after-tax-interest version of the sales return (Ratio 3)
- *AT*, the total assets turnover ratio (Ratio 12)
- *ROA(ATI)*, the "refined" return on assets (Ratio 2)
- *IN(ATI)*, an after-tax version of the average interest rate (Ratio 6)
- *ROA(ATI) – IN(ATI)*, the leverage potential
- *L/E*, the extent of borrowing, or the debt-equity ratio (Ratio 15)

The Scott formula uses after-tax interest to bring in the effects of income tax systematically, but it can be done without the tax adjustment as long as it is left out of *all three* of the ratios mentioning ATI above. Let's see how this formula is calculated from the financial statements and then, how to use it. A brief arithmetic proof of the formula is included in the endnotes, if you're interested.[6]

Scott Formula for CPR

To illustrate how to apply the Scott formula to a real company, let's use CPR's figures. *The formula can be applied to any set of balanced financial statement figures*: it works because the balance sheet balances, as long as SR, ROA, and IN are either all before tax or all after tax. (We'll do them all after tax.) To test your knowledge of the financial statements, put a piece of paper over the 2004 figures below and find them yourself in the financial statements at the beginning of Section 10.4. (You should recognize the ratios as the same ones calculated in Section 10.4, including ROA(ATI), but with SR(ATI) and IN(ATI) now adjusted for after-tax interest.)

	2004 Figures	Symbols
Total assets, end of 2004	$10,499.8	A
Total liabilities, end of 2004	6,517.4	L
Total equity, end of 2004	3,982.4	E
Total revenue for 2004	3,902.9	REV
Net income for 2004	413.0	NI
Interest expense for 2004	223.9	INT
Income tax rate for 2004 ($143.3 / ($413.0 + $143.3))	0.257	TR
After-tax 2004 interest expense (Expense × (1 – Tax rate))	166.4	ATI = INT × (1 – TR)
ROE (return on equity)	0.104	NI / E
SR(ATI) (sales return before interest)	0.149	(NI + ATI) / REV
AT (assets turnover)	0.372	REV / A
ROA(ATI) (return on assets)	0.055	(NI + ATI) / A
IN(ATI) (average interest rate after tax)	0.026	ATI / L
L/E (debt-equity ratio)	1.64	L / E

Result:

ROE = SR(ATI) × AT + (ROA(ATI) – IN(ATI)) × L/E
0.104 = 0.149 × 0.372 + (0.055 – 0.026) × 1.64
0.104 = 0.149 + 0.029 × 1.64
0.104 = 0.055 + 0.048 off by 0.01 due to rounding

For comparison, here is the result for CPR for 2003. If you are not sure how it all works, check the amounts below by calculating them from the 2003 figures.

0.110 = 0.166 × 0.368 + (0.061 – 0.032) × 1.72
0.110 = 0.061 + 0.029 × 1.72
0.110 = 0.061 + 0.050

(A good way to check your work as you're going is to make sure that the result of multiplying the first two terms after the equal sign is the same as the third term on the right, after the plus sign. Both terms are ROA(ATI).)

Summary Comments on Integrative and Leverage Analyses for CPR

ROE is explained exactly by the five other ratios.

The Scott formula result for CPR shows that the company's 10.4% return on equity in 2004 and 11% in 2003 were made up of:

2004	2003
• A 14.9% return on sales (adding back after-tax interest)	16.6%
• An asset turnover of 0.372	0.368
• Return on assets of 5.5% (adding back after-tax interest)	6.1%
• Average interest rate of 2.6% (after tax)	3.2%
• Leverage potential of 2.9% (5.5% – 2.6%) after tax	2.9%
• A debt-equity ratio of 1.64	1.72

This provides several points of comparison with other companies or other years. Those comparisons could have been made using the individual ratios listed earlier, but now the ratios are tied to one another so that you can see how each affects return on equity. The terms on the right of the equal sign can be collected together to summarize the two basic components of the return on equity:

- The first is the *operating return*, which indicates the company's ability to make a return on its assets before interest costs (2004: 0.149 × 0.372 = 0.055, the return on assets).
- The second is the *leverage return* (2004: (0.055 – 0.026) × 1.64 = 0.029 × 1.64 = 0.048, or 0.049 without the rounding error), which starts with the return on assets (0.055) and then subtracts the interest cost to get the *leverage potential* and adjusts for the degree of borrowing. The Scott formula's second term tells us about how the leverage return arose.

ROE = Operating return + Leverage return.

So, we have for CPR:

	Return on equity	=	Operating return	+	Leverage return
2004:	10.4%	=	5.5%	+	4.9%
2003:	11.0%	=	6.1%	+	5.0%

Thus, the Scott formula analysis indicates that CPR's ROE went down because the improvement in asset turnover was offset by the decline in sales return. The lower ROE is also the result of the decreased leverage component. This indicates a little less risk but these factors are not large.

HOW'S YOUR UNDERSTANDING?

Here are two questions you should be able to answer based on what you have just read. If you can't answer them, it would be best to reread the material.

1. You have prepared a leverage analysis for Pembina Manufacturing Ltd. for 2006 and determined that the return on equity was 12%, the return on assets was 7%, and the leverage return was 5%. Explain this result to the company's president.
2. Write a paragraph summarizing CPR's financial performance for 2004 compared with 2003. Use information from Sections 10.4, 10.5 and 10.6.

10.7 Future Cash Flows: Present Value Analysis

Management decision making must look to the future.

Cash flow is important to a company, and assessing cash flow is a significant part of the analysis of a company's financial performance and position. Sorting out the impact of interest rates on the company's returns is important to understanding how it has performed. Stock markets and other capital markets are concerned with the company's expected ability to generate returns in the future, especially cash returns that can be used to pay dividends or reinvest in the company. Many financial contracts, such as those for management compensation and supply or service arrangements, focus on future financial performance. Generally, management should be looking forward to the future and trying to combine its asset acquisition, borrowing, and income-generation strategies to produce a good future return for the owners.

An important way of thinking about future performance, especially future cash flows, is *present value* (*PV*) or *discounted cash flow* (*DCF*) analysis. Future cash flows are not the same as present ones, because you have to wait for them. Because you have to wait, you lose interest or other returns you could have earned if you had had the cash sooner.

Detailed PV or DCF techniques are examined in management accounting and finance courses, and you may well have seen them already in economics or business mathematics courses. In this section, basic ideas will be outlined to help you think about how managers can assess projects that promise future cash flows and how traders in capital markets may use expectations of future cash flows and future interest rates when deciding on prices of securities. (Such traders would rarely do explicit PV or DCF calculations, but research shows that capital market prices behave as if they were doing something like that.)

Interest and the Time Value of Money

The existence of interest gives money (cash flow) a time value.

In Western society, it is permissible—even expected—that the owner of capital should charge a person who wants to use that capital a fee for that use. That fee is called *interest* and is computed by applying a specified percentage rate to the amount lent, which can be referred to as either the *investment* or the *principal*. For example, an 8% interest rate on a $200 loan would produce annual interest of $16 ($200 × 0.08). The existence of interest, which builds up as time passes, gives money a *time value*. The *time value of money* is the principle behind all the calculations in this section.

Here are some interest formulas you probably already know (P = principal or investment, i = interest rate):

$$\text{Annual interest} = P \times i$$
$$\text{Amount due at the end of one year} = P \times (1 + i)$$
$$\text{Amount due after } n \text{ years, with annual compounding, if no payments are made} = P \times (1 + i)^n$$

Interest is added to the principal to compute the total future cash flow.

The amount due is the total future cash flow, consisting of repaying the principal *plus* paying the accumulated interest.

Suppose a loan provides for repayment of the principal plus interest after several years, with no payments in the meantime. Two examples of this are Canada Savings Bonds (when you buy them you are lending the government your money) and whole life insurance (some of the premiums you pay are invested on your behalf and you are entitled to the accumulated value if you don't die first). If the interest is *compounded*, which is normally the case, that means *interest builds up on the unpaid interest as well as on*

Interest's impact depends on how frequently it is compounded.

the unpaid principal. In order to know how this works, you need to know how frequently interest compounds. Do you get interest on the interest:

- as soon as any interest arises ("continuous *compounding*")? or
- after a day's interest has been added ("daily compounding")? or
- after a month's interest has been added ("monthly compounding")? or
- only after a year's interest has been added ("annual compounding")?

Here's an example of annual compounding. We have the same $200, 8% loan as above, which is to be repaid in five years with annual compounding. We can then calculate the amount that the loan has built up to at the end of each year (its "*future value*," *FV* below) as follows:

EXHIBIT 10•12

Year	FV at Beginning of Year	Annual Interest at 8%	FV at End of Year
1	$200.00	$16.00	$216.00
2	216.00	17.28	233.28
3	233.28	18.66	251.94
4	251.94	20.16	272.10
5	272.10	21.77	293.87

You can see that the FV increases every year. Using the third interest formula above, we can calculate the FV at the end of any year:

End of year 3:
$$FV = P \times (1 + i)^n$$
$$= \$200 \times (1 + 0.08)^3$$
$$= \$251.94$$

End of year 5:
$$FV = \$200 \times (1 + 0.08)^5$$
$$= \$293.87$$

Interest and Present Value

If you wait for your money, you lose the interest you could have earned if you had it now.

The concept of interest can be "turned on its head" by considering what you *lose* by waiting some period of time for your money, or, putting it another way, what a future payment is worth in present terms if you assume your money should earn interest between now and when you get it back.

Suppose someone promises to give you $100 a year from now. If you had the money now, instead, you'd be earning 9% interest on it.

- If you'd had some amount P now and earned 9% on it, you'd be in the same position as you will be after waiting the year for $100.
- Using the second interest formula above, $100 = P × (1 + 0.09), where P is the amount on which you could have earned interest.
- Solving for P, we get P = $100/(1.09) = $91.74.
- If you had $91.74, you could have invested it at 9% and ended up with $100 at the end of the year ($91.74 + 0.09 × $91.74 = $100).

Present value is the future cash flow minus the interest that could have been earned.

The $91.74 is the *present value* of $100 received after waiting one year, "discounted at 9%." Present value is another way of thinking of the time value of money: it reminds us that as long as we wait for cash that could have earned interest starting now, we *lose* that interest. As long as the interest rate is greater than zero, present value is *less than* the actual future amount of cash that will be received because the interest included in that future cash flow has been deducted.

The following present value formulas are analogous to the above interest formulas (here C = future cash flow and i = interest rate):

Present value waiting one year $= \frac{C}{1+i}$

Present value waiting *n* years with no payments in the meantime, interest compounded annually $= \frac{C}{(1+i)^n}$

Combining these two, present value of a constant cash payment over *n* years, interest compounded annually $= \frac{C}{i}\left[1 - \frac{1}{(1+i)^n}\right]$

(A comment on the derivation of the third formula is at the end of this chapter.[7])

Lost interest is the opportunity cost of waiting for the cash.

Therefore the present value of $1,000 received three years from now, discounted at an opportunity cost interest rate of 12%, would be $711.78 (this is $1,000 divided by $(1.12)^3$). The phrase "*opportunity cost*" is often used, because by waiting three years for the $1,000, the opportunity is lost to invest at 12% in the meantime.

The concepts of future value and present value are illustrated in Figure 10.1. The charts in the figure illustrate the difference between the future values of an investment made now and the present values of future cash flows. *Interest gets larger each period.* In the future values case, it becomes a larger component of the total value; in the present values case, it becomes a larger component of the cash flow.

FIGURE 10.1

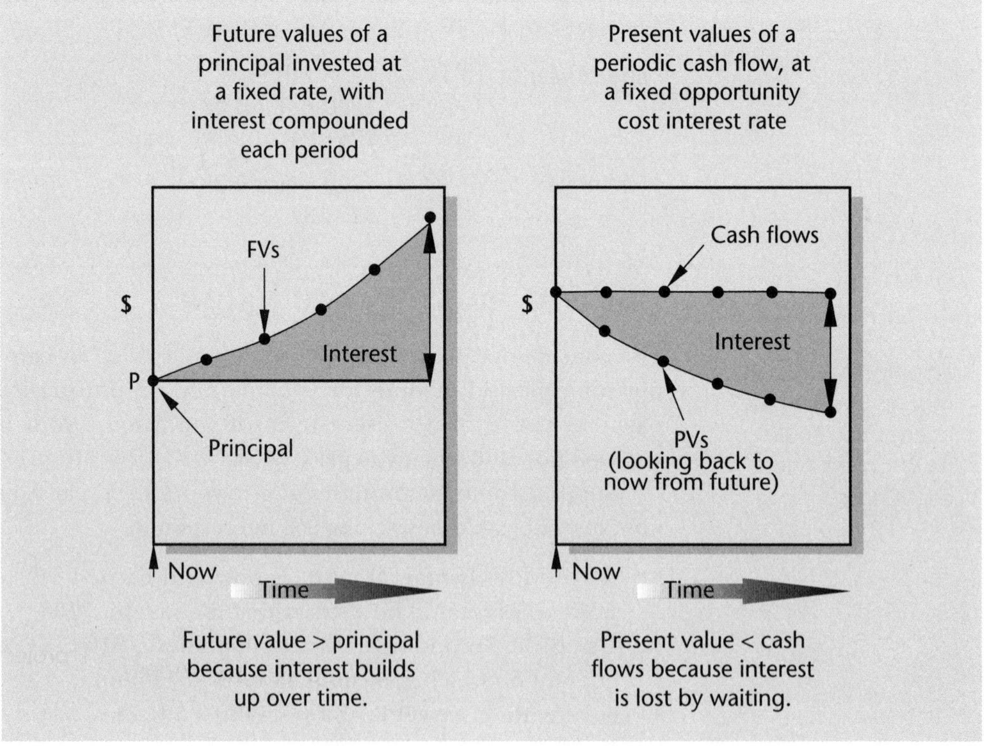
Future values of a principal invested at a fixed rate, with interest compounded each period
FVs
$
P
Interest
Principal
Now
Time
Future value > principal because interest builds up over time.
Present values of a periodic cash flow, at a fixed opportunity cost interest rate
Cash flows
$
Interest
PVs (looking back to now from future)
Now
Time
Present value < cash flows because interest is lost by waiting.

Here's a present value example. A company is considering an investment that will cost $10,000 now and will return $2,400 at the end of each year for five years. This looks good: 24% of the investment cost received each year, a total of $12,000 back on the $10,000 invested. To make the investment, the company will have to borrow at an interest rate of 7%. Should it go ahead?

Before we do the calculations, note three things about problems like this:

A project should earn a return that is at least equal to the rate paid to finance the project.

Present value has future interest removed and so can be compared to the project's cost.

1. We are trying to determine if the money coming in is *equivalent* to a *cost of capital* of 7%. If the company has to raise its money at 7%, it will want the investments it makes to return at least that. A greater rate of return would be desirable, otherwise there would be little point in investing, but 7% is the *minimum* acceptable return.
2. The idea of present value analysis is to take the future returns and subtract the 7% that the company has to pay on its borrowing, to determine if, after considering the borrowing cost, the returns equal the $10,000 that has to be invested. *Is the present value of the future cash flows equal to the present cost outlay that has to be made in order to get those flows?*
3. The 24% quoted above is *irrelevant* to the analysis. It compares the annual return to the investment cost, alright, but it does not consider the interest cost of waiting several years for some of that return. The whole idea of present value analysis is to build that interest cost, the time value of money, into the analysis.

Here's the present value analysis:

- Using the second present value formula above:

PV of first year's return is $\$2,400/(1.07)^1$	$2,242.99
PV of second year's return is $\$2,400/(1.07)^2$	2,096.25
PV of third year's return is $\$2,400/(1.07)^3$	1,959.11
PV of fourth year's return is $\$2,400/(1.07)^4$	1,830.95
PV of fifth year's return is $\$2,400/(1.07)^5$	1,711.17
Total PV	$9,840.47

- Since the annual flows are constant, the third present value formula above could have been used instead:

  $PV = (\$2,400/0.07)(1 - 1/(1.07)^5)$ = $9,840.48

  This is the same answer except for a minor rounding difference.

We can draw the needed conclusion from this and also see the effects of waiting for returns:

Present value is less than cost, which means the return is less than the financing rate.

Decision using present value: if PV > investment cost, project is attractive; if PV < investment cost, project is not attractive.

- The conclusion is that the investment is *not* a good idea. It will cost $10,000, but after calculating the interest cost of waiting for the money to be returned, the present value of the $12,000 returned is only $9,840. Therefore, the investment is returning *less* than the 7% rate the company has to pay to finance it. It's close, but still not attractive.
- You can estimate the "internal rate of return" (IRR) of the project by equating the cost of $10,000 to the third formula above and solving for i:

  $\$10,000 = (\$2,400 / i)(1 - 1 / (1 + i)^5)$

  This calculation produces an i of 6.4%.

A higher interest rate means more interest is lost by waiting, so the present value is lower.

So the return from the project is less than 7%. The lower interest rate of 6.4% produced a higher PV ($10,000) than the higher required interest rate of 7% ($9,840). (Don't worry about having to solve for the *n*th root of a denominator as above: there are theoretical problems with calculating the IRR, mainly that it assumes the returns are reinvested at the IRR rate, 6.4% above, so we will not use it further. But you can see the idea that if the IRR is not at least equal to the borrowing cost, the project is not attractive.)

Decision using rate of return: if project rate of return > cost of capital rate, project is attractive; if it is < than cost of capital rate, it is not attractive.

The farther into the future the cash flow is, the lower the present value is.

- From the annual calculations above, you can see that the present value of the $2,400 is smaller the longer we wait for it. The $2,400 received after one year has a PV of $2,243, but the $2,400 received after four years has a PV of $1,831. This is a necessary result: the longer the wait, the lower the PV because the greater is the amount of interest assumed included in the cash flow and, therefore, the lower is the residual PV. In the right-hand chart of Figure 10.1, you can see the PVs getting smaller as they go out further into the future.

Time value of money: the longer you wait for the money, the lower its present value and the less attractive it is.

Some Present Value Examples

Present value at 11% exceeds cost, so the project is attractive (it earns more than 11%).

As we have seen with the example above, the concept of present value is very useful in evaluating investment possibilities ahead of time. Here are some more examples.

1. Suppose you are offered the chance to invest $2,000 in a project that will pay you back $4,500 after six years. Is it a good deal? Suppose, alternatively, you could invest your $2,000 at 11%. The present value of the $4,500 is $\$4{,}500/(1 + 0.11)^6$, or $2,406. Therefore, the present value of what you'll get ($2,406) exceeds your cost ($2,000), and it does seem to be a good deal.
2. Gazplatz Ltd. issues bonds paying interest at 7% having a total face value of $100,000 that will pay interest every year in cash plus pay the principal back in 10 years. What would you pay for such a set of bonds if you could get 9% on your money elsewhere?

   a. Present value of annual interest
   $$= (\$7{,}000 / 0.09)\ (1 - 1/(1 + 0.09)^{10}) = \$44{,}924$$
   b. Present value of principal payment
   $$= \$100{,}000 / (1 + 0.09)^{10} = 42{,}241$$
   Total present value = $87,165

   (Note that the interest rate in the formula is the *opportunity* rate or *required* rate of 9%, the cost of raising the capital to make the investment or the returns forgone from other uses of the investment cost. The company's 7% rate just determines how much interest is paid each year—it does not represent the investor's interest expectations.)

   As a rational investor, you'd be willing to pay $87,165 for the bonds. If the bonds sold for $87,165, they'd be "*priced to yield*" 9%. They'd sell at a discount below $100,000 to make them sufficiently attractive to investors who want a better return than the stated 7% rate. By paying $87,165, you'd actually earn the 9% you want (the bonds' *yield*), as we can show by constructing a table of each year's return:

If the bonds were priced to yield 9%, they'd sell for $87,165.

Date	Cash Paid Each Year	Return on Investment Demanded (9%)	Residual (Growth in Debt)	Effective Principal Balance
Purchase date				$87,165
1 year later	$ 7,000	$ 7,845*	$ (845)	88,010
2 years later	7,000	7,921	(921)	88,931
3 years later	7,000	8,004	(1,004)	89,935
4 years later	7,000	8,094	(1,094)	91,029
5 years later	7,000	8,193	(1,193)	92,222
6 years later	7,000	8,299	(1,299)	93,521
7 years later	7,000	8,417	(1,417)	94,938
8 years later	7,000	8,544	(1,544)	96,482
9 years later	7,000	8,683	(1,683)	98,165
10 years later	107,000	8,835	98,165	0
	$170,000	$82,835	$87,165	

* $7,845 = $87,165 × 0.09; $7,921 = $88,010 × 0.09; and so on.

3. Usually, in modern financial arrangements, "blended" payments are made to cover the specified interest plus some payment on the principal. House mortgages and car loans are two common examples. In such cases, to understand what is going on, we have to separate the return *on* investment (the interest) from the return *of* investment (repayment of the principal). Here is an example: a loan of $7,998 carrying an interest rate of 10% is being repaid by a blended annual payment of $2,110, made at the end of each year, which will cover all interest and pay off the principal as well in five years. In such a case, the interest amount gets smaller every year because the principal balance is falling, but the rate of return on investment is a constant 10%.

Date	Total Blended Payment	Return on Investment (Interest)	Residual Paid on Principal	Principal Balance
Loan date				$ 7,998
1 year later	$ 2,110	$ 800*	$1,310	6,688
2 years later	2,110	669	1,441	5,247
3 years later	2,110	525	1,585	3,662
4 years later	2,110	366	1,744	1,918
5 years later	2,110	192	1,918	0
	$10,550	$2,552	$7,998	

* $800 = $7,998 × 0.10; $669 = $6,688 × 0.10; and so on.

The present value of the blended payments equals the principal amount of the loan.

Using this example, the present value of \$2,110 paid every year for five years, discounted at 10%, compounded annually, is \$7,998, the loan principal. This is $(\$2{,}110/0.10) \times (1 - 1/(1.10)^5)$: check it and see.

HOW'S YOUR UNDERSTANDING?

Here are two questions you should be able to answer based on what you have just read. If you can't answer them, it would be best to reread the material.

1. What is the present value of \$300 you will receive after two years if your opportunity cost of waiting is 11%?
2. Wildwood Inc. issued a set of \$1,000 face-value bonds carrying an interest rate of 10% and payable in eight years. The bonds were priced to yield 12%, which is what the capital market demanded for bonds of that risk and life. Did the bonds sell for more, or less, than \$1,000 each?

PV = \$243.49, which is $\$300/(1 + (0.11)^2)$

Less: the market wanted more return than 10% and so would offer a lower price than \$1,000 so that the price would be the bond's present value at 12% instead of 10%.

10.8 "What If" (Effects) Analysis

You may want to see what difference an accounting method you prefer would make.

Suppose you are a financial analyst trying to determine what a recently released set of financial statements tells you about the company's performance. You can do various standard analyses, but before you do that you find that the company's accounting isn't quite comparable to that of another company you want to compare it to, or that the company has used an accounting method you don't agree with. You therefore want to alter the numbers to show "what if" the company used the other company's accounting method, or a method you do agree with.

Doing this has been necessary rather too often in recent years, as company after company reported that its earnings or other financial statement quantities had been improperly stated when the financial statements first came out. Press releases that give the company's explanation of what happened can be given a "reasonableness check" by using the sorts of analyses shown here.

Analysis of the effects of a method choice helps in making the choice.

"What if" questions are very common in business. Answering them requires analysis of the accounting information: we'll call this "*what if*" (*effects*) *analysis*. The ability to analyze accounting information to tell managers, bankers, and others what difference various changes in *accounting policy choices* or detailed methods, correction of errors in the financial statements, or business events in general would make to the financial statements is very important to accountants. If you are going to be an accountant, you have to develop this skill. If you are not going to be an accountant, you should have some idea of what the accountants are doing in such analyses, so that you can evaluate the results they give you. You may even want to do some basic analysis yourself. Computer spreadsheets are particularly good for this sort of analysis, but you have to know what to tell the spreadsheet to do.

Examples of "What If" Effects Analysis

Effects analysis can often be done using shortcuts, once you understand the idea.

One way to think about what would result if one method were used instead of another, or one event happened instead of another, is to figure out the accounting numbers both ways and compare them. Another way is to use shortcuts, like the "net of tax" approach illustrated in Sections 1.12 and 10.2 or other forms of marginal analysis. If you see a shortcut in a given problem, including the examples below, go ahead and use it!

a. Cash Versus Accrual

Here's an example we've seen since Chapter 1. Suppose a company's president said, "I know we use accrual accounting, but what difference would it make to this year's income if we used the cash basis instead?"

We find that this year's accrual income is $11,800 (income statement), and this year's cash from operations is $13,400 (cash flow statement). Therefore, the answer to the president's question is that income would be $1,600 higher this year on a cash basis. No analysis is needed, because the financial statements provide the answer, if you know how to read them.

b. Revenue Recognition: During or After Production

Effects analysis can often be done from overall effects without knowing details.

Section 6.7 gives the example of Greenway Construction, which uses percentage of completion to recognize its construction revenues and expenses. Suppose the company's banker, more used to revenue recognition at completion of production (completion of the contract), wanted to know what difference there would be to income if the completion of production method were used instead. You can answer this without knowing the details of the accounting methods, as long as you know what the methods do to income. (If you have not yet studied Section 6.7, the necessary data are given below.)

The percentage of completion project income (totalling $600,000 over three years) was:

- $120,000 for Year 1;
- $270,000 for Year 2; and
- $210,000 for Year 3.

If revenue and expenses were recognized only at completion of the project, the project income would be:

- $0 in Year 1;
- $0 in Year 2; and
- $600,000 in Year 3.

So the answer to the banker's question would be that income would be:

- $120,000 lower in Year 1 ($0 – $120,000);
- $270,000 lower in Year 2 ($0 – $270,000); and
- $390,000 higher in Year 3 ($600,000 – $210,000).

There has been no change in the three-year total, but the yearly figures are rearranged if the completion of production method is used.

c. Franchise Revenue Recognition

Similarly, Section 6.8 compares the accrual and cash basis ways of recognizing income from WonderBurgers Ltd.'s franchising operations. Again, all we need to know is the effect of each method on income. If you have not yet studied Section 6.8, here are that section's results for the accrual versus the cash basis of recognizing income.

EXHIBIT 10·15

	Accrual Basis Income			Cash Basis Income		
	(a)	(b)	(c)	(d)	(e)	(f)
Year	Revenue	Expense	Income	Received	Spent	Income
1	$10,000	$3,200	$ 6,800	$15,000	$4,000	$11,000
2	7,500	2,400	5,100	5,000	3,000	2,000
3	7,500	2,400	5,100	5,000	1,000	4,000
	$25,000	$8,000	$17,000	$25,000	$8,000	$17,000

Difference			
Year	(a)–(d)	(b)–(e)	(c)–(f)
1	$(5,000)	$ (800)	$(4,200)
2	2,500	(600)	3,100
3	2,500	1,400	1,100
	0	0	0

If the cash basis were used instead of the accrual basis, the following income effects would result over the three years of the WonderBurgers example (see the (c) – (f) column under Difference):

- Year 1 income would be $4,200 higher;
- Year 2 income would be $3,100 lower; and
- Year 3 income would be $1,100 lower.

Examples of Income Tax Effects In This Analysis

d. Income Tax Effects on Examples (b) and (c)

Suppose Greenway Construction pays income tax at a rate of 35% and WonderBurgers pays at a rate of 30%. What effect would that have on the figures above? Income tax reduces all the effects by the tax rate, because that proportion goes to the government. As shown elsewhere in this book (and below), a useful rule is just to multiply the before-tax effect by (1 – Tax rate), in this case (1 – 0.35) = 0.65 for Greenway and (1 – 0.30) = 0.70 for WonderBurgers.

Here is a table of the effects, before and after income tax (for presentation purposes, Greenway's figures are in thousands of dollars):

EXHIBIT 10·16

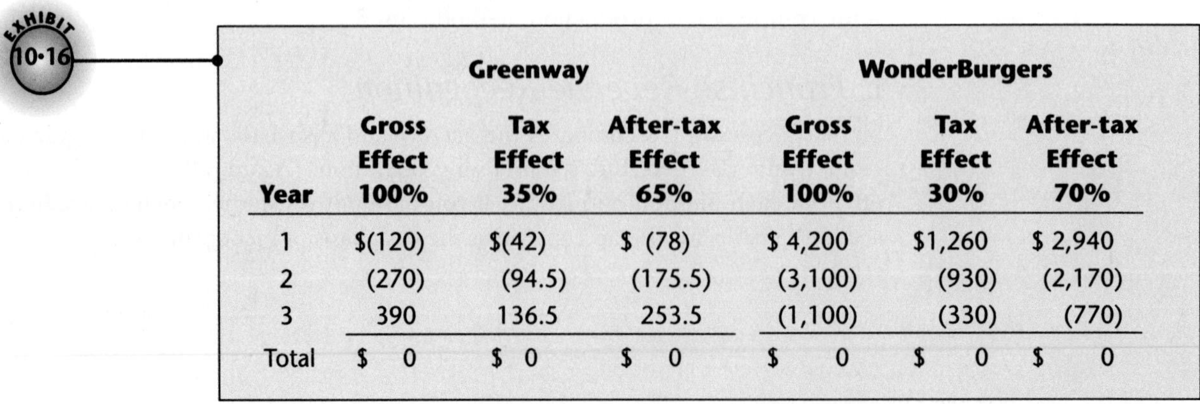

	Greenway			WonderBurgers		
Year	Gross Effect 100%	Tax Effect 35%	After-tax Effect 65%	Gross Effect 100%	Tax Effect 30%	After-tax Effect 70%
1	$(120)	$(42)	$ (78)	$ 4,200	$1,260	$ 2,940
2	(270)	(94.5)	(175.5)	(3,100)	(930)	(2,170)
3	390	136.5	253.5	(1,100)	(330)	(770)
Total	$ 0	$ 0	$ 0	$ 0	$ 0	$ 0

Income tax reduces both positive and negative differences:

- The assumption here is that an increased income is taxed, and
- A decreased income produces tax savings (by reducing tax payable on other income or creating tax credits that can be used to get refunds on past years' taxes or reduce future taxes).

Without knowing the details of the income tax law (which are beyond the scope of this book), we cannot say for sure how much of the income tax effect is current and how much is future. We know the effect on *total* income tax expense, as indicated above, but not how to allocate that effect between the current and future portions of the expense. We know the other side of the overall effect, the increase or decrease in *total* income tax liability, but not how to allocate that effect between the income tax payable liability and the future income tax liability.

e. "Net-of-Tax" Analysis and Interest Expense Net of Tax

Income tax tends to reduce both positive and negative effects on income.

Please review the net-of-tax material in Section 1.12 and, if you have not studied Section 10.2 yet, please read the latter part of it now. Those sections' analyses are examples of "what if" analysis, and net-of-tax analysis can be used to build tax effects into many evaluations.

HOW'S YOUR UNDERSTANDING?

Here are two questions you should be able to answer based on what you have just read. If you can't answer them, it would be best to reread the material.

1. A company is thinking of changing its accounting policies in a way that will increase revenue by $500,000 this year, with $300,000 of that coming from a reduction in last year's revenue and $200,000 coming from a reduction in next year's revenue. Expenses would change too, with last year's expenses going down $215,000, this year's expenses going up $320,000, and next year's expenses going down $105,000. Ignoring income tax, what would this change do to (a) net income this year, (b) retained earnings at the beginning of this year, (c) retained earnings at the end of this year, and (d) retained earnings at the end of next year?

(a) Up $180,000 ($500,000 – $320,000).

(b) Down $85,000 ($(300,000) – $(215,000)).

(c) Up $95,000 ($(85,000) + $180,000).

(d) No change. By that point, sum of revenue changes = 0, sum of expense changes = 0, so effect on retained earnings also = 0.

2. Answer part 1 assuming the company's income tax rate is 40%.

Just multiply each answer above by (1 – 0.40), with the results: (a) up $108,000; (b) down $51,000; (c) up $57,000; (d) still no effect.

10.9 Multi-Year "What If" (Effects) Analysis

The analysis approach outlined in Section 10.8 can be extended to as many years as you need. Some of this was illustrated above in the Greenway and WonderBurgers examples, but now let's develop a framework for a complete multi-year analysis.

An Example

Earth Fabrics Inc. manufactures several lines of environmentally friendly dress fabrics, hiking clothes, and other cloth goods. It has been in business three years. There have been more returns of fabrics by retail stores in the current year than in the first two, and because of this, the president is considering a suggestion by the external auditor to recognize revenue from shipments to retailers a little more conservatively. The company's income tax rate is 34%, and revenue and accounts receivable data for the company's first three years, presented in the usual financial statement presentation order of having the most recent year to the left, are:

	Year 3	Year 2	Year 1
Revenue for the year	$1,432,312	$943,678	$575,904
Year-end accounts receivable	194,587	148,429	98,346

The auditor suggests that a more appropriate revenue recognition policy would reduce revenues by reducing year-end accounts receivable by 10% at the end of Year 1, 15% at the end of Year 2, and 25% at the end of Year 3. (Recognizing revenue includes a debit to accounts receivable and a credit to revenue, so reducing receivables implies reducing revenue, and vice versa.)

What effect would this have on:

1. Accounts receivable at the end of each year?
2. Revenue in each year?
3. Net income for the year?
4. Income tax liability at the end of each year?
5. Shareholders' equity at the end of each year?

1. Effects on accounts receivable:

Year 1	Receivables down 10% = $ 9,835	New balance = $ 88,511
Year 2	Receivables down 15% = $22,264	New balance = $126,165
Year 3	Receivables down 25% = $48,647	New balance = $145,940

It's important to realize what these receivables changes do. By reducing the receivables at the end of any year, all revenue recognized up to that point is reduced—you might say that the recognition of some of it is being postponed to the next year. So, for example, the Year 1 revenue is reduced $9,835, but because that revenue is postponed to Year 2, that year's revenue is increased by $9,835. By the end of Year 3, all the prior revenues are reduced by $48,647. Let's see how that divides up into the three years.

2. Effects on revenue:

Year 1	Revenue down	$ 9,835
Year 2	Revenue down $22,264 and up $9,835, net down	12,429
Year 3	Revenue down $48,647 and up $22,264, net down	26,383
Total decrease in revenue over the three years		$48,647

3. Effects on net income:

Year 1	Net income down $9,835 × (1 – 0.34)	$ 6,491
Year 2	Net income down $12,429 × (1 – 0.34)	8,203
Year 3	Net income down $26,383 × (1 – 0.34)	17,413
Total decrease in net income over the three years		$32,107

We can check this. If accounts receivable are reduced by an accumulated amount of $48,647, then the accumulated net income must have gone down by this amount × (1 – 0.34). So, $48,647 × (1 – 0.34) = $32,107. The rest ($48,647 – $32,107 = $16,540) is the effect on income tax itself, which we will calculate directly next.

4. Effects on income tax liability:
   Income tax is saved on the lower incomes. The amount of the accumulated tax saving is just the tax rate (0.34) times the accumulated change in accounts receivable at the same time*:

Year 1	Year-end tax liability down $9,835 × (0.34)	$ 3,344
Year 2	Year-end tax liability down $22,264 × (0.34)	$ 7,570
Year 3	Year-end tax liability down $48,647 × (0.34)	$16,540**

* Or calculate the reduced revenue each year and multiply the revenue effect by 0.34.
** Check: this is the same as "the rest" of the receivable effect identified in answer 3.

5. Effects on shareholders' equity:
   Shareholders' equity is reduced by the reductions in net income, which reduce retained earnings. Therefore, the effects on shareholders' equity are the accumulations of those listed for income in part 3:

Year 1	Ending equity down	$ 6,491
Year 2	Ending equity down ($6,491 + $8,203)	$14,694
Year 3	Ending equity down ($6,491 + $8,203 + $17,413)	$32,107

An Analytical Framework

It may help you to keep multiple-year analyses straight if you use the analytical framework below. The framework relies on two important things:

- Because accounting is a double-entry system, all the effects at any point in time must balance out, so that the balance sheet stays in balance. This might help if, for example, you can't remember which way one effect goes; you know that it has to work so that everything stays in balance.
- Because each balance sheet is the accumulation of everything that has gone before, each balance sheet's effects are the sum of whatever the effects were on the previous balance sheet plus the effects on the income statement between the two balance sheets.

Figure 10.2 provides the framework, in blank. We'll fill it in shortly.

FIGURE 10.2

"What If" Effects Analytical Framework

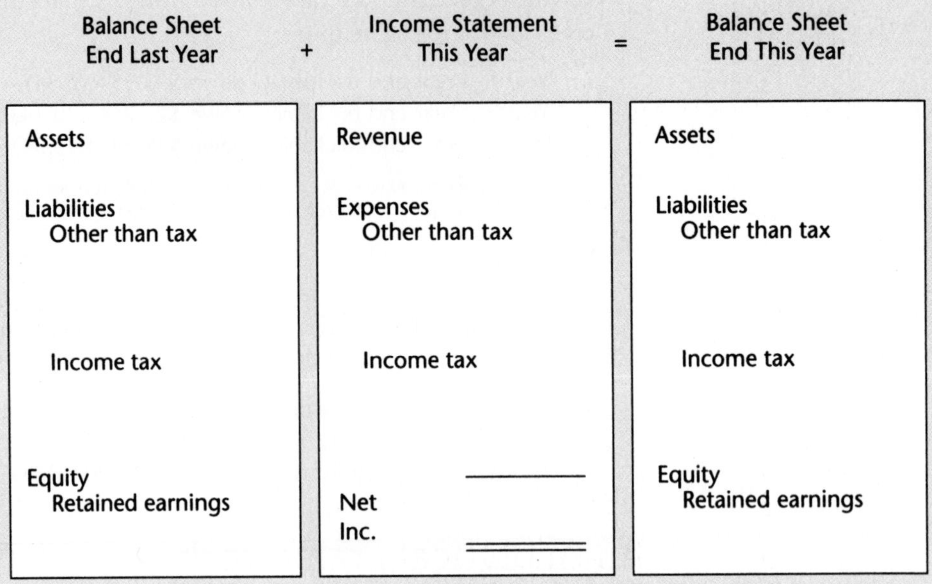

Balance Sheet End Last Year	+	Income Statement This Year	=	Balance Sheet End This Year
Assets		Revenue		Assets
Liabilities Other than tax		Expenses Other than tax		Liabilities Other than tax
Income tax		Income tax		Income tax
Equity Retained earnings		Net Inc.		Equity Retained earnings

Notes

1. Without knowledge of the tax law, it may be impossible to separate the tax effects into current and future portions.
2. For there to be a cash effect, some cash or cash equivalent account must be affected. For accounting policy changes, error corrections, and most other effects analyses, this will not happen.

Now let's fill the framework in three times, once for each of the three years of the Earth Fabrics example. Remember that the company has only existed for three years, so the "end of last year" figures for Year 1 are all zero.

	Balance Sheet End Last Year	+	Income Statement This Year		=	Balance Sheet End This Year	
Year 1							
Assets			*Revenue*			*Assets*	
Rec. down	$ 0		Down	$ 9,835		Rec. down	$ 9,835
Liabilities			*Expenses*			*Liabilities*	
Other than tax			*Other than tax*			*Other than tax*	
No effect			No effect			No effect	
Income tax			*Income tax*			*Income tax*	
Down	$ 0		Down	$ 3,344		Down	$ 3,344
Equity						*Equity*	
Retained earn.			*Net income*			*Retained earn.*	
Down	$ 0		Down	$ 6,491		Down	$ 6,491
Year 2							
Assets			*Revenue*			*Assets*	
Rec. down	$ 9,835		Down	$12,429		Rec. down	$22,264
Liabilities			*Expenses*			*Liabilities*	
Other than tax			*Other than tax*			*Other than tax*	
No effect			No effect			No effect	
Income tax			*Income tax*			*Income tax*	
Down	$ 3,344		Down	$ 4,226		Down	$ 7,570
Equity						*Equity*	
Retained earn.			*Net income*			*Retained earn.*	
Down	$ 6,491		Down	$ 8,203		Down	$14,694
Year 3							
Assets			*Revenue*			*Assets*	
Rec. down	$22,264		Down	$26,383		Rec. down	$48,647
Liabilities			*Expenses*			*Liabilities*	
Other than tax			*Other than tax*			*Other than tax*	
No effect			No effect			No effect	
Income tax			*Income tax*			*Income tax*	
Down	$ 7,570		Down	$ 8,970		Down	$16,540
Equity						*Equity*	
Retained earn.			*Net income*			*Retained earn.*	
Down	$14,694		Down	$17,413		Down	$32,107

The analysis can start from any point but has to add and cross-add in all directions.

You should note the following two points about the analytical framework:

- Each year's effects add vertically and horizontally. That is, vertically, the beginning and ending balance sheet effects and income statement effects work out exactly, and horizontally, the ending balance sheet effects are the sum of the beginning ones and the income statement ones.
- You can do the analysis at any point, working forward or backward from there. Probably, the most important analysis would be Year 3, because it accumulates everything from the beginning to now.

The analytical framework will help you think about effects analysis, but you have to consider the specific circumstances of each situation rather than hope for a general solution you can memorize. You have to exercise the knowledge and judgment you've acquired in your studies and experience! We'll do a further effects analysis example below to help you develop your analytical ability.

Journal Entry

You may be interested to know how the revenue recognition change would be entered in the accounts. It is quite straightforward, and uses the figures for the Year 3 analysis, because the company is just finishing Year 3 (let's assume the accounts for Year 3 have not yet been closed). Here is the entry, *in the order of the accounts in the analytical framework*:

CR Accounts receivable		48,647
DR Income tax liability (we don't know if this is current or future tax)	16,540	
DR Retained earnings (*prior* years' effects, aggregated)	14,694	
DR Revenue (Year 3)	26,383	
CR Income tax expense (Year 3)		8,970

Cash Effects

Cash is unlikely to be affected by accounting method changes.

You'll note that the analysis above and the journal entry to implement the change said nothing about cash. An important point to remember is that *analysis of accounting method changes almost never involves cash.* Accrual accounting, after all, is intended to go beyond cash flow, so accrual figures don't affect cash, before or after the change. If we are changing revenue, receivables, inventories, depreciation, etc., we will change net income, working capital, income tax liability, and/or owners' equity (retained earnings), but unless cash is being spent or received as part of the change, there is no cash effect. There will *eventually* be a cash effect through increased income tax or a tax refund, but at the time the accounting change is implemented, there is no tax effect.

It's pretty easy to see that if no cash (or cash equivalent) account is affected in the change, there is no cash effect. Remembering that may be enough for you! But you can also show, via examining effects on the cash flow statement's operations section, that even if there appears to be a cash effect because net income is affected, that effect is cancelled out by effects on other account changes used to determine cash from operations. Let's use the Earth Fabrics example to show you how this works.

	Year 1	Year 2	Year 3
Accounts receivable:			
Total reduction at the end of the year	$9,835	$22,264	$48,647
Total reduction at the beginning of the year	0	9,835	22,264
Asset reduction over the year	$9,835	$12,429	$26,383
Income tax liability:			
Total reduction at the end of the year	$3,344	$ 7,570	$16,540
Total reduction at the beginning of the year	0	3,344	7,570
Liability reduction over the year	$3,344	$ 4,226	$ 8,970
Retained earnings:			
Total reduction at the end of the year	$6,491	$14,694	$32,107
Total reduction at the beginning of the year	0	6,491	14,694
Income reduction over the year	$6,491	$ 8,203	$17,413
Cash flow statement's operations section changes:			
Income reduction appears to hurt cash	–$6,491	–$ 8,203	–$17,413
Receivables reduction appears to help cash	9,835	12,429	26,383
Liability reduction appears to hurt cash	–3,344	–4,226	–8,970
Net effect on cash from operations	$ 0	$ 0	$ 0

A Further Example

Rexdon Interiors Ltd. sells decorating supplies and does contract home and office decorating work. The company accounts for revenue at the point of delivery for ordinary sales and on the completed contract basis for contract work. Resulting accounts for 2004 and 2003 are:

	2004	2003
Revenue for 2004	$1,234,530	
Accounts receivable at the end of the year	114,593	$93,438
Bad debts expense for 2004	11,240	
Allowance for doubtful accounts at the end of the year	13,925	6,560

The president, Rex, is thinking of changing the revenue recognition method for contract work to the percentage of completion method. (You don't have to know the details of the method to do this analysis.) If this were done,

- accounts receivable would rise to $190,540 at the end of 2003 and $132,768 at the end of 2004;
- the controller advises that revenue/expense matching would also require raising the allowance for doubtful accounts to $14,260 at the end of 2003 and to $16,450 at the end of 2004. No other expense recognition changes would be anticipated.
- Rexdon's income tax rate is 32%.

Using the analytical framework described above, here is a summary of the effects of the policy change. ("ADA" is the allowance for doubtful accounts.) Explanations for the figures follow.

Balance Sheet End Last Year		+	Income Statement This Year		=	Balance Sheet End This Year	
Assets			*Revenue*			*Assets*	
Rec. up	$97,102		Down	$78,927		Rec. up	$18,175
ADA up	$(7,700)					ADA up	$(2,525)
Liabilities			*Expenses*			*Liabilities*	
Other than tax			*Other than tax*			*Other than tax*	
	No effect		BDs down	$ 5,175			No effect
Income tax			*Income tax*			*Income tax*	
Up	$28,609		Down	$23,601		Up	$ 5,008
Equity						*Equity*	
Retained earn.			*Net income*			*Retained earn.*	
Up	$60,793		Down	$50,151		Up	$10,642

The effects are much larger at the end of 2003 than at the end of 2004, resulting in effects on the 2004 income statement that might be opposite to what you expected. This is a warning to corporate executives contemplating earnings management: if a company does try to manipulate its net income through accounting policy changes, it can easily have such unexpected results. Financial statement manipulation is not for the faint of heart: unexpected effects are just one reason such manipulation is not a good idea. President Rex should only change revenue recognition policies if he believes the new policy is really better, more appropriate, and fairer, and if he is therefore willing to stick with the new policy even when it produces awkward results, as it does in 2004.

Here are details behind the above framework summary:

a. Retained earnings at the end of 2003 would rise by the increase in receivables minus the increase in income tax expense:

($190,540 – $93,438 – $14,260 – $6,560) × (1 – 0.32)
= $89,402 × (1 – 0.32)
= $60,793 increase.

b. The 2003 income tax liability would increase by

$89,402 × 0.32 = $28,609.

c. Revenue for 2004 would decrease because more revenue that is now in 2004 would be pushed back to 2003 than would revenue now in 2005 be pushed back to 2004.
   - The increase in 2003 accounts receivable ($190,540 – $93,438 = $97,102) would be transferred out of 2004 revenue;
   - The increase in 2004 accounts receivable ($132,768 – $114,593 = $18,175) would be transferred into 2004 revenue;
   - For a net decrease in 2004 revenue of $78,927 ($97,102 – $18,175).

d. Bad debts expense for 2004 would also decrease because of the corresponding revision in the timing of recognition of the expense.
   - The increase in 2003 allowance ($14,260 – $6,560 = $7,700) would be transferred out of 2004 expense to 2003;
   - The increase in 2004 allowance ($16,450 – $13,925 = $2,525) would be transferred into 2004 expense;
   - For a net decrease in 2004 expense of $5,175.

e. Net income for 2004 would decrease due to the combined effect of the revenue decrease and the bad debts expense decrease, minus the tax effect:

($78,927 – $5,175) × (1 – 0.32) = $73,752 × (1 – 0.32) = $50,151 decrease.

f. The 2004 income tax expense would decrease by $73,752 × 0.32 = $23,601.
g. Income tax liability at the end of 2004 would increase $5,008 ($28,609 increase from 2003, minus $23,601 decrease from 2004).
h. There would be no immediate effect on cash or on 2004 cash flow, but eventually the $5,008 increased income tax liability would have to be paid.

Following the above framework summary, the journal entry to record the policy change as at the end of 2004 would be:

DR Accounts receivable	18,175	
CR Allowance for doubtful accounts		2,525
CR Income tax liability (payable or future)		5,008
CR Retained earnings (*prior* period policy change effect)		60,793
DR Revenue for 2004	78,927	
CR Bad debts expense for 2004		5,175
CR Income tax expense for 2004		23,601

Note that these examples assume that policy changes and error corrections affecting prior years are entered directly into retained earnings and would be shown on the statement of retained earnings. That is consistent with present Canadian GAAP, as explained in Section 3.5. However, GAAP in the U.S. would require that most of these be adjusted to the current year's income statement instead. This means that in the U.S., the current year's income would include the prior years' effects also. The net effect on the balance sheet at the end of the current year would be the same under either country's GAAP.

HOW'S YOUR UNDERSTANDING?

Here are two questions you should be able to answer based on what you have just read. If you can't answer them, it would be best to reread the material.

1. Hinton Inc. has found an error in its revenue account: an invoice for $1,400 was recorded as revenue in 2002 when it should have been recorded in 2003. The company's income tax rate is 35% and there was no corresponding error in cost of goods sold. What is the effect of the error on: (a) 2002 net income; (b) 2002 cash from operations; (c) 2003 net income; (d) retained earnings at the end of 2002; (e) retained earnings at the end of 2003?

(a) $1,400 × (1 – 0.35) = $910 too high;

(b) no cash effect;

(c) $910 too low;

(d) $910 too high;

(e) no effect as the sum of 2002's and 2003's incomes is unaffected

2. Granby Industrial Inc. decided to change its accounting for warranties, to accrue warranty expense sooner than had been done. The effect on warranty liability as at the end of 2002 was to increase it by $121,000. By the end of 2003, the liability would go up $134,000. The company's income tax rate is 30%. What would be the effect of the change on: (a) 2003 net income; (b) 2003 cash from operations; (c) retained earnings at the end of 2003; (d) income tax liability at the end of 2003?

(a) ($134,000 – $121,000) × (1 – 0.30) = $9,100 lower;

(b) no cash effect;

(c) $134,000 × (1 – 0.30) = $93,800 lower;

(d) $134,000 × (0.30) = $40,200 lower.

10.10 Terms to Be Sure You Understand

Here is this chapter's list of terms introduced or emphasized. Make sure you know what they mean *in accounting*, and if any are unclear to you, check the chapter again or refer to the glossary of terms at the back of the book.

Accounting policy choices
Acid test ratio
AT
Average interest rate
Book value per share
Cash flow to total assets
Collection ratio
Common size financial statements
Compounded(ing)
Cost of capital
Current ratio
Days' sales in receivables
DCF
Debt to assets ratio
Debt-equity ratio
Discounted cash flow
Dividend payout ratio
Earnings per share
Earnings-price ratio
EPS
Financial statement analysis
Future value
FV
Gross margin
Gross profit ratio
IN(ATI)
Interest
Interest coverage ratio
Inventory turnover
L/E
Leverage
Leverage analysis
Leverage potential
Leverage return
Long-term debt-equity ratio
Management discussion and analysis
Market capitalization
MD&A
Net-of-tax analysis
Notes to the financial statements
Operating return
Opportunity cost
PE
Present value
Present value analysis
Price to book ratio
Priced to yield
Price-earnings ratio
Principal
Profit margin
PV
Quick ratio
Ratio analysis
Ratios
Refined ROA
Return on assets
Return on equity
Return on investment
ROA
ROA(ATI)
ROE
ROI
Sales return
Scott formula
SR(ATI)
Time value of money
Total assets turnover
"What if" (effects) analysis
Working capital
Working capital ratio
Yield

DATA FOR INSTALLMENT 10

In Installment 9, three financial statements for Mato Inc. were prepared: a statement of income and deficit for the year ended February 28, 2007 (which might have been called the statement of loss and deficit, because the company had a $54,066 loss); balance sheets at February 28, 2007, and March 1, 2006; and cash flow statement for the year ended February 28, 2007.

These statements are the data for this installment, which will illustrate the calculation of various financial ratios and the Scott formula. The illustration will not always be straightforward, because the company lost money and is not in a strong financial position. Unfortunately, you may well encounter such less-than-successful companies. So, seeing how to apply the analyses to them should increase your understanding of the analyses.

RESULTS FOR INSTALLMENT 10

To begin with, here are the ratios set out in Section 10.4, in the order given there. Refer to the statements in Installment 9 (Section 9.9), and make sure you know where the figures for the ratios below came from. Note that the company has made no provision for an income tax recovery on its first-year loss—such a recovery would depend on having future taxable income to deduct the loss against, and that is not likely enough to warrant creating an income tax recovery asset in the present circumstances.

Other versions of some of the ratios calculated below are quite possible. Dollar signs have been omitted and most ratios are rounded to three decimals.

Performance ratios:

1. Return on year-end equity: (54,066) / 70,934 = (0.762), negative.
   Return on beginning equity: (54,066) / 125,000 = (0.433), negative.
2. Return on ending assets: ((54,066) + 6,469) / 160,742 = (0.296), negative.
3. Sales return before interest: ((54,066) + 6,469) / 229,387 = (0.207), negative.
   Sales return after interest: (54,066) / 229,387 = (0.236), negative.
4. Common size financial statements: not illustrated here.
5. Gross margin: 90,620 / 229,387 = 0.395. Cost of goods sold is 0.605 of sales revenue, so the average markup is 0.395 / 0.605 = 65% of cost.
6. Average interest rate: 6,469 / 89,808 = 0.072.
7. Cash flow to total ending assets: (40,028) / 160,742 = (0.249), negative.
8. Earnings per share: number of shares not known, and EPS is not as meaningful for a private company as for a publicly traded one.
9. Book value per share: number of shares not known; however, the owners' original equity of $125,000 is now down to $70,934, which means the book value of the shares is only 56.7% of the amounts the owners contributed.
10. Price-earnings ratio: not determinable because the shares of a private company like this are not traded and their price, therefore, is not known.
11. Dividend payout ratio: no dividends declared since there was a loss.

Activity (turnover) ratios:

12. Total asset turnover: 229,387 / 160,742 = 1.427 times.
13. Inventory turnover: 138,767 / 33,612 = 4.128 times.
14. Collection ratio: 14,129 / (229,387/365) = 22.5 days.

Financing ratios:

15. Debt-equity ratio: 89,808 / 70,934 = 1.266.
    Beginning debt-equity ratio was: 16,100 / 125,000 = 0.129.
16. Long-term debt-equity ratio: zero (no long-term debt).
17. Debt to assets ratio: 89,808 / 160,742 = 0.559.

Liquidity and solvency warning ratios:

18. Working capital ratio: 54,684 / 89,808 = 0.609.
    Beginning working capital ratio was: 130,000 / 16,100 = 8.075.
19. Acid test ratio: (6,418 + 14,129) / 89,808 = 0.229.
20. Interest coverage ratio: not calculated because with this large a loss there is no coverage!

The ratios tell a grim story:

- The company has lost 43.3% of its beginning equity;
- Its working capital ratio is considerably less than 1 (its working capital is negative);
- Its acid test ratio is less than 25%; and
- Its cash and receivables would carry its operations for less than a month.

But, there are some positive signs:

- The collection ratio is low (only 22.5 days);
- The debt-equity ratio is not high, even though equity has been reduced by losses; and
- With a fairly low debt to assets ratio and no long-term debt, there may be room for some long-term borrowing, should that be necessary to improve the current position.

What does the Scott formula tell us? Using the year-end figures from the above ratios, we have (no tax adjustments to any ratios are necessary):

$$\begin{aligned}
ROE &= SR \times AT &&+ (ROA - IN) \times L/E \\
(0.762) &= (0.207) \times 1.427 &&+ ((0.296) - 0.072) \times 1.266 \\
(0.762) &= (0.295) &&+ (0.368) \times 1.266 \\
(0.762) &= (0.295) &&+ (0.466)
\end{aligned}$$

The formula works out to within a 0.001 rounding error. It indicates that the company's woeful ROE is due to the negative effects of leverage compounding poor operating performance: the company was already losing money, and by borrowing, made things worse. Normally, a high asset turnover indicates good performance. But here, as the company was losing on every sale, getting more sales also made things worse. Perhaps Mavis and Tomas tried to do too much in their first year.

This example illustrates that most ratios and such aggregations as the Scott formula can be calculated for losing companies. Financial statement analysis is not limited to profitable, financially solid companies. However, the interpretation of the statements must be made carefully, because negative relationships may exist where they're not expected, as we saw with the effects of asset turnover above.

We should wish Mavis and Tomas well in their second year. If they don't do better, there won't be a third year!

10.12 Homework and Discussion to Develop Understanding

The problems roughly follow the outline of the chapter. Three main categories of questions are presented.

- Asterisked problems (*) have an informal solution provided in the Student Solutions Manual.
- EXTENDED TIME problems grant a thorough examination of the material and may take longer to complete.
- CHALLENGING problems are more difficult.

For further explanation, please refer to Section 1.15.

Financial Statement Analysis and Interpretation • Sections 10.3–10.6

Discussing Financial Analysis Issues

*** PROBLEM 10.1** List advantages and disadvantages of ratio analysis

List the advantages and disadvantages you see of using ratio analysis of financial statements (including leverage analysis) as a way of evaluating management's performance. For the disadvantages, try to think of a way around each problem you identify.

PROBLEM 10.2 Comment on a complaint about financial statement analysis

A senior member of a large public company's management complained:

> Accountants' financial analyses don't seem very useful to me. The analyses don't reveal the business management factors that are important to my company's success. They are biased toward the past rather than the future. And, anyway, the stock market is way ahead of the accountants in judging the company's performance.

Comment on the manager's complaint.

PROBLEM 10.3 Ratios to measure different kinds of performance

1. Many financial performance measures are ratios of some return over some investment base. Why is such a concept of performance important in business?
2. With your answer to part 1 in mind, how might you measure the performance of each of the following investments owned by I. Investor?
   a. Her $1,200 in a savings account at Banker's Trust.
   b. Her investment of $15,000 in a little consulting business she runs in her spare time.
   c. Her Slapdash 210 ragtop sports car.
   d. Her investment of $300,000 in a stock-indexed mutual fund.

PROBLEM 10.4 How does financial statement analysis help users?

Many external parties rely on statements such as the balance sheet, the income statement, and the cash flow statement produced by a company. Identify two different types of major users of financial information and briefly explain how analysis of the three financial statements will help them. (This is a similar question to some asked about the value of financial statements in earlier chapters, but now you should be able to relate financial statement analysis to user value.)

PROBLEM 10.5 Draft a speech on analysis and the use of financial statements

Write the rough notes for a speech you have been asked to give to a local investment club. The members of the club are all experienced stock market investors and want a better understanding of companies' accounting information. The topic of your speech is "Analysis and Use of Financial Accounting Information."

Performing Ratio Analysis

* **PROBLEM 10.6** Use statement analysis to evaluate a president's claims

The president of a medium-sized manufacturing company wants to renew the company's operating loan. In discussions with the bank's lending officer, the president says, "As the accompanying financial statements show, our working capital position has increased during the past year, and we have managed to reduce operating expenses significantly."

The partial financial statements showed the following:

Titan Manufacturing Ltd.
Partial Balance Sheet
as at December 31, 2006 and 2005

	2006	2005
Current Assets		
Cash	$ 50,000	$200,000
Accounts receivable	250,000	100,000
Inventories	500,000	400,000
Total current assets	$800,000	$700,000
Current Liabilities		
Accounts payable	$250,000	$200,000
Operating loan	100,000	100,000
Total current liabilities	$350,000	$300,000

Titan Manufacturing Ltd.
Income Statement
for the Years Ended December 31, 2006 and 2005

	2006	2005
Sales	$1,200,000	$1,500,000
Less cost of goods sold	780,000	900,000
Gross profit	$ 420,000	$ 600,000
Operating expenses	350,000	400,000
Income before taxes	$ 70,000	$ 200,000
Income taxes	14,000	40,000
Net income	$ 56,000	$ 160,000

1. Evaluate the president's comments. Incorporate appropriate ratio analysis into your discussion.
2. What additional financial information (if any) would you request of the president? Why?

PROBLEM 10.7 Use ratios to evaluate relative performance

Your friend, Inna, has asked you to evaluate information about two companies in the same industry. Inna wants to invest in one or the other, but not both. Both companies are publicly traded, started with $10,000 of cash, have been in operation exactly one year, have paid the interest owing on their long-term debts to date, and have declared dividends of $1 per share.

The *beginning* balance sheets for the two companies at January 1, 2006, were as follows:

Alpha Company		Omega Company	
Total assets	$10,000	Total assets	$10,000
Long-term debt	$ 1,000	Long-term debt	$ 9,000
Shareholders' equity		Shareholders' equity	
(900 common shares issued)	9,000	(100 common shares issued)	1,000
Total	$10,000	Total	$10,000

In 2006, Alpha Company had a net income of $2,400, while Omega Company's net income was $1,600. Your friend says, "Alpha Company seems the better investment. Its return on investment is 24%, and Omega's is only 16%."

Comment on Inna's observation and on the relative performance of the companies, and give her some investment advice.

PROBLEM 10.8 Performance evaluation using ratios

International Business Computers (IBC) has enjoyed modest success in penetrating the personal computer market since it began operations a few years ago. A new computer line introduced recently has been received well by the general public. However, the president, who is well versed in electronics but not in accounting, is worried about the future of the company.

The company's operating loan is at its limit and more cash is needed to continue operations. The bank wants more information before it extends the company's credit limit.

The president has asked you, as vice-president of finance, to do a preliminary evaluation of the company's performance, using appropriate financial statement analysis, and to recommend possible courses of action for the company. The president particularly wants to know how the company can obtain additional cash. Use the following summary financial information to do your evaluation and make your recommendations.

International Business Computers
Balance Sheets as at December 31 (in 000s)

	2004	2003	2002
Current assets:			
Cash	$ 19	$ 24	$ 50
Marketable securities	37	37	37
Accounts receivable—trade	544	420	257
Inventory	833	503	361
Total current assets	$1,433	$ 984	$ 705
Fixed assets:			
Land	$ 200	$ 200	$ 100
Buildings	350	350	200
Equipment	950	950	700
	$1,500	$1,500	$1,000
Less: Accumulated amortization, buildings and equipment	(447)	(372)	(288)
Net fixed assets	1,053	1,128	712
Total assets	$2,486	$2,112	$1,417
Current liabilities:			
Bank loan	$ 825	$ 570	—
Accounts payable—trade	300	215	$ 144
Other liabilities	82	80	75
Income tax payable	48	52	50
Total current liabilities	$1,255	$ 917	$ 269
Shareholders' equity:			
Common stock	$1,000	$1,000	$1,000
Retained earnings	231	195	148
Total shareholders' equity	$1,231	$1,195	$1,148
Total liabilities and shareholders' equity	$2,486	$2,112	$1,417

International Business Computers
Combined Statements of Income and Retained Earnings
for the Years Ended December 31

	2004	2003	2002
Sales	$3,200	$2,800	$2,340
Cost of goods sold	2,500	2,150	1,800
Gross profit	$ 700	$ 650	$ 540
Expenses	584	533	428
Net income	$ 116	$ 117	$ 112
Opening retained earnings	195	148	96
	$ 311	$ 265	$ 208
Less: Dividends	80	70	60
Closing retained earnings	$ 231	$ 195	$ 148
Other related information included in total expenses:			
Interest expense	$ 89	$ 61	—
Income tax expense	$ 95	$ 102	$ 97

Performing Integrative Ratio Analysis

*** PROBLEM 10.9** Comments on leverage, risk, and Scott formula's analysis

Use nontechnical language to answer the following:

1. What is financial leverage?
2. Why is such leverage risky?
3. How does the Scott formula incorporate leverage?
4. Which is more risky, a company whose Scott formula leverage component is $(0.10 - 0.08) \times 2$, or one whose component is $(0.09 - 0.08) \times 1$? Explain.

PROBLEM 10.10 Answer various questions using ratio analysis

Company A is owned 100% by Mr. A. A summary of Company A's financial statement information is as follows:

Balance Sheet as at September 30, 2006:		
Total assets		$115,000
Total liabilities		$ 50,000
Total shareholder's equity		65,000
Total liabilities and shareholder's equity		$115,000
Income Statement for the year ending September 30, 2006:		
Revenue		$ 45,000
Expenses		
Interest	$ 3,000	
General and operating expenses	27,000	
Income tax (33⅓%)	5,000	35,000
Net income for the year		$ 10,000
Statement of Retained Earnings for the year ending September 30, 2006:		
Balance at beginning of year		$ 25,000
Net income for year		10,000
Balance at end of year		$ 35,000

1. Calculate Company A's return on equity for 2006.
2. What contributes more to return on equity: managerial performance (operating return) or leverage return (financial leverage)? Show all calculations.
3. Company A is considering borrowing $50,000 for additional assets that would earn the company the same return on assets it has historically earned, according to the financial statement information above. The cost of borrowing this money is 8%. Should the company borrow the money? (Assume there are no alternative sources of funding.) Show all calculations. Hint: this is not a present value question.
4. Place yourself in the role of the local bank manager. Mr. A has approached you to lend the company the required $50,000 mentioned above. Detailed financial statement information has already been presented to you.
   a. What additional information would you require, if any?
   b. What financial statement ratios, in addition to those calculated in previous parts of this problem, would be useful in aiding your decision? Do not calculate the ratios, just mention or describe them.

PROBLEM 10.11 Calculate and explain return on equity and effect of debt

A neighbour of yours finds out that you are taking business courses and engages you in a conversation to get some cheap investment advice. She was raised during the Depression and is very averse to debt, believing that solid companies should be debt-free and raise all their capital by issuing shares or by retaining earnings. You have handy a set of financial statements for a company she knows about, which you use to discuss the matter with her.

Use the financial information below, extracted from those financial statements, to calculate the company's return on equity. Explain to your neighbour the effect debt has on the company's return on equity, and, specifically, whether this return is helped or hindered by the company's debt.

Total assets	$410,090
Total liabilities	161,340
Interest-bearing long-term debt	69,400
Share capital	142,050
Income tax rate	43%
Retained earnings	$106,700
Total revenues	510,900
Interest expense	8,270
Income before-tax and unusual item	58,850
Net income	54,300

EXTENDED TIME

PROBLEM 10.12 Use the Scott formula to explain change in performance

The president of General Products Ltd. is curious about why—in spite of growth in revenue, assets, and net income since last year—the company's return on equity has gone down. Last year's ROE was 9.3%, but this year it is 9.0%.

This year's financial statement information shows the following:

- As at September 30, 2006: total assets, $7,500,000; total liabilities, $3,000,000; total owners' equity, $4,500,000.
- For the year ended September 30, 2006: revenue, $2,700,000; interest expense, $300,000; other expenses except income tax, $1,725,000; income tax expense (40%), $270,000; net income, $405,000; dividends declared, $75,000.

1. Prepare a Scott-formula analysis for the year ended September 30, 2006.
2. Explain to the president what the results you derived in part 1 indicate about the company's 2006 performance.
3. The president wants to know what the limitations of the Scott formula for assessing managerial performance are. Remembering that the formula is based on accounting figures, answer the president.
4. Last year's Scott formula for General Products Ltd. (rounded to three decimals) was: 0.093 = (0.164) (0.491) + (0.080 – 0.025) (0.240). Use this and your answer to part 1 to explain to the president why return on equity changed from last year to this year.

PROBLEM 10.13 Analysis of effects of events on Scott formula leverage analysis

You are the chief accountant for Yummy Cookies Inc. and have just calculated the following Scott-formula leverage analysis for the company:

$$\text{ROE} = \text{SR(ATI)} \times \text{AT} + (\text{ROA(ATI)} - \text{IN(ATI)}) \times \text{L/E}$$
$$0.095 = 0.04 \times 2.00 + (0.08 - 0.07) \times 1.5$$

The president is not happy with a return on equity of 9.5% and has asked you to estimate the effects of each of the following changes and events separately:

1. Raising selling prices to increase after-tax sales return by half and asset turnover by 5%.
2. Refinancing the company's debt to reduce the after-tax cost of borrowing to 6%.
3. Reducing operating costs to increase after-tax sales return to 5%.
4. Increasing long-term borrowing and reducing equity to increase the debt-equity ratio to 1.8.

Future Cash Flows: Present Value Analysis • Section 10.7

Understanding Present Value

PROBLEM 10.14 Basic present value analysis

You have just won a large lottery prize and must choose how you wish to receive your winnings. Which of the following will you choose?

1. An immediate payment of $25,000,000.
2. An initial payment of $1,000,000 now and a further 24 annual payments of $1,000,000 at the end of each year.
3. A monthly payment of $80,000 for 25 years. The first payment will be received one month from now.

PROBLEM 10.15 Basic ideas of present value analysis

1. Explain what the "time value of money" or "present value" concept is all about. Why would businesspeople be sensitive to it?
2. Calculate the present value of each of the following:
   a. $1,000 to be received a year from now. If it were on hand now, it would be invested at 10% interest.
   b. $1,000 to be received at the end of each of the next three years. The opportunity cost of interest or cost of capital in this case is 12%.
   c. Answer (b) again but assume a rate of 10%. Why is the present value higher when the rate is lower?

PROBLEM 10.16 Explain effects of some changes on present values

You are working on some project evaluations for your company's president, and have just completed present value calculations. The president asks you to consider some possible changes in the project plans. Explain the effect of each on the present values you have just calculated.

a. One project's time line is shortened by two years, with the total cash flow from the project being the same as originally predicted.
b. The required rate of return on another project is increased from 9% to 11%.
c. Some cash inflows on a third project are expected to be postponed so that they come in during the 5th to 8th years instead of the 3rd to 6th years, though the total cash inflow will remain the same and will still take place over the originally planned 15 years.
d. The company's cost of capital increases by 0.5% as a result of increases in market interest rates.

CHALLENGING

PROBLEM 10.17 Retirement planning

As a newly qualified chartered accountant, you feel it is time you started planning for your retirement. Now aged 25, you plan to retire after working for an additional 30 years. You expect to enjoy 35 years of retirement. After reviewing your desired retirement lifestyle, you feel you will need a pre-tax income of $100,000 per year during retirement.

Required:

1. How much must you save each year to achieve your goal if you achieve an after-tax return on your savings of 8%?
2. Assume you save the same amount as calculated above but achieve a 10% after-tax return. What pre-tax income would this provide for your retirement?
3. How much would you have to save annually to achieve your goal if you only achieve a 5% after-tax return?

Present Value Analysis in Making Decisions

PROBLEM 10.18 Present value analysis—how to finance your car?

Feeling the need for speed, you decide to purchase a Honda Civic Si with all the options as a graduation present to yourself. Your research on the Honda Canada Web site shows that the full price including taxes totals $41,874.29. You estimate that with your current funds and some cash presents from family, you will have to finance $35,000 at 5%.

1. What will your monthly payment be if you finance the vehicle over 48 months?
2. What will your monthly payment be if you finance the vehicle over 60 months?

PROBLEM 10.19 Present value analysis—proposed investment in shares

Surprising Sleepwear Ltd. is considering making an investment in shares of a company that makes fibreglass underwear. The investment will cost $175,000 and will return $8,000 cash per year for four years. At the end of four years, Surprising expects to be able to sell the shares for $200,000. Surprising pays 8% to raise financing for such ventures. Based just on this data, should Surprising buy the shares?

PROBLEM 10.20 Present value analysis—buy or lease a truck?

Speedy Trucking is trying to decide whether it should buy a new truck for its business or lease the truck from another company. If Speedy decides to buy the truck, it must pay $140,000 cash immediately, and the truck is expected to last for five years. At the end of the five years, the truck will have no remaining value and will be disposed of. If Speedy decides to lease the truck, it must pay $30,000 at the end of each year for five years, at which point the truck must be returned to the leasing company.

1. If the current market interest rate (which Speedy has to pay to borrow) is 8%, should Speedy lease or buy the truck?
2. Suppose Speedy discovers that if the truck were bought, it could be sold at the end of the five years for $25,000. Would your answer to part 1 change?
3. Identify one or two important assumptions made in your analyses and explain why those assumptions are important.

PROBLEM 10.21 Buy a kitchenette unit or not?

Harriett is thinking of buying a kitchenette unit for her "handmade goods" store, so that she may sell coffee, cappuccino, cookies, and other such things to browsing customers. She thinks the unit would be a great success, bringing in net cash of $4,500 per year (sales from the unit, less expenses, plus increased sales of handcrafts, less expenses). The unit would cost $20,000 and Harriett would plan to sell it in four years for about $6,500 and buy a bigger one if the idea is a success. Harriett's company would pay about 12% interest on a bank loan to cover the cost of the unit.

Should Harriett's company buy the kitchenette unit? Support your answer with relevant calculations.

PROBLEM 10.22 Answer questions about a blended payments mortgage

You are the accountant for Red River Jeans, which has just obtained a mortgage on its factory. The mortgage carries interest at 5% and requires 10 annual payments of $15,000 beginning a year from when the cash was provided. Answer the following questions:

1. How much cash did Red River receive for the mortgage?
2. What will be the interest expense on the mortgage for the first year?
3. What will be owing on the mortgage at the end of the sixth year?
4. You have to do a balance sheet on the day the mortgage was obtained. In that balance sheet, what will be the current portion of the mortgage, and what will be the noncurrent portion?

CHALLENGING

PROBLEM 10.23 Evaluate business disposition alternatives

A company has decided to discontinue one of its lines of business. It has put the business up for sale and has received three offers. The first is for $750,000 cash. The second is for $250,000 cash now and $75,000 for each of the next 10 years. The third is for a 10-year schedule of payments equalling $75,000 for each of the next five years and $125,000 for each of the remaining five years. The company has studied interest rates and believes it could earn 5% on the money for the next five years and 6% for the five years after that. Which offer is the best one?

Bond and Stock Price Analysis

* **PROBLEM 10.24** Bond pricing

Wescania Inc. plans to issue 100,000 $100 bonds, intending to use the bonds to invest in various business opportunities that are expected to earn an overall 10% return over the 10 years the bonds are outstanding. Bond markets are rather volatile right now, so the company is trying to set the interest rate on the bonds so that they will bring in the needed $10,000,000 without costing more interest than necessary. Right now, the bond market seems to price $100 bonds for companies like Wescania at $100 if they carry interest of 8%, so the company plans to pay 8% interest on the bonds.

1. What would the 8% bonds sell for if Wescania priced them to yield
   a. 8%?
   b. 7%?
   c. 9%?
2. If the company could sell the bonds priced to yield 7%, it would obtain about $700,000 more than the $10,000,000 needed. Does that mean the company would make a greater net income on the projects than it planned, or would it make less?

PROBLEM 10.25 Evaluate a possible investment

Rosie has been saving money for years and has it invested in bank investment certificates that earn 5%. She feels the rate of return is too low and has been looking around for other investment opportunities. She has been considering investing in Natural Body Oils Inc. (NBO), which has been doing very well in recent years. NBO's shares are selling for $15 right now on the Toronto Stock Exchange. Her investigation indicates that a share of NBO may be expected to pay an annual dividend of $1.00 per year and should sell for somewhere between $12 and $20 in five years, at which time Rosie plans to cash all her investments in and buy a condo in a warm place.

What advice would you give Rosie about investing in NBO?

PROBLEM 10.26 Present value analysis—investment choices

You are a rational investor facing a choice of two investment opportunities on December 31, 2004. Your required rate of return is 9%, the current market yield.

1. The first investment is in corporate bonds issued by Big Conglomerate, Inc. (an old and established firm), which have a face value of $100 and pay 8% annual interest on December 31 of each of the next four years, and repay the $100 principal on December 31 of the fourth year.

   What is the value of the $100 Big Conglomerate bond to you?
2. The second alternative is an investment in shares of a small gold mining company recently formed by your uncle. He is quite confident that the company will be able to pay cash dividends according to the following schedule:

Dec. 31/2005	Dec. 31/2006	Dec. 31/2007	Dec. 31/2008
$32 per share	$32 per share	$32 per share	$32 per share

   Based on this schedule, at what price per share would it not matter to you whether you invested some of your money in Big Conglomerate bonds or bought shares in your uncle's mining company?
3. What other factors might you want to consider before you make a decision?

What If Effects Analysis • Sections 10.8 and 10.9

Understanding What If Analysis

* **PROBLEM 10.27** Some effects analysis concepts

1. Why do changes in accounting methods usually have no effect on cash or cash flow?
2. Since the cash flow statement begins with net income, any method change that changes net income will appear to change cash flow. How can this happen when the cash flow statement's total cash flow is unaffected by the change?
3. Can you suggest a situation where an accounting method change *would* affect cash flow as reported on the cash flow statement?
4. Why is it important to take income tax into account when doing "what if" effects analysis?
5. If a company decides to recognize revenue earlier than had been its practice, its accounts receivable will increase. Does this mean that revenue and net income will increase for every year affected by the policy change?

PROBLEM 10.28 General effects analysis

Suppose that on December 31, the last day of its fiscal year, a large company sold bonds by which it borrowed $75,000,000 cash, to be paid back in six years. The money was used on the same day to reduce the company's short-term bank loans by $25,000,000 and buy additional equipment for $50,000,000.

Calculate the changes to the following that would result from the above:

a. Total current assets.
b. Total assets.
c. Total current liabilities.
d. Working capital ratio.
e. Total shareholders' equity.
f. Net earnings for the year ended on the day of the borrowing.
g. Cash and cash equivalents.
h. Cash used for investments.
i. Cash provided from financing.

Describe how predictions of the effects on the following could be made:

j. Return on equity for the period after the loan.
k. Leverage return.

PROBLEM 10.29 Effects on debt and equity changes

Suppose that a company decided to make a common share offering for $45,000,000. $15,000,000 would be used to expand and renovate an existing factory while the remainder would be used to pay down long-term debt. Calculate the change this would have upon the company's

a. Total assets
b. Total liabilities
c. Total shareholders' equity
d. Debt-equity ratio
e. Cash provided from financing activities
f. Cash provided from investing activities
g. Cash on hand

Performing What If Analysis

* **PROBLEM 10.30** Effects of changing doubtful accounts allowance, with tax

"Karl, we have a problem in our accounts receivable. We've provided an allowance for doubtful accounts of 2% of the gross receivables, but during this recession more customers are running into trouble. The allowance should be raised to 5%."

"Tanya, we can't do that. It would wipe out our profitability and ruin our cash flow."

Given the data below, prepare an analysis for Karl and Tanya. (If you have not yet studied the allowance for doubtful accounts, Tanya's proposal would reduce income by the indicated increase in the allowance.)

Data:	Gross accounts receivable at year-end	$8,649,000
	Net income for the year at present	$223,650
	Income tax rate	30%

PROBLEM 10.31 Effects of ending a policy of capitalizing advertising costs, with income tax

Checkup Auto Services Inc., which has been in business one year, has a chain of heavily advertised automobile service centres. The company's income tax rate is 35%. The company makes it a practice to capitalize a portion of its advertising costs as a "deferred asset." The amount of advertising cost capitalized this year was $100,000 and the new company's policy is to amortize the capitalized amount to expense at 20% per year. An accountant suggested to the company's vice-president of finance that the policy of capitalizing advertising should be ended because the future economic benefit from the expenditures is not clearly determinable. The vice-president wants to know what effect such policy changes would have.

PROBLEM 10.32 Effects of proposed policy of capitalizing improvement costs, with income tax

Senior management of Telemark Skiing Ltd. wishes to capitalize $2,650,000 in ski hill improvement costs expended this year and amortize the capitalized costs over 10 years, rather than just expensing them all as is now done. The company's income tax rate is 30%, and the company would plan to continue deducting the costs as expenses in computing income tax payable for this year, assuming the tax authorities would permit that. What would be the effect on this year's net income and cash flow from operations if the company capitalized those costs?

Performing What If Analysis with Income and Ratio Effects

*** PROBLEM 10.33** Effects analysis of truck fleet purchase and financing

Suppose that on May 1, 2006, Large Corporation decides to purchase a new fleet of delivery trucks at a total cost of $5,800,000. The trucks will be paid for in cash, which Large Corporation will raise by using $2,200,000 cash on hand, issuing shares for $2,000,000, and borrowing $1,600,000 over 20 years from the bank.

1. Using the preceding information, fill in the blanks below, indicating the magnitude and direction of the change in each category the truck purchase will cause.

Large Corporation
Changes in Balance Sheet at May 1, 2006

Cash equivalent assets	$______	Cash equivalent liabilities	$______
Other current assets	$______	Other current liabilities	$______
Noncurrent assets	$______	Noncurrent liabilities	$______
		Share capital	$______
		Retained earnings	$______
Total assets	$______	Total liabilities & owners' equity	$______

2. What effect (if any) will this event have on the financing activities section of the cash flow statement for the year?
3. What effect (if any) will this event have on the income statement for the year?
4. Which important financial statement ratios would you expect this event to affect?
5. Record the above event as a journal entry.

PROBLEM 10.34 Loan and policy change effects analyses

1. Strapped Ltd., which has $210,000 in current assets and $180,000 in current liabilities, borrows $50,000 from the bank as a long-term loan, repayable in four years. What is the effect of this loan on working capital? On the working capital ratio? On current net income?
2. Slipshod Inc. has discovered that it has not estimated enough warranty expenses because more customers are returning products for repair than had been expected. The company decides to recognize an additional $210,000 in noncurrent warranty liability, and therefore in corresponding expenses: $145,000 in respect to sales recognized in the current year and $65,000 in respect to prior years' sales. The company's income tax rate is 40%. What will this do to the current year's net income? To retained earnings? To cash from operations? To the working capital ratio?

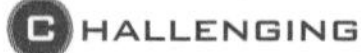

PROBLEM 10.35 Multiple-issue effects analysis, with tax

Cranberry Costumes Ltd. has been operating for several years now. So far the income for the current year is $75,000, before income tax at 30%. (The preceding year's income before tax was $62,000, and the tax rate then was also 30%.) Owner Jan Berry is considering a few changes and has asked your advice. The possible changes are:

- Change the revenue recognition policy to recognize revenue earlier in the process. This would increase accounts receivable by $26,000 immediately and $28,000 at the end of the previous year.
- Make a monthly accrual of the bonuses paid to employees at the end of each fiscal year. This would increase accounts payable by $11,000 immediately and $7,000 at the end of the preceding year.

- Postpone for five years repayment of a $19,000 loan (by Jan to the company), which has up to now been classified as a current liability.
- Capitalize as a trademark asset $14,000 of advertising supplies and wages expense recorded in the preceding year.

1. Calculate the net income after income tax for the current year that will result if all of the changes are adopted, and discuss the economic reasons for considering each change.
2. Calculate the effect on the amount of cash in the bank account of Cranberry Costumes Ltd. that these changes will have.
3. Explain any difference between results calculated for part 1 and part 2 above.

CHALLENGING

PROBLEM 10.36 Effects analysis, with ratios

Funtime Toys Inc. invents, manufactures, and sells toys and children's board games. In 2006, financial executives at Funtime decided to change two accounting methods.

- First, they decided to capitalize certain costs related to the development of new educational games, which had previously been expensed as incurred. It was thought that market demand for the games had been strong for several years, and that development costs were sure to provide future benefits.
- Second, the amortization method used on one class of equipment was changed to produce an annual amortization expense that was thought to better match the company's revenue generation process.

The effects of these changes on development and amortization expenses for the fiscal years 2005 and 2006 are shown below. The company's income tax rate is 30% and the method changes would affect future, not current, income tax.

Development Expense	**2005**	**2006**
Old method	$ 70,000	$ 90,000
New method	60,000	81,000
Amortization Expense	**2005**	**2006**
Old method	$160,000	$180,000
New method	175,000	170,000

Determine the combined impact the two method changes have on each of the following items for 2005 and 2006. Decide whether each item increases, decreases, or is not affected. (Check each ratio carefully to determine the impact on both the numerator and the denominator.)

a. Net income.
b. Working capital at the end of the year.
c. Total assets at the end of the year.
d. Debt-equity ratio at the end of the year.
e. Return on year-end equity.
f. Total asset turnover.

Multi-Year What-If Analysis

* **PROBLEM 10.37** Basic multi-year effects analysis, with income tax

Mistaya Ltd. has decided to change its revenue recognition policy to increase revenue $10,000 in the current year and by a total of $8,000 in prior years (accounts receivable are increased correspondingly). Matched expenses increase $4,000 in the current year and $3,000 in prior years (so accounts payable go up as well). The company's income tax rate is 35%.

Determine all effects of the change on the company's income statement and cash flow statement for the current year and balance sheet as at the end of the current year. Show your calculations and demonstrate that all the effects balance.

PROBLEM 10.38 Multi-year effects analysis without considering income tax

Record Sales Inc. has the following history for its first three years of existence:

	2006	2005	2004
Revenue:			
Credit sales	$1,100,000	$700,000	$500,000
Cash sales	100,000	90,000	40,000
Cash collected from customers*	1,050,000	740,000	420,000
Accounts receivable that became:			
Doubtful during the year	50,000	25,000	10,000
Worthless during the year	20,000	40,000	5,000

* Including cash sales

The president, John Record, is wondering what difference to the company's working capital and income before income tax it would make if the company used one of the following accounts receivable valuation methods:

a. Make no allowance for doubtful or bad debts and just keep trying to collect.
b. Write off worthless accounts, but make no allowance for doubtful ones.
c. Allow for doubtful and worthless accounts when they become known.

Provide an analysis for the president.

PROBLEM 10.39 Effects of recognizing supplies inventory, with tax

Magnic Manufacturing Co. has large amounts of manufacturing supplies that have been recorded as an expense when purchased. Now the company is considering recognizing the supplies on hand as an asset. If this were done, a new supplies inventory account would appear in the current assets. Its balance would be $148,650 at the end of last year and $123,860 at the end of this year. The company's income tax rate is 30%.

Calculate the effect on each of the following that would result if the company changed its accounting to recognize the supplies inventory:

1. Retained earnings at the end of last year.
2. Income tax liability at the end of last year.
3. Supplies expense for this year.
4. Net income for this year.
5. Current assets at the end of this year.
6. Income tax liability at the end of this year.
7. Retained earnings at the end of this year.
8. Cash flow for this year.
9. Cash flow for next year.

PROBLEM 10.40 Multi-year effects analysis, with tax

Kennedy Controls Inc. is considering a change in its accounting for maintenance costs. The chief financial officer proposes that the company capitalize 20% of its maintenance expenses, on the grounds that some of that expenditure has created additional plant assets. The company, the income tax rate for which is 40%, has existed for four years and amortizes its plant assets at 10% of year-end cost.

Here are some relevant account balances for the last four years, before considering the above proposal:

	Year 1	Year 2	Year 3	Year 4
Expenditures on plant assets	$1,243,610	$ 114,950	$ 34,770	$ 111,240
Balance in the plant assets account	1,243,610	1,358,560	1,393,330	1,504,570
Amortization expense	124,361	135,856	139,333	150,457
Accumulated amortization	124,361	260,217	399,550	550,007
Maintenance expense	43,860	64,940	73,355	95,440

Determine the effects of the proposed change on the *Year 4* income statement, cash flow statement, and balance sheet at the *end of Year 4.*

PROBLEM 10.41 Effects of an inventory error, with tax

On December 20, 2004, Profit Company Ltd. received merchandise amounting to $1,000, half of which was counted in its December 31 listing of all inventory items on hand. The invoice was not received until January 4, 2005, at which time the acquisition was recorded as of that date. The acquisition should have been recorded in 2004. Assume that the periodic inventory method is used (that is, the inventory asset is based on what was counted as being on hand, and the cost of goods sold expense is deduced as "beginning inventory + purchases – ending inventory" and that the company's income tax rate is 40%. Indicate the effect (overstatement, understatement, none) and the amount of the effect, if any, on each of the following:

1. Inventory as at December 31, 2004.
2. Inventory as at December 31, 2005.
3. Cost of goods sold expense, 2004.
4. Cost of goods sold expense, 2005.
5. Net income for 2004.
6. Net income for 2005.
7. Accounts payable as at December 31, 2004.
8. Accounts payable as at December 31, 2005.
9. Retained earnings as at December 31, 2004.
10. Retained earnings as at December 31, 2005.

Integrated Problems

Analyze Petro-Canada's Financial Statements

Information for Problems 10.42*, 10.43*, and 10.44*: Petro-Canada

Petro-Canada, headquartered in Calgary, is a national oil company with operations across Canada, including oil from the Grand Banks of Atlantic Canada and from the Syncrude project in Alberta, natural gas in various parts of Western Canada, and gas stations in most parts of the country. Below are its 2004 financial statements (without notes or accounting policies). Use those statements to answer the following three problems.

Petro-Canada
Consolidated Balance Sheet
(stated in millions of Canadian dollars)

As at December 31,	**2004**	**2003** (Note 2)
Assets		
Current assets		
Cash and cash equivalents (Note 13)	**$ 170**	$ 635
Accounts receivable (Note 11)	**1,254**	1,503
Inventories (Note 14)	**549**	551
Prepaid expenses	**13**	16
	1,986	2,705
Property, plant and equipment, net (Note 15)	**14,783**	10,943
Goodwill (Note 12)	**986**	810
Deferred charges and other assets (Note 16)	**345**	316
	$ 18,100	$ 14,774
Liabilities and shareholders' equity		
Current liabilities		
Accounts payable and accrued liabilities	**$ 2,223**	$ 1,822
Income taxes payable	**370**	300
Short-term notes payable	**299**	–
Current portion of long-term debt (Note 17)	**6**	6
	2,898	2,128
Long-term debt (Note 17)	**2,275**	2,223
Other liabilities (Note 18)	**646**	306
Asset retirement obligations (Note 19)	**834**	773
Future income taxes (Note 7)	**2,708**	1,756
Commitments and contingent liabilities (Note 25)		
Shareholders' equity (Note 20)	**8,739**	7,588
	$ 18,100	$ 14,774

Approved on behalf of the Board of Directors

Ron A. Brenneman, *Director* Brian F. MacNeill, *Director*

Petro-Canada
Consolidated Statement of Earnings
(stated in millions of Canadian dollars)

For the years ended December 31,	**2004**	2003 (Note 2)	2002 (Note 2)
Revenue			
Operating	**$14,687**	$12,887	$10,374
Investment and other income (Note 4)	**(310)**	12	–
	14,377	12,899	10,374
Expenses			
Crude oil and product purchases	**6,740**	5,620	4,837
Operating, marketing and general (Note 5)	**2,690**	2,557	2,222
Exploration (Note 15)	**235**	271	301
Depreciation, depletion and amortization (Notes 5 and 15)	**1,402**	1,560	977
Foreign currency translation (Note 6)	**(77)**	(251)	52
Interest	**142**	182	187
	11,132	9,939	8,576
Earnings before income taxes	**3,245**	2,960	1,798
Provision for income taxes (Note 7)			
Current	**1,461**	1,247	959
Future	**27**	63	(116)
	1,488	1,310	843
Net earnings	**$ 1,757**	$ 1,650	$ 955
Earnings per share (Note 8)			
Basic	**$ 6.64**	$ 6.23	$ 3.63
Diluted	**$ 6.55**	$ 6.16	$ 3.59

Petro-Canada
Consolidated Statement of Retained Earnings
(stated in millions of Canadian dollars)

For the years ended December 31,	**2004**	2003 (Note 2)	2002 (Note 2)
Retained earnings at beginning of year, as previously reported	**$3,943**	$2,380	$1,511
Retroactive application of change in accounting for asset retirement obligations (Note 2)	**(133)**	(114)	(95)
Retained earnings at beginning of year, as restated	**$3,810**	$2,266	$1,416
Net earnings	**1,757**	1,650	955
Dividends on common shares	**(159)**	(106)	(105)
Retained earnings at end of year	**$5,408**	$3,810	$2,266

Petro-Canada
Consolidated Statement of Cash Flows
(stated in millions of Canadian dollars)

For the years ended December 31,	2004	2003 (Note 2)	2002 (Note 2)
Operating activities			
Net earnings	**$ 1,757**	$ 1,650	$ 955
Items not affecting cash flow from operating activities before changes in noncash working capital (Note 9)	**1,755**	1,451	1,020
Exploration expenses (Note 15)	**235**	271	301
Cash flow from operating activities before changes in noncash working capital	**3,747**	3,372	2,276
Proceeds from sale of accounts receivable (Note 11)	**399**	–	–
Increase (decrease) in other noncash working capital related to operating activities (Note 10)	**133**	(164)	(226)
Cash flow from operating activities	**4,279**	3,208	2,050
Investing activities			
Expenditures on property, plant and equipment and exploration (Note 15)	**(4,073)**	(2,315)	(1,861)
Proceeds from sales of assets	**44**	165	26
Increase in deferred charges and other assets	**(36)**	(147)	(72)
Acquisition of Prima Energy Corporation (Note 12)	**(644)**	–	–
Acquisition of oil and gas operations of Veba Oil and Gas GmbH (Note 12)	**–**	–	(2,234)
(Increase) decrease in noncash working capital related to investing activities (Note 10)	**10**	94	(16)
	(4,699)	(2,203)	(4,157)
Financing activities			
Increase in short-term notes payable	**314**	–	–
Proceeds from issue of long-term debt	**533**	804	2,100
Repayment of long-term debt	**(299)**	(1,352)	(465)
Proceeds from issue of common shares	**39**	50	30
Purchase of common shares (Note 20)	**(447)**	–	–
Dividends on common shares	**(159)**	(106)	(105)
Increase in noncash working capital related to financing activities (Note 10)	**(26)**	–	–
	(45)	(604)	1,560
Increase (decrease) in cash and cash equivalents	**(465)**	401	(547)
Cash and cash equivalents at beginning of year	**635**	234	781
Cash and cash equivalents at end of year (Note 13)	**$ 170**	$ 635	$ 234

*** PROBLEM 10.42** Interpret Petro-Canada's cash flow statement

Use the above Petro-Canada cash flow statement, and other statements where relevant, to answer the following questions:

1. Why is the company's cash from operating activities ($4,279 million in 2004, for example) so much greater than its earnings ($1,757 million in 2004, for example)?
2. The notes to the financial statements are not included above. What kinds of accounts are likely to be mentioned in Notes 9 and 10?
3. Write a paragraph identifying the major components of the company's cash flows over the three years.
4. Interpret the company's cash flow and financial strategy, particularly for 2004, using for reference the points a–i set out in Section 10.5 and used there to comment on CPR.

*** PROBLEM 10.43** Analyze Petro-Canada's financial position

Prepare an analysis of and commentary on Petro-Canada's financial position at the end of 2004, as compared to 2003, using the balance sheet above and any relevant information from the other financial statements above.

EXTENDED TIME

*** PROBLEM 10.44** Do a performance analysis of Petro-Canada

1. Using the Petro-Canada financial statements above, prepare a few ratios relevant to analyzing the company's financial performance for 2004 as compared to 2003, and comment on what those ratios show.
2. Did Petro-Canada benefit from financial leverage in 2004? How did that compare to 2003? Answer these questions simply, without use of the Scott formula.
3. Answer the questions in part 2 using the Scott formula, and comment on the relative sizes of operating and leverage returns in 2004 and 2003.

Analyze Sleeman Breweries Ltd.'s Financial Statements

Information for Problems 10.45, 10.46 and 10.47: Sleeman Breweries Ltd.

Sleeman Breweries Ltd. is headquartered in Guelph, Ontario. According to Note 1 in the 2004 Annual Report, Sleeman "develops, produces, imports, markets and distributes beer for sale to provincial liquor distribution organizations and entities engaged in the food and beverage industries within Canada." Below are its financial statements (without notes or accounting policies) for the year ended January 1, 2005. Use those statements to answer the following three problems. (Note that Sleeman had 16,259,645 common shares outstanding at January 1, 2005, and 15,971,050 at December 27, 2003.)

Sleeman Breweries Ltd.
Consolidated Balance Sheets
(in thousands of dollars)

	January 1, 2005	December 27, 2003
ASSETS		
Current		
Accounts receivable –Trade	**$ 34,529**	$ 30,322
–Other (Note 5)	**9,196**	6,363
Income taxes recoverable	**697**	–
Inventories (Note 6)	**39,147**	31,054
Prepaid expenses	**6,589**	5,379
	90,158	73,118
Note receivable (Note 5)	**1,083**	2,166
Property, plant and equipment (Note 7)	**100,748**	74,691
Long-term investment and executive loans (Note 8)	**3,311**	6,337
Intangible assets (Note 9)	**104,852**	86,443
	$ 300,152	$ 242,755
LIABILITIES		
Current		
Bank indebtedness (Note 10)	**$ 9,634**	$ 555
Accounts payable and accrued liabilities	**39,146**	39,299
Income taxes payable	**–**	2,284
Current portion of long-term debt (Note 11)	**12,043**	13,374
	60,823	55,512
Long-term debt (Note 11)	**103,616**	71,916
Future income taxes (Note 12)	**13,929**	11,527
	178,368	138,955
SHAREHOLDERS' EQUITY		
Share capital (Note 13)	**48,353**	45,075
Contributed surplus	**308**	28
Retained earnings	**73,123**	58,697
	121,784	103,800
	$ 300,152	$ 242,755

Approved by the Board

Pierre Des Marais II, *Director* Ken Hallat, *Director*

Sleeman Breweries Ltd.
Consolidated Statements of Earnings and Retained Earnings
(in thousands of dollars except per share amounts)

	Fiscal Year Ended	
	January 1, 2005	December 27, 2003
Net revenue	**$ 213,354**	$ 185,036
Cost of goods sold	**106,207**	96,703
Gross margin	**107,147**	88,333
Gain on settlement of obligation (Note 4)	–	591
Selling, general and administrative	**71,204**	55,523
Earnings before the undernoted	**35,943**	33,401
Depreciation and amortization	**7,172**	6,301
Interest expense—net	**6,643**	6,097
Earnings before income taxes	**22,128**	21,003
Income taxes (Note 12)	**7,702**	8,750
Net earnings	**14,426**	12,253
Retained earnings, beginning of year	**58,697**	46,444
Retained earnings, end of year	**$ 73,123**	$ 58,697
Earnings per share (Note 15)		
Basic	**$ 0.89**	$ 0.77
Diluted	**$ 0.87**	$ 0.76

Sleeman Breweries Ltd.
Consolidated Statements of Cash Flow
(in thousands of dollars except per share amounts)

	Fiscal Year Ended	
	January 1, 2005	December 27, 2003
Net inflow (outflow) of cash related to the following activities:		
Operating		
Net earnings	**$ 14,426**	$ 12,253
Items not affecting cash		
Depreciation and amortization	**7,172**	6,301
Future income taxes	**2,184**	3,221
Gain on settlement of obligation (Note 4)	**–**	(591)
Noncash interest charges in income	**(314)**	(90)
Stock-based compensation expense	**280**	28
Loss (gain) on disposal of equipment	**(5)**	4
	23,743	21,126
Changes in noncash operating working capital items (Note 16)	**(10,544)**	(7,533)
	13,199	13,593
Investing		
Business acquisitions (net) (Note 3)	**(40,265)**	–
Proceeds from sale of agency agreement	**1,176**	980
Additions to property, plant and equipment	**(15,735)**	(8,652)
Additions to intangible assets	**(859)**	(2,105)
Proceeds from executive loans	**1,499**	249
Proceeds from disposal of equipment	**630**	19
	(53,554)	(9,509)
Financing		
Net increase in bank operating loans	**8,388**	(9,906)
Stock options exercised	**3,274**	1,322
Long-term debt—proceeds	**41,193**	90,000
Long-term debt—principal repayments	**(12,500)**	(85,500)
	40,355	(4,084)
Change in cash and cash balance, end of year	**$ –**	$ –
Supplemental disclosures of cash flows:		
Interest paid	**$ 7,433**	$ 6,121
Income taxes paid, net of cash refunds of $885 (2002 –$221)	**$ 7,439**	$ 3,332

PROBLEM 10.45 Analyze Sleeman's financial performance

Using the above financial statements, prepare an analysis and interpretation of Sleeman Breweries Ltd.'s 2004 financial performance in comparison to 2003. Use relevant performance-related ratios from Section 10.4 plus the company's cash flow information.

EXTENDED TIME

PROBLEM 10.46 Analyze Sleeman's financial position

Using the above financial statements, prepare an analysis and interpretation of Sleeman Breweries Ltd.'s financial position as at January 1, 2005 (2004 fiscal year), in comparison to 2003. Use any relevant ratios and cash flow information.

EXTENDED TIME

PROBLEM 10.47 Analyze Sleeman's leverage

Using the above financial statements, prepare an analysis, using the Scott formula, of whether, and to what extent, Sleeman benefited from leverage in 2004 as compared to 2003.

Analyze Canadian National Railway Company's Financial Statements

Information for Problems 10.48, 10.49, and 10.50: Canadian National Railway Company.

The Canadian National Railway Company (CN) is Canada's largest railway company and one of CPR's largest competitors. In order to answer the following questions, you will need to find CN's financial statements available on its Web site at **www.cn.ca**. Look for a link titled About CN and navigate to find the annual report section. If you are using the 2004 annual report as this question does, there are two complete sets of financial statements. Use only the Canadian GAAP statements of the 2004 annual report. You should be able to answer the same kinds of questions for years after 2004, depending on what information CN posts to its Web site in later years.

EXTENDED TIME

PROBLEM 10.48 Examine CN's cash flow and financial performance

Examine CN's financial statements.

1. Write a paragraph identifying the major components of the company's cash flows over the three years.
2. What caused financing activities to switch from a cash outflow in 2003 to a cash inflow in 2004? Why might this change have been necessary?
3. Using CN's financial statements, prepare an analysis of the company's financial performance in 2004 compared to 2003. Use any relevant ratios and information.

PROBLEM 10.49 Analyze CN's leverage

Using the above financial statements, prepare an analysis, using the Scott formula, of whether, and to what extent, CN benefited from leverage in 2004 as compared to 2003.

PROBLEM 10.50 Compare CN to CPR

The Canadian National Railway Company is one of the main competitors to the Canadian Pacific Railway Company. Compare the analysis you have just completed on CN in Problems 10.48 and 10.49 to the analysis of CPR presented in the chapter. Does each company display the same trends in terms of financial performance between 2004 and 2003? Do the companies' strategies of financing or growth seem to be similar? Discuss these issues and any other relevant information.

CASE 10A

USING ANALYSIS TO CATCH PROBLEMS

Read the article "Hide and Seek" below and then discuss its list of ten "red flags" that investors should beware of in evaluating the story told by the financial statements. Here are just some ideas to get you started:

- How has what you have learned about accounting helped you to recognize or avoid the red flags?
- How might the ratio and leverage analysis covered in this chapter be used to identify problems such as those identified in the article?
- Does the existence of such problems indicate weaknesses in financial accounting that should be addressed?
- Can you suggest other red flags in addition to the article's ten?

HIDE AND SEEK

Accounting tricks make it difficult for investors to get a true picture of a company's finances. Here are 10 red flags to watch out for.

By John Gray

So you thought it was safe to go back into the investing waters. For years, some companies have played fast and loose with their reported earnings. Analysts, shareholders and the media embraced the farce of pro forma earnings that often have only a casual relationship to standard accounting practices—and uncritical investors rewarded those companies with soaring share prices and huge management compensation packages. But that's all changed now, right? The collapse of Enron Corp., the Houston-based energy trading giant that used invisible ink to write its financial statements; the bankruptcy of Global Crossing, the Bermuda-based telecom giant; criticism over accounting practices at Tyco International and even IBM—it's put a stop to all those accounting shenanigans, hasn't it?

Wrong, warns Al Rosen, forensic accountant, chairman of Toronto-based Veritas Investment Research Corp. and one of Canada's staunchest critics of accounting monkey business. "That's a bunch of bull," he says. "There are still plenty of companies out there playing accounting dirty tricks, and they can't afford to stop." As we enter yet another earnings season, and gear up for the release of dozens of annual reports, Rosen and other independent financial analysts are predicting just as much accounting tomfoolery as in the past.

Rosen has often been a lone voice in the wilderness, accusing companies of misleading shareholders through a variety of ingenious—and, unfortunately, perfectly legal—accounting schemes. But the slowing economy and the end of the bull market last year made it more difficult for companies to hide their financial sins; as a result, shareholders have become hungry for more critical analysis of the companies in which they have invested. (In a recent study of 150 randomly chosen companies, the Ontario Securities Commission found fault with the interim financial reporting of 77.) The collapse of Enron—with its bogus financial statements given the seal of approval by auditor Arthur Andersen LLP (which has been indicted by a federal grand jury in Houston)—has shown that shareholders themselves must cast the first critical eye on a company's financials. As Wall Street giant Goldman Sachs stated in a recent report: "There is a need now, more than ever, for financial statements users to delve into company reports to ferret out accounting's 'smoke and mirrors.'"

It is a daunting task, but something shareholders now must do to protect themselves from the financial landmines planted in some company financial statements, says Robin Schwill, an insolvency lawyer with the Toronto-based law firm of Osler, Hoskin & Harcourt LLP, who also teaches an MBA course on financial statement interpretation at York University's Schulich School of Business. "This is hard work," Schwill concedes. "But if you don't do it, you are not an investor—you are a gambler who is taking a roll of the dice."

Not that an amateur analyst would have been able to uncover Enron's complex web of financial indiscretions.

Indeed, in the wake of the scandal, US President George W. Bush has proposed a 10-point corporate responsibility plan, which, among other things, would force CEOs to vouch for the veracity of information in their financial statements. In the meanwhile, there are plenty of red flags that investors should look for to ensure that earnings statements reflect the company's bottom line.

1 The Big Bath

Canadian investors have become all too familiar with the strategy known as "Big Bath Accounting." In the wake of the tech-stock meltdown, once-stellar companies such as Nortel Networks Corp. and JDS Uniphase Corp. broke records with the size of their writedowns. Last year, Nortel announced a staggering six-month net loss of more than US$19 billion; not to be outdone, JDS reported an annual loss of US$50.6 billion. Investors should prepare for more big baths this year, as companies try to account for the loss of revenue as a result of recession and the Sept. 11 terrorist attacks—and as they grapple with changes to the Canadian Institute of Chartered Accountants standards, which shorten the length of time in which firms can write down such charges as goodwill. "A lot of companies are going to take a vacuum cleaner to the books and take as big a hit as they can to get these charges off their books," says Rosen.

It has already started. In February, Montreal-based Quebecor Inc. warned investors that it might have to write off between $1.5 billion and $2 billion in goodwill related to their purchase of Le Groupe Vidéotron Ltée. Quebecor's $5.4-billion purchase of the cable company in late 2000 pushed its depreciation and amortization costs up by $174.1 million and increased its financial expenses to $214.2 million. That helped force the company to post a net loss of $241.7 million, or a whopping $3.74 per share, last year.

Now, taking a huge loss is not as bad as tweaking the numbers to boost profits. But it makes it just as difficult for investors to properly evaluate the company and compare it to its peers who have not taken a loss. After all, once a company has taken a multibillion-dollar charge, just about anything looks good. Taking a large writeoff in the wake of a bad transaction is appropriate, says Larry Woods, an independent financial analyst based in Hamilton, Ont. However, many companies write down every conceivable charge—even inventories on which they will eventually see some return. "The money they eventually earn from those transactions then seeps into the companies' operational earnings," Woods says, "making it impossible to determine if the revenue is from core businesses or from stuff they previously wrote off."

2 Everything-but-the-Bad-Stuff Accounting

A more common practice is for companies to highlight "everything but the bad stuff" in their quarterly earnings press releases, says Rosen. Companies in the tech sector perfected the practice, but it has spread well beyond Silicon Valley. Take the Toronto-Dominion Bank, which in February announced quarterly earnings of $526 million. That figure was based on what the bank describes as "operating cash basis," which excludes "items it doesn't consider to be part of its normal operations" such as acquisition funding costs associated with its purchase of Canada Trust in 2000. However, TD does not exclude the revenue that has flowed into the bank from the Canada Trust merger. The result is a distorted picture of the bank's performance. Lower down in the filing the bank reports that under standard accounting rules, net earnings are $355 million—a 32.5% drop.

Claude Lamoureux, president and CEO of the Ontario Teachers' Pension Plan (OTPP) Board, decries the practice of trumpeting pro forma earnings in press releases and public discussions with shareholders. He has called on Canadian firms to base all their press releases on financial statements that comply with generally accepted accounting principles (GAAP) and are approved by both the company's auditor and the audit committee of the board of directors.

3 Moving Debt off the Balance Sheet

The accounting technique made infamous by Enron was its use of special purpose entities (SPE) to move debt off its balance sheet. Use of off-balance-sheet financing has become increasingly popular in recent years, according to a recent Goldman Sachs report. This is perhaps the most dangerous accounting gimmick, because it is very difficult to determine from financial filings exactly when a company has entered into these agreements. As the Goldman Sachs report notes, "Accounting sleuths must delve through the investing company's audited financial statements in search of footnotes that may list financing-related associates, affiliates, or partnerships." The lack of disclosure makes it impossible for investors to determine how much the company must pay to fully service its debt or to fulfill other contractual obligations, says Woods. "Companies have been piling on debt for years now, and these off-balance-sheet entities can be the straw that breaks the camel's back."

4 Pension Plan Makeover

Pension plan accounting is complicated, esoteric and not entirely logical. But what every shareholder needs to understand is that most companies have obligations to fund their pension plan to a certain level. Any shortfall must eventually be made up by contributions from the company's coffers. During the bull market of the past few years, companies were able to cut back on contributions, as gains in the stock market helped keep pension plans healthy. But even as stock prices stumbled, or fell dramatically, many firms kept on predicting robust growth of their pension investments to help boost their bottom line.

Take Toronto-based Imperial Oil Ltd., which in its most recent annual report noted that expected gains in its pension plan were calculated at about 10%, allowing it to book a $259-million reduction in pension expense. At the same time, however, the company reported that the *actual* gains on its pension plan were more along the lines of $157 million.

Fiddling with the pension fund is a common accounting trick. With all markets down substantially from the previous years, most mutual funds showing negative returns, and a growing number of baby boomers poised to start collecting their pensions, shareholders have to ask themselves how long it will be before companies have to start dipping into revenue to top up those plans.

5 Turning Expenses into Assets

You have to spend money to make money, right? Well, not in the world of creative accounting. With a little sleight of hand you can easily turn costs (which your peers are listing as expenses) into assets. Laval, Que.-based BioChem Pharma Inc. (which merged with UK drug maker Shire Pharmaceuticals in May, 2001) used this audacious strategy in 1998 when it established CliniChem, a sister company, to handle all its research and development. By funnelling BioChem's R&D work through CliniChem, which then promptly hired BioChem to actually do the work, the company magically changed one of the most expensive costs for a biotech into revenue. (When Rosen publicly criticized the company in this magazine, he didn't get letters from shareholders thanking him for his analysis. Rather, he got inquiries from other companies looking for advice on how to set up similar schemes.)

6 Not All Earnings Are Created Equally

From what source does a company derive its income? Are earnings coming from core operations, or are they supplemented with a host of other sales from affiliated operations, tax credits, sale of assets or investing profits?

With the economy dragging and sales lagging, many companies are likely to post a loss this year. As a result, they will qualify for tax credits that can be manipulated to manage the bottom line. These credits can give a false impression of how successful a company is in selling its goods or services. Such is the case for Toronto-based Imax Corp., which reported more than 90% of a calculated US$46-million tax effect in 2000, helping reduce its net loss for the year. Such credits also have a nasty habit of disappearing as the company reassesses its finances. This was the case with Consumers Packaging Inc. The Toronto-based glass manufacturer, whose stock has been suspended from trading since December, recorded a $20-million tax asset in 1999, only to cancel it the next year.

7 Adding Water to the Wine

Few accounting subjects are as controversial as the issue of how companies account for stock-based compensation. Most stock option plans are not considered an expense and do not need to be accounted for on the books at all. But they can have a significant effect on the value of shareholders' investments. A recent survey by *Canadian Business* found company after company that would have seen reported earnings slashed by as much as 200% had they been forced to expense stock option plans.

Shareholders must constantly monitor the use of shares to compensate management or to acquire rival companies, or they run the risk of seeing their investment watered down as the profit pie gets cut into more and smaller pieces. As OTPP head Lamoureux points out, between 1998 and 2001 Nortel reported 14% sales growth; however, on a per-share basis, that translated into a decline of 26% over the same period. JDS Uniphase reported a staggering 586% increase in sales during that period. However, if calculated on a per-share basis, it dwindles to a relatively small 81% increase over the same four years.

8 Channel Stuffing

Nothing will destroy a company's ability to meet analysts' earnings expectations more than having a warehouse full of unsold goods. Rather than come clean and tell shareholders they have not met sales expectations, some companies are tempted to move their merchandise to the market knowing that much of it is going to come back unsold or will have to be sold at a massive discount. Investors looking for evidence of channel stuffing should look for large changes to stated inventory levels, or an increase in the contingencies set aside for bad accounts.

The most powerful example of the practice was the fall from grace of "Chainsaw" Al Dunlap, the former head of Sunbeam Corp., the US appliance maker. He allegedly moved millions of dollars in merchandise onto the backs of distributors and retailers using discounts and other inducements. That, along with the use of cash reserves to pump up the company's operating earnings, resulted in a record-breaking US$189 million in reported earnings in fiscal 1997. But when the scheme was uncovered, Sunbeam was forced to restate its earnings from the fourth quarter of 1996 to the first quarter of 1998; the US Securities and Exchange Commission (SEC) alleges that US$60 million of that record-breaking profit was the result of accounting fraud. An SEC lawsuit against Dunlap, other Sunbeam executives and a former partner of Arthur Andersen, its auditor, is still ongoing. Dunlap and a group of former Sunbeam executives recently settled a class action lawsuit, agreeing to pay more than US$15 million to shareholders.

9 Changing Horses

As the Canadian and US economies continue to grow closer, the stocks of many companies trade on both Canadian and US exchanges. These companies may make their primary financial reporting in accordance with either Canadian or US accounting principles, which allows them to shop around and see which set of standards provides the rosiest picture. "If a company suddenly changes which accounting standards it is reporting under," Rosen says, "you had better look pretty closely at the books to see why."

Depending on the industry, or the transaction, a switch from Canadian GAAP to US GAAP can subtract millions from the bottom line. "Much of Canadian GAAP income is not income at all under US GAAP," says Rosen.

10 Words to Live or Die by

There are certain words used by companies that are a major red flag for accounting sleuths. For instance, if you find a "going concern" note in the company's financial statements, pay close attention. This means the company may discuss some fundamental assumptions that could mean the difference between it staying in business or going out of business. Shareholders should also be concerned if the company changes auditors in the middle of an audit or announces the sudden resignation of its CEO or chief financial officer to "pursue other interests."

Just ask investors in Toronto-based e-commerce company Microforum Inc. On Sept. 21, 2000, the company announced the resignation of its CFO to pursue "an entrepreneurial start-up opportunity." One week later, Microforum announced an unexpected $3-million to $5-million loss, and said that it was investigating allegations levied by its former CFO against CEO Howard Pearl. Pearl stepped down amid reports he used company funds to take his family to Disney World and put his children's nanny on the company payroll. Microforum said it has investigated the allegations and found no evidence of wrongdoing by Pearl. Microforum is now under bankruptcy protection, and investors are left with a stock worth less than 10¢ per share, a far cry from the more than $14 it was trading at two years ago.

There are still many mini-Enrons waiting to be discovered, says Woods. "A lot of the profits companies have been reporting recently are bull," he says. An indication of this can be seen when you compare the value of the S&P 500 index to US corporate income tax. The two indicators usually move in tandem, but a few years ago they began to diverge, meaning that corporations were reporting higher profits to shareholders than they were to the tax man.

The bottom line for shareholders: look well beyond the bottom line to fully understand the companies you are investing in. "The footnotes to the financial statements are a treasure trove of information," says Rosen. "Read the footnotes first. After seeing all the ways a company has bent, spindled and mutilated its earnings, you may have an entirely different outlook on the company." Words to the wise.

Canadian Business, April 1, 2002, pp. 28, 30–32.

CASE 10B

ANALYSIS OF A COMPANY'S FAILURE

This case is about a company that went under 30 years ago. It's an "oldie but goodie": the insight it provides into using financial information to spot trouble is still valuable!

W.T. Grant Company was a large U.S. retailer that enjoyed considerable success but then went bankrupt in the mid-1970s. The company had grown rapidly in the ten years up to 1973, establishing over 600 new stores in that period. A Canadian subsidiary was Zellers, now owned by the Hudson's Bay Company. It made some strategy changes during this time; for example, moving "upscale" from low-priced soft goods to higher-priced goods in competition with several department store chains. Its strategy was also to lease store space rather than to buy the property.

The company's share price fell dramatically between January 31, 1973, and January 31, 1974. In 1974, the company lost its credit rating, and after rescue attempts by 143 banks, the company was declared bankrupt shortly after the end of its 1975 fiscal year. Within another year, all the company's assets had been liquidated and the company ceased to exist.

Summary financial statements, several ratios, and the Scott formula calculations for W.T. Grant over the period 1970–75 are shown below.[8] Use those to identify some reasons for the company's share price crash in 1973–74 and its ultimate failure.

W.T. GRANT COMPANY
Some Balance Sheet Items as of January 31 (in millions $)

	1970	1971	1972	1973	1974	1975
Cash and marketable securities	33	34	50	31	46	80
Accounts receivable	368	420	477	543	599	431
Inventory	222	260	299	400	451	407
Total current assets	628	720	831	980	1103	925
Total assets	707	808	945	1111	1253	1082
Total current liabilities	367	459	476	633	690	750
Total liabilities	416	506	619	776	929	968
Equity	291	302	326	335	324	114

Some Income, Cash Flow, and Dividend Numbers (in millions $)
Year Ended January 31

	1970	1971	1972	1973	1974	1975
Revenue	1220	1265	1384	1655	1861	1772
Cost of goods sold	818	843	931	1125	1283	1303
Income before interest and tax	85	92	76	85	60	(87)
Interest expense	15	19	16	21	51	199
Tax expense	28	33	26	26	1	(119)
Net income	42	40	35	38	8	(177)
Tax rate	0.40	0.45	0.43	0.41	0.11	0.40
Dividends declared	20	21	21	21	21	5
Cash flow from operations	(3)	(15)	(27)	(114)	(93)	(85)
Financing activities	25	33	76	121	138	140
Investment activities	(14)	(17)	(32)	(28)	(29)	(21)

W.T. GRANT COMPANY
Some Summary Numbers (Year Ended January 31)

	1970	1971	1972	1973	1974	1975
Return on equity	0.144	0.132	0.107	0.113	0.025	−1.553
Return on assets	0.072	0.062	0.047	0.045	0.042	−0.057
Sales return	0.042	0.040	0.032	0.030	0.028	−0.035
Total asset turnover	1.73	1.57	1.46	1.49	1.49	1.64
Cash flow to total assets	−0.004	−0.019	−0.029	−0.103	−0.074	−0.079
Average interest rate	0.022	0.038	0.026	0.027	0.055	0.205
Debt/equity ratio	1.43	1.68	1.90	2.32	2.87	8.49
Inventory turnover	3.68	3.24	3.21	2.81	2.84	3.20
Collection ratio	110.1	121.2	125.8	119.8	117.5	88.8
Working capital ratio	1.71	1.57	1.75	1.55	1.60	1.23
Acid test ratio	1.09	0.99	1.11	0.91	0.93	0.67
Gross margin	0.32	0.33	0.33	0.32	0.31	0.26
Interest coverage ratio	5.67	4.84	4.75	4.05	1.33	negative
Earnings per share in $	2.94	2.67	2.50	2.71	0.57	negative
Dividends per share in $	1.40	1.40	1.50	1.50	1.50	zero
January 31 closing share price in $	47.0	47.1	47.8	43.9	10.9	1.1

Scott Formula Components*

	ROE	=	SR	×	AT	+	(ROA	−	IN)	×	(D/E)
1970	0.144	=	0.042	×	1.73	+	(0.072	−	0.022)	×	1.43
1971	0.132	=	0.040	×	1.57	+	(0.062	−	0.021)	×	1.68
1972	0.107	=	0.030	×	1.46	+	(0.047	−	0.015)	×	1.90
1973	0.113	=	0.030	×	1.49	+	(0.045	−	0.016)	×	2.32
1974	0.025	=	0.028	×	1.49	+	(0.042	−	0.049)	×	2.87
1975	−1.553	=	−0.035	×	1.64	+	(−0.057	−	0.119)	×	8.49

*Because of rounding, the numbers don't all satisfy the relationship precisely.

NOTES

1. Canadian Tire Corporation, 2004 annual report, 42, 43.
2. Wal-Mart Inc., 2004 annual report summary, www.walmartstores.com, summary p. 16.
3. Canadian National Railway, 2004 annual report, Canadian GAAP version, 81–82.
4. Ibid., 81–82.
5. The booklet *Reporting Cash Flows: A Guide to the Revised Statement of Changes in Financial Position* (Toronto: Deloitte, Haskins & Sells now Deloitte & Touche, 1986) was helpful in developing points about interpreting cash flow information.
6. Proof of the Scott formula (A = Assets, L = Liabilities, E = Equity, and the "ATI" notation for ROA, SR, and IN is left out to avoid clutter):
   a. Define ROE = Net income / E
   b. Define ROA = (Net income + After-tax interest expense) / A
   c. Define IN = After-tax interest expense / L
   d. By double-entry accounting, A = L + E
   e. From (a), Net income = ROE × E
   f. From (b), Net income = (ROA × A) – After-tax interest expense
   g. Equate right sides of (e) and (f):
   ROE × E = (ROA × A) – After-tax interest expense
   h. From (d) and (c):
   ROE × E = (ROA × L + E) – (IN × L)

ROE × E = ROA × L + ROA × E – IN × L
ROE × E = ROA × E + (ROA – IN) × L

i. Dividing the last through by E produces:
ROE = ROA + (ROA – IN) × L / E

j. Break up the first term to the right of the equal sign into two terms by multiplying it by REV / REV:
ROA = (Net income + After-tax interest expense) / A
ROA = (Net income + After-tax interest expense) / REV × REV / A

k. Define the first new term as sales return SR and the second as asset turnover AT

l. This produces the final version of the formula:
ROE = SR × AT + (ROA – IN) × L / E
Putting in the ATI notation produces:
ROE = SR(ATI) × AT + (ROA(ATI) – IN(ATI)) × L / E

7. The formula for the present value of a constant cash payment comes from the sum of the following geometric series:

$$\frac{C}{(1+i)^1} + \frac{C}{(1+i)^2} + \frac{C}{(1+i)^3} + \dots + \frac{C}{(1+i)^n}$$

See an algebra textbook for proof of how this series sums to the formula given.

8. For more information on this case and some interesting charts of various ratios' performance over time, see J.A. Largey, III, and C.P. Stickney, "Cash Flows, Ratio Analysis and the W.T. Grant Company Bankruptcy," Financial Analysts Journal (July–August 1980): 51–54.

GLOSSARY OF TERMS

This glossary provides definitions for many terms in financial accounting[1] and refers readers back to those chapter sections in which the terms are discussed. If a good definition or discussion appears in a chapter section, the reference to that section may be provided without repeating the definition. Terms are cross-referenced to other terms where helpful. For additional help in finding things, consult the index at the end of the book. Technical terms used in any definition are themselves defined in their alphabetical location in the glossary.

Accelerated amortization (depreciation)

An amortization method, such as declining balance, that records more amortization in the earlier years of an asset's life, and less in later years, than does the straight-line method. See **Straight-line amortization**, **Declining balance amortization**, and Section 8.12.

Account

A summary record of an asset, liability, owners' equity, revenue, or expense, in which the effects of transactions, accruals, and adjustments are indicated in dollars (where dollars are the currency of the country). See **General journal**, **General ledger**, **Transaction**, and Sections 2.3, 2.4, and 2.5.

Accountant

A person who performs accounting functions. Professional accountants are those who are granted designations by self-regulating bodies on the basis of special training and successful examination. For example: CA or Chartered Accountant (Canada, the United Kingdom); CGA or Certified General Accountant (Canada); CMA or Certified Management Accountant (Canada, the United States); and CPA or Certified Public Accountant (the United States). See Section 1.5.

Accounting

"To account" is to provide a record, such as of funds paid or received for something. Being "accountable" is to be responsible for, as in to account for one's actions. These two ideas together describe the practice of accounting as the recordkeeping and reporting of an enterprise's performance and position in monetary terms. Management is responsible for the decisions made in an enterprise. Accounting provides the reports that summarize the economic results of these decisions for inside use and transmits them to outside, interested parties (such as investors, creditors, and regulatory agencies). See **Financial accounting**, **Management accounting**, and Section 1.1.

Accounting control

The practice of creating accounting records that provide expected quantities of important assets and liabilities and so improve the internal control over those assets. Used by most companies for cash, accounts receivable, sales taxes collected on behalf of governments and employee deductions, and by many companies for investments, inventories, property and equipment, and accounts payable. See **Internal control** and Section 7.9 for various examples of accounting control.

Accounting entity

The enterprise for which the accounting is being done. The entity may be a single legal corporation or other organization, an economic unit without legal standing (such as a proprietorship), or a group of corporations with connected ownership for which consolidated financial statements are prepared. See Sections 5.2 and 9.7.

Accounting policies

The chosen accounting methods used by a company to recognize economic events on an accrual basis, and to report the financial position and results of operations. For examples, see the notes immediately following the financial statements of any company. The first such note is usually a summary of significant accounting policies. See Sections 1.1, 5.5, 6.4, 8.4, and 9.2.

Accounting policy choice

A decision among acceptable accounting policies is often needed because more than one acceptable policy exists in many areas. See Sections 6.4, 8.1, and 10.8.

Accounting principles

See **Generally accepted accounting principles** and Sections 1.1 and 5.1.

Accounting research

The practice of studying accounting phenomena to determine their effects on other phenomena, such as share prices and the effects of those on accounting. Introduced in Section 1.5 and mentioned frequently throughout the book.

Accounting standards

The recommending of particular accounting methods or policies by an authoritative body. In Canada this is done by the Accounting Standards Board of the Canadian Institute of Chartered Accountants, in the United States, by the Financial Accounting Standards Board. See **Authoritative standards**, **Accounting policies**, **Generally accepted accounting principles,** and Section 5.1.

Accounting Standards Board

The committee of the Canadian Institute of Chartered Accountants that is responsible for setting financial accounting standards in Canada. See Section 5.4.

Accounts payable

Liabilities representing amounts owed to short-term trade creditors. (An account payable for the debtor is an account receivable for the creditor.) See Sections 2.3, 2.4, and 9.2.

Accounts receivable

Amounts owing by debtors (customers), usually arising from sales of goods or services. See Sections 2.3, 3.3, 6.3, 6.4, and 8.6.

Accrual accounting

The method of making an economically meaningful and comprehensive measurement of performance and position by recognizing economic events regardless of when cash transactions happen, as opposed to the simpler cash basis of accounting. Under this method, revenues and expenses (and related assets and liabilities) are reflected in the accounts in the period to which they relate. See Sections 1.9, 3.1, and 6.2.

Accrual basis

The use of accrual accounting in preparing financial statements. See Section 3.7.

Accrual income

The result of subtracting expenses from revenue(s), when both kinds of accounts are calculated by accrual accounting. See **Accrual accounting**, **Net income**, and Sections 1.9, 3.3, 3.7, 4.1, 6.2, and 6.3.

Accrue

To enter amounts in the accounts to reflect events or estimates that are economically meaningful but that do not (at present) involve the exchange of cash. Examples would be recording interest that is building up on a debt prior to paying it or recording revenue from credit sales prior to receipt of cash from customers. See Sections 1.9, 3.1, and 6.2, and **Accrual accounting**, **Revenue recognition**, and **Matching**; see also **Deferral**.

Accrued expense

An expense recognized in the accounts prior to paying for it. See Section 6.10.

Accumulated amortization (depreciation)

A balance sheet account that accumulates total amortization (depreciation) expense over a number of years. The account balance is a credit and so is opposite to the debit-balance asset cost account. The difference between cost and accumulated amortization is the "book value" of the asset. See **Book value**, **Contra accounts**, **Fixed assets**, **Amortization** and **Amortization expense**, and Sections 2.1, 2.3, and 7.7.

Accumulated foreign currency translation adjustment

An account arising as a consequence of the method used to convert foreign operations' accounting figures into Canadian dollars for the purpose of combining them with the figures for Canadian operations. Because income statement accounts are generally converted at average foreign exchange rates and balance sheet accounts are generally converted at year-end or historical rates, converted accounts do not quite balance. The difference is put into equity as a separate item because it does not seem to fit anywhere else and it is part of the (converted) residual equity of the owners. See Sections 2.9 and 9.4.

Acid test ratio

Cash, temporary investments, and accounts receivable divided by current liabilities. Also called the quick ratio. See **Ratios** and Sections 2.3 and 10.4 (Ratio 19), where the ratio is explained.

Acquisition

There are two related meanings in accounting. The first is just a purchase. Buying a new asset is often described as an acquisition of that asset, or acquiring it. See **Acquisition cost** and **Historical cost**. The second meaning applies to a **Business combination** in which one company buys enough of the voting shares of another company to get voting control and so become the **Parent** of that company, which becomes the acquiring company's **Subsidiary.** See Section 9.7. (A **Merger** is a business combination in which neither company controls the other. Accounting standards now require virtually all business combinations to be accounted for as acquisitions.)

Acquisition cost

See **Historical cost** and Section 8.2.

Adjusted trial balance

The list of accounts prepared after all the accrual accounting adjustments and corrections have been made and so representing the final account balances used in preparing the financial statements. See **Trial balance**, **Adjusting (journal) entry**, and Sections 3.8 and 3.9.

Adjusting (journal) entry

A journal entry to implement accrual accounting by recognizing in the accounts economic events not yet adequately accounted for by the routine transactional accounting system. (For example, if there is no transaction to reveal the gradual wear and tear of a fixed asset, an adjusting entry must be made to recognize this depreciation.) See Sections 3.8 and 3.9.

Adjustment(s)

See **Adjusting (journal) entry** and Section 1.7.

Adverse opinion

A type of **Auditor's opinion** in which the opinion is that the financial statements are *not* fairly presented. See Section 5.8.

Agent

A person who is party to a contract between that person and another, called the principal. The agent's role is to carry out the wishes of the principal as specified in the contract. Some examples of agents are managers, auditors, lawyers, and physicians, who are entrusted with acting on behalf of one or more others (the principals, such as owners, creditors, defendants, and patients). Agents have a stewardship responsibility to the principal. See **Contract**, **Principal**, **Stewardship**, and Section 5.11.

Aggressive accounting

Seeking out accounting methods and policy choices to meet management objectives for growth, financing, bonuses, or other purposes that seem to violate principles such as fairness and conservatism. See Section 6.4.

Aging of accounts receivable

The process of classifying accounts receivable by the time that has passed since the account came into existence. This classification is used as an aid to estimating the required allowance for doubtful accounts for the estimated amount of uncollectible accounts receivable. See Section 8.6.

Allocating, allocation

Spreading the impact of an event out over time, as in amortization of an asset's cost over its useful life or recognition of revenue for a long-term contract over several periods. See **Amortization** and Sections 6.5 and 6.10. See also **Interperiod tax allocation** and Section 9.3, and **Intraperiod tax allocation** and Section 3.5. (Allocation is also used, especially in management accounting, to refer to spreading the impact of an event across activities, such as in allocating the cost of repairs to different departments.)

Allowance for doubtful accounts

The estimated amount of accounts receivable that will not be collected (which are "doubtful"). The allowance, which is a contra account to accounts receivable, is used in order to recognize the bad debts expense related to such doubtful accounts but without removing those accounts from the books because the firm will still try to collect the amounts owing. See Section 7.7.

American Institute of Certified Public Accountants (AICPA)

The national self-regulating body in the United States that sets and monitors the auditing and professional standards by which CPAs practise.

Amortization

Allocation of the cost of a noncurrent asset to expense over several accounting periods to recognize the "consumption" of the asset's economic value as it helps to earn revenue over those periods. Amortization expense for a period thus is deducted from revenue in that period, recognizing it as a cost of earning the revenue. The term *amortization*, and especially the common term *depreciation*, is used for the allocation of the cost of tangible assets over time; amortization is also used for the allocation of the cost of intangible assets such as patents, franchise rights, and goodwill. See **Accumulated amortization**, **Intangible assets**, and Sections 1.10, 7.7, 8.10, and 8.12.

Amortization expense

The expense recorded to recognize asset amortization. See **Amortization**, **Accumulated amortization**, and Sections 7.7 and 8.10.

Amortize

To allocate the cost of noncurrent assets (and sometimes liabilities) to expense over several accounting periods. See **Amortization**, **Allocating**, and Sections 8.10 and 8.12.

Analysis, analyze

The technique, common in accounting, of comparing information derived from different sources or methods in order to understand what has happened, identify errors, and answer questions about the effects of possible actions or events. See **Reconciliation** and **"What if" (effects) analysis**. Also used to refer to the detailed study of accounting information, such as by using **Ratios**. See Sections 1.12 and 10.1–10.9.

Annual report

The document provided annually to the shareholders by the officers of a company. It includes the financial statements, the notes to the financial statements, the auditor's report, supplementary financial information such as multi-year summaries, and reports from the company's board of directors and management. See Sections 1.1, 1.3, and 5.6.

Articulate, Articulation

Of the income statement, retained earnings statement, and balance sheet; refers to the fact that because these three statements are prepared from one set of balanced accounts, changes in any one of the three normally affect the others. In particular, recognition of revenue and expense relies on the fact that a revenue causes a change in the balance sheet, as does an expense. See **Recognition**, **Revenue recognition**, and Sections 3.3, 3.6, 6.3, 6.4, and 8.2.

Asset(s)

An asset is a resource available to do business in the future, represented by an ownership of or right to expected future economic benefits. Assets have value because they are expected to bring benefits as they are used or sold. See Sections 1.1, 2.3, and 8.2, and **Cash equivalent assets**, **Inventory**, **Accounts receivable**, **Current assets**, **Fixed assets,** and **Intangible assets**.

Asset valuation

Determination of the amounts to be used for assets on the balance sheet. See **Balance sheet valuation** and Section 8.2.

Assumed cost flow

The practice in inventory accounting of determining the cost of inventories purchased at varying unit costs by assuming a specific order in which the inventory will be taken to have flowed into and out of the company. See **Cost flow assumption** and Section 8.7.

Assurance

A broader word than "audit," encompassing auditing and similar procedures to confirm or verify reports or events as fair and proper and assure users of such reports that they may be relied upon. See **Audit**, **Auditor's report**, and **Fairness** and Section 5.8.

AT

The total assets turnover ratio, defined and explained in Section 10.4, Ratio 12. Used in the Scott formula in Section 10.6.

Audit

The examination of accounting records and their supporting documentation with the objective of determining the fairness with which the financial statements present the financial position and performance of the company. See **Auditor**, **Auditor's report**, and Section 5.8.

Audit committee

A committee of a corporation's **Board of directors**, usually composed largely or entirely of directors not also having management positions, which reviews the company's accounting statements and communicates directly with the **External auditor**. See Sections 5.9 and 7.3.

Auditor

The person or firm who performs an audit for the purpose of preparing a report on the credibility of the financial statements, also called the **External auditor**. See Sections 1.4, 1.5, and 5.8. Compare **Internal auditor**.

Auditor's opinion

The portion of the **auditor's report** in which the auditor expresses a professional opinion that the financial statements are, or are not, fairly presented.

Auditor's report (or auditors' report)

The document accompanying the financial statements that expresses the auditor's opinion on the fairness of the financial statements. The auditor's report explains what the auditor did and states the **Auditor's opinion**. See Section 5.8.

Authoritative standards

Written rules and guidance established by official accounting standard-setters such as the CICA in Canada and the FASB in the United States. See ***CICA Handbook*** and Sections 5.1, 5.4, and 6.4.

Available cost

The total dollar amount represented by the sum of beginning inventory and purchases during the period, and thus representing the total dollar cost of inventory available for sale or use during the period. See Sections 8.7 and 8.8.

Average cost (AVGE)

An inventory cost-flow assumption where the cost of an individual unit of inventory is the weighted average cost of the beginning inventory and subsequent purchases. See **Weighted average** and Section 8.7.

Average interest rate

An average calculated by dividing interest expense by total liabilities. Defined and explained in Section 10.4 (Ratio 6). An after-tax version of this is used in the Scott formula in Section 10.6 (see **IN(ATI)**).

AVGE

See **Average cost** and **Weighted average**.

B

Bad debts expense

An expense account that results from the reduction in carrying value of those accounts receivable that have been projected to be uncollectible or doubtful. See **Allowance for doubtful accounts** and Section 7.7.

Balance (an account total)

The net sum of the amounts added to and subtracted from an account since the account began. In financial accounting's double-entry system, the balance is expressed as a net debit (DR) or net credit (CR). See **Account**, **Double-entry accounting**, and Sections 2.4 and 2.5.

Balance (in the balance sheet or the trial balance)

Refers to the double-entry accounting requirement that the sum of the accounts with debit balances and the sum of those with credit balances be equal. In the balance sheet, this means that the sum of the assets equals the sum of the liabilities and equity. See **Balance sheet**, **Balance sheet equation**, **Trial balance**, and Sections 2.3, 2.7, and 3.9.

Balance sheet

The "balanced" list of assets, liabilities, and owners' equity constituting the formal statement of a company's financial position at a specified date, summarizing by category the assets, liabilities, and owners' equity. See **Balance**, **Balance sheet equation**, **Balance sheet valuation**, **Statement of financial position,** and Sections 2.2, 2.7, and 2.11.

Balance sheet equation

The double-entry arithmetic by which Assets = Liabilities + Owners' Equity. See Sections 2.3, 2.4, 8.2, and 8.7.

Balance sheet valuation

Assigning numerical values to the balance sheet's assets, liabilities, and owners' equity accounts. See Section 8.2.

Bank overdraft

A negative bank account balance (withdrawals exceeding deposits), which banks may allow as a de facto loan as long as it is temporary. See **Line of credit** and Sections 2.7 and 4.3.

Bank reconciliation

An analysis conducted to determine if the bank account balance according to the accounting records corresponds with the balance as reported by the bank. The two balances seldom agree exactly, so the reconciliation is designed to set out the reasons for any disagreement. See **Analysis** and Sections 1.12 and 7.5.

Bankruptcy

The usually involuntary termination of an enterprise due to its inability to pay its debts and continue in operation. Bankruptcy usually involves significant losses to both creditors and owners. See **Going concern**.

Betterment

An expenditure to improve an asset's value to the business, more than just repairs and maintenance. See Section 8.4.

Big Bath

A way of manipulating reported income to show even poorer results in a poor year in order to enhance later years' results. See Sections 3.10 and 6.4.

Board of directors

The senior level of management, representing and directly responsible to the owners (shareholders). Normally elected annually by the shareholders, the board is responsible for hiring and supervising the operating management (president, chief executive officer, etc.). See Sections 2.3, 3.3, and 5.3.

Bond, bonded debt

A certificate of debt issued by an enterprise in return for cash, in which a promise is made to repay the debt (usually at a particular date or on a specified schedule) plus interest. Many bonds may be sold to other people by those who received them in return for the original cash provided to the enterprise. See Sections 2.7 and 9.3.

Bond markets

Capital markets in which debt instruments (bonds and similar items), rather than shares, are traded. See **Capital markets.**

Bookkeeping

The process of recording, classifying, and summarizing transactions in the books of account. See Sections 1.7, 2.2, and 2.4.

Books

Colloquial term for the accounting records, including computerized records, left over from the time when the records were written in bound books. See Sections 1.7 and 7.2.

Books of original entry

The journals in which transactions are first recorded. See Section 7.2.

Book value

The amount shown in the accounts for any individual asset, liability, or owners' equity item after deducting any related contra account (for example, the book value of a truck is the recorded cost minus accumulated amortization). The term is also commonly used for the whole enterprise, to refer to the net amount of total assets less total liabilities (the recorded value of the owners' residual interest, which equals total equity: Assets = Liabilities + Equity). See Sections 7.7 and 8.11 for the book value of individual assets and Sections 2.3, 9.4, and 9.7 for the book value of the whole enterprise. See also **Book value per share**.

Book value per share

Total shareholders' equity divided by the number of shares issued. It is defined and explained in Section 10.4, Ratio 9.

Bottom line

A colloquialism referring to the net income (the "bottom line" on the income statement). See **Net income**.

Business combination

A merger of separate corporations or an acquisition of control of one corporation by another, in which the corporations become a single economic entity. See **Accounting entity**, **Consolidation**, and Section 9.7.

CA

Chartered accountant. See **Canadian Institute of Chartered Accountants**. See Sections 5.8 and 5.9.

Callable debt

Debt, such as bonds, that might have to be repaid ahead of schedule at the option of the creditor. Most bank loans are callable, in that the bank can ask for repayment within a few days even if the original repayment plan extended over a longer period. See Section 9.2.

Canada Business Corporations Act (CBCA)

The federal corporations act that provides the authority for the incorporation of federally incorporated companies in Canada and generally sets the requirements for their activities. It requires any such company to prepare annual financial statements.

Canadian Certified General Accountants Association (CGA-Canada)

An association whose members (CGAs) have had training in accounting, taxation, auditing, and other areas of business and have passed qualifying exams. CGA-Canada and provincial associations of CGAs set and monitor standards by which CGAs practise. CGA-Canada is one of the three national professional accounting bodies. See **Accountant** and Sections 1.5, 5.8, and 5.9.

Canadian Institute of Chartered Accountants (CICA)

A national, self-regulating association of chartered accountants in which the accountants have met education and examination standards in Canada. The CICA and provincial institutes of CAs set and monitor the standards by which CAs practise. One of the three national professional accounting bodies. See **Accountant** and Sections 1.5, 5.8, and 5.9.

Capital

The owner's contribution to or interest in a business (the equity). Often used specifically to refer to the equity of unincorporated businesses (proprietorships and partnerships). See **Equity** and Sections 2.9 and 9.4.

Capital cost allowance

The Canadian Income Tax Act's version of amortization (depreciation), used in calculating taxable income for assessment of income tax. See Section 9.3.

Capitalization, capitalize

The recognition of an expenditure that may benefit a future period as an asset rather than as an expense of the period of its occurrence. Expenditures are capitalized if they are likely to lead to future benefits, and, thus, meet the criterion to be an asset. See Sections 3.8 and 8.4.

Capitalized costs

Costs that have been included with an asset on the balance sheet instead of being deducted as expenses on the income statement. See Sections 7.7, 8.4, and 8.14.

Capital lease

A lease having the economic character of asset ownership. See Sections 8.14 and 9.3.

Capital markets

Markets in which financial instruments such as shares and bonds are traded. See Sections 3.2 and 5.10, **Financial instruments**, and **Stock exchange**.

Cash

Currency and coin on hand, balances in bank accounts, and other highly liquid assets. See **Cash and equivalents** and Sections 4.3, 7.5, and 8.5.

Cash and equivalents

Cash and near-cash assets minus near-cash liabilities: cash equivalent assets minus cash equivalent liabilities. Changes in cash and equivalents are explained by the cash flow statement (SCFP). See **Cash flow statement**, **Cash**, and Sections 4.3 and 8.5.

Cash disbursements

Cash payouts, by cheque, currency, or direct deductions from the bank account. See **Cash payments**, **Cash disbursements journal**, **Cash receipts**, **Cash income**, and Section 4.4.

Cash disbursements journal

The record of cheques and other cash payments made. See **Books of original entry** and Section 7.2.

Cash equivalent assets

A term used to describe cash plus very liquid bank deposits and similar assets that can be converted into cash on demand. See Sections 4.3 and 8.5.

Cash equivalent liabilities

Liabilities that are payable on demand and so represent a reduction in the liquidity otherwise apparent from the amount of cash. Under current accounting standards, temporary bank overdrafts are the only common cash equivalent liabilities. See **Bank overdraft** and Section 4.3.

Cash flow

The inflows of cash (cash receipts) and outflows of cash (cash disbursements) over a period. Information about cash flow is presented in the **Cash flow statement**. See also Sections 4.2 and 4.3.

Cash flow analysis

A method of accounting **Analysis** directed at understanding the enterprise's cash inflows, outflows, and resulting balances. This analysis lies behind the **Cash flow statement**. See Section 4.2.

Cash flow statement

A statement that explains the changes in cash (and equivalent) balances during a fiscal period. Also referred to as "Statement of changes in financial position (SCFP)," "Funds statement," or "Statement of cash flows." See **Direct method of cash flow analysis**, **Indirect**

method of cash flow analysis, and Sections 1.1, 4.2, 4.3, and 10.5.

Cash flow to total assets

The ratio of cash from operations divided by total assets. It is defined and explained in Section 10.4, Ratio 7. See **Cash from operations**.

Cash from operations

Cash generated by day-to-day business activities and highlighted as the first section in the **Cash flow statement**. See Sections 4.2, 4.3, 4.9, and 10.5.

Cash income

Cash receipts minus cash disbursements, or that subset of both that relates to day-to-day operations. The operating subset is roughly equivalent to the Cash flow statement's **Cash from operations** figure. See **Cash receipts**, **Cash disbursements**, **Direct method of cash flow analysis,** and Sections 1.10 and 4.4.

Cash payments

Payments by currency, cheque, or other bank withdrawal. See **Cash transaction**, **Cash disbursements journal**, and Section 4.4.

Cash receipts

Cash inflows, by currency, others' cheques, or direct bank deposits. See **Cash transaction**, **Cash receipts journal,** and Section 4.4.

Cash receipts journal

The record of customers' cheques and other cash received. See **Books of original entry** and Section 7.2.

Cash received basis

Recognition of revenue only when the cash comes in. See **Revenue recognition**, **Conservatism**, and Section 6.7.

Cash transaction

The simplest kind of economic exchange routinely recorded by financial accounting, and an important starting point for the financial statements. See Sections 1.7 and 4.4.

CCA

See **Capital cost allowance.**

CGA

Certified general accountant. See Canadian Certified General Accountants Association (CGA-Canada) and Sections 5.8 and 5.9.

Change effects analysis

Analysis of the effects on financial statements of economic or accounting policy changes. See Sections 1.12 and 10.8 and **"What if" (effects) analysis**.

Change in cash

Demonstrating why cash changed as it did is the objective of the **Cash flow statement**'s analysis. **Cash income** is part of this change. See Sections 1.10 and 4.3–4.5.

Chart of accounts

An organized list of the accounts used in the accounting system. This can be contrasted with the "trial balance," which displays all the accounts and their debit or credit balances. See Section 7.2.

Cheque

A request by one party that the party's bank pay a specified amount to another party. See Section 7.2.

CICA Handbook

The authoritative source of financial accounting standards in Canada. See Section 5.4.

Classification

Choice of where in the financial statements to place an account, such as whether an investment asset should be shown as a current asset or a noncurrent asset. See Sections 2.7, 3.5, and 3.8.

Classification policies

Accounting policies covering where within a financial statement an account or description is to appear. See Sections 2.7, 3.5, 3.8, and 6.4 and **Accounting policies**.

Classified financial statements

Financial statement with accounts organized under headings that clarify the accounts' meaning, done to increase the information value of the statements. See Sections 2.3, 2.7, 3.5, and 4.3.

Clean opinion

An external auditor's report which states the auditor's opinion that the financial statements are fairly presented. This is the kind of auditor's report that most companies receive because it indicates the auditor found no problems. See **Auditor's report**, **Qualified opinion**, and Section 5.8.

Close, closing

Transfer(ring) the temporary accounts (revenues, expenses, and dividends declared) to retained earnings at the end of the fiscal period. See **Closing entry** and Sections 3.6 and 3.7.

Closing entry or entries

Journal entries recorded at year-end to transfer the balances in temporary accounts (revenues, expenses, and dividends) to the balance sheet account retained earnings and set those balances to zero in preparation for entering the next year's transactions. See Sections 3.6–3.8.

CMA

Certified management accountant. See **Society of Management Accountants of Canada** and Sections 5.8 and 5.9.

COGS

See **Cost of goods sold** and Sections 7.9 and 8.7.

COGS expense

See **Cost of goods sold expense** and Sections 7.9 and 8.7.

Collection ratio

The ratio of accounts receivable to the daily sales, expressed in number of days' sales represented by accounts receivable. Also called **Days' sales in receivables**. It is defined and explained in Section 10.4, Ratio 14.

Common shares

The basic voting ownership interests in a corporation. See **Corporation** and Sections 2.9 and 9.4.

Common size financial statements

A technique of analyzing financial statements in which income statement figures are expressed in percentages of revenue and balance sheet accounts are expressed in percentages of total asset. It is defined and explained in Section 10.4, Ratio 4.

Company

See **Corporation**.

Comparability

Information that enables users to identify similarities in and differences between two sets of economic phenomena, such as two different years of a company's financial statements. Comparability between companies and consistency of one company over time are major objectives of financial accounting. See **Fairness**, **Consistency**, and Sections 5.2, 5.3, and 6.4.

Compilation

A service performed by accountants practising public accounting, whereby they prepare financial statements for enterprises without taking responsibility for the quality of the accounting information used to prepare them and without auditing them. See Section 5.8.

Completed contract

A method of revenue recognition for long-term contracts in which the revenue is not reported on the income statement until the contract has been completed. See **Revenue recognition**, **Conservatism**, and Section 6.7.

Compound, compounded, compounding

These refer to the frequency with which interest calculated on a loan or other debt is periodically added to the principal and so attracts future interest itself. Annual compounding, for example, means that interest built up on a loan starts to bear interest itself on each annual anniversary of the loan. See **Present value** and Section 10.7.

Conditional sale contract

A form of borrowing whereby the title to an asset purchased on credit does not pass to the buyer until all the payments, usually plus interest, are made. See Section 9.3.

Conservatism, conservative

A prudent reaction to uncertainty to ensure that risks inherent in business situations are adequately considered—often phrased as "anticipate possible losses but not possible gains." In situations where the accountant cannot decide on the superiority of one of two accounting treatments on the basis of accounting principles alone, being conservative means choosing the treatment that has the least favourable impact on the income of the current period. See **Historical cost**, **Cash received basis**, **Completed contract** method, and **Lower of cost or market** for examples of conservatism, and see also Sections 5.2, 5.3, 6.4, 6.7, and 8.2.

Consistency

Treatment of like transactions in the same way in consecutive periods so that financial statements will be comparable. The reporting policy implying that procedures, once adopted, should be followed from period to period by a company. See **Accounting policies** and Sections 5.2, 5.3, and 6.4.

Consolidated financial statements, consolidation

Consolidation is a method of preparing financial statements for a group of corporations linked by ownership as if they were a single corporation. Consolidated financial statements recognize that the separate legal entities are components of one economic unit. They are distinguishable from the separate parent and subsidiary corporations' statements, and from combined statements of affiliated corporations. See **Pooling of interests method**, **Purchase method,** and Sections 1.1, 2.9, 9.6, and 9.7.

Consolidated goodwill

A form of **Goodwill** arising only when companies' financial statements are combined in **Purchase method** consolidation. See Sections 2.9 and 9.7.

Contingency, contingent asset, contingent liability

An economic event (especially a negative one) that is in the process of occurring and so is not yet resolved. Contingencies would include but are not limited to pending or threatened litigation, threat of expropriation of assets, guarantees of the indebtedness of others, and possible liabilities arising from discounted bills of exchange or promissory notes. See **Conservatism** and Section 9.3.

Contra accounts

Accounts established to accumulate certain deductions from an asset, liability, or owners' equity item. See **Book value**, **Amortization**, **Depreciation**, **Allowance for doubtful accounts**, and Sections 7.7 and 9.3.

Contract

A contract is an oral or written agreement between or among parties, setting out each party's responsibilities and specifying actions agreed to and resulting payments or other settlements. See **Agent** and **Principal** regarding one type of contract important in accounting, and Section 5.11.

Contributed surplus

The difference between the legal **Par value** (or **Stated value**) of a share and the cash or other consideration received by the company when the share was issued. Also referred to with terms like "capital in excess of par value." Does not apply to **No-par shares**, which are the usual kind in Canada. See Sections 2.9, 2.10, and 9.4.

Control account

An account used to contain the aggregate amounts of many detailed transactions and so help to prevent or detect errors in the detailed records. The accounts receivable control account, for example, should have the same total as the sum of all the individual customers' accounts receivable. Control accounts with detailed backup include cash, accounts receivable, inventory, accumulated amortization, accounts payable, sales tax due, employee deductions due, and share capital. See **Internal control**, **Accounting control**, and Sections 7.2, 7.6, and 7.7.

Convertible

A bond or share that can be changed into another kind of **Security**, usually a **Preferred share** that can be converted into a **Common share**. See Section 9.5.

Corporate governance

The arrangements by which the board of directors and top management operate the corporation on behalf of its shareholders. See Section 7.3.

Corporate group

A group of corporations linked by common or mutual ownership. See **Consolidation** and Sections 2.8, 9.6, and 9.7.

Corporation

A legal entity with or without share capital, legally separate from those who own it or work as a part of it. It enjoys most of the rights and responsibilities of a person except for those that only an actual person can enjoy. Its main feature is limited liability; in other words, only the assets of the company can be claimed by creditors, not the assets of owners. See **Partnership**, **Proprietorship**, and Sections 1.4, 2.9, 3.2, and 9.4.

Cost

The value of an asset when it is acquired by the business. See **Historical cost** and Sections 1.7, 8.2, and 8.4.

Cost allocation

Spreading the cost of an asset out over the periods in which it is useful. See **Allocating**, **Amortization**, and Sections 8.8 and 8.9. (Cost allocation is also used in managerial accounting to refer to spreading the cost of an activity out across various products or services affected by that activity.)

Cost basis

Usually used to account for a noncurrent intercorporate investment when a corporation owns less than 20% of another corporation. The investment is carried at cost, and any receipt of dividends or interest is recorded as "other income." See **Equity basis**, **Intercorporate investments**, and Section 9.6.

Cost-benefit

The idea of comparing the benefits of a particular action with its costs, and taking action only if the benefits exceed the costs. See Sections 1.5 and 5.2.

Cost flow assumption

An assumption made about the order in which units of inventory move into and out of an enterprise, used to compute inventory asset value and cost of goods sold expense in cases where the order of flow is not or cannot be identified. Possible assumptions include FIFO, LIFO, and weighted average. See **Cost of goods sold**, **FIFO**, **AVGE**, **Weighted average**, and **LIFO** for specific examples. See also Section 8.7.

Cost of capital

The cost of raising debt or equity funds (e.g., the cost of borrowed funds is mostly the interest to be paid to the lender). See Section 10.7.

Cost of goods sold (COGS) expense

An expense account that reflects the cost of goods that generated the revenue (also called cost of sales). The method of calculating COGS depends on the method of inventory costing. See **Cost flow assumption**, **Inventory costing**, and Sections 3.3, 3.4, 7.9, and 8.7.

Cost principle

The use of the historical cost of assets to value them on the balance sheet. See **Historical cost**, **Balance sheet valuation**, and Sections 5.2 and 8.2.

CPA

Certified public accountant (a designation used especially in the United States). See **American Institute of Certified Public Accountants** and Sections 5.8 and 5.9.

Credit (CR or Cr)

The right-hand side of double-entry accounting. The term *credit* can be used as a noun to refer to the right-hand side of a journal entry or account, or as a verb referring to the action of making an entry to the right-hand side of an account. Most accounts on the right-hand side of the balance sheets have credit balances (in other words, the credits to them exceed the debits to them). The term *credit* also refers to the right to buy or borrow on the promise of future payment. A credit journal entry to the liabilities and equity side of the balance sheet causes an increase in the account, while a credit to the assets side of the balance sheet causes a decrease. See **Double-entry accounting**, **Debit,** and Sections 2.4–2.6.

Creditor

One who extends credit (that is, gives someone the right to buy or borrow now in consideration of a promise to pay at a later date). See Sections 1.5 and 2.3.

Credit transaction

An economic exchange in which at least one party makes a promise to pay cash or other consideration later. This kind of transaction is recognized by most financial accounting systems, especially if it is a routine way of doing business. See **Accounts receivable**, **Accounts payable**, and Section 1.7.

Critical event

A point in the revenue generation and collection process chosen to represent the earning of the revenue, and so the point at which the revenue is recognized in the accounts. This is a simplification: a common critical event is the point at which the customer takes delivery of the goods sold. Not all revenue is accounted for this way: some is allocated over more than one point in the process: long-term construction projects and franchise revenue are examples where the critical event simplification is generally not used. See **Revenue recognition** and Section 6.6.

Current assets

Cash and other assets such as temporary investments, inventory, receivables, and current prepayments that are realizable or will be consumed within the normal operating cycle of an enterprise (usually one year). See such current asset categories as **Cash equivalent assets**, **Inventory**, and **Accounts receivable**. See also Sections 2.3, 2.10, 2.11, and 8.2.

Current liabilities

Debts or estimated claims on the resources of a firm that are expected to be paid within the normal operating cycle of an enterprise (usually one year). See **Cash equivalent liabilities**, **Accounts payable**, and Sections 2.3, 2.10, and 9.2.

Current or market value

The estimated sale value of an asset, settlement value of a debt, or trading value of an equity share. See Sections 8.2, 8.5, and 8.9.

Current portion of income tax expense

The part of the year's income tax expense that has been paid or is due to be paid within the next year. The rest of the income tax expense is the **Future portion of income tax expense**. See Section 9.3.

Current ratio

Also called **Working capital ratio**, equalling current assets divided by current liabilities. It is defined and explained in Section 10.4, Ratio 18. See also Section 2.3.

Current value accounting

A proposed accounting method that would use current or market values to value assets and liabilities and to calculate income. See Sections 2.9 and 8.2.

Cut off

The end of a fiscal period and the procedures used to ensure accuracy in measuring phenomena up to that date. See Section 6.5.

D

Days' sales in receivables

The ratio of accounts receivable to the daily sales, expressed in number of days' sales represented by accounts receivable. Also called **Collection ratio**. Defined and explained in Section 10.4, Ratio 14.

DCF

See **Discounted cash flows**, another phrase for "present value" analysis of future cash flows. See **Present value** and Section 10.7.

Debenture

A form of **Security** taken by a creditor on a loan or bond, in which the creditor has a general ability to influence or direct management decisions if the debt payments are not made on schedule; not a claim on a specific asset as a **Mortgage** has. See Sections 2.7 and 9.3.

Debit (DR or Dr)

The left-hand side of double-entry accounting. The term *debit* can be used as a noun to refer to the left-hand side of a journal entry or account or as a verb referring to the action of making an entry on the left-hand side of an account. Most accounts (except contra accounts) on the left-hand side of the balance sheet have debit balances, which means the debits to them exceed the credits to them. A debit will increase the amounts on the asset side of the balance sheet, but decrease the amounts on the liabilities and equity side. See **Double-entry accounting**, **Credit**, and Sections 2.4–2.6.

Debt

An obligation to make a future payment in return for a benefit already received. See Sections 2.3, 9.2, and 9.3.

Debt-equity ratio

Total liabilities divided by total equity. It is defined and explained in Section 10.4, Ratio 15. See also Section 2.3, and used in the Scott formula in Section 10.6.

Debt to assets ratio

Total liabilities divided by total assets. It is defined and explained in Section 10.4, Ratio 17.

Decelerated amortization

The opposite of accelerated amortization or depreciation. Not acceptable for most enterprises. See **Accelerated amortization** and Section 8.12.

Decision relevance

An accounting objective: information should be available to the user at a time and in a form that is useful to the user's decision making. See **Relevance** and Sections 5.2, 5.3, and 6.6.

Declining balance amortization

An accelerated amortization (depreciation) method in which the annual amortization (depreciation) expense is calculated as a fixed percentage of the book value of the asset, which declines over time as amortization is deducted. See **Accelerated amortization**, **Amortization**, and Section 8.12.

Deferral

Part of accrual accounting but often used as the opposite to an accrual. A deferral involves keeping a past cash receipt or payment on the balance sheet—in other words, putting it on the income statement as revenue or expense at a later time. An example is recognizing a deferred revenue liability resulting from a recent cash receipt, such as for a magazine subscription to be delivered later. (In contrast, accruals involve recording a revenue or expense before the cash receipt or payment occurs.) See Sections 6.2 and 6.3.

Deferral method

A way of accounting for future income tax expenses incurred by present activities, now largely replaced by future income tax liability estimates. See **Deferred income tax**.

Deferred charge

A noncurrent **Prepaid expense**, in which the costs of issuing bonds, incorporation costs, or other expenditures benefiting several future periods are shown as noncurrent assets and usually amortized to expense over several periods or otherwise charged to expenses in some future period. See Sections 2.10 and 8.14.

Deferred income tax (expense and liability)

An expense account and corresponding liability intended to recognize the future tax consequences of income reported on the current income statement but not to be reported on the tax return until a future period. Now largely replaced by future income tax liability estimates. See **Future income tax** and Section 9.3.

Deferred revenue

A liability account used for customer deposits or other cash receipts prior to the completion of the sale (for example, before delivery). See Section 9.3.

Deficit

Negative retained earnings, and sometimes also used to refer to negative earnings. See **Retained earnings**, **Net loss**, and Sections 2.3 and 3.3.

Delivery

The most common basis of recognizing revenue. Revenue is said to be earned when the product or service has been delivered to the customer. See **Revenue recognition** and Sections 6.6 and 6.7.

Demand loans

Loans that are repayable whenever the creditor wants. These are a form of **Callable debt**. See Section 9.2.

Denial of opinion

A form of **Auditor's opinion** in which the auditor reports that *no* opinion may be given about the financial statements' fairness. See Section 5.8.

Depletion

An amortization (depreciation) method used for physically wasting assets such as natural resources. See Section 8.10.

Depreciation

The recognition of the expense due to use of the economic value of fixed tangible assets (for example, trucks, building, or plant). Usage, at least in Canada, appears to be changing to replace the term **depreciation** with the more general term **amortization**. See **Amortization**, **Declining balance amortization**, **Straight-line amortization**, **Book value**, and **Accumulated amortization (depreciation)**. See also Sections 1.10, 7.7, 8.10, and 8.12.

Diminishing balance

Another name for **Declining balance amortization.** See Section 8.12.

Direct method of cash flow analysis

A method of preparing the **Cash flow statement**, especially the **Cash from operations** section, using records of cash receipts and disbursements instead of the adjustments to net income used in the more traditional **Indirect method of cash flow analysis**. See Sections 4.3 and 4.4.

Direct write-off

Transferring the cost of an asset to an expense or **Loss** account by removing the amount entirely from the asset account. Used in cases where there is no prior allowance for the expense or loss, so used when there is no **Contra account** such as **Accumulated amortization** or **Allowance for doubtful accounts**. See Section 7.7.

Disbursements

See **Cash disbursements** and Section 4.3.

Disclosure

Provision of information about economic events beyond that included in the financial statement figures. Usually given in the notes to the financial statements, but also provided outside the financial statements in press releases, speeches, and other announcements. See **Notes to the financial statements**, **Management of corporate financial disclosure**, and Sections 1.10, 4.7, 5.2, 5.3, and 6.4.

Discontinued operations

Portions of the business that the enterprise has decided not to keep going and/or to sell to others. It is good practice to separate the effects of discontinued operations from continuing operations when measuring income and cash flow. See Section 3.5.

Discount (on bonds)

Arises when bonds are issued at a price below their legal face value, such as a $100 bond being issued for $95 cash, indicating a $5 discount. See Section 9.3.

Discounted cash flows

"Present value" analysis of future cash flows by removing their presumed interest components. See **Present value** and Section 10.7.

Discretionary expenses

Expenses that depend on management's discretion rather than on the necessities of producing, selling, or shipping goods and services. Examples might be donations, political contributions, some maintenance and warranty costs, and bonuses not specifically called for in employment contracts. See Section 6.6.

DIT

See **Deferred income tax**.

Dividend payout ratio

The ratio of dividends declared to net income. It is defined and explained in Section 10.4, Ratio 11.

Dividends

Distributions of a portion of net income to shareholders in the company. Since this type of payment does not relate to the operating performance of the company, it is placed on the statement of retained earnings and not the income statement. See **Statement of retained earnings**, **Stock dividend,** and Sections 2.3, 3.3, 3.4, and 9.4.

Double declining balance

See **Declining balance amortization**, **Accelerated amortization**, **Amortization** and Section 8.12.

Double-entry accounting

The practice of recording two aspects of each transaction or event: the resource effect and the source or story of that effect. Though much expanded since its invention several hundred years ago, it is still the basis of bookkeeping and financial accounting. See Sections 2.2 and 2.3.

Double-entry bookkeeping

See **Double-entry accounting**.

E

Earnings

A common synonym for net income. See **Net income** and Sections 2.3 and 3.3.

Earnings management

Choosing accounting methods and/or making business deals with the specific objective of altering the size, trend, or interpretation of the company's earnings (net income). Usually frowned on as a form of **Manipulation of accounting information**. See Sections 3.10, 6.5, and 9.5.

Earnings per share (EPS)

The ratio of net income to the average number of common (voting) shares outstanding, used to allow the owner of the shares to relate the corporation's earning power to the size of his or her investment. The calculation of EPS can be quite complex, so most public companies calculate it for the users (as required by generally accepted accounting principles for such corporations) and report it on their income statements. See **Ratios**, Section 3.4, and Section 10.4, Ratio 8, where EPS is defined and explained.

Earnings-price ratio

The inverse of the **Price-earnings ratio**. Earnings per share divided by the market price of one share of a corporation. See **PE ratio**, **Ratios**, and Section 10.4, Ratio 10, where the ratio is defined and explained.

EBITDA

Earnings before interest, tax, depreciation and amortization. A more positive measure of net income for a company because it includes all revenues but not all expenses. See Section 3.10.

E-commerce

See **Electronic commerce** and Sections 1.7 and 7.2.

Economic entity

The financial accounting definition of an enterprise, used to determine what is to be included in transactions and in the financial statements. Also used to refer to a group of companies considered to be under the same control and, so, constituting a larger economic group. See **Accounting entity**, **Transaction**, **Consolidation**, and Sections 2.9, 3.2, 5.2, and 9.7.

Effective income tax rate

The income tax rate the company appears to incur, as deduced from the financial statements. Differs from the statutory or legal rate because of many possible tax incentives, varying rates across jurisdictions, etc. Can be estimated as the company's income tax expense divided by income before income tax, both from the income statement. See Section 9.3.

Effects analysis

See **"What if" (effects) analysis** and Sections 1.12 and 10.8.

Efficiency (of information use, or informational efficiency)

Refers to a market's prices quickly and appropriately changing to reflect new information. See Section 5.10.

Efficient capital market

A theoretical description of a capital market whose prices respond quickly and appropriately to information. See Section 5.10.

Efficient market hypothesis

The proposal that capital markets actually are "efficient," responding quickly, smoothly, and appropriately to information. Some seem to be efficient, and some do not. See **Efficient capital market** and Section 5.10.

Electronic commerce

Also called **e-commerce**, this is the conducting of financial transactions, and many of the business transactions behind them, over electronic media such as telecommunication lines or the Web. See Section 7.2.

Electronic funds transfer (EFT)

Transfer of money between a buyer's bank account and the seller's bank account without need to write cheques or make deposits. EFT is what is happening if a customer uses a bank card to pay for groceries in the supermarket and the amount is automatically deducted from the customer's bank account. See Section 7.2.

Employee deductions

Amounts an employer is required to deduct from an employee's pay and remit to someone else on behalf of the employee. Such deductions include income tax, pension contributions, union dues, and many other amounts the employee wants to or has to pay before receiving the net pay that is left over. See Section 7.6.

Entity

See **Accounting entity** and **Economic entity**.

Entry

See **Journal entry** and Sections 2.4, 2.6, and 3.6.

EPS

See **Earnings per share** and Section 10.4, Ratio 8.

Equities

A term sometimes used to refer to the right-hand side of the balance sheet (Equities = Liabilities + Owners' equity).

Equity

The net assets or residual interest of an owner or shareholder (Assets = Liabilities + Equity, or restated as Equity = Assets – Liabilities). See **Balance sheet equation** and the components of equity under **Shareholders' equity**, **Retained earnings**, and Sections 2.3, 2.9, and 9.4.

Equity basis

A method of accounting for intercorporate investments usually used when a company owns between 20% and 50% of another company. The investment is carried at cost, and any profit or loss, multiplied by the percentage ownership of the owned company, is added to or deducted from the investment. Any dividends received are deducted from the investment. See **Cost basis** and Section 9.6.

Exchange

A transfer of goods, services, or money between two parties. In financial accounting, the most significant kind of exchange is external—that is, between the enterprise and parties it deals with, such as customers, suppliers, owners, employees, and creditors. See **Transaction** and Sections 1.7 and 2.4.

Expenditure

The term can mean any **Cash payment**, but usually spending on noncurrent assets or debts is meant. Also used instead of the word **Expense** for governments and other nonbusiness organizations that may not use full accrual accounting and therefore do not have expenses as accountants usually mean them. See Sections 3.3 and 5.5.

Expense

The cost of assets used and/or obligations created in generating revenue, whether or not paid for in cash in the period they appear on the **Income statement**. See **Revenue**, **Matching**, **Expense recognition**, **Accrual accounting**, and Sections 1.10, 3.3, 3.4, 6.3, and 6.8.

Expense recognition

Incorporating measures of expenses incurred into the measurement of income by entering into the accounts the amount of expense determined, according to the firm's accounting policies, to be attributable to the current period. See **Matching**, **Revenue recognition**, and Sections 6.3 and 6.8.

Expensing

Classifying an expenditure or promised expenditure (accrual) as an expense rather than an asset. Opposite of **Capitalization**. See Section 8.4.

External audit

The audit conducted by an **External auditor**. See Section 5.8.

External auditor

An independent outside auditor appointed to review the financial statements. See **Auditor** and Sections 1.5, 5.1, 5.2 and 5.8.

Extraordinary items

Gains and losses that arise out of situations that are not normal to the operations of a firm, not under the control of management, and not expected to recur regularly in the future. See Section 3.5.

F

Fair market value

A value or price determined by an unrelated buyer and seller who are separate and acting rationally in their own self-interest. The value is considered more meaningful if established in an actual transaction than if estimated hypothetically. **Historical cost** is assumed to have been the fair market value of an asset when it was acquired. See forms of estimated fair market value under **Fair value accounting**, **Net realizable value** and **Replacement cost**, and Sections 8.2 and 9.7.

Fairness

Because of all the estimations, judgments, and policy choices that go into preparing financial statements, there is no one correct set of figures or disclosures. Instead, there is the idea of fairness, which means playing by the rules and preparing statements honestly, without any intent to deceive or to present any particular view. The opinion paragraph of the auditor's report states that the financial statements "present fairly ... in accordance with generally accepted accounting principles." Attention to fairness in the application of accounting principles requires care and judgment in distinguishing the substance from the form of a transaction and identifying the accepted principles and practices. See **Generally accepted accounting principles**, **Accounting standards**, and Sections 5.2, 5.3, and 6.4.

Fair value

An estimate of the fair market values of assets and liabilities of an acquired company used in the purchase method of consolidation accounting. See Sections 8.2 and 9.7.

Fair value accounting

Valuing assets on the balance sheet at their estimated value to the company, such as if sold in a fair transaction. Fair value accounting would use these values instead of **Historical cost** amounts on the balance sheet. See **Fair market value** and **Fair value**, and Section 6.3.

FASB

See **Financial Accounting Standards Board** and Section 5.4.

FIFO

An inventory cost flow assumption by which cost of goods sold is determined from the cost of the beginning inventory and the cost of the oldest purchases since; thus the acronym FIFO, which stands for "first in, first out." It follows therefore that under FIFO, ending inventory cost is determined from the cost of the most recent purchases. Since the older inventory is assumed to be sold first, FIFO in a period of inflation usually creates a smaller cost of goods sold and higher income and ending inventory asset value than **LIFO** or **Weighted average**. See **Cost flow assumption**, **Cost of goods sold**, and Section 8.7.

Financial accounting

The reporting in **Financial statements** of the financial position and performance of a firm to users external to the firm on a regular, periodic basis. See **Management accounting** and Section 1.3.

Financial Accounting Standards Board (FASB)

A U.S. body responsible for setting the standards that financial reporting must follow. The Canadian counterpart is the Canadian Institute of Chartered Accountants. See ***CICA Handbook*** and Section 5.4.

Financial assets

Near-cash assets such as traded shares, bonds, some kinds of loans, and accounts receivable, especially as would be held by financial institutions such as banks. Part of the general category of **Financial instruments**. See Section 8.2.

Financial instruments

Debts, shares, foreign exchange contracts, and other financial obligations and assets, many of which are traded on **Stock markets** and other **Capital markets**. See Sections 2.9, 5.10, and 9.5.

Financial leverage

See **Leverage** and Section 10.6.

Financial performance

The enterprise's ability to generate new resources from day-to-day operations over a period of time, via dealing with customers, employees, and suppliers. Measured by the **Net income** figure in the **Income statement** and the **Cash from operations** figure in the **Cash flow statement**, as well as by the details of both statements. See Sections 1.3 and 3.3.

Financial position

The enterprise's set of assets, liabilities, and owners' equity at a point in time. Measured by the **Balance sheet**, also called the **Statement of financial position**. See Sections 1.3 and 2.3.

Financial reporting

Use of **Financial statements** and **Disclosure** to report to people outside the enterprise on its **Financial performance** and **Financial position**. See Section 5.6.

Financial statement analysis

Use of the financial statements to develop summary measures (ratios) and interpretive comments about an enterprise's financial performance and position. See **Ratios** and Sections 10.3 and 10.4.

Financial statements

The reports, for people external to the enterprise but also of interest to management, referred to in the definition of **Accounting**, which generally comprise a **Balance sheet**, **Income statement**, **Statement of retained earnings**, **Cash flow statement**, and the **Notes** to these statements. See each of these statements in this glossary and Sections 1.3 and 5.6.

Financing

The combination of **Debt** and **Equity** that accounts for the company's assets. See Section 2.3. See also **Balance sheet equation**. Sometimes there is also **Off-balance-sheet financing**.

Financing activities

The category of the **Cash flow statement** that describes the cash obtained or used in connection with noncurrent debt and equity. See Section 4.3.

First-in, first-out

See **FIFO** and Section 8.7.

Fiscal

Refers to the finances of an entity, and so is used to designate the period covered by the financial statements, which may not accord with regular calendar periods. For example, some companies use a 52-week "fiscal year" in some years and 53 weeks in others, and such a **Fiscal period** may end at any time of the calendar year the company has chosen. See Section 2.10.

Fiscal period

The period (usually a year, a quarter, or a month) over which performance (net income) is measured and at the end of which position (balance sheet) is determined. See Section 6.5.

Fixed assets

Tangible, noncurrent, physical assets that are not expected to be used up in one operating cycle, but are expected to be used in generating revenue for many periods (for example, machines, buildings, land). See **Noncurrent assets** and Section 8.10.

Foreign currency translation, foreign currency translation adjustment

The conversion of foreign monies into domestic monies at a specific date—either a transaction date, if translating a single transaction, or a financial statement date, if translating a foreign operation for consolidation purposes. This process normally produces an adjustment to make the accounts balance, shown in the equity section of the balance sheet. See **Accumulated foreign currency translation adjustment** and Sections 2.9 and 2.10.

Form versus substance

A potential choice or conflict among accounting methods in which one possibility ("form") fits the accounting rules better and another possibility ("substance") reports the business and economic reality better. See Sections 5.2 and 5.3.

Franchising

A franchisor sells to a franchisee the right to use the franchisor's name, products, or other economic goods. See Section 6.8.

Fund accounting

A kind of accounting used by governments and other nonbusiness organizations to segregate groups of assets, liabilities, some forms of equity, revenues, and expenditures, in accordance with the purpose for which the funds were obtained. For example, donations received might be segregated from research grants received so that each kind of money is put to the use intended when it was obtained. See comments at the end of Section 9.4.

Funds statement

See **Cash flow statement** and Section 4.2.

Future income tax, future portion of income tax expense

Income tax expected to be paid in future years based on business events and income tax calculations done up to the present. The liability and associated expense are calculated by the **Liability method**, which estimates the likely future tax payments directly, and which has recently replaced the **Deferral method** and **Deferred income tax**. See Section 9.3.

Future income tax liability

Estimated income taxes due in the future, based on accounting income and income tax calculations done up to the present. The liability results from **Future income tax** accounting. This liability is usually noncurrent. (Future income tax assets also can arise from future income tax accounting.) See Section 9.3.

Future value (FV)

The amount to which presently held financial assets or liabilities will build up as interest is added to the principal amount invested or borrowed. Often contrasted with **Present value**, which is the future cash flows minus interest included in them. See Section 10.7.

GAAP

See **Generally accepted accounting principles** and Sections 5.1, 5.3, 6.4, 8.2, and 8.5.

GAAS

See **Generally accepted auditing standards** and Section 5.8.

Gain, gains

Usually refers to the profit (proceeds minus book value) obtained from the disposition of assets (or liabilities) not normally disposed of in the daily course of business, such as from selling land, buildings, or other noncurrent assets, or from refinancing debt. Gains are considered nonoperating items and so, if they are material, they are segregated from normal revenues and expenses on the income statement and the cash flows involved are included in the investing or financing sections of the cash flow statement. See Sections 7.7 and 8.11.

Gain (loss) on sale

A **Gain** on sale occurs when a company receives a larger amount of proceeds for an asset than its book value. An income statement account is then credited with the difference. A **Loss** on sale occurs when the asset's book value is more than the proceeds received from the sale. An income statement account is then debited with the difference. See **Book value** and Sections 7.7 and 8.11.

General journal

An accounting record used mainly to record accrual adjustments (journal entries) not provided for in separate specialized journals. See Sections 3.8 and 7.2.

General ledger

A collection of individual accounts that summarizes the entire financial accounting system of an enterprise. See Sections 2.5, 3.8, and 7.2.

Generally accepted accounting principles (GAAP)

Principles and methods of accounting that have the general support of standard-setting bodies, general practice, texts, and other sources. See **Accounting standards** and Sections 1.1, 5.1, and 5.3.

Generally accepted auditing standards (GAAS)

The professional standards of care and evidence compilation that external auditors are expected to follow when preparing their reports on financial statements. See **Auditor's report** and Section 5.8.

Going concern

A fundamental assumption in financial accounting that a firm will be financially viable and remain in business long enough to see all of its current plans carried out. If a firm is not a going concern, normal accounting principles do not apply. See **Liquidation value** and Sections 5.2, 8.2, and 9.2.

Goods and services tax

See **GST** and Sections 7.2 and 7.6.

Goodwill

The difference between the price paid for a group of assets and the sum of their apparent fair (market) values. Arises when a bundle of assets or a whole company is acquired and when the difference is positive. ("Badwill," a negative difference, is not recognized.) See Sections 2.9, 2.11, 8.14, and 9.7.

Goodwill arising on consolidation

Goodwill existing only in **Consolidated financial statements** accounted for using the **Purchase method**, indicating that the **Parent** corporation paid more for its investment in a **Subsidiary** corporation included in the consolidated statements than the fair values of the subsidiary's assets. See **Goodwill** and Sections 2.9 and 9.7.

Governmental accounting

Accounting procedures, usually different from **GAAP** for businesses but in recent years becoming more like GAAP, used to account for governments and their agencies. See Section 5.5.

Governments

In this book, governments are used mainly as an example of organizations that have accounting systems and prepare financial statements but do not have the characteristics of businesses, especially the goals and ownership structure. See Section 5.5. Governments also levy GST, income and other taxes and so have an influence on businesses' accounting. See Sections 7.6 and 9.3.

Gross margin or gross profit

Revenue minus cost of goods sold expense. See Sections 3.4 and 10.4.

Gross margin ratio or gross profit ratio

Equals (Revenue – Cost of goods sold expense) / Revenue. See **Ratios** and Section 10.4, Ratio 5, where the gross margin (or gross profit) ratio is defined and explained. See also Section 3.4.

GST (Goods and services tax)

The Canadian federal goods and services tax, a kind of sales tax which businesses must collect on most of their revenue and remit to the government after deducting any GST the businesses paid on their own purchases. See **HST**, **PST**, and Sections 7.2 and 7.6.

H

Harmonization

The movement toward making countries' accounting standards the same as those of other countries, which would strengthen the internationalization of accounting standards. See Section 5.5.

Historical cost

The dollar value of a transaction on the date it happens, normally maintained in the accounting records from then on because of accounting's reliance on transactions as the basis for recording events. The cost, or historical cost, of an asset is therefore the dollar amount paid for it or promised to be paid as of the date the asset was acquired. See **Cost**, **Lower of cost or market**, **Conservatism**, and Sections 1.7, 5.2, 8.2, and 9.2.

HST

Harmonized sales tax. See **GST** and Section 7.6.

I

IASB

See **International Accounting Standards Board** and Section 5.4.

IASC

See **International Accounting Standards Committee**.

Impaired assets

Assets whose value to the business has gone down since they were acquired. This is especially used in reference to **Investments** and **Goodwill**, which, if impaired, have to be reduced in value on the balance sheet, creating a **Write-off** or loss expense. See Sections 8.2 and 8.14.

IN(ATI)

The after-tax overall interest rate paid by an enterprise on its liabilities. Used in the **Scott formula**. See Section 10.6.

Income

The (net) income of a business is the residual after deducting expenses from revenues. Also referred to as profit or earnings. See **Accrual income**, **Cash income**, **Net income**, and Sections 1.9, 2.3, 3.3, 3.4, and 6.6.

Income before (income) tax

An amount equal to revenue plus other income minus all other ordinary expenses except income tax. Appears quite low down on the income statement. Some nontaxed or special items, such as **Extraordinary items**, are placed after income tax has been deducted, and are therefore not part of income before income tax. See Section 3.5.

Income from continuing operations

Income after deducting income tax but before adding gains or deducting losses from **Discontinued operations**. See Section 3.5.

Income measurement

A phrase used to describe financial accounting's way of calculating (net) income as shown on the income statement. The phrase is also used to describe the general problem of determining what income is and considering alternatives to the usual **Accrual accounting** basis. See Sections 3.2 and 8.2.

Income smoothing

The "manipulation" of net income so that the year-to-year variations in reported income are reduced. See Sections 3.10 and 6.4.

Income statement

A financial statement that summarizes revenues and expenses of a business for a stated period of time and computes the residual net income (revenues minus expenses). Sometimes referred to as "Statement of Earnings," "Statement of Operations," or "Statement of Income." See components of the income statement such as **Revenue**, **Expense**, and **Net income**; also **Financial performance** and Sections 1.1, 3.3, and 3.5.

Income tax

Tax assessed on income, according to laws about the computation of income for income tax purposes. See Sections 3.5 and 9.3.

Income tax allocation

The attempt to allocate income tax expense to the appropriate year or activity to which it applies, even if it is paid in another year or in aggregate across activities. See **Income tax expense**, **Deferred income tax**, **Future income tax**, **Intraperiod tax allocation,** and Sections 3.5 and 9.3.

Income tax expense

An estimate of the current and future income tax arising from the income as computed on the income statement and matched to the revenues and expenses shown on the statement. See **Income tax allocation** and Sections 3.5 and 9.3.

Income tax payable

The liability for the amount of income tax due on the year's income, calculated according to the income tax law whether or not that matches the Income tax expense. See Section 9.3.

Indenture

A contract signed by a borrower and lender under which the borrower undertakes to meet certain conditions, such as keeping the working capital ratio above a specified amount, violation of which would give the lender the right to ask for immediate repayment of the loan or to take other action. See Section 9.3.

Independence

Having no financial or other interest that would influence one's decisions. **External auditors** are expected to be independent of the enterprises they audit, and so can hold no shares, nor management positions, etc. See Sections 1.4, 5.8, and 5.9.

Indirect method of cash flow analysis

The traditional method of deriving the **Cash flow statement**, especially the **Cash from operations** section, by adjusting net income for noncash items. See Sections 4.3 and 4.5.

Information system

An organized and systematic way of providing information to decision makers. Accounting is an information system. See also **Management information system** and Section 1.7.

Input market value

The market value of an asset calculated as the amount it would cost to replace or reproduce it. See **Replacement cost** and Section 8.2.

Intangible assets

Nonphysical, noncurrent assets such as copyrights, patents, trademarks, import and export licences, other rights that give a firm an exclusive or preferred position in the marketplace, and goodwill. See **Assets**, **Amortization**, **Goodwill**, and Sections 2.11, 7.7, and 8.14.

Intercorporate investments

Investments by one corporation in other corporations. See **Consolidation**, **Equity basis**, **Cost basis**, and Section 9.6.

Interest

The amount charged by a lender for the use of borrowed money. See Sections 3.5, 10.2, and 10.7.

Interest coverage ratio

Usually calculated as (Income before interest expense + Income tax) / Interest expense. See **Ratios** and Section 10.4, Ratio 20, where the interest coverage ratio is defined and explained.

Interim financial reporting

Reporting financial position and performance at a shorter interval than one year. The most common example is the three-month "quarterly reporting" done by companies listed on stock exchanges. See Section 5.6.

Internal auditor

An auditor who works for the enterprise and thus verifies information for management's use and to help the enterprise perform better. See Section 1.5 and contrast with **External auditor**.

Internal control

Methods of providing physical security and management control over an enterprise's cash, inventories, and other assets. See Sections 7.2–7.9.

Internal financing

Financing provided from funds raised in day-to-day operations rather than by borrowing or issuing equity. See **Cash from operations** and Section 4.7.

International Accounting Standards Board (IASB)

The international accounting standard-setter, headquartered in London, England. See Sections 5.4 and 5.5.

International Accounting Standards Committee (IASC)

The predecessor of the **International Accounting Standards Board (IASB)**.

Interperiod tax allocation

Allocating the enterprise's income tax expenses over several years to match the expenses to the incomes shown in the income statement. Necessitated by timing differences between GAAP and the income tax law in the recognition of various revenues and expenses. See Sections 3.5 and 9.3. Contrast **Intraperiod tax allocation**.

Intraperiod tax allocation

The attempt to match income tax expense to the various items in the income statement, especially separating general income tax expense from that due to special items below that expense on the income statement, such as **Extraordinary items** and **Discontinued operations**. See Sections 3.5 and 9.3.

Inventory(ies)

The goods purchased or manufactured by a company for sale, resale, or further use in operations, including finished goods, goods in process, raw materials, and supplies. See **Current assets**, **Inventory costing**, and Sections 2.3, 2.4, 3.3, 7.9, and 8.7.

Inventory costing

Comprises various methods of determining the cost of inventory for balance sheet valuation purposes and of valuing cost of goods sold. The more common methods are **FIFO**, **LIFO**, and **Weighted average**. See also Sections 8.4 and 8.7.

Inventory turnover

Cost of goods sold expense / Average inventory assets. See **Ratios** and Section 10.4, Ratio 13, where inventory turnover is defined and explained.

Inventory valuation

The process of determining the amount at which inventory is shown on the balance sheet, normally the **Lower of cost or market**. See **Inventory costing** and Section 8.7.

Investing activities

The category of the **Cash flow statement** that describes the cash used to acquire, or the cash obtained by disposing of, noncurrent assets. See Section 4.3.

Investments

Usually refers to such assets as shares or bonds held for their financial return (interest or dividends), rather than for their use in the enterprise's operations. See Sections 8.5, 9.6, and 10.2.

Investors

People who own **Investments** and who, because of their interest in the value of those shares or bonds, are interested in information about the enterprises issuing such shares and bonds. See Sections 1.5 and 5.10.

J

Joint venture

A business arrangement between corporations that is like a corporate partnership. See Section 9.6.

Journal entry

A record of a transaction or accrual adjustment that lists the accounts affected and in which the total of the debits equals the total of the credits. See **Account** and Sections 2.4, 2.6, and 3.8.

Journals

Records in which accounting transactions of a similar nature are permanently recorded. See **Books of original entry**, **General journal**, and Section 7.2.

L

L/E

Total liabilities / Total equity, the **Debt-equity ratio** used in the **Scott formula**. See Section 10.6.

Last-in, first-out

See **LIFO** and Section 8.7.

Lease

A contract requiring the user of an asset to pay the owner of the asset a predetermined fee for the use of the asset. See Section 8.14.

Leasehold improvements

Assets such as fixtures, decorating, and alterations installed into rented (leased) premises and so being economic assets for the enterprise even though not strictly owned because they form part of the leased property. Such improvements are usually amortized over the period of the lease, as a reasonable estimate of their useful life. See Sections 3.12 and 8.4.

Ledger

Any book or electronic record that summarizes the transactions from the "books of original entry" in the form of accounts. See **Accounts**, **General ledger**, **Journals**, **Trial balance**, and Section 7.2.

Letter to the shareholders

Part of the **Annual report**, it is a letter from senior management to the shareholders, summarizing major decisions and strategies, commenting on the company's performance for the year and usually looking ahead to future performance. See Section 5.6.

Leverage

Leverage, or financial leverage, refers to the increased rate of return on owners' equity when assets earn a return larger than the interest rate paid for debt financing them. The **Scott formula** indicates how part of the **Return on equity** is made up of **Operating return** and **Leverage return**. See **Scott formula** and Sections 10.4 and 10.6.

Leverage analysis

Study of the financial statements and corporate financial structure in order to determine how, and how well, the company is making use of **Leverage**. See Section 10.6.

Leverage potential

The difference between operating return (return on assets) and borrowing cost, which produces **Leverage** when multiplied by the degree of borrowing in the Scott formula. See Section 10.6.

Leverage return

The portion of the **Return on equity** that is due to earning more return on borrowed funds than it costs in interest to borrow them. See **Scott formula**, **Operating return**, and Section 10.6.

Liability

A debt or obligation, legally existing or estimated via accrual accounting techniques, of the enterprise to another party (creditor) arising from a past transaction (for example, a bank loan, a shareholder loan, an account payable, a mortgage, an accrued expense, or deferred revenue). See **Creditor** and Sections 1.1, 2.3, 2.9, 2.10, 9.2, and 9.3.

Liability method

A method of **Income tax allocation** in which the impact of **Future income tax** is estimated according to what is expected to be paid rather than according to past timing differences as done in the former **Deferred income tax** accounting. The liability method is common in other countries, and Canada has recently adopted it. See Section 9.3.

LIFO

A cost flow assumption that is the opposite of FIFO. "Last in, first out" assumes that the units sold are from the most recent purchases and thus bases cost of goods sold on the most recent purchases and ending inventory on the oldest purchases. Because of this, in a period of inflation the LIFO cost of goods sold figure is usually the highest of the inventory costing methods, and the inventory value on the balance sheet is usually the lowest. See **Cost flow assumption**, **FIFO**, **Weighted average**, **Inventory costing**, and Section 8.7.

Line of credit

Advance approval from a bank to borrow money under agreed conditions. A line of credit usually means that the borrower can get the money as needed (for example, when the bank account is overdrawn), without further approval.

Liquidation value

The value of a firm's assets if they are all to be sold off when it is no longer a going concern. See Section 8.2.

Liquidity

The excess of very short-term assets over short-term debts, and so the measure of a company's ability to pay its immediate obligations in cash at the present moment. See **Solvency** and Sections 4.2, 4.8, and 10.4 (Ratios 18–20).

Listed (shares)

A listed company (corporation) is one whose shares are available for trading on a **Stock exchange**. See **Public company** and Sections 5.3 and 5.10.

Loans from shareholder(s)

Informal loans to the corporation by shareholder(s), who therefore act as creditors as well as owners. They are most common in private company corporations. See Section 9.3.

Long-term debt-equity ratio

Calculated as (Long-term loans + Mortgages + Bonds + Similar long-term debts) / Total equity. See **Ratios** and Section 10.4, Ratio 16, where the ratio is defined and explained.

Loss, losses

Usually refers to the case of a negative return (proceeds being less than book value) obtained from the disposition of assets (or liabilities) not normally disposed of in the daily course of business, such as from selling land, buildings or other noncurrent assets, or from refinancing debt. These are considered nonoperating items and so are, if material, segregated from normal revenues and expenses on the income statement, and the cash flows involved are included in the investing or financing sections of the cash flow statement. See Sections 2.3, 3.3, 7.7, and 8.11.

Loss on sale

Selling a noncurrent asset for less than its book value. See **Gain (loss) on sale**, **Book value**, **Loss**, and Sections 7.7 and 8.11.

Lower of cost or market

A method of valuing items of inventory, temporary investments, or other current assets, under which losses inherent in declines of the market prices of items held below their costs are recognized in the period in which such declines become apparent. Gains from market increases above cost are not recognized until the items are sold. Lower of cost or market is a conservative procedure. See **Conservatism** and Sections 8.2, 8.5, and 8.9.

M

Management

The people (managers) who run the day-to-day operations of an enterprise or other organization, in contrast to the shareholders (investors), members, and voters who own or legally control the enterprise. See Section 1.3.

Management accounting

Accounting information designed to aid management in its operation and control of the firm, and in its general decision making. It is different from **Financial accounting**, which is aimed primarily at users external to the firm. See Section 1.3.

Management discussion and analysis (MD&A)

A section of a company's annual report in which management reviews the results for the year and explains what happened in some detail. The MD&A is used by many analysts to supplement ratios and other forms of analysis. See **Annual report** and Sections 5.6 and 10.3.

Management information system

The accounting, marketing, production, employee, and other recordkeeping and reporting systems within the enterprise used by management in its internal decision making. Often abbreviated as MIS and often associated with computer systems. See **Management accounting**, **Electronic commerce**, and Section 7.3.

Management of corporate financial disclosure

Steps taken by management to manage the outward flow of information about an enterprise, much as other aspects of the enterprise are managed. See Section 3.10.

Managers

See **Management** and Section 1.3.

Manipulation

The accusation that management, in choosing its accounting and disclosure policies, attempts to make the performance and position measures suit its wishes. See Sections 3.10 and 6.4.

Marginal analysis

Focusing on revenues or expenses that change between two alternatives, rather than including all revenues and expenses, so as to highlight effects. See **"What if" (effects) analysis** and Section 1.12.

Marketable securities

Investments having a ready market for resale and held as a way of earning a return from temporarily unneeded cash. See **Temporary investments** and Sections 8.5 and 9.6.

Market capitalization

An estimate of the value of a listed public company made by multiplying the current share price times the number of shares issued and outstanding. See Section 2.3 and comments under Ratio 9 in Section 10.4.

Market value

See **Fair market value** and Sections 2.3, 8.2, and 8.3.

Markup

The difference between the enterprise's selling prices for its products and the unit costs it incurs for those products, often a function of a specific decision to add a profit margin to the cost incurred. See comments about markup in Section 3.4 regarding **Gross margin** and Sections 7.9 and 8.9 regarding the **Retail inventory control method**.

Matching, matching principle

The concept of recognizing expenses in the same accounting period in which the related revenues are recognized. See **Accrual accounting**, **Expense recognition**, **Revenue recognition**, and Sections 5.2, 5.3, 5.8, 6.3, 6.4, 8.6, and 9.3.

Material, materiality

In accounting, material means that the magnitude of an omission or misstatement of accounting information makes it probable that, in the light of surrounding circumstances, the judgment of a reasonable person relying on the information would have been changed or influenced by the omission or misstatement. Materiality and **Decision relevance** are both defined in terms of what influences or what makes a difference to a decision maker. A decision not to disclose certain information may be made because it is believed that investors or other users have no need for that kind of information (it is not relevant) or that the amounts involved are too small to make a difference (it is not material). See **Relevance** and Sections 3.5, 5.2, 5.3, and 6.4.

MD&A

See **Management discussion and analysis** and Sections 5.6 and 10.3.

Measurement, measuring

The attachment of dollar figures to assets, liabilities, revenues, and expenses in order to produce the figures (values) on the balance sheet and to enable the computation of income (revenues minus expenses) and equity (assets minus liabilities). See **Asset valuation**, **Balance sheet valuation**, **Income measurement**, **Recognition**, **Income**, and Section 8.2.

Merger

The joining together of two corporations such that the owners of both become the owners of the combined corporation and both corporations are approximately equal contributors to the combination. See Section 9.7.

Minority interest, noncontrolling interest

An account in the liabilities part of the consolidated balance sheet. The percentage of the subsidiary's equity not owned by the parent company is designated as minority (noncontrolling) interest liability. A minority (noncontrolling) interest expense calculated in a similar way is also deducted in computing consolidated net income. See **Consolidation** and Sections 2.9 and 9.7.

Mortgage

A form of **Security** on a loan in which the lender has a direct claim on title to property specified in the mortgage. Usually used to finance the acquisition of that property. See Sections 2.3, 2.7, and 9.3.

Moving average cost, moving weighted average

See **AVGE**, **Average cost**, and Section 8.7.

N

Net

In accounting, net means the residual after one quantity is subtracted from another. Examples are **Net book value**, **Net income**, **Net-of-tax analysis**, and **Net realizable value**. See Section 2.7.

Net book value

The cost of an asset minus any accumulated depreciation, amortization, allowance for doubtful accounts, and so on. See **Book value** and Sections 7.7 and 8.11.

Net income

Equals income minus income tax expense, plus or minus extraordinary and special items (each **Net** of any income tax). See **Income**, **Retained earnings**, **Matching**, and Sections 1.12, 3.3, 3.5, and 6.3.

Net loss

Negative **Net income**. See Section 3.3.

Net-of-tax analysis

A method of determining the impact of management decisions or accounting changes in which the effects of income tax are included to produce the net after-tax effect of the decision or change. See Sections 1.12, 10.2, and 10.8.

Net present value

The present value of future cash flows minus the initial investment required to obtain those cash flows. See Section 8.2.

Net realizable value

The fair market value that an asset will bring if it is sold through the usual product market minus any completion or disposal costs. See **Fair market value**, **Lower of cost or market**, and Sections 8.2 and 8.9.

Neutrality

An objective of preparing financial accounting information in which the information should represent phenomena neutrally, without attention to the particular interests of any party or parties. See **Objectivity**, **Independence**, and Section 5.2.

Noncontrolling interest

The portion of a **Subsidiary** corporation included in consolidated financial statements that is not owned by the controlling (majority) owners of the **Parent** corporation. See **Minority interest**, **Consolidation**, and Sections 2.9 and 9.7.

Noncurrent assets

Assets expected to bring benefit for more than one fiscal year. See **Fixed assets**, **Current assets**, and Sections 2.3 and 8.11.

Noncurrent liabilities

Liabilities expected to be repaid or otherwise removed more than one year in the future. See **Liability** and Sections 2.3 and 9.3.

Nonoperating cash flows

Cash inflows and outflows related to noncurrent investments, financing, and usually dividends, and so separate from the cash flows resulting from day-to-day operations. See **Cash flow statement** and Sections 4.2 and 4.3.

No-par (shares)

Shares having no legal minimum issue price (**Par value**) and whose proceeds are thus simply added to share capital at whatever price is obtained in each issue. See Section 2.9.

Notes, Notes to the financial statements

Notes appended to the statements, providing information about the accounting policies chosen and other supplementary information helpful to interpreting the figures. See Sections 1.3, 2.3, 2.7, 4.7, 5.6, 5.7, 6.4, and 10.3.

Notes payable

Accounts payable that are supported by signed contracts or other agreements and usually carry interest. Often used to describe financing obtained from banks and other financial institutions that is used to provide operating funds or funds for construction prior to completion of projects. Notes may be used prior to obtaining more secured financing like a **Mortgage**.

Notes receivable

Accounts receivable supported by signed contracts or other agreements specifying repayment terms, interest rate, and other conditions. See Section 8.6.

Not-for-profit accounting

Procedures used to account for nonbusiness, nongovernment entities. These procedures increasingly follow **GAAP**. See Section 5.5.

Not-for-profit organizations

In this book, another example of organizations, other than **Governments**, that have accounting systems and prepare financial statements but differ from businesses, especially in goals and ownership structure. See Section 5.5.

Objectivity

The notion that the information in financial statements must be as free from bias as possible, in order that all user groups can have confidence in it. An accountant attempts to record and report data that are based on objective sources to make the data more acceptable to outside parties. Because completed arm's-length transactions are supported by documents that can be verified by any interested observer, these constitute the preferred basis of measurement. See **Fairness**, **Neutrality**, **Relevance**, **Reliability**, and Sections 1.4, 5.2, 5.3, and 5.8.

Off-balance-sheet financing

Methods of obtaining financing that avoid having to record the sources as liabilities or equity. See Sections 2.9 and 9.5.

Ontario Securities Commission (OSC)

The securities-trading regulator for Ontario and the leading such regulator in Canada. See Section 5.4.

Operating activities

See **Cash from operations** and Section 4.2.

Operating income before tax

The income after deducting the day-to-day expenses incurred in earning revenues but before deducting expenses coming from other sources such as interest (based on borrowing), gains or losses on asset disposals, and income tax. See Section 3.10.

Operating lease

A contract to rent or use an asset that does not convey rights similar to ownership of the asset and that therefore is accounted for simply as rental expense. See **Capital lease** and Section 8.14.

Operating return

The return earned by an enterprise before considering the cost of financing and usually also before considering nonrecurring items. See **Leverage return**, **Scott formula**, and Section 10.6.

Opportunity cost

The return that could have been earned if funds were used in another way than the way they are being used or are proposed to be used. It is called a cost because it is the return given up by not adopting that other use. See Section 10.7.

OSC

See **Ontario Securities Commission** and Section 5.4.

Other assets

A catch-all category used for noncurrent (and occasionally current) assets that do not fit into other categories, are not material individually but aggregate to a material total. See Section 8.14.

Output market value

The market value of an asset if sold. See **Net realizable value** and Section 8.2.

Overdraft

See **Bank overdraft** and Section 2.7.

Overhead costs

Costs of manufacturing inventories or constructing other assets that are incurred indirectly, such as heat, power, and supervisors' salaries. See Section 8.4.

Owners

Parties who have contributed resources in return for the right to dividends and any residual value (equity) of the enterprise. See Sections 1.5, 2.9, and 9.4.

Owner's capital

The owner's equity of the proprietor of an unincorporated business. See **Capital**, **Equity**, and Sections 2.9 and 9.4.

Owners' equity

See **Equity**, **Shareholders' equity**, and Sections 2.3, 2.9, 2.10, and 9.4.

P

Pacioli

Luca Pacioli's *Suma* is the first known book describing double-entry bookkeeping. It was published in 1494 and quickly became influential in the development of accounting and business in Europe. See Section 2.2.

Packing slip

A document accompanying a shipment that describes the shipment's contents and can be used to verify the supplier's invoice for the cost of the shipment. See Section 7.2.

Parent

The dominant corporation in a corporate group linked by ownership, the name of which is usually used in the consolidated financial statements. See Sections 2.9 and 9.7.

Partners' capital, Partners' equity

The owners' equity section of a partnership's balance sheet. See **Partnership** and Sections 2.3, 2.9, and 9.4, and the example in Section 3.8.

Partnership

A contractual agreement among individuals to share resources and operations in a jointly run business. This form of business does not have the privilege of limited liability. See **Corporation**, **Proprietorship**, and Sections 2.9 and 9.4.

Par value

A value set as the legal minimum amount for which a corporation's shares may be issued. Used in earlier years to prevent "watering the stock" and other frauds in which managers sold shares cheaply to themselves or their friends and then outvoted more legitimate shareholders. With the protection to shareholders provided by greater regulation and scrutiny of companies' affairs in the present time, Canadian companies typically have **No-par** shares instead, but par value is still used in many other jurisdictions, including some in the United States. See **Contributed surplus** and Sections 2.9 and 9.4.

PE, PE ratio

The price-earnings ratio is calculated as the current price of a share in the corporation divided by its earnings per share. See **Price-earnings ratio**, **Ratios,** and Section 10.4, Ratio 10, where the ratio is defined and explained.

Percentage of completion

A method of allocating revenue (and associated expenses) over several fiscal periods during which the revenue is earned. Used for long-term construction contracts, franchise revenue, and similar multi-period revenues. See Sections 6.7 and 6.8.

Period expenses

Expenses that are related to the passage of time rather than to the level of sales volume or other activities. Examples are interest, many salaries, and portions of some **Overhead costs** such as heat, light, and property taxes. See Section 6.6.

Periodic inventory control method

A method of calculating inventory that uses data on beginning inventory, additions to inventory, and an end-of-period count to deduce the cost of goods sold. See **Perpetual inventory control method**, **Retail inventory control method**, and Section 7.9.

Periodic reporting

A basic convention of financial accounting that holds that accounting information must be assembled and presented to users at regular intervals (at least yearly and often quarterly or monthly). See Section 6.5.

Perpetual inventory control method

A method of controlling inventory that maintains continuous records on the flow of units of inventory. Thus, there are figures on record for beginning inventory, each unit added to inventory, and each unit removed from inventory for sale. From this, an ending inventory figure can be determined and checked against the figure from a physical count. This method provides better internal control than the periodic inventory method, but it is also more costly to maintain the extra records. See **Periodic inventory control method** and Section 7.9.

Personal guarantees

Additional **Security** on loans, often taken by banks lending to private corporations, in which some or all shareholders sign agreements to contribute personal assets if the corporation does not repay the loans or pay interest on schedule. See Section 9.3.

Petty cash

A small fund of cash kept on hand by an employee for paying small expenses such as postage, minor supplies, and courier charges. See Section 7.5.

Plug

The double-entry system requires that debits equal credits. If adding up all the debits and the credits does not produce two equal figures, the statements must be adjusted so that a balance occurs. The amount of adjustment needed is often called a "plug." This would only be needed if there had been an error somewhere, though sometimes the word *plug* is used in criticism of accrual, consolidation, or other adjustments that produce amounts the critic does not like.

Point of sale

Often used to refer to the point in time when a sale has been completed and the product or service has been delivered to the customer, which is the most common point of recognizing revenue. See **Revenue recognition** and Sections 6.6 and 6.7.

Pooling of interests method

A type of business combination (compare with **Purchase method**). In pooling of interests, the assets, liabilities, equities, revenues, and expenses of the firms are added together using their book values. See **Consolidation** and Section 9.7.

Post-closing accounts

The accounts as they exist after the revenues, expenses, and dividends accounts have been transferred to retained earnings ("closed"). See Sections 3.6 and 3.7.

Post-closing trial balance

A **Trial balance** of the **Post-closing accounts**. See Section 3.7.

Post, posting, posted

Transfer, transferring, or having transferred journal entries to ledger accounts and thereby making them permanent. The only way to fix a mistake is to use an adjusting or correcting entry and post that. See Sections 2.5, 2.6, 3.6, 3.8, and 7.2.

Preferred shares

Ownership shares having special rights in addition to (or instead of) those going with common shares. See Sections 2.9 and 9.4.

Premium

Arises when bonds are issued at a price above their legal face value, such as a $100 bond being issued for $105 cash, indicating a $5 premium. See Section 9.3.

Prepaid expense

An expenditure recorded as a current asset because the benefit will be obtained in the near future (for example, insurance coverage good for the next year). See Section 6.10.

Preparers

Managers and accountants who produce financial statements. See Section 1.5.

Present value

Future cash inflows or outflows reduced to their "present" amount by removing from them the interest that could have been earned or paid had the money been on hand for investment today. See Sections 8.6, 8.14, 9.3, and 10.7.

Present value analysis

Analysis of future cash flows done by removing the presumed interest components of those flows. See **Discounted cash flows** and Section 10.7.

Priced to yield

A reference to issuing a security such as a bond for different proceeds than the face value (the amount that will have to be repaid), so that, based on those proceeds, the bond's effective interest rate equals ("yields") some desired rate. For example, a $100 5% bond could be issued for less than $100 cash so that the bond's interest would amount to 6% on the lower amount the bond sold for. The bond would be said to yield 6%. See Section 10.7.

Price-earnings ratio

Market price of one share of a corporation divided by earnings per share. See **PE ratio**, **Ratios**, and Section 10.4, Ratio 10, where the ratio is defined and explained.

Price-level-adjusted historical cost

A rarely used asset valuation method in which the historical cost of each asset is revalued for inflation. See **Historical cost**, **Fair market value**, and Section 8.2.

Price to book ratio

The ratio of a share's current market value to its **Book value**, or in aggregate, the ratio of the company's total **Market capitalization** to the **Book value** of its equity. See Sections 2.3, 2.10, and 10.4, Ratio 9, where the ratio is defined and explained.

Principal

(1) In interest calculations, the principal is the amount of money initially borrowed, lent, or invested and on which interest is calculated. See Section 10.7. (2) In some kinds of **Contracts**, the principal is the person to whom the **Agent** is responsible. See Sections 5.11 and 10.7.

Prior-period adjustment

A method formerly used in Canada but not recommended anymore by **Accounting standards**, in which accounting is done separately for a gain or loss specifically identified with and directly related to the activities of particular prior periods, but not attributable to economic events occurring subsequent to those periods (so net income of those later periods is not increased or decreased because doing so could cause a distortion in the later results).

Professional ethics

Codes of conduct to guide professionals in applying their professional judgment and that are conducive to their professional activities. See Sections 5.8 and 5.9.

Professionalism

Acting according to the levels of competence, ethics, independence, etc., expected of professionals. See Section 5.9.

Professional judgment

The judgment of professionals about problems in their domain—for example, that of accountants or auditors about financial accounting matters. See Section 5.9.

Profit

See **Net income** and Section 2.3.

Profit margin

See **Sales return** ratio, **Ratios**, and Section 10.4, Ratio 3, where the sales return or profit margin ratio is defined and explained.

Pro forma earnings

An income number other than that reported as net income, which is suggested for use to evaluate a company's performance rather than net income. Pro forma earnings, like **EBITDA**, usually do not include various major expenses, especially losses and write-offs, and so are a more positive measure of income than net income. See Section 3.10.

Proprietor's equity

The **Equity** of an unincorporated business that is owned by a single person. See Section 2.9.

Proprietorship

A firm that is neither a corporation nor a partnership but is under the sole control of one individual. Such a firm is not legally separate from that individual. See **Partnership**, **Corporation**, and Sections 2.9 and 9.4.

Prospectus

A formal document that includes detailed financial information, which is required by law when a company invites the public to subscribe to its securities.

Provision

Another phrase for a usually noncurrent accrual such as for future pension costs or warranties (see Section 9.3). Particularly common when the liability is created to anticipate losses or major expenses involved in discontinuing a business line, refinancing debts, or disposing of major assets. See Section 9.3.

PST

Provincial sales tax. See Section 7.6.

Public accounting, Public accounting firms

Offering auditing, accounting, tax, consulting, and related services to the public on a professional basis. Some of these firms are very large, with thousands of professionals and staff, while others are very small one-person offices. See Sections 1.5 and 5.8.

Public company

A **Corporation** whose shares and related securities are sold widely to members of the public and other investors and whose securities are traded on **Stock exchanges** and other capital markets. See Sections 2.9 and 5.10.

Purchase method

A type of accounting for business combinations (compare with the **Pooling of interests method**). Under this method, which is the overwhelmingly dominant method of determining consolidated financial statement figures, the assets and liabilities of the acquired company are added to those of the parent at fair values and any difference between the portion of the sum of fair values acquired by the parent and the total price paid is accounted for as goodwill. See **Consolidation** and Section 9.7.

Purchase order

A document used when a formal request to buy products or services is made. See Section 7.2.

PV

See **Present value** and Section 10.7.

Qualified opinion

A report by the external auditors that indicates there is a deficiency in the financial statements. See Section 5.8.

Quarterly financial reporting

A form of **Interim financial reporting** in which the financial statements are issued to cover three-month periods. See Section 5.6.

Quarterly report

See **Quarterly financial reporting** and Sections 1.3 and 5.10.

Quick ratio

Cash, temporary investments, and accounts receivable divided by current liabilities. Also called the acid test ratio. See **Ratios** and Sections 2.3 and 10.4, Ratio 19, where the ratio is defined and explained.

R&D

Research and development activities, a controversial accounting problem because the activities are intended to lead to future benefits and thus their costs may be considered to be assets, yet GAAP require that generally such costs be charged to expense as incurred. See Section 8.14.

Ratios, ratio analysis

Numbers produced by dividing one financial statement figure by another figure; for example, the working capital ratio is the total current assets figure divided by the total current liabilities figure. Standard ratios are used to assess aspects of a firm, particularly profitability, solvency, and liquidity. See Sections 10.2, 10.4, and 10.6. Section 10.4 describes 20 common ratios. See Section 10.4.

Realized

Used in this book as a synonym of received, or collected. Revenue is recognized when earned, but that is usually before it is collected or realized. See **Revenue recognition** and Sections 6.3 and 6.6.

Receivable

Funds expected to be collected by the enterprise. The usual kind is trade **Accounts receivable**, but other kinds include taxes receivable, employee expense advances receivable, and **Notes receivable**. See Section 2.4.

Reclassification (entry)

A journal entry or repositioning of an account that changes the location of the account within the balance sheet or within the income statement but does not affect income. See **Classification policies** and Section 2.7.

Reclassified account

An account moved to a different place within a financial statement without changing income or equity. See Sections 2.7 and 8.5.

Recognition

Giving effect in the accounts to revenue believed to be earned, or expenses believed to be incurred, before (or after) the cash is collected or paid. See **Revenue recognition, Expense recognition**, and Sections 5.2, 6.4, 6.6, 6.7, and 6.8.

Recognized

Revenues or expenses (usually), entered into the accounts or given effect in the accounts. See **Recognition** and Section 6.2.

Reconcile, Reconciliation

The **Analysis** technique of comparing two sets of information that relate to the same account or activity and identifying differences that indicate errors in either or both records. See **Bank reconciliation** and Sections 1.12, 4.9, 7.5, and 7.9.

Recordkeeping

The bookkeeping and other methods used to create the underlying records on which accounting information is based. See Sections 5.2, 5.3, 6.2, and 6.3.

Redeemable

Shares or bonds that have the right to be sold back to the company. See Section 9.5.

Refined ROA

A version of the **Return on assets** ratio. See **ROA(ATI)**, **Ratios**, and Section 10.4, Ratio 2, where the ratio is defined and explained.

Relevance

The capacity of information to make a difference in a decision by helping users to form predictions about the outcomes of past, present, and future events, or to confirm or correct prior expectations. See **Decision relevance** and Sections 5.2 and 5.3.

Reliability

A characteristic of information that is represented faithfully and is free from bias and verifiable. See **Timeliness**, **Objectivity**, and Sections 5.2 and 5.3.

Replacement cost

The price that will have to be paid in order to replace an existing asset with a similar asset. This amount is likely to be different from that of **Fair market value** or **Net realizable value**. See also **Lower of cost or market** and Sections 8.2 and 8.9.

Resources

In financial accounting, the recognized assets of the enterprise as shown on the balance sheet. See Section 2.3.

Retail inventory control method

Providing internal control and deducing inventory amounts for financial statements by using ratios of cost to selling price; for example, deducing cost of goods sold from sales revenue minus the markup on cost. Ending inventory cost can be determined by measuring inventory at retail prices minus markup. See **Perpetual inventory method**, **Periodic inventory method**, **Inventory costing**, and Sections 7.9 and 8.9.

Retained earnings

Earnings not yet distributed to owners; the sum of net incomes earned over the life of a company, less distributions (dividends declared) to owners. See **Equity** and Sections 2.3, 2.9, 3.3, 3.5, and 9.4.

Retained earnings statement

See **Statement of retained earnings** and Sections 3.3, 3.4, 3.5, and 5.5.

Return

Some amount of gain (income or performance) usually measured in relation to the amount invested to get the return. See **Risk**, Sections 5.10 and 10.2, and such ratios as **Return on equity** and **Return on assets** in Sections 10.4 and 10.6.

Return on assets (ROA or ROA(ATI))

Net income, before considering interest expense or the tax saving provided by interest expense, divided by total assets. This measures the **Operating return** before the cost of financing. See **Ratios** and Sections 10.3 and 10.4, Ratio 2, where the ratio is defined and explained, and Section 10.6, where it is used in the **Scott formula**.

Return on equity (ROE)

Net income divided by owners' equity. The most frequently used ratio for measuring the business's return to owners. See **Ratios** and Sections 10.2 and 10.4, Ratio 1, where the ratio is defined and explained, and Section 10.6, where it is used in the **Scott formula**.

Return on investment (ROI)

A general term for measures of return related to the investment needed to earn the return. See **Return on assets**, **Return on equity**, and Section 10.2.

Revenue

The amount of benefit received or promised from the sale of goods or services, before any deductions for the cost of providing the goods or services. See **Income statement**, **Revenue recognition**, and Sections 1.10, 3.3, 3.5, 6.3, and 6.6.

Revenue recognition

The entering into the accounts of the amount of revenue determined, according to the firm's accounting policies, to be attributable to the current period. See **Accrual accounting**, **Accounts receivable**, **Revenue**, and Sections 6.3, 6.6, and 6.7.

Review

A report prepared on an enterprise's financial statements by a **Public accounting** firm that is less than an **Audit** but more than a **Compilation**: the accounting firm studies the statements' contents and compliance with GAAP to determine if there are any apparent problems but does not verify individual accounts or the underlying records. See Section 5.8.

Risk

The probable variability in possible future outcomes above and below the expected level of outcomes (for example, returns), but especially below. Risk and return go hand in hand, because a high risk should mean a higher potential return and vice versa. See Section 5.10 and **Return**, and Section 10.4, Ratios 14–20.

ROA

See **Return on assets**.

ROA(ATI)

See **Refined ROA**, **Return on assets**, and Sections 10.3, 10.4, and 10.6.

ROE

See **Return on equity** and Sections 10.4 and 10.6.

ROI

See **Return on investment** and Section 10.2.

Sales invoice

A document containing the details of a sale. See Section 7.2.

Sales journal

A record of sales made, used to produce the **Revenue** data in the accounts. See **Books of original entry** and Section 7.2.

Sales return

The ratio of net income to revenue. See **Ratios** and Section 10.4, Ratio 3, where the ratio is defined and explained, and Section 10.6, where a refined version **(SR(ATI))** is used in the **Scott formula**.

Sales taxes

Taxes the enterprise must charge its customers and remit to the government. See Section 7.6.

SCFP (Statement of changes in financial position)

See **Cash flow statement**.

Scott formula

A financial analysis technique for studying leverage effects by combining a group of ratios into a more comprehensive explanation of performance. The formula separates **Return on equity** into **Operating return** and **Leverage return**. See **Leverage**, **Ratios**, and Section 10.6.

SEC

See **Securities and Exchange Commission** and Sections 5.4 and 5.10.

Securities

Shares, bonds, and other financial instruments issued by corporations and governments and usually traded on **Capital markets**. See Sections 5.10 and 9.3.

Securities and Exchange Commission (SEC)

An agency of the U.S. government that supervises the registration of security issues, prosecutes fraudulent stock manipulations, and regulates securities transactions in the United States. See Sections 5.4 and 5.10.

Security

(1) Singular of **Securities**. (2) Protection to a lender or other creditor in which the lender is given rights to specific assets (as in a **Mortgage**), more general rights to monitor the borrower (**Debenture** or **Indenture**), or other promises (such as **Personal guarantees**).

Segmented information

Financial statement information desegregated by geographical or economic area of activity in order to provide greater insight into financial performance and position. Segmented information is usually placed at the end of the notes to the financial statements.

Segregation of duties

An internal control technique whereby tasks involved in sensitive assets such as cash, accounts receivable, or inventories are divided up so that no one both handles the asset and keeps the records of the asset. See Sections 7.3 and 7.5.

Share capital

The portion of a corporation's equity obtained by issuing shares in return for cash or other considerations. See Sections 2.3, 2.9, and 9.4.

Shareholders

The holders of a corporation's **Share capital**, and so the owners of the corporation. See Section 1.4.

Shareholders' equity

The sum of shareholders' direct investment (share capital) and indirect investment (retained earnings). See **Share capital**, **Equity**, **Retained earnings**, and Sections 2.3, 2.9, and 9.4.

Share split

Reissuing shares in which the number of new shares is some multiple of the previous number. For example, a two-for-one split results in a shareholder owning twice as many shares as before. Because there has been a change only in the number of shares but not in the underlying value of the corporation, the share price should fall in accordance with the split (e.g., the new shares above should have a share price about half the previous price). See Section 9.4.

Shares (stock)

Units of **Share capital**, evidenced by certificates and, for **Public companies**, traded on **Capital markets** with other **Securities**. See Sections 2.3 and 2.9.

Significant accounting policies

The main choices among possible accounting methods made by the enterprise in preparing its financial statements. These policies are usually summarized in the first note to the financial statements. See **Accounting policies, Notes to the financial statements**, and Sections 5.6, 5.7, and 6.4.

Significant influence

An investment in another corporation that is not large enough for voting control but is large enough to influence how that corporation does business. See **Equity basis** and Section 9.6.

Society of Management Accountants of Canada (SMA-Canada)

A society whose members have had training in tax, accounting, internal audit, and other related areas, with a particular focus on internal management accounting, and have passed qualifying exams. It is one of the three national professional accounting bodies. See **Accountant**.

Solvency

The condition of being able to meet all debts and obligations. See **Statement of changes in financial position, Liquidity**, Sections 3.4 and 4.2, and Section 10.4, Ratios 18–20.

Source documents

The evidence required to record a **Transaction**. See Section 7.2.

Sources

The right-hand side of the balance sheet (liabilities and equity) are the sources of the enterprise's assets. See Section 2.3.

Specialized ledgers

Ledgers used to keep track of particular assets, liabilities, or equities, such as accounts receivable, fixed assets, or share capital. See Section 7.2.

Specific identification

Accounting for inventories according to the specific cost of the items, which therefore requires some sort of identification of the items, such as by serial number. Contrast **Assumed cost flow** and see Section 8.7.

SR(ATI)

See **Sales return** and Section 10.4.

Standard cost

A method of determining manufactured inventory costs that uses expected normal production costs rather than actual costs. See Section 8.9.

Stated value

A value provided to shares that is similar to **Par value** but less legally binding. See Section 2.9.

Statement of cash flows

See **Cash flow statement** and Section 4.2.

Statement of changes in financial position (SCFP)

See **Cash flow statement** and Section 4.2.

Statement of financial position

A synonym for **Balance sheet**. See Section 2.3.

Statement of retained earnings

A financial statement that summarizes the changes in retained earnings for the year. Change in retained earnings equals **Net income** minus **Dividends** plus or minus any retained earnings adjustments. See Sections 3.3, 3.4, and 5.5.

Statement of source and application of cash

See **Cash flow statement** and Section 4.2.

Stewardship

The concept that some persons (for example, management) are responsible for looking after the assets and interests of other persons (for example, shareholders), and that reports should be prepared that will be suitable to allow the "stewards" to be held accountable for the actions taken on behalf of the other persons. See **Agent** and Sections 2.2, 3.2, and 5.11.

Stock-based compensation

A way of paying executives and other employees by giving them shares in the company or **Stock options** that allow them to acquire shares in the future at attractive prices. Such compensation is in addition to salaries and bonuses. See Section 9.5.

Stock dividend

A **Dividend** paid by issuing more shares to present shareholders rather than paying them cash. See Sections 3.3 and 9.4.

Stock exchange

A place where **Shares** and other **Securities** are traded. See Section 5.10.

Stockholder

An alternative term for **Shareholder**, particularly used in the United States.

Stock market

A **Capital market** in which equity shares are traded. Often used as a generic term for stock exchanges and capital markets. See Sections 1.5, 2.3, 3.2, and 5.10.

Stock option(s)

Promises, usually made to senior managers, to issue shares to them at specified prices. The prices are usually set to be higher than present prices but lower than expected future prices, to provide an incentive to work to increase those future prices. See Sections 3.10 and 9.5.

Stocks

Usually used to mean **Shares**, but also used to mean **Inventories**, as in "stocktaking" for counting inventories. See Section 2.3.

Straight-line amortization (depreciation)

A method of computing amortization (depreciation) simply by dividing the difference between the asset's cost and its expected salvage value by the number of years the asset is expected to be used. It is the most common amortization method used in Canada. See **Amortization** and Section 8.12.

Subsidiary

A company that is owned by another company (the **Parent**). The parent need not own all the subsidiary's shares, but does own at least a majority of the voting shares of the subsidiary. See **Consolidation** and Sections 2.9 and 9.7.

Subsidiary ledgers

See **Specialized ledgers.**

Sum-of-years'-digits

An accelerated method of computing amortization (depreciation) that produces a declining annual expense, which is used in the United States but is rare in Canada. See **Accelerated amortization** and Note 21 to Chapter 8.

Synoptic

A bookkeeping record listing cash transactions of the business.

T

T-account

A T-shaped representation of a ledger account used in analysis or demonstration. See Section 2.5.

Tangible assets

See **Fixed assets** and Section 8.4.

Taxable income

Income calculated according to income tax law and used as the basis for computing income tax payable. See Section 9.3.

Temporary differences

Differences between accounting calculations of income and calculations required for income tax purposes that will eventually net out to zero. These affect income tax expense calculations. See Section 9.3.

Temporary investments

Investments made for a short term, often used as a place to put temporarily excess cash to work. See Sections 8.5 and 9.6.

Term preferred shares

Preferred shares issued with a fixed term and dividend rate, and therefore having some of the characteristics of debt. See Section 9.5.

Timeliness

Timely information is usable because it relates to present decision needs. Information received late may be too late to be usable, since decisions pass it by. See **Relevance**, **Reliability**, and Section 5.2.

Time value of money

Money can earn interest, so money received in the future is worth less in "present value" terms because the lower amount can be invested to grow to the future amount. Money has a time value because interest accrues over time. See **Present value** and Section 10.7.

Toronto Stock Exchange

The leading **Stock exchange** in Canada. See Section 5.4.

Total assets turnover

The ratio of revenue to total assets. See **Ratios** and Section 10.4, Ratio 12, where the ratio is defined and explained. See also Section 10.6, where the ratio is used in the **Scott formula**.

Trade receivables

These are **Accounts receivable** arising in the normal course of business with customers. See Section 8.6.

Transaction

An accounting transaction is the basis of bookkeeping and is defined by four criteria described and explained in Section 1.7.

Transaction base

The idea that financial accounting is substantially defined by the use of the **Transaction** as the fundamental recordkeeping basis underlying the accounting data. See Section 1.7.

Treasury shares (stock)

Share capital issued and then reacquired by the firm that issued the shares. The result is a reduction of shareholders' equity because resources have been used to reduce the actual amount of outstanding equity. See Sections 2.9 and 9.4.

Trial balance

A list of all the general ledger accounts and their balances. The sum of the accounts with debit balances should equal the sum of those with credit balances. This is contrasted with the **Chart of accounts**, which lists only the account names. See **Account** and Sections 2.5, 3.6, 3.7, and 3.8.

TSX

The **Toronto Stock Exchange**. See Section 5.4.

Unadjusted trial balance

The **Trial balance** of the accounts prior to making various accrual adjustments in preparation for the financial statements. See Sections 3.8 and 3.9.

Unaudited

Refers to financial statements that have not received an **External audit** and so are not accompanied by an **Auditor's opinion**. See Section 5.8.

Units-of-production amortization

An amortization (depreciation) method in which the annual amortization expense varies directly with the year's production volume. See Section 8.12.

Unusual items

Unusual revenues or expenses that are large enough to be worth identifying separately in the income statement. See Section 3.5.

Users

People who use financial statements to assist them in deciding whether to invest in the enterprise, lend it money, or take other action involving financial information. See Section 1.5.

Valuation

Determining the amounts at which assets, liabilities, and equity should be shown in the balance sheet. See Section 8.2.

Value in use

The value of an asset determined by the future cash flows it brings in, or the future expenses that will be avoided by owning the asset. See Section 8.2.

Verifiability

Ability to trace an accounting entry or figure back to the underlying evidence of its occurrence and validity. See **Source documents** and Sections 1.7, 5.2, 5.3, and 5.8.

Warrants

Attachments to shares or bonds giving rights to acquire further shares or bonds on specified terms. See Section 9.5.

Weighted average

An inventory cost flow assumption that determines cost of goods sold and ending inventory cost by averaging the cost of all of the inventory available during the period. See **AVGE**, **Average cost**, **LIFO**, **FIFO**, **Inventory costing**, and Section 8.7.

"What if" (effects) analysis

Analyzing potential business decisions or accounting policies by determining their effects on income, cash flow, or other important items. See Sections 1.12, 10.8, and 10.9.

Working capital

The difference between current assets and current liabilities. See **Current assets**, **Current liabilities**, and Sections 2.3 and 9.2, and 10.4.

Working capital ratio

Current assets divided by current liabilities. See **Ratios** and Sections 2.3 and 9.2 and Section 10.4, Ratio 18, where the ratio is defined and explained.

Work order

A document specifying the components and assembly or other work to be done to provide a product ordered by a customer. See Section 7.2.

Write-down

Reducing an asset's value on the balance sheet but not removing the asset completely (which is a **Write-off**). See Sections 7.7 and 8.11.

Write-off

Refers to the elimination of an asset from the balance sheet. If there is a **Contra account** against the asset already, the write-off is made against the contra, so expense and income are not affected. If there is no contra account, the write-off (a **Direct write-off**,

Section 7.7) is made to an expense or a loss account and income is reduced. See Sections 7.7 and 8.11.

Write-off (bad debts)

Refers to eliminating an account receivable deemed to be uncollectible. If the elimination is done by deducting the amount from both the **Accounts receivable** asset and the **Allowance for doubtful accounts**, there is no effect on income. Otherwise, the write-off reduces income. See Section 7.7.

Write-off (noncurrent assets)

Refers to eliminating a noncurrent asset, such as land, buildings, equipment, investments or **Goodwill**, deemed not to have further value to the enterprise. The elimination is done by removing both the asset cost and the **Accumulated amortization** related to that asset, if any. Income is reduced by the amount by which the asset cost exceeds the accumulated amortization. Otherwise, the write-off reduces income. See Sections 7.7 and 8.11.

Yield

The effective interest rate a financial instrument such as a **Bond** earns, given the amount of money received when it was issued. See **Present value** and Section 10.7.

NOTES

1. Some supplementary help in developing this glossary originally came from the *CICA Handbook* (Toronto: Canadian Institute of Chartered Accountants, various versions); S. Davidson, C.L. Mitchell, C.P. Stickney, and R.L. Weil, *Financial Accounting: An Introduction to Concepts, Methods and Uses* (Toronto: Holt, Rinehart & Winston, 1986); *Funk & Wagnalls Canadian College Dictionary* (Markham: Fitzhenry & Whiteside, 1986); and Ross M. Skinner, *Accounting Standards in Evolution* (Toronto: Holt, Rinehart & Winston, 1987).

A

Text Credits

pp. 4–7, 271: Enbridge logo and financial information reprinted by permission of Enbridge Inc.;

p. 92, 712–714: Petro-Canada logo and financial information reprinted by permission of Petro-Canada;

pp. 104, 106, 151, 247, 248, 440, 647–651: Canadian Pacific Railway financial information reprinted by permission of Canadian Pacific Railway;

p. 110: RBC logo and Consolidated Balance Sheet reprinted courtesy of RBC Financial Group;

p. 187: Corporate earnings for ATI Technologies Inc., Cognos Inc., Printera Corp., and Research In Motion Ltd. Reprinted by permission of CNW Group and CCNMatthews;

p. 306: Condensed Statements of Shareholders' Equity, Tyson Food Inc. 2005 Annual Report reprinted by permission of Tyson Food Inc.;

pp. 307–310: Condensed Financial Statements of The Government of Canada and Notes (2004–2005) from "Annual Financial Report of the Government of Canada-Fiscal Year 2004–2005", Department of Finance Canada. Reproduced with the permission of the Minister of Public Works and Government Services Canada, 2006;

p. 313: The Canadian Academic Accounting Association Statement of Financial Position reprinted by permission of The Canadian Academic Accounting Association;

p. 319: Canadian Pacific Railway Limited Auditors' Report to the Shareholders and Comments reprinted by permission of PricewaterhouseCoopers Canada;

p. 350: "It's time to Narrow the GAAP Gap" reprinted by permission of *National Post*;

p. 405: "Tech firms' accounting methods assailed," by Simon Tuck, *The Globe and Mail*, March 29, 1999 reprinted by permission from *The Globe and Mail*;

pp. 420–422: "Lessons of the 90's" copyright 2002 Harris Collingwood. From *The New York Times Magazine*. Distributed by The New York Times Special Features.

pp. 428–433: Barcol Doors and Windows financial documents reprinted by permission of Barcol Doors and Windows;

pp. 565–566: "How to Hide $3.8 Billion in Expenses," by Peter Elstrom, *Business Week*, July 8, 2002, p.51;

pp. 716–718: Sleeman Breweries financial information reprinted courtesy of Sleeman Breweries Ltd.;

pp. 720–723: "Hide and Seek" by John Gray, *Canadian Business*, April 1, 2002, pp.28–32. Reprinted by permission of *Canadian Business*.

Photo Credits

Page 3: © Royalty-Free/Corbis;

Page 4: Reprinted by permission of Enbridge Inc.;

Page 11 top: CP PHOTO/Adrian Wyld;

Page 11 bottom: © 2006 JupiterImages and its Licensors. All Rights Reserved;

Page 59: The Globe & Mail/Tibor Kolley/CP Photo;

Page 62: © Copyright the Trustees of The British Museum;

Page 103: Canadian Pacific Railway Archives (E7926-13);

Page 133: © Peter Beck/CORBIS;

Page 135: © Historical Picture Archive/CORBIS;

Page 137: © Bettmann/CORBIS;

Page 138: Courtesy of Ursus Books and Prints Ltd., New York;

Page 139: © Duomo/CORBIS;

Page 229: © 2006 JupiterImages and its Licensors. All Rights Reserved.;

Page 287: PhotoDisc/Getty Images;

Page 357: © 2006 JupiterImages and its Licensors. All Rights Reserved.;

Page 423: PhotoDisc/Getty Images;

Page 487: PhotoDisc/Getty Images;

Page 571: Lifestyles Productions/Index Stock;

Page 639: Phil Cantor/Index Stock.